Explore the extensive retail career information at the Web site

• **General Information** – We discuss the career-preparation process in these steps: assessing yourself, acquiring job leads, writing a résumé and cover letter, and handling the personal interview and post-interview activities.

• **Internships** – A well-balanced approach to planning your career during college is often the key to long-run success. What does this mean? You should take your college education seriously, participate in co-curricular and extra-curricular activities, and begin to acquire meaningful work experience.

• **Job Hunting Guide** – The job-hunting process consists of several steps, which we discuss in detail: collecting information, applying for a job, using effective job-search methods, evaluating a job offer, and using job-hunt-related search engines.

• **Types of Retail Jobs** – We provide in-depth information on the nature of these retail jobs: buyers and merchandise managers, customer service representatives, restaurant and food service managers, retail managers, retail sales workers, and travel agents. We also cite numerous other positions in retailing, present several flow charts demonstrating career-path growth, and offer links to hundreds of retailers' career sites.

NEW! NEW! NEW! THE blog on retailing: www.bermanevansretail.com

In our continuing efforts to be cutting edge, we are extremely excited to engage you through our new blog.

What's in it for you?

- ALL aspects of the blog–from its design to the topical categories to each of the posts—have been and will continue to be 100% prepared by the authors. Not graduate assistants, not behind-the-scenes bloggers, or others. JUST the authors: Barry Berman and Joel Evans.
- Our blog is intended to satisfy a number of goals:
    - To provide current, ongoing material that covers all eight of the major parts in *Retail Management*.
    - To offer a large amount of information on careers in retailing, including job-hunting tips and links directly to the job section of numerous retailers' Web sites.
    - To be visually attractive and interactive; and to include multimedia content.
    - To encourage feedback and comments. For blog-related comments or questions, contact us directly at **bermanevansretail@gmail.com.** We promise to respond. Again, "we" means the authors—not a third party.
    - To be both informative and engaging (fun)!
- The emerging role of social media in retailing receives special coverage. There are a lot of interesting stories out.
- We will be looking at the good and the bad practices of retailers.
- There will be posts of interviews that we conduct with executives of leading retail companies.
- There will be direct links to many retail-related LinkedIn groups. LinkedIn is the leading online professional networking site.

Retail Management

Retail Management

A Strategic Approach

TWELFTH EDITION

Barry Berman
Hofstra University

Joel R. Evans
Hofstra University

PEARSON

Boston Columbus Indianapolis New York San Francisco Upper Saddle River
Amsterdam Cape Town Dubai London Madrid Milan Munich Paris Montréal Toronto
Delhi Mexico City São Paulo Sydney Hong Kong Seoul Singapore Taipei Tokyo

Editor-in-Chief: Stephanie Wall
Acquisitions Editor: Erin Gardner
Editorial Project Manager: Kierra Bloom
Editorial Assistant: Jacob Garber
Director of Marketing: Maggie Moylan
Executive Marketing Manager: Anne Fahlgren
Senior Managing Editor: Judy Leale
Production Project Manager: Becca Groves
Senior Operations Supervisor: Arnold Vila
Operations Specialist: Cathleen Petersen
Creative Director: Blair Brown
Senior Art Director: Janet Slowik
Interior and Cover Designer: Karen Quigley
Cover Photo: shutterstock images
Senior Editorial Media Project Manager: Denise Vaughn
Production Media Project Manager: Lisa Rinaldi
Full-Service Project Management and Composition: Integra
Printer/Binder: Courier/Kendallville
Cover Printer: Courier/Kendallville
Text Font: 10/12, Times LT Std

Credits and acknowledgments borrowed from other sources and reproduced, with permission, in this textbook appear on the appropriate page within text.

Library of Congress Cataloging-in-Publication Data
Berman, Barry.
Retail management: a strategic approach/Barry Berman, Joel R. Evans.—12th ed.
p. cm.
Includes bibliographical references and index.
ISBN 978-0-13-272082-3
1. Retail trade—Management. I. Evans, Joel R. II. Title.
HF5429.B45 2013
658.8'7—dc23

2012017351

10 9 8 7 6 5 4 3

ISBN 10: 0-13-272082-5
ISBN 13: 978-0-13-272082-3

To Linda; Glenna, Paul, Danielle, Sophie, and Joshua;
and Lisa, Ben, Philip, Emily, and Levi

To Linda, Stacey, and Jennifer

Thank you for your enduring patience
and understanding.

Brief Contents

Contents

Preface

Welcome to *Retail Management: A Strategic Approach.* Our major goal is to present you with the most current, comprehensive, reader-friendly book and supplements on retail management possible. We want you to get thoroughly immersed in the subject matter, see how retail strategies are formed, look at the activities of a wide range of actual retailers (large and small, goods and services, domestic and global), and explore the possibility of a full-time career in retail management. Read through this preface and see what's available to you.

The concept of a strategic approach to retailing is the cornerstone of this book. With a strategic approach, the fundamental principle is that the retailer has to plan for and adapt to a complex, changing environment. Both opportunities and constraints must be considered. A retail strategy is the overall plan or framework of action that guides a retailer. Ideally, it will be at least one year in duration and outline the mission, goals, consumer market, overall and specific activities, and control mechanisms of the retailer. Without a pre-defined and well-integrated strategy, the firm may flounder and be unable to cope with the environment that surrounds it. Through our text, we want you to become a good retail planner and decision maker and be able to adapt to change.

Since the first edition of *Retail Management: A Strategic Approach*, we have sought to be as contemporary and forward-looking as possible. We are proactive rather than reactive in our preparation of each edition. That is why we take this adage of Wal-Mart's founder, the late Sam Walton, so seriously: "Commit to your business. Believe in it more than anybody else."

WHAT'S NEW TO THIS EDITION

1. All data and examples are as current as possible and reflect the current economic situation. We believe it is essential that our book take into account the economic environment that has dramatically affected so many businesses and consumers.
2. NEW! Chapter opening vignettes—each relating to the evolving interaction of social media and retailing. We had a lot of fun writing these vignettes!
3. NEW! QR codes have been introduced throughout to link you directly to Web sites referenced in all NEW applied boxes within each chapter. Be sure to download a QR reader app on your smart phone to make use of this new feature! Topics include:
   a. *Technology in Retailing*
   b. *Retailing Around the World*
   c. *Ethics in Retailing*
   d. *Careers in Retailing*
4. NEW! Thirty shorter cases, as well as eight comprehensive cases. Every case is based on real companies and real situations.
5. NEW photos appear throughout—many with an international flavor (to further emphasize the global nature of retailing).
6. Our comprehensive Web site (www.pearsonhighered.com/bermanevans) has been completely updated.
7. We have a brand new, dynamic, current, interactive blog just for students and professors interested in retailing. There is a lot of cool stuff there. Please join us at www.bermanevansretail.com. Both our Web site and blog have a lot of career material.

THE BERMAN EVANS PRE-QUIZ

To highlight the interesting and useful information presented in *Retail Management: A Strategic Approach*, here's a brief pre-quiz. (Wow! Who ever heard of STARTING a book with a quiz?) It's a fun trivia quiz, based on one piece of information that we write about in each chapter. When you finish reading our book, you'll know the answers to all of these questions and a whole lot more. Text page references are provided for the trivia pre-quiz. Please: No peeking until after you complete the quiz. See how many questions you can answer:

1. **Chapter 1:** About how many people are employed by traditional retailers (including food and beverage service firms) in the United States? (see page 5)

2. **Chapter 2:** Who is the world's largest video game and software retailer? (see page 26)
3. **Chapter 3:** What percentage of all U.S. retail firms that file tax returns are sole proprietors? (see page 58)
4. **Chapter 4:** Suppose you want to open your own store and you decide to become a franchisee for Subway. What franchise fee will you have to pay? What percentage of your sales must you pay as an ongoing cost of doing business? (see page 108)
5. **Chapter 5:** What is scrambled merchandising? [Hint: It does not involve eggs or an omelet.] Why do so many retailers engage in it? (see page 115)
6. **Chapter 6:** Which age group is more likely to use the Web, 18- to 29-year-olds or those 65 and older? [This is a really easy question.] (see page 149)
7. **Chapter 7:** According to a recent global survey of shoppers, what is the number one reason why people shop at a specific retailer? (see page 182)
8. **Chapter 8:** What is the Universal Product Code? Why is it important for retailers? (see page 206)
9. **Chapter 9:** What is a parasite store? [No, it is not a bug.] (see page 234)
10. **Chapter 10:** Where is the world's largest shopping center (megamall)? (see page 260)
11. **Chapter 11:** Katherine Krill and Mary Sammons are female top executives of what two firms? (see page 293)
12. **Chapter 12:** What do Borders, Filene's Basement, and Syms all have in common? (see page 313)
13. **Chapter 13:** How many credit and debit cards are in use in the United States? (see page 332)
14. **Chapter 14:** In terms of dollar sales, what percentage of U.S. retail revenues are contributed by private brands such as Sears' Kenmore appliances and J.C. Penney's American Living apparel? (see page 364)
15. **Chapter 15:** TJX (the parent company of T.J. Maxx and Marshall's) attributes a large part of its merchandising success to its reliance on opportunistic buying. What is this? (see page 381)
16. **Chapter 16:** What are the FIFO and LIFO methods of accounting in inventory management? (see page 401)
17. **Chapter 17:** When manufacturers or wholesalers seek to control the retail prices of their goods and services, it is called vertical price fixing. Is this practice legal in the United States? (see page 427)
18. **Chapter 18:** Inside most supermarkets, a straight traffic flow places displays and aisles in a rectangular pattern. What U.S. football term is also used to denote this type of traffic flow? [This one is really easy for you sports fans.] (see page 468)
19. **Chapter 19:** Among these retail store types, which one spends the lowest percentage of its sales on advertising: apparel and accessories stores, department stores, eating places, grocery stores, hotels and motels, movie theaters, or shoe stores? (see page 482)
20. **Chapter 20:** In retail management, what is gap analysis? [Hint: It does not require a dental procedure at your local dentist.] (see page 523)
21. **Career Appendix (bonus question):** True or false? "Retail is one of the largest, most dynamic parts of the world economy. In good economic times, jobs in the retail sector are numerous and many entry-level positions are easy to get. Even during economic contractions, when some retailing sectors suffer, others—like groceries, drugstores, and discounters—thrive." (see page 541)

WHAT IS COVERED IN RETAIL MANAGEMENT

Retail Management: A Strategic Approach has eight parts.

Part One introduces the field of retailing, the basics of strategic planning, the importance of building and maintaining customer and supplier relations, and the decisions to be made in owning or managing a retail business.

In **Part Two**, retail institutions are examined in terms of ownership types, as well as store-based, nonstore-based, electronic, and nontraditional strategy mixes. The wheel of retailing, scrambled merchandising, the retail life cycle, and the Web are covered.

Part Three focuses on target marketing and information-gathering methods, including discussions of why and how consumers shop and the retailing information system and data warehouse.

Part Four presents a four-step approach to location planning: trading-area analysis, choosing the most desirable type of location, selecting a general locale, and deciding on a specific site.

Part Five discusses the elements involved in managing a retail business: the retail organization structure, human resource management, and operations management (both financial and operational).

Part Six deals with merchandise management—developing and implementing merchandise plans, the financial aspects of merchandising, and pricing.

In **Part Seven**, the ways to communicate with customers are analyzed, with special attention paid to retail image, atmosphere, and promotion.

Part Eight deals with integrating and controlling a retail strategy.

At the end of the text, **Appendix: Careers in Retailing**, highlights career opportunities in retailing. There is also a comprehensive **Glossary**.

To give you the best possible learning experience, these features are included in every chapter:

- A contemporary opening vignette that highlights the emerging interplay between retailers and social media.
- Chapter objectives.
- Chapter overview.
- Reader-friendly coverage of all the important topics pertaining to that chapter.
- A colorful design with numerous photos and figures that illustrate important points.
- Margin notes with links to key Web sites.
- Four real-world boxes on "Technology in Retailing," "Retailing Around the World," "Ethics in Retailing," and "Careers in Retailing" in each chapter. Use your phone to link to the sites, within each box, via QR codes throughout the text!
- A chapter summary tied directly to the chapter goals.
- A list of key terms and their page references.
- Questions for discussion.
- Online exercise to stimulate thought.
- Chapter endnotes.

To provide extra coverage for five special topics, we also include these chapter-ending appendixes: Chapter 1—"Understanding the Recent Economic Downturn in the United States and Around the Globe," Chapter 2—"Planning for the Unique Aspects of Service Retailing," Chapter 3—"The Special Dimensions of Strategic Planning in a Global Retailing Environment," Chapter 4—"The Dynamics of Franchising," and Chapter 6—"Multi-Channel Retailing."

At the end of each of the eight parts in *Retail Management*, there are a variety of short and long cases. They deal with such firms as Amazon.com, eBay, Forever 21, Gap, McDonald's, Perfumania, and Starbucks. In all, there are 30 shorts cases and eight long cases.

THE E-VOLUTION OF *RETAIL MANAGEMENT: A STRATEGIC APPROACH*

As music legend Bob Dylan once said, "The times, they are a changing." What does this all mean? The "E" word—electronic—now permeates our lives. From a consumer perspective, gone are the old electric typewriters, replaced by PCs, smart phones, and tablets. Snail mail is giving way to E-mail, texting, and Facebook. Looking for a new music CD? Well, we can go to the store—or order it from Amazon.com (www.amazon.com) or download some tracks from iTunes to create our own CDs/DVDs.

Are you doing research? Then hop on the Internet to gain access to millions of facts at your fingertips. The Web is an anytime (24/7/365), anywhere medium that is transforming—and will continue to transform—our behavior.

From a retailer perspective, we see four formats—all covered in *Retail Management*—competing in the new millennium (cited in descending order of importance):

- **Combined "bricks-and-mortar" and "clicks-and-mortar" retailers.** These are store-based retailers that also offer online shopping, thus providing customers the ultimate in choice and convenience. Virtually all of the world's largest retailers, as well as many medium and small firms, fall into this category. This is clearly the fast-growing format in retailing, exemplified by such different firms as Best Buy (www.bestbuy.com), Costco (www.costco.com), and Target (www.target.com).

- **Clicks-and-mortar retailers.** These are the new breed of online-only retailers that have emerged in recent years, led by Amazon.com (www.amazon.com). Rather than utilize their own physical store facilities, these companies promote a "virtual" shopping experience: wide selections, low prices, and convenience. Among the firms in this category are Blue Nile (www.bluenile.com), the jewelry retailer; Priceline.com (www.priceline.com), the discount airfare and hotel retailer; and Zappos (www.zappos.com), the retailer of shoes, apparel, and a whole lot more.
- **Direct marketers with clicks-and-mortar retailing operations.** These are firms that have relied on traditional nonstore media such as print catalogs, direct selling in homes, and TV infomercials to generate business. Almost all of them have added Web sites to enhance their businesses. Leaders include Lands' End (www.landsend.com) and QVC (www.qvc.com). These direct marketers will see a dramatic increase in the proportion of sales coming from the Web.
- **Bricks-and-mortar retailers.** These are companies that rely on their physical facilities to make sales. They do not sell online, but use the Internet for providing information, customer service, and image building. Auto dealers typically offer product information and customer service online, but conduct their sales transactions at retail stores. Firms in this category represent the smallest grouping of retailers. Many will need to rethink their approach as online competition intensifies.

We have access to more information sources than ever before, from global trade associations to government agencies. The information in *Retail Management*, Twelfth Edition, is more current than ever because we are using the original sources themselves and not waiting for data to be published months or a year after being compiled. We are also able to include a greater range of real-world examples because of the information at company Web sites.

Will this help you, the reader? You bet. Our philosophy has always been to make *Retail Management* as reader-friendly, up-to-date, and useful as possible. In addition, we want you to benefit from our experiences, in this case, our E-xperiences.

E-XCITING E-FEATURES

To reflect these E-xciting times, *Retail Management: A Strategic Approach*, Twelfth Edition, incorporates a host of E-features throughout the book—and at our wide-ranging, interactive Web site (www.pearsonhighered.com/bermanevans) and at our new blog (www.bermanevansretail.com).

The Twelfth Edition has a very strong integration of the book with this Web site:

- A special section of our Web site is devoted to each chapter.
- In each chapter, there are multiple references to Web links regarding particular topics (such as free online sources of secondary data).
- Every chapter has a number of margin notes that refer to company Web sites.
- Every chapter concludes with a short online exercise.
- At our Web site, for each chapter, there are chapter objectives, a chapter overview, a listing of key terms, interactive study guide questions, links to relevant Web sites, and more.
- Our Web site contains extra math exercises for Chapters 9, 12, 16, and 17.
- Our Web site includes in-depth exercises that apply key course concepts through free company downloads and demonstrations. There are several for each part of the book.
- The Web site even includes hints for solving cases, a listing of key online secondary data sources, and descriptions of retail job opportunities and career ladders.
- With regard to in-text content, each chapter includes important practical applications of the Web within the context of that chapter.

Our new blog includes many features that are intended to enrich your understanding and appreciation of retailing. The blog includes such topics as current events in retailing, examples of good and bad retailing practices, career information, social media and retailing, and much more. Check us out at (www.bermanevansretail.com).

But, that's not all! *Retail Management*, Twelfth Edition, is packed with other E-features:

- The interactive online study guide provides correct answers and text page references for more than 50 questions per chapter—about 1,100 in all!
- Our Web site (www.pearsonhighered.com/bermanevans) also includes:
  - More than 1,000 links.
  - A full glossary.
  - A lot of career material, including a directory of hundreds of retailers and their online addresses. We have links directly to the career sections of leading retailers.
  - A list of popular search engines.
  - A list of free online secondary data sources.
  - Hints on how to solve a case study.
  - Interactive computer exercises tied into the text.
  - An interactive strategic planning template that places the retail planning process into a series of steps that are integrated with Figure 3-1 in the book.
  - A list of major trade associations—with links to their Web sites.
  - Information from the Federal Trade Commission (useful for consumers and potential franchisees) and the Small Business Administration (useful for entrepreneurs).
- A number of "Technology in Retailing" boxes cover E-applications.
- Many cases have E-components.
- At the Web site (www.pearsonhighered.com/bermanevans):
  - The section entitled "Retail Careers" has four basic categories.
    - *General Information.* We discuss the career preparation process in terms of these steps: assessing yourself, acquiring job leads, writing a résumé and cover letter, and doing well with the personal interview and post-interview activities.
    - *Internships.* In planning a career, a well-balanced approach during college is often the key to long-run success. What does this mean? A person should take his or her college education seriously, participate in co-curricular and extracurricular activities, and begin to acquire meaningful work experience.
    - *Job Hunting Guide.* The job-hunting process consists of several steps, which are discussed in detail: collecting information, applying for a job, job-search methods, evaluating a job offer, and becoming familiar with job-hunt-related search engines.
    - *Types of Retail Jobs.* We provide in-depth information on these retail jobs: buyers and merchandise managers, customer service representatives, restaurant and food service managers, retail managers, retail sales workers, and travel agents. We also cite numerous other positions in retailing, present several flow charts demonstrating career path growth, and offer links to retailers' career sites.
  - Web addresses are provided for hundreds of U.S. and foreign retailers as well as more than 50 professional and trade associations.

CAREERS! CAREERS! CAREERS!

We recognize that many of you may be contemplating a career in retailing/retail management. We have a great deal of material that should help you decide whether such a career is for you, learn more about the broad range of careers in retailing, and obtain contact information about potential employers. Here are the major career-oriented features of *Retail Management: A Strategic Approach* and our Web site and blog:

- Our strategic approach to the field of retail management enables you to learn about the key concepts that should be grasped by anyone who wants to pursue a professional career in retailing/retail management.
- Each chapter has a "Careers in Retailing" box that traces the career path of real people in such areas as store management, operations, merchandising, information technology, human resource management, online retailing, loss prevention, finance, logistics, and advertising. The information in these boxes is from the National Retail Federation, the leading association in retailing.
- Chapter 11 covers retail organizations and human resource management.

- The appendix presents an overview of career opportunities, complete with salary ranges for a variety of jobs in retailing.
- The blog has a regular stream of current information on careers in retailing.

CONCLUDING REMARKS

We consider ourselves to be as reader-friendly as possible. Please feel free to send us feedback regarding any aspect of *Retail Management* or its package. We promise to reply to any correspondence.

Sincerely,

Professor Barry Berman (E-mail at **barry.berman@hofstra.edu**),
Zarb School of Business, Hofstra University, Hempstead, NY 11549

Professor Joel R. Evans (E-mail at **joel.r.evans@hofstra.edu**),
Zarb School of Business, Hofstra University, Hempstead, NY, 11549

About the Authors

Barry Berman

Joel R. Evans

Barry Berman (Ph.D. in Business with majors in Marketing and Behavioral Science) is the Walter H. "Bud" Miller Distinguished Professor of Business and Professor of Marketing and International Business in the Zarb School of Business at Hofstra University. He is also the director of Hofstra's Executive MBA program. **Joel R. Evans** (Ph.D. in Business with majors in Marketing and Public Policy) is the RMI Distinguished Professor of Business and Professor of Marketing and International Business in the Zarb School of Business at Hofstra University. He is also the coordinator for Hofstra's Master of Science programs in Marketing and Marketing Research. The Zarb School of Business at Hofstra University is fully accredited by AACSB International.

While at Hofstra, each has been honored as a faculty inductee in Beta Gamma Sigma honor society, has received multiple Dean's Awards for service, and has been selected as the Teacher of the Year by the Hofstra MBA Association. For several years, Drs. Berman and Evans were co-directors of Hofstra's Retail Management Institute and Business Research Institute. Both regularly teach undergraduate and graduate courses to a wide range of students.

Barry Berman and Joel R. Evans have worked together in co-authoring several best-selling texts, including *Retail Management: A Strategic Approach*, Twelfth Edition. They have also consulted for a variety of clients, from "mom-and-pop" retailers to *Fortune* 500 companies. They were co-founders of the American Marketing Association's Special Interest Group in Retailing and Retail Management. They co-chaired the Academy of Marketing Science/American Collegiate Retailing Association's triennial conference several times and edited the conference proceedings. They have been featured speakers at the annual meeting of the National Retail Federation, the world's largest retailing trade association. Barry has served as president of the American Collegiate Retailing Association.

Barry and Joel are both active Web practitioners (and surfers), and they have written and developed all of the content for the comprehensive Web site that accompanies *Retail Management* (www.pearsonhighered.com/bermanevans) and a new blog on all things retailing (www.bermanevansretail.com). They may be reached through the Web site, the blog, or E-mail: **barry.berman@hofstra.edu** and **joel.r.evans@hofstra.edu**.

Acknowledgments

Many people have assisted us in the preparation of this book, and to them we extend our warmest appreciation.

We thank the following reviewers, who have reacted to this or earlier editions of the text. Each has provided us with perceptive comments that have helped us to crystallize our thoughts and to make *Retail Management* the best book possible:

M. Wayne Alexander, Morehead State University
Larry Audler, University of New Orleans
Ramon Avila, Ball State University
Betty V. Balevic, Skidmore College
Stephen Batory, Bloomsburg University
Leta Beard, University of Washington
Joseph J. Belonax, Western Michigan University
Ronald Bernard, Diablo Valley College
Charles D. Bodkin, University of North Carolina at Charlotte
Charlane Bomrad, Onondaga Community College
John J. Buckley, Orange County Community College
David J. Burns, Youngstown State University
David A. Campbell, Southern Illinois University
John W. Carpenter, Lake Land College
Joseph A. Davidson, Cuyahoga Community College
Peter T. Doukas, Westchester Community College
Blake Escudier, San Jose State University
Jack D. Eure, Jr., Southwest Texas State University
Phyllis Fein, Westchester Community College
Letty Fisher, Westchester Community College
Myron Gable, Shippensburg University
Linda L. Golden, University of Texas at Austin
James Gray, Florida Atlantic University
Barbara Gross, California State University–Northridge
J. Duncan Herrington, Radford University
Mary Higby, University of Detroit, Mercy
Terence L. Holmes, Murray State University
Charles A. Ingene, University of Mississippi
Marvin A. Jolson, University of Maryland
David C. Jones, Otterbein College
Marilyn Jones, Bond University
Carol Kaufman-Scarborough, Rutgers University
Ruth Keyes, SUNY College of Technology
Maryon King, Southern Illinois University
Stephen Kirk, East Carolina University
John Lanasa, Duquesne University
Dana Lanham, University of North Carolina at Charlotte
J. Ford Laumer, Jr., Auburn University
Marilyn Lavin, University of Wisconsin–Whitewater
Dennis G. Lee, Southwest Georgia Technical College
Richard C. Leventhal, Metropolitan State College
Michael Little, Virginia Commonwealth University
John Lloyd, Monroe Community College
Ann Lucht, Milwaukee Area Technical College
Robert Lupton, Central Washington University
Vincent Magnini, Longwood University
James O. McCann, Henry Ford Community College
Frank McDaniels, Delaware County Community College
Sanjay S. Mehta, Sam Houston State University
Ronald Michman, Shippensburg University
Jihye Park, Iowa State University
Howard C. Paul, Mercyhurst College
Roy B. Payne, Purdue University
Susan Peters, California State Polytechnic University, Pomona
Dawn I. Pysarchik, Michigan State University
Julian Redfearn, Kilgore College
Curtis Reierson, Baylor University
Barry Rudin, Loras College
Julie Toner Schrader, North Dakota State University
Steven J. Shaw, University of South Carolina
Ruth K. Shelton, James Madison University
Gladys S. Sherdell, Bellarmine College

Jill F. Slomski, Gannon University
Randy Stuart, Kennesaw State University
John E. Swan, University of Alabama, Birmingham
Ruth Taylor, Texas State University–San Marcos
Lisa Taylor Weaver, Las Positas College
Moira Tolan, Mount Saint Mary College
Anthony Urbanisk, Northern State University
Anu Venkateswaran, Wilberforce University
Lillian Werner, University of Minnesota
Kaylene C. Williams, California State University, Stanislaus
Mathew C. Williams, Clover Park Technical College
Terrell G. Williams, Western Washington State University
Yingjiao Xu, Ohio University
Ugur Yucelt, Pennsylvania State University, Harrisburg

Special recognition is due to Trefis.com, *Chain Store Age*, *Progressive Grocer*, Platt Retail Institute, and Retail Image Consulting for their cooperation and assistance in providing case studies and photos for this edition. We also appreciate the efforts of our Pearson colleagues who have worked diligently on this edition: Kierra Bloom, Erin Gardner, and Becca Richter Groves. As always, thank you to Diane Schoenberg for the editorial assistance. And thanks to Christopher DeVivo and Brian Bluver.

Barry Berman
Joel R. Evans
Hofstra University

Retail Management

PART 1

An Overview of Strategic Retail Management

Welcome to *Retail Management: A Strategic Approach*, 12e. We hope you find this book to be informative, timely, action-oriented, and reader-friendly. Please visit our Web site (www.pearsonhighered.com/bermanevans) and our new blog (www.bermanevansretail.com) for interactive, useful, up-to-date features that complement the text—including chapter hot links, a study guide, and much more!

In Part One, we explore the field of retailing, establishing and maintaining relationships, and the basic principles of strategic planning and the decisions made in owning or managing a retail business.

Chapter 1 describes retailing, shows why it should be studied, and examines its special characteristics. We note the value of strategic planning, including a detailed review of Target Corporation (a titan of retailing). The retailing concept is presented, along with the total retail experience, customer service, and relationship retailing. The focus and format of the text are detailed.

Chapter 2 looks at the complexities of retailers' relationships—with both customers and other channel members. We examine value and the value chain, customer relationships and channel relationships, the differences in relationship building between goods and service retailers, the impact of technology on retailing relationships, and the interplay between ethical performance and relationships in retailing. The chapter ends with an appendix on planning for the unique aspects of service retailing.

Chapter 3 shows the usefulness of strategic planning for all kinds of retailers. We focus on the planning process: situation analysis, objectives, identifying consumers, overall strategy, specific activities, control, and feedback. We also look at the controllable and uncontrollable parts of a retail strategy. Strategic planning is shown as a series of interrelated steps that are continuously reviewed. A detailed computerized strategic planning template, available at our Web site, is described. At the end of the chapter, there is an appendix on the strategic implications of global retailing.

Source: Winthrop Brookhouse/Shutterstock.com. Reprinted by permission.

An Introduction to Retailing

Chapter Objectives

1. To define retailing, consider it from various perspectives, demonstrate its impact, and note its special characteristics

2. To introduce the concept of strategic planning and apply it

3. To show why the retailing concept is the foundation of a successful business, with an emphasis on the total retail experience, customer service, and relationship retailing

4. To indicate the focus and format of the text

Today, social media affect the business and social lives of more and more of us. Facebook alone is approaching one billion (yes, billion) users around the world. When we use the term "social media" in this book, we are referring to "the various online technology tools that enable people to communicate easily via the Internet and mobile devices to share information and resources. Social media can include text, audio, video, images, podcasts, and other multimedia communications."

Accordingly, in *Retail Management: A Strategic Approach*, we begin each chapter with a discussion of social media relevant to the retailing topics in that chapter. At www.bermanevansretail.com, we've set up a dynamic retailing blog with all sorts of interesting and current information—retailer links, career opportunities, news about the retail industry and individual retailers, and more. Check it out!!

Many different kinds of retailers, both large and small—from Aéropostale to Jiffy Lube to 7-Eleven to Zara—are actively involved with social media to communicate with customers, reinforce their images, introduce new locations and merchandise, sell products, run special promotions, and so much more.

According to Barbara Farfan of About.com: Retail Industry (www.retailindustry.about.com), being successful with social media in retailing requires that companies connect properly with those consumers who want a meaningful relationship and "not a pickup line." This means that retailers must interact in a way that is valued by consumers over a long time period. Thus, if a given retailer is unwilling to do that, it is doing a very poor job with social media. As Farfan notes: "Saying that marketing efforts in social spaces don't immediately result in sales is like saying that your U.S. blow dryer doesn't work when you plug it into the electrical outlet in Bali. Duh. It won't work because they're not wired the same. (Trust me, I saw the flames. It won't work.)"[1]

Source: BeTA-Artworks/fotolia.com.

Overview

Retailing encompasses the business activities involved in selling goods and services to consumers for their personal, family, or household use. It includes every sale to the *final* consumer—ranging from cars to apparel to meals at restaurants to movie tickets. Retailing is the last stage in the distribution process.

Retailing today is at a complex crossroads. On the one hand, retail sales are at their highest point in history (despite a dip during the recent "Great Recession"). Wal-Mart is the leading company in the world in terms of sales—ahead of ExxonMobil, Toyota, and other manufacturing giants. New technologies are improving retail productivity. There are lots of opportunities to start a new retail business—or work for an existing one—and to become a franchisee. Global retailing possibilities abound. On the other hand, retailers face numerous challenges. The weak economy in recent years has had a major impact on retailers, their suppliers, and consumers around the world. Many consumers are bored with shopping or do not have much time for it. Some locales have too many stores, and retailers often spur one another into frequent price cutting (and low profit margins). Customer service expectations are high at a time when more retailers offer self-service and automated systems. Some retailers remain unsure what to do with the Web; they are still grappling with the emphasis to place on image enhancement, customer information and feedback, and sales transactions. And the emerging influence of social media has been hard for many retailers to adapt to in their strategies.

These are among the key issues that retailers must resolve:

"How can we best serve our customers while earning a fair profit?"

"How can we stand out in a highly competitive environment where consumers have so many choices?"

"How can we grow our business while retaining a core of loyal customers?"

Our point of view: Retail decision makers can best address these questions by fully understanding and applying the basic principles of retailing in a well-structured, systematic, and focused retail strategy. That is the philosophy behind *Retail Management: A Strategic Approach*.

Visit Amazon.com's Web site (www.amazon.com) and see what drives one of the world's "hot" retailers.

Can retailers flourish in today's tough marketplace? You bet! Just look at your favorite restaurant, gift shop, and food store. Look at the popularity of Costco, Subway, and Amazon.com. What do they have in common? A desire to please the customer and a strong market niche. To prosper in the long term, they all need a strategic plan and a willingness to adapt, both central thrusts of this book. See Figure 1-1.

FIGURE 1-1
Boom Times for Subway

The Subway fast-food chain has been doing well around the world, largely because of its low-fat, inexpensive hero sandwiches. This Paris unit is only one of the more than 36,000 Subway stores that are located in about 100 different countries.

Source: Tupungato/Shutterstock.com. Reprinted by permission.

In Chapter 1, we look at the framework of retailing, the value of developing and applying a sound retail strategy, and the focus and format of the text. A special appendix at the end of this chapter looks at the impact of the recent economic downturn on retailers in the United States and around the world.

THE FRAMEWORK OF RETAILING

To appreciate retailing's role and the range of retailing activities, let's view it from three perspectives:

- Suppose we manage a manufacturing firm that makes cosmetics. How should we sell these items? We could distribute via big chains such as Sephora or small neighborhood stores, have our own sales force visit people in their homes as Mary Kay does, or set up our own stores (if we have the ability and resources to do so). We could sponsor TV infomercials or magazine ads, complete with a toll-free phone number.
- Suppose we have an idea for a new way to teach first graders how to use computer software for spelling and vocabulary. How should we implement this idea? We could lease a store in a strip shopping center and run ads in a local paper, rent space in a local YMCA and rely on teacher referrals, or do mailings to parents and visit children in their homes. In each case, the service is offered "live." But there is another option: We could use an animated Web site to teach children online.
- Suppose that we, as consumers, want to buy apparel. What choices do we have? We could go to a department store or an apparel store. We could shop with a full-service retailer or a discounter. We could go to a shopping center or order from a catalog. We could look to retailers that carry a wide range of clothing (from outerwear to jeans to suits) or look to firms that specialize in one clothing category (such as leather coats). We could surf around the Web and visit retailers around the globe. We could also stop by Facebook and see what other consumers are saying about various retailers.

Service businesses such as Jiffy Lube (www.jiffylube.com) are engaged in retailing.

There is a tendency to think of retailing as primarily involving the sale of tangible (physical) goods. However, retailing also includes the sale of services. And this is a big part of retailing! A service may be the shopper's primary purchase (such as a haircut) or it may be part of the shopper's purchase of a good (such as furniture delivery). Retailing does not have to involve a store. Mail and phone orders, direct selling to consumers in their homes and offices, Web transactions, and vending machine sales all fall within the scope of retailing. Retailing does not even have to include a "retailer." Manufacturers, importers, nonprofit firms, and wholesalers act as retailers when they sell to final consumers.

Let's now examine various reasons for studying retailing and its special characteristics.

Reasons for Studying Retailing

Learn more about the exciting array of retailing career opportunities (www.allretailjobs.com).

Retailing is an important field to study because of its impact on the economy, its functions in distribution, and its relationship with firms selling goods and services to retailers for their resale or use. These factors are discussed next. A fourth factor for students of retailing is the broad range of career opportunities, as highlighted with a "Careers in Retailing" box in each chapter, Appendix A at the end of this book, our Web site (www.pearsonhighered.com/bermanevans), and our blog (www.bermanevansretail.com). See Figure 1-2.

THE IMPACT OF RETAILING ON THE ECONOMY Retailing is a major part of U.S. and world commerce. Retail sales and employment are vital economic contributors, and retail trends often mirror trends in a nation's overall economy.

According to the Department of Commerce, annual U.S. retail store sales are nearly $5 trillion—representing one-third of the total economy. Telephone and mail-order sales by nonstore retailers, vending machines, direct selling, and the Web generate hundreds of billions of dollars in additional yearly revenues. And personal consumption expenditures on financial, medical, legal, educational, and other services account for another several hundred billion dollars in annual retail revenues. Outside the United States, retail sales are several trillions of dollars per year.

Durable goods stores—including motor vehicles and parts dealers; furniture, home furnishings, electronics and appliance stores; and building materials and hardware stores—make up 30 percent of U.S. retail store sales. Nondurable goods and services stores—including general merchandise stores; food and beverage stores; health- and personal-care stores; gasoline stations; clothing and

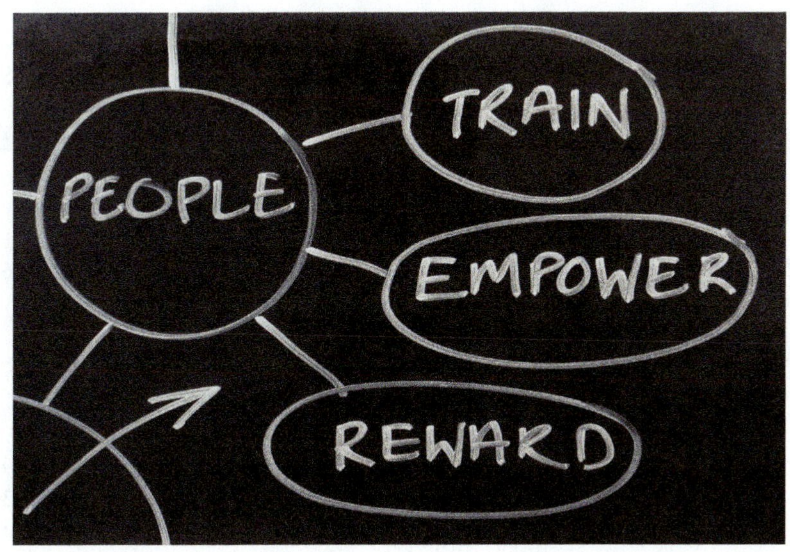

FIGURE 1-2

Encouraging People to Consider a Career in Retailing

To attract and retain high-quality, motivated workers, retailers should properly train them, empower them to be responsive to reasonable requests that may "break the rules" (without always having to ask the boss), and reward—and visibly recognize—superior performance. A key aspect of a meaningful reward system is an employee's opportunities for upward mobility in terms of a better job and a bigger paycheck (promoting from within).

Source: Thinglass/ Shutterstock.com. Reprinted by permission.

accessories stores; sporting goods, hobby, book, and music stores; eating and drinking places; and miscellaneous retailers—together account for 70 percent of U.S. retail store sales.

The world's 250 largest retailers generate more than $4 trillion in annual revenues. They represent 33 nations. Eighty-four of the largest 250 retailers are based in the United States, 32 in Japan, 19 in Germany, 15 in Great Britain, and 13 in France.[2] Table 1-1 shows the 10 largest U.S.-based retailers. In 2010, their U.S. sales exceeded $810 billion. During 2011, they operated over 34,000 U.S. stores with three million employees. Visit our Web site (www.pearsonhighered.com/bermanevans) and our blog (www.bermanevansretail.com) for links to a lot of current information on retailing.

The *Occupational Outlook Handbook* (www.bls.gov/oco) is a great source of information on employment trends.

Retailing is a major source of jobs. In the United States alone, 25 million people—about one-sixth of the total labor force—work for traditional retailers (including food and beverage service firms, such as restaurants). Yet this figure understates the true number of people who work in retailing because it does not include the several million persons employed by other service firms, seasonal employees, proprietors, and unreported workers in family businesses or partnerships.

CAREERS IN RETAILING

Carving Out a Career in Retailing

Retailing offers a number of exciting career opportunities in such diverse areas as store management, sales, human resources, supply chain management, merchandise buying and planning, and loss prevention. Let's look at some of these options.

Store management: These positions involve departmental or total store responsibility for the opening and closing of stores, store staffing, and meeting financial objectives.

Sales: Sales personnel range from basic sales positions where personnel receive little training to areas where extensive product knowledge is required (like jewelry, major appliances, and computers).

Human resources: Human resource managers recruit, train, and motivate retail employees at all levels in the firm. Retail staffing needs may be heavily seasonal.

Supply chain management: Personnel in this area often manage a firm's distribution centers, trucking operations, as well as monitor the shipment of imported goods. Some retailers outsource some supply chain management responsibilities to vendors and specialists.

Merchandise buying and planning: These managers arrange for the purchase of national brands as well as private-label goods. Vendor appraisal, negotiation skills, and a strong understanding of fashion trends and seasonality are key.

Loss prevention: These specialists concentrate on minimizing losses due to theft by consumers and employees, vendor fraud, and paperwork errors (such as failing to record markdowns).

Source: "Retail Career Areas," NRF Foundation www.nrffoundation.com/content/retail-career-areas (March 3, 2012).

TABLE 1-1 The 10 Largest Retailers Based in the United States

Rank	Company	Web Address	Major Retail Emphasis	2010 U.S. Sales (millions)	2011 Number of U.S. Stores	2011 Number of U.S Employees
1	Wal-Mart	www.walmart.com	Full-line discount stores, supercenters, membership clubs	$307,736	4,360	1,400,000
2	Kroger	www.kroger.com	Supermarkets, convenience stores, jewelry stores	78,326	4,100	320,000+
3	Target	www.target.com	Full-line discount stores, supercenters	65,815	1,760	355,000
4	Walgreens	www.walgreens.com	Drugstores	61,240	7,800	244,000
5	Home Depot	www.homedepot.com	Home centers	60,194	1,975	300,000+
6	Costco	www.costco.com	Membership clubs	58,983	435	108,000
7	CVS Caremark	www.cvscaremark.com	Drugstores	57,464	7,200	200,000
8	Lowe's	www.lowes.com	Home centers	48,175	1,725	230,000
9	Best Buy	www.bestbuy.com	Consumer electronics stores	37,110	1,320	165,000
10	Sears Holdings	www.sears.com	Department stores, specialty stores	35,362	3,500	275,000

Sources: "2011 Top 100 Retailers," www.stores.org/2011/Top-100-Retailers; and company reports.

From a cost perspective, retailing is a significant field of study. In the United States, on average, 33 cents of every dollar spent in department stores, 45 cents spent in furniture and home furnishings stores, and 28 cents spent in grocery stores go to the retailers to cover operating costs, activities performed, and profits. Costs include rent, displays, wages, ads, and maintenance. Only a small part of each dollar is profit. In 2010, the 10 largest U.S. retailers' after-tax profits averaged 3.5 percent of sales.[3] Figure 1-3 shows costs and profits for Walgreens, a drugstore chain.

RETAIL FUNCTIONS IN DISTRIBUTION Retailing is the last stage in a **channel of distribution**—all of the businesses and people involved in the physical movement and transfer of ownership of goods and services from producer to consumer. A typical distribution channel is shown in Figure 1-4. Retailers often act as the contact between manufacturers, wholesalers, and the consumer. Many manufacturers would like to make one basic type of item and sell their entire inventory to as

FIGURE 1-3
The High Costs and Low Profits of Retailing—Where the Typical $100 Spent with Walgreens Goes

Source: Computed by the authors from *Walgreens 2011 Annual Report.*

FIGURE 1-4
A Typical Channel of Distribution

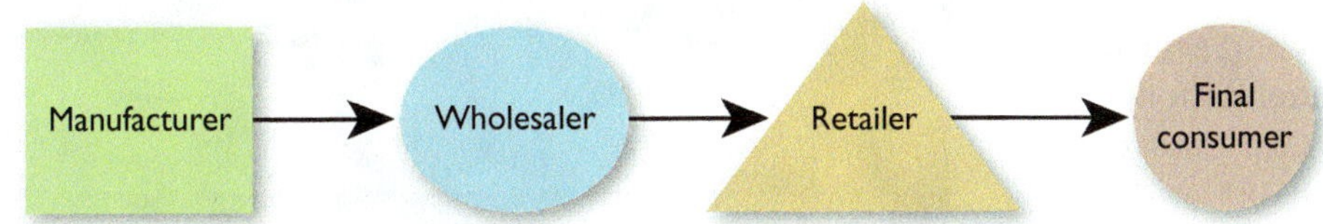

few buyers as possible, but consumers usually want to choose from a variety of goods and services and purchase a limited quantity. Retailers collect an assortment from various sources, buy in large quantity, and sell in small amounts. This is the **sorting process**. See Figure 1-5.

Another job for retailers is communicating both with customers and with manufacturers and wholesalers. Shoppers learn about the availability and characteristics of goods and services, store hours, sales, and so on from retailer ads, salespeople, and displays. Manufacturers and wholesalers are informed by their retailers with regard to sales forecasts, delivery delays, customer complaints, defective items, inventory turnover, and more. Many goods and services have been modified due to retailer feedback.

For small suppliers, retailers can provide assistance by transporting, storing, marking, advertising, and pre-paying for products. Small retailers may need the same type of help from their suppliers. The tasks performed by retailers affect the percentage of each sales dollar they need to cover costs and profits.

Retailers also complete transactions with customers. This means having convenient locations, filling orders promptly and accurately, and processing credit purchases. Some retailers also provide customer services such as gift wrapping, delivery, and installation. To make themselves even more appealing, many firms now engage in **multi-channel retailing**, whereby a retailer sells to consumers through multiple retail formats (points of contact). Most large retailers operate both physical stores and Web sites to make shopping easier and to accommodate consumer desires. Some firms even sell to customers through retail stores, mail order, a Web site, and a toll-free phone number. See Figure 1-6.

Sherwin-Williams (www.sherwin-williams.com) is not only a manufacturer but also a retailer.

For these reasons, products are usually sold through retailers not owned by manufacturers (wholesalers). This lets the manufacturers reach more customers, reduce costs, improve cash flow, increase sales more rapidly, and focus on their area of expertise. Select manufacturers such as Sherwin-Williams and Polo Ralph Lauren do operate retail facilities (besides selling at

FIGURE 1-5
The Retailer's Role in the Sorting Process

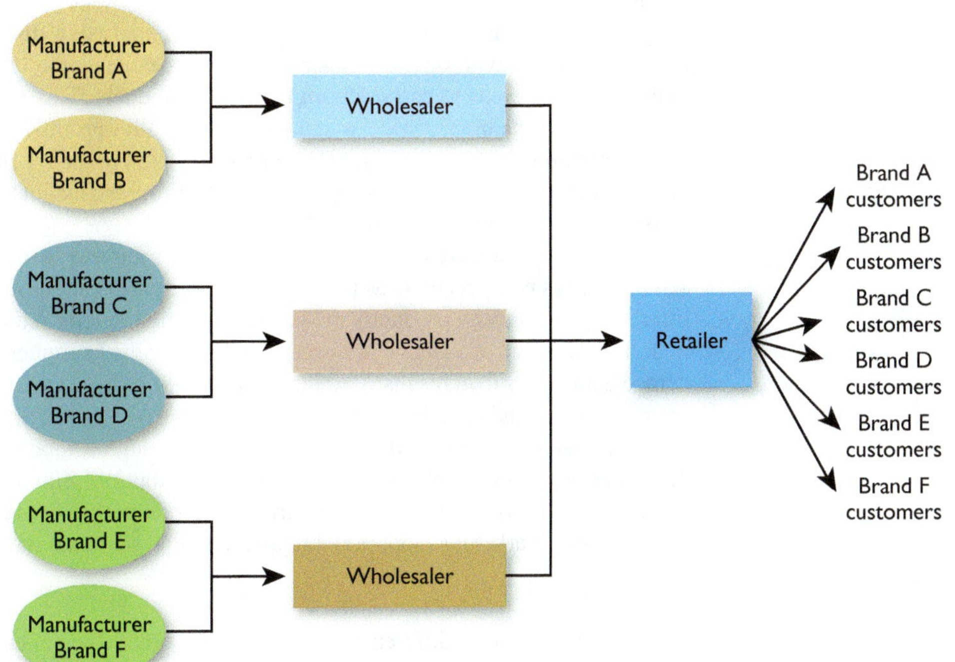

FIGURE 1-6

Apple and Multi-Channel Retailing

Apple Corporation sells its products at company-owned stores, such as the London shop shown here, at leading retailers such as Best Buy, and at its Web site (www.apple.com). The firm also has an easy-to-remember toll-free phone number—1-800-MY-APPLE.

Source: 1000 Words/Shutterstock.com. Reprinted by permission.

traditional retailers). In running their stores, these firms complete the full range of retailing functions and compete with conventional retailers.

THE RELATIONSHIPS AMONG RETAILERS AND THEIR SUPPLIERS Relationships among retailers and suppliers can be complex. Because retailers are part of a distribution channel, manufacturers and wholesalers must be concerned about the caliber of displays, customer service, store hours, and retailers' reliability as business partners. Retailers are also major customers of goods and services for resale, store fixtures, computers, management consulting, and insurance.

These are some issues over which retailers and their suppliers have different priorities: control over the distribution channel, profit allocation, the number of competing retailers handling suppliers' products, product displays, promotion support, payment terms, and operating flexibility. Due to the growth of large chains, retailers have more power than ever. Unless suppliers know retailer needs, they cannot have good rapport with them; as long as retailers have a choice of suppliers, they will pick those offering more.

Channel relations tend to be smoothest with **exclusive distribution**, whereby suppliers make agreements with one or a few retailers that designate the latter as the only ones in specified geographic areas to carry certain brands or products. This stimulates both parties to work together to maintain an image, assign shelf space, allot profits and costs, and advertise. It also usually requires that retailers limit their brand selection in the specified product lines; they might have to decline to handle other suppliers' brands. From the manufacturers' perspective, exclusive distribution may limit their long-run total sales.

Channel relations tend to be most volatile with **intensive distribution**, whereby suppliers sell through as many retailers as possible. This often maximizes suppliers' sales and lets retailers offer many brands and product versions. Competition among retailers selling the same items is high; retailers may use tactics not beneficial to individual suppliers, because they are more concerned about their own results. Retailers may assign little space to specific brands, set very high prices on them, and not advertise them.

With **selective distribution**, suppliers sell through a moderate number of retailers. This combines aspects of exclusive and intensive distribution. Suppliers have higher sales than in exclusive distribution, and retailers carry some competing brands. It encourages suppliers to provide some marketing support and retailers to give adequate shelf space. See Figure 1-7.

The Special Characteristics of Retailing

Three factors that most differentiate retailing from other types of business are noted in Figure 1-8 and discussed here. Each factor imposes unique requirements on retail firms.

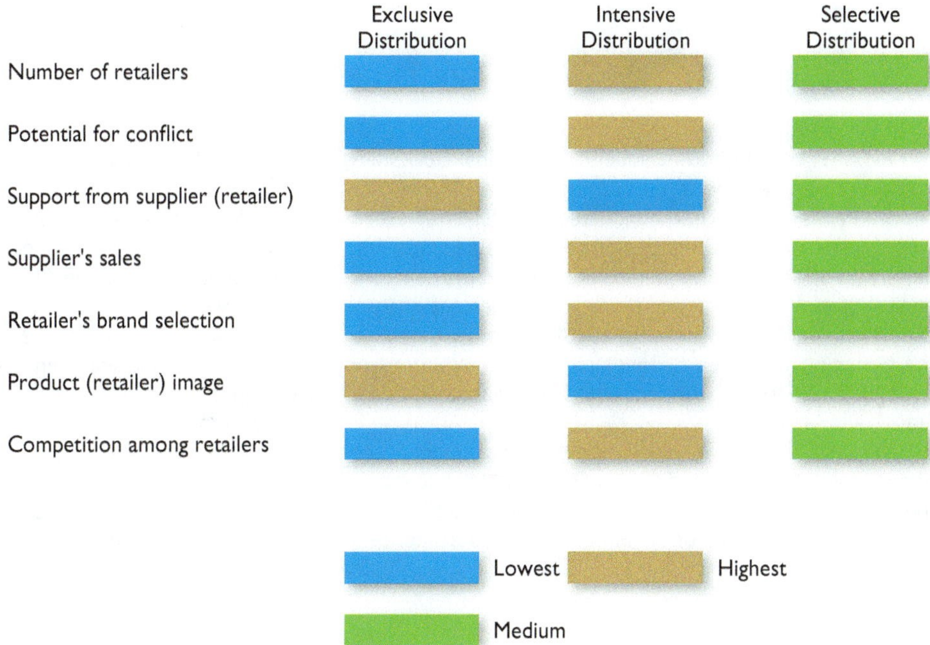

FIGURE 1-7
Comparing Exclusive, Intensive, and Selective Distribution

The average amount of a sales transaction for retailers is much less than for manufacturers. The average sales transaction per shopping trip is well under $100 for department stores, specialty stores, and supermarkets. This low amount creates a need to tightly control the costs associated with each transaction (such as credit verification, sales personnel, and bagging); to maximize the number of customers drawn to the retailer, which may place more emphasis on ads and special promotions; and to increase impulse sales by more aggressive selling. However, cost control can be tough. For instance, inventory management is often expensive due to the many small transactions to a large number of customers. A typical supermarket has several thousand customer transactions *per week*, which makes it harder to find the proper in-stock level and product selection. Thus, retailers are expanding their use of computerized inventory systems.

Final consumers make many unplanned or impulse purchases. Surveys show that a large percentage of consumers do not look at ads before shopping, do not prepare shopping lists (or do deviate from the lists) once in stores, and make fully unplanned purchases. This behavior indicates the value of in-store displays, attractive store layouts, and well-organized stores, catalogs, and Web sites. Candy, cosmetics, snack foods, magazines, and other items are sold as impulse goods when placed in visible, high-traffic areas in a store, catalog, or Web site. Because so many purchases are unplanned, the retailer's ability to forecast, budget, order merchandise, and have sufficient personnel on the selling floor is more difficult.

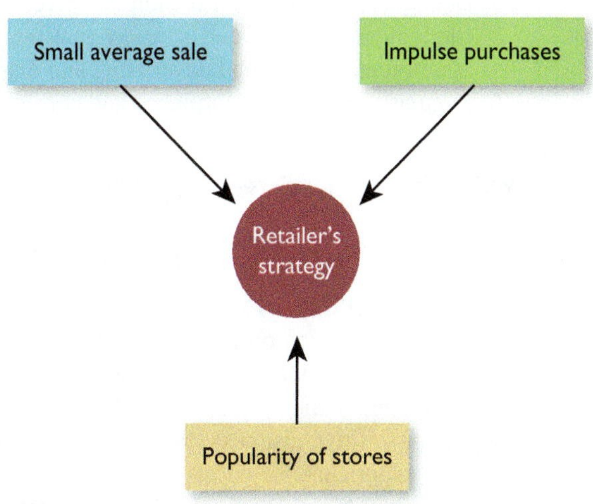

FIGURE 1-8
Special Characteristics Affecting Retailers

Countries That Chief Executive Officers (CEOs) Are Targeting for Retail Growth

As part of PricewaterhouseCoopers' 14th Global CEO study, 1,201 business leaders in 69 countries were surveyed. In-depth interviews were also conducted with 31 chief executive officers (CEOs). Ninety percent of the retail CEOs who participated in the survey were optimistic about their companies' growth prospects for 2011, and 93 percent of these executives were also optimistic about growth prospects in the following three years. Developed market countries on the retail CEOs top-growth lists include Germany, the United States, and France.

The International Monetary Fund predicted sluggish economic growth in developed economies for 2011. In contrast, the fund predicted that emerging markets such as China and India would experience better times. Increased affluence in China and India markets has created many opportunities in these markets.

Ninety-three percent of retail executives stated that they would expand their Asian operations in 2011. Although many firms began operating in China just for sourcing goods, China has now received increased attention as a marketplace for retail operations. Currently only single-brand foreign retailers are allowed to have a significant presence in India. Legislation that is proposed in India will allow foreign big-box store retailers to own up to 49 percent of a joint venture with a domestic Indian retailer as a partner.

Source: PricewaterhouseCoopers, "14th Annual Global CEO Survey," www.pwc.com/ceosurvey (2011).

Macy's (www.macys.com) has a Web site to accompany its traditional stores and catalogs.

Retail customers usually visit a store, even though mail, phone, and Web sales have increased. Despite the inroads made by nonstore retailers, most retail transactions are still conducted in stores—and will continue to be in the future. Many people like to shop in person; want to touch, smell, and/or try on products; like to browse for unplanned purchases; feel more comfortable taking a purchase home with them than waiting for a delivery; and desire privacy while at home. This store-based shopping orientation has implications for retailers; they must work to attract shoppers to stores and consider such factors as store location, transportation, store hours, proximity of competitors, product selection, parking, and ads.

THE IMPORTANCE OF DEVELOPING AND APPLYING A RETAIL STRATEGY

A **retail strategy** is the overall plan guiding a retail firm. It influences the firm's business activities and its response to market forces, such as competition and the economy. Any retailer, regardless of size or type, should utilize these six steps in strategic planning:

1. Define the type of business in terms of the goods or service category and the company's specific orientation (such as full service or "no frills").
2. Set long-run and short-run objectives for sales and profit, market share, image, and so on.
3. Determine the customer market to target on the basis of its characteristics (such as gender and income level) and needs (such as product and brand preferences).
4. Devise an overall, long-run plan that gives general direction to the firm and its employees.
5. Implement an integrated strategy that combines such factors as store location, product assortment, pricing, and advertising and displays to achieve objectives.
6. Regularly evaluate performance and correct weaknesses or problems when observed.

To illustrate these points, the background and strategy of Target Corporation—one of the world's foremost retailers—are presented. Then the retailing concept is explained and applied.

Target Corporation: The Winning Approach of an Upscale Discounter![4]

See the mass/class approach of Target Corporation (www.target.com).

COMPANY BACKGROUND Target Corporation describes itself as "an upscale discounter that provides high-quality, on-trend merchandise at attractive prices in clean, spacious, and guest-friendly stores. In addition, Target operates an online business, Target.com. The first Target store opened in 1962 in the Minneapolis suburb of Roseville, Minn., with a focus on convenient shopping at competitive discount prices. Today, Target remains committed to providing a one-stop shopping experience for guests by delivering differentiated merchandise and outstanding value with its Expect More. Pay Less.® brand promise."

Hoover's recent profile of Target reports that:

> The fashion-minded discounter operates Target and SuperTarget stores in 49 states, as well as an online business at Target.com. Target and its larger grocery-carrying incarnation, SuperTarget, have carved out a niche by offering more upscale, fashion-forward merchandise than rivals Wal-Mart and Kmart. Target also issues its proprietary Target credit card, good only at Target. After a reversal in fortune that coincided with the onset of the deep recession, Target is growing its grocery business, remodeling stores, and—in a few years—entering the Canadian market.

Today, Target Corporation has 1,760 stores with 355,000 employees. More than 250 of the stores are SuperTarget outlets, which are larger and carry more merchandise than typical Target stores. And the Target.com Web site is quite popular. The firm is the third largest U.S. retailer (in terms of revenues).

THE TARGET CORPORATION'S STRATEGY: KEYS TO SUCCESS Throughout its existence, Target has adhered to a consistent, far-sighted, customer-oriented strategy—one that has paved the way for its long-term achievements.

GROWTH-ORIENTED OBJECTIVES. "Our mission is to make Target the preferred shopping destination for our guests by delivering outstanding value, continuous innovation, and an exceptional guest experience by consistently fulfilling our Expect More. Pay Less. brand promise. To support our mission, we are guided by our commitments to great value, the community, diversity, and the environment."

APPEAL TO A PRIME MARKET. The firm is strong with middle-income, well-educated adults. The median age of customers is 40, the median annual household income is about $64,000, 43 percent have children at home, and 57 percent have completed college.

DISTINCTIVE COMPANY IMAGE. Target has done a superb job of positioning itself. See Figure 1-9. It is a discount department store chain with everyday low prices. It has linoleum floors, shopping carts, and a simple layout. But Target is also perceived as an upscale discounter: "Expect more of everything. More great design, more choices, and more designer-created items that you won't find anywhere else. And pay less. It's as simple as that." For 2012, Target reached an arrangement with the very popular young designer Jason Wu to carry "an affordable, limited-edition collection of women's apparel, handbags, and scarves."

FIGURE 1-9

"Expect More. Pay Less" at Target Stores

The Target bull's-eye logo represents the retailer's customer-focused strategy that combines a strong merchandise selection, popular brands, a guest-friendly shopping environment, and low prices—so, the image portrayed by the bull's-eye is right on target!

Source: SeanPavonePhoto/ Shutterstock.com. Reprinted by permission.

FOCUS. The chain never loses sight of its discount store niche: "In this increasingly competitive retail landscape, we strive to remain relevant to our guests by surprising and delighting them with a constant flow of affordable new merchandise, an evolving store design that meets their changing shopping needs, and a convenient array of goods and services that includes food, pharmacy, and Starbucks."

STRONG CUSTOMER SERVICE FOR ITS RETAIL CATEGORY. The firm prides itself on offering excellent customer service for a discount store: "We are committed to consistently delighting our guests. We strive to exceed their expectations, adding this and trying that to provide the perfect blend of style, substance, and oh-so-satisfying shopping."

MULTIPLE POINTS OF CONTACT. Target reaches its customers through extensive advertising, stores in 49 states, a toll-free telephone service center (open 7 days a week, 17 hours per day), a Web site, and the use of Facebook, Twitter, LinkedIn, MySpace, and other social media sites.

EMPLOYEE RELATIONS. Target calls its employees "team members" and says: "The pace is fast, the atmosphere is fun, and the people are friendly. Every team member—from stores to distribution centers to corporate offices—is empowered and encouraged to innovate, contribute ideas, and discover solutions. People at Target are respected and recognized for their work and know they are a unique and important part of a world-class team."

INNOVATION. Target often introduces clever, unique innovations. For example, "Innovative packaging helps differentiate our owned brands, including our popular resealable Archer Farms chip bag, featuring a zipper that helps chips stay fresher longer. Our new Archer Farms cereal box features rounded corners, larger graphics, and appealing images. An easy-to-peel seal and a hinged plastic cover ensure easy pouring and longer freshness. And, we're making it easier to entertain with Archer Farms appetizers that can all be cooked at the same temperature, helping alleviate the stress of preparing for a party."

COMMITMENT TO TECHNOLOGY. Target is devoted to new technologies: "We continue to invest in technology and infrastructure, including implementation of enhanced guest-service systems and construction of new perishable-food and general merchandise distribution centers and Target.com fulfillment centers."

COMMUNITY INVOLVEMENT. Target believes in giving back: "Community giving is and always has been a cornerstone of our company. Since 1946, Target has given 5 percent of our income—which today totals more than $3 million per week—to our communities. We listen, act and give locally, offering our individual time and talent in addition to our company resources."

CONSTANTLY MONITORING PERFORMANCE. "We strive for continuous improvement in everything we do. We are committed to efficient expense management with focused attention on both delivering results today and preparing for our future."

TARGET ADAPTS TO A DIFFICULT ECONOMY Due to the difficult economic conditions in recent years, even outstanding retailers such as Target have been affected. From 2007 through 2009, Target's sales growth and profit growth slowed considerably from 2006. Since then, Target's sales growth is better, but still affected by the weak economy. Target's sales per square foot are not expected to reach 2006 levels again until 2013, although they have been inching back up since 2010. This has put a strain on profit margins and net income.

Overall, Target's chief executive officer (CEO) is adapting to this environment by opening fewer stores and undertaking several other actions:

> To boost sales, it has been adding groceries to its product lineup at existing stores and giving 5 percent off on purchases made with a Target debit or credit card. To create a shopping experience guests can't find anywhere else, we remodeled 341 general merchandise stores in 2010, far more than any other year. These remodels added a broader grocery assortment, along with our latest merchandising innovations, including home, beauty, electronics, video games, and shoes. By 2011, we had 462 general merchandise locations with our expanded fresh food assortment, and we completed 380 remodels in 2011.

The Retailing Concept

As just described, Target has a sincere long-term desire to please customers. It uses a customer-centered, chainwide approach to strategy development and implementation, is value-driven, and has clear goals. Together, these four principles form the **retailing concept** (depicted in Figure 1-10), which should be understood and applied by all retailers:

1. *Customer orientation.* The retailer determines the attributes and needs of its customers and endeavors to satisfy these needs to the fullest.
2. *Coordinated effort.* The retailer integrates all plans and activities to maximize efficiency.
3. *Value driven.* The retailer offers good value to customers, whether it be upscale or discount. This means having prices appropriate for the level of products and customer service.
4. *Goal orientation.* The retailer sets goals and then uses its strategy to attain them.

Unfortunately, this concept is not grasped by every retailer. Some are indifferent to customer needs, plan haphazardly, have prices that do not reflect the value offered, and have unclear goals. Some are not receptive to change, or they blindly follow strategies enacted by competitors. Some do not get feedback from customers; they rely on supplier reports or their own past sales trends.

The retailing concept is straightforward. It means communicating with shoppers and viewing their desires as critical to the firm's success, having a consistent strategy (such as offering designer brands, plentiful sales personnel, attractive displays, and above-average prices in an upscale store); offering prices perceived as "fair" (a good value for the money) by customers; and working to achieve meaningful, specific, and reachable goals. However, the retailing concept is only a strategic guide. It does not deal with a firm's internal capabilities or competitive advantages but offers a broad planning framework.

Let's look at three issues that relate to a retailer's performance in terms of the retailing concept: the total retail experience, customer service, and relationship retailing.

THE TOTAL RETAIL EXPERIENCE One consumer may shop at a discounter, another at a neighborhood store, and a third at a full-service firm; yet, these diverse customers all have something crucial in common: They each encounter a total retail experience (including everything from parking to the checkout) in making a purchase. Consider:

> Today's merchants are well aware they can't afford to be perceived as a simple box of stuff sold by promotions, price cuts, and coupons. Value is everywhere; and the market is saturated with commodities. Consumers are shopping again, but in a different way. The dizzying choice between similar items offered by copycat promotions and like loyalty programs has diluted retail's options for competitive advantage. More than ever, shopping is about how it makes you feel, and the shift in consumer expectations is compelling retailers to look at aspects of "who" as opposed to "what" they want to be. Retailers with genuine character, definitive core values, and concern for community are likely to profit the most. The competition is now for share of life, as opposed to share of wallet.[5]

FIGURE 1-10
Applying the Retailing Concept

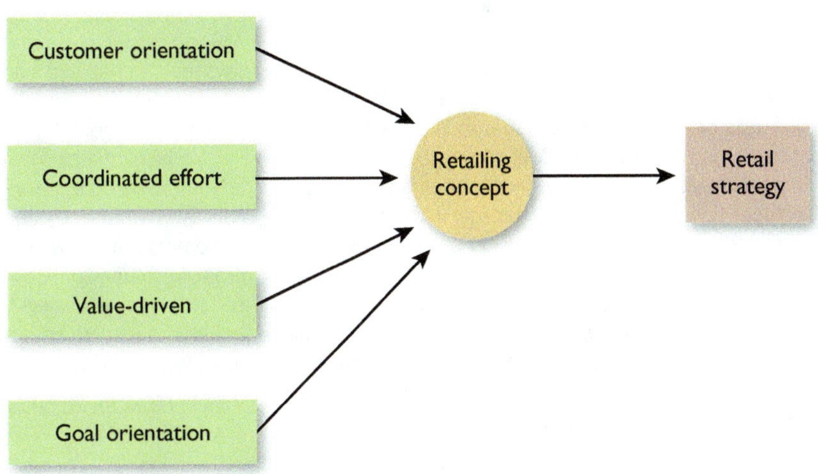

The **total retail experience** includes all the elements in a retail offering that encourage or inhibit consumers during their contact with a retailer. Many elements, such as the number of salespeople, displays, prices, the brands carried, and inventory on hand, are controllable by a retailer; others, such as the adequacy of on-street parking, the speed of a consumer's Internet connection, and sales taxes, are not. If some part of the total retail experience is unsatisfactory, consumers may not make a purchase—they may even decide not to patronize a retailer again. Retailers should strive not to "turn off" any customers: "Keeping stores neat and clean is not only easy to do; it is generally an inexpensive way to attract customers. Take a look around. Here are ten ways your store may be turning off shoppers: (1) dirty bathrooms; (2) messy dressing rooms; (3) loud music; (4) handwritten signs [that look unprofessional]; (5) stained floors or ceiling tiles; (6) burned-out or poor lighting; (7) offensive odors; (8) crowded aisles; (9) disorganized checkout counters; and (10) lack of shopping carts/baskets because there's not a single type of retailer that wouldn't need at least some sort of shopping basket."[6]

In planning its strategy, a retailer must be sure that all strategic elements are in place. For the shopper segment to which it appeals, the total retail experience must be aimed at fulfilling that segment's expectations. A discounter should have ample stock on hand when it runs sales but not plush carpeting; a full-service store should have superior personnel but not have them perceived as haughty by customers. Various retailers have not learned this lesson, which is why some theme restaurants are in trouble. The novelty has worn off, and many people believe the food is only fair while prices are high.

A big challenge for retailers is generating customer "excitement" because many people are bored with shopping or have little time for it. Here is what one retailer, highlighted in Figure 1-11, does:

Build-A-Bear Workshop (www.buildabear.com) even offers a great online shopping experience.

> Build-A-Bear Workshop is the leading and only global company that offers an interactive make-your-own stuffed animal retail-entertainment experience. The company currently operates more than 400 Build-A-Bear Workshop stores worldwide, including company-owned stores in the United States, Puerto Rico, Canada, Great Britain, and Ireland, and franchise stores in Europe, Asia, Australia, Africa, Mexico, and the Middle East. In 2007, the interactive experience was enhanced—all the way to CyBEAR® space—with the launch of Bearville.com (www.bearville.com), our entertainment destination and virtual world. Guests who visit a Build-A-Bear Workshop store enter a recognizable and distinctive teddy bear themed environment consisting of eight stuffed animal-making stations: Choose Me, Hear Me, Stuff Me, Stitch Me, Fluff Me, Dress Me, Name Me, and Take Me Home. Store associates, known as master Bear Builder associates, share the experience with Guests at each phase of the bear-making process. Regardless of age, Guests enjoy this special place where they create a memory with their friends and family.[7]

Nowhere to Hide

According to Kyle Scott, an author with an interest in ethics, "When times are hard, people may be willing to take bigger risks, with ethics often taking a back seat to the need to survive." Yet, despite the current weak economic climate, retailers should not behave unethically simply because it's easier than doing the "right thing" or because a manager is too motivated or self-interested to say "no" to a decision path you know is morally incorrect.

A major change in the ethical environment involves the transparency relating to business decisions arising from social media. As a result of social media, reports of unethical behavior can spread among consumers, the general public, shareholders, and regulatory authorities with lightning-like speed. Kyle Scott says that "social media and the unprecedented dissemination of information may indeed serve as the watchdog we need to curb ethical violations."

Social media blogs are becoming much more prominent as an ethical watchdog. For example, blogs reported that Amazon.com (www.amazon.com) was charging higher prices to loyal customers than new customers, that various retailers were not properly testing some of the statements on product labels, that certain new car dealers were providing poor warranty service, and that a leading department store was refusing to accept returns within the designated time period.

Source: Laura Bruck, "Business Ethics: Shades of Grey," *Distributor Focus* (April 2011), pp. A–D.

FIGURE 1-11

The Build-A-Bear Experience: Never Boring

High shopper interactivity and customized products—in a child-friendly store environment—make Build-A-Bear Workshop a fun place to shop.

Source: Reprinted by permission of Susan V. Berry, Retail Image Consulting, Inc.

CUSTOMER SERVICE **Customer service** refers to the identifiable, but sometimes intangible, activities undertaken by a retailer in conjunction with the basic goods and services it sells. It has a strong impact on the total retail experience. Among the factors comprising a customer service strategy are store hours, parking, shopper friendliness of the store layout, credit acceptance, salespeople, amenities such as gift wrapping, restrooms, employee politeness, delivery policies, the time shoppers spend in checkout lines, and customer follow-up. This list is not all inclusive, and it differs in terms of the retail strategy undertaken. Customer service is discussed further in Chapter 2.

At Lands' End (www.landsend.com), customer service means "Guaranteed. Period."

Satisfaction with customer service is affected by expectations (based on the type of retailer) and past experience, and people's assessment of customer service depends on their perceptions—not necessarily reality. Different people may evaluate the same service quite differently. The same person may even rate a firm's customer service differently over time due to its intangibility, although the service stays constant:

> Costco shoppers don't expect anyone to help them to their car with bundles of commodities. Teens at Abercrombie & Fitch would be pretty turned off if a tuxedo-clad piano player serenaded them while they shopped. And Wal-Mart customers would protest loudly if the company traded its shopping carts for oversized nylon tote bags. On the other hand, helping shoppers to their cars when they have an oversized purchase is part of the service package at P.C. Richard & Sons, piano music sets the mood at Nordstrom, and nylon totes jammed full of value-priced apparel are in sync with the Old Navy image. The challenge for retailers is to ask shoppers what they expect in the way of service, listen to what they say, and then make every attempt to satisfy them.[8]

Interestingly, despite a desire to provide excellent customer service, a number of outstanding retailers now wonder if "the customer is always right." Are there limits? Consider that consumers come in all sorts of sizes, shapes, and personalities: "They can be enchanting, funny, and delightful. Or, they can be hostile, aggressive, and impossible to please. Obviously, when you've dealt with a difficult customer, you know first-hand that they're not always right. Sometimes, they are just plain old *wrong*. But, here's the problem. Research suggests that your customers are going to share their experiences (good or bad) with their friends. Here are a few ways to keep the peace in dealing with an aggressive customer: remain in control, be friendly, never argue, and sometimes it's necessary to cut ties with your difficult customers and part ways."[9]

As with the retailers profiled in this book, we want to engage in relationship retailing. So please visit our Web site (www.pearsonhighered.com/bermanevans) or blog (www.bermanevansretail.com).

RELATIONSHIP RETAILING The best retailers know it is in their interest to engage in **relationship retailing**, whereby they seek to establish and maintain long-term bonds with customers, rather than act as if each sales transaction is a completely new encounter. This means concentrating on the total retail experience, monitoring satisfaction with customer service, and staying in touch with customers. Figure 1-12 shows a customer respect checklist that retailers could use to assess their relationship efforts.

To be effective in relationship retailing, a firm should keep two points in mind: (1) Because it is harder to lure new customers than to make existing ones happy, a "win–win" approach is critical. For a retailer to "win" in the long run (attract shoppers, make sales, earn profits), the customer must also "win" in the long run (receive good value, be treated with respect, feel welcome by the firm). Otherwise, that retailer loses (shoppers patronize competitors) and customers lose (by spending time and money to learn about other retailers). (2) Due to advances in computer technology, it is now much easier to develop a customer data base with information on people's attributes and past shopping behavior. Ongoing customer contact can be better, more frequent, and more focused. This is covered further in Chapter 2.

THE FOCUS AND FORMAT OF THE TEXT

There are various approaches to the study of retailing: an institutional approach, which describes the types of retailers and their development; a functional approach, which concentrates on the activities that retailers perform (such as buying, pricing, and personnel practices); and a strategic approach, which centers on defining the retail business, setting objectives, appealing to an

FIGURE 1-12
A Customer Respect Checklist

- ✓ When interacting with customers, do employees always say "How may I help you?" "Please?" "Thank you?"
- ✓ Are employees properly trained to service the retailer's customers?
- ✓ Do employees listen carefully when customers state their preferences and not push goods and services that are beyond the shoppers' interest or budget?
- ✓ Are employees patient and not condescending when talking to customers?
- ✓ Is the customer's time valued?
- ✓ Do the hours that the retailer is open correspond with the hours sought by customers?
- ✓ Do the retailer and its employees honor all promises that are made to customers—and strive not to mislead shoppers?
- ✓ Do employees avoid being confrontational with customers if the latter make a complaint about merchandise or service?
- ✓ Are customer phone calls, E-mails, and other contacts with the retailer directed to the right employees and handled promptly?
- ✓ For a retailer that operates both store and online businesses, are policies clearly stated and distinctions between the two formats with regard to purchase, shipping, and return policies noted in the store and online?
- ✓ Does the retailer monitor online customer reviews and social media discussions and work to resolve any problems that are noted there?
- ✓ Does the retailer treat every customer respectfully, regardless of age, gender, race, ethnicity, and other factors?
- ✓ Does the retailer recognize and reward its most loyal customers?
- ✓ Does the retailer's employee review process include how well the employees are rated by customers?

TECHNOLOGY IN RETAILING

Enhancing the Shopping Experience Through Mobile Devices

By using Scan-It (www.scan-it.com), a device that resembles a smart phone which is attached to a shopping cart handle, consumers can scan and bag their groceries as they go through the aisles of a supermarket. If a shopper decides to change a scanned purchase, he or she can simply check "Remove" from the menu and scan the item again after it is removed from the cart. Not only does Scan-It keep a running total of a consumer's purchases, but also it prints relevant coupons based on a consumer's purchases. For example, a shopper that scanned coffee could receive an electronic coupon for coffee creamer.

Scan-It is currently in use in about one-half of Ahold USA's (www.ahold.com) Stop & Shop and Giant supermarkets. According to an Ahold USA executive, shoppers who use Scan-It spend about 10 percent more than the average shopper. The executive attributes the additional sales to the system's targeted coupons and the control over their spending that consumers feel. Scan-It shoppers also save considerable time at the checkout since the time-consuming tasks of scanning and packing groceries have already been completed. Research by an information technology firm has also found that shoplifting losses by firms that use mobile device technology are far less than losses based on cashier error.

Source: Ann Zimmerman, "Check Out the Future of Shopping," *Wall Street Journal* (May 18, 2011), pp. D1, D2.

appropriate customer market, developing an overall plan, implementing an integrated strategy, and regularly reviewing operations.

We will study retailing from each perspective but center on a *strategic approach.* Our basic premise is that the retailer has to plan for and adapt to a complex, changing environment. Both opportunities and threats must be considered. By engaging in strategic retail management, the retailer is encouraged to study competitors, suppliers, economic factors, consumer changes, marketplace trends, legal restrictions, and other elements. A firm prospers if its competitive strengths match the opportunities in the environment, weaknesses are eliminated or minimized, and plans look to the future (as well as the past). Look at the appendix to Chapter 1, which examines the impact of a weak economic situation on retailers and consumers alike.

Retail Management: A Strategic Approach is divided into eight parts. The rest of Part One looks at building relationships and strategic planning in retailing. Part Two examines retailing institutions on the basis of their ownership; store-based strategy mix; and Web, nonstore-based, and other nontraditional retailing formats. Part Three deals with consumer behavior and information gathering in retailing. Parts Four through Seven discuss the specific elements of a retailing strategy: planning the store location; managing a retail business; planning, handling, and pricing merchandise; and communicating with the customer. Part Eight shows how a retailing strategy may be integrated, analyzed, and improved. These topics have special end-of-chapter appendixes: the impact of the economy (Chapter 1), service retailing (Chapter 2), global retailing (Chapter 3), franchising (Chapter 4), and multi-channel retailing (Chapter 6). There is also an end-of-text appendix on retailing careers and a glossary with text page references. Our Web site includes "How to Solve a Case Study" (www.pearsonhighered.com/bermanevans), which will aid you in your case analyses.

To underscore retailing's exciting nature, four real-world boxes appear in each chapter: "Careers in Retailing," "Ethics in Retailing," "Retailing Around the World," and "Technology in Retailing."

Chapter Summary

In this and every chapter, the summary is related to the objectives stated at the beginning of the chapter.

1. *To define retailing, consider it from various perspectives, demonstrate its impact, and note its special characteristics.* Retailing comprises the business activities involved in selling goods and services to consumers for personal, family, or household use. It is the last stage in the distribution process. Today, retailing is at a complex crossroads, with many challenges ahead.

Retailing may be viewed from multiple perspectives. It includes tangible and intangible items, does not have to involve a store, and can be done by manufacturers and others—as well as retailers.

Annual U.S. store sales are approaching $5 trillion, with other forms of retailing accounting for hundreds of billions of dollars more. The world's 250 largest retailers account for more than $4 trillion in yearly revenues. About 25 million people in the United States work for retailers (including food and beverage service firms), which understates the number of those actually employed in a retailing capacity. Retail firms receive up to 40 cents or more of every sales dollar as compensation for operating costs, the functions performed, and the profits earned.

Retailing encompasses all of the businesses and people involved in physically moving and transferring ownership of goods and services from producer to consumer. In a distribution channel, retailers perform valuable functions as the contact for manufacturers, wholesalers, and final consumers. They collect assortments from various suppliers and offer them to customers. They communicate with both customers and other channel members. They may ship, store, mark, advertise, and pre-pay for items. They complete transactions with customers and often provide customer services. They may offer multiple formats (multi-channel retailing) to facilitate shopping.

Retailers and their suppliers have complex relationships because retailers serve in two capacities. They are part of a distribution channel aimed at the final consumer, and they are major customers for suppliers. Channel relations are smoothest with exclusive distribution; they are most volatile with intensive distribution. Selective distribution is a way to balance sales goals and channel cooperation.

Retailing has several special characteristics. The average sales transaction is small. Final consumers make many unplanned purchases. Most customers visit a store location.

2. *To introduce the concept of strategic planning and apply it.* A retail strategy is the overall plan guiding the firm. It has six basic steps: defining the business, setting objectives, defining the customer market, developing an overall plan, enacting an integrated strategy, and evaluating performance and making modifications. Target Corporation's strategy has been particularly well designed and enacted, even though it has been affected by the tough economy in recent years.

3. *To show why the retailing concept is the foundation of a successful business, with an emphasis on the total retail experience, customer service, and relationship retailing.* The retailing concept should be understood and used by all retailers. It requires a firm to have a customer orientation, use a coordinated effort, and be value driven and goal oriented. Despite its straightforward nature, many firms do not adhere to one or more elements of the retailing concept.

The total retail experience consists of all elements in a retail offering that encourage or inhibit consumers during their contact with a retailer. Some elements are controllable by the retailer; others are not. Customer service includes identifiable, but sometimes intangible, activities undertaken by a retailer in association with the basic goods and services sold. It has an effect on the total retail experience. In relationship retailing, a firm seeks long-term bonds with customers rather than acting as if each sales transaction is a totally new encounter with them.

4. *To indicate the focus and format of the text.* Retailing may be studied by using an institutional approach, a functional approach, and a strategic approach. Although all three approaches are covered in this book, our focus is on the strategic approach. The underlying principle is that a retail firm needs to plan for and adapt to a complex, changing environment.

Key Terms

retailing (p. 3)
channel of distribution (p. 6)
sorting process (p. 7)
multi-channel retailing (p. 7)
exclusive distribution (p. 8)
intensive distribution (p. 8)
selective distribution (p. 8)
retail strategy (p. 10)
retailing concept (p. 13)
total retail experience (p. 14)
customer service (p. 15)
relationship retailing (p. 16)

Questions for Discussion

1. What is your favorite consumer electronics retailer? Discuss the criteria you use in making your selection. What can a competing firm do to lure you away from your favorite firm?
2. What kinds of information do retailers communicate to customers? To suppliers?
3. What are the pros and cons of a firm such as Apple having its own retail stores and E-commerce Web site (www.apple.com) as well as selling through traditional retailers?
4. Why would one retailer seek to be part of an exclusive distribution channel while another seeks to be part of an intensive distribution channel?
5. Describe how the special characteristics of retailing offer unique opportunities and problems for local gift shops.

6. What is the purpose of developing a formal retail strategy? How could a strategic plan be used by a restaurant chain?
7. On the basis of the chapter description of Target Corporation, present five suggestions that a new retailer should consider.
8. Explain the retailing concept. Apply it to your school's bookstore.
9. Define the term "total retail experience." Then describe a recent retail situation in which your expectations were surpassed, and state why.
10. Do you believe that customer service in retailing is improving or declining? Why?
11. How could a small Web-only retailer engage in relationship retailing?
12. What checklist item(s) in Figure 1-12 do you think would be most difficult for Ikea, the global furniture retailer, to address? Why?

Web-Based Exercise

Visit our blog (www.bermanevansretail.com). Describe the elements of the blog and give several examples of what you learn at the site.

Note: Also stop by our Web site (www.pearsonhighered.com/bermanevans) to experience a number of highly interactive, appealing Web exercises based on actual company demonstrations, and sample materials related to retailing.

APPENDIX Understanding the Recent Economic Downturn in the United States and Around the Globe

From 2008 through 2011, the economies of the United States and many other countries around the globe either declined or were stagnant. In some instances, the effects were devastating. Millions of people lost their jobs, had trouble paying their mortgages (with many having to give up their homes), and became pessimistic about the future. Long-time firms such as Borders, Blockbuster, and Great Atlantic & Pacific Tea declared bankruptcy or went out of business. Numerous other retailers suffered losses and had to run frequent sales to generate business or to close unprofitable stores.

In this appendix, we present a brief overview of the events leading to the economic downturn, the impact of the downturn on economies around the world, and the effect of the downturn on retailing. We also discuss some of the strategic options that retailers are pursuing and should pursue to sustain their business amid a weak economy.

The Current Economic Downturn

In 2011, the Census Bureau reported that the average U.S. family's income, when adjusted for inflation, had dropped to the same level as in 1996.[1] Median household income dropped for the third consecutive year in 2010, to a $49,455 level. Clearly, the gains in income of the boom times of the early 2000s were eliminated. The percentage of Americans living in poverty was 15.1 percent of the population as of 2011, with 22 percent of all American children living in poverty—the largest percentage since 1993.[2]

Especially noteworthy was the growing gap between the "best-off" and "worst-off" Americans. The top one-fifth of households accounted for 50.2 percent of total pre-tax income; while the bottom one-fifth received 11.8 percent of total income.[3] One widely accepted measure of the income inequality is the Gini index, which ranges from zero (if all households have the same earnings) to one (when all of the income goes to one person). Today, the Gini index is well below 0.47. This represents a 20 percent rise in the disparity over the past 40 years, based on calculations from the Census Bureau.[4] According to a Procter & Gamble executive, "We [the United States] now have a Gini index similar to the Philippines and Mexico—you'd never have imagined that. I don't think we've typically thought about America as a country with big income gaps to this extent."[5]

With over 14 million people unemployed, many of them for extended time periods, consumer spending has dropped significantly in the United States. As of 2012, the unemployment rate was still hovering at nearly 9 percent. In contrast, from 1948 to 2010, the unemployment rate averaged 5.7 percent. The number of long-term unemployed (those jobless for 27 weeks or more) was 6 million as of 2012. This accounted for 43 percent of those unemployed. These numbers do not reflect individuals who are not looking for work although they would like a job and those working part-time who would prefer full-time positions. The broader definition of unemployment/underemployment rate was about 16 percent in 2012. This computation of unemployment corresponds to the way in which Japan, Canada, and Western Europe calculate their unemployment rate.

The lack of jobs and concern over job security have resulted in both less spending (and increased savings) as well as reduced consumer confidence (due to lower levels of home equity and losses in stock market investments). The personal savings rate, the percent of each paycheck that is not spent, increased to 6.4 percent in 2011, the highest rate since June 2009. Because consumer spending constitutes 70 percent of the U.S. economy, this reduction in spending is a major drag on economic growth. Further evidence of increased savings has been the increased use of debit cards instead of credit cards.

By late 2011, consumer confidence, as measured by The Conference Board Research Center, had deteriorated sharply. The consumer confidence index was the lowest level in over two years.[5] Likewise, the University of Michigan measure of consumer expectations for March 2012 dropped to the lowest level since May 1980.[6] About 60 percent of those surveyed in the Michigan study anticipated that their incomes would fall in 2012, after adjusting for inflation. This is the most pessimistic expectation in the history of the University of Michigan study of consumer confidence.

Home prices continued to fall, dropping 2.5 percent in 2011. These prices are only expected to go up by 1.1 percent per year through 2015, based on a study of over 100 economists. As of 2011, housing values had dropped 31.6 percent from their peak values in 2005 according to Standard & Poor's Case Shiller 20-city index. One in five Americans with a mortgage owes more than their home is worth and $7 trillion in homeowner equity has been lost in the housing bust. This number is very significant because for most Americans, their home is their largest asset. In 2011, banks held close to 500,000 foreclosed homes on their books and an additional 4 million homes were in some stage of the foreclosure process or were "seriously delinquent" (having missed three or more mortgage payments).[7] This housing crisis had the greatest impact in Nevada, Arizona, and Florida.

The housing bust weighs heavily on the economy in various ways. Low housing prices for existing homes reduces new construction (since existing homes compete with new homes), lessens the number of home renovation projects, and lastly, makes banks become more hesitant to provide mortgages.

The Impact of the Downturn on Economies Around the World

In its flagship report, *World Economic Outlook*, the International Monetary Fund (IMF) warned that the U.S. and European economies face a continuing recession and a "lost decade of growth" unless governments take concerted actions to revamp their economic policies. The IMF forecast world economic growth for 2011 at 4 percent. The IMF forecast U.S. growth at 1.5 percent per year, slightly less than the European zone, at 1.6 percent. China, in contrast, was forecast to grow at 9.5 percent in 2011 (versus 10.3 percent in 2010) and India at 7.8 percent (versus 10.1 percent in 2010).[8]

During 2011, Europe was in the midst of a financial crisis that, according to some economists, made the U.S. financial crisis seem tame. Greece, Ireland, and Portugal required bailouts from European Union member nations. Faced with reduced tax revenues due to declining economic growth and higher interest payments because of their diminished credit ratings, these counties had difficulties in making necessary debt payments. Italy and Spain also encountered financial difficulties. Europe's banks and insurers held about $200 billion in Greek debt. The fallout from the situation in Greece, Portugal, and Spain in terms of direct losses from investments has been called "one of the worst sovereign debt disasters ever."[9]

A major problem related to the downgrading of Greek bonds to junk status by Standard & Poor's was that Greek bonds could not be used as collateral by the European Central Bank if they rated below investment grade. This problem will greatly expand if Spain and Portugal lose their investment-grade status. Another major concern is that investors may decide to stop buying European nation debt.

The Effect of the Economic Downturn on Retailing

The effect of the economic downturn has been especially hard on home- and appliance-based retailers such as Home Depot, Lowe's, and Sears. Each of these retailers highly relies on the sale of tools, home renovation supplies, and large appliances. Standard & Poor's projected that each of these retailers would have same store sales declines for 2011.[10]

On the other hand, retailers such as Dollar General and Family Dollar have benefitted from increased purchases from two different market segments: the "trade down" and the "trade in." The first segment, which was affected by increased gasoline prices and food costs, traded down to these stores. On the other hand, although trade-ins could afford to shop elsewhere, they increasingly shopped at discount stores to exercise their frugality and smart shopping skills.[11] Off-price apparel chains such as Marshalls, Burlington Coat Factory, and T.J. Maxx also drew new shoppers because many people became more value-driven. In addition, these off-price chains had significant buying opportunities due to overstocked channel members and cancellations of purchases from bankrupt retailers.

The 2008–2011 retail bankruptcies were undertaken under a tougher set of rules than in the previous economic downturn. Prior to 2005, U.S. firms had an unlimited amount of time to file a restructuring plan after filing for bankruptcy. Since 2005, these filings have had to be submitted within 18 months. Under earlier laws, retailers had two years or more (via extensions) to determine which store locations to keep. Today, retailers under bankruptcy protection must make store-closing decisions within 210 days. Retailers in bankruptcy also now need to pay suppliers and utilities during the retailers' bankruptcy period. Under the older laws, suppliers and utilities had to wait until a company emerged from bankruptcy before being paid. Lastly, due to concerns from lenders who were burnt with mortgage-backed securities, troubled retailers have found it much more difficult to get financing. As a result of these factors, many retailers that entered bankruptcy were unable to restructure and, thus, were forced to close.

Among the bankruptcies that were quickly followed by company closings were: Borders, Blockbuster (which was sold off), Anchor Blue, and Syms. While all of these retailers were adversely affected by the overall economic conditions in the United States, the specific causes of their declines were somewhat different.

The bankruptcy of Borders, like Blockbuster, probably was caused more by the firm's inability to adapt to technological developments than the country's economic plight. Borders was a latecomer to E-commerce, having established its Web site in 2008, long after www.barnesandnoble.com and www.amazon.com. Borders was also late in developing and marketing E-reader technology. Amazon.com first marketed its Kindle reader in November 2007, and Barnes & Noble began to sell its Nook reader in November 2009 without competition from Borders until 2010 (when Borders came out with its Kobo reader). Borders' bankruptcy resulted ultimately in its closing all of its 399 stores and laying off 10,700 employees.

Some analysts also argued that Borders opened too many stores, despite the chain's lackluster sales. Many of these stores were too large and too many leases involved long-term 15- to 20-year leases that were difficult to close. While these stores may have been profitable before the Internet, the Internet is far more efficient at selling a large selection of titles than a bricks-and-mortar store.[12]

When Blockbuster U.S. declared bankruptcy in September 2010, the Canadian Blockbuster unit became the guarantor. On May 20, 2011, Blockbuster Canada sought bankruptcy and stated that it planned to close 140 Blockbuster stores in Canada. Industry observers stated that the availability of movies via on demand from cable and satellite television providers, via the mail or streaming from firms such as Netflix, and even through vending machines, very effectively competed with Blockbuster's "go out and rent" way of renting movies. Unlike Blockbuster, which charged consumers for each video rental, Netflix offered subscriptions entitling members to unlimited viewing for one monthly fee. And Redbox has 25,000 video kiosks (over three times the amount that Blockbuster had) that enabled consumers to rent videos at convenient neighborhood locations at $1 per DVD. In 2011, after a bankruptcy court auction, Blockbuster was acquired by Dish Networks for $321 million. At its peak, Blockbuster operated more than 9,000 stores; now, the figure is about 1,500.

Great Atlantic & Pacific Tea (A&P) filed for Chapter 11 bankruptcy in December 2010. In addition to stores operated under its A&P brand designation, A&P operated almost 400 supermarkets in eight states under the A&P, Waldbaum's, Food Emporium, Super Fresh, Food Basics, and Pathmark brands. Some analysts attributed the chain's problems to the loss of sales to supercenters and membership clubs, as well as lower sales revenues as a result of the general economic climate. A&P also suffered losses as a result of purchasing Pathmark Stores in 2007 (just as the U.S. economy fell into a recession) with a $1.7 billion financing agreement. Lastly, A&P had a supply agreement that required it to obtain 70 percent of its purchases from C&S Wholesale Grocers. Prior to bankruptcy, A&P tried unsuccessfully to renegotiate its contract with C&S. A&P is trying to revitalize its operations by restructuring its debt, reducing its cost structure, and closing unprofitable locations.[13] It secured $800 million in debtor-in-possession financing that enabled it to pay suppliers of new merchandise.

Some analysts believed that retailers that were number two or three in market share in their respective markets were particularly vulnerable to bankruptcy or liquidation. This was especially the case for retailers that used heavy debt to fund their expansion during the period when interest rates were low and credit availability was high. Retailers owned by private equity firms that were acquired during the pre-2008 boom years—due to their strong cash flow and property assets—were also financially stressed.

Due to shoppers' concern about the viability of retailers in bankruptcy, the sales of gift cards were affected. It was widely publicized by the media that gift card recipients would be treated as unsecured creditors when a retailer entered into bankruptcy protection.

Strategic Options for Retailers in Weak Economic Times

Let's look at several strategic options that are available to retailers to increase their performance during troubled economic times:

- *Rethink existing store formats.* At Wal-Mart, smaller-format stores will play a larger role in the future in order to grow the chain's urban presence, increase sales per square foot, and lower rent and utility costs. As of 2011, only about 50 of Wal-Mart's 4,300 U.S. stores were located in urban centers. Wal-Mart's average supercenter is now 140,000 to 170,000 square feet, versus 195,000 square feet a few years ago. Wal-Mart's small format store prototypes are Neighborhood Market and Wal-Mart Express. Its Neighborhood Markets, which average 40,000 square feet, include supermarket-type goods, and generally include a pharmacy. Wal-Mart's Express stores average 15,000 square feet and offer food and key general merchandise goods. To make this small-store format strategy work, Wal-Mart needs to reduce product assortments and maximize supply chain efficiencies so stockouts are minimized despite lower in-store inventory levels. Wal-Mart is also offering a site-to-store program to enable customers to order goods online from Wal-Mart's extensive merchandise assortment and then have these goods delivered to a nearby Wal-Mart store.[14]
- *Increased use of pop-up stores.* The use of temporary pop-up stores has been intensifying due to several interrelated developments: a large vacancy rate for prime retail space, the need for additional income by commercial property owners, and increased consumer search for bargains. Although some pop-up stores focus on holiday shopping (such as Christmas tree accessories or Halloween costumes), others are open for longer time periods and focus on the sale of manufacturer overstocks, discontinued merchandise, and designer samples.
- *Low inventory levels to reduce markdowns.* Shoppers make fewer trips to stores when gasoline prices are relatively high. With access to the Web, many shoppers are also likely to research their destinations and determine their purchases at home versus in the store. According to ShopperTrak, consumer store traffic was 2.2 percent less in 2011 than in 2010. To avoid higher markdowns, retailers need to buy right—special deals, closeouts, manufacturer overstocks, etc. They need to better plan their inventory levels to avoid the need for large markdowns to clear unsold inventories. Foot Locker and Champs Sports have expanded their inventory at a slower rate than their sales levels to keep their inventory position in check. They also focus more of their purchases on popular items such as Nike's Michael Jordan– and Kobe Bryant–branded sneakers.[15]
- *Increased promotions using coupons.* In 2010, marketers distributed 332 billion coupons, the largest distribution quantity ever. The 2010 level exceeded 2009's level by 6.8 percent. In total, 87.7 percent of these coupons were distributed in free-standing insert fliers. NCH Marketing Services reported that 78.3 percent of U.S. consumers regularly used coupons in 2010, compared with a 77 percent of the population in 2009.[16]
- *Shopper discounts based on credit card purchases.* Target and Lowe's each have store-branded credit cards that offer customers a 5 percent discount on all purchases. Target's CEO has commented that shoppers who use these cards spend on average 50 percent more each visit.[17]
- *Begin the holiday season earlier.* One estimate is that stores typically place orders up to four to seven months in advance. Thus, due to the combined effects of a recession, poor

credit availability, and an atmosphere of consumer caution, stores may have 15 to 20 percent or more excess holiday inventory. As a result, many retailers promote major holidays well ahead of time and conduct special sales events even before a holiday season begins. Many retailers now reduce prices on Christmas items before Thanksgiving.

- *Re-introduce layaway plans.* The concept of layaways started during the Great Depression as a way of enabling customers to purchase items without using a credit card. Through a layaway plan, a customer pays the product's total cost (plus a small fee) in installments before being allowed to take the item home. In a traditional layaway program, a customer has 30 days to pay for an item after making an initial payment. Although layaway programs deny instant gratification to the purchaser, the customer receives the attraction of credit cards (being able to purchase an item without paying the full price up front), but without the risk of overextending his or her credit. Until the 2008–2009 economic downturn, Kmart was the only major U.S. retailer with a layaway program. Now, Sears, T.J. Maxx, Marshalls, Burlington Coat Factory, and Wal-Mart—along with many regional chains and local stores—offer layaway programs. In September 2011, Wal-Mart began to offer a layaway option for electronics and toys priced at $15 or more.[18] According to Wal-Mart's chief merchandising officer, "It [the popularity of the layaway program] just tells us that the customer is still struggling. There's a fragile economy, and our customer needs our help."[19]

2 Building and Sustaining Relationships in Retailing

In Chapter 2, we emphasize the importance of "value" and "relationships" for retailers. A good social media strategy can enhance any retailer's efforts to provide value and create and maintain customer relationships. As Awareness, Inc. (www.awarenessnetworks.com) notes, social media "involve connecting directly with customers, being social, and engaging in conversation." This includes "both a strategy and a set of tools and tactics that are then rolled into a social media marketing program."

According to Awareness, Inc., building value and relationships through social media entails many factors, including these:

- A social media strategy includes determining who and where your customers are, the best ways to connect with them, your social media goals and how you'll measure success for these goals, and aligning social media plans with the overall business strategy.
- Social media, unlike traditional advertising, are bi-directional. Consumers want to share their feedback and opinions, not just hear from the retailer.
- The best social media sites encourage regular, ongoing bi-directional communication. They engage their participants.
- Accurate, consumer-oriented, value-laden content is a must: "To keep your audience's attention, you've got to offer them valuable information. It means substantial content that makes people's lives easier and gives more meaning to their decision. How does that help you? By providing the content they seek, people associate your brand with being knowledgeable, helpful, and welcoming, making it that much easier for them to think of you at decision time."

In sum, customers want to have access to retailers on a 24-hour-per-day basis through multiple media platforms—and to be able to offer comments, feedback, questions, complaints, and praise that get prompt and helpful responses from the retailers.[1]

Chapter Objectives

1. To explain what "value" really means and highlight its pivotal role in retailers' building and sustaining relationships
2. To describe how both customer relationships and channel relationships may be nurtured in today's highly competitive marketplace
3. To examine the differences in relationship building between goods and service retailers
4. To discuss the impact of technology on relationships in retailing
5. To consider the interplay between retailers' ethical performance and relationships in retailing

Source: BeTA-Artworks/ fotolia.com.

Overview

To prosper, a retailer must properly apply the concepts of "value" and "relationship" so (1) customers strongly believe the firm offers a good value for the money and (2) both customers and channel members want to do business with that retailer. Some firms grasp this well. Others still have some work to do. Consider GameStop's forward-thinking view:

GameStop (www.gamestop.com) is—first and foremost—a customer-driven retailer.

> GameStop is the world's largest video game and entertainment software retailer. GameStop stores around the globe are exciting places to be. From teens and young adults to parents and grandparents, our customers come from all different countries and continents, with interests ranging from sword fighting to sudoku, and from drag racing to dancing. The company operates more than 6,500 retail stores worldwide, as well as GameStop.com and EBgames.com. *Game Informer* magazine, a leading multi-platform video game publication, is also an important part of the GameStop family. We offer customers the most popular new software, hardware, and game accessories for next generation video game systems and the PC. In addition, our used game trade program creates value for customers while recycling products no longer being played.[2]

As retailers look to the future, this is the looming bottom line on value: "Consumers will demand more for less from the shopping experience. Time and budget constrained consumers will spend less time shopping, make fewer trips, visit fewer stores, and shop more purposefully. Different strokes will satisfy different folks. Consumers will shop different formats for different needs. Specifically, they will split the commodity shopping trip from the value-added shopping trip. Consumers are becoming more skeptical about price. Under the barrage of sales, price has lost its meaning; gimmicks have lost their appeal. To regain consumer confidence, pricing by retailers and manufacturers alike will become clearer, more sensible, and more sophisticated."[3] See Figure 2-1.

This chapter looks at value and the value chain, relationship retailing with regard to customers and channel partners, the differences in relationship building between goods and service retailers, technology and relationships, and ethics and relationships. There is also a chapter appendix on service retailing.

VALUE AND THE VALUE CHAIN

In many channels of distribution, there are several parties: manufacturer, wholesaler, retailer, and customer. These parties are most apt to be satisfied with their interactions when they have similar beliefs about the value provided and received, and they agree on the payment for that level of value.

FIGURE 2-1

The Key to Long-Term Customer Satisfaction: Meeting Expectations

In today's highly competitive retailing environment, companies must do everything they can to generate and maintain a distinctive edge. To attract customers and gain their loyalty, it is no longer enough to "satisfy" them; they need to be "wowed." This requires (a) an in-depth understanding of target shoppers' desires; (b) the proper mix of merchandise, customer service, and prices for those shoppers; and (c) supportive, ongoing customer interaction. These are not easy tasks.

Source: iQoncept/ Shutterstock.com. Reprinted by permission.

From the perspective of the manufacturer, wholesaler, and retailer, **value** is embodied by a series of activities and processes—a value chain—that *provides* a certain value for the consumer. It is the totality of the tangible and intangible product and customer service attributes offered to shoppers. The level of value relates to each firm's desire for a fair profit and its niche (such as discount versus upscale). Firms may differ in rewarding the value each provides and in allocating the activities undertaken.

From the customer's perspective, **value** is the *perception* the shopper has of a value chain. It is the customer's view of all the benefits from a purchase (formed by the total retail experience). Value is based on the perceived benefits received versus the price paid. It varies by type of shopper. Price-oriented shoppers want low prices, service-oriented shoppers will pay more for superior customer service, and status-oriented shoppers will pay a lot to patronize prestigious stores.

Why is "value" such a meaningful concept for every retailer in any kind of setting?

- Customers must always believe they get their money's worth, whether the retailer sells $45,000 Patek Phillipe watches or $40 Casio watches.
- A strong retail effort is required so that customers perceive the level of value provided in the manner the firm intends.
- Value is desired by all customers; however, it means different things to different customers.
- Consumer comparison shopping for prices is easy through ads and the World Wide Web. Thus, prices have moved closer together for different types of retailers.
- Retail differentiation is essential so a firm is not perceived as a "me too" retailer.
- A specific value/price level must be set. A retailer can offer $100 worth of benefits for a $100 item or $125 worth of benefits (through better ambience and customer service) for the same item with a $125 price. Either approach can work if properly enacted and marketed.

Peapod (www.peapod.com) offers a unique value chain with its home delivery service.

A retail **value chain** represents the total bundle of benefits offered to consumers through a channel of distribution. It comprises shopping location and parking, retailer ambience, the level of customer service, the products/brands carried, product quality, the retailer's in-stock position, shipping, prices, the retailer's image, and other elements. As a rule, consumers are concerned with the results of a value chain, not the process. Food shoppers who buy online via Peapod care only that they receive the brands ordered when desired, not about the steps needed for the home delivery of food at the neighborhood level.

Some elements of a retail value chain are visible to shoppers, such as display windows, store hours, sales personnel, and point-of-sale equipment. Other elements are not visible, such as store location planning, credit processing, company warehouses, and many merchandising decisions. In the latter case, various cues are surrogates for value: upscale store ambience and plentiful sales personnel for high-end retailers; shopping carts and self-service for discounters.

There are three aspects of a value-oriented retail strategy: expected, augmented, and potential. An *expected retail strategy* represents the minimum value chain elements a given customer segment (e.g., young women) expects from a type of retailer (e.g., a mid-priced apparel retailer). In most cases, the following are expected value chain elements: store cleanliness, convenient hours, well-informed employees, timely service, popular products in stock, parking, and return privileges. If applied poorly, expected elements cause customer dissatisfaction and relate to why shoppers avoid certain retailers.

Compare T.J. Maxx (www.tjmaxx.com) and Lord & Taylor (www.lordandtaylor.com).

An *augmented retail strategy* includes the extra elements in a value chain that differentiate one retailer from another. As an example, how is Sears different from Saks? The following are often augmented elements: exclusive brands, superior salespeople, loyalty programs, delivery, personal shoppers and other special services, and valet parking. Augmented features complement expected value chain elements, and they are the key to continued customer patronage with a particular retailer.

A *potential retail strategy* comprises value chain elements not yet perfected by a competing firm in the retailer's category. For example, what customer services could a new upscale apparel chain offer that no other chain offers? In many situations, the following are potential value chain elements: 24/7 store hours (an augmented strategy for supermarkets), unlimited customer return privileges, full-scale product customization, instant fulfillment of rain checks through in-store

CAREERS IN RETAILING

Glen Senk: Urban Outfitters

Glen T. Senk is chief executive officer (CEO) of Urban Outfitters (www.urbanoutfitters.com). Urban Outfitters has a number of successful retail operations, including Urban Outfitters stores aimed at 18- to 30-year-old females, Anthropologie (www.anthroplogie.com) that focuses on women aged 28 to 40, Free People (www.freepeople.com), a fashion-forward line aimed at women in their 20s, and the brand Liefsdoittir, Scandinavian-inspired apparel and footwear sold at Anthropologie stores.

Senk has an educational background that consists of an undergraduate degree from New York University and an MBA degree from the University of Chicago. After graduating from business school in 1981, he started at Bloomingdale's, where he worked for nine years. In the early 1990s, Senk was working at Williams-Sonoma, where he was senior vice-president and general merchandise manager, when he decided to open his own business. While raising money for that new venture, Senk met Richard Hayne, the founder of Urban Outfitters. In 1994, Senk began working at Urban Outfitters as manager of a prototype store for Anthropologie. Senk assumed his current CEO position in 2007.

According to Senk, "I love the theater of retail. I love that I can control every part of the experience—the product itself, the pricing, the way the product is sold, the way we communicate and so on."

Source: "Urban Outfitters' Glen Senk: Look for the Right Culture, Diverse Opinions and 'Bad News,'" http://knowledge.wharton.upenn.edu/article.cfm?articleid=2785 (May 25, 2011).

Today Barnes & Noble (www.bn.com) relies on both its stores and its Web site for revenues.

orders accompanied by free delivery, and in-mall trams to make it easier for shoppers to move through enormous regional shopping centers. The first firms to capitalize on potential features typically gain a head start over their adversaries. Barnes & Noble and Borders accomplished this by opening the first book superstores, and Amazon.com became a major player by opening the first online bookstore. Yet, even as pioneers, firms must excel at meeting customers' basic expectations and offering differentiated features from competitors if they are to grow, which is why Borders was forced out of business—it did not adapt fast enough.

There are five potential pitfalls to avoid in planning a value-oriented retail strategy:

- *Planning value with just a price perspective.* Value is tied to two factors: benefits and prices. All major discounters now accept credit cards because shoppers want to purchase with them.
- *Providing value-enhancing services that customers do not want or will not pay extra for.* Ikea knows most of its customers want to save money by assembling furniture themselves.
- *Competing in the wrong value/price segment.* Neighborhood retailers generally have a tough time competing in the low-price part of the market. They are better off providing augmented benefits and charging somewhat more than large chains.
- *Believing augmented elements alone create value.* Many retailers think that if they offer a benefit not available from competitors that they will automatically prosper. Yet, they must never lose sight of the importance of expected benefits. A movie theater with limited parking will have problems even if it features first-run movies.
- *Paying lip service to customer service.* Most firms say, and even believe, customers are always right. Yet, they may act contrary to this philosophy—by having a high turnover of salespeople, charging for returned goods that have been opened, and not giving rain checks if items are out of stock.

To sidestep these pitfalls, a retailer could use the checklist in Figure 2-2, which poses a number of questions that must be addressed. The checklist can be answered by an owner/corporate president, a team of executives, or an independent consultant. It should be reviewed at least once a year or more often if a major development, such as the emergence of a strong competitor, occurs.

RETAILER RELATIONSHIPS

In Chapter 1, we introduced the concept of *relationship retailing,* whereby retailers seek to form and maintain long-term bonds with customers, rather than act as if each sales transaction is a new encounter with them. For relationship retailing to work, enduring value-driven relationships are needed with other channel members, as well as with customers. Both jobs are challenging. See Figure 2-3. Visit our Web site for links related to relationship retailing issues (www.pearsonhighered.com/bermanevans).

FIGURE 2-2
A Value-Oriented Retailing Checklist

Answer yes or no to each question.

- ✓ Is value defined from a consumer perspective?
- ✓ Does the retailer have a clear value/price point?
- ✓ Is the retailer's value position competitively defensible?
- ✓ Are channel partners capable of delivering value-enhancing services?
- ✓ Does the retailer distinguish between expected and augmented value chain elements?
- ✓ Has the retailer identified meaningful potential value chain elements?
- ✓ Is the retailer's value-oriented approach aimed at a distinct market segment?
- ✓ Is the retailer's value-oriented approach consistent?
- ✓ Is the retailer's value-oriented approach effectively communicated to the target market?
- ✓ Can the target market clearly identify the retailer's positioning strategy?
- ✓ Does the retailer's positioning strategy consider trade-offs in sales versus profits?
- ✓ Does the retailer set customer satisfaction goals?
- ✓ Does the retailer periodically measure customer satisfaction levels?
- ✓ Is the retailer careful to avoid the pitfalls in value-oriented retailing?
- ✓ Is the retailer always looking out for new opportunities that will create customer value?

Customer Relationships

Loyal customers are the backbone of a business. Thus, it is important that they be cultivated. Here's why: "Are your customers satisfied? That's good, right? Well, yes for the short term. But in the long term, it's not necessarily enough. While a loyal customer is a satisfied customer, the converse is not necessarily true. Real loyalty—much harder to earn than mere satisfaction—tells you that your customer wants to stick with you over the long haul and will share that feeling with others. Loyalty derives not from hum-drum 'good' transactions but from exceeding customer expectations on a repeated basis. It is delightful experiences that make someone—emotionally devoted to you—want to tell others."[4]

In relationship retailing, there are four factors to keep in mind: the customer base, customer service, customer satisfaction, and loyalty programs and defection rates. Let's explore these next.

THE CUSTOMER BASE Retailers must regularly analyze their customer base in terms of population and lifestyle trends, attitudes toward and reasons for shopping, the level of loyalty, and the mix of new versus loyal customers.

The U.S. population is aging. One-fourth of households have only one person, one-seventh of people move annually, most people live in urban and suburban areas, the number of working women is high, middle-class income has been rising very slowly, and African American, Hispanic American, and Asian American segments are expanding. Thus, gender roles are changing, shoppers demand more, consumers are more diverse, there is less interest in shopping, and time-saving goods and services are desired.

Consider the following about consumers around the world:

- "There's no overlooking the fact that many consumers in mature markets like Europe, Japan, and Northern America are at the very least fearful of their financial futures, meaning that any kind of deal or discount is welcomed with open arms. But even those consumers who don't need to scrimp and save (including the middle classes in emerging markets) are still enthusiastically seeking out deals in almost every purchase, from everyday staples to

FIGURE 2-3
Sony's Relationship Challenges

As one of the world's leading consumer electronics companies, Sony wants to have good relationships with both the customers who buy the firm's products and the thousands of retailers around the world that sell Sony products. By opening its own stores, such as this one in Paris, Sony is enhancing its customer relationships. But, at the same time, Sony now competes with some of the retailers stocking its goods.

Source: Tupungato/Shutterstock.com. Reprinted by permission.

one-off indulgences. Why? Because for consumers driven by collecting as many and as varied experiences as possible, every cent, yen, or penny saved, means more to spend on new goods, services, and ultimately experiences."

- When surveyed about money saving strategies, buying on sale (59 percent) or using coupons (48 percent) were the top two answers from shoppers globally.
- About 60 percent of U.S. and British consumers say they do not like paying full price.
- In India, 10 percent of online shoppers access a deal site each month.
- In China, leisure, movies, and dining account for more than 50 percent of daily deals.[5]

It is more worth nurturing relationships with some shoppers than with others; they are the retailer's **core customers**—its best customers. And they should be singled out:

> Most businesses have a mix of good, better, and best customers. Unfortunately, there are bad customers as well, and they can be a waste of time and money. Good customers might be good because they spend lots of money. They might be good because they come back often. Bad customers are the ones who are never satisfied and almost always cost more to serve than they spend. The trick is to identify the best customers and see what characteristics differentiate these profitable customers from all the rest. Then focus your strategies on the segments most apt to produce the new best customers.[6]

A retailer's desired mix of new versus loyal customers depends on that firm's stage in its life cycle, goals, and resources, as well as competitors' actions. A mature firm is more apt to rely on core customers and supplement its revenues with new shoppers. A new firm faces the dual tasks of attracting shoppers and building a loyal following; it cannot do the latter without the former. If goals are growth-oriented, the customer base must be expanded by adding stores, increasing advertising, and so on; the challenge is to do this in a way that does not deflect attention from core customers. Although it is more costly to attract new customers than to serve existing ones, core customers are not cost-free. If competitors try to take away a firm's existing customers with price cuts and special promotions, a retailer may feel it must pursue competitors' customers in the same way. Again, it must be careful not to alienate core customers.

CUSTOMER SERVICE As described in Chapter 1, *customer service* refers to the identifiable, but sometimes intangible, activities undertaken by a retailer in conjunction with the goods and services it sells. It has an impact on the total retail experience. Consistent with a value chain philosophy, retailers must apply two elements of customer service: **Expected customer service** is the service level that customers want to receive from any retailer, such as basic employee courtesy. **Augmented customer service** includes the activities that enhance the shopping experience and give retailers a competitive advantage. AutoZone does a good job with both expected and augmented customer services. Even though the retailer sells several thousand parts and accessories, it considers its best product to be customer service; and

AutoZone (www.autozone.com) has a unique style of customer service.

> you get that free of charge. Our stores have friendly, knowledgeable people who are glad to help you. "AutoZoners always put customers first!" That's the first line of our pledge and it's the most important thing we do. We go the extra mile to make sure you get the help you need. We have created our shopping experience with the customer in mind. We're constantly changing our stores to bring you the newest and most exciting products. And you always know when you enter our stores you'll find a great selection of quality merchandise at low prices.[7]

The attributes of personnel who interact with customers (such as politeness and knowledge), as well as the number and variety of customer services offered, have a strong effect on the relationship created. Although planning a superior customer service strategy can be complex, a well-executed strategy can pay off in a big way. Just a decade ago, independent pharmacies were perceived by many experts as an "endangered species." But today, they have found a strong marketplace niche based on personal service, as praised recently by *Consumer Reports*:

> Ninety-four percent of readers are highly satisfied with their experiences at neighborhood independent drugstores. Although generally satisfied with their pharmacies, some were irked by long waits and lagging service at some big box stores. "Chalk one up for the little guy," said Tod Marks, senior editor, *Consumer Reports*. "We found that the independents made fewer errors, offered swifter service at the pharmacy counter, and were more likely to have medications ready for pick up when promised." Readers gave independent drugstores top scores across the board for pharmacists' knowledge about drugs and other products, helpfulness and courtesy, speed, accuracy, and personal service. Those who shopped at independents were twice as likely as chain drugstore shoppers to characterize their druggist as easy to talk to and able to give them a one-on-one consultation.[8]

Nordstrom (www.nordstrom.com) really believes in empowering its employees to better serve customers.

Some retailers realize customer service is better if they utilize **employee empowerment**, whereby workers have the discretion to do what they believe is necessary—within reason—to satisfy the customer, even if this means bending the rules. Nordstrom is well known for its employee empowerment: "Our people and the passion they have for service make all the difference. We trust one another's integrity and ability. Our only rule: use good judgment in all situations. Be empowered. Want to go above and beyond for a customer? Make a suggestion? Try something new? We want you to take the initiative and we'll support your efforts to deliver exceptional service. Have an idea? Want to talk? If it's important to you, we're listening. And if you've got a great idea, we want to hear it."[9]

To apply customer service effectively, a firm must first develop an overall service strategy and then plan individual services. Figure 2-4 shows one way a retailer may view the customer services it offers.

DEVELOPING A CUSTOMER SERVICE STRATEGY. A retailer must make the following vital decisions.

What customer services are expected and what customer services are augmented for a particular retailer? Examples of expected customer services are credit for a furniture retailer, new-car preparation for an auto dealer, and a liberal return policy for a gift shop. Those retailers could not stay in business without them. Because augmented customer services are extra elements, a firm could serve its target market without such services; yet, using them enhances its competitive standing. Examples are delivery for a supermarket, an extra warranty for an auto dealer, and gift wrapping for a toy store. Each firm needs to learn which customer services are expected and which are augmented for its situation. Expected customer services for one retailer, such as delivery, may be augmented for another. See Figure 2-5.

What level of customer service is proper to complement a firm's image? An upscale retailer would offer more customer services than a discounter because people expect the upscale firm to have a wider range of customer services as part of its basic strategy. Performance would also be different. Customers of an upscale retailer may expect elaborate gift wrapping, valet parking, a

FIGURE 2-4
Classifying Customer Service

Source: Adapted by the authors from Albert D. Bates, "Rethinking the Service Offer," *Retailing Issues Letter* (December 1986), p. 3. Reprinted by permission.

Value of the Customer Service to the Shopper / Cost of Offering the Customer Service	High	Low
High	**Patronage Builders** High-cost activities that are the primary factors behind customer loyalties. Examples: transaction speed, credit, gift registry	**Patronage Solidifiers** The "low-cost little things" that increase loyalty. Examples: courtesy (referring to the customer by name and saying thank you), suggestion selling
Low	**Disappointers** Expensive activities that do no real good. Examples: weekday deliveries for two-earner families, home economists	**Basics** Low-cost activities that are "naturally expected." They don't build patronage, but their absence could reduce patronage. Examples: free parking, in-store directories

restaurant, and a ladies' room attendant, whereas discount shoppers may expect cardboard gift boxes, self-service parking, a lunch counter, and an unattended ladies' room. Customer service categories are the same; performance is not.

Should there be a choice of customer services? Some firms let customers select from various levels of customer service; others provide only one level. A retailer may honor several credit cards or only its own. Trade-ins may be allowed on some items or all. Warranties may

FIGURE 2-5
The Walking Company: Providing Extra Value for Customers

As The Walking Company (www.thewalkingcompany.com) says, "We search the world over, so you can walk the world in comfort. Whether you purchase a fashion comfort sandal to wear while dining out, comfortable dress shoes to commute to the city, an ultimate comfort clog to use while on your feet all day at work, or a new pair of performance shoes to reach your personal fitness goals, our highly trained sales staff can help you with all of your comfort shoe needs. Customer service is our number one priority, and your satisfaction is guaranteed." The firm has stores around the country and a shopper-friendly Web site.

Source: Reprinted by permission of Susan V. Berry, Retail Image Consulting, Inc.

have optional extensions or fixed lengths. A firm may offer one-, three-, and six-month payment plans or insist on immediate payment.

Amazon.com (www.amazon.com) offers free delivery on orders of $25 or more.

Should customer services be free? Two factors cause retailers to charge for some customer services: (1) Delivery, gift wrapping, and some other customer services are labor intensive. (2) People are more apt to be home for a delivery or service call if a fee is imposed. Without a fee, a retailer may have to attempt a delivery twice. In settling on a free or fee-based strategy, a firm must determine which customer services are expected (these are often free) and which are augmented (these may be offered for a fee), monitor competitors and profit margins, and study the target market. In setting fees, a retailer must also decide if its goal is to break even or to make a profit on certain customer services.

How can a retailer measure the benefits of providing customer services against their costs? The purpose of customer services is to enhance the shopping experience in a manner that attracts and retains shoppers—while maximizing sales and profits. Thus, augmented customer services should not be offered unless they raise total sales and profits. A retailer should plan augmented customer services based on its experience, competitors' actions, and customer comments; when the costs of providing these customer services increase, higher prices should be passed on to the consumer.

How can customer services be terminated? Once a customer service strategy is set, shoppers are likely to react negatively to any customer service reduction. Nonetheless, some costly augmented customer services may have to be dropped. In that case, the best approach is to be forthright by explaining why the customer services are being terminated and how customers will benefit via lower prices. Sometimes a firm may use a middle ground, charging for previously free customer services (such as clothing alterations) to allow those who want the services to still receive them.

PLANNING INDIVIDUAL CUSTOMER SERVICES. Once a broad customer service plan is outlined, individual customer services are planned. A department store may offer credit, layaway, gift wrapping, a bridal registry, free parking, a restaurant, a beauty salon, carpet installation, dressing rooms, clothing alterations, pay phones, rest rooms and sitting areas, the use of baby strollers, delivery, and fur storage. The range of typical customer services is shown in Table 2-1 and described next. Most retailers let customers make credit purchases; and many firms accept personal checks with proper identification. Consumers' use of credit rises as the purchase amount goes up. Retailer-sponsored credit cards have three key advantages: (1) The retailer saves the fee it would pay for outside card sales. (2) People are encouraged to shop with a given retailer because its card is usually not accepted elsewhere. (3) Contact can be maintained with customers and information learned about them. There are also disadvantages to retailer cards: Startup costs are high, the firm must worry about unpaid bills and slow cash flow, credit checks and follow-up tasks must be performed, and customers without the firm's card may be discouraged from shopping. Bank and other commercial credit cards enable small and medium retailers to offer credit, generate added business for all types of retailers, appeal to mobile shoppers, provide advertising support from the sponsor, reduce bad debts, eliminate startup costs for the retailer, and provide data. Yet, these cards charge a transaction fee and do not yield loyalty to the retailer.

TABLE 2-1 Typical Customer Services

Credit	Miscellaneous	
Delivery	• Bridal registry	• Rest rooms
Alterations and installations	• Interior designers	• Restaurant
Packaging (gift wrapping)	• Personal shoppers	• Babysitting
Complaints and returns handling	• Ticket outlets	• Fitting rooms
Gift certificates	• Parking	• Beauty salon
Trade-ins	• Water fountains	• Fur storage
Trial purchases	• Pay phones	• Shopping bags
Special sales for regular customers	• Baby strollers	• Information
Extended store hours	• Company-sponsored social media	• Layaways
Mail and phone orders		

Most bank cards and retailer cards involve a **revolving credit account**, whereby a customer charges items and is billed monthly on the basis of the outstanding cumulative balance. An **option credit account** is a form of revolving account; no interest is assessed if a person pays a bill in full when it is due. When a person make a partial payment, he or she is assessed interest monthly on the unpaid balance. Some credit card firms (such as American Express) and some retailers offer an **open credit account**, whereby a consumer must pay the bill in full when it is due. Partial, revolving payments are not permitted. A person with an open account also has a credit limit (although it may be more flexible).

For a retailer that offers delivery, there are three decisions: the transportation method, equipment ownership versus rental, and timing. The shipping method can be car, van, truck, rail, mail, and so forth. The costs and appropriateness of the methods depend on the products. Large retailers often find it economical to own their delivery vehicles. This also lets them advertise the company name, have control over schedules, and use their employees for deliveries. Small retailers serving limited trading areas may use personal vehicles. Many small, medium, and even large retailers use shippers such as UPS if consumers live away from a delivery area and shipments are not otherwise efficient. Finally, the retailer must decide how quickly to process orders and how often to deliver to different locales.

For some retailers, alterations and installations are expected customer services—although more retailers now charge fees. However, many discounters have stopped offering alterations of clothing and installations of heavy appliances on both a free and a fee basis. They feel the services are too ancillary to their business and not worth the effort. Other retailers offer only basic alterations: shortening pants, taking in the waist, and lengthening jacket sleeves. They do not adjust jacket shoulders or width. Some appliance retailers may hook up washing machines but not do plumbing work.

Within a store, packaging (gift wrapping)—as well as complaints and returns handling—can be centrally located or decentralized. Centralized packaging counters and complaints and returns areas have key advantages: They may be situated in otherwise dead spaces, the main selling areas are not cluttered, specialized personnel can be used, and a common policy is enacted. The advantages of decentralized facilities are that shoppers are not inconvenienced, people are kept in the selling area (where a salesperson may resolve a problem or offer different merchandise), and extra personnel are not required. In either case, clear guidelines as to the handling of complaints and returns are needed.

Gift certificates encourage shopping with a given retailer. Many firms require certificates to be spent and not redeemed for cash. Trade-ins also induce new and regular shoppers to shop. People may feel they are getting a bargain. Trial purchases let shoppers test products before purchases are final to reduce risks.

The State of Retailing in the Czech Republic

The Czech Republic is one of the wealthiest of the newer European Union members. Its per capita gross domestic product (GDP) at purchasing power parity is $25,450 ($ U.S.), as compared with Poland's at $18,880 ($ U.S.). And although the Czech retail industry is less developed than that of western Europe, it is more mature than its eastern European neighbors.

Retail sales (not counting vehicles) constitutes 45 percent of spending in the Czech Republic. Since about one-half of retail spending goes to food, Czech consumers have less money to spend on such nonessential items as electronics and entertainment. Retail analysts predict that the share of food sales will decline as Czech Republic income levels increase. The increased use of credit cards (more than 1.6 million credit cards were issued in the Czech Republic in 2010) and online transactions will also spur growth in the Czech retail sector.

Retail ownership in the Czech Republic is dominated by foreign-owned hypermarkets (combination discount department stores and supermarkets) and food superstores. These retailers include Schwarz Group (Germany), REWE Group (Germany, www.rewe-group.com/en), Ahold (Netherlands, www.ahold.com), Tesco (Great Britain, www.tesco.com), and Metro (Germany, www.metrogroup.de). Competition is intense and the hypermarket segment appears to be saturated, especially in major cities. Several of these retailers have begun to expand in less urban markets with smaller store formats.

Source: "Czech Republic: Industry Forecast: Consumer Goods & Retail," *Economist Intelligence Unit-Business Eastern Europe* (March 14, 2011), p. 6.

Retailers increasingly offer special customer services to regular customers. Sales events (not open to the general public) and extended hours are provided. Mail and phone orders are handled for convenience.

Other useful customer services include a bridal registry, interior designers, personal shoppers, ticket outlets, free (or low-cost) and plentiful parking, water fountains, pay phones, baby strollers, company-sponsored social media, rest rooms, a restaurant, babysitting, fitting rooms, a beauty salon, fur storage, shopping bags, information counters, and layaway plans.

A retailer's willingness to offer some or all of these services indicates to customers a concern for them. Therefore, firms need to consider the impact of excessive self-service. For example, about one-third of the units in the Albertson's supermarket chain recently decided to remove all self-checkout lanes from its stores. Why? "We just want the opportunity to talk to customers more."[10]

CUSTOMER SATISFACTION **Customer satisfaction** occurs when the value and customer service provided through a retailing experience meet or exceed consumer expectations. If the expectations of value and customer service are not met, the consumer will be dissatisfied: "Retail satisfaction consists of three categories: *shopping systems satisfaction*, which includes availability and types of outlets; *buying systems satisfaction*, which includes selection and actual purchasing of products; and *consumer satisfaction*, which is derived from the use of the product. Dissatisfaction with any of the three aspects could lead to customer disloyalty, decrease in sales, and erosion of the market share."[11]

Only "very satisfied" customers are likely to remain loyal in the long run. How well are retailers doing in customer satisfaction? Many have much work to do. The American Customer Satisfaction Index (www.theacsi.org) annually questions thousands of people to link customer expectations, perceived quality, and perceived value to satisfaction. Overall, retailers consistently score about 75 to 77 on a scale of 100. Gasoline stations usually rate lowest in the retailing category (with scores around 70). To improve matters, retailers should engage in the process shown in Figure 2-6.

Most consumers do not complain to the retailer when dissatisfied. They just shop elsewhere. Why don't shoppers complain more? (1) Most people feel complaining produces little or no positive results, so they do not bother to complain. (2) Complaining is not easy. Consumers have to find the party to whom they should complain, access to that party may be restricted, and written forms may have to be completed.

Try out some of StatPac's surveys (www.statpac.com/online-surveys/examples.htm) for measuring customer satisfaction.

To obtain more feedback, retailers must make it easier for shoppers to complain, make sure shoppers believe their concerns are addressed, and sponsor ongoing customer satisfaction surveys. As suggested by software firm StatPac, retailers should ask such questions as these and then take corrective actions:

1. "Overall, how satisfied or dissatisfied are you with the store?"
2. "How satisfied or dissatisfied are you with the *price* of the items you purchased?"
3. "How satisfied or dissatisfied are you with the *quality* of the merchandise?"
4. "Please tell us something we could do to improve our store."[12]

LOYALTY PROGRAMS **Consumer loyalty (frequent shopper) programs** reward a retailer's best customers, those with whom it wants long-lasting relationships. According to Gallup, customers who are actively involved in a department store or grocery store loyalty

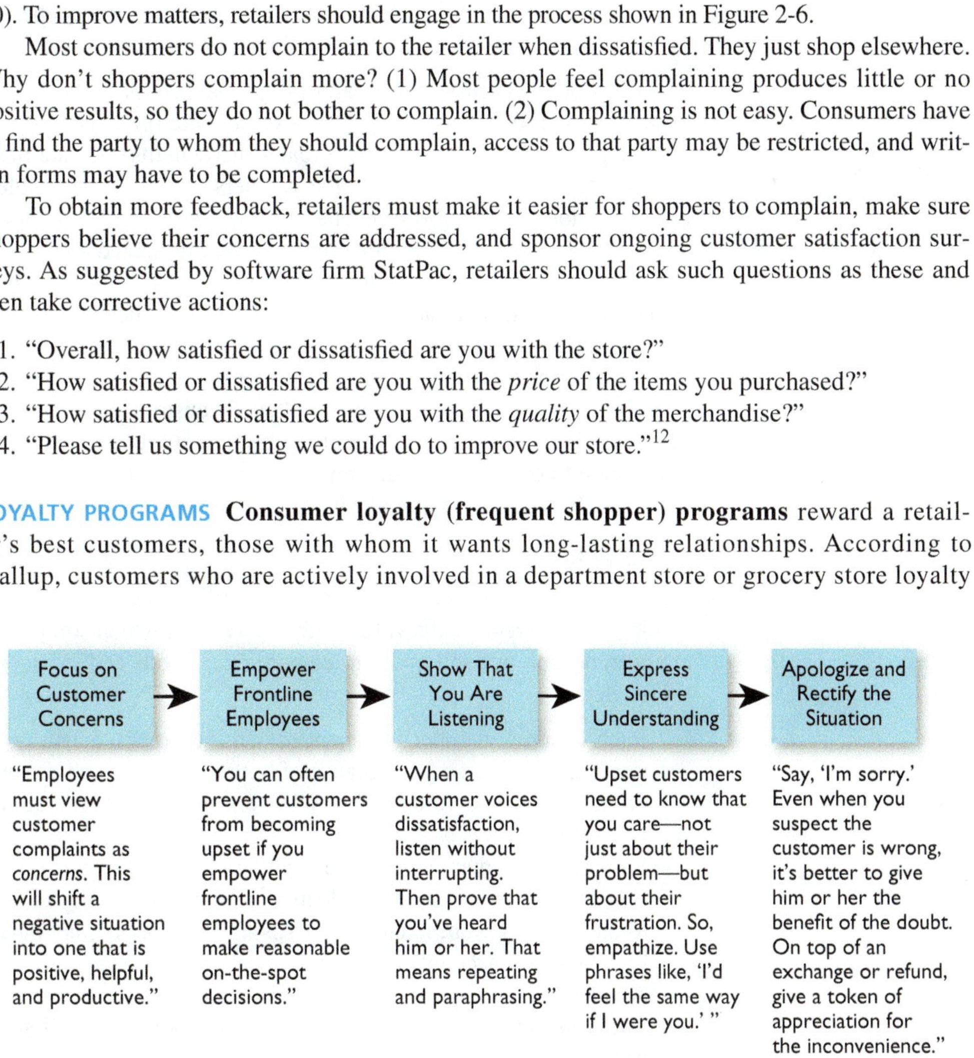

FIGURE 2-6
Turning Around Weak Customer Service

Source: Figure and its discussion developed by the authors from information in Jeff Mowatt, "Keeping Customers When Things Go Wrong," *Canadian Manager* (Summer 2001), pp. 23, 28.

Focus on Customer Concerns →	Empower Frontline Employees →	Show That You Are Listening →	Express Sincere Understanding →	Apologize and Rectify the Situation
"Employees must view customer complaints as *concerns*. This will shift a negative situation into one that is positive, helpful, and productive."	"You can often prevent customers from becoming upset if you empower frontline employees to make reasonable on-the-spot decisions."	"When a customer voices dissatisfaction, listen without interrupting. Then prove that you've heard him or her. That means repeating and paraphrasing."	"Upset customers need to know that you care—not just about their problem—but about their frustration. So, empathize. Use phrases like, 'I'd feel the same way if I were you.' "	"Say, 'I'm sorry.' Even when you suspect the customer is wrong, it's better to give him or her the benefit of the doubt. On top of an exchange or refund, give a token of appreciation for the inconvenience."

program do 80 to 85 percent of their category shopping in those stores. And here's what these consumers want:

> Activating and fully engaging customers is the key to maximizing investment in loyalty programs. But how do you get them to participate in the first place? And how do you satisfy this captive customer base? Among loyalty program participants, the main drivers of engagement and activation vary by category: For activated and fully engaged department store and grocery store participants in their primary store's loyalty program, the program itself is a key driver, followed by the quality of discounts, and the quality of rewards. The marketing message surrounding these loyalty programs might be rooted in rewarding customers or offering exclusive perks for frequent shoppers. But companies wouldn't engage in these initiatives without the potential for a significant payout.[13]

From the shopper's perspective, there are five types of reward categories:

- *Economic rewards* include things such as price reductions and purchase vouchers. People most concerned about their budgets will perceive these types of rewards as valuable.
- *Hedonistic rewards* include things such as points that can be exchanged for spa services or participation in games or sweepstakes. These rewards have more emotional value and will attract people who shop for pleasure.
- *Social-relational rewards* include things such as mailings about special events or the right to use special waiting areas at airports. Consumers who want to be identified with a privileged group will value these kinds of rewards.
- *Informational rewards* include things such as personalized beauty advice or information about new goods or services. They will attract consumers who like to stick with one brand or store.
- *Functional rewards* include things such as access to priority checkout counters or home delivery. Consumers who want to reduce the time they spend shopping will value these most.[14]

Great Britain's Tesco (www.tesco.com/clubcard) has a strong loyalty program (Tesco Clubcard) for its supermarket customers.

What do good customer loyalty programs have in common? Their rewards are useful and appealing, and they are attainable in a reasonable time. The programs honor shopping behavior (the greater the purchases, the greater the benefits). A data base tracks behavior. There are features that are unique to particular retailers and not redeemable elsewhere. Rewards stimulate both short- and long-run purchases. Customer communications are personalized. Frequent shoppers feel "special." Participation rules are publicized and rarely change.

When a retailer studies customer defections (by tracking data bases or surveying consumers), it can learn how many customers it is losing and why they no longer patronize the firm. Customer defections may be viewed in absolute terms (people who no longer buy from the firm at all) and in relative terms (people who shop less often). Each retailer must define its acceptable defection rate. Furthermore, not all shoppers are "good" customers. A retailer may feel it is okay if shoppers who always look for sales, return items without receipts, and expect fee-based services to be free decide to defect. Unfortunately, too few retailers review defection data or survey defecting customers because of the complexity of doing so and an unwillingness to hear "bad news."

Channel Relationships

Within a value chain, the members of a distribution channel (manufacturers, wholesalers, and retailers) jointly represent a **value delivery system**, which comprises all the parties that develop, produce, deliver, and sell and service particular goods and services. These are the ramifications for retailers:

- Each channel member is dependent on the others. When consumers shop with a certain retailer, they often do so because of both the retailer and the products it carries.
- All activities in a value delivery system must be enumerated and responsibility assigned for them.
- Small retailers may have to use suppliers outside the normal distribution channel to get the products they want and gain adequate supplier support. Although large retailers may be able to buy directly from manufacturers, smaller retailers may have to buy through wholesalers handling such accounts.
- A value delivery system is as good as its weakest link. No matter how well a retailer performs its activities, it will still have unhappy shoppers if suppliers deliver late or do not honor warranties.

- The nature of a given value delivery system must be related to target market expectations.
- Channel member costs and functions are influenced by each party's role. Long-term cooperation and two-way information flows foster efficiency.
- Value delivery systems are complex due to the vast product assortment of superstores, the many forms of retailing, and the use of multiple distribution channels by some manufacturers.
- Nonstore retailing (such as mail order, phone, and Web transactions) requires a different delivery system than store retailing.
- Due to conflicting goals about profit margins, shelf space, and so on, some channel members are adversarial—to the detriment of the value delivery system and channel relationships.

When they forge strong positive channel relationships, members of a value delivery system better serve each other and the final consumer. Here's how:

> At Wal-Mart and Sam's Club, we're 100 percent committed to giving customers unbeatable value, reliable quality, and friendly service. Working closely with suppliers to drive out unnecessary costs allows us to pass savings to our shoppers. We realize it takes a lot of time and effort to become a Wal-Mart or Sam's Club supplier; therefore, we may not be the proper fit for every business. In the end, whether we do business or not, we're confident the steps outlined here will enhance your overall business development. To initiate the partnership process, please visit Walmartstores.com and apply online.[15]

Ace (www.acehardware.com) prides itself on strong relationships with its suppliers.

> Since the Ace Hardware cooperative structure allows our buyers to negotiate with combined buying power of over 4,800 locations, our store owners have a significant advantage over nonaffiliated stores. Our regional and state-of-the-art distribution centers and computerized ordering give you efficient access to more than 70,000 items in every major hardware category. Your Ace Hardware store will also be equipped with a proprietary computerized management system, which will provide accurate sales transaction processing, detailed sales and expense information, and extensive inventory management and ordering features to help you run a "tight ship."[16]

One relationship-oriented practice that some manufacturers and retailers use, especially supermarket chains, is *category management*, whereby channel members collaborate to manage products by category rather than by individual item. Successful category management is based on these actions: (1) Retailers listen better to customers and stock what they want. (2) Profitability is improved because inventory matches demand more closely. (3) By being better focused, shoppers find each department to be more desirable. (4) Retail buyers have more responsibility and accountability for category results. (5) Retailers and suppliers share data and are more computerized. (6) Retailers and suppliers plan together. Category management is discussed further in Chapter 14.

Figure 2-7 shows various factors that contribute to effective channel relationships.

THE DIFFERENCES IN RELATIONSHIP BUILDING BETWEEN GOODS AND SERVICE RETAILERS

Consumer interest in services makes it crucial to understand the differences in relationship building between retailers that market services and those that market goods. This applies to store-based and nonstore-based firms, those offering only goods *or* services, and those offering goods *and* services.

Goods retailing focuses on the sale of tangible (physical) products. **Service retailing** involves transactions in which consumers do not purchase or acquire ownership of tangible products. Some retailers engage in either goods retailing (such as hardware stores) or service retailing (such as travel agencies); others offer a combination of the two (such as Best Buy selling PCs and offering fee-based Geek Squad services). The latter format is growing. Consider how many drugstores offer film developing, how many department stores have beauty salons, how many hotels have gift shops, and so on.

Service retailing encompasses such diverse businesses as personal services, hotels and motels, auto repair and rental, and recreational services. In addition, although several services have not been commonly considered a part of retailing (such as medical, dental, legal, and educational services), they should be when they entail final consumer sales. There are three basic kinds of service retailing:

- **Rented-goods services**, whereby consumers lease and use goods for specified periods of time. Tangible goods are leased for a fixed time, but ownership is not obtained and the goods

FIGURE 2-7
Elements Contributing to Effective Channel Relationships

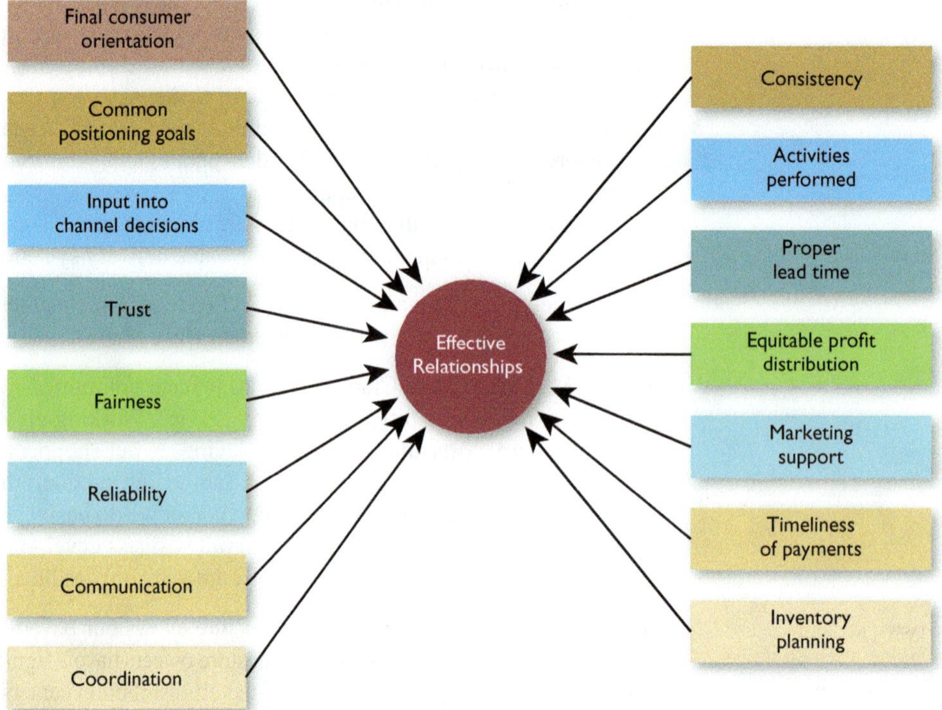

must be returned when the rental period is up. Examples are Hertz car rentals, carpet cleaner rentals at a supermarket, and video rentals at Redbox kiosks.

- **Owned-goods services**, whereby goods owned by consumers are repaired, improved, or maintained. In this grouping, the retailer providing the service never owns the good involved. Illustrations include watch repair, lawn care, and an annual air-conditioner tune-up.
- **Nongoods services**, whereby intangible personal services are offered to consumers who then experience the services rather than possess them. The seller offers personal expertise for a specified time in return for a fee; tangible goods are not involved. Some examples are stockbrokers, travel agents, real-estate brokers, and personal trainers.

Please note: The terms *customer service* and *service retailing* are not interchangeable. Customer service refers to the activities undertaken *in conjunction with* the retailer's main business; they are part of the total retail experience. Service retailing refers to situations in which services *are sold to* consumers.

Cheap Tickets (www.cheaptickets.com) makes itself more tangible through its descriptive name.

There are four unique aspects of service retailing that influence relationship building and customer retention: (1) The intangibility of many services makes a consumer's choice of competitive offerings tougher than with goods. (2) The service provider and his or her services are sometimes inseparable (thus localizing marketing efforts). (3) The perishability of many services prevents storage and increases risks. (4) The human nature involved in many services makes them more variable.

The intangible (and possibly abstract) nature of some services makes it harder for a firm to develop a clear consumer-oriented strategy, particularly because many retailers (such as opticians, repairpeople, and landscapers) start service businesses on the basis of their product expertise. The inseparability of the service provider and his or her services means the owner-operator is often indispensable and good customer relations are pivotal. Perishability presents a risk that in many cases cannot be overcome. Thus, revenues from an unrented hotel room are forever lost. Variability means service quality may differ for each shopping experience, store, or service provider. See Figure 2-8.

Service retailing is much more dependent on personal interactions and word-of-mouth communication than goods retailing. According to Leonard Berry, building customer–firm relationships benefits both parties: "For services that are personally important, variable in quality, and/or complex, many customers will desire to be relationship customers." For example, financial, insurance, and hairstyling services have characteristics "that would cause many customers to desire continuity with

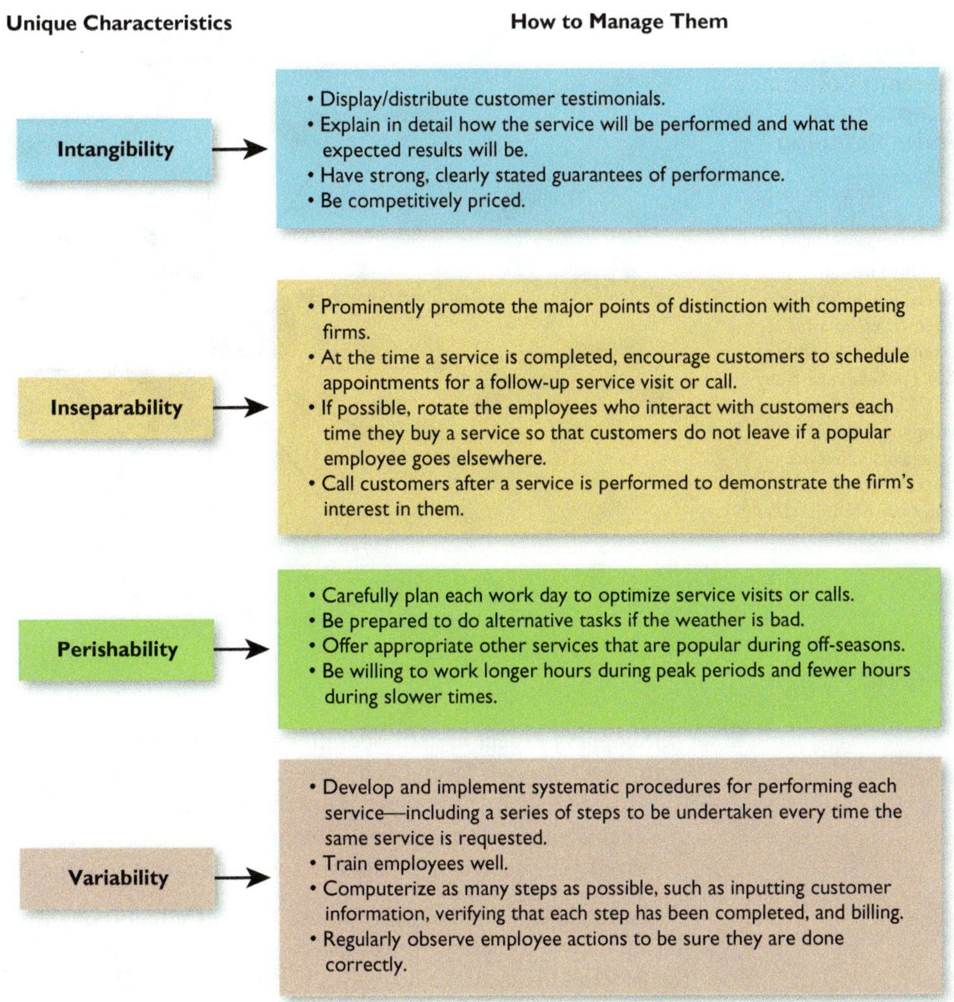

FIGURE 2-8
The Unique Characteristics of Service Retailing and How to Manage Them

the same provider, a proactive service attitude, and customized service delivery." As Berry notes, service intangibility makes it harder for customers to evaluate performance before a purchase. The variability of services that are labor intensive "encourages customer loyalty when excellent service is experienced. Not only does the auto repair firm want to find customers who will be loyal, but customers want to find an auto repair firm that evokes their loyalty." Understanding customers and building a social rapport "over a series of service encounters facilitates the tailoring of service to customer specifications." Relationship retailing may not apply to every service scenario: "However, for those services distinguished by the characteristics discussed here, it is potent."[17]

Figure 2-9 highlights several factors that consumers may consider in forming their perceptions about the caliber of the service retailing experience offered by a particular firm. The appendix at the end of this chapter presents an additional discussion on the unique aspects of operating a service retailing business.

TECHNOLOGY AND RELATIONSHIPS IN RETAILING

Technology is beneficial to retailing relationships if it facilitates a better communication flow between retailers and their customers, as well as between retailers and their suppliers, and there are faster, more dependable transactions.

These two points are key in studying technology and its impact on relationships in retailing:

1. In each firm, the roles of technology and "humans" must be clear and consistent with the goals and style of that business. Although technology can facilitate customer service, it may become overloaded and break down. It is also viewed as impersonal by some consumers. New technology must be set up efficiently with minimal disruptions to suppliers, employees, and customers.

FIGURE 2-9
Selected Factors Affecting Consumer Perceptions of Service Retailing

Sources: Adapted by the authors from Leonard L. Berry, Kathleen Seiders, and Dhruv Grewal, "Understanding Service Convenience," *Journal of Marketing*, Vol. 66 (July 2002), pp. 1–17; and Hung-Chang Chiu, "A Study on the Cognitive and Affective Components of Service Quality," *Total Quality Management*, Vol. 13 (March 2002), pp. 265–274.

2. Shoppers expect certain operations to be in place, so they can rapidly complete credit transactions, get feedback on product availability, and so on. Firms have to deploy some advances (such as a computerized checkout system) simply to be competitive. By enacting other advances, they can be distinctive. For instance, consider the paint store with computerized paint-matching equipment for customers who want to touch up old paint jobs.

Throughout this book, we devote a lot of attention to technological advances via our "Technology in Retailing" boxes and in-chapter discussions. Here, we look at technology's effects in terms of electronic banking and customer–supplier interactions.

Electronic Banking

Electronic banking involves both the use of automatic teller machines (ATMs) and the instant processing of retail purchases. It allows centralized recordkeeping and lets customers complete transactions 24 hours a day, 7 days a week at bank and nonbank locations—including home or office. Besides its use in typical financial transactions (such as check cashing, deposits, withdrawals, and transfers), electronic banking is now used in retailing. Many retailers accept some form of electronic debit payment plan (discussed further in Chapter 13), whereby the purchase price is immediately deducted from a consumer's bank account by computer and transferred to the retailer's account.

Worldwide, there are more than 2.4 billion ATMs—425,000 in the United States alone—and people make several billion ATM transactions yearly.[18] ATMs are located in banks, shopping centers, department stores, supermarkets, convenience stores, hotels, and airports; on college campuses; and at other sites. With sharing systems, such as the Cirrus, Maestro, and Plus networks, consumers can make transactions at ATMs outside their local banking areas and around the world.

A highly touted new version of electronic payment is called the *smart card* by industry observers. The smart card contains an electronic strip that stores and modifies customer information as transactions take place. Its acceptance is important for retailers and shoppers alike:

> A smart card includes an embedded integrated circuit chip and communicates with a reader through physical contact or with a remote contactless electromagnetic field that energizes the chip and transfers data between the card and the reader. Smart cards can store large amounts of data, carry out data storage and management, encryption, decryption, and digital signature calculations, and interact intelligently with a smart card reader. Smart card

technology conforms to international standards and is available in a variety of form factors, including plastic cards, key fobs, watches, subscriber identification modules used in GSM mobile phones, and USB-based tokens.[19]

Customer and Supplier Interactions

Technology is changing the nature of retailer–customer and retailer–supplier interactions. See Figure 2-10. If applied well, benefits accrue to all parties. If not, there are negative ramifications. Here are several illustrations.

Retailers widely use point-of-sale scanning equipment. Why? By electronically scanning products (rather than having cashiers "ring up" each product), retailers can quickly complete transactions, amass sales data, give feedback to suppliers, place and receive orders faster, reduce costs, and adjust inventory. There is a downside to scanning: the error rate. This can upset consumers, especially if they perceive scanning as inaccurate. Yet, according to research on scanning, scanner errors in reading prices occur very infrequently; although consumers believe most errors result in overcharges, overcharges and undercharges are equally likely. One way to assure consumers is to display more information at the point of purchase.

One type of point-of-sale system involves self-scanning (which is discussed further in Chapter 13). Although some retailers now believe that self-scanning is too impersonal, about one-sixth of U.S. supermarkets utilize self-scanning equipment. Here's how a basic customer-operated point-of-sale (POS) system—a self-scanning checkout—works:

> Customers pay for and bag their own merchandise without interacting with a human cashier, although a support person is typically nearby and available. The station includes a touch-screen display, barcode scanner, weighing scale, credit card reader and cash reader,

FIGURE 2-10

Advances in Technology Aid Retailer Interactions

Retailer interactions with their customers and suppliers are faster and more multi-platform than ever. Communications "anywhere, anytime" are now a reality. The new world of technology affects both large and small retailers.

Source: Samer/Shutterstock.com. Reprinted by permission.

and deposit unit. After the customer scans the item's barcode, the item is placed in the bag, which is hanging on a scale. If the weight of the additional item does not jive with the item just scanned, the customer is asked to rescan it, otherwise an alarm will notify the attendant.[20]

Neiman Marcus pioneered the electronic gift card (www.neimanmarcus.com).

Other technological innovations are also influencing retail interactions. Here are three examples:

- Many retailers think they have the answer to the problem of finding the perfect gift—the electronic gift card. Its sales have risen sharply in recent times: "With electronic or virtual gift cards and mobile applications that allow consumers to purchase and redeem gift cards from their mobile/smart phones, sales only continue to grow. While consumers flock to them for their flexibility, businesses have embraced them as a means to increase sales. Not only are buyers spurred into making new purchases, but they often spend more than the gift card amount. For retailers, gift cards can also be instrumental to improving cash flow and managing inventory."[21]
- Interactive electronic kiosks (discussed in Chapter 6) are gaining in use. For example, the Nordic Choice Hotel chain is the first in Norway to use "a 100 percent automated check-in and departure system at a major hotel. The Comfort Xpress Hotel in Oslo allows guests to reserve, check in, and check out without having to deal with a pesky human. Using a system by Ariane Systems, guests check in prior to arrival using the Allegro Web/mobile check-in platform. They click a link received via E-mail or text and set a check-in time, manage room preferences, update their profile, and pay."[22]
- More retailers are using Web portals to exchange information with suppliers: "ChainDrugStore.net (www.chaindrugstore.net) is the network for manufacturers, wholesalers, and others that need to analyze, understand, and manage their pharmacy activity to achieve increased profitability and business efficiencies. We work with more than 300 manufacturers, wholesalers, and managed care organizations to positively impact pharmacy purchasing, dispensing, reimbursement, and contracting strategy by secure online communications, analytics, and proprietary business intelligence tools."[23] ChainDrugStore.net is the link with more than 100,000 stores and pharmacies.

ETHICAL PERFORMANCE AND RELATIONSHIPS IN RETAILING

Ethical challenges fall into three interconnected categories: *Ethics* relates to the retailer's moral principles and values. *Social responsibility* involves acts benefiting society. *Consumerism* entails protecting consumer rights. "Good" behavior depends not only on the retailer but also on the expectations of the community in which it does business.

TECHNOLOGY IN RETAILING

Customer Relations Management and Apparel Retailing

Diane Ferraez, the marketing manager of Jesta I.S. (www.jestais.com), a software company specializing in customer relationship management (CRM) solutions, states that the use of CRM software depends on the nature of an apparel retailer's business. "Apparel retailers that cater to the budget-conscious shopper may not use a full CRM package because the nature of the merchandise is entirely on 'opportunistic buying' and not on purchasing a particular line of merchandise." In addition, many low-end retailers focus on minimizing checkout waiting lines, so there is little opportunity to capture information. Lastly, some low-end shoppers do not want to be identified as "low-end shoppers."

Ferraez warns apparel retailers to be aware of three common pitfalls in planning and implementing a technology-based CRM solution:

- Seeking to capture customer data on the customer's first store visit. Data should be captured slowly, a little at a time, until complete.
- Forcing the CRM system to ask the customer questions at a specific point in time. The system must recognize that some customers may feel uncomfortable proving phone numbers, for example, to male sales associates.
- Offering promotions to customers that cannot be acted upon in the store environment. The CRM system needs to reflect a store's inventory availability.

Source: Jessica Binns, "CRM: Helping Apparel Companies Compete," *Apparel Magazine* (April 2011), pp. 12–14.

Throughout this book, in "Ethics in Retailing" boxes and chapter discussions, we look at many ethical issues. Here we study the broader effects of ethics, social responsibility, and consumerism. Visit our Web site for links on retailers' ethical challenges (www.pearsonhighered.com/bermanevans).

Ethics

In dealing with their constituencies (customers, the general public, employees, suppliers, competitors, and others), retailers have a moral obligation to act ethically. Furthermore, due to the media attention paid to firms' behavior and the high expectations people have today, a failure to be ethical may lead to adverse publicity, lawsuits, the loss of customers, and a lack of self-respect among employees.

When a retailer has a sense of **ethics**, it acts in a trustworthy, fair, honest, and respectful manner with each of its constituencies. Executives must articulate to employees and channel partners which kinds of behavior are acceptable and which are not. The best way to avoid unethical acts is for firms to have written ethics codes, to distribute them to employees and channel partners, to monitor behavior, and to punish poor behavior—and for top managers to be highly ethical in their own conduct. See Figure 2-11.

Society often may deem certain behavior to be unethical even if laws do not forbid it. Most observers would agree that practices such as these are unethical (and sometimes illegal, too):

- Raising prices on scarce products after a natural disaster such as a hurricane.
- Not having adequate merchandise on hand when a sale is advertised.
- Charging high prices in low-income areas because consumers there do not have the transportation mobility to shop out of their neighborhoods.
- Selling alcohol and tobacco products to children.
- Having a salesperson pose as a market researcher when engaged in telemarketing.
- Defaming competitors.
- Selling refurbished merchandise as new.
- Pressuring employees to push high-profit items, even if these items are not the best products.
- Selling information from a customer data base to other parties.

The Direct Marketing Association makes its complete ethics code available at its Web site (www.dmaresponsibility.org/Guidelines).

Many trade associations promote ethics codes to member firms. For example, here are some provisions of the Direct Marketing Association's ethics code:

Article 1: "All offers should be clear, honest, and complete."

Article 8: "All contacts should disclose the name of the sponsor and each purpose of the contact; no one should make offers or solicitations in the guise of one purpose when the intent is a different purpose."

FIGURE 2-11
"Ethics" in Retailing

Some retailers are less ethical than they should be. They need to do better. Use this photo as an example. It is pretty easy to read the large print in the store sign: "WEEKEND SALE. ENTIRE STORE. TAKE 40% OFF." It is almost impossible to read the small print at the bottom: "excludes dress shirts, neckwear, handbags, & accessories."

Source: Chin-Hong, Cheah/Shutterstock.com. Reprinted by permission.

Article 24: "No sweepstakes promotion should represent that a recipient or entrant has won a prize or that any entry stands a greater chance of winning a prize than any other entry when this is not the case."

Article 32: "Firms should be sensitive to the issue of consumer privacy."[24]

Social Responsibility

A retailer exhibiting **social responsibility** acts in the best interests of society—as well as itself. The challenge is to balance corporate citizenship with a fair level of profits for stockholders, management, and employees. Some forms of social responsibility are virtually cost-free, such as having employees participate in community events or disposing of waste products in a more careful way. Some are more costly, such as making donations to charitable groups or giving away goods and services to a school. Still others mean going above and beyond the letter of the law, such as having free loaner wheelchairs for persons with disabilities besides legally mandated wheelchair accessibility to retail premises.

Most retailers know socially responsible acts do not go unnoticed. Although the acts may not stimulate greater patronage for firms with weak strategies, they can be a customer inducement for those otherwise viewed as "me too" entities. It may also be possible to profit from good deeds. If a retailer donates excess inventory to a charity that cares for the ill, it can take a tax deduction equal to the cost of the goods plus one-half the difference between the cost and the retail price. To do this, a retailer must be a corporation and the charity must use the goods and not sell or trade them.

The Ronald McDonald House program (www.rmhc.org) is one of the most respected community outreach efforts in retailing.

This is what some retailers are doing. McDonald's founded Ronald McDonald House so families can stay at a low-cost facility instead of a costly hotel when seriously ill children get medical treatment away from home. Target is among the firms that no longer sells cigarettes. Wal-Mart's environmental goals "are simple and straightforward: to be supplied 100 percent by renewable energy, to create zero waste, and to sell products that sustain people and the environment."[25] J.C. Penney requires all suppliers to sign a code of conduct that underage labor is not used. Hannaford Bros.' pledge sums up the role of a socially involved retailer:

> A Hannaford supermarket is a part of the community, and our associates are your friends and neighbors. We're committed to the towns and cities in which we do business, dedicating time and resources to support schools, groups, and organizations that enrich all our lives. Each year, Hannaford gives more than $4 million in charitable donations and sponsorships directly to programs that help families and children—and donates more than 8 million pounds of groceries to hunger-relief programs. And that's not to mention the time and money donated individually by our associates.[26]

ETHICS IN RETAILING

Adapting to the Latest ADA Requirements

In July 2010, the Americans with Disabilities Act (ADA) underwent a major revision. As of March 15, 2012, when these changes are effective, retail facilities need to meet new requirements relating to rest-room space and configuration, aisle width, and the slope of floor space. ADA standards for parking lots and shopping center mall entrances have also been upgraded.

Penalties for not complying with ADA regulations can exceed $100,000. In addition, the ADA is empowered to force retailers to renovate their current facilities so as to comply with its revised requirements. Retail facilities completed prior to March 15, 2012 could be built to either the old or new ADA standards.

Under the old standard, retailers were also fined and required to upgrade their facilities to meet the ADA standards in effect. For example, QuikTrip (www.quiktrip.com), a convenience store chain with over 550 locations, was fined $55,000 and required to establish a $1.5 million fund to cover damages to handicapped individuals. In addition, that chain needed to improve parking accessibility and upgrade its fuel pumps within a three-year period. JoAnn Fabrics & Craft Stores (www.joann.com) agreed, under the old standards, to renovate its entrances, aisles, displays, cutting areas, and checkout counters at its 840 U.S. stores.

Source: Kevin Hughes, "New Disabilities Act Requirements Loom," www.nrei.com (January–February 2011), p. 48.

Consumerism

Consumerism involves the activities of government, business, and other organizations to protect people from practices infringing upon their rights as consumers. These actions recognize that consumers have basic rights that should be safeguarded. As President Kennedy said about 50 years ago, consumers have the *right to safety* (protection against unsafe conditions and hazardous goods and services), the *right to be informed* (protection against fraudulent, deceptive, and incomplete information, advertising, and labeling), the *right to choose* (access to a variety of goods, services, and retailers), and the *right to be heard* (consumer feedback, both positive and negative, to the firm and to government agencies).

Learn more about ADA (www.ada.gov).

Retailers and their channel partners need to avoid business practices violating these rights and to do all they can to understand and protect them. These are some reasons:

- Some retail practices are covered by legislation. One major law is the **Americans with Disabilities Act (ADA)**, which mandates that persons with disabilities be given appropriate access to retailing facilities. As Title III of the Act states (www.ada.gov/cguide.htm): "Public accommodations [retail stores] must comply with basic nondiscrimination requirements that prohibit exclusion, segregation, and unequal treatment. They also must comply with specific requirements related to architectural standards for new and altered buildings; reasonable modifications to policies, practices, and procedures; effective communication with people with hearing, vision, or speech disabilities; and other access requirements. Additionally, public accommodations must remove barriers in existing buildings where it is easy to do so without much difficulty or expense, given the public accommodation's resources." ADA affects entrances, vertical transportation, width of aisles, and store displays. See Figure 2-12.
- People are more apt to patronize firms perceived as customer-oriented and not to shop with ones seen as "greedy."
- Consumers are more knowledgeable, price-conscious, and selective than in the past. Online customer reviews and social media now attract a lot of shopper interest.
- Large retailers may be viewed as indifferent to consumers. They may not provide enough personal attention for shoppers or may have inadequate control over employees.
- For some shoppers, the increasing use of self-service causes frustration.
- Innovative technology is unsettling to many consumers, who must learn new shopping behavior (such as how to use electronic video kiosks).
- Retailers are in direct customer contact, so they are often blamed for and asked to resolve problems caused by manufacturers (such as defective products).

FIGURE 2-12

Understanding the Americans with Disabilities Act

The Americans with Disabilities Act requires that retailers provide reasonable access—both inside and outside—their stores. As highlighted here, aisles must be wide enough to accommodate shoppers who use scooters or wheelchairs to maneuver around.

Source: imageegami/Shutterstock.com. Reprinted by permission.

One troublesome issue for consumers involves how retailers handle *customer privacy*. A consumer-oriented approach, comprising these elements, can reduce negative shopper feelings: (1) Notice—"A company should provide consumers with a clear and conspicuous notice regarding its information practices." (2) Consumer choice—"A company should provide consumers with an opportunity to decide whether it may disclose personal information about them to unaffiliated third parties." (3) Access and correction—"Companies should provide consumers with an opportunity to access and correct personal information that they have collected about the consumers." (4) Security—"Companies should adopt reasonable security measures to protect the privacy of personal information." (5) Enforcement—"The firm should have in place a system by which it can enforce its privacy policy."[27]

To avoid customer relations problems, many retailers have devised programs to protect consumer rights without waiting for government or consumer pressure to do so. Here are examples.

For 100 years, J.C. Penney has adhered to the general principles of the "Penney Idea":

> To serve the public, as nearly as we can, to its complete satisfaction; to expect for the service we render a fair remuneration and not all the profit the traffic will bear; to do all in our power to pack the customer dollar with value, quality, and satisfaction; to continue training ourselves and our associates so the service we give will be more intelligently performed; to improve constantly the human factor in our business; to reward men and women in our firm by participation in what the business produces; and to test our every policy, method, and act—"Does it square with what is right and just?"[28]

More than 40 years ago, the Giant Food supermarket chain devised a consumer bill of rights (based on President Kennedy's), which it still follows today: (1) Right to safety—Giant's product safety standards, such as age-labeling toys, go beyond those required by the government. (2) Right to be informed—Giant has a detailed labeling system. (3) Right to choose—Consumers who want to purchase possibly harmful or hazardous products (such as foods with additives) can do so. (4) Right to be heard—A continuing dialog with reputable consumer groups is in place. (5) Right to redress—There is a money-back guarantee policy on products. (6) Right to service—Customers should receive good in-store service.[29]

A number of retailers have enacted their own programs to test merchandise for such attributes as value, quality, misrepresentation of contents, safety, and durability. Sears, Wal-Mart, A&P, Macy's, and Target are just a few of those doing testing. Among the other consumerism activities undertaken by many retailers are setting clear procedures for handling customer complaints, sponsoring consumer education programs, and training personnel to interact properly with customers.

Consumer-oriented activities are not limited to large chains; small firms can also be involved. A local toy store can separate toys by age group. A grocery store can set up displays featuring environmentally safe detergents. A neighborhood restaurant can cook foods in low-fat vegetable oil. A sporting goods store can give a money-back guarantee on exercise equipment, so people can try it at home.

Chapter Summary

1. *To explain what "value" really means and highlight its pivotal role in retailers' building and sustaining relationships.* Sellers undertake a series of activities and processes to provide a given level of value for the consumer. Consumers then perceive the value offered by sellers, based on the perceived benefits received versus the prices paid. Perceived value varies by type of shopper.

   A retail value chain represents the total bundle of benefits offered by a channel of distribution. It comprises shopping location, ambience, customer service, the products/brands carried, product quality, the in-stock position, shipping, prices, the retailer's image, and so forth. Some elements of a retail value chain are visible to shoppers. Others are not. An expected retail strategy represents the minimum value chain elements a given customer segment expects from a given retailer type. An augmented retail strategy includes the extra elements that differentiate retailers. A potential retail strategy includes value chain elements not yet perfected in the retailer's industry category.

2. *To describe how both customer relationships and channel relationships may be nurtured in today's highly competitive marketplace.* For relationship retailing to work, enduring relationships are needed with other channel members, as well as with customers. More retailers now realize loyal customers are the backbone of their business.

To engage in relationship retailing with consumers, these factors should be considered: the customer base, customer service, customer satisfaction, and loyalty programs and defection rates. In terms of the customer base, all customers are not equal. Some shoppers are more worth nurturing than others; they are a retailer's core customers.

Customer service has two components: expected services and augmented services. The attributes of personnel who interact with customers, as well as the number and variety of customer services offered, have a big impact on the relationship created. Some firms have improved customer service by empowering personnel, giving them the authority to bend some rules. In devising a strategy, a retailer must make broad decisions and then enact specific tactics as to credit, delivery, and so forth.

Customer satisfaction occurs when the value and customer service provided in a retail experience meet or exceed expectations. Otherwise, the consumer will be dissatisfied.

Loyalty programs reward the best customers, those with whom a retailer wants to develop long-lasting relationships. To succeed, they must complement a sound value-driven retail strategy. By studying defections, a firm can learn how many customers it is losing and why they no longer patronize it.

Members of a distribution channel jointly represent a value delivery system. Each one depends on the others; and every activity must be enumerated and responsibility assigned. Small retailers may have to use suppliers outside the normal channel to get the items they want and gain supplier support. A delivery system is as good as its weakest link. A relationship-oriented technique that some manufacturers and retailers are trying, especially supermarket chains, is category management.

3. *To examine the differences in relationship building between goods and service retailers.* Goods retailing focuses on selling tangible products. Service retailing involves transactions where consumers do not purchase or acquire ownership of tangible products.

There are three kinds of service retailing: rented-goods services, where consumers lease goods for a given time; owned-goods services, where goods owned by consumers are repaired, improved, or maintained; and nongoods services, where consumers experience personal services rather than possess them. Customer service refers to activities that are part of the total retail experience. With service retailing, services are sold to the consumer.

The unique features of service retailing that influence relationship building and retention are the intangible nature of many services, the inseparability of some service providers and their services, the perishability of many services, and the variability of many services.

4. *To discuss the impact of technology on relationships in retailing.* Technology is advantageous when it leads to an improved information flow between retailers and suppliers, and between retailers and customers, and to faster, smoother transactions.

Electronic banking involves both the use of ATMs and the instant processing of retail purchases. It allows centralized records and lets customers complete transactions 24 hours a day, 7 days a week at various sites. Technology is also changing the nature of supplier–retailer–customer interactions via point-of-sale equipment, self-scanning, electronic gift cards, interactive kiosks, and other innovations.

5. *To consider the interplay between retailers' ethical performance and relationships in retailing.* Retailer challenges fall into three related categories: Ethics relates to a firm's moral principles and values. Social responsibility has to do with benefiting society. Consumerism entails the protection of consumer rights. "Good" behavior is based not only the firm's practices but also on the expectations of the community in which it does business.

Ethical retailers act in a trustworthy, fair, honest, and respectful way. Firms are more apt to avoid unethical behavior if they have written ethics codes, communicate them to employees, monitor and punish poor behavior, and have ethical executives. Retailers perform in a socially responsible manner when they act in the best interests of society through recycling and conservation programs and other efforts. Consumerism activities involve government, business, and independent organizations. Four consumer rights are basic: to safety, to be informed, to choose, and to be heard.

Key Terms

value (p. 27)
value chain (p. 27)
core customers (p. 30)
expected customer service (p. 31)
augmented customer service (p. 31)
employee empowerment (p. 31)
revolving credit account (p. 34)
option credit account (p. 34)
open credit account (p. 34)
customer satisfaction (p. 35)
consumer loyalty (frequent shopper) programs (p. 35)
value delivery system (p. 36)
goods retailing (p. 37)
service retailing (p. 37)
rented-goods services (p. 37)
owned-goods services (p. 38)
nongoods services (p. 38)
electronic banking (p. 40)
ethics (p. 43)
social responsibility (p. 44)
consumerism (p. 45)
Americans with Disabilities Act (ADA) (p. 45)

Questions for Discussion

1. When a consumer shops at an upscale apparel store, what factors determine whether the consumer feels that he or she got a fair value? How does the perception of value differ when that same consumer shops at a low-end apparel store?
2. What are the expected and augmented value chain elements for each of these retailers?
   a. Home Depot.
   b. Ikea.
   c. Local fruit-and-vegetable store.
3. Why should a retailer devote special attention to its core customers? How should it do so?
4. What is the connection between customer service and employee empowerment? Is employee empowerment always a good idea? Why or why not?
5. How would you measure the level of customer satisfaction with your favorite restaurant?
6. Devise a consumer loyalty program for Barnes & Noble.
7. What are the unique aspects of service retailing? Give an example of each.
8. What are the pros and cons of ATMs? As a retailer, would you want an ATM in your store? Why or why not?
9. Will the time come when most consumer purchases are made with self-scanners? Explain your answer.
10. Describe three unethical, but legal, acts on the part of retailers that you have recently encountered. How have you reacted in each case?
11. Differentiate between social responsibility and consumerism from the perspective of a retailer.
12. How would you deal with consumer concerns about privacy in their relationships with retailers?

Web-Based Exercise

Visit the Web site of Sephora (www.sephora.com), the perfume and cosmetics chain with stores in 25 countries. Click on "Customer Service" at the bottom of the home page. Comment on the information you find there. Does Sephora have customer-oriented policies? Explain your answer.

Note: Also stop by our Web site (www.pearsonhighered.com/bermanevans) to experience a number of highly interactive, appealing Web exercises based on actual company demonstrations, and sample materials related to retailing.

APPENDIX Planning for the Unique Aspects of Service Retailing

We present this appendix because service retailing in the United States and around the world is growing steadily and represents a large portion of overall retailing. In the United States, consumers spend 60 percent of their after-tax income on such services as travel, recreation, personal care, education, medical care, and housing. About 80 percent of the labor force works in services. Consumers spend billions of dollars each year to rent such products as power tools and party goods (coffee urns, silverware, wine glasses, etc.). People annually spend $150 billion to maintain their cars. There are 82,000 beauty and barber shops, 40,000 dry cleaning and laundry outlets, 48,000 hotels and motels, and 27,000 private fitness and recreation clubs. During the past 40 years, the prices of services have risen more than the prices of many goods. Due to technological advances, automation has substantially reduced manufacturing labor costs, but many services remain labor-intensive due to their personal nature.[1]

Here, we look at the abilities required to be a successful service retailer, how to improve the performance of service retailers, and the strategy of a Baldrige Award winner.

Abilities Required to Be a Successful Service Retailer

The personal abilities required to succeed in service retailing are usually quite distinct from those in goods retailing:

- With service retailing, the major value provided to the customer is some type of retailer service, not the ownership of a physical product produced by a manufacturer.
- Specific skills are often required, and these skills may not be transferable from one type of service to another. TV repairpeople, beauticians, and accountants cannot easily change businesses or transfer skills. The owners of appliance stores, cosmetics stores, and toy stores (all goods retailers) would have an easier time than service retailers in changing and transferring their skills to another area.
- More service operators must possess licenses or certification to run their businesses. Barbers, real-estate brokers, dentists, attorneys, plumbers, and others must pass exams in their fields.
- Owners of service businesses must enjoy their jobs and have the aptitude for them. Because of the close personal contact with customers, these elements are essential and difficult to feign.

Many service retailers can operate on lower overall investments and succeed on less yearly revenues than goods retailers. A firm with four outdoor tennis courts can operate with one worker who functions as clerk/cashier and maintenance person. A tax-preparation firm can succeed with one accountant. A watch repair business needs one repairperson. In each case, the owner may be the only skilled worker. Operating costs can be held down accordingly. On the other hand, a goods retailer needs a solid product assortment and inventory on hand, which may be costly and require storage facilities.

The time commitment of a service retailer differs by type of business opportunity. Some businesses, such as a self-service laundromat or a movie theater, require a low time commitment. Other businesses, such as house painting or a travel agency, require a large time commitment because personal service is the key to profitability. More service firms are in the high rather than the low time-investment category.

Improving the Performance of Service Retailers

Service tangibility can be increased by stressing service provider reliability, promoting a continuous theme (the Hertz #1 Club Gold), describing specific results (a car tune-up's improving gas consumption by one mile per gallon), and offering warranties (hotels giving automatic refunds to unhappy guests). Airlines have Web sites where customers can select flights and make their reservations interactively. These sites are a tangible representation of the airlines and their logos.

Demand and supply can be better matched by offering similar services to market segments with different demand patterns (Manhattan tourists versus residents), new services with demand patterns that are countercyclical from existing services (cross-country skiing during the winter at Denver golf resorts), new services that complement existing ones (beauty salons adding tanning booths), special deals during nonpeak times (midweek movie theater prices), and new services not subject to existing capacity constraints (a 10-table restaurant starting a home catering service).

Standardizing services reduces their variability, makes it easier to set prices, and improves efficiency. Services can be standardized by clearly defining each task, determining the minimum and maximum times needed to complete each task, selecting the best order for tasks to be done, and noting the optimum time and quality of the entire service. Standardization has been successfully applied to such firms as quick-auto-service providers (oil change and tune-up firms), legal services (for house closings and similar proceedings), and emergency medical care centers. If services are standardized, there is often a trade-off (e.g., more consistent quality and convenience in exchange for less of a personal touch).

Besides standardizing services, retailers may be able to make services more efficient by automating them and substituting machinery for labor. Thus, real-estate attorneys often use computerized word-processing templates for common paragraphs in house closings. This means more consistency in the way documents look, time savings, and neater documents with fewer errors. Among the service firms that automate at least part of their operations are banks, car washes, bowling alleys, airlines, phone services, real-estate brokers, and hotels.

One way that services can increase customer loyalty is by better understanding and reacting to shopper complaints. This strategy enables a service operator to rectify problem areas that would otherwise be unknown. It also enables the service operator to offer restitution to the consumer so that he/she will remain loyal. Unfortunately, too often, a dissatisfied customer will find it easier to switch to a competitor (or complain to friends and family) as opposed to complaining to the service operator.[2] A recent study found that Web-based retailers can reduce the negative effect of a service-related failure by communicating with these customers and treating them in a fair manner. Employee politeness and sincerity are closely related to customer satisfaction following a service failure.[3]

Other research has found that a retailer's service support, service-related training, and rewards and recognition for good service all motivate the firm's employees to provide higher levels of service quality. And employees are more likely to practice good service when service quality is consistently communicated within the retail organization.[4]

The location of a service retailer must be carefully considered. Sometimes, as with TV repairs, house painting, and lawn care, the service is "delivered" to the customer. The firm's location becomes a client's home, and the actual retail office is rather insignificant. Many clients might never even see a service firm's office; they make contact by phone or personal visits, and customer convenience is optimized. The firm incurs travel expenses, but it also has low (or no) rent and does not have to maintain store facilities, set up displays, and so on. Other service retailers are visited on "specific-intent" shopping trips. Although a customer may be concerned about the convenience of a service location, he or she usually does not select a skilled practitioner such as a doctor or a lawyer based on the location. It is common for doctors and attorneys to have offices in their homes or near hospitals or court buildings. A small store can often be used because little or no room is needed for displaying merchandise. A travel agency may have six salespeople and book millions of dollars in trips, but fit into a 500-square-foot store.

To improve their pricing decisions, service retailers can apply these principles to "capture and communicate value through their pricing":[5] Satisfaction-based pricing recognizes and reduces customer perceptions of uncertainty that service intangibility magnifies. It involves service guarantees, benefit-driven pricing, and flat-rate pricing. Relationship pricing encourages long-term relationships with valuable customers. It entails long-term contracts and price bundling. Efficiency pricing shares cost savings with customers that arise from the firm's efficiently executing service tasks. It is related to the concept of cost leadership.

Negotiated pricing occurs when a retailer works out pricing arrangements with individual customers because a unique or complex service is involved and a one-time price must be agreed on. Unlike traditional pricing (whereby each consumer pays the same price for a standard service), each consumer may pay a different price under negotiated pricing (depending on the nature of the unique service). A moving company charges different fees, depending on the

FIGURE A2-1
Lessons in Service Retailing from the Best Firms

Source: Figure developed by the authors based on information in Robert C. Ford, Cherrill P. Heaton, and Stephen W. Brown, "Delivering Excellent Service: Lessons from the Best Firms," *California Management Review*, Vol. 44 (Fall 2001), pp. 39–56.

distance of the move, who packs the breakable furniture, the use of stairs versus an elevator, access to highways, and the weight of furniture.

Contingency pricing is an arrangement whereby the retailer does not get paid until after the service is performed and payment is contingent on the service's being satisfactory. A real-estate broker earns a fee only when a house purchaser (who is ready, willing, and able to buy) is presented to the house seller. Several brokers may show a house to prospective buyers, but only the broker who actually sells the house earns a commission. This technique presents risks to a retailer because considerable time and effort may be spent without payment. A broker may show a house 25 times, not sell it, and, therefore, not be paid.

One customer type is often beyond the reach of some service firms: the do-it-yourselfer. And the number of do-it-yourselfers in the United States is growing, as service costs increase (and due to the weak economy). The do-it-yourselfer does a car tune-up, paints the house, mows the lawn, makes all vacation plans, and/or sets up a darkroom for developing film. Goods-oriented discount retailers do well by selling supplies to these people, but service retailers suffer because the labor is done by the customer.

Figure A2-1 highlights 10 lessons that service retailers can learn from the best in the business, such as Walt Disney Company, Marriott International, Ritz-Carlton, and Southwest Airlines.

The Strategy of Pal's Sudden Service: A Baldrige Award Winner[6]

The Baldrige Award is given by the president of the United States to businesses—manufacturing and service, small and large—and to education and healthcare organizations that apply and are judged to be outstanding in seven areas: leadership; strategic planning; customer and market focus; measurement, analysis, and knowledge management; human resource focus; process management; and business results. One of the few retailers to win this award is Pal's Sudden Service—based in Kingsport, Tennessee—a privately owned, quick-service restaurant chain with 23 locations (as of 2011). The firm distinguishes itself by offering competitively priced food of consistently high quality, delivered rapidly, cheerfully, and without error.

Only one other restaurant, K&N Management, a Texas-based operator of seven fast-food restaurants, has won the Baldrige Award; and K&N made 13 trips to Pal's over a nine-year period to view Pal's operation. According to K&N's co-owner, its sales were around $3 million per unit when they first observed Pal's and were around $7.5 million per unit in 2011.

Hop over to Pal's Sudden Service (www.palsweb.com). See why it's a big winner!

For every organizational and operational activity, Pal's has a process. Its Business Excellence Process is the key integrating element and ensures that customer needs are met in each transaction. Carried out under the leadership of Pal's top executives and its owner-operators, the Business Excellence Process spans all facets of operations from strategic planning (done annually) to online quality control.

Pal's goal is to provide the "quickest, friendliest, most accurate service available." Achieving this is a challenge in an industry with very high employee turnover rates. The company's success in significantly reducing turnover among frontline production and service personnel, most of whom are between the ages of 16 and 32, is a key advantage. Owner-operators and assistant managers have primary responsibility for training based on a four-step model: show it, do it, evaluate it, and perform it again. Employees must demonstrate 100 percent competence before they can work at a specific job task.

Pal's order handout speed has improved more than 30 percent since 1995, decreasing to 20 seconds, almost four times faster than its top competitor. As a result, Pal's is able to serve one car every 18 seconds at its drive-thru windows. Order errors are rare, averaging less than 1 for every 3,500 transactions. The firm aims to reduce its error rate even more. In addition, Pal's has consistently received the highest health inspection scores in its market.

Strategic Planning in Retailing

As we show in Chapter 3, strategic planning in retailing is a complex process with a number of intertwined factors, both controllable and uncontrollable. And the Internet and social media are dramatically altering the way that retailers plan out their strategies.

Let us consider the impact of technology on how retailers plan their in-store displays and layouts. Previously, "in-store marketing—the practice of trying to influence consumers' buying decisions as they shop—typically consisted of flashy product displays, special promotions at the end of the aisle, and attention-grabbing packaging on the shelf."

Today, many consumers approach their shopping much differently; and retailers need to plan and adapt their strategies accordingly. Consumers not only go online to shop; they also go online to begin the shopping process and, sometimes, just to hear what others have to say. Until recently, consumers spent most of their online shopping activities on such items as electronics, travel, and apparel. Now, they even look for the comments of fellow shoppers for more routine products. In a recent survey, WSL Strategic Retail (a consulting firm) found that many post-recession consumers spend more time researching everyday merchandise, including diapers, beverages, and pet products.

As reported in the *Wall Street Journal*, this change in consumer behavior:

> has led retailers and brands to target customers via blogs, social media sites such as Facebook and Twitter, and campaigns on retail sites, in addition to in-store campaigns. Brands including household goods are reacting by trying to be visible online where deal hunters research. "Buy now" buttons on social media sites like Facebook, product reviews on retailer and manufacturer Web sites, online circulars, digital coupons, and blogger buzz are now crucial for products to make it on to the shopping list and ultimately into the cart, marketers say.[1]

Chapter Objectives

1. To show the value of strategic planning for all types of retailers
2. To explain the steps in strategic planning for retailers: situation analysis, objectives, identification of consumers, overall strategy, specific activities, control, and feedback
3. To examine the individual controllable and uncontrollable elements of a retail strategy, and to present strategic planning as a series of integrated steps
4. To demonstrate how a strategic plan can be prepared

Source: BeTA-Artworks/fotolia.com.

Overview

In this chapter, we cover strategic retail planning—the foundation of our book—in detail. As noted in Chapter 1, a **retail strategy** is the overall plan or framework of action that guides a retailer. Ideally, it will be at least one year long and outline the retailer's mission, goals, consumer market, overall and specific activities, and control mechanisms. Without a defined and well-integrated strategy, a firm may be unable to cope with the marketplace. This is the advice offered by the U.S. Small Business Administration:

> Do you really need to make a business plan? The short answer is yes. The importance of a comprehensive, thoughtful business plan cannot be overemphasized. Many factors critical to business success depend upon your plan: outside funding, credit from suppliers, management of your operation and finances, promotion and marketing of your business, and achievement of your goals and objectives. Some people assume that if they are not going to seek financial support from lenders or investors to open their business that they don't need to prepare a business plan, but *every* business should have one. Writing a business plan serves as a roadmap for your venture when you're starting out. It can help you figure out many key business elements, including: (1) What you will need to do to get started and what resources (time, money, etc.) you will need to expend. (2) What it will take for your business to make a profit and how long that will take. (3) What information potential customers, vendors, and investors will need to know in order for you to market your business effectively. Writing your business plan also forces you to think about your business objectively.[2]

My Strategic Plan (www.mystrategicplan.com) has a lot of useful planning tools for retailers at its Web site. Click on "Resources."

The process of strategic retail planning has several attractive features: It provides a thorough analysis of the requirements for doing business for different types of retailers. It outlines retailer goals. A firm determines how to differentiate itself from competitors and develop an offering that appeals to a group of customers. The legal, economic, and competitive environment is studied. A firm's total efforts are coordinated. Crises are anticipated and often avoided.

Strategic planning can be done by the owner of a firm, professional management, or a combination of the two. Even among family businesses, the majority of high-growth companies have strategic plans.

The steps in planning and enacting a retail strategy are interdependent; a firm often starts with a general plan that gets more specific as options and payoffs become clearer. In this chapter, we cover each step in developing a retail strategy, as shown in Figure 3-1. Given the importance of global retailing, a chapter appendix explores the special dimensions of strategic planning in a global environment. Visit our Web site (www.pearsonhighered.com/bermanevans) for several links on strategic planning.

SITUATION ANALYSIS

Situation analysis is a candid evaluation of the opportunities and threats facing a prospective or existing retailer. It seeks to answer two general questions: What is the firm's current status? In which direction should it be heading? Situation analysis means being guided by an organizational mission, evaluating ownership and management options, and outlining the goods/service category to be sold.

A good strategy anticipates and adapts to both the opportunities and threats in the changing business environment. **Opportunities** are marketplace openings that exist because other retailers have not yet capitalized on them. Ikea does well because it is the pioneer firm in offering a huge selection of furniture at discount prices. **Threats** are environmental and marketplace factors that can adversely affect retailers if they do not react to them (and, sometimes, even if they do). Single-screen movie theaters have virtually disappeared because they have been unable to fend off multi-screen theaters.

A firm needs to spot trends early enough to satisfy customers and stay ahead of competitors, yet not so early that shoppers are not ready for changes or that false trends are perceived. Merchandising shifts—such as stocking fad items—are more quickly enacted than changes in a

FIGURE 3-1
Elements of a Retail Strategy

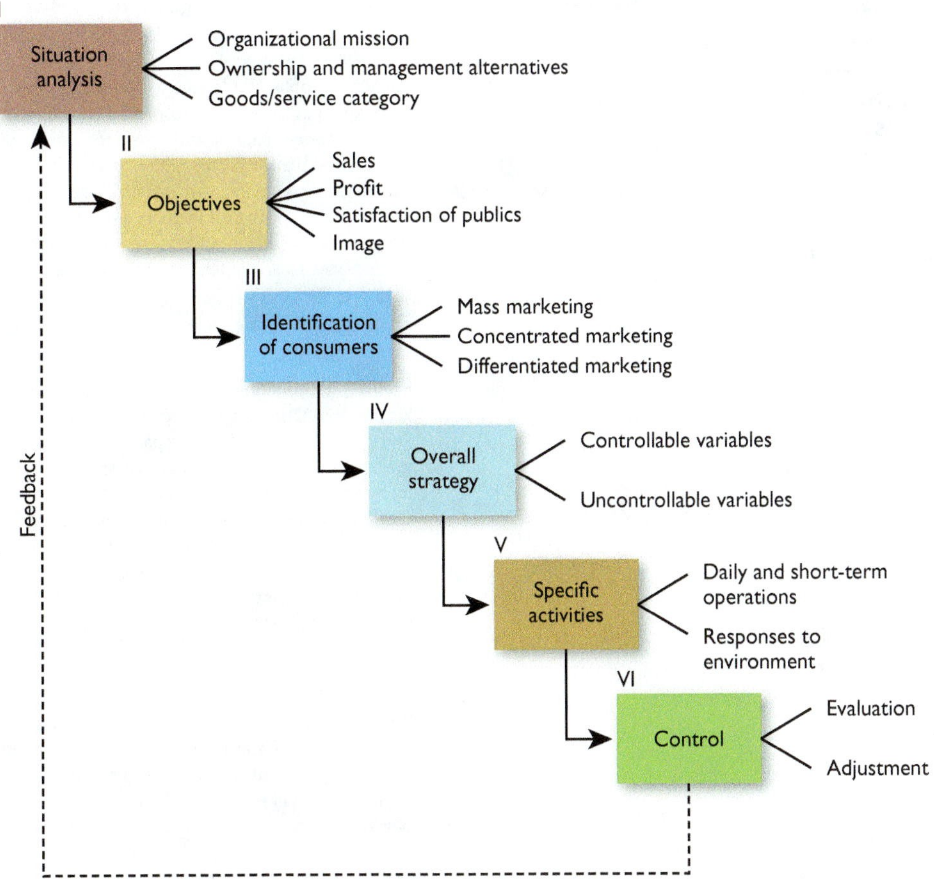

firm's location, price, or promotion strategy. A new retailer can adapt to trends easier than existing ones with established images, ongoing leases, and space limitations. Well-prepared small firms can compete with large retailers.

During situation analysis, especially for a new retailer or one thinking about making a major strategic change, an honest, in-depth self-assessment is vital. It is all right for a person or company to be ambitious and aggressive, but overestimating one's abilities and prospects may be harmful—if the results are entry into the wrong retail business, inadequate resources, or misjudgment of competitors.

Organizational Mission

An **organizational mission** is a retailer's commitment to a type of business and to a distinctive role in the marketplace. It is reflected in the firm's attitude toward consumers, employees, suppliers, competitors, government, and others. A clear mission lets a firm gain a customer following and distinguish itself from competitors. See Figure 3-2.

One major decision is whether to base a business around the goods and services sold or around consumer needs. A person opening a hardware business must decide if, in addition to hardware products, a line of bathroom vanities should be stocked. A traditionalist might not carry vanities because they seem unconnected to the proposed business. But if the store is to be a do-it-yourself home improvement center, vanities are a logical part of the mix. That store would carry any relevant items the consumer wants.

A second major decision is whether a retailer wants a place in the market as a leader or a follower. It could seek to offer a unique strategy, such as Taco Bell becoming the first national quick-serve Mexican food chain. Or it could emulate the practices of competitors but do a better job in executing them, such as a local fast-food Mexican restaurant offering five-minute guaranteed service and a cleanliness pledge.

FIGURE 3-2
Examples of Well-Conceived Organizational Missions

Source: Adapted by the authors from the company mission statements as stated at their Web sites (March 9, 2012).

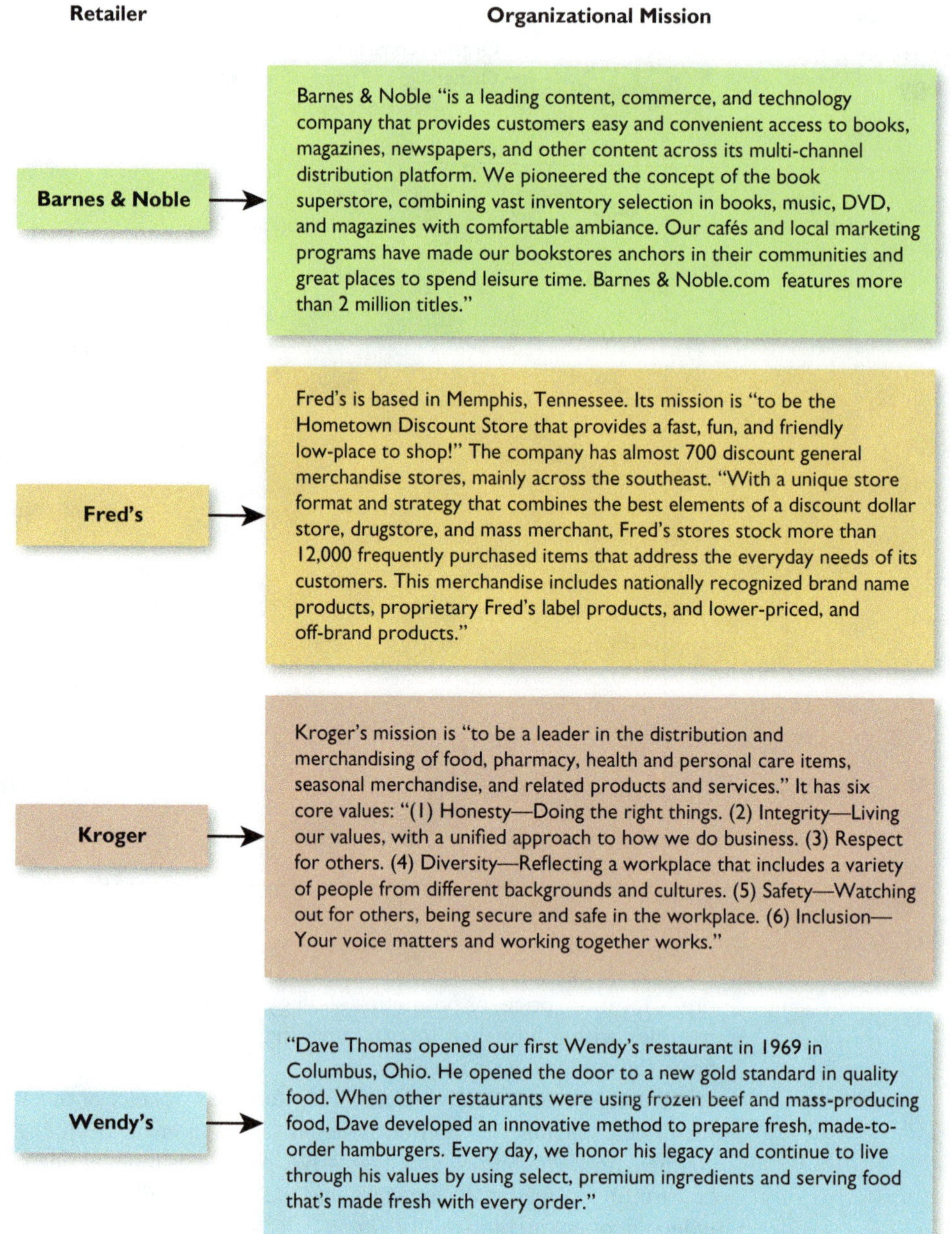

See how the Neiman Marcus Web site (www.neimanmarcus.com) is consistent with its upscale mission.

A third decision involves market scope. Large chains often seek a broad customer base (due to their resources and recognition). It is often best for small retailers and startups to focus on a narrower customer base, so they can compete with bigger firms that tend not to adapt strategies, as well as to local markets.

Although the development of an organizational mission is the first step in the planning process, the mission should be continually reviewed and adjusted to reflect changing company goals and a dynamic retail environment. Here are examples of well-conceived retail organizational missions:[3]

> At McDonald's, our customers are the reason for our existence. We demonstrate our appreciation by providing them with high-quality food and superior service, in a clean, welcoming environment, at a great value. Our goal is QSC&V (quality, service, cleanliness, and value) for each and every customer, each and every time.

CAREERS IN RETAILING

The Skills Needed for Future Retail Executives

Let us summarize the findings of a survey among 135 presidents and chief executive officers concerning the skills needs for the future generation of retail leaders. Although most of the survey respondents came from fashion- and beauty-based specialty stores, about one-third of respondents had their most recent experience with hard goods retailers.

When they were asked what leadership skills are most important for success over the next five years, 80 percent of the responses were "strong vision for the company." Other key skills are "understanding of the consumer" (79 percent of responses), the ability to "team build/foster talent" (72 percent), "good communications skills" (70 percent), "strategic skills" (66 percent), and the "ability to foster innovation in others" (62 percent).

Interestingly, 74 percent of the respondents stated that they will look beyond the retail sector when recruiting for leadership positions in the next five years. When asked why they will be looking at other industries for key retail personnel, the most common response was that they "want leaders with a new perspective" (69 percent of responses), followed by "wanting leaders who are better prepared for new ways business is conducted" (52 percent), and "wanting leaders with skills/expertise not currently available in the industry" (45 percent).

Source: Arnold J. Karr, "Retail CEO Survey: Future Leaders Need Different Skillset," *Women's Wear Daily* (November 1, 2011), p. 1.

PetSmart is the largest specialty retailer of services and solutions for the lifetime needs of pets. It operates pet stores, in-store pet dog and cat boarding facilities, Doggie Day Camps, and is a leading online provider of pet supplies and pet care information. PetSmart provides a broad range of competitively priced pet food and supplies and offers complete pet training and adoption services.

At Zumiez, we do what others have only dreamed of! We provide you with cutting edge clothing, footwear, accessories, DVDs, and hard goods for skate and snow for active lifestyles. Everything we do revolves around the customer—you are the heart of our company. We love and support the skate and snow industries that our customers live and ride for. With the success of our retail Zumiez shops, we've opened our online store for the world to experience, zumiez.com.

Ownership and Management Alternatives

An essential aspect of situation analysis is assessing ownership and management alternatives, including whether to form a sole proprietorship, partnership, or corporation—and whether to start a new business, buy an existing business, or become a franchisee.[4] Management options include owner-manager versus professional manager and centralized versus decentralized structures. Consider that "There is no single best form of ownership for a business. That's partly because the limitations of a particular form of ownership can often be compensated for. For instance, a sole proprietor can often buy insurance coverage to reduce liability exposure. Even after you have established your business as a particular entity, you may need to re-evaluate your choice of entity as the business evolves. An experienced attorney and tax advisor can help you decide which form of ownership is best for your business."[5]

A **sole proprietorship** is an unincorporated retail firm owned by one person. All benefits, profits, risks, and costs accrue to that individual. It is simple to form, fully controlled by the owner, operationally flexible, easy to dissolve, and subject to single taxation by the government. It makes the owner personally liable for legal claims from suppliers, creditors, and others; it can also lead to limited capital and expertise.

A **partnership** is an unincorporated retail firm owned by two or more persons, each with a financial interest. Partners share benefits, profits, risks, and costs. Responsibility and expertise are divided among multiple principals, there is a greater capability for raising funds than with a proprietorship, the format is simpler to form than a corporation, and it is subject to single taxation by the government. Depending on the type of partnership, it, too, can make owners personally liable for legal claims, can be dissolved due to a partner's death or a disagreement, binds all partners to actions made by any individual partner acting on behalf of the firm, and usually has less ability to raise capital than a corporation.

A **corporation** is a retail firm that is formally incorporated under state law. It is a legal entity apart from individual officers (or stockholders). Funds can be raised through the sale of stock, legal claims against individuals are not usually allowed, ownership transfer is relatively easy, the firm is assured of long-term existence (if a founder leaves, retires, or dies), the use of professional managers is encouraged, and unambiguous operating authority is outlined. Depending on the type of corporation, it is subject to double taxation (company earnings and stockholder dividends), faces more government rules, can require a complex process when established, may be viewed as impersonal, and may separate ownership from management. A closed corporation is run by a limited number of persons who control ownership; stock is not available to the public. In an open corporation, stock is widely traded and available to the public.

Sole proprietorships account for 74 percent of all U.S. retail firms that file tax returns, partnerships for 6 percent, and corporations for 20 percent. In terms of sales volume, sole proprietorships account for just 5 percent of total U.S. retail store sales, partnerships for 10 percent, and corporations for 85 percent.[6]

Starting a new business—being entrepreneurial—offers a retailer flexibility in location, operating style, product lines, customer markets, and other factors, and a strategy is fully tailored to the owner's desires and strengths. There may be high construction costs, a time lag until the business is opened and then until profits are earned, beginning with an unknown name, and having to form supplier relationships and amass an inventory of goods. Figure 3-3 presents a checklist to consider when starting a business.

FIGURE 3-3
A Checklist to Consider When Starting a New Retail Business

Source: Adapted by the authors from *Small Business Management Training Instructor's Guide*, No. 109 (Washington, DC: U.S. Small Business Administration, n.d.).

Name of Business ____________________

A. Self-Assessment and Business Choice

✓ Evaluate your strengths and weaknesses.
✓ Commitment paragraph: Why should you be in business for yourself? Why open a new business rather than acquire an existing one or become a member of a franchise chain?
✓ Describe the type of retail business that fits your strengths and desires. What will make it unique? What will the business offer customers? How will you capitalize on the weaknesses of competitors?

B. Overall Retail Plan

✓ State your philosophy of business.
✓ Choose an ownership form (sole proprietorship, partnership, or corporation).
✓ State your long- and short-run goals.
✓ Analyze your customers from their point of view.
✓ Research your market size and store location.
✓ Quantify the total retail sales of your goods/service category in your trading area.
✓ Analyze your competition.
✓ Quantify your potential market share.
✓ Develop your retail strategy: store location and operations, merchandising, pricing, and store image and promotion.

C. Financial Plan

✓ What level of funds will you need to get started and to get through the first year? Where will they come from?
✓ Determine the first-year profit, return on investment, and salary that you need/want.
✓ Project monthly cash flow and profit-and-loss statements for the first two years.
✓ What sales will be needed to break even during the first year? What will you do if these sales are not reached?

D. Organizational Details Plan

✓ Describe your personnel plan (hats to wear), organizational plan, and policies.
✓ List the jobs you like and want to do and those you dislike, cannot do, or do not want to do.
✓ Outline your accounting and inventory systems.
✓ Note your insurance plans.
✓ Specify how day-to-day operations would be conducted for each aspect of your strategy.
✓ Review the risks you face and how you plan to cope with them.

FIGURE 3-4
A Checklist for Purchasing an Existing Retail Business

NAME OF BUSINESS ____________________

- ✓ Why is the seller placing the business up for sale?
- ✓ How much are you paying for goodwill (the cost of the business above its tangible asset value)?
- ✓ Have sales, inventory levels, and profit figures been confirmed by your accountant?
- ✓ Will the seller introduce you to his or her customers and stay on during the transition period?
- ✓ Will the seller sign a statement that he or she will not open a directly competing business in the same trading area for a reasonable time period?
- ✓ If sales are seasonal, are you purchasing the business at the right time of the year?
- ✓ In the purchase of the business, are you assuming existing debts of the seller?
- ✓ Who receives proceeds from transactions made prior to the sale of the business but not yet paid by customers?
- ✓ What is the length of the lease if property is rented?
- ✓ If property is to be purchased along with the business, has it been inspected by a professional engineer?
- ✓ How modern are the storefront and store fixtures?
- ✓ Is inventory fresh? Does it contain a full merchandise assortment?
- ✓ Are the advertising policy, customer service policy, and pricing policy of the past owner similar to yours? Can you continue old policies?
- ✓ If the business is to be part of a chain, is the new unit compatible with existing units?
- ✓ How much trading-area overlap is there with existing stores?
- ✓ Has a lawyer examined the proposed contract?
- ✓ What effect will owning this business have on your lifestyle and on your family relationships?

Buying an existing business allows a retailer to acquire an established company name, a customer following, a good location, trained personnel, and facilities; to operate immediately; to generate ongoing sales and profits; and to possibly get good lease terms or financing (at favorable interest rates) from the seller. Fixtures may be older, there is less flexibility in enacting a strategy tailored to the new owner's desires and strengths, and the growth potential of the business may be limited. Figure 3-4 shows a checklist to consider when purchasing an existing retail business.

By being a franchisee, a retailer can combine independent ownership with franchisor support: strategic planning assistance; a known company name and loyal customer following; cooperative advertising and buying; and a regional, national, or global (rather than local) image. However, a franchisee contract may specify rigid operating standards, limit the product lines sold, and restrict supplier choice; the franchisor company is usually paid continuously (royalties); advertising fees may be required; and there is a possibility of termination by the franchisor if the agreement is not followed satisfactorily.

Strategically, the management format also has a dramatic impact. With an owner-manager, planning tends to be less formal and more intuitive, and many tasks are reserved for that person (such as employee supervision and cash management). With professional management, planning tends to be more formal and systematic. Yet, professional managers are more constrained in their authority than an owner-manager. In a centralized structure, planning clout lies with top management or ownership; managers in individual departments have major input into decisions with a decentralized structure.

A comprehensive discussion of independent retailers, chains, franchises, leased departments, vertical marketing systems, and consumer cooperatives is included in Chapter 4.

Entrepreneur magazine (www.entrepreneur.com) addresses many of the issues facing new and growing firms as they plan their strategies.

Goods/Service Category

Before a prospective retail firm can fully design a strategic plan, it selects a **goods/service category**—the line of business—in which to operate. Figure 3-5 shows the diversity of goods/service categories. Chapter 5 examines the attributes of food-based and general merchandise store retailers. Chapter 6 focuses on Web, nonstore, and other forms of nontraditional retailing.

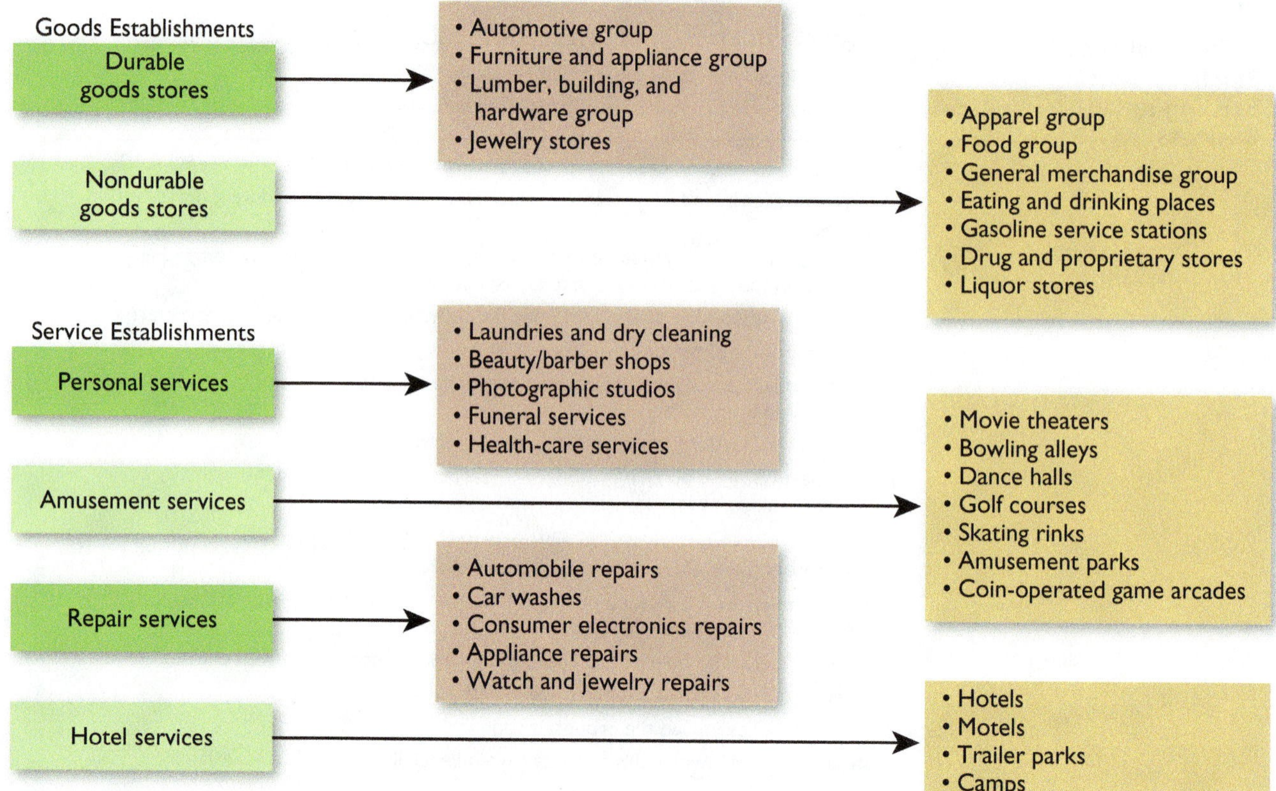

FIGURE 3-5
Selected Kinds of Retail Goods and Service Establishments

It is advisable to specify both a general goods/service category and a niche within that category. Mercedes dealers are luxury auto retailers catering to upscale customers. Wendy's is an eating and drinking chain known for its quality fast food with a menu that emphasizes hamburgers. Motel 6 is a chain whose forte is inexpensive rooms with few frills.

A potential retail business owner should select a type of business that will allow him or her to match personal abilities, financial resources, and time availability with the requirements of that kind of business. Visit our Web site (www.pearsonhighered.com/bermanevans) for links to many retail trade associations, which represent various goods/service categories.

Personal Abilities

Personal abilities depend on an individual's aptitude—the preference for a type of business and the potential to do well; education—formal learning about retail practices and policies; and experience—practical learning about retail practices and policies.

An individual who wants to run a business, likes to use initiative, and has the ability to react quickly to competitive developments will be suited to a different type of situation than a person who depends on others for advice and does not like to make decisions. The first individual could be an independent operator, in a dynamic business such as apparel; the second might seek partners or a franchise and a stable business, such as a stationery store. Some people enjoy customer interaction; they would dislike the impersonality of a self-service operation. Others enjoy the impersonality of mail-order or Web retailing.

In certain fields, education and experience requirements are specified by law. Stockbrokers, real-estate brokers, beauticians, pharmacists, and opticians must all satisfy educational or experience standards to show competency. For example, real-estate brokers are licensed after a review of their knowledge of real-estate practices and their ethical character. The legal designation "broker" does not depend on the ability to sell or have a customer-oriented demeanor.

Some skills can be learned; others are inborn. Accordingly, potential retail owners have to assess their skills and match them with the demands of a given business. This involves careful reflection about oneself. Partnerships may be best when two or more parties possess complementary skills. A person with selling experience may join with someone who has the operating skills to start a business. Each partner has valued skills, but he or she may be unable to operate a retail entity without the expertise of the other.

Financial Resources

Many retail enterprises, especially new, independent ones, fail because the owners do not adequately project the financial resources needed to open and operate the firm. Table 3-1 outlines some of the typical investments for a new retail venture.

Novice retailers tend to underestimate the value of a personal drawing account, which is used for the living expenses of the owner and his or her family in the early, unprofitable stage of a business. Because few new ventures are immediately profitable, the budget must include such expenditures. In addition, the costs of renovating an existing facility often are miscalculated. Underfunded firms usually invest in only essential renovations. This practice reduces the initial investment, but it may give the retailer a poor image. Merchandise assortment, as well as the types of goods and services sold, also affects the financial outlay. Finally, the use of a partnership, corporation, or franchise agreement will affect the investment.

Table 3-2 illustrates the financial requirements for a hypothetical used-car dealer. The initial personal savings investment of $300,000 would force many potential owners to rethink the choice of product category and the format of the firm: (1) The plans for a 40-car inventory reflect this owner's desire for a balanced product line. If the firm concentrates on subcompact, compact, and intermediate cars, it can reduce inventory size and lower the investment. (2) The initial investment can be reduced by seeking a location whose facilities do not have to be modified. (3) Fewer financial resources are needed if a partnership or corporation is set up with other individuals, so that costs—and profits—are shared.

Wells Fargo (https://www.wellsfargo.com/biz) offers financial support and advice for small firms.

The U.S. Small Business Administration (www.sba.gov/category/navigation-structure/loans-grants) assists businesses by guaranteeing thousands of loans each year. Such private companies as Wells Fargo and American Express also have financing programs specifically aimed at small businesses.

Time Demands

Time demands on retail owners (or managers) differ significantly by goods or service category. They are influenced both by consumer shopping patterns and by the ability of the owner or manager to automate operations or delegate activities to others.

TABLE 3-1 Some Typical Financial Investments for a New Retail Venture

Use of Funds	Source of Funds
Land and building (lease or purchase)	Personal savings, bank loan, commercial finance company
Inventory	Personal savings, manufacturer credit, commercial finance company, sales revenues
Fixtures (display cases, storage facilities, signs, lighting, carpeting, etc.)	Personal savings, manufacturer credit, bank loan, commercial finance company
Equipment (cash register, marking machine, office equipment, computers, etc.)	Personal savings, manufacturer credit, bank loan, commercial finance company
Personnel (salespeople, cashiers, stockpeople, etc.)	Personal savings, bank loan, sales revenues
Promotion	Personal savings, sales revenues
Personal drawing account	Personal savings, life insurance loan
Miscellaneous (equipment repair, credit sales [bad debts], professional wholesaler credit, bank services, repayment of loans)	Personal savings, manufacturer and credit plan, bank loan, commercial finance company

Note: Collateral for a bank loan may be a building, fixtures, land, inventory, or a personal residence.

TABLE 3-2 Financial Requirements for a Used-Car Dealer

Total investments (first year)	
Lease (10 years, $60,000 per year)	$ 60,000
Beginning inventory (40 cars, average cost of $10,000)	400,000
Replacement inventory (40 cars, average cost of $10,000)[a]	400,000
Fixtures and equipment (painting, paneling, carpeting, lighting, signs, heating and air-conditioning system, electronic cash register, service bay)	60,000
Replacement parts	75,000
Personnel (one mechanic)	45,000
Promotion (brochures and newspaper advertising)	35,000
Drawing account (to cover owner's personal expenses for one year; all selling and operating functions except mechanical ones performed by the owner)	40,000
Accountant	15,000
Miscellaneous (loan payments, etc.)	100,000
Profit (projected)	40,000
	$1,270,000
Source of funds	
Personal savings	$ 300,000
Bank loan	426,000
Sales revenues (based on expected sales of 40 cars, average price of $13,600)	544,000
	$1,270,000

[a] Assumes that 40 cars are sold during the year. As each type of car is sold, a replacement is bought by the dealer and placed in inventory. At the end of the year, inventory on hand remains at 40 units.

Many retailers must have regular weekend and evening hours to serve time-pressed shoppers. Gift shops, toy stores, and others have extreme seasonal shifts in their hours. Mail-order firms and those selling through the Web, which can process orders during any part of the day, have more flexible hours.

Some businesses require less owner involvement, including gas stations with no repair services, coin-operated laundries, and movie theaters. The emphasis on automation, self-service, standardization, and financial controls lets the owner reduce the time investment. Other businesses, such as hair salons, restaurants, and jewelry stores, require more active owner involvement.

Intensive owner participation can be the result of several factors:

- The owner may be the key service provider, with patrons attracted by his or her skills (the major competitive advantage). Delegating work to others will lessen consumer loyalty.
- Personal services are not easy to automate.
- Due to limited funds, the owner and his or her family must often undertake all operating functions for a small retail firm. Spouses and/or children work in 40 percent of family-owned businesses.
- In a business that operates on a cash basis, the owner must be around to avoid being cheated.

Off-hours activities are often essential. At a restaurant, some foods must be prepared in advance of the posted dining hours. An owner of a small computer store cleans, stocks shelves, and does the books during the hours the firm is closed. A prospective retail owner also has to examine his or her time preferences regarding stability versus seasonality, ideal working hours, and personal involvement.

OBJECTIVES

After situation analysis, a retailer sets **objectives**, the long-run and short-run performance targets it hopes to attain. This helps mold a strategy and translates the organizational mission into action. A firm can pursue goals related to one or more of these areas: sales, profit, satisfaction of publics, and image. Some retailers strive to achieve all these goals; others attend to a few and want to achieve them really well. Think about this array of goals for the Kroger Company:

Kroger (www.kroger.com) is one of the leading food-based retailers in the United States.

> Our strategy focuses on improving our customers' shopping experiences through improved service, product selection, and price. Successful execution of this strategy requires a balance between sales growth and earnings growth. Maintaining this strategy requires the ability to develop and execute plans to generate cost savings and productivity improvements that can be invested in the merchandising and pricing initiatives necessary to support our customer-focused programs, as well as recognizing and implementing organizational changes as required. If we are unable to execute our plans, or if our plans fail to meet our customers' expectations, our sales and earnings growth could be adversely affected.[7]

Sales

Sales objectives are related to the volume of goods and services a retailer sells. Growth, stability, and market share are the sales goals most often sought.

Some retailers set sales growth as a top priority. They want to expand their business. There may be less emphasis on short-run profits. The assumption is that investments in the present will yield future profits. A firm that does well often becomes interested in opening new units and enlarging revenues. However, management skills and the personal touch are sometimes lost with overly fast expansion.

Stability is the goal of retailers that emphasize maintaining their sales volume, market share, price lines, and so on. Small retailers often seek stable sales that enable the owners to make a satisfactory living every year without downswings or upsurges. And certain firms develop a loyal customer following and are intent not on expanding but on continuing the approach that attracted the original consumers.

For some firms, market share—the percentage of total retail-category sales contributed by a given company—is another goal. It is often an objective only for large retailers or retail chains. The small retailer is more concerned with competition across the street than with total sales in a metropolitan area.

Sales objectives may be expressed in dollars and units. To reach dollar goals, a retailer can engage in a discount strategy (low prices and high unit sales), a moderate strategy (medium prices and medium unit sales), or a prestige strategy (high prices and low unit sales). In the long run, having unit sales as a performance target is vital. Dollar sales by year may be difficult to compare due to changing retail prices and inflation; unit sales are easier to compare. A firm with sales of $350,000 three years ago and $500,000 today might assume it is doing well, until unit sales are computed: 10,000 then and 8,000 now.

Profit

With profitability objectives, retailers seek at least a minimum profit level during a designated period, usually a year. Profit may be expressed in dollars or as a percentage of sales. For a firm with yearly sales of $5 million and total costs of $4.2 million, pre-tax dollar profit is $800,000 and profits as a percentage of sales are 16 percent. If the profit goal is equal to or less than $800,000, or 16 percent, the retailer is satisfied. If the goal is higher, the firm has not attained the minimum desired profit and is dissatisfied.

Firms with large capital expenditures in land, buildings, and equipment often set return on investment (ROI) as a goal. ROI is the relationship between profits and the investment in capital items. A satisfactory rate of return is pre-defined and compared with the actual return at the end of the year or other period. For a retailer with annual sales of $5 million and expenditures (including payments for capital items) of $4 million, the yearly profit is $1 million. If the total capital investment is $10 million, ROI is $1 million/$10 million, or 10 percent per year. The goal must be 10 percent or less for the firm to be satisfied.

Operating efficiency may be expressed as 1 – (operating expenses/company sales). The higher the result, the more efficient the firm. A retailer with sales of $2 million and operating costs of $1 million has a 50 percent efficiency rating ([1 – ($1 million/$2 million)]). Of every sales dollar, 50 cents goes for nonoperating costs and profits, and 50 cents for operating expenses. The retailer might set a goal to increase efficiency to 60 percent. On sales of $2 million, operating costs would have to drop to $800,000 ([1 – ($800,000/$2 million)]). Sixty cents of every sales dollar would then go for nonoperating costs and profits, and 40 cents for operations, which would lead to better profits. If a firm cuts expenses too much, customer service may decline; this may lead to a decline in sales and profit.

Satisfaction of Publics

Retailers typically strive to satisfy their publics: stockholders, customers, suppliers, employees, and government. Stockholder satisfaction is a goal for any publicly owned retailer. Some firms set policies leading to small annual increases in sales and profits (because these goals can be sustained over the long run and indicate good management) rather than ones based on innovative ideas that may lead to peaks and valleys in sales and profits (indicating risky decisions). Stable earnings lead to stable dividends.

Customer satisfaction with the total retail experience is a well-entrenched goal at most firms now. A policy of *caveat emptor* ("Let the buyer beware") will not work in today's competitive marketplace. Retailers must listen to criticism and adapt. If shoppers are pleased, other goals are more easily reached. Yet, for many retailers, other objectives rate higher in their list of priorities.

Good supplier relations is also a key goal. Retailers must understand and work with their suppliers to secure favorable purchase terms, new products, good return policies, prompt shipments, and cooperation. Relationships are very important for small retailers due to the many services that suppliers offer them.

Cordial labor relations is another goal that is often critical to retailers' performance. Good employee morale means less absenteeism, better treatment of customers, and lower staffing turnover. Relations can be improved by effective selection, training, and motivation.

Because all levels of government impose rules affecting retailing practices, another goal should be to understand and adapt to these rules. In some cases, firms can influence rules by acting as members of large groups, such as trade associations or chambers of commerce.

Image (Positioning)

An **image** represents how a given retailer is perceived by consumers and others. A firm may be seen as innovative or conservative, specialized or broad-based, discount-oriented or upscale. The key to a successful image is that consumers view the retailer in the manner the firm intends.

Through **positioning**, a retailer devises its strategy in a way that projects an image relative to its retail category and its competitors and that elicits a positive consumer response. A firm selling women's apparel could generally position itself as an upscale or mid-priced specialty retailer, a traditional department store, a discount department store, or a discount specialty retailer, and it could specifically position itself with regard to other retailers carrying women's apparel.

Two opposite positioning philosophies have gained popularity in recent years: mass merchandising and niche retailing. **Mass merchandising** is a positioning approach whereby retailers offer a discount or value-oriented image, a wide and/or deep merchandise selection, and large store facilities. Wal-Mart has a wide, deep merchandise mix whereas Dick's Sporting Goods has a narrower, deeper assortment. These firms appeal to a broad customer market, attract a lot of customer traffic, and generate high stock turnover. Because mass merchants have relatively low operating costs, achieve economies in operations, and appeal to value-conscious shoppers, their continuing popularity is forecast.

Babies "R" Us (www.babiesrus.com) has a very focused strategy and an online tie-in with Toys "R" Us.

In **niche retailing**, retailers identify specific customer segments and deploy unique strategies to address the desires of those segments rather than the mass market. Niching creates a high level of loyalty and shields retailers from more conventional competitors. Babies "R" Us appeals to parents with very young children, whereas Catherines Stores has fashions for plus-size women. A niche retailing approach will have a strong future since it lets retailers stress factors other than price and have a better focus. See Figure 3-6.

Because both mass merchandising and niche retailing are now popular, some observers call this the era of **bifurcated retailing**. They believe this may mean the decline of

TECHNOLOGY IN RETAILING

Supply Chain Management and Cloud Technology

For many retailers, improving efficiency is a key goal. According to Marshall Fisher, a professor of operations and information management at the Wharton School, "cloud computing [technology] is a hugely important development" that enables companies to access third-party software "in a much more convenient way. You can run software, and it looks like it's on your computer."

One major application of cloud technology enables retail executives to better manage international shipments by sea and air transport, to comply with customs requirements, and to use mobile devices like iPhones to track shipments as they go from one truck dispatching center to another. As Chris Jones, an executive at Descartes, a major software supplier, says: "This is a complex process to plan because there are so many vehicle breakdowns, traffic jams, missing shipments, and other unpredictable events."

In a related cloud-technology application, several thousand sales and merchandising employees of Kraft Foods can track the firm's products over various mobile devices including iPhones, Android phones, and even Java-based phones. Inventory management decisions can be made on the basis of sales data by store and warehouse location. As mobile devices become more widely used and have greater storage capacity, graphics capability, and power, the importance of cloud technology will increase.

Source: "Supply-Chain Management: Growing Global Complexity Drives Companies into the 'Cloud,'" http://knowledge.wharton.upenn.edu/article.cfm?articledi=2669 (January 12, 2011).

middle-of-the-market retailing. Firms that are neither competitively priced nor particularly individualistic may have more difficulty competing.

Let's further examine the concept of positioning through these examples:

- The bebe apparel chain "designs, develops, and produces a distinctive line of contemporary women's apparel and accessories. The company uses these brand names:bebe, BEBE SPORT, 2b bebe, and bebe outlet brands." The first bebe boutique was opened in San Francisco in 1976. Today, bebe is "one of the top women's retailers—having developed the contemporary market for the masses. The firm has forever changed the landscape of the women's retail fashion world." By using "an edgy, high-impact, visual ad campaign combining print, outdoor, in-store, and direct mail communication, we attract customers who are intrigued

FIGURE 3-6
Niche Retailing by Babies "R" Us

As the Babies "R" Us Web site (www.babiesrus.com) notes, the chain "features a wide selection of products for newborns and infants, including cribs and furniture, car seats, strollers, formula, diapers, bedding, clothing for preemies through size 48 months, toys, and plenty of unique gift ideas."

Source: Reprinted by permission of Susan V. Berry, Retail Image Consulting, Inc.

FIGURE 3-7
Selected Retail Positioning Strategies

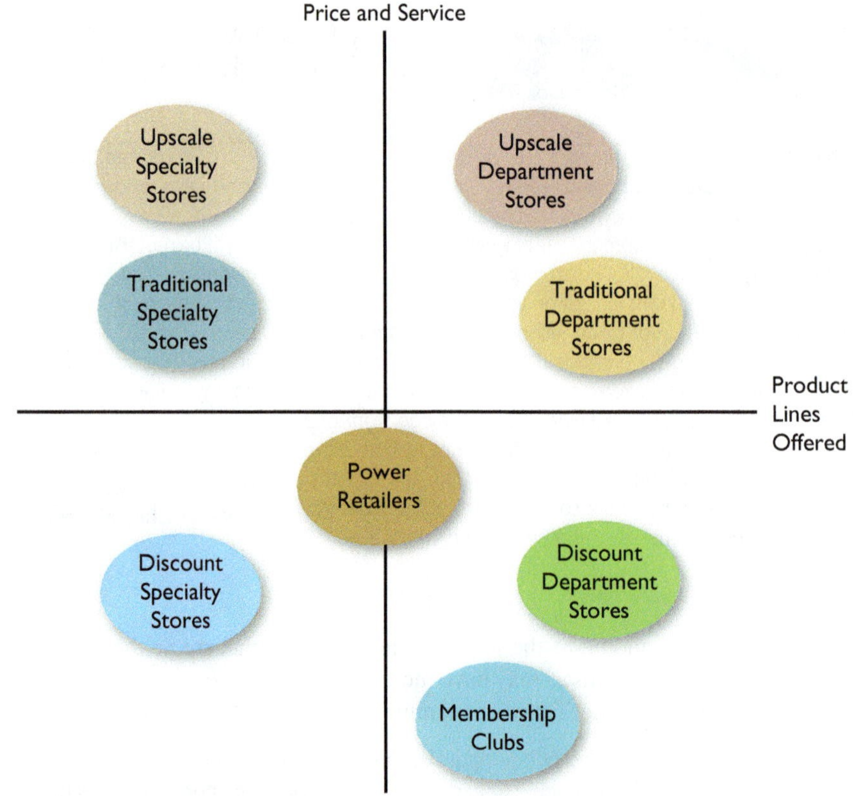

by the playfully sensual and evocative imagery of the bebe lifestyle. We also offer a line of merchandise branded with the distinctive bebe logo to increase brand awareness."[8]

Trader Joe's (www.traderjoes.com) is a shopping haven for consumers looking for distinctive, fairly priced food items.

- At Trader Joe's food stores, providing "value" is the underpinning of its strategy. The company offers everyday low prices on all of the items it sells—"no sales, no gimmicks, no clubs to join, no special cards to swipe." Trader Joe's buys directly from suppliers whenever it can and bargains hard, thereby passing the savings on to its customers: "If an item doesn't pull its weight, it goes away. We buy in volume and contract early to get the best prices. Most grocers charge their suppliers fees for putting an item on the shelf. This means higher prices, so we don't do it. We keep costs low—every penny *we* save is a penny *you* save. It's not complicated. We just focus on what matters—great food + great prices = value."[9]

Figure 3-7 shows a retail positioning map based on two shopping criteria: (1) price and service and (2) product lines offered. Our assumption: There is a link between price and service (high price equals excellent service). Upscale department stores (Neiman Marcus) offer outstanding customer service and carry several product lines. Traditional department stores (Sears) carry more electronics and other product lines than upscale stores. They have a trained sales staff to help customers. Discount department stores (Wal-Mart) carry a lot of product lines and rely on self-service. Membership clubs (Costco) have a limited selection in a number of product categories. They have very low prices and plain surroundings. Upscale specialty stores (Tiffany) offer outstanding customer service and focus on one general product category. Traditional specialty stores (Gap) have a trained sales staff to help customers and focus on one general product category. Discount specialty stores (Old Navy) rely more on self-service and focus on one general product category. Power retailers (Home Depot) offer moderate service and prices and a huge assortment within one general product category.

Selection of Objectives

A firm that clearly sets its goals and devises a strategy to achieve them improves its chances of success.

An example of a retailer with clear goals and a proper strategy to attain them is Papa John's, the 3,700-outlet pizza chain that has outlets in all 50 U.S. states and more than 30 countries. As reported at its Web site (www.papajohns.com/about/pj_mission.shtm), Papa John's focuses on customers. It seeks to generate strong brand loyalty via "(a) authentic, superior-quality products, (b) legendary customer service, and (c) exceptional community service." Papa John's views employees as team members, who represent its most important asset. The firm provides "clear, consistent, strategic leadership and career opportunities for team members who (a) exhibit passion toward work, (b) uphold core values, (c) take pride of ownership in building the long-term value of the Papa John's brand, and (d) have ethical business practices." Papa John's also recognizes the importance of its franchisees. It strives to "create continued opportunity for outstanding financial returns to those franchisees who (a) adhere to proven core values and systems, (b) exhibit passion in running their businesses, and (c) take pride of ownership in building the long-term value of the Papa John's brand." A good return to shareholders rounds out Papa John's strategy.

IDENTIFICATION OF CONSUMER CHARACTERISTICS AND NEEDS

The customer group sought by a retailer is called the **target market**. In selecting its target market, a firm may use one of three techniques: **mass marketing**, selling goods and services to a broad spectrum of consumers; **concentrated marketing**, zeroing in on one specific group; or **differentiated marketing**, aiming at two or more distinct consumer groups, with different retailing approaches for each group.

Supermarkets and drugstores define their target markets broadly. They sell a wide assortment of medium-quality items at popular prices. In contrast, a small upscale men's shoe store appeals to a specific consumer group by offering a narrow, deep product assortment at above-average prices (or in other cases, below-average prices). A retailer aiming at one segment does not try to appeal to everyone.

Department stores are among those seeking multiple market segments. They cater to several customer groups, with unique goods and services for each. Apparel may be sold in a number of distinct boutiques in the store. Large chains frequently have divisions that appeal to different market segments. Darden Restaurants operates Red Lobster (seafood), Olive Garden (Italian), LongHorn Steakhouse (emphasis on beef entrées), Capital Grill (American-style with "relaxed elegance"), Seasons 52 (seasonal grill and wine bar), and Bahama Breeze (Caribbean-style) restaurants for customers with different food preferences.

After choosing the target market, a firm can determine its best competitive advantages and devise a strategy mix. See Table 3-3. The significance of **competitive advantages**—the distinct competencies of a retailer relative to competitors—must not be overlooked. Some examples will demonstrate this:

TABLE 3-3 Target Marketing Techniques and Their Strategic Implications

	Target Market Techniques		
Strategic Implications	Mass Marketing	Concentrated Marketing	Differentiated Marketing
Retailer's location	Near a large population base	Near a small or medium population base	Near a large population base
Goods and service mix	Wide selection of medium-quality items	Selection geared to market segment—high- or low-quality items	Distinct goods/services aimed at each market segment
Promotion efforts	Mass advertising subscription	Direct mail, E-mail, media and messages	Different for each segment
Price orientation	Popular prices	High or low	High, medium, and low—depending on market segment
Strategy	One general strategy for a large homogeneous (similar) group of consumers	One specific strategy directed at a specific, limited group of customers	Multiple specific strategies, each directed at different (heterogeneous) groups of consumers

FIGURE 3-8

La Boqueria Market: A Shopper's Delight

La Boqueria Market in Barcelona is Spain's most famous indoor marketplace. It is especially popular with tourists and local residents who are attracted by the fresh foods and wide variety: "It's been here since medieval times and is the largest market in Spain. The iconic Modernist stained glass entrance attracts millions of visitors every year to this Aladdin's cave of tantalizing food, exotic fruits, and spices." People eat, shop, and gossip together doing what the Spanish excel at—living life and enjoying a sense of community" (www.barcelona-tourist-travel-guide.com/la-boqueria.html).

Source: Borodaev/Shutterstock.com. Reprinted by permission.

Is the T.J. Maxx Web site (www.tjmaxx.com) on target for the customers it wants to reach?

- Tiffany seeks affluent, status-conscious consumers. It puts stores in prestigious shopping areas, offers high-quality products, uses elegant ads, has extensive customer services, and has rather high prices.
- Kohl's targets middle-class, value-conscious shoppers. It locates mostly in suburban shopping areas, offers national brands and Kohl's brands of medium quality, features good values in ads, has some customer services, and charges below-average to average prices.
- T.J. Maxx, an off-price store chain, aims at extremely price-conscious consumers. It locates in low-rent strip shopping centers or districts, offers national brands (sometimes overruns and seconds) of average to below-average quality, emphasizes low prices, offers few customer services, and sets very low prices.

The key to the success of each of these retailers is its ability to define customers and cater to their needs in a distinctive manner. See Figure 3-8.

Retailers are better able to select a target market and satisfy customer needs if they have a good understanding of consumer behavior. This topic is discussed in Chapter 7.

OVERALL STRATEGY

Next, the retailer develops an in-depth overall strategy. This involves two components: the aspects of business the firm can directly affect and those to which the retailer must adapt. The former are called **controllable variables**, and the latter are called **uncontrollable variables**. See Figure 3-9.

A strategy must be devised with both variables in mind. The ability of retailers to grasp and predict the effects of controllable and uncontrollable variables is greatly aided by the use of suitable data. In Chapter 8, information gathering and processing in retailing are described.

FIGURE 3-9
Developing an Overall Retail Strategy

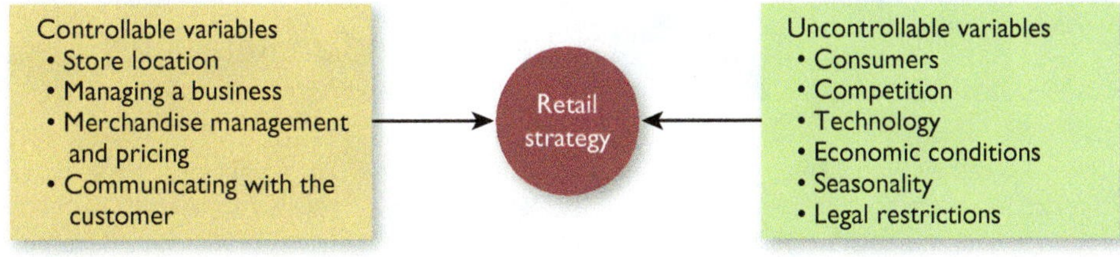

Controllable Variables

The controllable parts of a retail strategy consist of the categories shown in Figure 3-9: store location, managing a business, merchandise management and pricing, and communicating with the customer. A good strategy integrates these areas. These elements are covered in depth in Chapters 9 through 19.

STORE LOCATION A retailer has several store location decisions to make. The initial one is whether to use a store or nonstore format. Then, for store-based retailers, a general location and a specific site are determined. Competitors, transportation access, population density, the type of neighborhood, nearness to suppliers, pedestrian traffic, and store composition are considered in picking a location. See Figure 3-10.

The terms of tenancy (such as rent and operating flexibility) are reviewed and a build, buy, or rent decision is made. The locations of multiple outlets are considered if expansion is a goal.

MANAGING A BUSINESS Two major elements are involved in managing a business: the retail organization and human resource management, and operations management. Tasks, policies, resources, authority, responsibility, and rewards are outlined via a retail organization structure. Practices regarding employee hiring, training, compensation, and supervision are instituted through human resource management. Job descriptions and functions are communicated, along with the responsibility of all personnel and the chain of command.

Operations management oversees the tasks that satisfy customer, employee, and management goals. The financial aspects of operations involve asset management, budgeting, and

FIGURE 3-10
Pushcart Retailing: Stores on Wheels

Djemaa el Fna Square in Marrakech, Morocco is a popular destination for Moroccans and tourists—complete with a mix of retail shops and stalls.

Source: Philip Lange/ Shutterstock.com. Reprinted by permission.

Trends in Indian Retailing

The A.T. Kearney Global Retail Development Index (GRDI) ranks the top 30 emerging countries for retail development. For the fourth time in the past five years, India has been ranked as the most attractive country for retail investment. For 2011, the annual Indian retail market was estimated at $425 billion ($ U.S.). Three major trends characterize retailing in India: the rise in private-label sales, the continued entry of global brands, and the increased role of licensed merchandise.

Private labels currently make up 10 to 12 percent of retail sales. For example, while retailers such as Trent have 90 percent of their sales in private labels, others such as Spencers (with more than 6,000 items covering such diverse goods as food, apparel, and electronics) has 10 percent of its sales in private-label goods.

For the past five years, such luxury global brands as Cartier (www.cartier.com), Armani (www.armani.com), and Prada (www.prada.com) have been targeting India's affluent consumers. Many of these shoppers have become more familiar with these brands from their travel abroad.

Smaller retailers have increasingly turned to licensed brands as a means of building their image. One licensed brand, Born to Shop, is targeted at 25- to 35-year-old females with significant disposable incomes who have hectic schedules.

Source: Dwijorani Senjam, "Consolidation Phase in Indian Retail Industry," *Licensing Journal* (April 2011), pp. 1–6.

resource allocation. Other elements include store format and size, personnel use, store maintenance, energy management, store security, insurance, credit management, computerization, and crisis management.

MERCHANDISE MANAGEMENT AND PRICING In merchandise management, the general quality of the goods and services offering is set. Decisions are made as to the width of assortment (the number of product categories carried) and the depth of assortment (the variety of products carried in any category). Policies are set with respect to introducing new items. Criteria for buying decisions (how often, what terms, and which suppliers) are established. Forecasting, budgeting, and accounting procedures are outlined, as is the level of inventory for each type of merchandise. Finally, the retailer devises procedures to assess the success or failure of each item sold.

With regard to pricing, a retailer chooses from among several techniques; and it decides what range of prices to set, consistent with the firm's image and the quality of goods and services offered. The number of prices within each product category is determined, such as how many prices of luggage to carry. And the use of markdowns is planned in advance.

COMMUNICATING WITH THE CUSTOMER An image can be created and sustained by applying various techniques.

The physical attributes, or atmosphere, of a store and its surrounding area greatly influence consumer perceptions. The impact of the storefront (the building's exterior or the home page for a Web retailer) should not be undervalued, as it is the first physical element seen by customers. Once inside, layouts and displays, floor colors, lighting, scents, music, and the kind of sales personnel also contribute to a retailer's image. Customer services and community relations generate a favorable image for the retailer.

The right use of promotional tools enhances sales performance. These tools range from inexpensive flyers for a take-out restaurant to an expensive national ad campaign for a franchise chain. Three forms of paid promotion are available: advertising, personal selling, and sales promotion. In addition, a retailer can obtain free publicity when stories about it are written, televised, broadcast, or blogged.

While the preceding discussion outlined the controllable parts of a retail strategy, uncontrollable variables (discussed next) must also be kept in mind.

Uncontrollable Variables

The uncontrollable parts of a strategy consist of the factors shown in Figure 3-9: consumers, competition, technology, economic conditions, seasonality, and legal restrictions. Farsighted retailers adapt the controllable parts of their strategies to take into account elements beyond their immediate control.

CONSUMERS A skillful retailer knows it cannot alter demographic trends or lifestyle patterns, impose tastes, or "force" goods and services on people. The firm learns about its target market and forms a strategy consistent with consumer trends and desires. It cannot sell goods or services that are beyond the price range of customers, that are not wanted, or that are not displayed or advertised in the proper manner.

COMPETITION There is often little that retailers can do to limit the entry of competitors. In fact, a retailer's success may encourage the entry of new firms or cause established competitors to modify their strategies to capitalize on the popularity of a successful retailer. A major increase in competition should lead a company to re-examine its strategy, including its target market and merchandising focus, to ensure that it sustains a competitive edge. A continued willingness to satisfy customers better than any competitor is fundamental.

TECHNOLOGY Computer systems are available for inventory control and checkout operations. There are more high-tech ways to warehouse and transport merchandise. Toll-free 800 numbers are popular for consumer ordering. And, of course, there is the Web. Nonetheless, some advancements are expensive and may be beyond the reach of small retailers. For example, although small firms might have computerized checkouts, they will probably be unable to use fully automated inventory systems. As a result, their efficiency may be less than that of larger competitors. They must adapt by providing more personalized service.

ECONOMIC CONDITIONS Economic conditions are beyond any retailer's control, no matter how large it is. Unemployment, interest rates, inflation, tax levels, and the annual economic growth (known as gross domestic product or GDP) are just some economic factors with which a retailer copes. In outlining the controllable parts of its strategy, a retailer needs to consider forecasts about international, national, state, and local economies.

SEASONALITY A constraint on certain retailers is their seasonality, as well as the possibility that unpredictable weather will play havoc with sales forecasts. Retailers selling sports equipment, fresh food, travel services, and car rentals cannot control the seasonality of demand or bad weather. They can diversify offerings to carry a goods/service mix with items that are popular in different seasons. Thus, a sporting goods retailer can emphasize ski equipment and snowmobiles in the winter, baseball and golf equipment in the spring, scuba equipment and fishing gear in the summer, and basketball and football supplies in the fall.

LEGAL RESTRICTIONS Table 3-4 shows how each controllable aspect of a retail strategy is affected by the legal environment.

The FTC has a publication on why "Competition Counts" (http://www.ftc.gov/bc/edu/pubs/consumer/general/zgen01.pdf).

Retailers that operate in more than one state are subject to federal laws and agencies. The Sherman Act and the Clayton Act deal with monopolies and restraints of trade. The Federal Trade Commission deals with unfair trade practices and consumer complaints. The Robinson-Patman Act prohibits suppliers from giving unjust merchandise discounts to large retailers that could adversely affect small ones. The Telemarketing Sales Rule protects consumers.

At the state and local levels, retailers have to deal with many restrictions. Zoning laws prohibit firms from operating at certain sites and demand that building specifications be met. Blue laws limit the times during which retailers can conduct business. Construction, smoking, and other codes are imposed by the state and city. The licenses to operate some businesses are under state or city jurisdiction.

For more information, contact the Federal Trade Commission (www.ftc.gov), state and local bodies, the Better Business Bureau (www.bbb.org), the National Retail Federation (www.nrf.com), or a group such as the Direct Marketing Association (www.the-dma.org).

Integrating Overall Strategy

What do you think about the overall strategy of Kmart (www.kmart.com)?

At this point, the firm has set an overall strategy. It has chosen a mission, an ownership and management style, and a goods/service category. Goals are clear. A target market has been designated and studied. Decisions have been made about store location, managing the business, merchandise management and pricing, and communications. These factors must be coordinated to have a consistent, integrated strategy and to account for uncontrollable variables (consumers,

TABLE 3-4 The Impact of the Legal Environment on Retailing[a]

Controllable Factor Affected	Selected Legal Constraints on Retailers
Store location	*Zoning laws* restrict the potential choices for a location and the type of facilities constructed.
	Blue laws restrict the days and hours during which retailers may operate.
	Environmental laws limit the retail uses of certain sites.
	Door-to-door (direct) selling laws protect consumer privacy.
	Local ordinances involve fire, smoking, outside lighting, capacity, and other rules.
	Leases and mortgages require parties to abide by stipulations in tenancy documents.
Managing the business	*Licensing provisions* mandate minimum education and/or experience for certain personnel.
	Personnel laws involve nondiscriminatory hiring, promoting, and firing of employees.
	Antitrust laws limit large firm mergers and expansion.
	Franchise agreements require parties to abide by various legal provisions.
	Business taxes include real-estate and income taxes.
	Recycling laws mandate that retailers participate in recycling for various materials.
Merchandise management and pricing	*Trademarks* provide retailers with exclusive rights to the brand names they develop.
	Merchandise restrictions forbid some retailers from selling specified goods or services.
	Product liability laws allow retailers to be sued if they sell defective products.
	Lemon laws specify consumer rights if products, such as autos, require continuing repairs.
	Sales taxes are required in most states, although *tax-free days* have been introduced in some locales to encourage consumer shopping.
	Unit-pricing laws require price per unit to be displayed (most often applied to supermarkets).
	Collusion laws prohibit retailers from discussing selling prices with competitors.
	Sale prices must be a reduction from the retailer's normal selling prices.
	Price discrimination laws prohibit suppliers from offering unjustified discounts to large retailers that are unavailable to smaller ones.
Communicating with the customer	*Truth-in-advertising* and *-selling laws* require retailers to be honest and not omit key facts.
	Truth-in-credit laws require that shoppers be informed of all terms when buying on credit.
	Telemarketing laws protect the privacy and rights of consumers regarding telephone sales.
	Bait-and-switch laws make it illegal to lure shoppers into a store to buy low-priced items and then to aggressively try to switch them to higher-priced ones.
	Inventory laws mandate that retailers must have sufficient stock when running sales.
	Labeling laws require merchandise to be correctly labeled and displayed.
	Cooling-off laws let customers cancel completed orders, often made by in-home sales, within three days of a contract date.

[a] This table is broad in nature and omits a law-by-law description. Many laws are state or locally oriented and apply only to certain locations; the laws in each locale differ widely. The intent here is to give the reader some understanding of the current legal environment as it affects retail management.

competition, technology, economy, seasonality, and legal restrictions). The firm is then ready to do the specific tasks to carry out its strategy productively.

SPECIFIC ACTIVITIES

Short-run decisions are now made and enacted for each controllable part of the strategy in Figure 3-9. These actions are known as **tactics** and encompass a retailer's daily and short-term operations. They must be responsive to the uncontrollable environment. Here are some tactical moves a retailer may make:

Stores (www.stores.org) tracks all kinds of tactical moves made by retailers.

- *Store location.* Trading-area analysis gauges the area from which a firm draws its customers. The level of competition in a trading area is studied regularly. Relationships with nearby retailers are optimized. A chain carefully decides on the sites of new outlets. Facilities are actually built or modified.

Reaching Out in Times of Tragedy

On a monthly basis, *Franchising World* reports on instances of the franchising industry's community outreach programs. For example, one issue described the franchising community's efforts in assisting those who suffered as a result of the earthquake and tsunami that hit Japan in 2011.

The nature of the retailers' efforts varied: Some provided collection boxes, others made direct contributions from retailer-based charitable foundations, and still others developed cause-related marketing programs, which donated a portion of profits on specific items.

7-Eleven (www.7-eleven.com) installed in-store collection boxes in nearly 39,000 of its store locations to assist relief organizations in Japan. McDonald's (www.mcdonalds.com) decided to contribute $2 million to the International Federation of the Red Cross for the charity's disaster relief efforts in Japan. Auntie Anne's (www.auntieannes.com), the pretzel chain, donated the profits for its sales of lemonade over one entire month to relief efforts in Japan. As a result of this commitment, sales of lemonade almost tripled at Auntie Anne's outlets. Marriott International (www.marriott.com) offered Marriott Rewards members the opportunity to redeem points for donations to the International Federation of Red Cross and Red Crescent Societies Japan Earthquake and Tsunami relief programs.

Source: "Franchise Community Reaches Out to Japan," *Franchising World* (June 2011), p. 70.

- *Managing the business.* There is a clear chain of command from managers to workers. An organization structure is set into place. Personnel are hired, trained, and supervised. Financial management tracks assets and liabilities. The budget is spent properly. Operations are systemized and adjusted as required.
- *Merchandise management and pricing.* The assortments within departments and the space allotted to each department require constant decision making. Innovative firms look for new merchandise and clear out slow-moving items. Purchase terms are negotiated and suppliers sought. Selling prices reflect the firm's image and target market. Price ranges offer consumers some choice. Adaptive actions are needed to respond to higher supplier prices and react to competitors' prices.
- *Communicating with the customer.* The storefront and display windows, store layout, and merchandise displays need regular attention. These elements help gain consumer enthusiasm, present a fresh look, introduce new products, and reflect changing seasons. Ads are placed during the proper time and in the proper media. The deployment of sales personnel varies by merchandise category and season.

The essence of retailing excellence is building a sound strategy and fine-tuning it. A firm that stands still is often moving backward. Tactical decision making is discussed in detail in Chapters 9 through 19.

CONTROL

In the **control** phase, a review takes place (Step VI in Figure 3-1), as the strategy and tactics (Steps IV and V) are assessed against the business mission, objectives, and target market (Steps I, II, and III). This procedure is called a retail audit, which is a systematic process for analyzing the performance of a retailer. The retail audit is covered in Chapter 20.

The strengths and weaknesses of a retailer are revealed as performance is reviewed. The aspects of a strategy that have gone well are maintained; those that have gone poorly are revised, consistent with the mission, goals, and target market. The adjustments are reviewed in the firm's next retail audit.

FEEDBACK

At each stage in a strategy, an observant management receives signals or cues, known as **feedback**, as to the success or failure of that part of the strategy. Refer to Figure 3-1. Positive feedback includes high sales revenue, no problems with the government, and low employee turnover. Negative feedback includes falling sales revenue, government sanctions (such as fines), and high employee turnover.

Retail executives look for positive and negative feedback so they can determine the causes and then capitalize on opportunities or rectify problems.

A STRATEGIC PLANNING TEMPLATE FOR RETAIL MANAGEMENT

A detailed, user-friendly strategic planning template, *Computer-Assisted Strategic Retail Management Planning*, appears at our Web site (www.pearsonhighered.com/bermanevans). This template uses a series of drop-down menus, based on Figure 3-1, to build a strategic plan. You may apply the template to one of the retail scenarios provided—or devise your own scenario. You have the option of printing each facet of the planning process individually, or printing the entire plan as an integrated whole.

Table 3-5 highlights the steps used in *Computer-Assisted Strategic Retail Management Planning* as the basis for preparing a strategic plan. Table 3-6 presents an example of how the template may be used.

TABLE 3-5 Outline of the Computerized Strategic Planning Template

1. **Situation Analysis**
   - Current organizational mission
   - Current ownership and management alternatives
   - Current goods/service category
2. **SWOT Analysis**
   - Strengths: Current and long term
   - Weaknesses: Current and long term
   - Opportunities: Current and long term
   - Threats: Current and long term
3. **Objectives**
   - Sales
   - Profit
   - Positioning
   - Satisfaction of publics
4. **Identification of Consumers**
   - Choice of target market
     - Mass marketing
     - Concentrated marketing
     - Differentiated marketing
5. **Overall Strategy**
   - Controllable variables
     - Goods/services strategy
     - Location strategy
     - Pricing strategy
     - Promotion strategy
   - Uncontrollable variables
     - Consumer environment
     - Competitive environment
     - Legal environment
     - Economic environment
     - Technological environment
6. **Specific Activities**
   - Daily and short-term operations
   - Responses to environment
7. **Control**
   - Evaluation
   - Adjustment

TABLE 3-6 Sample Strategic Plan: A High-Fashion Ladies Clothing Shop

Sally's is a small, independently owned, high-fashion ladies clothing shop located in a suburban strip mall. It is a full-price, full-service store for fashion-forward shoppers. Sally's carries sportswear from popular designers, has a personal shopper for busy executives, and has an on-premises tailor. The store is updating its strategic plan as a means of getting additional financing for an anticipated expansion.

1. **Situation Analysis**
   - Current organizational mission: A high-fashion clothing retailer selling high-quality and designer-label clothing and accessories in an attractive full-service store environment.
   - Current ownership and management alternatives: Sole proprietor, independent store.
   - Current goods/service category: Ladies coats, jackets, blouses, and suits from major designers, as well as a full line of fashion accessories (such as scarves, belts, and hats).
2. **SWOT Analysis**
   - Strengths
     - Current
       - A loyal customer base.
       - An excellent reputation for high-fashion clothing and accessories within the community.
       - Little competition within a target market concerned with high fashion.
       - Acceptance by a target market more concerned with fashion, quality, and customer service than with price.
       - Unlike consumers favoring classic clothing, Sally's fashion-forward customers spend a considerable amount of money on clothing and accessories per year.
       - Sally's has a highly regarded personal shopper (who assembles clothing based on customer preferences, visits customers, and arranges for a tailor to visit customers).
     - Long term
       - A fashion-forward image with the store's target market.
       - Exclusive relationships with some well-known and some emerging designers.
       - A low-rent location in comparison to a regional shopping center.
       - Excellent supplier relationships.
       - Loyal employees.
       - Excellent relationships within the community.
   - Weaknesses
     - Current
       - Difficulty in recruiting appropriate part-time personnel for peak seasonal periods.
       - The store's small space limits assortment and depth. Too often, the tailor has to perform major alterations.
       - Delivery times for certain French and Italian designers are too long.
       - The retailer does not have a computer-based information system which would better enable it to access key information concerning inventory, sales, customer preferences, and purchase histories.
     - Long term
       - Sally's small orders limit bargaining power with vendors. This affects prices paid, as well as access to "hot-selling" clothing.
       - The store's suburban strip mall location substantially reduces its trading area. The store gets little tourist trade.
       - Over-reliance on the owner-manager, and on several key employees.
       - No long-term management succession plan.
   - Opportunities
     - Current
       - Sally's can hire another experienced tailor with a following to create a custom-made clothing department.
       - The store can hire an assistant to better coordinate trunk and fashion shows. This would solidify Sally's reputation among fashion-forward shoppers and in the community.
       - An adjacent store is vacant. Taking over this space would enable Sally's to increase its size by 50 percent.
       - Sally's is considering enhancing its Web site. This would enable it to appeal to a larger trading area, promote more events (such as a fashion show), and provide links to designers.
     - Long term
       - The larger store would allow Sally's to expand the number of designers, as well as the product lines carried. This would also improve Sally's bargaining power with suppliers.
       - A custom-made clothing department would enable Sally's to appeal to customers who dislike "ready-to-wear apparel" and to customers with highly individualized tastes.
       - The enhanced Web site should expand Sally's market.
   - Threats
     - Current
       - There are rumors that Bloomingdale's, a fashion-based department store, may soon locate a new store within 10 miles of Sally's. This could affect relationships with suppliers, as well as customers. Bloomingdale's offers one-stop shopping and has a flexible return policy for unaltered merchandise with its labels intact.
       - The current local recession has reduced revenues significantly as many customers have cut back on purchases.

Continued

TABLE 3-6 Sample Strategic Plan: A High-Fashion Ladies Clothing Shop (*Continued*)

- Long term
  - Many of Sally's customers are in their 50s and 60s. Some are close to retirement; others intend to spend more time in Florida and Arizona during the winter. The store needs to attract and retain younger shoppers.

3. **Objectives**
   - Sales: Achieve sales volume of $4 million per year.
   - Profit: (a) Achieve net profit before tax of $300,000. (b) Increase inventory turnover from 4 times a year to 6 times a year. (c) Increase gross margin return on inventory (GMROI) by 50 percent through more effective inventory management.
   - Positioning: (a) Reposition store to appeal to younger shoppers without losing current clientele. (b) Increase acceptance by younger shoppers. (c) Establish more of a Web presence.
   - Satisfaction of publics: (a) Maintain store loyalty among current customers. (b) Increase relationship with younger designers selling less costly, younger apparel. (c) Maintain excellent relationship with employees.
4. **Identification of Consumers**
   - Choice of target market approach
     - Mass marketing: This is not a mass-market store.
     - Concentrated marketing: This is Sally's current target market strategy.
     - Differentiated marketing: Sally's might consider attracting multiple target markets: its current fashion-forward customers seeking designer apparel and accessories in a full-service environment; younger, professional customers who desire more trendy clothing; and fashion-forward customers who desire custom-made clothing.
5. **Overall Strategy**
   - Controllable variables
     - Goods/service strategy: Merchandise is fashion-forward from established and emerging designers. Fashion accessories include such items as scarves, belts, and hats. The retailer has no plans to sell ladies' shoes or pocketbooks. Most of the designer merchandise is selectively distributed. A planned custom-made clothing department would enable Sally's to attract hard-to-fit and hard-to-please shoppers. Custom-made clothing shoppers would have a wide variety of swatches and fashion books from which to choose.
     - Location strategy: Sally's currently occupies a single location in a suburban strip mall. This site has comparatively low rent, is within 10 miles of 80 percent of the store's customers, has adequate parking, and has good visibility from the road.
     - Pricing strategy: Sally's charges list price for all of its goods. Included in the price are full-tailoring service, as well as a personal shopper for important customers. Twice a year, the store has a 50 percent off sale on seasonal goods. This is followed by 70 percent off sales to clear the store of remaining off-season inventory.
     - Promotion strategy: Sally's sales personnel are well-trained and highly motivated. They know key customers by name and by their style, color, and designer preferences. Sally's plans to upgrade its regular fashion and trunk shows where new styles are exhibited to current customers and potential customers. Sally's also maintains a customer data base. The best customers are called when suitable merchandise arrives and are allowed to preview it. Some other customers are contacted by mail. The improved Web site will feature the latest styles, the Web address of major designers, color availability, and more. Sally's has a display listing in the Yellow Pages.
   - Uncontrollable variables
     - Consumer environment: Business is subject to the uncertainty of the acceptance of new fashions by the target market. Although Sally's wants to attract two additional segments (custom-made clothing buyers and younger buyers), there is no assurance that it will be successful with these target markets. The store needs to be careful that in seeking these new segments, it does not alienate its current shoppers.
     - Competitive environment: The rumored opening of a fashion-oriented department store in the area would significantly affect sales.
     - Legal environment: Sally's is careful in fully complying with all laws. Unlike some competitors, it does not eliminate sales taxes for cash purchases or ship empty boxes out-of-state to avoid sales tax.
     - Economic environment: Local recessions can reduce sales substantially.
     - Technological environment: Sally's is in the process of investigating a new retail information system to track purchases, inventories, credit card transactions, and more.
6. **Specific Activities**
   - Daily and short-term operations: Sally's policy is to match competitors' prices, promptly correct alteration problems, have longer store hours during busy periods, and offer exclusive merchandise.
   - Responses to environment: Sally's acts appropriately with regard to trends in the economy, competitor actions, and so forth.
7. **Control**
   - Evaluation: The new retail information system will better enable Sally's to ascertain fashion trends, adjust inventories to reduce markdowns, and contact customers with specific offerings. Sales by color, size, style, and designer will be more carefully monitored.
   - Adjustment: The retail information system will enable Sally's store to reduce excess inventories, maximize sales opportunities, and better target individual customers.

Chapter Summary

1. *To show the value of strategic planning for all types of retailers.* A retail strategy is the overall plan that guides a firm. It consists of situation analysis, objectives, identification of a customer market, broad strategy, specific activities, control, and feedback. Without a well-conceived strategy, a retailer may be unable to cope with environmental factors.

2. *To explain the steps in strategic planning for retailers.* Situation analysis is the candid evaluation of opportunities and threats. It looks at the firm's current marketplace position and where it should be heading. This analysis includes defining an organizational mission, evaluating ownership and management options, and outlining the goods/service category.

   An organizational mission is a commitment to a type of business and a place in the market. Ownership/management options include sole proprietorship, partnership, or corporation; starting a business, buying an existing one, or being a franchisee; owner management or professional management; and being centralized or decentralized. The goods/service category depends on personal abilities, finances, and time resources.

   A firm may pursue one or more of these goals: sales (growth, stability, and market share), profit (level, return on investment, and efficiency), satisfaction of publics (stockholders, consumers, and others), and image/positioning (customer and industry perceptions).

   Next, consumer characteristics and needs are determined, and a target market is selected. A firm can sell to a broad spectrum of consumers (mass marketing); zero in on one customer group (concentrated marketing); or aim at two or more distinct groups of consumers (differentiated marketing), with separate retailing approaches for each.

   A broad strategy is then formed. It involves controllable variables (aspects of business a firm can directly affect) and uncontrollable variables (factors a firm cannot control and to which it must adapt).

   After a general strategy is set, a firm makes and implements short-run decisions (tactics) for each controllable part of that strategy. Tactics must be forward-looking and respond to the environment.

   Through a control process, strategy and tactics are evaluated and revised continuously. A retail audit systematically reviews a strategy and its execution on a regular basis. Strengths are emphasized and weaknesses minimized or eliminated.

   An alert firm seeks out signals or cues, known as feedback, that indicate the level of performance at each step in the strategy.

3. *To examine the individual controllable and uncontrollable elements of a retail strategy, and to present strategic planning as a series of integrated steps.* There are four major controllable factors in retail planning: store location, managing the business, merchandise management and pricing, and communicating with the customer. The principal uncontrollable factors affecting retail planning are consumers, competition, technology, economic conditions, seasonality, and legal restrictions.

   Each stage in the strategic planning process needs to be performed, undertaken sequentially, and coordinated in order to have a consistent, integrated, unified strategy.

4. *To demonstrate how a strategic plan can be prepared.* A comprehensive, user-friendly strategic planning template, *Computer-Assisted Strategic Retail Management Planning,* appears at our Web site. This template uses a series of drop-down menus to build a strategic plan.

Key Terms

retail strategy (p. 54)
situation analysis (p. 54)
opportunities (p. 54)
threats (p. 54)
organizational mission (p. 55)
sole proprietorship (p. 57)
partnership (p. 57)
corporation (p. 58)
goods/service category (p. 59)
objectives (p. 62)
image (p. 64)
positioning (p. 64)
mass merchandising (p. 64)
niche retailing (p. 64)
bifurcated retailing (p. 64)
target market (p. 67)
mass marketing (p. 67)
concentrated marketing (p. 67)
differentiated marketing (p. 67)
competitive advantages (p. 67)
controllable variables (p. 68)
uncontrollable variables (p. 68)
tactics (p. 72)
control (p. 73)
feedback (p. 73)

Questions for Discussion

1. Why is it necessary for a small retailer to develop a thorough, well-integrated strategy? What could happen if the firm does not develop such a strategy?
2. How would situation analysis differ for a shoe store chain and an online shoe retailer?
3. What are the pros and cons of starting a new hair salon versus buying an existing one?
4. Develop a checklist to help a prospective service retailer choose the proper service category in which to operate. Include personal abilities, financial resources, and time demands.
5. Why do retailers frequently underestimate the financial and time requirements of a business?
6. Draw and explain a positioning map showing the kinds of retailers selling tablets such as the iPad and Kindle Fire.
7. Discuss local examples of retailers applying mass marketing, concentrated marketing, and differentiated marketing.
8. Marsha Hill is the store manager at a popular camera shop. She has saved $100,000 and wants to open her own store. Devise an overall strategy for Marsha, including each of the controllable factors listed in Figure 3-9 in your answer.
9. A competing bicycle store has a better location than yours. It is in a modern shopping center with a lot of customer traffic. Your store is in an older neighborhood and requires customers to travel farther to reach you. How could you use a merchandising, pricing, and communications strategy to overcome your disadvantageous location?
10. Describe how a retailer can use fine-tuning in strategic planning.
11. How are the control and feedback phases of retail strategy planning interrelated? Give an example.
12. Should a catalog-based men's wear retailer use the strategic planning process differently from an Internet retailer? Why or why not?

Web-Based Exercise

Visit the Web site of Angie's List (www.angieslist.com): "More than a million members use Angie's List to find high quality service companies and health care professionals in over 500 categories." Describe and evaluate the company's strategy based on the information you find there. Why do you think that Angie's List has been so successful?

Note: Also stop by our Web site (www.pearsonhighered.com/bermanevans) to experience a number of highly interactive, appealing Web exercises based on actual company demonstrations, and sample materials related to retailing.

APPENDIX The Special Dimensions of Strategic Planning in a Global Retailing Environment

There are about 270 countries and dependent areas—with 7 billion people and a $65 trillion economy—in the world. The United States accounts for less than 5 percent of the world's population and more than one-fifth of the worldwide economy. Although the United States is a huge marketplace, there are also many other opportunities. Annual worldwide retailing sales have reached $15 trillion—and they are growing. In 2011, developing countries accounted for 42 percent of retail sales globally.[1] When we talk about the global environment of retailing, we mean both U.S. firms operating in foreign markets and foreign retailers operating in U.S. markets.

The global strategic planning challenge is clear:

Michigan State University has a Web site (www.globaledge.msu.edu) that is an excellent source of information on global business practices.

> It is time to focus on a portfolio of countries—with different levels of risk, at different stages of maturity, and with distinctive consumer profiles—to balance short- and long-term opportunities. South America has jumped in our Global Retail Development Index (GRDI), based on continued growth through the global meltdown. Asia has dropped in the rankings even though India and China continue to lead the way out of the global recession. The Middle East and North Africa—although dominating headlines with political unrest—account for eight of the top 20 countries in the GRDI.[2]

In embarking on an international retailing strategy, firms should consider the various factors shown in Figure A3-1.

The Strategic Planning Process and Global Retailing

Retailers looking to operate globally should follow these seven steps *in conjunction with* the strategic planning process described in Chapter 3:

1. *Choose a strategy—then execute it:* Retailers cannot just decide to go into a growing market. They need appropriate strategies, consistent with the market.
2. *Find a competitive advantage:* In developing countries without modern retail institutions, "bringing modern supply chain management and merchandising, as well as financial resources, might be sufficient" to succeed. However, in more developed markets, better competitive advantages are required, such as popular brands, low prices, and so forth.
3. *Learn much about local tastes and customs:* Retailers must learn about the different supply chains, laws, and consumer interests.
4. *Use mostly local talent:* "The ideal situation is for most stores to have local managers." Unfortunately, many foreign firms do not necessarily grasp this.
5. *Develop local relationships:* "In China, a major European food retailer had trouble achieving success largely because of a failure to build strong local supplier relations."
6. *Be prepared to make big mistakes:* "The capacity to learn and change is critical, and a commitment of time is necessary to do that."
7. *Be prepared to invest on a large scale.* "A profitable enterprise will only come about with sufficient economies of scale."[3]

Opportunities and Threats in Global Retailing

For participating firms, there are wide-ranging opportunities and threats in global retailing.

Opportunities

- Foreign markets may be used to complement domestic sales.
- Foreign markets may represent growth opportunities if domestic markets are saturated or stagnant.

FIGURE A3-1
Factors to Consider When Engaging in Global Retailing

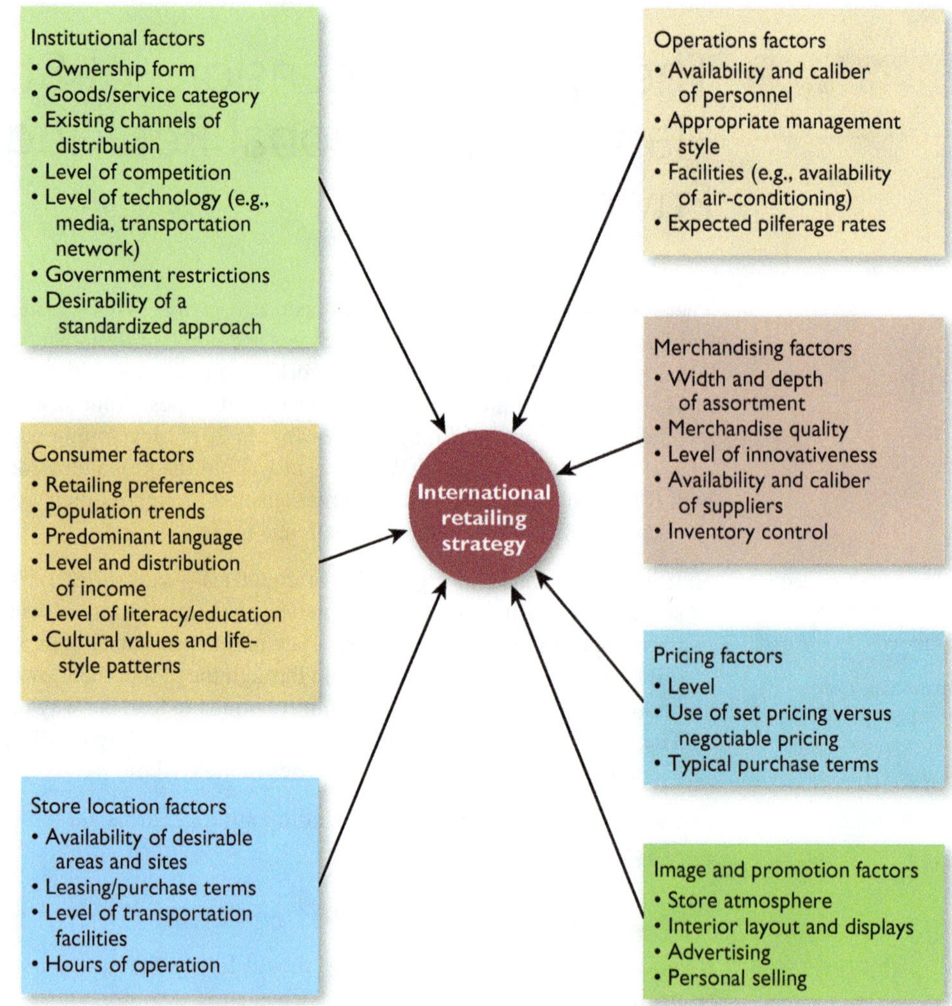

- A retailer may be able to offer goods, services, or technology not yet available in foreign markets.
- Competition may be less in some foreign markets.
- There may be tax or investment advantages in foreign markets.
- Due to government and economic shifts, many countries are more open to the entry of foreign firms.
- Communications are easier than before. The Internet enables retailers to reach customers and suppliers well outside their domestic markets.

Threats

- There may be cultural differences between domestic and foreign markets.
- Management styles may not be easily adaptable.
- Foreign governments may place restrictions on some operations.
- Personal income may be poorly distributed among consumers in foreign markets.
- Distribution systems and technology may be inadequate (e.g., poor roads and lack of refrigeration). This may minimize the effectiveness of the Web as a selling tool.
- Institutional formats vary greatly among countries.
- Currencies are different. The countries in the European Union have sought to alleviate this problem through the euro, a common currency, in most of their member nations.

Standardization: An Opportunity and a Threat

When devising a global strategy, a retailer must pay attention to the concept of *standardization.* Can the home market strategy be standardized and directly applied to foreign markets, or do personnel, physical facilities, operations, advertising messages, product lines, and other factors have to be adapted to local conditions and needs? Table A3-1 shows how the economies differ in 15 countries. And consider this comment from a global retailing expert:

> It shouldn't be a shock that retailers have to work hard to understand the international consumer when they have already worked very hard to understand the domestic consumer. We just tend to forget because it has become automatic. The things retailers learn might make [international consumers] look different for different reasons. But the effort that goes into understanding them and really fine-tuning the market to who they are, is the same principle American retailers have been using for 100 years.[4]

Ten Trends in Global Retailing

Several factors can affect the level of success of an international retailing strategy:

1. *Social responsibility.* "More consumers are becoming concerned about the impact that companies have on society. This includes the impact on the physical environment, on workers in countries that supply products, and the impact that products have on the consumers who purchase them."
2. *Global consumer growth shifts away from the United States.* "For the world's largest retailers, this means increased growth opportunities in Asia. It also means that the U.S. market will be a bit more challenging. Retailers in the U.S. market will increasingly face a market share battle."
3. *Commoditization run amok.* "Consumers are jaded. To demonstrate differentiation from competitors, it is no longer sufficient for retailers to simply do everything right. Those that differentiate on the basis of something other than price will be the winners of the future."

TABLE A3-1 The Global Economy, Selected Countries

Country	2011 Population (millions)	2011 Population Density (per square kilometer)	2011 Per Capita GDP (U.S. $)	2010 Per Capita Retail Sales-Excluding Autos & Food Service (U.S. $)	2010–2016 Projected Annual Retail Growth Rate—After Inflation (%)	2011 World Competitiveness Ranking Among the 15 Countries Listed
Brazil	203	24	10,800	2,733	7.7	14
Canada	34	3	39,400	10,294	2.9	2
China	1,337	139	7,600	874	8.4	4
France	65	101	33,100	10,382	1.5	8
Germany	81	228	35,700	10,847	1.3	3
Great Britain	62	257	34,800	10,239	2.5	5
India	1,189	362	3,500	412	4.4	9
Indonesia	245	129	4,200	1,164	3.4	10
Italy	61	202	30,500	9,131	0.1	13
Japan	126	335	34,000	8,901	0.0	7
Mexico	113	58	13,900	2,841	3.0	11
Philippines	101	339	3,500	904	4.7	12
Russia	138	8	15,900	3,468	4.1	15
South Korea	48	489	30,000	4,139	2.4	6
United States	313	32	47,200	9,879	2.9	1

GDP is a country's gross domestic product. Per capita GDP is expressed in terms of purchasing power parity.

World Competitiveness Ranking is based on a country's economic performance, government efficiency, business efficiency, and infrastructure.

Sources: Compiled by the authors from *CIA World Factbook*, https://www.cia.gov/library/publications/the-world-factbook (February 15, 2012); Frank Badillo, "The Global Macroeconomic Outlook for Retail: Danger from Europe to China," www.kantarretailiq.com (September 15, 2011); and *IMD World Competitiveness Yearbook 2011.*

4. *The rise of "long tail" retailing.* "The long tail means focusing on niche opportunities that can be quite lucrative. Consider how consumer income in any country is distributed. The mass market is where the greatest share of income exists and where most retailers compete. The ends of the tail are smaller, representing a smaller share of income. Yet, these ends have often been ignored by retailers intent on reaping the economies of scale associated with the mass market in the middle."
5. *The fight to plant the flag in India.* "India has become the next big thing for the world's leading retailers. Even though India remains relatively closed to foreign retail investment, its business environment is riddled with obstacles, and its rapid economic growth is so new that it is not clear whether it can be sustained, it is a country with more than a billion people."
6. *Retail investment in services.* "As countries grow and achieve economic affluence, consumer spending on goods as a share of GDP tends to decline while spending on services grows disproportionately."
7. *Emerging market investment in developed retailers.* "One of the notable aspects of the global economy lately has been the huge surpluses of key emerging countries. Not only may funds in such countries seek to acquire retail companies, but in some cases they may invest in the development of startup retailers as well."
8. *Multi-channel integration.* "The best retailers will most likely focus on enriching the brand experience for distinct customer segments across multiple channels. They will use Web sites not just to sell, but to build brand identity, engage consumers in dialog, and obtain feedback from consumers."
9. *Focus on customer experience.* "One way to tackle the problem of a lack of retailer differentiation is to focus on improving the experience of consumers in the store. This encompasses far more than customer service and includes all the elements influencing consumers (such as store layout, signage, lighting, service, and the ease and speed of transactions)."
10. *Retailers as world-class marketers.* "Today, some of the world's top retailers are aggressively hiring top marketers away from manufacturing companies. Their goal is to become marketing powerhouses, to build strong brand identity in order to compete with other retailers and, increasingly, to compete with branded suppliers through private label sales."[5]

U.S. Retailers in Foreign Markets

Here are three of the many examples of U.S. retailers with high involvement in foreign markets.

Toys "R" Us has more than 600 Toys "R" Us, Babies "R" Us, and Side-by-Side stores abroad. Among the 35 nations in which it has stores are Australia, France, Germany, Great Britain, Japan, Singapore, Spain, and Sweden. In some markets, such as Indonesia, South Africa, Turkey, and United Arab Emirates, the firm emphasizes franchising rather than direct corporate ownership. Why? This enables it to better tap the local knowledge of franchisees in certain markets while still setting corporate policies.[6]

The majority of McDonald's restaurants are outside the United States. Sales at the 19,400 outlets in 120 foreign nations account for two-thirds of total revenues. Besides Europe, McDonald's has outlets in such nations as Argentina, Australia, Austria, Brazil, Canada, China, Colombia, Egypt, Greece, India, Japan, Malaysia, Mexico, New Zealand, Pakistan, Russia, South Africa, South Korea, Spain, and Uruguay. The McDonald's restaurant located in Moscow's Pushkin Square is its largest with 28 cash registers and a seating capacity of 700 customers. This restaurant serves over 20,000 customers on a daily basis. To better appeal to Russian customers, McDonald's features such specialties as potato wedges, cherry pie, and cabbage pie.[7]

Amazon.com has rapidly expanded globally by introducing dedicated Web sites for specific nations. They include Canada (www.amazon.ca), China (www.joyo.com), France (www.amazon.fr), Germany (www.amazon.de), Great Britain (www.amazon.co.uk), Japan (www.amazon.co.jp), and Spain (www.amazon.es). Although these sites all have the familiar Amazon Web design, they differ by language, products offered, and currency.

Foreign Retailers in the U.S. Market

A large number of foreign retailers have entered the United States to appeal to the world's most affluent mass market. Here are three examples.

Ikea is a Swedish-based home-furnishings retailer operating more than 300 stores in 37 nations. In 1985, Ikea opened its first U.S. store in Pennsylvania. Since then, it has added nearly 40 other U.S. stores in such cities as Baltimore, Chicago, Elizabeth (New Jersey), Hicksville (Long Island, New York), Houston, Los Angeles, San Diego, Seattle, and Washington, DC. The firm offers durable, stylish, ready-to-assemble furniture at low prices. Stores are huge, have enormous selections, and include a playroom for children and other amenities. Today, Ikea generates 94 percent of its sales from international operations, and 15 percent of total company sales are from its North American stores.[8]

The Netherlands' Royal Ahold (also known as Ahold) ranks among the world's top retailers with annual worldwide retail sales of $40 billion from its 3,000 stores, and serves millions of shoppers weekly. In the United States, the firm has acquired several chains, making it the leading supermarket firm on the East Coast. Its 725 U.S. stores include Stop & Shop, Giant Food, and Martin's. The firm also owns Peapod, the online food retailer.[9]

PricewaterhouseCoopers publishes an annual survey of global retailing executives (www.pwc.com/gx/en/ceo-survey/industry/retail.jhtml).

Luxottica, an Italian firm, operates more than 7,000 eyeglass and sunglass stores in North America, Asia-Pacific, China, South Africa, Latin America, and Europe. It has the highest market share in the U.S. optical retail market with its LensCrafters, Pearle Vision, and Sunglass Hut stores. Luxottica also operates leased departments at Sears Optical and at Target Optical stores in the United States. Luxottica's annual total revenue (including eyeglass and sunglass manufacturing) exceeds $8 billion (U.S.).[10]

Although the revenues of U.S.-based retailers owned by foreign firms are hard to measure, they are several hundred billion dollars annually. Foreign ownership in U.S. retailers is highest for general merchandise stores, food stores, and apparel and accessory stores. Examples of U.S.-based retailers owned by foreign firms are shown in Table A3-2.

TABLE A3-2 Selected Ownership of U.S. Retailers by Foreign Firms

U.S. Retailer	Principal Business	Foreign Owner	Country of Owner
Circle K	Convenience stores	Couche-Tard	Canada
Claire's	Fashion accessories stores	Monsoon	Great Britain
Crate & Barrel	Housewares stores	Otto GmbH	Germany
Food Lion	Supermarkets	Delhaize Group	Belgium
Giant Food	Supermarkets	Royal Ahold	Netherlands
Great Atlantic & Pacific (A&P)	Supermarkets	Tengelmann	Germany
Hannaford Bros.	Supermarkets	Delhaize Group	Belgium
LensCrafters	Optical stores	Luxottica	Italy
Motel 6	Economy motels	Accor	France
Peapod	Online grocery delivery	Royal Ahold	Netherlands
7-Eleven	Convenience stores	Seven & I Holdings	Japan
Stop & Shop	Supermarkets	Royal Ahold	Netherlands
Sunglass Hut	Sunglass stores	Luxottica	Italy
Talbots	Apparel	Aeon	Japan

PART 1 Short Cases

Case 1: Howard Schultz on Starbucks' Future Plans to Grow[c-1]

Howard Schultz, the founder of Starbucks (www.starbucks.com), returned to the company as CEO in 2008, after not being involved with day-to-day responsibilities with Starbucks for almost eight years. Shortly after his return, he began to question the appropriateness of the company's strategy in the recessionary environment. Evidence of a major problem at Starbucks was that many of its underperforming shops had been open for business for less than 18 months.

Schultz believes that too many retailers manage their companies on the basis of same store sales growth objectives. Although this measure focuses on sales growth in existing (versus new stores), too much reliance on same-store growth may cause a store manager to increase sales in ways that can undermine a brand's long-term image and reputation. To illustrate this point, Schultz found that one of his managers decided to sell teddy bears to grow sales, even though the stuffed animals had no relationship whatsoever to coffee. As a result, Schultz decided to stop reporting same-store sales each month.

As a vehicle for long-term growth, Starbucks introduced new products and brands within its stores. Instead of first selling VIA, a new instant coffee, in grocery stores and drugstores, Starbucks decided to first sell VIA in its own stores over a six to eight-month time period. After VIA's success was proven, it was then sold through the other traditional channels. The initial sales success of VIA reduced the need for stocking payments (slotting allowances) to the grocery stores and drugstores. It also enabled the new product to achieve additional credibility among consumers.

Starbucks has also had great success with its loyalty card program, which accounts for one-fifth of all store-based transactions. Its program lets customers receive rewards for purchasing Starbucks-branded products in grocery and drug stores.

Starbucks is counting on China as a major growth market. As of 2011, Starbucks had about 800 stores in China. In the long run, it plans to have thousands of stores there. Starbucks' first Chinese stores were located in Shanghai and Beijing. It now has locations in secondary and tertiary markets such as Fuzhou. Although many Westerners have never heard of Fuzhou, it has a population of over 5 million people. On its opening day there, Chinese consumers lined up to try Starbucks coffee despite inclement weather. China has 140 cities with more than 1 million people each. Unlike other retailers, Starbucks plans to develop territories before moving to new markets. Starbucks is also looking at expanding in other emerging markets including India, Brazil, and Vietnam.

Starbucks is careful to modify its products to reflect the unique tastes of foreign palates, as well as to be respectful of cultural differences among consumers. For example, Chinese customers prefer black sesame seed to blueberry as a topping or filling for muffins. To successfully implement its strategy, Starbucks needs to decentralize planning and decision making on a regional or even county-based level.

Acquisitions represent another potential vehicle of growth for Starbucks. With $2 billion in cash on its balance sheet, Starbucks is financially capable of buying successful companies in both the United States and abroad.

Questions

1. Discuss the pros and cons of evaluating a retailer's success using same store sales growth data.
2. Comment on Starbucks' introduction of VIA in its own stores before attempting to sell it in grocery and drugstores.
3. Evaluate Starbucks' strategy of developing (saturating) existing foreign markets before expanding into new countries.
4. Describe the pros and cons of growing through acquisitions as opposed to internal expansion to Starbucks.

Case 2: Manufacturer–Retailer Relations in the Chocolate Business[c-2]

Eric Heinbockel and his two friends, Fabian Kaempfer and Nick LaCava, launched Chocomize (www.chocomize.com), a mass-customized chocolate company in late 2009. The partners launched the company with an investment of $80,000 in capital, mostly from friends and family members. Under mass customization, a consumer is able to choose the combination of ingredients and toppings (such as marshmallows, raisins, and coconut pieces) that they desire to be mixed into their candy bars. A similar mass customization strategy has been successfully used by Chocri (www.chocri.co.uk), a Berlin-based European chocolate maker.

During summer 2010, a European luxury retailer contacted Chocomize's partners with an offer to purchase 15,000 chocolate bars. This retailer planned to sell Chocomize's mass-customized products in its New York City, Miami, and Los Angeles stores during the Christmas holiday season. Chocomize carefully evaluated this proposal since it occurred during a time period when it was selling less than 150 chocolate bars daily.

Even though the potential order seemed very appealing, the owners of Chocomize had some major concerns. One, the retailer wanted to buy the chocolate at cost, arguing that this purchase would have tremendous publicity value to the small firm. Two, Chocomize's three chocolate machines and 1,500-square-foot facility would only be able to produce 10,000 customized bars—not the 15,000 desired by the retailer. Third, the order was so large that it could affect Chocomize's ability to fulfill the orders from its loyal Web-based customers. Four, Chocomize's reputation could be irreparably damaged if its product quality were compromised as a result of taking this large order.

[c-1]The material in this case is drawn from Allen Webb, "Starbucks' Quest for Healthy Growth: An Interview with Howard Schultz," *McKinsey Quarterly* (March 2011), pp. 1–8.

[c-2]The material in this case is drawn from Amy Barrett, "Their Business Was Doing O.K. Then These Chocolaters Got a Dream They Couldn't Ignore—Or Could They?" www.inc.com (June 2011).

One way of properly filling the order was to find a subcontractor to help Chocomize produce the required quantity. Unfortunately, Chocomize's partners could not find a suitable contractor experienced in the kind of melted toppings that Chocomize used.

In October 2010, two of the partners presented their dilemma to two classes at the Harvard Business School. Many of the Harvard students believed that accepting the offer would be a mistake for the same reasons the partners were concerned. In addition, two potential subcontractors that were contacted based on a student's recommendation also did not work out. One required a minimum order of 50,000 bars. The other could not use the same imported Belgium chocolate that Chocomize utilized. This second subcontractor also had difficulties with reproducing Chocomize's packaging. As a result, Chocomize's partners decided to decline the retailer's order.

Things are now looking up for Chocomize. In November 2010, the partners appeared on three morning network television programs. Chocomize's products were also described in articles that appeared in *New York Times* and *USA Today*. The company sales in the time period from Thanksgiving to New Years accounted for almost 40 percent of the company's annual $400,000 revenue.

The European retailer then again expressed interest in placing a large order, this time for the 2011 holiday season. By then, Chocomize had worked out arrangements with a contract manufacturer to supply the required purchase quantities for these bulk order sales.

Questions

1. Under what circumstances should Chocomize have accepted the European retailer's initial offer?
2. Comment on the conflicting goals of the European luxury retailer and Chocomize.
3. Discuss the concept of value and the value chain for Chocomize.
4. How can the European retailer utilize relationship retailing for its chocolate products?

Case 3: Carrefour's and Best Buy's Chinese Adventures[c-3]

Both Carrefour (www.carrefour.com) and Wal-Mart (www.walmart.com) were recently charged with conducting bait-and-switch tactics in China. The two retailers were accused by China's National Development and Reform Commission of attracting shoppers into their stores with massive promotions and then charging these customers more than the advertised prices. Carrefour and Wal-Mart were fined the equivalent of $76,000 for each offending store—a total of 19 stores for the two companies combined. This was the largest fine ever assessed in China against any retailer.

Carrefour's difficulties are based on an imbalance of power that exists between retailers and suppliers in China. According to a Commerce Ministry spokesperson, China has too many suppliers and too few major retailers. As a result, Chinese retailers have been able to exert their power by forcing suppliers to accept low prices based on bidding wars, stretched out payment terms, and the required payment of fees and commissions.

While fees and commissions have been customarily set at 4 percent of sales, some merchants have secured commissions of between 10 and 20 percent. As a manager of a Carrefour supplier says: "Only big manufacturers are tough enough to stop supplying Carrefour when it asks for higher rebates. Small suppliers like us just have to do as we're told if it asks us to pay more rebates." Some retail analysts familiar with the Chinese market also suggest that the pricing issue has been partially caused by the autonomy given to Chinese retail managers. In an effort to attract price-sensitive Chinese consumers, many managers sought low prices by requiring kickbacks from suppliers. Recently, Carrefour began to reduce the power of regional and individual store managers.

Carrefour and Wal-Mart, two of the world's largest retailers and among China's top five retailers, are not the only global retailers with problems in China. Home Depot (www.homedepot.com) recently closed its sole remaining store in Beijing. Likewise, Mattel closed its Shanghai Barbie doll flagship store just two years after it opened. Best Buy (www.bestbuy.com), the electronics giant, also recently announced its plans to close all of its nine Chinese stores.

According to Barbara E. Kahn, a Wharton marketing professor, Best Buy's problems in China were largely the result of its using the same marketing strategy in China as in the United States. While Best Buy has high brand recognition in the United States, it is virtually unknown in China. And unlike the U.S. market, China's market for electronics is fragmented with a large number of small electronics retailers. In China, stores are located so close to one another that a new Best Buy store could have three competitors virtually next door.

Because Chinese customers are very price sensitive, Best Buy's U.S.-based strategy of for high customer service accompanied by higher price levels was inappropriate for the Chinese market. In contrast, to keep prices low, two Chinese competitors—Gome (www.gome.com.hk) and Suning (www.cnsuning.com/include/english)—purchase goods on a consignment basis and pay suppliers only after goods are sold. These Chinese retailers also require their suppliers to provide sales personnel for each of their stores.

Questions

1. How else could a foreign retailer exert additional power with its Chinese suppliers (and not face government restrictions)?
2. How can foreign retailers successfully position themselves in China?
3. Discuss the pros and cons of a retailer's use of a standardized versus a nonstandardized retail strategy throughout the world.
4. How can a global retailer exert greater oversight with the personnel in its foreign stores?

[c-3]The material in this case is drawn from "Carrefour in China: When the Price Isn't Right," www.knowledgeatwharton.com.cn (March 16, 2011).

Case 4: Ahold: A European Powerhouse Facing Tough Times[c-4]

Royal Ahold, also known as Ahold (www.ahold.com), is a Dutch-based global retailer with about 3,000 stores worldwide. Its Dutch brands include Albert Heijn (supermarkets, convenience stores, and online shopping), Etos (drugstores and online shopping), Gall & Gall (wine and liquor stores and online shopping), and Albert (online groceries). Ahold's USA brands include various supermarkets and superstores, including Stop & Shop, Giant Food, and Martin's Food Markets—as well as Peapod (online groceries and deliveries for Stop & Shop). In addition, Ahold operates hypermarkets (which combine discount department stores and supermarkets), supermarkets, convenience stores, and banking services in The Czech Republic, Slovakia, Sweden, Norway, Estonia, Latvia, Lithuania, and Portugal.

Ahold had overall sales growth of 4.4 percent between 2009 and 2010 (after adjusting for exchange rates and the effect of an additional week in 2009). However, its profitability dropped during this time period. Ahold's gross profit margin (net revenues less cost of goods sold/net revenues) decreased from 27.2 percent to 26.8 percent, and its operating profit margin (gross profit less operating expenses/net revenues) declined slightly from 4.6 percent to 4.5 percent over this time period. Ahold attributed these declines to two factors: increases in costs that could not be passed onto customers and the need to reduce prices to attract customers in a recessionary economic environment.

Ahold's overall corporate strategy focuses on its brands, shoppers, and operations. These strategies are interconnected. Ahold seeks to be either the market leader or the number two share position holder in each market area in which it operates. The retailer believes that a high market share can reduce competition and provide it with cost advantages via quantity discounts, bargaining power with suppliers, and distribution economies.

Ahold strives to attract and retain consumers through better-quality products and customer services, and by being positioned as a price leader. Cost reduction programs by trimming operating expenses are part of its overall strategy. According to Dick Boer, Ahold's chief executive: "We will continue to reduce costs so that we can invest in our offering to improve the value we provide, while managing the balance between sales and margin." Specific financial goals associated with these strategies are to have long-term net sales increases of 5 percent (up from its 4.4 percent levels) and operating profits of 5 percent (an increase from 4.5 percent).

Although Ahold's U.S. operations accounted for slightly more than 60 percent of its revenues in 2010, the European operations are critical to its profit, market share, and consumer loyalty goals. One of the reasons that Ahold's U.S. operations have been growing at a faster rate than its European units is the company's decision to focus on new stores and acquisitions in the American market. In terms of same-store sales growth (from stores open at least one year), Ahold's European operations have consistently outperformed its U.S.-based units. In particular, its Albert Heijn units have done better than Ahold's U.S. units due to Heijn being a market leader in the Dutch market with about a 25 percent market share. Ahold Europe has also benefitted from centralized buying economies of scale and from being a member of AMS, Europe's second largest buying group.

Questions

1. Evaluate Ahold's overall retail strategy.
2. Discuss appropriate cost reduction strategies for Ahold using the patronage builders, patronage solidifiers, disappointers, and basics model in Figure 2-4.
3. Are there any disadvantages with Ahold having a high market share in some of its markets? Explain your answer.
4. Comment on Ahold's decision to grow its U.S. operations through adding stores and making acquisitions rather than same store sales growth.

[c-4]The material in this case is drawn from Himanshu Pal, "Measuring Ahold Europe's FY 2010 Performance—A Tale of Contrasting Fortunes," www.kantarretailiq.com (March 9, 2011).

Comprehensive Case

Abercrombie & Fitch Co.: Looking to the Future*

Introduction

Abercrombie & Fitch Co. (www.abercrombie.com) is a specialty retailer that operates stores and Web sites that sell casual sportswear apparel, including knitted and woven shirts, graphic T-shirts, fleece, jeans and woven pants, shorts, sweaters, outerwear, personal care products, and accessories for men, women, and kids under the Abercrombie & Fitch, Abercrombie, and Hollister store names. It also has stores and a Web site selling underwear, personal care items, sleepwear, and home products for women under the Gilly Hicks brand.

Company Background

Abercrombie & Fitch Co. (A&F) has three main store divisions. Its Abercrombie & Fitch stores are more valuable than Hollister stores and Gilly Hicks & abercrombie kids stores for the following reasons:

- Hollister stores are more in number, but A&F stores are larger in size. Hollister has about 1.5 times the number of A&F stores, but the average size of an A&F store is around 1.3 times the average size of a Hollister store.
- Abercrombie & Fitch stores are positioned as a premium-priced brand, targeting women in the upper income segment. The company views the "in-store experience" as the primary vehicle for communicating the spirit of the brand. To ensure this, the company is acquiring larger retail spaces for its new stores as well as remodeling some of the existing ones to increase their retail space.
- The average revenue per square foot for A&F stores was $451 as of 2010 compared to $368 for Hollister stores and $317 for Gilly Hicks & abercrombie kids stores. As the economic environment improves and consumer spending increases, we expect revenue per square foot for A&F stores to cross pre-recession levels and reach nearly $550 by the end of our forecast period of 2017.
- Abercrombie & Fitch stores have profit margins of 15 percent or more, which are considerably more than profit margins for Hollister stores or Gilly Hicks and abercrombie kids stores. The unique identity of the A&F brand as being premium—as well as exclusive—enables it to sell products at higher price points than the Hollister brand, thus obtaining higher profit margins.

Key Trends

Declining Apparel Demand Due to Economic Downturn The apparel industry witnessed a short-term decrease in demand because of the economic downturn during 2008–2009 that led to a considerable fall in consumer spending. This significantly impacted the revenues of major specialty retailers such as Abercrombie & Fitch, whose revenues declined at an annual rate of 11.6 percent of from 2007 to 2009.

Increasing Competition from Department and Discount Stores In the competitive apparel industry, the local department stores and discount store chains have been scaling up their operations. As a result, the larger national department stores and specialty store chains such as Abercrombie & Fitch, faced with shrinking margins, need to increase their operational efficiency to remain profitable.

International Expansion With strong comparable sales growth at its international stores, particularly in Great Britain, Abercrombie & Fitch is looking to further expand its presence in Europe. In addition to this, the firm plans to take advantage of the growing Asian market, which is becoming a focal point of the global retail industry, with major retailers across the globe speeding their plans of growing their presence there. As Asian consumers, backed by good disposable income, are showing an interest in luxury goods, Abercrombie & Fitch can leverage its image to gain a foothold in this market.

Retail Store Divisions

Abercrombie & Fitch Stores

The Abercrombie & Fitch stores (AFS) division has solid sales per square foot of retail store space, with 2010 revenues of $451 per square foot. This figure is projected to reach $548 per square foot as of 2017.

The revenue per square foot for AFS had crossed the $450 mark before the recent economic downturn. Unlike many other retailers, AFS did not offer discounts to boost sales during the downturn. Though this impacted its sales, it helped to maintain the luxury image of the brand, which would help to boost its comparable store sales as the economic environment improves.

The company's international AFS unit has been reporting strong sales; and the firm believes that there is tremendous upside in its international business. The Asian market presents a great opportunity for the company to expand its A&F brand as there is a growing demand for luxury apparel in this region and an increasing percentage of population in the age group 15 years to 25 years, which the firm primarily targets. It opened a flagship store in Tokyo, Japan, in fiscal 2009 and is planning to add more stores at up-market shopping destinations in these regions. Currently, international store sales account for 8 percent to 9 percent of its total sales; but, as noted, the company sees significant potential.

To succeed in the future, AFS needs to correctly gauge rapidly changing trends in a highly competitive fashion industry—and adjust its product offering accordingly. In the first quarter of 2009, AFS missed some key trends, which significantly contributed to a fall in sales compared to quarter one of 2008. In addition, the pace of the economic recovery impacts the company's revenue per square foot. Because of the slow and prolonged economic recovery process, the demand for the brand's products has been slow to pick up, as customers have shifted to lower priced brands. During the worst of the economic slowdown during 2008–2009, spending by upper income consumers declined by 9 percent and spending by teens dropped 20 percent.

*The material in this case is adapted by the authors from *Trefis Analysis for Abercrombie & Fitch Co.* (Boston, MA: Insight Guru Inc, May 26, 2011). Reprinted by permission of Trefis.com.

It is expected that the average square feet per store for AFS will continue to rise into the future, as it is in line with the company's plans of having a larger retail space for its new stores. AFS views the "in-store experience" as the primary vehicle for communicating the spirit of the brand. To ensure this, the company is acquiring larger retail spaces for its new stores as well as remodeling some of the existing ones to increase their retail space. On the other hand, AFS has seen a consistent increase in its operating expenses since 2005, which has significantly cut down on its operating margins. To increase margins and reduce average unit costs, the company is looking to consolidate its business by closing down some underperforming stores and increase the size of strategic stores.

When acquiring new retail space at a location, the company has to trade off between the cost of retail space and the expected demand for its products. In the current economic environment, and with the real-estate market being volatile, the company may have to be more economical in obtaining space.

Hollister Stores

The revenue per square foot for Hollister stores increased to around $520 in 2007. This was largely due to a positive macroeconomic environment during this period, which was driving demand in the apparel industry, and the company's success in marketing the Hollister brand. However, it decreased to about $326 in 2009, an annual negative growth rate of roughly 20 percent from 2007. This was largely due to falling demand in the apparel industry, especially in the luxury segment, as a result of the economic downturn. The revenue per square foot increased to $368 in 2010. Going forward, it is expected that the division's revenue per square foot will show a positive trend and reach the $490 mark as of 2017.

Hollister's strategy is driven by innovative marketing. For its Hollister brand, A&F uses the walking self-advertisement technique, wherein people who are wearing the company's clothes advertise the products because there are usually large prints of the brand's name, logo, initials, and fictional date of establishment on most of their clothing items. In addition to this, many of the models who advertise the brand's products also sell the products in the stores. These marketing tactics had been working successfully for the brand before the economic slowdown and are expected to further contribute to generating demand once consumer spending picks up.

Hollister's 2007–2009 sales decline was not only due to falling consumer spending; the brand lost market share to competitors such as American Eagle and Aéropostale, which also offer trendy clothing, but at a discount to Hollister prices. These competitors, which are becoming increasingly popular in the teen clothing segment, will be adopting aggressive marketing strategies to hold on to their increasing market share as the economic environment improves.

As the company aggressively marketed its Hollister brand in the United States, it increased the number of stores from around 320 in 2005 to 540 in 2010 (compared with 325 for AFS). Going forward, a further increase in the number of Hollister stores is projected, though at a slower rate, as the company expands its business both in the United States and internationally. As the economy recovers, A&F expects demand for Hollister products to pick up and cross historical levels. A&F would have to expand its capacity to meet the future expected demand by increasing the number of stores. Currently, the firm only has a few Hollister stores in Europe, which have been giving encouraging results. The growing Asian retail market is where A&F predicts maximum growth potential and is planning to expand its presence in the region.

The square feet per store for Hollister stores rose slightly between 2005 and 2010. It is projected that this trend will continue into the future, in line with the company's plans of having a larger retail space for its new Hollister stores, especially at international shopping locations. A&F will be adding flagship stores and mall-based stores in Europe and Asia. These stores are expected to have larger retail space that will help A&F to sell the brand's luxury image in these new global markets. The company is also remodeling better-performing existing stores to increase their selling space and further improve their productivity.

To promote its Hollister brand globally, A&F has identified specific up-market shopping destinations, especially in growing Asian markets. However, commercial real-estate at these locations is becoming very expensive, and in the current economic environment, the company may have to be more economical when acquiring retail space.

A&F put controls on Hollister's operating costs by reducing its marketing, general, and distribution expense by nearly 13 percent in 2009 and keeping its store and distribution expense almost flat through 2010. The company sees further opportunities for optimizing its operations to reduce costs.

The Hollister brand operates in a very competitive environment. Revenues are largely driven by its ability to successfully gauge changing fashion trends and consumer preferences.

Gilly Hicks and abercrombie kids Stores

Gilly Hicks is a newer store concept that features apparel and undergarment items for young women. As its Facebook page (www.facebook.com/gillyhicks) notes: "Fun, casual, and sexy with a Sydney [Australia] sensibility, Gilly never takes herself too seriously. Free-spirited and beautiful—perfect for the All-American girl." The abercrombie kids stores offers Abercrombie & Fitch style clothing that is targeted especially for boys and girls.

The revenue per square foot for these stores decreased from $460 in 2005 to $286 in 2009, before rebounding to $317 in 2010. Not only was this due to falling demand in the apparel industry, especially in the luxury segment, as a result of the economic downturn, but the unsuccessful launch and marketing of the now-defunct Ruehl store brand. Going forward, it is expected that sales per square foot will rise to nearly $400 as of 2017. A&F has successfully established a marketing platform for its newly launched Gilly Hicks store brand.

Increasing demand for luxury wear in the children's apparel market is projected largely because of the trickle-down effect from growth in the luxury market for women's and men's wear, into the luxury market for children. The abercrombie kids store brand can leverage the luxury heritage of the established Abercrombie & Fitch brand to grow in this market.

The Gilly Hicks store brand is operating in a very competitive market segment. The intimate apparel marketplace already has a large number of established players. Before it can capture a significant portion of that customer base, A&F would need to build the brand's image considerably.

Between 2005 and 2010, A&F gradually increased the number of abercrombie kids and Ruehl stores and launched Gilly Hicks stores. Although the company discontinued its Ruehl store brand in fiscal 2009, it is forecast that A&F will continue to expand its abercrombie kids and Gilly Hicks business in the United States and then internationally by increasing its fleet of stores for these brands.

Despite the competition, there is huge potential in the intimate apparel market. The global lingerie market, which declined at an annual growth rate of 1.6 percent between 2007 and 2009, is expected to increase at an annual growth rate of 1.5 percent and reach a value of $32 billion by 2016. By aggressively growing its Gilly Hicks store, A&F feels that these stores can leverage the strength of its already established brands and capture sizeable market share by 2016.

Again, if the economic recovery is slower in the next few quarters, the company would have to significantly reduce its annual sales target. This would affect its plans for expansion as A&F would only be comfortable with increasing its capital expenditure only if it sees a comparable growth in revenues.

A&F gradually increased the square feet per store for Gilly Hicks and abercrombie kids from 2005 to 2010. This trend is expected to continue into the future. This is in line with the company's plan of remodeling better-performing stores to increase their capacity and also develop new stores, which would be larger than existing average stores. However, if revenue per square foot from these stores does not increase in the near term, A&F may have to cut down on plans for expanding their average size.

A&F wants to enhance the marketing platform for these brands. To aggressively expand its abercrombie kids and Gilly Hicks store brands, the company expects to adopt a similar marketing strategy to that used by the AFS and Hollister brands.

Internet and Catalog Orders

The Internet and Catalog Orders division revenues increased from $120 million in 2005 to $352 million in 2010, driven by growth in online sales due to increasing Internet penetration. It is forecast that these revenues will increase to more than $930 million as of 2017 due to the continuing rise in the direct (online) channel and the popularity of E-commerce. This business represents a major revenue expansion opportunity for Abercrombie & Fitch.

A&F is gaining popularity through social media channels. It has a growing following on social networking sites such as Facebook and a growing customer base on its mobile commerce channel. The company is making significant investments in new marketing initiatives, which includes offering engaging offers and promotions through its direct channels. The aggregate number of unique visitors to the company's retail Web sites has been increasing strongly on an annual basis.

The benchmark key performance indicators (KPIs) for the direct-to-consumer channel are expected to become more competitive. To do this, the company needs to continuously optimize its supply chain to keep in line with industry benchmarks like lead time, turnaround time, and so forth. Already, the Internet and Catalog Orders business has been able to scale up operations efficiently, benefiting from the operating resources of the company's store divisions.

Between 2008 and 2010, A&F reduced the operating expenses related to its Internet and catalog business by about 10 percent annually. This was largely due to the business benefiting from the company's large operating resources. The company believes that there is further scope for optimizing these operations. However, going forward, efficiency may decrease slightly and then remain flat as A&F incurs higher operating expenses as this business expands outside the United States. The company has made plans for expanding its online business to Canada and Europe.

Summing It Up—By the Numbers

Companywide, Abercrombie & Fitch generated total revenues of $3.47 billion in calendar year 2010. This is forecast to rise to $5.48 billion in calendar year 2017. Its overall gross profit as a percentage of revenue is projected to increase from 15.6 percent in 2010 to 23.3 percent in 2017, due to operating efficiencies in each of the firm's divisions, higher sales per square foot, and the greater importance of the high margin Internet and catalog business.

Table 1 shows 2007–2017 actual and projected performance for each of A&F's key businesses. Growth prospects and profitability forecasts vary widely among the business units.

Questions

1. What can *any* retailer learn from this case?
2. How could A&F enhance the total retail experience at each of its store brands?
3. Describe several uncontrollable factors that impact A&F.
4. Analyze A&F's overall retail strategy, based on the steps discussed in Chapter 3.
5. What kind of loyalty program(s) should A&F offer? Present details in your answer.
6. What recommendations would you suggest to A&F as it looks to the future?
7. Look at Table 1 and note at least five key points to be learned from the data in that table.

TABLE 1 Selected Abercrombie & Fitch Data by Division, Actual and Projected

	2007	2008	2009	2010	2011	2012	2013	2014	2015	2016	2017
Abercrombie & Fitch Stores											
Total Revenue (Bil. $)	1.51	1.39	1.16	1.38	1.41	1.44	1.5	1.56	1.62	1.66	1.69
Revenue per Square Foot ($)	476	440	371	451	487	506	516	527	537	543	548
Square Feet per Store (000)	8.82	8.85	8.89	9.11	9.16	9.2	9.25	9.29	9.34	9.39	9.43
Number of Stores	359	356	346	325	305	311	317	321	324	325	325
Gross Profits (Mil. $)	393	258	185	199	227	261	300	334	370	397	420
Gross Profits (%)	26.0	18.6	15.9	14.4	16.1	18.1	20.0	21.4	22.8	23.9	24.9
Hollister Stores											
Total Revenue (Bil. $)	1.46	1.38	1.15	1.35	1.54	1.68	1.80	1.91	2.02	2.09	2.15
Revenue per Square Foot ($)	520	425	326	368	404	421	437	455	473	483	490
Square Feet per Store (000)	6.67	6.72	6.75	6.88	6.91	6.95	6.98	7.02	7.05	7.09	7.12
Number of Stores	450	515	525	540	561	584	595	606	607	613	619
Gross Profits (Mil. $)	264	200	137	146	187	228	270	309	346	369	388
Gross Profits (%)	18.1	14.6	12.0	10.9	12.2	13.6	15.0	16.2	17.2	17.7	18.0
Gilly Hicks and abercrombie kids Stores											
Total Revenue (Bil. $)	479	450	374	389	418	470	534	588	636	675	703
Revenue per Square Foot ($)	462	355	286	317	342	356	370	378	385	393	397
Square Feet per Store (000)	4.97	5.29	5.45	5.72	5.84	5.95	6.07	6.19	6.32	6.44	6.57
Number of Stores	226	254	225	204	214	229	245	257	265	267	270
Gross Profits (Mil. $)	101	70.2	52.6	49.3	59.3	74.8	93.3	110	123	134	140
Gross Profits (%)	21.1	15.6	14.0	12.7	14.2	15.9	17.5	18.7	19.5	19.8	20.0
Internet and Catalog Orders Business											
Total Revenue (Bil. $)	298	315	250	352	458	549	632	727	814	871	932
Gross Profits (Mil. $)	126	129	100	146	180	206	232	261	288	306	327
Gross Profits (%)	42.3	41.2	40.4	41.6	39.5	37.5	36.8	36.0	35.5	35.1	35.1

Note: Abercrombie & Fitch Co. reports financial information for fiscal year ended January 31st. This table calendarizes Abercrombie & Fitch Co.'s reported financial data for the year ended December 31st and uses existing data and Trefis assumptions to project future performance.

PART 2

Situation Analysis

In Part Two, we talk about the organizational missions, ownership and management alternatives, goods/service categories, and objectives of a broad range of retail institutions. By understanding the unique attributes of these institutions, better retail strategies can be developed and implemented.

Chapter 4 examines the characteristics of retail institutions on the basis of ownership type: independent, chain, franchise, leased department, vertical marketing system, and consumer cooperative. We also discuss the methods used by manufacturers, wholesalers, and retailers to obtain control in a distribution channel. A chapter appendix has additional information on franchising.

Chapter 5 describes retail institutions in terms of their strategy mix. We introduce three key concepts: the wheel of retailing, scrambled merchandising, and the retail life cycle. Strategic responses to the evolving marketplace are noted. Several strategy mixes are then studied, with food and general merchandise retailers reviewed separately.

Chapter 6 focuses on nonstore retailing, electronic retailing, and nontraditional retailing approaches. We cover direct marketing, direct selling, vending machines, the World Wide Web, video kiosks, and airport retailing. The dynamics of Web-based retailing are featured. A chapter appendix covers the emerging area of multi-channel retailing in more depth.

Source: Tupungato/Shutterstock.com. Reprinted by permission.

4 Retail Institutions by Ownership

Chapter Objectives

1. To show the ways in which retail institutions can be classified
2. To study retailers on the basis of ownership type and to examine the characteristics of each
3. To explore the methods used by manufacturers, wholesalers, and retailers to exert influence in the distribution channel

Store-based retail firms may operate as few as one facility—such as a local pizza shop—or as many as several thousand locations—such as the Subway fast-food chain with more than 35,000 outlets around the world. Yet, despite their differences in scale, small and mid-sized retailers, like the larger retail chains with which they compete, are finding that the use of social media can be quite worthwhile.

In a recent survey of small and mid-sized U.S. firms, Pitney Bowes found that social media now rival E-mail as a key communication method. Why? The majority of respondents think that the use of social media is cost effective and easy to use; only slightly more of the respondents say this about E-mail. About 40 percent of the respondents now feel almost as comfortable and knowledgeable with social media as they do with E-mail.

According to Pitney Bowes, it is the value for the money spent that is driving the adoption and use of social media by small and mid-sized businesses. This is the main reason that social media have moved ahead of direct (snail) mail as a communication tool for these firms. And, during the last couple of years, social media spending by small and mid-sized firms has risen by a greater percentage than their spending on any other form of communication. However, overall spending on social media still lags behind the money allocated to E-mail and other types of advertising by small and mid-sized firms.

A study of small businesses by American Express determined that during a recent one-and-a-half-year period, the percentage of responding firms involved with social media increased from 15 percent to 35 percent; and one in eight respondents said they now use blogs to communicate—double the prior number. Facebook is the dominant social media point of contact for small businesses, far ahead of Twitter, YouTube, and other social media forums.[1]

Source: BeTA-Artworks/fotolia.com.

Overview

A **retail institution** is the basic format or structure of a business. In the United States, there are 2.4 million retail firms (including those with no payroll, whereby only the owner and/or family members work for the firm), and they operate 3.2 million establishments. An institutional discussion shows the relative sizes and diversity of different kinds of retailing, and indicates how various retailers are affected by the external environment. Institutional analysis is important in strategic planning when selecting an organizational mission, choosing an ownership alternative, defining the goods/service category, and setting objectives.

We examine retail institutions from these perspectives: ownership (Chapter 4); store-based strategy mix (Chapter 5); and nonstore-based, electronic, and nontraditional retailing (Chapter 6). Figure 4-1 shows a breakdown. An institution may be correctly placed in more than one category: A department store may be part of a chain, have a store-based strategy, accept mail-order sales, and operate a Web site.

Please interpret the data in Chapters 4, 5, and 6 carefully. Because some institutional categories are not mutually exclusive, care should be taken in combining statistics so double counting does not occur. We have drawn in the data in these chapters from a number of government and nongovernment sources. Although data are as current as possible, not all information corresponds to a common date. *Census of Retail Trade* data are only collected twice a decade. Furthermore, our numbers are based on the broad interpretation of retailing used in this book, which includes auto repair shops, hotels and motels, movie theaters, real-estate brokers, and others who sell to the final consumer.

RETAIL INSTITUTIONS CHARACTERIZED BY OWNERSHIP

Retail firms may be independently owned, chain-owned, franchisee-operated, leased departments, owned by manufacturers or wholesalers, or consumer-owned.

Although retailers are primarily small (three-quarters of all stores are operated by firms with one outlet and more than one-half of all firms have two or fewer paid employees), there are also

FIGURE 4-1
A Classification Method for Retail Institutions

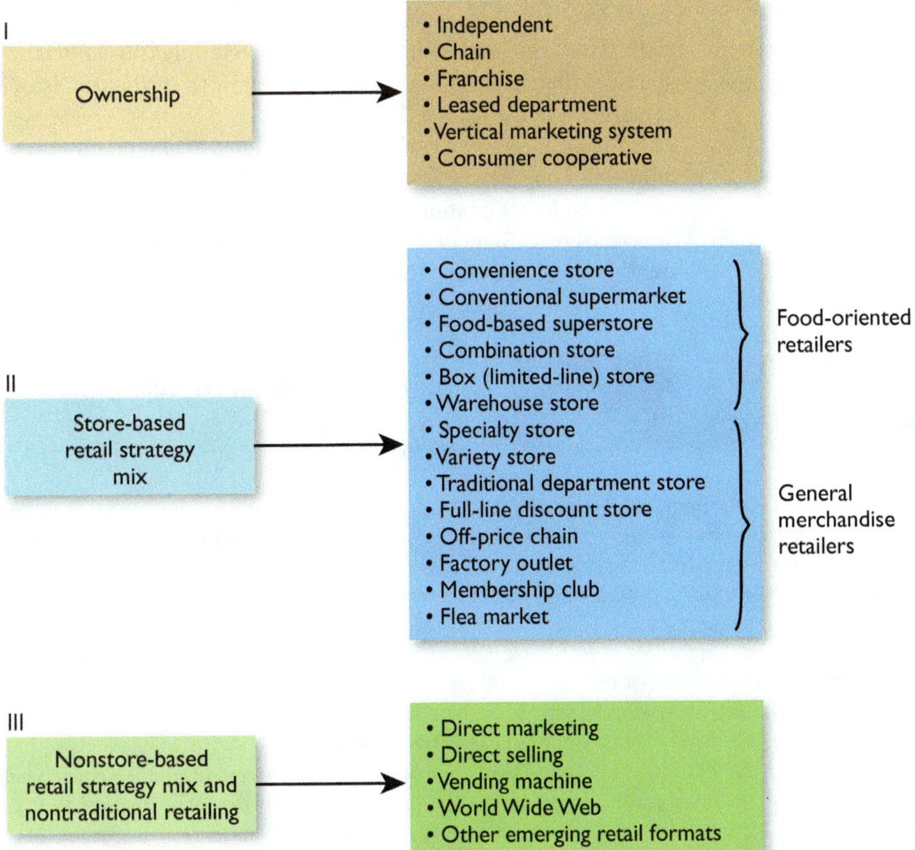

very large retailers. The five leading U.S.-based retailers annually total $575 billion in U.S. sales alone and employ more than 2.6 million people in the United States. Ownership opportunities abound. According to the U.S. Census Bureau (www.census.gov), women own nearly one million retail firms, African Americans (men and women) 110,000 retail firms, Hispanic Americans (men and women) 175,000 retail firms, and Asian Americans (men and women) 190,000 retail firms.

Each ownership format serves a marketplace niche, if the strategy is executed well:

- Independent retailers capitalize on a very targeted customer base and please shoppers in a friendly, informal way. Word-of-mouth communication is important. These retailers should not try to serve too many customers or enter into price wars.
- Chain retailers benefit from their widely known image and from economies of scales and mass promotion possibilities. They should maintain their image chainwide and not be inflexible in adapting to changes in the marketplace.
- Franchisors have strong geographic coverage—due to franchisee investments—and the motivation of franchisees as owner-operators. They should not get bogged down in policy disputes with franchisees or charge excessive royalty fees.
- Leased departments enable store operators and outside parties to join forces and enhance the shopping experience, while sharing expertise and expenses. They should not hurt the image of the store or place too much pressure on the lessee to bring in store traffic.
- A vertically integrated channel gives a firm greater control over sources of supply, but it should not provide consumers with too little choice of products or too few outlets.
- Cooperatives provide members with price savings. They should not expect too much involvement by members or add facilities that raise costs too much.

Independent

The Business Owner's Toolkit (www.toolkit.com) is an excellent resource for the independent retailer.

An **independent** retailer owns one retail unit. There are 2.3 million independent U.S. retailers—accounting for about one-quarter of total store sales. Seventy percent of independents are run by the owners and their families; and those firms generate just 3 percent of U.S. store sales (averaging under $100,000 in annual revenues) and have no paid workers (there is no payroll).

The high number of independents is associated with the **ease of entry** into the marketplace, due to low capital requirements and no, or relatively simple, licensing provisions for many small retail firms. The investment per worker in retailing is usually much lower than for manufacturers, and licensing is pretty routine. Each year, tens of thousands of new retailers, mostly independents, open in the United States.

The ease of entry—which leads to intense competition—is a big factor in the high rate of failures among newer firms. One-third of new U.S. retailers do not survive the first year, and two-thirds do not continue beyond the third year. Most failures involve independents. Annually, thousands of U.S. retailers (of all sizes) file for bankruptcy protection—besides the thousands of small firms that simply close.[2]

The Participation of Women in Retailing

A research study was recently conducted of about 2,500 college-educated men and women regarding their views about women's participation in the workforce. Among the topics covered were reasons why too few women progressed up the management ladder in the United States.

The study found that the lack of female executives was due to both mindsets and behaviors—at companies and among women employees. The situation was especially critical at the point when female middle managers would normally become senior managers.

According to the study, gender diversity was simply not an important enough priority at most companies and that there was great variability in the number of gender-based diversity policies that firms developed. Most companies that responded to the survey had female role models and informal networks of female executives. In addition, many companies had shifted work hours to meet female workers' concern for a balance among work, family, and leisure. Among the issues that need to be addressed are the incorrect perception that certain jobs should not be available to women or that women should be rewarded only for performance, while men should be rewarded for potential.

Source: Charlotte Werner, Sandrine Devillard, and Sandra Sancier-Sultan, "How Women Can Contribute More to the U.S. Economy," *McKinsey Quarterly* (April 2011).

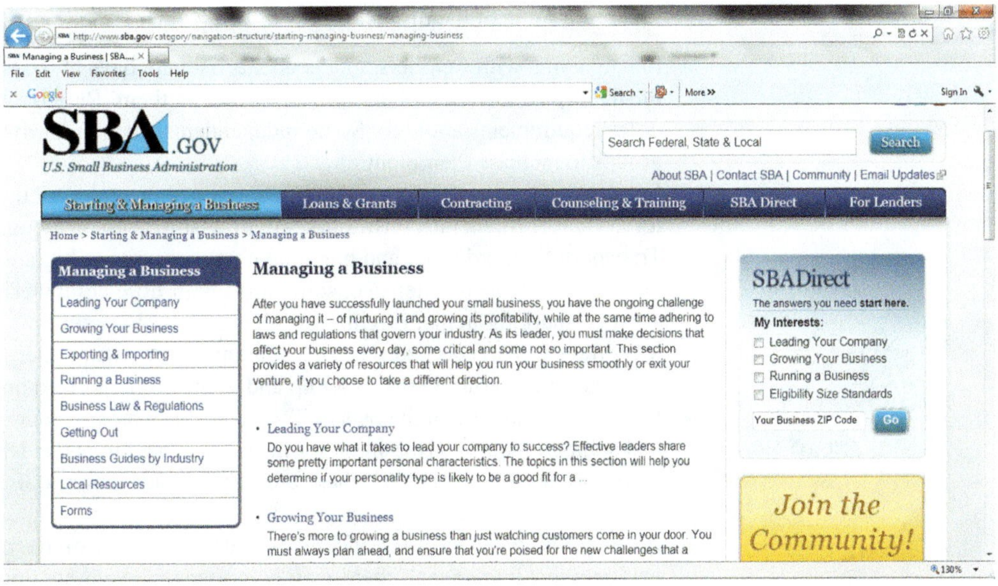

FIGURE 4-2

Useful Online Information for Small Retailers

Go to www.sba.gov/category/navigation-structure/starting-managing-business and download any of the U.S. Small Business Administration's online information at this Web site. It's free!

The U.S. Small Business Administration (SBA) has a Small Business Development Center (SBDC) to assist current and prospective small business owners (www.sba.gov/content/small-business-development-centers-sbdcs). There are 63 lead SBDCs (at least one in every state) and about 1,000 local SBDCs, satellites, and specialty centers. The purpose is to assist "small businesses with financial, marketing, production, organization, engineering, and technical problems and feasibility studies." Centers offer free counseling, seminars and training sessions, conferences, and information through the Internet, as well as in person and by phone. The SBA also has a lot of free downloadable information at its Web site (www.sba.gov). See Figure 4-2.

Read the Aunt Annie's story (www.auntieannes.com/corporate_ingredients.aspx)—from a farmer's market to a worldwide chain.

COMPETITIVE ADVANTAGES AND DISADVANTAGES OF INDEPENDENTS Independent retailers have a variety of advantages and disadvantages. These are among their advantages:

- There is flexibility in choosing retail formats and locations and in devising strategy. Because only one location is involved, detailed specifications can be set for the best site and a thorough search undertaken. Uniform location standards are not needed, as they are for chains, and independents do not have to worry about stores being too close together. Independents have great latitude in selecting target markets. Because they often have modest goals, small segments may be selected rather than the mass market. Assortments, prices, hours, and other factors are then set consistent with the segment.
- Investment costs for leases, fixtures, workers, and merchandise can be held down; and there is no duplication of stock or personnel functions. Responsibilities are clearly delineated within a store.
- Independents frequently act as specialists in a niche of a particular goods/service category. They are then more efficient and can lure shoppers interested in specialized retailers.
- Independents exert strong control over their strategies, and the owner-operator is typically on the premises. Decision making is centralized and layers of management personnel are minimized.
- There is a certain image attached to independents, particularly small ones, that chains cannot readily capture. This is the image of a personable retailer with a comfortable atmosphere in which to shop.
- Independents can easily sustain consistency in their efforts because only one store is operated.
- Independents have "independence." They do not have to fret about stockholders, board of directors meetings, and labor unrest. They are often free from unions and seniority rules.
- Owner-operators typically have a strong entrepreneurial drive. They have made a personal investment and there is a lot of ego involvement: "No matter what the size, to succeed in your business you will need to be good at what you do, know how to market it to get customers, be able to keep proper records of expenses and payments, and plan for weeks and even months ahead."[3]

These are some of the disadvantages of independent retailing:

- In bargaining with suppliers, independents may not have much power because they often buy in small quantities. Suppliers may even bypass them. Reordering may be hard if minimum order requirements are high. Some independents, such as hardware stores, belong to buying groups to increase their clout.
- Independents generally cannot gain economies of scale in buying and maintaining inventory. Due to financial constraints, small assortments are bought several times per year. Transportation, ordering, and handling costs per unit are high.
- Operations are labor intensive, sometimes with little computerization. Ordering, taking inventory, marking items, ringing up sales, and bookkeeping may be done manually. This is less efficient than computerization. In many cases, owner-operators are unwilling or unable to spend time learning how to set up and apply computerized procedures.
- Due to the relatively high costs of TV ads and the broad geographic coverage of magazines and some newspapers (too large for firms with one outlet), independents are limited in their access to certain media. Yet, there are various promotion tools available for creative independents (see Chapter 19).
- A crucial problem for independents is overdependence on the owner. All decisions may be made by that person, and there may be no management continuity when the owner-boss is ill, on vacation, or retires. Long-run success and employee morale can be affected by this. As one small business consultant said: "Owners stay awake at night worrying about how to pay their bills, collect accounts receivables, and make payroll or the bank loan."[4]
- A limited amount of time is allotted to long-run planning because the owner is intimately involved in daily operations of the firm.

Chain

A **chain** retailer operates multiple outlets (store units) under common ownership; it usually engages in some level of centralized (or coordinated) purchasing and decision making. In the United States, there are roughly 110,000 retail chains that operate about 950,000 establishments.

There are 7,300 U.S. and international Radio Shack (www.radioshack.com) stores and 1,400 wireless kiosks. See if there is one near you.

The relative strength of chain retailing is great, even though the number of firms is small (less than 5 percent of all U.S. retail firms). Chains today operate about 30 percent of retail establishments, and because stores in chains tend to be considerably larger than those run by independents, chains account for roughly three-quarters of total U.S. store sales and employment. Although the majority of chains have 5 or fewer outlets, the several hundred firms with 100 or more outlets account for more than 60 percent of U.S. retail sales. Some big U.S. chains have at least 1,000 outlets each. There are also many large foreign chains. See Figure 4-3.

FIGURE 4-3
Louis Vuitton: A Powerhouse of Upscale Retailing
Louis Vuitton is a huge French-based chain with stores around the world, including this one in Stockholm, Sweden. Its Web site (www.louisvuitton.com) may be accessed in nine languages.

Source: Tupungato/Shutterstock.com. Reprinted by permission.

TECHNOLOGY IN RETAILING

American Express and Facebook for Small Retailers

American Express (Amex) (www.americanexpress.com) has recently began offering small retailers and other small business owners advertising credits on Facebook. Any Amex customer with a membership rewards card can redeem these points for advertising on American Express' OPEN's Facebook page (www.facebook.com/americanexpress) in amounts of $50, $100, and $250.

This promotion by American Express provides a more convenient way for small retailers to pay for Facebook advertising. Since nearly one billion people use Facebook, these ads enable small firms to facilitate word-of-mouth communication at unprecedented rates. About 35 percent of the 728 small businesses surveyed by Amex used Facebook to promote their company; about 10 percent use Twitter.

According to a research analyst, in order for the Amex Facebook offer to succeed, small-business owners need to be better informed as to how to use social media most effectively. Another analyst notes that Amex's program will not necessarily transform retailers into social media experts.

In November 2010, Amex hosted "Small Business Saturday," an event that offered small firms a free Facebook ad. According to Amex, 10,000 firms signed up for this offer. American Express also sponsors Open Forum, a social network that focuses on providing advice to small businesses.

Source: Jeremy Quittner, "Amex Small-Biz Reward: Facebook Ads," *American Banker* (June 30, 2011), pp. 1–9.

The dominance of chains varies by type of retailer. Chains generate at least 75 percent of total U.S. category sales for department stores, discount department stores, and grocery stores. On the other hand, stationery, beauty salon, furniture, and liquor store chains produce far less than 50 percent of U.S. retail sales in their categories.

Sears' own Kenmore brand (www.kenmore.com) is so powerful that many different appliances are sold under the Kenmore name.

COMPETITIVE ADVANTAGES AND DISADVANTAGES OF CHAINS There are numerous competitive advantages for chain retailers:

- Many chains have bargaining power due to their purchase volume. They receive new items when introduced, have orders promptly filled, get sales support, and obtain volume discounts. Large chains may also gain exclusive rights to certain items and have goods produced under the chains' brands.
- Chains achieve cost efficiencies when they buy directly from manufacturers and in large volume, ship and store goods, and attend trade shows sponsored by suppliers to learn about new offerings. They can sometimes bypass wholesalers, with the result being lower supplier prices.
- Efficiency is gained by sharing warehouse facilities, purchasing standardized store fixtures, and so on; by centralized buying and decision making; and by other practices. Chains typically give headquarters executives broad authority for personnel policies and for buying, pricing, and advertising decisions.
- Chains use computers in ordering merchandise, taking inventory, forecasting, ringing up sales, and bookkeeping. This increases efficiency and reduces overall costs.
- Chains, particularly national or regional ones, can take advantage of a variety of media, from TV to magazines to newspapers to online blogs.
- Most chains have defined management philosophies, with detailed strategies and clear employee responsibilities. There is continuity when managerial personnel are absent or retire because there are qualified people to fill in and succession plans in place. See Figure 4-4.
- Many chains expend considerable time on long-run plans and assign specific staff to planning on a permanent basis. Opportunities and threats are carefully monitored.

Chain retailers do have a number of disadvantages:

- Once chains are established, flexibility may be limited. New nonoverlapping store locations may be hard to find. Consistent strategies must be maintained throughout all units, including prices, promotions, and product assortments. It may be difficult to adapt to local diverse markets.
- Investments are higher due to multiple leases and fixtures. The purchase of merchandise is more costly because a number of store branches must be stocked.
- Managerial control is complex, especially for chains with geographically dispersed branches. Top management cannot maintain the control over each branch that independents have over

FIGURE 4-4

Mini: One Part of the BMW Three-Brand Mix

BMW produces BMW, Mini (including the Mini Cooper), and Rolls-Royce vehicles. Through three distinct worldwide retail chains, there are 3,100 BMW dealerships, 1,300 Mini dealerships, and 80 Rolls-Royce dealerships. The Mini dealership shown here is in Birmingham, England.

Source: Tupungato/ Shutterstock.com. Reprinted by permission.

their single outlet. Lack of communication and delays in making and enacting decisions are particular problems.

- Personnel in large chains often have limited independence because there are several management layers and unionized employees. Some chains empower personnel to give them more authority.

Franchising[5]

The International Franchise Association (www.franchise.org) is a leading source of information about franchising.

Franchising involves a contractual arrangement between a *franchisor* (a manufacturer, wholesaler, or service sponsor) and a retail *franchisee*, which allows the franchisee to conduct business under an established name and according to a given pattern of business. The franchisee typically pays an initial fee and a monthly percentage of gross sales in exchange for the exclusive rights to sell goods and services in an area. Small businesses benefit by being part of a large, chain-type retail institution.

In **product/trademark franchising**, a franchisee acquires the identity of a franchisor by agreeing to sell the latter's products and/or operate under the latter's name. The franchisee operates rather autonomously. There are certain operating rules, but the franchisee sets store hours, chooses a location, and determines facilities and displays. Product/trademark franchising represents 60 percent of retail franchising sales. Examples are auto dealers and many gasoline service stations.

With **business format franchising**, there is a more interactive relationship between a franchisor and a franchisee. The franchisee receives assistance on site location, quality control, accounting systems, startup practices, management training, and responding to problems besides the right to sell goods and services. Prototype stores, standardized product lines, and cooperative advertising foster a level of coordination previously found only in chains. Business format franchising arrangements are common for restaurants and other food outlets, real-estate, and service retailing. Due to the small size of many franchisees, business formats account for about 80 percent of franchised outlets, although just 40 percent of total sales (including auto dealers).

McDonald's (www.aboutmcdonalds.com/mcd/franchising.html) is a good example of a business format franchise arrangement. The firm provides franchisee training at "Hamburger U," a detailed operating manual, regular visits by service managers, and brush-up training. In return for a 20-year franchising agreement with McDonald's, a traditional franchisee generally must put up a minimum of $500,000 of nonborrowed personal resources and typically pays ongoing royalty fees totaling at least 12.5 percent of gross sales to McDonald's. See Figure 4-5.

SIZE AND STRUCTURAL ARRANGEMENTS[6] Although auto and truck dealers provide more than one-half of all U.S. retail franchise sales, few sectors of retailing have been unaffected by franchising's growth. In the United States, there are more than 3,000 retail franchisors doing business

FIGURE 4-5
McDonald's Qualifications for Potential Franchisees

Source: Figure developed by the authors based on information in McDonald's "Frequently Asked Questions—Qualifications," **www.mcdonalds.com/corp/franchise/faqs2/qualifications. html** (February 19, 2009).

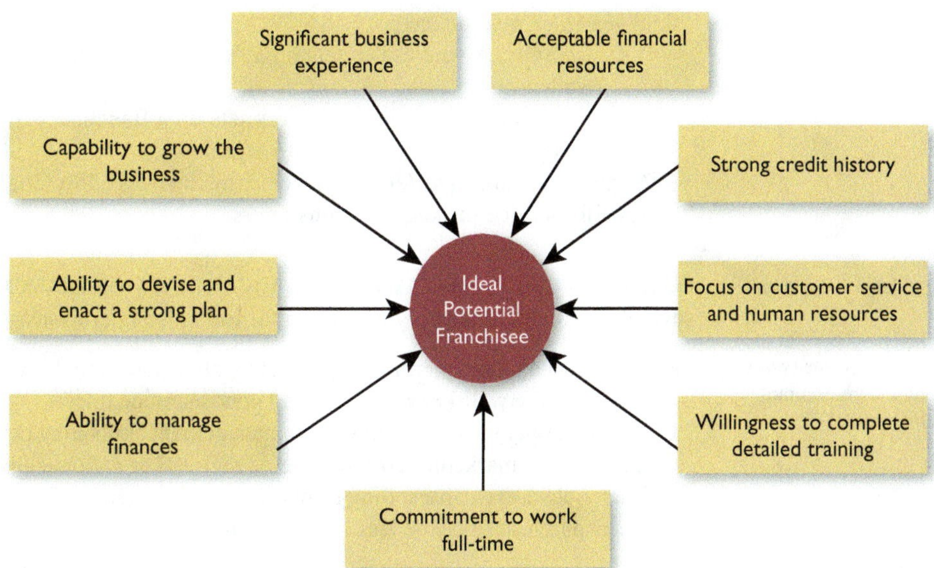

with 350,000 franchisees. They operate 800,000 franchisee- and franchisor-owned outlets, employ several million people, and generate one-third of total store sales. In addition, hundreds of U.S.-based franchisors have foreign operations, with tens of thousands of outlets.

About 85 percent of U.S. franchising sales and franchised outlets involve franchisee-owned units; the rest involve franchisor-owned outlets. If franchisees operate one outlet, they are independents; if they operate two or more outlets, they are chains. Today, a large number of franchisees operate as chains.

Three structural arrangements dominate retail franchising. See Figure 4-6.

1. *Manufacturer-retailer.* A manufacturer gives independent franchisees the right to sell goods and related services through a licensing agreement.

FIGURE 4-6
Structural Arrangements in Retail Franchising

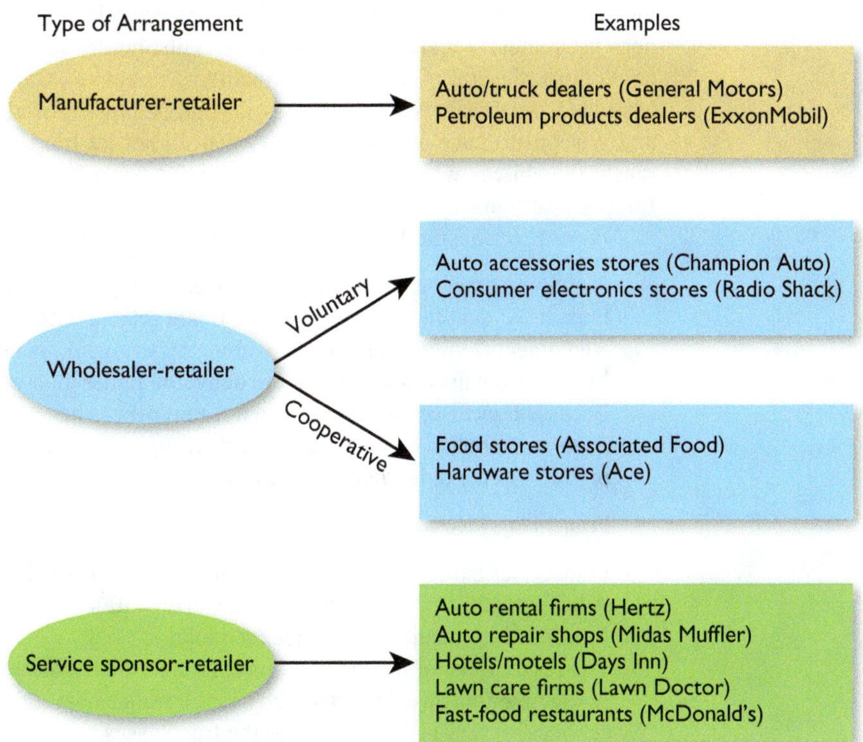

2. *Wholesaler-retailer.*
   a. *Voluntary.* A wholesaler sets up a franchise system and grants franchises to individual retailers.
   b. *Cooperative.* A group of retailers sets up a franchise system and shares the ownership and operations of a wholesaling organization.
3. *Service sponsor-retailer.* A service firm licenses individual retailers so they can offer specific service packages to consumers.

Want to learn more about what it takes to be a franchisee? Check out the Jazzercise Web site (www.jazzercise.com/become_franchise.htm).

COMPETITIVE ADVANTAGES AND DISADVANTAGES OF FRANCHISING *Franchisees* receive several benefits by investing in successful franchise operations:

- They own a retail enterprise with a relatively small capital investment.
- They acquire well-known names and goods/service lines.
- Standard operating procedures and management skills may be taught to them.
- Cooperative marketing efforts (such as regional or national advertising) are facilitated.
- They obtain exclusive selling rights for specified geographical territories.
- Their purchases may be less costly per unit due to the volume of the overall franchise.

Some potential problems do exist for franchisees:

- Oversaturation could occur if too many franchisees are in one geographic area.
- Due to overzealous selling by some franchisors, franchisees' income potential, required managerial ability, and investment may be incorrectly stated.
- They may be locked into contracts requiring purchases from franchisors or certain vendors.
- Cancellation clauses may give franchisors the right to void agreements if provisions are not satisfied.
- In some industries, franchise agreements are of short duration.
- Royalties are often a percentage of gross sales, regardless of franchisee profits.

The preceding factors contribute to **constrained decision making**, whereby franchisors limit franchisee involvement in the strategic planning process.

The Federal Trade Commission (FTC) has a recently revised rule regarding disclosure requirements and business opportunities (http://business.ftc.gov/sites/default/files/pdf/bus70-franchise-rule-compliance-guide.pdf) that applies to all U.S. franchisors. It is intended to provide adequate information to potential franchisees prior to their investment. Although the FTC does not regularly review disclosure statements, nearly 20 states check them and may require corrections. Several of those states (including Arkansas, California, Hawaii, Illinois, Indiana, Maryland, Michigan, Minnesota, Mississippi, Nebraska, South Dakota, Virginia, Washington, and Wisconsin) have fair practice laws that do not let franchisors terminate, cancel, or fail to renew franchisees without just cause. The FTC has a franchising Web site (www.ftc.gov/bcp/franchise/netfran.shtm), as highlighted in Figure 4-7.

Franchisors accrue lots of benefits by having franchise arrangements:

- A national or global presence is developed more quickly and with less franchisor investment.
- Franchisee qualifications for ownership are set and enforced.
- Agreements require franchisees to abide by stringent operating rules set by franchisors.
- Money is obtained when goods are delivered rather than when they are sold.
- Because franchisees are owners and not employees, they have a greater incentive to work hard.
- Even after franchisees have paid for their outlets, franchisors receive royalties and may sell products to the individual proprietors.

Franchisors also face potential problems:

- Franchisees harm the overall reputation if they do not adhere to company standards.
- A lack of uniformity among outlets adversely affects customer loyalty.
- Intrafranchise competition is not desirable.
- The resale value of individual units is injured if franchisees perform poorly.
- Ineffective franchised units directly injure franchisors' profitability that results from selling services, materials, or products to the franchisees and from royalty fees.
- Franchisees, in greater numbers, are seeking to limit franchisors' rules and regulations.

FIGURE 4-7
The FTC on Franchise and Business Opportunities
At the FTC's franchising site, www.ftc.gov/bcp/franchise/netfran.shtm, there are many free downloads about opportunities—and warnings, as well.

Further information on franchising is contained in the appendix at the end of this chapter. Also, visit our Web site for a lot of links on this topic (www.pearsonhighered.com/bermanevans).

Leased Department

A **leased department** is a department in a retail store—usually a department, discount, or specialty store—that is rented to an outside party. The leased department proprietor is responsible for all aspects of its business (including fixtures) and normally pays a percentage of sales as rent. The store sets operating restrictions for the leased department to ensure overall consistency and coordination.[7]

Leased departments (sometimes called "stores within a store") are used by store-based retailers to broaden their offerings into product categories that often are on the fringe of the store's major product lines. They are most common for in-store beauty salons; banks; photographic studios; and shoe, jewelry, cosmetics, watch repair, and shoe repair departments. Leased departments are also popular in shopping center food courts. They account for $20 billion in annual department store sales. More luxury brands, such as Gucci and Dior, are leasing out departments to have greater control over the way their products are sold. Data on overall leased department sales are not available.

Consider that it may sometimes be in the retailer's best interest to let other parties handle certain store departments:

> Sears is carving out about 15 percent of the square footage in its Costa Mesa, California, store to house the much trendier retailer Forever 21. Target has 1,450 Radio Shack-run mobile phone shops in its stores. And Wal-Mart Realty says it has almost 400 in-store leases ready for some well-matched retailer who sees the benefit of letting "Wal-Mart's repeat customers become [their] repeat customers." Retailers in Europe and Asia have used the concept extensively—nearly all major Chinese retailers are really a conglomeration of ever-changing smaller stores which stand up in competition, or are pruned from the landscape.[8]

COMPETITIVE ADVANTAGES AND DISADVANTAGES OF LEASED DEPARTMENTS From the *stores' perspective*, leased departments offer a number of benefits:

- The market is enlarged by providing one-stop customer shopping.
- Personnel management, merchandise displays, and reordering items are undertaken by lessees.
- Regular store personnel do not have to be involved.
- Leased department operators pay for some expenses, thus reducing store costs.
- A percentage of revenues is received regularly.

There are also some potential pitfalls, from the stores' perspective:

- Leased department operating procedures may conflict with store procedures.
- Lessees may adversely affect stores' images.
- Customers may blame problems on the stores rather than on the lessees.

For *leased department operators*, there are these advantages:

- Stores are known, have steady customers, and generate immediate sales for leased departments.
- Some costs are reduced through shared facilities, such as security equipment and display windows.
- Their image is enhanced by their relationships with popular stores.
- The operators have greater control over their own image and selling strategy than if the retailers act as the resellers.

Lessees face these possible problems:

- There may be inflexibility as to the hours they must be open and the operating style.
- The goods/service lines are usually restricted.
- If they are successful, stores may raise rent or not renew leases when they expire.
- In-store locations may not generate the sales expected.

CPI (www.cpicorp.com) has flourished with its leased department relationship at Sears and Wal-Mart.

An example of a thriving long-term lease arrangement is one between CPI Corporation and Sears. In exchange for space in about 1,000 U.S. and Canadian Sears stores, CPI pays 15 percent of its sales. Its annual sales per square foot are much higher than Sears' overall average. CPI's agreement with Sears has been renewed several times. Annual revenues through Sears are $200 million. Since 2007, CPI has also operated portrait studios in Wal-Mart stores.[9]

Understanding Ethical Behavior in Family Businesses

The traditional thinking is that nonfamily businesses generally seek to make a profit, increase market share, and reach given return-on-investment goals. In contrast, family-run businesses are more committed to providing employment for family and friends and to aid the community.

Nonetheless, based on their research, two experts state that face-to-face interactions (social exchanges) that occur in an organization's daily routine can be used to explain the ethical behavior in both family and nonfamily businesses. Family members' social interactions produce a distinctive ethical frame of reference. There are two contrasting forms of exchange within an organization: restricted exchange systems (RES) and generalized exchange systems (GES). RES are characterized by individualism, competition, and impersonality. GES focus more on the long-term relationships among individuals, on altruistic goals, and on the community. In GES, the obligation is not to a single exchange partner, but to the group as a whole.

Although some firms use pure RES and others use pure GES, others can be in the middle on these dimensions (RES/GES). These firms may seek out economic goals within moral constraints. The RES and GES frameworks can be used to explain both relationships within family-run businesses and a large organization's ethical perspective.

Source: Rebecca G. Long and K. Michael Mathews, "Ethics in the Family Firm: Cohesion Through Reciprocity and Exchange," *Business Ethics Quarterly*, Vol. 21 (April 2011), pp. 287–308.

Vertical Marketing System

A **vertical marketing system** consists of all the levels of independently owned businesses along a channel of distribution. Goods and services are normally distributed through one of these systems: independent, partially integrated, and fully integrated. See Figure 4-8.

In an *independent vertical marketing system*, there are three levels of independently owned firms: manufacturers, wholesalers, and retailers. Such a system is most often used if manufacturers or retailers are small, intensive distribution is sought, customers are widely dispersed, unit sales are high, company resources are low, channel members seek to share costs and risks, and task specialization is desirable. Independent vertical marketing systems are used by many stationery stores, gift shops, hardware stores, food stores, drugstores, and many other firms. They are the leading form of vertical marketing system.

With a *partially integrated system*, two independently owned businesses along a channel perform all production and distribution functions. It is most common when a manufacturer and a retailer complete transactions and shipping, storing, and other distribution functions in the absence of a wholesaler. This system is most apt if manufacturers and retailers are large, selective or exclusive distribution is sought, unit sales are moderate, company resources are high, greater channel control is desired, and existing wholesalers are too expensive or unavailable. Partially integrated systems are often used by furniture stores, appliance stores, restaurants, computer retailers, and mail-order firms.

Kroger, the food retailer, manufactures 5,000 food and nonfood products in its 40 plants (www.thekrogerco.com/operations/operations_manufacturing.htm).

Through a *fully integrated system*, one firm performs all production and distribution functions. The firm has total control over its strategy, direct customer contact, and exclusivity over its offering; it also keeps all profits. This system can be costly and requires a lot of expertise. In the past, vertical marketing was employed mostly by manufacturers, such as Avon and Sherwin-Williams. At Sherwin-Williams, its own 3,400 paint stores account for nearly 60 percent of total company sales.[10] Today, more retailers (such as Kroger) use fully integrated systems for at least some products.

Some firms use **dual marketing** (a form of *multi-channel retailing*) and engage in more than one type of distribution arrangement. In this way, firms appeal to different consumers, increase sales, share some costs, and retain a good degree of strategic control. Here are two

FIGURE 4-8
Vertical Marketing Systems: Functions and Ownership

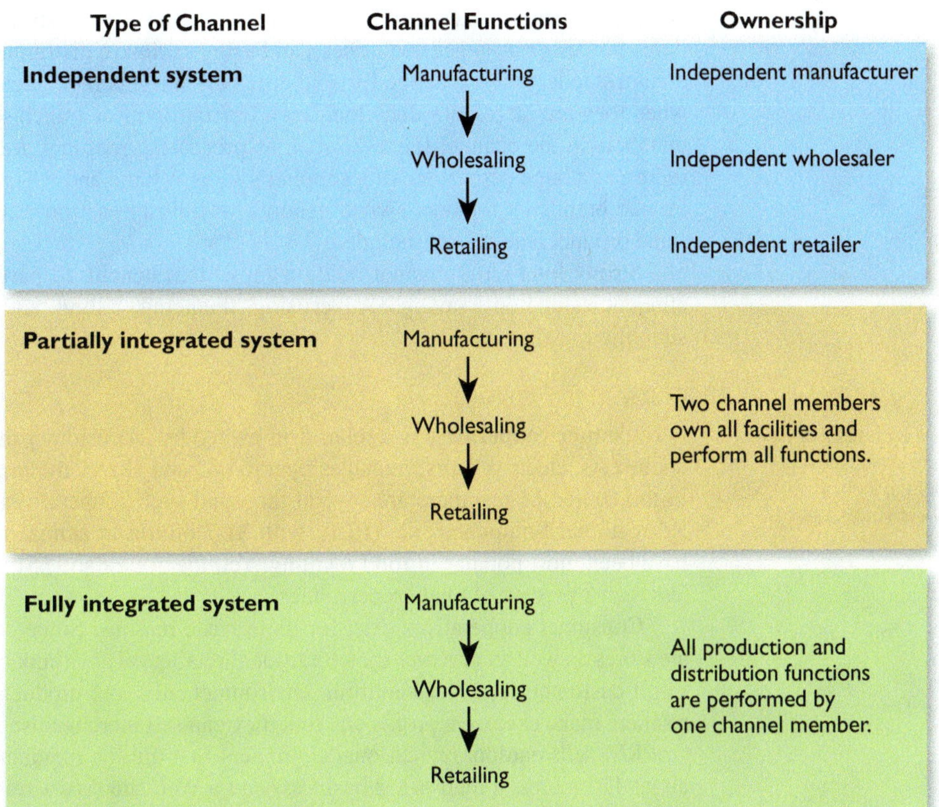

FIGURE 4-9
Sherwin-Williams' Dual Marketing System

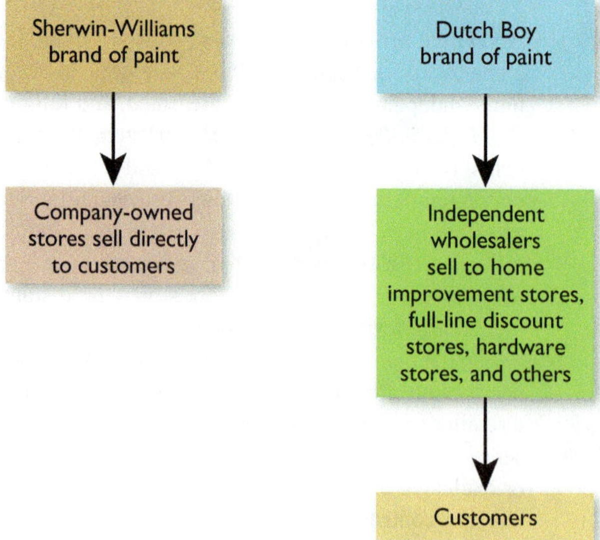

examples. (1) Sherwin-Williams sells Sherwin-Williams' paints at company stores. It sells Dutch Boy paints in home improvement stores, full-line discount stores, hardware stores, and others. See Figure 4-9. (2) In addition to its traditional standalone outlets, Dunkin' Donuts and Baskin-Robbins share facilities in a number of locations, so as to attract more customers and increase the revenue per transaction.

Besides partially or fully integrating a vertical marketing system, a firm can exert power in a distribution channel because of its economic, legal, or political strength; superior knowledge and abilities; customer loyalty; or other factors. With **channel control**, one member of a distribution channel dominates the decisions made in that channel due to the power it possesses. Manufacturers, wholesalers, and retailers each have a combination of tools to improve their positions relative to one another.

Manufacturers exert control by franchising, developing strong brand loyalty, pre-ticketing items (to designate suggested prices), and using exclusive distribution with retailers that agree to certain standards in exchange for sole distribution rights in an area. *Wholesalers* exert influence when they are large, introduce their own brands, sponsor franchises, and are the most efficient members in the channel for tasks such as processing reorders. *Retailers* exert clout when they represent a large percentage of a supplier's sales volume and when they foster their own brands. Private brands let retailers switch vendors with no impact on customer loyalty, as long as the same product features are included.

Strong long-term channel relationships often benefit all parties. They lead to scheduling efficiencies and cost savings. Advertising, financing, billing, and other tasks are dramatically simplified.

Consumer Cooperative

As an REI member (www.rei.com/membership/benefits), look at what $20 will get you!

A **consumer cooperative** is a retail firm owned by its customer members. A group of consumers invests, elects officers, manages operations, and shares the profits or savings that accrue.[11] In the United States, there are several thousand such cooperatives, from small buying clubs to Recreational Equipment Inc. (REI), with $1.7 billion in annual sales. Consumer cooperatives have been most popular in food retailing. Yet, the 500 or so U.S. food cooperatives account for less than 1 percent of total grocery sales.

Consumer cooperatives exist for these basic reasons: Some consumers feel they can operate stores as well as or better than traditional retailers. They think existing retailers inadequately fulfill customer needs for healthful, environmentally safe products. They also assume existing retailers make excessive profits and that they can sell merchandise for lower prices.

REI sells outdoor recreational equipment to 4 million members and other customers. It has about 125 stores, a mail-order business, and a Web site (www.rei.com). Unlike other cooperatives, REI is run by a professional staff that adheres to policies set by the member-elected board.

Asda Turns to Small-Box Stores

Although Wal-Mart's Asda (www.asda.com) supermarket chain in Great Britain traditionally used a large store format, it recently has begun to also open small-box formats. These smaller stores have been increasingly situated in locations where getting zoning approval for larger stores was difficult to obtain. Wal-Mart's competitors, Tesco (www.tesco.com), Sainsbury's (www.sainsburys.co.uk), and Marks & Spencer (www.marksandspencer.com), already have a large number of small-format stores. And two other British chains, Morrisons (www.morrisons.co.uk) and Waitrose (www.waitrose.com), are introducing small-store operations.

Developing profitable small stores is not as easy as it may seem at first glance for Wal-Mart. Due to size restrictions in comparison to its typical stores, Wal-Mart needs to heavily edit its assortment to ensure that the right brands are stocked in the right sizes and varieties. Tesco, with its shopper loyalty program, has an advantage over Wal-Mart due to its data on customer preferences by store location. Wal-Mart does not have a loyalty program.

Many of Wal-Mart's smaller stores are also in urban locations where the cost of doing business is higher. These stores need to have their inventory replenished more frequently, which places an additional burden on costs. To reduce shipping costs, many small Asda stores are located close to larger Wal-Mart supercenters.

Source: Natalie Berg and David Gray, "First Look at the Asda Supermarket," www.stores.org (July 2011).

There is a $20 one-time membership fee, which allows customers to shop at REI, vote for directors, and share in profits (based on the amount spent by each member). REI's goal is to distribute a regular dividend to members.

Cooperatives are only a small part of retailing because they involve consumer initiative and drive, consumers are usually not expert in retailing functions, cost savings and low selling prices are often not as expected, and consumer boredom in running a cooperative frequently occurs.

Chapter Summary

1. *To show the ways in which retail institutions can be classified.* There are 2.4 million retail firms in the United States operating 3.2 million establishments. They can be grouped on the basis of ownership, store-based strategy mix, and nonstore-based and nontraditional retailing. Many retailers can be placed in more than one category. This chapter deals with retail ownership. Chapters 5 and 6 report on the other classifications.

2. *To study retailers on the basis of ownership type, and to examine the characteristics of each.* About 70 percent of U.S. retail establishments are independents, each with one store. This is mostly due to the ease of entry. Independents' competitive advantages include their flexibility, low investments, specialized offerings, direct strategy control, image, consistency, independence, and entrepreneurial spirit. Disadvantages include limited bargaining power, few economies of scale, labor intensity, reduced media access, overdependence on owner, and limited planning.

   Chains are multiple stores under common ownership, with some centralized buying and decision making. They account for 30 percent of U.S. retail outlets but 75 percent of retail sales. Chains' advantages are bargaining power, functional efficiencies, multiple-store operations, computerization, media access, well-defined management, and planning. They face these potential problems: inflexibility, high investments, reduced control, and limited independence of personnel.

   Franchising embodies arrangements between franchisors and franchisees that let the latter do business under established names and according to detailed rules. It accounts for one-third of U.S. store sales. Franchisees benefit from small investments, popular company names, standardized operations and training, cooperative marketing, exclusive selling rights, and volume purchases. They may face constrained decision making, resulting in oversaturation, lower than promised profits, strict contract terms, cancellation clauses, short-term contracts, and royalty fees. Franchisors benefit by expanding their businesses, setting franchisee qualifications, improving cash flow, outlining procedures, gaining motivated franchisees, and receiving ongoing royalties. They may suffer if franchisees hurt the company image, do not operate uniformly, compete with one another, lower resale values and franchisor profits, and seek greater independence.

Leased departments are in-store locations rented to outside parties. They usually exist in categories on the fringe of their stores' major product lines. Stores gain from the expertise of lessees, greater traffic, reduced costs, merchandising support, and revenues. Potential store disadvantages are conflicts with lessees and adverse effects on store image. Lessee benefits are well-known store names, steady customers, immediate sales, reduced expenses, economies of scale, an image associated with the store, and more control over their strategy. Potential lessee problems are operating inflexibility, restrictions on items sold, lease nonrenewal, and poorer results than expected.

Vertical marketing systems consist of all the levels of independently owned firms along a channel of distribution. Independent systems have separately owned manufacturers, wholesalers, and retailers. In partially integrated systems, two separately owned firms, usually manufacturers and retailers, perform all production and distribution functions. With fully integrated systems, single firms do all production and distribution functions. Some firms use dual marketing, whereby they are involved in more than one type of system.

Consumer cooperatives are owned by their customers who invest, elect officers, manage operations, and share savings or profits. They account for a tiny piece of retail sales. Cooperatives are formed because consumers think they can do retailing functions, traditional retailers are inadequate, and prices are high. They have not grown much because consumer initiative is required, expertise may be lacking, expectations have frequently not been met, and boredom occurs.

3. *To explore the methods used by manufacturers, wholesalers, and retailers to exert influence in the distribution channel.* Even without an integrated vertical marketing system, channel control can be exerted by the most powerful firm(s) in a channel. Manufacturers, wholesalers, and retailers each have ways to increase their impact. Retailers' influence is greatest when they are a large part of their vendors' sales and private brands are used.

Key Terms

retail institution (p. 93)
independent (p. 94)
ease of entry (p. 94)
chain (p. 96)
franchising (p. 98)
product/trademark franchising (p. 98)
business format franchising (p. 98)
constrained decision making (p. 100)
leased department (p. 101)
vertical marketing system (p. 103)
dual marketing (p. 103)
channel control (p. 104)
consumer cooperative (p. 104)

Questions for Discussion

1. What are the characteristics of each of the ownership forms discussed in this chapter?
2. Do you believe that independent retailers will soon disappear from the retail landscape? Explain your answer.
3. Why does the concept of ease of entry usually have less impact on chain retailers than on independent retailers?
4. How can an independent retailer overcome the problem of little computerization?
5. What difficulties might an independent encounter if it tries to expand into a chain?
6. What competitive advantages and disadvantages do regional chains have in comparison with national chains?
7. What are the similarities and differences between chains and franchising?
8. From the *franchisee's* perspective, under what circumstances would product/trademark franchising be advantageous? When would business format franchising be better?
9. Why would a supermarket want to lease space to an outside operator rather than run a business, such as dry cleaning, itself? What would be its risks in this approach?
10. What are the pros and cons of Sherwin-Williams using dual marketing?
11. How could a small independent restaurant increase its channel power?
12. Would REI be as successful if it operated as a traditional chain? Explain your answer.

Web-Based Exercise

Visit the Web site of 7-Eleven (www.franchise.7-eleven.com), one of the leading retail franchisors in the world. Based on the information you find there, would you be interested in becoming a 7-Eleven franchisee? Why or why not?

Note: Also stop by our Web site (www.pearsonhighered.com/bermanevans) to experience a number of highly interactive, appealing Web exercises based on actual company demonstrations, and sample materials related to retailing.

APPENDIX The Dynamics of Franchising

This appendix is presented because of franchising's strong retailing presence and the exciting opportunities in franchising. Over the past two decades, annual U.S. franchising sales have more than tripled! We go beyond the discussion of franchising in Chapter 4 and provide information on managerial issues in franchising and on franchisor–franchisee relationships.

Look at the "Franchise" section of Edible Arrangements' Web site (www.ediblearrangements.com).

Consider this, for example: In 1999, Tariq and Kamran Farid open their first Edible Arrangements store in East Haven, Connecticut. The initial franchised store opened during 2001 in Waltham, Massachusetts. Now, due to franchising, Edible Arrangements has about 1,100 stores worldwide, mostly franchised. The firm was recently ranked number nine on *Forbes* magazine's "Top Franchises for the Money" and number one in its category in "*Entrepreneur* Magazine's Franchise 500" (for the fourth consecutive year). The firm's niche is clear, as described at its Web site (www.ediblearrangements.com): "Edible Arrangements brings joy to our customers on a daily basis by featuring fruit juices, smoothies, fruit salads, and dipped fruit."[1]

How about Dunkin' Donuts? It is the number one retailer of hot and iced regular coffee-by-the-cup in the United States and the largest coffee and baked goods chain in the world. Dunkin' Donuts serves more than 3 million customers per day with 52 varieties of donuts and over a dozen coffee beverages (as well as bagels, breakfast sandwiches, and other baked goods). There are about 10,000 franchised Dunkin' Donuts in the United States and an additional 3,000 shops in 30 countries throughout the world. Financial requirements are a minimum net worth of $500,000 and a minimum liquidity of $250,000 for the first store.[2]

U.S. franchisors are situated in over 170 countries, a number that is rising due to these factors: U.S. firms see the foreign market potential. Franchising is accepted as a retailing format in more nations. Trade barriers are fewer due to such pacts as the North American Free Trade Agreement, which makes it easier for firms based in the United States, Canada, and Mexico to operate in each other's marketplaces.

Here are three Web sites for you to get more information on franchising. And remember, we have a special listing of franchising links at our Web site (www.pearsonhighered.com/bermanevans):

- Federal Trade Commission (http://business.ftc.gov/documents/inv05-buying-franchise-consumer-guide).
- International Franchise Association (www.franchise.org).
- Small Business Administration (www.sba.gov/category/navigation-structure/starting-managing-business/starting-business/establishing-business/buying-franchise).

Managerial Issues in Franchising

Franchising appeals to franchisees for several reasons. Most franchisors have easy-to-learn, standardized operating methods that they have perfected. New franchisees do not have to learn from their own trial-and-error method. Franchisors often have facilities where franchisees are trained to operate equipment, manage employees, keep records, and improve customer relations; there are usually follow-up field visits.

A new outlet of a nationally advertised franchise (such as Burger King) can attract a large customer following rather quickly and easily because of the reputation of the firm. And not only does franchising result in good initial sales and profits, it also reduces franchisees' risk of failure *if the franchisees affiliate with strong, supportive franchisors.*

What kind of individual is best suited to being a franchisee? This is what one expert says:

> While the franchisor will give the start-up training and offer ongoing support, you, the franchisee, must be prepared to manage the business. While some franchises may lend themselves to absentee ownership, most are best run by hands-on management. You must be willing to work harder than you have perhaps ever worked before. Forty-hour weeks are also a myth,

particularly in the start-up phase of the business. It is more like 60- to 70-hour weeks. You must also be willing to mop floors, empty garbage, fire employees, and handle upset customers.[3]

What makes McDonald's such an admired franchise operator? The company provides its franchisees with training, operations support, advertising support, and much more:

- Own and operate your own business. "You are in business for yourself, but not by yourself."
- Be able to use "the trademarks and operating system of the number one brand in the world."
- Gain " local and national support in the areas of operations, training, advertising, marketing, human resources, real-estate, construction, purchasing, and equipment purchasing and maintenance."
- Enjoy "working with people, from your restaurant crew to your customers and community."
- Be able to "contribute to the success of McDonald's: Big Mac, Filet-O-Fish, and Egg McMuffin sandwiches have all been developed by owner/operators."
- Achieve "personal growth and business knowledge from your experience as an owner/operator."[4]

Investment and startup costs for a franchised outlet can be as low as a few thousand dollars for a personal service business to as high as several million dollars for a hotel. In return for its expenditures, a franchisee gets exclusive selling rights for an area; a business format franchisee gets training, equipment and fixtures, and support in site selection, supplier negotiations, advertising, and so on. One-half of U.S. business format franchisors require franchisees to be owner-operators and work full-time. Besides receiving fees and royalties from franchisees, franchisors may sell goods and services to them. This may be required; more often, for legal reasons, such purchases are at the franchisees' discretion (subject to franchisor specifications). Each year, franchisors sell billions of dollars worth of items to franchisees.

Table A4-1 shows the franchise fees, startup costs, and royalty fees for new franchisees at 10 leading franchisors in various business categories. Financing support—either through in-house financing or third-party financing—is offered by most of the firms cited in Table A4-1. In addition, with its guaranteed loan program, the U.S. Small Business Administration is a good financing option for prospective franchisees, and some banks offer special interest rates for franchisees affiliated with established franchisors.

Franchised outlets can be bought (leased) from franchisors, master franchisees, or existing franchisees. Franchisors sell either new locations or company-owned outlets (some

TABLE A4-1 The Costs of Becoming a New Franchisee with Selected Franchisors (as of 2011)

Franchising Company	Total Startup Costs (Including Franchise Fee)	Franchise Fee	Royalty Fee as a % of Sales	Franchisee-Owned Outlets as a % of All Outlets	Offers Financing Support
Aamco Transmissions	$225,536–$299,631	$17,500–$39,500	7.5	100	Third party
H&R Block	$34,440–$110,030	No initial fee	30	43	Third party
Carvel Ice Cream	$234,375–$354,550	$30,000	$2.11/gallon	97	Third party
Fantastic Sams	$115,000–$228,600	$30,000	$350/wk	99	Third party
Jazzercise	$2,980–$75,500	$500–$1,000	20	99+	None
Pearle Vision	$300,000	$30,000	5.5	52	In-house and third party
Petland	$299,000–$1,050,000	$30,000	4.5	95	Third party
Subway	$84,300–$258,300	$15,000	8	100	In-house and third party
Super 8 Motels	$178,270–$3,572,460	$25,000–$26,500	5.5	100	Third party
UPS Store	$150,200–$371,020	$29,950	5	100	In-house and third party

Source: Computed by the authors from "2011 Franchise 500 Rankings," www.entrepreneur.com/franchise500.

FIGURE A4-1
A Checklist of Questions for Prospective Franchisees Considering Franchise Opportunities

- ✓ What are the required franchise fees: initial fee, advertising appropriations, and royalties?
- ✓ What degree of technical knowledge is required of the franchisee?
- ✓ What is the required investment of time by the franchisee? Does the franchisee have to be actively involved in the day-to-day operations of the franchise?
- ✓ How much control does the franchisor exert in terms of materials purchased, sales quotas, space requirements, pricing, the range of goods sold, required inventory levels, and so on?
- ✓ Can the franchisee tolerate the regimentation and rules of the franchisor?
- ✓ Are the costs of required supplies and materials purchased from the franchisor at market value, above market value, or below market value?
- ✓ What degree of name recognition do consumers have of the franchise? Does the franchisor have a meaningful advertising program?
- ✓ What image does the franchise have among consumers and among current franchisees?
- ✓ What are the level and quality of services provided by the franchisor: site selection, training, bookkeeping, human relations, equipment maintenance, and trouble-shooting?
- ✓ What is the franchisor policy in terminating franchisees? What are the conditions of franchise termination? What is the rate of franchise termination and nonrenewal?
- ✓ What is the franchisor's legal history?
- ✓ What is the length of the franchise agreement?
- ✓ What is the failure rate of existing franchises?
- ✓ What is the franchisor's policy with regard to company-owned and franchisee-owned outlets?
- ✓ What policy does the franchisor have in allowing franchisees to sell their business?
- ✓ What is the franchisor's policy with regard to territorial protection for existing franchisees? With regard to new franchisees and new company-owned establishments?
- ✓ What is the earning potential of the franchise during the first year? The first five years?

of which may have been taken back from unsuccessful franchisees). At times, they sell the rights in entire regions or counties to master franchisees, which then deal with individual franchisees. Existing franchisees usually have the right to sell their units if they first offer them to their franchisor, if potential buyers meet all financial and other criteria, and/or if buyers undergo training. Of interest to prospective franchisees is the emphasis a firm places on franchisee-owned outlets versus franchisor-owned ones. This indicates the commitment to franchising. As indicated in Table A4-1, leading franchisors typically own a small percentage of outlets.

One last point regarding managerial issues in franchising concerns the failure rate of new franchisees. For many years, it was believed that success as a franchisee was a "sure thing"—and much safer than starting a business—due to the franchisor's well-known name, its experience, and its training programs. However, some recent research has shown franchising to be as risky as opening a new business. Why? Some franchisors have oversaturated the market and not provided promised support, and unscrupulous franchisors have preyed on unsuspecting investors.

With the preceding in mind, Figure A4-1 has a checklist by which potential franchisees can assess opportunities. In using the checklist, franchisees should also obtain full prospectuses and financial reports from all franchisors under consideration, and talk to existing franchise operators and customers.

Franchisor–Franchisee Relationships

Taco John's (www.tacojohns.com/aboutus/becomeafranchisee/franchisefaqs) prides itself on its supportive relationships with franchisees.

Many franchisors and franchisees have good relationships because they share goals for company image, operations, the goods and services offered, cooperative ads, and sales and profit growth. This two-way relationship is illustrated by the actions of Taco John's International (www.tacojohns.com), a firm with about 400 franchised pizza restaurants in more than 25 states:

> Restaurant chains often claim to have amazing opportunities. They promise big profits, great growth, and minimal management. The thing is they aren't always true. At Taco John's we have an honest, and family-centered approach. When it comes to your franchise, you're really in charge. You will own and manage your own restaurant. Sound scary? It shouldn't. As a Taco John's franchisee, you will have access to our Franchise Support Center in Cheyenne, Wyoming. You'll work with professionals experienced in:
>
> - Franchise Development
> - Marketing and Advertising
> - Franchise Business Consultants
> - Human Resources
> - Training
>
> We require every franchisee to attend an intensive training program that covers the ins and outs of our restaurant operations and teaches just how to achieve our standards of hometown hospitality, boldly flavored food, and spotless, friendly restaurants. We also teach you the skills that will make you more comfortable in your new role and will help you be more successful from the start, like employee selection processes, coaching skills, financial management, and local store marketing! You won't always see us. But we'll always have your back![5]

Nonetheless, for several reasons, tensions do sometimes exist between various franchisors and their franchisees:

- The franchisor–franchisee relationship is not one of employer to employee. Franchisor controls are often viewed as rigid.
- Many agreements are considered too short by franchisees. Nearly half of U.S. agreements are 10 years or less (one-sixth are 5 years or less), usually at the franchisor's request.
- The loss of a franchise generally means eviction, and the franchisee gets nothing for "goodwill."
- Some franchisors believe their franchisees do not reinvest enough in their outlets or care enough about the consistency of operations from one outlet to another.
- Franchisors may not give adequate territorial protection and may open new outlets near existing ones.
- Franchisees may refuse to participate in cooperative advertising programs.
- Franchised outlets up for sale must usually be offered first to franchisors, which also have approval of sales to third parties.
- Some franchisees believe franchisor marketing support is low.
- Franchisees may be prohibited from operating competing businesses.
- Restrictions on suppliers may cause franchisees to pay higher prices and have limited choices.
- Franchisees may band together to force changes in policies and exert pressure on franchisors.
- Sales and profit expectations may not be realized.

Tensions can lead to conflicts—even litigation. Potential negative franchisor actions include terminating agreements; reducing marketing support; and adding red tape for orders, information requests, and warranty work. Potential negative franchisee actions include terminating agreements, adding competitors' products, refusing to promote goods and services, and not complying with data requests. Each year, business format franchisors terminate the contracts of 10 percent of the franchisee-owned stores that opened within the preceding five years.

Although franchising has been characterized by franchisors having more power than franchisees, this inequality is being reduced. First, franchisees affiliated with specific franchisors have joined together. For example, the Association of Kentucky Fried Chicken Franchisees and National Coalition of Associations of 7-Eleven Franchisees represent thousands of franchisees. Second, large umbrella groups, such as the American Franchisee Association (www.franchisee.org) and the American Association of Franchisees & Dealers (www.aafd.org), have been formed. Third, many franchisees now operate more than one outlet, so they have greater clout. Fourth, there has been a substantial rise in litigation.

Better communication and better cooperation help resolve problems. Here are two progressive tactics: First, the International Franchise Association has an ethics code for its franchisor and franchisee members, founded on the principle that each franchisor–franchisee relationship requires the mutual commitment of both parties (www.franchise.org/industrysecondary.aspx?id=3554):

> Each party will fulfill its obligations, will act consistent with the interests of the brand, and will not act so as to harm the brand and system. This willing interdependence between franchisors and franchisees, and the trust and honesty upon which it is founded, has made franchising a worldwide success as a strategy for business growth. Honesty embodies openness, candor, and truthfulness. Franchisees and franchisors commit to sharing ideas and information and to face challenges in clear and direct terms. Our members will be sincere in word, act, and character—reputable and without deception.

Second, the National Franchise Mediation Program seeks to resolve franchisor–franchisee disagreements. All mediation efforts are voluntary, confidential, nonbinding, and informal: "Typically, disputes that are mediated are concluded expeditiously at moderate cost compared to disputes that are arbitrated or litigated. Since inception [1994], a success rate of approximately 80 percent has been achieved in mediations in which the franchisee agreed to participate, with many more cases resolved without intervention of a mediator. Parties report that, as a result of the program, they are resolving substantially more disputes through informal negotiations without either party needing to report to formal mediation through the program."[6]

5 Retail Institutions by Store-Based Strategy Mix

Chapter Objectives

1. To describe the wheel of retailing, scrambled merchandising, and the retail life cycle, and to show how they can help explain the performance of retail strategy mixes

2. To discuss ways in which retail strategy mixes are evolving

3. To examine a wide variety of food-oriented retailers involved with store-based strategy mixes

4. To study a wide range of general merchandise retailers involved with store-based strategy mixes

As we discuss in Chapter 5, although facing strong competition from big-box chains such as Wal-Mart, Costco, and Target, supermarkets remain a vital part of retailing with hundreds of billions of dollars of annual sales in the United States alone. Safeway, one of the leaders among supermarket chains, is very active in its digital marketing efforts.

After a thorough analysis of Safeway's activities, the consulting firm Kantar Retail concluded that "Safeway currently uses several interactive resources to communicate with the new wave of shoppers. Each social medium—blogs, Twitter, and Facebook—has a different role in Safeway's digital marketing strategy. Safeway has gained a strong understanding of how to utilize each effectively and is continuing to further develop its social media strategy as usage trends evolve."

Safeway's social media approach has changed over time. When the firm began its social media activities, it set up a rather simple blog at its Web site. Now, the "Today at Safeway Blog" (www.safeway.com/IFL/Grocery/Community) has many features, including information about product ingredients, nutrition, recipes, and a lot more. The company asks store associates and customer relations personnel to contribute to the blog. These are its goals, as stated at the blog: "In a nutshell, it's about family, food, value, and fun. Of course, what makes this blog really exciting is YOU—so join the conversation!"

Safeway is heavily involved with Twitter and Facebook. Each of Safeway's store formats, such as Safeway (http://twitter.com/#!/safeway), Vons (http://twitter.com/#!/vonsglendale), and Tom Thumb (http://twitter.com/#!/tomthumb_stores) has its own Twitter account to foster regional and local customized information. Tweets are targeted at consumers' pre-shop, in-store, and post-shop needs. At Facebook (www.facebook.com/Safeway), Safeway has hundreds of thousands of followers. The retailer seeks to promote brand awareness and to encourage customers to provide feedback and to generate their own content—both positive and negative. Safeway actively engages shoppers about their experiences to stimulate loyalty to the retailer.[1]

Source: BeTA-Artworks/ fotolia.com.

Overview

In Chapter 4, retail institutions were described by type of ownership. In this chapter, we discuss three key concepts in planning retail strategy mixes: the wheel of retailing, scrambled merchandising, and the retail life cycle. We then look at how retail strategies are evolving and study the basic strategies of several store-based institutions. Chapter 6 deals with nonstore-based, electronic, and nontraditional strategies.

CONSIDERATIONS IN PLANNING A RETAIL STRATEGY MIX

A retailer may be categorized by its **strategy mix**, the firm's particular combination of store location, operating procedures, goods/services offered, pricing tactics, store atmosphere and customer services, and promotional methods.

Store location refers to the use of a store or nonstore format, placement in a geographic area, and the kind of site (such as a shopping center). Operating procedures include the kinds of personnel employed, management style, store hours, and other factors. The goods/services offered may encompass several product categories or just one; quality may be low, medium, or high. Pricing refers to a retailer's use of prestige pricing (creating a quality image), competitive pricing (setting prices at the level of rivals), or penetration pricing (underpricing other retailers). Store atmosphere and customer services are reflected by the physical facilities and personal attention provided, return policies, delivery, and other factors. Promotion involves activities in such areas as advertising, displays, personal selling, and sales promotion. By combining these elements, a retailer can develop a unique strategy.

To flourish today, a retailer should strive to be dominant in some way. The firm may then reach **destination retailer** status—whereby consumers view the company as distinctive enough to become loyal to it and go out of their way to shop there. We tend to link "dominant" with "large." Yet, both small and large retailers can dominate in their own way. As follows, there are many ways to be a destination retailer, and combining two or more approaches can yield even greater appeal for a given retailer:

- Be price-oriented and cost-efficient to attract price-sensitive shoppers.
- Be upscale to attract full-service, status-conscious consumers.
- Be convenient to attract those wanting shopping ease, nearby locations, or long hours.
- Offer a dominant assortment in the product lines carried to appeal to consumers interested in variety and in-store shopping comparisons.
- Offer superior customer service to attract those frustrated by the decline in retail service.
- Be innovative or exclusive and provide a unique way of operating (such as kiosks at airports) or carry products/brands not stocked by others to reach people who are innovators or bored.

Before looking at specific strategy mixes, let's look at three concepts that help explain the use of these mixes: the wheel of retailing, scrambled merchandising, and the retail life cycle—as well as the ways in which retail strategies are evolving.

The Wheel of Retailing

According to the **wheel of retailing** theory, retail innovators often first appear as low-price operators with low costs and low profit margin requirements. Over time, the innovators upgrade the products they carry and improve their facilities and customer service (by adding better-quality items, locating in higher-rent sites, providing credit and delivery, and so on), and prices rise. As innovators mature, they become vulnerable to new discounters with lower costs, hence, the wheel of retailing.[2] See Figure 5-1.

The wheel is grounded on four principles: (1) There are many price-sensitive shoppers who will trade customer services, wide selections, and convenient locations for lower prices. (2) Price-sensitive shoppers are often not loyal and will switch to retailers with lower prices. However, prestige-oriented customers enjoy shopping at retailers with high-end strategies. (3) New institutions are frequently able to have lower operating costs than existing institutions. (4) As retailers move up the wheel, they typically do so to increase sales, broaden the target market, and improve their image.

For example, when traditional department store prices became too high for many consumers, the growth of the full-line discount store (led by Wal-Mart) was the result. The full-line discount store stressed low prices because of such cost-cutting techniques as having a small

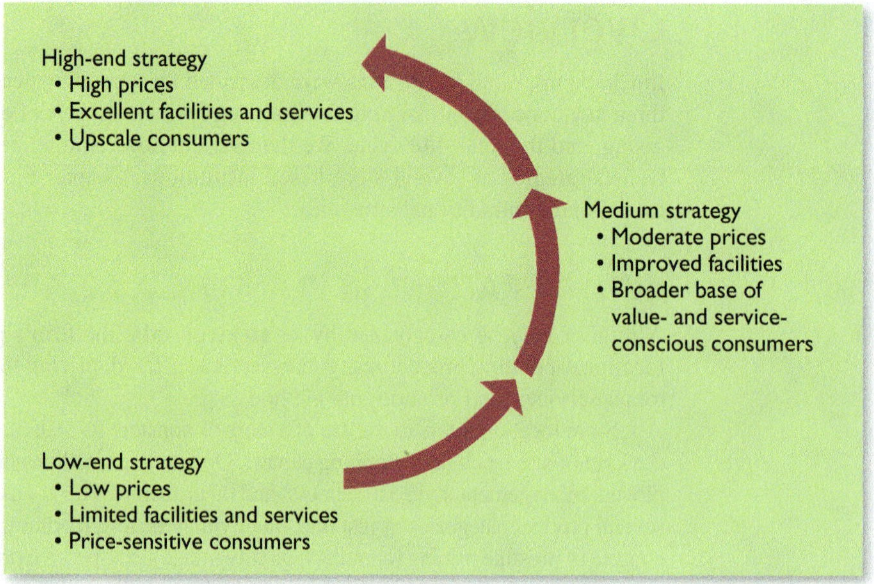

FIGURE 5-1
The Wheel of Retailing
As a low-end retailer upgrades its strategy to increase sales and profit margins, a new form of discounter takes its place.

sales force, situating in lower-rent store locations, using inexpensive fixtures, emphasizing high stock turnover, and accepting only cash or check payments for goods. Then, as full-line discount stores prospered, they typically sought to move up a little along the wheel. This meant enlarging the sales force, improving locations, upgrading fixtures, carrying a greater selection of merchandise, and accepting credit. These improvements led to higher costs, which led to somewhat higher prices. The wheel of retailing again came into play as newer discounters, such as off-price chains, factory outlets, and permanent flea markets, expanded to satisfy the needs of the most price-conscious consumer. More recently, we have witnessed the birth of discount Web retailers, some of which have very low costs because they do not have "bricks-and-mortar" facilities.

Where would you place CarMax (www.carmax.com) along the wheel of retailing?

As indicated in Figure 5-1, the wheel of retailing reveals three basic strategic positions: low end, medium, and high end. The medium strategy may have some difficulties if retailers in this position are not perceived as distinctive: "An unfocused firm stuck in the mushy middle of its category is ripe picking for competition. As an industry matures, competitors come in and steal market share from above you as well as below you. This is what happened to Sears. While Sears stayed in the middle of the department-store market, the department-store industry was diverging into two separate industries, one at the low end and one at the high end."[3] Figure 5-2 shows the opposing alternatives in considering a strategy mix.

Outlet Mall 66: A Discount Shopper's Haven

The Outlet Mall 66 (www.theoutlet66mall.com) in Canóvas, Puerto Rico is a 428,000-square-foot discount shopping center that targets price-conscious shoppers. This mall is located near the intersection of PR-3 (Puerto Rico's second longest highway) and PR-66. It currently has 73 stores and 53 smaller shops located in the corridor.

Major tenants include Burlington Coat Factory, Nike Factory Outlet, Polo Ralph Lauren, and Nautica. Other retailers located there are Perry Ellis, Crocs, Levi's, and Gymboree. The mall rose from number 324 in 2008 to 267 in 2011 among the *Caribbean Business* Top 400 companies. It was also named among the 100 Fastest Growing Companies.

According to Yesenia Serrano, Outlet Mall 66's marketing director, "Puerto Rican customers love shopping and following the latest fashion and consumer trends. When given the option, they will select outlet products that offer brand-name-quality products at a more affordable price." Serrano states that there is no specific demographic profile among outlet customers. The single shared shopper characteristic is a high level of price consciousness. The Outlet Mall 66 offers customers a discount card, which provides savings as high as 30 percent. Purchases made with this card are analyzed by Outlet 66's management to better understand shopping behavior.

Source: James Ferré, "The Outlet Mall 66 Bets on Price-Conscious Consumers," *Caribbean Business* (June 23, 2011), pp. 34–35.

FIGURE 5-2
Retail Strategy Alternatives

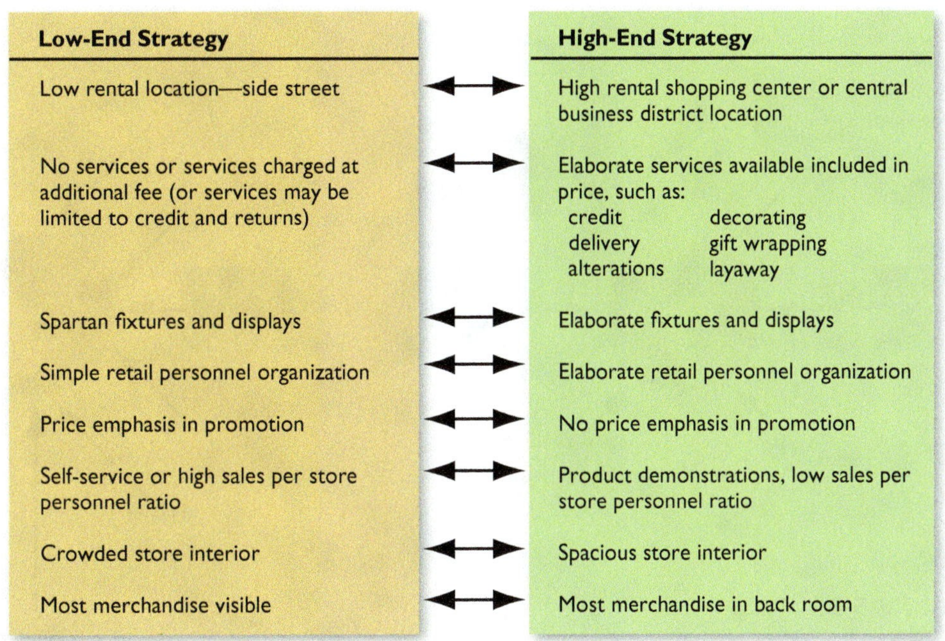

The wheel of retailing suggests that established firms should be wary in adding services or converting a strategy from low end to high end. Because price-conscious shoppers are not usually loyal, they are apt to switch to lower-priced firms. Furthermore, retailers may then eliminate the competitive advantages that have led to profitability. This occurred with the retail catalog showroom, a now defunct retail format.

Scrambled Merchandising

Whereas the wheel of retailing focuses on product quality, prices, and customer service, scrambled merchandising involves a retailer increasing its width of assortment (the number of different product lines carried). **Scrambled merchandising** occurs when a retailer adds goods and services that may be unrelated to each other and to the firm's original business. See Figure 5-3.

Scrambled merchandising is popular for many reasons: Retailers want to increase overall revenues; fast-selling, highly profitable goods and services are usually the ones added; consumers make more impulse purchases; people like one-stop shopping; different target markets may be reached; and the impact of seasonality and competition is reduced. In addition, the popularity of a retailer's original product line(s) may fall, causing it to scramble to maintain and grow the customer base. For example, even though Starbucks' in-store coffee sales are still strong, it now faces more competition in the coffee market from Dunkin' Donuts, McDonald's, and other chains that have upgraded their offerings. Today, Starbucks carries many items outside its original coffee business, including pastries, hot breakfasts, salads, sandwiches, and smoothies.

How much of a practitioner of scrambled merchandising is Brookstone (www.brookstone.com)?

Scrambled merchandising is contagious. Drugstores, bookstores, florists, video renters, and gift shops are all affected by supermarkets' scrambled merchandising. A significant amount of U.S. supermarket sales are from general merchandise, health and beauty aids, and other non-grocery items, such as pharmacy items, magazines, flowers, and video rentals (often through vending machines from Redbox). In response, drugstores and others are pushed into scrambled merchandising to fill the sales void caused by supermarkets. Drugstores have added toys and gift items, greeting cards, batteries, and cameras. This then creates a void for additional retailers, which are also forced to scramble.

The prevalence of scrambled merchandising means greater competition among different types of retailers and that distribution costs are affected as sales are dispersed over more retailers. There are other limitations to scrambled merchandising, including the potential lack of retailer expertise in buying, selling, and servicing unfamiliar items; the costs associated with a broader assortment (including lower inventory turnover); and the possible harm to a retailer's image if scrambled merchandising is ineffective.

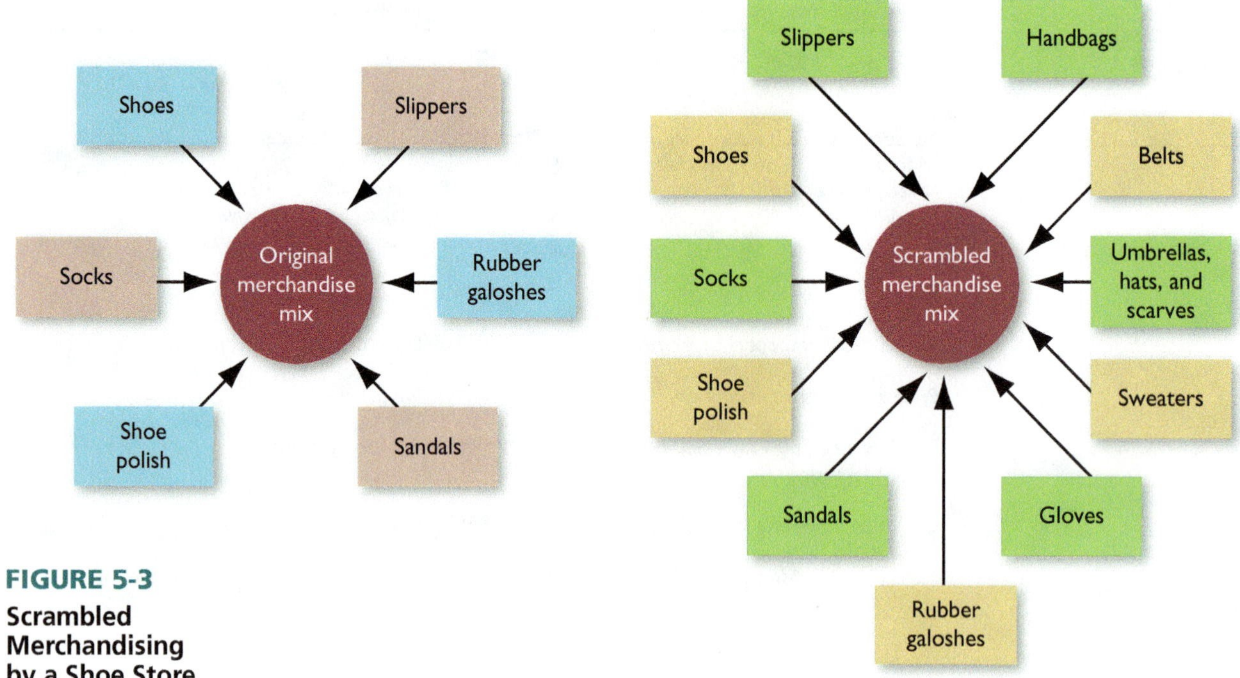

FIGURE 5-3
Scrambled Merchandising by a Shoe Store

The Retail Life Cycle

The **retail life cycle** concept states that retail institutions—like the goods and services they sell—pass through identifiable life stages: introduction (early growth), growth (accelerated development), maturity, and decline. The direction and speed of institutional changes can be interpreted from this concept.[4] Take a look at Figure 5-4. Figure 5-4 (a) shows the business characteristics of the four stages, and Figure 5-4(b) indicates the stages in which several mall-based retail formats are now operating.

FIGURE 5-4
The Retail Life Cycle
Source: Reprinted by permission of Kantar Retail.

(a) Key Business Characteristics During the Stages of the Retail Life Cycle

	Life Cycle Stage			
	Introduction	Growth	Maturity	Decline
Sales	Low/growing	Rapid acceleration	High, leveling off	Dropping
Profitability	Negative to break even	High yield	High/declining	Low to break even
Positioning	Concept innovation	Special need	Broad market	Niche
Competition	None	Limited	Extensive/ saturation	Intensive/ consolidated

(b) Applying the Retail Life Cycle to Mall Retailers

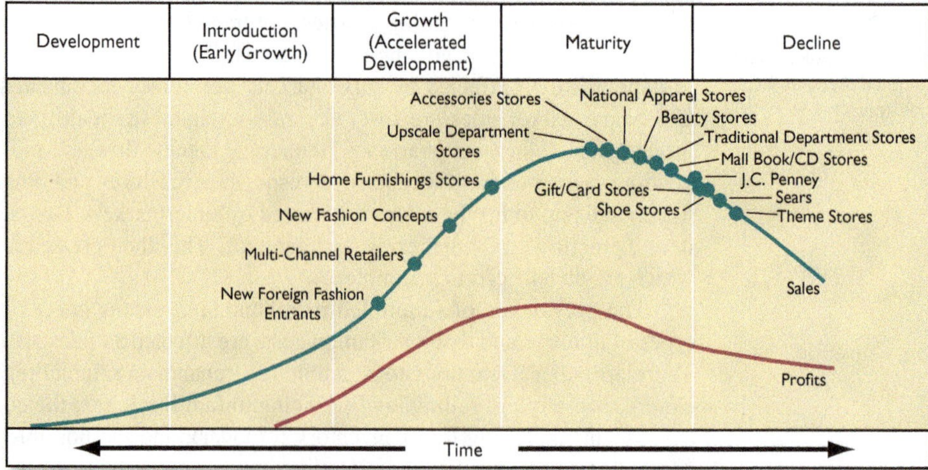

Let's examine the stages of the retail life cycle as they apply to individual institutional formats and show specific examples. During the first stage of the cycle (introduction), there is a strong departure from the strategy mixes of existing retail institutions. A firm in this stage significantly alters at least one element of the strategy mix from that of traditional competitors. Sales and then profits often rise sharply for the first firms in a category. There are risks that new institutions will not be accepted by shoppers, and there may be large initial losses due to heavy investments. At this stage, long-run success is not assured.

One institution in the innovation stage is the online streaming of movies, a retail service. How quickly will this business catch on—and at what price? The early category leader is Netflix:

> Netflix is the leading online subscription service streaming movies and TV episodes over the Internet. For only $7.99 a month, members can instantly watch unlimited movies and TV episodes streamed to their TVs and computers. There are no commercials, and you can pause, rewind, fast forward, or re-watch as often as you like. It's that easy. Use your Xbox 360, PS3, Wii, or any other device that streams from Netflix. There are no dues or late fees ever! Netflix membership is a month-to-month subscription and begins at sign-up. You can cancel anytime, online, 24 hours a day.[5]

See Intouch Interactive's (www.intouchinteractive.com) view of the future for video kiosks.

In the second stage (growth), both sales and profits exhibit rapid growth. Existing firms expand geographically, and newer companies of the same type enter. Toward the end of accelerated development, cost pressures (to cover a larger staff, a more complex inventory system, and extensive controls) may begin to affect profits.

The interactive electronic video kiosk is an institution in the growth stage. Today, kiosks sell everything from clothing to magazines to insurance to personal computers (PCs). According to various sources, U.S. retail sales revenues generated by kiosks rose from $1.1 billion in 2001 to more than $12 billion in 2012. Worldwide, the number of installed interactive kiosks is projected to rise to more than 2.5 million kiosks in 2014 (up from 250,000 kiosks in 2001).[6] This format is examined further in Chapter 6.

The third stage (maturity) is characterized by slow sales growth for the institutional type. Although overall sales may continue to go up, that rise is at a much lower rate than during prior stages. Profit margins may have to be reduced to stimulate purchases. Maturity is brought on by market saturation caused by the high number of firms in an institutional format, competition from newer institutions, changing societal interests, and inadequate management skills to lead mature or larger firms. Once maturity is reached, the goal is to sustain it as long as possible and not to fall into decline.

The liquor store, a form of specialty store, is an institution in the maturity stage; sales are rising, but slowly as compared with earlier times. From 1992 to 2011, U.S. liquor store sales increased at a far lower annual percentage rate than the rate for the U.S. retailing industry overall. This was due to competition from membership clubs, mail-order wine retailers, and supermarkets (in states allowing wine or liquor sales); changing lifestyles and attitudes regarding liquor; the national 21-year-old drinking age requirement; and limits on the nonalcoholic items that liquor stores are permitted to sell in some locales.

The final stage in the retail life cycle is decline, whereby industrywide sales and profits for a format fall off, many firms abandon the format, and newer formats attract consumers previously committed to that retailer type. In some cases, a decline may be hard or almost impossible to reverse. In others, it may be avoided or postponed by repositioning the institution.

After peaking in the 1980s, the retail catalog showroom declined thereafter; it vanished in the United States in 1998 as the leading firms went out of business. With this format, consumers chose items from a catalog, shopped in a warehouse setting, and wrote up orders. Why did it fade away? Many other retailers cut costs and prices, so showrooms were no longer low-price leaders. Catalogs had to be printed far in advance. Many items were slow-sellers or had low margins. Some consumers found showrooms crowded and disliked writing orders, the lack of displays reduced browsing, and the paucity of apparel goods held down revenues. Note: Great Britain's Argos chain still operates more than 700 catalog showrooms.[7]

On the other hand, conventional supermarkets have slowed their decline by placing new units in suburban shopping centers, redesigning interiors, lengthening store hours, having low prices, expanding the use of scrambled merchandising, closing unprofitable smaller units, and converting to larger outlets.

The life-cycle concept highlights the proper retailer response as institutions evolve. Expansion should be the focus initially, administrative skills and operations become critical in maturity, and adaptation is essential at the end of the cycle.

HOW RETAIL INSTITUTIONS ARE EVOLVING

Forward-looking firms know their individual strategies must be modified as retail institutions evolve over time. Complacency is not appropriate. Many retailers have witnessed shrinking profit margins due to intense competition and consumer interest in lower prices. This puts pressure on them to tighten internal cost controls and to promote higher-margin goods and services while eliminating unprofitable items. Let's see how firms are reacting to this formidable challenge through mergers, diversification, and downsizing, as well as cost containment and value-driven retailing.

Mergers, Diversification, and Downsizing

Some firms use mergers and diversification to sustain sales growth in a highly competitive environment (or when the institutional category in which they operate matures). For stronger firms, this trend is expected to carry over into the future.

Mergers involve the combination of separately owned retail firms. Some mergers take place between retailers of different types, such as the ones between Sears (the department store chain) and Kmart (the full-line discount store chain). Other mergers occur between similar types of retailers, such as two banks (as took place when Bank of America acquired Commerce Bank). By merging, retailers hope to jointly maximize resources, enlarge their customer base, improve productivity and bargaining power, limit weaknesses, and gain competitive advantages. It is a way for resourceful retailers to grow more rapidly and for weaker ones to enhance their long-term prospects for survival (or sell assets).

Through its various retail chains, Bed Bath & Beyond (www.bedbathandbeyond.com/about_us.asp) is a retailing dynamo.

With **diversification**, retailers become active in businesses outside their normal operations—and add stores in different goods/service categories. That is why Bed Bath & Beyond now owns and operates Christmas Tree Shops (a bargain store chain), Harmon and Harmon Face Values (discount store chains that emphasize cosmetics and health and beauty aids), and buybuy BABY (a store chain with 20,000-plus items targeted to parents of infants and young children).

The size of many retail chains has grown due to mergers and diversification. Not all firms have done well with that approach. Thus, even though stronger firms are expanding, we are also witnessing **downsizing**—whereby unprofitable stores are closed or divisions are sold off—by retailers unhappy with performance. Because Kmart's diversification efforts had poor results, it closed or sold its ventures outside the general merchandise store field (including Borders bookstores, Builders Square, Office Max, Payless shoe stores, and Sports Authority). It also closed many Kmart stores after merging with Sears.

The interest in downsizing should continue. Various retailers have overextended themselves and do not have the resources or management talent to succeed without retrenching. In their quest to open new stores, certain firms have chosen poor sites (having already saturated the best locations). Retailers such as Barnes & Noble are more interested in operating fewer, but much larger, stores and using the Web. Retailers such as supermarkets are finding they can do better if they are regional rather than national.

Cost Containment and Value-Driven Retailing

With a cost-containment approach, retailers strive to hold down both initial investments and operating costs. Many firms use this strategy because of intense competition from discounters, the need to control complicated chain or franchise operations, high land and construction costs, the volatility of the economy, and a desire to maximize productivity. Today, "a mature, highly saturated market, a slow-growth environment, and firms' inability to raise prices makes it imperative to drive down costs." Retailers "are examining every aspect of their businesses in order to streamline processes and costs."[8] See Figure 5-5.

Save-On-Closeouts.com has a cost-containment approach that even extends to its austere Web site (www.save-on-closeouts.com).

Cost containment can be accomplished by one or more of these approaches:

- Standardizing operating procedures, store layouts, store size, and product offerings.
- Using secondary locations, freestanding units, and locations in older strip centers and by occupying sites abandoned by others (second-use locations).

FIGURE 5-5
Cutting Costs Wherever Possible
Given the thin profit margins for supermarkets and many other retailers, every penny of costs saved really matters. With regard to shopping carts, there are two associated costs that retailers want to reduce: paying employees to scour the parking lot to collect stray carts and the replacement costs of stolen and damaged carts.

Source: Stacie Stauff Smith Photography/Shutterstock.com. Reprinted by permission.

- Placing stores in smaller communities where building regulations are less strict, labor costs are lower, and construction and operating costs are reduced.
- Using inexpensive construction materials, such as bare cinder-block walls and concrete floors.
- Using plainer fixtures and lower-cost displays.
- Buying refurbished equipment.
- Joining cooperative buying and advertising groups.
- Encouraging manufacturers to finance inventories.

A driving force behind cost containment is the quest to provide good value to customers:

> Value is the key factor in the "new normal." The word's meaning, however, is subjective; it can mean price, quality, service, convenience, or a combination thereof. Price clearly plays a big role in what consumers buy and where they buy it. Indeed, the pricing policies of retailers—particularly discounters—have encouraged consumers to shop for bargains and to distrust traditional sales and sale prices. Pragmatic consumers have discovered that price is no longer an accurate reflection of quality and that they can get reasonable quality at everyday low prices.[9]

RETAIL INSTITUTIONS CATEGORIZED BY STORE-BASED STRATEGY MIX

Selected aspects of the strategy mixes of 14 store-based retail institutions, divided into food-oriented and general merchandise groups, are highlighted in this section and Table 5-1. Although not all-inclusive, the strategy mixes do provide a good overview of store-based strategies. Please note that *width of assortment* is the number of different product lines carried by a retailer; *depth of assortment* is the selection within the product lines stocked. Visit our Web site (www.pearsonhighered.com/bermanevans) for many links related to retail institutions' strategies.

Food-Oriented Retailers

The following food-oriented strategic retail formats are described next: convenience store, conventional supermarket, food-based superstore, combination store, box (limited-line) store, and warehouse store.

TABLE 5-1 Selected Aspects of Store-Based Retail Strategy Mixes

Type of Retailer	Location	Merchandise	Prices	Atmosphere and Services	Promotion
Food-Oriented					
Convenience store	Neighborhood	Medium width and low depth of assortment; average quality	Average to above average	Average	Moderate
Conventional supermarket	Neighborhood	Extensive width and depth of assortment; average quality; manufacturer, private, and generic brands	Competitive	Average	Heavy use of newspapers, flyers, and coupons; self-service
Food-based superstore	Community shopping center or isolated site	Full assortment of supermarket items, plus health and beauty aids and general merchandise	Competitive	Average	Heavy use of newspapers and flyers; self-service
Combination store	Community shopping center or isolated site	Full selection of supermarket and drugstore items or supermarket and general merchandise; average quality	Competitive	Average	Heavy use of newspapers and flyers; self-service
Box (limited-line) store	Neighborhood	Low width and depth of assortment; few perishables; few national brands	Very low	Low	Little or none
Warehouse store	Secondary site, often in industrial area	Moderate width and low depth; emphasis on manufacturer brands bought at discounts	Very low	Low	Little or none
General Merchandise					
Specialty store	Business district or shopping center	Very narrow width and extensive depth of assortment; average to good quality	Competitive to above average	Average to excellent	Heavy use of displays; extensive sales force
Traditional department store	Business district, shopping center, or isolated store	Extensive width and depth of assortment; average to good quality	Average to above average	Good to excellent	Heavy ad and catalog use, direct mail; personal selling
Full-line discount store	Business district, shopping center, or isolated store	Extensive width and depth of assortment; average to good quality	Competitive	Slightly below average to average	Heavy use of newspapers; price-oriented; moderate sales force
Variety store	Business district, shopping center, or isolated store	Good width and some depth of assortment; below-average to average quality	Average	Below average	Use of newspapers; self-service
Off-price chain	Business district, suburban shopping strip, or isolated store	Moderate width but poor depth of assortment; average to good quality; lower continuity	Low	Below average	Use of newspapers; brands not advertised; limited sales force
Factory outlet	Out-of-the-way site or discount mall	Moderate width but poor depth of assortment; some irregular merchandise; lower continuity	Very low	Very low	Little; self-service

TABLE 5-1 Selected Aspects of Store-Based Retail Strategy Mixes (*Continued*)

Type of Retailer	Location	Merchandise	Prices	Atmosphere and Services	Promotion
Membership club	Isolated store or secondary site (industrial park)	Moderate width but poor depth of assortment; lower continuity	Very low	Very low	Little; some direct mail; limited sales force
Flea market	Isolated site, racetrack, or arena	Extensive width but poor depth of assortment; variable quality; lower continuity	Very low	Very low	Limited; self-service

CONVENIENCE STORE A **convenience store** is typically a well-located, food-oriented retailer that is open long hours and carries a moderate number of items. The store facility is small (only a fraction of the size of a conventional supermarket) and has average to above-average prices and average atmosphere and customer services. The ease of shopping at convenience stores and the impersonal nature of many large supermarkets make convenience stores particularly appealing to their customers, many of whom are male.

7-Eleven (www.7-eleven.com) leads the convenience store category.

There are 146,000 U.S. convenience stores (excluding stores where food is a small fraction of revenues), and total annual sales are $190 billion (excluding gasoline).[10] 7-Eleven, Circle K, and Casey's General Store are major food-based U.S. convenience store chains. Speedway is a leading gasoline service station-based convenience store chain with 1,350 outlets.

Items such as milk, eggs, and bread once represented the major portion of sales; now sandwiches, tobacco products, snack foods, soft drinks, general merchandise, beer and wine, ATMs, and lottery tickets are also key items. And gasoline generates 30 percent or more of total sales at most of the convenience stores that carry it.

This format's advantages are its usefulness when a person does not want to travel to or shop at a supermarket, sales of both fill-in items and gas, long hours, and drive-thru windows. Many shoppers visit multiple times a week, and the average transaction is small. Due to limited space, stores get frequent deliveries and have high handling costs. Buyers are less price-sensitive than at other food-oriented stores.

The industry does have problems: Some areas are saturated with stores; supermarkets have longer hours and more nonfood items; some stores have become too big, making shopping less convenient; the traditional market (blue-collar workers) has shrunk; and some chains have had financial woes.

The Food Marketing Institute (www.fmi.org) is the leading industry association for food retailers.

CONVENTIONAL SUPERMARKET A **supermarket** is a self-service food store with grocery, meat, and produce departments and minimum annual sales of $2 million. Included are conventional supermarkets, food-based superstores, combination stores, box (limited-line) stores, and warehouse stores. See Figure 5-6.

A **conventional supermarket** is a departmentalized food store with a wide range of food and related products; sales of general merchandise are rather limited. This institution started more than 80 years ago when it was recognized that large-scale operations would let a retailer combine volume sales, self-service, and low prices. Self-service enabled supermarkets to both cut costs and increase volume. Personnel costs were reduced, and impulse buying increased. The car and the refrigerator contributed to the supermarket's success by lowering travel costs and adding to the life span of perishables.

For several decades, overall supermarket sales have been about 70 to 75 percent of U.S. grocery sales, with conventional supermarkets now yielding one-sixth of total supermarket sales. There are 17,000 conventional units, with annual sales of $105 billion.[11] Chains account for the great majority of sales. Among the leaders are Kroger, Safeway, and Loblaw, although a number of these firms' stores are now food-based superstores. Many independent supermarkets are affiliated with cooperative or voluntary organizations such as IGA and Supervalu.

Conventional supermarkets generally rely on high inventory turnover (volume sales). Their profit margins are low. In general, average gross margins (selling price less merchandise cost) are 20 to 22 percent of sales, and net profits are 1 to 3 percent of sales.

FIGURE 5-6

Supermarkets Have a Lot to Offer

Supermarkets are well-designed, with a plentiful assortment of food and related items, good parking, and fair prices. The self-service environment is easy to maneuver.

Source: Fedor Kondratenko/ Shutterstock.com. Reprinted by permission.

They face intense competition from other food stores: Convenience stores offer easier shopping; food-based superstores and combination stores have more product lines and greater variety within them, as well as better margins; and box and warehouse stores have lower operating costs and prices. Membership clubs (discussed later), with low prices, also provide competition—especially now that they have much expanded food lines. Variations of the supermarket are covered next.

FOOD-BASED SUPERSTORE A **food-based superstore** is larger and more diversified than a conventional supermarket but usually smaller and less diversified than a combination store. This format originated in the 1970s as supermarkets sought to stem sales declines by expanding store size and the number of nonfood items carried. Some supermarkets merged with drugstores or general merchandise stores, but more grew into food-based superstores. There are 11,000 food-based U.S. superstores, with sales of \$270 billion.[12]

The typical food-based superstore occupies at least 30,000 to 50,000 square feet of space, and 20 to 25 percent of sales are from general merchandise, including garden supplies, flowers,

CAREERS IN RETAILING

David Kahn: A Serial Retail Entrepreneur

In 2002, David Kahn at age 49 owned 45 Blockbuster (www.blockbuster.com) franchises in Alabama and Mississippi. Kahn estimates that his group of stores was the seventh-largest video-rental chain in the United States and that its market value was over \$15 million at its peak. Ultimately, Kahn's business model was doomed by Netflix (www.netflix.com). Unlike Blockbuster, with Netflix, consumers could always secure their first choice option. The Netflix model also offered unlimited movies at one price. Lastly, Netflix did not require the annoying trip to the video rental store to return a video. As of Spring 2006, Kahn left the video business.

Kahn's second venture into retailing was also franchise-based. In mid-2007, he purchased six Subway franchises. Six-months later, Subway (www.subway.com) rolled out its "\$5 Footlong" hero; this drastically slashed Kahn's profit margins. He soon sold his Subway units earning a small profit.

In September 2009, Kahn founded Yogurt Mountain (www.yogurtmountain.com), a self-service yogurt store where consumers can mix over 50 toppings in their choice of 16 flavors of yogurt. The price is based on the weight. In March 2010, Kahn sold 40 percent of this business to an investment group for \$3 million. By 2012, Yogurt Mountain had more than 40 locations (many franchised) in 15 states.

Source: Douglas Alden Warshaw, "Pulling Off the Ultimate Career Makeover," http://management.fortune.cnn.com/2011/06/21/pulling-off-the-ultimate-career-makeover (June 21, 2011).

small appliances, and DVDs. It caters to consumers' complete grocery needs, along with fill-in general merchandise.

Like combination stores, food-based superstores are efficient, offer a degree of one-stop shopping, stimulate impulse purchases, and feature high-profit general merchandise. But they also offer other advantages: It is easier and less costly to redesign and convert supermarkets into food-based superstores than into combination stores. Many consumers feel more comfortable shopping in true food stores than in huge combination stores. Management expertise is better focused.

Over the past two decades, U.S. supermarket chains have turned more to food-based superstores. They have expanded and remodeled existing supermarkets and built numerous new stores. Many independents have also converted to food-based superstores.

Meijer's (www.meijer.com) combination stores are quite popular with shoppers. They carry 120,000 items.

COMBINATION STORE A **combination store** unites supermarket and general merchandise in one facility, with general merchandise accounting for 25 to 40 percent of sales. The format began in the late 1960s and early 1970s, as common checkout areas were used for separately owned supermarkets and drugstores or supermarkets and general merchandise stores. The natural offshoot was integrating operations under one management. The 4,500 U.S. combination stores (including supercenters) have per year sales of $160 billion.[13] Combination store leaders include Meijer, Fred Meyer, and Albertson's.

Combination stores are large, from 30,000 up to 100,000 or more square feet. This leads to operating efficiencies and cost savings. Consumers like one-stop shopping and will travel to get there. Impulse sales are high. Many general merchandise items have better margins than food items. Supermarkets and drugstores have commonalities in the customers served and the low-price, high-turnover items sold. Drugstore and general merchandise customers are drawn to the store more often.

A **supercenter** is a combination store blending an economy supermarket with a discount department store. It is the U.S. version of the even larger **hypermarket** (the European institution pioneered by firms such as Carrefour that did not succeed in the United States). As a rule, the majority of supercenter sales are from nonfood items. Stores usually range from 75,000 to 150,000 square feet in size, and they stock up to 50,000 and more items—much more than the 30,000 or so items carried by other combination stores. Wal-Mart and Target both operate a growing number of supercenters.

BOX (LIMITED-LINE) STORE The **box (limited-line) store** is a food-based discounter that focuses on a small selection of items, moderate hours of operation (compared with other supermarkets), few services, and limited manufacturer brands. They carry fewer than 2,000 items, few refrigerated perishables, and few sizes and brands per item. Prices are on shelves or overhead signs. Items are displayed in cut cases. Customers bag purchases. Box stores rely on low-priced private-label brands. Their prices are 20 to 30 percent below supermarkets.

The box store originated in Europe and was exported to the United States in the mid-1970s. The growth of these stores has not been as anticipated, and sales have actually fallen modestly in recent years. Some other food stores have matched box-store prices. Many people are loyal to manufacturer brands, and box stores cannot fulfill one-stop shopping needs. There are 2,800 box stores in the United States, with sales of $14 billion.[14] The leading box store operators are Save-A-Lot and Aldi.

WAREHOUSE STORE A **warehouse store** is a food-based discounter offering a moderate number of food items in a no-frills setting. It appeals to one-stop food shoppers, concentrates on special purchases of popular brands, uses cut-case displays, offers little service, posts prices on shelves, and locates in secondary sites. These stores began in the late 1970s. There are now 1,700 U.S. stores with $70 billion in annual sales.[15]

The largest warehouse store is known as a super warehouse. There are more than 600 of them in the United States. They have annual sales exceeding $20 million each, and they contain a variety of departments, including produce. High ceilings accommodate pallet loads of groceries. Shipments are made directly to the store. Customers pack their own groceries. Super warehouses are profitable at gross margins far lower than for conventional supermarkets. The leading super warehouse chain is Cub Foods.

Many consumers do not like shopping in warehouse settings. Furthermore, because products are usually acquired when special deals are available, brands may be temporarily or permanently out of stock.

Table 5-2 shows selected operating data for the food-oriented retailers just described.

TABLE 5-2 Selected Typical Operating Data for Food-Oriented Retailers, as of 2011

Factor	Convenience Stores	Conventional Supermarkets	Food-Based Superstores	Combination Stores	Box (Limited-Line) Stores	Warehouse Stores
Number of stores	146,000	17,000	11,000	4,500	2,800	1,700
Total annual sales	$190 billion[a]	$105 billion	$270 billion	$160 billion[b]	$14 billion	$70 billion[c]
Average store selling area (sq. ft.)	5,000 or less	15,000–20,000	30,000–50,000+	30,000–100,000+	5,000–9,000	15,000+
Number of checkouts per store	1–3	6–10	10+	10+	3–5	5+
Gross margin	25–30%	20–22%	20–25%	25%	10–12%	12–15%
Number of items stocked per store	3,000–4,000	12,000–17,000	20,000+	30,000+	Under 2,000	2,500+
Major emphasis	Daily fill-in needs; dairy, sandwiches, tobacco, gas, beverages, magazines	Food; only 5–10% of sales from general merchandise	Positioned between supermarket and combo store; 20–25% of sales from general merchandise	One-stop shopping; general merchandise is 25–40% of sales (higher at supercenters)	Low prices; few or no perishables	Low prices; variable assortments; may or may not stock perishables

[a] Excluding gasoline.

[b] Including supermarket-item sales at the supercenters of Wal-Mart, Target, and Kmart (which are more heavily oriented to general merchandise than other combination stores).

[c] Including supermarket-item sales at Costco, Sam's, and other membership clubs.

Sources: Various issues of *Progressive Grocer,* www.progessivegrocer.com; Food Marketing Institute, "Facts & Figures," www.fmi.org/facts_figs; *Convenience Store Decisions,* www.csdecisions.com; and authors' estimates.

General Merchandise Retailers

We now examine these general merchandise strategic retail formats highlighted in Table 5-1: specialty store, traditional department store, full-line discount store, variety store, off-price chain, factory outlet, membership club, and flea market.

SPECIALTY STORE A **specialty store** concentrates on selling one goods or service line, such as young women's apparel. It usually carries a narrow but deep assortment in the chosen category and tailors the strategy to a given market segment. This enables the store to maintain a better selection and sales expertise than competitors, which are often department stores. Investments are controlled, and there is a certain amount of flexibility. Among the most popular categories of specialty stores are apparel, personal care, auto supply, home furnishings, electronics, books, toys, home improvement, pet supplies, jewelry, and sporting goods.

Consumers often shop at specialty stores because of the knowledgeable sales personnel, the variety of choices within the given category, customer service policies, intimate store size and atmosphere (although this is not true of the category killer store), the lack of crowds (also not true of category killer stores), and the absence of aisles of unrelated merchandise that they must pass through. Some specialty stores have elaborate fixtures and upscale merchandise for affluent shoppers, whereas others are discount-oriented and aim at price-conscious consumers.

Total specialty store sales are difficult to determine because these retailers sell virtually all kinds of goods and services, and aggregate specialty store data are not compiled by the government. We do estimate that annual nonfood specialty store sales in the United States are $2.5 trillion (including auto dealers). The top 50 specialty store chains (excluding auto dealers) have sales of $450 billion. Among those chains, about one-third are involved with

FIGURE 5-7

Home Depot: A Power Retailer

As a power retailer, "Home Depot has more than 2,200 convenient locations throughout the United States (including the territories of Puerto Rico and the Virgin Islands), Canada, China, and Mexico. Stores average 105,000 square feet with approximately 23,000 additional square feet of outside garden area. Our store inventory consists of up to 40,000 different kinds of building materials, home improvement supplies, appliances, and lawn and garden products for all of your project needs." (https://corporate.homedepot.com/OurCompany/Pages/default.aspx)

Source: Reprinted by permission of Susan V. Berry, Retail Image Consulting, Inc.

apparel. Specialty store leaders include Home Depot (home improvement), Best Buy (consumer electronics), TJX (apparel), Toys "R" Us (toys), GameStop (video games), and Barnes & Noble (books).[16]

As noted earlier in the chapter, one type of specialty store—the category killer—has gained particular strength. A **category killer** (also known as a **power retailer**) is an especially large specialty store. It features an enormous selection in its category and relatively low prices. Consumers are drawn from wide geographic areas. Home Depot, Barnes & Noble, Sephora, Sports Authority, and Staples are among the chains almost fully based on the concept. See Figure 5-7. At Sephora's more than 1,000 stores around the world (including 60 in China), the "unique, open-sell environment features over 200 classic and emerging brands across a broad range of product categories including skincare, color, fragrance, bath & body, smilecare, and haircare, in addition to Sephora's own private label."[17]

The focus of specialty stores is sometimes as narrow as the Joy of Socks (www.joyofsocks.com).

Nonetheless, smaller specialty stores (even ones with under 1,000 square feet of space) can prosper if they are focused, offer strong customer service, and avoid imitating larger firms. Many consumers do not like going to category killer stores: "Shoppers looking for just one or a few basic items and a quick checkout may not want to scour a cavernous warehouse to find what they need." Furthermore, "some categories of merchandise, such as high-tech consumer electronics products, require greater support at retail, from specially trained, knowledgeable employees, than the support typically offered at category killer stores."[18]

Any size specialty store can be adversely affected by seasonality or a decline in the popularity of its product category. This type of store may also fail to attract consumers who are interested in one-stop shopping for multiple product categories.

TRADITIONAL DEPARTMENT STORE A **department store** is a large retail unit with an extensive assortment (width and depth) of goods and services that is organized into separate departments for purposes of buying, promotion, customer service, and control. It has the most selection of any general merchandise retailer, often serves as the anchor store in a shopping center or district, has strong credit card penetration, and is usually part of a chain. To be classified as a department store, a retailer must sell a wide range of products (such as apparel, furniture, appliances, and home furnishings), and selected other items (such as paint, hardware, toiletries, cosmetics, photo equipment, jewelry, toys, and sporting goods) with no one merchandise line predominating.

Two basic types of retailers meet the preceding criteria: the traditional department store and the full-line discount store. They account for $500 billion in annual sales (including supercenters, where general merchandise sales exceed food sales and leased departments), about one-tenth of all U.S. retail sales.[19] The traditional department store is discussed here; the full-line discount store is examined next.

At a **traditional department store**, merchandise quality ranges from average to quite good. Pricing is moderate to above average. Customer service ranges from medium levels of sales help,

Belk, Inc. (www.belk.com) is the nation's largest privately owned department store company, with more than 300 fashion department stores in 16 states.

credit, delivery, and so forth to high levels of each. For example, Macy's targets middle-class shoppers interested in assortment and moderate prices, whereas Bloomingdale's aims at upscale consumers through more trendy merchandise and higher prices. Few traditional department stores sell all of the product lines that the category used to carry. Many place greater emphasis on apparel and may not carry such lines as furniture, electronics, and major appliances.

Over its history, the traditional department store has contributed many innovations, such as advertising prices, enacting a one-price policy (whereby all shoppers pay the same price for the same item), developing computerized checkouts, offering money-back guarantees, adding branch stores, decentralizing management, and moving into suburban shopping centers. However, in recent years, the performance of traditional department stores has lagged far behind that of full-line discount stores. Today, traditional department store sales ($100 billion annually) represent one-fifth of total department store sales. These are some reasons for traditional department stores' difficulties:

- Price-conscious consumers are more attracted to discounters than to traditional department stores.
- These stores no longer have as much brand exclusivity for a lot of the items they sell.
- The growth of shopping centers has aided specialty stores because consumers can engage in one-stop shopping at several specialty stores in the same shopping center. Department stores do not dominate the smaller stores around them as they once did.
- Specialty stores often have better assortments in the lines they carry.
- Customer service has deteriorated. Often, store personnel are not as loyal, helpful, or knowledgeable as in prior years.
- Some stores are too big and have too much unproductive selling space and low-turnover merchandise.
- Many department stores have had a weak focus on market segments and a fuzzy image.
- Such chains as Sears have repeatedly changed strategic orientation, confusing consumers as to their image. (Is Sears a traditional department store chain or a full-line discount store chain?)
- Some companies are not as innovative in their merchandise decisions as they once were.

Traditional department stores need to clarify their niche in the marketplace (retail positioning); place greater emphasis on customer service and sales personnel; present more exciting, better-organized store interiors; use space better by downsizing stores and eliminating slow-selling items (such as J.C. Penney dropping consumer electronics); and open outlets in smaller,

TECHNOLOGY IN RETAILING

Gas Station TV Pumps Up Business

The GSTV network (www.gstv.com) reaches 27 million viewers per month in over 100 U.S. markets. Another gas-station-based network, Outcast (www.outcast.net), is viewed by 23 million people on more than 12,000 screens nationwide. A third network, PumpTV (www.pumptotv.com), reaches 20 million viewers on 10,000 screens in major U.S. markets. Companies that advertise at gas station pumps include American Express, CVS Pharmacy, Subway, Dunkin' Donuts, and Verizon.

Generally, gas pump television networks utilize a format that consists of a television segment followed by a promotion. The television segment is custom produced by companies such as ESPN, NBCU news, and AccuWeather. Promotions can be either product- or image-based. Promotional schedules are developed specially for each retailer.

Research on pump TV ads shows their impact for gas stations and convenience stores with gas:

- Ninety-three percent of consumers surveyed preferred gas stations with GSTV.
- Ninety percent of fuel consumers noticed the TV screens, more than 70 percent of respondents considered at-the-pump advertising as a good source of product information, and 75 percent could recall at least one advertisement.
- A Nielsen study for GSTV found that sales of advertised windshield washer fluid increased by 42 percent and sales of advertised candy increased by 69 percent.

Source: Laura Glass and Mark Ward Sr., "TV at the Pump," *NPN Magazine* (January–February 2011), pp. 22–24.

FIGURE 5-8

Harrods: One of the World's Great Department Stores

The Harrods department store in London has been at its current location for about 110 years. The store occupies more than one-million square feet of selling space, sits on a five-acre site, and is comprised of more than 330 individual departments.

Source: dutourdumonde/ Shutterstock.com. Reprinted by permission.

less developed towns and cities (as Sears has done). They can also centralize more buying and promotion functions, do better research, and reach customers more efficiently (by such tools as targeted mailing pieces). See Figure 5-8.

In recent years, this format has been making something of a comeback due to more brand exclusives:

> Part of the success has come from a renewed push to line up exclusive collections, a change from the prior "homogeneous" offerings. Goods that can't be found anywhere else, especially those branded with well-known or celebrity names, make the store a destination. It also helps a department-store chain avoid the pricing wars that come with selling commoditized goods.[20]

For example, Macy's recently gained sole rights to the Tommy Hilfiger apparel brand and J.C. Penney now has exclusive rights to the Liz Claiborne apparel brand.

FULL-LINE DISCOUNT STORE A **full-line discount store** is a type of department store with these features:

- It conveys the image of a high-volume, low-cost outlet selling a broad product assortment for less than conventional prices.
- It is more apt to carry the range of general merchandise once expected only at department stores, including electronics, furniture, and appliances—as well as auto accessories, gardening tools, and housewares.
- Shopping carts and centralized checkout service are provided.
- Customer service is not usually provided within store departments but at a centralized area. Products are normally sold via self-service with minimal assistance in any single department.
- Nondurable (soft) goods often feature private brands, whereas durable (hard) goods emphasize well-known manufacturer brands.
- Less fashion-sensitive merchandise is carried.

- Buildings, equipment, and fixtures are less expensive; and operating costs are lower than for traditional department stores and specialty stores.

Annual U.S. full-line discount store revenues are $400 billion (including general merchandise-based supercenters and leased departments), roughly 80 percent of all U.S. department store sales. Together, Wal-Mart, Target, and Kmart operate 7,000 full-line discount stores (including supercenters), with $330 billion in full-line discount store sales.[21]

The success of full-line discount stores is due to many factors. They have a clear customer focus: middle-class and lower-middle-class shoppers looking for good value. The stores feature popular brands of average- to good-quality merchandise at competitive prices. They have expanded their goods and service categories and often have their own private brands. Firms have worked hard to improve their image and provide more customer services. The average outlet (not the supercenter) tends to be smaller than a traditional department store, and sales per square foot are usually higher, which improves productivity. Some full-line discount stores are located in small towns where competition is less intense. Facilities may be newer than those of many traditional department stores.

The greatest challenges facing full-line discount stores are the competition from other retailers (especially lower-priced store discounters, category killer stores, and Web-based retailers such as Amazon.com and eBay), too rapid expansion of some firms, saturation of prime locations, and the dominance of Wal-Mart and Target (as Kmart has fallen off dramatically over the past decade). The industry has undergone a number of consolidations, bankruptcies, and liquidations.

VARIETY STORE A **variety store** handles an assortment of inexpensive and popularly priced goods and services, such as apparel and accessories, costume jewelry, notions and small wares, candy, toys, and other items in the price range. There are open displays and few salespeople. The stores do not carry full product lines, may not be departmentalized, and do not deliver products. Although the conventional variety store format has faded away, there are two successful spin-offs from it: dollar discount stores and closeout chains.

Dollar discount stores sell similar items to those in conventional variety stores but in plainer surroundings and at much lower prices. They generate $25 billion in yearly sales. Dollar General and Family Dollar are the two leading dollar discount store chains. The two firms operate a total of 17,000 stores and have $22 billion in annual sales. *Closeout chains* sell similar items to those in conventional variety stores but feature closeouts and overruns. They account for $8 billion annually. Big Lots is the leader in that category with more than 1,400 stores and annual sales of $5 billion.[22]

The conventional variety store format (which included Woolworth and McCrory) pretty much disappeared from the U.S. marketplace in the mid-1990s after a long, successful run. What happened? There was heavy competition from specialty stores and discounters, most of the stores were older facilities, and some items had low profit margins. At one time, Woolworth had 1,200 variety stores with annual sales of $2 billion.

OFF-PRICE CHAIN An **off-price chain** features brand-name (sometimes designer) apparel and accessories, footwear (primarily women's and family), linens, fabrics, cosmetics, and/or housewares and sells them at everyday low prices in an efficient, limited-service environment. It frequently has community dressing rooms, centralized checkout counters, no gift wrapping, and extra charges for alterations. The chains buy merchandise opportunistically, as special deals occur. Other retailers' canceled orders, manufacturers' irregulars and overruns, and end-of-season items are often purchased for a fraction of their original wholesale prices. The total sales of U.S. off-price apparel stores are $50 billion. The biggest chains are T.J. Maxx and Marshalls (both owned by TJX), Ross Stores, and Burlington Coat Factory.

TJX (www.tjx.com) operates two of the biggest off-price apparel chains: T.J. Maxx and Marshalls.

Off-price chains aim at the same shoppers as traditional department stores—but with prices reduced by 40 to 50 percent. Shoppers are also lured by the promise of new merchandise on a regular basis. TJX is an off-price retailer that seeks to "deliver a rapidly changing assortment of fashionable, quality, brand name merchandise at prices that are 20 to 60 percent less than department and specialty store regular prices, every day." The retailer's main target group consists of "a middle- to upper-middle-income shopper who is fashion and value conscious and fits the same profile as a department or specialty store shopper."[23] Off-price shopping centers now appeal to people's interest in one-stop shopping.

The most crucial strategic element for off-price chains involves buying merchandise and establishing long-term relationships with suppliers. To succeed, the chains must secure large quantities of merchandise at reduced wholesale prices and have a regular flow of goods into the stores. Sometimes, manufacturers use off-price chains to sell samples, products that are not doing well when they are introduced, and merchandise remaining near the end of a season. At other times, off-price chains employ a more active buying strategy. Instead of waiting for closeouts and canceled orders, they convince manufacturers to make merchandise during off-seasons and pay cash for items early. Off-price chains are less demanding in terms of the support requested from suppliers, they do not return products, and they pay promptly.

Off-price chains face some market pressure because of competition from other institutional formats that run frequent sales throughout the year, the discontinuity of merchandise, poor management at some firms, insufficient customer service for some shoppers, and the shakeout of underfinanced companies.

FACTORY OUTLET A **factory outlet** is a manufacturer-owned store selling closeouts; discontinued merchandise; irregulars; canceled orders; and, sometimes, in-season, first-quality merchandise. Manufacturers' interest in outlet stores has risen for four basic reasons:

1. Manufacturers can control where their discounted merchandise is sold. By placing outlets in out-of-the-way spots with low sales penetration of the firm's brands, outlet revenues do not affect sales at key specialty and department store accounts.
2. Outlets are profitable despite prices up to 60 percent less than customary retail prices due to low operating costs—few services, low rent, limited displays, and plain store fixtures—and selling more merchandise made especially for outlet stores.
3. The manufacturer decides on store visibility, sets promotion policies, removes labels, and ensures that discontinued items and irregulars are disposed of properly.
4. Because many specialty and department stores are increasing private-label sales, manufacturers need revenue from outlet stores to sustain their own growth.

More factory stores now operate in clusters or in outlet malls to expand customer traffic, and they use cooperative ads. Large outlet malls are in Connecticut, Florida, Georgia, New York, Pennsylvania, Tennessee, and other states. There are 14,000 U.S. factory outlet stores representing hundreds of manufacturers, many in the 180 outlet malls nationwide. These stores have $23 billion in yearly sales, with three-quarters from apparel and accessories. There are 360 outlet malls worldwide.[24] Firms with a major presence include Bass (footwear), Polo Ralph Lauren (apparel), Levi's (apparel), Nike (apparel and footwear), Samsonite (luggage), and Totes (rain gear). See Figure 5-9.

FIGURE 5-9
Polo Ralph Lauren: Realizing the Value of Outlet Centers

Polo Ralph Lauren has about 200 factory outlet stores around the world, including this one in San Marcos, Texas. These stores sell men's, women's, and children's apparel, as well as accessories and fragrances.

Source: Ahmad Faizal Yahya/Shutterstock.com. Reprinted by permission.

The Men's Warehouse Guarantee

One of every five suits purchased in the United States is bought at a Men's Warehouse store (www.menswarehouse.com). George Zimmer, the founder of Men's Warehouse, has also been the company's spokesperson for more than 25 years. When Zimmer filmed his first commercial in 1986, he intended to use the tag line "That's the fact, Jack." Instead, he used the expression "I guarantee it." The guarantee stated that consumers who shop at a Men's Warehouse store would like the way they look. Obviously, this tag line worked well as it is still being used by Zimmer in the firm's advertising.

According to the retailer's senior vice president of marketing, Matthew Stringer, Zimmer took "a common phrase and turned it into a tag line that is immediately recognizable. Everyone knows it." Zimmer noted that, "if you distill it down [our competitive advantage] is [based on] the founder's guarantee and promise of satisfaction."

Based on company research conducted in March 2011, 91 percent of Americans think dressing well can make a man appear to be more physically attractive than he really is. The research study also concluded that 78 percent of women think that one of the sexiest things a guy can do is dress well. Men's Warehouse's recent commercials were based around these survey results.

Source: Jean E. Palmieri, "The Men's Warehouse Promise," *Women's Wear Daily* (June 2, 2011), p. 12.

When deciding whether to utilize factory outlets, manufacturers must be cautious. They must evaluate their retailing expertise, the investment costs, the impact on existing retailers that buy from them, and the response of consumers. Manufacturers do not want to jeopardize their products' sales at full retail prices.

MEMBERSHIP CLUB A **membership (warehouse) club** appeals to price-conscious consumers, who must be members to shop there. It straddles the line between wholesaling and retailing. Some members are small business owners and employees who pay a membership fee to buy merchandise at wholesale prices. They make purchases for use in operating their firms or for personal use and yield 60 percent of club sales. Most members are final consumers who buy for their own use; they represent 40 percent of club sales. They must pay an annual fee to be a member. Prices may be slightly more than for business customers. There are 1,400 U.S. membership clubs, with annual sales to final consumers of more than $60 billion. Costco and Sam's Club generate 90 percent of industry sales.[25]

Sam's (www.samsclub.com) is Wal-Mart's membership club division. It has lower prices and plainer settings than Wal-Mart's full-line discount stores.

The operating strategy of the modern membership club centers on large stores (up to 100,000 or more square feet), inexpensive isolated or industrial locations, opportunistic buying (with some merchandise discontinuity), a fraction of the items stocked by full-line discount stores, little advertising, plain fixtures, wide aisles to give forklift trucks access to shelves, concrete floors, limited delivery, fewer credit options, and very low prices. A typical club carries general merchandise, such as consumer electronics, appliances, computers, housewares, tires, and apparel (35 to 60 percent of sales); food (20 to 35 percent of sales); and sundries, such as health and beauty aids, tobacco, liquor, and candy (15 to 30 percent of sales). It may also have a pharmacy, photo developing, a car-buying service, a gasoline service station, and other items once viewed as frills for this format. Inventory turnover is several times that of a department store.

The major retailing challenges relate to the allocation of company efforts between business and final consumer accounts (without antagonizing one group or the other and without presenting a blurred store image), the lack of interest by many consumers in shopping at warehouse-type stores, the power of the two industry leaders, and the potential for saturation caused by overexpansion.

FLEA MARKET At a **flea market**, many retail vendors sell a range of products at discount prices in plain surroundings. It is rooted in the centuries-old tradition of street selling—shoppers touch and sample items, and they haggle over prices. Vendors used to sell only antiques, bric-a-brac, and assorted used merchandise. Today, they also frequently sell new goods, such as clothing, cosmetics, watches, consumer electronics, housewares, and gift items. See Figure 5-10.

Many flea markets are located in nontraditional sites such as racetracks, stadiums, and arenas. Some are at sites abandoned by other retailers. Typically, vendors rent space. A flea market might rent individual spaces for $30 to $100 or more per day, depending on location. Some flea markets impose a parking fee or admission charge for shoppers.

FIGURE 5-10

The Grand Bazaar in Istanbul, Turkey

The Grand Bazaar in Istanbul is one of the largest covered flea markets in the world. It has 60 streets and 5,000 shops and attracts 250,000 to 400,000 visitors per day. It is best known for the jewelry, hand-painted ceramics, carpets, embroideries, spices, and antique shops. Many of the stalls in the bazaar are grouped by type of goods. The bazaar has been an important trading center since 1461. It was enlarged in the 16th century, and underwent major restorations following an earthquake in the 1890s and a fire in 1954.

Source: Ahmad Faizal Yahya/Shutterstock.com. Reprinted by permission.

There are a few hundred major U.S. flea markets, but overall sales data are not available. The credibility of permanent flea markets, consumer interest in bargaining, the broader product mix, the availability of brand-name goods, and the low prices all contribute to the format's appeal. One of the best-known businesses in this genre is the Rose Bowl Flea Market, which is open the second Sunday of each month. It regularly features 2,500 vendors and attracts 20,000 shoppers a day. "The only restricted items are food, animals, guns, ammunition, pornography, and services requiring physical contact." The costs of vendor spaces range from $25 to $250 for one day.[26]

At a flea market, price haggling is encouraged, cash is the predominant currency, and many vendors gain their first real experience as retail entrepreneurs. One recent trend involves nonstore, Web-based flea markets such as eBay (www.ebay.com), eBid (www.ebid.com), OnlineAuction (www.onlineauction.com), and Skoreit! (www.skoreit.com). Online auction sites account for several billion dollars in sales annually and are popular among bargain hunters.

Many traditional retailers believe flea markets represent an unfair method of competition because the quality of merchandise may be misrepresented, consumers may buy items at flea markets and return them to other retailers for higher refunds, suppliers are often unaware their products are sold there, sales taxes can be easily avoided, and operating costs are quite low. Flea markets may also cause traffic congestion.

The high sales volume from off-price chains, factory outlets, membership clubs, and flea markets is explained by the wheel of retailing. These institutions are low-cost operators appealing to price-conscious consumers who are not totally satisfied with other retail formats that have upgraded their merchandise and customer service, raised prices, and moved along the wheel.

Chapter Summary

1. *To describe the wheel of retailing, scrambled merchandising, and the retail life cycle, and to show how they can help explain the performance of retail strategy mixes.* In Chapter 4, retail institutions were examined by ownership. Chapter 5 takes a store-based strategic retailing perspective. A retail strategy mix involves a combination of factors: location, operations, goods/services offered, pricing, atmosphere and customer services, and promotion. To flourish, a firm should strive to be dominant in some way and, thus, reach destination retailer status.

Three important concepts help explain the performance of diverse retail strategies. According to the wheel of retailing, retail innovators often first appear as low-price operators with low costs and low profit margins. Over time, they upgrade their offerings and customer services and raise prices. They are then vulnerable to new discounters with lower costs that take their place along the wheel. With scrambled merchandising, a retailer adds goods and services that are unrelated to each other and its original business to increase overall sales and profits. Scrambled merchandising is contagious and often used in self-defense. The retail life cycle states that institutions pass through identifiable stages of introduction, growth, maturity, and decline. Strategies change as institutions mature.

2. *To discuss ways in which retail strategy mixes are evolving.* Many institutions are adapting to marketplace dynamics. These approaches have been popular for various firms, depending on their strengths, weaknesses, and goals: mergers, by which separately owned retailers join together; diversification, by which a retailer becomes active in businesses outside its normal operations; and downsizing, whereby unprofitable stores are closed or divisions sold. Sometimes, single companies use all three approaches. More firms also utilize cost containment and value-driven retailing. They strive to hold down both investment and operating costs. There are many ways to do this.

3. *To examine a wide variety of food-oriented retailers involved with store-based strategy mixes.* Retail institutions may be classified by store-based strategy mix and divided into food-oriented and general merchandise groups. Fourteen store-based strategy mixes are covered in this chapter.

These are the food-oriented store-based retailers: A convenience store is well located, is open long hours, and offers a moderate number of fill-in items at average to above-average prices. A conventional supermarket is departmentalized and carries a wide range of food and related items, there is little general merchandise, and prices are competitive. A food-based superstore is larger and more diversified than a conventional supermarket but smaller and less diversified than a combination store. A combination store unites supermarket and general merchandise in a large facility and sets competitive prices; the food-based supercenter (hypermarket) is a type of combination store. The box (limited-line) store is a discounter focusing on a small selection, moderate hours, few services, and few manufacturer brands. A warehouse store is a discounter offering a moderate number of food items in a no-frills setting that can be quite large.

4. *To study a wide range of general merchandise retailers involved with store-based strategy mixes.* A specialty store concentrates on one goods or service line and has a tailored strategy; the category killer is a special kind of specialty store. A department store is a large retailer with an extensive assortment of goods and services. The traditional one has a range of customer services and average to above-average prices. A full-line discount store is a department store with a low-cost, low-price strategy. A variety store has inexpensive and popularly priced items in a plain setting. An off-price chain features brand-name items and sells them at low prices in an austere environment. A factory outlet is manufacturer-owned and sells closeouts, discontinued merchandise, and irregulars at very low prices. A membership club appeals to price-conscious shoppers who must be members to shop. A flea market has many vendors offering items at discount prices in nontraditional venues.

Key Terms

strategy mix (p. 113)
destination retailer (p. 113)
wheel of retailing (p. 113)
scrambled merchandising (p. 115)
retail life cycle (p. 116)
mergers (p. 118)
diversification (p. 118)
downsizing (p. 118)
convenience store (p. 121)
supermarket (p. 121)
conventional supermarket (p. 121)
food-based superstore (p. 122)
combination store (p. 123)
supercenter (p. 123)
hypermarket (p. 123)
box (limited-line) store (p. 123)
warehouse store (p. 123)
specialty store (p. 124)
category killer (power retailer) (p. 125)
department store (p. 125)
traditional department store (p. 125)
full-line discount store (p. 127)
variety store (p. 128)
off-price chain (p. 128)
factory outlet (p. 129)
membership (warehouse) club (p. 130)
flea market (p. 130)

Questions for Discussion

1. Describe how a small shoe store could be a destination retailer.
2. Explain the wheel of retailing. Is this theory applicable today? Why or why not?
3. Develop a high-end retail strategy mix for a toy store. Include location, operating procedures, goods/services offered, pricing tactics, and promotion methods.
4. How could these retailers best apply scrambled merchandising? Explain your answers.
   a. Kay Jewelers.
   b. 1-800 Flowers.
   c. A local delicatessen.
   d. Dunkin' Donuts.

5. What strategic emphasis should be used by institutions in the growth stage of the retail life cycle compared with the emphasis by institutions in the maturity stage?
6. Contrast the strategy mixes of convenience stores, conventional supermarkets, food-based superstores, and warehouse stores. Is there room for each? Explain your answer.
7. Do you think U.S. combination stores (supercenters) will dominate grocery retailing? Why or why not?
8. What are the pros and cons of Sephora carrying more than 200 brands of personal-care products?
9. Contrast the strategy mixes of specialty stores, traditional department stores, and full-line discount stores.
10. What must the off-price chain do to succeed in the future?
11. Do you expect factory outlet centers to keep growing? Explain your answer.
12. Comment on the decision of many membership clubs to begin selling gasoline.

Web-Based Exercise

Visit the Web site of Dillard's (www.dillards.com). In your view, (a) where is Dillard's positioned along the wheel of retailing, and (b) how would you describe its use of scrambled merchandising? Explain whether you think that Dillard's is doing the right thing in terms of these two concepts.

Note: Also stop by our Web site (www.pearsonhighered.com/bermanevans) to experience a number of highly interactive, appealing Web exercises based on actual company demonstrations, and sample materials related to retailing.

6 Web, Nonstore-Based, and Other Forms of Nontraditional Retailing

Chapter Objectives

1. To contrast single-channel and multi-channel retailing
2. To look at the characteristics of the three major retail institutions involved with nonstore-based strategy mixes: direct marketing, direct selling, and vending machines—with an emphasis on direct marketing
3. To explore the emergence of electronic retailing through the World Wide Web
4. To discuss two other nontraditional forms of retailing: video kiosks and airport retailing

As both multi-channel and Web-only retailers look to ramp up their online revenues, many of them may be missing out on a huge opportunity. Why? A big challenge is for retailers to effectively coordinate their E-commerce efforts with their social media activities. Too often, the two formats are not integrated well—and, sometimes, not interrelated at all.

Verdict Research, a leading European consultancy, says that retailers often overlook the vast possibilities that can arise when they transform their Web-based stores "into entertainment destinations by integrating social media." Verdict concludes that even though E-commerce and social media are typically operated as separate entities, the retailers that see the benefits of combining the entities will be rewarded.

According to Charlotte Woods, a Verdict analyst, most retail firms understand the importance of social media. However, relatively few have used social media for the greatest benefit. By managing their physical and online stores separately, companies are missing out. They can attract more customer traffic to their online shops by utilizing social media "to create entertainment destinations which consumers can get excited about." This means that the retailers can "create retail theater online." Thus, "this concept would work particularly well for entertainment retailers, which could use interviews with authors and actors in the content of their home page." As Woods also notes:

> This sort of strategy will become increasingly important as competition continues to grow. Retailers will therefore have to work harder to engage customers, and integrating social media with their online stores could prove lucrative to those that get on the front foot.

Verdict Research notes that inserting appropriate retailer-created YouTube videos at online store sites and showing short video clips which feature interviews with celebrities, store executives, and designers are quite effective. RVCA, a clothing chain, includes blogs, YouTube videos, and music tour dates right at its Web site (www.rvca.com). As a result, consumers spend more time at the site.[1]

Source: BeTA-Artworks/fotolia.com.

Overview

In this chapter, we contrast single-channel and multi-channel retailing and then examine nonstore-based retailing, electronic retailing, and two other types of nontraditional retailing: video kiosks and airport retailing. These formats affect the strategies of current and new store retailers. Visit our Web site (www.pearsonhighered.com/bermanevans) for links to nonstore and nontraditional topics.

When it begins, a retailer often relies on **single-channel retailing**, whereby it sells to consumers through one retail format. That one format may be store-based (a corner shoe store) or nonstore-based (catalog retailing, direct selling, or Web retailing). As the firm grows, it may turn to **multi-channel retailing**, whereby a retailer sells to consumers through multiple retail formats. According to recent research, many small firms are engaged in multi-channel retailing through their stores and Web sites.[2]

From its roots as a full-line discount store chain, Wal-Mart (www.walmart.com) has become a master of multi-channel retailing.

Multi-channel retailing enables firms to reach different customer groups, share costs among various formats, and diversify its supplier base. Retail leader Wal-Mart sells at stores (including Wal-Mart, Sam's Club, and Neighborhood Market), a Web site (www.walmart.com), and a Web-to-store format whereby customers purchase online and pick up products at the store. Figure 6-1 shows examples of single- and multi-channel retailing. An end-of-chapter appendix explores multi-channel retailing in more detail.

Why have we introduced this concept here? Because even though some nonstore-based firms are "pure players" (single-channel retailers), a rapidly growing number of firms are combining store and nonstore retailing to actively pursue multi-channel retailing: "Customer channel preferences are constantly evolving. As new digital channels emerge, retailers should explore new ways to reach the right customer with the right message through the right channel at the right time. Best-in-class retailers have shown that the secret to multi-channel marketing success is to invest in new channels, develop a channel integration roadmap, and use customer analytics as the backbone for marketing communications."[3]

The ever-popular eBay (www.ebay.com) is a pure Web retailer.

Retailers—single-channel or multi-channel—engage in **nonstore retailing** when they use strategy mixes that are not store-based to reach consumers and complete transactions. U.S. nonstore retailing sales exceed $525 billion annually, with 80 percent of that from direct marketing (hence, the direct marketing emphasis in this chapter). The fastest-growing form of direct marketing involves electronic (Web-based—including mobile) retailing. U.S. Web retailing revenues are now $250 billion per year.[4] See Figure 6-2.

Nontraditional retailing also comprises video kiosks and airport retailing, two key formats not fitting neatly into "store-based" or "nonstore-based" retailing. Sometimes they are store-based; other times they are not. What they have in common is their departure from traditional retailing strategies.

FIGURE 6-1
Approaches to Retailing Channels

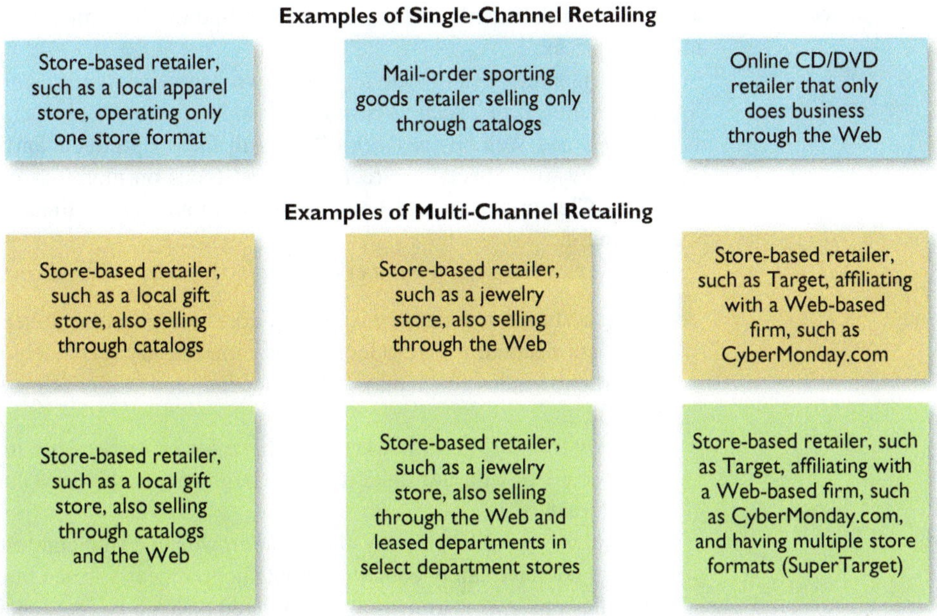

Examples of Single-Channel Retailing

Store-based retailer, such as a local apparel store, operating only one store format

Mail-order sporting goods retailer selling only through catalogs

Online CD/DVD retailer that only does business through the Web

Examples of Multi-Channel Retailing

Store-based retailer, such as a local gift store, also selling through catalogs

Store-based retailer, such as a jewelry store, also selling through the Web

Store-based retailer, such as Target, affiliating with a Web-based firm, such as CyberMonday.com

Store-based retailer, such as a local gift store, also selling through catalogs and the Web

Store-based retailer, such as a jewelry store, also selling through the Web and leased departments in select department stores

Store-based retailer, such as Target, affiliating with a Web-based firm, such as CyberMonday.com, and having multiple store formats (SuperTarget)

FIGURE 6-2

Aldo: Combining Bricks-and-Mortar with Clicks-and-Mortar

Retailers of every size and type are stepping up their use of Web retailing. Aldo Shoes has a carefully constructed Web site (www.aldoshoes.com) to complement its 1,000 stores in 60 countries.

Source: Reprinted by permission of Susan V. Berry, Retail Image Consulting, Inc.

DIRECT MARKETING

In **direct marketing**, a customer is first exposed to a good or service through a nonpersonal medium (direct mail, TV, radio, magazine, newspaper, computer, or tablet) and then orders by mail, phone, or fax—and increasingly by computer, smart phone, or tablet. Annual U.S. sales are more than $425 billion (including the Web), and more than half of adults make at least one such purchase a year. Japan, Germany, Great Britain, France, and Italy are among the direct marketing leaders outside the United States. Popular products are gift items, apparel, magazines, books and music, sports equipment, home accessories, food, and insurance.

Direct magazine (www.directmag.com) is a vital source of direct marketing information.

In the United States, direct marketing customers are more apt to be middle class. Mail shoppers are more likely to live in areas away from malls. Phone shoppers are more likely to live in upscale metropolitan areas; they want to avoid traffic and save time. The share of direct marketing purchases made by men has grown: The average consumer who buys direct spends several hundred dollars per year; and he or she wants convenience, unique products, and good prices.

Direct marketers can be divided into two broad categories: general and specialty. General direct marketing firms, such as Sears (with its mail-order and Web businesses) and QVC (with its cable TV and Web businesses), offer a full line of products and sell everything from clothing to housewares. Specialty direct marketers focus on more narrow product lines. L.L. Bean, Publishers Clearinghouse, and Franklin Mint are among the thousands of U.S. specialty firms. See Figure 6-3.

Direct marketing has a number of strategic business advantages:

- Many costs are reduced—low startup costs are possible; inventories are reduced; no displays are needed; a prime location is unnecessary; regularly staffed store hours are not important; a sales force may not be needed; and business may be run out of a garage or basement.
- It is possible for direct marketers to have lower prices (due to reduced costs) than store-based retailers with the same items. A huge geographic area can be covered inexpensively and efficiently.
- Customers shop conveniently—without crowds, parking congestion, or checkout lines. And they do not have safety concerns about shopping early in the morning or late at night.
- Specific consumer segments are pinpointed through targeted mailings.

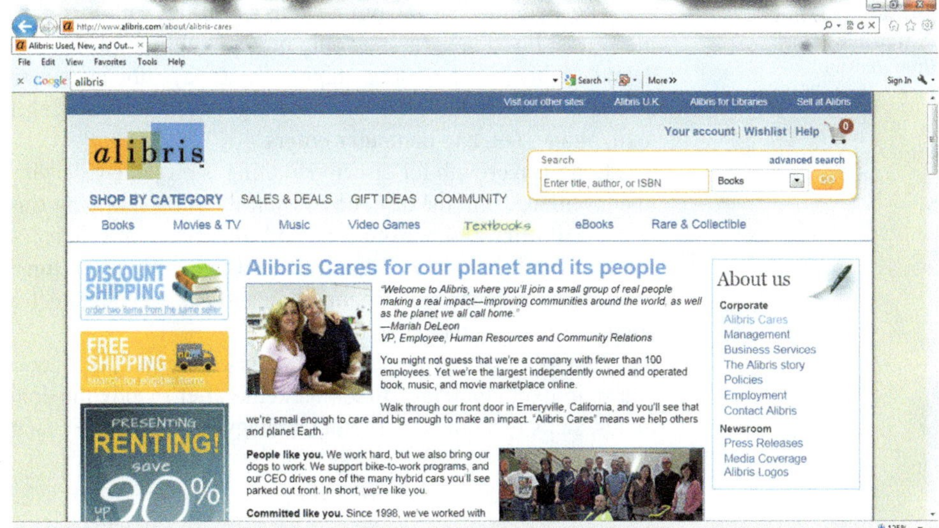

FIGURE 6-3

Alibris: A Socially Conscious Online Retailer of Books, Music, and Movies

Alibris is a specialized online marketplace for thousands of independent sellers of new and used books, music, and movies, as well as rare and collectible titles.

Source: Reprinted by permission of Alibris.

- Consumers may sometimes legally avoid sales tax by buying from direct marketers not having retail facilities in their state (however, some states want to eliminate this loophole).
- A store-based firm can supplement its regular business and expand its trading area (even becoming national or global) without adding outlets.

Direct marketing also has its limits, but they are not as critical as those for direct selling:

- Products cannot be examined before purchase. Thus, the range of items purchased is more limited than in stores, and companies need liberal return policies to attract and keep customers.
- Firms may underestimate costs. Catalogs can be expensive. A computer system is required to track shipments, purchases, and returns, and to keep lists current. A 24-hour phone staff may be needed.
- Even successful catalogs often draw purchases from less than 10 percent of recipients.
- Clutter exists. Each year, billions of E-mails and catalogs are mailed in the United States alone.
- Printed catalogs are prepared well in advance, causing difficulties in price and style planning.
- Some firms have given the industry a bad name due to delivery delays and shoddy goods.

Shauna Mei: AHAlife.com

Shauna Mei is the founder and CEO of AHAlife.com (www.ahalife.com), an online retailer that features hard-to-find luxury products. Mei has an unusual background for a retailer, since she graduated from Massachusetts Institute of Technology with an electrical engineering/computer science degree. Prior to establishing AHAlife, she worked at Goldman Sachs in investment banking and co-founded a research and investment firm specializing in luxury goods. Mei also served as chief operating officer of a Swedish wellness and activewear company.

AHAlife introduces one new product each day. Through an editorial-type format, the retailer's Web site tells a story about the product's manufacture, who made it, and where it was made. Products are chosen by such celebrity taste-makers as Bobbi Brown (make-up artist), Cynthia Rowley (fashion designer), Tina Brown (journalist and talk-show host), and Daniel Boulud (chef and restaurant owner).

Unlike department and specialty stores that employ professional buyers who scour the market for goods in a given merchandise category, AHAlife uses these and other experts to suggest goods based on their knowledge and experience. AHAlife also changes its featured products every day to generate continued interest in its site. Lastly, many of AHAlife's products are tied to social causes as they are made by groups such as Afghani widows or women in the Congo.

Source: Janet Groeber, "Curating the Conversation," *Stores* (June 2011).

The full 30-day rule is available online (http://business.ftc.gov/print/85).

The Federal Trade Commission's "30-day rule" is a U.S. regulation that affects direct marketers. It requires firms to ship orders within 30 days of their receipt or notify customers of delays. If an order cannot be shipped in 60 days, the customer must be given a specific delivery date and offered the option of canceling an order or waiting for it to be filled. The rule covers mail, phone, fax, and computer orders.

Long-run growth for direct marketing is projected, despite its limitations. Consumer interest in convenience and the difficulty in setting aside shopping time will continue. More direct marketers will offer 24-hour ordering and improve their efficiency. Greater product standardization and the prominence of well-known brands will reduce consumer perceptions of risk when buying from a catalog or the Web. Technological breakthroughs, such as purchases on smart phones, will attract more consumer shopping.

Due to its vast presence and immense potential, our detailed discussion is intended to give you an in-depth look into direct marketing. Let's study the domain of direct marketing, emerging trends, steps in a direct marketing strategy, and key issues facing direct marketers.

The Domain of Direct Marketing

As defined earlier, *direct marketing* is a form of retailing in which a consumer is exposed to a good or service through a nonpersonal medium and then orders by mail, phone, fax, or computer. It may also be viewed as a "data-driven, cross media, interactive, multi-channel process for building and cultivating mutually beneficial relationships between companies and their customers and prospects."[5]

Accordingly, we *do* include these as forms of direct marketing: any catalog; any mail, TV, radio, magazine, newspaper, phone directory, fax, or other ad; any computer-based transaction; or any other nonpersonal contact that stimulates customers to place orders by mail, phone, fax, or computer (counting interactive TV).

We *do not* include these as forms of direct marketing: (1) Direct selling—consumers are solicited by in-person sales efforts or seller-originated phone calls and the firm uses personal communication to initiate contact. (2) Conventional vending machines, whereby consumers are exposed to nonpersonal media but do not complete transactions via mail, phone, fax, or computer; they do not interact with the firm in a manner that allows a data base to be generated and kept.

Direct marketing *is* involved in many computerized kiosk transactions; when items are shipped to consumers, there is a company–customer interaction and a data base can be formed. Direct marketing is also in play when consumers originate phone calls, based on catalogs or ads they have seen.

The Customer Data Base: Key to Successful Direct Marketing

Because direct marketers often initiate contact with customers (in contrast to store shopping trips that are initiated by the consumer), it is imperative that they develop and maintain a comprehensive customer data base. They can then pinpoint their best customers, make offers aimed at specific customer needs, avoid costly mailings to nonresponsive shoppers, and track sales by customer. A good data base is the major asset of most direct marketers, and *every* thriving direct marketer has a strong data base.

Data-base retailing is a way to collect, store, and use relevant information about customers. Such information typically includes a person's name, address, background data, shopping interests, and purchase behavior. Although data bases are often compiled through large computerized information systems, they may also be used by small firms that are not overly computerized.

Here's an example of how data-base retailing can be beneficial:

> When a company can link customers' purchases to the offers that spurred them, the data provide valuable clues as to which goods and services should be offered next to those particular customers and prospects. Knowing more about target audiences' particular attitudes, propensities, and household composition provides clues about the channels, messages, and timing for the next offer. By understanding both customers' online and onsite shopping behavior, content can be further personalized to increase the likelihood of purchase while improving the customer experience.[6]

Data-base retailing is discussed further in Chapter 8.

Emerging Trends

Several trends are relevant for direct marketing: the evolving activities of direct marketers, changing consumer lifestyles, increased competition, the greater use of multi-channel retailing, the newer roles for catalogs and TV, technological advances, and the interest in global direct marketing. Online retailing is discussed in depth later in this chapter.

EVOLVING ACTIVITIES OF DIRECT MARKETERS Over the past 40 years, these direct marketing activities have evolved:

- Technology has moved to the forefront in all aspects of direct marketing—from lead generation to order processing.
- Multiple points of customer contact are offered by many more firms today.
- There is an increased focus on data-base retailing.
- Many more firms now have well-articulated and widely communicated privacy policies.

CHANGING CONSUMER LIFESTYLES Consumer lifestyles in America have shifted dramatically over the past several decades, mostly due to the large number of women who are now in the labor force and the longer commuting time to and from work for suburban residents. Many consumers no longer have the time or inclination to shop at stores. They are attracted by the ease of purchasing through direct marketing.

These are some of the factors consumers consider in selecting a direct marketer:

- Company reputation (image).
- Ability to shop whenever the consumer wants.
- Types of goods and services as well as the assortment and brand names carried.
- Availability of a toll-free phone number or Web site for ordering.
- Credit card acceptance.
- Speed of promised delivery time.
- Competitive prices.
- Satisfaction with past purchases and good return policies.
- Customer reviews and comments at retail sites and through social media.

INCREASED COMPETITION AMONG FIRMS As direct marketing sales have risen, so has competition; although there are a number of big firms, such as Sears and Spiegel, there are also thousands of small ones. According to the Direct Marketing Association, there are thousands of U.S. mail-order (and E-mail-based) companies alone.

Spiegel (www.spiegel.com) has largely been a direct marketer since the early 1900s. It faces more competition now than ever before.

Intense competition exists because entry into direct marketing is easier and less costly than entry into store retailing. A firm does not need a store; can operate with a small staff; and can use low-cost one-inch magazine ads, send brochures to targeted shoppers, and have an inexpensive Web site. It can keep a low inventory and place orders with suppliers after people buy items (as long as it meets the 30-day rule).

About one out of every two new direct marketers fails. Direct marketing lures many small firms that may poorly define their market niche, offer nondistinctive goods and services, have limited experience, misjudge the needed effort, have trouble with supplier continuity, and attract many consumer complaints.

GREATER USE OF MULTI-CHANNEL RETAILING Today, many stores add to their revenues by using ads, brochures, catalogs, and Web sites to obtain mail-order, phone, and computer-generated sales. They see that direct marketing is efficient, targets specific segments, appeals to people who might not otherwise shop with those firms, and needs a lower investment to reach other geographic areas than opening branch outlets.

REI—the outdoor recreational equipment chain—is a good example of a store-based retailer that has flourished with its distinctive multi-channel approach, winning several accolades along the way: For millions of "active members and other customers, REI provides the knowledge and confidence to explore and discover new adventures. We do this through frequent educational clinics and expert advice at our retail stores and at REI.com from trusted REI staff who share our members' passion for outdoor recreation. Above all, we provide a convenient and seamless shopping experience, whether at an REI retail store, online, by phone, or by mail order."[7]

NEWER ROLES FOR CATALOGS AND TV Direct marketers are recasting how they use their catalogs and their approach to TV retailing. We are witnessing three key changes in long-standing catalog tactics: (1) Many firms now print "specialogs" in addition to or instead of the annual catalogs showing all of their products. With a **specialog**, a retailer caters to a particular customer segment, emphasizes a limited number of items, and reduces production and postage costs (as a specialog is much shorter than a general catalog). Each year, such firms as Spiegel, L.L. Bean, and Travelsmith send out separate specialogs by market segment or occasion. (2) To help defray costs, some companies accept ads from noncompeting firms that are compatible with their image. (3) To stimulate sales and defray costs, some catalogs are sold in bookstores, supermarkets, and airports, and at company Web sites. The percentage of consumers buying a catalog who actually make a purchase is far higher than that for those who get catalogs in the mail.

TV retailing has two major components (not including interactive TV shopping, which is just getting off the ground): shopping networks and infomercials. On a *shopping network*, the programming focuses on merchandise presentations and their sales (usually by phone). The two biggest players are cable giants QVC and Home Shopping Network (HSN), with combined annual worldwide revenues of $11 billion. QVC has access to a global TV audience of 200 million households, and HSN has access to 100 million households. About 10 percent of U.S. consumers buy goods through TV shopping programs each year. Once regarded as a medium primarily for shut-ins and the lower middle class, the typical TV-based shopper is now younger, more fashion-conscious, and as apt to be from a high-income household as the overall U.S. population. QVC and HSN feature jewelry, women's clothing, and personal-care items and do not focus on leading brands. Most items must be bought when they are shown to encourage shoppers to act quickly. Both firms have active Web sites (www.qvc.com and www.hsn.com).[8]

George Foreman became a very rich man through his infomercials for grills (www.georgeforemancooking.com).

An **infomercial** is a program-length TV commercial (typically, 30 minutes) for a specific good or service that airs on cable or broadcast television, often at a fringe time. As they watch an infomercial, shoppers call in orders, which are delivered to them. Infomercials work well for products that benefit from demonstrations. Good infomercials present detailed information, include customer testimonials, are entertaining, and are divided into timed segments (since the average viewer watches only a few minutes at a time) with ordering information displayed in every segment. Infomercials account for several billion dollars in annual U.S. revenues. Popular infomercials include those for the Bowflex Home Gym, Proactiv Acne Treatment, Ronco Showtime Rotisserie, Iconic Breeze Air purifier, Snuggie, and ShamWow.[9] The Electronic Retailing Association (www.retailing.org) is the trade association for infomercial firms.

TECHNOLOGICAL ADVANCES The technology revolution is improving operating efficiency and offering enhanced sales opportunities:

- Market segments can be better targeted. Through selective binding, bigger catalogs are sent to the best customers and shorter catalogs to new prospects.
- Firms inexpensively use computers to enter mail and phone orders, arrange for shipments, and monitor inventory on hand.
- It is simple to set up and maintain computerized data bases using inexpensive software.
- Huge, automated distribution centers efficiently accumulate and ship orders.
- Customers dial toll-free phone numbers or visit Web sites to place orders and get information. The cost per call for the direct marketer is quite low.
- Consumers can conclude transactions from more sites, including kiosks at airports and train stations.
- Cable and satellite programming and the Web offer 24-hour shopping and ordering.
- In-home, at-work, and leisure-time Web-based shopping transactions can be conducted.

Lands' End has many different Web sites to service customers around the world, such as its French site (www.fr.landsend.com). Because of Lands' End's customer commitment, this site is in French.

MOUNTING INTEREST IN GLOBAL DIRECT MARKETING More retailers are involved with global direct marketing because of the growing consumer acceptance of nonstore retailing in other countries. Among the U.S.-based direct marketers with a significant international presence are Brookstone, Eddie Bauer, Lands' End, and Williams-Sonoma.

Outside the United States, annual direct marketing sales (by both domestic and foreign firms) are hundreds of billions of dollars. Direct marketing trade associations—each representing many member firms—exist in such diverse countries as Australia, Brazil, China, France, Germany, Japan,

ETHICS IN RETAILING

Rising Concerns About Online Privacy

As a result of a recent federal U.S. district court case, retailers need to pay more attention to the way they present their online privacy policies. In that case, Bresnan Communications (www.bresnan.com), an Internet service provider, allowed NebuAd Inc. to install a device on Bresnan's network that tracked and analyzed customers' Web surfing behavior. NebuAd then was able to create a profile of Bresnan's customers based on their specific Web-browsing history.

The district court concluded that Bresnan accessed customers' computers with proper authorization because the customers had consented to give their E-mail addresses to third parties. However, it also ruled that Bresnan "exceeded authorization" since it did not inform customers that its cookies would alter their privacy and security settings. In a related case, the Federal Trade Commission charged that Sears and Kmart did not adequately disclose the amount of personal information collected from users who downloaded a certain software application.

As a result of these cases, legal experts believe that retailers seeking to access customer Web data must have a specific privacy policy, transmit multiple notices to their customers (such as a privacy policy and an online subscriber agreement), and provide customers with an opt-out option.

Source: David Mirchin, "Getting Down to the Basics of a Solid Privacy Policy," *Information Today* (February 2011), pp. 34–35.

Russia, and Spain. In Europe alone, there are well over 10,000 direct marketing companies; and the emerging Indian direct marketing arena features hundreds of firms, domestic and international.[10]

The Steps in a Direct Marketing Strategy

A direct marketing strategy has eight steps: business definition, generating customers, media selection, presenting the message, customer contact, customer response, order fulfillment, and measuring results and maintaining the data base. See Figure 6-4.

BUSINESS DEFINITION First, a company makes two decisions regarding its business definition: (1) Is the firm going to be a pure direct marketer, or is it going to engage in multi-channel retailing? If the firm chooses the latter, it must clarify the role of direct marketing in its overall retail strategy. (2) Is the firm going to be a general direct marketer and carry a broad product assortment, or will it specialize in one goods/service category?

GENERATING CUSTOMERS A mechanism for generating business is devised next. A firm can:

- Buy a printed mailing list or an E-mail list from a broker. For one mailing, a list usually costs up to $50 to $100 or more per 1,000 names and addresses; if printed, it is supplied in mailing-label format. Lists may be broad or broken down by gender, location, and so on. In purchasing a list, the direct marketer should check its currency.
- Download a mailing list from the Web that is sold by a firm such as infoUSA (www.infousa.com), which has data on the home addresses of 100 million U.S. households. With a download, a retailer can use the list multiple times, but it is responsible for selecting names and printing labels.

FIGURE 6-4
Executing a Direct Marketing Strategy

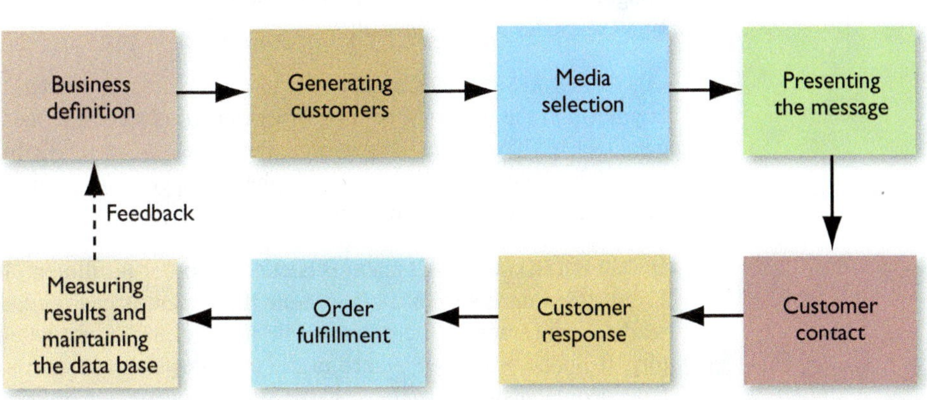

- Send out a blind mailing to all the residents in a particular area. This method can be expensive (unless done through E-mail) and may receive a very low response rate.
- Advertise in a newspaper, magazine, Web site, or other medium, and ask customers to order by mail, phone, fax, or computer.
- Contact consumers who have bought from the firm or requested information. This is efficient, but it takes a while to develop a data base. To grow, a firm cannot rely solely on past customers.

MEDIA SELECTION Several media are available to the direct marketer:

- Printed and/or online catalogs.
- Direct mail ads and brochures.
- Inserts with monthly credit card and other bills ("statement stuffers").
- Freestanding displays with coupons, brochures, or catalogs (such as magazine subscription cards at the supermarket checkout counter).
- Ads or programs in the mass media—newspapers, magazines, radio, TV.
- Banner ads or "hot links" on the World Wide Web.
- Video kiosks.

In choosing among media, costs, distribution, lead time, and other factors should be considered.

PRESENTING THE MESSAGE Now, the firm prepares and presents its message in a way that engenders interest, creates (or sustains) the proper image, points out compelling reasons to purchase, and provides data about goods or services (such as prices and sizes). The message must also contain ordering instructions, including the payment method; how to designate the chosen items; shipping fees; and a firm's address, phone number, and Web address.

The message, and the medium in which it is presented, should be planned in the same way that a traditional retailer plans a store. The latter uses a storefront, lighting, carpeting, the store layout, and displays to foster an image. In direct marketing, the headlines, message content, use of color, paper quality, personalization of mail, space devoted to each item, and other elements affect a firm's image.

CUSTOMER CONTACT For each campaign, a direct marketer decides whether to contact all customers in its data base or to seek specific market segments (with different messages and/or media for each). It can classify prospective customers as *regulars* (those who buy continuously), *nonregulars* (those who buy infrequently), *new contacts* (those who have never been sought before by the firm), and *nonrespondents* (those who have been contacted but never made a purchase).

Regulars and nonregulars are the most apt to respond to a firm's future offerings, and they can be better targeted because the firm has their purchase histories. For example, customers who have bought clothing before are prime prospects for specialogs. New contacts probably know little about the firm. Messages to them must build interest, accurately portray the firm, and present meaningful reasons for consumers to buy. This group is important if growth is sought.

Nonrespondents who have been contacted repeatedly without purchasing are unlikely to ever buy. Unless a firm can present a very different message, it is inefficient to pursue this group. Firms such as Publishers Clearinghouse send mailings to millions of people who have never bought from them; this is okay because they sell inexpensive impulse items and need only a small response rate to succeed.

CUSTOMER RESPONSE Customers respond to direct marketers in one of three ways: (1) They buy through the mail, phone, fax, or computer. (2) They request further information, such as a catalog. (3) They ignore the message. Purchases are generally made by no more than 2 to 3 percent of those contacted. The rate is higher for specialogs, mail-order clubs (e.g., for music), and firms focusing on repeat customers.

ORDER FULFILLMENT A system is needed for order fulfillment. If orders are received by mail or fax, the firm must sort them, determine if payment is enclosed, see whether the item is in stock, mail announcements if items cannot be sent on time, coordinate shipments, and replenish inventory. If phone orders are placed, a trained sales staff must be available when people may call. Salespeople answer questions, make suggestions, enter orders, note the payment method, see whether items are in stock, coordinate shipments, and replenish inventory. If orders are placed by computer, there must be a process to promptly and efficiently handle credit transactions, issue receipts, and forward orders to a warehouse. In all cases, names, addresses, and purchase data are added to the data base for future reference.

In peak seasons, additional warehouse, shipping, order processing, and sales workers supplement regular employees. Direct marketers that are highly regarded by consumers fill orders promptly, have knowledgeable and courteous personnel, do not misrepresent quality, and provide liberal return policies.

MEASURING RESULTS AND MAINTAINING THE DATA BASE The last step is analyzing results and maintaining the data base. Direct marketing often yields clear outcomes:

- *Overall response rate*—the number and percentage of people who make a purchase after receiving or viewing a particular brochure, catalog, or Web site.
- *Average purchase amount*—by customer location, gender, and so forth.
- *Sales volume by product category*—revenues correlated with the space allotted to each product in brochures, catalogs, and so forth.
- *Value of list brokers*—the revenues generated by various mailing lists.

After measuring results, the firm reviews its data base and makes sure that new shoppers are added, address changes are noted for existing customers, purchase and consumer information is current and available in segmentation categories, and nonrespondents are purged (when desirable).

This stage provides feedback for the direct marketer as it plans each new campaign.

Key Issues Facing Direct Marketers

In planning and applying their strategies, direct marketers must keep the following in mind.

Many people dislike one or more aspects of direct marketing. They are the most dissatisfied with late delivery or nondelivery, deceptive claims, broken or damaged items, the wrong items being sent, and the lack of information. Nonetheless, in most cases, leading direct marketers are rated well by consumers.

Most U.S. households report that they open all direct mail, but many would like to receive less of it. Because the average American household receives numerous catalogs each year, besides hundreds of other mailings, firms must be concerned about clutter. It is hard to be distinctive in this environment.

A lot of consumers are concerned that their names and other information are being sold by list brokers, as well as by some retailers. They feel this is an invasion of privacy and that their decision to purchase does not constitute permission to pass on personal data. To counteract this, members of the Direct Marketing Association remove people's names from list circulation if they make a request.

Multi-channel retailers need a consistent image for both store-based and direct marketing efforts. They must also perceive the similarities and differences in each approach's strategy. The steady increase in postal rates makes mailing catalogs, brochures, and other promotional materials costly for some firms. Numerous direct marketers are turning more to newspapers, magazines, and cable TV—and the Web.

Direct marketers must monitor the legal environment. They must be aware that, in the future, more states will probably require residents to pay sales tax on out-of-state direct marketing purchases; the firms would have to remit the tax payments to affected states. New laws will be contested by retailers.

DIRECT SELLING

Direct selling includes both personal contact with consumers in their homes (and other nonstore locations such as offices) and phone solicitations initiated by a retailer. See Figure 6-5. Cosmetics, jewelry, vitamins, household goods and services (such as carpet cleaning), vacuum cleaners, and magazines and newspapers are among the items sometimes sold in this way. The industry has $29 billion in annual U.S. sales and employs 16 million people (more than 90 percent part-time). Annual foreign direct selling revenues are an additional $105 billion, generated by 72 million salespeople.[11] Table 6-1 shows a U.S. industry overview.

FIGURE 6-5

Direct Selling Via Telemarketing

With telemarketing, trained salespeople interact with customers virtually anywhere. They describe product features, answer questions, arrange for payment and shipping, and follow-up to see if customers are satisfied after purchasing. However, today, many people feel that telemarketing is too intrusive.

Source: Yuri Arcurs/ Shutterstock.com. Reprinted by permission.

TABLE 6-1 A Snapshot of the U.S. Direct Selling Industry

Major Product Groups (as a percent of sales dollars)	
Home and family care products/home durables	24.4
Wellness (weight loss products, vitamins, etc.)	23.0
Personal care	19.4
Services (travel, real-estate) and other	19.2
Clothing and accessories	11.0
Leisure/educational (books, encyclopedias, toys/games, etc.)	3.0
Sales Strategy (method used to generate sales, as a percent of sales dollars)	
Individual/one-to-one selling	63.5
Party plan/group sales	27.9
Customer placing order directly with firm	7.5
Other	1.1
Demographics of Salespeople (as a percent of all salespeople)	
Female/male	81.8/18.2
Part time/full time	91.1/8.9
Education (high school grad or less/at least some college)	28.0/72.0
Married/not married	77.0/23.0
Place of Sales (as a percent of sales dollars)	
In the home	73.0
Over the Internet	7.0
Over the phone	6.0
Automatic shipments to customers	5.0
At a temporary location (such as a fair, exhibition, shopping mall, etc.)	3.0
In a workplace	2.0
Other locations	4.0

Sources: "Fact Sheet: U.S. Direct Selling in 2010," http://dsa.org/research/industry-statistics/10gofactsheet.pdf; and authors' estimates.

The Direct Selling Association (www.dsa.org) is working hard to promote the image and professionalism of this retail format.

A direct-selling strategy emphasizes convenient shopping and a personal touch, and detailed demonstrations can be made. Consumers often relax more in their homes than in stores. They are also apt to be attentive and are not exposed to competing brands (as in stores). For some, such as older consumers and those with young children, in-store shopping is hard due to limited mobility. For the retailer, direct selling has lower overhead costs because stores and fixtures are not necessary.

Despite its advantages, direct selling in the United States is growing slowly:

- Online transactions are easier and offer many more seller product options for shoppers.
- More women work, and they may not be interested in or available for at-home selling.
- The desire for full-time careers and job opportunities in other fields have reduced the pool of people interested in direct selling jobs.
- A firm's market coverage is limited by the size of its sales force.
- Sales productivity is low because the average transaction is small and most consumers are unreceptive—many will not open their doors to salespeople or talk to telemarketers.
- Sales force turnover is high because employees are often poorly supervised part-timers.
- To stimulate sales personnel, compensation is usually 25 to 50 percent of the revenues they generate. This means average to above-average prices.
- There are various legal restrictions due to deceptive and high-pressure sales tactics. One such restriction is the FTC's Telemarketing Sales Rule (www.ftc.gov/bcp/rulemaking/tsr), which mandates that firms must disclose their identity and that the purpose of the call is selling.
- Because *door-to-door* has a poor image, the industry prefers the term *direct selling*.

Firms are reacting to these issues. Avon places greater emphasis on workplace sales, offers free training to sales personnel, rewards the best workers with better territories, pursues more global sales, and places cosmetics kiosks in shopping centers. Mary Kay hires community residents as salespeople and has a party atmosphere rather than a strict door-to-door approach; this requires networks of family, friends, and neighbors. And every major direct selling firm has a Web site to supplement revenues.

Among the leading direct sellers are Avon and Mary Kay (cosmetics), Amway (household supplies), Tupperware (plastic containers), Shaklee (health products), Fuller Brush (small household products), and Kirby (vacuum cleaners). Some stores, such as J.C. Penney, also use direct selling. Penney's decorator consultants sell a complete line of furnishings, not available in its stores, to consumers in their homes (www.jcpenneycustomdecorating.com).

TECHNOLOGY IN RETAILING

Internet Retail 2.0

Internet Retail 2.0 (www.retail20.com) comprises Web-based retail startups that work with Amazon.com or other major online retailers. Unlike Internet retailers that closed down after the 2000 dot.com bust, these new retailers utilize cloud computing, have advanced delivery systems, and/or have strong social relationships with their customers.

One Internet Retail 2.0 client is Quidsi (www.quidsi.com), an online retailer that sells diapers, baby products, soap, and cosmetics. According to Leonard Lodish, a Quidsi board member who is also a marketing professor, the retailer has a highly efficient distribution system characterized by the use of robots to fulfill orders. It also uses software technology that automatically calculates the proper box size for individual orders. Lodish views Quidsi's most important asset as its relationship with new parents, who often need advice on their purchases. Quidsi was acquired by Amazon.com for $500 million in November 2010.

Other examples of Internet 2.0 retailers are Zappos (www.zappos.com) and Warby Parker (www.warbyparker.com). Zappos reduces the perceived risk of consumers in buying shoes through its liberal return policy. It was acquired by Amazon.com in July 2009 for $850 million. Warby Parker's site enables consumers to upload photos so they can see how they will look wearing different eyeglass styles and colors.

Source: "Many-Stop Shopping? How Niche Retailers Are Thriving on Internet 2.0," http://knowledge.wharton.upenn.edu (May 11, 2011).

VENDING MACHINES

The Canteen Corporation (www.canteen.com) has vending machines at thousands of client locations.

A **vending machine** is a cash- or card-operated retailing format that dispenses goods (such as beverages) and services (such as electronic arcade games). It eliminates the use of sales personnel and allows 24-hour sales. Machines can be placed wherever convenient for consumers—inside or outside stores, in motel corridors, at train stations, or on street corners. See Figure 6-6.

Although there have been many attempts to "vend" clothing, magazines, and other general merchandise, more than 95 percent of the $45 billion in annual U.S. vending machine sales involve hot and cold beverages and food items. Because of health issues, over the past 40 years, cigarettes' share of sales has gone from 25 to less than 1 percent. The greatest sales at are public places such as service stations and at offices; colleges, universities, and elementary schools; factories; and hospitals and nursing homes. Newspapers on street corners and sidewalks, various machines in hotels and motels, and candy machines in restaurants and at train stations are visible aspects of vending but account for a small percentage of U.S. vending machine sales.[12] Leading vending machine operators are Canteen Corporation and Aramark Refreshment Services.

Items priced above $1.50 have not sold well; too many coins are required, and some vending machines do not have dollar bill changers. Consumers are reluctant to buy more expensive items that they cannot see displayed or have explained. However, their expanded access to and

FIGURE 6-6

Vending Machines: Popular Around the Globe

Vending machines can pop up everywhere, including this food-and-beverage vending machine in Moscow, Russia.

Source: nikshor/Shutterstock.com. Reprinted by permission.

use of debit cards are having an impact on resolving the payment issue, and the video-kiosk type of vending machine lets people see product displays and get detailed information (and then place a credit or debit card order). Popular brands and standardized nonfood items are best suited to increasing sales via vending machines.

To improve productivity and customer relations, vending operators are applying several innovations. Popular products such as French fries are being made fresh in vending machines. Machine malfunctions are reduced by applying electronic mechanisms to cash-handling controls. Microprocessors track consumer preferences, trace malfunctions, and record receipts. Some machines have voice synthesizers that are programmed to say "Thank you, come again" or "Your change is 25 cents."

Operators must still deal with theft, vandalism, stockouts, above-average prices, and the perception that vending machines should be patronized only when a fill-in convenience item is needed.

ELECTRONIC RETAILING: THE EMERGENCE OF THE WORLD WIDE WEB

We are living through enormous changes from the days when retailing simply meant visiting a store, shopping from a printed catalog, greeting the Avon lady in one's home, or buying candy from a vending machine. Who would have thought that a person could "surf the Web" (sometimes, on the phone, no less) to research a stock, learn about a new product, search for bargains, save a trip to the store, and complain about customer service? These activities are real and they're here to stay. Let's look at the World Wide Web from a retailing perspective, remembering that selling on the Web is a form of direct marketing.

Let's define two terms that may be confusing: The **Internet** is a global electronic superhighway of computer networks that use a common protocol and that are linked by telecommunications lines and satellite. It acts as a single, cooperative virtual network and is maintained by universities, governments, and businesses. The **World Wide Web (Web)** is one way to access information on the Internet, whereby people work with easy-to-use Web addresses (sites) and pages. Users see words, charts, pictures, and video, and hear audio—which turn their computers, smart phones, and tablets into interactive multimedia centers. People can easily move from site to site by pointing at the proper spot on the screen and clicking a mouse button. Browsing software, such as Microsoft Internet Explorer, Mozilla Firefox, Google Chrome, and Apple Safari facilitate Web surfing.

Both *Internet* and *World Wide Web* convey the same central theme: online interactive retailing. Because almost all online retailing is done via the World Wide Web, we use *Web* in our discussion, which is comprised of these topics: the role of the Web, the scope of Web retailing, characteristics of Web users, factors to consider in planning whether to have a Web site, and examples of Web retailers. Visit our Web site (www.pearsonhighered.com/bermanevans) for valuable links on E-retailing.

The Role of the Web

From the vantage point of the retailer, the World Wide Web can serve one or more roles:

- Project a retail presence and enhance the retailer's image.
- Generate sales as the major source of revenue for an online retailer or as a complementary source of revenue for a store-based retailer.
- Reach geographically dispersed consumers, including foreign ones.
- Provide information to consumers about products carried, store locations, usage information, answers to common questions, customer loyalty programs, and so on.
- Promote new products and fully explain and demonstrate their features.
- Furnish customer service in the form of E-mail, "hot links," and other communications.
- Be more "personal" with consumers by letting them point and click on topics they choose.
- Conduct a retail business in a cost-efficient manner.
- Obtain customer feedback and reviews, and encourage "conversations" via social media.
- Promote special offers and send coupons to Web customers.
- Describe employment opportunities.
- Present information to potential investors, potential franchisees, and the media.

The role a retailer assigns to the Web depends on (1) whether its major goal is to communicate interactively with consumers, sell goods and services, or emphasize both of these activities; (2) whether it is predominantly a traditional retailer that wants to have a Web presence or a newer firm that wants to derive most or all of its sales from the Web; and (3) the level of resources the retailer wants to commit to site development and maintenance. There are millions of Web sites worldwide and hundreds of thousands in retailing.

The Scope of Web Retailing

Internet Retailer (www.internetretailer.com) tracks online retailing.

The potential for online retailing is enormous: As of 2012, there were 275 million Web users in North America, 475 million in Europe, 950 million in Asia-Pacific, 225 million in Latin America, and 125 million in Africa/the Middle East. More than 90 percent of U.S. Web users have made at least one online purchase; and more than three-quarters have made at least one online purchase in the last six months. A decade ago, U.S. shoppers generated 75 percent of worldwide online retail sales; the amount is now one-third and falling.

Despite the recent weak economy, Web-generated revenues have steadily increased; and in the United States, 90 percent of current purchases are made by those with broadband connections (rather than dial-up). Mobile U.S. Web retailing is expected to reach more than $30 billion annually by 2016. Globally, 44 percent of Internet users do less than 5 percent of their total monthly shopping online, 29 percent do 6 to 10 percent of shopping online, 18 percent do 11 to 25 percent of shopping online, 7 percent do 26 to 50 percent of shopping online, and 2 percent do more than one-half of their shopping online.[13] Figure 6-7 indicates the percentage of global consumers intending to make online purchases by selected product category.

Despite the foregoing data, the Web accounts for only 5 percent or so of U.S. retail sales! It will not be the death knell of store-based retailing but another choice for shoppers, like other forms of direct marketing. There is much higher sales growth for "clicks-and-mortar" Web retailing (multi-channel retailing) than "bricks-and-mortar" stores (single-channel retailing) and "clicks-only" Web firms (single-channel retailing). Store-based retailers account for more than three-quarters of U.S. online sales.

FIGURE 6-7
Global Consumers' Online Retail Purchase Intent (Selected Product Categories)

Source: Chart developed by the authors from data in "Gobal Trends in Online Shopping" www.nielsen.com (June 2010).

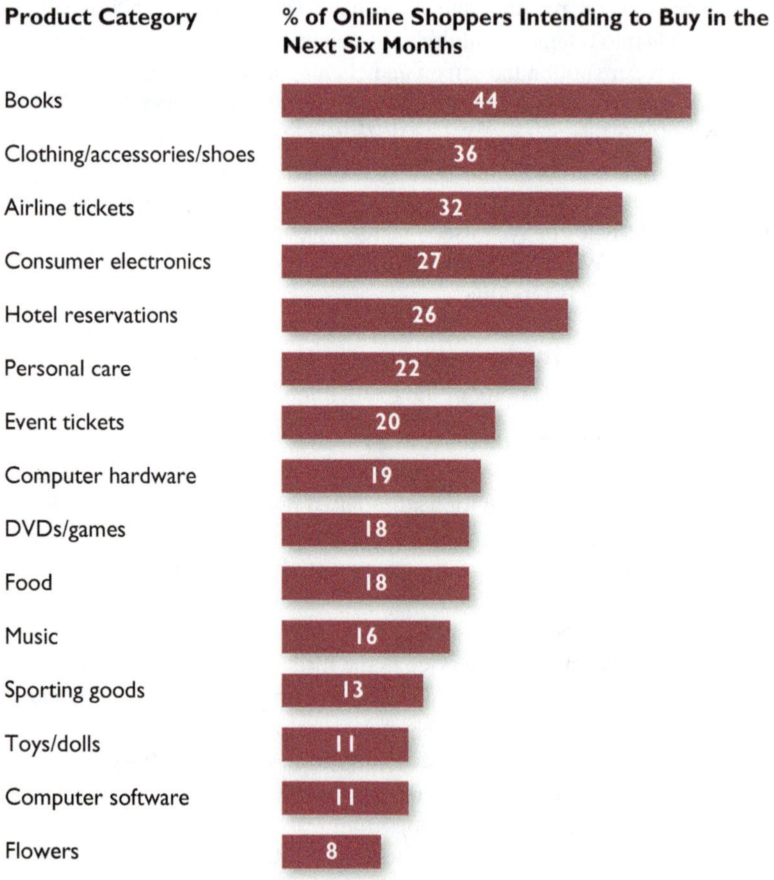

Product Category	% of Online Shoppers Intending to Buy in the Next Six Months
Books	44
Clothing/accessories/shoes	36
Airline tickets	32
Consumer electronics	27
Hotel reservations	26
Personal care	22
Event tickets	20
Computer hardware	19
DVDs/games	18
Food	18
Music	16
Sporting goods	13
Toys/dolls	11
Computer software	11
Flowers	8

There will be times when the consumer will buy from the retailer online, and times when they buy when visiting the store. "Grab and go" is a very profitable retail option. This is where the customer orders online and then drops in to grab the product as they pass the store. As retailers, we need to get into the same "head space" as consumers and their changing habits. The future may mean that less stock is displayed in-store, but it is displayed with more flair as the space is now available for you to create displays that make the consumer go Wow![14]

Characteristics of Web Users

U.S. Web users have these characteristics, which are highlighted in Figure 6-8:

- *Gender.* There are almost as many males as females on the Web; however, females shop more often.
- *Age.* Eighteen- to 29-year-olds are most likely to use the Web; those 65 and older are least likely.
- *Community type.* Suburban and urban residents are somewhat more apt to use the Web than rural residents.
- *Income.* Just over three-fifths of households with an annual income under $30,000 use the Web; in contrast, 96 percent of households with an annual income of at least $75,000 use the Web.
- *Education.* Those who have attended college are more likely to use the Internet as those who have not, especially those with less than a high school degree.

These are some key factors to online shoppers with regard to their continued patronage: (1) *Web site design/interaction*—"Includes all elements of the consumer's experience at the Web site (except for customer service), including navigation, information search, order processing, shipment tracking, product availability, and product and price offerings." (2) *Fulfillment/reliability*—"Customers receive what they thought they ordered based on the display and description provided at the Web site and/or delivery of the right product at the right price (i.e., billed correctly) in good condition within the time frame promised." (3) *Customer service*—"Helpful, responsive service that responds to customer inquiries and returns/complaints quickly during or after the sale." (4) *Security/privacy*—"The security of credit-card payments and the privacy of shared information during or after the sale."[15]

Web users can be enticed to shop more often if they are assured of privacy, retailers are perceived as trustworthy, sites are easy to maneuver, prices are lower than at stores, there are strong money-back guarantees, they can return a product to a store, shipping costs are not hidden until the end of the purchase process, transactions are secure, they can speak with sales representatives, download time is fast, and the retailer has smart phone and tablet apps available.

FIGURE 6-8
A Snapshot of U.S. Web Users

Source: Charts developed by the authors from data in "Demographics of Internet Users," www.pewinternet.org (May 2011).

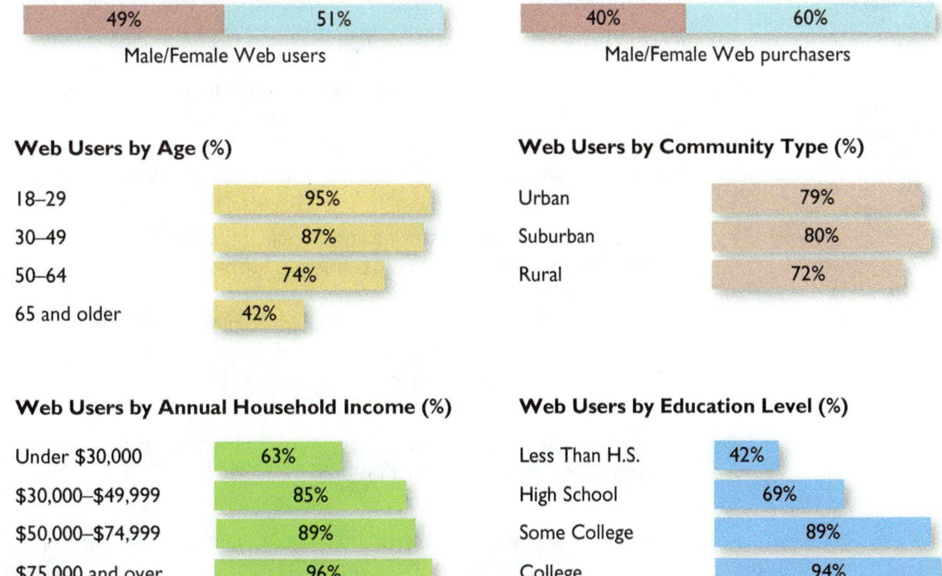

Factors to Consider in Planning Whether to Have a Web Site

The Web generally offers many *advantages* for retailers. It is usually less costly to operate a Web site than a store. The potential marketplace is huge and dispersed, yet relatively easy to reach. Web sites can be quite exciting, due to their multimedia capabilities. People can visit Web sites at any time, and their visits can be as short or as long as they desire. Information can be targeted, so that, for example, a person visiting a toy retailer's Web site could click on the icon labeled "Educational Toys—ages three to six." A customer data base can be established and customer feedback obtained.

The Web also has *disadvantages* for retailers: If consumers do not know a firm's Web address, it may be hard to find. For various reasons, some people are not yet willing to buy online. There is tremendous clutter with regard to the number of Web sites. Because Web surfers are easily bored, a Web site must be regularly updated to ensure repeat visits. The more multimedia features a Web site has, the slower it may be for people with dial-up connections to access. Some firms have been overwhelmed with customer service requests and questions from E-mail. It may be hard to coordinate store and Web transactions. There are few standards or rules as to what may be portrayed at Web sites. Consumers expect online services to be free and are reluctant to pay for them.

There is a large gulf between full-scale, integrated Web selling and a basic "telling"—rather than "selling"—Web site. A "telling" site emphasizes information about the retailer and where its stores are located; little attention is devoted to making transactions. A "selling" site includes the features of a telling site, but is also a dynamic transaction-oriented approach; it has all the bells and whistles that online shoppers have come to expect. In developing and implementing the proper online retailing strategy, a well-conceived and step-by-step approach is imperative, as shown in Figure 6-9. The retailer needs to determine everything from the customer base

FIGURE 6-9

The Stages in Devising and Implementing an Online Retailing Strategy

Sources: Chart developed by the authors from tips at "Six Things to Consider If You Are New to E-Commerce," www.networksolutions.com/e-commerce/new-to-ecommerce.jsp (March 3, 2012); "Key Issues in Implementing an E-Commerce Strategy," www.powerhomebiz.com/vol103/implement.htm (December 29, 2011); and Diane Buzzeo, "Retail Online Integration: Four Steps Every Online Retailer Can Take Right Now to Drive Sales," www.retailonlineintegration.com (June 20, 2011).

1. Be sure there is a customer base interested in your having an online retail business: Who will shop online? Why? What do they want in online shopping?
2. The two options in starting out are (a) going from store-based retailing to a store-plus-online presence, or (b) beginning as an online retailer. Note: The first option has a customer following and name recognition—at least among its store-based customers.
3. Select a Web address (URL) that is distinctive and easy-to-remember. This may be hard given that many addresses have already been taken. So, be creative.
4. Design the Web site through do-it-yourself software (or have the site professionally designed by a specialist) and prepare content to appear on the site. "Your Web site design must do far more than appeal to the eye—it must convince visitors to stick around and complete transactions."Be sure to use navigation that is simple and clear. Have your competitive advantages stand out. Use photos with good resolution. Have "about us," "products," "buy," "add to cart," and "shipping" buttons be highly visible. Regularly update content for both visitors and search engines.
5. Make purchasing easy and secure. Offer multiple payment options, with PayPal the simplest format for smaller retailers (it accepts leading credit/debit cards). Have an SSL (secure sockets layer) certificate and display it to allay shoppers' privacy fears. State policies for cancellations, returns, and shipping. Send E-mails confirming orders and enable customers to track their orders.
6. Have logistics in place for storing and shipping merchandise. Have shippers lined up. Monitor order fulfillment and inventory. Coordinate store and online transactions, if engaged in both.
7. Promote the Web site as much as possible—online and offline. Be sure the site is search engine optimized (SEO) for Google, Bing, etc., with regard to key words, headings, and so forth. Use opt-in E-mail to stay in touch with customers.
8. After the online business is running well, become more engaged with social media. This presents a "networking opportunity that no online retailer can afford to miss."
9. Measure performance and revise the strategy as needed. If shopping cart abandonment (whereby the shopper stops when at the payment stage of the process) is high, the causes must be remedied.

to the Web site design to the purchase process to shipping to social media, and then measure performance.[16]

Sign up for eMarketer's free daily newsletter with regular summaries of E-retailing news (www.emarketer.com/Newsletter.aspx).

Web retailers should carefully consider these recommendations, which build on Figure 6-9, compiled from several industry experts:

- Develop (or exploit) a well-known, trustworthy retailer name.
- Tailor the product assortment for Web shoppers, and keep freshening the offerings.
- With download speed in mind, provide pictures and ample product information.
- Enable the shopper to make as few clicks as possible to get product information and place orders.
- Provide the best possible search engine at the firm's Web site.
- Capitalize on customer information and relationships.
- Integrate online and offline businesses, and look for partnering opportunities.
- With permission, save customer data to make future shopping trips easier.
- Indicate shipping fees upfront and be clear about delivery options.
- Do not promote items that are out of stock; and let shoppers know immediately if items will not be shipped for a few days.
- Offer online order tracking.
- Use a secure order entry system for shoppers.
- Prominently state the firm's return and privacy policies.

See the checklist in Figure 6-10.

A firm cannot just put up a site and wait for consumers to visit it in droves and then expect them to happily return. In many cases: (1) It is still difficult for people to find exactly what they are looking for. (2) Once the person finds what he or she wants, it may be hard to envision the product. "Subtleties of color and texture often don't come across well on the Web. Until someone figures out how to send a cashmere scarf digitally, you won't be able to touch it." (3) Customer service may be lacking. (4) Web sites and their store siblings may not be in sync. "Send someone

FIGURE 6-10

A Checklist of Retailer Decisions in Utilizing the Web

✓ What are the company's Web goals? At what point is it expected that the site will be profitable?
✓ What budget will be allocated to developing and maintaining a Web site?
✓ Who will develop and maintain the Web site, the retailer itself or an outside specialist?
✓ Should the firm set up an independent Web site for itself or should it be part of a "cybermall?"
✓ What features will the Web site have? What level of customer service will be offered?
✓ What information will the Web site provide?
✓ How will the goods and services assortment differ at the Web site from the firm's store?
✓ Will the Web site offer benefits not available elsewhere?
✓ Will prices reflect a good value for the consumer?
✓ How fast will the user be able to download the text and images from the Web site, and point and click from screen to screen?
✓ How often will Web site content be changed?
✓ What staff will handle Web inquiries and transactions?
✓ How fast will turnaround time be for Web inquiries and transactions?
✓ How will the firm coordinate store and Web transactions and customer interactions?
✓ What will be done to avoid crashes and slow site features during peak shopping hours and seasons?
✓ How will online orders be processed?
✓ How easy will it be for shoppers to enter and complete orders?
✓ What online payment methods will be accepted?
✓ What search engines (such as Yahoo!) will list the retailer's Web site?
✓ How will the site be promoted: (a) on the Web and (b) by the company?
✓ How will Web data be stored and arranged? How will all of the firm's information systems be integrated?
✓ How will Web success be measured?
✓ How will the firm determine which Web shoppers are new customers and which are customers who would otherwise visit a company store?
✓ How will the firm ensure secure (encrypted) transactions?
✓ How will consumer privacy concerns be handled?
✓ How will returns and customer complaints be handled?

a gift from CompanyA.com and the recipient may be surprised to find it can't be returned or exchanged at a Company A store." (5) Privacy policies may not be not consumer-oriented. "Order from a site, fill out a survey, or merely browse, and you find your E-mail box swamped with unsolicited ads and other junk."[17]

Examples of Web Retailing in Action

These examples show the breadth of retailing on the World Wide Web.

Amazon.com (www.amazon.com) is probably the most famous pure Web retailer in the world, with revenues exceeding $8 billion and tens of millions of customers purchasing from the firm each year. This is how *Hoover's* sums up the Amazon.com phenomenon:

> What began as Earth's biggest bookstore has become Earth's biggest everything store. Expansion has propelled Amazon.com in innumerable directions. While the Web site still offers millions of books, movies, games, and music, Amazon.com's electronics and other general merchandise categories, including apparel and accessories, auto parts, home furnishings, health and beauty aids, toys, and groceries ring up more than 50 percent of sales. Shoppers can also download E-books, games, MP3s, and films, including the Kindle [which now has a tablet version]. In addition, Amazon.com offers self-publishing, online advertising, an E-commerce platform, Web hosting, and a co-branded credit card.[18]

At the opposite end of the spectrum from Amazon.com is the specialty business of SeamlessWeb.com (www.seamlessweb.com):

> Seamless is the best way to order food for delivery and pickup from over 7,500 restaurants and 40+ cuisine types. Seamless is the nation's largest online and mobile food ordering company and has made ordering food fun and easy for more than one million members. You can browse menus, view ratings, read reviews, and discover great new restaurants. On the go? Download our mobile applications for Apple iPhone, Android, and BlackBerry to order food for delivery or pickup. Seamless features in New York, Washington D.C., Boston, Chicago, San Francisco, Los Angeles, Philadelphia, London, and other U.S. cities.[19]

Newegg (www.newegg.com), as highlighted in Figure 6-11, is a very successful online retailer of technology and related products that was started in 2001:

> Newegg Inc. is the second-largest online-only retailer in the United States. It owns and operates Newegg.com and regularly earns industry-leading customer service ratings. The award-winning Web site has more than 16 million registered users and offers customers

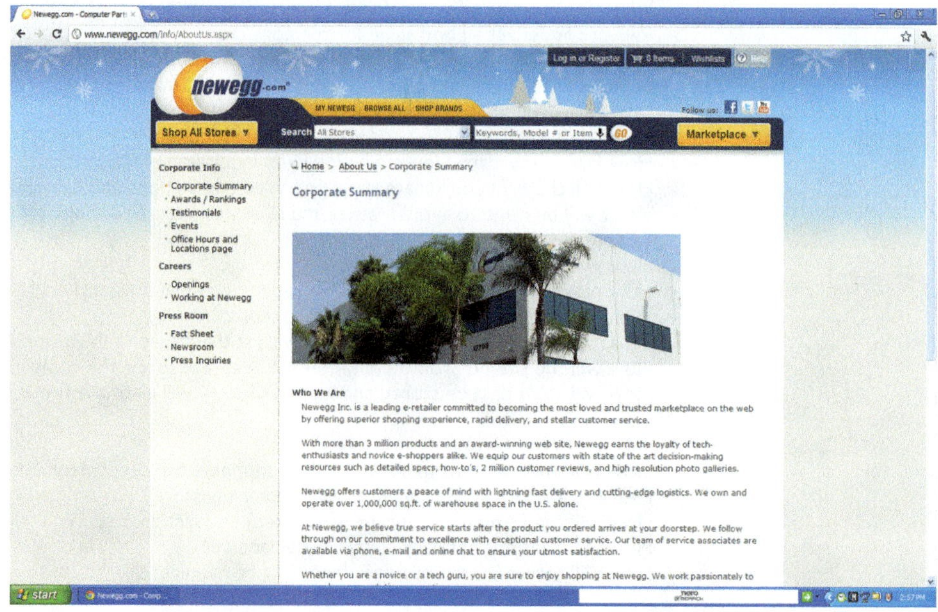

FIGURE 6-11
Newegg: A Well-Liked Online Retailer

Source: Reprinted by permission. © Newegg Inc.

FIGURE 6-12
Priceline.com: Online Auctions for Travel

Source: Reprinted by permission. © Priceline.com.

a comprehensive selection of the latest consumer electronics products, detailed product descriptions, and images, as well as how-to information and customer reviews. Using the site's online tech community, customers can interact with other computer, gaming, and consumer electronics enthusiasts. With more than 570,000 products, Newegg earns the loyalty of tech-enthusiasts and novice E-shoppers alike.[20]

Here are three other interesting Web retailing illustrations: First, eBay (www.ebay.com), Priceline.com (www.priceline.com), and uBid.com (www.ubid.com) offer online auctions, with everything from consumer electronics and textbooks to hotel rates and air fares. See Figure 6-12. Even nonprofit Goodwill has an auction Web site (www.shopgoodwill.com) to sell donated items. Second, Starbucks offers high-speed wireless Internet service at thousands of stores: "Enjoy great coffee and the Internet at your fingertips. Starbucks offers free, one-click, unlimited Wi-Fi at all company-owned stores in the United States, including instant access to the Starbucks Digital Network. There's no purchase or subscription required, no password needed, and no time limit on your session. Just open a browser on your laptop or mobile device and click Connect."[21] Third, J.C. Penney has an optimal multi-channel mix, by offering store, catalog, and online options to shoppers.

OTHER NONTRADITIONAL FORMS OF RETAILING

Two other nontraditional institutions merit discussion: video kiosks and airport retailing. Although both formats have existed for years, they are now much more popular. They appeal to retailers' desires to use new technology (video kiosks) and to locate in sites with high pedestrian traffic (airports).

Video Kiosks

The Digital Screen Media Association (www.digitalscreenmedia.org) tracks trends involving video kiosks.

The **video kiosk** is a freestanding, interactive, electronic computer terminal that displays products and related information on a video screen; it often has a touch screen for consumers to make selections. Some kiosks are located in stores to enhance customer service; others let consumers place orders, complete transactions (typically with a credit card), and arrange for shipping. Kiosks can be linked to retailers' computer networks or to the Web. There are 2.5 million video kiosks in use throughout the world, more than one million of which are Internet connected. In the United States, they generate $15 billion in annual retail sales. It is estimated that kiosks *influence* $100 to $200 billion in global retail sales—by providing product and warranty information, showing product assortments, displaying out-of-stock products, listing products by price, and so forth—and *generate* $25 billion globally in retail sales annually. North America accounts for the majority of kiosk sales, followed by the Pacific Rim, Europe, and the rest of the world.[22]

How exactly do video kiosks work? They are self-contained, computer-style terminals through which shoppers can access information and facilitate transactions. Video kiosks can enable self-check-ins at airports, demonstrate products in stores, offer DVD rentals, and do a whole lot more. Kiosk systems utilize:

> hardware designs that can be expanded to include numerous peripherals, such as touch screens, thermal printers, and card scanners. You will typically see a touch screen and on-screen keyboard used for data entry, along with card readers and barcode scanners. A thermal printer is the most common output device. Interactive kiosks may have a customized, hardened enclosure, or may simply be a standard PC that has been repurposed. Virtually any kiosk application in this context will be "interactive," to reduce confusion among the different kinds of kiosks (both high-tech and low-tech) that are in use today.[23]

Video kiosks can be placed almost anywhere (from a store aisle to the lobby of a college dormitory to a hotel lobby), require few employees, and are an entertaining and easy way to shop. Many shopping centers and individual stores are putting their space to better, more profitable use by setting up video kiosks in previously underutilized areas. These kiosks carry everything from gift certificates to concert tickets to airline tickets. Take the case of Macy's: Since 2009, it has deployed consumer electronics kiosks in more than 400 stores: "The kiosks sell an array of small consumer electronics, including iPods, accessories, and digital cameras from top manufacturers such as Sony and Apple."[24] In late 2011, Macy's began testing cosmetics kiosks.

The average hardware cost to a retailer per video kiosk is several thousand dollars plus ongoing content development and kiosk maintenance. Hardware prices range from under $500 per kiosk to $10,000 to $15,000 per kiosk, depending on its functions—the more features, the higher the price.[25]

Airport Retailing

In the past, the leading airport retailers were fast-food outlets, tiny gift stores, and newspaper/magazine stands. Today, airports are a major mecca of retailing. At virtually every large airport, as well as at many medium ones, there are full-blown shopping areas. And most small airports have at least a fast-food retailer and vending machines for newspapers, candy, and so forth.

The potential retail market is huge. Worldwide, more than 1,200 commercial airports handle nearly 5 billion passengers each year—with North America accounting for one-third of global passenger traffic. U.S. airports alone fly millions of passengers each day and employ nearly 2 million people (who often buy something for their personal use at the airport). There are more than 400 primary commercial U.S. airports. Overall, airport retailing generates $35 billion in global sales annually, and many airports generate annual retail revenues of at least $50 million.[26] See Figure 6-13.

Consider this:

> While luxury stores set up in airports long ago to attract duty-free international shoppers, retailing in many domestic terminals was limited to newsstands and shops selling coffee mugs and local smoked meat. No more. "Airports are becoming, really, a service facility, like a shopping mall," said Jose Gomez of Mango, the fashion retailer. The new wave of stores targets teenagers, women, and bargain shoppers. Domestic travelers spend more than an hour, on average, waiting in airports once passing security. At large airports, retailing (including food) is the second-biggest source of revenue, at 19 percent.[27]

New York's Kennedy Airport (www.ifly.com/john-f-kennedy-international-airport/shops-stores) typifies the retailing environment at the world's major airports.

FIGURE 6-13
Airport Retailing: Bigger Than Ever

Source: Tan Wei Ming/ Shutterstock.com. Reprinted by permission.

These are some of the distinctive features of airport retailing:

- There is a large group of prospective shoppers. In an average year, a big airport may have 20 million or more people passing through its concourses. In contrast, a typical regional shopping mall attracts 5 million to 6 million annual visits.
- Air travelers are a temporarily captive audience at the airport and looking to fill their waiting time, which could be up to several hours. They tend to have above-average incomes.
- Sales per square foot of retail space are much higher than at regional malls. Rent is about 20 to 30 percent higher per square foot for airport retailers.
- Airport stores are smaller, carry fewer items, and have higher prices than traditional stores.
- Replenishing merchandise and stocking shelves may be difficult at airport stores because they are physically removed from delivery areas and space is limited.
- The sales of gift items and forgotten travel items, from travelers not having the time to shop elsewhere, are excellent. Brookstone, which sells garment bags and travel clocks at airport shops, calls these products "I forgot" merchandise.

RETAILING AROUND THE WORLD

Kuala Lampur International Airport: A Master of Wi-Fi

Kuala Lumpur International Airport (KLIA) (www.klia.com.my) is one of the largest airports in the world. KLIA accommodates more than 34 million passengers and 1.2 million tons of cargo each year. KLIA's main terminal building alone is the size equivalent of 72 football fields.

Operated by Malasia Airports, in 2000, KLIA was the first airport in the world to offer free Wi-Fi. This service was upgraded in 2006 to expand Wi-Fi coverage to such higher density areas as passenger concourses. It was again upgraded in 2011 when the airport's management found that passengers wanted Wi-Fi throughout the airport and expected faster and more reliable performance. This system provides free hotspot services to airport passengers.

Forrester Research, a marketing research firm, reports that more than 35 percent of business airline passengers and 12 percent of leisure travelers go online at airports. According to the general manager of Malaysia Airports Technologies, "Airport travelers are among the most sophisticated users of technology and are now equipped with a variety of powerful Wi-Fi enabled devices." Wi-Fi is also used by airline, ground-handling and aircraft maintenance, and cargo-handling personnel. New aircraft, such as the Airbus A380, need Wi-Fi connections to retrieve and load data during layovers and turnaround flights.

Source: "One of World's Largest Airports Takes Off with Smarter Wi-Fi Across Massive Indoor/Outdoor Facility," www.ruckuswireless.com/press/releases/20110613-kuala-lumpur-international-airport (July 23, 2011).

- Passengers are at airports at all times of the day. Thus, longer store hours are possible.
- International travelers are often interested in duty-free shopping.
- There is much tighter security at airports than before, which has had a dampening effect on some shopping.

Chapter Summary

1. *To contrast single-channel and multi-channel retailing.* A new retailer often relies on single-channel retailing, whereby it sells to consumers through one retail format. As the firm grows, it may turn to multi-channel retailing and sell to consumers through multiple retail formats. This allows the firm to reach different customers, share costs among various formats, and diversify its supplier base.

2. *To look at the characteristics of the three major retail institutions involved with nonstore-based strategy mixes: direct marketing, direct selling, and vending machines—with an emphasis on direct marketing.* Firms employ nonstore retailing to reach customers and complete transactions. Nonstore retailing encompasses direct marketing, direct selling, and vending machines.

   In direct marketing, a consumer is exposed to a good or service through a nonpersonal medium and orders by mail, phone, fax, or computer. Annual U.S. retail sales from direct marketing (including the Web) exceed $425 billion. Direct marketers fall into two categories: general and specialty. Among the strengths of direct marketing are its reduced operating costs, large geographic coverage, customer convenience, and targeted segments. Among the weaknesses are the shopper's inability to examine items before purchase, the costs of printing and mailing, the low response rate, and marketplace clutter. Under the "30-day rule," there are legal requirements that a firm must follow as to shipping speed. The long-run prospects for direct marketing are strong due to consumer interest in reduced shopping time, 24-hour ordering, the sales of well-known brands, improvements in operating efficiency, and technology.

   The key to successful direct marketing is the customer data base, with data-base retailing being a way to collect, store, and use relevant information. Several trends are vital to direct marketers: their attitudes and activities, changing consumer lifestyles, increased competition, the use of dual distribution, the roles for catalogs and TV, technological advances, and the growth in global direct marketing. Specialogs and infomercials are two tools being used more by direct marketers.

   A direct marketing plan has eight stages: business definition, generating customers, media selection, presenting the message, customer contact, customer response, order fulfillment, and measuring results and maintaining the data base. Firms must consider that many people dislike shopping this way, feel overwhelmed by the amount of direct mail, and are concerned about privacy.

   Direct selling includes personal contact with consumers in their homes (and other nonstore sites) and phone calls by the seller. It yields $29 billion in annual U.S. retail sales, covering many goods and services. The strategy mix stresses convenience, a personal touch, demonstrations, and relaxed consumers. U.S. sales are not going up much due to the rise in working women, the labor intensity of the business, sales force turnover, government rules, and the poor image of some firms.

   A vending machine uses coin- and card-operated dispensing of goods and services. It eliminates salespeople, allows 24-hour sales, and may be put almost anywhere. Beverages and food represent 95 percent of the $45 billion in annual U.S. vending revenues. Efforts in other product categories have met with customer resistance, and items priced above $1.50 have not done well.

3. *To explore the emergence of electronic retailing through the World Wide Web.* The Internet is a global electronic superhighway that acts as a single, cooperative virtual network. The World Wide Web (Web) is a way to access information on the Internet, whereby people turn their computers into interactive multimedia centers. The Web can serve one or more retailer purposes, from projecting an image to presenting information to investors. The purpose chosen depends on the goals and focus. There is a great contrast between store retailing and Web retailing.

   The growth of Web-based retailing has been enormous. Annual U.S. revenues from retailing on the Web are $250 billion. Nonetheless, the Web still garners only a small percentage of total U.S. retail sales.

   Somewhat more females than males shop on the Web. Web usage declines by age group and increases by income and education level. Shoppers are attracted by Web site design, reliability, customer service, and security. Nonshoppers worry about the trustworthiness of online firms, want to see and handle products first, and do not like shipping cost surprises.

The Web offers these positive features for retailers: It can be inexpensive to have a Web site. The potential marketplace is huge and dispersed, yet easy to reach. Sites can be quite exciting. People can visit a site at any time. Information can be targeted. A customer data base can be established and customer feedback obtained. Yet, if consumers do not know a firm's Web address, it may be hard to find. Many people will not buy online. There is clutter with regard to the number of retail sites. Because Web surfers are easily bored, a firm must regularly update its site to ensure repeat visits. The more multimedia features a site has, the slower it may be to access. Some firms have been deluged with customer service requests. Improvements are needed to coordinate store and Web transactions. There are few standards or rules as to what may be portrayed at Web sites. Consumers expect online services to be free and are reluctant to pay for them.

A well-developed Web strategy would move through nine stages, from determining the customer base to measuring performance. A systematic approach is vital.

4. *To discuss two other nontraditional forms of retailing: video kiosks and airport retailing.* The video kiosk is a freestanding, interactive computer terminal that displays products and other information on a video screen; it often has a touchscreen for people to make selections. Although some kiosks are in stores to upgrade customer service, others let consumers place orders, complete transactions, and arrange shipping. Kiosks can be put almost anywhere, require few personnel, and are an entertaining and easy way for people to shop. They yield $15 billion in annual U.S. revenues.

Due to the huge size of the air travel marketplace, airports are popular as retail shopping areas. Travelers (and workers) are temporarily captive at the airport, often with a lot of time to fill. Sales per square foot, as well as rent, are high. Gift items and "I forgot" merchandise sell especially well. Globally, annual retail revenues are $35 billion at airports.

Key Terms

single-channel retailing (p. 135)
multi-channel retailing (p. 135)
nonstore retailing (p. 135)
direct marketing (p. 136)
data-base retailing (p. 138)
specialog (p. 140)
infomercial (p. 140)
direct selling (p. 143)
vending machine (p. 146)
Internet (p. 147)
World Wide Web (Web) (p. 147)
video kiosk (p. 153)

Questions for Discussion

1. Contrast single-channel and multi-channel retailing. What do you think are the advantages of each?
2. Do you think nonstore retailing will continue to grow faster than store-based retailing? Explain your answer.
3. How would you increase a direct marketer's response rate from less than 1 percent of those receiving E-mail sales offers by the firm to 3 percent?
4. Explain the "30-day rule" for direct marketers.
5. What are the two main decisions to be made in the business definition stage of planning a direct marketing strategy?
6. How should CVS/pharmacy (www.cvs.com) handle consumer concerns about their privacy?
7. Differentiate between direct selling and direct marketing. What are the strengths and weaknesses of each?
8. Select a product not heavily sold through vending machines, and present a brief plan for doing so.
9. From a consumer's perspective, what are the advantages and disadvantages of the World Wide Web?
10. From a retailer's perspective, what are the advantages and disadvantages of having a Web site?
11. What must retailers do to improve customer service on the Web?
12. What future role do you see for video kiosks? Why?

Web-Based Exercise

Visit the "Trends & Data" section of Internet Retailer's Web site (www.internetretailer.com) by clicking on the tab. Describe four key current facts that a retailer could learn from this section of the site.

Note: Also stop by our Web site (www.pearsonhighered.com/bermanevans) to experience a number of highly interactive, appealing Web exercises based on actual company demonstrations and sample materials related to retailing.

APPENDIX Multi-Channel Retailing*

As we noted at the beginning of Chapter 6, a retail firm relies on single-channel retailing if it sells to consumers through one format. A firm uses multi-channel retailing if it sells to consumers through multiple formats. We devote this appendix to multi-channel retailing because so many firms are combining store and nonstore retailing—as well as using multiple store formats.

Multi-channel retailing enables consumers to conveniently shop in a number of different ways, including stores, catalogs, a Web site, kiosks, and smart phones and tablets with Internet access. Some firms have even developed advanced multi-channel retailing systems that enable consumers to examine products at one format, buy them at another format, and pick them up—and possibly return them—at a third format.

Consider Cabela's, an outdoor lifestyle retailer. The firm has 32 stores in 22 states and 2 stores in Canada, publishes a catalog, operates a Web site (www.cabelas.com), and offers in-store kiosks. During the course of a year, Cabela's stocks as many as 225,000 different items. The retailer:

> fosters multi-channel initiatives through in-store kiosks to provide its customers with access to its full product assortments and to purchase items that are out-of-stock in its stores. Its store pick-up program enables customers to order products online or through its catalogs and pick them up at a nearby Cabela's store. This not only saves delivery costs to the customers, but also increases traffic at stores. The multi-channel model uses the same merchandising teams, distribution centers, customer data bases, and infrastructure for all channels.[1]

In recognition of the increasing importance of multi-channel retailing, *Catalog Age* was renamed and repositioned as *Multi-Channel Merchant* (www.multichannelmerchant.com).

Planning and maintaining a well-integrated multi-channel strategy is not easy. At a minimum, it requires setting up an infrastructure that can effectively link multiple channels. A retailer that accepts a Web purchase for exchange at a retail store needs an information system to verify the purchase, the price paid, the method of payment, and the date of the transaction. That firm also needs a mechanism for delivering goods regardless of which channel was used by a customer to purchase.

These are just some of the strategic and operational issues for multi-channel retailers to address:

- What multi-channel cross-selling opportunities exist? A firm could list its Web site on business cards, store invoices, and shopping bags. It could also list the nearest store locations when a consumer inputs a ZIP code at the Web site.
- How should the product assortment/variety strategy be adapted to each channel? How much merchandise overlap should exist across channels?
- How well can a distribution center handle both direct-to-store and direct-to-consumer shipments?
- Should prices be consistent across channels (except for shipping and handling, as well as closeouts)?
- How can a consistent image be devised and sustained across all channels?
- What is the role of each channel? Some consumers prefer to search the Web to determine pricing and product information, and then they purchase in a store due to their desire to see the product, try it on, and gain the immediacy that accompanies an in-store transaction.
- What are the best opportunities for leveraging a firm's assets through a multi-channel strategy? Many catalog-based retailers have logistics systems that can be easily adapted to Web-based sales.
- Do relationships with current suppliers prevent the firm from expanding into new channels?

*The material in this appendix is updated and adapted by the authors from Barry Berman and Shawn Thelen, "A Guide to Developing and Managing a Well-Integrated Multi-Channel Retail Strategy," *International Journal of Retail & Distribution Management*, Vol. 32 (No. 3, 2004), pp. 147–156. Used by permission of Barry Berman and Shawn Thelen.

Advantages of Multi-Channel Retail Strategies

There are several advantages to a retailer's enacting a multi-channel approach, including the selection of specific channels based upon their unique strengths, opportunities to leverage assets, and opportunities for increased sales and profits by appealing to multi-channel shoppers.

Selecting Among Multiple Channels Based on Their Unique Strengths

A retailer with a multi-channel strategy can use the most appropriate channels to sell particular goods or services or to reach different target markets. Because each channel has a unique combination of strengths, a multi-channel retailer has the best opportunities to fulfill its customers' shopping desires.

Store-based shopping enables customers to see an item, feel it, smell it (e.g., candles or perfumes), try it out, and then pick it up and take it home on the same shopping trip without incurring shipping and handling costs. Catalogs offer high visual impact, a high-quality image, and portability (they can be taken anywhere by the shopper). The Web offers high-quality video/audio capabilities, an interactive format, a personalized customer interface, virtually unlimited space, the ability for a customer to verify in-stock position and order status, and, in some cases, tax-free shopping. In-store kiosks are helpful for shoppers not having Web access, can lead to less inventory in the store (and reduce the need to stock low-turnover items in each store), facilitate self-service by providing information, and offer high video/audio quality.

To plan an appropriate channel mix and the role of each channel, retailers must recognize how different channels complement one another. Best Buy (www.bestbuy.com), Costco (www.costco.com), and Staple's (www.staples.com) are just a few of the retailers that have a broader selection of items on the Web to encourage consumers to shop online. They also send customer mailings to encourage them to place orders on their Web sites or to visit stores.

Pottery Barn (www.potterybarn.com) has built a multi-channel strategy around its catalog business. The firm distributes 140 million print copies of its catalogs yearly in addition to making them available. These include "best buys" and seasonal catalogs for lighting, dining, media, and storage. According to one analyst: "If it stops mailing catalogs, the Web traffic and Internet orders are slow. The catalog is really the catalyst that gets someone to go to the Pottery Barn Web site and place an order."[2]

Macy's (www.macys.com), Abercrombie & Fitch (www.abercrombie.com), and Gap (www.gap.com) have obtained high conversion rates (the percent of site visits that result in orders) from customers that have accessed their sites via tablets. These tablets enable retailers to add videos, slideshows, product demonstrations, and "order" buttons. Many customers find these visuals and graphics to be compelling. According to one research study, the conversion rate for tablet viewers is 4 to 5 percent versus 3 percent for shoppers viewing a Web site on a PC. Many retailers also report that the average purchase quantity via tablets is 10 to 20 percent above a PC or smart phone transaction.[3]

Opportunities to Leverage Assets

Multi-channel retailing presents opportunities for firms to leverage both tangible assets and intangible assets. A store-based retailer can leverage tangible assets by using excess capacity in its warehouse to service catalog or Web sales; that same firm can leverage its well-known brand name (an intangible asset) by selling online in geographic areas where it has no stores.

Retailers can also work with channel partners to leverage their collective assets. Checkout by Amazon (https://payments.amazon.com) is a service by Amazon.com that enables other Web-based retailers to use Amazon.com's one-click ordering system, and it enables customers to easily determine applicable sales tax and track their orders until delivered. Amazon.com has extended this offering to Checkout by Amazon Mobile. This service enables mobile shoppers to complete purchases without the need to re-enter shipping and payment information. With Checkout by Amazon Mobile, mobile shoppers can stay on Amazon.com's Web site throughout the shopping process.

Opportunities for Increased Sales and Profits by Appealing to Multi-Channel Shoppers

A large-scale research study found that multi-channel consumers, on average, spend more and have a higher lifetime value than single-channel consumers. The authors also reported on other studies that discovered offering multi-channel capability increased customer satisfaction and loyalty to retailers.[4]

In 2010, Sears (www.sears.com) launched digital versions of its "Wish Book" catalog to reach new customer segments. It made its holiday Wish Book available on Facebook, iPhone, and as an iPad app. According to a Sears executive: "We feel by going through mobile and iPad we've hit a new demographic that may not have been interested in Sears before. By enabling these digital capabilities, we can interact with customers and that allows us to socially connect with them through the feedback channels we offer."[5]

Developing a Well-Integrated Multi-Channel Strategy

A well-integrated multi-channel strategy requires linkages among all of the channels. Customers should be able to easily make the transition from looking up products on the Web or in a catalog to picking up the products in a retail store.

If these linkages are not properly established, sales can be lost. A study of 2,000 British consumers found that just 40 percent of them would visit a retailer's Web site if they could not find an item in the store. The study's authors recommended that retail salespeople need to be trained and motivated to use multi-channel strategies to avoid this unnecessary loss of sales.[6]

There should be a good deal of commonality in the description and appearance of each item regardless of channel. For example, in-store personnel should be able to verify a Web or catalog purchase and arrange for returns or exchanges. At Brooks Brothers' Web site (www.brooksbrothers.com), shoppers can access copies of current catalogs by page number. In addition, salespeople in stores have copies of catalogs available so that customers can place orders for items not carried in a particular outlet.

These are characteristics common to superior multi-channel strategies: integrated promotions across channels; product consistency across channels; an integrated information system that shares customer, pricing, and inventory data across multiple channels; a store pickup process for items purchased on the Web or through a catalog; and the search for multi-channel opportunities with appropriate partners.

Integrating Promotions Across Channels

Cross-promotion enables consumers to use each promotional forum in its best light. Here is a list of some cross-promotion tactics:

- Include the Web site address on shopping bags, in catalogs, and in newspaper ads.
- Provide in-store kiosks so customers can order out-of-stock merchandise without a shipping fee.
- Include store addresses, phone numbers, hours, and directions on the Web site and in catalogs.
- Make it possible for customers to shop for items on the Web using the catalog order numbers.
- Distribute store coupons by direct mail and online; offer catalogs in stores and at the Web site.
- Target single-channel customers with promotions from other channels.
- Send store-based shoppers targeted E-mails (on an opt-in basis) for selected goods and services.
- Have a strong social media presence.

Ensuring Product Consistency Across Channels

Too little product overlap across channels may result in an inconsistent image. However, too much overlap may result in the loss of sales opportunities. Multi-channel retailers often use the Web as a way to offer very specialized merchandise that cannot be profitably offered in stores. For example, Williams-Sonoma's (www.williams-sonoma.com) and Radio Shack's (www.radioshack.com) Web sites offer consumers highly specialized items not stocked in these chains' local retail stores. This maximizes store space while, at the same time, fulfills specialized needs of niche market segments.

Having an Information System That Effectively Shares Data Across Channels

To best manage a multi-channel system, a retailer needs an information system that shares customer, pricing, and inventory information across channels:

- The director of merchandising for Patagonia (www.patagonia.com), the outdoor clothing retailer, says this about its multi-channel philosophy: "Patagonia believes in one brand, one message, one customer philosophy. We all support the company in total. We want our customers to get inventory wherever it suits them best—whatever channel is best for them. We don't compete against ourselves. We're all on the same page."[7]
- Best Buy (www.bestbuy.com) and Sears (www.sears.com) have Web sites that enable shoppers to not only confirm whether merchandise is in stock, but also to set up in-store pickup.

Enacting a Store-Pickup Process for Items Purchased on the Web or Through a Catalog

In-store pickup requires that a retailer's inventory data base be integrated and that the firm has a logistics infrastructure that can pick and route merchandise to customers. Increasingly, shoppers are ordering big-ticket items such as digital cameras, computers, and appliances online but picking them up at nearby stores. Consumers favor this approach to avoid shipping and handling charges, to reduce their having to navigate through a big-box store, and to avoid wasting time looking for items that may be out-of-stock.

Pier 1 (www.pier1.com), the home furnishings and décor retailer, recently re-launched its Web site-to-store sales model. It now lists all of the items that it sells on the Web site, so "customers will be able to go online, check inventory at their local store, reserve the item, and then pick it up and pay for it in-store." This site-to-store model enables Pier 1 "to leverage our store base without any of the complexities around online payment or fulfillment."[8]

Store pickup often enables shoppers to get items on the same day they make a purchase. Many customers also favor in-store pickup so that they can more easily return goods that do not meet their expectations. Best Buy reports that 40 percent of its online purchases are now picked up by customers at one of its stores as opposed to being delivered.[9]

Searching for Multi-Channel Opportunities with Appropriate Partners

The retailer needs to understand that in almost all cases a multi-channel strategy requires additional resources and competencies that are significantly greater than those demanded by a single-channel strategy. Although some retailers may conclude that they do not have these competencies or resources, others look for strategic partnerships with firms having complementary resources.

Special Challenges

A multi-channel strategy is not appropriate for every retailer. Not all retailers possess the financial and managerial resources to do so—or have the same potential synergies.

A key challenge for many retailers, particularly small to middle size firms, is the consolidation of their disparate retail management systems into one customer-focused system. Many retailers started out with a single channel—typically bricks-and-mortar—and then added telephone sales, Web sales, and maybe even eBay sales. As a result, these retailers often developed separate information systems for each channel. Thus, each of these channels had a distinct information system with its own set of customer, product, sales, and inventory data. With a multi-channel-based system, a retailer's overall information center must be unified. In this way, a retailer can determine whether a large Web site or catalog user base exists within the trading area of a proposed retail location. According to an analysis published by the Harvard Business School, "creating the appropriate organizational structure is arguably the greatest challenge facing all multichannel retailers."[10]

Multi-channel retailers need to maintain the same branding identity for their products across diverse channels. Graphics designers need to establish specific guidelines and templates so that type fonts, colors, and key design elements are shared across channels. To complicate matters, products often look differently in a catalog versus on a computer screen due to Web sites and smart phones having lower resolutions than print. Colors are also depicted differently on computers than in catalogs due to a user's color preferences. This may especially affect the purchase of apparel or furniture.[11]

A final potential difficulty is the management of a retailer's distribution center. Such a center requires efficient procedures for handling both large orders that are shipped directly to stores and small shipments that are made to thousands or tens of thousands of customers. The system for handling large store-based retail purchase orders (which are often full-case loads) are quite different than shipping individual items to a customer's home.

PART 2 Short Cases

Case 1: Ernie's Auto Body: Utilizing the Key Choice Collision Center Network[c-1]

John Magowan, owner of Ernie's Auto Body Care, is a founding member of the Key Choice Collision Center. Key Choice is a retail cooperative of 15 noncompeting body shops located in the Upper Midwest. Unlike other cooperatives, group purchasing is just the initial step used by Key Choice members in an overall strategy to reduce total costs.

Through Key Choice, participating retailers seek to identify the best practices used by each member and then adapt them for use by other members. These best practices have been applied to such issues as estimating repair costs, office procedures, and even shop techniques. As a result, Key Choice members have standardized about 85 percent of their repair and restoration processes. Members not only use a common brand of paint products to reduce costs (through quantity discounts and better bargaining power), but also standardize paint-spray-gun settings.

Key Choice cooperative members stress the need for continuous improvement. According to Magowan: "If a shop or a person says they're lean [very cost efficient], they're far from it. You'll never be 100 percent lean. It's about constant, continual improvement." This improvement often results in higher customer satisfaction index scores.

Members also share personnel in emergency situations, such as when a severe hail storm generates demand that cannot be planned for or satisfied. As an example, two cooperative members recently flew to another member's location to help write up estimates for hail damage and spent four full days (from dawn to dusk).

Cooperative members benefit from sharing financial data and from comparing their shops' performance against national and group averages. This enables an individual shop to determine whether its material cost is too high or whether its labor utilization is as productive as a "best practice" body shop. Based on this data, members are encouraged to develop specific goals related to shop size, market area, and individual circumstances. Members further benefit from social contacts that are based on friendships and common experiences associated with work and business ownership.

Ernie's Auto Body shop is in Hayward, Wisconsin, a town with 1,800 people. Because Hayward is rural, the shop draws customers from a 50- to 75-mile range. Customers include both local residents and tourists attracted by the area's fishing, snowmobiling, cross-country skiing, and golf attractions.

Two particular challenges that John Magowan faces are high seasonality and finding skilled labor. His business can be very strong in key seasons, but very slow during off-seasons. High seasonality leads to problems relating to capacity usage, staffing, and customer waiting time. While the area is very scenic, it has been difficult hiring qualified technicians to work there. As a result, Magowan has had to hire staff from as far as 600 miles away. Since Magowan feels that his sales have approached a peak level, he has devoted much effort to reducing costs by streamlining car repair and restoration processes. As Magowan says: "If you can't grow sales, you have to focus on net improvement, or it'll shrink because of inflation."

[c-1]The material in this case is drawn from James E. Guyette, "Growth Mode," www.searchautoparts.com (July 2011).

Questions

1. What additional cost savings and opportunities exist for Key Choice Collision members that have not been discussed in this case?
2. Explain the differences and similarities between franchising and cooperatives from a retailer's perspective.
3. Discuss the pros and cons of a cooperative member comparing its financial performance against national and group averages.
4. How can Key Choice members better manage the inherent seasonality in their business? Look at both demand and supply-related issues.

Case 2: Family Dollar: Reinventing the Discount Store[c-2]

When 21-year-old Leon Levine founded Family Dollar Stores (www.familydollar.com) in 1959, his first store was located in Charlotte, North Carolina, and it focused on selling fabrics and apparel. Over time, the growing chain's selection of goods expanded to include holiday decorations, home-cleaning products, pet-related goods, and health and beauty aids. Currently, there are more than 6,800 Family Dollar stores in 44 states.

Central to Family Dollar's overall retail strategy are these factors:

- An emphasis on merchandise priced at less than $2.
- All stores being laid out in exactly the same way (to enable customers to easily find merchandise).
- A high-value orientation.
- Good customer service.

The recent recessionary economic climate forced Family Dollar to re-examine its product selection and store layout. As a result of the poor economy, many of Family Dollar's lower-income core customers reduced their apparel and footwear expenditures. Instead, they concentrated their purchases on more basic needs. On the other hand, middle-income consumers increasingly shopped at Family Dollar for such basic commodity items as home-cleaning supplies and refrigerated foods.

Due to the increased popularity of refrigerated and frozen foods, each renovated Family Dollar store now has 5 to 10 refrigerator/freezer units. Family Dollar has also reduced the number of brands it carries to increase its bargaining power with suppliers and to simplify its ordering and stocking processes. However, Family Dollar has increased the number of products stocked within a brand.

[c-2]The material in this case is drawn from Jordan K. Speer, "Family Dollar Doubles Down on Apparel," *Apparel Magazine* (February 2011), pp. 24–26.

Family Dollar's new layout, which has been applied to several hundred stores, "is more intuitive, with clean lines of sight," according to Family Dollar's manager of public relations. It also incorporates lifestyle-oriented displays. In the past, sweatpants and matching tops were placed on separate racks. As a result, many customers were unaware that these items could be combined to form a matching outfit. Since Family Dollar's new layout makes it easier for customers to walk around a store, it encourages impulse purchases. The new layout also provides more selling space for the stores' best-selling items. Family Dollar is completing its renovation program over a four-year period.

Based on market research, Family Dollar found that many of its customers were concerned with sizing inconsistencies and had some quality issues regarding apparel items (such as poor stitching on seams). Family Dollar discovered that many of its customers were unwilling to reduce purchases for children's clothing despite the recession's effect on their disposable income. As a result, Family Dollar's sales of children's clothing have been strong. Family Dollar plans to expand into other areas of children's clothing such as bibs, diapers, and footwear.

Recently, sales of apparel and accessories have been increasing. As a result, Family Dollar plans to focus more attention on men's and women's apparel. The chain is now using market research data to position stores into clusters based on consumer expenditures. Some stores have been more successful in the sale of fashion apparel, while others are better sellers of basic items like socks.

Questions

1. Evaluate Family Dollar's retail strategy. Will it work in both good and bad economic times?
2. Discuss the pros and cons of Family Dollar's reducing the number of brands but increasing the selection within a brand.
3. Describe Family Dollar's competitive advantages and disadvantages with respect to competition from conventional supermarkets and box stores.
4. How can a full-line discount store do better in competing against a variety store like Family Dollar?

Case 3: Amazon.com's Mom Program[c-3]

The Amazon Mom membership program (www.amazon.com/gp/mom/signup/info) began in fall 2010 after a successful test market in June 2010. The Amazon Mom program is targeted at parents, relatives (such as grandparents, aunts, and uncles), and caretakers who regularly purchase such goods as diapers and baby wipes for babies and young infants. Because these items are bought with high frequency, Amazon.com views this as a major opportunity to "lock in" these consumers to a pattern of regular purchasing at Amazon.com.

Even though Amazon.com (www.amazon.com) customizes its home page for any customer based on his or her purchase history, Amazon Mom goes a step further by suggesting related products. An Amazon Mom member, for example, may see selections of baby monitors (which transmit sounds from a baby's room to another area), nursery furniture, and a full selection of diapers.

Amazon.com sees Amazon Mom as a gateway to make consumers aware of and experience the benefits associated with Amazon's Prime and Subscribe & Save programs. Under the Amazon Prime program (www.amazon.com/prime), members pay a $79 yearly fee for unlimited two-day shipping with no minimum purchase requirement. Amazon Mom members receive an additional month of Amazon Prime every time they purchase $25 of baby products. Amazon Prime is advantageous to Amazon.com because it rewards the most loyal customers. At the same time, Amazon Prime encourages members to purchase more goods through Amazon.com. According to a former Amazon Prime team member, Prime membership "was never about the $79. It was really about changing people's mentality so they wouldn't shop anywhere else."

Subscribe & Save (www.amazon.com/gp/subscribe-and-save/details) is an Amazon.com program that provides an additional discount to consumers who elect to purchase an item at selected intervals. Subscribe & Save members also receive free shipping on every shipment. While Subscribe & Save was originally targeted at consumer purchases of laundry supplies, coffees, and paper goods, Amazon Mom extends this program to products aimed at babies and infants. Amazon.com hopes that the Amazon Mom program will yield continual use of its Subscribe & Save program as both children and their parents get older.

Amazon.com believes Amazon Mom is an effective strategy to attract parents, relatives, and caretakers who often have little time and patience for purchasing consumables. For many young parents, the purchase of diapers, baby wipes, and other consumables is viewed as a routine purchase with little perceived risk. In addition, many Amazon Mom members fear running out of these supplies, and see home delivery as a positive alternative to carrying several boxes of diapers at a time.

Some analysts believe that Amazon.com's strategy for Amazon Mom is to lure consumers with low-price products such as diapers and then encourage them to purchase goods with higher profit margins, such as car seats. An analysis of Amazon Mom's prices for two popular brands of diapers—Huggies Snug & Dry and Pampers Cruisers Dry Max—found that Amazon.com's price with its 30 percent discount was only 5 to 7 cents less than the next lowest-priced retailer, Sam's Club (www.samsclub.com).

Questions

1. Discuss the pros and cons of Amazon Mom's membership program from a consumer's perspective.
2. Evaluate the pros and cons of Amazon Mom's membership program from Amazon's perspective.
3. List appropriate products for Amazon to market with its Subscribe & Save program.
4. Evaluate the pros and cons of Amazon Mom's low price strategy.

[c-3]The material in this case is drawn from Amy Koo and Stephen Mader, "Amazon.mom: Driving & Stealing Trips," www.kantarretailiq.com (March 10, 2011).

Case 4: The Status of E-Tailing in China[c-4]

In April 2011, Gome (www.gome.com.hk), one of China's largest brick-and-mortar consumer electronics and home appliance retailers, set up an online presence. Gome's move into the Web was significant as few of China's stores had a Web presence. A study by iResearch, an Internet research firm, found that of the 30 largest Chinese Web-based merchants in terms of revenue, 26 were Web only. This is in sharp contrast to the United States, where only five of the largest Web-based retailers are clicks only.

Research by the China Chain Store and Franchise Association (CCFA) examined the current status of E-tailing in China. One of its major findings was that only 34 of the top 100 retail chains in China even had a Web presence. Furthermore, most of these retailers had Web sites that only described product attributes as opposed to selling. As a CCFA executive noted: "Most traditional Chinese retailers have no clear idea why they're going online, how big their online business should be, and how it [functions within] their overall business."

Unfortunately, too many large Chinese retailers do not understand the synergies associated with multi-channel retailing. According to the founder of a Shanghai-based online supermarket, "offline and online retail are very different industries. There is a huge disparity between the two, particularly in terms of IT [information technology] expertise, supply chain structure, human capital management, and marketing. Offline retailers that want to build an online channel are essentially starting from scratch."

In order to succeed, Chinese bricks-and-mortar retailers need to better understand how IT and logistics need to be managed in a multi-channel environment. Unfortunately, too many Chinese store-based retailers have planned their Web-based operations using existing IT personnel. These personnel typically do not have the skill set and experience to manage order processing, payment processing, customer monitoring, and other tasks that are unique to Web operations.

One way for Chinese store-based retailers to transition into multiple channels is through partnerships with suppliers. Suning (www.suning.com/include/english), a large electronics and home appliance retailer, worked with IBM in the development of its Web site. It also collaborated with Baidu (http://ir.baidu.com), China's largest search engine, to generate traffic. Likewise, Uniglo (www.uniglo.com), a Japanese casual clothing chain, formed a partnership with Taobao (www.taobao.com/index_global.php), China's largest Internet retailer. As a result, Uniglo's site attracted 400,000 visitors within 10 days after its initial launch.

Many Chinese retailers have long-term relationships with major suppliers that provide them with top-selling goods, as well as lower costs due to more bargaining power with suppliers. Leading Chinese retailers also have warehouses that result in speedy delivery throughout China and have high awareness and trust levels among Chinese consumers.

Questions

1. Comment on the statement: "Offline and online retail are very different industries. There is a huge disparity between the two, particularly in terms of IT expertise, supply chain structure, human capital management, and marketing. Offline retailers that want to build an online channel are essentially starting from scratch."
2. Discuss the pros and cons of a multi-channel retail strategy for Chinese retailers.
3. Describe the special logistics of a Web-based merchant in China.
4. What are some other opportunities for partnerships between retailers and their suppliers in China?

[c-4]The material in this case is drawn from "Reluctant E-Tailers: What's Keeping China's Big Chains Offline?" http://knowledge.wharton.upenn.edu (May 4, 2011).

PART 2 Comprehensive Case

Retailing Around the Globe*

Introduction

Although store retailers around the world face many of the same issues involving changing shopping behavior, government regulation, and technology, companies in each country are operating at different stages of their life cycle. That was a key message supplied by National Association of Convenience Stores (NACS, www.nacsonline.com) president and chief executive Hank Armour at a question-and-answer session with Insight Managing Director Dan Munford during the Insight NACS Future of International Convenience conference held in London last year.

As an example of the different life cycles, Armour pointed out that self-checkout is further advanced in Great Britain and many other countries in Europe than it is in the United States. However, U.S. retailers are much further down the road with pay-at-the-pump gasoline technology than their European counterparts.

The Future of International Convenience conference focused on global consumer trends and the winning strategies of several best-in-class retailers from around the world.

Looking Outward

Debbie Robinson, former director of marketing for Great Britain's Cooperative Group and a pioneer in "responsible" retailing, provided opening comments at the Future of International Convenience conference, noting that retailers around the world were operating against the backdrop of global population growth, climate change, the growing affluence of the BRIC nations (Brazil, Russia, India, China), and the increased multi-ethnicities and aging populations in markets around the world. "With the massive increase in population, growth isn't the problem. It's how you sustain that growth," said Robinson.

Armour of NACS went on to discuss what he called a "bifurcation" of retail shopping experiences between consumer demand for large one-stop-shop hypermarkets and supercenters versus smaller, quality shopping experiences. "I think convenience retailing is the most personable type," said Armour, who was a retailer for many years and is a member of the *Convenience Store News* Hall of Fame. "To be successful in this business, you have to like people—we can build small store formats, but the magic is in how you run them."

The chief executive of NACS also spoke about the importance of advocacy and getting out early in front of key issues, such as tobacco bans and restrictions. "It's amazing that people wait for it to happen before doing something about it," he said. Armour also praised retailers for being able to operate successfully despite government regulations, pointing to two U.S. retailers—Sheetz and Rutter's—for being able to operate profitably in markets where they cannot sell beer, a convenience-store staple in many other parts of the United States. "Whatever the regulations, customers expect us to deliver a convenient shopping mission," he said.

Sheetz and Rutter's

The chief executives of both Sheetz (www.sheetz.com), the Altoona, Pennsylvania-based convenience store chain, and Rutter's (www.rutters.com), based in York, Pennsylvania, were on hand at the Future of International Convenience conference to discuss their company's success secrets.

In a sit-down with Insight's Munford, Stan Sheetz talked about how he's grown up in the business. "My father started the company before I was born," said Sheetz. "I look forward to going to work every day and meeting great people. If you don't enjoy people, you're in the wrong industry. This industry is all about people—customers and employees."

The first secret to success, according to Sheetz, is to pay appropriate salaries to attract the best workers. "We pay above market wages," said the executive. "But it doesn't stop there. That just gets them in the door. Once they are here, we have to provide them with the culture. Success lies in providing career opportunities to people." Sheetz said that 80 percent of his company's store managers have been promoted from store level employee. "The real point of differentiation is the people you have running your business," he emphasized.

Sheetz also spoke about the role fuel has played in the retailer's success: "We sell over $1 billion of fuel a year. We use it as a draw to get people on our property." Sheetz sells unbranded fuel and buys directly from refiners, does its own blending at terminals, and controls the delivery right to the stores, where many of its stations have 20 pumps in the forecourt. Serving "the road warrior" is the retailer's goal, said Sheetz. "We want to provide that on-the-go customer with the ability to fill his tank, fill his tummy, and empty his bladder," said the executive, emphasizing the critical and important role that clean restrooms play in attracting the road warrior.

Sheetz acknowledged that technology will also play a big role in the industry's future. "Technology is the great enabler," he said. "By increasing efficiencies, it allows you to transfer time to more productive, customer-facing uses."

Scott Hartman, chief of Rutter's Farm Stores, picked up on the technology theme and described how Rutter's was reaching customers with new technologies. Hartman said 55 Pennsylvania-based stores operate in one of the most competitive convenience markets in the world. "Four of the top six convenience stores in sales per store are located in Pennsylvania," said Hartman, listing Rutter's among Sheetz, Wawa, and Giant Eagle as among the top industry performers.

Rutter's has been an early adopter of new technology in the industry and was the second convenience chain in the United States to launch a Web site, claimed Hartman. Like Sheetz, Rutter's utilizes touch screen ordering for food service. "The customers who most love it are the younger customers—they trust technology more than people to get the order right," said Hartman.

*The material in this case is adapted by the authors from Don Longo, "Convenience Store Retailing Goes Through Stages Around the Globe," *Convenience Store News* (January 10, 2011), pp. 41–48. Reprinted by permission of *Convenience Store News*, www.csn.com.

Rutter's loyalty rewards program, launched a year ago, now has 200,000 active card users and 1,000 customers have signed up to receive special offers, E-mails, and texts from the retailer. Mobile phone apps are the retailer's current focus. Rutter's has been a first mover in convenience, teaming up with GasBuddy, a Canadian company, which sends information on local gas prices to customers' mobile phones.

The Rutter's apps are now on three platforms: Blackberry, iPhone, and Android; and they enable the retailer to attract shoppers to its stores with offers and challenge competitors on prices. According to Hartman, the apps also offer details of store opening hours and services, sign-up features for promotions and deals, menu lists, a membership card access via the phone, feedback functions, and digital couponing. Rutter's is also adding a games feature with a "spin to win" format that features sponsor logos and digital coupons as prizes. Hartman said consumer-facing technologies were a journey, not a destination, and he urged delegates to enjoy and embrace them.

International Retailers

Joe Barrett, director of the Irish convenience store chain Applegreen (www.applegreen.ie), spoke at the Future of International Convenience conference about the chain's focus on continuous improvement. A night earlier, Applegreen was named the International Convenience Retailer of the Year by a panel of international judges. "We build on mistakes, trying to improve each store as we go," said Barrett.

Applegreen was founded in Ireland in 2004 and entered the Great Britain market—where it now has 13 stores—in 2008. Barrett noted that the company's biggest strategic moves took place in the middle of a financial crisis in Ireland. One of those key strategic moves was opening a distribution warehouse for frozen, chilled, and ambient food. "It's difficult to be seen to be green but we have significantly reduced the number of trucks delivering to sites," said Barrett, adding that Applegreen promotes its own private-label products on the side of its trucks. "Private label is really important to us," he said. Applegreen retails milk and water at one Euro per liter and offers two for three Euros on other lines such as cooked meats. Savings have also been secured by outsourcing the firm's accounts function, reducing the wage bill, and reinvesting it in the management team to analyze data and grow business.

Other big news in the British retail industry has been the expansion of upscale grocer Waitrose (www.waitrose.com) into the convenience market. In its large convenience store prototype, Waitrose is focusing on fresh foods, which accounts for 70 percent of sales. In the smaller prototype, the focus is on what the retailer calls "healthy options."

Kate Smith-Bingham, head of offer development at Waitrose, told the audience that the grocer's push into convenience was designed to reach customers with whom it previously had little access through its larger supermarkets. She estimated that market as worth 31 million pounds in annual sales and said it was growing. She also noted that Waitrose was late to the party, following other British grocers such as Tesco and Sainsbury's into the convenience arena.

The first large Waitrose convenience store opened in December 2008. It's about 6,000 square feet, with two-thirds of the space devoted to fresh food, including serving counters for meat and fish, cheese, and deli. Waitrose opened its first smaller convenience store in Cambridge in June 2010. At just 3,000 square feet, it offers fresh, healthy meals, but no food counters. Smith-Bingham said Waitrose will continue testing the convenience market and has plans for more stores.

The retail director for Ireland's leading forecourt store retailer (which combines convenience store and gasoline sales), Topaz (www.topaz.ie), spoke about the company's use of price optimization technology to improve sales and profits at the pump. "It's a mathematical equation," said Frank Gleeson. "We know what's going to happen when prices change. We can change prices more quickly, the information is quicker, and with historical data we can optimize sales and profits." Topaz has been working on price optimization with KSS Fuels since 2009.

The Convenience Store of the Future

When it comes to the convenience store of the future, the president of international design firm CBX encouraged retailers to get out of their comfort zones. "Think big," said Joe Bona, as he presented a concept for a future convenience store based on the layout of an airport. The futuristic concept provides five zones offering fuel, convenience, amenities, dining, and vehicle-related services:

- In the fuel zone, the store could sell replaceable cartridges to power cars, an electric charger for electric cars, and a variety of different fuels.
- The convenience zone could feature online ordering and pickup service, and even a pharmacy department as Bona pointed out that drugstores such as Duane Reade were adding food and competing with convenience stores more aggressively.
- The amenities zone could include a remote office for customers to use, a spa, and gym facilities, as well as pet stay areas.
- The dining zone could feature "chef pods" where customers would assemble their own ingredients, but not heat or cook products. "You could partner with a celebrity chef, like Jaime Oliver, to give the store's food offering more credibility," said Bona.
- The vehicle zone could include auto diagnostics, a green car wash, and other services.

Worldwide Regulation

"Regulation will be the next big thing to hit you hard," said Mark Wohltmann of USP Market Intelligence, a German research firm acquired by Nielsen Co. in early 2010. Without prejudging whether the regulations were good or bad, Wohltmann listed the core categories where regulatory activity would increase for convenience stores: tobacco, sweets, fizzy drinks, and food service.

Wohltmann urged retailers to research and evaluate the expected impact of new regulations, validate the findings, organize and work with partners, and take action ahead of competitors. "Prepare today, the regulations will come," he warned.

Touring London's Convenience Store Scene

The Future of Convenience and Petroleum Retailing conference, sponsored by Insight and NACS, included tours of innovative small format stores in Ireland, Great Britain, and Paris,

France. Doing good and tasting good seemed to be the theme of the tours as most of the stores visited were leading examples of serving local community needs and offering the freshest available product. *Convenience Store News* tagged along on the tour to convenience stores at the St. Pancras railroad station in London and stores in other parts of the city.

At the St. Pancras station, tour-goers were treated to a look at two Marks & Spencer Simply Food stores—one a small convenience store and the other a larger store that included a department for M&S branded apparel, general merchandise, and gift items. Also at the station, delegates visited Sourced Market (www.sourcedmarket.com), an independent convenience store that aims to replicate the ambience and food selection of an open-air market. See Figure 1.

In the north London area called Maide Vale, the tour visited a Tesco Express allied with an Esso fuel forecourt. This store, in an upper-income area of the city, sells more fuel and food than any other Tesco Express alliance store. More like a small grocery store than a convenience store, this Tesco Express has a relatively high average ticket of 5.7 pounds.

Then, the London tour moved on to Crouch End, described by some as the most competitive food retailing area of Great Britain. Within a few blocks, there are numerous food retailers including Tesco Express, M&S Simply Food, Waitrose's convenience store concept, and Budgens (www.budgens.co.uk), among others. See Figures 2 and 3.

The Waitrose store represents the relatively new convenience store division of the sixth largest British grocer. Like its supermarket parent, Waitrose's convenience store gets high marks from customers for its fresh food and modern look, with low fixtures and an emphasis on its front-of-the-store serviced food departments. The store does 190,000 to 200,000 British pounds in sales per week and its average ticket is an eye-opening 10.60 pounds.

Budgens is located just a few doors away from Waitrose. It is a franchise owned by Andrew Thornton. This store illustrated how an independent with clarity of vision can differentiate itself and compete against the chains. Thornton told the group he focuses on three things: first, locally sourced and specialty food; second, community; and third, the environment

FIGURE 1

Sourced Market

Located in the St. Pancras railroad station in northern London, Sourced Market is one of several British food and convenience stores that tries to replicate the ambience of an open air market.

Source: Reprinted by permission of *Convenience Store News*, www.csn.com.

FIGURE 2

Tesco Express

The Tesco Express concept, shown here in London's Crouch End, appears much more successful than Tesco's U.S. convenience store format, Fresh & Easy.

Source: Reprinted by permission of *Convenience Store News*, www.csn.com.

FIGURE 3

Budgens

Andrew Thornton, owner of Budgens in London, has a rooftop organic garden above the store. Produce from the garden are used in sandwiches and salads sold in the store.

Source: Reprinted by permission of *Convenience Store News*, www.csn.com.

and sustainability. Thornton's Budgens features what he calls the world's first store with a rooftop garden that provides vegetables for sale at the store. "It's the most local source you can get," said Thornton as he treated tour-goers to lunch on the rooftop, which he calls Food from the Sky.

Questions

1. What can *any* retailer learn from this case?
2. Discuss the advantages and disadvantages of independent stores or small chains that compete with large chains.
3. How can a convenience store become a destination retailer?
4. Relate the wheel of retailing and scrambled merchandising to at least two of the retailers highlighted in this case.
5. At what stage in the retail life cycle are most convenience stores? Explain your answer.
6. Visit the Web sites of at least two retailers noted in this case and assess their online retailing efforts.
7. What actions must the retailers you examined for Question 6 undertake to better coordinate their store-based and Web-based efforts (multi-channel retailing)?

PART 3

Targeting Customers and Gathering Information

In Part Three, we first present various key concepts for retailers to better identify and understand consumers and develop an appropriate target market plan. Information-gathering methods—which can be used in identifying and understanding consumers as well as in developing and implementing a retail strategy—are then described.

Chapter 7 discusses many influences on retail shoppers: demographics, lifestyles, needs and desires, shopping attitudes and behavior, retailer actions that influence shopping, and environmental factors. We place these elements within a target marketing framework, because it is critical for retailers to recognize what makes their customers and potential customers tick—and for them to act accordingly.

Chapter 8 deals with information gathering and processing in retailing. We first consider the information flows in a retail distribution channel and review the difficulties that may arise from basing a retail strategy on inadequate information. Then we examine in depth the retail information system, its components, and recent advances in information systems—with particular emphasis on data warehousing and data mining. The last part of the chapter describes the marketing research process.

Source: Kenishirotie/Shutterstock.com. Reprinted by permission.

7 Identifying and Understanding Consumers

Chapter Objectives

1. To discuss why it is important for a retailer to properly identify, understand, and appeal to its customers

2. To enumerate and describe a number of consumer demographics, lifestyle factors, and needs and desires—and to explain how these concepts can be applied to retailing

3. To examine consumer attitudes toward shopping and consumer shopping behavior, including the consumer decision process and its stages

4. To look at retailer actions based on target market planning

5. To note some of the environmental factors that affect consumer shopping

Source: BeTA-Artworks/ fotolia.com.

Identifying the characteristics of their customers and understanding their behavior patterns are vital tasks for retailers to be able to devise and implement the correct strategy and tactics. Because social media activities are changing the ways in which retailers communicate with customers, retailers need to learn how different consumer groups are using social media as part of their shopping process.

Greystripe, a mobile advertising network, regularly publishes an "Advertiser's Insights Report," which tracks mobile phone users' behavior. One recent report examined how U.S. moms are using smart phones for some aspects of shopping. These are some of the findings from that study:

- Use of smart phones by moms of all ages has increased rapidly. These devices are almost as popular among moms ages 45 years and older as they are among younger moms (those 18 to 44 years old).
- Across several different smart phone shopping activities, younger and older moms have similar participation levels. However, younger moms are more apt to use their smart phones to research new products, download digital coupons, track sale items, and actually make purchases.
- The two most popular smart phone shopping activities for both younger and older moms are locating the nearest store and conducting price comparisons.
- "Apps" are more popular among younger moms and there is a large gap between younger and older moms with regard to using smart phones for social networking purposes.

In a separate study (not broken out by age) conducted by BabyCenter, a parenting Web site, the majority of moms said that they regularly use the mobile Internet. Nearly one-half use their smart phones in shopping and a greater percentage of moms do social networking through their smart phones than the general U.S. population. Coupons and locating nearby deals are especially appealing to moms compared to the general population.[1]

Overview

The success of a retail strategy depends on how well a firm identifies and understands its customers and how well it forms a strategy mix to appeal to them. This entails identifying consumer characteristics, needs, and attitudes; recognizing how people make decisions; and then devising the proper target market plan. See Figure 7-1. It also means studying environmental factors that affect decisions. Consider this:

Today's consumers are more empowered than ever before. They have numerous options with regard to when they shop, where they shop, and how they go about shopping. As a result, consumers now have higher expectations about the retailers with which they do business. In such a competitive environment, retailers must better understand and service their customers. This requires strong research and listening skills by retail personnel:

> Customers select their shopping destination based upon their particular needs for that specific shopping occasion. Are they looking to purchase groceries, a wedding outfit, or a gift? On top of this, a customer's expectations for a shopping trip differ greatly depending upon very specific needs, for example, a customer visiting a supermarket for a pint of milk wants speedy, efficient service, whereas a customer looking for menu inspiration for a dinner party desires an entirely different experience. Retailers are judged on the range, availability, quality, and ease with which customers can access and use the services they offer.[2]

In this chapter, we explore—from a retailing perspective—the impact on shoppers of each of the elements shown in Figure 7-2: demographics, lifestyles, needs and desires, shopping attitudes and behavior, retailer actions that influence shopping, and environmental factors. By studying

FIGURE 7-1

Recognizing Consumer Diversity in the Marketplace

Good retailers realize that customers (and potential customers) have varying backgrounds, interests, fashion sense, shopping behavior, and so on—even the young adult market. Thus, the best retail strategies cater to the needs and desires of a specific group of customers.

Source: Kurhan/Shutterstock.com. Reprinted by permission.

FIGURE 7-2
What Makes Retail Shoppers Tick

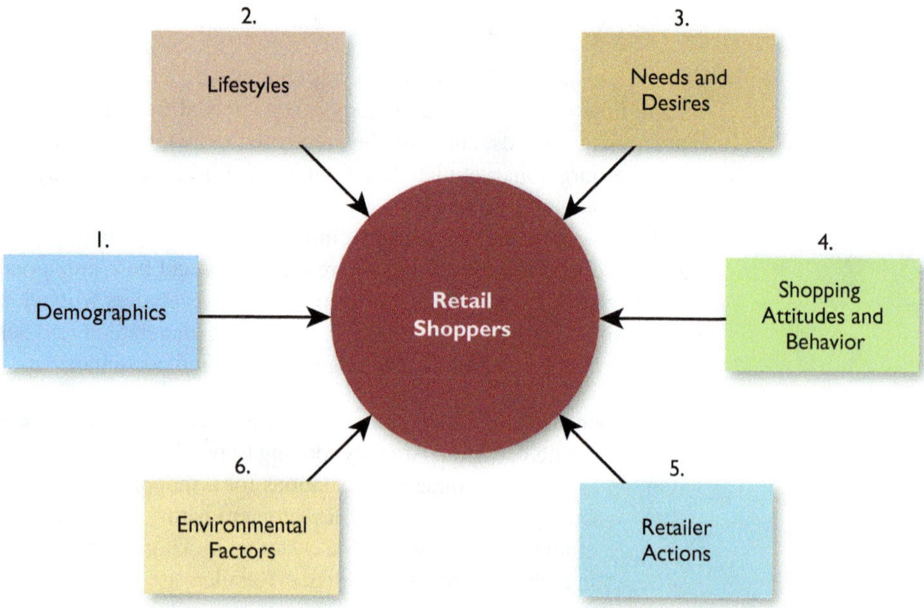

these elements, a retailer can devise the best possible target market plan and do so in the context of its overall strategy.

Please note: We use *consumer*, *customer*, and *shopper* interchangeably in this chapter.

CONSUMER DEMOGRAPHICS AND LIFESTYLES

Demographics are objective, quantifiable, easily identifiable, and measurable population data. **Lifestyles** are ways in which individual consumers and families (households) live and spend time and money. Visit our Web site (www.pearsonhighered.com/bermanevans) for links on these topics.

Consumer Demographics

At *The Rite Site* (www.easidemographics.com/cgi-bin/login_free.asp), retailers can access lots of useful demographic data. Take a look at the free reports.

Both groups of consumers and individual consumers can be identified by such demographics as gender, age, population growth rate, life expectancy, literacy, language spoken, household size, marital and family status, income, retail sales, mobility, place of residence, occupation, education, and ethnic/racial background. These factors affect people's retail shopping and retailer actions.

A retailer should have some knowledge of overall trends, as well as the demographics of its own target market. Table 7-1 indicates broad demographics for 10 nations around the world, and Table 7-2 shows U.S. demographics by region. Regional data are useful since most retailers are local and regional.

In understanding U.S. demographics, it is helpful to know these facts:

- The typical household has an annual income of $50,000. The top one-fifth of households earn $100,000 or more; the lowest one-fifth earn $20,000 or less. If income is high, people are apt to have **discretionary income**—money left after paying taxes and buying necessities.
- About 12 percent of people move each year; two-thirds of all moves are in the same county.
- There are 5 million more females than males; three-fifths of adult females are in the labor force.
- Most U.S. employment is in services. In addition, there are now more professionals and white-collar workers than before and fewer blue-collar and agricultural workers.
- Thirty percent of all U.S. adults aged 25 and older have at least a four-year college degree.
- The population comprises many ethnic and racial groups. African Americans, Hispanic Americans, and Asian Americans account for one-third of U.S. residents—a steadily rising figure. Each of these groups represents a large potential target market; their total annual buying power is $2 trillion.[3]

Although the preceding gives an overview of the United States, demographics vary by area (as Table 7-2 indicates). Within a state or city, some locales have larger [or smaller] populations

TABLE 7-1 Population Demographics: A Global Perspective—Selected Countries

Country	Male/ Female (%)	Age Distribution(%) 0–14 Years	15–64 Years	65 Years and Over	2011 Population Growth (%)	Life Expectancy in Years	Literacy Rate (%)	Principal Languages Spoken
Canada	49.5/50.5	16	68	16	0.79	81.4	99	English, French
China	51.3/48.7	18	73	9	0.49	74.7	92	More than a dozen versions of Chinese
Great Britain	49.5/50.5	17	66	17	0.56	80.1	99	English, Welsh
India	51.9/48.1	30	65	5	1.34	66.8	61	Hindi, English, 14 other official languages
Italy	49.0/51.0	14	66	20	0.42	81.8	98	Italian, German, French, Slovene
Japan	48.7/51.3	13	64	23	−0.28	82.3	99	Japanese
Mexico	49.0/51.0	28	65	7	1.10	76.5	86	Spanish
Poland	48.5/51.5	15	71	14	−0.06	76.1	99+	Polish
South Africa	49.7/50.3	28	66	6	−0.38	49.3	86	Afrikaans, IsiZulu, IsiXhosa, 8 other official languages
United States	49.2/50.8	20	67	13	0.96	78.4	99	English, Spanish

The literacy rate is the percentage of people who are 15 and older who can read and write.

Sources: Compiled by the authors from *World Factbook*, https://www.cia.gov/library/publications/the-world-factbook (November 15, 2011).

TABLE 7-2 Selected 2010 U.S. Demographics by Region

Region	Percent of Household Income	Percent of Population	Percent Ages 18–24	Percent Ages 62 and Older	Population Per Square Mile
ENC	15.0	15.6	9.7	16.0	160
ESC	6.0	5.5	9.4	16.7	106
M	7.1	7.3	9.9	15.5	30
MA	13.2	14.5	9.6	17.4	388
NE	4.7	5.2	9.6	17.3	215
P	16.2	16.7	10.7	14.7	55
SA	19.4	17.6	9.7	17.4	238
WNC	6.6	6.9	9.7	16.7	42
WSC	11.8	10.7	10.0	14.2	94

ENC (East North Central) = Illinois, Indiana, Michigan, Ohio, Wisconsin

ESC (East South Central) = Alabama, Kentucky, Mississippi, Tennessee

M (Mountain) = Arizona, Colorado, Idaho, Montana, Nevada, New Mexico, Utah, Wyoming

MA (Middle Atlantic) = New Jersey, New York, Pennsylvania

NE (New England) = Connecticut, Maine, Massachusetts, New Hampshire, Rhode Island, Vermont

P (Pacific) = Alaska, California, Hawaii, Oregon, Washington

SA (South Atlantic) = Delaware, District of Columbia, Florida, Georgia, Maryland, North Carolina, South Carolina, Virginia, West Virginia

WNC (West North Central) = Iowa, Kansas, Minnesota, Missouri, Nebraska, North Dakota, South Dakota

WSC (West South Central) = Arkansas, Louisiana, Oklahoma, Texas

Source: Computed and estimated by the authors from U.S. Bureau of the Census, http://2010.census.gov/2010census.

and more [or less] affluent, older [younger], and better-educated [or less-educated] residents. Because most retailers are local or operate in only part of a region, they must compile data about the people living in their trading areas and those most apt to shop there. *For a given business and location*, the characteristics of the target market (the customer group to be sought by the retailer) can be studied on the basis of some combination of these demographic factors—and a retail strategy planned accordingly:

- *Market size*—How many people are in the potential target market?
- *Gender*—Is the potential target market more male or female, or are they equal in proportion?
- *Age*—What are the prime age groups to which the retailer wants to appeal?
- *Household size*—What is the average household size of potential consumers?
- *Marital and family status*—Are potential consumers single or married? Do families have children?
- *Income*—Is the potential target market lower income, middle income, or upper income? Is discretionary income available for luxury purchases?
- *Retail sales*—What is the area's sales forecast for the retailer's goods/services category?
- *Birth rate*—How important is the birth rate for the retailer's goods/services category?
- *Mobility*—What percent of the potential target market moves into and out of the trading area yearly?
- *Where people live*—How large is the trading area from which potential customers can be drawn?
- *Employment status*—Does the potential target market include working women?
- *Occupation*—In what industries and occupations are people in the area working? Are they professionals, office workers, or of some other designation?
- *Education*—Are potential customers college-educated?
- *Ethnic/racial background*—Does the potential target market cover a distinctive racial or ethnic group?

Great Britain's *Customer Insight Magazine* (www.customer-insight.co.uk) provides a good perspective on emerging consumer trends.

Consumer Lifestyles

Consumer lifestyles are based on social and psychological factors and are influenced by demographics. As with demographics, a retailer should first have some knowledge of consumer lifestyle concepts and then determine the lifestyle attributes of its own target market.

Succeeding in Developing Markets

In contrast to many multi-nationals that have been slow to understand consumers outside Europe and North America, local retailers have been quick to understand their customers and develop offerings specifically for them. The best of these retailers have been successful in taking sales from street vendors, mom-and-pop stores, and even multi-national retail chains.

One recent study illustrates this point. The study looked at large retailers in six areas: Beijing Hualian Group (China), Biedronka (a Polish firm owned by a Portuguese retailer), BIM (Turkey), Magazine Luiza (Brazil), Pick n Pay (South Africa), and Supermercados Peruanos (Peru).

The researchers found that several of the strategies used by these retailers have been successful in emerging markets:

- **Aim low**—Target products at the low-income segments from the beginning. By initially aiming at a more affluent segment, it would be difficult to make the product affordable to the mass market.
- **Adapt to consumer habits**—Provide decent quality at the low end and aspirational choices at the high end.
- **Don't just sell, educate**—Devote resources to turning salespeople into educators.
- **Focus on your brands appropriately**—Concentrate on brands that represent quality and reliability to consumers.
- **Develop quick reflexes**—Be nimble, quickly adapt to change, and be prepared for the unexpected.

Source: Guillermo D'Andrea, David Marcotte, and Gwen Dixon Morrison, "Let Emerging Market Customers Be Your Teachers," *Harvard Business Review* (December 2010), pp. 115–120.

These *social factors* are useful in identifying and understanding consumer lifestyles.

- A **culture** is a distinctive heritage shared by a group of people that passes on a series of beliefs, norms, and customs. The U.S. culture stresses individuality, success, education, and material comfort; there are also various subcultures (such as African, Asian, and Hispanic Americans) due to the many countries from which residents have come.
- **Social class** involves an informal ranking of people based on income, occupation, education, and other factors. People often have similar values in each social class.
- **Reference groups** influence people's thoughts and behavior: aspirational groups—a person does not belong but wishes to join; membership groups—a person does belong; and dissociative groups—a person does not want to belong. Face-to-face groups, such as families, have the most impact. Within reference groups, there are opinion leaders whose views are well respected and sought.
- The **family life cycle** describes how a traditional family moves from bachelorhood to children to solitary retirement. At each stage, attitudes, needs, purchases, and income change. Retailers must also be alert to the many adults who never marry, divorced adults, single-parent families, and childless couples. The **household life cycle** incorporates life stages for both family and nonfamily households.
- *Time utilization* refers to the activities in which a person is involved and the amount of time allocated to them. The broad categories are work, transportation, eating, recreation, entertainment, parenting, sleeping, and (retailers hope) shopping. Today, many consumers allocate less time to shopping.

These *psychological factors* help in identifying and understanding consumer lifestyles:

Consumer psychology can be studied with tools such as the Keirsey Temperament Sorter. Take the online test (www.keirsey.com/sorter/instruments2.aspx?partid=0) to learn about yourself.

- A **personality** is the sum total of an individual's traits, which make that individual unique. They include a person's level of self-confidence, innovativeness, autonomy, sociability, emotional stability, and assertiveness.
- **Class consciousness** is the extent to which a person desires and pursues social status. It helps determine the use of reference groups and the importance of prestige purchases. A class-conscious person values the status of goods, services, and retailers.
- **Attitudes (opinions)** are the positive, neutral, or negative feelings a person has about different topics. They are also feelings consumers have about a given retailer and its activities. Does the consumer feel a retailer is desirable, unique, and fairly priced?
- **Perceived risk** is the level of risk a consumer believes exists regarding the purchase of a specific good or service from a given retailer, whether or not the belief is correct. There are six types: *functional* (Will a good or service perform well?), *physical* (Can a good or service hurt me?), *financial* (Can I afford it?), *social* (What will peers think of my shopping here?), *psychological* (Am I doing the right thing?), and *time* (How much shopping effort is needed?). Perceived risk is high if a retailer or its brands are new, a person is on a budget or has little experience, there are many choices, and an item is socially visible or complex. See Figure 7-3. Firms can reduce perceived risk with information.
- *The importance of a purchase* to the consumer affects the amount of time he or she will spend to make a decision and the range of alternatives considered. If a purchase is important, perceived risk tends to be higher, and the retailer must adapt to this.

A retailer can develop a lifestyle profile of its target market by answering these questions and then using the answers in developing its strategy:

- *Culture*—What values, norms, and customs are most important to the potential target market?
- *Social class*—Are potential consumers lower, middle, or upper class? Are they socially mobile?
- *Reference groups*—To whom do people look for purchasing advice? Does this differ by good or service category? How can a firm target opinion leaders?
- *Family (or household) life cycle*—In what stage(s) of the cycle are the bulk of potential customers?
- *Time utilization*—How do people spend time? How do they feel about their shopping time?

FIGURE 7-3
The Impact of Perceived Risk on Consumers

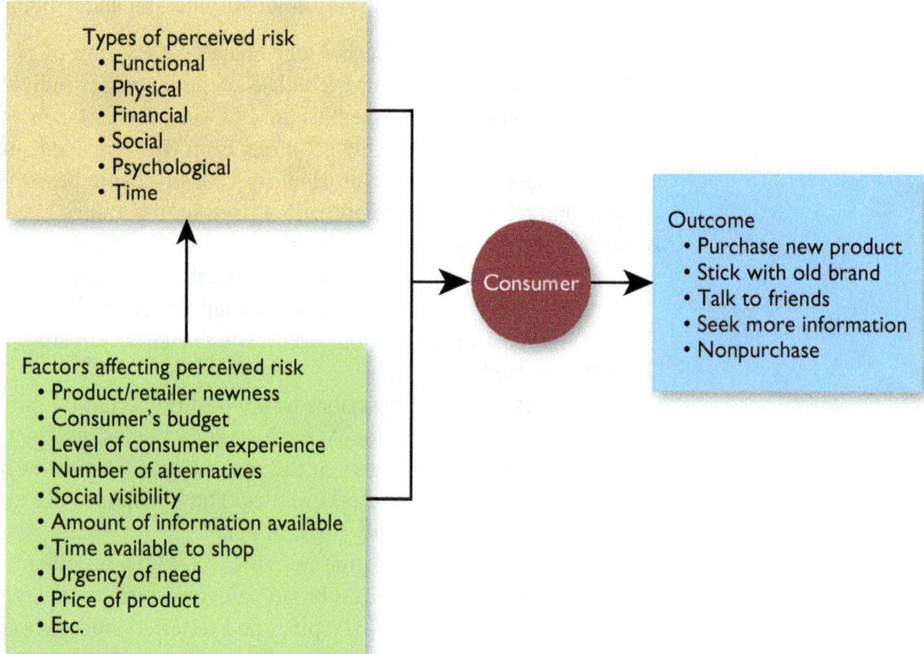

- *Personality*—Do potential customers have identifiable personality traits?
- *Class consciousness*—Are potential consumers status-conscious? How does this affect purchases?
- *Attitudes*—How does the potential target market feel about the retailer and its offerings in terms of specific strategy components?
- *Perceived risk*—Do potential customers feel risk in connection with the retailer? Which goods and services have the greatest perceived risk?
- *Importance of the purchase*—How important are the goods/services offered to potential customers?

Retailing Implications of Consumer Demographics and Lifestyles

Demographic and lifestyle factors need to be considered from several perspectives. Here are some illustrations. By no means do the examples cover the full domain of retailing.

Gender Roles: The huge number of working women, who put in 60 to 70 hours or more each week between their job and home responsibilities, has altered lifestyles significantly. Compared with women who have not worked outside the home, they tend to be more self-confident and individualistic, more concerned with convenience, more interested in sharing household and family tasks with spouses or significant others, more knowledgeable and demanding as consumers, more interested in leisure activities and travel, more involved with self-improvement and education, more appearance-conscious, and more indifferent to small price differences among retailers. They are less interested in unhurried shopping trips.

Due to the trend toward working women, male lifestyles are also changing. More men now take care of their children, shop for food, do laundry, wash dishes, cook, vacuum, and clean the bathroom. Thirty-five percent of U.S. grocery and mass merchandise shoppers are now men.[4] In the future, there will be still more changes in men's and women's roles. The clout and duties of husbands and wives will be shared more often. Retailers need to appreciate this trend. See Figure 7-4.

Consumer Sophistication and Confidence: Many shoppers are now more knowledgeable and cosmopolitan; more aware of trends in tastes, styles, and goods and services; and more sophisticated. Nonconforming behavior is accepted when consumers are self-assured and better appreciate the available choices. Confident shoppers experiment more. For example, according to one retailing expert: Today, "being 'cheap' could be considered an asset. Consumers have started thinking differently about their purchases, paying only for attributes they really want in a product

FIGURE 7-4
Blurring Gender Roles
Due to changing lifestyles, more men and women now shop together.

Source: iofoto/Shutterstock.com. Reprinted by permission.

and sacrificing other elements. Retailers who figure out a way to 'design it up and price it down' appeal to consumers looking for something fun that's cheap. Furniture retailer Ikea is able to offer style at low prices, in part because shoppers must put the furniture together themselves. Customers of fashion retailer Zara may accept cheaper fabrics or simple construction as long as clothing reflects the latest styles."[5]

Poverty of Time: The increase in working women, the desire for personal fulfillment, the daily job commute, and the need for some people to have second jobs contribute to many consumers feeling time-pressured: "No matter how rich or poor consumers are, time is the great social equalizer. A new priority of making the most of the limited time we have is taking over. Consumers are looking at all the ways they spend their time, including shopping, and demanding a more time-efficient, time-conscious way to shop."[6] There are ways for retailers to respond to the poverty-of-time concept. Firms can add branch stores to limit customer travel time; be open longer hours; add on-floor sales personnel; reduce checkout time; and use mail order, Web sites, and other direct marketing practices. See Figure 7-5.

FIGURE 7-5
Addressing the Poverty of Time
The 24/7, anywhere, anything nature of online shopping is a big attraction for people who are pressed for time.

Source: iofoto/Shutterstock.com. Reprinted by permission.

What Bothers Consumers About Retailing?

Consumer Reports (www.consumerreports.com) recently surveyed close to 1,000 consumers to determine what specific customer service issues got them the most upset. Respondents rated 12 practices on a 10-point scale ranging from not annoying at all (0) to tremendously annoying (10). The three most annoying complaints of in-store customers, and their scores, were: the salesperson is rude (8.7), the salesperson is too pushy (8.2), and the customer cannot find a salesperson (7.5). The three most annoying issues for phone-based customers were: can't get a human on the phone (8.9), many phone steps needed (8.5), and long wait on hold (8.2).

The inability to speak to a real person on the phone was particularly annoying to women and to both men and women aged 50 years and older. Women were also more likely to be annoyed by unapologetic employees, the need to go through multiple prompts for assistance, and the difficulty in finding a salesperson in a store. Men, on the other hand, were more likely to be annoyed by pitches for goods and services that were unrelated to their purchase.

Sixty-four percent of respondents stated that during the previous 12 months they had left a store because of poor customer service and 67 percent had hung up on a customer service phone call without having their problem addressed.

Source: "What's Wrong with Customer Service?" *Consumer Reports* (July 2011), pp. 16–18.

Component Lifestyles: In the past, shoppers were typecast, based on demographics and lifestyles. Now, it is recognized that shopping is less predictable and more individualistic. It is more situation-based, hence, the term *component lifestyle:* "Have you wondered what's going on with consumers? Why the contradictions when it comes to spending money? Why they will buy a $500 leather jacket at full price but wait for a $50 sweater to go on sale? Will buy a top-line sports utility vehicle then go to Costco for tires? Will pay $3.50 for a cup of coffee but think $1.29 is too much for a hamburger? Will spend $2.00 for a strawberry-smelling bath soap but wait for a coupon to buy a $0.99 twin pack of toilet soap?"[7]

Consumer Profiles

VALS (www.strategicbusinessinsights.com/vals) classifies lifestyles into several profiles. Visit the site to learn about the profiles and take the "VALS Survey" to see where you fit.

Considerable research has been aimed at describing consumer profiles in a way that is useful for retailers. Here are three examples:

- Boston Proper is an online and catalog retailer appealing to a customer group that is not well served. This is the "35- to 55-year-old woman who wants to dress in an age-appropriate, fit-appropriate way that is sexy and on trend. The company centers solely on that demographic, and this focused approach is working. As its chief executive says: 'We need both the Web and catalog because that is what works for our customer. The catalog breaks through in the mailbox and captures her attention. After folding over pages or circling what she wants, she can go to the Web where it is easy and convenient to buy what she wants.'"[8]
- Those people living in the United States who identify themselves as Hispanic or Latino went up by 43 percent—about 51 million people—from 2000 to 2010. Today, Hispanics comprise 16.3 percent of the total U.S. population; and this group is expected to grow to 58 million people as of 2015. *Women's Wear Daily* says that: "Retailers such as Macy's, Wal-Mart, Dillard's, J.C. Penney, Kohl's, Kmart, and Sears have been paying close attention to the significant spending power of Hispanic shoppers. Stores have been aggressively courting the Hispanic customer with specific apparel collections, TV and radio ad campaigns, and bilingual direct mailers, credit card applications, and in-store signage. Kohl's signed a megadeal with Jennifer Lopez and Marc Anthony for a lifestyle fashion venture."[9]
- Claritas' Prism segmentation system divides American households into various lifestyle categories. These are the four wealthiest groups: (1) Upper crust—America's wealthiest lifestyle and a "haven for empty-nesting couples ages 45 to 64. No segment has a more opulent standard of living. Shop at Saks Fifth Avenue." (2) Blue-blood estates—This group represents suburban wealth. It consists of "married couples with children, significant percentage of Asian Americans, and six-figure incomes earned by business executives and professionals. Shop at Thomasville." (3) Movers & shakers—This group consists of up-and-comers. It is "a wealthy suburban world of dual-income couples who are highly educated, typically between the ages of 35 and 54. Shop at J. Crew." (4) Young digerati—This group contains tech-savvy

individuals who reside in "fashionable neighborhoods on the urban fringe." They are "affluent, highly educated, and ethnically mixed and interested in trendy apartments, fitness clubs and boutiques, casual restaurants, and all types of bars—juice, coffee, and microbrew."[10]

CONSUMER NEEDS AND DESIRES

Lane Bryant (www.lanebryant.com), a retailer of fashionable plus-size women's apparel, seeks to satisfy both consumer needs and desires, especially the latter.

When developing a target market profile, a retailer should identify key consumer needs and desires. From a retailing perspective, *needs* are a person's basic shopping requirements consistent with his or her present demographics and lifestyle. *Desires* are discretionary shopping goals that have an impact on attitudes and behavior. A person may need a new car to get to and from work, and he or she may seek a dealer with Saturday service hours. The person may desire a Porsche and a free loaner car when the vehicle is serviced but be satisfied with a Toyota that can be serviced on the weekend and fits within the budget.

Consider this: "The upheaval in the marketplace caused by demographic and economic changes is creating challenges and opportunities. The biggest threat to an auto brand might be the monthly cable bill. The fast-food industry might get a boost from bad weather in Georgia, which causes the price of peanuts to skyrocket. Laptop sales can be hurt when women of a certain life stage instead commit cash to garish bridesmaid dresses. For retailers, the question becomes: How do you move your product from a 'want' to a 'need' and then keep it from slipping back to a 'could live without'?"[11] And this: "Lauren Liggett, a college student, found herself hooked the moment she saw the pilot episode of the TLC reality show "Extreme Couponing." She began scouring the Internet for couponing Web sites, bought copies of the Sunday newspaper for the circulars, and headed to the grocery store to shop for her family. On that first shopping trip, she presented her coupons to the cashier and felt the adrenaline rush of watching her total drop from $263 to $50. 'Pretty good for my first time!' she recalls. Today, Lauren has slashed her family's monthly grocery bill from $400 to $100."[12]

When a retail strategy aims to satisfy consumer needs and desires, it appeals to consumer **motives**, the reasons for their behavior. These are just a few of the questions to resolve:

- How far will customers travel to get to the retailer?
- How important is convenience?
- What hours are desired? Are evening and weekend hours required?
- What level of customer services is preferred?
- How extensive a goods/service assortment is desired?
- What level of goods/service quality is preferred?
- How important is price?
- What retailer actions are necessary to reduce perceived risk?
- Do different market segments have special needs? If so, what are they?

Let's address the last question by looking at three particular market segments that attract retailer attention: in-home shoppers, online shoppers, and outshoppers.

In-Home Shopping: The in-home shopper is not always a captive audience. Shopping is often discretionary, not necessary. Convenience in ordering an item, without traveling for it, is important. These shoppers are often active store shoppers, and they are affluent and well educated. Many in-home shoppers are self-confident, younger, and venturesome. They like in-store shopping but have low opinions of local shopping. For some catalog shoppers, time is not important. In households with young children, in-home shopping is more likely if the woman works part-time or not at all than if she works full-time. In-home shoppers may be unable to comparison shop; may not be able to touch, feel, handle, or examine products firsthand; are concerned about service (such as returns); and may not have a salesperson to ask questions.

Check out the Pew Internet & American Life Project Web site (www.pewinternet.org/Topics.aspx) to find out more about Web users.

Online Shopping: People who shop online are often well-educated and have above-average incomes (as stated in Chapter 6). As we noted earlier, Web shopping encompasses more than just purchasing online. At Toys "R" Us, online shoppers can research items, check out prices, and place orders. Some shoppers have items shipped to them, while others go to the store. The retailer has a very strong portfolio of E-commerce Web sites that include Toysrus.com, Babiesrus.com, eToys.com, and FAO.com, As a result, the firm offers customers a large online choice of toys and baby products. In addition, the retailer operates Toys.com, "which offers customers exclusive deals." Products are sold at about 875 Toys "R" Us and Babies "R" Us stores in the United States and Puerto Rico, 600-plus company-owned international stores, and more than 140 licensed stores in 35 countries and jurisdictions.[13]

Outshopping: Out-of-hometown shopping, **outshopping**, is important for both local and surrounding retailers. The former want to minimize this behavior, whereas the latter want to maximize it. Outshoppers are often young, members of a large family, and new to the community. Income and education vary by situation. Outshoppers differ in their lifestyles from those who patronize hometown stores. They enjoy fine foods, like to travel, are active, like to change stores, and read out-of-town newspapers. They also downplay hometown stores and compliment out-of-town stores. This is vital data for suburban shopping centers. Outshoppers have the same basic reasons for out-of-town shopping whether they reside in small or large communities—easy access, liberal credit, store diversity, product assortments, prices, the presence of large chains, entertainment facilities, customer services, and product quality.

SHOPPING ATTITUDES AND BEHAVIOR

In this section, we look at people's attitudes toward shopping, where they shop, and the way in which they make purchase decisions. Table 7-3 shows why shoppers around the world patronize specific retailers and their primary reasons for buying at specific grocery stores.

Attitudes Toward Shopping

Considerable research has been done on people's attitudes toward shopping. Such attitudes have a big impact on the ways in which people act in a retail setting. Retailers must strive to turn around some negative perceptions that now exist. Let us highlight some research findings.

Shopping Enjoyment: In general, people do not enjoy shopping as much as in the past. So, what does stimulate a pleasurable shopping experience—a challenge that retailers must address? "Customers derive shopping enjoyment from an assessment of accessibility, atmosphere, environment, and personnel. If a shopping center facilitates fast, efficient shopping, this would

TABLE 7-3 Global Shopping Attitudes and Behavior

Why Consumers in 51 Countries Shop at a Specific Retailer (% saying highly influential):

Reason	%
Good value for the money	61
Lowest prices	58
Convenient location	57
Great sales and promotions	55
Desired products in stock	54
Organized store layout (ease of shopping)	42
Friendly, knowledgeable employees	40
Fast checkout	38
Customer loyalty program	28

Primary Reasons for Shopping at a Grocery Store by Region (%)

	Africa/ Middle East	Asia Pacific	Europe	Latin America	North America
Stocking up	19	18	37	19	60
Making a quick replenishing trip	33	32	25	25	7
Buying a few essentials	28	29	21	32	18
Buying for a meal today	6	9	5	4	4
Buying only nonfood products	5	4	3	5	1
Buying only an advertised product	6	6	7	9	7
Other	3	2	2	6	3

Source: Compiled by the authors from Nielsen, "Shopping & Saving Strategies Around the World," http://nielsen.com/us/en/insights/reports-downloads.html (October 2011).

appeal to men, who would enjoy shopping in that region, and may therefore be more likely to return to the location in the future. At the same time, since women comprise a higher proportion of shoppers, there is a need to promote aspects of the shopping center as a relaxing and fun leisure activity to increase female enjoyment, to retain these customers, and to increase the likelihood of repatronage."[14]

Attitudes Toward Shopping Time: Retail shopping is often viewed as a chore. "Retailers should not lose sight of the importance of time-related factors in catering to customers. No matter how much effort the retailer invests in order to improve store ambience, the effects of those efforts can be tempered by the consumer's level of chronic time pressure. Therefore, retailers should not only invest more in store atmospherics (e.g., music, color, lighting, smell, and visual merchandising) but pay equal attention to the efficiency of store location, parking, and sales personnel assistance that may deactivate shoppers' chronic time pressure."[15]

Shifting Feelings About Retailing: There has been a major change in attitudes toward spending, value, and shopping with established retailers: "The same shopper who buys commodity goods at Target may also buy expensive apparel at Nordstrom. This shift does not appear to be transitory, but rather seems to define a more enduring pattern of behavior." In addition, the "rapid expansion of specialty chains, combined with heightened competition from mass merchandisers and department stores, has led to price wars and homogenization in several subsegments. Specialty retailers must therefore constantly try to find ways to distinguish themselves from competitors."[16]

Why People Buy or Do Not Buy on a Shopping Trip: It is critical for retailers to determine why shoppers leave without making a purchase. Is it prices? A rude salesperson? Not accepting the consumer's credit card? Not having an item in stock? Or some other factor? According to one retail consulting company, here are the top 10 reasons shoppers leave an apparel store without buying:

1. Cannot find an appealing style.
2. Cannot find the right size or the item is out of stock.
3. Nothing fits.
4. No sales help is available.
5. Cannot get in and out of the store easily.
6. Prices are too high.
7. In-store experience is stressful.
8. Cannot find a good value.
9. Store is not merchandised conveniently.
10. Seasonality is off.[17]

Attitudes by Market Segment: Research has shown that shoppers may be classified into several types based on their outlook to shopping. For example, according to one classification, shoppers can be broken into four types. "Thrifties" are most interested in price and convenience. They are apt to shop at Wal-Mart. "Allures" want a "fun, social shopping experience." They gravitate toward retailers such Bloomingdale's and Limited Brands. "Speedsters" want to shop quickly. They shop disproportionately at Target and Costco. "Elites" want quality merchandise, an unhurried shopping experience, and the ability to be educated about products. They patronize retailers such as Neiman Marcus and Amazon.com. Many "retailers don't know how their customers prefer their shopping experience and compete by doing what their competitors do. But that doesn't work. Customer insight will allow a retailer not only to survive but to thrive against even the toughest competition."[18]

Attitudes Toward Private Brands: Many consumers believe private (retailer) brands are as good as or better than manufacturer brands. According to a recent study by Mintel: "Some 44 percent of grocery shoppers believe store brands are of better quality today than they were five years ago and 39 percent would recommend a store brand. One-third say they don't feel like they're giving anything up (such as flavor or prestige) by using store brands. Only 19 percent say it's 'worth paying more for name brands.' "[19]

Where People Shop

Consumer patronage differs sharply by type of retailer. Thus, it is vital for firms to recognize the venues where consumers are most likely to shop and plan accordingly.

Why do some people shop at both upscale Tiffany (www.tiffany.com) and a membership club such as BJ's (www.bjswholesale.com)?

Many consumers do **cross-shopping**, whereby they (1) shop for a product category at more than one retail format during the year or (2) visit multiple retailers on one shopping trip. The first scenario occurs because these consumers feel comfortable shopping at different formats during the year, their goals vary by occasion (they may want bargains on everyday clothes and fashionable items for weekend wear), they shop wherever sales are offered, and they have a favorite format for themselves and another one for other household members. Visiting multiple outlets on one trip occurs because consumers want to save travel time and shopping time. Here are cross-shopping examples:

- Some supermarket customers also regularly buy items carried by the supermarket at convenience stores, full-line department stores, drugstores, and specialty food stores.
- Some department-store customers also regularly buy items carried by the department store at factory outlets and full-line discount stores.
- The majority of Web shoppers also buy from catalog retailers, mass merchants, apparel chains, and department stores.
- Cross-shopping is high for apparel, home furnishings, shoes, sporting goods, and personal-care items.

The Consumer Decision Process

Besides identifying target market characteristics, a retailer should know how people make decisions. This requires familiarity with **consumer behavior**, which is the process by which people determine whether, what, when, where, how, from whom, and how often to purchase goods and services. Such behavior is influenced by a person's background and traits.

The consumer's decision process must be grasped from two different perspectives: (1) what good or service the consumer is thinking about buying and (2) where the consumer is going to purchase that item (if the person opts to buy). A consumer can make these decisions separately or jointly. If made jointly, he or she relies on the retailer for support (information, assortments, and knowledgeable sales personnel) over the entire decision process. If the decisions are made independently—what to buy versus where to buy—the person gathers information and advice before visiting a retailer and views the retailer merely as a place to buy (and probably more interchangeable with other firms).

The U.S. government facilitates consumer decision making for such products as food by providing free online information (http://publications.usa.gov/USAPubs.php?CatID=6).

In choosing whether or not to buy a given item (*what*), the consumer considers features, durability, distinctiveness, value, ease of use, and so on. In choosing the retailer to patronize for that item (*where*), the consumer considers location, assortment, credit availability, sales help, hours, customer service, and so on. Thus, the manufacturer and retailer have distinct challenges: The manufacturer wants people to buy its brand (*what*) at any location carrying it (*where*). The

Vince Camuto: Targeting Consumer Niches

Vince Camuto has had a remarkable career in retailing. It began after high school when he worked as a service manager in the early 1960s at I. Miller, a women's shoe and accessories store. In 1999, as chief executive officer and creative director for Nine West (www.ninewest.com), Camuto sold this firm to Jones Apparel (www.jonesapparel.com) for $2 billion.

A week after his noncompete period ended with Jones Apparel, Vince Camuto started working with Dillard's department stores on brand development. As the Camuto Group (www.camutogroup.com), Camuto's firm purchased BCBG's (www.bcbg.com) footwear license. It also purchased the license for the Jessica Simpson (www.jessicasimpson.com) brand for $15 million. Annual sales of the Jessica Simpson brand currently equal $750 million.

Camuto is credited with several important consumer behavior innovations:

- In the 1970s, he combined Japanese financing, Italian design, and low-cost Brazilian manufacturing. He recognized the importance of giving women great-looking shoes at reasonable prices.
- After his low-cost shoes caught on and became a hot-selling brand, Camuto repositioned the brand to attract more affluent shoppers.
- The Camuto brand includes nine categories from footwear to jewelry, with additional lines to come. The use of a family brand reduces promotional costs and spreads a positive image among its newer products.

Source: Dinah Eng, "The Nine West Founder Looks Back," *Fortune International* (Europe) (July 4, 2011), pp. 19–20.

retailer wants people to buy the product, not necessarily the manufacturer's brand (*what*), at its store or nonstore location (*where*).

The **consumer decision process** has two parts: the process itself and the factors affecting the process. There are six steps in the process: stimulus, problem awareness, information search, evaluation of alternatives, purchase, and post-purchase behavior. The consumer's demographics and lifestyle affect the process. The complete process is shown in Figure 7-6.

The best retailers assist consumers at each stage in the process: stimulus (newspaper ads), problem awareness (stocking new models), information search (point-of-sale displays and good salespeople), evaluation of alternatives (clearly noticeable differences among products), purchase (acceptance of credit cards), and post-purchase behavior (extended warranties and money-back returns). The greater the role a retailer assumes in the decision process, the more loyal the consumer will be.

Each time a person buys a good or service, he or she goes through a decision process. In some cases, all six steps in the process are utilized; in others, only a few steps are employed. For example, a consumer who has previously and satisfactorily bought luggage at a local store may not use the same extensive process as one who has never bought luggage.

The decision process outlined in Figure 7-6 assumes that the end result is a purchase. However, at any point, a potential customer may decide not to buy; the process then stops. A good or service may be unneeded, unsatisfactory, or too expensive. Before discussing the ways in which retail consumers use the decision process, we explain the entire process.

Stimulus: A **stimulus** is a cue (social or commercial) or a drive (physical) meant to motivate or arouse a person to act. When a person talks with friends, fellow employees, and others, a social cue is received. The special attribute of a social cue is that it involves an interpersonal, noncommercial source. A commercial cue is a message sponsored by a retailer or some other seller. Ads, sales pitches, and store displays are commercial stimuli. Such cues may not be regarded as highly as social ones by consumers because they are seller-controlled. A third type of stimulus is a physical drive. It occurs when one or more of a person's physical senses are affected. Hunger, thirst, cold, heat, pain, or fear could cause a physical drive. A potential consumer may be exposed to any or all three types of stimuli. If aroused (motivated), he or she goes to the next step in the process. If a person is not sufficiently aroused, the stimulus is ignored—terminating the process for the given good or service.

Problem Awareness: At **problem awareness**, the consumer not only has been aroused by social, commercial, and/or physical stimuli but also recognizes that the good or service under consideration may solve a problem of shortage or unfulfilled desire. It is sometimes hard to learn

FIGURE 7-6
The Consumer Decision Process

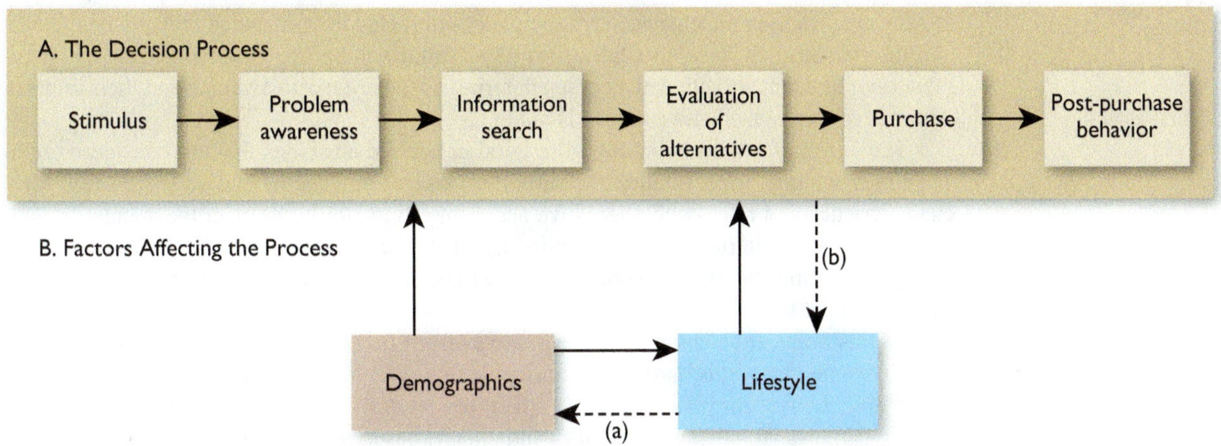

Note: Solid arrows connect all the elements in the decision process and show the impact of demographics and lifestyle upon the process. Dashed arrows show feedback. (a) shows the impact of lifestyle on certain demographics, such as family size, location, and marital status. (b) shows the impact of a purchase on elements of lifestyle, such as social class, reference groups, and social performance.

why a person is motivated enough to move from a stimulus to problem awareness. Many people shop with the same retailer or buy the same good or service for different reasons; they may not know their own motivation, and they may not tell a retailer their real reasons for shopping there or buying a certain item.

Recognition of shortage occurs when a person discovers a good or service should be repurchased. A good could wear down beyond repair, or the person might run out of an item such as milk. Service may be necessary if a good such as a car requires a repair. Recognition of unfulfilled desire takes place when a person becomes aware of a good or service that has not been bought before or a retailer that has not been patronized before. An item (such as contact lenses) may improve a person's lifestyle, self-image, and so on in an untried manner, or it may offer new performance features (such as a voice-activated computer). People are more hesitant to act on unfulfilled desires. Risks and benefits may be tougher to see. When a person becomes aware of a shortage or an unfulfilled desire, he or she acts only if it is a problem worth solving. Otherwise, the process ends.

Nonprofit Consumer World is an online, noncommercial guide with more than 2,000 sources to aid the consumer's information search (www.consumerworld.org).

Information Search: If problem awareness merits further thought, information is sought. An **information search** has two parts: (1) determining the alternatives that will solve the problem at hand (and where they can be bought) and (2) ascertaining the characteristics of each alternative.

First, the person compiles a list of goods or services that address the shortage or desire being considered. This list does not have to be formal. It may be a group of alternatives the person thinks about. A person with a lot of purchase experience normally uses an internal memory search to determine the goods or services—and retailers—that are satisfactory. A person with little purchase experience often uses an external search to develop a list of alternatives and retailers. This search can involve commercial sources such as retail salespeople, noncommercial sources such as *Consumer Reports*, and social sources such as friends. Second, the person gathers information about each alternative's attributes. An experienced shopper searches his or her memory for the attributes (pros and cons) of each alternative. A consumer with little experience or a lot of uncertainty searches externally for information.

The extent of an information search depends, in part, on the consumer's perceived risk regarding a specific good or service. Risk varies among individuals and by situation. For some, it is inconsequential; for others, it is quite important. The retailer's role is to provide enough information for a shopper to feel comfortable in making decisions, thus reducing perceived risk. Point-of-purchase ads, product displays, and knowledgeable sales personnel can provide consumers with the information they need.

Once the consumer's search for information is completed, he or she must decide whether a current shortage or unfulfilled desire can be met by any of the alternatives. If one or more are satisfactory, the consumer moves to the next step in the decision process. The consumer stops the process if no satisfactory goods or services are found.

Evaluation of Alternatives: Next, a person selects one option from among the choices. This is easy if one alternative is superior on all features. An item with excellent quality and a low price is a certain pick over expensive, average-quality ones. However, a choice may not be that simple, and the person then does an **evaluation of alternatives** before making a decision. If two or more options seem attractive, the person determines the criteria to evaluate and their importance. Alternatives are ranked and a choice is made.

The criteria for a decision are those good or service attributes that are considered relevant. They may include price, quality, fit, durability, and so on. The person sets standards for these characteristics and rates each alternative according to its ability to meet the standards. The importance of each criterion is also determined, and attributes are usually of differing importance to each person. One shopper may consider price to be most important while another places greater weight on quality and durability.

At this point, the person ranks alternatives from most favorite to least favorite and selects one. For some items, it is hard to rate attributes of available alternatives because they are technical, intangible, new, or poorly labeled. When this occurs, shoppers often use price, brand name, or store name as an indicator of quality and choose based on this criterion. Once a person ranks alternatives, he or she chooses the most satisfactory good or service. In situations where no alternative is adequate, a decision not to buy is made.

Purchase Act: A person is now ready for the **purchase act**—an exchange of money or a promise to pay for the ownership or use of a good or service. Important decisions are still made

FIGURE 7-7
Key Factors in the Purchase Act

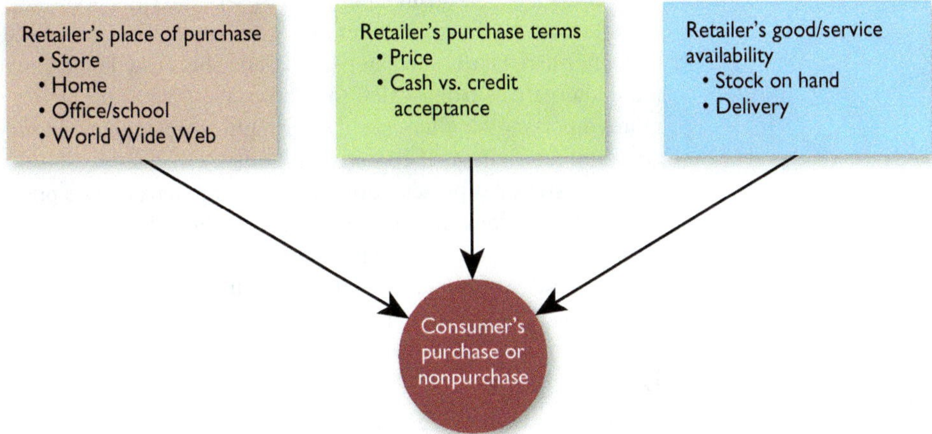

in this step. For a retailer, the purchase act may be the most crucial aspect of the decision process because the consumer is mainly concerned with three factors, as highlighted in Figure 7-7:

1. *Place of purchase*—this may be a store or a nonstore location. Many more items are bought at stores than through nonstore retailing, although the latter are growing more quickly. The place of purchase is evaluated in the same way as the good or the service: alternatives are listed, their traits are defined, and they are ranked. The most desirable place is then chosen. Criteria for selecting a store retailer include store location, store layout, service, sales help, store image, and prices. Criteria for selecting a nonstore retailer include image, service, prices, hours, interactivity, and convenience. A consumer will shop with the firm that has the best combination of criteria, as defined by that consumer.
2. *Purchase terms*—these include the price and method of payment. Price is the dollar amount a person must pay to achieve the ownership or use of a good or service. Method of payment is the way the price may be paid (cash, short-term credit, long-term credit).
3. *Availability*—this relates to stock on hand and delivery. Stock on hand is the amount of an item that a place of purchase has in stock. Delivery is the time span between placing an order and receiving an item and the ease with which an item is transported to its place of use.

If a person is pleased with all aspects of the purchase act, the good or service is bought. If there is dissatisfaction with the place of purchase, the terms of purchase, or availability, the consumer may not buy, although there is contentment with the item itself:

> Kylie wanted to buy a new car. But, after a month of trying, she gave up: "The model I wanted was sold only at a dealer 50 miles away and through an online third-party firm. The dealer overpriced the car by $750. The Web retailer had a good deal on the model I wanted, but insisted that I had to buy an upgrade package for $500. When I heard that, I decided to keep my old car for another year."

Post-Purchase Behavior: After buying a good or service, a consumer may engage in **post-purchase behavior**, which falls into either of two categories: further purchases or re-evaluation. Sometimes, buying one item leads to further purchases and decision making continues until the last purchase is made. For instance, a car purchase leads to insurance; a retailer using scrambled merchandising may stimulate a shopper to make further purchases after the primary good or service is bought.

A person may also re-evaluate a purchase. Is performance as promised? Do actual attributes match the expectations the consumer had? Has the retailer acted as expected? Satisfaction typically leads to contentment, a repurchase when a good or service wears out, and positive ratings to friends. Dissatisfaction may lead to unhappiness, brand or store switching, and unfavorable conversations with friends and negative online postings. The latter situation (dissatisfaction) may result from **cognitive dissonance**—doubt that the correct decision has been made. A consumer may regret that the purchase was made at all or may wish that another choice had been made. To overcome cognitive dissonance and dissatisfaction, the retailer must realize that the decision process does not end with a purchase. After-care (by phone, a service visit, or E-mail) may be as important as anything a retailer does to complete the sale. When items are expensive or important, after-care takes on greater significance because the person really wants to be right. Also, the more alternatives from which to choose, the greater the doubt after a decision is made and the more important the after-care. Department stores pioneered money-back guarantees so customers could return items if cognitive dissonance occurred.

Realistic sales presentations and ad campaigns reduce post-sale dissatisfaction because consumer expectations do not then exceed reality. If overly high expectations are created, a consumer is more apt to be unhappy because performance is not at the level promised. Combining an honest sales presentation with good customer after-care reduces or eliminates cognitive dissonance and dissatisfaction.

Types of Consumer Decision Making

Every time a person buys a good or service or visits a retailer, he or she uses a form of the decision process. The process is often undertaken subconsciously, and a person is not even aware of its use. And, as indicated in Figure 7-6, the process is affected by consumer characteristics. Older people may not spend as much time as younger ones in making some decisions due to their experience. Well-educated consumers may consult many information sources—and, increasingly, the Internet—before making a decision. Upper-income consumers may spend less time making a decision because they can afford to buy again if they are dissatisfied. In a family with children, each member may have input into a decision, which lengthens the process. Class-conscious shoppers may be more interested in social sources, including social media. Consumers with low self-esteem or high perceived risk may use all the steps in detail. People under time pressure may skip steps to save time.

The use of the decision process differs by situation. The purchase of a new home usually means a thorough use of each step in the process; perceived risk is high regardless of the consumer's background. In the purchase of a fast-food meal, the consumer often skips certain steps; perceived risk is low regardless of the person's background. There are three types of decision processes: extended decision making, limited decision making, and routine decision making.

Extended decision making occurs when a consumer makes full use of the decision process. A lot of time is spent gathering information and evaluating alternatives—both what to buy and where to buy it—before a purchase. The potential for cognitive dissonance is great. In this category are expensive, complex items with which the person has had little or no experience. Perceived risk of all kinds is high. Items requiring extended decision making include a house, a first car, and life insurance. At any point in the process, a consumer can stop, and for expensive, complex items, this occurs often. Consumer traits (such as age, education, income, and class consciousness) have the most impact with extended decision making.

Because their customers tend to use extended decision making, such retailers as real-estate brokers and auto dealers emphasize personal selling, printed materials, and other communication to provide as much information as possible. A low-key informative approach may be best, so shoppers do not feel threatened. Various financing options may be offered. In this way, the consumer's perceived risk is minimized.

With **limited decision making**, a consumer uses each step in the purchase process but does not spend a great deal of time on each of them. It requires less time than extended decision making because the person typically has some experience with both the what and the where of the purchase. This category includes items that have been bought before but not regularly. Risk is moderate, and the consumer spends some time shopping. Priority may be placed on evaluating known alternatives according to the person's desires and standards, although information search is important for some. Items requiring limited decision making include a second car, clothing, a vacation, and gifts. Consumer attributes affect decision making, but the impact lessens as perceived risk falls and experience rises. Income, the importance of the purchase, and motives play strong roles in limited decision making.

This form of decision making is relevant to such retailers as department stores, specialty stores, and nonstore retailers that want to sway behavior and that carry goods and services that people have bought before. The shopping environment and assortment are very important. Sales personnel should be available for questions and to differentiate among brands or models.

Routine decision making takes place when the consumer buys out of habit and skips steps in the purchase process. He or she wants to spend little or no time shopping, and the same brands are usually repurchased (often from the same retailers). This category includes items that are bought regularly. They have little risk because of consumer experience. The key step is problem awareness. When the consumer realizes a good or service is needed, a repurchase is often automatic. Information search, evaluation of alternatives, and post-purchase behavior are unlikely. These steps are not undertaken as long as a person is satisfied. Items involved with routine decision making include groceries, newspapers, and haircuts. Consumer attributes have little impact. Problem awareness almost inevitably leads to a purchase.

This type of decision making is most relevant to such retailers as supermarkets, dry cleaners, and fast-food outlets. For them, these strategic elements are crucial: a good location, long hours, clear product displays, and, most important, product availability. Ads should be reminder-oriented. The major task is completing the transaction quickly and precisely.

Impulse Purchases and Customer Loyalty

Impulse purchases and customer loyalty merit our special attention.

Impulse purchases arise when consumers buy products and/or brands they had not planned on buying before entering a store, reading a mail-order catalog, seeing a TV shopping show, turning to the Web, and so forth. At least part of consumer decision making is influenced by the retailer. There are three kinds of impulse shopping:

- *Completely unplanned.* Before coming into contact with a retailer, a consumer has no intention of making a purchase in a goods or service category.
- *Partially unplanned.* Before coming into contact with a retailer, a consumer has decided to make a purchase in a goods or service category but has not chosen a brand or model.
- *Unplanned substitution.* A consumer intends to buy a specific brand of a good or service but changes his or her mind about the brand after coming into contact with a retailer.

With the partially unplanned and substitution kinds of impulse purchases, some decisions take place before a person interacts with a retailer. In these cases, a shopper may be involved with extended, limited, or routine decision making. Completely unplanned shopping is often related to routine decision making or limited decision making; there is little or no time spent shopping, and the key step is problem awareness.

According to recent research from OgilvyAction, about 72 percent of North American shoppers "make at least one decision in-store." For European, Middle Eastern, and African shoppers, the figure is 59 percent. For shoppers in various Asian markets, the number is 54 percent. Roughly 51 percent of Latin American shoppers make at least one purchase decision in the store.[20]

Impulse purchases are more influenced by retail displays and in-store interactions than are pre-planned purchases: "Sales in a category with displays often will rise, although sales of the brand on display may not enjoy the same percentage increase. Shoppers can seldom resist stocking up on quality brands that slash the price to sustain volume sales. Brands that engage shoppers, experientially or emotionally, tend to turn shoppers into buyers. Engagement can range from having brand ambassadors interacting in-store to demonstrations and sampling."[21] See Figure 7-8.

In studying impulse buying, these are some of the consumer attitudes and behavior patterns that retailers should take into consideration:

- In-store browsing is positively affected by the amount of time a person has to shop.
- Some individuals are more predisposed toward making impulse purchases than others.
- The leading reason given by consumers for impulse shopping is to take advantage of a low price/bargain. "Impulse should no longer be viewed of as frivolous behavior—increasingly, it is savvy opportunism."
- Impulse shopping is affected by how stores are arranged. "Old Navy has remodeled many stores so customers can [get around the store more easily] and see more merchandise."
- Impulse shopping is influenced by whether consumers believe that discounts are real. "Shoppers are now seeing through half-hearted initiatives, some of which aren't a bargain at all."[22]

L.L. Bean (www.llbean.com) has some of the most loyal customers around. See why.

When **customer loyalty** exists, a person regularly patronizes a particular retailer (store or nonstore) that he or she knows, likes, and trusts. This lets a person reduce decision making

FIGURE 7-8
Stimulating Impulse Shopping
Could you resist spending more if an in-store circular featured deals such as the ones shown here?

Source: trekandshoot/ Shutterstock.com. Reprinted by permission.

because he or she does not have to invest time in learning about and choosing the retailer from which to purchase. Loyal customers tend to be time-conscious, like shopping locally, do not often engage in outshopping, and spend more per shopping trip. In a service setting, such as an auto repair shop, customer satisfaction often leads to shopper loyalty; price has less bearing on decisions.

Applying the retailing concept certainly enhances the chances of gaining and keeping loyal customers: customer orientation, coordinated effort, value-driven, and goal orientation. Relationship retailing also helps!

According to one expert, customer loyalty can be placed into four categories (from worst to best):

1. **Inertia Loyalty**—These shoppers are loyal because it is inconvenient to switch retailers or brands. This occurs with loyalty programs offered by airlines, banks, and grocery retailers. Patrons "have no incentive to stay once a competitor makes it easy to switch."
2. **Mercenary Loyalty**—"Just as a mercenary will swear allegiance for a price, retailers can pay customers for their loyalty." Points and discount-based loyalty programs usually are in this tier. "Yes, the tactic may work, but its major weakness is that the loyalty generated is emotionally shallow, and there's little to stop your competitor from taking customers simply by paying more."
3. **True Loyalty**—Retailers get to this tier when customers feel compelling reasons to resist offers from competitive offers. A retailer "with true loyalty won't lose customers because the relationship is based on a deeper connection of trust and shared value."
4. **Cult Loyalty**—For customers at this tier, "rejecting the brand would be like rejecting your own values. Commitment becomes a virtual lock. Cult loyalty can be cultivated, particularly through an effective social-media program."[23]

Unfortunately, a number of retailers use a one-size-fits-all loyalty program, typically monetary rewards to stimulate repeat visits:

> Product discounts won't change buying behavior in the long run in shoppers who value personalized service, convenience, or shopping pleasure more. They may change their behavior to access the price promotion, but likely will revert back to their regular brands or buying habits shortly thereafter. A more effective way to woo customers and maintain their patronage is to offer them individualized rewards, based on what they value. Providing access to a speedy checkout lane would be a better way to win the loyalty of a person who hates grocery shopping than a discount on a future purchase.[24]

Pasta Pomodoro's New-Fashioned Loyalty Program

Pasta Pomodoro (www.pastapomodoro.com), a 26-unit California-based Italian casual restaurant chain, uses Punchh (www.punchh.com), a mobile app loyalty program that is compatible with the chain's older card-based program. Although the older loyalty program requires members to present their member card or telephone number, with the Punchh-based program, members can download this information directly from their smart phone.

After patrons complete their meals, they can use their camera app to take a digital photo of their bill. The photos are uploaded to the computer server and stored in Punchh's data base. The photos include such details of the transaction as the total bill, the waiter's name, and the total loyalty points earned during each visit. Guests are eligible to receive restaurant rewards for redemption once they have earned the required number of points. Members can also share their restaurant experiences with Pasta Pomodoro management, as well as others, on Facebook. The Punchh system can also be used by consumers to locate all nearby restaurants that participate in this loyalty program.

While both the card- and app-based loyalty programs are still available to the restaurant's guests, four times more guests have signed up for the new program. Members of the Punchh program also have a higher visit frequency rate than card-based program members.

Source: Deena M. Amato-McCoy, "New Generation of Loyalty," *Stores* (May 2011), pp. 34–35.

RETAILER ACTIONS

As noted in Chapter 3, in *mass marketing*, a firm such as a supermarket or a drugstore sells to a broad spectrum of consumers; it does not really focus efforts on any one kind of customer. In *concentrated marketing*, a retailer tailors its strategy to the needs of one distinct consumer group, such as young working women; it does not attempt to satisfy people outside that segment. With *differentiated marketing*, a retailer aims at two or more distinct consumer groups, such as men and boys, with a different strategy mix for each; it can do this by operating more than one kind of outlet (such as separate men's and boys' clothing stores) or by having distinct departments grouped by market segment in a single store (as a department store might do). In deciding on a target market approach, a retailer considers its goods/service category and goals, competitors' actions, the size of various segments, the efficiency of each target market alternative for the particular firm, the resources required, and other factors. See Figure 7-9.

After choosing a target market method, the retailer selects the target market(s) to which it wants to appeal; identifies the characteristics, needs, and attitudes of the target market(s); seeks to understand how its target customers make purchase decisions; and acts appropriately. The process to devise a target market strategy is shown in Figure 7-10. Visit our Web site (www.pearsonhighered.com/bermanevans) for several useful links on target marketing.

We now present several examples of retailers' target market activities.

Retailers with Mass Marketing Strategies

Walgreens drugstore chain and Kohl's Department Stores engage in mass marketing.

Walgreens is a national chain with 8,000 drugstores. The firm attracts a broad array of customers. About 6.1 million people visit a Walgreens store daily. The firm "provides the most convenient access to consumer goods and services, and pharmacy, health and wellness services, in America. We are transforming into a more efficient and customer-focused firm. We offer patients a way to stretch their dollars and maintain prescriptions in one place without sacrificing the safety, service, or convenience of their nearby neighborhood drugstore. We have expanded our private brands, which provide greater value to customers. We continue to offer competitively priced consumables, whose sales have been very strong, particularly for fast, easy, midweek fill-in needs in our conveniently located retail stores."[25]

Kohl's is a popular general merchandise retailer. And it is capitalizing on a mass marketing approach: "If you've ever shopped one of our clean, bright department stores, you've already experienced our commitment to family, value, and national brands. Our stores are stocked with everything you need for yourself and your home—apparel, shoes, and accessories for women, children, and men, plus home products like small electronics, bedding, luggage, and more. Online, we've taken our commitment to convenience even further, and you'll find there's more to like at Kohls.com with every click of your mouse."[26]

Find out why Kohl's is appealing (www.kohls.com).

FIGURE 7-9

Contrasting Target Market Strategies

Givenchy is an upscale retailer of perfume, cologne, and cosmetics. Shown here is its Paris, France, store (top); this Venice, Italy, street vendor appeals mostly to tourists looking for bargains (bottom).

Sources: Tupungato/ Shutterstock.com; and Paul Prescott/Shutterstock.com. Reprinted by permission.

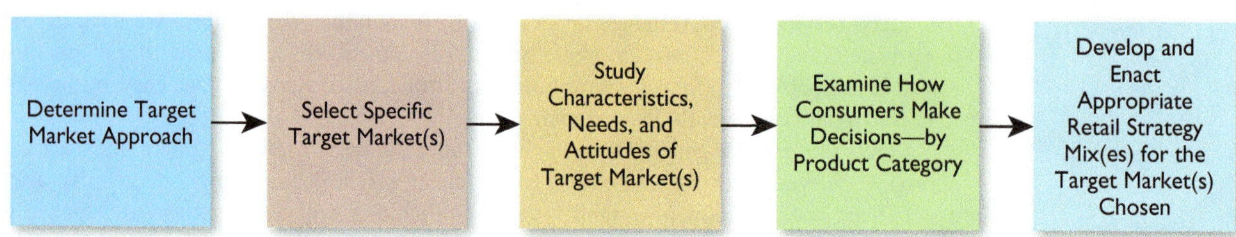

FIGURE 7-10

Devising a Target Market Strategy

Retailers with Concentrated Marketing Strategies

Family Dollar and Wet Seal engage in concentrated marketing.

Family Dollar (www.familydollar.com) has carved out a distinctive, narrow niche for itself.

Family Dollar operates 7,200 dollar stores (a type of variety store) in 45 states. It has a very focused target market strategy: The average Family Dollar customer is a female with an annual income of less than $40,000 who shops for her family. Customers depend on Family Dollar for the good prices they need to stretch their budgets. Stores are rather small and often situated in rural areas and small towns, as well as in urban areas. "Our merchandise is sold at everyday low prices in a no-frills, low overhead, self-service environment. Most merchandise is priced under $10.00."[27]

Wet Seal is a 460-store apparel chain that caters to young women. According to the company, "Wet Seal is the junior apparel brand for teenage girls that seek trend-focused and value competitive clothing with a target customer age of 13 to 19 years old. Wet Seal seeks to provide its customer base with a balance of affordably priced fashionable apparel and accessories. Wet Seal stores average approximately 4,000 square feet in size."[28] Wet Seal brings in new apparel and accessories on a regular basis.

Retailers with Differentiated Marketing Strategies

Foot Locker, Inc. and Gap Inc. engage in differentiated marketing.

Limited Brands (www.limitedbrands.com) is another retailer practicing differentiated marketing—with its Victoria's Secret, Pink, Bath & Body Works, La Senza, C.O. Bigelow, White Barn Candle Co., and Henri Bendel units.

Besides its mainstream Foot Locker stores, the parent company (Foot Locker, Inc.) also operates chains geared specially toward women and children. Lady Foot Locker offers "major athletic footwear and apparel brands, as well as casual wear and an assortment of apparel designed for a variety of activities, including running, walking, toning, and fitness." Kids Foot Locker carries "the largest selection of brand-name athletic footwear, apparel, and accessories for children. Stores feature an environment geared to appeal to both parents and children."[29]

For many years, Gap Inc. has applied differentiated marketing through its Gap ("clean, classic clothing and accessories to help customers express their individual sense of style—includes Gap, Gap Kids, Baby Gap, Gap Maternity, and Gap Body"), Banana Republic ("accessible luxury that brings modern, soulful, effortless, and versatile style for men and women around the world"), Old Navy ("brings fun fashion and value to the whole family" and "ensures that our customers find great, quality products at good value"), Piperlime ("an online fashion boutique that inspires customers with a fresh and unique mix of products, brands, and price points"), and Athleta ("the ultimate performance apparel and gear for every active woman, from the weekend warrior to the committed yogini to the driven competitive athlete") divisions.[30]

ENVIRONMENTAL FACTORS AFFECTING CONSUMERS

Several environmental factors influence shopping attitudes and behavior, including:

- State of the economy.
- Consumer confidence about the future.
- Country of residence (industrialized versus developing).
- Cost of living in the person's region or city of residence.
- Rate of inflation (how quickly prices are rising).
- Infrastructure where people shop, such as traffic congestion, the crime rate, and the ease of parking.
- Price wars among retailers.
- Emergence of new retail formats.
- Trend toward more people working at home.
- Government and community regulations regarding shopping hours, new construction, consumer protection, and so forth.
- Evolving societal values and norms.

Although all of these elements may not necessarily have an impact on any particular shopper, they do influence the retailer's overall target market.

When considering the retail strategy that they offer their customers, companies should consider these observations about the standard of living. It:

> includes not only the material articles of consumption but also the size of a family, the environment, educational opportunities, and spending for health, recreation, and social services. Unemployment, low wages, crowded living conditions, and physical calamities may bring a drop in the standard of living; and an increase in social benefits and higher wages may bring a rise. The standard of living varies from nation to nation; and international comparisons are sometimes made by analyzing per capita income or any number of other indicators. Industrialized nations tend to have a higher standard of living.[31]

> While consumers are still reeling from the the global economic crisis, lessons have been learned, behaviors have changed, and consumers have adapted. As Alexandra Smith of Mintel said, "The effects of the global economic crisis have had long-reaching implications. Indeed, these consumer trends are a legacy created by economics, but now gathering." In Great Britain, 43 percent of consumers say: "Trying to add to my rainy day savings" is a priority. One-third of U.S. consumers say they're using debit rather than credit transactions. They want to know what they're getting themselves into: no hidden costs and no pricey upgrades.[32]

Chapter Summary

1. *To discuss why it is important for a retailer to properly identify, understand, and appeal to its customers.* To properly develop a strategy mix, a retailer must identify the characteristics, needs, and attitudes of consumers; understand how consumers make decisions; and enact the proper target market plan. It must study environmental influences, too.

2. *To enumerate and describe a number of consumer demographics, lifestyle factors, and needs and desires—and to explain how these concepts can be applied to retailing.* Demographics are easily identifiable and measurable population statistics. Lifestyles are the ways in which consumers live and spend time and money.

   Consumer demographics include gender, age, life expectancy, literacy, languages spoken, income, retail sales, education, and ethnic/racial background. These data usually have to be localized to be useful for retailers. Consumer lifestyles comprise social and psychological elements and are affected by demographics. Social factors include culture, social class, reference groups, the family life cycle, and time utilization. Psychological factors include personality, class consciousness, attitudes, perceived risk, and purchase importance. As with demographics, a firm can generate a lifestyle profile of its target market by analyzing these concepts.

   There are several demographic and lifestyle trends that apply to retailing. These involve gender roles, consumer sophistication and confidence, the poverty of time, and component lifestyles. Research has enumerated consumer profiles in a useful way for retailers.

   When preparing a target market profile, consumer needs and desires should be identified. Needs are basic shopping requirements, and desires are discretionary shopping goals. A retail strategy geared toward satisfying consumer needs is appealing to their motives—the reasons for behavior. The better needs and desires are addressed, the more apt people are to buy.

3. *To examine consumer attitudes toward shopping and consumer shopping behavior, including the consumer decision process and its stages.* Many people do not enjoy shopping and no longer feel high prices reflect value. Different segments have different attitudes. More people now believe private brands are of good quality. Consumer patronage differs by retailer type. People often cross-shop, whereby they shop for a product category at more than one retail format during the year or visit multiple retailers on the same shopping trip.

   Retailers should have an awareness of consumer behavior—the process individuals use to decide whether, what, when, where, how, from whom, and how often to buy. The consumer's decision process must be grasped from two perspectives: (a) the good or service the consumer thinks of buying and (b) where the consumer will buy that item. These decisions can be made separately or jointly.

   The consumer decision process consists of stimulus, problem awareness, information search, evaluation of alternatives, purchase, and post-purchase behavior. It is influenced by a person's background and traits. A stimulus is a cue or drive meant to motivate a person to act. At problem awareness, the consumer not only has been aroused by a stimulus but also recognizes that a good or service may solve a problem of shortage or unfulfilled desire. An information search determines the available alternatives and their characteristics. Alternatives are then evaluated and ranked. In the purchase act, a consumer considers the place of purchase, terms, and availability. After a purchase, there may be post-purchase behavior in the form of additional purchases or re-evaluation. The consumer may have cognitive dissonance if there is doubt that a correct choice has been made.

In extended decision making, a person makes full use of the decision process. In limited decision making, each step is used, but not in depth. In routine decision making, a person buys out of habit and skips steps. Impulse purchases occur when shoppers make purchases they had not planned before coming into contact with the retailer. With customer loyalty, a person regularly patronizes a retailer.

4. *To look at retailer actions based on target market planning.* Retailers can deploy mass marketing, concentrated marketing, or differentiated marketing. Several examples are presented.

5. *To note some of the environmental factors that affect consumer shopping.* Consumer attitudes and behavior are swayed by the economy, the inflation rate, the infrastructure where people shop, and other factors. Retailers also need to consider how the standard of living is changing.

Key Terms

demographics (p. 174)
lifestyles (p. 174)
discretionary income (p. 174)
culture (p. 177)
social class (p. 177)
reference groups (p. 177)
family life cycle (p. 177)
household life cycle (p. 177)
personality (p. 177)
class consciousness (p. 177)
attitudes (opinions) (p. 177)
perceived risk (p. 177)
motives (p. 181)
outshopping (p. 182)
cross-shopping (p. 184)
consumer behavior (p. 184)
consumer decision process (p. 185)
stimulus (p. 185)
problem awareness (p. 185)
information search (p. 186)
evaluation of alternatives (p. 186)
purchase act (p. 186)
post-purchase behavior (p. 187)
cognitive dissonance (p. 187)
extended decision making (p. 188)
limited decision making (p. 188)
routine decision making (p. 189)
impulse purchases (p. 189)
customer loyalty (p. 189)

Questions for Discussion

1. Comment on this statement: "A competitive retail sector, facing an uncertain economic future, is being challenged by consumers to compete for their business. In this environment, only the fittest and those really listening to what their customers really want are likely to survive."
2. Analyze the global population data in Table 7-1 from a retailing perspective.
3. How could a national auto parts chain use the U.S. population data presented in Table 7-2?
4. Explain how a retailer selling expensive furniture could reduce the six types of perceived risk.
5. Why is it important for retailers to know the difference between needs and desires?
6. Why do some consumers engage in outshopping? What could be done to encourage them to shop closer to home?
7. Is cross-shopping good or bad for a retailer? Explain your answer.
8. Describe how the consumer decision process would operate for these goods and services. Include "what" and "where" in your answers: a smart phone, a lawn care service, and an everyday watch. Which elements of the decision process are most important to retailers in each instance? Explain your answers.
9. Differentiate among the three types of impulse purchases. Give an example of each.
10. Contrast the mass-market approach used by a supermarket with the concentrated marketing approach used by a fruit-and-vegetable store. What is the key to each firm succeeding?
11. Visit a nearby Radio Shack or look at its Web site (www.radioshack.com), and then describe its target market strategy.
12. Why is it worthwhile for retailers to understand the complexity of the standard-of-living concept?

Web-Based Exercise

Macy's (www.macys.com) and Bloomingdale's (www.bloomingdales.com) are two department store chains operated by Macy's Inc. (www.macysinc.com). Visit these three Web sites and evaluate the target marketing efforts that you find described there, in terms of the concepts in this chapter. How do the target market strategies differ for Macy's and Bloomingdale's?

Note: Also stop by our Web site (www.pearsonhighered.com/bermanevans) to experience a number of highly interactive, appealing Web exercises based on actual company demonstrations and sample materials related to retailing.

8 Information Gathering and Processing in Retailing

Chapter Objectives

1. To discuss how information flows in a retail distribution channel
2. To show why retailers should avoid strategies based on inadequate information
3. To look at the retail information system, its components, and the recent advances in such systems
4. To describe the marketing research process

The best retailers recognize that their decisions should be made after gathering and analyzing key information and not just made based on intuition or a "gut feeling." What we are seeing more often is that social media can play a vital ongoing role in this process—especially with regard to acquiring competitive intelligence.

Here's what Kristi Hines, a consultant and blogger, says about the information value of social media:

> Are you looking for that competitive edge? Want to know what your peers are doing? Using social media to research competitors can provide useful information for any business. Learning about your competitors' activities can give you insight into what works and what doesn't. The beauty of social media is that there's a ton of information about competitors that is public. And not only is their strategy public, but the reaction to that strategy is public as well. Think about the things you can learn about your competitors through different social networks, search engines, and other outlets.

Monika Hansen, another consultant and blogger, suggests what to look for when visiting competitors' social media sites: At Twitter, review what other retailers are tweeting, how many followers these retailers have, and what kinds of mentions are being left by followers. At Facebook, see how other retailers are using their "wall" to energize customers, how many people "like" the firms, and what makes people happy and unhappy. At YouTube, view video clips from other retailers—some even have their own YouTube channels—to learn what they are doing and how many views they are getting. As Hansen says: "This is a great way to see what is and what is not working for your competitors on social media. No need to repeat someone else's mistakes, right?"[1]

Source: BeTA-Artworks/ fotolia.com.

Overview

When a retailer sets a new strategy or modifies an existing one, gathering and analyzing information is crucial because it reduces the chances of wrong decisions. The firm can study the attributes and buying behavior of current and potential customers, alternative store and nonstore sites, store management and operations, product offerings, prices, and store image and promotion to prepare the best plan. See Figure 8-1.

Research activity should, to a large degree, be determined by the risk involved. Although it may be risky for a department store to open a new branch store, there is much less risk if that retailer is deciding whether to carry a new line of sweaters. In the branch store situation, thousands of research dollars and months of study may be necessary. In the case of the new sweaters, limited research may be sufficient.

iTools (www.itools.com) offers very useful research tools, including multiple search engines, a dictionary, a thesaurus, a language translator, and more.

Information gathering and processing should be conducted in an ongoing manner, yielding enough data for planning and analysis. Consider these two examples:

> For many retailers, determining where to spend precious capital requires input from a number of departments—and combining their data into usable information. This includes comparing store sales and overall performance with the store's condition so that finances can be directed to where they will be most effective. Technology can help ensure that information gathering can be standardized and repeated for multiple stores, and that the resulting data can be combined and streamlined into a form that can help decision makers act.[2]

> A few years ago, Dunkin' Donuts chief marketing officer Ken Kimmel wanted to use cell phone cameras to capture images of doughnut cases that needed improvement, but the technology just wasn't up to the task—until the iPhone came along. Now On The Spot Systems, Kimmel's firm, has an app to survey customers. Customers complete the survey on smart phones while waiting for their payment to be processed. To review results, clients access a secure Web portal. They receive reports with all data compiled—stores compared, pie charts, graphs, etc.; and they receive verbatim customer responses.[3]

FIGURE 8-1

Be Informed, But Not Overloaded

Today, more information is available—for both large and small retailers—than ever before. So, even though it is imperative to gather and analyze sufficient data to make the best decisions, retailers also must be careful not to become overwhelmed by the data.

Source: Angela Waye/Shutterstock.com. Reprinted by permission.

This chapter first looks at the information flows in a retail distribution channel and notes the ramifications of inadequate research. We then describe the retail information system, data-base management and data warehousing, and the marketing research process in detail.

INFORMATION FLOWS IN A RETAIL DISTRIBUTION CHANNEL

In an effective retail distribution channel, information flows freely and efficiently among the three main parties: supplier (manufacturer and/or wholesaler), retailer, and consumer. This enables the parties to better anticipate and address each other's performance expectations. We highlight the flows in Figure 8-2 and describe the information needs of the parties next.

A *supplier* needs these kinds of information: (1) from the retailer—estimates of category sales, inventory turnover rates, feedback on competitors, the level of customer returns, and so on; and (2) from the consumer—attitudes toward given styles and models, the extent of brand loyalty, the willingness to pay a premium for superior quality, and so on. A *retailer* needs these kinds of information: (1) from the supplier—advance notice of new models and model changes, training materials for complex products, sales forecasts, justification for price hikes, and so on; and (2) from the consumer—why people shop with the retailer, what they like and dislike about the retailer, where else people shop, and so on. A *consumer* needs these kinds of information: (1) from the supplier—assembly and operating instructions, the extent of warranty coverage, where to send a complaint, and so on; and (2) from the retailer—how various alternatives compare, where specific merchandise is stocked in the store, the methods of payment accepted, the rain check policy when a sale item is out of stock, and so on.

Retailers often play a crucial role in collecting data for other members of the value delivery chain because they have the most direct contact with shoppers. Retailers can assist other channel members by:

- Permitting data to be gathered on their premises. Many research firms like to conduct surveys at shopping centers because of the large and broad base of shoppers.
- Gathering specific data requested by suppliers, such as how shoppers react to displays.
- Passing along information on the attributes of consumers buying particular brands and models. Because many credit transactions involve retailer cards, these retailers can link purchases with consumer age, income, occupation, and other factors.

For the best information flows, collaboration and cooperation are necessary—especially between suppliers and retailers. This is not always easy, as the view of one supply chain analyst indicates: "In a growing number of instances, a [retailer's] success is now highly reliant on the performance of its suppliers and on the efficient workings of those relationships. However, the information on suppliers available to buyers is often fragmented, erroneous, incomplete, insufficient, and frequently duplicated across the enterprise. In the vast majority of instances, there is no single source of supplier information."[4]

Fortunately, many retailers are working to improve their information-sharing efforts. And as in many aspects of retailing, Wal-Mart is leading the way. Thousands of suppliers have online access to Wal-Mart's data base through its password-protected Retail Link system (https://retaillink.wal-mart.com), which handles hundreds of thousands of information queries weekly. Retail Link was developed to promote more collaboration in inventory planning and product shipping, and it is a linchpin of Wal-Mart's information efforts today:

> Retail Link provides information and an array of products that allow a supplier to impact all aspects of their business. By using the information available in Retail Link, you can easily plan, execute, and analyze your business—thus providing better service to our common

FIGURE 8-2
How Information Flows in a Retail Distribution Channel

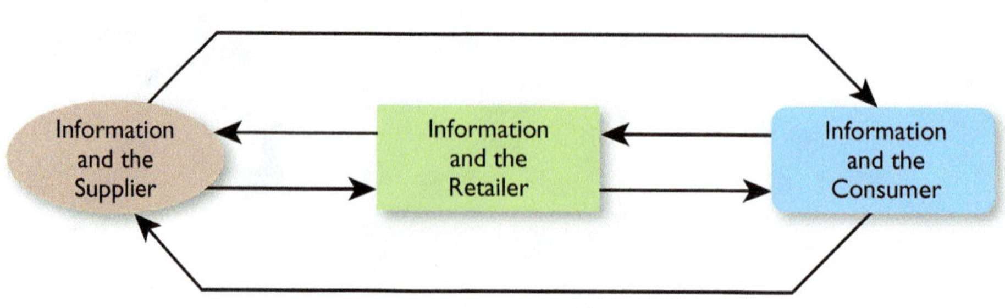

CAREERS IN RETAILING

Carol Tomé: Home Depot Information Guru

Carol Tomé, Home Depot's (www.homedepot.com) chief financial officer, is a leading contender to be the home improvement chain's next chief executive officer (CEO). Her chances of replacing Frank Blake, the current CEO, at his retirement depend to a large degree on whether she is successful in updating Home Depot's in-store technology and its Web-based sales. Although technology has not been a major priority at Home Depot until recently, the company recently introduced a mobile app that enables customers to order goods on their iPhone or iPad. And in 2010, under her leadership, Home Depot invested $60 million to replace the retailer's in-store computers with 40,000 handheld devices.

Carol Tomé has been the only senior Home Depot executive who has reported to all four of its CEOs. In 2001, she was promoted from treasurer to chief financial officer (CFO). As CFO, her responsibilities were broadened to include store operations and customer service. She also headed a corporate-wide committee that planned and implemented Home Depot's store expansion program.

Ms. Tomé annually earns several million dollars from Home Depot. In addition to her responsibilities at Home Depot, she is a director of United Parcel Service and chairperson of the Federal Reserve Bank of Atlanta.

Source: Chris Burritt, "Home Depot's Fix-It Lady," www.businessweek.com (January 17, 2011).

customers. The Retail Link Web site is accessible to any area within your company. We require all suppliers to participate in Retail Link because of the benefits it provides. Should you become one of our suppliers, you'll be provided with the requirements for accessing Retail Link.[5]

AVOIDING RETAIL STRATEGIES BASED ON INADEQUATE INFORMATION

Retailers are often tempted to rely on nonsystematic or incomplete ways of obtaining information due to time and costs, as well as a lack of research skills. The results can be devastating. Here are examples.

Using intuition. A movie theater charges $10 for tickets at all times. The manager feels that because all patrons are seeing the same movie, prices should be the same for a Monday matinee as a Saturday evening. Yet, by looking at data stored in the theater's information system, she would learn attendance is much lower on Mondays. Because people prefer Saturday evening performances, they will pay $10 to see a movie then. Weekday customers have to be lured, and a lower price is a way to do so.

Continuing what was done before. A toy store orders conservatively for the holiday season because prior year sales were weak. The store sells out two weeks before the peak of the season, and more items cannot be received in time for the holiday. The owner assumed that last year's poor sales would occur again. Yet, a consumer survey would reveal a sense of optimism and an increased desire to give gifts.

Copying a successful competitor's strategy. A local bookstore decides to cut the prices of best-sellers to match the prices of a nearby chain bookstore. The local store then loses a lot of money and has to go out of business. Its costs are too high to match the chain's prices. The firm lost sight of its natural strengths (personal service, a more customer-friendly atmosphere, and long-time community ties).

Devising a strategy after speaking to a few individuals about their perceptions. A family-run gift store decides to have a family meeting to determine the product assortment for the next year. Each family member gives an opinion, and an overall "shopping list" is then compiled. Sometimes, the selections are right on target; other times, they result in a lot of excess inventory. The family would do better by also attending trade shows and reading industry publications.

Automatically assuming that a successful business can easily expand. A Web retailer does well with small appliances and portable TVs. It has a good reputation and wants to add other product lines to capitalize on its customer goodwill. However, the addition of custom furniture yields poor results. The firm did not first conduct research, which would have indicated that people buy standard, branded merchandise via the Web but are more reluctant to buy custom furniture that way.

Not having a good read on consumer perceptions. A florist cuts the price of two-day-old flowers from $17 to $5 a dozen because they have a shorter life expectancy, but they don't sell. The florist assumes bargain-hunting consumers will want the flowers as gifts or for floral arrangements. What the florist does not realize (due to a lack of research) is that people perceive the older flowers to be of poor quality. The extremely low price actually turns off customers!

What conclusion should we draw from these examples? Inadequate information can cause a firm to devise and enact a bad strategy. These situations can be avoided by using a well-conceived retail information system and properly executing marketing research.

THE RETAIL INFORMATION SYSTEM

A retail information system requires a lot of background information, which makes the SecondaryData.com Web site (www.secondarydata.com/marketing/retailing.asp) valuable.

Data gathering and analysis should not be regarded as a one-shot resolution of a single retailing issue. They should be part of an ongoing, integrated process. A **retail information system (RIS)** anticipates the information needs of retail managers; collects, organizes, and stores relevant data on a continuous basis; and directs the flow of information to the proper decision makers.

These topics are covered next: building and using a retail information system, data-base management, and gathering information via the UPC (Universal Product Code) and EDI (electronic data interchange).

Building and Using a Retail Information System

Figure 8-3 presents a general RIS. A retailer begins with its business philosophy and goals, which are influenced by environmental factors (such as competitors and the economy). The philosophy and goals provide broad guidelines that direct strategic planning. Some aspects of plans are routine and need little re-evaluation. Others are nonroutine and need evaluation each time they arise.

Once a strategy is outlined, the data needed to enact it are collected, analyzed, and interpreted. If data already exist, they are retrieved from files. When new data are acquired, files are updated. All of this occurs in the information control center. Based on data in the control center, decisions are enacted.

Performance results are fed back to the information control center and compared with preset criteria. Data are retrieved from files or further data are collected. Routine adjustments are made promptly. Regular reports and exception reports (to explain deviations from expected

FIGURE 8-3
A Retail Information System

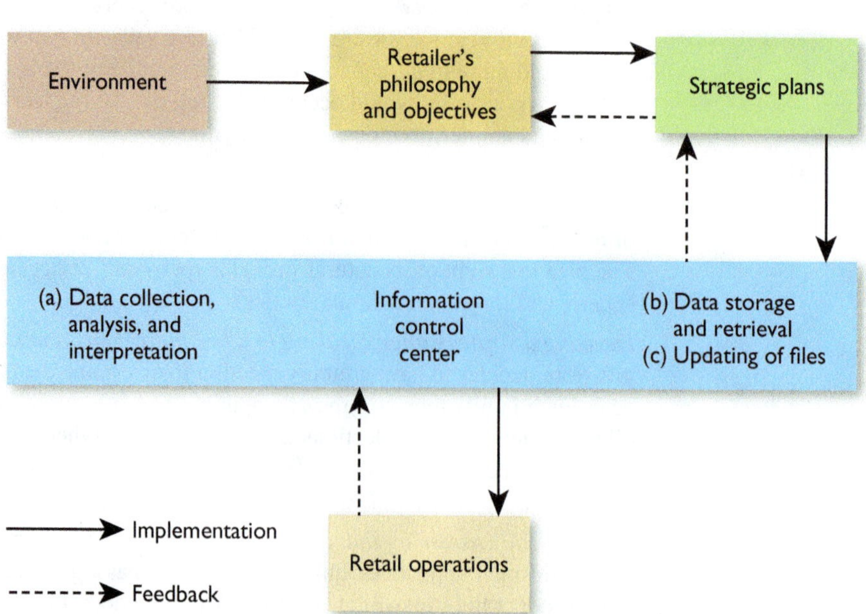

Protecting Wireless Communications at Modell's

Modell's (www.modells.com) is a 140-store family-owned sporting goods, apparel, and footwear retailer. It recently launched a Wi-Fi system that was to be used for such store management functions as inventory management, price lookup, returns processing with vendors, and a communication link with field supervisors and district managers.

A major concern to Modell's has been the protection of its Wi-Fi system from hacking and other breaches. The PCI Security Council (www.pcisecuritystandards.org) has issued compliance guidelines for retailers and other organizations that process electronic payments through local area networks (LANs) to protect these data. The council has also recommended that large firms use automated anti-intrusion systems.

By using wireless anti-intrusion systems, retailers and other organizations can check for unauthorized devices, bogus files, and rogue clients (where intruders pull files to another location) on their networks. During a test of its new system at its Manhattan headquarters, Modell's identified several security issues that needed to be resolved.

Modell's also plans to adapt its Wi-Fi system for consumer usage. Potential consumer applications include hotspot access points, multi-channel capabilities (such as ordering merchandise online that is out of stock in the store), and in-store payment processing. Modell's will have to expand its online security system even further to cover these new applications.

Source: M. V. Greene, "Defending Data," www.stores.com (March 2011).

performance) are given to the right managers. Sometimes, managers may react in a way that affects the overall philosophy or goals (such as revising an old-fashioned image or sacrificing short-run profits to introduce a computer system).

All types of data should be stored in the control center for future and ongoing use, and the control center should be integrated with the firm's short- and long-run plans and operations. Information should not be gathered sporadically and haphazardly but systematically.

Retail Info Systems News (www.risnews.com) provides good insights for retailers.

A good RIS has several strengths. Information gathering is organized and company focused. Data are regularly collected and stored so opportunities are foreseen and crises averted. Strategic elements can be coordinated. New strategies can be devised more quickly. Quantitative results are accessible, and cost-benefit analysis can be done. Information is routed to the right personnel. Yet, deploying an RIS may require high initial time and labor costs, and complex decisions may be needed to set up such a system.

In building a retail information system, a number of decisions have to be made:

- *How active a role should be given to the RIS?* Will it be used to proactively search for and distribute any relevant information or will it be used to reactively respond to requests from managers when problems arise? The best systems are more proactive, because they anticipate events.
- *Should an RIS be managed internally or be outsourced?* Although many retailers engage in RIS functions, some use outside specialists. Either style can work, as long as the RIS is guided by the retailer's information needs. Several firms have their own RIS and use outside firms for specific tasks (such as conducting surveys or managing networks).
- *How much should an RIS cost?* Retailers typically spend 0.5 to 2.0 percent of their sales on an RIS. This lags behind most of the suppliers from which retailers buy goods and services.[6]
- *How technology-driven should an RIS be?* Although retailers can gather data from trade associations, surveys, and so forth, more firms now rely on technology to drive the information process. With the advent of low-cost personal computers and tablets, inexpensive networks, cloud computing, and low-priced software, technology is easy to use. Even a neighborhood deli can generate sales data by product and offer specials on slow-sellers. See Figure 8-4.
- *How much data are enough?* The purpose of an RIS is to provide enough information, on a regular basis, for a retailer to make the proper strategy choices—not to overwhelm retail managers. This means a balancing act between too little information and information overload. To avoid overload, data should be carefully edited to eliminate redundancies.
- *How should data be disseminated throughout the firm?* This requires decisions as to who receives various reports, the frequency of data distribution, and access to data bases. When a firm has multiple divisions or operates in several regions, information access and distribution must be coordinated.
- *How should data be stored for future use?* Relevant data should be stored in a manner that makes information retrieval easy and allows for adequate longitudinal (period-to-period) analysis.

FIGURE 8-4

It's Time to Turn from the Old Ways of Collecting and Storing Data

With all of the inexpensive, easy-to-use technology and related software on the market today, even the smallest retailers are able to utilize computerized retail information systems; they should not rely primarily on calculators, notebooks, and pens and pencils.

Source: Olga Constantin/ Shutterstock.com. Reprinted by permission.

Larger retailers tend to have a chief information officer (CIO) overseeing their RIS. Their information systems departments often have formal, written annual plans. Computers are used by virtually all companies that conduct information systems analysis, and many firms use the Web for some RIS functions. Further growth in the use of retail information systems is still expected. There are many differences in information systems among retailers, on the basis of revenues and retail format.

Thirty years ago, most computerized retail systems were used only to reduce cashier errors and improve inventory control. Today, they often form the foundation for a retail information system and are used in surveys, ordering, merchandise transfers between stores, and other tasks. These activities are conducted by both small and large retailers. The vast majority of small and medium retailers—as well as large retailers—have computerized financial management systems, analyze sales electronically, and use computerized inventory management systems. Here are illustrations of the ways in which retailers are using the latest technological advances to computerize their information systems.

Retail Pro, Inc. markets Retail Pro management information software to retailers. This software is used at stores around the world. Although popular with large retailers, Retail Pro software also has an appeal among smaller retailers due to flexible pricing based on the number of users and stores, the type of hardware, and so forth:

To see the various applications of Retail Pro, visit this Web site (www.retailpro.com/solutions).

> Retail Pro is the leading point-of-sale and inventory management software used by specialty retailers worldwide. Over 10,000 retail companies have purchased Retail Pro since 1986. Retailers in almost every sector are experiencing the benefits of Retail Pro on a daily basis, such as a best-of-breed point-of-sales system, sophisticated business intelligence tools for stock replenishment, and an easy-to-use fully-integrated report designer module. The software is an integrated system for point-of-sales and store operations, merchandising planning and analysis, and customer management. 25,000+ installations. Running in 70+ countries. Available in 18 languages.[7]

MicroStrategy typically works with larger retailers—including two-thirds of the top 500 retailers in the world—to prepare computerized information systems. Clients include Container Store, eBay, Groupon, Lowe's, and Yum! One of the firm's leading products is MicroStrategy Desktop, which enables clients to acquire data via extensive, user-friendly analytical applications. The software can handle various business problems or issues in a manner that leads to cost-cutting decisions and better financial performance: "Within Desktop's intuitive Windows-based interface, users interactively build reports, retrieve and display results, and navigate information to areas of interest. Although Desktop is a comprehensive development and reporting interface, it can also be customized for different users' skill levels and security profiles."[8]

Brinker International owns or franchises more than 1,500 casual dining places under the Chili's Grill & Bar, Romano's Macaroni Grill, and Maggiano's Little Italy names:

> Margins are slim in the restaurant industry, forcing companies to constantly scrutinize labor, food, and other operating costs. Kenny Sullivan of Brinker International admits that pleasing customers while maintaining profitability is a constant balancing act. That's why Brinker uses WebFOCUS business intelligence technology from Information Builders. "Managers at all levels of our organization depend on business intelligence technology to plan, manage, and control many aspects of our business," says Sullivan. "We're in a low-margin, high-volume business where a single percentage point increase in productivity will drive a million dollars to the bottom line."[9]

Data-Base Management

In **data-base management**, a retailer gathers, integrates, applies, and stores information related to specific subject areas. It is a major element in an RIS and may be used with customer data bases, vendor data bases, product category data bases, and so on. A firm may compile and store data on customer attributes and purchase behavior, compute sales figures by vendor, and store records by product category. Each of these would represent a separate data base. Among retailers that have data bases, most use them for frequent shopper programs, customer analysis, promotion evaluation, inventory planning, trading-area analysis, joint promotions with manufacturers, media planning, and customer communications.

Data-base management should be approached as a series of five steps:

1. Plan the particular data base and its components and determine information needs.
2. Acquire the necessary information.
3. Retain the information in a usable and accessible format.
4. Update the data base regularly to reflect changing demographics, recent purchases, and so forth.
5. Analyze the data base to determine company strengths and weaknesses.

Information can come from internal and external sources. A retailer can develop data bases internally by keeping detailed records and arranging them. It could generate data bases *by customer*—purchase frequency, items bought, average purchase, demographics, and payment method; *by vendor*—total retailer purchases per period, total sales to customers per period, the most popular items, retailer profit margins, average delivery time, and service quality; and *by product category*—total category sales per period, item sales per period, retailer profit margins, and the percentage of items discounted.

Pitney Bowes (www.pbinsight.com/products/data) offers a number of useful products to help firms build and manage their data bases.

There are firms that compile data bases and make them available for a fee. Pitney Bowes is a leader in this field: "As organizations strive to gain and retain customers in today's ultra-competitive environment, target marketing is no longer a luxury—it's a necessity. Enterprises must quickly identify their highest-valued customers and prospects and predict their behavior at the neighborhood level—the most stable, statistically viable geographic area in our mobile society. Retailers can then decisively develop fine-tuned campaigns with optimal returns to draw these customers and win their loyalty. To achieve these goals easily and affordably, Pitney Bowes Business Insight pioneered PSYTE Advantage—the industry's most complete and customizable neighborhood segmentation solution."[10]

To effectively manage a retail data base, these are vital considerations:

- What are the firm's data-base goals?
- Who will be responsible for data management?
- What type of information will be collected and produced? What will be its format (images, data files, and so on)? Where do you plan to store the data?
- Is every data-base initiative analyzed to see if it is successful?
- Is there a mechanism to flag data that indicates potential problems or opportunities?
- Are customer purchases of different products or from different company divisions cross-linked?
- How will data be communicated?
- Is there a clear privacy policy that is communicated to those in a data base? Are there opt-out provisions for those who do not want to be included in a data base?
- Is the data base updated each time there is a customer interaction?
- Are customers, personnel, suppliers, and others invited to update their personal data?
- Is the data base periodically checked to eliminate redundant files?
- Roughly how long should the data be retained? Is it permanent? Will it be updated?[11]

Let's now discuss two aspects of data-base management: Data warehousing is a mechanism for storing and distributing information. Data mining and micromarketing are ways in which information can be utilized. Figure 8-5 shows the interplay of data warehousing with data mining and micromarketing.

Teradata Magazine Online (www.teradatamagazine.com) explores data warehousing in depth.

DATA WAREHOUSING One advance in data-base management is **data warehousing**, whereby copies of all the data bases in a firm are maintained in one location and are accessible to employees at any locale. A data warehouse is a comprehensive compilation of the data used to support management decision making:

> It is a subject-oriented, integrated, time-variant, and nonvolatile collection of data in support of management's decision-making process. *Subject-Oriented*—It can be used to analyze a particular subject area, such as "sales." *Integrated*—It integrates data from multiple data sources. *Time-Variant*—Historical data is kept, such as 3 months, 6 months, 12 months, or even older data. This contrasts with a transactions system, where often only the most recent data is kept. *Nonvolatile*—Once data are in a data warehouse, they will not change. So, historical data in a data warehouse should never be altered.[12]

FIGURE 8-5
Retail Data-Base Management in Action

The data warehouse is where information is collected, sorted, and stored centrally. Information is disseminated to retailer personnel, as well as to channel partners (such as alerting them to what merchandise is hot and what is not hot) and customers (such as telling them about order status). In data mining, retail executives and other employees—and sometimes channel partners—analyze information by customer type, product category, and so forth in order to determine opportunities for tailored marketing efforts. With micromarketing, the retailer applies differentiated marketing. Focused retail strategy mixes are planned for specific customer segments—or even for individual customers.

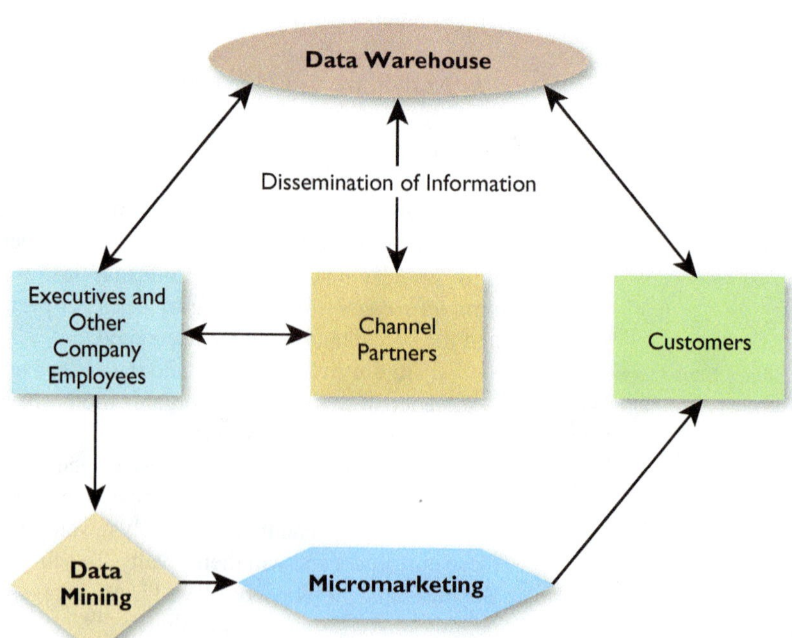

A data warehouse has the following components: (1) the data warehouse, where data are physically stored; (2) software to copy original data bases and transfer them to the warehouse; (3) interactive software to process inquiries; and (4) a directory for the categories of information kept in the warehouse.

Data warehousing has several advantages. Executives and other employees are quickly, easily, and simultaneously able to access data wherever they may be. There is more companywide entrée to new data when they are first available. Data inconsistencies are reduced by consolidating records in one location. Better data analysis and manipulation are possible because information is stored in one location.

Computerized data warehouses were once costly to build (an average of $2.2 million in the 1990s) and, thus, feasible only for the largest retailers. This has changed. A simple data warehouse can now be put together for less than $25,000, making it affordable to all but very small retailers (which do not have to deal with far-flung executives, making data warehousing less necessary for them).

Macy's, Pacific Sunwear, 7-Eleven, Sears, and Wal-Mart are just a few of the multitude of retailers that use data warehousing: "As an early adopter of data warehousing technologies in the 1990s, the retail industry has gained years of experience with now-mission-critical data warehousing systems. From the first (and rudimentary) store-item-day historical sales reporting data bases, retailers have greatly expanded the use of analytical systems to support the business and drive vital operational decisions."[13]

Helzberg Diamonds (www.helzberg.com), with more than 230 U.S. jewelry stores, is one of the many retailers positioning itself for long-term growth and focusing on cost reductions via a constantly updated data warehousing structure. The company has a point-of-sale system developed especially for specialty retailers. This system:

> uploads data nightly from individual stores, performs data quality checks to ensure that numbers are accurate, and loads the information into a data warehouse. After data are loaded and cleansed, reports are automatically refreshed. "This process is the pulse of the operation. The data flow through all of our systems, informing just about everyone about the latest metrics; and it also flows into the merchandise system." The same data are provided to store managers to help them examine product category sales and identify trends in promotions and information like individual associate performance and credit sales.[14]

DATA MINING AND MICROMARKETING **Data mining** is the in-depth analysis of information to gain specific insights about customers, product categories, vendors, and so forth. The goal is to learn if there are opportunities for tailored marketing efforts that would lead to better retailer performance. One application of data mining is **micromarketing**, whereby the retailer uses differentiated marketing and develops focused retail strategy mixes for specific customer segments, sometimes fine-tuned for the individual shopper.

For an in-depth discussion, go to About Retail Industry (http://retailindustry.about.com), and type "customer data mining" in the search engine.

Data mining relies on special software to sift through a data warehouse to uncover patterns and relationships among different factors. The software allows vast amounts of data to be quickly searched and sorted. That is why many firms, such as supermarkets, have made the financial commitment to data mining. For example: "Grocers can combine third-party demographic and behavioral data with transactional data for a more complete picture of how customers think and shop. Traditional segments are now giving way to sub-segments that allow grocers to further define their shopper base. Thus, they can build on the traditional segmentation practice of promoting to the 'young families' segment of shoppers. Using a sub-segment marketing approach, grocers can promote directly to the 'young families with dogs' sub-segment to capture additional revenue."[15]

Look at how Gilt Groupe uses data mining in the firm's micromarketing efforts:

> Sales move quickly, as each event typically lasts less than 36 hours. While that adds to the exclusivity of Gilt, it makes it more vital that the firm understand individual customer preferences. [According to Gilt], "it is important to marry the product to the customer at the right time. We may not have a particular brand, but something in a similar style and at a price point we think you might like." Having access to good information results in a significant lift for cross-marketing campaigns that, for example, target an apparel buyer who hasn't yet made a home décor purchase.[16]

Gathering Information Through the UPC and EDI

To be more efficient with their information systems, most retailers rely on the Universal Product Code (UPC) and many now utilize electronic data interchange (EDI).

With the **Universal Product Code (UPC)**, products (or tags attached to them) are marked with a series of thick and thin vertical lines, representing each item's identification code. An item's UPC includes both numbers and lines. The lines are "read" by scanners at checkout counters. Cashiers do not enter transactions manually—although they can, if needed. Because the UPC itself is not readable by humans, the retailer or vendor must attach a ticket or sticker to a product specifying its size, color, and other information (if not on the package or the product). Given that the UPC does not include price information, this too must be added by a ticket or sticker.

By using UPC-based technology, retailers can record data instantly on an item's model number, size, color, and other factors when it is sold, as well as send the data to a computer that monitors unit sales, inventory levels, and so forth. The goals are to produce better merchandising data, improve inventory management, speed transaction time, raise productivity, reduce errors, and coordinate information.

Since its inception, UPC technology has improved substantially. It is now the accepted retailing standard: "There are about five billion scans every day. The UPC allows all stores in the retail sector to identify products and capture information about them. Stores can control inventory more efficiently, provide a faster and more accurate checkout for customers, and easily gather information for accurate and immediate marketing reports."[17]

Virtually every time sales or inventory data are scanned by a computer, UPC technology is involved. More than 200,000 U.S. manufacturers and retailers belong to GS1 US (formerly known as the Uniform Code Council), a group that has taken the lead in setting and promoting inter-industry product identification and communication standards. Figure 8-6 shows how far UPC technology has come. The UPC is discussed further in Chapter 16.

GXS is one of the leaders in EDI technology (http://edi.gxs.com).

With **electronic data interchange (EDI)**, retailers and suppliers regularly exchange information through their computers with regard to inventory levels, delivery times, unit sales, and so on of particular items. As a result, both parties enhance their decision-making capabilities, better control inventory, and are more responsive to demand. UPC scanning is often the basis for product-related EDI data. Hundreds of thousands of firms around the world (including 60,000 in the United States alone) use some form of the EDI system. Consider this scenario:

> EDI is the common language between retailers and their suppliers. Through EDI, traditional documents such as purchase orders, invoices, inventory reports, advanced shipping notifications, routing requests, and routing instructions are exchanged by electronic means from one computer system to another. Every stage of the fulfillment cycle is reliant on accurate and timely information being passed on electronically. Companies can also leverage EDI to make their supply chains flow more smoothly and strengthen relationships with customers and vendors by improving the timing and accuracy in the delivery of goods and services.[18]

Today, more retailers are expanding their EDI efforts to incorporate Internet communications with suppliers. This is known as *I-EDI (Internet electronic data interchange)*. The retailer use of I-EDI was ushered in by Wal-Mart a little over a decade ago. Today, I-EDI "allows small- to medium-sized businesses to receive, create, send, and manage electronic documents using just a Web browser. I-EDI works by replicating the contents of a paper-based document onto a Web page." Through simple forms, retailers and suppliers can communicate and comply with each other's requirements by applying built-in business rules. After key information has been entered into the forms, data are automatically converted into EDI messages and sent out by an Internet-based communication protocol.[19] EDI is covered further in Chapter 15; CPFR (collaborative planning, forecasting, and replenishment) is also discussed there.

THE MARKETING RESEARCH PROCESS

Marketing research in retailing entails the collection and analysis of information relating to specific issues or problems facing a retailer. At farsighted firms, marketing research is just one element in a retail information system. At others, marketing research may be the only type of data gathering and processing.

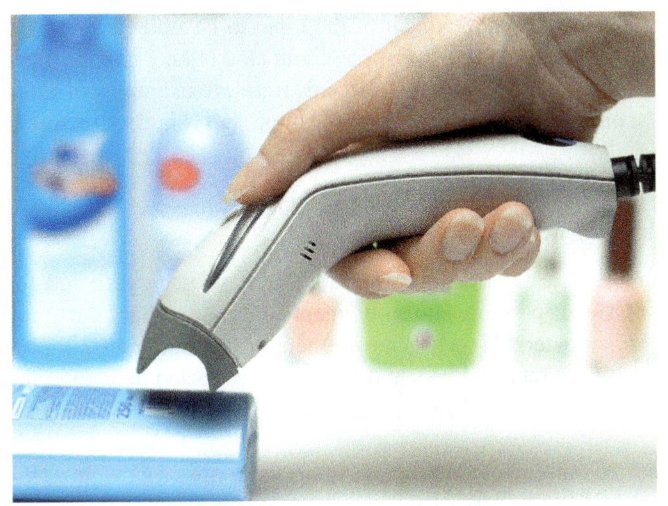

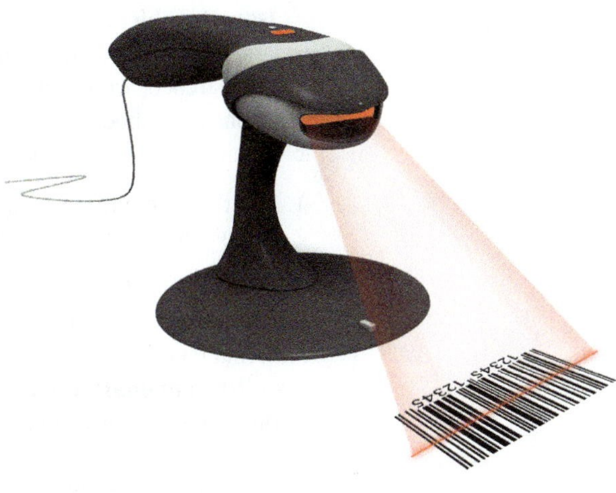

FIGURE 8-6

Applying UPC Technology to Gain Better Information

Portable UPC scanners are lightweight, highly mobile, and come in various shapes and colors. They all have the same purpose—to "read" the information on the UPC label, transmit the data to a computer, compile and store the data, and provide up-to-the-minute and detailed reports to retail employees who analyze the data and act accordingly.

Sources: Voznikevich Konstantin/Shutterstock.com, erzetic/Shutterstock.com, Ruslan Anatolevich Kuzmenkov/Shutterstock.com, and Andrey Bandurenko/Shutterstock.com. Reprinted by permission.

The **marketing research process** embodies a series of activities: defining the issue or problem to be studied, examining secondary data, generating primary data (if needed), analyzing data, making recommendations, and implementing findings. It is not a single act; it is a systematic process. Figure 8-7 outlines the research process. Each activity is done sequentially. Secondary data are not examined until after an issue or problem is defined. The dashed line around the primary data stage means these data are generated only if secondary data do not yield actionable information. The process is described next.

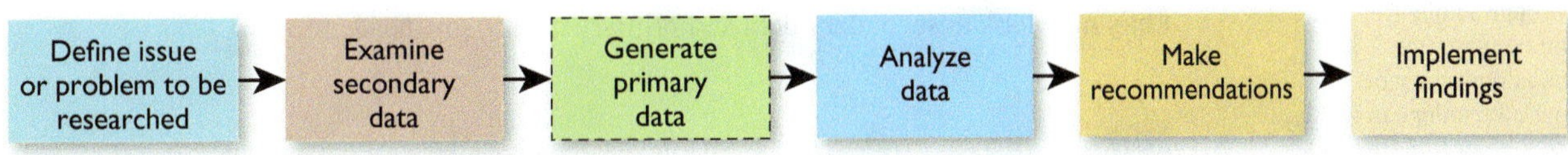

FIGURE 8-7

The Marketing Research Process in Retailing

Issue (problem) definition involves a clear statement of the topic to be studied. What information does the retailer want to obtain to make a decision? Without clearly knowing the topic to be researched, irrelevant and confusing data could be collected. Here are examples of issue definitions for a shoe store. The first one seeks to compare three locations and is fairly structured; the second is more open-ended:

1. "Of three potential new store locations, which should we choose?"
2. "How can we improve the sales of our men's shoes?"

When **secondary data** are involved, a retailer looks at data that have been gathered for purposes other than addressing the issue or problem currently under study. Secondary data may be internal (such as company records) or external (such as government reports and trade publications). When **primary data** are involved, a retailer looks at data that are collected to address the specific issue or problem under study. This type of data may be generated via survey, observation, experiment, and simulation.

Secondary data are sometimes relied on; other times, primary data are crucial. In some cases, both are gathered. It is important that retailers keep these points in mind: (1) There is great diversity in the possible types of data collection (and in the costs). (2) Only data relevant to the issue being studied should be collected. (3) Primary data are usually acquired only if secondary data are inadequate (thus, the dashed box in Figure 8-7). Both secondary and primary data are described further in the next sections.

These kinds of secondary and primary data can be gathered for the shoe store issues just stated:

Issue (Problem) Definition	Information Needed to Solve Issue (Problem)
1.Which store location?	1. Data on access to transportation, traffic, consumer profiles, rent, store size, and types of competition are gathered from government reports, trade publications, and observation by the owner for each of the three potential store locations.
2. How to improve sales of shoes?	2. Store sales records for the past five years by product category are gathered. A consumer survey in a nearby mall is conducted.

After data are collected, data analysis is performed to assess that information and relate it to the defined issue. Alternative solutions are also clearly outlined. For example:

Issue (Problem) Definition	Alternative Solutions
1. Which store location?	1. Each site is ranked for all of the criteria (access to transportation, traffic, consumer profiles, rent, store size, and types of competition).
2. How to improve sales of shoes?	2. Alternative strategies to boost sales are analyzed and ranked.

At this point, the pros and cons of each alternative are enumerated. See Table 8-1. Recommendations are then made as to the best strategy for the retailer. Of the available options, which is best? Table 8-1 also shows recommendations for the shoe-store issues discussed in this section.

Last, but not least, the recommended strategy is implemented. If research is to replace intuition in strategic retailing, a decision maker must follow the recommendations from research studies, even if they seem to contradict his or her own ideas.

Let's now look at secondary data and primary data in greater depth.

Through Public Register Online (www.annualreportservice.com), a retailer can learn about other firms around the globe. Get an annual report here. [A free login is required.]

Secondary Data

ADVANTAGES AND DISADVANTAGES Secondary data have several advantages:

- Data assembly is inexpensive. Company records, trade journals, and government publications are all rather low cost. No data collection forms, interviewers, and tabulations are needed.

TABLE 8-1 Research-Based Recommendations

Issue (Problem)	Alternatives	Pros and Cons of Alternatives	Recommendation
1. Which store location?	Site A	Best transportation, traffic, and consumer profiles. Highest rent. Smallest store space. Extensive competition.	Site A: the many advantages far outweigh the disadvantages.
	Site B	Poorest transportation, traffic, and consumer profiles. Lowest rent. Largest store space. No competition.	
	Site C	Intermediate on all criteria.	
2. How to improve sales of shoes?	Increased assortment	Will attract and satisfy many more customers. High costs. High level of inventory. Reduces turnover for many items.	Lower prices and increase ads: additional customers offset higher costs and lower margins; combination best expands business.
	Drop some lines and specialize	Will attract and satisfy a specific consumer market. Excludes many segments. Costs and inventory reduced.	
	Slightly reduce prices	Unit sales increase. Markup and profit per item decline.	
	Advertise	Will increase traffic and new customers. High costs.	

- Data can be gathered quickly. Company records, library sources, and Web sites can be accessed immediately. Many firms store reports in their retail information systems.
- There may be several sources of secondary data—with many perspectives.
- A secondary source may possess information that would otherwise be unavailable to the retailer. Government publications often have statistics no private firm could acquire.
- When data are assembled by a source such as *Progressive Grocer*, A.C. Nielsen, *Stores*, or the government, results are usually quite credible.
- The retailer may have only a rough idea of the topics to investigate. Secondary data can then help to define issues more specifically. In addition, background information about a given issue can be gathered from secondary sources before undertaking a primary study.

TECHNOLOGY IN RETAILING

Harnessing Customer Data Through CART

Green Hills (www.greenhills.com) is a Syracuse, New York–based supermarket chain that tests new technologies and merchandising plans in its Center for Advancing Retail & Technology (CART) (www.advancingretail.org), a learning center based in one of its stores. Although there are many benefits of running a laboratory in a live-store environment, occasionally there are conflicts that arise as to the relative importance of the store versus the lab.

CART is used by Green Hills' vendors as both a test marketing and education center where knowledge is shared with other retailers. CART, for example, provides an environment where retailers can test the value of providing information on a customer's mobile phone while he/she is shopping. This is a much more sophisticated type of analysis than conducting an overall store traffic count or counting the number of consumers who travel a given aisle.

These are some of the other areas which CART researches:

- Shopper traffic flow throughout the store.
- The effect of sign location on product sales.
- The effectiveness of vendor and retailer collaborative promotions on brand loyalty.

CART regularly publishes the results of its research findings on the Web site. It also offers custom research for retailers, wholesalers, and vendors.

Source: Joseph Tranowski, "Retail 3.0," www.progressivegrocer.com (May 2011).

Secondary data also have several potential disadvantages:

- Available data may not suit the purposes of the current study because they have been collected for other reasons. Neighborhood statistics may not be found in secondary sources.
- Secondary data may be incomplete. A service station owner would want car data broken down by year, model, and mileage driven, so as to stock parts. A motor vehicle bureau could provide data on the models but not the mileage driven.
- Information may be dated. Statistics gathered every two to five years may not be valid today. The *U.S. Census of Retail Trade* is conducted every five years. Furthermore, there is often a long time delay between the completion of a census and the release of information.
- The accuracy of secondary data must be carefully evaluated. Thus, a retailer needs to decide whether the data have been compiled in an unbiased way. The purpose of the research, the data collection tools, and the method of analysis should each be examined—if they are available for review.
- Some secondary data sources are known for poor data collection techniques; they should be avoided. If there are conflicting data, the source with the best reputation for accuracy should be used.
- In retailing, many secondary data projects are not retested and the user of secondary data has to hope results from one narrow study are applicable to his or her firm.

Whether secondary data resolve an issue or not, their low cost and availability require that primary data not be amassed until after studying secondary data. Only if secondary data are not actionable should primary data be collected. We now present various secondary data sources for retailers.

SOURCES There are many sources and types of secondary data. The major distinctions are between internal and external sources.

Internal secondary data are available within the company, sometimes from the data bank of a retail information system. Before searching for external secondary data or primary data, the retailer should look at information available inside the firm.

At the beginning of the year, most retailers develop budgets for the next 12 months. They are based on sales forecasts and outline planned expenditures for that year. A firm's prior budget and its performance in attaining budgetary goals are good sources of secondary data in preparing a new budget.

Retailers use sales and profit-and-loss reports to judge performance. Many have data from electronic registers that can be studied by store, department, and item. By comparing data with prior periods, a firm gets a sense of growth or contraction. Overdependence on sales data may be misleading. Sales should be examined along with profit-and-loss data to indicate strengths and weaknesses in operations and management and to help lead to improvements.

Through customer billing reports, a retailer learns about inventory movement, sales by different personnel, and sales volume. For credit customers, sales by location, repayment time, and types of purchases can be reviewed. Purchase invoices show the retailer's own buying history and let it evaluate itself against budgetary goals. See Figure 8-8.

Inventory records indicate the merchandise carried throughout the year and the turnover of these items. Knowing the lead time to place and receive orders from suppliers, as well as the extra merchandise kept on hand to prevent running out at different times during the year, aids planning.

If a firm does primary research, the resultant report should be kept for future use (hopefully in the retail information system). When used initially, a report involves primary data. Later reference to it is secondary in nature since the report is no longer used for its primary purpose.

Written reports on performance are another source of internal secondary data. They may be prepared and filed by senior executives, buyers, sales personnel, or others. All phases of retail management can be improved through formal report procedures.

External secondary data are available from sources outside the firm. They should be consulted if internal information is insufficient for a decision to be made on a defined issue. These sources are comprised of government and nongovernment categories.

To use external secondary data well, appropriate online data bases should be consulted. They contain all kinds of written materials, usually by subject or topic heading, for a specified time. Here

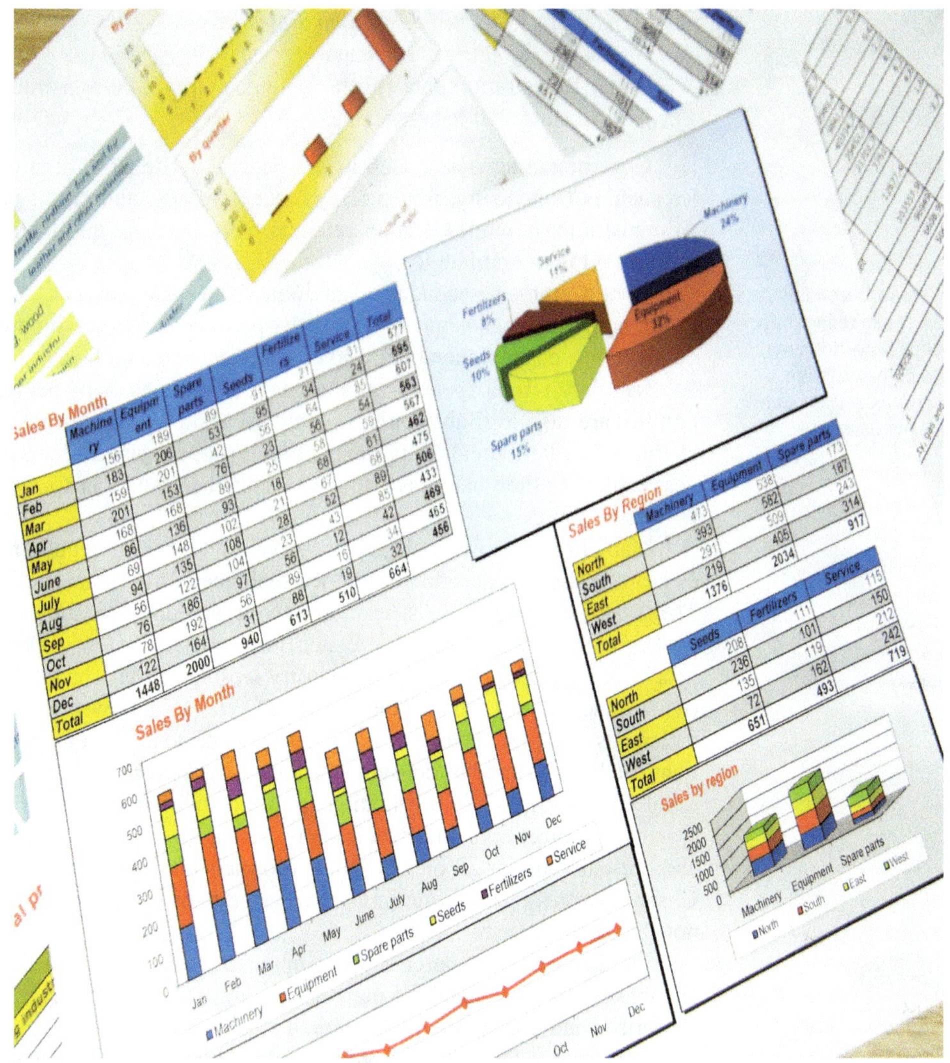

FIGURE 8-8

Internal Secondary Data: A Valuable Source of Knowledge

Every retailer retains a variety of records that indicate past performance, typically by season, product category, and store unit (if a chain)—and, increasingly, by specific customer and product item. This information is useful in comparing past and current performance and in making future forecasts.

Source: Nataliiap/Shutterstock.com. Reprinted by permission.

are several data bases, chosen for their retailing relevance. They are available through the Internet (for online access, you must use your company, college, or local library Web connection—direct entry to the sites is password-protected):

- Academic Search Premier/EBSCOhost.
- Business Source Premier/EBSCOhost.
- Dow Jones Factiva.
- Gale Business & Company Resource Center.
- Gale Virtual Reference Library.
- IngentaConnect.
- LexisNexis Academic Universe.
- Mergent Online.
- Plunkett Research Online.
- Standard & Poor's NetAdvantage.

The U.S. Census Bureau has a Web site (www.census.gov/econ/www/retmenu.html) listing recent retailing reports, which can be viewed and downloaded.

The government distributes a wide range of materials. Here are several publications, chosen for their retailing value. They are available in any business library or other large library or through the Web:

- *Annual Retail Trade Survey.*
- *U.S. Census of Retail Trade.* Every five years ending in 2 and 7.
- *U.S. Census of Service Industries.* Every five years ending in 2 and 7.
- *Monthly Retail Trade and Food Services Sales.*

- *Statistical Abstract of the United States.*
- *U.S. Survey of Current Business.*
- *Other*: Registration data (births, deaths, automobile registrations, etc.). Available through federal, state, and local agencies.

Government agencies, such as the Federal Trade Commission, provide pamphlets on topics such as franchising, unit pricing, deceptive ads, and credit policies. The Small Business Administration provides smaller retailers with literature and advice. Pamphlets are distributed free or sold for a nominal fee.

Looking for secondary data on direct marketing (http://directmag.com/research) or E-commerce (www.wilsonweb.com/research)? Check out these sites.

Nongovernment secondary data come from many sources, often cited in reference guides. Major nongovernment sources are regular periodicals; books, monographs, and other nonregular publications; channel members; and commercial research houses.

Regular periodicals are available at most libraries or by personal subscription. A growing number are also available online; some Web sites provide free information, whereas others charge a fee. Periodicals may have a broad scope (such as *Fortune*) and discuss diverse business topics, or they may have narrower coverage (such as *Chain Store Age*) and deal mostly with retail topics.

Many firms publish books, monographs, and other nonregular retailing materials. Some, such as Pearson Higher Education (www.pearsonhighered.com), have textbooks and practitioner books. The American Marketing Association (www.marketingpower.com) offers information to enhance readers' business knowledge. The Better Business Bureau (www.bbb.org) wants to improve the public's image of business and expand industry self-regulation. The International Franchise Association (www.franchise.org) and the National Retail Federation (www.nrf.com) describe industry practices and trends, and they act as spokespersons to advocate the best interests of members. Other associations can be uncovered by consulting Gale's *Encyclopedia of Associations.*

Retailers often get information from channel partners such as ad agencies, franchise operators, manufacturers, and wholesalers. When these firms do research for their own purposes and present some or all of the findings to their retailers, external secondary data are involved. Channel partners pass on findings to enhance their sales and retailer relations. They usually do not charge for the information.

The last external source is the commercial research house that conducts ongoing studies and makes results available to many clients for a fee. This source is secondary if the retailer is a subscriber and does not request tailored studies. Information Resources Inc., A.C. Nielsen, and Standard Rate & Data Service provide subscriptions at lower costs than a retailer would incur if data were collected only for its use.

Our Web site (www.pearsonhighered.com/bermanevans) has links to about 50 online sources of free external secondary data—both government and nongovernment.

Primary Data

ADVANTAGES AND DISADVANTAGES After exhausting the available secondary data, a defined issue may still be unresolved. In this instance, primary data (collected to resolve a specific topic at hand) are needed. When secondary data are sufficient, primary data are not collected. There are several advantages associated with primary data:

- They are collected to fit the retailer's specific purpose.
- Information is current.
- The units of measure and data categories are designed for the issue being studied.
- The firm either collects data itself or hires an outside party. The source is known and controlled, and the methodology is constructed for the specific study.
- There are no conflicting data from different sources.
- When secondary data do not resolve an issue, primary data are the only alternative.

There are also several possible disadvantages often associated with primary data:

- They are normally more expensive to obtain than secondary data.
- Information gathering tends to be more time-consuming.
- Some types of information cannot be acquired by an individual firm.
- If only primary data are collected, the perspective may be limited.
- Irrelevant information may be collected if the issue is not stated clearly enough.

In sum, a retailer has many criteria to weigh in evaluating the use of primary data. In particular, specificity, currency, and reliability must be weighed against high costs, time, and limited access to materials. A variety of primary data sources for retailers are discussed next.

Want to learn about conducting an Internet survey? Go to this Business Research Lab Web site (www.busreslab.com/onlinesurvey.htm).

SOURCES The first decision is to determine who collects the data. A retailer can do this itself (internal) or hire a research firm (external). Internal collection is usually quicker and cheaper. External collection is usually more objective and formal. Second, a sampling method is specified. Instead of gathering data from all stores, all products, and all customers, a retailer may obtain accurate data by studying a sample of them. This saves time and money. With a **probability (random) sample**, every store, product, or customer has an equal or known chance of being chosen for study. In a **nonprobability sample**, stores, products, or customers are chosen by the researcher—based on judgment or convenience. A probability sample is more accurate but is also more costly and complex. Third, the retailer chooses among four methods of data collection: survey, observation, experiment, and simulation. All of the methods are capable of generating data for each element of a strategy.

SURVEY. With a **survey**, information is systematically gathered from respondents by communicating with them. Surveys are used in many retail settings. In a low-key, interactive manner, Sunglass Hut surveys its shoppers and encourages them to share their experiences through an interactive device known as Social Sun. Food Lion uses in-store surveys to learn how satisfied customers are and what their attitudes are on various subjects.

A survey may be conducted in person, over the phone, by mail, or online. Typically, a questionnaire is used. A *personal survey* is face-to-face, flexible, and able to elicit lengthy responses; unclear questions can be explained. It may be costly, and interviewer bias is possible. A *phone survey* is fast and rather inexpensive. Responses are often short, and nonresponse may be a problem. A *mail survey* can reach a wide range of respondents, has no interviewer bias, and is not costly. Slow returns, high nonresponse rates, and participation by incorrect respondents are potential problems. An *online survey* is interactive, can be adapted to individuals, and yields quick results. Yet, only certain customers shop online or answer online surveys. The technique chosen depends on the goals and requirements of the research project.

A survey may be nondisguised or disguised. In a nondisguised survey, the respondent is told the real purpose of the study. In a disguised survey, the respondent is not told the true purpose so that person does not answer what he or she thinks a firm wants to hear. Disguised surveys use word associations, sentence completions, and projective questions (such as, "Do your friends like shopping at this store?").

The **semantic differential**—a listing of bipolar adjective scales—is a survey technique that may be disguised or nondisguised. A respondent is asked to rate one or more retailers on several criteria, each evaluated by bipolar adjectives (such as unfriendly–friendly). By computing the average rating of all respondents for each criterion, an overall profile is developed. Figure 8-9 shows a semantic differential comparing two furniture retailers. Store A is a prestige, high-quality store and Store B is a mid-quality, family-run store. The semantic differential graphically portrays their images.

OBSERVATION. The form of research in which present behavior or the results of past behavior are noted and recorded is known as **observation**. Because people are not questioned, observation may not require respondents' cooperation, and survey biases are minimized. Many times, observation is used in actual situations. The key disadvantage of using observation alone is that attitudes are not elicited.

Retailers use observation to determine the quality of sales presentations (by having researchers pose as shoppers), to monitor related-item buying, to determine store activity by time and day, to make pedestrian and vehicular traffic counts (to measure the potential of new locations), and to determine the proportion of patrons using mass transit.

With **mystery shoppers**, retailers hire people to pose as customers and observe their operations, from sales presentations to how well displays are maintained to service calls. One research firm, Michelson & Associates (www.michelson.com/mystery), has a pool of more than 80,000 mystery shoppers: "We qualify, train, and manage our shoppers to gather factual information and provide objective observations based on their experiences on the front line. Our field reps range from 21 to 70 years of age with the majority being women between the ages of 30 and 45. Our shoppers can be pre-selected based on specific client criteria such as demographics, type of car, shopping habits, etc."[20]

FIGURE 8-9
A Semantic Differential for Two Furniture Stores

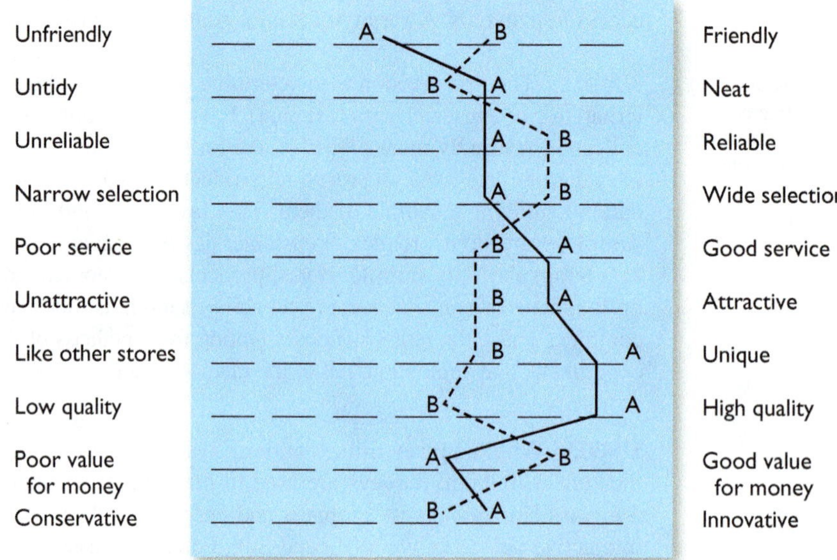

Observation may be disguised or nondisguised, structured or unstructured, direct or indirect, and human or mechanical. In disguised observation, the shopper or company employee is not aware he or she is being watched by a two-way mirror or hidden camera. In nondisguised observation, the participant knows he or she is being observed—such as a department manager watching a cashier's behavior. Structured observation calls for the observer to note specific behavior. Unstructured observation requires the observer to note all of the activities of the person being studied. With direct observation, the observer watches people's present behavior. With indirect observation, the observer examines evidence of past behavior such as food products in consumer pantries. Human observation is carried out by people. It may be disguised, but the observer may enter biased notations and miss behavior. Mechanical observation, such as a camera filming in-store shopping, eliminates viewer bias and does not miss behavior.

EXPERIMENT. An **experiment** is a type of research in which one or more elements of a retail strategy mix are manipulated under controlled conditions. An element may be a price, a shelf display, or store hours. If a retailer wants to find out the effects of a price change on a brand's sales, only the price of that brand is varied. Other elements of the strategy stay the same, so the true effect of price is measured.

An experiment may use survey or observation techniques to record data. In a survey, questions are asked about the experiment: Did you buy Brand Z because of its new shelf display? Are you buying more ice cream because it's on sale? In observation, behavior is watched during the experiment: Sales of Brand Z rise by 20 percent when a new display is used. Ice cream sales go up 25 percent during a special sale.

Surveys and observations are experimental if they occur under closely controlled situations. When surveys ask broad attitude questions or unstructured behavior is observed, experiments are not involved. Experimentation can be difficult since many uncontrollable factors (such as the weather, competition, and the economy) come into play. Yet, a well-controlled experiment yields a lot of good data.

The major advantage is an experiment's ability to show cause and effect (a lower price results in higher sales). It is also systematically structured and enacted. The major potential disadvantages are high costs, contrived settings, and uncontrollable factors.

SIMULATION. A type of experiment whereby a computer program is used to manipulate the elements of a retail strategy mix rather than test them in a real setting is called **simulation**. Two kinds of simulation are now being applied in retail settings: those based on mathematical models and those involving "virtual reality."

Wing Zone Spreads Its Wings

A couple of years ago, Matt Friedman, the co-founder and CEO of the 100-unit and growing Wing Zone (www.wingzone.com) restaurant chain, analyzed the U.S. franchise market and clearly did not like what he found. Even though his U.S. restaurants were doing well, Friedman was concerned that the opportunities for domestic expansion would be low due to the lack of financing on the part of its franchisees. Friedman also concluded that competition in many foreign markets was less than in the United States where a number of firms were direct competitors.

After analyzing the core elements of Wing Zone's strategy, its management decided upon the characteristics necessary for a foreign market to be successful. Wing Zone found these included residents who appreciate the spiciness associated with its hot wings, who had experience with home or office delivery of food products, who appreciated poultry products, and whose countries had a large middle-class population.

In November 2010, Wing Zone opened its first international restaurant in Panama City, Panama. Subsequently, Wing Zone sold franchises in El Salvador, the Bahamas, Great Britain, Ireland, Scotland, Saudi Arabia, and Japan. A major difference between Wing Zone's U.S. and foreign franchised units is that foreign franchises need to stock sauces and other condiments in large quantities since they are produced in the United States.

Source: Jason Daley, "No Boundaries," www.entrepreneur.com (May 2011).

With the first kind of simulation, a model of the expected controllable and uncontrollable retail environment is constructed. Factors—such as the projected effects of a price cut or longer store hours—are manipulated by computer (rather than in the marketplace) so their impact on the overall strategy and specific elements of it are learned. No consumer cooperation is needed, and many combinations of factors can be analyzed in a controlled, rapid, inexpensive, and risk-free manner. This format is gaining popularity because good software is available. However, it is still somewhat difficult to use.

In the second kind of simulation, a retailer devises or buys interactive software that lets participants simulate actual behavior in as realistic a format as possible. This approach creates a "virtual shopping environment." At present, there is limited software for these simulations and personnel must be trained to interpret it. One newer application of a virtual reality simulation is from Vision Critical:

> ShelfsetPlus lets you analyze consumer reactions as they browse a virtual retail shelf, window display, or menu. Participants zoom in and out, read labels, compare prices, buy items, or return them to the shelf. Evaluate how brands, product descriptions, placement, and price affect buying decisions. Combine shopping behavior with surveys and purchase history to get a holistic understanding of customers. Once you've determined the optimal shelf-set factors, you can test the effectiveness of the overall shopping experience. Study such things as entrance, lighting, and signage to pinpoint opportunities to improve response rates. VirtualPlus uses the latest virtual 3D modeling.[21]

Chapter Summary

1. *To discuss how information flows in a retail distribution channel.* In an effective retail distribution channel, information flows freely and efficiently among the three main parties (supplier, retailer, and consumer). As a result, the parties can better anticipate and address each other's performance expectations. Retailers often have a vital role in collecting data because they have the most direct contact with shoppers.

2. *To show why retailers should avoid strategies based on inadequate information.* Whether developing a new strategy or modifying an existing one, good data are necessary to reduce a retailer's chances of making incorrect decisions. Retailers that rely on nonsystematic or incomplete research, such as intuition, increase their probabilities of failure.

3. *To look at the retail information system, its components, and the recent advances in such systems.* Useful information should be acquired through an ongoing, well-integrated process. A retail information system anticipates the data needs of retail managers; continuously collects, organizes, and stores relevant data; and directs the flow of information to decision makers. Such a system has several components: environment, retailer's philosophy, strategic plans, information control center, and retail operations. The most important component is the information control center. It directs data collection, stores and retrieves data, and updates files.

   Data-base management is used to collect, integrate, apply, and store information related to specific topics (such as customers, vendors, and product categories). Data-base information can come from internal (company-generated) and external (purchased from outside firms) sources. A key advance in data-base management is data warehousing, whereby copies of all the data bases in a firm are kept in one location and can be accessed by employees at any locale. It is a huge repository separate from the operational data bases that support departmental applications. Through data mining and micromarketing, retailers use data warehouses to pinpoint the specific needs of customer segments.

   Retailers have increased their use of computerized retail information systems, and the Universal Product Code (UPC) is now the dominant technology for processing product-related data. With electronic data interchange (EDI) and Internet electronic data interchange (I-EDI), the computers of retailers and their suppliers regularly exchange information, sometimes through the Web.

4. *To describe the marketing research process.* Marketing research in retailing involves these sequential activities: defining the issue or problem to be researched, examining secondary data, gathering primary data (if needed), analyzing the data, making recommendations, and implementing findings. It is systematic in nature and not a single act.

   Secondary data (gathered for other purposes) are inexpensive, can be collected quickly, may have several sources, and may yield otherwise unattainable information. Some sources are very credible. When an issue is ill defined, a secondary data search can clarify it. There are also potential pitfalls: These data may not suit the purposes of the study, units of measurement may not be specific enough, information may be old or inaccurate, a source may be disreputable, and data may not be reliable.

   Primary data (gathered to resolve the specific topic at hand) are collected if secondary data do not adequately address the issue. They are precise and current, data are collected and categorized with the units of measures desired, the methodology is known, there are no conflicting results, and the level of reliability can be determined. When secondary data do not exist, primary data are the only option. The potential disadvantages are the cost, time, limited access, narrow perspective, and amassing of irrelevant information.

Key Terms

retail information system (RIS) (p. 200)
data-base management (p. 203)
data warehousing (p. 204)
data mining (p. 205)
micromarketing (p. 205)
Universal Product Code (UPC) (p. 206)
electronic data interchange (EDI) (p. 206)
marketing research in retailing (p. 206)
marketing research process (p. 207)
issue (problem) definition (p. 208)
secondary data (p. 208)
primary data (p. 208)
internal secondary data (p. 210)
external secondary data (p. 210)
probability (random) sample (p. 213)
nonprobability sample (p. 213)
survey (p. 213)
semantic differential (p. 213)
observation (p. 213)
mystery shoppers (p. 213)
experiment (p. 214)
simulation (p. 214)

Questions for Discussion

1. Relate the information flows in Figure 8-1 to a florist near your college or university.
2. What would you recommend to guard against this comment? "Traditionally, retailers and suppliers just don't like to share supply-chain information with each other."
3. Can a retailer ever have too much information? Explain your answer.
4. How could a small retailer devise a retail information system?
5. Explain the relationship among the terms *data warehouse*, *data mining*, and *micromarketing*. How can F.Y.E. (For Your Entertainment, www.fye.com) apply these concepts?
6. What are the opportunities and potential problems with electronic data interchange (EDI) for a drugstore chain?
7. Cite the major advantages and disadvantages of secondary data.

8. As a casual dining restaurant owner, what kinds of secondary data would you use to learn more about your industry and consumer trends in dining out?
9. Describe the major advantage of each method of gathering primary data: survey, observation, experiment, and simulation.
10. Develop a 10-item semantic differential for a local hardware store to judge its image. Who should be surveyed? Why?
11. Why would a retailer use mystery shoppers rather than other forms of observation? Are there any instances when you would not recommend their use? Why or why not?
12. Why do you think that "virtual shopping" has not taken off faster as a research tool for retailers?

Web-Based Exercise

Visit the Web site of the Coca-Cola Retailing Research Council (www.ccrrc.org), an online resource for information about strategic issues impacting grocery and convenience store retailers. Describe some of the information the site offers for retailers. Which would you most recommend? Why?

Note: Also stop by our Web site (www.pearsonhighered.com/bermanevans) to experience a number of highly interactive, appealing Web exercises based on actual company demonstrations and sample materials related to retailing.

PART 3 Short Cases

Case 1: The Costco Mindset: Appealing to Consumers' Interest in Quantity Discounts[c-1]

A major issue for many retailers is determining the quantity discount level to offer consumers that maximizes profits. The use of such discounts is central to the pricing strategy of membership clubs that often strap multiple cans and bottles of the same brand together. It is also important for supermarkets to examine their quantity discount strategy to combat lost sales from membership clubs and supercenters.

To manufacturers, quantity discounts encourage loyal customers to stock up on their brands. This approach may discourage consumers from purchasing competing brands during a time when their homes are amply stocked. To retailers, quantity discounts increase sales volume. Often, the value of the quantity discount offered to consumers is based on the retailers' lower wholesale costs. As an alternative to large package sizes, consumers may prefer purchasing multiple quantities of smaller package sizes versus one larger size due to perishability concerns.

Using advanced statistical analysis, two researchers developed a mathematical model that uncovers how consumers modify their purchase decisions for goods and services based on the quantity discounts offered. This model enables retailers to study the effect of quantity discounts on sales and profits without the need for costly and time-consuming experiments or trial-and-error pricing tactics. According to the researchers, the logic behind quantity discounts is based on the average consumer's obtaining diminishing satisfaction from each additional unit purchased. As a result, consumers are less willing to pay the same price for additional units as for prior units purchased at the same time.

The research model was based on an online movie rental business with two scenarios: no competition and competition. Using a sample of 250 consumers, subjects were offered different monthly pricing plans for movies based on the number of movies they wanted to view at a time. The level of the discount was varied to allow the researchers to determine the optimal price levels for the rental firms.

The study found that the price consumers were willing to pay for DVD rentals declined after renting the first DVD and took a major price drop on additional units thereafter. The researchers saw that DVD rental retailers must offer dramatic discounts to retain customers interested in renting two or more DVDs. Based on these findings, the hypothetical movie rental firm would maximize profit at a monthly fee of $13 for a one-DVD-at-a-time plan, $23 per month for a two-DVD plan, and $31 for a three–DVD plan—assuming no competition. A second model looked at optimal pricing that reflected competition from both Netflix and Blockbuster. Under this scenario, the profit maximizing price would be $8.22 per month for a one-DVD-at-a-time plan, $12.69 for two DVDs, $16.40 for three DVDs, and $21.82 for a four-DVD plan.

The retailer's brand name and the product's features both had an impact on the price that consumers were willing to pay. Consumers would be willing to pay a price premium of $1 per month for Netflix over Blockbuster and about 65 cents more for a Blu-ray alternative.

Questions

1. Discuss the pros and cons of quantity discount-based promotions from a manufacturer's perspective.
2. Describe the pros and cons of quantity discount-based promotions from a retailer's perspective.
3. Explain the concept of diminishing satisfaction with each additional unit consumed.
4. Evaluate the applicability of these research findings to a membership club such as BJ's.

Case 2: 7-Eleven: A New Focus on the Customer ("the Guest")[c-2]

In 2006, Joe DePinto, the chief executive of 7-Eleven (www.7-eleven.com), realized that to remain top of mind among consumers, the 7,200-unit chain (with stores in the United States and Canada) had to undergo some major changes. As a result, DePinto developed a new strategy based around what 7-Eleven refers to as "servant leadership."

The key to the overall servant leadership strategy is to place 7-Eleven's customers ("guests") at the top of the pyramid, its employees and store operators in the middle, and its management team at the bottom. This is because the success of 7-Eleven is largely determined by how well it can respond to changing consumer needs. After finding out that its loyal customers were aging, 7-Eleven began to target a younger audience that DePinto calls "millennials." To better appeal to this group, 7-Eleven increased the emphasis on its Slurpee-flavored frozen-drink beverage, as well as its Big Gulp, 32-ounce fountain drink.

7-Eleven also introduced 7-Select, a private-label brand with over 3,000 items. This brand was developed to appeal to price-conscious consumers affected by the recession. According to DePinto, "There was a need for a private-label offering with high quality, strong appeal for consumers, and a sharper retail price point." The 7-Select brand was originally planned as a response to consumer demand for a quick snack at a low cost. The brand was launched with 7-Select chips, expanded to other snack items, and now includes health-and-beauty aids.

Another important aspect of 7-Eleven's consumer-centric strategy is based on an upgraded store image, new hot food offerings, and new lighting. Within a four-year period, over one-half of 7-Eleven's U.S. and Canadian stores were remodeled.

[c-1]The material in this case is drawn from "Catering to the Costco Mindset: Finding the 'Sweet Spot' in Quantity Discounts," http://knowledge.wharton.upenn.edu (October 27, 2010).

[c-2]The material in this case is drawn from "7-Eleven: Contemporary Convenience," *Retail Merchandiser* (May–June 2011), pp. 5–7.

Because 7-Eleven sells over one million cups of coffee daily, a vital part of the upgraded image dealt with its coffee bar.

The final essential aspect of 7-Eleven's new strategy involved the balance between corporate and franchise ownership. When DePinto took over as CEO in late 2005, 7-Eleven's North American locations were 50 percent corporate-owned and 50 percent franchise-based. After a management team studied both types of ownership arrangements, it discovered that franchise operators outperformed the company stores and had a closer relationship with their customers (including knowing many customers by name). Currently, 77 percent of the chain's North American stores are franchise operated.

Today, 7-Eleven has also given more autonomy to franchisees based on their superior market knowledge. Franchisees are now empowered to choose roughly 30 new products presented by the chain's category managers each week, to stop stocking slow-selling goods, and to even choose 15 percent of their inventory from local or regional resellers that are not customary suppliers to 7-Eleven. This flexibility enables 7-Eleven's franchisees to better respond to the demographic, lifestyle, and ethnic characteristics of the population surrounding their stores.

At 7-Eleven, the company and the franchisee split a store's gross profits. In contrast, at most franchises, franchisor royalties are based on sales, not franchisee profits. While the traditional sales-based model may generate channel conflict (as franchisors may be more concerned with sales than profits), at 7-Eleven the focus is on cooperation since profits are shared by both parties.

Questions

1. Explain the importance of the 7-Select private-label program in 7-Eleven's consumer-centric focus strategy.
2. Describe the pros and cons of corporate versus franchisee ownership to 7-Eleven.
3. From the customer's perspective, discuss the pros and cons of giving franchisees more autonomy.
4. Why do so few franchise companies tie royalties to sales, not profits? Are sales easier to monitor through a retail information system than profits? Why or why not?

Case 3: Testing Channel Formats at Wal-Mart[c-3]

After eight quarters with negative comparable store sales, Wal-Mart (www.walmart.com) began to look more seriously at multi-channel alternatives as a means of reversing this decline. Wal-Mart hopes that its thousands of retail stores and its online operations can become better integrated to increase shopper convenience. Wal-Mart's CEO believes that better coordination between the stores and the Internet can deliver "immediacy" in a way that clicks-only retailers cannot match. As an example, a Wal-Mart consumer can search the Web for product information, determine if a local store has the item in stock, order the good online, and then pick it up in a convenient local store.

The following illustrate some of the research initiatives Wal-Mart has undertaken with regard to expanding its multi-channel capabilities:

- "Wal-Mart to Go" grocery delivery—Wal-Mart tested home delivery of online groceries in San Jose, California. Customers could browse Wal-Mart's product availability by brand and type of product. Online orders were delivered for a $5 to $10 fee. This concept has now been expanded into several areas served by Wal-Mart.
- Mobile shopping—With Wal-Mart's "My Holiday" app, shoppers can purchase goods through their mobile Walmart.com page. In early 2011, Wal-Mart introduced a Mobile Pharmacy that enables consumers to refill prescriptions by placing orders from their phone.
- Free delivery to FedEx locations—As of March 2011, Wal-Mart began a delivery program that ships goods to 180 FedEx locations in New York City, San Francisco, Chicago, Boston, Washington, D.C., and Los Angeles. This program is aimed at delivering goods to shoppers in areas where customers prefer not to leave the package at their door.
- "Pick-Up Today" online order-to-store service—Customers can order online and then pick up the merchandise at a local Wal-Mart. In March 2011, Wal-Mart expanded this service to cover 40,000 items, including electronics, toys, baby goods, and hardware.
- Mobile commerce—Wal-Mart is experimenting with mobile checkouts that enable smart phone owners to check out using their phone instead of a store-based self-checkout unit.
- Social commerce—Wal-Mart recently bought Kosmix, a social media filtering company.

While Wal-Mart's strategies reflect changes in technology and in the ways consumers shop, they are not guaranteed to be successful. Some are copies of successful strategies used by competitors (such as Peapod's grocery delivery or Best Buy's order online and pickup in the store). Other strategies can only work in selected areas. For example, "Walmart to Go" Grocery Delivery is most feasible in markets with high-population densities, such as cities and nearby suburbs. It also remains to be seen whether consumers will order perishables like fruits and vegetables from a Wal-Mart Web site without being able to inspect these goods for freshness or ripeness. Lastly, in some of these activities, like mobile apps, Wal-Mart is not a technological leader; and some retail analysts feel that Free Delivery to FedEx locations better enable Wal-Mart to serve urban areas where it does not have sufficient stores.

Questions

1. From the customer's perspective, evaluate Wal-Mart's "Wal-Mart to Go" and mobile shopping multi-channel strategies.
2. From the customer's perspective, discuss the relative benefits of Wal-Mart's free delivery to FedEx locations and its "Pick-Up Today online order-to-store service strategies."
3. What customer-based criteria would you use to evaluate whether Wal-Mart succeeds with its new efforts?
4. What information should Wal-Mart compile about smart phone transactions? How should it use the information?

[c-3]The material in this case is drawn from Robin Sherk, "Walmart Continues Multi-Channel Tests: What Are Its Prospects?" www.kantarretailiq.com (June 17, 2011).

Case 4: Growth Reimagined: Prospects in Emerging Markets[c-4]

Let us examine the findings of a recent Pricewaterhouse Coopers (PwC) Annual Global CEO study. In particular, that report looked at how 75 retail CEOs (chief executive officers) in 30 countries are approaching growth prospects at a time when economic growth is uncertain. At the time this study was conducted, the global economy was still recovering from the worst economic crisis in the past 75 years.

PwC found that, in general, retail CEOs have renewed confidence in their firms' growth prospects. Ninety percent of the CEOs expect to have higher sales within a one-year period, and 93 percent expect sales to climb over the next three years. This shows more confidence than the prior year's study when only 74 percent of retail CEOs were either somewhat or very confident of having increased sales over the next fiscal year. The respondents were particularly positive about their Asian operations, with 93 percent of the respondents stating that they should be able to expand their Asian operations over the next year. In addition, 55 percent of the CEOs also saw promise in their West European retail operations.

In the recent study, the CEOs were also very positive about emerging markets, such as China and India, due to rising consumer affluence, the growing middle class, good economic growth (especially as compared with developed economies), and new legal developments. Indian regulators, for example, have been considering whether to allow foreign "big-box" retailers to own up to 49 percent of joint ventures with Indian retailers as majority partners. Before this development, foreign retailers could only sell one brand in each store. Thirty-three percent of retail CEOs view China as one of the three foreign countries most critical to their companies' growth.

[c-4]The material in this case is drawn from "Growth Reimagined: Retail Industry Summary," www.pwc.com/ceosurvey (2011).

In earlier PwC studies, retail CEOs viewed their best opportunities for growth to be obtaining higher market shares in their core markets. The latest study shows the shift to developing new products and services relating to mobile devices and social networks, green products, and achieving shared priorities with governments.

Globally, retail CEOs are aware of the greater importance of mobile devices and social networks that affect the shopping process and information search. Fifty-three percent of the respondents stated that they are making major changes in their retail strategies to capitalize on these developments. Fifty-seven percent of the retail CEOs stated that one of the major reasons they are investing in information technology is to support mobile devices and social networks. Interesting, even though all of the retailers had Web sites, only two-thirds of the retail firms could handle an E-commerce transaction.

While only 52 percent of the respondents view their responsibilities to include developing green products, many CEOs have become more involved with using sustainable products, developing products with low emissions, and becoming more active with product recycling. These retailers are working closely with suppliers to develop ecologically suitable products.

Lastly, retail CEOs are concerned about the impact of reduced local, state, and federal budgets on economic growth, employment, and consumer spending.

Questions

1. Discuss the pros and cons of a retailer's developing new stores in domestic markets instead of China and India.
2. Develop a research study proposal to evaluate the impact of mobile devices on a consumer's information search behavior.
3. What factors explain the relatively low percent of retailers capable of handling an E-commerce transaction?
4. Devise a brief survey to show how much interest that people have in shopping with retailers that are environmentally conscious.

PART 3 Comprehensive Case

Starbucks' Customer Appeal*

Introduction

Starbucks (www.starbucks.com) is the world's leading roaster and retailer of specialty coffee. Through its global network of owned and franchised coffee retail outlets, Starbucks offers a wide range of products such as high-quality whole bean coffees, freshly brewed coffees, Italian-style espresso beverages, cold-blended beverages, premium teas, food items including sandwiches, and coffee-making equipment.

Starbucks' own stores are located near offices and residential areas and are larger in size, compared to its licensed (franchised) stores that are much smaller and mostly located at airports and supermarkets. In addition to selling packaged coffee beans through its retail outlets, Starbucks also sells packaged and ready-to-drink products through retailers such as Costco and Target.

Starbucks' company-operated stores generate more dollar profits than the franchised stores, which have a higher profit margin. It makes money through both sales at company-owned stores and through franchise fees and royalties from franchised stores. The firm earns higher profit margins from franchised stores compared to company-owned stores because there are no operational and employee costs to Starbucks that are incurred with franchised stores; hence, Starbucks gets to keep entire royalty and rent fees without owing any costs.

In 2010, profit per company-owned store was $107,800, which is expected to reach $182,000 as of 2018. By comparison, profit per franchised store for Starbucks was $70,000 in 2010, expected to reach $96,000 as of 2018. At the end of 2010, Starbucks' own store count was 8,870 compared to 8,130 franchised stores.

Key Trends

Franchises and international markets will continue to drive Starbucks' expansion. The saturation of the U.S. beverage market has resulted in self-cannibalization of a large number of Starbucks' stores. The company closed nearly 890 underperforming stores between 2008 and 2010. In contrast, international markets such as China have shown strong positive growth even during bad economic times.

Starbucks actively uses social media to connect with the younger population. The firm is expanding its target audience to teen coffee drinkers, as this segment is believed to be one of the major growth drivers for the company. Starbucks is using the Internet on a massive scale to connect with teenagers on a personal level through blogs, dedicated communities, forums, and Web sites. For example, "My Starbucks Idea" (http://mystarbucksidea.force.com) is a Web-based community where customers can post new ideas and provide feedback on beverages and store services.

Starbucks recently entered the single-serve and instant coffee markets with the launch of the VIA brand, which has been well received by consumers in the United States and Canada. Key attributes such as high quality, portability, and ease of use are driving customers to VIA. Starbucks has also entered the instant coffee market in Europe and Asia, and will compete with Nestlé, a dominant player in these markets. Currently, the global instant coffee market is worth about $21 billion annually, presenting a huge opportunity for VIA.

Company-Owned Stores

Beverage spending per customer visit represents the average amount spent on beverages at a Starbucks store by one customer during one visit. This figure increased by more than half a dollar from 2005 to 2010, with the average reaching $4.77 in 2010. This may be attributed to rising prices of raw materials (beverage ingredients such as coffee beans, milk, sugar, artificial sweeteners, and flavors) that are eventually passed on to the customers. The increase can also be attributed to the introduction of new and costlier beverages in the menu, and the favorable response they have generated among customers. It is expected that the beverage spending per customer visit will increase steadily, as Starbucks keeps on adding innovative and slightly higher-priced premium beverages to its menu, reaching $6.09 as of 2018.

To be as innovative as possible, Starbucks has invested a lot on research and development. A majority of this spending has been for the development, testing, and improvement of new beverage products that can be sold at higher prices.

Diet and health concerns are driving the size of the beverages chosen by some customers. Starbucks serves drinks in various sizes—short (8 ounces), tall (12 ounces), grande (16 ounces), and Venti (20-ounce and 24-ounce versions), along with a choice of caffeine levels (decaf, single shot, double shot, triple shot). For example, a short-brewed coffee has 180 milligrams of caffeine in comparison to 415 milligrams in a Venti. Diet and health concerns play a role in not only how frequently people consume caffeinated beverages but also how much they consume with each serving. Thus, consumer discretion driven by health concerns impact the dollars shelled out for a drink.

The choice of ingredients and exotic blends have an impact on the beverage price paid by customers. At Starbucks, customers can choose coffee ingredients and blends according to their personal desires. For example, you can choose to have coffee with milk (nonfat milk, 2 percent fat milk, whole milk, or soy milk), sugar or artificial sweetener, whipped cream, and so forth. Some ingredients increase the beverage price, while others do not. The total beverage price may even vary due to add-on flavors preferred by customers. For example, Frappuccino buyers have to shell out an additional 70 cents to get add-on flavors, while adding a vanilla or mocha syrup may cost 30 cents extra.

Promotional offers such as lower prices during happy hours and a free drink during the second visit on the same day are good to increase customers. However, they also negatively impact the average spending per customer visit. The number of daily customers per store increased to 432 in 2010 and going forward, this daily figure is expected to exceed 500 by 2017.

Starbucks will continue to differentiate itself from premium coffees offered by McDonald's and other chains with lower-priced beverages that cut into Starbucks' customer

*The material in this case is adapted by the authors from *Trefis Analysis for Starbucks* (Boston, MA: Insight Guru Inc., September 7, 2011). Reprinted by permission of Trefis.com.

segment. This was amplified further by lower spending by consumers during the recession. However, in the long run, it is expected that there will be ample market space for both types of business models, as their target audiences will be different. Customers seeking a premium-quality experience at a luxury price are likely to keep on visiting Starbucks.

For a while, Starbucks expanded very aggressively in the United States, which led to some self-cannibalization by nearby Starbucks outlets. At one point, an average of 8.5 new locations were opened weekly. Starbucks dealt with this issue by undergoing a restructuring in 2008 and 2009, closing down more than 890 stores. This drive has reflected positively and factored out cannibalization.

Starbucks has spent a great deal of effort and money to ensure a better customer experience. Employee training is conducted very seriously and innovative ways are being sought to improve customer convenience. The retailer relies heavily on information technology systems across its operations, including supply chain management, point-of-sale processing at stores, and streamlined processes and transactions. These systems enable the firm to offer faster and better service to customers.

Historically, Starbucks avoided traditional television advertising, relying primarily on word of mouth to build its brand. However, in recent years, the company has increased its advertisement budgets and has started using more conventional advertising media such as television and newspaper. Starbucks also announced that it would be launching its first national advertising campaign.

As noted, due to the recession, many U.S. customers became more cautious in spending and turned to lower-priced beverages at Starbucks' stores. However, in international markets, especially where the recession did not hit as hard as compared to the United States, Starbucks' new overseas outlets got a great response from customers. Future growth is expected to be driven by its existing international markets such as Canada, Great Britain, China, Japan, France, Spain, and potential new markets such as India, Brazil, and Russia. In China, where stores provide higher profitability and margins compared to U.S. units, Starbucks has a target of increasing its store count to 1,500 very quickly.

An important consideration in international markets is gaining enough information to adapt the basic Starbucks' strategy. A failure to understand local tastes and to blend with local cultures is a potential risk to Starbucks' international expansion plans.

Franchised Stores

For franchised (licensed) stores, the average beverage spending per customer visit and the number of daily customer visits per store closely parallel the figures for company-owned stores. From $4.77 in 2010, the average beverage spending is expected to reach $6.09 in 2018; and the average number of daily customer visits per store will rise from 432 in 2010 to 516 in 2018.

Starbucks collects royalties (fees) from each franchised store in return for the latter being able to use the Starbucks name and logo, to sell Starbucks products, and to participate in training and other programs sponsored by Starbucks. The fees charged by Starbucks to its franchise (licensing) partners represent a percentage of the total sales generated by the franchisees.

The royalties collected by Starbucks as a percentage of the total revenue of franchised stores were consistent at 14.3 to 14.6 percent from 2005 to 2010, with slight variations. It is expected that future fees as a percentage of total revenue for franchisees will be in line with the historical average. See Figure 1.

The franchising agreements with outside partners have created a lot of new locations, such as supermarkets and airports, accessible to Starbucks. Leveraging the partners' infrastructure, Starbucks opened new stores at a very aggressive rate until 2008. The number of franchised U.S. stores increased from 2,633 in 2005 to 4,424 in 2010. Owing to the economic slowdown and saturation of the U.S. market, the growth rate has slowed since 2009.

The number of international franchised stores grew from 1,824 in 2005 to 3,600 in 2010. Starbucks is shifting its international focus to opening more franchised stores rather than fully owned stores. Growth should continue for franchised stores in the coming years, as the company ventures into new international locales. The growth of U.S. franchised stores will be very slow as the firm seeks new strategic locations that will not bring self-cannibalization. Starbucks selects international partners very carefully. They must have an in-depth understanding of the local customers' taste and preferences and also be able to match the high standards of customer satisfaction delivered by Starbucks-owned stores.

Franchised stores' gross profits (as a percentage of royalty revenues) were consistently in the range of 60 to 65 percent from 2005 to 2010 except for 2008, where it saw a strong decline. This is much higher than for company-owned stores, for which Starbucks incurs all operating costs.

Packaged Coffee and Tea

In recent years, Starbucks has branched out into selling packaged beverages through stores outside the company's owned and franchised Starbucks stores. Starbucks generates revenues by selling packaged coffee and tea globally under its name and logo through arrangements with grocery stores, such as

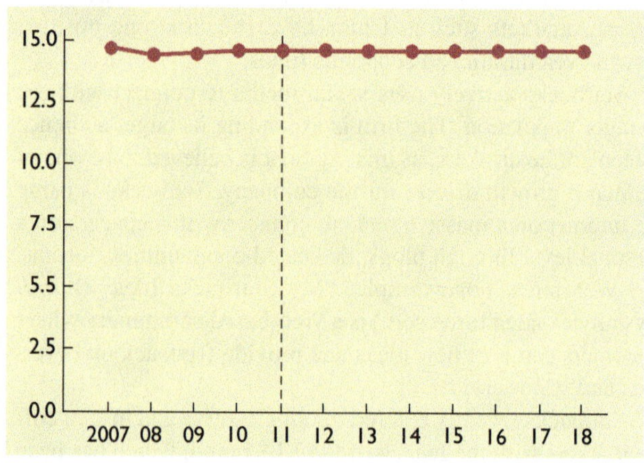

FIGURE 1
Royalty Collected from Franchisees as a Percentage of Their Total Revenues

supermarkets, and warehouse club stores, such as Costco. Currently, Starbucks packaged coffee and tea are available in around 37,000 stores worldwide.

Starbucks packaged coffee and tea revenues increased from $254.2 million in 2005 to $393 million in 2010. It is projected that packaged coffee and tea revenues for Starbucks will continue to increase in the coming years at a substantial rate with consumer spending expected to increase in favorable economic conditions. Revenues in 2018 are expected to reach $769 million—nearly double the 2010 amount.

International markets are attractive destinations for Starbucks retail stores, as well as partnerships with other companies. Since 2009, there has been an increase in partnerships between Starbucks and other retail companies to market Starbucks processed and packaged products internationally. Starbucks wants to actively leverage these partnerships and expand into new locations in the coming years.

Packaged coffee revenues have seen significant growth in the international markets, driven by aggressive pricing, new packaging graphics, new sizes, and new partners. Starbucks expects this trend to continue with the same momentum.

Starbucks is trying to come up with new products and innovative concepts to earn more revenues from this packaged coffee and tea due to their high profitability. Starbucks VIA, an instant coffee brand, is one example that is proving to be beneficial for the company.

To succeed with packaged goods, Starbucks is reliant on the marketing prowess and support from its partners. Revenues are dependent on the reputation of their selling partners and their reach among customers, over which Starbucks has no direct control.

Food Service

Starbucks also generates revenues by selling whole bean and ground coffees, as well as a selection of premium Tazo teas, to institutional food-service companies that are targeted toward service businesses and industries such as education, health care, office coffee distributors, hotels, restaurants, airlines, and other retailers. These firms sell beverages rather than packaged goods under the Starbucks' name and logo.

Food-service revenues increased from $307 million in 2005 to $406 million in 2008. However, 2009 saw a dip in the food-service revenues to $369 million, owing to continued softness in the hospitality industry led by the recession. The food-service revenues improved slightly in 2010; and going forward, these revenues are expected to further increase. The forecast is that revenues will reach $577 million in 2018.

As with the sales of packaged products through third parties, food-service revenues are closely linked with the selling partners' reputation and reach among customers, which Starbucks cannot directly control.

Other Branded Products

In partnership with leading companies such as Pepsi, Unilever, and Dreyer's, Starbucks obtains additional revenue by developing and distributing its branded products. Most of its ready-to-drink beverages (Frappuccino, DoubleShot espresso, and Discoveries) and ice creams are sold under this partnership arrangement.

Revenues from these products increased from $53 million in 2005 to $97.5 million in 2008. The year 2009 saw a dip due to the inability of partners to maintain high sales in bad economic times as compared to the previous years. However, this category improved slightly in 2010 as the economic environment improved. We expect Starbucks' revenues from these partnerships to increase to $116 million in 2018. Though this division has a great growth potential, it won't be reflected sooner as the growth is invariably dependent on the performance of the company's primary business of retail stores, and currently the company is focusing to strategically rebuild that. Once the goal is achieved, it is anticipated that Starbucks management will show more focus on these secondary revenue sources.

The gross profit margins for packaged coffee and tea, food service, and other branded products have been strong, consistently averaging in the range of 60 to 65 percent from 2005 to 2010—except for 2008 when it saw a decline. That decline can be attributed to the increase in raw material prices, mainly for coffee beans, and Starbucks' inability to pass on the rising prices to the customers as the recession was at its peak. The gross profit margins are expected to be relatively stable at 65 percent through 2018.

Table 1 has data for Starbucks by division—from company-owned stores to other branded products.

Questions

1. What can *any* retailer learn from this case?
2. Based on the information in this case and at Starbucks' Web site (www.starbucks.com), describe the market segment(s) to which the firm appeals. What attracts the segment(s) to Starbucks?
3. Apply the concept of the consumer decision process to Starbucks.
4. Do you think that consumers know—or care—which outlets are owned by Starbucks and which are franchised? Explain your answer.
5. What customer information should Starbucks keep in its retail information system? How could it use this information?
6. Are there any risks to Starbucks selling its brands in food stores? Explain your answer.
7. Make several recommendations for Starbucks based on the data in Figure 1 and Table 1.

TABLE 1 Selected Starbucks Data by Division, Actual and Projected

	2007	2008	2009	2010	2011	2012	2013	2014	2015	2016	2017	2018
Company-Owned Stores												
Total Revenues (Bil. $)	8.34	8.6	8.3	8.74	9.42	10.4	11.5	12.6	13.6	14.7	15.8	16.9
Beverage Revenue (Bil. $)	6.29	6.53	6.31	6.64	7.14	7.84	8.6	9.35	10.1	10.8	11.6	12.4
Beverage Spending Per Customer Visit ($)	4.73	4.60	4.57	4.77	5.05	5.25	5.46	5.63	5.74	5.85	5.97	6.09
Daily Customers Per Store	408	423	427	432	449	458	467	476	486	496	506	516
Number of Stores (000s)	8.92	9.19	8.85	8.83	8.61	8.91	9.23	9.55	9.88	10.2	10.5	10.8
Food and Other Revenue (Bil. $)	2.05	2.07	1.99	2.1	2.28	2.57	2.91	3.22	3.57	3.87	4.18	4.53
Food and Other Spend Per Customer Visit ($)	1.55	1.46	1.44	1.51	1.61	1.73	1.85	1.94	2.04	2.10	2.16	2.23
Gross Profits (Bil. $)	0.67	0.34	0.66	0.96	1.13	1.35	1.50	1.64	1.77	1.91	2.05	2.20
Gross Profits (%)	8.0	4.0	8.0	11.0	12.0	13.0	13.0	13.0	13.0	13.0	13.0	13.0
Franchised Stores												
Total Revenue for Starbucks (Bil. $)	0.71	0.79	0.81	0.88	1.01	1.14	1.28	1.43	1.56	1.7	1.86	2.03
Royalty Collected by Starbucks as a % of Total Revenue of Franchised Stores	14.6	14.4	14.4	14.6	14.6	14.6	14.6	14.6	14.6	14.6	14.6	14.6
Daily Customers Per Store	408	423	427	432	449	458	467	476	486	496	506	516
Number of Stores (000s)	6.84	7.69	7.86	8.02	8.39	8.89	9.42	9.99	10.5	11.00	11.6	12.1
Gross Profits (Bil. $)	0.44	0.39	0.48	0.57	0.66	0.74	0.83	0.93	1.01	1.11	1.21	1.32
Gross Profits (%)	61.8	50.0	60.0	65.0	65.0	65.0	65.0	65.0	65.0	65.0	65.0	65.0
Packaged Coffee, Tea, and Other Businesses												
Total Revenue (Bil. $)	0.78	0.84	0.80	0.83	0.90	0.96	1.02	1.09	1.16	1.25	1.35	1.46
Packaged Coffee and Tea Revenue (Mil. $)	336	341	364	393	441	485	533	576	622	672	719	769
Food Service Revenue (Mil. $)	380	406	369	373	388	400	412	433	454	477	525	577
Branded Products and Other Revenue (Mil. $)	58.5	97.5	63.3	66.0	69.3	72.7	76.4	81.7	87.4	96.2	105	116
Gross Profits (Mil. $)	479	422	478	541	584	623	664	709	757	810	877	951
Gross Profits (%)	61.8	50.0	60.0	65.0	65.0	65.0	65.0	65.0	65.0	65.0	65.0	65.0

PART 4

Choosing a Store Location

Once a retailer has conducted a situation analysis, set its goals, identified consumer characteristics and needs, and gathered adequate information about the marketplace, it is ready to develop and enact an overall strategy. In Parts Four through Seven, we examine the elements of such a strategy: choosing a store location, managing a business, merchandise management and pricing, and communicating with the customer. Part Four concentrates on store location.

Chapter 9 deals with the crucial nature of store location for retailers and outlines a four-step approach to location planning. In this chapter, we focus on Step 1, trading-area analysis. Among the topics we look at are the use of geographic information systems, the size and shape of trading areas, how to determine trading areas for existing and new stores, and the major factors to consider in assessing trading areas. Several data sources are described.

Chapter 10 covers the last three steps in location planning: deciding on the most desirable type of location, selecting a general location, and choosing a particular site within that location. We first contrast isolated store, unplanned business district, and planned shopping center locales. Criteria for rating each location are then outlined and detailed.

Source: Ibne Handel/Shutterstock.com. Reprinted by permission.

9 Trading-Area Analysis

Chapter Objectives

1. To demonstrate the importance of store location for a retailer and outline the process for choosing a store location
2. To discuss the concept of a trading area and its related components
3. To show how trading areas may be delineated for existing and new stores
4. To examine three major factors in trading-area analysis: population characteristics, economic base characteristics, and competition and the level of saturation

Retailers choose their store locations based on a wide range of factors, including the attributes of various trading areas, the nearness to other units operated by the same firm and to stores operated by competing firms, population characteristics, and more. Likewise, consumers choose the locations where they like to shop based on a wide range of factors, including the overall appeal of the area, the distance to the store, the availability of a choice of retailers and brands, the ease of parking, and more.

Today, with the growing popularity of location-based social media applications via the GPS software built into smart phones, the dynamics are certainly changing from the shopper's perspective. A survey by Wi-Fi hot spot provider JiWire found that mobile Wi-Fi users in North America are most interested in these location-based services: the distance and directions to nearby stores, points of interest, checking-in so others know where you are geographically, and reviews. JiWire also discovered that many users are concerned about privacy issues, with women worrying more than men.

Vons, a supermarket chain owned by Safeway, has tested—in partnership with PepsiCo—the effectiveness of location-based marketing through Foursquare, one of the leaders in the field. As Kantar Retail's Alida Destrempe puts it: Blogs enable firms to communicate "What's new," Twitter can describe "What's happening," and Facebook enables users to say "What's on my mind." Foursquare focuses on a different issue: "Where am I?" Destrempe notes that "Foursquare adds value to social networking in ways that other social media can't, as it bridges the gap between social media and the physical world."

At Vons (www.vons.com/IFL/Grocery/Foursquare), Foursquare users "check in" by scanning their store loyalty card at the checkout counter. By checking in, customers accumulate points that can be converted into discount coupons for PepsiCo products as such Pepsi Max and Tropicana juices. This allows the retailer to provide a more personalized shopping experience and stimulate greater loyalty toward Vons.[1]

Source: BeTA-Artworks/ fotolia.com.

Overview

Because well over 90 percent of retail sales are made at stores, the selection of a store location is one of the most significant strategic decisions in retailing. Consider the detailed planning of Aldi, the German-based discount food chain with more than 1,150 stores in 31 U.S. states.

Recently, Aldi decided to open its first shopping-mall-based U.S. supermarket at Westfield Chicago Ridge in suburban Chicago. Except for its shopping mall location, the 20,000-square-foot Aldi store is typical of the retailer. Aldi's Michael Jessen says that:

> On the exterior, we worked closely with the developer and were able to provide a good presentation of the store on the footage we were given. Supermarkets in malls are much more uncommon in the United States than in Europe. But, there are lots of benefits to malls. Between the flow of regular mall traffic and the employees who work in the shops, this location gives us the opportunity to introduce Aldi to a whole new group of customers. There are still lots of people who have never set foot in an Aldi. A mall gives you a captive audience.[2]

This chapter and the next explain why the proper store location is so crucial, as well as the steps a retailer should take in choosing a store location and deciding whether to build, lease, or buy facilities. Visit our Web site (www.pearsonhighered.com/bermanevans) for links on store location.

THE IMPORTANCE OF LOCATION TO A RETAILER

A lot of good information on location planning is available at this Web site (http://retail.about.com/od/location/a/selecting_site.htm).

Location decisions are complex, costs can be quite high, there is little flexibility once a site is chosen, and locational attributes have a big impact on a strategy. One of the oldest retailing adages is that "location, location, location" is the major factor leading to a firm's success or failure. See Figure 9-1.

A good location may let a retailer succeed even if its strategy mix is mediocre. A hospital gift shop may do well, although its assortment is limited, its prices are high, and it does not advertise. On the other hand, a poor location may be such a liability that even superior retailers cannot overcome it. A mom-and-pop store may do poorly if it is across the street from a category killer store; although the small firm features personal service, it cannot match the selection and prices. At a different site, it might prosper.

The choice of a location requires extensive decision making due to the number of criteria considered, including population size and traits, the competition, transportation access, parking

FIGURE 9-1

The Importance of Location to Foot Locker

The Foot Locker chain is the leading store brand of Foot Locker, Inc. There are 1,150 Foot Locker units in the United States and 800 in twenty other countries. The U.S. stores occupy an average of roughly 2,400 selling square feet; the international stores occupy an average of about 1,500-selling-square-feet. Foot Locker stores are largely in located regional and neighborhood shopping centers, with some stores in popular business districts and city streets. Shown here is a city street store in Copenhagen, Demark.

Source: Tupungato/Shutterstock.com. Reprinted by permission.

availability, the nature of nearby stores, property costs, the length of the agreement, legal restrictions, and other factors.

A store location typically necessitates a sizable investment and a long-term commitment. Even a retailer that minimizes its investment by leasing (rather than owning a building and land) can incur large costs. Besides lease payments, the firm must spend money on lighting, fixtures, a storefront, and so on.

Although leases of less than 5 years are common in less desirable retailing locations, leases in good shopping centers or shopping districts are often 5 to 10 years or more. It is not uncommon for a supermarket lease to be 15 or 20 years. Department stores and large specialty stores on major downtown thoroughfares occasionally sign leases longer than 20 years.

Due to its fixed nature, the investment, and the length of the lease, store location is the least flexible element of a retail strategy. A firm cannot easily move to another site or convert to another format. It may also be barred from subleasing to another party during the lease period; if a retailer breaks a lease, it may be responsible to the property owner for financial losses. In contrast, ads, prices, customer services, and assortment can be modified as the environment (consumers, competition, the economy) changes.

Even a retailer that owns its store's building and land may also find it hard to change locations. It has to find an acceptable buyer, which might take several months or longer, and it may have to assist the buyer with financing. It may incur a loss, should it sell during an economic downturn.

A firm moving from one locale to another faces three potential problems. (1) Some loyal customers and employees may be lost; the greater the distance between the old and new locations, the bigger the loss. (2) A new site may not have the same traits as the original one. (3) Store fixtures and renovations at an old site usually cannot be transferred; their value is lost if they have not been fully depreciated.

Store location affects long- and short-run planning. In the *long run*, the choice of location influences the overall strategy. A retailer must be at a site that is consistent with its mission, goals, and target market for an extended time. It also must regularly study and monitor the status of the location as to population trends, the distances people travel to the store, and competitors' entry and exit—and adapt accordingly.

In the *short run*, the location has an impact on the specific elements of a strategy mix. A retailer in a downtown area with many office buildings may have little pedestrian traffic on weekends. It would probably be improper to sell items such as major appliances there (these items are often bought jointly by adult household members). The retailer could either close on weekends and not stock certain products or remain open and try to attract customers to the area by aggressive promotion or pricing. If the retailer closes on weekends, it adapts its strategy mix to the attributes of the location. If it stays open, it invests additional resources in an attempt to alter shopping habits. A retailer that strives to overcome its location, by and large, faces greater risks than one that adapts.

Retailers should follow these four steps in choosing a store location:

1. Evaluate alternate geographic (trading) areas in terms of the characteristics of residents and existing retailers.
2. Determine whether to locate as an isolated store in an unplanned business district or in a planned shopping center within the geographic area.
3. Select the general isolated store, unplanned business district, or planned shopping center location.
4. Analyze alternate sites contained in the specified retail location type.

This chapter concentrates on Step 1. Chapter 10 details Steps 2, 3, and 4. The selection of a store location is a process involving each of these steps.

TRADING-AREA ANALYSIS

The first step in the choice of a retail store location is to describe and evaluate alternate trading areas and then decide on the most desirable one. A **trading area** is a geographical area containing the customers and potential customers of a particular retailer or group of retailers for

Shopping Center Interest Among Puerto Rico Developers

Puerto Rico, with more than 45 shopping centers, nearly 32 million square feet of shopping space, and at least 50 successful national and international retailers is the undisputed "shopping-center mecca" of the Caribbean. The island will soon gain an additional 1.5 million square feet of new shopping center and mixed-use space. These two new developments represent a total investment of $850 million by Michigan-based Taubman Centers, Inc. (www.taubman.com) and South American Constructora Sambil of Venezuela (www.tusambil.com). Both projects combine tourism and entertainment (adding 464 hotel rooms) along with the shopping center space.

A number of factors have spurred developers' interest in Puerto Rico. These include higher sales per square foot of retail space than in the United States, a large base of middle-class shoppers, and the island's recovery from a long recession. The use of English as the island's official language of conducting business and the existence of the same tax codes as in the United States also contribute to Puerto Rico's attractiveness.

As compared to the U.S. mainland, until recently, there was less competition in many product categories. For example, before CVS pharmacy's arrival, Walgreens had been the unchallenged leader in the pharmacy sector. And for almost 25 years, Kmart was the only U.S. discounter on the island. Wal-Mart, Marshalls, and T.J. Maxx now compete in this segment.

Source: Frances Ryan, "Stateside and Latin American Shopping-Center Developers Eye Puerto Rico Market as New Frontier," *Caribbean Business* (February 17, 2011), pp. 16–20.

specific goods and/or services. The size of a trading area typically reflects the boundaries within which it is profitable to sell and/or deliver products.[3] After a trading area is picked, it should be reviewed regularly.

A thorough analysis of trading areas provides several benefits:

- Consumers' demographic and socioeconomic characteristics are examined. For a new store, the study of proposed trading areas reveals opportunities and the retail strategy necessary to succeed. For an existing store, it can be determined if the current strategy still matches consumer needs.
- The focus of promotional activities is ascertained, and the retailer can look at media coverage patterns of proposed or existing locations. If 95 percent of customers live within three miles of a store, it would be inefficient to advertise in a paper with a citywide audience.
- A chain retailer learns whether the location of a proposed new store will service additional customers or take business from its existing stores. Suppose a supermarket chain has a store in Jackson, Mississippi, with a trading area of two miles, and it considers adding a new store, three miles from the Jackson branch. Figure 9-2 shows the distinct trading areas and expected overlap of the stores. The shaded portion represents the **trading-area overlap**, where the same customers are served by both branches. The chain must look at the overall net increase in sales if it adds the proposed store (total revised sales of existing store + total sales of new store—total previous sales of existing store).
- Chains anticipate whether competitors want to open nearby stores if the firm does not do so itself. That is why TJX has two of its chains, T.J. Maxx and Marshalls, situate within 1.5 miles of each other in more than 100 U.S. markets, even though they are both off-price apparel firms.
- The best number of stores for a chain to operate in a given area is calculated. How many outlets should a retailer have in a region to provide good service for customers (without raising costs too much or having too much overlap)? When CVS pharmacy entered Atlanta, it opened nine new drugstores in one day. This gave it enough coverage of the city to service residents, without placing stores too close together. A major competitive advantage for Canadian Tire Corporation is that four-fifths of the Canadian population live within a 15-minute drive of a Canadian Tire store.
- Geographic weaknesses are highlighted. Suppose a suburban shopping center does an analysis and discovers that most of those residing south of town do not shop there, and a more comprehensive study reveals that people are afraid to drive past a dangerous railroad crossing. Due to its research, the shopping center could exert political pressure to make the crossing safer.

FIGURE 9-2

The Trading Areas of Current and Proposed Supermarket Outlets

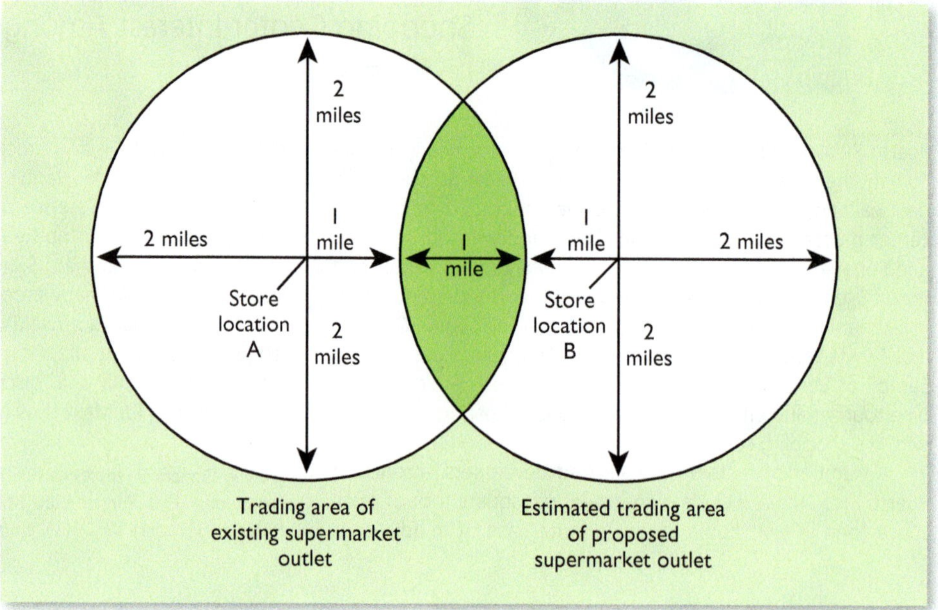

- The impact of the Internet is taken into account. Store-based retailers must examine trading areas more carefully than ever to see how their customers' shopping behavior is changing due to the Web.
- Other factors are reviewed. The competition, financial institutions, transportation, labor availability, supplier location, legal restrictions, and so on can each be learned for the trading area(s) examined.

The Use of Geographic Information Systems in Trading-Area Delineation and Analysis

Increasingly, retailers are using **geographic information system (GIS)** software, which combines digitized mapping with key locational data to graphically depict trading-area characteristics such as population demographics; data on customer purchases; and listings of current, proposed, and competitor locations. Commercial GIS software lets firms quickly research the attractiveness of different locations and access computer-generated maps. Before, retailers often placed different color pins on paper maps to show current and proposed locales—and competitors' sites—and had to collect and analyze data.[4]

Learn more about TIGER mapping at its Web site (www.census.gov/geo/www/tiger).

Most GIS software programs are extrapolated from the decennial *Census of Population* and the U.S. Census Bureau's national digital map (known as TIGER—topologically integrated geographic encoding and referencing). TIGER incorporates all streets and highways in the United States. TIGER files may be ordered free of charge by calling 301-763-4636. Commercial GIS software can be bought and accessed through Web site downloads or by DVDs or CDs.

TIGER maps may be adapted to reflect census tracts, railroads, highways, waterways, and other physical attributes of any U.S. area. They do not show retailers, other commercial entities, or population traits, and the Web site is hard to use. The federal government recently invested several hundred million dollars to upgrade the TIGER program.

Mapping software from private firms has many more enhancements than TIGER. These firms often offer free demonstrations, but they expect to be paid for their software packages. Although GIS software differs by vendor, it generally can be accessed or bought for as little as $100 (or less) or for as much as several thousand dollars, is designed to work with personal computers, and allows for some manipulation of trading-area data. Illustrations appear in Figure 9-3.

FIGURE 9-3
GIS Software in Action

(A) This map shows the relative location of customers who patronize a particular store. Desire lines (spider lines) indicate the relationship between the location of each customer and the store location. The analysis examines the relationship between total purchase behavior and the distance each customer travels to patronize the store. (B) This map illustrates the impact on existing customers if the location of a store/site (in this case, a bank) is changed. The "x" represents the proposed location and the "check" represents the existing location. The red and yellow polygons represent a 9-minute drive around each location. This 9-minute value represents 80 percent of the customer base.

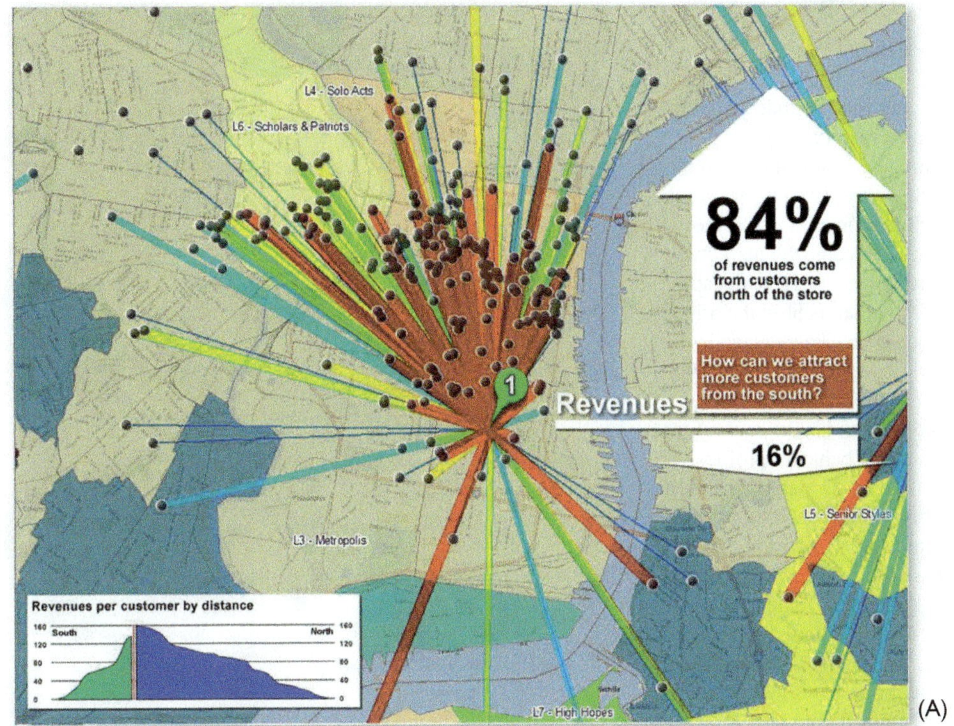

(A)

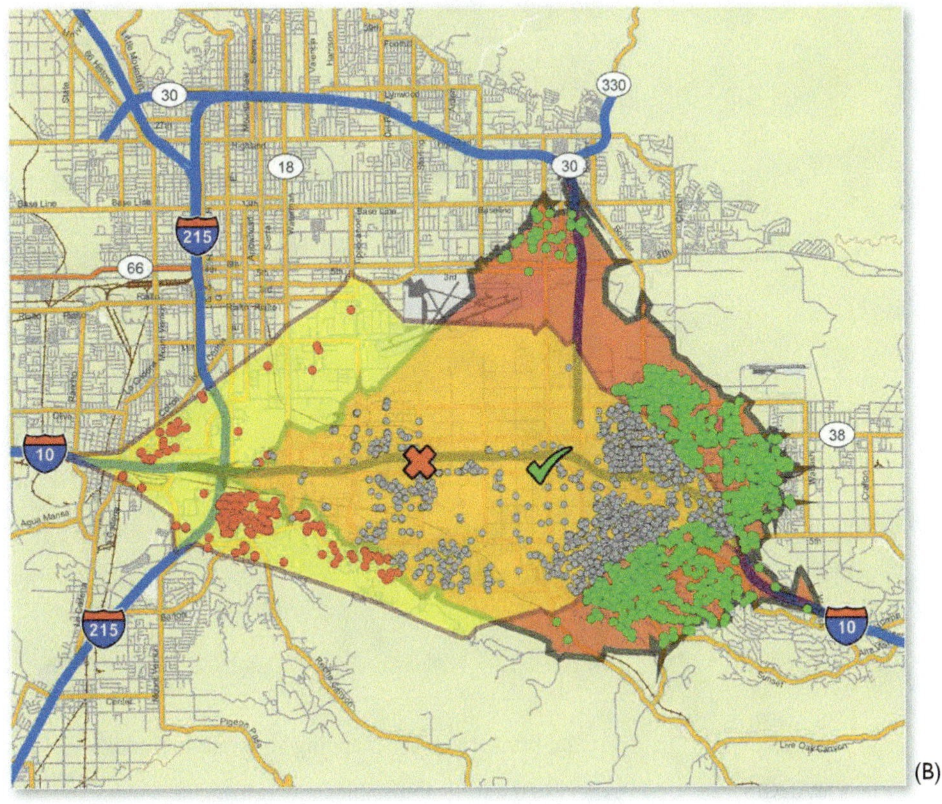

(B)

(Continued)

FIGURE 9-3
(Continued)

(C) In this map, a retail location is interested in understanding the correlation between the purchase behavior of customers and the lifestyle segment of the neighborhood in which they live. The company markets a customized message to each lifestyle segment in the primary trade area. The message is tailored to reflect the historic product purchases in each segment and is the basis of the customer behavior profile.
(D) This 3-D map is a synthesis of customer spending for one retail site. The customer data base (with customer spending) is "geocoded." The number of customers who live in each grid cell is calculated and their total dollar purchases aggregated or summed. The result is a polygonal grid with a count of customers and the total dollars spent at the store/site/location.

Source: © Esri, Tele Atlas, HandsOn-BI. Used by permission. All rights reserved.

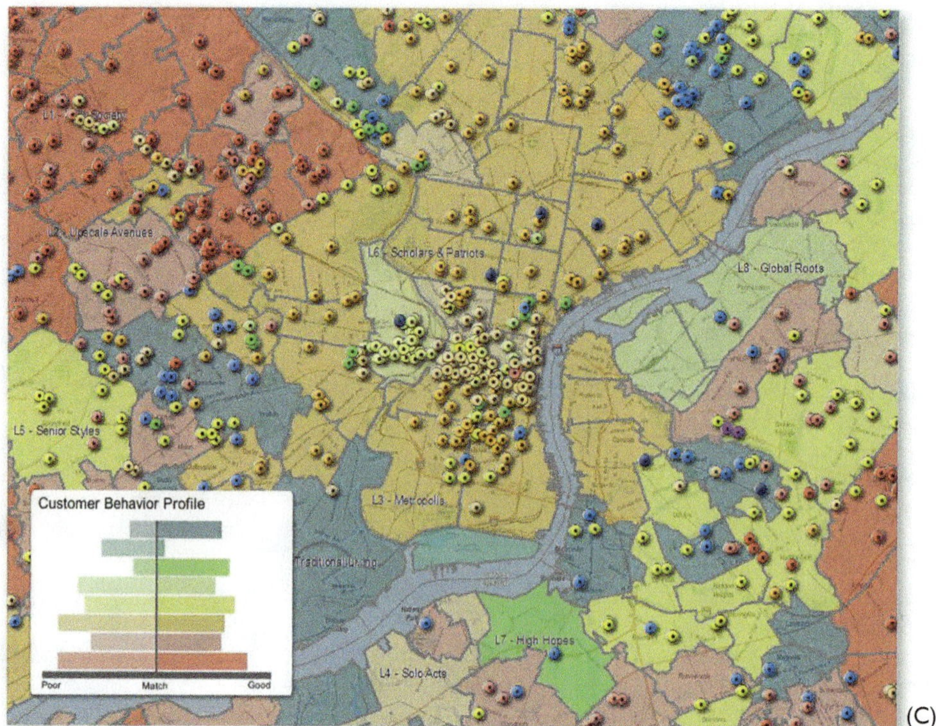

(C)

(D)

Private firms that offer mapping software include:

Take a look at ArcGIS from Esri (www.arcgis.com/home).

- Alteryx (www.demographicsnow.com).
- Autodesk (http://usa.autodesk.com).
- Caliper Corporation (www.caliper.com).
- Esri (www.esri.com).

TECHNOLOGY IN RETAILING

ShopperTrak and RetailNEXT

ShopperTrak (www.shoppertrak.com) has 70,000 shopper traffic-counting devices that have been installed in 70 countries around the world. ShopperTrak devices count shopper visits and can refine the counts to exclude children and retail employees from its overall count. ShopperTrak's traffic counts are between 96 percent and 98 percent accurate.

Traffic-counting data can also be used by retailers in various ways to increase their operating efficiency. Traffic counts can be deployed by apparel retailers to better staff fitting rooms. And ShopperTrak's new FlashTraffic system conveys traffic data on an hourly basis to retailers' point-of-sale systems to enable retail managers to adjust and optimize store staffing levels.

BVI Networks (www.bvinetworks.com) offers a RetailNEXT solution that allows retailers to determine how many consumers visit a particular aisle and who looks at a particular display. According to BVI's founder and chief executive: "We can match a specific product item to a display and tell you how much time shoppers spent at the display and how many ended up purchasing from it. If you make a merchandise layout change, you can see how it impacts what happens traffic-wise throughout the store." Like ShopperTrak, BVI can monitor traffic in and out of fitting rooms and help store personnel determine when dressing rooms need to be cleaned.

Source: Jessica Binns, "700 Million and Counting," *Apparel Magazine* (February 2011), pp. 14–15.

- geoVue (www.geovue.com).
- MPSI (www.mpsisolutions.com).
- Nielsen Site Reports (www.claritas.com/sitereports/Default.jsp).
- Pitney Bowes Business Insight (www.pbinsight.com/products/location-intelligence/applications/mapping-analytical).
- TeleAtlas Map Insight (http://mapinsight.teleatlas.com).
- Tetrad Computer Applications (www.tetrad.com).

At our Web site (www.pearsonhighered.com/bermanevans), we provide links to descriptions of the GIS software for all of these firms. Many of the companies have free demonstrations at their sites.

Pitney Bowes offers a wide range of MapInfo GIS software (www.pbinsight.com/products/location-intelligence). Click "Applications" on the left toolbar.

GIS software can be applied in various ways. A chain retailer could learn which of its stores have trading areas containing households with a median annual income of more than $50,000. That firm could derive the sales potential of proposed new store locations and their potential effect on sales at existing stores. It could use GIS software to learn the demographics of customers at its best locations and set up a computer model to find potential locations with the most desired attributes. A retailer could even use the software to pinpoint its geographic areas of strength and weakness.

These two examples show how retailers benefit from GIS software:

- Starbucks utilizes GIS software as part of its site-selection planning. It evaluates trading areas within each market. As Patrick O'Hagan, the retailer's manager of global market planning, says: "My team provides analytics, decision support, business intelligence, and geospatial intelligence to our real-estate partners. Our in-house group is lean, but we provide data to hundreds of people globally. So, we need tools that provide decision support to answer critical questions—what's going on in this trade area; what are general retail trends in this area; where are competitors; who are those competitors; where is business generated; where's the highest traffic volume; where are people living; where are they working; and how are they traveling to work?" Starbucks uses ArcGIS from Esri to create data, maps, and models on employee desktops and then use these tools on desktops, in browsers, or on mobile devices, "depending on the needs of real-estate partners."[5]
- GFK GeoMarketing offers GIS software services that assist international retailers wanting to expand into such countries as China. The firm recently did a location analysis in Peking to determine customer buying power for a German clothing firm seeking to do business in China: "Using the GIS software RegioGraph, population data were prepared, analyzed, and differentiated according to region. With the help of these data, consumer potential was determined, providing the first objective benchmark for the company. This served as a foundation so that the company could gain insight into the proposed location's full market potential. Further calculations on location-related factors were carried out, including site location characteristics, accessibility, nearby competition, and the nature and structure of existing businesses in the immediate vicinity. The results yielded detailed information regarding the most suitable locations, as well as regions to be avoided."[6]

The Size and Shape of Trading Areas

Each trading area has three parts: The **primary trading area** encompasses 50 to 80 percent of a store's customers. It is the area closest to the store and possesses the highest density of customers to population and the highest per capita sales. There is little overlap with other trading areas. The **secondary trading area** contains an additional 15 to 25 percent of a store's customers. It is located outside the primary area, and customers are more widely dispersed. The **fringe trading area** includes all the remaining customers, and they are the most widely dispersed. A store could have a primary trading area of 4 miles, a secondary trading area of 5 miles, and a fringe trading area of 10 miles. The fringe trading area typically includes some outshoppers who travel greater distances to patronize certain stores.

Visit this site to see the complexity of factors in site selection (www.conway.com/cheklist).

Figure 9-4 shows the makeup of trading areas and their segments. In reality, trading areas do not usually follow such circular patterns. They adjust to the physical environment. The size and shape of a trading area are influenced by store type, store size, the location of competitors, housing patterns, travel time and traffic barriers (such as toll bridges), and media availability. These factors are discussed next.

Two stores can have different trading areas even if they are in the same shopping district or shopping center. Situated in one shopping center could be a branch of an apparel chain with a distinctive image and people willing to travel up to 20 miles and a shoe store seen as average and people willing to travel up to 5 miles. When one store has a better assortment, promotes more, and/or creates a stronger image, it may then become a **destination store** and generate a trading area much larger than that of a competitor with a "me-too" appeal. That is why Dunkin' Donuts uses the slogan "America Runs on Dunkin." A **parasite store** does not create its own traffic and

FIGURE 9-4
The Segments of a Trading Area

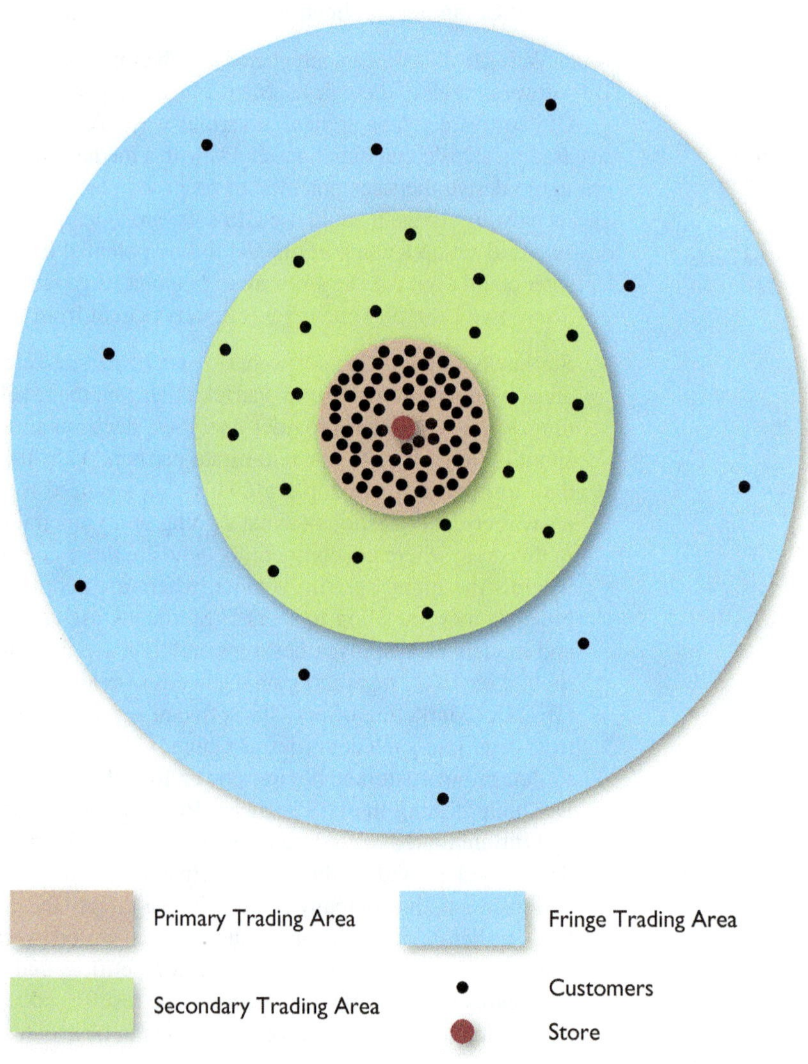

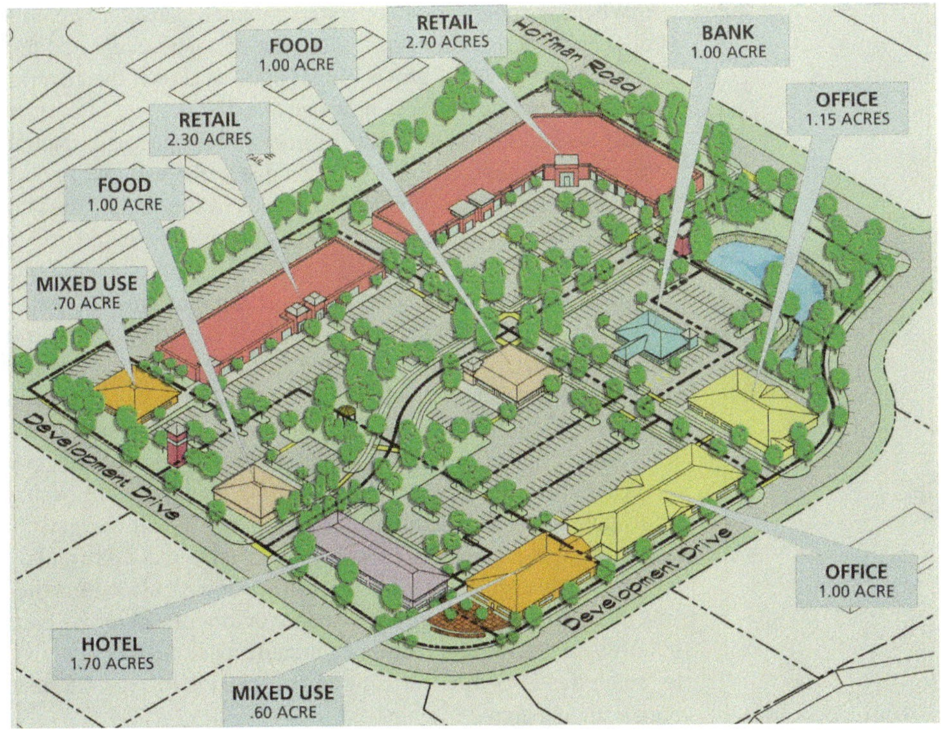

FIGURE 9-5

Planning a Mixed-Use Center

A mixed-use center combines retail facilities with other types of businesses, such as the hotel, bank, and office space shown here. In this instance, five acres of retail space are planned—which amount to almost 220,000 square feet of retail properties—in addition to the two full acres allocated to food. As a result, the retailers (nonfood and food) will attract local workers, hotel guests, and other tourists and shoppers (some of whom will be willing to travel to the center because of its size and variety).

Source: Donald Joski/ Shutterstock.com. Reprinted by permission.

has no real trading area of its own. This store depends on people who are drawn to the location for other reasons. A magazine stand in a hotel lobby and a snack bar in a shopping center are parasites. While they are there, customers patronize these shops.

The extent of a store's or center's trading area is affected by its own size. As a store or center gets larger, its trading area usually increases, because store or center size generally reflects the assortment of goods and services. Yet, trading areas do not grow proportionately with store or center size. As a rule, supermarket trading areas are bigger than those of convenience stores. Supermarkets have a better product selection, and convenience stores appeal to the need for fill-in merchandise. In a regional shopping center, department stores usually have the largest trading areas, followed by apparel stores; gift stores have comparatively small trading areas. See Figures 9-5 and 9-6.

FIGURE 9-6

Informal Retailing: A Local Neighborhood Draw

At times, many people think of themselves as "retailers" with valuable mementos and other used (vintage) items to sell. But, garage sales are usually not a draw outside of the immediate surrounding neighborhood. Shown here is a garage sale in Ottawa, Canada.

Source: Feng Yu/ Shutterstock.com. Reprinted by permission.

Whenever potential shoppers are situated between two competing stores, the trading area is often reduced for each store. The size of each store's trading area normally increases as the distance between stores grows (target markets do not then overlap as much). On the other hand, when stores are situated very near one another, the size of each store's trading area does not necessarily shrink. This store grouping may actually increase the trading area for each store if more consumers are attracted to the location due to the variety of goods and services. Yet, each store's market penetration (its percentage of sales in the trading area) may be low with such competition. Also, the entry of a new store may change the shape or create gaps in the trading areas of existing stores.

In many urban communities, people are clustered in multi-unit housing near the center of commerce. With such population density, it is worthwhile for a retailer to be quite close to consumers; trading areas tend to be small because there are several shopping districts in close proximity to one another, particularly for the most densely populated cities. In many suburbs, people live in single-unit housing—which is more geographically spread out. To produce satisfactory sales volume there, a retailer needs to attract shoppers from a greater distance.

The influence of travel or driving time on a trading area may not be clear from the population's geographic distribution. Physical barriers (toll bridges, poor roads, railroad tracks, one-way streets) usually reduce trading areas' size and contribute to their odd shapes. Economic barriers, such as different sales taxes in two towns, also affect the size and shape of trading areas.

In a community where a newspaper or other local media are available, a retailer could afford to advertise and enlarge its trading area. If local media are not available, the retailer would have to weigh the costs of advertising in countywide or regional media against the possibilities of a bigger trading area.

Delineating the Trading Area of an Existing Store

The size, shape, and characteristics of the trading area for an existing store—or shopping district or shopping center—can usually be delineated quite accurately. Store records (secondary data) or a special research study (primary data) can measure the trading area. And many firms offer computer-generated maps that can be tailored to individual retailers' needs.

Store records can reveal customer addresses. For credit customers, the data can be obtained from a retailer's billing department; for cash customers, addresses can be acquired by analyzing deliveries, cash sales slips, store contests (sweepstakes), and checks. In both instances, the task is relatively inexpensive and quick because the data were originally collected for other purposes and are readily available.

Because many big retailers have computerized credit card systems, they can delineate primary, secondary, and fringe trading areas in terms of the:

- Frequency with which people from various geographic locales shop at a particular store.
- Average dollar purchases at a store by people from given geographic locales.
- Concentration of a store's credit card holders from given geographic locales.

Although it is easy to get data on credit card customers, the analysis may be invalid if cash customers are not also studied. Credit use may vary among shoppers from different locales, especially if consumer traits in the locales are dissimilar. A firm reduces this problem if both cash and credit customers are studied.

MetroCount (www.metrocount.com) offers software to provide vehicular traffic counts. Click on "Products."

A retailer can also collect primary data to determine trading-area size. It can record the license plate numbers of cars parked near a store, find the general addresses of those vehicle owners by contacting the state motor vehicle office, and then note them on a map. Typically, only the ZIP code and street of residence are provided to protect people's privacy. When using license plate analysis, nondrivers and passengers—customers who walk to a store, use mass transit, or are driven by others—should not be omitted. To collect data on these customers, questions must often be asked (survey).

Visit this site (www.claritas.com/MyBestSegments/Default.jsp) to study your area's lifestyles and purchasing preferences. Click on "You Are Where You Live."

If a retailer desires more demographic and lifestyle information about consumers in particular areas, it can buy the data. PRIZM (now owned by Nielsen) is a system for identifying communities by lifestyle clusters. It identifies 66 neighborhood types, including "Upward Bound," "Blue-Chip Blues," and "Suburban Sprawl." This system was originally based on ZIP codes; it now also incorporates census tracts, block groups and enumeration districts, phone exchanges, and postal routes. Online PRIZM reports can be downloaded for as little as a few hundred dollars; costs are higher if reports are tailored to the individual retailer.

No matter how a trading area is delineated, a time bias may exist. A downtown business district is patronized by different customers during the week (those who work there) than on weekends (those who travel there to shop). Special events may attract people from great distances for only a brief time. Thus, an accurate estimate of a store's trading area requires complete and continuous investigation.

After delineating a trading area, the retailer should map people's locations and densities—either manually or with GIS software. In the manual method, a paper map of the area around a store is used. Different color dots or pins are placed on this map to represent *population* locations and densities, incomes, and other factors. *Customer* locations and densities are then indicated; primary, secondary, and fringe trading areas are denoted by ZIP code. Customers can be lured by promotions aimed at particular ZIP codes. With GIS software, vital customer data (such as purchase frequencies and amounts) are combined with other information sources (such as census data) to yield computer-generated digitized maps depicting primary, secondary, and fringe trading areas.

Delineating the Trading Area of a New Store

A new store opening in an established trading area can use the methods just cited. The discussion in this section refers to a trading area with less-defined shopping and traffic patterns. Such an area must normally be evaluated in terms of opportunities rather than current patronage and traffic (pedestrian and vehicular) patterns. Accordingly, additional tools must be utilized.

Trend analysis—projecting the future based on the past—can be employed by examining government and other data for predictions about population location, auto registrations, new housing starts, mass transportation, highways, zoning, and so on. Through consumer surveys, information can be gathered about the time and distance people would be willing to travel to various possible retail locations, the factors attracting people to a new store, the addresses of those most apt to visit a new store, and other topics. Either technique may be a basis for delineating alternate new store trading areas.

Three computerized trading-area analysis models are available for assessing new store locations:

- An **analog model** is the simplest and most popular trading-area analysis model. Potential sales for a new store are estimated on the basis of revenues for similar stores in existing areas, the competition at a prospective location, the new store's expected market share at that location, and the size and density of the location's primary trading area.
- A **regression model** uses a series of mathematical equations showing the association between potential store sales and several independent variables at each location, such as population size, average income, the number of households, nearby competitors, transportation barriers, and traffic patterns.
- A **gravity model** is based on the premise that people are drawn to stores that are closer and more attractive than competitors' stores. The distance between consumers and competitors, the distance between consumers and a given site, and store image can be included in this model.

Computerized trading-area models offer several benefits to retailers: They operate in an objective and systematic way. They offer insights as to how each locational attribute should be weighted. They are useful in screening a large number of locations. They can assess management performance by comparing forecasts with results.

More specific methods for delineating new trading areas are described next.[7]

REILLY'S LAW The traditional means of trading-area delineation is **Reilly's law of retail gravitation.**[8] It establishes a point of indifference between two cities or communities, so the trading area of each can be determined. The **point of indifference** is the geographic breaking point between two cities (communities) at which consumers are indifferent to shopping at either. According to Reilly's law, more consumers go to the larger city or community because there are more stores; the assortment makes travel time worthwhile. Reilly's law rests on these assumptions: Two competing areas are equally accessible from a major road, and retailers in the two areas are equally effective. Other factors (such as population dispersion) are held constant or ignored.

The law may be expressed algebraically as:[9]

$$D_{ab} = \frac{d}{1 + \sqrt{P_b/P_a}}$$

where

D_{ab} = Limit of city (community) A's trading area, measured in miles along the road to city (community) B

d = Distance in miles along a major roadway between cities (communities) A and B

P_a = Population of city (community) A

P_b = Population of city (community) B

A city with a population of 90,000 (A) would draw people from three times the distance as a city with 10,000 (B). If the cities are 20 miles apart, the point of indifference for the larger city is 15 miles, and for the smaller city, it is 5 miles:

$$D_{ab} = \frac{20}{1 + \sqrt{10{,}000/90{,}000}} = 15\,\text{miles}$$

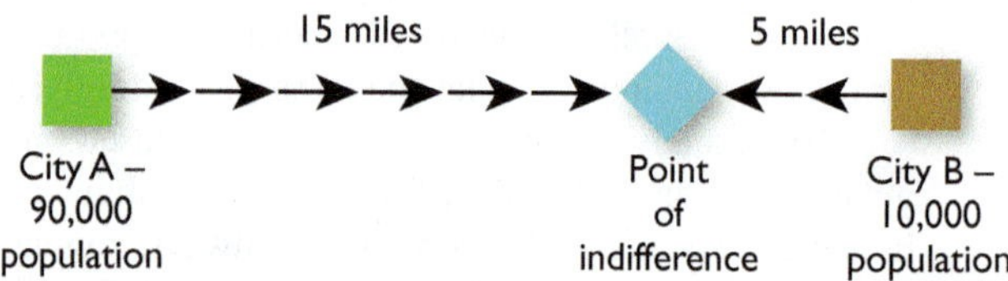

Reilly's law is an important contribution to trading-area analysis because of its ease of calculation. It is most useful when other data are not available or when compiling other data is costly. Nonetheless, Reilly's law has three limitations: (1) Distance is only measured by major thoroughfares; some people will travel shorter distances along cross streets. (2) Travel time does not necessarily reflect the distance traveled. Many people are more concerned about time than distance. (3) Actual distance may not correspond with the perceptions of distance. A store with few services and crowded aisles is apt to be a greater perceived distance from a person than a similarly located store with a more pleasant atmosphere.

HUFF'S LAW **Huff's law of shopper attraction** delineates trading areas on the basis of the product assortment (of the items desired by the consumer) carried at various shopping locations, travel times from the shopper's home to alternative locations, and the sensitivity of the kind of shopping to travel time. Assortment is rated by the total square feet of selling space a retailer expects all firms in a shopping area to allot to a product category. Sensitivity to the kind of shopping entails the trip's purpose (restocking versus shopping) and the type of good/service sought (such as clothing versus groceries).[10]

Huff's law is expressed as:

$$P_{ij} = \frac{\dfrac{S_j}{(T_{ij})^{\lambda}}}{\displaystyle\sum_{j}^{n} \dfrac{S_j}{(T_{ij})^{\lambda}}}$$

where

P_{ij} = Probability of a consumer's traveling from home i to shopping location j

S_j = Square footage of selling space in shopping location j expected to be devoted to a particular product category

T_{ij} = Travel time from consumer's home i to shopping location j

λ = Parameter used to estimate the effect of travel time on different kinds of shopping trips

n = Number of different shopping locations

λ must be determined through research or by a computer program.

Assume a leased department operator studies three possible locations with 200, 300, and 500 total square feet of store space allocated to men's cologne (by all retailers in the areas). A group of potential customers lives 7 minutes from the first location, 10 minutes from the second, and 15 minutes from the third. The operator estimates the effect of travel time to be 2. Therefore, the probability of consumers' shopping is 43.9 percent for Location 1, 32.2 percent for Location 2, and 23.9 percent for Location 3:

$$P_{i1} = \frac{(200)/(7)^2}{(200)/(7)^2 + (300)/(10)^2 + (500)/(15)^2} = 43.9\%$$

$$P_{i2} = \frac{(300)/(10)^2}{(200)/(7)^2 + (300)/(10)^2 + (500)/(15)^2} = 32.2\%$$

$$P_{i3} = \frac{(500)/(15)^2}{(200)/(7)^2 + (300)/(10)^2 + (500)/(15)^2} = 23.9\%$$

If 200 shoppers for men's cologne live 7 minutes from Location 1, about 88 of them will shop there.

These points should be considered in using Huff's law:

- To determine Location 1's trading area, similar computations would be made for shoppers living at a driving time of 10, 15, 20 minutes, and so on. The number of shoppers at each distance who would shop there are then summed. Thus, stores in Location 1 could estimate their total market, the trading-area size, and the primary, secondary, and fringe areas for a product category.
- If new retail facilities in a product category are added to a locale, the percentage of shoppers living at every travel time from that location who would shop there goes up.
- The probability of people shopping at a location depends on the effect of travel time. If a product is important, such as dress watches, consumers are less travel sensitive. A λ of 1 leads to these figures: Location 1, 31.1 percent; Location 2, 32.6 percent; and Location 3, 36.3 percent (based on the space in the cologne example). Location 3 would be popular for the watches due to its assortment.
- All the variables are rather hard to calculate; for mapping purposes, travel time must be converted to miles. Travel time also depends on the transportation form used.
- Since people buy different items on different shopping trips, the trading area varies by trip.

Today, the Huff model is incorporated in such GIS software as Esri's ArcGIS Business Analyst.

Learn more about the current use of the Huff model (www.esri.com/library/whitepapers/pdfs/calibrating-huff-model.pdf).

OTHER TRADING-AREA RESEARCH Over the years, many researchers have examined trading-area size in a variety of settings. They have introduced additional factors and advanced statistical techniques to explain the consumer's choice of shopping location.

In his model, Gautschi added to Huff's analysis by including shopping-center descriptors and transportation conditions. Weisbrod, Parcells, and Kern studied shopping center appeal on the basis of expected population changes, store characteristics, and the transportation network. LeBlang demonstrated that consumer lifestyles could be used to predict sales at new department store locations. Albaladejo-Pina and Aranda-Gallego looked at the effects of competition among stores in different sections of a trading area. Bell, Ho, and Tang devised a model with fixed and variable store choice factors. Rogers examined the role of human decision making versus computer-based models in site choice. Smith and Hay reviewed the role of competition in trading areas. ReVelle, Murray, and Serra examined the impact of a firm's reducing the number of facilities in an area. Wood and Browne focused on the specifics of convenience store location planning. Diep and Sweeney studied shopping trip value. Rajagopal examined shopping attractions, routes to shopping, and establishing customer-centric strategies. Russell and Heidkamp, aided by GIS methodology, found that the loss of just one supermarket in a city had a dramatic effect on shoppers.[11]

CHARACTERISTICS OF TRADING AREAS

PCensus for MapInfo (www.tetrad.com/industry/franchising.html) is a useful tool for scrutinizing potential franchise locations.

After the size and shape of alternative trading areas are determined, the characteristics of those areas are studied. Of special interest are the attributes of residents and how well they match the firm's definition of its target market. An auto repair franchisee may compare opportunities in several locales by reviewing the number of car registrations; a hearing aid retailer may evaluate the percentage of the population 60 years of age or older; and a bookstore retailer may be concerned with residents' education level.

Among the trading-area factors that should be studied by most retailers are the population size and characteristics, availability of labor, closeness to sources of supply, promotion facilities, economic base, competition, availability of locations, and regulations. The **economic base** is an area's industrial and commercial structure—the companies and industries that residents depend on to earn a living. The dominant industry (company) in an area is important because its drastic decline may have adverse effects on a large segment of residents. An area with a diverse economic base, where residents work for a variety of nonrelated industries, is more secure than an area with one major industry. Table 9-1 summarizes a number of factors to consider in evaluating retail trading areas.

Much of the data needed to describe an area can be obtained from the U.S. Bureau of the Census, the *American Community Survey, Editor & Publisher Market Guide, Survey of Buying Power, Rand McNally Commercial Atlas & Marketing Guide, Standard Rate & Data Service,*

TABLE 9-1 Chief Factors to Consider in Evaluating Retail Trading Areas

Population Size and Characteristics	
Total size and density	Total disposable income
Age distribution	Per capita disposable income
Average educational level	Occupation distribution
Percentage of residents owning homes	Trends
Availability of Labor	
Management	
Management trainee	
Clerical	
Closeness to Sources of Supply	
Delivery costs	Number of manufacturers and wholesalers
Timeliness	Availability and reliability of product lines
Promotion Facilities	
Availability and frequency of media	
Costs	
Waste	
Economic Base	
Dominant industry	Freedom from economic and seasonal fluctuations
Extent of diversification	Availability of credit and financial facilities
Growth projections	
Competitive Situation	
Number and size of existing competitors	Short-run and long-run outlook
Evaluation of competitor strengths/weaknesses	Level of saturation
Availability of Store Locations	
Number and type of locations	Zoning restrictions
Access to transportation	Costs
Owning versus leasing opportunities	
Regulations	
Taxes	Minimum wages
Licensing	Zoning
Operations	

regional planning boards, public utilities, chambers of commerce, local government offices, shopping-center owners, and renting agents. In addition, GIS software provides data on potential buying power in an area, the location of competitors, and highway access. Both demographic and lifestyle information may also be included in this software.

Although the yardsticks in Table 9-1 are not equally important in all location decisions, each should be considered. The most important yardsticks should be "knockout" factors: If a location does not meet minimum standards on key measures, it should be immediately dropped from further consideration.

These are examples of desirable trading-area attributes, according to several retailers:

- Perfumania's prime target market is 25- to 45-year-old women. So, it likes to be near high-traffic retailers. Approximately 80 percent of the retailer's 275 stores are in regional shopping centers, and most of the rest of its stores are in strip shopping centers and urban areas. It is especially interested in the rents charged when comparing different locales. As Perfumania's real-estate consultant notes: "Growth is restricted only to finding the right locations for the right price."
- At the 5,000-store AutoZone chain, top management wants to expand in new markets where it has no stores, as well as in areas where further growth is possible. The company seeks high visibility sites in locations with a lot of traffic and does considerable research before going into new markets. AutoZone includes these criteria in choosing locations: area demographics, types of vehicles, buying trends on auto-related products, the level of competition, and the costs of real-estate. As the retailer says: "In reviewing the vehicle profile, we consider the number of vehicles that are seven years old and older, or 'our kind of vehicles'; these vehicles are generally no longer under the original manufacturer warranties and require more maintenance and repair than younger vehicles."
- Stride Rite's 360 shoe stores have a dual location approach. The traditional children's stores are situated mostly in "larger regional shopping centers, clustered in the major U.S. market areas. The average size of a children's store is approximately 1,300 square feet." The company's discount stores average 2,800 square feet because they offer an assortment of adult footwear in addition to children's shoes: "Most of our outlet stores are located in shopping centers consisting only of outlet stores."
- Dollar General operates nearly 10,000 stores, "conveniently located in a variety of rural, suburban, and urban communities." Almost 70 percent of the stores serve communities with populations of less than 20,000 people. "The majority of our customers live within three to five miles, or a 10-minute drive, of our stores. Our close proximity to customers drives their loyalty and trip frequency and makes us an attractive alternative to large retail stores which are often located farther away."[12]

Tax Policy and Online Retailers

Many large retail chains, including Wal-Mart (www.walmart.com), Best Buy (www.bestbuy.com), Sears Holdings (www.searsholdings.com), Home Depot (www.homedepot.com), and Target (www.target.com), have joined the Alliance for Main Street Fairness (www.standwithmainstreet.com), a group that is seeking to change the sales tax laws relating to online sales. The alliance argues that in states with high state, city, and/or county sales tax rates (such as Alabama, Arizona, Arkansas, California, Kansas, Louisiana, New York, Oklahoma, Texas, and Washington—all of which have combined sales taxes of over 8 percent), online firms have an unfair major price advantage over bricks-and-clicks firms (that must collect sales tax even online if they have stores in those states).

Currently, online retailers without a physical presence in a state are not required to collect state sales taxes. Based on this law, as of mid-2012, Amazon.com (www.amazon.com) collected sales tax only on sales from customers in six states: Kansas, Kentucky, New York, North Dakota, Texas, and Washington.

The alliance group was instrumental in getting Illinois to amend its laws so that online retailers would have to collect sales taxes if they had an Illinois-based marketing affiliate. Amazon quickly severed ties with several of its Illinois-based affiliates to retain its sales tax advantage. Similarly, Amazon.com closed its distribution center located in Irving, Texas, after the state controller sent Amazon.com a bill for $269 million in uncollected sales tax.

Sources: Miguel Bustillo and Stu Woo, "Retailers Push Amazon on Taxes: Wal-Mart, Target, and Others Look to Close Loophole for Online Sellers Amid State-Budget Crises," www.wallstreetjournal.com (March 17, 2011); and Alison Fitzgerald, Catherine Dodge, Rich Miller, and Richard Rubin, "Wanted a Tax Code for the Digital Age," www.businessweek.com (April 11, 2011).

Several stages of the process for gathering data to analyze trading areas are shown in Figure 9-7, which includes not only the attributes of residents but also those of the competition. By studying these factors, a retailer sees how desirable an area is for its business.

We next discuss three elements in trading-area selection: population characteristics, economic base characteristics, and the nature of competition and the level of saturation.

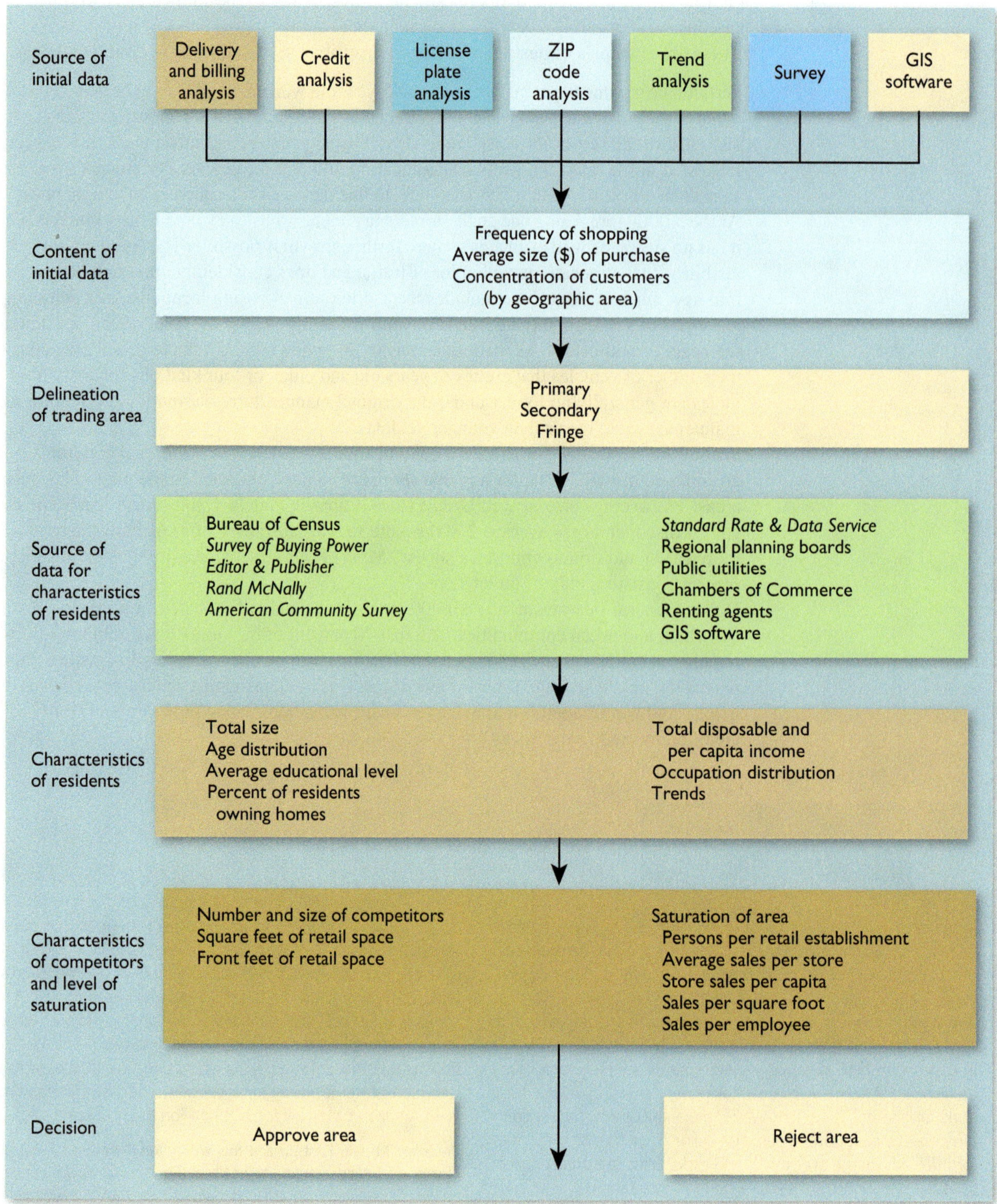

FIGURE 9-7
Analyzing Retail Trade Areas

Characteristics of the Population

Extensive knowledge about population characteristics can be gained from secondary sources. They offer data on population size, number of households, income distribution, education level, age distribution, and more. Since *Census of Population* and other public sources are so valuable, we briefly discuss them next.

Find in-depth information regarding the 2010 U.S. Census (www.census.gov/2010census).

CENSUS OF POPULATION The **Census of Population** supplies a wide range of demographic data for all U.S. cities and surrounding vicinities. Data are organized on a geographic basis, starting with blocks and continuing to census tracts, cities, counties, states, and regions. There are less data for blocks and census tracts than for larger units due to privacy issues. The major advantage of census data is the information on small geographic units. Once trading-area boundaries are outlined, a firm can look at data for each geographic unit in that area and study aggregate demographics. There are also data categories especially helpful for retailers interested in segmenting the market—including racial and ethnic data, small-area income data, and commuting patterns. Census data come in many formats, including online.

The U.S. Census Bureau's TIGER computerized data base contains extremely detailed physical breakdowns of areas in the United States. The data base has digital descriptions of geographic areas (area boundaries and codes, latitude and longitude coordinates, and address ranges). Because TIGER data must be used in conjunction with population and other data, GIS software is necessary. As noted earlier in this chapter, many private firms have devised location analysis programs, based in large part on TIGER. These firms also usually project data to the present year and into the future.

The major drawbacks of the *Census of Population* are that it is done only once every 10 years and all data are not immediately available. The last full set of U.S. census data is the 2010 *Census of Population*, with data released in phases from 2011 through 2013. Thus, census material can be out of date and inaccurate. Other sources, such as municipal building departments or utilities, state governments, other Census reports (such as the *Current Population Survey*), and computerized projections by private firms such as Dun & Bradstreet must be used to update *Census of Population* data.

The value of the *Census of Population*'s actual 2010 census tract data can be shown by an illustration of Long Beach, New York, which is 30 miles east of New York City on Long Island's south shore. Long Beach includes the six census tracts highlighted in Figure 9-8—4164, 4165, 4166, 4167.01, 4167.02, and 4168. Although tract 4163 is contiguous with Long Beach, it represents another community. Table 9-2 shows various population statistics for each Long Beach census tract. Overall, Long Beach is above average in most demographics. However, resident characteristics in each tract do differ; thus, a retailer might choose to locate in one or more tracts but not in others.

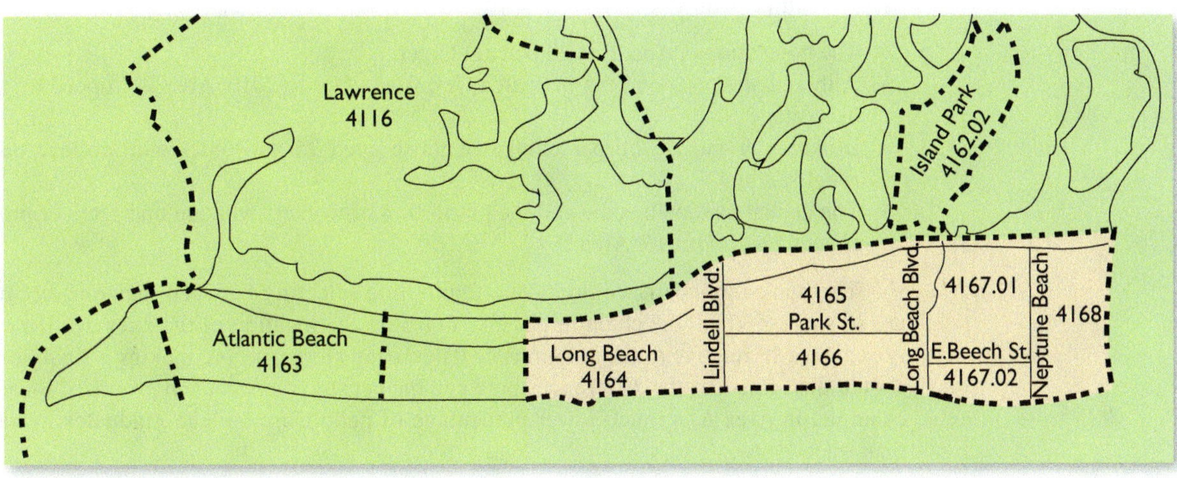

FIGURE 9-8
The Census Tracts of Long Beach, New York

TABLE 9-2 Selected Characteristics of Long Beach, New York, Residents by Census Tract, 2000 and 2010

	Tract Number					
	4164	4165	4166	4167.01	4167.02	4168
Total Population						
2000	7,406	6,231	6,326	4,471	4,443	6,585
2000 population 25 and older	5,772	4,073	4,904	3,163	3,739	5,173
2010	7,140	6,158	5,392	4,329	4,155	6,101
2010 population 25 and older	5,471	4,295	4,230	3,149	3,615	4,968
2010 median age (years)	44.4	52.7	44.6	41.6	46.6	48.2
Number of Households						
2000	3,138	2,002	2,592	1,601	2,440	3,165
2010	3,096	2,009	2,571	1,593	2,474	3,066
2010 average size	2.31	3.07	2.10	2.72	1.68	1.99
Education						
College graduates (% of population 25 and older), 2010	38.4	26.7	60.8	41.4	57.4	53.6
Income						
Median household income, 2010 (estimate)	$92,167	$84,208	$97,922	$96,713	$70,335	$99,150
Annual household of $50,000 or more (% of households)	76.1	70.4	79.6	78.9	68.2	75.8
Selected Occupations						
Managerial, professional, and related occupations (% of employed persons 16 and older), 2010	39.4	35.1	56.3	45.6	57.4	54.6

Sources: 2010 Census of Population (Washington, DC: U.S. Bureau of the Census); "2010 Census Data," www.easidemographics.com (December 30, 2011); and authors' computations.

Suppose a local bookstore wants to evaluate two potential trading areas based on the demographic data of the census tracts described in Table 9-2. Trading-area A corresponds with tracts 4164 and 4166. Area B corresponds to tracts 4167.01 and 4168. Population data for these areas (extracted from Table 9-2) are presented in Table 9-3. Area A is somewhat different from Area B, despite their proximity:

- The population in Area B is 20 percent larger.
- Although the population in both areas fell from 2000 to 2010, Area B dropped by a smaller percentage.
- In Areas A and B, the percentage of those aged 25 and older with college degrees is roughly equal.
- The annual median income and the proportion of workers who are managers or professionals are a bit higher for Area B.

The bookstore chain would have a tough time selecting between the areas because they are so similar. Thus, the chain might also consider the location of the sites available in Area A and Area B, relative to the locations of its existing stores, before making a final decision. It should also consider the differences between the census tracts in each proposed location. For example, in Area A, a much lower percentage of people are college graduates in tract 4164 than tract 4166.

OTHER PUBLIC SOURCES There are many other useful, easily accessible public sources for current population information, in addition to the *Census of Population*—especially on a city or county basis. These sources typically update their data annually. They also provide some data

TABLE 9-3 Selected 2010 Population Statistics for Long Beach Trading-Areas A and B

	Area A (Tracts 4164 and 4166)	Area B (Tracts 4167.01 and 4168)
Total population, 2010	12,532	10,430
Population change, 2000–2010 (%)	−8.7	−5.7
College graduates, 25 and older, 2010 (%)	48.2	48.9
Median household income, 2010	$94,778	$98,317
Managerial and professional specialty occupations (% of employed persons 16 and older), 2010	47.1	51.5

not available from the *Census of Population*—total annual retail sales by area, annual retail sales for specific product categories, and population projections. The biggest disadvantage of these sources is their use of geographic territories that are often much larger than a store's trading area and that cannot be broken down easily.

One newer national source of annual population data is the *American Community Survey*, which provides "demographic, social, economic, and housing data" for almost 1,000 geographical areas. The survey has an excellent, user-friendly Web site (www.census.gov/acs/www). On the state and local level, public data sources include planning commissions, research centers at public universities, county offices, and many other institutions.

Let us demonstrate the usefulness of public sources through the following example. Note: We obtained all of the information for our example on the Internet—free!

Suppose a prospective new car dealer investigates three counties near Chicago: DuPage, Kane, and Lake. The dealer decides to focus on one source of data available in print and online versions: *Northern Illinois Market Facts* (prepared by the Center for Government Studies, Northern Illinois University). Table 9-4 lists selected population and retail sales data for these counties.

What can the car dealer learn? DuPage is by far the largest county; Kane is the smallest. However, the population growth rate from 2000 to 2010 was much higher for Kane. Lake has the highest median household income; DuPage has the most adult college graduates. On a per capita basis, DuPage residents account for 60 percent more retail sales than Kane residents and 21 percent more than Lake residents. Lake and DuPage residents both allocate more than one-fifth of their retail spending to autos and gas stations, while Kane residents account for the highest percentage of retail spending at apparel and food stores.

A Cadillac dealer using these data might select DuPage or Lake, and a Ford dealer might select Kane. But because the data are broad in nature, several subsections of Kane may actually be superior choices to subsections in DuPage or Lake for the Cadillac dealer. The competition in each area also must be noted.

The location decision for a fast-food franchise usually requires less data than for a bookstore or an auto dealer. Fast-food franchisors often seek communities with many people living or working within a three- or four-mile radius of their stores. However, bookstore owners and auto dealers cannot locate merely on the basis of population density. They must consider a more complex set of population factors.

Economic Base Characteristics

The economic base reflects a community's commercial and industrial infrastructure and residents' sources of income. A firm seeking stability normally prefers an area with a diversified economic base (a large number of nonrelated industries) to one with an economic base keyed to a single major industry. The latter area is more affected by a strike, declining demand for an industry, and cyclical fluctuations.

In assessing a trading area's economic base, a retailer should investigate the percentage of the labor force in each industry, transportation, banking facilities, the impact of economic

TABLE 9-4 Selected Data Relating to Three Illinois Counties (2010, unless otherwise specified)

	County		
	DuPage	Kane	Lake
Total population	954,215	525,966	732,619
Annual population growth, 2000–2010	0.54%	2.67%	1.29%
Number of households	356,437	179,532	254,774
People 20 and over (%)	73.0%	68.2%	69.9%
Median household income	$ 67,066	$ 65,752	$ 70,368
Households with $50,000 or more in annual income	65.60%	63.90%	66.30%
College graduates, 25 and older (%)	45.10%	32.30%	42.00%
Total retail sales	$15,887,679,750	$5,456,897,250	$10,039,810,776
Annual per-capita retail sales	$ 16,650	$ 10,375	$ 13,704
Employment in retail trade	102,500	49,655	76,489
Total Retail Sales by Category			
Apparel			
Automotive and gas stations	$ 3,688,040,975	$ 983,556,420	$ 2,116,536,291
Eating, drinking, and hotel	$ 1,549,645,160	$ 564,361,518	$ 967,057,080
Food (grocery)	$ 1,767,206,180	$ 770,014,224	$ 1,178,051,352
General merchandise	$ 1,708,044,850	$ 676,918,242	$ 1,239,591,348
Home improvement and hardware	$ 680,355,295	$ 330,306,648	$ 539,940,203
Household goods	$ 917,954,830	$ 233,528,904	$ 734,084,238
Pharmaceutical	$ 2,377,903,780	$ 788,423,034	$ 1,786,125,122
Other	$ 2,546,799,835	$ 752,131,380	$ 1,147,281,354
Percentage of Total Retail Sales by Category			
Apparel	4.1%	6.6%	3.3%
Automotive and gas stations	23.2%	18.0%	21.1%
Eating, drinking, and hotel	9.8%	10.3%	9.6%
Food (grocery)	11.1%	14.1%	11.7%
General merchandise	10.7%	12.4%	12.4%
Home improvement and hardware	4.3%	6.1%	5.4%
Household goods	5.8%	4.3%	7.3%
Pharmaceutical	15.0%	14.5%	17.8%
Other	16.0%	13.7%	11.4%

Source: Computed by the authors from *Northern Illinois Market Facts 2010* (DeKalb, IL: Center for Governmental Studies, Northern Illinois University).

fluctuations, and the future of individual industries (firms). Data can be obtained from such sources as Easy Analytic Software, *Editor & Publisher Market Guide*, regional planning commissions, industrial development organizations, and chambers of commerce.

Easy Analytic Software (www.easidemographics.com) offers several inexpensive economic reports. It also produces "Census 2010 Reports" that can be downloaded free (after a simple sign-in), including Quick Reports, Quick Tables, Quick Maps, Site Analysis, Rank Analysis, and Profile Analysis.

Editor & Publisher Market Guide offers annual economic base data for cities, including employment sources, transportation networks, financial institutions, auto registrations, newspaper circulation, and shopping centers. It also has data on population size and total households. *Editor & Publisher Market Guide* data cover broad geographic areas. The bookstore chain noted earlier would find the information on shopping centers to be helpful. The auto dealer would find the information on the transportation network, the availability of financial institutions, and the number of passenger cars to be useful. *Editor & Publisher Market Guide* is best used to supplement other sources.

The Nature of Competition and the Level of Saturation

A trading area may have residents who match the characteristics of the desired market and a strong economic base, yet still be a poor location for a new store if competition is too intense. A locale with a small population and a narrow economic base may be a good location if competition is minimal.

When examining competition, these factors should be analyzed: the number of existing stores, the size distribution of existing stores, the rate of new store openings, the strengths and weaknesses of all stores, short-run and long-run trends, and the level of saturation.

Over the past 25 years, more U.S. retailers have entered foreign markets due to less competition there. That is why Wal-Mart has entered into 30 countries, including Argentina, Brazil, China, Mexico, and Nigeria; Home Depot is now in China, Guam, and Mexico; and Baskin-Robbins has stores in Australia, Greece, Indonesia, Malaysia, Russia, and Thailand. Yet, in the future, even these locales may become oversaturated due to all the new stores. Furthermore, although the Northeast population in the United States has been declining relative to the Southeast and the Southwest—and is often considered to be saturated with stores—its high population density (the number of persons per square mile) is crucial for retailers. According to the *2010 Census*, in New Jersey, there are 1,196 people per square mile; in Massachusetts, 840; in Florida, 351; in Louisiana, 105; in Arizona, 57; and in Utah, 34.

An **understored trading area** has too few stores selling a specific good or service to satisfy the needs of its population. An **overstored trading area** has so many stores selling a specific good or service that some retailers cannot earn an adequate profit. A **saturated trading area** has the proper amount of stores to satisfy the needs of its population for a specific good or service, and to enable retailers to prosper.

Despite the large number of areas in the United States that are overstored, there still remain plentiful opportunities in understored communities. For example, CVS/pharmacy, the huge drugstore chain (with more than 7,200 stores):

> looks for highly-visible locations in high-traffic areas that are easily accessible and are in a trade area of at least 18,000 people. We prefer sites that can support a freestanding store with drive-thru capability, between 1.5 to 2 acres, with parking for at least 80 vehicles. An aging population and the increased utilization of prescription drugs are fueling the demand for more pharmacy services. Several markets in the United States with high-growth population rates are relatively understored and need more pharmacies. We will meet this demand by opening new stores in these high-growth markets.[13]

Wendy Bentkoski: Niche Retail Strategies

Wendy Bentkoski, a certified shopping center manager (CSM), is the founder and head of Niche Retail Strategies, LLC (www.niche-retail-strategies.com), a consulting firm that manages shopping centers and mixed-use properties located on the West Coast of the United States.

One of Bentkoski's major projects involved planning and managing the grand opening of The Americana at Brand (www.americanaatbrand.com), a $400 million mixed-use project in Glendale, California, that includes 75 boutiques (comprising 375,000 square feet of retail space), apartments, and an 18-screen movie theater.

Prior to her work on that project, Bentkoski was general manager of Two Rodeo (www.2rodeo.com), a 130,000-square-foot shopping center in Beverly Hills, California, with such upscale tenants as Tiffany, Gianni Versace, Breguet, Jimmy Chou, Judith Ripka, Lalique, and Gucci Fine Jewelry. As general manager of this center, she increased common area maintenance charges, grew parking revenues, and reduced fraudulent insurance claims. These and other initiatives resulted in an annual rise in shopping-center income of $700,000. She also supervised the installation of new energy management and fire alarm systems and the planning and installation of all new landscaping.

To retain Two Rodeo's image as a prestigious center, Bentkoski has worked with its retailers to build store traffic through such activities as wine-tasting classes and a pet adoption program.

Source: "Welcome to Niche Retail Strategies, LLC," www.niche-retail-strategies.com (March 27, 2012).

MEASURING TRADING-AREA SATURATION Because any trading area can support only a given number of stores or square feet of selling space per goods/service category, these ratios can help to quantify retail store saturation:

- Number of persons per retail establishment.
- Average sales per retail store.
- Average sales per retail store category.
- Average store sales per capita or household.
- Average sales per square foot of selling area.
- Average sales per employee.

The saturation level in a trading area can be measured against a goal or compared with other trading areas. An auto accessory chain might find that its current trading area is saturated by computing the ratio of residents to auto accessory stores. On the basis of this calculation, the owner could then decide to expand into a nearby locale with a lower ratio rather than to add another store in its present trading area.

Data for saturation ratios can be obtained from a retailer's records on its performance, city and state records, phone directories, consumer surveys, economic census data, *Editor & Publisher Market Guide*, *County Business Patterns*, trade publications, and other sources. Sales by product category, population size, and number of households per market area can be found with other national and state sources.

When investigating an area's saturation for a specific good or service, ratios must be interpreted carefully. Differences among areas are not always reliable indicators of saturation. For instance, car sales per capita are different for a suburban area than an urban area because suburbanites have a much greater need for cars. Each area's level of saturation should be evaluated against distinct standards—based on optimum per capita sales figures in that area.

In calculating saturation based on sales per square foot, a new or growing retailer must take its proposed store into account. If that store is not part of the calculation, the relative value of each trading area is distorted. Sales per square foot decline most if new outlets are added in small communities. The retailer should also consider if a new store will expand the total consumer market for a good or service category in a trading area or just increase its market share in that area without expanding the total market.

These are three examples of how retailers factor trading-area saturation into their decisions:

- Kroger knows that the "operating environment for food retailing continues to be characterized by intense price competition, aggressive supercenter expansion, increasing fragmentation of retail formats, entry of nontraditional competitors, and market consolidation. We have developed a strategic plan that we believe is a balanced approach that will enable Kroger to meet the wide-ranging needs and expectations of our customers in this challenging economic environment. However, the nature and extent to which our competitors implement various pricing and promotional activities in response to increasing competition, including our execution of our strategic plan, and our response to these competitive actions, will affect our profitability."[14]
- Kohl's operates department stores in 49 states: "Our primary competitors are traditional department stores, upscale mass merchandisers, and specialty stores. Our specific competitors vary from market to market. We compete for customers, associates, locations, merchandise, services, and other important aspects of our business. Those competitors, some of which have a greater market presence than Kohl's, include traditional store-based retailers, Internet and catalog businesses, and others. Our management considers style, quality, and price to be the most significant competitive factors in the industry. Merchandise mix, service, and convenience are also key competitive factors."[15]
- Retailers selling food can acquire annual data from *Marketing Guidebook* (www.marketingguidebook.com)—including population size, number of households, total food store sales, number of food stores by type of retailer (such as supermarkets versus membership clubs), and more—that can be used to measure the level of saturation by U.S. city and community.

Look at the *Marketing Guidebook* sample (www.marketingguidebook.com/samples.html) to see the saturation levels of supermarkets. Click "County Level Data."

Chapter Summary

1. *To demonstrate the importance of store location for a retailer and outline the process for choosing a store location.* The location choice is critical because of the complex decision making, the high costs, the lack of flexibility once a site is chosen, and the impact of a site on the strategy. A good location may let a retailer succeed even if its strategy mix is relatively mediocre.

   The selection of a store location includes (1) evaluating alternative trading areas, (2) determining the best type of location, (3) picking a general site, and (4) settling on a specific site. This chapter looks at Step 1. Chapter 10 details Steps 2, 3, and 4.

2. *To discuss the concept of a trading area and its related components.* A trading area is the geographical area from which customers are drawn. When shopping locales are nearby, they may have trading-area overlap.

   Many retailers utilize geographic information system (GIS) software to delineate and analyze trading areas. The software combines digitized mapping with key data to graphically depict trading areas. This lets retailers research alternative locations and display findings on computerized maps. Several vendors market GIS software, based on TIGER mapping by the U.S. government.

   Each trading area has primary, secondary, and fringe components. The farther people live from a shopping area, the less apt they are to travel there. The size and shape of a trading area depend on store type, store size, competitor locations, housing patterns, travel time and traffic barriers, and media availability. Destination stores have larger trading areas than parasites.

3. *To show how trading areas may be delineated for existing and new stores.* The size, shape, and characteristics of the trading area for an existing store or group of stores can be learned accurately—based on store records, contests, license plate numbers, surveys, and so on. Time biases must be considered in amassing data. Results should be mapped and customer densities noted.

   Potential trading areas for a new store must often be described in terms of opportunities, rather than current patronage and traffic. Trend analysis and consumer surveys may be used. Three computerized models are available for planning a new store location: analog, regression, and gravity. They offer several benefits.

   Two techniques for delineating new trading areas are Reilly's law, which relates the population size of different cities to the size of their trading areas; and Huff's law, which is based on each area's shopping assortment, the distance of people from various retail locales, and sensitivity to travel time.

4. *To examine three major factors in trading-area analysis: population characteristics, economic base characteristics, and competition and the level of saturation.* The best sources for population data are the *Census of Population* and other publicly available sources. Census data are detailed and specific, but become dated. Information from public sources such as the *American Community Survey* may be more current, but they report on broader geographic areas.

   An area's economic base reflects the community's commercial and industrial infrastructure, as well as residents' income sources. A retailer should look at the percentage of the labor force in each industry, the transportation network, banking facilities, the potential impact of economic fluctuations on the area, and the future of individual industries. Easy Analytic and *Editor & Publisher Market Guide* are good sources of data on the economic base.

   A trading area cannot be properly analyzed without studying the nature of competition and the level of saturation. An area may be understored (too few retailers), overstored (too many retailers), or saturated (the proper number of retailers). Saturation may be measured in terms of the number of persons per store, average sales per store, average store sales per capita or household, average sales per square foot of selling space, and average sales per employee.

Key Terms

trading area (p. 228)
trading-area overlap (p. 229)
geographic information system (GIS) (p. 230)
primary trading area (p. 234)
secondary trading area (p. 234)
fringe trading area (p. 234)
destination store (p. 234)
parasite store (p. 234)
analog model (p. 237)
regression model (p. 237)
gravity model (p. 237)
Reilly's law of retail gravitation (p. 237)
point of indifference (p. 237)
Huff's law of shopper attraction (p. 238)
economic base (p. 240)
Census of Population (p. 243)
understored trading area (p. 247)
overstored trading area (p. 247)
saturated trading area (p. 247)

Questions for Discussion

1. Comment on this statement: "A poor location may be such a liability that even superior retailers cannot overcome it." Is it always true? Give examples.
2. If a retailer has a new 10-year store lease, does this mean the next time it studies the characteristics of its trading area should be 5 years from now? Explain your answer.
3. What is trading-area overlap? Are there any advantages to a chain retailer's having some overlap among its various stores? Why or why not?
4. Describe three ways in which a consumer electronics store chain could use geographic information system (GIS) software in its trading-area analysis.
5. How could an off-campus store selling textbooks and supplies near a college campus determine its primary, secondary, and fringe trading areas? Why should the store obtain this information?
6. How could a parasite store increase the size of its trading area?
7. Explain Reilly's law. What are its advantages and disadvantages?
8. Use Huff's law to compute the probability of consumers' traveling from their homes to each of three shopping areas: Square footage of selling space—Location 1, 15,000; Location 2, 20,000; Location 3, 25,000. Travel time—to Location 1, 15 minutes; to Location 2, 21 minutes; to Location 3, 25 minutes. Effect of travel time on shopping trip—2. Explain your answer.
9. What are the major advantages and disadvantages of *Census of Population* data in delineating trading areas?
10. Look at the most recent online data from the *American Community Survey* (www.census.gov/acs/www) for the area in which your college is located. What retailing-related conclusions do you draw?
11. If a retail area is acknowledged to be "undersaturated," what does this signify for existing retailers? For prospective retailers considering this area?
12. How could a Web-based retailer determine the level of saturation for its product category? What should this retailer do to lessen the impact of the level of saturation it faces?

Note: At our Web site (www.pearsonhighered.com/bermanevans), there are several math questions related to the material in this chapter so that you may review these concepts.

Web-Based Exercise

Visit the Web site of Site Selection Online (www.siteselection.com). What could a retailer learn from the two most recent issues of *Site Selection Magazine*? What Web site feature do you like best? Why?

Note: Also stop by our Web site (www.pearsonhighered.com/bermanevans) to experience a number of highly interactive, appealing Web exercises based on actual company demonstrations and sample materials related to retailing.

10 Site Selection

In recent years, shopping centers have faced intense competition from big-box stores in isolated or strip locations, outlet shopping areas, and online retailers—including those with traditional store locales. As a result, more shopping center operators are utilizing social media to lure and retain customers.

Consider this observation from *Chain Store Age*'s Katherine Field:

> Even some of the savviest mall owners admit there was a time when they considered social media participation optional. But by 2010, most major shopping center developers, managers, and owners had jumped on the Facebook and Twitter bandwagons—and social media programs have since eclipsed traditional marketing methods at many properties. A study by Alexander Babbage, "Shopping Center Social Media Benchmark Report," found that social media tools and networks are making it easier for shopping centers to relay information, interact with customers, and generally stay connected—and that is what is largely driving mall buy-in.

In 2011, Cleveland-based Forest City Enterprises (a leading national operator of shopping centers) partnered with PlaceWise Media to introduce the Shoptopia Network (www.shoptopia.com), a social media site that "combines online, social, mobile, and digital screen-based communications into an interactive experience and relationship with consumers." At launch, Shoptopia featured 16 Forest City shopping malls and reached 12 million monthly shoppers.

For 2012, the goal was for Shoptopia to encompass at least 150 shopping centers (including many not operated by Forest City) and attract more than 100 million monthly shoppers. The expansion of Shoptopia is intended to "enhance the relationship among malls, retailers, brands, and shoppers with an interactive experience before, during, and after shopping." According to Forest City's Jane Lisey, "The Shoptopia Network engages our shoppers with insights to all things fashionable, special offers, and feedback from their peers. It's a perfect integration of all the digital and physical shopping experiences. Shoppers are engaged, informed, and rewarded for their participation."[1]

Chapter Objectives

1. To thoroughly examine the types of locations available to a retailer: isolated store, unplanned business district, and planned shopping center
2. To note the decisions necessary in choosing a general retail location
3. To describe the concept of the one-hundred percent location
4. To discuss several criteria for evaluating general retail locations and the specific sites within them
5. To contrast alternative terms of occupancy

Source: BeTA-Artworks/ fotolia.com.

Overview

After a retailer investigates alternative trading areas (Step 1), it determines what type of location is desirable (Step 2), selects the general location (Step 3), and evaluates alternative specific store sites (Step 4). Steps 2, 3, and 4 are discussed in this chapter.

Consider these tips from an interview by *Progressive Grocer* with Robert Tack, chief executive of real-estate firm Capital Retail Group: "Finding the right location and the right price can be the secret path to success for any retailer. While planning conservatively and within a reasonable budget is always smart, retailers need to include five other key components of site selection that are just as important":

The Small Business Administration offers lots of advice on site selection (www.sba.gov/content/tips-choosing-business-location).

1. Know the customer. This is critical in site selection. Such retailers as Starbucks and Target use specific location and shopper profiles that incorporate numerous data points. New retailers can utilize free data. Firms can set up grading systems by rating factors like visibility, access, population size, household income, and traffic. "A minimum acceptable score can be applied as a guideline helping a retailer avoid choosing poor performing locations."
2. Seek out locales with the highest sales potential. The rent charged for a site should reflect the sales revenue that can be generated there. High rents may sometimes, but not necessarily, be worth the investment.
3. Understand the current state of the retail leasing market to see whether a landlord's rent is fair (reasonable). "Having several qualified choices readily available as a backup helps alleviate the frustration if negotiations break down on the first choice."
4. Research the co-tenants in a shopping center or shopping district to see if they are compatible and a customer attraction. Pedestrian and vehicular traffic counts indicate whether co-tenants are good for the newly arriving retailer. Anchor stores "often establish the basic customer profile, but the type of smaller tenants is as important."
5. Be aware of the long-term commitment that must be made, because leases typically are in force for at least five years—and many times, longer than that.[2]

TYPES OF LOCATIONS

There are three different location types: isolated store, unplanned business district, and planned shopping center. Each has its own attributes as to the composition of competitors, parking, nearness to nonretail institutions (such as office buildings), and other factors. Step 2 in the location process is to determine which type of location to use.

The Isolated Store

An **isolated store** is a freestanding retail outlet located on either a highway or a street. There are no adjacent retailers with which this type of store shares traffic.

The advantages of this type of retail location are many:

- There is no competition in close proximity.
- Rental costs are relatively low.
- There is flexibility; no group rules must be followed in operations, and larger space may be obtained.
- Isolation is good for stores involved in one-stop or convenience shopping.
- Better road and traffic visibility is possible.
- Facilities can be adapted to individual specifications.
- Easy parking can be arranged.
- Cost reductions are possible, leading to lower prices.

There are also various disadvantages to this retail location type:

- Initial customers may be difficult to attract.
- Many people will not travel very far to get to one store on a continuous basis.
- Most people like variety in shopping.
- Advertising expenses may be high.
- Costs such as outside lighting, security, grounds maintenance, and trash collection are not shared.

FIGURE 10-1
At Starbucks, Isolated Locations Are a Key Part of the Mix
These days, Starbucks (www.starbucks.com) has stores at all types of locations—including standalone sites, shopping centers, downtown business districts, and other sites. In this way, it efficiently reaches different geographic markets—and consumers who are working, shopping, traveling, and so forth.

Source: Reprinted by permission of Susan V. Berry, Retail Image Consulting, Inc.

- Other retailers and community zoning laws may restrict access to desirable locations.
- A store must often be built rather than rented.
- As a rule, unplanned business districts and planned shopping centers are much more popular among consumers; they generate most of retail sales.

Large-store formats (such as Wal-Mart supercenters and Costco membership clubs) and convenience-oriented retailers (such as 7-Eleven) are usually the retailers best suited to isolated locations because of the challenge of attracting a target market. A small specialty store would probably be unable to develop a customer following; people would be unwilling to travel to a store that does not have a large assortment of products or a strong image for merchandise and/or prices.

Years ago, numerous shopping centers forbade the entry of discounters because discount operations were frowned on by their traditional anchor retailers. This forced the discounters to seek isolated sites or to build their own centers, and they have been successful. Today, diverse retailers are in isolated locations as well as at business district and shopping center sites. Retailers using a mixed-location strategy include McDonald's, Target, Sears, Starbucks, Toys "R" Us, Wal-Mart, and 7-Eleven. Some retailers, including many gas stations and convenience stores, still emphasize isolated locations. See Figure 10-1.

The Unplanned Business District

An **unplanned business district** is a type of retail location where two or more stores situate together (or in close proximity) in such a way that the total arrangement or mix of stores is not due to prior long-range planning. Stores locate based on what is best for them, not the district. Four shoe stores may exist in an area with no pharmacy. There are four kinds of unplanned business district: central business district, secondary business district, neighborhood business district, and string. A discussion of each follows.

CENTRAL BUSINESS DISTRICT A **central business district (CBD)** is the hub of retailing in a city. It is synonymous with the term *downtown*. The CBD exists where there is the greatest density of office buildings and stores. Both vehicular and pedestrian traffic are very high. The core of a CBD is often no more than a square mile, with cultural and entertainment facilities surrounding it. Shoppers are drawn from the whole urban area and include all ethnic groups and all classes of people. The CBD has at least one major department store and a number of specialty and convenience stores. The arrangement of stores follows no pre-set format; it depends on history (first come, first located), retail trends, and luck.

Here are some strengths that allow CBDs to draw a large number of shoppers:

- Excellent goods/service assortment.
- Access to public transportation.
- Variety of store types and positioning strategies within one area.

- Wide range of prices.
- Variety of customer services.
- High level of pedestrian traffic.
- Nearness to commercial and social facilities.

In addition, chain headquarters stores are often situated in CBDs.

These are some of the inherent weaknesses of the CBD:

- Inadequate parking, as well as traffic and delivery congestion.
- Travel time for those living in the suburbs.
- Frail condition of some cities—such as aging stores—compared with their suburbs.
- Relatively poor image of central cities to some potential consumers.
- High rents and taxes for the most popular sites.
- Movement of some popular downtown stores to suburban shopping centers.
- Discontinuity of offerings (such as four shoe stores and no pharmacy).

The CBD remains a major retailing force, although its share of overall sales has fallen over the years, as compared with the planned shopping center. Besides the weaknesses cited, much of the drop-off is due to suburbanization. In the first half of the twentieth century, most urban workers lived near their jobs. Gradually, many people moved to suburbs—where they are often served by planned shopping centers.

A number of CBDs are doing quite well, and many others are striving to return to their former stature. They use such tactics as modernizing storefronts and equipment, forming cooperative merchants' associations, modernizing sidewalks and adding brighter lighting, building vertical malls (with several floors of stores), improving transportation networks, closing streets to vehicular traffic (sometimes with disappointing results), bringing in "razzmatazz" retailers such as Nike Town, and integrating a commercial and residential environment known as mixed-use facilities. As Carol Coletta, the head of CEOs for Cities, has noted: "Every metro area has good suburbs, but if you don't have a strong downtown and close-in neighborhoods, then you're not offering a choice that many people are seeking. Offering that choice is a real competitive advantage for cities. Clearly, the next generation of Americans is looking for different kinds of lifestyles—walkable, art, culture, entertainment."[3]

A good example of the value of a revitalized CBD is Philadelphia, where there has been a strong long-term effort under way to make the central city more competitive with suburban shopping centers:

> It became clear that the story of how Center City Philadelphia transformed itself was relevant to the issues facing Downtown Denver. Consider these facts about Philadelphia's CBD: $55 million in streetscape, façade, and public area improvements have been made since 1997. The CBD has added 12,265 new housing units, converting vacant office buildings, factories, and lots into new condos, apartments, and single-family housing, transforming neighborhoods, increasing density, and attracting new retail development. Within a five-minute walk from City Hall, there are 67,000 workers, 11,000 residents, and 416,000 annual overnight visitors who together generate over $150 million in annual sales.[4]

Boston's Faneuil Hall is another long-term CBD renovation success. When developer James Rouse took over the site, it had three 150-year-old, block-long former food warehouses that were abandoned for nearly a decade. Rouse used landscaping, fountains, banners, open-air courts, street performers, and colorful graphics to enable Faneuil Hall to capture a festive spirit. Faneuil Hall now combines shopping, eating, and entertainment. Today, it has 100 shops and pushcarts, 13 full-service restaurants, 35 food stalls, and regular outdoor events and entertainment. It attracts 18 million shoppers and visitors yearly.[5]

Other major CBD revitalization projects include Annapolis Town Centre (Maryland), Branson Landing (Missouri), City Center District (Dallas), Harborplace Baltimore, Peabody Place (Memphis), Pioneer Place (Portland, Oregon), Times Square (New York City), Tower City Center (Cleveland), and Union Station (Washington, DC). See Figure 10-2.

Visit our Web site (www.pearsonhighered.com/bermanevans) for links to all of the CBD projects mentioned in this section.

Grand Central Terminal (www.grandcentralterminal.com) is all dressed up and open for business.

FIGURE 10-2

Times Square: A Revitalized Central Business District

For a while, the Times Square district in Manhattan, New York, was in serious decline. Now, after years of billions of dollars in renovations and new construction, the area is thriving again (day and night) with retailers, hotels, Broadway shows, restaurants, and a whole lot more—and tourists from around the world visit and shop.

Source: Songquan/ Shutterstock.com. Reprinted by permission.

SECONDARY BUSINESS DISTRICT A **secondary business district (SBD)** is an unplanned shopping area in a city or town that is usually bounded by the intersection of two major streets. Cities—particularly larger ones—often have multiple SBDs, each with at least a junior department store (a branch of a traditional department store or a full-line discount store) and/or some larger specialty stores, besides many smaller stores. This format is now more important because cities have "sprawled" over larger geographic areas.

The kinds of goods and services sold in an SBD mirror those in the CBD. However, an SBD has smaller stores, less width and depth of merchandise assortment, and a smaller trading area (consumers will not travel as far), and it sells a higher proportion of convenience-oriented items.

The SBD's major strengths include a good product selection, access to thoroughfares and public transportation, less crowding and more personal service than a CBD, and placement nearer to residential areas than a CBD. The SBD's major weaknesses include the discontinuity of offerings, the sometimes high rent and taxes (but not as high as in a CBD), traffic and delivery congestion, aging facilities, parking difficulties, and fewer chain outlets than in the CBD. These weaknesses have generally not affected the SBD as much as the CBD—and parking problems, travel time, and congestion are less for the SBD.

ETHICS IN RETAILING

Jersey City Moves Forward

During the past 40 years, Jersey City, New Jersey, has undergone a major change from a city that had an older population and an economic base that relied on manufacturing and shipping to one with a younger population and a retail-based economy. Many of the city's apartment and office building redevelopment projects are now zoned to require that a minimum percentage of a complex's ground floor be devoted to retail facilities. And several of the restaurants also have open sidewalk cafés.

Jersey City currently has 82 redevelopment projects in 33 redevelopment areas in the city's 11 neighborhoods. These plans cover about one-half of the city. According to Robert Cotter, Jersey City's director of planning: "We want density; density drives it all. The more density you have, the more likely you'll have shops and restaurants to serve the new population."

A key to the success of many of these retail projects is the high percentage of Jersey City residents who rely on bicycles for transportation. Forty percent of Jersey City residents do not own a car and another 39 percent of households own only one car. As a result, many of Jersey City's residents find it quite convenient to shop locally as they need to rely on walking and bicycle transportation.

Source: "Jersey City Successfully Creates an Environment that Caters to Retail and Restaurants," *Jersey City: A Vibrant Renaissance Retail Traffic* (May–June 2011), pp. JC4–JC6.

NEIGHBORHOOD BUSINESS DISTRICT A **neighborhood business district (NBD)** is an unplanned shopping area that appeals to the convenience shopping and service needs of a single residential area. An NBD contains several small stores, such as a dry cleaner, a stationery store, a barber shop and/or a beauty salon, a liquor store, and a restaurant. The leading retailer is typically a supermarket or a large drugstore. This type of business district is situated on the major street(s) of its residential area.

An NBD offers a good location, long store hours, good parking, and a less hectic atmosphere than a CBD or SBD. On the other hand, there is a limited selection of goods and services, and prices tend to be higher because competition is less than in a CBD or SBD.

STRING A **string** is an unplanned shopping area comprising a group of retail stores, often with similar or compatible product lines, located along a street or highway. There is little extension of shopping onto perpendicular streets. A string may start with an isolated store, success then breeding competitors. Car dealers, antique stores, and apparel retailers often situate in strings.

A string location has many of the advantages of an isolated store site (lower rent, more flexibility, better road visibility and parking, and lower operating costs), along with some disadvantages (less product variety, increased travel for many consumers, higher advertising costs, zoning restrictions, and the need to build premises). Unlike an isolated store, a string store has competition at its location. This draws more people to the area and allows for some sharing of common costs. It also means less control over prices and less loyalty toward each outlet. An individual store's increased traffic flow, due to being in a string rather than an isolated site, may be greater than the customers lost to competitors. This explains why four gas stations locate on opposing corners.

Figure 10-3 shows a map with various forms of unplanned business districts and isolated locations.

FIGURE 10-3
Unplanned Business Districts and Isolated Locations

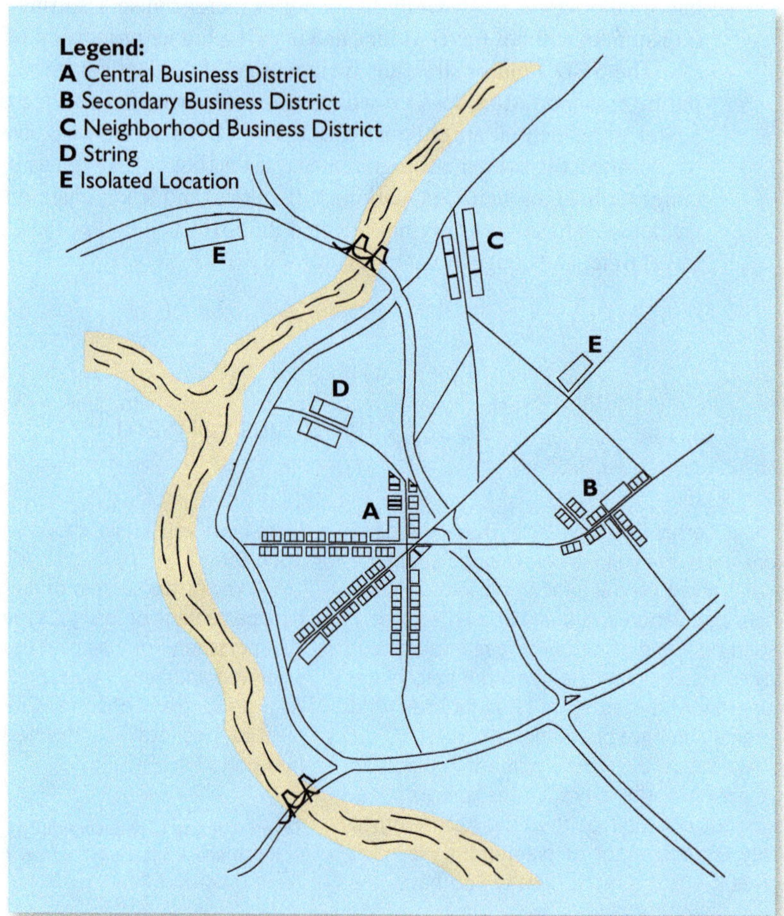

The Planned Shopping Center

A **planned shopping center** consists of a group of architecturally unified commercial establishments on a site that is centrally owned or managed, designed and operated as a unit, based on balanced tenancy, and accompanied by parking facilities. Its location, size, and mix of stores are related to the trading area served. Through **balanced tenancy**, the stores in a planned shopping center complement each other as to the quality and variety of their product offerings, and the kind and number of stores are linked to overall population needs. To ensure balanced tenancy, the management of a planned center usually specifies the proportion of total space for each kind of retailer, limits the product lines that can be sold by every store, and stipulates what kinds of firms can acquire unexpired leases. At a well-run center, a coordinated and cooperative long-run retailing strategy is followed by all stores.

Shopping centers in some form have existed for more than 1,000 years. Learn more about this phenomenon (www.icsc.org/srch/about/impactofshoppingcenters).

The planned shopping center has several positive attributes:

- Well-rounded assortments of goods and services based on long-range planning.
- Strong suburban population.
- Interest in one-stop, family shopping.
- Cooperative planning and sharing of common costs.
- Creation of distinctive, but unified, shopping center images.
- Maximization of pedestrian traffic for individual stores.
- Access to highways and availability of parking for consumers.
- More appealing than city shopping for some people.
- Generally lower rent and taxes than CBDs (except for enclosed regional malls).
- Generally lower theft rates than CBDs.
- Popularity of malls—both *open* (shopping area off-limits to vehicles) and *closed* (shopping area off-limits to vehicles and all stores in a temperature-controlled facility).
- Growth of discount malls and other newer types of shopping centers.

There are also some limitations associated with the planned shopping center:

- Landlord regulations that reduce each retailer's flexibility, such as required hours.
- Generally higher rent than an isolated store.
- Restrictions on the goods/services that can be sold by each store.
- A competitive environment within the center.
- Required payments for items that may be of little or no value to an individual retailer, such as membership in a merchants' association.
- Too many malls in a number of areas ("the malling of America").
- Rising consumer boredom with and disinterest in shopping as an activity.
- Aging facilities of some older centers.
- Domination by large anchor stores.

Shopping Centers Today, in print and online (www.icsc.org/sct/index.php), is the bible of the industry.

How important are planned shopping centers? According to recent research, there are almost 108,000 U.S. shopping centers, about 1,100 of which are fully enclosed shopping malls. Shopping center revenues are about $2.35 trillion annually and account for nearly one-half of total U.S. retail-store sales (including autos and gasoline). About 14.5 million people work in shopping centers. Eighty-five percent of Americans over age 18 visit some type of center in an average month. Nordstrom, Radio Shack, Macy's, Foot Locker, Sephora, and Body Shop are among the vast number of chains with a strong presence at shopping centers. Some big retailers have also been involved in shopping center development. Sears has participated in the construction of dozens of shopping centers, and Publix Supermarkets operates centers with hundreds of small tenants. Each year, numerous new centers of all kinds and sizes are built, and retail space is added to existing centers.[6] See Figure 10-4.

To sustain their long-term growth, shopping centers are engaging in these practices:

- Several older centers have been renovated, expanded, and/or repositioned. The Cherry Hill Mall in Philadelphia; Hamilton Place Mall in Chattanooga; Kentucky Oaks Mall in Paducah, Kentucky; McCain Mall in Little Rock, Arkansas; Westfield Trumbull Shopping Center in Trumbull, Connecticut; and Yorkdale Shopping Centre Mall in Toronto, Canada, have all recently been revitalized. Visit our Web site (www.pearsonhighered.com/bermanevans) for links to these centers.

FIGURE 10-4

Macy's: A Dominant Shopping Center Retailer

Macy's has department stores in planned shopping centers around the United States. It is usually one of the lead anchors in these shopping centers, with multiple entrances/ exits and easy access from parking lots.

Source: Reprinted by permission of Susan V. Berry, Retail Image Consulting, Inc.

- Certain derivative types of centers have fostered consumer interest and enthusiasm. Three of these, megamalls, lifestyle centers, and power centers, are discussed a little later in this chapter.
- Shopping centers are responding to shifting consumer lifestyles. They have made parking easier; added ramps for baby strollers and wheelchairs; and included more distinctive retailers such as the Apple Store, Apricot Lane, BCBG Max Azira, Juicy Couture, MaxMara, Michael Kors, Rue 21, and Zumiez. They have also introduced more information booths and center directories.
- The retailer mix has broadened at many centers to attract people interested in one-stop shopping. More centers now include banks, stockbrokers, dentists, doctors, beauty salons, TV repair outlets, and/or car rental offices. Many centers also include "temporary tenants," retailers that lease space (often in mall aisles or walkways) and sell from booths or moving carts. The tenants benefit from the lower rent and short-term commitment; the centers benefit by creating more excitement and diversity in shopping. Consumers often happen on new vendors in unexpected places.

CAREERS IN RETAILING

Christina Norsig: PopUpInsider.com

As a result of successfully developing eight pop-up—also known as temporary—stores (ranging from 1,500 square feet to as large as 6,000 square feet) in New York City, a leading trade magazine referred to Christina Norsig as "The Queen of Pop-Ups." Norsig started her first pop-up store in 2003 as an extension of her online store that sold fine china and housewares. Based on the positive experience for her and her temporary landlords, she then began to match retailers needing temporary space with property owners looking to fill their vacant retail space. Many of the leases that Norsig sets up are for two- to eight-week time periods.

At one time, pop-up stores were most common in highly seasonal product categories such as Halloween costumes and Christmas decorations and toys. Today, the product categories sold at these stores have greatly expanded.

Some pop-up stores specialize in the sales of closeouts, in nostalgic items such as CDs and vintage T-shirts, and events such as local street fairs. In addition, many retailers use temporary locations to test consumer interest in new retail formats or in new product categories without the need to commit to a 10- to 20-year lease. On the supply side, with recent commercial real-estate vacancy rates close to 13 percent, numerous property owners have become more willing to accept short-term retail tenants.

Source: "Christina Norsig," http://popupinsider.com/about-us (April 9, 2012).

- Open-air malls are gaining popularity since they are less expensive to build, which means lower rents and common area costs. Many people also like the outdoor shopping experience. A popular example is the Mall at Partridge Creek, an open-air regional center in Clinton Township, Michigan. It is anchored by Nordstrom, Parisian, and a 14-screen cinema. The center has 90 stores and restaurants. What gives it a special flair? "Partridge Creek has amenities unique to malls in Michigan, including: Bocce ball courts, free Wi-Fi, pop-jet fountains, a TV court, and a 30-foot fireplace."[7]
- More shopping center developers are striving to build their own brand loyalty. Simon and Westfield are among the developers that have spent millions of dollars to boost their images by advertising their own names—with slogans such as "Simon Malls—More Choices." Simon (www.simon.com) owns and manages more than 390 properties in 41 states, Europe, Japan, and elsewhere.
- Some shopping centers use frequent-shopper programs to retain customers and track spending. Prizes range from pre-paid calling cards to Caribbean vacations.

There are three types of planned shopping centers: regional, community, and neighborhood. Their characteristics are noted in Table 10-1, and they are described next.

REGIONAL SHOPPING CENTER A **regional shopping center** is a large, planned shopping facility appealing to a geographically dispersed market. It has at least one or two department stores (each with at least 100,000 square feet) and 50 to 150 or more smaller retailers. A regional center offers

TABLE 10-1 Characteristics of Typical Regional, Community, and Neighborhood Types of U.S. Planned Shopping Centers

Features of a Typical Center	Type of Center		
	Regional	Community	Neighborhood
Total site area (acres)	30–100+	10–40	3–15
Total sq. ft. leased to retailers	400,001–2,000,000+	100,001–400,000	30,000–100,000
Principal tenant	One, two, or more full-sized department stores	Branch (traditional or discount), department store variety store, and/or category killer store	Supermarket or drugstore
Number of stores	50–150 or more	15–25	5–15
Goods and services offered	Largest assortment for customers, focusing on goods that encourage careful shopping and services that enhance the shopping experience (such as a food court)	Moderate assortment for customers, focusing on a mix of shopping- and convenience-oriented goods and services	Lowest assortment for customers, emphasizing convenience-oriented goods and services
Minimum number of people living/working in trading area needed to support center	100,000+	20,000–100,000	3,000–50,000
Trading area in driving time	Up to 30 minutes	Up to 20 minutes	Fewer than 15 minutes
Location	Outside central city, on arterial highway or expressway	Close to one or more populated residential area(s)	Along a major thoroughfare in a single residential area
Layout	Mall, often enclosed with anchor stores at major entrances/exits	Strip or L-shaped	Strip
Percentage of all centers	3	15	82
Percentage of all centers' selling space	27	41	32

Source: Adapted by the authors from International Council of Shopping Centers, "2011 Economic Impact of Shopping Centers," www.icsc.org/ICSC%20PressKit_FINAL_11_9_11.pdf.

a very broad and deep assortment of shopping-oriented goods and services intended to enhance the consumer's visit. The market is 100,000+ people who live or work up to a 30-minute drive away. On average, people travel under 20 minutes.

The regional center is the result of a planned effort to re-create the shopping variety of a central city in suburbia. Some regional centers have even become the social, cultural, and vocational focal point of an entire suburban area. Frequently, it is used as a town plaza, a meeting place, a concert hall, and a place for a brisk indoor walk. Despite the declining overall interest in shopping, on a typical visit to a regional shopping center, many people spend an average of an hour or more there.

The first outdoor regional shopping center opened in 1950 in Seattle, anchored by a branch of Bon Marche, a leading downtown department store. Southdale Center (outside Minneapolis), built in 1956 for the Target Corporation (then Dayton Hudson), was the first fully enclosed, climate-controlled mall. Today, there are about 2,755 U.S. regional centers, and this format is also popping up around the world (where small stores still remain the dominant force) from Australia to Brazil to India to Malaysia.

Mall of America's attractions (www.mallofamerica.com/attractions) are as impressive as the mall itself.

One type of regional center is the **megamall**, an enormous planned shopping center with 1 million+ square feet of retail space, multiple anchor stores, up to several hundred specialty stores, food courts, and entertainment facilities. It seeks to heighten interest in shopping and expand the trading area. There are 515 U.S. megamalls, including Mall of America (www.mallofamerica.com) in Minnesota. It has four anchors (Bloomingdale's, Macy's, Nordstrom, and Sears), 520 other stores, a 14-screen movie theater, a health club, 50 restaurants, a Nickelodeon Universe indoor amusement park, an aquarium, and 12,550 parking spaces—with 4.2 million square feet of building space. The mall has stores for every budget, attracts 40 percent of visitors from outside a 150-mile radius, and draws 40 million visitors annually. Beijing, China's Jin Yuan shopping center is the largest megamall in the world. See Figure 10-5 for another leading regional center.

COMMUNITY SHOPPING CENTER A **community shopping center** is a moderate-sized, planned shopping facility with a branch department store (traditional or discount) and/or a category killer store, as well as several smaller stores (similar to those in a neighborhood center). It offers a moderate assortment of shopping- and convenience-oriented goods and services to consumers from one or more nearby, well-populated, residential areas. About 20,000 to 100,000 people, who live or work within a 10- to 20-minute drive, are served by this location. There are nearly 16,500 community shopping centers in the United States.

FIGURE 10-5
Galereya Afina

The Galereya Afina is a vertical regional shopping center in Odessa, Russia. It is quite modern and relatively new. As a result, it attracts shoppers and visitors from quite a distance. There are numerous nearby hotels that promote their proximity to the center.

Source: Brendan Howard/Shutterstock.com. Reprinted by permission.

There is better long-range planning for a community shopping center than a neighborhood shopping center. Balanced tenancy is usually enforced, and cooperative promotion is more apt. Store composition and the center's image are kept pretty consistent with pre-set goals.

Two noteworthy types of community center are the power center and the lifestyle center. A **power center** is a shopping site with (1) up to a half-dozen or so category killer stores and a mix of smaller stores or (2) several complementary stores specializing in one product category. A power center usually occupies 200,000 to 400,000 square feet on a major highway or road intersection. It seeks to be quite distinctive to draw shoppers and better compete with regional centers. See Figure 10-6. There are more than 2,500 U.S. power centers, such as Pennsylvania's Whitehall Square. That 315,000-square-foot center is a category killer center with a 55,000-square-foot Raymour & Flanigan Furniture Store, a 52,000-square-foot Redner's Warehouse Market, a 49,000-square-foot Sports Authority, a 30,000-square-foot Ross Dress for Less, a 23,000-square-foot PetSmart, and a 21,000-square-foot Staples, as well as several smaller stores.

Brixmor (www.brixmor.com/PropertySearch.asp) is a leading retail-estate developer with several power centers. Visit its properties online.

A **lifestyle center** is an open-air shopping site that typically includes 150,000 to 500,000 square feet of space dedicated to upscale, well-known specialty stores. The focus is often on apparel, home products, books, music, and restaurants. Popular stores at lifestyle centers include Ann Taylor, Banana Republic, Barnes & Noble, Bath & Body Works, Gap, GapKids, Pottery Barn, Talbots, Victoria's Secret, and Williams-Sonoma. Aspen Grove in Littleton, Denver; Deer Park Town Center in Illinois; Rookwood Commons in Cincinnati, Ohio; and CocoWalk in Coconut Grove, Florida, are examples of lifestyle shopping centers. At present, there are about 400 such centers in the United States.

NEIGHBORHOOD SHOPPING CENTER A **neighborhood shopping center** is a planned shopping facility, with the largest store being a supermarket or a drugstore. Other retailers often include a bakery, a laundry, a dry cleaner, a stationery store, a barbershop or beauty parlor, a hardware store, a restaurant, a liquor store, and a gas station. This center focuses on convenience-oriented goods and services for people living or working nearby. It serves 3,000 to 50,000 people who are within a 15-minute drive (usually less than 10 minutes).

A neighborhood center is usually arranged in a strip. Initially, it is carefully planned and tenants are balanced. Over time, the planned aspects may lessen and newcomers may face fewer restrictions. Thus, a liquor store may replace a barbershop—leaving a void. A center's ability to maintain balance depends on its attractiveness to potential tenants (expressed by the extent of store vacancies). In number, but not in selling space or sales, neighborhood centers account for 80 percent of all U.S. shopping centers (with nearly 89,000 such centers in existence as of 2011).

FIGURE 10-6

Target: A Power Center Anchor

Most Target stores are in power centers; and among the other retailers that are situated in such centers with Target are Home Depot, Staples, and Walgreens. The average Target store has about 135,000 square feet of space; and its supercenters (which combine a discount department store and a supermarket in the same facility) are even larger.

Source: Reprinted by permission of Susan V. Berry, Retail Image Consulting, Inc.

THE CHOICE OF A GENERAL LOCATION

The last part of Step 2 in location planning requires a retailer to select a locational format: isolated, unplanned district, or planned center. The decision depends on the firm's strategy and a careful evaluation of the advantages and disadvantages of each alternative.

Next, in Step 3, the retailer chooses a broadly defined site. Two decisions are needed here. First, the specific kind of isolated store, unplanned business district, or planned shopping center location is picked. If a firm wants an isolated store, it must decide on a highway or side street. Should it desire an unplanned business area, it must decide on a CBD, an SBD, an NBD, or a string. A retailer seeking a planned area must choose a regional, community, or neighborhood shopping center—and whether to use a derivative form such as a megamall or power center. Here are the preferences of three retailers:

- Radio Shack operates about 4,500 company-owned stores, 1,200 franchise stores, and 1,250 kiosks (in Target and Sam's units) in the United States. These stores are located in strip centers and major shopping malls, as well as at individual store sites. Each location offers an assortment of name brand and private brand consumer electronics products. Radio Shack stores are about 2,500 square feet; and they are located in malls, open-air centers, and strip centers, as well as at individual sites. About 90 percent of Americans either live or work within five minutes of a Radio Shack store. And its "small-box format enables customers to generally get in and out of a store quickly without having to deal with the hassles associated with big-box shopping—including parking issues, navigating a large store to find the exact items you need, and the occasional lengthy checkout lines."[8]

Guitar Center (www.guitarcenter.com) has a well-conceived location plan.

- The Guitar Center operates more than 220 Guitar Center stores in 43 states and 102 Music & Arts stores in 19 states. Among the Guitar Center stores, 65 percent are primary format units, 33 percent are secondary format units, and 2 percent are tertiary format units. According to the retailer: "The store format is determined primarily by the size of the market in which it is located. Our primary format stores serve major metropolitan population centers and generally range in size from 13,000 to 30,000 square feet. Our secondary format stores serve metropolitan areas not served by primary format stores and generally range from 8,000 to 14,000 square feet. Tertiary market stores serve smaller populations and are about 5,000 square feet."[9]
- Apple Stores are usually placed at high-traffic locations in better shopping malls and urban shopping districts in about a dozen countries, including the United States. By owning and operating 400 of its own stores and situating them in prominent high-traffic locations, the firm "is better positioned to ensure a high-quality customer buying experience and attract new customers. Stores are designed to simplify and enhance the presentation and marketing of Apple products and related solutions. To that end, store configurations have evolved into various sizes to accommodate market-specific demands."[10]

Second, a firm must select its general store placement. For an isolated store, this means picking a specific highway or side street. For an unplanned district or planned center, this means picking a specific district (e.g., downtown Los Angeles) or center (e.g., La Gran Plaza in Fort Worth, Texas).

In Step 3, the retailer narrows down the decisions made in the first two steps and then chooses a general location. Step 4 requires the firm to evaluate specific alternative sites, including their position on a block (or in a center), the side of the street, and the terms of tenancy. The factors to be considered in assessing and choosing a general location and a specific site within that location are described together in the next section because many strategic decisions are similar for these two steps.

LOCATION AND SITE EVALUATION

The assessment of general locations and the specific sites within them requires extensive analysis. In any area, the optimum site for a particular store is called the **one-hundred percent location**. Because different retailers need different kinds of sites, a location labeled as 100 percent for one firm may be less desirable for another. An upscale ladies' apparel shop would seek a location unlike one sought by a convenience store. The apparel shop would benefit from heavy pedestrian traffic, closeness to major department stores, and proximity to other specialty stores. The convenience store would rather be in an area with ample parking and heavy vehicular traffic. It does not need to be close to other stores.

FIGURE 10-7
A Location/Site Evaluation Checklist

Rate each of these criteria on a scale of 1 to 10, with 1 being excellent and 10 being poor.

Pedestrian Traffic	Number of people	________
	Type of people	________
Vehicular Traffic	Number of vehicles	________
	Type of vehicles	________
	Traffic congestion	________
Parking Facilities	Number and quality of parking spots	________
	Distance to store	________
	Availability of employee parking	________
Transportation	Availability of mass transit	________
	Access from major highways	________
	Ease of deliveries	________
Store Composition	Number and size of stores	________
	Affinity	________
	Retail balance	________
Specific Site	Visibility	________
	Placement in the location	________
	Size and shape of the lot	________
	Size and shape of the building	________
	Condition and age of the lot and building	________
Terms of Occupancy	Ownership or leasing terms	________
	Operations and maintenance costs	________
	Taxes	________
	Zoning restrictions	________
	Voluntary regulations	________
Overall Rating	General location	________
	Specific site	________

Figure 10-7 has a location/site evaluation checklist. A retailer should rate each alternative location (and specific site) on all the criteria and develop overall ratings for them. Two firms may rate the same site differently. This figure should be used in conjunction with the trading-area data in Chapter 9, not instead of them.

Pedestrian Traffic

The most crucial measures of a location's and site's value are the number and type of people passing by. Other things being equal, a site with the most pedestrian traffic is often best. See Figure 10-8.

Not everyone passing a location or site is a good prospect for all types of stores, so many firms use selective counting procedures, such as counting only those carrying shopping bags. Otherwise, pedestrian traffic totals may include too many nonshoppers. It would be improper for an appliance retailer to count as prospective shoppers all people passing a downtown site on the way to work. In fact, much downtown pedestrian traffic may be from people who are there for nonretailing activities.

A proper pedestrian traffic count should encompass these four elements:

- Separation of the count by age and gender (with very young children not counted).
- Division of the count by time (this allows the study of peaks, low points, and changes in the gender of the people passing by the hour).
- Pedestrian interviews (to find out the proportion of potential shoppers).
- Spot analysis of shopping trips (to verify the stores actually visited).

Vehicular Traffic

The quantity and characteristics of vehicular traffic are very important for retailers that appeal to customers who drive there. Convenience stores, outlets in regional shopping centers, and car washes are retailers that rely on heavy vehicular traffic. Automotive traffic studies are essential in suburban areas, where pedestrian traffic is often limited.

As with pedestrian traffic, adjustments to the raw count of vehicular traffic must be made. Some retailers count only homeward-bound traffic, some exclude vehicles on the other side of a

TECHNOLOGY IN RETAILING

Vitamin Shoppe and Site-Selection Technology

Since 2004, Buxton (www.buxtonco.com), a site-selection software firm, has worked with Vitamin Shoppe (www.vitaminshoppe.com) in developing and fine-tuning a model that identifies new markets and specific sites. The model is also useful in predicting the performance of new stores. In 2004, Vitamin Shoppe had about 235 locations in 20 states. As of 2011, its store count had grown to about 500 stores in 39 states. Michael Archbold, Vitamin Shoppe's president, estimates that the chain has the potential of 900 U.S. stores.

Buxton's analysis of retail sites and market areas is based on such general factors as population density, the composition of nearby retailers, and demographic data on an area's residents. Buxton also uses data from Vitamin Shoppe's loyalty program; this is particularly valuable since 87 percent of the retailer's overall sales are loyalty plan members. Consumer lifestyle and behavior from more than 120 million households are also part of Buxton's data base.

The Vitamin Shoppe forecasts sales based on its classifying consumers into about 60 categories. This analysis is then adjusted by a customer's distance from each store. Customers living within one mile of a store are expected to spend much more than those living three miles away.

Source: Karen M. Kroll, "Zeroing in on Success," www.stores.org (July 2011).

divided highway, and some omit out-of-state cars. Data may be available from the state highway department, the county engineer, or the regional planning commission.

Besides traffic counts, the retailer should study the extent and timing of congestion (from traffic, detours, and poor roads). People normally avoid congested areas and shop where driving time and driving difficulties are minimized.

Parking Facilities

Most U.S. retail stores include some provision for nearby off-street parking. In many business districts, parking is provided by individual stores, arrangements among stores, and local government. In planned shopping centers, parking is shared by all stores there. The number and quality of parking spots, their distances from stores, and the availability of employee parking should all be evaluated.

The need for retailer parking facilities depends on the store's trading area, the type of store, the proportion of shoppers using a car, the existence of other parking, the turnover of spaces (which depend on the length of a shopping trip), the flow of shoppers, and parking by nonshoppers. A shopping center normally needs 4 to 5 parking spaces per 1,000 square feet of gross floor area, a supermarket 10 to 15 spaces, and a furniture store 3 or 4 spaces.

FIGURE 10-8
Pedestrian Traffic Rules!

In heavily-populated Suzhou, China, the pedestrian traffic count is enormous—which is great news for retailers. Even if many passersby are not shoppers, the massive number of pedestrians makes the area shown here popular with retailers.

Source: Tan Wei Ming/Shutterstock.com. Reprinted by permission.

Free parking sometimes creates problems. Commuters and employees of nearby businesses may park in spaces intended for shoppers. This problem can be lessened by validating shoppers' parking stubs and requiring payment from nonshoppers. Another problem may occur if the selling space at a location increases due to new stores or the expansion of current ones. Existing parking may then be inadequate. Double-deck parking or parking tiers save land and shorten the distance from a parked car to a store—a key factor because customers at a regional shopping center may be unwilling to walk more than a few hundred feet from their cars to the center.

Transportation

Mass transit, access from major highways, and ease of deliveries must be examined.

In a downtown area, closeness to mass transit is important for people who do not own cars, who commute to work, or who would not otherwise shop in an area with traffic congestion. The availability of buses, taxis, subways, trains, and other kinds of public transit is a must for any area not readily accessible by vehicular traffic.

Locations dependent on vehicular traffic should be rated on their nearness to major thoroughfares. Driving time is a consideration for many people. In addition, drivers heading eastbound on a highway often do not like to make a U-turn to get to a store on the westbound side of that highway.

The transportation network should be studied for delivery truck access. Many thoroughfares are excellent for cars but ban large trucks or cannot bear their weight.

Store Composition

The number and size of stores should be consistent with the type of location. A retailer in an isolated site wants no stores nearby; a retailer in a neighborhood business district wants an area with 10 to 15 small stores; and a retailer in a regional shopping center wants a location with many stores, including large department stores (to generate customer traffic).

If the stores at a given location (be it an unplanned district or a planned center) complement, blend, and cooperate with one another, and each benefits from the others' presence, **affinity** exists. When affinity is strong, the sales of each store are greater, due to the high customer traffic, than if the stores are apart. The practice of similar or complementary stores locating near each other is based on two factors: (1) Customers like to compare the prices, styles, selections, and services of similar stores. (2) Customers like one-stop shopping and purchase at different stores on the same trip. Affinities can exist among competing stores, as well as among complementary stores. More people travel to shopping areas with large selections than to convenience-oriented areas, so the sales of all stores are enhanced.

One measure of compatibility is the degree to which stores exchange customers. Stores in these categories are very compatible with each other and have high customer interchange:

- Supermarket, drugstore, bakery, fruit-and-vegetable store, meat store.
- Department store, apparel store, hosiery store, lingerie shop, shoe store, jewelry store.

Retail balance, the mix of stores within a district or shopping center, should also be considered. Proper balance occurs when the number of store facilities for each merchandise or service classification is equal to the location's market potential, a range of goods and services is provided to foster one-stop shopping, there is an adequate assortment within any category, and there is a proper mix of store types (balanced tenancy).

Specific Site

Visibility; placement in the location, size, and shape of the lot; size and shape of the building; and condition and age of the lot and building should be reviewed for the specific site.

Visibility is a site's ability to be seen by pedestrian or vehicular traffic. A site on a side street or at the end of a shopping center is not as visible as one on a major road or at the center's entrance. High visibility aids store awareness; and some people hesitate to go down a side street or to the end of a center.

Placement in the location is a site's relative position in the district or center. A corner location may be desirable because it is situated at the intersection of two streets and has "corner influence." It is usually more expensive because of the greater pedestrian and vehicular passersby due to traffic flows from two streets, increased window display area, and less traffic congestion through

FIGURE 10-9
Corner Influence and Hershey's
Consider the pedestrian and vehicular traffic—and the eyecatching appeal—generated by this Hershey's store in Ohio.

Source: Reprinted by permission of Susan V. Berry, Retail Image Consulting, Inc.

multiple entrances. Corner influence is greatest in high-volume locations. That is why some Pier 1 stores, Starbucks restaurants, and various other retailers seek corner sites. See Figure 10-9.

A convenience-oriented firm, such as a stationery store, is very concerned about the side of the street, the location relative to other convenience-oriented stores, nearness to parking, access to a bus stop, and the distance from residences. A shopping-oriented retailer, such as a furniture store, is more interested in a corner site to increase window display space, proximity to wallpaper and other related retailers, the accessibility of its pickup platform to consumers, and the ease of deliveries to the store.

When a retailer buys or rents an existing building, its size and shape should be noted. The condition and age of the lot and the building should also be studied. A department store requires significantly more space than a boutique, and it may desire a square site, while the boutique seeks a rectangular one. Any site should be viewed in terms of total space needs: parking, walkways, selling, nonselling, and so on.

Due to the saturation of many desirable locations and the lack of available spots in others, some firms have turned to nontraditional sites—often to complement their existing stores. T.G.I. Friday's, Staples, and Bally have airport stores. Subway has outlets in many Wal-Marts, and Subway and some other fast-food retailers share facilities to provide more variety and to share costs. See Figure 10-10.

Terms of Occupancy

Terms of occupancy—ownership versus leasing, the type of lease, operations and maintenance costs, taxes, zoning restrictions, and voluntary regulations—must be evaluated for each prospective site.

OWNERSHIP VERSUS LEASING A retailer with adequate funding can either own or lease premises. Ownership is more common in small stores, in small communities, or at inexpensive locations. It has several advantages. There is no chance that a property owner will not renew a lease or double the rent when a lease expires. Monthly mortgage payments are stable. Operations are flexible; a retailer can engage in scrambled merchandising and break down walls. It is also likely that property value will appreciate over time, resulting in a financial gain if the business is sold. Ownership disadvantages are the high initial costs, the long-term commitment, and the inability to readily change sites. Home Depot owns about 89 percent of its store properties.[11]

The National Trust for Historic Preservation (www.preservationnation.org) has revitalized communities across the United States.

If a retailer chooses ownership, it must decide whether to construct a new facility or buy an existing building. The retailer should consider the purchase price and maintenance costs, zoning restrictions, the age and condition of existing facilities, the adaptability of existing facilities, and the time to erect a new building. To encourage building rehabilitation in towns with 5,000 to 50,000 people, Congress enacted the Main Street program (www.mainstreet.org) of the National Trust for Historic Preservation. There is currently a network of 46 statewide, citywide, and regional Main Street programs actively serving more than 2,000 towns. These towns benefit from planning support, tax credits, and low-interest loans.

FIGURE 10-10

Multi-Store Locations

To draw more customers and split overhead costs, various retailers are sharing store locations. The location shown here includes Starbucks, Popeye's, Pizza Hut, and Taco Bell.

Source: Reprinted by permission of Susan V. Berry, Retail Image Consulting, Inc.

The great majority of stores in central business districts and regional shopping centers are leased (with Home Depot being one of the exceptions), mostly due to the high investment for ownership. Department stores tend to have renewable 20- to 30-year leases, supermarkets usually have renewable 15- to 20-year leases, and specialty stores often have 5- to 10-year leases with options to extend. Some leases give the retailer the right to end an agreement before the expiration date—under given circumstances and for a specified retailer payment.

Leasing minimizes the initial investment, reduces risk, allows access to prime sites that cannot hold more stores, leads to immediate occupancy and traffic, and reduces the long-term commitment. Many retailers also feel they can open more stores or spend more on other aspects of their strategies by leasing. Firms that lease accept limits on operating flexibility, restrictions on subletting and selling the business, possible nonrenewal problems, rent increases, and not gaining from rising real-estate values.

Through a *sale-leaseback*, some large retailers build stores and then sell them to real-estate investors who lease the property back to the retailers on a long-term basis. Retailers using sale-leasebacks build stores to their specifications and have bargaining power in leasing—while lowering capital expenditures.

TYPES OF LEASES Property owners do not rely solely on constant rent leases, partly due to their concern about interest rates and the related rise in operating costs. Terms can be quite complicated.[12]

Tiffany (www.tiffany.com), a name synonymous with glamour, is one of the cornerstone retailers on New York's high-rent Fifth Avenue.

The simplest, most direct arrangement is the **straight lease**—a retailer pays a fixed dollar amount per month over the life of the lease. Rent usually ranges from \$1 to \$75 annually per square foot, depending on the site's desirability and store traffic. At some sites, rents can be much higher. On New York's Fifth Avenue, the average yearly rental rate ranges up to \$2,250 per square foot! This is the world's highest retail rental rate.[13]

A **percentage lease** stipulates that rent is related to sales or profits. This differs from a straight lease, which provides for constant payments. A percentage lease protects a property owner against inflation and lets it benefit if a store is successful; it also allows a tenant to view the lease as a variable cost—rent is lower when its performance is weak and higher when performance is good. The percentage rate varies by type of shopping district or center and by type of store.

Percentage leases have variations. With a specified minimum, low sales are assumed to be partly the retailer's responsibility; the property owner receives minimum payments (as in a straight lease) no matter what the sales or profits. With a specified maximum, it is assumed that a very successful retailer should not pay more than a maximum rent. Superior merchandising, promotion, and pricing should reward the retailer. Another variation is the sliding scale: The ratio

Fashion Retailing and Montreal

Montreal is the largest city in Quebec and the second-largest city in Canada. While the average retail space in Montreal rented for $117 per square foot as of mid-year 2010, Montreal's most sought-after retail space was priced as high as $500 per square foot. Montreal's Ste. Catherine Street is the 32nd most expensive retail location in the world with retail space averaging about $300 (U.S.) per square foot.

Many upscale retailers consider this a bargain as compared with space on the Champs Elysees in Paris or on Fifth Avenue in New York City. Fashion-based stores located on Ste. Catherine Street include H&M, Lululemmon Athletica, Max Mara, La Maison Simons, and Banana Republic, as well as Centre Eaton (a fashion-based shopping center with a large number of restaurants).

According to Georges Renaud, a Certified Property Manager: "Montreal is rich in culture, fashion, and active people. We're fortunate to be an international, multicultural city." It offers "a huge amount of theater, dining, and nightlife. It is also a fashionable city. A lot of money is spent on fashion here." Montreal's fashion forwardness, its ties to Europe, and relatively reasonable rental costs have drawn a number of major fashion-based retailers to the area.

Source: Kristin Gunderson Hunt, "Fashion Retailers Keep Montreal Moving," *Journal of Property Management*, Vol. 76 (January–February 2011), pp. 26–27.

of rent to sales changes as sales rise. A sliding-down scale has a retailer pay a lower percentage as sales go up and is an incentive to the retailer.

A **graduated lease** calls for precise rent increases over a stated period of time. Monthly rent may be $4,800 for the first five years and $5,600 for the last five years of a lease. Rent is known in advance by the retailer and the property owner, and it is based on expected increases in sales and costs. There is no problem auditing sales or profits, as there is for percentage leases. This lease is often used with small retailers.

A **maintenance-increase-recoupment lease** has a provision allowing rent to increase if a property owner's taxes, heating bills, insurance, or other expenses rise beyond a certain point. This provision most often supplements a straight rental lease agreement.

A **net lease** calls for all maintenance costs (such as heating, electricity, insurance, and interior repair) to be paid by the retailer. It frees the property owner from managing the facility and gives the retailer control over store maintenance. It is used to supplement a straight lease or a percentage lease.

OTHER CONSIDERATIONS After assessing ownership and leasing opportunities, a retailer must look at the costs of operations and maintenance. The age and condition of a facility may cause a retailer to have high monthly costs, even though the mortgage or rent is low. Furthermore, the costs of extensive renovations should be calculated.

What is the sales tax in Utah? California? Go to this site (www.salestaxinstitute.com/rates.html) to find out the sales tax in all 50 states and the District of Columbia.

Differences in sales taxes (those customers pay) and business taxes (those retailers pay) among alternative sites must be weighed. Business taxes should be broken down into real-estate and income categories. The highest statewide sales tax is in Indiana, Mississippi, New Jersey, Rhode Island, and Tennessee (7 percent); Alaska, Delaware, Montana, New Hampshire, and Oregon have no state sales tax.

There may be zoning restrictions as to the kind of stores allowed, store size, building height, the type of merchandise carried, and other factors that have to be hurdled (or another site chosen). For example, many communities believe that their local retail economies can handle only so many new stores without causing some existing firms to fail. Therefore, they have passed zoning regulations that forbid retail stores from exceeding a given size. This helps to:

> sustain the vitality of small, pedestrian-oriented business districts and nurture local retailers. Size caps prevent traffic congestion and over-burdened public infrastructure. They require all retailers to build stores that are appropriately sized for the community. Wal-Mart, Home Depot, and other chains can open stores so long as they do not exceed the size limit—a limit for local businesses also. Cities that have adopted size caps find that, in some cases, retailers that typically build larger stores will opt not to open and, in other cases, they will design smaller stores.[14]

Voluntary restrictions—not mandated by the government—are most prevalent in planned shopping centers and may include required membership in merchant groups, uniform hours, and cooperative security forces. Leases for many stores in regional shopping centers have included clauses protecting anchor tenants from too much competition—especially from discounters. These clauses involve limits on product lines, bans against discounting, fees for common services, and so forth. Anchors are protected by developers because the developers need their long-term commitments to finance the centers. The Federal Trade Commission discourages "exclusives"—whereby only a particular retailer in a center can carry specified merchandise—and "radius clauses"—whereby a tenant agrees not to operate another store within a certain distance.

Because of overbuilding, some retailers are in a good position to bargain over the terms of occupancy. This differs from city to city and from shopping location to shopping location.

Overall Rating

The last task in choosing a store location is to compute overall ratings: (1) Each location under consideration is given an overall rating based on the criteria in Figure 10-7. (2) The overall ratings of alternative locations are compared, and the best location is chosen. (3) The same procedure is used to evaluate the alternative sites within the location.

Lease agreements used to be so simple that they could be written on a napkin—not today (http://www.maclw.com/articles/45_Retail_Lease_Nego_Tips.pdf).

It is often difficult to compile and compare composite evaluations because some attributes may be positive while others are negative. The general location may be a good shopping center, but the site in the center may be poor, or an area may have excellent potential but take two years to build a store. The attributes in Figure 10-7 should be weighted according to their importance. An overall rating should also include *knockout factors*—those that preclude consideration of a site. Possible knockout factors are a short lease, little or no evening or weekend pedestrian traffic, and poor tenant relations with the landlord.

Chapter Summary

1. *To thoroughly examine the types of locations available to a retailer: isolated store, unplanned business district, and planned shopping center.* After a retailer rates alternative trading areas, it decides on the type of location, selects the general location, and chooses a particular site. There are three basic locational types.

   An isolated store is freestanding, not adjacent to other stores. It has no competition, low rent, flexibility, road visibility, easy parking, and lower property costs. It also has a lack of traffic, no variety for shoppers, no shared costs, and zoning restrictions.

   An unplanned business district is a shopping area with two or more stores located together or nearby. Store composition is not based on planning. There are four categories: central business district, secondary business district, neighborhood business district, and string. An unplanned district generally has these favorable points: variety of goods, services, and prices; access to public transit; nearness to commercial and social facilities; and pedestrian traffic. Yet, its shortcomings have led to the growth of the planned shopping center: inadequate parking, older facilities, high rents and taxes in popular CBDs, discontinuity of offerings, traffic and delivery congestion, high theft rates, and some declining central cities.

   A planned shopping center is centrally owned or managed and well balanced. It usually has one or more anchor stores and many smaller stores. The planned center is popular, due to extensive goods and service offerings, expanding suburbs, shared strategic planning and costs, attractive locations, parking facilities, lower rent and taxes (except for regional centers), lower theft rates, the popularity of malls (although some people are now bored with them), and the lesser appeal of inner-city shopping. Negative aspects include operations inflexibility, restrictions on merchandise carried, and anchor store domination. There are three forms: regional, community, and neighborhood centers.

2. *To note the decisions necessary in choosing a general retail location.* First, the specific form of isolated store, unplanned business district, or planned shopping center location is determined, such as whether to be on a highway or side street; in a CBD, an SBD, an NBD, or a string; or in a regional, community, or neighborhood shopping center. Then the general store location is specified—singling out a particular highway, business district, or shopping center.

3. *To describe the concept of the one-hundred percent location.* Extensive analysis is required when evaluating each general location and specific sites within it. Most importantly, the optimum site for a given store must be determined. This is the one-hundred percent location, and it differs by retailer.

4. *To discuss several criteria for evaluating general retail locations and the specific sites within them.* Pedestrian traffic, vehicular traffic, parking facilities, transportation, store composition, the attributes of each specific site, and terms of occupancy should be studied. An overall rating is then computed for each location and site, and the best one selected.

   Affinity occurs when the stores at the same location complement, blend, and cooperate with one another; each benefits from the others' presence.

5. *To contrast alternative terms of occupancy.* A retailer can opt to own or lease. If it leases, terms are specified in a straight lease, percentage lease, graduated lease, maintenance-increase-recoupment lease, and/or net lease. Operating and maintenance costs, taxes, zoning restrictions, and voluntary restrictions also need to be reviewed.

Key Terms

isolated store (p. 252)
unplanned business district (p. 253)
central business district (CBD) (p. 253)
secondary business district (SBD) (p. 255)
neighborhood business district (NBD) (p. 256)
string (p. 256)
planned shopping center (p. 257)
balanced tenancy (p. 257)
regional shopping center (p. 259)
megamall (p. 260)
community shopping center (p. 260)
power center (p. 261)
lifestyle center (p. 261)
neighborhood shopping center (p. 261)
one-hundred percent location (p. 262)
affinity (p. 265)
retail balance (p. 265)
terms of occupancy (p. 266)
straight lease (p. 267)
percentage lease (p. 267)
graduated lease (p. 268)
maintenance-increase-recoupment lease (p. 268)
net lease (p. 268)

Questions for Discussion

1. A cell-phone-service chain has decided to open outlets in a combination of isolated locations, unplanned business districts, and planned shopping centers. Comment on this strategy.
2. From the retailer's perspective, compare the advantages of locating in unplanned business districts versus planned shopping centers.
3. Differentiate among the central business district, the secondary business district, the neighborhood business district, and the string.
4. Develop a brief plan to revitalize a neighborhood business district near your campus.
5. What is a megamall? What is a lifestyle center? Describe the strengths and weaknesses of each.
6. Evaluate a regional shopping center near your campus.
7. Explain why a one-hundred percent location for a discount apparel chain may not be a one-hundred percent location for a moderate-priced local apparel store.
8. What criteria should a small retailer use in selecting a general store location and a specific site within it? A large retailer?
9. What difficulties are there in using a rating scale such as that shown in Figure 10-7? What are the benefits?
10. How do the parking needs for a fine restaurant, a computer repair store, and a luggage store differ?
11. Under what circumstances would it be more desirable for a retailer to buy or lease an existing facility rather than to build a new store?
12. What are the pros and cons of a straight lease versus a percentage lease for a prospective retail tenant? For the landlord?

Web-Based Exercise

Visit the Web site of MainStreet.org (www.preservationnation.org/main-street). What could the retailers in a small community learn from this site?

Note: Also stop by our Web site (www.pearsonhighered.com/bermanevans) to experience a number of highly interactive, appealing Web exercises based on actual company demonstrations and sample materials related to retailing.

PART 4 Short Cases

Case 1: Adapting Store Size to the Type of Location[c-1]

A significant trend among mass merchants is the greater use of small prototype stores rather than their big-box format. Wal-Mart (www.walmart.com) is opening a number of smaller stores (ranging in size from 30,000 to 60,000 square feet), mostly in urban areas. An extreme example of this new store format is a 3,500-square-foot "Wal-Mart on Campus" store located at the University of Arkansas.

Target Corporation (www.target.com) is using small-store formats as part of its expansion plans in Seattle, Baltimore, and San Francisco. Target's prototype store for these urban markets ranges in size from 60,000 to 100,000 square feet. Target currently has about 150 stores in urban areas, including a location in New York City's East Harlem area. In addition, Kohl's (www.kohls.com), Old Navy (www.oldnavy.com), Gap (www.gap.com), and numerous other retailers are looking at downsized stores at their newer locations.

For many big-box store chains, smaller prototypes are an ideal way to capitalize on opportunities in urban cities, where rents are generally high. These areas are densely populated, accessible by mass transportation, and have available full-time and part-time help. Despite their potential, only about 50 of Wal-Mart's thousands of U.S. stores are located in major cities. Wal-Mart also has no store in New York City, and only two stores in Los Angeles.

Smaller stores are also an ideal way for retailers to open new units in locations that were vacated by such defunct retailers as Circuit City, Steve & Barry's, Borders, and Mervyn's. When Kohl's took over locations that were formerly used by Mervyn's, Kohl's was compelled to reduce its store footprint.

The Limited (www.limited.com) and Home Depot (www.homedepot.com) have used reduced-size store prototypes as a means of utilizing small, but highly desirable, locations. And there are other reasons why smaller stores make sense. These stores have lower rental and operating expenses. Older shoppers often like smaller stores because they reduce shopping time and the need to walk through larger stores. For major retail chains, smaller-store formats have less trading-area overlap with existing stores than bigger stores. Small stores can meet the demands of markets that could not be economically feasible with a larger store. Lastly, smaller stores in existing market areas can better utilize a chain's existing distribution centers than larger stores located in more distant locations.

A vital strategic issue involving the use of smaller-store formats relates to the appropriate level of merchandise selection. One potential problem associated with small stores is the need for faster inventory replenishment due to their smaller storage areas. Merchandise selection in smaller formats also needs to be more carefully planned to ensure that it includes relevant goods and services appropriate for the store's customers. Some reductions in inventory selection are simple to implement. For example, urban apartment dwellers have limited capabilities to store bulk purchases of paper towels and no need for patio furniture, snow blowers, and garden supplies. Other reductions that are more difficult to plan include color choices, size distributions, and so forth. One way of providing sufficient assortment in a small space is to enable customers to order merchandise on the Web (via an in-store kiosk) and have it shipped to the store for pickup by consumers or shipped directly to shoppers' homes.

Questions

1. Under what conditions should a large box store retailer like a Best Buy pursue a small-store strategy?
2. Would the population characteristics of a small store's trading area differ from that of a larger store? Why or why not?
3. Discuss the concept of trading-area overlap from the perspective of small- versus large-store formats.
4. Explain how small-store formats could be a means of capitalizing on trading areas where a large-format retailer is understored.

Case 2: Examining Perfumania's Site-Selection Strategy[c-2]

Perfumania (www.perfumania.com) is a fragrance retailer with 350 value-priced fragrance stores in the United States and an additional 20 stores in Puerto Rico. Despite the weak economy, Perfumania opened 59 stores in 2009, nine in 2010, and 10 to 15 locations in 2011 (including its first stores in Canada). Ultimately, the retailer plans to have as many as 600 stores.

In 2009, Perfumania decided to outsource its real-estate activities and hired RCS Real Estate Advisors (www.rcsrealestate.com) to handle site selection and lease negotiation for its new retail locations, as well as lease renewals and lease termination negotiations for its existing stores. In evaluating Perfumania's stores, RCS found that the chain had a number of locations where it was committed to paying above-market rental rates due to changes in rental market conditions. As a result, many of these locations were unprofitable. To the extent possible, RCS renegotiated lease terms at these locations and/or refused to renew these leases at the old rents when they expired.

Most of Perfumania's locations range from 1,500 to 2,000 square feet. Its regional mall locations are 1,500 square feet (of which 1,200 square feet comprises selling space) and its outlet mall stores are 2,000 square feet in size (1,700 square feet of which is selling space). According to Michael Katz, Perfumania's president and chief executive: "About 80 percent of our stores are in regional malls, outlet malls, or strip centers, and we have a few lifestyle center stores, though those

[c-1]The material in this case is drawn from Debra Hazel, "Small Formats: Big Opportunities," www.chainstoreage.com (February 2011).

[c-2]The material in this case is drawn from Katherine Field, "Focus On: Site Selection and Optimization," www.chainstoreage.com (January 2011) and Katherine Field, "Sweet Smell of Success," www.chainstoreage.com (February 2011).

haven't been as successful." Perfumania also has some stores located in major urban shopping districts. The challenge with the urban locations is being able to achieve sufficient volume to offset higher rental and operating costs.

In general, retail locations close to high-traffic destination retailers (which do not have to be apparel-based) have been the most successful for Perfumania. According to Katz, "If every one of our stores could be next to an Apple store, we would be happy!" In some instances, the chain has placed multiple stores in the same center. Currently, Perfumania has two stores with the same inventory, store exterior, and interior design and inventory in the Mall of America (a Minnesota mall with over 500 stores that attracts 40 million visitors per year). These stores are so successful that Perfumania's management is seeking a third location there. As the president and chief executive of RCS says: "The product is so much of an impulse purchase that if you're on two sides of a really big mall, and it's a great mall, why not?"

The expansion of its highly profitable locations into outlet malls is Perfumania's most recent growth strategy. Other targeted areas for new locations are western, southeastern, and southwestern states. Canada represents a major opportunity since it does not have a national fragrance retailer. Perfumania is targeting three to four Canadian cities for new store development.

Perfumania is rolling out a new prototype store for its regional shopping center locations. It plans to apply this new contemporary design to its stores located in strip centers and lifestyle centers, but will only make minor changes in its outlet mall locations.

Questions

1. Describe the pros and cons of Perfumania's outsourcing its site selection and leasing operations versus conducting these activities in-house.
2. With what types of stores would Perfumania have an affinity? Explain your answer.
3. Describe how Perfumania could seek to renegotiate a lease with an above-market rent with a major mall.
4. Comment on Perfumania's seeking a third location in Mall of America from the perspective of trading-area overlap.

Case 3: Examining Rue 21's Location Strategy[C-3]

Rue 21 (www.rue21.com) is the fast-growing specialty retailer that sells fashion items (including footwear, fragrance and beauty items, jewelry, intimate apparel and sleepwear, and accessories) to girls and young men at value-oriented prices. Most of Rue 21's merchandise is trendy and priced below $35. According to the retailer's annual report, "Our merchandise is designed to appeal to 11- to 17-year-olds who aspire to be '21.'"

As of the end of its 2011 fiscal year, the chain operated 740 stores in 45 states. Rue 21 opened 110 stores in 2011 alone; and it ultimately plans to have more than 1,000 U.S. retail stores. Its average store is 5,000 square feet. Most of its new stores will be in strip centers and regional malls in small- and middle-market communities.

Rue 21 credits its success to its flexible real-estate strategy as well as its sourcing model. Rue 21's overall location strategy is not based on market area or location type. Although many of Rue 21's stores are in rural markets, where it has little direct competition, it also has many successful stores in urban locations. As of the beginning of 2012, 52 percent of Rue 21's stores were located in strip centers, 31 percent in regional malls, and 17 percent in outlet centers. Rue 21 favors locations that share customer traffic with adjacent retailers such as Wal-Mart, Target, and Kohl's.

Unlike some other retailers, Rue 21 does not own any real-estate. Most store leases have initial terms of five to ten years, with additional five-year renewal options. Many of these leases have early cancellation clauses that permit Rue 21 to terminate the lease if certain sales levels are not achieved or if a strip center does not meet specific overall occupancy levels.

The retailer's store leases also provide for additional rental payments, based on a percentage of net sales, if Rue 21's sales at a given location exceed specified levels. Leases also require payment of common maintenance charges, real-estate insurance, and real-estate taxes. This shifts the burden of higher operating expenses from the property owner to Rue 21. Renewal options generally require higher rental payments in subsequent years.

Rue 21 faces several risks with regard to its real-estate strategy. In some instances, even with an early cancellation clause, it may be unable to get out of a lease at an unsuccessful location. In these cases, the chain would be bound to continue rental payments. Bankruptcies and store closings in adjacent locations can reduce store traffic in a shopping center and adversely affect the remaining tenants, including Rue 21. In addition, Rue 21 may not be able to renew a lease at a very successful location.

Rue 21 relies on more than 450 domestic suppliers and importers for product sourcing. Although most of its clothing and accessories are made by overseas suppliers, domestic suppliers are used when quick deliveries are needed to capitalize on a fast-moving fashion trend. Goods are shipped daily to each store to motivate shoppers to constantly visit the store location. Rue 21 also maintains its products' distinctiveness through its private-label brands: Rue 21 etc!, Carbon Elements, Ruse Beauté, and Tarea.

Questions

1. Evaluate the pros and cons to Rue 21 of each location type: strip center, regional mall, and outlet center.
2. Describe the pros and cons of Rue 21 not owning any real-estate.
3. How could Rue 21 reduce the risks associated with its real-estate strategy?
4. Should Rue 21 expand beyond the United States? Explain the complexities of doing so.

[c-3]The material in this case is drawn from Marianne Wilson, "Rue 21 in Expansion Mode," www.chainstoreage.com (June–July 2011), p. 22; and *Rue 21 2011 Annual Report.*

Case 4: Coach Expands into China's Tier 2 and Tier 3 Cities[c-4]

Until now, most foreign retailers have used heavily populated Tier 1 Chinese cities such as Beijing, Shanghai, Guangzhou, and Shenzen as their initial entry points into the Chinese consumer marketplace. In contrast, over the next twenty years, retail analysts predict that a large number of foreign retailers will increasingly seek out retail sites in Tier 2 and Tier 3 Chinese cities. Bain & Co., a global management consulting firm, lists 330 Tier 2 cities in China; they have populations of 500,000 to 2 million people. There are more than 1,200 smaller county-level communities that are considered to be Tier 3. Lang LaSalle, a global real-estate services firm, has identified 15 of China's Tier 2 cities and 25 of its Tier 3 cities, most of which are provincial capitals, as leading candidates for retailers.

What most researchers agree upon is that the relative importance of the Tier 1 cities in China will diminish over time in terms of population and spending power. China has more than 200 cities that each have a population of at least 1 million people. In contrast, there are only 35 cities this size in all of Europe.

Let's examine the expansion strategy of Coach (www.coach.com), a U.S.-based luxury leather fashion accessories designer and retailer, in China. Coach initially entered China in 2003 through licensing agreements. When Coach discovered that the locally managed retail outlets were very profitable, it purchased back these rights in 2009. Direct control of its image, expansion plans, and pricing was essential to Coach. The firm also realized that it needed to better understand the Chinese market and the important differences between Chinese and American consumers. Its research showed that Chinese consumers desire very conspicuous brand marking on all of Coach's apparel and accessory items.

Coach initially focused its attention on establishing its brand in such affluent Tier 1 cities as Beijing and Shanghai. The company then expanded into newer market locations such as Chongqing after it was firmly established in Tier 1 markets. This strategy is referred to as a "beachhead to a disperse location strategy." Of Coach's initial 28 Chinese stores, 12 are in Tier 1 cities and 16 are in Tier 2 cities or beyond. Coach opened 13 new stores in 2010; this represented an increase in square footage of 50 percent. It planned to open 30 new locations in 2011, representing another increase of 60 percent in square footage. Some of these stores will be Coach flagship stores to focus attention on Coach's presence in these new provincial markets, despite their having lower profitability than Coach's traditional stores.

In a conference call with financial analysts, Coach cited the Chinese market as its "largest geographic opportunity." Coach is seeking to more than double its sales in China, with a goal of $250 million (U.S.) as of fiscal year 2012, as compared with $100 million (U.S.) in fiscal year 2010.

Coach and other retailers are hoping that the lessons learned from their Tier 1 market experiences will be applicable to Tier 2 and Tier 3 cities. These retailers further believe that as first movers into Tier 2 and Tier 3 cities, they will be able to solidify their image as innovators, secure the best retail locations, and be able to obtain sourcing agreements with the best logistics and materials suppliers. On the other hand, they will be assuming high risk to their image and profits, because they may not be as successful in these smaller market areas.

Questions

1. Evaluate Tier 2 and Tier 3 cities in contrast to Tier 1 Chinese cities from the perspectives of economic base characteristics, as well as the nature of competition and the level of saturation.
2. Discuss the pros and cons of Coach's "beachhead to a disperse location" strategy.
3. Describe the location-based advantages of being a first mover into Tier 1 and Tier 2 cites.
4. Explain the location-based disadvantages of being a first mover into Tier 1 and Tier 2 cites.

[c-4]The material in this case is drawn from Stephane Lesaffre and Amy Wang, "Multinational Retailers' Quest for Gold in China's Tier 2 and Tier 3 Cities," http://knowledge.wharton.upenn.edu (January 26, 2011).

PART 4 Comprehensive Case

The Growing Appeal of Nontraditional Retail Locations*

Introduction

Today, retailers are increasingly likely to locate their stores at sites that were typically avoided in the past. This shift is partly due to the saturation of many traditional retail locales—especially in the United States—and partly due to the interest to expand business by seeking out underutilized areas. Retailers are more apt to "push the envelope" and be more open minded about where they open new stores. Smaller stores, such as convenience stores, are especially suited to some of the sites now being developed.

While many retailers scramble for in-demand high-traffic corners, some are leveraging nontraditional locations for growth, brand positioning, and other competitive advantages. Sports stadiums, airports, dorm complexes, office buildings, and malls all have housed convenience stores, most often featuring a spin on the traditional convenience store offer.

"This is an interesting part of the industry; it's often mom-and-pops opening up a single store in a unique location or a location that is ancillary to another business, such as a restaurant operator in a business park opening a convenience location," said Mike Lawshe, president and CEO of Fort Worth, Texas-based Paragon Solutions, who has designed a number of nontraditional locations. "The traditional site selection model does not often work in many of these environments. It takes a new look at different demographics in a different setting. Nontraditional sites can be great opportunities, but sometimes big chains and others in the industry get tunnel vision."

Avoiding Tunnel Vision

Certainly Tulsa, Oklahoma-based QuikTrip (www.quiktrip.com) does not have tunnel vision—more like concourse vision. The convenience store operator acquired naming rights to the Grand Prairie AirHogs minor league baseball stadium in the Dallas market in 2008 and became a founding sponsor of the Sprint Center in Kansas City, Missouri, in late 2007, operating stores in both venues.

The naming rights and concession at the AirHog's home, now called QuikTrip Park, were meant to cement the chain's brand in a very competitive market it had operated in for about a decade, according to Jim Denny, vice-president of marketing for the 575-store chain. "This allowed us to reach a middle class demographic, but was much less expensive than partnering with Major League Baseball."

With 80 stores in the market, QuikTrip management thought that the partnership would be a good branding opportunity—and one that would reinforce the chain's positioning, which includes high-quality private-label packaged products and food-service items. The concession gives the chain an opportunity to promote its QT Kitchens sandwiches, pastries, and roller grill times—except for hot dogs, which are sold by another concessioner. The chain also sells coffee, hot chocolate, and other hot beverages; frozen drinks; Wally kid's drinks; and proprietary Rooster Booster and other packaged energy drinks. Soft drinks are sold elsewhere in the park. "That's one issue with any of these deals—if you are going to run a concession, you have to sell something no one else is selling," he noted.

Unfortunately, the early results at QuikTrip Park have been rather lackluster. "It is not doing as much for us as we would have liked, in terms of positioning our brand. It's been okay. But attendance figures are not as robust as we had hoped. When the Texas Rangers caught fire and started competing against us for fans with deals on their ticket prices, it hurt our business there," said Denny.

A much more successful venue for QuikTrip has been the Sprint Center, in Kansas City, a market the chain has operated in for more than 40 years. "Branding was not as big a strategy," Denny said. "We went into this more to promote and give exposure to QT Kitchens [food items]." See Figure 1.

The venue books a huge variety of attractions—some 90 events a year—from Sesame Street productions to Ozzie Osbourne concerts. The Sprint Center averages a million visitors per year. "We're reaching customers who would not normally stop in the stores, so it is almost like paid-for sampling because they are buying our products," the executive said. The store there is in the venue's premier location, at the main entrance that leads to escalators to go to the second level. "Everyone lands in front of our store," Denny said.

With the arena averaging 11,000 people per event, the QuikTrip store runs an average of 1,000 transactions per event. QuikTrip's longtime presence in the market has helped drive sales. The convenience store retailer has the greatest market share of any convenience-store operator in the city.

Unlike the strategy of many other retailers at indoor arenas and outdoor stadiums, the QuikTrip Sprint Center store sells products at the same retail prices found in other QuikTrip stores. "We didn't think it was fair to the customers to come in for a drink and then have it priced three times the amount they pay in our stores," Denny said, adding the decision was a key negotiating point with AEG Worldwide, which runs the Sprint Center venue.

The result: QuikTrip sells 22-ounce frozen drinks for $1 including tax, while another concessionaire is selling fountain drinks for nearly $5 each. (The retailer includes tax in the prices and rounds retail prices up or down to the nearest quarter, to keep the line moving.)

With customers coming in waves before the events and during intermissions, QuikTrip has set up the store as a self-serve location, keeping wait times to a minimum. The store is equipped with 20 frozen drink machines positioned on the outside perimeter of the 900-square-foot store. Three registers are kept open, while one or two other employees—all regular QuikTrip store associates, assistant managers, or managers—keep shelves stocked and the store clean and well maintained.

The chain pays Levy Restaurants, the arena's concessionaire, a percentage of the store's sales as it operates through

*The material in this case is adapted by the authors from Barbara Grondin Francella, "Retailers Leverage Unusual Locales," *Convenience Store News* (May 23, 2011), pp. 80–89. Reprinted by permission of *Convenience Store News*, www.csn.com.

FIGURE 1
QuikTrip at the Sprint Center
The QuikTrip store at the Sprint Center rings up an average of 1,000 transactions per event.

Source: Reprinted by permission of *Convenience Store News*, www.csn.com.

Levy's point-of-sale and cash handling system. "It's a good deal for us," Denny said. "We don't have to worry about making deposits."

For its support as a founding partner, QuikTrip is promoted through signage. The retailer has leveraged its relationship with the other founding sponsors, including Price Chopper supermarkets; United Missouri Bank, which partners with the chain on in-store ATMs; and the local MillerCoors distributor, which has worked with QuikTrip on a number of promotional events inside and outside the Sprint Center.

With a primary goal of brand positioning, food trial, and promotion, QuikTrip hoped to break even at the site. It has done that. Exit survey results revealed that QuikTrip has the highest brand recognition at the venue—higher, even, than Sprint.

In other sports venue news, such as the American Airlines Center, home of the Dallas Mavericks, 7-Eleven is selling Slurpees in 32-ounce souvenir cups. According to one review on yelp.com, the price is $7. (The chain had no comment.)

Big Store on Campus

In another high-traffic spot, 136-store Royal Farms (www.royalfarms.com), based in Baltimore, opened a store in August 2011 on the street level of a luxury student housing complex on the campus of the University of Maryland. The complex, called The Varsity, houses the first Royal Farms store to open in the area.

The 24-hour location offers takeout breakfast sandwiches, subs, wraps, and fresh brewed coffee, plus Royal Farms' signature takeout chicken, according to The Varsity's Web site (www.varsitycollegepark.com). "We thought this was a great opportunity to have a presence on a college campus," said Ed Stronski, a spokesperson for Royal Farms. The complex offers 20,000 square feet of retail space on the ground level, covered parking for retail customers and residents, and a fitness center, business center, and game room for students.

Meanwhile, a Wawa (www.wawa.com) college store in Princeton, New Jersey, has practically become an institution and made news when writer/actress Ellie Kemper, who plays a receptionist on NBC's long-running show *The Office*, blogged about "The Wa," which operates adjacent to the Princeton University campus. Kemper wrote an article entitled "Ode to Wawa" for the Princeton Paw, pledging her undying love for Wawa. "How do I put into words one of the most enduring relationships I have in this world? I'm not sure I know. How do I come to terms with the fact that whenever I come back to Princeton, it is the Wa that I am happiest to see?" she wrote. "I do appreciate Blair Arch and smile politely at my former professors, and give my friends half-hearted hugs; but it is the Wa that holds my undying adoration. The Wa was my Cheers (the bar in NBC's one-time hit comedy series). It made me feel like someone was taking care of me; even though I was no longer at home, somebody still cared enough to make sure I had a hot dog before going to bed."

Sky-High Sales

Another nontraditional venue with built-in traffic counts is an airport, where stores are either catering to employees of the airport, car rental services, and other nearby companies outside the terminal or to employees and passengers inside the terminal.

"For convenience/service centers on airport property, it is not necessarily the travelers you are attracting, it is the people who work there—hotel shuttle bus drivers, taxis, limos, and business and leisure rental car customers, as well as vendors, suppliers, and daily visitors to the complex. There could be 22,000 people working in the complex every day," noted Jim Fisher, chief executive of IMST Corporation, a Houston-based retail sales analysis firm that serves nontraditional retail organizations. "They are cities within themselves."

Airport Plazas LLC (www.airportplazas.com), the Jericho, New York-based developer and operator of convenience store and gasoline plazas at airports, has several major projects completed or in development, including Southwest Florida Airport (in Fort Meyers), JFK International Airport (in New York), Lambert-St. Louis International Airport (in Missouri), Dallas/Ft. Worth International Airport (in Texas), and Nashville International Airport (in Tennessee). These sites typically include a convenience store, light auto repair, car wash, and restaurant. The Airport Plaza store at Newark Liberty International that opened in 2010 features a gasoline and compressed natural gas station, 7-Eleven, auto repair, towing, and a two-bay car wash.

According to Airport Plazas' President and CEO George Abi Zeid, dealing with airports has its own challenges and rewards: "It's a long and tedious process, but at the end of the day you know you will get the approval for a mutually beneficial project. In addition to bringing income to the airport, these stores are a great convenience to the employees and customers. It's a beautiful captive market for us."

Airport Plazas LLC funded the Newark Project with its own capital and resources. The company has a funding commitment for the pending and future airport plazas. In each case, 20 percent of a project's capital will be provided by Airport Plazas, with the balance provided by the investors. The company will own and operate all plaza services except the food court and quick-serve restaurants, Abi Zeid said. The 7-Eleven at Newark airport is subleased, but future convenience stores will be operated by Airport Plazas itself.

Despite the challenges of operating on airport grounds, most of Airport Plazas' sites are "amazing locations" at the main entrance of the airport, Abi Zeid said. The 7-Eleven convenience store at Newark Liberty is reporting double the chain's national average in food sales.

Operating inside an airport brings another slew of challenges. The Camden Food Co. (www.camdenfoodco.com), which focuses on healthy food choices in a quick-serve setting, is a recent English import, now found inside airports in Indianapolis, Raleigh-Durham, and Vancouver. Expansion plans will also put Camden Food Co. sites in airport terminals in Houston, Milwaukee, Sacramento, Toronto, and New York (JFK). The chain's food offerings include sandwiches, salads, fruit, packaged snacks, and beverages that are fat-free, gluten-free, organic, and/or kosher.

"For us, operating in an airport does present a set of challenges," said Darleen Nascimento, a spokesperson for SSP America, the Landsdowne, Virginia-based division of SSP, which develops food concepts in travel locations worldwide. "We are highly impacted by what happens with the TSA (Transportation Security Administration) and the airlines themselves. We have a captive audience, which is the good news—that reduces the amount of competition compared to street-side stores. On the downside, the customers are limited to the number of people inside the terminal and that fluctuates up or down and is impacted by so many things—weather, the number of flights, how flights are scheduled, flight delays, cancellations, even things like the volcanic ash across the ocean."

Knowing how much food to prepare at what time can be difficult. Customers often do not follow their normal day-part eating patterns and Camden Food's policy is to stay open no matter what happens with flights. The chain also faces airport-related expenses, such as the fee it pays to get its product from its delivery spot at the airport to the actual site inside the terminal. "You need to consider the time it takes to do that, also," Nascimento added.

Because its locations are post-security points, hiring can be challenging too. "Think about how much you look forward to going to the airport, parking, getting a tram to the terminal, going through security—not every potential employee wants to deal with that every day," Nascimento said. Employees also face detailed security screenings for ID badges that allow them to go through security checks more quickly. "That process can cause hiring delays and plays into the recruiting process as well," she noted.

Still, she said, the process pays off. "Pre-security locations usually aren't as profitable as post-security locations, because travelers want to get through security before they relax and know they have time to think about food."

The Camden Food Co. concept especially appeals to traveling women and families, who are interested in something more nutritious than standard packaged snacks and fast food, she said. The chain is starting to incorporate more local fare, partnering with farmers and artisans within 100 miles of each airport. "Healthier fare is not commonplace in the airport, so we want to be a benchmark with what is happening street-side in terms of greener locations," Nascimento said. Cups are made of corn syrup to be biodegradable, for example.

Still, operating inside a retail store at an airport means making a huge capital investment in locations that are often built into older buildings, taking a certain amount of risk. "Some people don't understand the upfront investment, the process of getting governmental agency approval, and all of the extra fees," Nascimento said. See Figure 2.

Creating a Destination

Other operators of nontraditional locations don't have built-in foot traffic—they create it. The Nambe Falls Travel Center, built on Nambe Pueblo tribal land, is 15 minutes north of

FIGURE 2

Camden Food at the Airport

The Camden Food Co. positions itself as a healthy alternative for packaged snacks, beverages, and fast food in an airport terminal setting.

Source: Reprinted by permission of *Convenience Store News*, www.csn.com.

Santa Fe, New Mexico, off U.S. 84. The site, which sells Alta-branded E10 and E85 gasoline and B5 and B20 Blue Sun biodiesel, was the first retail business of the Nambe Pueblo Development Corp.

"Native American convenience stores are often built on remote locations and have to become destinations in their own right, being built in conjunction with other activities, such as a hotel, a casino, or further retail development," said IMST's Jim Fisher, whose firm has advised on more than 130 projects with Native American tribes.

The 6,100-square-foot Nambe Falls Travel Center houses a convenience store, Arby's, and Java City coffee bar that features a stacked-stone fireplace, free wireless Internet, and flat screen television. The store also has a postal station; beer, wine, and liquor section; discounted tobacco shop; and two drive-through windows. Open since 2008, the travel center saw first-year sales of just under $10 million, with 40 to 50 percent of that attributed to motor fuels.

"Our goal was to make the store memorable and give it multiple profit centers so that the travelers and the short-haul truckers who are going down the road would drive six-tenths of a mile around the loop when there are other convenience stores closer to the exit," said Matt Doyle of Development Services Group of Albuquerque. "We spent a lot of time making sure that we had warm colors and great concepts." Two of the advantages of developing tribal stores: Tribal land can be used as equity to gain financing, and because the tribe does not pay excise taxes, it is easier to price competitively with chain stores that are nearby.

Still, it can be a challenge to move a tribe's governing body to make timely decisions, Doyle said. "Our goal is to make them move quickly and understand the opportunity cost. They don't always understand the revenues they could be making on the land while it sits empty for a year."

Questions

1. What can *any* retailer learn from this case?
2. How would you determine the trading area for QuikTrip Park at the Grand Prairie AirHogs minor league baseball field?
3. Is QuikTrip Park a destination retailer or a parasite? Does your answer differ for its more traditional locations? Explain your answer.
4. Is The Varsity at the University of Maryland a destination store or a parasite? Explain your answer.
5. Should the retailers at airports care about the concept of balanced tenancy? Why?
6. Based on what criteria could Camden Food Co. determine if an airport was a one-hundred percent location for one of its stores?
7. What terms of occupancy are especially important for retailers locating at nontraditional sites?

PART 5

Managing a Retail Business

In Part Five, the elements of managing a retail enterprise are discussed. We first look at the steps in setting up a retail organization and the special human resource management environment of retailing. Operations management is then examined—from both financial and operational perspectives.

Chapter 11 reports how a retailer can use its organizational structure to assign tasks, policies, resources, authority, responsibilities, and rewards to satisfy the needs of the target market, employees, and management. We also show how human resource management can be applied so that the structure works properly. Human resource management consists of recruiting, selecting, training, compensating, and supervising personnel.

Chapter 12 focuses on the financial dimensions of operations management in enacting a retail strategy. We discuss these topics: profit planning, asset management (including the strategic profit model, other key ratios, and financial trends in retailing), budgeting, and resource allocation.

Chapter 13 presents the operational aspects of operations management. We cover these specific concepts: operations blueprint; store format, size, and space allocation; personnel utilization; store maintenance, energy management, and renovations; inventory management; store security; insurance; credit management; computerization; and crisis management.

Source: iofoto/Shutterstock.com. Reprinted by permission.

11 Retail Organization and Human Resource Management

Chapter Objectives

1. To study the procedures involved in setting up a retail organization

2. To examine the various organizational arrangements utilized in retailing

3. To consider the special human resource environment of retailing

4. To describe the principles and practices involved with the human resource management process in retailing

Superior human resource management in retailing not only requires that a firm hire and train good employees, but also keep them motivated. With the high employee turnover rate in retailing, this is not an easy task. Now, social media are emerging as a creative way to assist retailers in their human resource management. Let's see how.

PeopleMatter (www.peoplematter.com) is a new firm that has developed what it calls hire-to-retire software-as-a-service (SaaS) that is geared toward restaurants, hospitality firms, and other retailers. As Nate DaPore, PeopleMatter's president and CEO, puts it: "We want to really change the way the employer and the employee interact in the workplace. We use culture as a catalyst to build a company's brand. The system focuses on identifying those traits, developing them, engaging them, and helping build the company's brand, which leads to higher profits, sales, and viral marketing of that brand." DaPore adds that his software "allows the CEO to have a distribution channel to communicate with employees and also to provide structure and metrics around that brand-building and culture."

The PeopleMatter Rewards program is an innovative system to engage employees by using social media. This is how PeopleMatter describes the program at its Web site:

> Customers reward employees when they provide good service. Are you [the employer] following suit? You can't always count on a tip or high-five to boost workers' morale. A good manager knows the importance of employee recognition and rewards for quality customer service. We make online employee rewards simple to set up and easy to manage. We also make rewards social. Engage your connected work force with rewards that integrate recognition and feedback into social medias. Broadcast your brand to thousands, motivate people with the social tools they use every day, and tout your excellent service to the Web.[1]

Source: BeTA-Artworks/ fotolia.com.

Overview

Managing a retail business comprises three steps: setting up an organization structure, hiring and managing personnel, and managing operations—financially and nonfinancially. In this chapter, the first two steps are covered. Chapters 12 and 13 deal with operations management.

SETTING UP A RETAIL ORGANIZATION

Through a **retail organization,** a firm structures and assigns tasks (functions), policies, resources, authority, responsibilities, and rewards to efficiently and effectively satisfy the needs of its target market, employees, and management. Figure 11-1 shows various needs that should be taken into account when planning and assessing an organization's structure.

As a rule, a firm cannot survive unless its organization's structure satisfies the target market, regardless of how well employee and management needs are met. A structure that reduces costs through centralized buying but that results in a firm's being insensitive to geographic differences in customer preferences would be improper. Although many retailers perform similar tasks or functions (buying, pricing, displaying, and wrapping merchandise), there are many ways of organizing to carry out these functions. The process of setting up a retail organization, outlined in

FIGURE 11-1
Selected Factors That Must Be Considered in Planning and Assessing a Retail Organization

TARGET MARKET NEEDS

Are there sufficient personnel to provide appropriate customer service?
Are personnel knowledgeable and courteous?
Are store facilities well maintained?
Are the specific needs of branch store customers met?
Are changing needs promptly addressed?

EMPLOYEE NEEDS

Are positions challenging and satisfying enough?
Is there an orderly promotion program from within?
Is the employee able to participate in the decision making?
Are the channels of communication clear and open?
Is the authority-responsibility relationship clear?
Is each employee treated fairly?
Is good performance rewarded?

MANAGEMENT NEEDS

Is it relatively easy to obtain and retain competent personnel?
Are personnel procedures clearly defined?
Does each worker report to only one supervisor?
Can each manager properly supervise all of the workers reporting to him or her?
Do operating departments have adequate staff support (e.g., marketing research)?
Are the levels of organization properly developed?
Are the organization's plans well integrated?
Are employees motivated?
Is absenteeism low?
Is there a system to replace personnel in an orderly manner?
Is there enough flexibility to adapt to changes in customers or the environment?

FIGURE 11-2
The Process of Organizing a Retail Firm

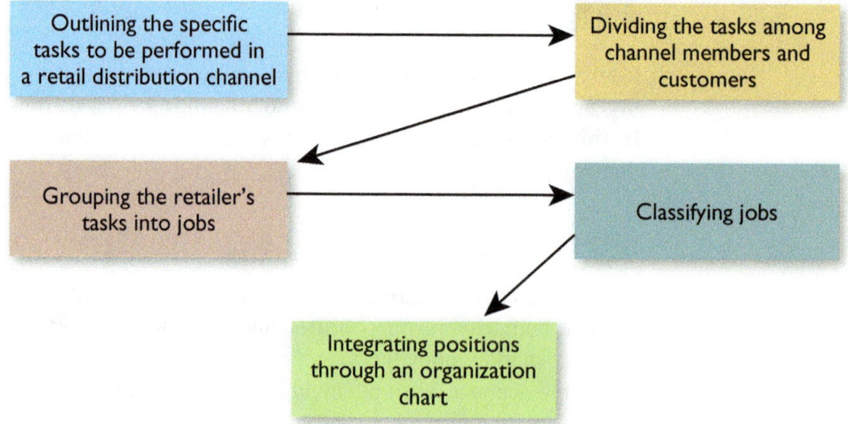

Figure 11-2, is described next. Visit our Web site (www.pearsonhighered.com/bermanevans) for several links on running a retail business.

Specifying Tasks to Be Performed

The tasks in a distribution channel must be enumerated, and then keyed to the chosen strategy mix, for effective retailing to occur:

- Buying merchandise on behalf of the retailer.
- Shipping merchandise to the retailer.
- Receiving merchandise and checking incoming shipments.
- Setting prices.
- Marking merchandise.
- Inventory storage and control.
- Preparing merchandise and window displays.
- Facilities maintenance (e.g., keeping the store clean).
- Customer research and exchanging information.
- Customer contact (e.g., advertising, personal selling).
- Facilitating shopping (e.g., convenient site, short checkout lines).
- Customer follow-up and complaint handling.
- Personnel management.
- Repairs and alteration of merchandise.
- Billing customers.
- Handling receipts and financial records.
- Credit operations.
- Gift wrapping.
- Delivery to customers.
- Returning unsold or damaged merchandise to vendors.
- Sales forecasting and budgeting.
- Coordination.

Dividing Tasks Among Channel Members and Customers

Sysco is a wholesaler serving 400,000 restaurants, hotels, schools, and other locales. It offers them a wide range of support services (www.sysco.com/customer-solutions.html).

Although the preceding tasks are typically performed in a distribution channel, they do not all have to be done by a retailer. Some can be completed by the manufacturer, wholesaler, specialist, or consumer. Figure 11-3 shows the types of activities that could be carried out by each party. Following are some criteria to consider in allocating the functions related to consumer credit.

A task should be carried out only if desired by the target market. For some retailers, liberal credit policies may provide significant advantages over competitors. For others, a cash-only policy may reduce their overhead and lead to lower prices.

A task should be done by the party with the best competence. Credit collection may require a legal staff and detailed digitized records—most affordable by medium or large retailers.

FIGURE 11-3
The Division of Tasks in a Distribution Channel

Performer	Tasks
Retailer	Can perform all or some of the tasks in the distribution channel, from buying merchandise to coordination.
Manufacturer or Wholesaler	Can take care of few or many functions, such as shipping, marking merchandise, inventory storage, displays, research, etc.
Specialist(s)	Can undertake a particular task: buying office, delivery firm, warehouse, marketing research firm, ad agency, accountant, credit bureau, computer service firm.
Consumer	Can be responsible for delivery, credit (cash purchases), sales effort (self-service), product alterations (do-it-yourselfers), etc.

Smaller retailers are likely to rely on bank credit cards. There is a loss of control when an activity is delegated to another party. A credit collection agency, pressing for past-due payments, may antagonize customers.

The retailer's institutional framework can have an impact on task allocation. Franchisees are readily able to get together to have their own private-label brands. Independents cannot do this as easily.

Task allocation depends on the savings gained by sharing or shifting tasks. The credit function is better performed by an outside credit bureau if it has expert personnel and ongoing access to financial data, uses tailored computer software, pays lower rent (due to an out-of-the-way site), and so on. Many retailers cannot attain these savings themselves.

This site (http://retailindustry.about.com/od/retailjobscareers) highlights the range of jobs available in retailing.

Grouping Tasks into Jobs

After the retailer decides which tasks to perform, they are grouped into jobs. The jobs must be clearly structured. Here are examples of grouping tasks into jobs:

Tasks	Jobs
Displaying merchandise, customer contact, gift wrapping, customer follow-up	Sales personnel
Entering transaction data, handling cash and credit purchases, gift wrapping	Cashier(s)
Receiving merchandise, checking incoming shipments, marking merchandise, inventory storage and control, returning merchandise to vendors	Inventory personnel
Window dressing, interior display setups, use of mobile displays	Display personnel
Billing customers, credit operations, customer research	Credit personnel
Merchandise repairs and alterations, resolution of complaints, customer research	Customer service personnel
Cleaning store, replacing old fixtures	Janitorial personnel
Employee management, sales forecasting, budgeting, pricing, coordinating tasks	Management personnel

Devising a Diversity Plan

During the previous 25 years, diversity planning for retailers focused largely on understanding and appreciating race, gender, and ethnic differences that exist among retail workers. Recently, diversity planning issues have also focused on age, sexual orientation, and nationality-related issues, as well. Effective diversity planning needs to take into account that although retail employees may be very similar in age, they may be very different in terms of nationality or gender.

There are significant benefits to having a diverse work force with people who can work well together. The availability schedules of different age groups may complement each other. Some Hispanic consumers also tend to favor retail salespersons with whom they can communicate in Spanish and who better understand their culture. Diverse retail personnel can be more effective in planning assortments for the variety of ethnic-based holidays during the year. And there may be less conflict due to retail personnel better understanding and appreciating differences among fellow employees.

In developing a diversity plan, retail executives need to

- define what is meant by diversity and diversity management.
- incorporate diversity management into their firms' mission and strategy.
- determine the type of diversity issues to address within the retail organization.
- develop a transition- and implementation-based diversity plan.
- audit the company culture from a diversity perspective.

Source: R. Roosevelt Thomas Jr. "Developing and Implementing a Diversity Plan," www.franchise.org/Franchise-Industry-Fran-World.aspx (June 2011).

While grouping tasks into jobs, specialization should be considered so each employee is responsible for a limited range of functions (as opposed to performing many diverse tasks). Specialization has the advantages of clearly defined tasks, greater expertise, reduced training, and hiring people with narrow education and experience. Problems can result due to extreme specialization: poor morale (boredom), people not being aware of their jobs' importance, and the need for more employees. Specialization means assigning explicit duties to individuals so a job position encompasses a homogeneous cluster of tasks.

Once tasks are grouped, job descriptions are constructed. These outline the job titles, objectives, duties, and responsibilities for every position. They are used as a hiring, supervision, and evaluation tool. Figure 11-4 contains a job description for a store manager.

Classifying Jobs

Jobs are then broadly grouped into functional, product, geographic, or combination classifications. *Functional classification* divides jobs by task—such as sales promotion, buying, and store operations. Expert knowledge is utilized. *Product classification* divides jobs on a goods or service basis. A department store hires different personnel for clothing, furniture, appliances, and so forth. This classification recognizes the differences in personnel requirements for different products.

Geographic classification is useful for chains operating in different areas. Employees are adapted to local conditions, and they are supervised by branch managers. Some firms, especially larger ones, use a *combination classification.* If a branch unit of a chain hires its selling staff, but buying personnel for each product line are hired by headquarters, the functional, product, and geographic formats are combined.

Developing an Organization Chart

The format of a retail organization must be designed in an integrated, coordinated way. Jobs must be defined and distinct; yet, interrelationships among positions must be clear. As one human resources software consultancy recently noted:

> Productivity and profitability depend on making sure all workers perform to their potential. The need to effectively leverage the skills of employees is even more critical for small and mid-sized firms since most cannot compete with large companies in technology, infrastructure, or financial resources. Small to mid-sized businesses must be smarter, more productive, and more cohesive. Studies show an increase in worker and business performance when a company sets and closely ties individual employee goals to its strategy. Yet, only seven percent of employees fully understand their company's strategies and what's expected of them to help achieve company goals.[2]

FIGURE 11-4
A Job Description for a Store Manager

JOB TITLE: Store Manager for 34th Street Branch of Pombo's Department Stores

POSITION REPORTS TO: Senior Vice-President

POSITIONS REPORTING TO STORE MANAGER: All personnel in the 34th Street store

OBJECTIVES: To properly staff and operate the 34th Street store

DUTIES AND RESPONSIBILITIES:
- Sales forecasting and budgeting
- Personnel recruitment, selection, training, motivation, and evaluation
- Merchandise display, inventory management, and merchandise reorders
- Transferring merchandise among stores
- Handling store receipts, preparing bank transactions, opening and closing store
- Reviewing customer complaints
- Reviewing computer data forms
- Semi-annual review of overall operations and reports for top management

COMMITTEES AND MEETINGS:
- Attendance at monthly meetings with Senior Vice-President
- Supervision of weekly meetings with department managers

The **hierarchy of authority** outlines the job interactions within a company by describing the reporting relationships among employees (from the lowest level to the highest level). Coordination and control are provided by this hierarchy. A firm with many workers reporting to one manager has a *flat organization.* Its benefits are good communication, quicker handling of problems, and better employee identification with a job. The major problem tends to be the number of people reporting to one manager. A *tall organization* has several management levels, resulting in close supervision and fewer workers reporting to each manager. Problems include a long channel of communication, the impersonal impression given to workers regarding access to upper-level personnel, and inflexible rules.

With these factors in mind, a retailer devises an **organization chart**, which graphically displays its hierarchical relationships. Table 11-1 lists the principles to consider in establishing an organization chart. Figure 11-5 shows examples of basic organization charts.

ORGANIZATIONAL PATTERNS IN RETAILING

An independent retailer has a simple organization. It operates only one store, the owner-manager usually supervises all employees, and workers have access to the owner-manager if there are problems. In contrast, a chain must specify how tasks are delegated, coordinate

TABLE 11-1 Principles for Organizing a Retail Firm

An organization should show interest in its employees. This can be accomplished through job rotation, promotion from within, participatory management, recognition, job enrichment, and so forth.

Employee turnover, lateness, and absenteeism should be monitored, because they may indicate personnel problems.

The line of authority should be traceable from the highest to the lowest positions. In this way, employees know to whom they report and who reports to them (*chain of command*).

A subordinate should only report to one direct supervisor (*unity of command*). This avoids the problem of workers receiving conflicting orders.

There is a limit to the number of employees a manager can directly supervise (*span of control*).

A person responsible for a given objective needs the power to achieve it.

Although a supervisor can delegate authority, he or she is still responsible for subordinates.

The greater the number of organizational levels, the longer the time for communication to travel and the greater the coordination problems.

An organization has an informal structure aside from the formal organization chart. Informal relationships exercise power in the organization and may bypass formal relationships and procedures.

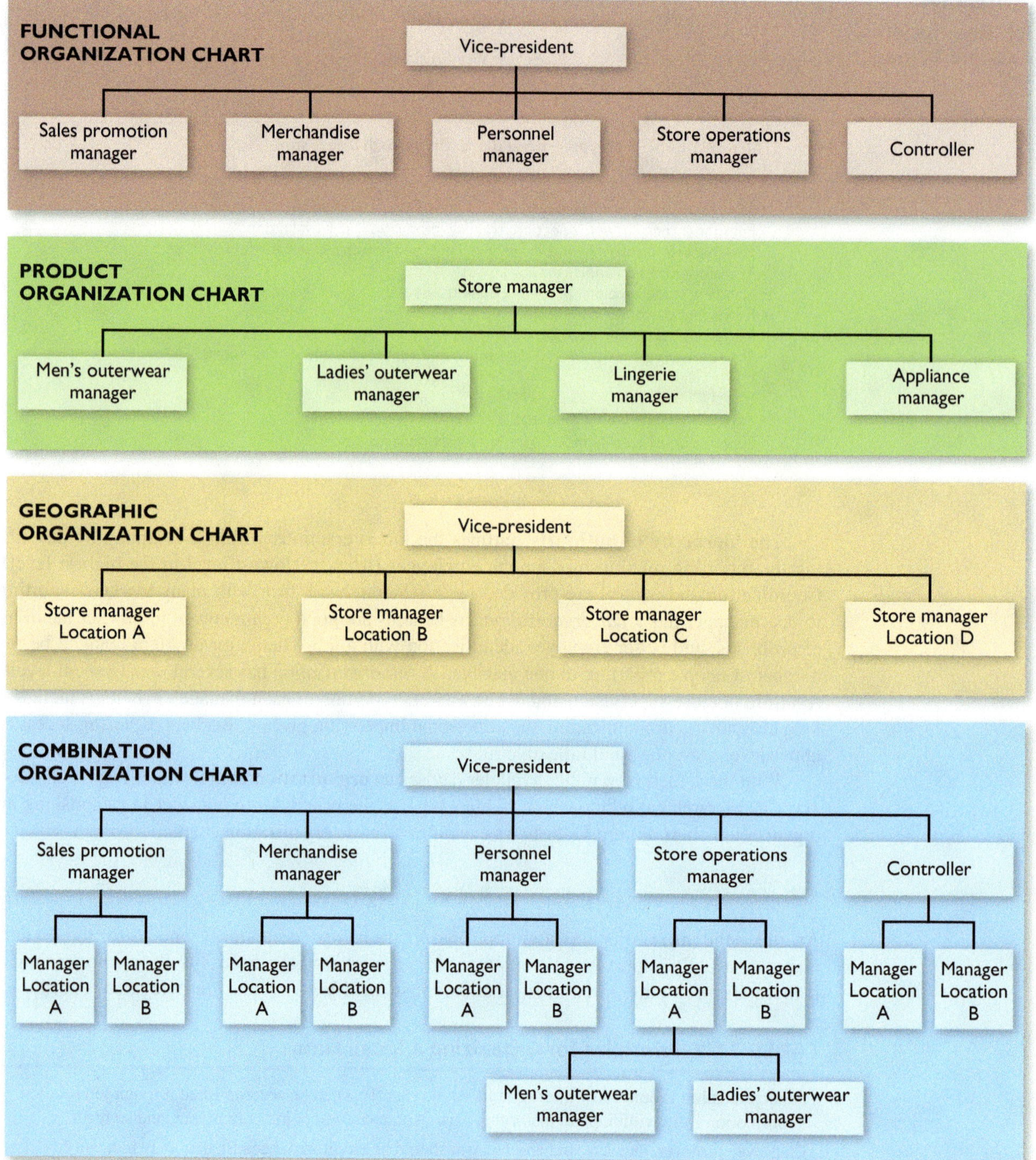

FIGURE 11-5
Different Forms of Retail Organization

multiple stores, and set common policies for employees. As examples, the organizational arrangements used by independent retailers, department stores, chain retailers, and diversified retailers are discussed next.

Organizational Arrangements Used by Small Independent Retailers

Small independents use uncomplicated arrangements with only two or three levels of personnel (owner-manager and employees), and the owner-manager personally runs the firm and oversees workers. There are few employees, little specialization, and no branch units. This does not mean

FIGURE 11-6
Organization Structures Used by Small Independents

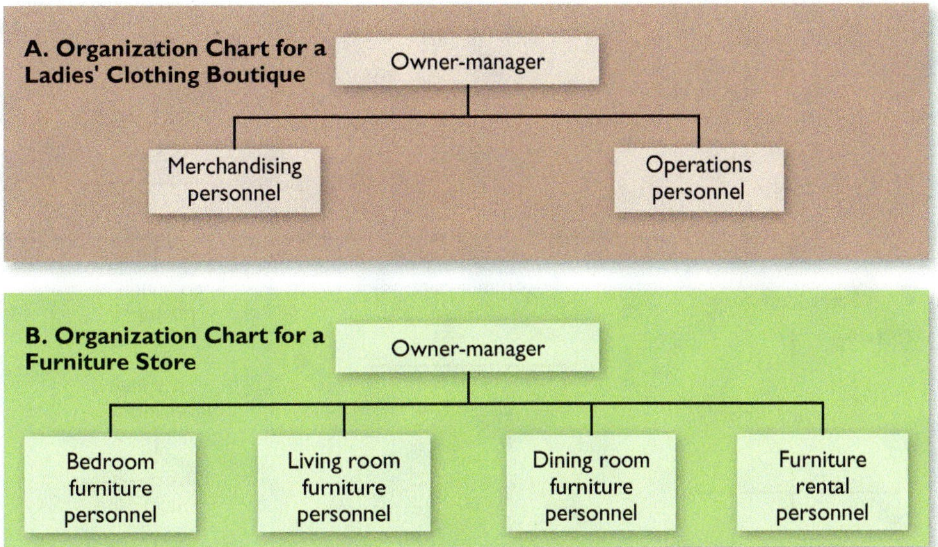

fewer activities must be performed but that many tasks are performed relative to the number of workers. Each employee must allot part of his or her time to several duties.

Figure 11-6 shows the organizations of two small firms. In A, a boutique is organized by function. Merchandising personnel buy and sell goods and services, plan assortments, set up displays, and prepare ads. Operations personnel are involved with store maintenance and operations. In B, a furniture store is organized on a product-oriented basis, with personnel in each category responsible for selected activities. All products get proper attention, and some expertise is developed. This is important because different skills are necessary to buy and sell each type of furniture.

Organizational Arrangements Used by Department Stores

Many department stores continue to use an organizational arrangement that is an adaptation of the **Mazur plan**, which divides all retail activities into four functional areas.[3] In twenty-first century terms, these are merchandising, communications, store management, and financial accounting:

1. *Merchandising*—buying, selling, stock planning and forecasting, and product-position (image-related) planning with regard to the mix of goods and services offered by the retailer.
2. *Communications*—public relations, advertising, window and interior displays, promotions, and online efforts.
3. *Store management*—operations management, inventory management, human resources, "backroom" activities, and store maintenance.
4. *Financial accounting (overseen by the controller)*—maintaining, monitoring, assessing the retailer's financial performance, including accounting, inventory control, credit and collections, and auditing.

These areas are organized into *line* (direct authority and responsibility) and *staff* (advisory and support) components. Thus, a controller and a communications manager often staff services to merchandisers; but within their disciplines, personnel are organized on a line basis. Figure 11-7 shows the modern version of the Mazur plan.

The merchandising division is responsible for buying and selling. It is headed by a merchandising manager, who is often viewed as the most important area executive. He or she supervises buyers, devises financial goals for each department, coordinates merchandise plans (so there is a consistent image among departments), and interprets the effects of economic data. In some cases, divisional merchandise managers are utilized, so the number of buyers reporting to a single manager does not become unwieldy.

In the basic Mazur plan, the buyer has complete accountability for expenses and profit goals within a department. Duties include preparing preliminary budgets, studying trends, negotiating

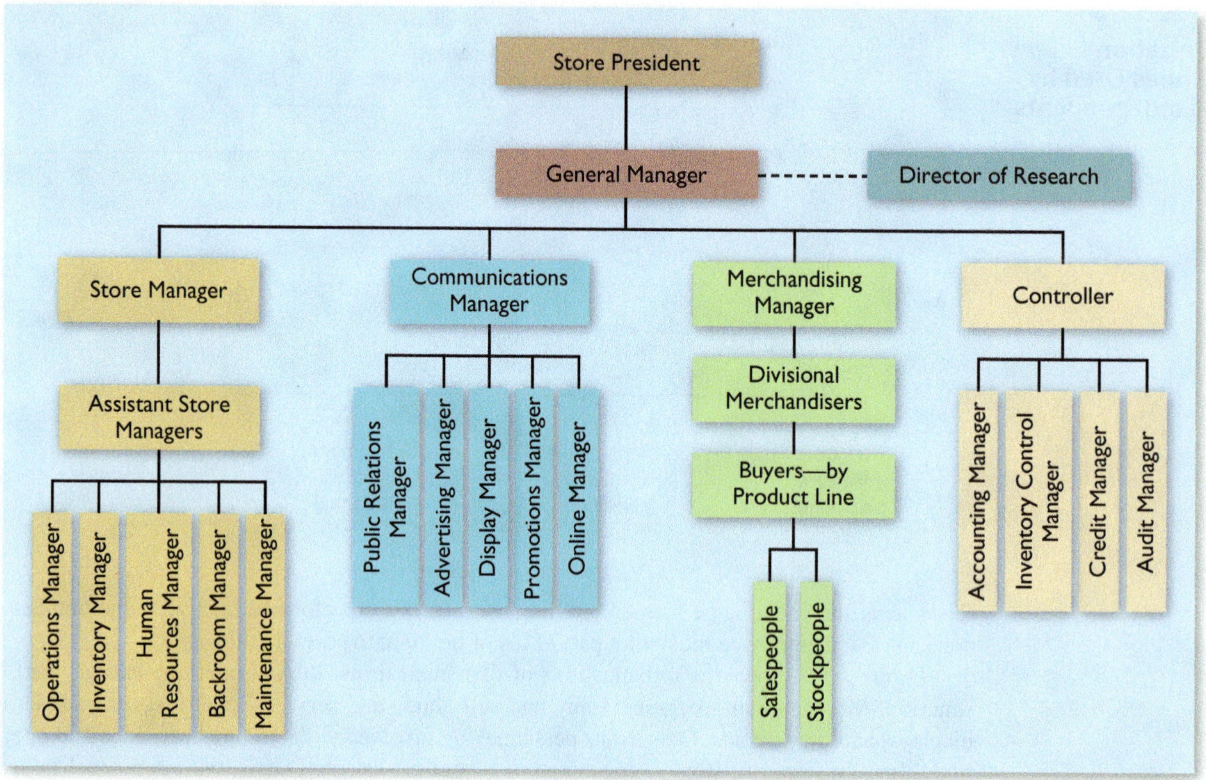

FIGURE 11-7

A Modern Version of the Basic Mazur Organizational Plan for Department Stores

Source: Adapted and updated by the authors from Paul Mazur, *Principles of Organization Applied to Modern Retailing* (NY: Harper & Brothers, 1927).

with vendors over price, planning the number of salespeople, and informing sales personnel about the merchandise purchased. Grouping buying and selling activities into one job (buyer) may present a problem. Because buyers are not constantly on the selling floor, training, scheduling, and supervising personnel may suffer.

The growth of branch stores led to three Mazur plan derivatives: *main store control*, by which headquarters executives oversee and operate branches; *separate store organization*, by which each branch has its own buying responsibilities; and **equal store organization,** by which buying is centralized and branches become sales units with equal operational status. The latter is the most popular format.

In the main store control format, most authority remains at headquarters. Merchandise planning and buying, advertising, financial controls, store hours, and other tasks are centrally managed to standardize the performance. Branch store managers hire and supervise employees, but daily operations conform to company policies. This works well if there are few branches and the preferences of their customers are similar to those at the main store. As branch stores increase, buyers, the advertising manager, and others may be overworked and give little attention to branches. Because headquarters personnel are not at the branches, differences in customer preferences may be overlooked.

The separate store format places merchandise managers in branch stores, which have autonomy for merchandising and operations. Customer needs are quickly noted, but duplication of tasks is possible. Coordination can also be a problem. Transferring goods between branches is more complex and costly. This format is best if stores are large, branches are dispersed, or local customer tastes vary widely.

In the equal store format, the benefits of both centralization and decentralization are sought. Buying—forecasting, planning, purchasing, pricing, distribution to branches, and promotion—is centralized. Selling—presenting merchandise, selling, customer services, and operations—is managed locally. All stores, including headquarters, are treated alike. Buyers are freed from managing so many workers. Data gathering is critical since buyers have less customer contact.

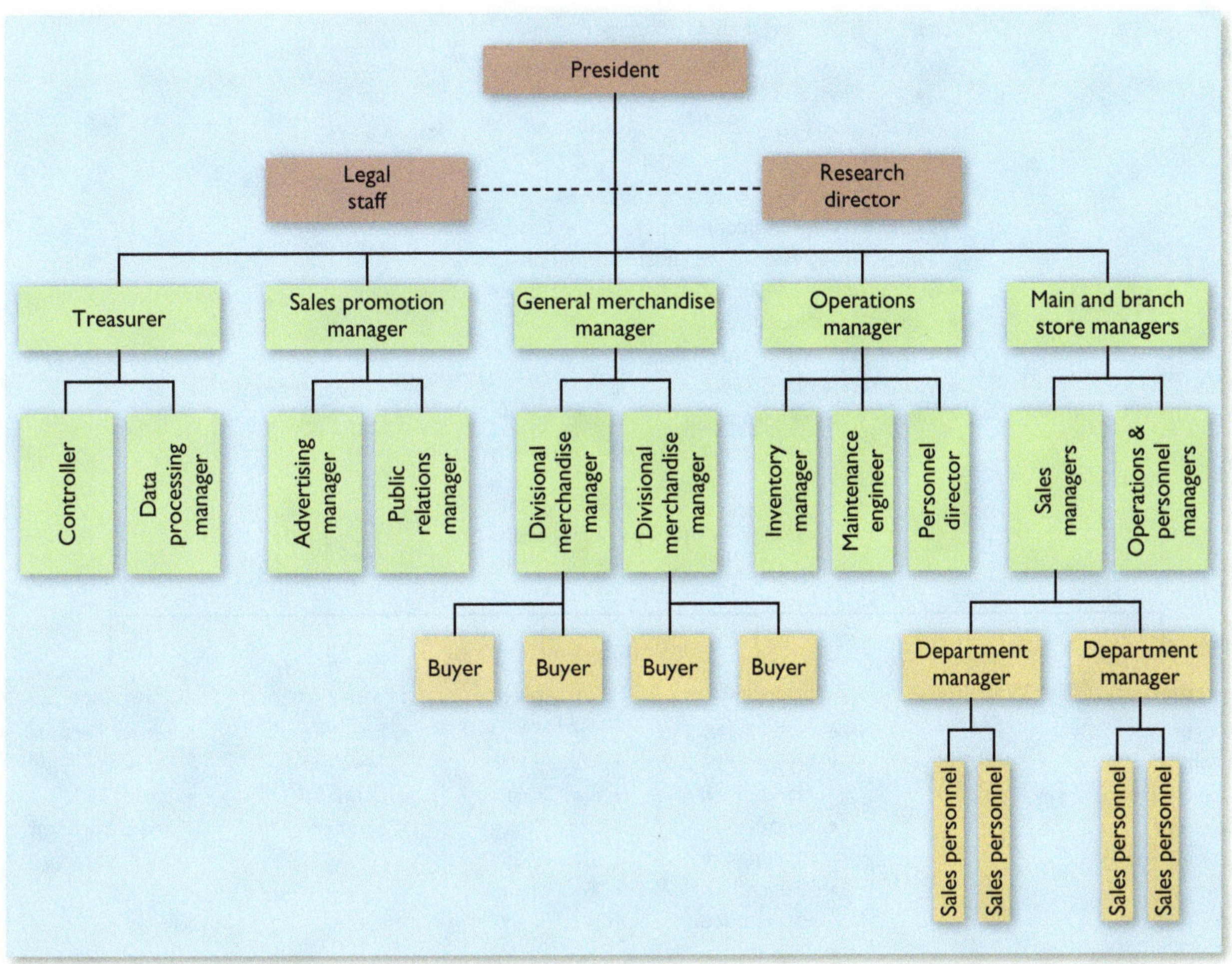

FIGURE 11-8
The Equal Store Organizational Format Used by Many Chain Stores

Organizational Arrangements Used by Chain Retailers

Various chain retailers use a version of the equal store organization, as depicted in Figure 11-8. Although chains' organizations may differ, they generally have these attributes:

- There are many functional divisions, such as sales promotion, merchandise management, distribution, operations, real-estate, personnel, and information systems.
- Overall authority is centralized. Store managers have selling responsibility.
- Many operations are standardized (fixtures, store layout, building design, merchandise lines, credit policy, and store service).
- An elaborate control system keeps management informed.
- Some decentralization lets branches adapt to localities and increases store manager responsibilities. Although large chains standardize most of the items their outlets carry, store managers often fine-tune the rest of the strategy mix for the local market. This is empowerment at the store manager level.

Organizational Arrangements Used by Diversified Retailers

A **diversified retailer** is a multi-line firm operating under central ownership. Like other chains, a diversified retailer operates multiple stores; unlike typical chains, a diversified firm is involved with different types of retail operations. Here are two examples:

To discover more about Kroger, go to this section of its Web site (www.thekrogerco.com/operations/operations.htm).

- Kroger Co. (www.kroger.com) operates supermarkets, warehouse stores, supercenters, convenience stores, jewelry stores, and service businesses; it also has a manufacturing group. The firm owns multiple store chains in each of its retail categories. See Figure 11-9.

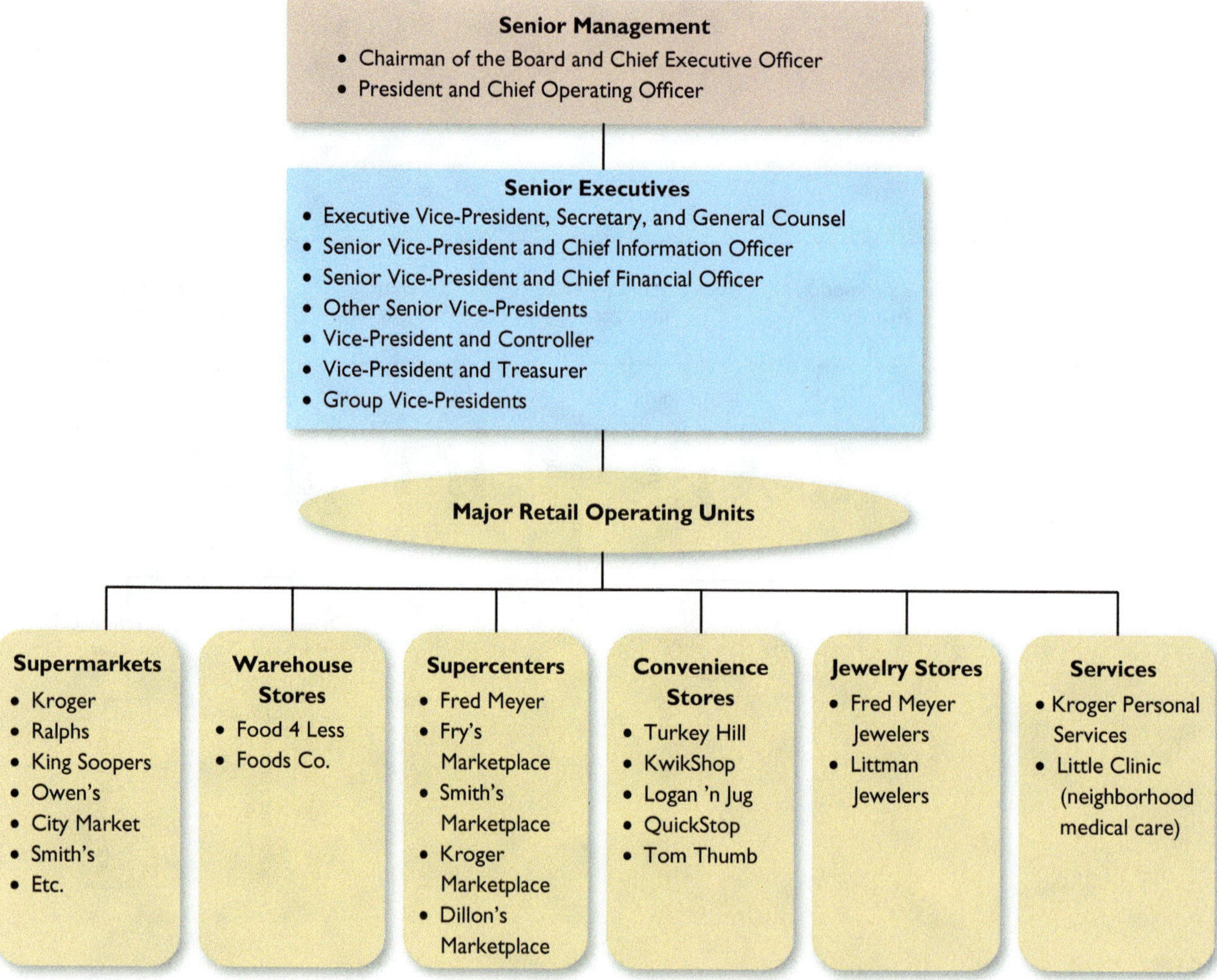

FIGURE 11-9

The Organizational Structure of Kroger Co. (Selected Store Chains and Positions)

Source: Compiled by the authors from the *Kroger Co. 2011 Annual Report.*

- Japan's Aeon Co. (www.aeon.info/en) comprises superstores, supermarkets, discount stores, home centers, specialty stores, convenience stores, financial services stores, restaurants, and more. Besides Japan, Aeon has facilities in numerous other countries. It is also a shopping center developer.

Due to their multiple strategy mixes, diversified retailers face complex organizational considerations. Interdivision control is needed, with operating procedures and goals clearly communicated. Interdivision competition must be coordinated. Resources must be divided among different divisions. Potential image and advertising conflicts must be avoided. Management skills must adapt to different operations.

HUMAN RESOURCE MANAGEMENT IN RETAILING

Human resource management involves recruiting, selecting, training, compensating, and supervising personnel in a manner consistent with the retailer's organization structure and strategy mix. Personnel practices are dependent on the line of business, number of employees, location of outlets, and other factors. Because good personnel are needed to develop and carry out retail strategies, and labor costs can amount to 50 percent or more of expenses, the value of human resource management is clear.

TABLE 11-2 The True Cost of Employee Turnover

Costs of using fill-in employees until permanent replacements are found.

Severance pay for exiting employees.

Costs of hiring new employees: advertising, interviewing time, travel expenses, testing, screening.

Training costs: trainers, training materials and technology, trainee compensation, supervisor time (on-the-job training).

Costs of mistakes and lower productivity while new employees gain experience.

Customer dissatisfaction due to the departure of previous employees and the use of inexperienced workers.

Loss of continuity among co-workers.

Poor employee morale when turnover is high.

Lower employee loyalty to retailer when turnover is high.

U.S. retailing employs 25 million people. Thus, there is a constant need to attract new employees—and retain existing ones. For example, as many as 2 million fast-food workers are aged 16 to 20, and they stay in their jobs for only short periods. In general, retailers need to reduce the turnover rate; when workers quickly exit a firm, the results can be disastrous. See Table 11-2.

Consider the approaches of Target, Uno Chicago Grill, Nordstrom, and Whole Foods:

- Target is committed to employee development and retention: "Goals are clear, challenging, and met through teamwork. In our stores, guests find a clean, organized, welcoming atmosphere, and smart, stylish merchandise. Creating this shopping experience for guests begins with creating a great workplace for team members. Every team member—from stores to distribution centers to corporate offices—is empowered and encouraged to innovate, contribute ideas, and discover solutions. People at Target are respected and recognized for their work and know they are a unique and important part of a world-class team." With regard to employee diversity, Target says: "We know that an inclusive environment, where all contributions are valued, is critical to ensuring future success."[4]
- Uno Chicago Grill regularly recruits college graduates for its management training program: "If you're ready to move ahead with a dynamic national chain, team up with Uno today. Each restaurant has a team made up of a general manager, assistant general manager, and 1 to 3 managers. In building this team, Uno works hard to offer the right mix to meet career aspirations, training opportunities, work/family considerations, and pay and benefits expectations."[5]

Uno Chicago Grill (http://unos.com/mgmtJobs.php) has a clear employee development plan.

Employee Turnover Facing International Hotels

A study of the reasons for employee turnover at Taiwanese hotels classified the causes into three categories: internal contentment, external contentment, and organization proffer. Internal contentment relates to the mentoring process for career enhancement, emotional exhaustion, and co-worker trust. External contentment includes such variables as the wage rate, the length of working time, fringe benefits, and the existence of a training program. Organization proffer relates to career advancement opportunities and the commitment to the organization, career, and job.

This research involved two stages. In the first stage, nine human resource managers of international hotels were designated as subject matter experts (SMEs). Each SME had at least 10 years of experience in the international hotel sector. They were asked to establish criteria to predict employee turnover. The second stage involved determining the weights (importance) for each criterion in the model. These weights were used to predict the highest turnover-risk hotels.

The SMEs predicted the turnover risk for new employees at international hotels based on the following weightings: internal contentment (0.343), external contentment (0.333), and organizational proffer (0.323). The differences among these criteria weights are small. These weights can also change with major shifts in the environment, such as increased economic uncertainty.

Source: Huang-Wei Su, Li-Tze Lee, and Chiang-Ku Fan, "Turnover Determinants of New Employees in International Hotels," *Journal of Service Science and Management*, Vol. 4 (June 2011), pp. 158–164.

- At Nordstrom, buying is decentralized and salespeople have considerable input. They can place special orders and are empowered to resolve customer problems: "Our goal is to provide outstanding service every day, one customer at a time. The 'Inverted Pyramid' represents our philosophy and our structure, with our customers at the top. Next are those who directly serve our customers—our salespeople and those who support them. Department managers, buyers, merchandise managers, store managers, regional managers, our executive team, and our board of directors all support those above them on the pyramid. We work hard to make decisions in the best interest of our customers and those serving them."[6]
- Whole Foods Market has been widely honored for its employee-nurturing environment. It mentors employees via education and on-the-job experience. It encourages worker participation and involvement at all levels of the business. The retailer strives to foster employee creativity and self-responsibility: "We encourage qualified team members to apply for any available opportunity in their store, region, or division as they expand their product knowledge, develop their skills, and enhance their value. All openings for positions at team leader level and higher are listed on our internal job site. Many other openings are posted as well, from all around the company."[7]

The Special Human Resource Environment of Retailing

The Bureau of Labor Statistics compiles current employment data on such jobs as retail sales worker supervisors and managers (www.bls.gov/oco).

Retailers face a human resource environment characterized by a large number of inexperienced workers, long hours, highly visible employees, a diverse work force, many part-time workers, and variable customer demand. These factors complicate employee hiring, staffing, and supervision.

The need for a large retail labor force often means hiring those with little or no prior experience. Sometimes, a position in retailing represents a person's first "real job." People are attracted to retailing because they find jobs near to home; and retail positions (such as cashiers, stock clerks, and some types of sales personnel) may require limited education, training, and skill. Also, the low wages paid for some positions result in the hiring of inexperienced people. Thus, high employee turnover and cases of poor performance, lateness, and absenteeism may result.

The long working hours in retailing, which may include weekends, turn off certain prospective employees; many retailers now have longer hours since more shoppers want to shop during evenings and weekends. Accordingly, some retailers require at least two shifts of full-time employees.

Retailing employees are highly visible to the customer. Therefore, when personnel are selected and trained, special care must be taken with regard to their manners and appearance. Some small retailers do not place enough emphasis on employee appearance (neat grooming and appropriate attire).

It is common for retailers to have a diverse labor force, with regard to age, work experience, gender, race, and other factors. This means that firms must train and supervise their workers so that they interact well with one another—and are sensitive to the perspectives and needs of one another. Consider the employee strategy of Home Depot: "We have partnered with national nonprofit and government agencies and educational organizations to reach out to the communities in which we operate and to provide us with a broad range of qualified candidates with diverse backgrounds." Home Depot has partnerships with the U.S. military, AARP (American Association of Retired Persons), and several Hispanic groups.[8]

Due to their long hours, retailers regularly hire part-time workers. In many supermarkets, more than one-half of the workers are part-time, and problems may arise. Some part-time employees are more lackadaisical, late, absent, or likely to quit than full-time employees. They must be closely monitored.

Variations in customer demand by day, time period, or season may cause difficulties. A significant number of U.S. shoppers make their major supermarket trips on Saturday or Sunday. So, how many employees should there be on Monday through Friday and how many on Saturday and Sunday? Demand differences by day part (morning, afternoon, evening) and by season (fall, holidays) also affect planning. When stores are very busy, even administrative and clerical employees may be needed on the sales floor.

As a rule, retailers should consider these points:

- Recruitment and selection procedures must efficiently generate sufficient applicants.
- Some training must be short because workers are inexperienced and temporary.
- Compensation must be perceived as "fair" by employees.

- Advancement opportunities must be available to employees who view retailing as a career.
- Employee appearance and work habits must be explained and reviewed.
- Diverse workers must be taught to work together well and amicably.
- Morale problems may result from high turnover and the many part-time workers.
- Full- and part-time workers may conflict, especially if some full-timers are replaced.

Various retail career opportunities are available to women and minorities. There is still some room for improvement.

See why Avon calls itself "The Company for Women" (http://avoncompany.com/aboutavon/careers).

WOMEN IN RETAILING Retailing has made a lot of progress in career advancement for women. According to the "2011 Catalyst Census: *Fortune 500* Women Board Directors," these retailers are among the U.S. public firms with at least 25 percent of corporate officers who are women: Avon, Macy's, Target, Barnes & Noble, BJ's, Publix Super Markets, Sunoco, Office Depot, Walt Disney, Advance Auto Parts, Nordstrom, TJX, CVS, Sears, and Staples.[9] In the lodging and food service sectors, the female-to-male mix for managerial jobs is nearly 50 percent. More than two-thirds of supervisors at eating and drinking establishments are women. Bank of America, Capital One, Ikea, Marriott, Patagonia, Sears, Target, and other retailers are regularly rated as excellent companies for working mothers.

As part of her legacy, Mary Kay Ash left behind a charitable foundation (www.mkacf.org).

Women have more career options in retailing than ever before, as the following examples show. Mary Kay Ash (Mary Kay cosmetics), Debbi Fields (Mrs. Fields' Cookies), and Lillian Vernon (the direct marketer) founded retailing empires. As of 2012, women were chief executive officers and/or chairpersons of the board of such U.S.-based retailers as Ann Taylor, Avon, BJ's, Jack in the Box, PC Connection, Rite Aid, Sunoco, and TJX.

At Ann Taylor, a retailer with $2 billion in annual sales and more than 950 stores, Katherine Krill is the chief executive officer, and 40 percent of the firm's board of directors are women:

> Katherine Lawther Krill has been chief executive officer of Ann Taylor Stores Corporation since October 2005 and its president since November 8, 2004. She is responsible for all three of the company's concepts—Ann Taylor Stores, Ann Taylor Loft, and Ann Taylor Factory Stores, as well as all aspects of marketing. Krill has been with Ann Taylor Corporation since 1994, when she joined as merchandising vice-president of separates, suits, dresses, and petites at Ann Taylor Stores.[10]

Rite Aid's chairperson of the board is Mary Sammons. She became chairperson in 2007, and served as chief executive officer from 2003 until 2010. Sammons joined Rite Aid in late 1999 as president and chief operating officer. Before joining Rite Aid, Sammons was president and chief executive officer of Fred Meyer Stores, which became a subsidiary of Kroger. In total, she worked at Fred Meyer for 26 years and held several senior-level positions. Today, Sammons also is a member of the Board of the National Association of Chain Drug Stores and the president of the Rite Aid Foundation.[11]

Despite recent progress, women still account for only a small percentage of corporate officers at publicly owned retail firms. These are some actions for retailers to take with regard to female workers:

- Meaningful training programs.
- Advancement opportunities.
- Flex time—the ability of employees to adapt their hours.
- Job sharing among two or more employees who each work less than full-time.
- Child care.

Fortune annually lists the best employers among public companies (http://money.cnn.com/magazines/fortune/bestcompanies).

MINORITIES IN RETAILING As with women, retailers have done many good things in the area of minority employment, with more still to be accomplished. Consider these examples of retailers cited in *Fortune*'s "100 Best Companies to Work for 2011: Minorities:"[12]

- CarMax recognizes the "value that diversity contributes to our organization and the competitive advantage we can maintain by having a broad range of talents, perspectives, and ideas. We believe that each associate brings valuable talents to the company, and we have a commitment to recruiting, hiring, training, and promoting qualified associates with diverse backgrounds; educating all associates on the importance of diversity and its impact on our business through our 'Treating Associates with Respect' policy; recognizing the value and importance of our associates' diverse attributes; and providing benefits to support a diverse work force and its needs."

- At Whole Foods Market, employees are "side by side with fun, friendly, and diverse team members and leadership, in an exciting and fast-paced setting; learning about natural and organic products from experts; feeling empowered to serve customers the way you'd expect to be served; letting your individual style show with our generous dress code; taking advantage of opportunities to grow personally and professionally; and experiencing daily the pride and satisfaction of contributing to the well-being of people and the planet. Our team members represent many nations, backgrounds, and perspectives, and speak many languages—yet all work together to meet the needs of customers."
- Zappos encourages "diversity in thoughts, opinions, and backgrounds. The more widespread and diverse your relationships, the bigger the positive impact you can make and the more valuable you will be to the company. It is critical for relationship-building to have effective, open, and honest communication. As the company grows, communication becomes more and more important because everyone needs to understand how his/her team connects to the big picture of what we're trying to accomplish. Communication is always a weak spot, no matter how good it is."[13]

At Wal-Mart, the labor force includes more than 248,000 African American associates, more than 42,000 Asian and 5,000 Pacific Islander associates, more than 167,000 Hispanic associates, and more than 14,000 American Indian and Alaskan Native associates. Enterprise Rent-A-Car not only has a diverse work force itself, but it also requires the same for its suppliers: "Enterprise wants its supplier base to bear a reasonable relationship to the communities in which we do business. Our supplier diversity program identifies and encourages equal opportunities for minority-owned, women-owned, and other types of disadvantaged businesses. National partnerships with organizations such as the National Minority Supplier Development Council, Women's Business Enterprise Council, and Airport Minority Advisory Council assist us in reaching our goals." Walgreens even has a special Web site devoted to employee diversity (www.walgreens.com/topic/sr/sr_diversity_home.jsp).[14]

These are some of the ways for retailers to even better address the needs of minority workers:

McDonald's (www.aboutmcdonalds.com/mcd/our_company/inclusion_and_diversity.html) actively encourages diversity and understanding.

- Have clear policy statements from top management as to the value of employee diversity.
- Engage in active recruitment programs to stimulate minority applications.
- Offer meaningful training programs.
- Provide advancement opportunities.
- Have zero tolerance for insensitive workplace behavior.

The Human Resource Management Process in Retailing

The **human resource management process** consists of these interrelated personnel activities: recruitment, selection, training, compensation, and supervision. The goals are to obtain, develop, and retain employees. When applying the process, diversity, labor laws, and privacy should be considered.

Diversity involves two premises: (1) that employees be hired and promoted in a fair and open way, without regard to gender, ethnic background, and other related factors; and (2) that in a diverse society, the workplace should be representative of such diversity.

There are several aspects of labor laws for retailers to satisfy. They must not:

- Hire underage workers.
- Pay workers "off the books."
- Require workers to engage in illegal acts (such as bait-and-switch selling).
- Discriminate in hiring or promoting workers.
- Violate worker safety regulations.
- Disobey the Americans with Disabilities Act.
- Deal with suppliers that disobey labor laws.

Retailers must also be careful not to violate employees' privacy rights. Only necessary data about workers should be gathered and stored, and such information should not be freely disseminated.

We now discuss each activity in human resource management for sales and middle-management jobs. For further insights, go to our Web site (www.pearsonhighered.com/bermanevans).

RECRUITING RETAIL PERSONNEL **Recruitment** is the activity whereby a retailer generates a list of job applicants. Table 11-3 indicates the features of several key recruitment sources. In addition to these sources, the Web now plays a bigger role in recruitment. Many retailers have a career or job section at their Web site, and some sections are as elaborate as the overall sites. Visit Target's Web site (www.target.com), for example. Scroll down to the bottom of the home page and click on "Careers."

With entry-level sales jobs, retailers rely on educational institutions, ads, walk-ins (or write-ins), Web sites (including social media), and employee recommendations. With middle-management positions, retailers rely on employment agencies, competitors, ads, and employee referrals. The retailer's typical goal is to generate a list of potential employees, which is reduced during selection. Retailers that only accept applications from those who meet minimum background standards save a lot of time and money.

SELECTING RETAIL PERSONNEL The firm next selects new employees by matching the traits of potential employees with specific job requirements. Job analysis and description, the application blank, interviewing, testing (optional), references, and a physical exam (optional) are tools in the process; they should be integrated.

In **job analysis,** information is amassed on each job's functions and requirements: duties, responsibilities, aptitude, interest, education, experience, and physical tasks. It is used to select personnel, set performance standards, and assign salaries. For example, department managers often act as the main sales associates for their areas, oversee other sales associates, have some administrative duties, report to the store manager, are eligible for bonuses, and are paid $25,000 to $45,000+ annually.

Job analysis should lead to written job descriptions. A **traditional job description** contains a position's title, relationships (superior and subordinate), and specific roles and tasks.

TABLE 11-3 Recruitment Sources and Their Characteristics

Sources	Characteristics
Outside the Company	
Educational institutions	a. High schools, business schools, community colleges, universities, graduate schools b. Good for training positions; ensure minimum educational requirements are met; especially useful when long-term contacts with instructors are developed
Other channel members, competitors	a. Employees of wholesalers, manufacturers, ad agencies, competitors; leads from each of these b. Reduce extent of training; can evaluate performance with prior firm(s); must instruct in company policy; some negative morale if current employees feel bypassed for promotions
Advertisements	a. Newspapers, trade publications, professional journals, Web sites b. Large quantity of applicants; average applicant quality may not be high; cost/applicant is low; additional responsibility placed on screening; can reduce unacceptable applications by noting job qualifications in ads
Employment agencies	a. Private organizations, professional organizations, government, executive search firms b. Must be carefully selected; must be determined who pays fee; good for applicant screening; specialists in personnel
Unsolicited applicants	a. Walk-ins, write-ins b. Wide variance in quality; must be carefully screened; file should be kept for future positions
Within the Company	
Current and former employees	a. Promotion or transfer of existing full-time employees, part-time employees; rehiring of laid-off employees b. Knowledge of company policies and personnel; good for morale; honest appraisal from in-house supervisor
Employee recommendations	a. Friends, acquaintances, relatives b. Value of recommendations depend on honesty and judgment of current employees

Figure 11-4 showed a store manager description. Yet, using a traditional description alone has been criticized. It may limit a job's scope, as well as its authority and responsibility; not let a person grow; limit activities to those listed; and not describe how jobs are coordinated. To complement a traditional description, a **goal-oriented job description** enumerates basic functions, the relationship of each job to overall goals, the interdependence of positions, and information flows. See Figure 11-10.

An **application blank** is usually the first tool used to screen applicants; it provides data on education, experience, health, reasons for leaving prior jobs, outside activities, hobbies, and references. It is usually short, requires little interpretation, and can be used as the basis for probing in an interview. With a **weighted application blank**, factors having a high relationship

FIGURE 11-10
A Goal-Oriented Job Description for a Management Trainee

Attributes Required	Ability	Desire	In the Retailing Environment
ANALYTICAL SKILLS: ability to solve problems; strong numerical ability for analysis of facts and data for planning, managing, and controlling.			Retail executives are problem solvers. Knowledge and understanding of past performance and present circumstances form the basis for action and planning.
CREATIVITY: ability to generate and recognize imaginative ideas and solutions; ability to recognize the need for and be responsive to change.			Retail executives are idea people. Successful buying results from sensitive, aware decisions, while merchandising requires imaginative, innovative techniques.
DECISIVENESS: ability to make quick decisions and render judgments, take action, and commit oneself to completion.			Retail executives are action people. Whether it's new fashion trends or customer desires, decisions must be made quickly and confidently in this ever-changing environment.
FLEXIBILITY: ability to adjust to the ever-changing needs of the situation; ability to adapt to different people, places, and things; willingness to do whatever is necessary to get the task done.			Retail executives are flexible. Surprises in retailing never cease. Plans must be altered quickly to accommodate changes in trends, styles, and attitudes, while numerous ongoing activities cannot be ignored.
INITIATIVE: ability to originate action rather than wait to be told what to do and ability to act based on conviction.			Retail executives are doers. Sales volumes, trends, and buying opportunities mean continual action. Opportunities for action must be seized.
LEADERSHIP: ability to inspire others to trust and respect your judgment; ability to delegate and to guide and persuade others.			Retail executives are managers. Running a business means depending on others to get the work done. One person cannot do it all.
ORGANIZATION: ability to establish priorities and courses of action for self and/or others; skill in planning and following up to achieve results.			Retail executives are jugglers. A variety of issues, functions, and projects are constantly in motion. To reach your goals, priorities must be set and work must be delegated to others.
RISK-TAKING: willingness to take calculated risks based on thorough analysis and sound judgment and to accept responsibility for the results.			Retail executives are courageous. Success in retailing often comes from taking calculated risks and having the confidence to try something new before someone else does.
STRESS TOLERANCE: ability to perform consistently under pressure, to thrive on constant change and challenge.			Retail executives are resilient. As the above description should suggest, retailing is fast-paced and demanding.

with job success are given more weight than others. Retailers that use such a form analyze the performance of current and past employees and determine the criteria (education, experience, and so on) best correlated with job success (as measured by longer tenure, better performance, and so on). After weighted scores are awarded to all job applicants (based on data they provide), a minimum total score becomes a cutoff point for hiring. An effective application blank aids retailers in lessening turnover and selecting high achievers.

An application blank should be used along with a job description. Those meeting minimum job requirements are processed further; others are immediately rejected. In this way, the application blank provides a quick and inexpensive method of screening.

The interview seeks information that can be amassed only by personal questioning and observation. It lets an employer determine a candidate's verbal ability, note his or her appearance, ask questions keyed to the application, and probe career goals. Interviewing decisions must be made about the level of formality, the number and length of interviews, the location, the person(s) to do the interviewing, and the interview structure. These decisions often depend on the interviewer's ability and the job's requirements.

Small firms tend to hire an applicant who has a good interview. Large firms may add testing. In this case, a candidate who does well in an interview then takes a psychological test (to measure personality, intelligence, interest, and leadership) and/or achievement tests (to measure learned knowledge).[15]

Tests must be administered by qualified people. Standardized exams should not be used unless proven effective in predicting job performance. Because achievement tests deal with specific skills or information (like the ability to make a sales presentation), they are easier to interpret than psychological tests, and direct relationships between knowledge and ability can be shown. In administering tests, retailers must not violate any federal, state, or local law. The federal Employee Polygraph Protection Act bars retailers from using lie detector tests in most hiring situations (drugstores are exempt).

CVS (http://info.cvscaremark.com/careers) encourages potential employees to apply online.

To save time and operate more efficiently, some retailers—large and small—use computerized application blanks and testing. Advance Auto Parts, Babies "R" Us, Best Buy, Blockbuster, CVS, Family Dollar, Lowe's, PetSmart, and Sports Authority are among those with in-store kiosks that allow people to apply for jobs, complete application blanks, and answer several questions. This speeds up the hiring process and attracts a lot of applicants.

Many retailers get references from applicants that can be checked either before or after an interview. References are contacted to see how enthusiastically they recommend an applicant, check the applicant's honesty, and ask why an applicant left a prior job. Mail and phone checks are inexpensive, fast, and easy.

Some firms require a physical exam because of the physical activity, long hours, and tensions involved in many retailing positions. A clean bill of health means the candidate is offered a job. Again, federal, state, and local laws must be followed.

Virtual Job Applications

TravelCenters of America (TA) (www.tatravelcenters.com) is a 165-unit retailer consisting of gas stations, quick-serve restaurants, and heavy truck maintenance shops. In the past, job applicants would typically walk into a retail location and be given an application form to complete. In many cases, the application form was never forwarded to the store manager or a manager at a nearby store who may have been short-staffed.

Now, applicants are directed to apply either via a toll-free phone number or a Web site maintained by JobApp (www.jobappnetwork.com). JobApp handles such tasks as I-9 compliance that conducts background checks on employees who handle cash and verifies the immigration status of new hires. JobApp also rates all candidates on a scale of one to five stars based on their suitability for each position. This enables hiring managers to contact potential new hires with four star or higher ratings. The online application process also provides job candidates with important information on the job description and the job-related responsibilities.

In an analysis of data from 20 percent of its locations, TA found that JobApp helped reduce employee turnover within the first 21 days after being hired by 40 percent. Total annual turnover rate was reduced by 14 percent.

Source: Sandy Smith, "Recruitment Resource," www.stores.org (August 2010).

Each step in the selection process complements the others; together they give the retailer a good information package for choosing personnel. As a rule, retailers should use job descriptions, application blanks, interviews, and reference checks. Follow-up interviews, psychological and achievement tests, and physical exams depend on the retailer and the position. Inexpensive tools (such as application blanks) are used in the early screening stages; more costly, in-depth tools (such as interviews) are used after reducing the applicant pool. Equal opportunity, nondiscriminatory practices must be followed.

TRAINING RETAIL PERSONNEL Every new employee should receive **pre-training**, an indoctrination on the firm's history and policies, as well as a job orientation on hours, compensation, the chain of command, and job duties. New employees should also be introduced to co-workers: It is essential for employees to "learn as soon as possible what is expected of them, and what to expect from others, in addition to learning about the values and attitudes of the organization. While people can learn from experience, they will make many mistakes that are unnecessary and potentially damaging. The main reasons orientation programs fail: The program was not planned; the employee was unaware of the job requirements; the employee does not feel welcome."[16]

Training programs teach new (and existing) personnel how best to perform their jobs or how to improve themselves. Training can range from one-day sessions on operating a computerized cash register, personal selling techniques, or compliance with affirmative action programs to two-year programs for executive trainees on all aspects of the retailer and its operations:

- For each new employee, Container Store provides extensive formal training, which includes learning about how to perform multiple jobs: "We place so much importance on service that every first-year, full-time salesperson receives about 263 hours of training—in a retail industry where the average is about 7 hours. And our trainers are in stores every day ensuring that employees are knowledgeable and empowered to offer the unparalleled customer service that we are known for in the industry."[17]
- Best Buy now uses an online "Learning Lounge" (www.bestbuylearninglounge.com) to help facilitate employee training for new and continuing workers, to keep employees current on the company's best practices, and to let employees easily communicate with one another. The password-protected portal is under the auspices of Best Buy's Retail Training & Development group, whose slogan is "grow. perform. succeed."
- At Costco, the majority of the managers have been internally promoted: "Sixty-eight percent of warehouse managers started out as hourly employees, for instance. So they know firsthand the motivational power of career tracks. You may lose a percentage of people who move on to higher-level jobs, but you have everybody doing better work. To get reluctant supervisors enthused about career tracks for lower-level workers, one expert recommends educating them about the program: 'We traveled across the state. We trained them on the benefits of the program, on why we were doing it. We did a lot more than give out handouts. We did role-playing. We did scenarios.' "[18]

Training should be an ongoing activity. New equipment, legal changes, new product lines, job promotions, low employee morale, and employee turnover necessitate not only training but also retraining. Macy's has a program called "clienteling," which tutors sales associates on how to have better long-term relations with specific repeat customers. Core vendors of Macy's teach sales associates about the features and benefits of new merchandise when it is introduced.

There are several training decisions, as shown in Figure 11-11. They can be divided into three categories: identifying needs, devising appropriate training methods, and evaluation.

Short-term training needs can be identified by measuring the gap between the skills that workers already have and the skills desired by the firm (for each job). This training should prepare employees for possible job rotation, promotions, and changes in the company. A longer training plan lets a firm identify future needs and train workers appropriately.

There are many training methods for retailers: lectures, demonstrations, videos, programmed instruction, conferences, sensitivity training, case studies, role playing, behavior modeling, and competency-based instruction. Some techniques may be computerized—as more firms are doing. The methods' attributes are noted in Table 11-4. Retailers often use more than one technique to reduce employee boredom and cover the material better.

Take a look at Centurion Systems' "Our Résumé" of retail training solutions (www.centurionsys.com).

Computer-based training software is available from a variety of vendors. For example, Centurion Systems has devised more than 100 training modules that have been used to train more

FIGURE 11-11
A Checklist of Selected Training Decisions

- ✓ When should training occur? (At the time of hiring and/or after being at the workplace?)
- ✓ How long should training be?
- ✓ What training programs should there be for new employees? For existing employees?
- ✓ Who should conduct each training program? (Supervisor, co-worker, training department, or outside specialist?)
- ✓ Where should training take place? (At the workplace or in a training room?)
- ✓ What material (content) should be learned? How should it be taught?
- ✓ Should audiovisuals be used? If yes, how?
- ✓ Should elements of the training program be computerized? If yes, how?
- ✓ How should the effectiveness of training be measured?

than 1 million retail employees in such areas as point-of-sales systems, labor scheduling, customer service, manager training, store operations, merchandise management, and more. Among its many clients are Big Lots, BJ's, Domino's, Godiva, Gymboree, Kohl's, Macy's, Starbucks, and Tiffany.

For training to succeed, a conducive environment is needed, based on several principles:

- All people can learn if taught well; there should be a sense of achievement.
- A person learns better when motivated; intelligence alone is not sufficient.
- Learning should be goal-oriented.
- A trainee learns more when he or she participates and is not a passive listener.
- The teacher must provide guidance, as well as adapt to the learner and to the situation.
- Learning should be approached as a series of steps rather than a one-time occurrence.
- Learning should be spread out over a reasonable period of time rather than be compressed.
- The learner should be encouraged to do homework or otherwise practice.
- Different methods of learning should be combined.
- Performance standards should be set and good performance recognized.

TABLE 11-4 The Characteristics of Retail Training Methods

Method	Characteristics
Lectures	Factual, uninterrupted presentations of material; can use professional educator or expert in the field; no active participation by trainees
Demonstrations	Good for showing how to use equipment or do a sales presentation; applies relevance of training; active participation by trainees
Videos	Highly visual, good for demonstration; can be used many times; no active participation by trainees
Programmed instruction	Presents information in a structured manner; requires response from trainees; provides performance feedback; adjustable to trainees' pace; high initial investment
Conferences	Useful for supervisory training; conference leaders must encourage participation; reinforce training
Sensitivity training	Extensive interaction; good for supervisors as a tool for understanding employees
Case studies	Actual or hypothetical problems presented, including circumstances, pertinent information, and questions; learning by doing; exposure to a wide variety of problems
Role playing	Trainees placed into real-life situations and act out roles
Behavior modeling	Trainees taught to imitate models shown in videos or in role-playing sessions
Competency-based instruction	Trainees given a list of tasks or exercises that are presented in a self-paced format

A training program must be regularly evaluated. Comparisons can be made between the performance of those who receive training and those who do not, as well as among employees receiving different types of training for the same job. Evaluations should always be made in relation to stated training goals. In addition, training effects should be measured over different time intervals (such as immediately, 30 days later, and six months later), and proper records maintained.

COMPENSATING RETAIL PERSONNEL Total **compensation**—direct monetary payments (salaries, commissions, and bonuses) and indirect payments (paid vacations, health and life insurance, and retirement plans)—should be fair to both the retailer and its employees. To better motivate employees, some firms also have profit-sharing. Smaller retailers often pay salaries, commissions, and/or bonuses and have fewer fringe benefits. Bigger ones generally pay salaries, commissions, and/or bonuses and offer more fringe benefits.

This site (www.dol.gov/esa/minwage/america.htm) shows the minimum wage in every state.

Since July 2009, the hourly federal minimum wage has been $7.25 (up from $6.55 as of July 2008 and $5.85 as of July 2007). Forty-five states also have their own laws—18 are higher than the federal minimum and four are lower. In 2012, Arizona, Colorado, Florida, Montana, Ohio, Oregon, Vermont, and Washington—all of which already had above-federal-minimum-wage rates—further raised their state minimum wages. The minimum wage has the most impact on retailers hiring entry-level, part-time workers. Full-time, career-track retailing jobs are paid an attractive market rate; to attract part-time workers in good economic times, retailers must often pay salaries above the minimum.

At some large firms, compensation for certain positions is set through collective bargaining. According to the U.S. Bureau of Labor Statistics, about 800,000 retail employees are represented by labor unions. However, union membership varies greatly. Unionized grocery stores account for more than one-half of total U.S. supermarket sales, while independent supermarkets are not usually unionized.

With a *straight salary*, a worker is paid a fixed amount per hour, week, month, or year. Advantages are retailer control, employee security, and known expenses. Disadvantages are retailer inflexibility, the limited productivity incentive, and fixed costs. Clerks and cashiers are usually paid salaries. With a *straight commission*, earnings are directly tied to productivity (such as sales volume). Advantages are retailer flexibility, the link to worker productivity, no fixed costs, and employee incentive. Disadvantages are the retailer's potential lack of control over the tasks performed, the risk of low earnings to employees, cost variability, and the lack of limits on worker earnings. Sales personnel for autos, real-estate, furniture, jewelry, and other expensive items are often paid a straight commission—as are direct-selling personnel.

To combine the attributes of salary and commission plans, retailers may pay employees a *salary plus commission*. Shoe salespeople, major appliance salespeople, and some management personnel are among those paid this way. Sometimes, bonuses supplement salary and/or commission, normally for outstanding performance. At Finish Line footwear and apparel stores, regional, district, and store managers receive fixed salaries and earn bonuses based on sales, the size of the payroll, and theft rate goals. In certain cases, retail executives are paid via a "compensation cafeteria" and choose their own combination of salary, bonus, deferred bonus, fringe benefits, life insurance, stock options, and retirement benefits.

Sears (www.searsholdings.com/careers/why us/benefits.htm) has a generous employee benefits package.

A thorny issue facing retailers today involves the benefits portion of employee compensation, especially as related to pensions and healthcare. It is a challenging time due to intense price competition, the use of part-time workers, and escalating medical costs as retailers try to balance their employees' needs with company financial needs.

SUPERVISING RETAIL PERSONNEL **Supervision** is the manner of providing a job environment that encourages employee accomplishment. The goals are to oversee personnel, attain good performance, maintain morale, motivate people, control costs, communicate, and resolve problems. Supervision is provided by personal contact, meetings, and reports.

Every firm wants to continually motivate employees so as to harness their energy on behalf of the retailer and achieve its goals. **Job motivation** is the drive within people to attain work-related goals. It may be positive or negative. These 10 attitude questions can be used to help predict employee behavior, based on their motivation:

1. Do you like the kind of work you do?
2. Does your work give you a sense of accomplishment?
3. Are you proud to say you work with us?

CAREERS IN RETAILING

Motivating Employees in Routine Jobs

Motivating retail employees who work in laundromats and in similar settings is especially difficult. This work is tedious, opportunities for advancement are limited, and many employees do not see their jobs as particularly meaningful. Yet, the owners of laundromats and many other retail facilities need to effectively motivate their employees if their businesses are to be successful. Here are some tips to help inspire employees to work hard in these environments.

At an employee's initial interview, it is important to tell the prospective employee about the store's history, its differential advantages over key competitors, and its role in the community. It should be further explained that no business owns consumer loyalty and that it is very easy for a consumer to switch to a competing retailer if not fully satisfied. The loss of a single customer can be significant when measured on a yearly or customer-lifetime basis.

Employees also must understand their role in providing customer satisfaction. Little things—such as phone calling customers when their laundry is ready or hunting down lost items—are positive examples of how one employee can make a real difference in a customer's experience. These little things can translate into positive word-of-mouth communication among the customer's friends and family.

Source: Scott Howard, "Imparting a Success Ethic," *American Coin-Op* (April 2011), pp. 26–27.

4. How does the amount of work expected from you influence your overall job attitude?
5. How do physical working conditions influence your overall job attitude?
6. How does the way you are treated by supervisors influence your overall job attitude?
7. Do you feel good about the future of the company?
8. Do you think the company is making the changes necessary to compete effectively?
9. Do you understand the company's business strategy?
10. Do you see a connection between your work and the company's strategic objectives?[19]

Employee motivation should be approached from two perspectives: What job-related factors cause employees to be satisfied or dissatisfied with their positions? What supervision style is best for both the retailer and its employees? See Figure 11-12.

Each employee looks at job satisfaction in terms of minimum expectations ("dissatisfiers") and desired goals ("satisfiers"). A motivated employee requires fulfillment of both factors. *Minimum expectations* relate mostly to the job environment, including a safe workplace, equitable treatment for those with the same jobs, some flexibility in company policies (such as not docking pay if a person is 10 minutes late), an even-tempered boss, some freedom in attire, a fair compensation package, basic fringe benefits (such as vacation time and medical coverage), clear communications, and

FIGURE 11-12

Demotivated Employees Result in Lower Productivity

Today, there are a lot of older adults working in retailing—to supplement their retirement benefits, to be active, and/or to be in a social setting. It is important that these workers be treated with respect and not be placed into menial, boring jobs that do not make use of their skill set. If they are unhappy, it may rub off on customers.

Source: Lisa F. Young/ Shutterstock.com. Reprinted by permission.

job security. These elements can generally influence motivation in only one way—negatively. If minimum expectations are not met, a person will be unhappy. If these expectations are met, they are taken for granted and do little to motivate the person to go "above and beyond."

Desired goals relate more to the job than to the work environment. They are based on whether an employee likes the job, is recognized for good performance, feels a sense of achievement, is empowered to make decisions, is trusted, has a defined career path, receives extra compensation when performance is exceptional, and is given the chance to learn and grow. These elements can have a huge impact on job satisfaction and motivate a person to go "above and beyond." Nonetheless, if minimum expectations are not met, an employee might still be dissatisfied enough to leave, even if the job is quite rewarding.

There are three basic styles of supervising retail employees:

- Management assumes that employees must be closely supervised and controlled and that only economic inducements really motivate. Management further believes that the average worker lacks ambition, dislikes responsibility, and prefers to be led. This is the traditional view of motivation and has been applied to lower-level retail positions.
- Management assumes employees can be self-managers and assigned authority, motivation is social and psychological, and supervision can be decentralized and participatory. Management also thinks that motivation, the capacity for assuming responsibility, and a readiness to achieve company goals exist in people. The critical supervisory task is to create an environment so people achieve their goals by attaining company objectives. This is a more modern view and applies to all levels of personnel.
- Management applies a self-management approach and also advocates more employee involvement in defining jobs and sharing overall decision making. There is mutual loyalty between the firm and its workers, and both parties enthusiastically cooperate for the long-term benefit of each. This is also a modern view and applies to all levels of personnel.

It is imperative to motivate employees in a manner that yields job satisfaction, low turnover, low absenteeism, and high productivity. Consider these suggestions from one leading consultant:

> **(1) Motivate Employees to Find Solutions**—Encourage employees to be solution creators instead of problem creators. When employees communicate a problem, look at it as an opportunity to empower the employees. **(2) Motivate Employees by Soliciting Opinions**—Just asking for opinions tells employees that you value their input. **(3) Motivate Employees by Managing to Their Level**—Learn employees' skills, experience, and motivation levels for performing workplace tasks. Follow-up based on your findings. **(4) Motivate Employees by Delegating Tasks**—Delegating a task shows employees you have confidence that they can do the job. **(5) Motivate Employees by Encouraging Ideas**—Create a safe environment for employees to share their ideas. Always give them credit for the ideas they express. **(6) Motivate Employees by Embracing Mistakes**—Allowing employees to make mistakes allows them to grow, be creative, and be empowered. **(7) Motivate Employees by Assigning Leadership Roles**—Leadership comes at all levels and doesn't require a title. Take the time to align employees' skills with leadership opportunities. **(8) Motivate Employees by Rewarding Initiative**—Publicly recognize employees during meetings, with reward bonuses, etc., so other employees are motivated to take initiative. (9) **Motivate Employees by Getting Goal Setting Buy-In**—Employees will be more motivated to achieve your goals if they help develop those goals.[20]

Chapter Summary

1. *To study the procedures involved in setting up a retail organization.* A retail organization structures and assigns tasks, policies, resources, authority, responsibilities, and rewards to satisfy the needs of its target market, employees, and management. There are five steps in setting up an organization: outlining specific tasks to be performed in a distribution channel, dividing tasks, grouping tasks into jobs, classifying jobs, and integrating positions with an organization chart.

Specific tasks include buying, shipping, receiving and checking, pricing, and marking merchandise; inventory control; display preparation; facilities maintenance; research; customer contact and follow-up; and a lot more. These tasks may be divided among retailers, manufacturers, wholesalers, specialists, and customers.

Tasks are next grouped into jobs, such as sales personnel, cashiers, inventory personnel, display personnel, customer service personnel, and management. Then jobs are arranged by functional, product, geographic, or combination classification. An organization chart displays the hierarchy of authority and the relationship among jobs, and it helps coordinates personnel.

2. *To examine the various organizational arrangements utilized in retailing.* Retail organization structures differ by institution. Small independents use simple formats with little specialization. Many department stores use a version of the Mazur plan and place functions into four categories: merchandising, communications, store management, and financial accounting. The equal store format is used by numerous chain stores. Diversified firms have very complex organizations.

3. *To consider the special human resource environment of retailing.* Retailers are unique due to the large number of inexperienced workers, long hours, highly visible employees, a diverse work force, many part-time workers, and variations in customer demand. There is a broad range of career opportunities available to women and minorities, although improvement is still needed.

4. *To describe the principles and practices involved with the human resource management process in retailing.* This process comprises several interrelated activities: recruitment, selection, training, compensation, and supervision. In applying the process, diversity, labor laws, and employee privacy should be kept in mind.

Recruitment generates job applicants. Sources include educational institutions, channel members, competitors, ads, employment agencies, unsolicited applicants, employees, and Web sites (including social media).

Personnel selection requires thorough job analysis, creating job descriptions, using application blanks, interviews, testing (optional), reference checking, and physical exams. After personnel are selected, they go through pre-training and job training. Good training identifies needs, uses proper methods, and assesses results. Training is usually vital for continuing as well as new, personnel.

Employees are compensated by direct monetary payments and/or indirect payments. The direct compensation plans are straight salary, straight commission, and salary plus commission and/or bonus. Indirect payments involve such items as paid vacations, health benefits, and retirement plans.

Proper supervision is needed to sustain superior employee performance. A main task is employee motivation. The causes of job satisfaction/dissatisfaction and the supervisory style must be reviewed.

Key Terms

retail organization (p. 281)
hierarchy of authority (p. 285)
organization chart (p. 285)
Mazur plan (p. 287)
equal store organization (p. 288)
diversified retailer (p. 289)
human resource management (p. 290)
human resource management process (p. 294)
recruitment (p. 295)
job analysis (p. 295)
traditional job description (p. 295)
goal-oriented job description (p. 296)
application blank (p. 296)
weighted application blank (p. 296)
pre-training (p. 298)
training programs (p. 298)
compensation (p. 300)
supervision (p. 300)
job motivation (p. 300)

Questions for Discussion

1. Cite at least five objectives a large consumer electronics store chain should set when setting up its organization structure.
2. Why are employee needs important in developing a retail organization?
3. Are the steps involved in setting up a retail organization the same for small and large retailers? Explain your answer.
4. Describe the greatest similarities and differences in the organization structures of small independents, chain retailers, and diversified retailers.
5. How can retailers attract and retain more women and minority workers?
6. How would small and large retailers act differently for each of the following?

   a. Diversity.
   b. Recruitment.
   c. Selection.
   d. Training.
   e. Compensation.
   f. Supervision.
7. Why are the job description and the application blank so important in employee selection?
8. What problems can occur while interviewing and testing prospective employees?
9. Present a plan for the ongoing training of both existing lower-level and middle-management employees without making it seem punitive.
10. Describe the goals of a compensation plan (both direct and indirect components) in a retail setting.
11. Are the minimum job expectations of entry-level workers and middle-level managers similar or dissimilar? What about the desired goals? Explain your answers.
12. How would you supervise and motivate a 19-year-old Old Navy employee? A 55-year-old Old Navy employee?

Web-Based Exercise

Visit the revitalized Web site that Macy's, Inc. has dedicated to "Careers After College" (www.macyscollege.com/college) for its Macy's and Bloomingdale's department store chains. What do you think of this site as a mechanism for attracting new college graduates to Macy's and Bloomingdale's? Why?

Note: Also stop by our Web site (www.pearsonhighered.com/bermanevans) to experience a number of highly interactive, appealing Web exercises based on actual company demonstrations and sample materials related to retailing.

12 Operations Management: Financial Dimensions

Retailers are always on the lookout for ways to improve their financial performance by more efficiently handling their operations. Consumers are also interested in making sure that their shopping experience is as secure as possible. PayPal (owned by eBay) can be used to accomplish both goals. It already handles $70 billion in annual shopper payments to retailers.

How does PayPal (www.paypal.com) work? Customers register credit card numbers with PayPal. When buying online, they access PayPal as an option at the retailer's Web site by typing their E-mail address. Payment is electronically sent without consumer credit-card data being inserted. While once primarily used by small retailers, today PayPal is also increasingly popular among larger retailers.

PayPal is quite active with social media, both to communicate with retail clients and to promote the payment system's availability—and to announce special promotions by these retailers. According to PayPal's president, Scott Thompson, the firm has rolled out a one-stop system for retailers to interact directly with their shoppers:

> during every part of the shopping life cycle—generating demand from consumers through location-based offers, making payments accessible from any device (not just from the mobile phone), and offering more flexibility to customers even *after* they've checked out. Nobody likes waiting for their bill at the restaurant. At PayPal, we want to free you from the cash register. The act of paying for something should be as seamless as a person's decision to buy it. The future is about creating real consumer choice, flexibility, and control over how people shop and pay.

To engage its retail clients and the clients' shoppers, PayPal is active with a blog (www.thepaypalblog.com), Facebook (www.facebook.com/paypal), Twitter (http://twitter.com/#!/PayPal), and YouTube (www.youtube.com/paypal). All of these efforts enable retailers to be more efficient for their shoppers to feel more secure.[1]

Chapter Objectives

1. To define operations management
2. To discuss profit planning
3. To describe asset management, including the strategic profit model, other key business ratios, and financial trends in retailing
4. To look at retail budgeting
5. To examine resource allocation

Source: BeTA-Artworks/fotolia.com.

Overview

After devising an organization structure and a human resource plan, a retailer concentrates on **operations management**—the efficient and effective implementation of the policies and tasks necessary to satisfy the firm's customers, employees, and management (and stockholders, if a public company). This has a major impact on sales and profits. High inventory levels, long hours, expensive fixtures, extensive customer services, and widespread advertising may lead to higher revenues. But at what cost? If a store pays night-shift workers a 25 percent premium, is being open 24 hours per day worthwhile (do the higher sales justify the costs and add to overall profit)?

This chapter covers the financial aspects of operations management, with emphasis on profit planning, asset management, budgeting, and resource allocation. The operational dimensions of operations management are explored in detail in Chapter 13. A number of useful financial operations links may be found at our Web site (www.pearsonhighered.com/bermanevans).

PROFIT PLANNING

Learn more about the profit-and-loss statement (www.scoreknox.org/library/profit.htm).

A **profit-and-loss (income) statement** is a summary of a retailer's revenues and expenses over a given period of time, usually a month, quarter, or year. It lets the firm review overall and specific revenues and costs for similar periods (such as January 1, 2012, to December 31, 2012, versus January 1, 2011, to December 31, 2011) and analyze profits. With frequent statements, a firm can monitor progress on goals, update performance estimates, and revise strategies and tactics.

In comparing profit-and-loss performance over time, it is crucial that the same time periods be used (such as the third quarter of 2012 with the third quarter of 2011) due to seasonality. Some fiscal years may have an unequal number of weeks (53 weeks one year versus 51 weeks another). Retailers that open new stores or expand existing stores between accounting periods should also take into account the larger facilities. Yearly results should reflect total revenue growth and the rise in same-store sales.

A profit-and-loss statement consists of these major components:

- **Net sales**—the revenues received by a retailer during a given period after deducting customer returns, markdowns, and employee discounts.
- **Cost of goods sold**—the amount a retailer pays to acquire the merchandise sold during a given time period. It is based on purchase prices and freight charges, less all discounts (such as quantity, cash, and promotion).
- **Gross profit (margin)**—the difference between net sales and the cost of goods sold; it consists of operating expenses plus net profit.
- **Operating expenses**—the cost of running a retail business.
- **Taxes**—the portion of revenues turned over to the federal, state, and/or local government.
- **Net profit after taxes**—the profit earned after all costs and taxes have been deducted.

Table 12-1 shows the most recent annual profit-and-loss statement for Donna's Gift Shop, an independent retailer. The firm uses a fiscal year (September 1 to August 31) rather than a calendar year in preparing its accounting reports. These observations can be drawn from the table:

- Annual net sales were $330,000—after deducting returns, markdowns on the items sold, and employee discounts from total sales.
- The cost of goods sold was $180,000, computed by taking the total purchases for merchandise sold, adding freight, and subtracting quantity, cash, and promotion discounts.
- Gross profit was $150,000, calculated by subtracting the cost of goods sold from net sales. This went for operating and other expenses, taxes, and profit.
- Operating expenses totaled $95,250, including salaries, advertising, supplies, shipping, insurance, maintenance, and other expenses.
- Unassigned costs were $20,000.
- Net profit before taxes was $34,750, computed by deducting total costs from gross profit. The tax bill was $15,500, leaving a net profit after taxes of $19,250.

Overall, fiscal 2012 was pretty good for Donna; her personal salary was $43,000 and the store's after-tax profit was $19,250. A further analysis of Donna's Gift Shop's profit-and-loss statement appears in the budgeting section of this chapter.

TABLE 12-1 Donna's Gift Shop, Fiscal 2012 Profit-and-Loss Statement

Net sales	$330,000
Cost of goods sold	$180,000
Gross profit	$150,000
Operating expenses	
Salaries	$ 75,000
Advertising	4,950
Supplies	1,650
Shipping	1,500
Insurance	4,500
Maintenance	5,100
Other	2,550
Total	$ 95,250
Other costs	$ 20,000
Total costs	$115,250
Net profit before taxes	$ 34,750
Taxes	$ 15,500
Net profit after taxes	$ 19,250

ASSET MANAGEMENT

Try out the Business Owner's Toolkit's downloadable Excel-based balance sheet template (www.toolkit.com/tools/bt.aspx?tid=balshe_m).

Each retailer has assets to manage and liabilities to control. This section covers the balance sheet, the strategic profit model, and other ratios. A **balance sheet** itemizes a retailer's assets, liabilities, and net worth at a specific time—based on the principle that Assets = Liabilities + Net worth. Table 12-2 has a balance sheet for Donna's Gift Shop.

Assets are any items a retailer owns with a monetary value. Current assets are cash on hand (or in the bank) and items readily converted to cash, such as inventory on hand and accounts receivable (amounts owed to the firm). Fixed assets are property, buildings (a store, warehouse, and so on), fixtures, and equipment such as cash registers and trucks; these are used for a long period.

TABLE 12-2 A Retail Balance Sheet for Donna's Gift Shop (as of August 31, 2012)

Assets		Liabilities	
Current		Current	
Cash on hand	$ 19,950	Payroll expenses payable	$ 6,000
Inventory	36,150	Taxes payable	13,500
Accounts receivable	1,650	Accounts payable	32,100
Total	$ 57,750	Short-term loan	1,050
		Total	$ 52,650
Fixed (present value)			
Property	$187,500	Fixed	
Building	63,000	Mortgage	$ 97,500
Store fixtures	14,550	Long-term loan	6,750
Equipment	2,550	Total	$104,250
Total	$267,600	Total liabilities	$156,900
Total assets	$325,350		
		Net Worth	$168,450
		Liabilities + net worth	$325,350

The major fixed asset for many retailers is real-estate. Unlike current assets, which are recorded at cost, fixed assets are recorded at cost less accumulated depreciation. Thus, records may not reflect the true value of these assets. Many retailing analysts use the term **hidden assets** to describe depreciated assets, such as buildings and warehouses, that are noted on a retail balance sheet at low values relative to their actual worth.

Liabilities are financial obligations a retailer incurs in operating a business. Current liabilities are payroll expenses payable, taxes payable, accounts payable (amounts owed to suppliers), and short-term loans; these must be paid in the coming year. Fixed liabilities comprise mortgages and long-term loans; these are generally repaid over several years.

A retailer's **net worth** is computed as assets minus liabilities. It is also called owner's equity and represents the value of a business after deducting all financial obligations.

In operations management, the retailer's goal is to use its assets in the manner providing the best results possible. There are three basic ways to measure those results: net profit margin, asset turnover, and financial leverage. Each component is discussed next.

Net profit margin is a performance measure based on a retailer's net profit and net sales:

$$\text{Net profit margin} = \frac{\text{Net profit after taxes}}{\text{Net sales}}$$

At Donna's Gift Shop, fiscal year 2012 net profit margin was 5.83 percent—a very good percentage for a gift shop. To enhance its net profit margin, a retailer must either raise gross profit as a percentage of sales or reduce expenses as a percentage of sales.[2] It could lift gross profit by purchasing opportunistically, selling exclusive products, avoiding price competition through excellent service, and adding items with higher margins. It could reduce operating costs by stressing self-service, lowering labor costs, refinancing the mortgage, cutting energy costs, and so on. The firm must be careful not to lessen customer service to the extent that sales and profit would decline.

Asset turnover is a performance measure based on a retailer's net sales and total assets:

$$\text{Asset turnover} = \frac{\text{Net sales}}{\text{Total assets}}$$

Donna's Gift Shop had a very low asset turnover, 1.0143—meaning it averaged \$1.01 in sales per dollar of total assets. To improve the asset turnover ratio, a firm must generate increased sales from the same level of assets or keep the same sales with fewer assets. A firm might increase sales by having longer hours, accepting online orders, training employees to sell additional products, or stocking better-known brands. None of these tactics requires expanding the asset base. Or a firm might maintain its sales on a lower asset base by moving to a smaller store, simplifying fixtures (or having suppliers install fixtures), keeping a lower inventory, and negotiating for the property owner to pay part of the costs of a renovation.

By looking at the relationship between net profit margin and asset turnover, **return on assets (ROA)** can be computed:

$$\text{Return on assets} = \text{Net profit margin} \times \text{Asset turnover}$$

$$\text{Return on assets} = \frac{\text{Net profit after taxes}}{\text{Net sales}} \times \frac{\text{Net sales}}{\text{Total assets}}$$

$$= \frac{\text{Net profit after taxes}}{\text{Total assets}}$$

Donna's Gift Shop had an ROA of 5.9 percent ($0.0583 \times 1.0143 = 0.059$). This return is below average for gift stores; the firm's good net profit margin does not adequately offset its low asset turnover.

Financial leverage is a performance measure based on the relationship between a retailer's total assets and net worth:

$$\text{Financial leverage} = \frac{\text{Total assets}}{\text{Net worth}}$$

Donna's Gift Shop's financial leverage ratio was 1.9314. Assets were just under twice the net worth, and total liabilities and net worth were almost equal. This ratio was slightly lower than the average for gift stores (a conservative group). The store is in no danger.

RETAILING AROUND THE WORLD

The Global Talent Shortage

According to a study by the World Economic Forum (www.weforum.org) and the Boston Consulting Group (www.bcg.com), entitled *Global Talent Risk—Seven Responses*, the scarcity of management talent will persist for decades. According to the director of the Georgetown University Center on Education and the Work Force, unless there are major changes in the current education-to-employment system, there could be at least 20 million vacant jobs in the United States alone.

Here are some proposed solutions for retailers to meet their staffing needs of the future:

- Develop a work-force strategy—Retailers need to contrast their employees' current skill sets with their long-term needs.
- Treat training as an investment—Newly hired retail employees should be required to attend classes as part of their orientation period. Retailers also need continuous education programs for their more experienced employees.
- Collaborate with industry and business partners—Retailers can participate in exchange programs with major suppliers. With one type of a plan, NCR (www.ncr.com) employees are better able to understand their clients' needs, while the clients are able to develop better knowledge of a technology's capabilities.
- Establish stronger relationships with educational institutions—Retailers can provide more internship experiences for students uncertain about a retail career.
- Strengthen community-based organizations—Retailers can work with economic development agencies by providing training programs and internships.

Source: Eric Krell, "The Global Talent Mismatch," *HR Magazine* (June 2011), pp. 68–73.

A retailer with a high financial leverage ratio has substantial debt, while a ratio of 1 means it has no debt—assets equal net worth. If the ratio is too high, there may be an excessive focus on cost-cutting and short-run sales so as to make interest payments, net profit margins may suffer, and a firm may be forced into bankruptcy if debts cannot be paid. When financial leverage is low, a retailer may be overly conservative—limiting its ability to renovate and expand existing stores and to enter new markets. Leverage is too low if owner's equity is relatively high; equity could be partly replaced by increasing short- and long-term loans and/or accounts payable. Some equity funds could be taken out of a business by the owner (stockholders, if a public firm).

The Strategic Profit Model

The relationship among net profit margin, asset turnover, and financial leverage is expressed by the **strategic profit model**, which reflects a performance measure known as **return on net worth (RONW)**. See Figure 12-1. The strategic profit model can be used in planning or controlling assets. Thus, a retailer could learn that the major cause of its poor return on net worth is weak asset turnover or financial leverage that is too low. A firm can raise its return on net worth by lifting the net profit margin, asset turnover, or financial leverage. Because these measures are multiplied to determine return on net worth, doubling *any* of them would double the return on net worth.

This is how the strategic profit model can be applied to Donna's Gift Shop:

$$\text{Return on net worth} = \frac{\text{Net profit after taxes}}{\text{Net sales}} \times \frac{\text{Net sales}}{\text{Total assets}} \times \frac{\text{Total assets}}{\text{Net worth}}$$

$$= \frac{\$19{,}250}{\$330{,}000} \times \frac{\$330{,}000}{\$325{,}350} \times \frac{\$325{,}350}{\$168{,}450}$$

$$= 0.0583 \times 1.0143 \times 1.9314$$

$$= 0.1142 = 11.4\%$$

Overall, Donna's return on net worth was above average for gift stores.

FIGURE 12-1
The Strategic Profit Model

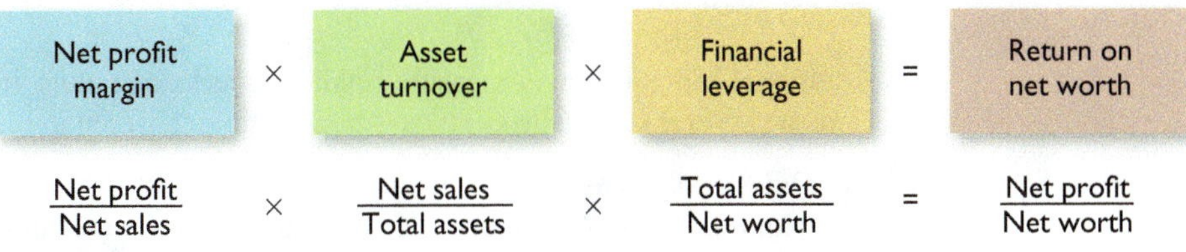

TABLE 12-3 Application of Strategic Profit Model to Selected Retailers (2010 Data)

Retailer	Net Profit Margin	×	Asset Turnover	×	Financial Leverage	=	Return on Net Worth
Apparel Retailers							
TJX	6.12%		2.75		2.57		43.25%
Gap, Inc.	8.21%		2.08		1.73		29.54%
Consumer Electronics Retailers							
Best Buy	2.54%		2.82		2.45		17.55%
Drugstore Retailers							
Walgreens	3.10%		2.57		1.82		14.50%
CVS Caremark	3.55%		1.55		1.65		9.08%
Food Retailers							
Publix	5.32%		2.47		1.40		18.40%
Safeway	1.44%		2.71		3.03		11.82%
General Merchandise Retailers							
Wal-Mart	3.89%		2.34		2.54		23.12%
Target	4.44%		1.51		2.82		18.91%
Sears Holdings	0.35%		1.79		2.82		1.77%
Costco	1.67%		3.27		2.18		11.90%
Macy's, Inc.	3.39%		1.21		3.73		15.30%
J.C. Penney	2.19%		1.36		2.39		7.12%
Home Improvement Retailers							
Home Depot	4.91%		1.69		2.12		17.59%
Lowe's	4.12%		1.49		1.86		11.42%
Office Supplies Retailers							
Staples	3.59%		1.76		2.01		12.70%
Office Depot	0.32%		2.50		5.97		4.78%

Note: The data in this table take into account the weakened performance of many retailers during the 2008–2009 economic downturn that continued through 2010.

Source: Computed by the authors from data in company annual reports.

Visit this site (www.pnwassoc.com/issues/codbanalysis.htm) to see how the strategic profit model can be applied to a hardware store.

Table 12-3 applies the strategic profit model to various retailers. It is best to make comparisons among firms within given retail categories. For example, the net profit margins of general merchandise retailers have historically been higher than those of food retailers. Because financial performance differs from year to year, caution is advised in studying these data. Furthermore, the individual components of the strategic profit model must be analyzed, not just the return on net worth. For example,

- TJX had the highest return on net worth among all 17 retailers shown in Table 12-3. Its net profit margin was lower than Gap, Inc., but its asset turnover was quite strong. TJX was also more financially leveraged than Gap, Inc.
- Sears Holdings (including Sears and Kmart) had a return on net worth that lagged well behind other general merchandise retailers. Its profit margin was especially weak.
- Staples outperformed Office Depot. It had a stronger profit margin and was not as leveraged.

Other Key Business Ratios

Additional ratios can also measure retailer success or failure in reaching performance goals. Here are several key business ratios—besides those covered in the preceding discussion:

- *Quick ratio*—cash plus accounts receivable divided by total current liabilities, those due within one year. A ratio above 1-to-1 means the firm is liquid and can cover short-term debt.

- *Current ratio*—total current assets (cash, accounts receivable, inventories, and marketable securities) divided by total current liabilities. A ratio of 2-to-1 or more is good.
- *Collection period*—accounts receivable divided by net sales and then multiplied by 365. If most sales are on credit, a collection period one-third or more over normal terms (such as 40.0 for a store with 30-day credit terms) means slow-turning receivables.
- *Accounts payable to net sales*—accounts payable divided by annual net sales. This compares how a retailer pays suppliers relative to volume transacted. A figure above the industry average indicates that a firm relies on suppliers to finance operations.
- *Overall gross profit*—net sales minus the cost of goods sold and then divided by net sales. This companywide average includes markdowns, discounts, and shortages.[3]

The Census Bureau, online, provides more than a decade of gross profit (gross margin) percentage data by line of business (www.census.gov/svsd/retlann/pdf/gmper.pdf).

For any retailer, large or small, the goal is to do as well as possible on these key business ratios. Areas of weakness must be identified and corrected for the firm to enhance its long-term results—and to avoid negative financial results. Table 12-4 describes ways to improve performance for each of the preceding ratios, as well as asset turnover and return on net worth.

At our Web site (www.pearsonhighered.com/bermanevans), we have links to Yahoo! Finance sites related to retailers' financial performance.

Financial Trends in Retailing

Entrepreneur's "Money" section (www.entrepreneur.com/money) has a lot of valuable advice for small businesses.

Several trends relating to asset management merit discussion: the state of the economy; funding sources (including initial public offerings); mergers, consolidations, and spin-offs; bankruptcies and liquidations; and questionable accounting and financial reporting practices.

Many retailers are affected by the strength or weakness of the economy. During a strong economy, high consumer demand may mask retailer weaknesses. But when the economy is weak, sales stagnate, cash flow problems may occur, heavy markdowns may be needed (which cut profit margins), consumers are more reluctant to buy big-ticket items, and public firms may see their stock prices adversely affected.

TABLE 12-4 Selected Ways for a Retailer to Improve Its Key Business Ratios

Ratios	Causes of Poor Performance	Suggestions to Improve Performance
Quick ratio	Too low a quick ratio indicates too much current liabilities relative to cash and accounts receivable.	Reduce current liabilities by outsourcing delivery and installation, leasing equipment (instead of purchasing), and turning over inventory more quickly.
Current ratio	Too low a current ratio indicates too much current liabilities relative to cash, accounts receivable, inventories, and marketable securities.	Reduce current liabilities. Consider outsourcing delivery and installation, as well as leasing equipment (instead of purchasing).
Collection period	Too long a collection period indicates too many slow-paying accounts.	Increase payment requirements for store-credit accounts and encourage marginal shoppers to use debit cards, layaway programs, and bank cards.
Accounts payable to net sales	Too high an accounts-payable-to-net-sales ratio indicates that a firm heavily relies on suppliers to finance inventories.	Increase inventory turnover of key items by reducing slow-turnover items, paying accounts payable on time, and purchasing more goods on consignment.
Overall gross profit margin	Too low an overall gross profit margin indicates a combination of low net sales and a high cost of goods sold.	Increase profit margins through better negotiation with vendors to reduce the cost of goods sold, lessen the use of discounting, avoid "meeting the price" of competition tactics, and better focus on merchandise with higher profit margins (such as private-label items).
Asset turnover	Too low an asset turnover indicates insufficient sales per dollar of assets.	Improve asset turnover by extending store hours, using central warehousing, outsourcing delivery and other services, and leasing instead of purchasing.
Return on net worth	Too low a return on net worth indicates insufficient profit as a percent of net worth.	Increase gross profit (through better negotiation and by selling a mix of more profitable goods) and lower operating expenses (by eliminating costly services that are not valued by consumers).

Consider these observations about the economy's impact: "'Most retailers have had to use deep price discounts to increase sales revenue, taking a bath on per-unit profits—sales up, margins down,' said Chris Christopher Jr., of IHS Global Insight. 'There are too many retailers chasing frugal and fatigued shoppers.' According to Ken Perkins of Retail Metrics, the end of 2011 'marked the most intense discounting in a decade—excluding the 2008 economic meltdown. Margins were under pressure from discounting, free shipping, price matching, greater expenses for ads, and expanded store hours.' Retail analysts said the gulf between weak and strong merchants was widening."[4]

Three sources of funding are important to retailers. First, because interest rates have remained quite low, many firms have sought to refinance their mortgages and leases—which can dramatically decrease their monthly payments. Even though funding has been tight since 2008, due to the tougher restrictions imposed by the financial markets retailers have retained some leverage. Because of the weak economy, many retail store vacancies occurred, and the rental marketplace has not bounced back from that. Furthermore, before the recession, retail developers overbuilt, which created even more vacancies. As one real-estate expert noted: "We do not expect rents to get back to their 2008 levels until early 2017."[5]

Second, shopping center developers often use a retail real-estate investment trust (REIT) to fund construction. With this strategy, investors buy shares in a REIT as they would a stock. Until the 2008 recession, investors liked REITs because property had historically been a good investment. Then, during the worst of the economic decline, many REITs struggled and their value fell. Nonetheless, the long-term forecast for REITs is good: "The property sector rode out the global financial crisis. Hence, while there could emerge some rental pressure in select segments of the market, the office segment for instance, overall expectations for property prices remain on a fairly even keel. Most market observers are fairly upbeat on the prospects for retail properties, particularly for shopping malls that are well managed in choice locations, on the back of expectations that domestic consumer spending will continue to expand."[6]

Third, a funding source that has gained retailing acceptance over the past 25 years is the initial public offering (IPO), whereby a firm raises money by selling stock. An IPO is typically used to fund expansion. What do investors look for in an IPO? "In general, you want profitable companies with unique goods or services that have high barriers to entry." After a slow period for IPOs due to the weak economy, things started to pick up again in 2011—Angie's List, Dunkin' Brands, Groupon, and Zipcar are retailers that became public companies.[7]

Mergers and consolidations represent a way for retailers to add to their asset base without building new facilities or waiting for new business units to turn a profit. They also present a way for weak retailers to receive financial transfusions. For example, in the last several years, Kmart acquired Sears and became Sears Holdings, Dick's Sporting Goods acquired Gaylan's, TD Bank acquired Commerce Bancorp, and Foot Locker acquired Foot Action. All of these deals were driven by the weakness of the acquired firms. Typically, mergers and consolidations lead to some stores being shut, particularly those with trading-area overlap, and cutbacks among management personnel.

The leveraged buyout (LBO) is a type of acquisition in which a retail ownership change is mostly financed by loans from banks, investors, and others. The LBO phenomenon has had a big effect on retail budgeting and cash flow. At times, because debts incurred with LBOs can be high, some well-known retailers have had to focus more on paying interest on their debts than on investing in their businesses, run sales to generate enough cash to cover operating costs and buy new goods, and sell store units to pay off debt. Two major retailers involved with LBOs were weakened: Toys "R" Us and Barneys New York.

Retailers sometimes consolidate their businesses to streamline operations and improve profits. Winn-Dixie, Eddie Bauer, Kmart, Macy's, Pier 1, Michaels, Sears, and many others have shut underperforming stores. Other times, retailers use spin-offs to generate more money or to sell a division that no longer meets expectations. Macy's sold off Lord & Taylor a short time after acquiring the upscale chain, Sears Holding sold its stake in Orchard Supply Hardware, and Limited Inc. spun off its original Limited Stores division to focus on its other businesses. Lexlie Wexner founded The Limited in 1963. This chain grew substantially and also diversified: "The Limited provided the seed for what has become Limited Brands, a retailing empire that includes Victoria's Secret, Bath & Body Works, and Henri Bendel. All those other names remain part of Limited Brands. But as the shopping conglomerate began to focus on higher-margin intimate apparel and beauty products, executives at its original franchise found it harder to amass the cash for operations like E-commerce."[8] Thus, The Limited was spun off.

When they want to continue in business, weak retailers file Chapter 11. If they want to liquidate, they file Chapter 7 (www.uscourts.gov/FederalCourts/Bankruptcy.aspx).

To safeguard themselves against mounting debts, as well as to continue in business, faltering retailers may seek bankruptcy protection under Chapter 11 of the Federal Bankruptcy Code (which was toughened in 2005). In November 2006, when the economy was quite strong, only 3.8 percent of the large retailers tracked by a turnaround consulting firm were facing a high possibility of bankruptcy or financial distress. By November 2008, the figure had risen to 25.8 percent.[9] Today, the figure is much lower (and closer to pre-recession percentages).

With bankruptcy protection, retailers can renegotiate bills, get out of leases, and work with creditors to plan for the future. Declaring bankruptcy has major ramifications: "Some say bankruptcy results in the loss of key executives, disruptions in supply, and demoralization on those who stay; but others say it fends off creditors and lets firms pay off debt and survive what may be a temporary upheaval. Executives not in favor of filing also cite the legal and financial advisory fees of bankruptcy protection."[10]

Here's a recent retail bankruptcy example involving Harry & David, a food company. It entered bankruptcy in March 2011 and successfully emerged from it in September 2011. During the 2010 holiday season, the firm anticipated stronger sales performance than it was achieving, which did not happen:

> To clear inventory, we had to discount heavily, which decreased net profits—and we failed to generate enough cash flow. After losing the ability to borrow and facing a significant liquidity shortfall, a Chapter 11 bankruptcy filing became necessary to (a) address our liquidity needs and (b) provide the opportunity to right-size our business through (i) structural improvements and (ii) the evaluation and elimination of liabilities that only serve to drain profitability. We filed for Chapter 11 on March 28, 2011. We emerged from bankruptcy on September 13, 2011.[11]

Not all bankruptcies end up with rejuvenated retailers. Many end up in liquidations, where the firms ultimately go out of business. This has happened with Borders, Filene's Basement, Linens 'n Things, Syms, and other firms. When a retailer goes out of business, it is painful for all parties: the owner/stockholders, employees, creditors, landlords (who then have vacant store sites), and customers. See Figure 12-2.

As with several other sectors of business, over the last few years, some retailers have been heavily criticized for questionable accounting and financial practices. Sometimes, the practices have been illegal. For example, in 2011, Don Watson, the former chief financial officer of CSK Auto (the parent company of Checker Auto Parts, Schucks Auto Supply, and Kragen Auto Parts) pleaded guilty in U.S. District Court to "conspiracy to commit securities and mail fraud in

The High Cost of Employee Turnover

Franchisees often compute the costs of employee turnover with regard to their advertising job positions, screening applicants, and then training new hires. In reality, the actual costs of turnover are considerably greater when lost sales due to poor customer service are taken into account. Harold Jackson, an owner of a variety of franchise operations in the Great Lakes area of Ohio, has calculated his firm's costs of a lost employee at between $700 and $1,000.

According to Jackson, a strategy to retain good employees starts with the hiring process. Unfortunately, too many franchise owners limit the hiring process to a basic interview and to verifying references. Instead, the franchise manager or owner needs to better explain the applicant's job position, including his or her customer service responsibilities.

One tool to better assess and match potential employees to their position is a behavioral assessment questionnaire that evaluates the key personality traits and attitudes needed for each job. When the owner of a seven-unit Subway (www.subway.com) group used an employee assessment tool, the franchise operator found that many employees were in the wrong positions. As an example, an order taker might have been happier working in a food-preparation environment with little or no customer contact. After examining the results from the behavioral assessment questionnaire, that franchise operator was able to reduce annual employee turnover from 70 to 42 percent.

Source: Harold Jackson, "Strategies to Combat Employee Turnover," *Franchising World* (May 2011), pp. 18–21.

FIGURE 12-2

The Demise of Linens 'n Things

After a long, successful run (with billions of dollars in annual sales) as a leading store-based retailer of household goods, Linens 'n Things went out of business in late 2008. The firm was adversely affected by the weak economy, heavy competition, and its unsuccessful conversion from a publicly owned to a privately owned company in 2006. At the end, it was unable to get support from its creditors or to find a buyer to keep the store-based business going. The Web domain name was sold; and in 2009, new owners opened an online-only business (www.lnt.com).

Source: Lori Martin/Shutterstock.com. Reprinted by permission.

connection with a scheme to misstate the company's reported earnings." He admitted that, from 2001 to 2006, he misstated CSK's earnings "by concealing that the company had tens of millions of dollars in vendor rebates that CSK had claimed as income but were never collected. The rebates were in fact not owed to the company or could not be collected and therefore should have been written off CSK's books. As a result of the fraud scheme, CSK reported tens of millions of dollars more in pre-tax income than it in fact earned."[12] In September 2011, Watson received a two-year jail sentence.

To avoid questionable or illegal practices, many retailers have enacted formal policies. At Home Depot, there is a detailed "Code of Ethics for Senior Financial Officers," as highlighted here. The code applies to Home Depot's chief executive, chief financial officer, and many other high-ranking personnel. Every one of these executives must adhere to such practices as these:

- Act in all financial and accounting matters as a model of honesty, integrity, and fair dealing;
- Owe and fulfill the highest care to the company over any personal or other interests;
- Avoid actual or apparent conflict of interest;
- Report any proposals or attempts by others to record transactions inaccurately;
- Provide assurance that the financial and accounting aspects of all proposed project activities is lawful, accurate, complete, and not intended to mislead;
- Proactively promote ethical behavior as a responsible partner; and
- Achieve responsible use of and control over all company assets and resources.[13]

BUDGETING

Why should a small business know about budgeting? Type "Budgeting" at this site (www.inc.com).

Budgeting outlines a retailer's planned expenditures for a given time based on expected performance. Costs are linked to satisfying target market, employee, and management goals. What should personnel costs be to attain a certain level of customer service? What compensation amount will motivate salespeople? What operating expenses will generate intended revenues and reach profit goals?

There are several benefits from a retailer's meticulously preparing a budget:

- Expenditures are clearly related to expected performance, and costs can be adjusted as goals are revised. This enhances productivity.
- Resources are allocated to the right departments, product categories, and so on.
- Spending for various departments, product categories, and so on is coordinated.
- Because planning is structured and integrated, the goal of efficiency is prominent.
- Cost standards are set, such as advertising equals 5 percent of sales.
- A firm prepares for the future rather than reacts to it.

- Expenditures are monitored during a budget cycle. If a firm allots $50,000 to buy new merchandise, and it has spent $33,000 halfway through a cycle, it has $17,000 remaining.
- A firm can analyze planned budgets versus actual budgets.
- Costs and performance can be compared with industry averages.

A retailer should be aware of the effort involved in the budgeting process, recognize that forecasts may not be fully accurate (due to unexpected demand, competitors' tactics, and so on), and modify plans as needed. The process should not be too conservative (or inflexible) or simply add a percentage to each expense category to arrive at the next budget, such as increasing spending by 3 percent across the board based on anticipated sales growth of 3 percent. The budgeting process is shown in Figure 12-3 and described next.

Preliminary Budgeting Decisions

There are six preliminary decisions.

First, budgeting authority is specified. In top-down budgeting, senior executives make centralized financial decisions and communicate them down the line to succeeding levels of managers. In bottom-up budgeting, lower-level executives develop departmental budget requests; these requests are assembled, and a company budget is designed. Bottom-up budgeting includes varied perspectives, holds managers more accountable, and enhances employee morale. Many firms combine aspects of the two approaches.

Second, the time frame is defined. Most firms have budgets with yearly, quarterly, and monthly components. Annual spending is planned, while costs and performance are regularly reviewed. This responds to seasonal or other fluctuations. Sometimes, the time frame is longer than a year or shorter than a month. When a firm opens new stores over a five-year period, it sets construction costs for the entire period. When a supermarket orders perishables, it has weekly budgets for each item.

Third, budgeting frequency is determined. Many firms review budgets on an ongoing basis, but most plan them yearly. In some firms, several months may be set aside each year for the

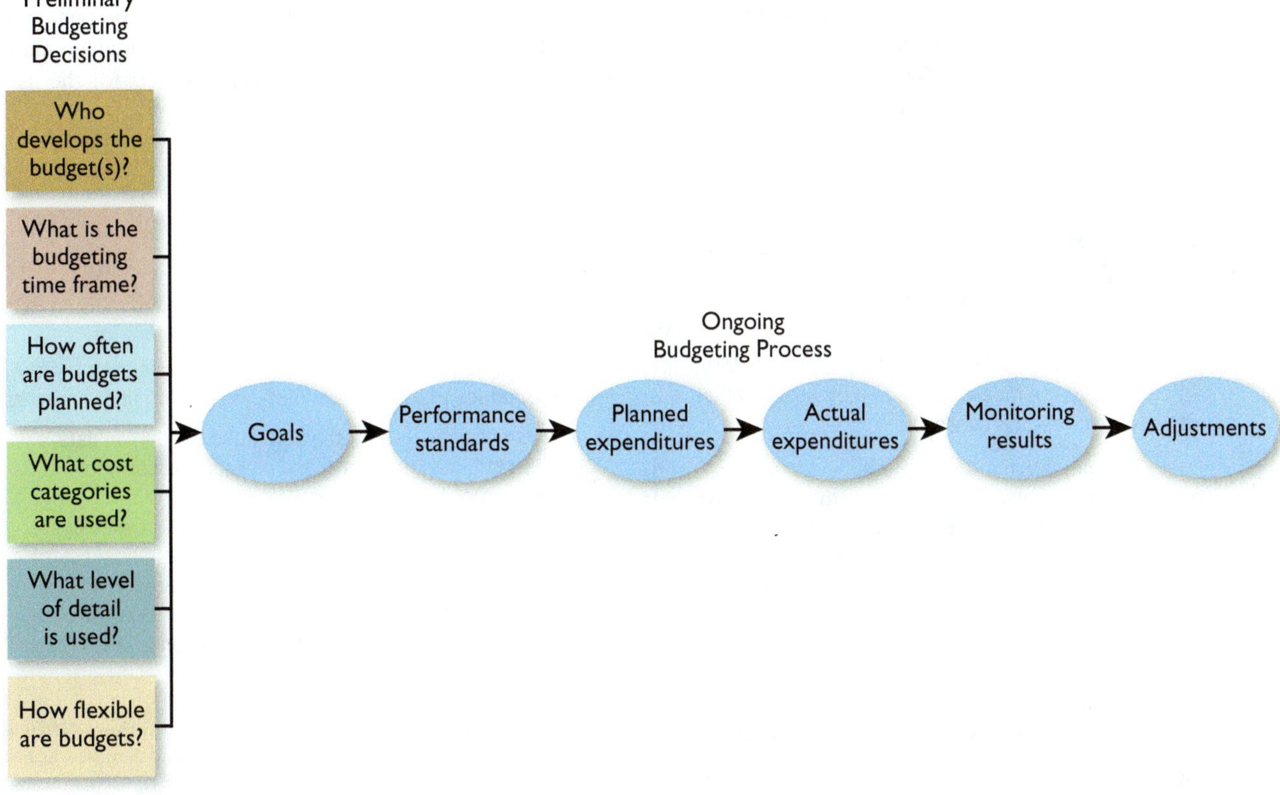

FIGURE 12-3
The Retail Budgeting Process

budgeting process; this lets all participants have time to gather data and facilitates taking the budgets through several drafts.

Fourth, cost categories are established:

- *Capital expenditures* are long-term investments in land, buildings, fixtures, and equipment. *Operating expenditures* are the short-term expenses of running a business.
- *Fixed costs*, such as store security, remain constant for the budget period regardless of the retailer's performance. *Variable costs*, such as sales commissions, are based on performance. If performance is good, these expenses often rise.
- *Direct costs* are incurred by specific departments, product categories, and so on, such as the earnings of department-based salespeople. *Indirect costs*, such as centralized cashiers, are shared by multiple departments, product categories, and so on.
- *Natural account expenses* are reported by the names of the costs, such as salaries, and not assigned by purpose. *Functional account expenses* are classified on the basis of the purpose or activity for which expenditures are made, such as cashier salaries.

Fifth, the level of detail is set. Should spending be assigned by department (produce), product category (fresh fruit), product subcategory (apples), and/or product item (McIntosh apples)? With a very detailed budget, every expense subcategory must be adequately covered.

Sixth, budget flexibility is prescribed. A budget should be strict enough to guide planned spending and link costs to goals. Yet, a budget that is too inflexible may not let a retailer adapt to changing market conditions, capitalize on new opportunities, or modify a poor strategy (if further spending is needed to improve matters). Budget flexibility is often expressed in quantitative terms, such as allowing a buyer to increase a quarterly budget by a certain maximum percentage if demand is higher than anticipated.

Ongoing Budgeting Process

After making preliminary budgeting decisions, the retailer engages in the ongoing budgeting process shown in Figure 12-3:

- Goals are set based on customer, employee, and management needs.
- Performance standards are specified, including customer service levels, the compensation needed to motivate employees, and the sales and profits needed to satisfy management. Typically, the budget is related to a sales forecast, which projects revenues for the next period. Forecasts are usually broken down by department or product category.

Dealing with Online Security Issues

According to many online security experts, information breaches, leaks to the media, fraud, and other issues that must be resolved. Consider this observation:

> Direct E-commerce fraud rates have decreased significantly over the last several years, in part due to major investments in security and fraud prevention. However, fraud still costs E-commerce merchants billions in losses. Despite the [large sums of money invested], merchants remain vulnerable to fraud committed using stolen information compromised in data breaches, highlighting a unique challenge to tighten security both in the physical and electronic environments. This becomes even more important given the emerging mobile commerce industry, which introduces additional security challenges.

Security experts recommend that firms focus their security strategies on three areas: restricting access, cleaning up the corporate culture, and developing a crisis communication plan to reduce the chances and magnitude of major breaches:

- *Restrict access*—Limit the access to confidential data, restrict E-mail recipients, and prohibit the copying and pasting of sensitive documents.
- *Clean up the corporate culture*—Discourage employees and managers from making potentially damaging statements concerning competitors or customers.
- *Develop a crisis communications plan*—Assess the company's security risks, develop likely scenarios, and create plans to manage communications.

Sources: Margaret Weichert, "Prevention Options?" www.merchantriskcouncil.org (December 2010); and "New Year, New Scams, New Risks—What to Watch for Now" (February 2011), www.iofm.com/security.

- Expenditures are planned in terms of performance goals. In **zero-based budgeting**, a firm starts each new budget from scratch and outlines the expenditures needed to reach that period's goals. All costs are justified each time a budget is done. With **incremental budgeting**, a firm uses current and past budgets as guides and adds to or subtracts from them to arrive at the coming period's spending. Most firms use incremental budgeting; it is easier, less time-consuming, and not as risky.
- Actual expenditures are made. The retailer pays rent and employee salaries, buys merchandise, places ads, and so on.
- Results are monitored: (1) Actual expenditures are compared with planned spending for each expense category, and reasons for any deviations are reviewed. (2) The firm learns if performance standards have been met and tries to explain deviations.
- The budget is adjusted. Revisions are major or minor, depending on how closely a firm has come to reaching its goals. The funds allotted to some expense categories may be reduced, while greater funds may be provided to other categories.

Table 12-5 compares budgeted and actual revenues, expenses, and profits for Donna's Gift Shop during fiscal 2012. The actual data come from Table 12-1. The variance figures compare expected and actual results for each profit-and-loss item. Variances are positive if performance is better than expected and negative if it is worse.

As Table 12-5 indicates, in *dollar terms*, net profit after taxes was $7,250 higher than budgeted. Sales were $30,000 higher than expected; thus, the cost of goods sold was $15,000 higher. Actual operating expenses were $750 lower than expected, while other costs were $2,000 higher. Table 12-5 also shows results in *percentage terms.* This lets a firm evaluate budgeted versus actual performance on a percent-of-sales basis. In Donna's case, actual net profit after taxes was 5.83 percent of sales—better than planned. The higher net profit was mostly due to the actual operating costs percentage being lower than planned.

Learn more about cash flow management at this site (www.entrepreneur.com/tag/392).

A firm must closely monitor its **cash flow**, which relates the amount and timing of revenues received to the amount and timing of expenditures for a specific time. In cash flow management,

TABLE 12-5 Donna's Gift Shop, Fiscal 2012 Budgeted Versus Actual Profit-and-Loss Statement (in Dollars and Percent)

	Budgeted		Actual		Variance[a]	
	Dollars	*Percent*	*Dollars*	*Percent*	*Dollars*	*Percent*
Net sales	$300,000	100.00	$330,000	100.00	+$30,000	—
Cost of goods sold	$165,000	55.00	$180,000	54.55	−$15,000	+0.45
Gross profit	$135,000	45.00	$150,000	45.45	+$15,000	+0.45
Operating expenses:						
Salaries	$ 75,000	25.00	$ 75,000	22.73	—	+2.27
Advertising	5,250	1.75	4,950	1.50	+$ 300	+0.25
Supplies	1,800	0.60	1,650	0.50	+$ 150	+0.10
Shipping	1,350	0.45	1,500	0.45	−$ 150	—
Insurance	4,500	1.50	4,500	1.36	—	+0.14
Maintenance	5,100	1.70	5,100	1.55	—	+0.15
Other	3,000	1.00	2,550	0.77	+$ 450	+0.23
Total	$ 96,000	32.00	$ 95,250	28.86	+$ 750	+3.14
Other costs	$ 18,000	6.00	$ 20,000	6.06	−$ 2,000	−0.06
Total costs	$114,000	38.00	$115,250	34.92	−$ 1,250	+3.08
Net profit before taxes	$ 21,000	7.00	$ 34,750	10.53	+$13,750	+3.53
Taxes	$ 9,000	3.00	$ 15,500	4.70	−$ 6,500	−1.70
Net profit after taxes	$ 12,000	4.00	$ 19,250	5.83	+$ 7,250	+1.83

There are small rounding errors.

[a] Variance is a positive number if actual sales or profits are higher than expected or actual expenses are lower than expected. Variance is a negative number if actual sales or profits are lower than expected or actual expenses are higher than expected.

TABLE 12-6 The Effects of Cash Flow

A.

A retailer has rather consistent sales throughout the year. Therefore, the cash flow in any given month is positive. This means no short-term loans are needed, and the owner can withdraw funds from the firm if she so desires:

Linda's Luncheonette, Cash Flow for January

Cash inflow:		
Net sales		$26,000
Cash outflow:		
Cost of goods sold	$9,500	
Operating expenses	8,000	
Other costs	2,500	
Total		$20,000
Positive cash flow		$6,000

B.

A retailer has highly seasonal sales that peak in December. Yet, to have a good assortment of merchandise on hand during December, it must order merchandise in September and October and pay for it in November. As a result, it has a negative cash flow in November that must be financed by a short-term loan. All debts are paid off in January, after the peak selling season is completed:

Dave's Party Favors, Cash Flow for November

Cash inflow:		
Net sales		$19,000
Cash outflow:		
Cost of goods sold	$22,500	
Operating expenses	3,000	
Other costs	2,100	
Total		$27,600
Net cash flow		–$8,600
Short-term loan (to be paid off in January)		$8,600

the usual intention is to make sure revenues are received before expenditures are made.[14] Otherwise, short-term loans may be needed or profits may be tied up in inventory and other expenses. For seasonal retailers, this may be unavoidable. Underestimating costs and overestimating revenues, both of which affect cash flow, are leading causes of new business failures. Table 12-6 has cash flow examples.

RESOURCE ALLOCATION

In allotting financial resources, both the magnitude of various costs and productivity should be examined. Each has significance for asset management and budgeting.

The Magnitude of Various Costs

To easily study the financial operating performance of publicly owned retailers, go to AnnualReports.com (www.annualreports.com), enter a company name, and download its annual report.

As noted before, spending can be divided into two categories. **Capital expenditures** are long-term investments in fixed assets. **Operating expenditures** are short-term selling and administrative costs in running a business. It is vital to have a sense of the magnitude of various capital and operating costs.

In 2011, these were the average capital expenditures (for the basic building shell; heating, ventilation, and air-conditioning; lighting; flooring; fixtures; ceilings; interior and exterior

The Computerized Checkout as an Operations Aid

Even though the checkout display area may be the most valuable space in a typical retail store, many retailers have not taken advantage of all the opportunities this space can provide. According to one retail analyst, a well-run checkout display area can add 1.5 to 1.8 percent to a firm's gross sales. In addition, goods sold at checkouts tend to have very high profit margins.

One major obstacle retailers need to overcome to more effectively use their checkout space is the resistance to new ideas. Another is the rivalry among store departments to include their goods in the checkout area. Lastly, magazine publishers, candy manufacturers, and beverage companies have convinced many retailers to include their goods, resulting in the exclusion of other suitable items.

Hiller's Markets (www.hillers.com) in Southfield, Michigan, has a successful checkout-based coupon program that enables shoppers to receive digital coupons on its Web site or on a customer's mobile phone. A customer's selected coupons are stored in a digital wallet and can be viewed any time. At the checkout, the shopper can instantaneously redeem these coupons by entering his/her home or mobile telephone number. These coupons are then matched against the consumer's purchases and are automatically deducted from the customer's bill. No loyalty card or special display at the checkout area is required.

Source: Edward Novick, "The Front-End Checkout: A Micro-Economic Model of the Store," www.progressivegrocer.com (January 2011).

signage; and roofing) for erecting a single store for a range of retailers: big-box stores (including department stores)—$3.7 million; supermarkets—$3.5 million; home centers—$1.6 million; apparel specialty stores—$400,000; and convenience stores—$300,000.[15] Thus, a typical home center chain must be prepared to invest $1.6 million to build each new store (which averaged 30,300 square feet industrywide in 2011), not including land and merchandise costs; the total could be higher if a bigger store is built.

Remodeling can also be expensive. It is prompted by competitive pressures, mergers and acquisitions, consumer trends, the requirement of complying with the Americans with Disabilities Act, environmental concerns, and other factors.

To reduce their investments, some retailers insist that real-estate developers help pay for building, renovating, and fixture costs. These demands by retail tenants reflect some areas' oversaturation, the amount of retail space available due to the liquidation of some retailers (as well as mergers), and the interest of developers in gaining retailers that generate consumer traffic (such as category killers).

Operating expenses, usually expressed as a percentage of sales, range from 20 percent or so in supermarkets to more than 40 percent in some specialty stores. To succeed, these costs must be in line with competitors' costs. Costco has an edge over many rivals due to lower SGA (selling, general, and administrative costs as a percentage of sales): Costco, 10 percent; Wal-Mart, 19 percent; Target, 20 percent; Kohl's, 23 percent; Dillard's, 27 percent; and Macy's, Inc., 33 percent. However, BJ's SGA is 9 percent.[16]

Resource allocation must also take into account **opportunity costs**—the possible benefits a retailer forgoes if it invests in one opportunity rather than another. If a supermarket chain renovates 15 existing stores at a total cost of $3.5 million, it cannot open a new outlet requiring a $3.5 million investment (excluding land and merchandise). Financial resources are finite, so firms often face either/or decisions.

Productivity

Look at the various ways in which retailers can improve their financial performance (www.toolkit.cch.com/text/P06_0100.asp).

Due to erratic sales revenues, mixed economic growth, high labor costs, intense competition, and other factors, many retailers place great priority on their **productivity**, the efficiency with which a retail strategy is carried out. Productivity can be described in terms of costs as a percentage of sales, the time it takes a cashier to complete a transaction, profit margins, sales per square foot, inventory turnover, and so forth. The key question is: How can sales and profit goals be reached while keeping control over costs?

Because different retail strategy mixes have distinct resource needs as to store location, fixtures, personnel, and other elements, productivity must be based on norms for each type of strategy mix (such as department stores versus full-line discount stores). Sales growth should also be measured on the basis of comparable seasons, using the same stores. Otherwise, the data will be affected by seasonality and/or the increased square footage of stores.

There are two ways to enhance productivity: (1) A firm can improve employee performance, sales per foot of space, and other factors by upgrading training programs, increasing advertising, and so forth. (2) It can reduce costs by automating, having suppliers do certain tasks, and so forth. A retailer could use a small core of full-time workers during nonpeak times, supplemented with part-timers in peak periods.

Productivity must not be measured from a cost-cutting perspective alone. This may undermine customer loyalty. One of the more complex dilemmas for store retailers that are also online is how to handle customer returns. To control costs, some of them have decided not to allow online purchases to be returned at their stores. This policy has gotten a lot of customers upset and resulted in most of these firms changing their policies.

These are two examples of strategies that diverse retailers have used to raise productivity:

- Many firms are using computer software to improve their allocation of shelf space to be more productive per square foot. The Winn-Dixie and ShopKo supermarket chains are among those that utilize SAS Retail Space Management software.
- Tuesday Morning is an 865-store chain selling quality closeouts. Its strategy is very cost-focused: "We have attractive store-level economics due to low store operating expenses and the low initial investment required to open new stores. Our destination-oriented retail format allows us to open stores in a wide range of locations, generally resulting in lower lease rates compared to other retailers. In addition to low real-estate costs, we maintain low operating and depreciation costs due to our no-frills, self-service format. Because we use low-cost store fixtures and have low pre-opening costs, new stores require a low initial investment and have historically generated a solid return on investment in their first full year."[17]

Tuesday Morning uses a variety of E-mail formats (http://etreasures.tuesdaymorning.com) to offer bargains to consumers and to reduce its costs by minimizing the need for printed circulars and newspaper ads.

It is vital that retailers, in their quest to become more productive, do not alienate their customers and diminish the shopping experience: "Increasing retail sales productivity is important, but the true challenge—and the true benchmark of retail management performance—is to build productivity profitably."[18]

Chapter Summary

1. *To define operations management.* Operations management involves efficiently and effectively implementing the tasks and policies to satisfy the retailer's customers, employees, and management. This chapter covered the financial aspects of operations management. Operational dimensions are studied in Chapter 13.

2. *To discuss profit planning.* The profit-and-loss (income) statement summarizes a retailer's revenues and expenses over a specific time, typically on a monthly, quarterly, and/or yearly basis. It consists of these major components: net sales, cost of goods sold, gross profit (margin), operating expenses, and net profit after taxes.

3. *To describe asset management, including the strategic profit model, other key business ratios, and financial trends in retailing.* Each retailer has assets and liabilities to manage. A balance sheet shows assets, liabilities, and net worth at a given time. Assets are items with a monetary value owned by a retailer; some appreciate and may have a hidden value. Liabilities are financial obligations. The retailer's net worth, also called owner's equity, is computed as assets minus liabilities.

   Asset management may be measured by reviewing the net profit margin, asset turnover, and financial leverage. Net profit margin equals net profit divided by net sales. Asset turnover equals net sales divided by total assets. By multiplying the net profit margin by asset turnover, a retailer can find its return on assets—which is based on net sales, net profit, and total assets. Financial leverage equals total assets divided by net worth. The strategic profit model incorporates asset turnover, profit margin, and financial leverage to yield the return on net worth. It allows a retailer to better plan and control its asset management.

   Other key ratios for retailers are the quick ratio, current ratio, collection period, accounts payable to net sales, and overall gross profit (in percent).

   Important financial trends involve the state of the economy; funding sources; mergers, consolidations, and spin-offs; bankruptcies and liquidations; and questionable accounting and financial reporting practices.

4. *To look at retail budgeting.* Budgeting outlines a retailer's planned expenditures for a given time based on expected performance; costs are linked to goals.

There are six preliminary decisions: (a) Responsibility is defined by top-down and/or bottom-up methods. (b) The time frame is specified. (c) Budgeting frequency is set. (d) Cost categories are established. (e) The level of detail is ascertained. (f) Budgeting flexibility is determined.

The ongoing budgeting process then proceeds: goals, performance standards, planned spending, actual expenditures, monitoring results, and adjustments. With zero-based budgeting, each budget starts from scratch; with incremental budgeting, current and past budgets are guides. The budgeted versus actual profit-and-loss statement and the percentage profit-and-loss statement are vital tools. In all budgeting decisions, cash flow, which relates the amount and timing of revenues received with the amount and timing of expenditures made, must be considered.

5. *To examine resource allocation.* Both the magnitude of costs and productivity need to be examined. Costs can be divided into capital and operating categories; both must be regularly reviewed. Opportunity costs mean forgoing possible benefits if a retailer invests in one opportunity rather than another. Productivity is the efficiency with which a retail strategy is carried out; the goal is to maximize sales and profits while keeping costs in check.

Key Terms

operations management (p. 306)
profit-and-loss (income) statement (p. 306)
net sales (p. 306)
cost of goods sold (p. 306)
gross profit (margin) (p. 306)
operating expenses (p. 306)
taxes (p. 306)
net profit after taxes (p. 306)
balance sheet (p. 307)
assets (p. 307)
hidden assets (p. 308)
liabilities (p. 308)
net worth (p. 308)
net profit margin (p. 308)
asset turnover (p. 308)
return on assets (ROA) (p. 308)
financial leverage (p. 308)
strategic profit model (p. 309)
return on net worth (RONW) (p. 309)
budgeting (p. 314)
zero-based budgeting (p. 317)
incremental budgeting (p. 317)
cash flow (p. 317)
capital expenditures (p. 318)
operating expenditures (p. 318)
opportunity costs (p. 319)
productivity (p. 319)

Questions for Discussion

1. Describe the relationship of assets, liabilities, and net worth for a retailer. How is a balance sheet useful in examining these items?
2. A retailer has net sales of $1,075,000, net profit of $185,000, total assets of $600,000, and a net worth of $225,000.
   a. Calculate net profit margin, asset turnover, and return on assets.
   b. Compute financial leverage and return on net worth.
   c. Evaluate the financial performance of this retailer.
3. How can a convenience store increase its asset turnover?
4. Is too low a financial leverage ratio good or bad? Why?
5. Differentiate between an IPO and an LBO.
6. Present five recommendations for retailers to improve their accounting and financial reporting practices with regard to disclosure ("transparency") of all relevant information to stockholders and others.
7. What is zero-based budgeting? Why do most retailers utilize incremental budgeting, despite its limitations?
8. What is the value of a percentage profit-and-loss statement?
9. How could a seasonal retailer improve its cash flow during periods when it must buy goods for future selling periods?
10. Distinguish between capital spending and operating expenditures. Why is this distinction important to retailers?
11. What factors should retailers consider when assessing opportunity costs?
12. How can these retailers improve their productivity?
    a. Travel agency.
    b. Neighborhood restaurant.
    c. College bookstore.
    d. Upscale apparel store.

Note: At our Web site (www.pearsonhighered.com/bermanevans), there are several math problems related to the material in this chapter so that you may review these concepts.

Web-Based Exercise

Visit the Web site of QuickBooks (http://support.qbo.intuit.com/interactive_tour_movie.cfm) to take the online interactive tour. What are benefits of a product such as this for a small retailer?

Note: Also stop by our Web site (www.pearsonhighered.com/bermanevans) to experience a number of highly interactive, appealing Web exercises based on actual company demonstrations and sample materials related to retailing.

13 Operations Management: Operational Dimensions

Chapter Objectives

1. To describe the operational scope of operations management

2. To examine several specific aspects of operating a retail business: operations blueprint; store format, size, and space allocation; personnel utilization; store maintenance, energy management, and renovations; inventory management; store security; insurance; credit management; computerization; outsourcing; and crisis management

As we've shown with each of our chapter-opening vignettes, social media are influencing virtually every aspect of retailing. This is quite evident with regard to store operations, the focus of Chapter 13.

According to *Stores* magazine's Susan Reda:

> The vision of a shopper roaming aisles, with smart phone in hand and receiving targeted messages and relevant coupons, is coming into focus quicker than anticipated. Customers are using their mobile phones to scan a barcode and perform price comparisons, to read online product reviews while they're in the store, and to check inventory at a nearby location when the item they're looking for is not in stock. These scenarios are being played out at retail stores across the country, and experts predict similar versions of the story to increase tenfold in the years to come.

Some retailers have found shoppers' increasing use of mobile technology to present a difficult task for them from an operations perspective; others are innovating. J.C. Penney is one of the forward-looking retailers, as highlighted in the book *Branded!: How Retailers Engage Consumers with Social Media and Mobility*. Here is what the authors conclude about Penney and its technological prowess:

> In many large corporations, a marketer's nemesis is often the information technology (IT) organization, but in J.C. Penney's push to expand its digital word of mouth, the CEO has found his closest partner to be his IT executive vice-president. As Penney's CEO notes: "We work hand-in-glove on all of these initiatives."

Because Penney was involved in E-commerce early, the firm had to build much of its Web site itself. It did not benefit from today's advanced Web design software packages. Recently, Penney's Web site was redesigned to include more social media and better support for mobile devices. Penney's CEO says, "We have a tremendous amount of innovation going on in the entire digital space. This is an infrastructure that will support every customer touch point—regardless of where they are, including J.C. Penney stores"[1]

Source: BeTA-Artworks/ fotolia.com.

Overview

For a good operations overview, go to the About.com: Retailing Web site (http://retail.about.com/od/storeoperations).

As defined in Chapter 12, *operations management* is the efficient and effective implementation of the policies and tasks that satisfy a retailer's customers, employees, and management (and stockholders, if it is publicly owned). While Chapter 12 examined the financial dimensions of operations management, this chapter covers the operational aspects.

For firms to succeed in the long term, operational areas need to be managed well. A decision to change a store format or to introduce new anti-theft equipment must be carefully reviewed because these acts greatly affect performance. In running their businesses, retail executives must make a wide range of operational decisions, such as these:

- What operating guidelines are used?
- What is the optimal format and size of a store? What is the relationship among shelf space, shelf location, and sales for each item in the store?
- How can personnel best be matched to customer traffic flows? Would increased staffing improve or reduce productivity? What impact does self-service have on sales?
- What effect does the use of various building materials have on store maintenance? How can energy costs be better controlled? How often should facilities be renovated?
- How can inventory best be managed?
- How can the personal safety of shoppers and employees be ensured?
- What levels of insurance are required?
- How can credit transactions be managed most effectively?
- How can computer systems improve operating efficiency?
- Should any aspects of operations be outsourced?
- What kinds of crisis management plans should be in place?

OPERATING A RETAIL BUSINESS

To address these questions, we now look at the operations blueprint; store format, size, and space allocation; personnel utilization; store maintenance, energy management, and renovations; inventory management; store security; insurance; credit management; computerization; outsourcing; and crisis management.

Operations Blueprint

To encourage more compatibility among different retail hardware and software systems, the National Retail Federation has established its ARTS program (www.nrf-arts.org).

An **operations blueprint** systematically lists all operating functions to be performed, their characteristics, and their timing. When developing a blueprint, the retailer specifies, in detail, every operating function from the store's opening to closing—and those responsible for them.[2] For example, who opens the store? When? What are the steps (turning off the alarm, turning on the power, setting up the computer, and so forth)? The performance of these tasks must not be left to chance.

A large or diversified retailer may use multiple blueprints and have separate blueprints for such areas as store maintenance, inventory management, credit management, and store displays. Whenever a retailer modifies its store format or operating procedures (such as relying more on self-service), it must also adjust the operations blueprint(s).

Figure 13-1 has an operations blueprint for a quick-oil-change firm. It identifies employee and customer tasks (in order) and expected performance times for each activity. Among the advantages of this blueprint—and others—are that it standardizes activities (within a location and between locations), isolates points at which operations may be weak or prone to failure (Do employees actually check transmission, brake, and power-steering fluids in one minute?), outlines a plan that can be evaluated for completeness (Should customers be offered different grades of oil?), shows personnel needs (Should one person change the oil and another wash the windshield?), and helps identify productivity improvements (Should the customer or an employee drive a car into and out of the service bay?).

Store Format, Size, and Space Allocation

The Benchmark Group (www.bgark.com) has collaborated with a number of retailers to develop their stores. Click on "Project Experience."

With regard to store format, it should be decided if productivity can be raised by such tactics as locating in a planned shopping center rather than in an unplanned business district, using prefabricated materials in construction, and applying certain kinds of store design and layouts.

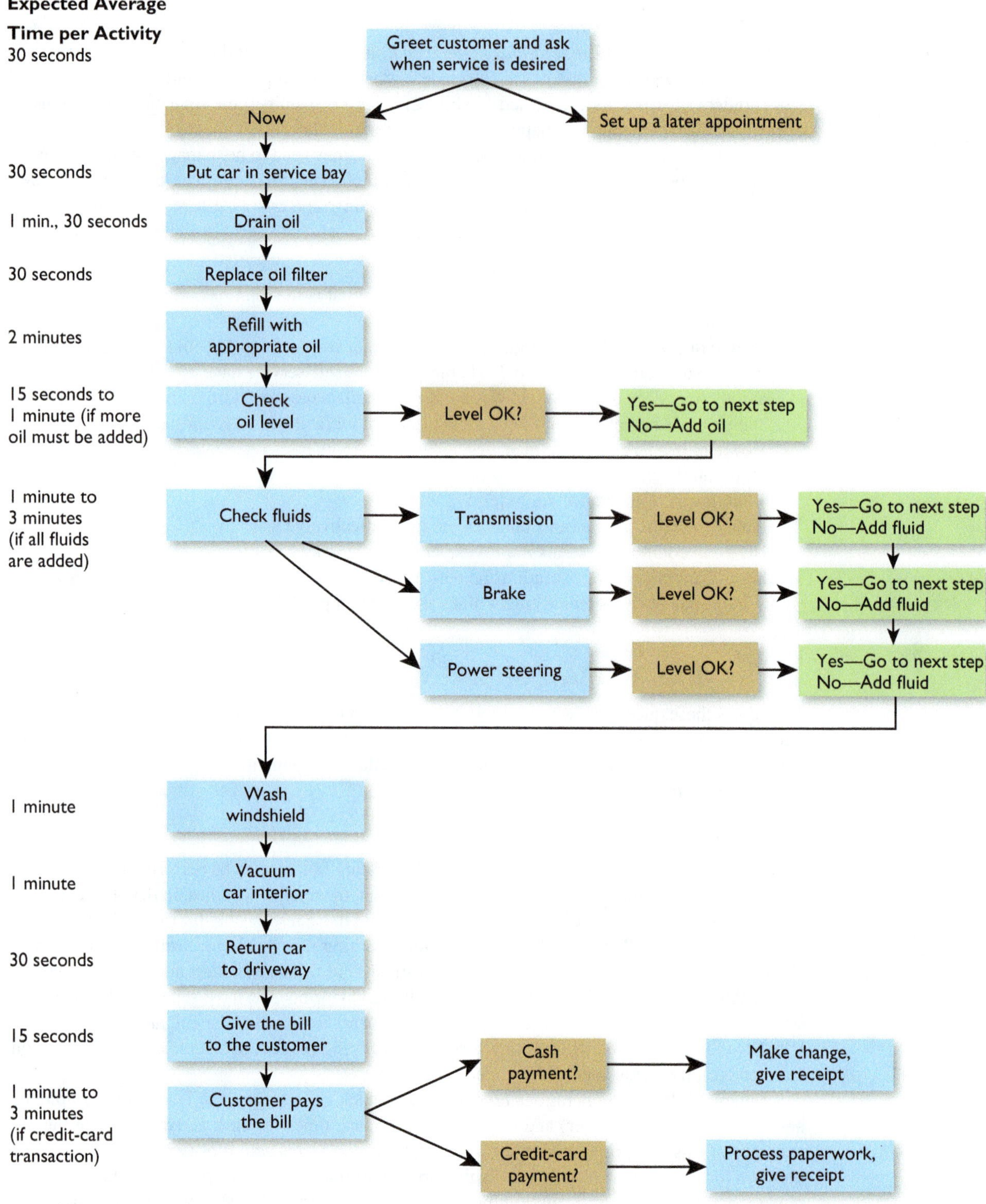

FIGURE 13-1

A Operations Blueprint for a Quick-Oil-Change Firm's Employees

Marriott's Global Plans

Growth in the developing countries of Asia is particularly important for Marriott International (www.marriott.com). Arne Sorenson, president and chief operating officer of Marriott International, believes that the Chinese economy will be as large as the U.S. economy (or larger) in the next 10 to 15 years. He estimates that China's current inventory of 1 million hotel rooms will double in the next 10 years. Marriott currently has about 60 hotels in China under its Marriott, Ritz-Carlton, JW Marriott, Renaissance, and Courtyard brands.

A second major part of Marriott's global expansion involves India. India, with 100,000 to 150,000 hotels, will experience a 10-times growth in hotel capacity over the next 10 to 15 years.

Marriott also recently added 50 "green" Fairfield Inns in Brazil in a partnership arrangement with PDG Realty. A stable government and the 2016 Olympics, which will be based in Rio de Janeiro, contribute to Brazil's attraction to Marriott.

Although the growth rate in Europe is small as compared with developing economies, Marriott's market share is tiny—between 1 and 2 percent of the hotel market. To build up its presence in Spain, Italy, and Portugal, Marriott recently signed a joint venture agreement that added 90 AC Hotels by Marriott (www.marriott.com/ac-hotels/travel.mi) to these countries.

Sources: Ruthanne Terrero, "One-on-One: Marriott International's Arne M. Sorenson," www.nxtbook.com/nxtbooks/questex/hm_201106/index.php?startid=24 (June 6, 2011); and Marriott Web site (January 19, 2012).

A key store format decision for chain retailers is whether to use **prototype stores,** whereby multiple outlets conform to relatively uniform construction, layout, and operations standards. Such stores make centralized management control easier, reduce construction costs, standardize operations, facilitate the interchange of employees among outlets, allow fixtures and other materials to be bought in quantity, and display a consistent chain image. Yet, a strict reliance on prototypes may lead to inflexibility, failure to adapt to or capitalize on local customer needs, and too little creativity. McDonald's, Pep Boys, Office Depot, Starbucks, and most supermarket chains are among those with prototype stores.

Together with prototype stores, some chains use **rationalized retailing** programs to combine a high degree of centralized management control with strict operating procedures for every phase of business. Most of these chains' operations are performed in a virtually identical manner in all outlets. Rigid control and standardization make this technique easy to enact and manage, and a firm can add a significant number of stores in a short time. Dunkin' Donuts, Old Navy, and Radio Shack use rationalized retailing. They operate many stores that are similar in size, layout, and merchandising. See Figure 13-2.

Many retailers use one or both of two contrasting store-size approaches to be distinctive and to deal with high rents in some metropolitan markets. Home Depot, Barnes & Noble, and Sports Authority have category killer stores with huge assortments that try to dominate smaller stores. Food-based warehouse stores and large discount-oriented stores often situate in secondary sites, where rents are low—confident that they can draw customers. Cub Foods (a warehouse chain) and Wal-Mart engage in this approach. At the same time, some retailers believe large stores are not efficient in serving saturated (or small) markets; they have been opening smaller stores or downsizing existing ones because of high rents. For example:

> Tiffany's U.S. stores over the years have evolved toward smaller-sized formats, as a result of more effective product category space utilization, visual merchandising, improved inventory replenishment to the stores, and reduced nonselling office space. This has also contributed to higher store productivity. New stores [that recently] opened range from 3,500 to 4,000 gross square feet, and management currently expects that new U.S. stores in the future will likely be in that approximate size range. In addition, management currently does not anticipate any meaningful change in future store sizes or formats for locations outside the United States.[3]

Retailers often focus on allocating store space. They use facilities productively by determining the amount of space, and its placement, for each product category. Sometimes, retailers drop merchandise lines because they occupy too much space. That is why J.C. Penney eliminated home electronics, large sporting goods, and photo equipment from its department stores. With a

FIGURE 13-2

Rationalized Retailing and Toys "R" Us

To present a uniform look for its stores and to be more efficient, Toys "R" Us frequently utilizes rationalized retailing as part of its prototype store formats.

Source: Reprinted by permission of Susan V. Berry, Retail Image Consulting, Inc.

top-down space management approach, a retailer starts with its total available store space (by outlet and for the overall firm, if a chain), divides the space into categories, and then works on product layouts. In contrast, a **bottom-up space management approach** begins planning at the individual product level and then proceeds to the category, total store, and overall company levels.

These are among the tactics that some retailers use to improve store space productivity: Vertical displays, which occupy less room, hang on store walls or from ceilings. Formerly free space now has small point-of-sale displays and vending machines; sometimes, product displays are in front of stores. Open doorways, mirrored walls, and vaulted ceilings give small stores a larger appearance. Up to 75 percent or more of total floor space may be used for selling; the rest is for storage, restrooms, and so on. Scrambled merchandising (with high-profit, high-turnover items) occupies more space in stores, in catalogs, and at Web sites than before. By staying open longer, retailers use space better.

Our Web site (www.pearsonhighered.com/bermanevans) has many links on these topics.

Personnel Utilization

From an operations perspective, efficiently utilizing retail personnel is vital: (1) Labor costs are high. For various retailers, wages and benefits may account for up to one-half of operating costs. (2) High employee turnover means increased recruitment, training, and supervision costs. (3) Poor personnel may have weak sales skills, mistreat shoppers, mis-ring transactions, and make other errors. (4) Productivity gains in technology have exceeded those in labor; yet, some retailers are labor intensive. (5) Labor scheduling is often subject to unanticipated demand. Although retailers know they must increase staff in peak periods and reduce it in slow ones, they may still be over- or understaffed if weather changes, competitors run specials, or suppliers increase promotions. (6) There is less flexibility for firms with unionized employees. Working conditions, compensation, tasks, overtime pay, performance measures, termination procedures, seniority rights, and promotion criteria are generally specified in union contracts.

These are among the tactics that can maximize personnel productivity:

- *Hiring process.* By very carefully screening potential employees before they are offered jobs, turnover is reduced and better performance secured.

CAREERS IN RETAILING

At Macy's, Diversity Makes Sense

Macy's (www.macys.com) views diversity as an all-encompassing term that includes hiring practices, vendor selection, promotional strategy, and community involvement. Macy's commitment to diversity is so strong that it has a position, senior vice-president for diversity strategies, especially devoted to this issue. Macy's also has an Executive Diversity Council, headed by the retailer's chief executive. The council is responsible for meeting companywide diversity-related goals.

At the employee recruitment level, Macy's has executives who are responsible for driving its diversity initiatives within their areas of specialty. As an example, the head of college recruitment is required to attract personnel who reflect the diversity of the people in the communities in which Macy's operates. As part of this initiative, Macy's has developed long-term relationships with major historically Black colleges and universities such as Morehouse and Spelman.

Diversity planning at Macy's even involves specialized promotions that reflect its diverse customer base. For instance, in 2010, Macy's held a two-day R & B festival that attracted between 20,000 and 25,000 people, most of whom were African American. Macy's also hosted in-store events and displayed merchandise that publicized the event. Diversity also is a vital part of Macy's vendor selection process. This is not only socially responsible, but also assures that these vendors better understand the needs of minorities and ethnic populations that Macy's serves.

Source: Sandy Smith, "All for One," http://www.stores.org (November 2010).

Kronos' Workforce Scheduler (www.kronos.com/scheduling-software/scheduling.aspx) allows retailers to better manage employee scheduling.

- *Workload forecasts.* For each time period, the number and type of employees are predetermined. A drugstore may have one pharmacist, one cashier, and one stockperson from 2 P.M. to 5 P.M. on weekdays and add a pharmacist and a cashier from 5 P.M. to 7:30 P.M. (to accommodate people shopping after work). In doing workload forecasts, costs must be balanced against the possibilities of lost sales if customer waiting time is excessive. The key is to be both efficient (cost-oriented) and effective (service-oriented). Many retailers use computer software as an aid in scheduling personnel.
- *Job standardization and cross-training.* Through **job standardization,** the tasks of personnel with similar positions in different departments, such as cashiers in clothing and candy departments, are rather uniform. With **cross-training,** personnel learn tasks associated with more than one job, such as cashier, stockperson, and gift wrapper. A firm increases personnel flexibility and reduces the number of employees needed at any time by job standardization and cross-training. If one department is slow, a cashier could be assigned to a busy one; and a salesperson could process transactions, set up displays, and handle complaints. Cross-training even reduces employee boredom.
- *Good communications.* Employees work best when they are clear about their responsibilities and well informed about policies and current company news. See Figure 13-3.
- *Employee performance standards.* Each worker is given clear goals and is accountable for them. Cashiers are judged on transaction speed and mis-rings, buyers on department revenues and markdowns, and senior executives on the firm's reaching sales and profit targets. Personnel are more productive when working toward specific goals.
- *Compensation.* Financial remuneration, promotions, and recognition that reward good performance help to motivate employees. A cashier is motivated to reduce mis-rings if there is a bonus for keeping mistakes under a certain percentage of all transactions.
- *Self-service.* Costs are reduced with self-service. However: (1) Self-service requires better displays, popular brands, ample assortments, and products with clear features. (2) By reducing sales personnel, some shoppers may feel service is inadequate. (3) There is no cross-selling (whereby customers are encouraged to buy complementary goods they may not have been thinking about).
- *Length of employment.* Generally, full-time workers who have been with a firm for an extended time are more productive than those who are part-time or who have worked there for a short time. They are often more knowledgeable, are more anxious to see the firm succeed, need less supervision, are popular with customers, can be promoted, and are adaptable to the work environment. The superior productivity of these workers normally far outweighs their higher compensation.

FIGURE 13-3
Communicating Productively with Employees
From both cost and time perspectives, videoconferencing is quite an effective way to communicate. An executive at an off-site location can communicate interactively with retail personnel at a store location—at a convenient time and without travel. This approach is more personal than E-mail or other written formats.

Source: iofoto/Shutterstock.com. Reprinted by permission.

Store Maintenance, Energy Management, and Renovations

Store maintenance encompasses all the activities in managing physical facilities. These are just some of the facilities to be managed: exterior—parking lot, points of entry and exit, outside signs and display windows, and common areas adjacent to a store (e.g., sidewalks); interior—windows, walls, flooring, climate control and energy use, lighting, displays and signs, fixtures, and ceilings. See Figure 13-4.

Visit this Web site (www.bltllc.com/commercial_industrial_floor.htm) to learn more about commercial flooring.

The quality of store maintenance affects consumer perceptions, the life span of facilities, and operating costs. Consumers do not like stores that are decaying or otherwise poorly maintained. This means promptly replacing burned-out lamps and periodically repainting room surfaces.

Thorough, ongoing maintenance may extend current facilities for a longer period before having to invest in new ones. At home centers, the heating, ventilation, and air-conditioning

FIGURE 13-4
A Checklist of Selected Store Maintenance Decisions

- ✓ What responsibility should the retailer have for maintaining outside facilities? For instance, does a lease agreement make the retailer or the property owner accountable for snow removal in the parking lot?
- ✓ Should store maintenance activities be done by the retailer's personnel or by outside specialists? Will that decision differ by type of facility (e.g., air-conditioning versus flooring) and by type of service (e.g., maintenance versus repairs)?
- ✓ What repairs should be classified as emergencies? How promptly should nonemergency repairs be made?
- ✓ What should be the required frequency of store maintenance for each type of facility (e.g., daily vacuuming of floors versus weekly washing of exterior windows)? How often should special maintenance activities be done (e.g., restriping spaces in a parking lot)?
- ✓ How should store maintenance vary by season and by time of day (e.g., when a store is open versus when it is closed)?
- ✓ How long should existing facilities be utilized before acquiring new ones? What schedule should be followed?
- ✓ What performance standards should be set for each element of store maintenance? Do these standards adequately balance costs against a desired level of maintenance?

equipment lasts an average of 15 years; display fixtures an average of 12 years; and interior signs an average of 7 years. But maintenance is costly.[4] In a typical year, a home center spends $15,000 on floor maintenance alone.

Due to rising costs over the last 40-plus years, energy management is a major factor in retail operations. For firms with special needs, such as food stores, it is especially critical. To manage their energy resources more effectively, many retailers now:

- Use better insulation in constructing and renovating stores.
- Carefully adjust interior temperature levels during nonselling hours. In summer, air-conditioning is reduced at off-hours; in winter, heating is lowered at off-hours.
- Use computerized systems to monitor temperature levels. Some chains' systems even allow operators to adjust the temperature, lighting, heat, and air-conditioning in multiple stores from one office.
- Substitute high-efficiency bulbs and fluorescent ballasts for traditional lighting.
- Install special air-conditioning systems that control humidity levels in specific store areas, such as freezer locations—to minimize moisture condensation.

Here is an example of how seriously some retailers take energy management:

> With long operating hours and lots of equipment for storing and cooking food, restaurants devour energy. Add lighting, estimated to account for 25 percent of the load, and you can understand why many operators are finding a place for light-emitting diode (LED) bulbs. Denny's recently tested LED lights from manufacturer Cree in various applications, and the results were such that Cree LEDs are now the preferred lighting standard for all new and remodeled units in the full-service family restaurant chain. In addition to reduced energy and maintenance costs, the LR6 downlights provide "the quality of light customers want," says Cree vice-president Craig Lofton. "High color rendering is especially critical in the food service industry, where steaks need to be beautifully red, peppers should pop with color, and the wood tones of the décor can create a warm, home-like atmosphere."[5]

Besides everyday maintenance and energy management, retailers need decision rules regarding renovations: How often are renovations necessary? What areas require renovations more frequently than others? How extensive will renovations be at any one time? Will the retailer be open for business as usual during renovations? How much money must be set aside in anticipation of future renovations? Will renovations result in higher revenues, lower operating costs, or both?

Improving Energy Management in a High-Cost Era

The owners and managers of enclosed shopping centers have historically focused their energy management efforts on heating, ventilating, and air-conditioning (HVAC) systems. In contrast, the owners and managers of strip centers have been less concerned about HVAC since their tenants are typically responsible for these costs.

Currently, owners and managers of both types of properties are focusing more on lighting costs. For example, at Regency Centers (www.regencycenters.com), a Florida-based real-estate firm that owns nearly 400 grocery-anchored strip centers and other community shopping centers, lighting accounts for 90 percent of the firm's energy-related costs. Efficient lighting pays off two ways: on a direct basis through lower energy costs and indirectly through lower HVAC costs since new bulbs give off less heat. The Department of Energy (www.energy.gov) estimates that new lighting fixtures can reduce electricity usage by 30 to 50 percent; in addition, they can provide a 10 to 20 percent annual cost savings from lower air-conditioning costs.

Although light-emitting diode (LED) bulbs cost three times more than other lighting sources, these bulbs are up to five times more efficient than standard incandescent bulbs. In addition, they also last up to 20 times longer; this results in significant labor savings. Some LED fixtures have even been designed to replace traditional incandescent and fluorescent fixtures.

Source: Jennifer Popovec, "Light Years Ahead," *Retail Traffic* (March–April 2011), pp. 69–71.

Sometimes, store renovations are extremely expensive and complex. For example, in spring 2012, Macy's embarked on a multi-year $400 million plan to renovate its Herald Square, New York, flagship store (which occupies millions of square feet):

> The store will stay open during construction. Upgrades include a 100,000-square-foot expansion of selling space, a new hall of luxury brands, creation of the world's largest women's shoe department with as many as 300,000 pairs of shoes available on any given day, and "an infusion" of technology and new media into the shopping experience throughout the store. The retailer will build interactive store directories, a system to stream live video feeds of events nationwide, digital product information, an enhanced shoe locator system, new signage, and a new mobile app to guide customers as they shop.[6]

Inventory Management

A retailer uses inventory management to maintain a proper merchandise assortment while ensuring that operations are efficient and effective. See Figure 13-5. Although the role of inventory management in merchandising is covered in Chapter 15, these are some operational issues to consider:

- How can the handling of merchandise from different suppliers be coordinated?
- How much inventory should be on the sales floor versus in a warehouse or storeroom?
- How often should inventory be moved from nonselling to selling areas of a store?
- What inventory functions can be done during nonstore hours?
- What are the trade-offs between faster supplier delivery and higher shipping costs?
- What supplier support is expected in storing merchandise or setting up displays?
- What level of in-store merchandise breakage is acceptable?
- Which items require customer delivery? When? By whom?

Store Security

Store security relates to two basic issues: personal security and merchandise security. Personal security is examined here. Merchandise security is covered in Chapter 15.

Many shoppers and employees feel less safe at retail shopping locations than before, with these results: Some people are unwilling to shop at night. Some shoppers believe malls are not as safe as they once were. Parking is a source of anxiety for people who worry about walking through a dimly lit parking lot. In response, retailers need to be proactive. For example, the

FIGURE 13-5

Inventory Management and Grocery Retailing

Inventory management for grocery stores is quite complex, regardless of the size of the store. For this retailer in Spain, food items come from a number of suppliers, they need to be nicely displayed, and the items must be regularly inspected and pruned out for appearance and freshness. Fruits and vegetables such as those highlighted here are highly perishable, which makes the timeliness of ordering and delivery crucial.

Source: iofoto/Shutterstock.com. Reprinted by permission.

FIGURE 13-6

Retail Security Means Vigilance

More retailers use video security cameras than ever before—partly because of declining equipment costs and partly due to the confidence that visible security measures have on customer perceptions of safety.

Source: mats/Shutterstock.com. Reprinted by permission.

75-acre Arden Fair Mall, near Sacramento, California, has a sophisticated surveillance network: "In addition to security officers on foot, Segways, bicycles, and by car, and under the watchful eye of Nick Novo (assistant security and guest services manager), security video is now key to the mall's success in reducing risk and preventing incidents." Arden Fair has even "upgraded to an analog DVR-based system and, at the same time, installed license plate readers on two staff vehicles to monitor activity in its parking lots."[7]

These are among the practices that a broad range of retailers are utilizing to address this issue:

- Uniformed security guards provide a visible presence that reassures customers and employees, and it is a warning to potential thieves and muggers. Some shopping areas even have horse-mounted guards or guards who patrol on motorized Segway Personal Transporters. As one security expert noted: "The standard practice is for guards to walk the floor to provide a visual reminder that they are there, and report unusual behavior to superiors or directly to police."[8]
- Undercover personnel are used to complement uniformed guards.
- Brighter lighting is used in parking lots, which are also patrolled more frequently by guards. These guards more often work in teams.
- TV cameras and other devices scan the areas frequented by shoppers and employees. See Figure 13-6. 7-Eleven has an in-store cable TV and alarm monitoring system, complete with audio.
- Some shopping areas have curfews for teenagers. This is a controversial tactic.
- Access to store backroom facilities (such as storage rooms) has been tightened.
- Bank deposits are made more frequently—often by armed security guards.

Insurance

Among the types of insurance that retailers buy are workers' compensation, product liability, fire, accident, property, and officers' liability. Many firms also offer health insurance to full-time employees; sometimes, they pay the entire premiums, other times, employees pay part or all of the premiums.

Insurance decisions can have a big impact on a retailer: (1) In recent years, premiums have risen dramatically. (2) Several insurers have reduced the scope of their coverage; they now require higher deductibles or do not provide coverage on all aspects of operations (such as the professional liability of pharmacists). (3) There are fewer insurers servicing retailers today than a decade ago; this limits the choice of carrier. (4) Insurance against environmental risks (such as leaking oil tanks) is more important due to government rules.

To protect themselves financially, a number of retailers have enacted costly programs aimed at lessening their vulnerability to employee and customer insurance claims due to unsafe conditions, as well as to hold down premiums. These programs include no-slip carpeting, flooring, and rubber entrance mats; more frequently mopping and inspecting wet floors; doing more elevator and escalator checks; having regular fire drills; building more fire-resistant facilities; setting up separate storage areas for dangerous items; discussing safety in employee training; and keeping records showing proper maintenance activity.

Credit Management

Visa presents a lot of advice (http://usa.visa.com/merchants/merchant_resources) for retailers. Scroll down to "Tips & Tools" and click on "Downloads."

These are the operational decisions to be made in the area of credit management:

- What form of payment is acceptable? A retailer may accept cash only, cash and personal checks, cash and credit card(s), cash and debit cards, or all of these.
- Who administers the credit plan? The firm can have its own credit system and/or accept major credit cards (such as Visa, MasterCard, American Express, and Discover). It may also work with PayPal and Google Checkout for online payments.
- What are customer eligibility requirements for a check or credit purchase? With a check purchase, a photo ID might be sufficient. To open a new credit account, a customer must meet age, employment, income, and other conditions; an existing customer would be evaluated in terms of the outstanding balance and credit limit. A minimum purchase amount may be specified for a credit transaction.
- What credit terms will be used? A retailer with its own plan must determine when interest charges begin to accrue, the rate of interest, and minimum monthly payments.
- How are late payments or nonpayments to be handled? Some retailers with their own credit plans rely on outside collection agencies to follow up on past-due accounts.

The retailer must weigh the ability of credit to increase revenues against the costs of processing payments—screening, transaction, and collection costs, as well as bad debts. If a retailer completes credit functions itself, it incurs these costs; if outside parties (such as Visa) are used, the retailer covers the costs by its fees to the credit organization.

The *Nilson Report* presents information on retail payment methods. At its site (www.nilsonreport.com), you can access highlights.

In the United States, there are 1.5 billion credit and debit cards in use. Annually, customers use their Visa, MasterCard, American Express, and Discover credit and debit cards to process $2 trillion in transactions. The average transaction involving a credit/debit card or a check is far higher than a cash one. One-third of all U.S. retail transactions are in cash, one-sixth are by check, and one-half are by credit and debit card. Among retailers accepting credit and debit cards, one-third have their own card, virtually all accept MasterCard and/or Visa, 80 percent accept Discover, and more than one-half accept American Express. Most firms accepting credit cards handle two or more cards.[9]

Credit card fees paid by retailers typically range from 1.5 percent to 5.0 percent of sales for Visa, MasterCard, Discover, and American Express—depending on volume and the card provider. There may also be transaction and monthly fees. With retailers' own credit operations, they incur all the processing costs; but they also get to collect the interest on unpaid balances. Costco offers a merchant credit-processing program in partnership with Elavon so that small firms may carry Visa or MasterCard. It charges a 1.37 percent of sales fee plus 12 cents per transaction for store retailers with an average transaction amount of $15 or less; 1.64 percent of sales plus 20 cents per transaction for other store retailers; and 1.99 percent plus 27 cents per transaction for nonstore retailers.[10]

Many retailers—of all types—now place great emphasis on a **debit card system,** whereby the purchase price is immediately deducted from a consumer's bank account and entered into a retailer's account through a computer terminal. The retailer's risk of nonpayment is eliminated, and its costs are reduced with debit rather than credit transactions. For traditional credit cards, monthly billing is employed; with debit cards, monetary account transfers are made at the time of the purchase. There is some resistance to debit transactions by consumers who like the delayed-payment benefit of conventional credit cards. On the other hand, the pre-paid gift card, a form of debit card, is popular.

Click on "About Deluxe" (www.deluxe.com) to learn about one of the premier payment systems support companies for retailers.

As the payment landscape evolves, new operational issues must be addressed:

- Retailers have more payment options. For example, online retailers offer an average of 3.5 payment choices.[11] At store-based retailers, training cashiers is more complex due to all the payment formats, such as cash, third-party and retailer credit and debit cards, personal checks, gift cards, and more.
- Hardware and software are available to process paper checks electronically. This means cost savings for the retailer and faster payments from the bank.
- Visa and MasterCard have been sued for requiring retailers to accept both credit and debit cards, and for the higher retailer fees with debit cards.
- Nonstore retailers have less legal protection against credit card fraud than store retailers that secure written authorization.
- Credit card transactions on the Web must instantly take into account different sales tax rates and currencies (for global sales).
- In Europe, retailers are still grappling with the intricacies of using the euro as currency because the euro is not the standard currency for countries such as Great Britain.

Computerization

CAM Commerce Solutions (www.camcommerce.com) offers very inexpensive operations software to small retailers in the hope that as these retailers grow, they will upgrade to advanced software.

Many retailers have substantially improved their individual operations productivity through computerization; with the continuing decline in the prices of computer systems and related software, even more small firms will do so in the near future. At the same time, retailers must consider the role of the supply chain: "Many leading retailers are converting to demand-driven supply chains where the focus is on meeting the demand of consumers and collaborating with suppliers to most effectively meet that demand. The power of the demand-driven supply chain (DDSC) is really compelling: It both increases product availability and inventory turns while reducing cash-to-cash cycle times and costs to serve."[12] Let's look at various examples of the operational benefits of computerization.

Retailers such as Home Depot, Wal-Mart, and J.C. Penney use videoconferencing. This lets them link store employees with central headquarters, as well as interact with vendors. Videoconferencing can be done through satellite technology and by computer (with special hardware and software). In both cases, audio/video communications train workers, spread news, stimulate employee morale, and so on.

Polycom (www.polycom.com/usa/en/products/voice/wireless_solutions) has a variety of wireless communications products.

In-store telecommunications aid operations via low-cost, secure in-store transmissions. Polycom, with its SpectraLink product line, is one of the firms that markets lightweight phones so workers can talk to one another anywhere in a store. There are no time charges or monthly

Corporate Responsibility as a Key Business Practice

Best Buy (www.bestbuy.com), Hennes & Mauritz (H&M) AB (www.hm.com), McDonald's (www.mcdonalds.com), Starbucks (www.starbucks.com), and Zara (www.zara.com) are among the retailers that have embraced corporate social responsibility and sustainability as a major part of their overall business strategy.

Best Buy has hosted a "Tech It Away" E-waste drive at three Vancouver, Canada, schools that collect and recycle used electronic equipment in exchange for grants from Best Buy. Each participating school has received $10,000 in grants from Best Buy. The recycling operation also resulted in reductions of 120,000 pounds from Canadian landfills.

In 2010, H&M launched a "Conscious Collection" clothing line for men, women, and children. These clothes are made from organic and recycled fabrics. By 2020, H&M plans to use only cotton derived from sustainable sources.

McDonald's was the recipient of the 2010 Catalyst Award that acknowledged the chain's commitment to advancing women in management positions. More than 25 percent of McDonald's vice-president or higher positions are filled by women.

Starbucks is a founding member of the Business for Innovative Climate and Energy Policy. Members of this group are committed to more stringent regulations concerning clean energy and climate change.

Zara has replaced its older gas-fueled delivery fleet with zero-emissions electric vehicles.

Source: Annie White, Dayna Linley, Emily Joldersma, et al., "Better Business," *Maclean's* (June 20, 2011), pp. 46–54.

FIGURE 13-7
How Computerization Improves Productivity

"Do you and your employees have enough time to manage staff, help customers, check inventory, stock shelves, set the store, process returns and product transfers, make sales, conduct cycle counts, and handle all of the other small tasks that come up in any given day? If not, the use of LXE's rugged mobile computers can improve your store's efficiency and accuracy in many areas. Get rid of those manual, paper processes and increase the speed and precision of your tasks that take away from helping customers and making sales."

Source: Reprinted by permission of LXE, now part of Honeywell.

fees. Polycom clients—for a variety of its products—have included America's Incredible Pizza Company, Barnes & Noble, Giant Food, Ikea, Kmart, Neiman Marcus, Rite Aid, and Toys "R" Us.

Software provides computerized inventory control and order tracking. For example, Park City Group's Fresh Market Manager "is a fully-integrated software application that manages produce and fresh foods in supermarkets and convenience stores. The application identifies the true cost of goods sold and provides hourly forecasts and production plans in real time. With Fresh Market Manager, you never have to worry about your food going to waste! With our software, you can accurately forecast demand for bakery and deli items, hot foods, seafood, produce, dairy, meat, frozen food, floral items, and more. You will not have to worry about production and inventory issues that cause problems for so many retailers."[13] LXE hardware and software (www.lxe.com) also enable retailers to be more efficient in performing a wide variety of functions. See Figure 13-7.

Nowhere is computerization more critical than in the checkout process. Let's examine the computerized checkout, the electronic point-of-sale system, and scanning formats.

The **computerized checkout** is used by both large and small retailers so they can efficiently process transactions and monitor inventory. Firms rely on UPC-based systems; cashiers manually ring up sales or pass items over or past scanners. Computerized registers instantly record and display sales, provide detailed receipts, and store inventory data. This type of checkout lowers costs by reducing transaction time, employee training, mis-rings, and the need for item pricing. Retailers also have better inventory control, reduced spoilage, and improved ordering. They even get item-by-item data—which aid in determining store layout and merchandise plans, shelf space, and inventory replenishment. Recent technological developments related to computerized checkouts include wireless scanners that let workers scan heavy items without lifting them, radio frequency identification tags (RFID) that emit a radio frequency code when placed near a receiver (which is faster than UPC codes and better for harsh climates), speech recognition (that can tally an order on the basis of a clerk's verbal command), and portable card readers. See Figure 13-8.

Retailers do face two potential problems with computerized checkouts. First, UPC-based systems do not reach peak efficiency unless all suppliers attach UPC labels to merchandise; otherwise, retailers incur labeling costs. Second, because UPC symbols are unreadable by humans, some states have laws that require price labeling on individual items. This lessens the labor savings of posting only shelf prices.

Many retailers have upgraded to an **electronic point-of-sale system,** which performs all the tasks of a computerized checkout and verifies check and charge transactions, provides instantaneous sales reports, monitors and changes prices, sends intra- and inter-store messages, evaluates personnel and profitability, and stores data. A point-of-sale system is often used along with a retail information system. Point-of-sale terminals can stand alone or be integrated with an in-store or a headquarters computer.

Retail scanning equipment comes in a wide variety of models and price ranges (www.barcodediscount.com).

Retailers have specific goals for scanning equipment: "Since the barcode scanner's first commercial use over 30 years ago, they have proven their value in automating workflow. Barcode scanners read SKUs [stock-keeping units], which allow data management for a multitude of inventory items in an efficient and simplified way. In retail outlets, barcode scanners are put to use receiving stock to the outlet, tracking the location on the sales floor (when used with inventory management software), counting inventory, and ringing up sales while lowering fatigue and human error."[14] Among the recent advances in scanning technology are hand-held scanners; wearable, hands-free scanners; miniaturized data transceivers; wireless scanners; and scanning via smart phones.

As noted in Chapter 2, another scanning option with retailer interest is **self-scanning,** whereby the consumer himself or herself scans items being purchased at a checkout counter, pays by credit or debit card, and bags items. According to the London-based RBR consulting firm:

> The global market for self-checkout has continued to thrive despite a difficult retail environment. This is one of the findings of new research by strategic research and consulting firm RBR (www.rbrlondon.com/retail). Self-checkout was introduced two decades ago and still has a long way to go before it can boast the level of penetration achieved by assisted E-POS. Nevertheless, it can no longer be called a niche product, now that it is mainstream in some parts of the world, primarily North America and western Europe, which account for the vast majority of the world's self-checkout installations. RBR forecasts that by 2016 the installed base of self-checkout terminals will be 325,000 worldwide, and annual shipments will exceed 60,000.[15]

Outsourcing

More retailers have turned to outsourcing for some of the operating tasks they previously performed themselves. With **outsourcing,** a retailer pays an outside party to undertake one or more of its operating functions. The goals are to reduce the costs and employee time devoted to particular tasks. For example, Limited Brands uses outside firms to oversee its energy use and facilities maintenance. Crate & Barrel outsources the management of its E-mail programs. Apple Stores, Payless Shoes, and Sports Chalet outsource their information technology services. Kmart

FIGURE 13-8
An Innovative Use of Checkout Technology

Portable credit- and debit-card readers make it easy for shoppers to checkout.

Source: Neil Speers/Shutterstock.com. Reprinted by permission.

uses logistics firms to consolidate small shipments and to process returned merchandise; it also outsources electronic data interchange tasks. Home Depot outsources most trucking operations. GE Capital handles credit-card processing for Wal-Mart's company-branded credit cards.

GE Capital (www.gogecapital/en/business) handles credit operations for a number of retailers.

This comment, from Accenture—a leading consulting firm—sums up the benefits of outsourcing:

> Retail executives believe outsourcing delivers operational efficiencies and the ability to quickly respond to customer needs. To combat low margins and commoditization, high-performance retailers leverage outsourcing to increase operational effectiveness and lower costs. Outsourcing can range from IT infrastructure through applications to a business process. Many companies see outsourcing as a phased process, beginning with infrastructure and ending with business processes being managed by a third party. The outsourcer can bring industrywide experience, along with specialist knowledge. Economies of scale drive down unit costs, as do shared resources. Unpredictable capital costs are replaced with variable operational costs.[16]

Crisis Management

Despite the best intentions, retailers may sometimes be faced with crisis situations that need to be managed as smoothly as feasible. Crises may be brought on by an in-store fire or broken water pipe, access to a store being partially blocked due to picketing by striking workers, a car accident in the parking lot, a burglary, a sudden illness by the owner or a key employee, a storm that knocks out a retailer's power, unexpectedly high or low consumer demand for a good or service, a sudden increase in a supplier's prices, a natural disaster such as a flood or an earthquake, or other factors.

Although many crises may be anticipated, and some adverse effects may occur regardless of retailer efforts, these principles are important:

1. There should be contingency plans for as many different types of crisis situations as possible. That is why retailers buy insurance, install backup generators, and prepare management succession plans. A firm can have a checklist to follow if there is an incident such as a store fire or a parking-lot accident.
2. Essential information should be communicated to all affected parties, such as the fire or police department, employees, customers, and the media, as soon as a crisis occurs.
3. Cooperation—not conflict—among the involved parties is essential.
4. Responses should be as swift as feasible; indecisiveness may worsen the situation.
5. The chain of command should be clear and decision makers given adequate authority.

Crisis management is a key task for both small and large retailers: "Some might say, 'It won't happen to us.' But without a thorough plan for responding to a multitude of potential events, organizations are leaving themselves wide open to the risks of poor crisis management."[17] And consider this: "Anything that unexpectedly disrupts a company's expected operation can harm the company even if the disruption is because of a windfall. That is why companies create contingency plans for many possible situations, so company management has a pre-researched plan of action to immediately follow."[18]

Visit our Web site (www.pearsonhighered.com/bermanevans) for several links on crisis management.

Chapter Summary

1. *To describe the operational scope of operations management.* Operations management efficiently and effectively seeks to enact the policies needed to satisfy customers, employees, and management. In contrast to Chapter 12, which dealt with financial aspects, Chapter 13 covered operational facets.

2. *To examine several specific aspects of operating a retail business.* An operations blueprint systematically lists all operating functions, their characteristics, and their timing, as well as the responsibility for performing the functions.

   Store format and size considerations include the use of prototype stores and store dimensions. Firms often use prototype stores in conjunction with rationalized retailing. Some retailers emphasize category killer stores; others open smaller stores. In space allocation, retailers deploy a top-down or a bottom-up approach. They want to optimize the productivity of store space.

Personnel utilization activities that improve productivity range from better screening applicants to workload forecasts to job standardization and cross-training. Job standardization routinizes the tasks of people with similar positions in different departments. With cross-training, people learn tasks associated with more than one job. A firm can advance its personnel flexibility and minimize the total number of workers needed at any given time by these techniques.

Store maintenance includes all activities in managing physical facilities. It influences people's perceptions of the retailer, the life span of facilities, and operating costs. To better control energy resources, retailers are doing everything from using better-quality insulation materials when building and renovating stores to substituting high-efficiency bulbs. Besides everyday facilities management, retailers need decision rules as to the frequency and manner of store renovations.

Good inventory management requires that retailers acquire and maintain the proper merchandise while ensuring efficient and effective operations. This encompasses everything from coordinating different supplier shipments to planning customer deliveries (if needed).

Store security measures protect both personal and merchandise safety. Because of safety concerns, fewer people now shop at night and some avoid shopping in areas they view as unsafe. In response, retailers are employing security guards, using better lighting in parking lots, tightening access to facilities, and deploying other tactics.

Among the insurance that retailers buy are workers' compensation, product liability, fire, accident, property, and officers' liability. Many firms also have employee health insurance.

Most U.S. adults use credit cards. Check and credit payments generally mean larger transactions than cash payments. One-third of retail transactions are in cash, one-sixth by check, and one-half by credit or debit card. Retailers pay various fees to be able to offer non-cash payment options to customers, and there is a wide range of payment systems available for retailers.

A growing number of retailers have computerized elements of operations. Videoconferencing and wireless in-store telephone communications are gaining in popularity. Computerized checkouts and electronic point-of-sale systems are quite useful. Electronic point-of-sale systems perform all the tasks of computerized checkouts and verify check and charge transactions, provide instant sales reports, monitor and change prices, send intra- and inter-store messages, evaluate personnel and profitability, and store data. Self-scanning is gaining in popularity.

With outsourcing, the retailer pays another party to handle one or more operating functions. The goals are to reduce costs and better utilize employees' time.

Crisis management must handle unexpected situations as smoothly as possible. There should be contingency plans, information should be communicated to those affected, all parties should cooperate, responses should be swift, and the chain of command for decisions should be clear.

Key Terms

operations blueprint (p. 323)
prototype stores (p. 325)
rationalized retailing (p. 325)
top-down space management approach (p. 326)
bottom-up space management approach (p. 326)
job standardization (p. 327)
cross-training (p. 327)
store maintenance (p. 328)
debit card system (p. 332)
computerized checkout (p. 334)
electronic point-of-sale system (p. 335)
self-scanning (p. 335)
outsourcing (p. 335)

Questions for Discussion

1. Present a brief operations blueprint for a consumer electronics repair service.
2. What are the pros and cons of prototype stores? For which kind of firms is this type of store *most* desirable?
3. Why would a retailer be interested in job standardization and cross-training for its employees?
4. Comment on this statement: "The quality of store maintenance efforts affects consumer perceptions of the retailer, the life span of facilities, and operating expenses."
5. Talk to two local retailers and ask them what they have done to maximize their energy efficiency. Present your findings.
6. As a luggage store owner, you are planning a complete renovation of the attaché case department. What operations decisions must you make?
7. Present a five-step plan for a retailer to reassure customers that it is safe to shop there.
8. A gas station does not accept checks because of the risks involved. However, it does accept Visa and MasterCard. Evaluate this strategy.

9. What potential problems may result if a retailer relies on its computer system to implement too many actions (such as employee scheduling or inventory reordering) automatically?
10. What operations criteria would you use to evaluate the success of self-scanning at a supermarket?
11. Are there any operating functions that should *never* be outsourced? Explain your answer.
12. Outline the contingency plan a retailer could have in the event of each of these occurrences:
    a. A shopper's accidentally setting off the burglar alarm.
    b. A flood in the store caused by a ruptured water pipe.
    c. A firm's Web site inadvertently making personal customer information available to a mailing list company.
    d. The bankruptcy of a key supplier.

Web-Based Exercise

Visit the Web site of Fifth Gear (www.infifthgear.com), an outsourcing company that provides order fulfillment services. What functions does Fifth Gear offer to retailers? As a retailer, what criteria would you use in deciding whether or not to hire Fifth Gear?

Note: Also stop by our Web site (www.pearsonhighered.com/bermanevans) to experience a number of highly interactive, appealing Web exercises based on actual company demonstrations and sample materials related to retailing.

PART 5 Short Cases

Case 1: Predicting Retail Worker Engagement[c-1]

In ten of the twelve reports published to date by the U.S. Census Bureau, retailing has been cited as one of the top ten industries that employ workers age 65 and older. As a consequence, one team of researchers decided to study the job engagement of older workers in a retail workplace.

Job engagement is the extent to which an employee places extra effort and goes beyond his/her job responsibilities. Three of the key areas explored by the researchers were the impact of age on job engagement, the factors that predict engagement, and how the factors that affect engagement are influenced by a worker's age. This study had a sufficiently large sample of retail workers who were more than 55 years old to examine how job engagement varies over a worker's life span.

The researchers invited all employees (8,433) in three U.S. regions of a large national *Fortune* 500 retailer (encompassing 352 of the firm's 6,000 stores) to participate in this study. Of this group, 6,085 employees responded, a 72 percent return rate. Respondents were given time off on their jobs to complete the questionnaire. The respondents were broken into three groups of younger workers—"emerging adults" (ages 18–24), "settling in adults" (25–39), and "adults in their prime working years" (40–54)—and the older workers were classified as "approaching retirement" (ages 55–64) and "retirement eligible" (66 and older).

The research project found that both older worker categories (approaching retirement and retirement eligible) were more engaged than the younger workers. The study's authors concluded that older workers were more highly obligated to their employer and had a stronger work ethic. The findings clearly suggest that older workers are not "checked out" or awaiting the time before retirement.

As also suggested by other research, the emerging adults were the least engaged of all the age groups studied. Other studies have found that emerging adults are less engaged because they are in transition to adult roles and commitments.

The factors that predict engagement generally do not differ by age group. Both older and younger workers who feel that their immediate supervisors are supportive—by being concerned with their well-being and recognizing their achievements—are more likely to be engaged than workers who do not experience these feelings. Workers of all ages who experience job clarity are also more engaged than those who do not. Both older and younger workers who have flexibility in managing their work and personal responsibilities are more engaged than those who feel conflicts among these commitments.

Lastly, this study determined that the factors affecting engagement do differ by age. Retirement-eligible workers were more oriented toward authority and more loyal to their employer than younger workers. Higher engagement levels among older workers may be due to the fact that when they have supervisor support and clarity they can more easily align the supervisor's goals with their own goals. Younger workers, on the other hand, may be more interested in getting training for promotions and, thus, become more engaged when they find the work to be interesting and challenging.

Questions

1. What is the managerial significance of the higher level of worker engagement among workers approaching retirement and retirement eligible employees?
2. How should a retailer respond to the findings of worker engagement being associated with immediate supervisors who are supportive and that recognize the accomplishment of employees?
3. How should a retailer motivate younger workers to become better engaged?
4. How should a retailer motivate older workers to become better engaged?

Case 2: Buying Local Cuts Costs for Wal-Mart[c-2]

Wal-Mart (www.walmart.com), with more than $120 billion in annual food sales, is the largest seller of grocery products in the United States. Although the firm is known for scouring the globe for the lowest-cost producers, Wal-Mart has recently begun purchasing fruits and vegetables from local farmers in order to reduce shipping costs and product spoilage. Locally grown produce also does not have to be stored in distribution centers as it can be shipped multiple times per day, if necessary, directly to each store. Local farmers can more easily handle emergency shipments so that there are fewer stockouts and lost sales. The availability of fresh local produce offers a significant benefit for many consumers who view fresh fruits and vegetables as a major competitive advantage in their store choice.

Wal-Mart is encouraging its produce managers to purchase fruits and vegetables grown within 450 miles of its distribution centers. Ten years ago, almost all of Wal-Mart's jalapeño peppers came from Florida, California, and Mexico. Now, Wal-Mart has suppliers of these hot peppers in 30 states. According to Wal-Mart's senior manager for produce: "I'm going to pay a higher price in Ohio for peppers, but if I don't have to ship them halfway across the country to store, it's a better deal."

Recently, Wal-Mart made a commitment to double its purchases of locally grown fruits and vegetables. Wal-Mart plans for local produce to comprise 9 percent of its U.S. total produce sales as of 2015. This strategy will ultimately shift sales from large far-away farms to smaller local farms. Similarly, Kroger (www.kroger.com), which operates about 2,400 grocery stores, is purchasing more produce in Texas to send to stores in the Southwest, as opposed to getting these crops from California or Colorado. As a Kroger spokesperson notes: "We use less energy and fuel to store, transport, and refrigerate

[c-1]The material in this case is drawn from Jacquelyn Boon James, Sharon McKechnie, and Jennifer Swanberg, "Predicting Employee Engagement in an Age-Diverse Retail Workforce," *Journal of Organizational Behavior*, Vol. 32 (January 4, 2011), pp. 173–196.

[c-2]The material in this case is drawn from Miguel Bustillo and David Kesmodel, " 'Local' Grows on Wal-Mart," www.wallstreetjournal.com (August 1, 2011).

the products." Supervalu (www.supervalu.com), the owner of more than 1,000 Jewel-Osco, Albertsons, and Luck supermarket stores, estimates that it uses local suppliers for between 25 and 40 percent of its produce purchases.

Interestingly, there is no federal standard or consensus among grocery managers as to what constitutes "locally grown" produce. At Safeway (www.safeway.com), the term "local" means that the produce is grown less than an eight-hour drive from a store. Kroger defines the term more loosely, designating "local" as being grown in the same state or even the same region as a store location. At Supervalu, the meaning of "local" varies by store. Some stores use this term to describe produce grown in neighboring states. At Wal-Mart, "locally grown" means the produce is grown in the same state where it is sold. A problem with this definition is that in a large state like Texas, "locally grown" can be used to describe produce grown a 12-hour drive from a supercenter location.

These varying definitions have generated criticism among consumer advocates who state that some chains are engaging in misleading promotions. A secondary issue is that there are limits to what can be produced locally in the winter in the northern United States due to climate considerations.

Questions

1. Discuss the pros and cons of purchasing locally grown produce from the perspective of the retailer and from the perspective of the consumer.
2. How would you educate store employees to understand why the retailer carries local produce and how they should explain these benefits to consumers?
3. Do you think the cash flow needs of small local produce firms are different from those of large produce firms? What are the implications of your answer for retailers?
4. Explain the implications of the different meanings of "local." What definition would you use? Why?

Case 3: 1-800-Flowers.com Teams with IBM's E-Commerce Platform[c-3]

1-800-Flowers.com (www.1800flowers.com) is the world's largest floral and gift shop, with annual revenues of about $670 million. 1-800-Flowers.com was one of the first retailers to brand itself, and it did so based on its easy-to-remember toll-free phone number. It was also one of the first retailers to partner with AOL, at the inception of the Internet.

A major part of 1-800-Flowers.com's overall retail strategy is its sale of multiple brands of gift items. This strategy provides consumers with a choice and appeals to multiple market segments. Among 1-800-Flowers.com's brands are Cheryl's (gourmet cookies), Popcorn Factory, Fannie May (chocolates), Winetasting.com, and Celebrations (party ideas). Because many of these brands involved acquisitions, business processes and information management systems were far from integrated in the past. This lack of coordination was costly for 1-800-Flowers.com due to the complex requirements necessary to coordinate these systems. Each brand used different methods to record shipping and warehousing data, which were hard to integrate into a single companywide report. Some acquisitions were for products that were sold primarily by catalog. The information systems for these brands were not directly applicable to Web-based businesses.

Even though the firm's basic information system worked well, it was not designed to handle a portfolio of 14 brands. Under the old system, 1-800-Flowers.com would have to individually revise product descriptions, add new product reviews, or record price changes for each brand platform. Under its new integrated system, the changes would only have to be recorded once. A single platform also enables 1-800-Flowers.com to more easily apply its best practices in one brand, to complementary brands.

1-800 Flowers.com chose IBM WebSphere Commerce as a unified technology platform to replace its multiple, diverse, and independent E-commerce systems. According to Steve Bozzo, the retailer's chief information officer:

> Being competitive today means being a lot smarter about all facets of commerce, from initial marketing efforts to customer interaction in the buying and selling phase to the product delivery and subsequent service that ensures customer satisfaction. We are optimizing our entire order life cycle and improving the customer experience with a comprehensive solution from IBM that manages information from multiple channels in a timely and accurate way. With WebSphere Commerce, basically you've got a single Web site that handles all of the transactions. This central engine supports as many customer-facing Web stores as you like, and it's easy to add new ones or roll new features across brands.

For consumers, IBM's E-commerce platform provides a seamless cross-channel customer experience. The system uses one shopping cart, one user ID, one password, and a single bill regardless of how many categories a purchase spans. For the retailer, the platform provides cross-selling opportunities. Consumers buying one type of product can be offered specials on another. Data on customer purchases could also be shared across all brands. Order confirmations can also be standardized across brands.

Since 1-800 Flowers.com placed Popcorn Factory on its new platform, the number of site visitors who make a purchase has improved. Customer experience ratings about the Web site's ease of use and appearance have also increased.

Questions

1. Discuss the potential cost savings in inventory management arising from a single integrated system.
2. Describe how customer data from one 1-800 Flowers.com division can be shared across divisions using the single platform.
3. What are the pros and cons of 1-800 Flowers.com's outsourcing software development, training, and implementation?
4. Develop a checklist to judge the effectiveness of the single integrated system versus the previous 14 separate systems.

[c-3]The material in this case is drawn from "1-800-Flowers.com: Creating an E-Commerce Platform for the Future," http://bx.businessweek.com (September 7, 2010); and D. H. Kass, "IBM Offers New Software and Consulting Services for $70 Billion Smarter Commerce Market," www.itchannelplanet.com (March 23, 2011).

Case 4: Chico's Steps Up Its Technology[c-4]

Chico's (www.chicos.com) is a women's specialty retailer with a past history of multiple store formats, shifting target markets, and "boom" or "bust" successes and failures. At the end of 2008, Chico's board of directors recruited David Dyer as its new chief executive. Dyer's immediate past position was as chief executive of Tommy Hilfiger Corporation. In turn, Dyer hired a number of key executives from Lands' End (www.landsend.com) to help restructure Chico's.

Immediately on taking the presidency of the company, David realized that Chico's information technology (IT) system was insufficient to handle its 1,000+ stores and its direct-to-consumer business. As a result, in 2010, Chico's invested more than $30 million (over one-third of its total capital budget) in a new IT system based on the JDA Merchandising suite (www.jda.com/solutions/merchandise-operations-overview), which is integrated with SAP (www.sap.com).

According to Gary King, Chico's chief information officer, the new system "allows us to hold as much product as possible in the distribution centers until the last minute, so we don't overwhelm the back room of the store and have to mark it down or move it to outlet stores to liquidate it. And selling online is a much more profitable way to handle slow-moving items."

Another component of this system is a work-force management component. This component not only handles labor scheduling and staff training, but also tracks shipments, handles home deliveries, and locates merchandise across stores. To reduce conflict between Chico's store and its online divisions, inventory is not attributed to a specific channel until it is sold. Thus, merchandise can be sold across channels. Markdowns can also be reduced as each channel has an equal opportunity to sell all goods.

In addition, Chico's has implemented SAS OnDemand: Marketing Automation software. This program has been used by Chico's to analyze data from its customer loyalty program to better understand important trends and opportunities. Among the key findings of this loyalty data were that Chico's had a lower share of its Northeast customers' disposable income than in other regions (due to extensive competition and product choice in this region). As a result, Chico's Northeast stores needed to stock a greater variety of merchandise than stores at other locations. Another important observation was that a majority of Chico's customers first went online to evaluate available styles and then visited the store to shop. In some instances, Chico's in-store customers ordered goods online only after visiting a store and determining that the goods are not available at the store.

Besides fine-tuning its current systems, Chico's plans to develop and implement a product-to-consumer life-cycle management system. Then, programs can track the development of Chico's private-label products from their inception to the creation of a purchase order for specific styles, colors, fabrics, and sizes. The product life-cycle management effort is very important to Chico's as it designs all of its products in-house. Other new software applications that are being planned include RFID (radio frequency identification) item-level tagging, point-of-sale automation, apps for smart phones, and evaluation of customer feedback via social media.

Questions

1. Describe the potential improvements in productivity that would warrant Chico's spending more than one-third of its total capital budget on a new IT system.
2. Discuss the value of labor scheduling for a retailer such as Chico's.
3. List ten different types of customer data that Chico's can obtain from its customer loyalty data base.
4. Comment on this statement: "A majority of Chico's customers first go online to evaluate available styles and then visit the store to shop."

[c-4]The material in this case is drawn from Masha Zager, "Chico's Comeback," *Apparel Magazine* (February 2011), pp. 6–8.

PART 5 Comprehensive Case

Automated Retailing: A Driver of Profits and Cost Savings*

Introduction

This case discusses the performance and the growing popularity of automated retail kiosks in the United States. These kiosks' transactions have risen quite significantly in the past few years, and they are reported to have increased the sales of any stores where they are deployed. In addition, with the advancement of technologies such as touch-screen displays and card readers, these kiosks provide a cost-effective, fast, and user-friendly experience to both shoppers and store owners. Also presented is a detailed analysis on the kiosks.

Automated Retailing Drives Profits

From the lottery to DVD rental and coin counting, automated retail kiosks increase store traffic and drive incremental sales. Automated retail kiosks are helping store operators boost traffic, incremental sales, and consumers' purchasing of high-margin convenience categories. They are also profit centers unto themselves.

Consumers first became familiar with automated kiosks in the early 1970s when ATM machines were introduced. Since then, the category has continued to grow. In 2008, self-service kiosk transactions in North America totaled $607 billion across all categories; in 2009, they exceeded $775 billion. By 2012, they were expected to reach $1.7 trillion, according to predictions by the Information Technology and Innovation Foundation (ITIF) in a report titled, "Embracing the Self-Service Economy." More kiosks (47 percent) are deployed by the retail sector than any other business category. Supermarkets and convenience stores are among the heaviest users.

Automated retail machines allow customer transactions to be performed via a self-serve, interactive kiosk. The kiosk handles all functions, from the selection to the transaction to the delivery of goods or services. Kiosks can be located inside or outside a store.

Advances in technology, such as touch-screen displays, card readers, and scanners, have made automated kiosks extremely cost-effective and user-friendly, says the ITIF. Neither consumers nor store employees need any special knowledge in order to use these kiosks. Some machines even have multilingual capabilities. See Figure 1.

With these advances and increased consumer adoption, it is no surprise that 75 percent of the convenience store and supermarket operators that participated in *Progressive Grocer's* [PG] and *Convenience Store News'* [CSN] "Supermarket and Convenience Channel Automated Retail Study" said that they currently offer some type of automated machine(s). Among the convenience stores, the rate is 68 percent; for the supermarkets, it is 85 percent. Lottery (48 percent), followed by soda (47 percent), DVD rental (34 percent), and coin-counting machines (21 percent) are the types of automated retail most frequently found in both channels. See Table 1.

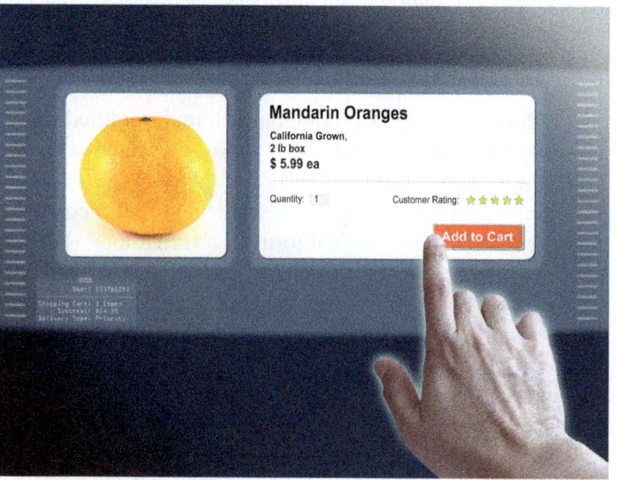

FIGURE 1

Automated Kiosks: Easy to Use

Touch-screen kiosks are extremely easy to use; and they also present pictures or videos of products—and sometimes, even include customer ratings.

Source: AlexAndra/Shutterstock.com. Reprinted by permission.

Besides the convenience for shoppers, automated kiosks expand a retailer's product or service offerings and contribute to the bottom line. Since units are self-serve, they can reduce labor costs, indicates the PG/CSN study.

Automated kiosks can also help retailers differentiate from competition with services—such as lottery tickets, coin counting, and DVD rental—that make their stores into shopper destinations. Consumers who use these kiosks often purchase snacks, beverages, and other impulse items. Many also pick up milk, tobacco, and other frequently replenished products. "DVD rentals create a destination for our store, as do lottery-ticket machines, which are heavily used," says Karen Jackson, store director for a Fred Meyer (www.fredmeyer.com) in Kent, Washington. The Kent location also has ATM, soda, and coin-counting machines.

Benefitting from Automated Kiosks

The benefits of automated machines are determined by the type of unit, the retail channel, and the store location. Among supermarkets and convenience stores, 71 percent of respondents to the PG/CSN study say lottery machines add value to their business, followed by coin counting (63 percent), DVD rental (58 percent), and cosmetics, photo processing, and electronics (each 46 percent). Refer to Table 1.

There are several reasons why retailers may view lottery machines as most valuable to their business. For starters, retailers are more likely to have lottery machines than other type units. Among retailers that have lottery machines, 58 percent say customer satisfaction is the most important attribute

*The material in this case is adapted by the authors from "Automated Retail Drives Profits," *Convenience Store News* (April 11, 2011), pp. C1–C8. Reprinted by permission of *Convenience Store News*, www.csn.com.

TABLE 1 The Use of Automated Retail Machines—and Their Perceived Value

Type of Automated Machine	% of Total Stores Offering	% of C-Stores Offering	% of Supermarkets Offering	% of C-Stores Finding Value	% of Total Stores Finding Value	% of Supermarkets Finding Value
Lottery	48	44	53	72	71	70
Soda machine	47	29	72	54	44	39
DVD rental	34	24	50	51	58	63
Coin-counting	21	8	40	100	63	61
Cosmetics	10	9	11	50	46	40
Photo-processing	9	4	17	40	46	47
Electronics	6	6	5	63	46	20

Source: Convenience Store News/Progressive Grocer Market Research, 2011.

considered when deciding to add an automated retail program to their store(s). Fifty-one percent cite the increase in store traffic these machines will promote as the most important attribute. See Table 2.

Coin-counting and DVD rental kiosks also rank high among survey respondents in terms of the value they bring. DVD rental kiosks offer flexibility in that they can be placed indoors or outdoors. This makes them suitable for both supermarkets and convenience stores that may have limited indoor floor space. The outdoor installation option has enabled many convenience stores to enter the DVD category for the first time. In the past, the square footage of "live" DVD or video rental counters (which are mainly display space) often made the segment prohibitive. DVD rental is also attractive to both channels because consumers make two stops, one to rent and one to return the DVD. This benefits the retailer on both ends of the transaction.

Coin-counting machines have greater penetration in supermarkets than convenience stores (c-stores). In part, this is due to convenience stores' space constraints and the fact that coin-counting machines can only be placed indoors. Only 8 percent of the convenience stores queried by PG/CSN have coin machines. However, coin counting is a revenue and traffic driver. It is also a destination service that provides consumers with incremental dollars. Often, shoppers use these funds to increase the value of their shopping basket.

At Jacksonville, Florida-based Winn-Dixie Stores (www.winndixie.com), DVD rental, water, and coin-counting machines, followed by lottery machines, generate the most traffic and the heftiest profits, says Tom Barr, the $7 billion chain's alternate source manager. Machines are located in many of the retailer's 484 stores in Florida, Georgia, Alabama, Mississippi, and Louisiana.

TABLE 2 How Supermarkets and Convenience Stores Value Automated Retail Machine Attributes

Value Attributes	% of Stores with Any Type of Machines That Value Attribute	% of Stores with Coin-Counting Machines That Value Attribute	% of Stores with DVD Rental Machines That Value Attribute	% of Stores with Lottery Machines That Value Attribute	% of Stores with Soda Machines That Value Attribute
Customer satisfaction	58	48	53	59	56
Increases store traffic	50	51	47	51	46
Drives profits	43	37	40	43	39
Maximizes retail space	43	41	42	43	40
Shrink/theft control	43	32	34	44	40
Provides a competitive edge	42	42	37	42	40
Low investment for high return	42	40	37	40	42
Labor savings	38	37	38	35	36
Merchandising support from vendor	38	32	36	39	37
Turnkey operation	34	37	37	33	35
Offers unique products not currently stocked	29	34	30	30	27

Source: Convenience Store News/Progressive Grocer Market Research, 2011.

TABLE 3 Automated Retail Machines Offered, by Company Size

		% of Convenience Stores Offering				% of Supermarkets Offering			
Type of Automated Machine	% of Total Stores Offering	All C-Stores	Single C-Store Operated	2 to 10 C-Stores Operated	11 or More C-Stores Operated	All Supers	Single Super Operated	2 to 10 Supers Operated	11 or More Supers Operated
Any automated retail	75	68	61	72	83	85	87	85	84
Lottery	48	44	45	47	41	53	53	41	64
Soda machine	47	29	34	29	14	72	71	74	73
DVD rental	34	24	15	22	48	50	40	32	73
Coin-counting	21	8	5	9	14	40	18	29	66
Cosmetics	10	9	10	5	14	11	11	6	16
Photo-processing	9	4	3	5	7	17	18	12	21
Electronics	6	6	5	7	7	5	3	3	9

Source: Convenience Store News/Progressive Grocer Market Research, 2011.

DVD machines also lead the charge in terms of types of machines that retailers plan to install over the next year. Across both channels, 14 percent will add DVD rental kiosks, followed by coin counting (5 percent), and photo processing (3 percent), according to the PG/CSN study. In total, 21 percent of respondents plan to add more automated machines of some kind.

Large chains are not the only ones that benefit from automated retail kiosks. According to the PG/CSN study, 61 percent of single location convenience-store operators offer automated machines of some kind. Among supermarket respondents, 87 percent of single store owners feature automated retail. See Table 3.

Happy Shoppers

Customer satisfaction is the area in which automated kiosks have the most impact or success, notes the PG/CSN study. This benefit is cited by 69 percent of retailers with coin-counting machines and 75 percent of retailers with DVD kiosks. Customer satisfaction is followed by labor savings (62 percent and 64 percent, respectively), maximizing retail space (61 percent and 62 percent, respectively), and increasing store traffic (55 percent and 58 percent, respectively).

Convenience is the key driver behind customer satisfaction. Some supermarkets, such as Winn-Dixie, place machines both inside and outside to maximize shopper convenience. This meets the needs of people who are grocery shopping, as well as those who are rushed and do not want to enter the store, says Winn-Dixie's Barr. "Everybody uses them," he adds. "They transcend everything. Convenience and price are the lures."

At Jacksons Food Stores, the kiosks are often the only place in small towns to rent DVDs, says Rich Levin, vice-president of marketing. Some of the locations have done so well that Jacksons has added a second machine. Since the machines are destinations, the locations are listed on Jacksons' Web site (www.jacksonsfoodstores.com). Jacksons began offering Redbox kiosks about 18 months ago. Today, the Meriden, Idaho-based convenience-store chain has DVD kiosks outside 80 of its 215 locations. Jacksons, which also has lottery machines, operates in Idaho, Oregon, Washington, and Nevada.

For other retailers, DVD kiosks give consumers a "one-stop shopping" experience. They also replace some of the DVD rental options that have disappeared from the retail landscape. "When the Redbox units first came in, I thought, 'Who would use those?'" says Fred Meyer's Jackson. "But Hollywood Video is gone, as are many Blockbusters." Certain DVD rental kiosk providers even allow their consumers to reserve movies online or via their mobile phones. This adds to the convenience. Movies are then picked up at the stores.

Labor and Cost Savings

Some automated kiosks help eliminate errors and control labor and other costs. This is particularly important during challenging economic times. "Self-service technology frees up workers who can be reassigned to more profitable jobs," indicates the ITIF report. In the case of many DVD and coin machines, the retailers do not have to stock, empty, or maintain kiosks; everything is handled by the machine provider. "We have no responsibility," says Winn-Dixie's Barr in discussing the retailer's role. "It's turnkey."

When considering adding an automated retail kiosk, retailers should explore the different operating models and related services offered by various suppliers. Some suppliers provide services that are completely turnkey and pay retailers a share of machine revenue.

Brand Awareness

Retailers are more familiar with some automated kiosk brands than others. On both an aided recall and total (unaided plus aided) recall basis, the vendor that convenience-store and supermarket respondents are most aware of is Redbox (www.redbox.com). Total awareness is 76 percent. Coinstar (www.coinstar.com) is second at 62 percent. It is followed by Blockbuster Express at 60 percent (www.blockbusterexpress.com) and Kodak at 41 percent (www.kodak.com). See Table 4.

TABLE 4 Awareness of Automated Retail Brands

Automated Retail Brands	% of All Stores Aware of Brand	% of C-Stores Aware of Brand	% of Supermarkets Aware of Brand
Redbox	76	74	78
Coinstar	62	56	72
Blockbuster Express (NCR)	60	59	61
Kodak	41	37	46
DVDXpress	29	28	30
CoinMaster	28	24	35
CoinMax (Cummins)	27	22	22
DVDPlay (NCR)	22	22	22
Zoom Systems	11	12	61

Source: Convenience Store News/Progressive Grocer Market Research, 2011.

Redbox's high brand awareness stems from its deep market penetration: The company operates more than 30,000 kiosks nationwide. Coinstar coin-counting machines number nearly 19,000 in the United States, Great Britain, Canada, and Puerto Rico. According to the retailers interviewed for this article, Redbox kiosks also have broader demographic appeal than many other machines.

Looking Ahead

With an eye toward the future, retailers and kiosk suppliers are developing new types of machines and new twists for old standbys. Coca-Cola's VideoVendor has a 46-inch touch-screen display with video, sound, and graphics. It lets consumers obtain more product information, such as nutritional value. Freestyle, another Coke product, is a robotics-enabled kiosk whose 30 flavor cartridges let users mix unique beverages.

Other machines increase employee efficiency and decrease errors and food waste. Stop & Shop (www.stopandshop.com), an East Coast grocery chain, and Quick Chek (www.quickchek.com), a regional New Jersey convenience-store operator, have implemented kiosks that allow shoppers to order prepared food. The consumer's order is printed out and read by the food preparation staff. Since consumers can make choices in areas like condiments, somebody who wants mustard will not wind up with mayonnaise.

On the personal finance side, 7-Eleven (www.7-eleven.com) has installed over 2,000 units that let shoppers cash checks, buy money orders, transfer funds abroad, and pay bills. Consumers do not have to "join" a store program. Services are attractive to lower-income shoppers and immigrants who may not have bank accounts and/or want to send/receive money. Generally, retail-based check-cashing operations command lower fees than traditional check-cashing establishments.

There is no question that the self-service category is growing. But it remains to be seen which of the newer machine concepts will experience the most growth. In addition to being popular among consumers, successful kiosks must operate efficiently and be easy and affordable for retailers to service and maintain. If they can truly revolutionize the customer experience, some concepts could end up rivaling the unprecedented success level and worldwide penetration of the ATM machine.

Questions

1. What can *any* retailer learn from this case?
2. Comment on the findings in Table 1.
3. Explain how automated retail machines can be best used in human resource management.
4. Discuss how automated retail machines can be best used in operations management. Relate your answer to Table 2.
5. What is the impact of company size on the use of automated retail machines? Refer to Table 3 in your answer.
6. Based on the data in Table 4, would you select Redbox for placement in a supermarket? What are the pros and cons of doing so?
7. What other ways could retailers use kiosks?

PART 6

Merchandise Management and Pricing

In Part Six, we present the merchandise management and pricing aspects of the retail strategy mix. Merchandise management consists of the buying, handling, and financial aspects of merchandising. Pricing decisions deal with the financial aspects of merchandise management and affect their interaction with other retailing elements.

Chapter 14 covers the development of merchandise plans. We begin by discussing the concept of a merchandising philosophy. We then look at buying organizations and their processes, as well as the major considerations in formulating merchandise plans. The chapter concludes by describing category management and merchandising software.

Chapter 15 focuses on implementing merchandise plans. We study each stage in the buying and handling process: gathering information, selecting and interacting with merchandise sources, evaluation, negotiation, concluding purchases, receiving and stocking merchandise, reordering, and re-evaluation. We also examine logistics and inventory management, as well as their effects on merchandising.

Chapter 16 concentrates on financial merchandise management. We introduce the cost and retail methods of accounting. The merchandise forecasting and budgeting process is presented. Unit control systems are discussed. Dollar and unit financial inventory controls are integrated.

Chapter 17 deals with pricing. We review the outside factors affecting price decisions: consumers, government, suppliers, and competitors. A framework for developing a price strategy is then shown: objectives, broad policy, basic strategy, implementation, and adjustments.

Source: Sylvie Bouchard/Shutterstock.com. Reprinted by permission.

14 Developing Merchandise Plans

Chapter Objectives

1. To demonstrate the importance of a sound merchandising philosophy
2. To study various buying organization formats and the processes they use
3. To outline the considerations in devising merchandise plans: forecasts, innovativeness, assortment, brands, timing, and allocation
4. To discuss category management and merchandising software

As we discuss in Chapter 14, merchandising decisions must reflect target market desires, the retailer's intended marketplace positioning, and more. Utilized actively as a merchandising tool, social media can help retailers be better merchandisers and reach out in a dynamic way to their customers.

Burberry is a British-based global luxury brand designer and retailer of apparel and accessories. The company has its own stores around the world, including the United States, and also sells through Bloomingdale's, Neiman Marcus, Nordstrom, and other upscale retailers. In its social media efforts, Burberry has a huge presence on Facebook (www.facebook.com/burberry) with more than 10 million likes from people. Photos on its Facebook wall are vital in Burberry's merchandising strategy.

The firm has increased its merchandising emphasis targeting young adults known as Millennials. In targeting this group, Burberry is most interested in twenty-somethings to thirty-somethings—which can be a challenging segment to reach and satisfy. As *Stores* magazine's Fiona Soltes describes the situation:

> Millennials are more interested in value than heritage and authenticity versus tactical marketing that rings untrue. Watching the way they've influenced fashion, technology, and workplace attitudes, the outspoken, anything-is-possible generation will leave its mark on luxury, too. "One thing I've found is that, if you look at the younger audience, it tends to be a harbinger of the entire audience," says Paul Hurley, CEO of ideeli, which offers members-only access to luxury brands online. "What they do now, they will likely do when they're older. But what they're doing now gets communicated to other segments of the population."

What drives apparel purchases by younger consumers? The CEO of research company Luxury Institute reports that many of these shoppers are attracted to "legacy" products such as luxury brands. Luxury products are important to Millennials because they may perceive expensive goods as investments in themselves. This helps to convert the Millennials' "want" for upscale brands into more of a "need" for those seeking the approval of others and to show that they are successful.[1]

Source: BeTA-Artworks/ fotolia.com.

Overview

Retail Detail Merchandising (www.rdmerchandising.com) is a third-party vendor of several merchandising services.

Retailers must have the proper product assortments and sell them in a manner consistent with their overall strategy. **Merchandising** consists of the activities involved in acquiring particular goods and/or services and making them available at the places, times, and prices and in the quantity that enable a retailer to reach its goals. Merchandising decisions can dramatically affect performance. Consider these observations—from three different perspectives:

- Often, the biggest competitive advantages of an independent retailer is the way in which it can focus on and adapt to consumer needs—thus, offering superior expertise and a high level of customer service. In contrast, the big-box retailer is better at cutting costs and, thereby, at offering lower prices (sometimes, extremely low prices) for shoppers. They recognize that for many products "the vast majority of shoppers are highly price sensitive. But for any item, and especially for those that are not commodities, there is a critical segment of customers who are not price shoppers, who focus instead on product quality, service, and a relaxed, friendly experience. Selling higher quality, specialty products on the basis of their intrinsic value, insulates a small retailer from price competition, and enables the retailer to obtain a higher initial markup, and avoid corrosive sales, price promotions, and other incentives that eat into margins."[2]
- Department stores typically appeal to consumers with "broader product assortments based on local demographics, versus an across-the-board assortment strategy by brand based on store size. Department store chains are also looking at more grassroots marketing to build a more loyal customer base. Many use viral marketing tools and social networking sites to reach out to their consumers with targeted promotions. Regarding specialty stores, there are more chains with product assortments that have expanded to accept a more alternative shopper; for example, Hot Topic or Torrid. This alternative shopper is also forcing malls to consider more mom-and-pop retailers that cater to this demographic as tenants."[3]
- In multi-channel supply chains, companies require an efficient, adaptable supply chain that can get products to the proper place, on time, and in good condition: "True multi-channel retailing involves managing online and in-store in an integrated way." It is critical to "consolidate the way stock is managed across all the channels, which gives maximum flexibility, and can help cut costs and working capital." Also important "is the greater use of international or offshore locations as retailers use the Web to drive an offer across more markets potentially as part of a market entry strategy." Lastly, "returns or reverse logistics must be made easy for shoppers. If people feel it will be a hassle or expensive to return an item, they're likely to go somewhere else."[4]

In this chapter, the planning aspects of merchandising are discussed. The implementation aspects of merchandising are examined in Chapter 15. The financial aspects of merchandising are described in Chapter 16. Retail pricing is covered in Chapter 17.

Visit our Web site (www.pearsonhighered.com/bermanevans) for a broad selection of links related to merchandising strategies and tactics.

MERCHANDISING PHILOSOPHY

At Cost Plus World Market, you never know what you'll find (www.worldmarket.com).

A **merchandising philosophy** sets the guiding principles for all the merchandise decisions that a retailer makes. It must reflect target market desires, the retailer's institutional type, the marketplace positioning, the defined value chain, supplier capabilities, costs, competitors, product trends, and other factors. The retail merchandising philosophy drives every product decision, from what product lines to carry to the shelf space allotted to different products to inventory turnover to pricing—and more: Many retailers think they have a good merchandising strategy: "However, filling in top sellers or having an open-to-buy is not a strategy. A merchandising strategy defines a company's future in terms of what you want your assortments to be, regardless of what you currently have in stock. A merchandise plan then articulates your desired outcome by product groups—revenue, gross profit percentage and dollars, and inventory turn. Tactical actions are necessary for day-to-day running operations or to stay afloat, but strategic actions

FIGURE 14-1

The Unique Merchandising Philosophy of Stew Leonard's

Stew Leonard's (www.stewleonards.com/html/about.cfm), which began as a small dairy store with 7 employees, has expanded into meats, fish, produce, bakery, cheese, and wine. Today, the company has 2,000 employees and 4 huge stores. Yet, unlike traditional supermarkets and superstores that sell 30,000 or more items, each Stew Leonard's food store carries just 2,000 items, chosen for their freshness, quality, and value.

Source: Reprinted by permission of Susan V. Berry, Retail Image Consulting, Inc.

ensure a thriving future. Start by asking yourself questions about the vision for your store, and the merchandise required to get you there."[5] See Figure 14-1.

Costco, the membership club giant, flourishes with its individualistic merchandising philosophy, whereby it offers members very low prices on a limited selection, but broad assortment, of national and private brands. Costco's approach yields high sales revenue through quick inventory turnover:

> This turnover, when combined with volume purchasing, efficient distribution, and reduced handling of merchandise in no-frills, self-service warehouse facilities, enables us to operate profitably at significantly lower gross margins than traditional wholesalers, mass merchandisers, supermarkets, and supercenters. We limit specific items in each product line to fast-selling models, sizes, and colors—and carry an average of 3,600 active stock keeping units (SKUs) per warehouse in our core warehouse business, as opposed to 45,000 to 140,000 SKUs or more at discount retailers, supermarkets, and supercenters. Many consumable products are offered for sale in case, carton, or multiple-pack quantities only.[6]

In forming a merchandising philosophy, the scope of responsibility for merchandise personnel must be stated. Are these personnel to be involved with the full array of *merchandising functions*, both buying and selling goods and services (including selection, pricing, display, and customer transactions)? Or are they to focus on the *buying function*, with others responsible for displays, personal selling, and so on? Many firms consider merchandising to be the foundation for their success, and buyers (or merchandise managers) engage in both buying and selling tasks. Other retailers consider their buyers to be skilled specialists who should not be active in the selling function, which is done by other skilled specialists. For example, store managers at full-line discount stores often have great influence on product displays but have little impact on whether to stock or promote particular brands.

With a merchandising-oriented philosophy, the buyer's expertise is used in selling, responsibility and authority are clear, the buyer ensures that items are properly displayed, costs are reduced (fewer specialists), and the buyer is close to consumers due to selling involvement. When buying and selling are separate, specialized skills are applied to each task, the morale of store personnel goes up as they get more authority, selling is not viewed as a secondary task, salesperson–customer interaction is better, and buying and selling personnel are distinctly supervised. Each firm must see which format is best for it.

To capitalize on opportunities, more retailers now use micromerchandising and cross-merchandising. With **micromerchandising**, a retailer adjusts shelf-space allocations to respond to customer and other differences among local markets. Dominick's supermarkets assign shelf space to children's and adult's cereals to reflect demand patterns at different stores. Wal-Mart allots the space to product lines at various stores to reflect differences in demographics, weather, and shopping. Micromerchandising is easier today due to the data generated. Consider this observation: "Getting the products to the store that the local market wants, in the right quantity, in the right color, in the right size, and priced to sell to maximize sell-through and profitability is the 'Holy Grail' of any retailer. The ability to keep your finger on the pulse of local changing consumer demands will be the key to growth."[7]

In **cross-merchandising**, a retailer carries complementary goods and services to encourage shoppers to buy more. That is why apparel stores stock accessories and auto dealers offer extended warranties. Cross-merchandising, like scrambled merchandising, can be ineffective if taken too far. Yet, it has tremendous potential. Consider this from the perspective of pharmacies, which use cross-merchandising to increase their revenues by making it easy for consumers to buy complementary items and by generating in-store (impulse) purchases. According to retailing consultant Neil Stern:

> People buy solutions, not products; and retailers tend to sell products, not solutions. So they need to combine things that tend to cross departments. A classic case for cross-merchandising is in cold and flu season. Cross-merchandising items like cough drops, Kleenex, and medications helps consumers easily find these items if they come in for one of them. During holidays, an aisle can be permanently devoted to specific occasions and change as the seasons do, so the aisle is a big draw with lots of cross-merchandising. Don't cross-merchandise items that don't go together.[8]

Assortment Planning as a Competitive Edge

Hibbett Sports (www.hibbett.com) is a big retail chain with more than 800 stores in 26 states as of 2012. However, its average store is only about 5,000 square feet in size. Its large number of stores, the small store size, and the need to tailor its assortment to each community makes assortment planning particularly complex. According to Mike McAbee, Hibbett Sports' vice-president of merchandise planning and replenishment: "Until we hit store number 500, we were able to use home-grown [software] programs and a lot of spreadsheets to figure out the individual personalities of each store."

Since 2005, Hibbett has been using JDA's Merchandise Management System (www.jda.com). As a result, the chain has been able to reduce its SKUs (stock-keeping units) by 10 to 30 percent in certain categories such as cleated footwear and for some basketball and women's apparel. This system has also enabled Hibbett to have deeper selections in its core product categories.

Hibbett's merchandise assortment planning is based on 26 attributes—including distance from a military base or a big-box competitor, whether the store is located in a shopping mall or strip center, and store demographics such as disposable income and population density. As McAbee says: "We cut through these attributes to find out what products do in certain markets."

Sources: Len Lewis, "Sporting Chance," www.stores.org (December 2010); and "About Us," www.hibbett.com/about (May 30, 2012).

BUYING ORGANIZATION FORMATS AND PROCESSES

A merchandising plan cannot be properly devised unless the buying organization and its processes are well defined: Who is responsible for decisions? What are their tasks? Do they have sufficient authority? How does merchandising fit with overall operations? Figure 14-2 highlights the range of organizational attributes from which to choose.

Level of Formality

With a *formal buying organization*, merchandising (buying) is a distinct retail task and a separate department is set up. The functions involved in acquiring merchandise and making it available for sale are under the control of this department. A formal organization is most often used by larger firms and involves distinct personnel. In an *informal buying organization*, merchandising (buying) is not a distinct task. The same personnel handle both merchandising (buying) and other retail tasks; responsibility and authority are not always clear-cut. Informal organizations generally occur in smaller retailers.

The advantages of a formal organization are the clarity of responsibilities and the use of full-time, specialized merchandisers. The disadvantage is the cost of a separate department. The advantages of an informal format are the low costs and flexibility. The disadvantages are less-defined responsibilities and the lesser emphasis on merchandise planning. Both structures exist in great numbers. It is not critical for a firm to use a formal department. It is crucial that the firm recognizes the role of merchandising (buying) and ensures that responsibility, activities, and operational relationships are aptly defined and enacted.

Degree of Centralization

Multi-unit retailers must choose whether to have a centralized buying organization or a decentralized one. In a *centralized buying organization*, all purchase decisions emanate from one office. A chain may have eight stores, with all merchandise decisions made at the headquarters store. In a *decentralized buying organization*, purchase decisions are made locally or regionally. A 40-store chain may allow each outlet to select its own merchandise or divide the branches into geographic territories (such as four branches per region) with regional decisions made by the headquarters store in each territory.

The advantages of centralized buying are the integration of effort, strict controls, consistent image, proximity to top management, staff support, and volume discounts. Possible disadvantages are the inflexibility, time delays, poor morale at local stores, and excessive uniformity. Decentralized

FIGURE 14-2
The Attributes and Functions of Buying Organizations

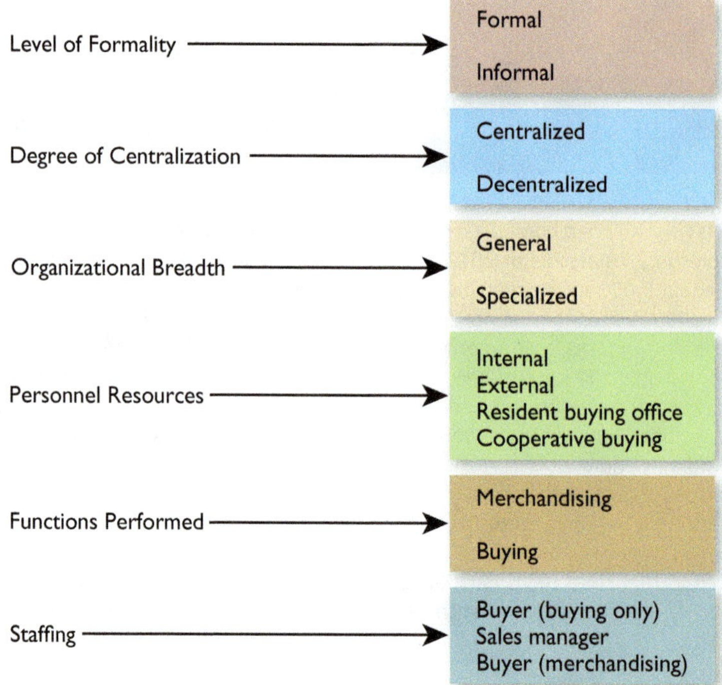

buying has these advantages: adaptability to local conditions, quick order processing, and improved morale because of branch autonomy. Potential disadvantages are disjointed planning, an inconsistent image, limited controls, little staff support, and a loss of volume discounts.

See what Zara's merchandisers think is "hot" (www.zara.com).

Many chains combine the formats by deploying a centralized buying organization while also giving store managers some input. This is how Zara, the Madrid-based global apparel chain with more than 1,600 stores in nearly 80 countries, operates:

> This international footprint proves that national borders are no hindrance to a shared fashion culture. Zara's approach to design is closely linked to our customers. A nonstop flow of data from stores conveys shoppers' desires and demands, inspiring our 200-person-strong creative team. Zara is in tune with its customers, who help it give shape to the ideas, trends, and tastes developing in the world. This is the secret to its success among a wide range of people, cultures, and generations, who, despite their differences, all share a special fondness for fashion.[9]

Organizational Breadth

In a general buying organization, one or several people buy all of a firm's merchandise. The owner of a small hardware store may buy the merchandise for his or her store. With a specialized organization, each buyer is responsible for a product category. A department store usually has separate buyers for girls', juniors', and women's clothes.

A general approach is better if the retailer is small or there are few products involved. A specialized approach is better if the retailer is large or many products are carried. By specializing, there is greater expertise and responsibility is well defined; however, costs are higher and extra personnel are required.

Personnel Resources

A retailer can choose an inside or outside buying organization. An *inside buying organization* is staffed by a retailer's personnel, and merchandise decisions are made by permanent employees. See Figure 14-3. With an *outside buying organization*, a firm or personnel external to the retailer are hired, usually on a fee basis. Most retailers use either an inside or an outside organization; some employ a combination.

An inside buying organization is most often used by large retailers and very small retailers. Large retailers do this to have greater control over merchandising decisions and to be more distinctive. They have the financial clout to employ their own specialists. At very small retailers, the owner or manager does all merchandising functions to save money and keep close to the market.

Ross Stores has merchandising career opportunities in New York and Los Angeles. Scroll down to "corporate/buying office/distribution opportunities" (www.rossstores.com/job_search.aspx).

Ross Stores (www.rossstores.com), the off-price apparel chain with about 1,000 stores in 27 states, is an example of a retailer with an inside buying organization. Ross operates buying offices in New York City and Los Angeles, the two largest U.S. apparel markets: "These strategic locations allow our buyers to be in the market on a daily basis, sourcing opportunities and negotiating purchases with vendors and manufacturers. These locations also enable our buyers to strengthen vendor relationships—a key element to the success of our off-price buying strategies." Ross employs 450 merchants, who include merchandise managers, buyers, and assistant buyers. These personnel average about 12 years of experience.[10]

An outside organization is most frequently used by small or medium-sized retailers or those far from supply sources. It is more efficient for them to hire outside buyers than to use company personnel. An outside organization has purchase volume clout in dealing with suppliers, usually services noncompeting retailers, offers research, and may sponsor private brands. Outside buying organizations may be paid by retailers that subscribe to their services or by vendors that give commissions. An individual retailer may set up its own internal organization if it feels its outside group is dealing with direct competitors or the firm finds it can buy items more efficiently on its own.

Learn more about the services provided by Doneger Group (www.doneger.com/web/89357.htm).

The Doneger Group (www.doneger.com), founded in 1946, is one of the leading outside buying firms, with hundreds of retailer clients. As its Web site notes, the company: "is the fashion industry's leading source of global trend intelligence, focused merchandising direction, expert analysis of the retail business, and comprehensive market information. Our goal is to move our clients forward in an increasingly competitive, consumer-oriented world with a companywide culture of innovation, creativity, and a deep level of trust and personal engagement in our client relationships. Building on our rich heritage and reputation, we strategically grow the business

FIGURE 14-3

Nike: An Illustration of an Inside Buying Organization

Nike has an extensive inside buying organization that stocks its own stores, such as the one shown here, as well as thousands of retail outlets around the world. As it says in the *Nike 2011 Annual Report:* "Our principal business activity is the design, development, and worldwide marketing and selling of high-quality footwear, apparel, equipment, and accessory products. Virtually all of our products are manufactured by independent contractors. Virtually all footwear and apparel products are produced outside the United States, while equipment products are produced both in the United States and abroad."

Source: Reprinted by permission of Susan V. Berry, Retail Image Consulting, Inc.

through the addition of new services and the development of specific divisions in support and anticipation of the ever-changing direction of the industry."[11]

A **resident buying office**, which can be an inside or outside organization, is used when a retailer wants to keep in close touch with key market trends and cannot do so through just headquarters buying staff. Such offices are situated in vital merchandise centers and provide data and contacts. Worldwide, several specialized firms operate resident buying offices. For instance, Milan, Italy-based VIB Group has a major resident buying office for international retailers: "Clients demand a local eye and ear on the Italian market, in touch with developing trends, brands, and merchandise. They value the importance of managing the supply chain via a local, experienced, and proven partner, to have an edge over competition and direct access to people who count. We help clients negotiate for the best prices and terms, leveraging our relationship with suppliers and the overall volume of business with them. We buy merchandise on behalf of the client, providing suppliers with all necessary guarantees."[12] Besides the large players, there are many smaller outside resident buying offices that assist retailers.

The Federation of Pharmacy Networks (www.fpn.org) provides many services for its members.

Today, independent retailers and small chains are involved with cooperative buying to a greater degree than before to compete with large chains. In **cooperative buying**, a group of retailers gets together to make quantity purchases from suppliers and obtain volume discounts. It is most popular among consumer electronics, food, hardware, and drugstore retailers. For example, more than 75 percent of independent consumer electronics stores belong to a buying group. One such entity is BrandSource, which represents 4,500 member stores that together account for well over $1 billion in annual sales. In addition to consumer electronics, BuyingSource handles furniture, floor coverings, plumbing items, and more. Other consumer electronics buying groups include Mega Group USA, Nationwide Marketing Group, and NATM Buying Corporation.[13]

As another cooperative buying illustration, the Federation of Pharmacy Networks (FPN) comprises 22 buying groups across the United States. It represents more than 14,000 independent drugstore owners: "Just as independent buying groups leverage the combined volume and voice of independent pharmacy owners, so does FPN utilize the collective business of its members to access the most aggressively negotiated programs and contracts available to independents today."[14]

Functions Performed

At this juncture, the responsibilities and functions of merchandise and in-store personnel are assigned. With a "merchandising" view, merchandise personnel oversee all buying and selling functions, including assortments, advertising, pricing, point-of-sale displays, employee utilization, and personal selling approaches. With a "buying" view, merchandise personnel oversee the buying of products, advertising, and pricing, while in-store personnel oversee assortments, displays, employee utilization, and sales presentations. The functions undertaken must reflect the retailer's level of formality, the degree of centralization, and personnel resources.

Staffing

The last organizational decision involves staffing. What positions must be filled and with what qualifications? Firms with a merchandising viewpoint are most concerned with hiring good buyers. Firms with a buying perspective are concerned about hiring sales managers, as well. Many large firms hire college graduates, train them, and promote them to buyers and sales managers.

A **buyer** is responsible for selecting the merchandise to be carried by a retailer and setting a strategy to market that merchandise. He or she devises and controls sales and profit projections for a product category (generally for all stores in a chain); plans proper merchandise assortments, styling, sizes, and quantities; negotiates with and evaluates vendors; and often oversees in-store displays. He or she must be attuned to the marketplace, be able to bargain with suppliers, and be capable of preparing detailed plans; and he or she may travel to the marketplace. A **sales manager** typically supervises the on-floor selling and operational activities for a specific retail department. He or she must be a good organizer, administrator, and motivator. A *merchandising buyer* must possess the attributes of each. Most retailers feel the critical qualification for good merchandisers is their ability to relate to customers and methodically anticipate future needs. In addition, to some extent, buyers are involved with many of the remaining tasks described in this and the next chapter.

Macy's, Inc. (www.macyscollege.com/college) has exciting career paths in both merchandising and operations.

Macy's, Inc., which operates the Macy's and Bloomingdale's department store chains, has career tracks that recognize the value of both merchandising and in-store personnel. Figure 14-4 shows two distinct career tracks.

FIGURE 14-4
Merchandising Versus Store Management Career Tracks at Macy's, Inc.

Note: Macy's has a flexible approach to career development after college. The merchandising and operations tracks depicted here are illustrative of the job progression through two different paths.

Source: Figure developed by the authors based on information at "Career Paths," www.macysjobs.com/college/careers/careerpaths (March 11, 2009).

Merchandising Track	*Store Management Track*
Divisional Merchandise Manager Oversees merchandise selection and procurement for a particular business segment. Sets the merchandise direction to ensure continuity on the selling floor. Develops strategy to ensure customer satisfaction and maximize performance and profits.	**Store Manager** Responsible for all aspects of running a profitable store. Sets the tone to ensure success in customer service, profits, operations, people development, merchandise presentation, and merchandise assortment.
Buyer Expected to maximize sales and profitability of a given business area by developing and implementing a strategy, analyzing it, and reacting to trends. Overall support of company sales, gross margin, and turnover objectives.	**Assistant Store Manager** Directs merchandise flow, store maintenance, expense management, shortage prevention, and store sales support activities for a large portion of store volume. Acts as Store Manager in his or her absence.
Associate Buyer Responsible for merchandise development, marketing, and financial management of a particular business area. This is a developmental step to buyer.	**Sales Manager** In charge of store activities in a specific merchandise area. Includes merchandise presentation, employee development, customer service, operations, and inventory control.
Assistant Buyer Aids buyer in selecting and procuring merchandise, which supports overall sales, gross margin, and turnover goals. Provides operational support to buyers. Assumes some buying responsibility, once buyer determines proficiency.	**Assistant Sales Manager** Responsible for supervising daily store activities in a specific merchandise area. Includes selling and service management, selecting and developing associates, merchandising, and business management.

Here's what it's like at the top of the merchandising world:

> Elizabeth Sweney is executive vice-president and senior general merchandise manager of J.C. Penney, overseeing women's apparel, accessories, handbags and shoes, and fine jewelry divisions. She also oversees the company's juniors and Sephora inside J.C. Penney businesses. Under her leadership, Penney has become a leading destination for discovering great style at compelling prices with the launch of successful private and exclusive brands that can only be found at J.C. Penney, such as Liz Claiborne, MNG by Mango, City Streets, Decree, I "Heart" Ronson by Charlotte Ronson, and more. Before joining Penney in 2000, she held senior-level positions at Kellwood, after serving in merchandising positions of increasing responsibility at Montgomery Ward for 17 years.[15]

DEVISING MERCHANDISE PLANS

There are several factors to consider in devising merchandise plans, as discussed next. See Figure 14-5.

Forecasts

Forecasts are projections of expected retail sales for given periods. They are the foundation of merchandise plans and include these components: overall company projections, product category projections, item-by-item projections, and store-by-store projections (if a chain). Consider the case of Ikea, the global furniture chain:

Ikea (www.ikea.com/ms/en_US/about_ikea) scours the globe for interesting new items that will be popular in its stores.

> To reduce costs, Ikea uses JDA Software's supply and demand optimization solutions, including JDA Demand and JDA Fulfillment. "Planners have been enthusiastic about this because it gives them better visibility into sales patterns and it has improved their global view," said Jimmy Biesert, head of supply chain planning. There are 11,000 products in the total Ikea product range. Each store carries a selection depending on store size. More than 2,000 suppliers in over 50 countries manufacture Ikea products. The profile of its well-designed and high-quality range is distinctively Swedish/Scandinavian. All products are labeled "Design and Quality, Ikea of Sweden."[16]

In this section, forecasting is examined from a general planning perspective. In Chapter 16, the financial dimensions of forecasting are reviewed.

When preparing forecasts, it is essential to distinguish among different types of merchandise. **Staple merchandise** consists of the regular products carried by a retailer. For a supermarket, staples include milk, bread, canned soup, and facial tissues. For a department store, staples include everyday watches, jeans, glassware, and housewares. Because these items

FIGURE 14-5
Considerations in Devising Merchandise Plans

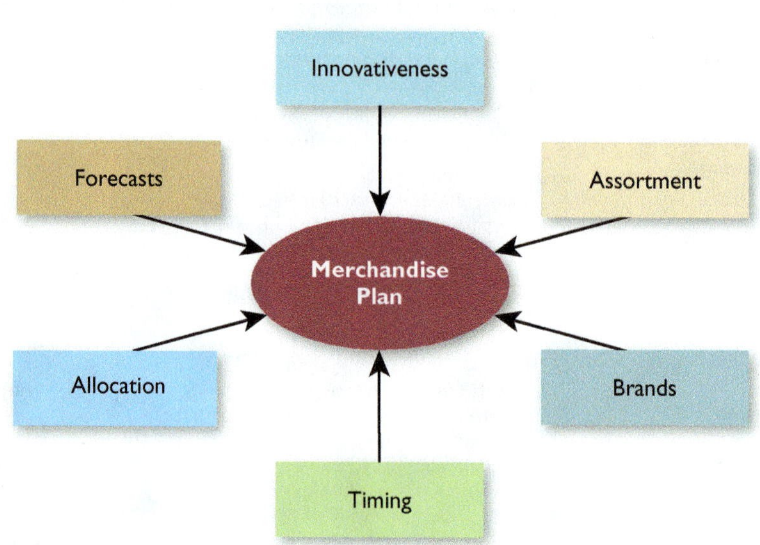

Fay Ricotta: Fifth Avenue Club

Fay Ricotta is one of eighteen personal shoppers employed in the women's wear department at Saks Fifth Avenue's (www.saksfifthavenue.com) New York flagship store. Previously, she worked at such high-fashion stores as Jeffrey (www.jeffreynewyork.com) and Bergdorf Goodman (www.bergdorfgoodman.com). To keep current on fashion trends, Ricotta travels to Paris' fashion week twice a year, attending 20 shows each visit.

As a personal shopper, Ricotta aids her clients in selecting, fitting, and coordinating appropriate clothing selections. She also provides her customers with access to sought-after labels, some of which are not stocked at Saks Fifth Avenue. Ricotta has access to such designers as Thom Browne, Lanvin, Yves Saint Laurent, and Calvin Klein.

Ricotta's 27 clients have two common characteristics: They are trim; and they are big spenders on clothing. Ninety percent wear a size 4, and only one is a size 12. Fay Ricotta's average client also buys between $150,000 and $200,000 of merchandise from her per year. Although Ricotta is paid on a commission basis, her fee is paid by Saks Fifth Avenue, not her clients.

Source: Christina Binkley, "Inside a Department Store's Secret Shopping Service," www.wallstreetjournal.com (August 11, 2011).

have relatively stable sales (sometimes seasonal) and their nature may not change much over time, a retailer can clearly outline the quantities for these items. A **basic stock list** specifies the inventory level, color, brand, style category, size, package, and so on for every staple item carried by the retailer.

Assortment merchandise consists of apparel, furniture, autos, and other products for which the retailer must carry a variety of products in order to give customers a proper selection. This merchandise is harder to forecast than staples due to demand variations, style changes, and the number of sizes and colors to be carried. Decisions are two-pronged: (1) Product lines, styles, designs, and colors are projected. (2) A **model stock plan** is used to project specific items, such as the number of green, red, and blue pullover sweaters of a certain design by size. With a model stock plan, many items are ordered for popular sizes and colors, and small amounts of less popular sizes and colors fill out the assortment.

Fashion merchandise consists of products that may have cyclical sales due to changing tastes and lifestyles. For these items, forecasting can be hard because styles may change from year to year. "Hot" colors often change back and forth. **Seasonal merchandise** consists of products that sell well over nonconsecutive time periods. Items such as ski equipment and air-conditioner servicing have excellent sales during one season per year. Because the strongest sales of seasonal items usually occur at the same time each year, forecasting is straightforward.

With **fad merchandise,** high sales are generated for a short time. Often, toys and games are fads, such as Harry Potter toys that flew off store shelves each time a related movie was released. It is hard to forecast whether such products will reach specific sales targets and how long they will be popular. Sometimes, fads turn into extended fads—and sales continue for a long period at a fraction of earlier sales. Trivial Pursuit board games are in the extended fad category.

In forecasting for best-sellers, many retailers use a **never-out list** to determine the amount of merchandise to purchase for resale. The goal is to purchase enough of these products so they are always in stock. Products are added to and deleted from the list as their popularity changes. Before a new James Patterson novel is released, stores order large quantities to be sure they meet anticipated demand. After it disappears from best-seller lists, smaller quantities are kept. It is a good strategy to use a combination of a basic stock list, a model stock plan, and a never-out list. These lists may overlap.

Innovativeness

The innovativeness of a merchandise plan depends on a number of factors. See Table 14-1.

An innovative retailer has a great opportunity—distinctiveness (by being first in the market)—and a great risk—possibly misreading customers and being stuck with large inventories. By assessing each factor in Table 14-1 and preparing a detailed plan for merchandising new goods and services, a firm can better capitalize on opportunities and reduce risks. As shown in

TABLE 14-1 Factors to Bear in Mind When Planning Merchandise Innovativeness

Factor	Relevance for Planning
Target market(s)	Evaluate whether the target market is conservative or innovative.
Goods/service growth potential	Consider each new offering on the basis of rapidity of initial sales, maximum sales potential per time period, and length of sales life.
Fashion trends	Understand vertical and horizontal fashion trends, if appropriate.
Retailer image	Carry goods/services that reinforce the firm's image. The level of innovativeness should be consistent with this image.
Competition	Lead or follow competition in the selection of new goods/services.
Customer segments	Segment customers by dividing merchandise into established-product displays and new-product displays.
Responsiveness to consumers	Carry new offerings when requested by the target market.
Amount of investment	Consider all of the possible investment for each new good/service: product costs, new fixtures, and additional personnel (or further training for existing personnel).
Profitability	Assess each new offering for potential profits.
Risk	Be aware of the possible tarnishing of the retailer's image, investment costs, and opportunity costs.
Constrained decision making	Restrict franchisees and chain branches from buying certain items.
Declining goods/services	Delete older goods/services if sales and/or profits are too low.

Figure 14-6, the Next apparel retailer takes innovativeness quite seriously. So do companies such as Brookstone and 7-Eleven:

Check out Brookstone's (www.brookstone.com) unique product offerings.

- Brookstone offers an eclectic mix of products—ranging from massage chairs to travel electronics to blood pressure monitors—that are "functional in purpose, distinctive in quality and design, and not widely available from other retailers. From the start, Brookstone created a fun, interactive shopping experience. At our stores, customers are encouraged to try products out for true, hands-on shopping. Every visit to Brookstone is an opportunity to discover new and ingenious items of superior quality—all in a friendly environment that simply can't be found anywhere else."
- The convenience store format is quite innovative, as shown by 7-Eleven, which began as Southland Ice Company in 1927. At that time, "products people wanted were pretty simple—milk, eggs, and bread." Today, 7-Eleven introduces new products virtually every week; and its product mix is quite different. Milk, eggs, and bread are still offered; but customers can also buy "a fresh salad, chicken wings for a tailgate party, wine, a pre-paid iTunes card, or a Slurpee drink in a cool, collectible cup. Whatever the need, we want to be the friendly, convenient, one-stop shop of choice."[17]

Retailers should assess the growth potential for each new good or service they carry: How fast will a new item generate significant sales? What are the most sales (dollars and units) to be reached in a season or year? Over what period will an item continue selling? One tool to assess potential is the **product life cycle**, which shows the expected behavior of a good or service over its life. The basic cycle comprises introduction, growth, maturity, and decline stages—shown in Figure 14-7 and described next.

During introduction, the retailer should anticipate a limited target market. The good or service will probably be supplied in one basic version. The manufacturer (supplier) may limit distribution to "finer" stores. Yet, new convenience items such as food and housewares products are normally mass distributed. Items initially distributed selectively tend to have high prices. Mass-distributed products typically involve low prices to foster faster consumer acceptance. Early promotion must be explanatory, geared to informing shoppers. At this stage, there are very few possible suppliers.

FIGURE 14-6
Innovativeness the Next Way
British-based Next (www.nextplc.co.uk) is known for its innovative approach to coordinated collections of private-branded women's wear and accessories that are sold in a boutique-style shopping environment. The brand is "aspirational yet affordable, with an appealing combination of distinctive style, good quality, and value. Next also carries menswear, home interior products, and children's wear. Next was chosen as the official clothing and home wear supplier for the London 2012 Olympic and Paralympic Games.

Source: Tupungato/Shutterstock.com. Reprinted by permission.

As innovators buy a new product and recommend it to friends, sales increase rapidly and the growth stage is entered. The target market includes middle-income consumers who are more innovative than average. The assortment expands, as do the number of retailers carrying the product. Price discounting is not widely used, but competing retailers offer a range of prices and customer service. Promotion is more persuasive and aimed at acquainting shoppers with availability and services. There are more suppliers.

FIGURE 14-7
The Traditional Product Life Cycle

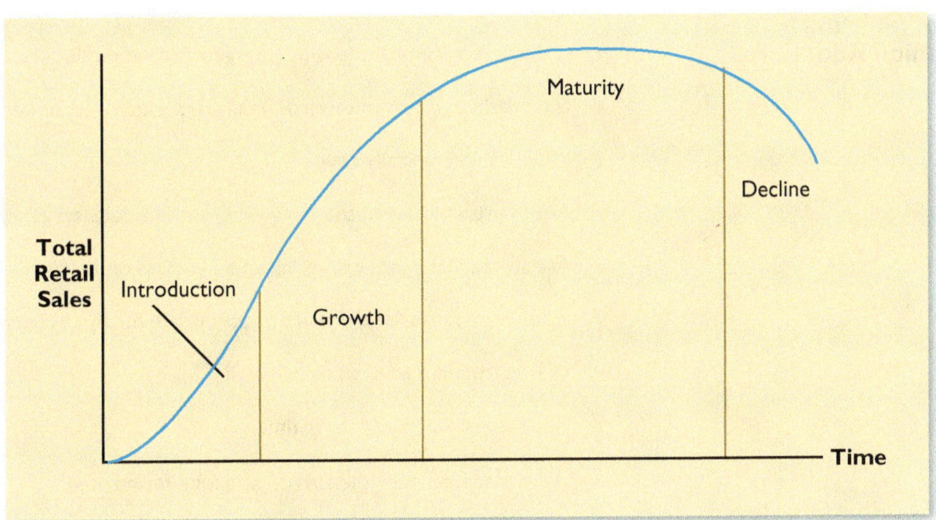

In maturity, sales reach their maximum, the largest portion of the target market is attracted, and shoppers select from very broad product offerings. All types of retailers (discount to upscale) carry the good or service in some form. Prestige retailers stress brand names and customer service, while others use active price competition. Price is more often cited in ads. Competition is intense.

The decline stage is brought on by a shrinking market (due to product obsolescence, newer substitutes, and boredom) and lower profit margins. The target market may become the lowest-income consumers and laggards. Some retailers cut back on the assortment; others drop the good or service. At retailers still carrying the items, promotion is reduced and geared to price. There are fewer suppliers.

Many retailers pay a lot of attention to new-product additions but not enough to deciding whether to drop existing items. Yet, because of limited resources and shelf space, some items have to be dropped when others are added. Instead of intuitively pruning products, a retailer should use structured guidelines:

- Select items for possible elimination on the basis of declining sales, prices, and profits, as well as the appearance of substitutes.
- Gather and analyze detailed financial and other data about these items.
- Consider nondeletion strategies such as cutting costs, revising promotion efforts, adjusting prices, and cooperating with other retailers.
- After making a deletion decision, do not overlook timing, parts and servicing, inventory, and holdover demand.

Sometimes, a seemingly obsolete good or service can be revived. An innovative retailer recognizes the potential in this area and merchandises accordingly. Direct marketers heavily promote "greatest hits" recordings featuring individual music artists and compilations of multiple artists.

Apparel retailers must be familiar with fashion trends. A *vertical trend* occurs when a fashion is first introduced to and accepted by upscale consumers and then undergoes changes in its basic form before it is sold to the general public. This type of fashion goes through three stages: distinctive—original designs, designer stores, custom-made, worn by upscale shoppers; emulation—modification of original designs, finer stores, alterations, worn by middle class; and economic emulation—simple copies, discount stores, mass-produced, mass-marketed.

With a *horizontal trend*, a new fashion is marketed to a broad spectrum of people upon its introduction while retaining its basic form. Within any social class, there are innovative customers who act as opinion leaders. New fashions must be accepted by these leaders, who then convince other members of the same social class (who are more conservative) to buy the items. Fashion is sold across the class and not from one class to another. Figure 14-8 has a checklist for predicting fashion adoption.

FIGURE 14-8

A Selected Checklist for Predicting Fashion Adoption

- ✓ Does the fashion satisfy a consumer need?
- ✓ Is the fashion compatible with emerging consumer lifestyles?
- ✓ Is the fashion oriented toward the mass market or a market segment?
- ✓ Is the fashion radically new?
- ✓ Are the reputations of the designer(s) and the retailers carrying the fashion good?
- ✓ Are several designers marketing some version of the fashion?
- ✓ Is the price range for the fashion appropriate for the target market?
- ✓ Will appropriate advertising be used?
- ✓ Will the fashion change over time?
- ✓ Will consumers view the fashion as a long-term trend?

Assortment

An **assortment** is the selection of merchandise a retailer carries. It includes both the breadth of product categories and the variety within each category.

A firm first chooses the quality of merchandise. Should it carry top-line, expensive items and sell to upper-income customers? Or should it carry middle-of-the-line, moderately priced items and cater to middle-income customers? Or should it carry lesser-quality, inexpensive items and attract lower-income customers? Or should it try to draw more than one market segment by offering a variety, such as middle- and top-line items for middle- and upper-income shoppers? The firm must also decide whether to carry promotional products (low-priced closeout items or special buys used to generate store traffic). Several factors must be reviewed in choosing merchandise quality. See Table 14-2.

Dollar Tree has an overall strategy that is very consistent with its approach to merchandise quality. The retailer is:

Look at Dollar Tree's (www.dollartree.com) targeted merchandising approach. Click on "About Us" at the bottom of the screen.

> a customer-oriented, value-driven variety store operating at a one dollar price point. Some of the product departments you'll find at Dollar Tree include housewares, glassware, dinnerware, cleaning supplies, candy, snacks, food, health and beauty, toys, gifts, gift bags and wrap, party supplies, stationery, craft supplies, teaching supplies, books, seasonal décor, and more! Everything you need for every day, every holiday, every occasion—and every single item is only $1 (or less)![18]

After deciding on product quality, a retailer determines its width and depth of assortment. **Width of assortment** refers to the number of distinct goods/service categories (product lines)

TABLE 14-2 Factors to Take into Account When Planning Merchandise Quality

Factor	Relevance for Planning
Target market(s)	Match merchandise quality to the wishes of the desired target market(s).
Competition	Sell similar quality (follow the competition) or different quality (to appeal to a different target market).
Retailer's image	Relate merchandise quality directly to the perception that customers have of a retailer.
Store location	Consider the impact of location on the retailer's image and the number of competitors, which, in turn, relate to quality.
Stock turnover	Be aware that high quality and high prices usually yield a lower turnover than low quality and low prices.
Profitability	Recognize that high-quality goods generally bring greater profit per unit than lesser-quality goods; turnover may cause total profits to be greater for the latter.
Manufacturer versus private brands	Understand that, for many consumers, manufacturer brands connote higher quality than private brands.
Customer services offered	Know that high-quality goods require personal selling, alterations, delivery, and so on. Lesser-quality merchandise may not.
Personnel	Employ skilled, knowledgeable personnel for high-quality merchandise. Self-service may be used with lesser-quality merchandise.
Perceived goods/ service benefits	Analyze consumers. Lesser-quality goods attract customers who desire functional product benefits. High-quality goods attract customers who desire extended product benefits (e.g., status, services).
Constrained decision making	Face reality. a. Franchisees or chain store managers often have limited or no control over product decisions. b. Independent retailers that buy from a few large wholesalers are limited to the range of quality offered by those wholesalers.

a retailer carries. **Depth of assortment** refers to the variety in any one goods/service category (product line) a retailer carries. As noted in Chapter 5, an assortment can range from wide and deep (department store) to narrow and shallow (box store). Figure 14-9 shows advantages and disadvantages for each basic strategy.

Assortment strategies vary widely. Web retailer Discount Art (www.discountart.com) says it is geared to "the artist who demands good-quality art materials, but also appreciates good prices." But even small retailers with a narrow product assortment, like the one in Figure 14-10, need a good selection to draw shoppers. KFC's thousands of worldwide outlets emphasize chicken and related products. They do not sell hamburgers, pizza, or many other popular fast-food items. Macy's department stores feature thousands of general merchandise items, and Amazon.com is

Advantages	Disadvantages
Wide and Deep (many goods/service categories and a large assortment in each category)	
Broad market	High inventory investment
Full selection of items	General image
High level of customer traffic	Many items with low turnover
Customer loyalty	Some obsolete merchandise
One-stop shopping	
No disappointed customers	
Wide and Shallow (many goods/service categories and a limited assortment in each category)	
Broad market	Low variety within product lines
High level of customer traffic	Some disappointed customers
Emphasis on convenience customers	Weak image
Less costly than wide and deep	Many items with low turnover
One-stop shopping	Reduced customer loyalty
Narrow and Deep (few goods/service categories and a large assortment in each category)	
Specialist image	Too much emphasis on one category
Good customer choice in category(ies)	No one-stop shopping
Specialized personnel	More susceptible to trends/cycles
Customer loyalty	Greater effort needed to enlarge the size of the trading area
No disappointed customers	Little (no) scrambled merchandising
Less costly than wide and deep	
Narrow and Shallow (few goods/service categories and a limited assortment in each category)	
Aimed at convenience customers	Little width and depth
Least costly	No one-stop shopping
High turnover of items	Some disappointed customers
	Weak image
	Limited customer loyalty
	Small trading area
	Little (no) scrambled merchandising

FIGURE 14-9
Retail Assortment Strategies

FIGURE 14-10

Product Assortment Is a Key to Sales—Regardless of the Retailer

To attract its tourist shoppers and spur impulse sales, this small Oxford Street, London retailer of soccer shirts, hats, and related gear has a good—and colorful—selection in its chosen few product categories.

Source: Ahmad Faizal Yahya/Shutterstock.com. Reprinted by permission.

an online department store with millions of items for sale. This is the dilemma that retailers may face in determining how big an assortment to carry:

> Twenty years ago, retailers made decisions based on budgets; ten years ago, they looked to make everything more efficient. Now, Ning Chiu [an assortment planning expert] says that "unless you buy right to begin, everything else is hindsight." Yet, merchants must trust their gut. "They're out at market; they see what trends are taking off and those that may not be." A retailer with stores five miles apart could have different customers. "A small store might trend much faster than a large store. Even within the same store, the clientele could change in the summer because of tourists."[19]

Retailers should take several factors into account in planning their assortment: If variety is increased, will overall sales go up? Will overall profits? How much space is required for each product category? How much space is available? Carrying 10 varieties of cat food will not necessarily yield greater sales or profits than stocking 4 varieties. The retailer must look at the investment costs that occur with a large variety. Because selling space is limited, it should be allocated to those goods and services generating the most customer traffic and sales. The inventory turnover rate should also be studied.

A distinction should be made among scrambled merchandising, complementary goods and services, and substitute goods and services. With *scrambled merchandising*, a retailer adds unrelated items to generate more revenues and lift profit margins (such as a florist carrying umbrellas). Handling *complementary goods and services* lets the retailer sell both basic items and related offerings (such as stereos and CDs) via cross-merchandising. Although scrambled merchandising and cross-merchandising both increase overall sales, carrying too many *substitute goods and services* (such as competing brands of toothpaste) may shift sales from one brand to another and have little impact on overall retail sales.

These factors are also key as a retailer considers a wider, deeper assortment: (1) Risks, merchandise investments, damages, and obsolescence may rise dramatically. (2) Personnel may be spread too thinly over dissimilar products. (3) Both the positive and negative ramifications of scrambled merchandising may occur. (4) Inventory control may be difficult; overall turnover probably will slow down.

A retailer may not have a choice about stocking a full assortment within a product line if a powerful supplier insists that the retailer carry its entire line or it will not sell at all to that retailer. But large retailers—and smaller ones belonging to cooperative buying groups—are now standing up to suppliers, and many retailers stock their own brands next to manufacturers'.

Brands

As part of its assortment planning, a retailer chooses the proper mix of manufacturer, private, and generic brands—a challenge made more complex with the proliferation of brands. **Manufacturer (national) brands** are produced and controlled by manufacturers. They are usually well known, supported by manufacturer ads, somewhat pre-sold to consumers, require limited retailer investment in marketing, and often represent maximum quality to consumers. Such brands dominate sales in many product categories. Popular manufacturer brands include Apple, Coke, Gillette, Levi's, Microsoft, Nike, Nintendo, Revlon, and Sony. The retailers likely to rely most heavily on manufacturer brands are small firms, Web firms, discounters, and others that want the credibility associated with well-known brands or that have low-price strategies (so consumers can compare the prices of different retailers on name-brand items).

Although they face extensive competition from private bands, manufacturer brands remain the dominant type of brand, accounting for more than 80 percent of all retail sales worldwide: "What would a supermarket without national brands look like? I can describe it in one lonely word—empty. It's hard to imagine a store with no Pepsi, Cheerios, Fritos, or Tide. No Colgate, Oreos, Tylenol, or Hellmann's. No Hershey bars, Campbell's soup, Heinz ketchup, Quaker oatmeal, or Tropicana orange juice. Where are this imaginary store's shoppers? At a supermarket where the aisles are lined with national brands."[20]

Private (dealer) brands, also known as **store brands,** contain names designated by wholesalers or retailers, are more profitable to retailers, are better controlled by retailers, are not sold by competing retailers, are less expensive for consumers, and lead to customer loyalty to retailers. With most private brands, retailers must line up suppliers, arrange for distribution and warehousing, sponsor ads, create displays, and absorb losses from unsold items. This is why retailer interest in private brands is growing:

- In *dollar sales*, private brands account for about 17 percent of U.S. retail revenues; they account for 22 percent of *unit sales.* Private brands represent 19 percent of dollar sales at food stores, 15 percent at drugstores (excluding prescription drugs), and 14 percent at mass merchandisers in the United States. In Europe, the dollar sales figure for private brands at grocery stores ranges from 16 percent of retail store revenues in Italy to 49 percent in Great Britain.[21]

Why Isn't Venezuelan Chocolate Selling Abroad?

The "provenance paradox" explains that consumers associate certain countries with the best products in a given product category. As examples, Swiss watches, German beer, and Italian clothing are viewed as high quality. Conversely, competing products from developing countries may be perceived as inferior, despite their actual quality ingredients and craftsmanship.

This explains why Chocolates El Rey (www.chocolates-elrey.com), a Venezuelan cacao bean and chocolate producer, is able to get a 30 percent price premium for its cacao (which is used as an ingredient in making Swiss and Belgium chocolate), but El Rey's own chocolate brand is difficult to sell outside of Venezuela due to low demand. Other examples of the provenance paradox include wines from Chilean-based Concha y Toro, refrigerators produced by Arcelik in Turkey, and goods from such emerging markets as China and India.

Firms from developing countries need to combat the provenance paradox through one or more of these tactics:

- Focus on basic commodities such as Egyptian cotton and Indian spices. Firms can continue as low-cost suppliers of basic commodities.
- Build strong brand names through aggressive promotions and focusing on building products with value-added features. Nissan, Honda, and Toyota are examples of this strategy.
- Seek to reposition the present country-of-origin's image.
- Create a new local brand that downplays the country of origin.

Source: Rohit Deshpandé, "Why You Aren't Buying Venezuelan Chocolate," *Harvard Business Review* (December 2010), pp. 25–27.

TABLE 14-3 The Berman/Evans Private Brand Test

Think you know a lot about private brands? Then take our test. Match the retailers and the brand names. The answers are at the bottom of the table. No peeking. First, take the test.

Please note: Retailers may have more than one brand on the list.

Retailer	Brand
1. A&P	a. Alfani men's apparel
2. Bloomingdale's	b. America's Choice cookies
3. Costco	c. Craftsman tools
4. Kmart	d. Jaclyn Smith bed and bath accessories
5. Kohl's	e. Joseph & Lyman men's apparel
6. Macy's	f. Kirkland Signature coffee
7. J.C. Penney	g. Master Choice jams and preserves
8. Sears	h. Mossimo women's apparel
9. Target	i. Ol' Roy dog food
10. Wal-Mart	j. Roadhandler tires
	k. Simply Vera sleepwear
	l. Stafford men's apparel

Answers: 1—b, g; 2—e; 3—f; 4—d; 5—k; 6—a; 7—l; 8—c, j; 9—h; 10—i

- Private brands are typically priced 20 to 30 percent below manufacturer brands. This benefits consumers, as well as retailers (costs are lower and revenues are shared by fewer parties). Retailer profits are higher from private brands, despite the lower prices.
- Most U.S. shoppers are aware of private brands—80 percent buy them regularly.
- At Gap, Old Navy, The Limited, McDonald's, and many other retailers, private brands represent most or all of company revenues.

The best-selling U.S. appliance brand (www.kenmore.com) is not GE or Whirlpool.

- At virtually all large retailers, both private brands and manufacturer brands are strong. Sears' Kenmore appliance line is the market-leading brand—ahead of GE, Maytag, and others. J.C. Penney private brands include American Living (created by Polo Ralph Lauren), Liz Claiborne (now sold exclusively at Penney), St. John's Bay, and Worthington. Amazon.com sells private brands, such as its Kindle product line, along with millions of manufacturer-branded items. Great Britain's Tesco supermarkets has four different private brands (known as "own brands") that encompass at least 500 product items *each*. Take our private brand challenge in Table 14-3.

In the past, private brands were only discount versions of mid-tier products. They are now seen in a different light: "Most shoppers are more alert to the concept of quality and value. Retailers recognize that price is not the single differentiator for all shoppers and cannot tempt everyone away from manufacturer brands. Thus, they have invested in the development of a wider variety of competitive offerings. Multi-tiered private label offers meet consumers at the premium, standard, and value points often with differentiated features at the higher-priced levels. In some categories, the premium private label will be the most expensive and innovative product."[22] See Figure 14-11.

For example, a *premium private brand* offered by Harris Teeter (the supermarket chain) is H.T. Traders, which is exclusive to the chain: "Our H.T. Traders search the world to bring you delicious and unexpected surprises in every aisle. From the finest olive oils to aromatic gourmet coffees to remarkable frozen desserts, each selection is chosen because it is a step above the ordinary. Whatever you enjoy, H.T. Traders products will add that little something extra to make it special to you and your family."[23]

Care must be taken in deciding how much to emphasize private brands. As previously noted, many consumers are loyal to manufacturer brands and would shop elsewhere if those brands are not stocked or their variety is pruned. See Figure 14-12.

Generic brands feature products' generic names as brands (such as canned peas); they are no-frills goods stocked by some retailers. They are a form of private brand. These items usually

FIGURE 14-11
Chico's Approach to Private Brands

Chico's (www.chicos.com) is a 660-store women's apparel chain. The retailer only sells its own private brand of "sophisticated, casual-to-dressy" apparel, accessories, and other nonclothing gift products.

Source: Reprinted by permission of Susan V. Berry, Retail Image Consulting, Inc.

receive secondary shelf locations, have little or no promotion support, may be of lesser quality, are stocked in limited assortments, and have plain packages. Retailers control generics and price them well below other brands. In supermarkets, generics account for under 1 percent of sales. For prescription drugs, where the quality of manufacturer brands and generics is similar, generics provide 60 percent of sales.

The competition between manufacturers and retailers for shelf space and profits has led to a **battle of the brands**, whereby manufacturer, private, and generic brands fight each other for more space and control. Nowhere is this battle clearer than at large retail chains: "Walk down the aisle of a Staples store, and you'll see a lot of big-name brands—Avery, Duracell,

FIGURE 14-12
Lowe's Distinctive Branding Strategy

Lowe's (www.lowes.com) carries a full assortment of both manufacturer brands and private brands to reach multiple customer segments: "We offer great values with national brands like StainMaster carpet and Valspar paint, and with our private brands like allen + roth home décor and Kobalt tools that offer exceptional style and function at a great price."

Source: Reprinted by permission of Susan V. Berry, Retail Image Consulting, Inc.

Hewlett-Packard, 3M, and more. But you'll also find more than two thousand products [as of 2011] sold under the retailer's own brand: Staples' yellow self-stick notes, Staples' stainless-steel shears, even Staples' ink cartridges for laser printers."[24] In 2011, Staples' own brand's sales exceeded 24 percent of its total sales.

Timing

For new products, the retailer must decide when they are first purchased, displayed, and sold. For established products, the firm must plan the merchandise flow during the year. The retailer should take into account its forecasts and other factors: peak seasons, order and delivery time, routine versus special orders, stock turnover, discounts, and the efficiency of inventory procedures.

Some goods and services have peak seasons. These items (such as winter coats) require large inventories in peak times and less stock during off seasons. Because some people like to shop during off seasons, the retailer should not eliminate the items.

With regard to order and delivery time, how long does it take the retailer to process an order request? After the order is sent to the supplier, how long does it take to receive merchandise? By adding these two periods together, the retailer can get a good idea of the lead time to restock shelves. If it takes a retailer 7 days to process an order and the supplier another 14 days to deliver goods, the retailer should begin a new order at least 21 days before the old inventory runs out.

Routine orders involve restocking staples and other regularly sold items. Deliveries are received weekly, monthly, and so on. Planning and problems are minimized. Special orders involve merchandise not sold regularly, such as custom furniture. They need more planning and cooperation between retailer and supplier. Specific delivery dates are usually arranged.

Stock turnover (how quickly merchandise sells) greatly influences how often items must be ordered. Convenience items such as milk and bread (which are also highly perishable) have a high turnover rate and are restocked quite often. Shopping items such as refrigerators and color TVs have a lower turnover rate and are restocked less often.

In deciding when and how often to buy merchandise, the availability of quantity discounts should be considered. Large purchases may result in lower per-unit costs. Efficient inventory procedures, such as electronic data interchange and quick response planning procedures, also decrease costs and order times while raising merchandise productivity.

Allocation

The last part of merchandise planning is the allocation of products. A single-unit retailer chooses how much merchandise to place on the sales floor, how much to place in a stockroom, and whether to use a warehouse. A chain also apportions products among stores. Allocation is covered further in Chapter 15.

Some retailers rely on warehouses as distribution centers. Products are shipped from suppliers to these warehouses, and then they are assigned and shipped to individual stores. Other

What's a Fair Return Policy?

According to the Retail Equation (www.theretailequation.com), a retailing consulting firm, approximately 8 percent of all customer returns may be classified as either unfair or fraudulent. The impact of excessive customer returns is so high that it forces retail managers to walk a fine line between customer satisfaction arising from a positive return policy and the loss of customer loyalty.

Tom Richman, vice-president of marketing for the Retail Equation, states that: "Anyone who says, 'No sale is ever final' is setting themselves up for fraud and abuse." Richman feels that the easiest way to curb abuse is for a store to require receipts, impose strict time limits on returns, require managers to sign off on returns, and provide store credits instead of money back for returned goods. The Retail Equation also recommends that retailers keep a data base of customers and their return behavior.

The Retail Equation further recommends that a retailer modify its return policy based on a customer's loyalty and purchases within a given merchandise category. A customer who purchases a high amount of merchandise in a given product category and rarely returns goods should get preferential treatment as opposed to an infrequent consumer who is not a member of the retailer's loyalty program.

Source: Michael Hartnett, "Restricting Returns, Satisfying Shoppers," www.stores.org (September 2010).

retailers, including many supermarket chains, do not rely as much on warehouses. They have at least some goods shipped directly from suppliers to individual stores.

It is vital for chains, whether engaged in centralized or decentralized merchandising, to have a clear store-by-store allocation plan. Even if merchandise lines are standardized across the chain, store-by-store assortments must reflect the variations in the size and diversity of the customer base, in store size and location, in the climate, and in other factors.

CATEGORY MANAGEMENT

As noted in Chapter 2, **category management** is a merchandising technique that some firms—including supermarkets, drugstores, hardware stores, and general merchandise retailers—use to improve productivity. It is a way to manage a retail business that focuses on the performance of product category results rather than individual brands. It arranges product groupings into strategic business units to better meet consumer needs and to achieve sales and profit goals. Retail managers make merchandising decisions that maximize the total return on the assets assigned to them.

This is how category management typically works. It is:

> a retailing process in which all like-minded products in a retailer's total portfolio are lumped together into product "categories." Some examples would be toothpaste, washing-up liquids, baked beans, dog foods, cosmetics, and walking shoes. Each category is then run like a "mini-business," managed by both the retailer and suppliers, with its own category turnover and/or profitability targets. The relationship between retailer and supplier is more collaborative in nature with more openness and information sharing. Suppliers are expected to propose actions (such as new products or promotions) only if they add to total category sales and shopper satisfaction.[25]

According to the A.C. Nielsen research company, good category management involves these steps:

1. Define the category based on the needs of the target market.
2. Assign a role to the category based on several questions: How important is the category to the consumer? How important is the category to the retailer? How important is the category to the retailer's competitors? What is the category's outlook in the marketplace?
3. Assess the category to find opportunities for improvement.
4. Set performance targets and measure progress with a category scorecard.
5. Create a marketing strategy that draws the overarching picture of how to achieve the category role and scorecard targets.
6. Choose tactics for category assortment, pricing, promotion, merchandising, and supply chain strategies.
7. Roll out the plan.
8. Review performance regularly and adjust as needed.[26]

A fundamental premise is that a retailer must empower specific personnel to be responsible for the financial performance of each product category. As with micromerchandising, category management means adapting merchandise for each store or region to best satisfy customers. In deciding on the space per product category, there are several crucial measures of performance. Comparisons can be made by studying company data from period to period and by looking at categorical statistics in trade magazines:

- *Sales per linear foot of shelf space*—annual sales divided by the total linear footage devoted to the product category.
- *Gross profit per linear foot of shelf space*—annual gross profit divided by the total linear footage devoted to the product category.
- *Return on inventory investment*—annual gross profit divided by average inventory at cost.

- *Inventory turnover*—the number of times during a given period, usually one year, that the average inventory on hand is sold.
- *Days' supply*—the number of days of supply of an item on the shelf.
- *Direct product profitability (DPP)*—an item's gross profit less its direct retailing costs (warehouse and store support, occupancy, inventory, and direct labor costs, but not general overhead).

Some collaborative aspects of category management are working well, while other aspects are not—due to the differing roles of manufacturers and retailers in the channel of distribution:[27]

What Manufacturers Feel About Retailers

SUCCESSFUL APPLICATIONS OF CATEGORY MANAGEMENT

- Retailers act as equal partners.
- Retailers get input from manufacturers so they put the best possible plan together.
- Retailers are open minded and willing to change.
- Retailers that give manufacturers proper lead time—and timely goals and suggestions—receive the highest-quality work.

UNSUCCESSFUL APPLICATIONS OF CATEGORY MANAGEMENT

- Different goals among the retailers' senior managers, category managers, and operations managers impede the process.
- Retailers have a "template fixation." Yet, a template alone cannot explain why shoppers choose a given product or category.
- Retailers expect manufacturers to do more than their share or to pay more than their share for gathering and analyzing data.

What Retailers Feel About Manufacturers

SUCCESSFUL APPLICATIONS OF CATEGORY MANAGEMENT

- Manufacturers gather data on consumer purchases and make recommendations to retailers.
- Manufacturers with clearly defined and supported plans are viewed favorably.
- Manufacturers help the retailers understand how to get more out of shopper traffic and build shopper loyalty, incremental volume, and return on merchandising assets.

UNSUCCESSFUL APPLICATIONS OF CATEGORY MANAGEMENT

- Manufacturers make recommendations that consistently favor their brands.
- Manufacturers just drop a completed template off with their retailers.
- Manufacturers do not maintain confidentiality for shared data or recommendations.

Figure 14-13 indicates how a retailer could use category management to better merchandise liquid detergent. One axis relates to direct product profitability. For the supermarket in this example, $0.69 per item is the average DPP for all liquid detergents. Those with higher amounts are placed in the top half of the grid and those with lower amounts in the bottom half. The other axis classifies detergents in terms of unit sales (an indicator of inventory turnover), with 12.3 items weekly being the dividing line between slow- and fast-moving detergents. All detergents can be placed into one of four categories: high potential ("sleepers"), products with high profitability but low sales; winners, products with high profitability and high sales; underachievers ("dogs"), products with low profitability and low sales; and traffic builders, products with low profitability and high sales. Specific strategies are recommended in the figure.

FIGURE 14-13

Applying Category Management to Heavy-Duty Liquid Detergent

Note: The criteria are based on the average profit and movement of the items in the product category of heavy-duty liquid detergent. The averages change for each product category.

Source: Walter H. Heller, "Profitability; Where It's Really At" (December 1992), p. 27. Copyright *Progressive Grocer*. Reprinted by permission.

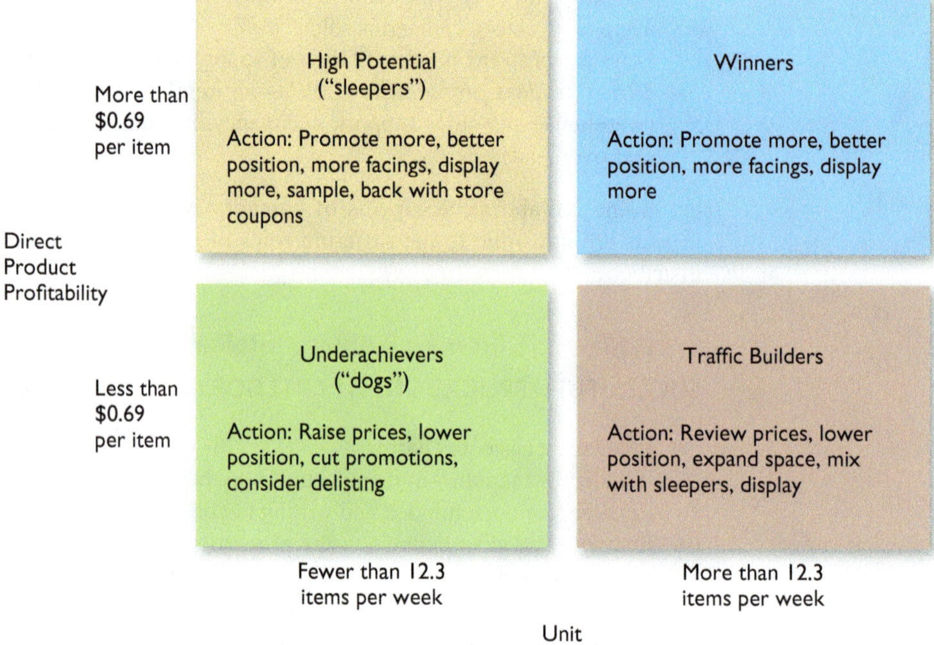

MERCHANDISING SOFTWARE

This site (www.business.com/directory/retail_and_consumer_services/software) provides a directory of retail software providers.

One of the most significant advances in merchandise planning is the widespread availability of computer software that gives retailers an excellent support mechanism to systematically prepare forecasts, try out various assortment scenarios, coordinate the data for category management, and so forth. In an era when many retailers carry thousands of items, merchandising software is a part of everyday business life.

Some merchandising software is provided by suppliers and trade associations at no charge—as part of the value delivery chain and relationship retailing. Other software is sold by marketing firms, often for $1,500 or less (although some software sells for $25,000 or more). Let's now discuss the far-reaching nature of merchandising software. Links to several retail merchandising software products, including category management, are at our Web site (www.pearsonhighered.com/bermanevans).

General Merchandise Planning Software

Some retailers prefer functionally driven software, while others use integrated software packages. Groupon, the online deal-of-the-day retailer, is an example of the latter. It utilizes MicroStrategy (www.microstrategy.com) software "to analyze its daily deals and gain a deeper understanding of consumer behavior by examining the types of goods and services purchased, discounts offered, location, and purchaser demographics. The MicroStrategy-based reports and dashboards give Groupon visibility into trends that can help to optimize and maximize the deals for improved performance. In addition, Groupon uses MicroStrategy to analyze and evaluate the effectiveness of its advertising expenditures."[28]

Forecasting Software

Many retailers use their data warehouses to make merchandise forecasts. JDA Software (www.jda.com) is one of the firms that produces software that lets them do so. DSW, the shoe chain with more than 300 of its own stores and leased departments in many others, is a major retail client: "DSW uses a core item planning system within JDA Enterprise Planning that allows the company to project the right inventory levels, keep stores optimally stocked, and purchase the right products—even the right mix of shoe sizes. 'JDA has provided us with technology capabilities that are robust enough to manage the complexity of our supply chain, while also supporting our critical business processes.'"[29]

Firms such as SAS (www.sas.com) offer sophisticated software for retail forecasting purposes: This software can be used to analyze and forecast events that occur over time. Retailers are able to discern trends that were not previously noticeable; and they can anticipate ups and downs to better plan future activities: "Whether you want to understand past trends, forecast the future, or better understand how your business functions, we provide a wide range of analytical tools that ensure your success."[30]

Innovativeness Software

Today's software provides detailed data rapidly, because it allows retailers to monitor and more quickly react to trends. Processes that once took months now are done in weeks or days. Instead of missing a selling season, retailers are prepared for the latest craze.

Overstock.com (the online retailer) is one of several firms that uses social collaboration from Spigit (www.spigit.com): Overstock.com offers brand-name products at discounted prices: "With more than 1,500 employees, the global retailer is always looking for ways to tap the creative thought of its employees, partners, and customers in order to manage new, innovative ideas around cost-savings, revenue generation, process improvements, and customer service. Utilizing a robust set of idea management software solutions, Overstock.com has created open and engaging communities that allow collaboration and innovation by all stakeholders across its entire organization. The new and novel method of engaging associates, partners, and customers has added significant value to the business, and has become an integral component in the company's competitive strategy."[31]

Assortment Software

Learn more about SAS retail software (www.sas.com/industry/retail).

A number of retailers employ merchandising software to better plan assortments. One such retailer is Sport Chalet, which uses SAS (www.sas.com) software. It is a specialty chain that has branched out from California to other states over the past decade or so. If you "need scuba gear, rental skis, a package of golf lessons, or mountain climbing gear," Sport Chalet has them all. Through SAS Merchandise Intelligence Solutions software, Sport Chalet is doing a better job with assortments, pricing, promotions, space plans, and allocations—and better selecting and managing inventory. That allows Sport Chalet's buying personnel to concentrate on uncovering the right products to sell: "This is critical as some sports gear has very long lead times for placing orders. The company is also able to make better decisions about what items to put on sale or put on clearance and when to do that. And it is easier to spot regional differences."[32]

Allocation Software

Chains of all sizes and types want to improve how they allocate merchandise to stores. There are several software programs to let them do so. Consider the Allocation software from JustEnough. Most retail planners would like to better tailor their merchandise to local needs. JustEnough's Allocation software "takes all the guesswork out of allocating products to stores where the products have the best chance of selling. JustEnough forecasts customer demand and, then—taking into account the current stock at each location and what has been sold—calculates both the optimal inventory to send to each location and how much to reorder across the supply chain." This tool enables the retailer "to define the rules on how to best allocate inventory for the fastest return on investment."[33]

Category Management Software

Harbor Wholesale supports its retailers—2,000 convenience stores, grocery stores, restaurants, and drugstores—with a category management team (www.harborwholesale.com/Page.aspx?nid=45) that uses sophisticated software.

A wide range of software programs is available to help manufacturers and retailers deal with category management's complexities. A few retailers have even developed their own software. Programs typically base space allocation on sales, inventory turnover, and profits at individual stores. Because data are store specific, space allocations reflect actual sales. These are examples of category management software:

- SAP for Retail (www.sap.com/software/category_management.epx) from SAP.
- Apollo Space Management & Planning (www.aldata.com/com/products/aldata-apollo) from Aldata.
- Shelf Logic Enterprise (www.shelflogic.com/Enterprise.htm) and Shelf Logic Master (www.shelflogic.com/Masteredit.htm). The Enterprise version is $4,995; the Master is $995.
- JDA Space Planning (www.jda.com/solutions/space-planning). See Figure 14-14.

FIGURE 14-14

JDA Space Planning: Software for Category Management Planning

Source: Reprinted by permission of JDA Software Group.

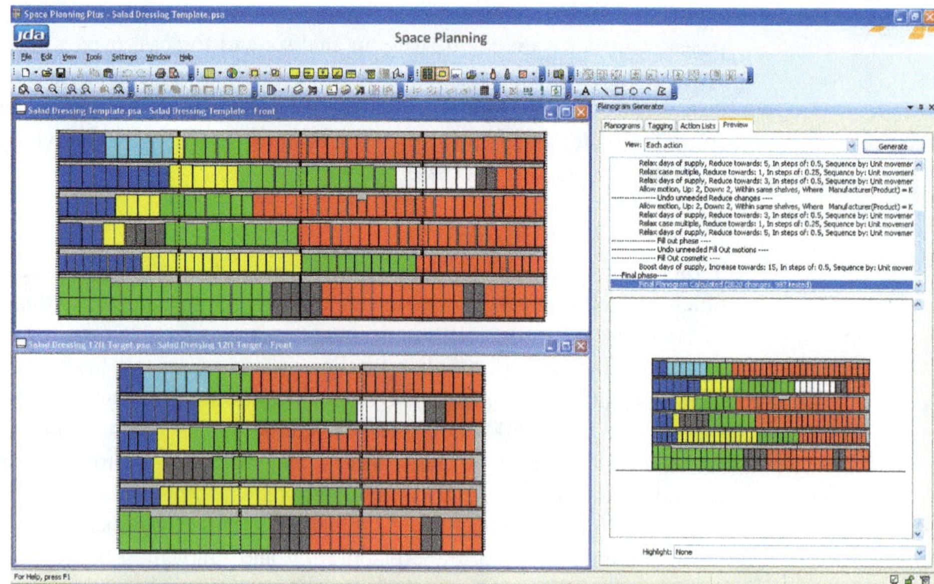

Chapter Summary

1. *To demonstrate the importance of a sound merchandising philosophy.* Developing and implementing a merchandise plan is a key element in a successful retail strategy. Merchandising consists of the activities involved in a retailer's buying goods and services and making them available for sale. A merchandising philosophy sets the guiding principles for all merchandise decisions and must reflect the desires of the target market, the retailer's institutional type, its positioning, its defined value chain, supplier capabilities, costs, competitors, product trends, and other factors.

2. *To study various buying organization formats and the processes they use.* The buying organization and its processes must be defined in terms of its formality, degree of centralization, organizational breadth, personnel resources, functions performed, and staffing.

   With a formal buying organization, merchandising is a distinct task in a separate department. In an informal buying organization, the same personnel handle both merchandising and other retail tasks. Multi-unit retailers must choose whether to have a centralized or a decentralized buying organization. In a centralized organization, all purchases emanate from one office. In a decentralized organization, decisions are made locally or regionally. For a general organization, one person or a few people buy all merchandise. For a specialized organization, each buyer is responsible for a product category.

   An inside buying organization is staffed by a retailer's personnel and decisions are made by its permanent employees. An outside buying organization involves a company or personnel external to the retailer. Most retailers use either an inside or an outside buying organization; some employ a combination. A resident buying office, which can be an inside or outside organization, is used when a retailer wants to keep in close touch with key markets and cannot do so through headquarters buying staff. Independents and small chains often use cooperative buying to compete with large chains.

   If a retailer has a "merchandising" view, merchandise personnel oversee all buying and selling functions. If it has a "buying" view, merchandise personnel oversee buying, advertising, and pricing, while store personnel oversee assortments, displays, personnel deployment, and sales presentations.

   A buyer is responsible for selecting merchandise and setting a strategy to market that merchandise. He or she devises and controls sales and profit projections for a product category; plans assortments, styling, sizes, and quantities; negotiates with and evaluates vendors; and oversees store displays. A sales manager supervises the on-floor selling and operational activities for a specific retail department. He or she must be a good organizer, administrator, and motivator.

3. *To outline the considerations in devising merchandise plans: forecasts, innovativeness, assortment, brands, timing, and allocation.* Forecasts are projections of expected retail sales and form the foundation of merchandise plans. Staple merchandise consists of the regular products a retailer carries. A basic stock list specifies the inventory level, color, brand, and so on for every staple item carried. Assortment merchandise consists of products for which there must be a variety so customers have a proper selection. A model stock plan projects levels of specific assortment merchandise. Fashion merchandise has cyclical sales due to changing tastes and lifestyles. Seasonal merchandise sells well over nonconsecutive periods. With fad merchandise, sales are high for a short time. When forecasting for best-sellers, many retailers use a never-out list.

   A retailer's innovativeness is related to the target market(s), product growth potential, fashion trends, the retailer's image, competition, customer segments, responsiveness to consumers, investment costs, profitability, risk, constrained decision making, and declining goods and services. Three issues are of particular interest: How fast will a new good or service generate sales? What are the most sales to be achieved in a season or a year? Over what period will a good or service continue to sell? A useful tool is the product life cycle.

   An assortment is the merchandise selection carried. The retailer first chooses the quality of merchandise. The assortment is then determined. Width of assortment refers to the number of distinct product categories carried. Depth of assortment refers to the variety in any category. As part of assortment planning, a retailer chooses its mix of brands. Manufacturer brands are produced and controlled by manufacturers. Private brands contain names designated by wholesalers or retailers. Generic brands feature generic names as brands and are a form of private brand. The competition between manufacturers and retailers is called the battle of the brands.

   For new goods and services, it must be decided when they are first to be displayed and sold. For established goods and services, the firm must plan the merchandise flow during the year. In deciding when and how often to buy merchandise, quantity discounts should be considered. A single-unit retailer chooses how much merchandise to allocate to the sales floor and how much to the stockroom, and whether to use a warehouse. A chain also allocates items among stores.

4. *To discuss category management and merchandising software.* Category management is a technique for managing a retail business that focuses on product category results rather than the performance of individual brands. It arranges product groups into strategic business units to better address consumer needs and meet financial goals. Category management helps retail personnel make the merchandising decisions that maximize the total return on the assets. There is now plentiful PC- and Web-based merchandising software available for retailers, in just about every aspect of merchandise planning.

Key Terms

merchandising (p. 349)
merchandising philosophy (p. 349)
micromerchandising (p. 351)
cross-merchandising (p. 351)
resident buying office (p. 354)
cooperative buying (p. 354)
buyer (p. 355)
sales manager (p. 355)
forecasts (p. 356)
staple merchandise (p. 356)
basic stock list (p. 357)
assortment merchandise (p. 357)
model stock plan (p. 357)
fashion merchandise (p. 357)
seasonal merchandise (p. 357)
fad merchandise (p. 357)
never-out list (p. 357)
product life cycle (p. 358)
assortment (p. 361)
width of assortment (p. 361)
depth of assortment (p. 362)
manufacturer (national) brands (p. 364)
private (dealer, store) brands (p. 364)
generic brands (p. 365)
battle of the brands (p. 366)
category management (p. 368)

Questions for Discussion

1. Describe and evaluate the merchandising philosophy of your favorite online retailer.
2. What is the distinction between *merchandising functions* and the *buying function*?
3. Is micromerchandising a good approach? Why or why not?
4. What are the advantages and disadvantages of a centralized buying organization?
5. Interview a local store owner and determine how he or she makes merchandise decisions. Evaluate that approach.
6. How could a convenience store use a basic stock list, a model stock plan, and a never-out list?
7. Under what circumstances could a retailer carry a wide range of merchandise quality without hurting its image? When should the quality of merchandise carried be quite narrow?
8. How could a major appliance repair service apply the product life-cycle concept?
9. What are the trade-offs in a retailer's deciding how much to emphasize private brands rather than manufacturer brands?

10. Present a checklist of five factors for a chain retailer to review in determining how to allocate merchandise among its stores.
11. What is the basic premise of category management? Why do you think that supermarkets have been at the forefront of the movement to use category management?
12. What do you think are the risks of placing too much reliance on merchandising software? Do the risks outweigh the benefits? Explain your answer.

Web-Based Exercise

Visit this section of the Planning Factory's Web site (www.planfact.co.uk/merchandise_planning_impact.htm). Review the merchandise planning templates described there. Would you recommend that a retailer use these templates? Why or why not?

Note: Also stop by our Web site (www.pearsonhighered.com/bermanevans) to experience a number of highly interactive, appealing Web exercises based on actual company demonstrations and sample materials related to retailing.

15 Implementing Merchandise Plans

In implementing its merchandise plans, Express—the apparel chain—has come up with one of the most aggressive uses of social media of any retailer. Since May 2011, Express has encouraged customers to browse its full product line and buy items at its Facebook page (www.facebook.com/express).

The Facebook page enables shoppers to not only buy any product that Express carries but to also recommend products and share purchase experiences by posting comments at the Express Facebook page; furthermore, customers can post information at their own Facebook pages. Just six months after launching the purchase option at Facebook, Express more than doubled the number of people posting "likes."

Jim Wright, the head of E-commerce for Express, says that "we see the integration of social shopping as the next step. If you look at what's happening today, top-down marketing and driving people to places to [transact] has changed. We need to be where customers are having their experiences and sharing information. We need to take down the barriers preventing a shopping experience." Wright adds that even though Express is using information from Facebook customers for E-mail purposes, the firm is doing everything possible to ensure that the privacy of personal customer information is respected.

As reported by *Chain Store Age*, inventory and pricing activities are consistent across the firm's online sites and mobile sites; and information is seamlessly updated in real time:

> The page provides a new product zoom technology and secure checkout; and it was developed in-house. Using Facebook lets customers engage in feedback of items by "liking" pieces, posting comments, recommending to friends, and posting purchases. Shoppers also have the capability to add products to their wish list that are shared with the Web site and mobile platforms. The customer's single wish list is accessible from all three shopping platforms. Additionally, Express' Facebook page provides users with the ability to purchase gift cards and E-gift cards for last minute in-person or virtual gifts.[1]

Chapter Objectives

1. To describe the steps in the implementation of merchandise plans: gathering information, selecting and interacting with merchandise sources, evaluation, negotiation, concluding purchases, receiving and stocking merchandise, reordering, and re-evaluation

2. To examine the prominent roles of logistics and inventory management in the implementation of merchandise plans

Source: BeTA-Artworks/ fotolia.com.

Overview

Enter the 7-Eleven Web site (http://corp.7-eleven.com) and click on "News Room" to find out what this creative retailer is doing.

This chapter builds on Chapter 14 and covers the implementation of merchandise plans, including logistics and inventory management. Sometimes, it is simple to enact merchandise plans. Other times, it requires a lot of hard work. A big challenge that food stores must face is reaching the proper balance between out-of-stock (OOS) and too much stock.

> U.S. grocers lose almost $20 billion annually in OOS. On the other end, there is margin erosion from markdowns on excess inventory. The problem is accentuated by perishables. Advanced supply-chain solutions can help; but grocers have typically underinvested in them. Failing to correct this hurts competitiveness and the ability to capitalize on next-generation supply-chain opportunities. A lot of factors (such as weather, seasonality, shelf life, etc.) impact demand and have to be factored simultaneously during forecasts. Lack of supplier collaboration further constrains retailers. Suppliers contribute almost 10 to 20 percent of OOS in grocery retail.[2]

IMPLEMENTING MERCHANDISE PLANS

The implementation of merchandise plans comprises the eight sequential steps shown in Figure 15-1 and discussed next.

Gathering Information

After overall merchandising plans are set, more information about target market needs and prospective suppliers is required before buying or rebuying merchandise. In gathering data *about the marketplace*, a retailer has several possible sources. The most valuable is the consumer. By regularly researching target market demographics, lifestyles, product preferences, and potential shopping plans, a retailer can learn about consumer demand directly. Loyalty programs and social media comments are especially useful in tracking consumer purchases and interests.

Other information sources can be used when direct consumer data are insufficient. Suppliers (manufacturers and wholesalers) usually do their own sales forecasts and marketing research (such as test marketing). They also know how much outside promotional support a retailer will get. In closing a deal with the retailer, a supplier may present charts and graphs, showing forecasts and promotional support. Yet, the retailer should remember that it is the party with direct access to the target market and its needs.

Retail sales and display personnel interact with consumers and can pass their observations along to management. A **want book (want slip)** system is a formal way to record consumer requests for unstocked or out-of-stock merchandise. It is very helpful to a retailer's buyers. Outside of customers, salespeople may provide the most useful information for merchandising decisions.

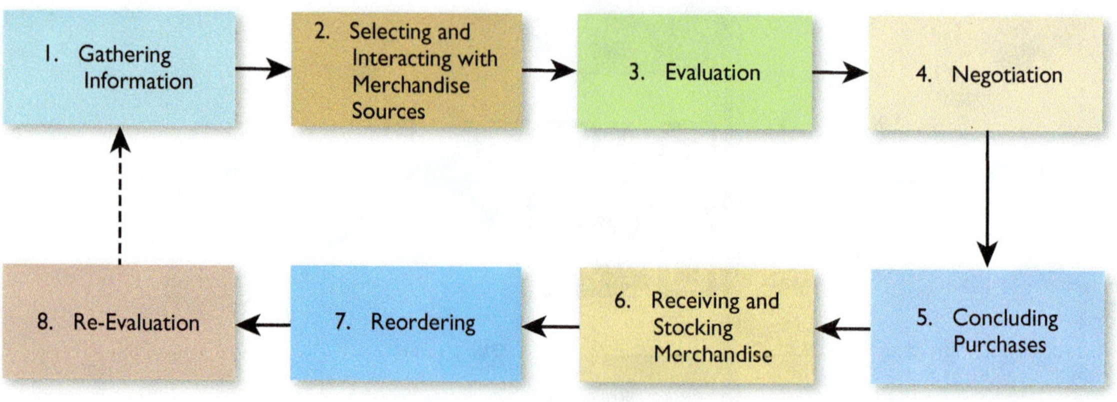

FIGURE 15-1
The Process for Implementing Merchandise Plans

See how mySimon (www.mysimon.com) can help retailers track competitors.

Competitors represent another information source. A risk-averse retailer may not stock an item until competitors do and may employ comparison shoppers to study the offerings and prices of competitors. The most sophisticated comparison shopping involves the use of Web-based shopping bots such as mySimon.com, whereby competitors' offerings and prices are tracked electronically. Buy.com, for one, constantly checks its prices to make sure that it is not undersold. In addition, trade publications report on trends in each aspect of retailing and provide another way of gathering data from competitors. See Figure 15-2 for an example of a competition shopping report.

In addition, government sources indicate unemployment, inflation, and product safety data; independent news sources conduct their own consumer polls and do investigative reporting; and commercial data can be purchased.

To learn about the attributes of *specific suppliers* and their merchandise, retailers can

Learn why High Point (www.highpointmarket.org) is a world-class trade show.

California Market Center (www.californiamarketcenter.com) offers a lot of online information for retailers. Click on "exhibitor/tenant."

- Talk to suppliers, get specification sheets, read trade publications, and seek references.
- Attend trade shows that feature numerous exhibitors (suppliers). There are hundreds of trade shows yearly in New York. In Paris, the semiannual Prêt à Porter show attracts representatives of more than 600 apparel brands and 40,000 attendees. The National Hardware Show in Las Vegas has 2,300 exhibitors and 30,000 attendees each year. The High Point Furniture Market in North Carolina has semiannual shows that attract more than 2,000 manufacturers and 80,000 attendees—from all 50 states and 110 countries.
- Visit year-round merchandise marts such as AmericasMart Atlanta (www.americasmart.com), California Market Center in Los Angeles (www.californiamarketcenter.com), Dallas Market Center (www.dallasmarketcenter.com), and Merchandise Mart in Chicago (www.merchandisemart.com/mmart). These marts have daily hours for permanent vendor showrooms and large areas for trade shows.

FIGURE 15-2
A Competition Shopping Report

COMPETITION SHOPPING REPORT

Store #_____ Date_____

Dept. #_____ Qualified Competition Shopped:

1._____
2._____

Our Style No.	Mfr. Model or Style	Description	Our Price	1st Compet. Price	2nd Compet. Price	Store's Recom. Price	Buyer's Recom. Price

Item Seen at Our Competitor's Store Which We Should Carry:					
Manufacturer	Mfr. Model or Style	Description	Reg. or List Price	Sale Price	Buyer's Comments

Signature of Shopper *Store Manager*

- Search the Web. One newer application is GoExhibit (www.goexhibit.com). A trade show coordinator "puts all the sights and sounds of a physical show right on your Web site." A 3-D virtual trade show lets the coordinator "add and design the booths, modify the exhibit hall layout, and manage the exhibit hall features." Trade show attendees "can move anywhere on the trade show floor, visiting exhibiting booths, the hall information center, or other attendees in the exhibit hall."[3]

Whatever the information acquired, a retailer should feel comfortable that it is sufficient for making good decisions. For routine decisions (staple products), limited information may be adequate. On the other hand, new fashions' sales fluctuate widely and require extensive data for forecasts.

At our Web site (www.pearsonhighered.com/bermanevans), we have more than a dozen links to leading trade shows and merchandise marts.

Selecting and Interacting with Merchandise Sources

The next step is to select sources of merchandise and to interact with them. Three major options exist:

- *Company-owned.* A large retailer owns a manufacturing and/or wholesaling facility. A company-owned supplier handles all or part of the merchandise the retailer requests.
- *Outside, regularly used supplier.* This supplier is not owned by the retailer but used regularly. A retailer knows the quality of merchandise and the reliability of the supplier from its experience.
- *Outside, new supplier.* This supplier is not owned by the retailer, which has not bought from it before. The retailer may be unfamiliar with merchandise quality and supplier reliability.

A retailer can rely on one kind of supplier or utilize a combination (the biggest retailers often use all three formats). The types of outside suppliers (regularly used and new) are described in Figure 15-3. In choosing vendors, the criteria listed in the Figure 15-4 checklist should be considered.

Big Lots places emphasis on supplier relations (www.biglotscorporate.com/vendor/index.asp).

Big Lots, which buys merchandise to stock its national chain of closeout stores, is a good example of how complicated choosing suppliers can be:

> An integral part of our business is purchasing quality brand-name merchandise directly from manufacturers and other vendors typically at prices substantially below those paid by traditional retailers. We purchase significant quantities of a vendor's closeout merchandise in specific product categories and control distribution in accordance with vendor instructions. Our sourcing channels also include bankruptcies, liquidations, and insurance claims. We supplement our purchases with direct import and domestically-sourced merchandise in departments. Our top ten vendors account for 16 percent of total purchases. We buy 25 percent of merchandise directly from overseas vendors, including 21 percent from vendors in China.[4]

Retailers and suppliers often interact well together, as highlighted in Figure 15-5. Other times, there are conflicts. As noted earlier, relationship building can be invaluable. Yet, there remain sore points between retailers and suppliers. On the one hand, many retailers have beefed up their use of private brands because they are upset when suppliers such as Gucci open their own stores in the same shopping centers. Most Gucci sales now come from company-owned and franchised shops. On the other hand, many suppliers are distressed by what they believe is retailers' excessive use of **chargebacks,** whereby retailers, at their sole discretion, make deductions in their bills for infractions ranging from late shipments to damaged and expired goods. Some suppliers have even taken their retailers to court over the practice. Attain Consulting Group divides chargebacks into three categories:

- *Intentional deductions* are proactively offered by manufacturers to their retailers with the objective of increasing the revenue of the manufacturer. Examples are discounts, rebates, advertising, and markdown allowances that provide retailers with an extra incentive to promote products.
- *Unauthorized deductions* are not foreseen by manufacturers. Examples are retailer chargebacks for alleged merchandise shortages, customer returns to the retailer, and allegations of price discrepancies from what the retailer agreed to pay. Some retailers are very aggressive in applying unauthorized deductions.
- *Preventable deductions* can be avoided by manufacturers with better performance. Such deductions are due suppliers failing to fully comply with retailers' rules regarding order fulfillment, carrier routing, container labeling, shipment documentation, or E-commerce practices. For example, a retailer might require that shipments be labeled with a specific type of barcode or that every item be folded and marked with the manufacturer's suggested retail price.[5]

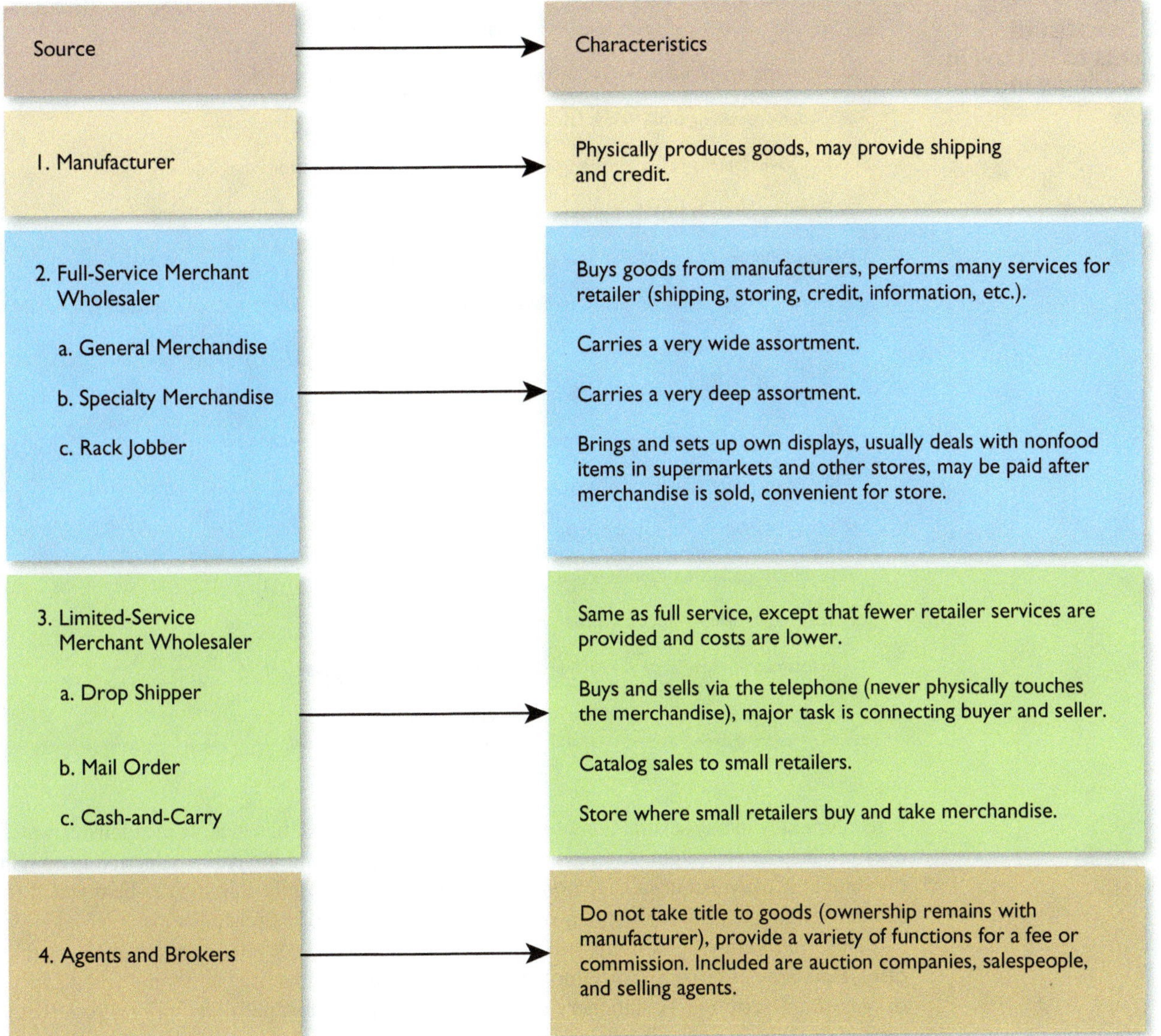

FIGURE 15-3
Outside Sources of Supply

Selecting merchandise sources must be viewed as a two-way street. For example, Apple is selective about the retailers carrying some of its products: For the past decade, Target has stocked a number of Apple products and "in keeping with Apple's typical deals with retailers, Apple's products get some special space set aside for themselves. But unlike more than 600 Best Buy locations, Target's retail locations didn't feature Apple Shops with staffing and more extensive product offerings." Since 2012, this approach has been changing. with Apple supporting mini stores "in larger Target stores in cities that can't support a standalone Apple Store."[6]

Evaluating Merchandise

Whatever source is chosen, there must be a procedure to evaluate the merchandise under consideration. Three procedures are possible: inspection, sampling, and description. The technique depends on the item's cost, its attributes, and purchase regularity.

Inspection occurs when every single unit is examined before purchase and after delivery. Jewelry and art are examples of expensive, rather unique purchases for which the retailer carefully inspects all items.

Sampling is used with regular purchases of large quantities of breakable, perishable, or expensive items. Because inspection is inefficient, items are sampled for quality and condition.

FIGURE 15-4

A Checklist of Points to Review in Choosing Vendors

- ✓ Reliability—Will a supplier consistently fulfill all written promises?
- ✓ Price–quality—Who provides the best merchandise at the lowest price?
- ✓ Order-processing time—How fast will deliveries be made?
- ✓ Exclusive rights—Will a supplier give exclusive selling rights or customize products?
- ✓ Functions provided—Will a supplier undertake shipping, storing, and other functions, if needed?
- ✓ Information—Will a supplier pass along important data?
- ✓ Ethics—Will a supplier fulfill all verbal promises and not engage in unfair business or labor practices?
- ✓ Guarantee—Does a supplier stand behind its offerings?
- ✓ Credit—Can credit purchases be made from a supplier? On what terms?
- ✓ Long-term relationships—Will a supplier be available over an extended period?
- ✓ Reorders—Can a supplier promptly fill reorders?
- ✓ Markup—Will markup (price margins) be adequate?
- ✓ Innovativeness—Is a supplier's line innovative or conservative?
- ✓ Local advertising—Does a supplier advertise in local media?
- ✓ Investment—How large are total investment costs with a supplier?
- ✓ Risk—How much risk is involved in dealing with a supplier?

A retailer ready to buy several hundred light fixtures, bunches of bananas, or inexpensive watches does not inspect each item. A number of units are sampled, and the entire selection is bought if the sample is okay. An unsatisfactory sample might cause a whole shipment to be rejected (or a discount negotiated). Sampling may also occur upon receipt of merchandise.

Description buying is used with standardized, nonbreakable, and nonperishable merchandise. Items are not inspected or sampled; they are ordered in quantity based on a verbal, written, or pictorial description. A stationery store can order paper clips, pads, and printer paper from a catalog or Web site. After it receives an order, only a count of those items is conducted.

FIGURE 15-5

Brooks Brothers: A Collaborative Supplier–Retailer Program

Brooks Brothers has strong relationships with several suppliers. One of these is the Hong Kong-based Tal Group. Brooks Brothers and Tal collaborate on innovations such as wrinkle-free, stain-resistant, moisture-wicking fabrics. Tal is viewed as a strategic supplier.

Source: Reprinted by permission of Susan V. Berry, Retail Image Consulting, Inc.

Negotiating the Purchase

Next, a retailer negotiates the purchase and its terms. A new or special order usually results in a negotiated contract, and a retailer and a supplier carefully discuss all aspects of the purchase. A regular order or reorder often involves a uniform contract, because terms are standard or have already been set and the order is handled routinely.

Off-price retailers and other deep discounters may require negotiated contracts for most purchases. These firms employ **opportunistic buying,** by which especially low prices are negotiated for merchandise whose sales have not lived up to expectations, end-of-season goods, items consumers have returned to the manufacturer or another retailer, and closeouts. TJX is different from typical retailers that place merchandise orders well in advance of the selling season: "Our merchant organization of over 700 people constantly covers the marketplace, buying great brands close to need and into current fashion and pricing trends. Opportunistic buying is core to our flexibility and allows us to offer customers better brands, more excitement, and continuous freshness."[7]

Several purchase terms must be specified, whether a negotiated or a uniform contract is involved. These include the delivery date, quantity purchased, price and payment arrangements, discounts, form of delivery, and point of transfer of title, as well as special clauses.

The delivery date and the quantity purchased must be clear. A retailer should be able to cancel an order if either provision is not carried out. The purchase price, payment arrangements, and permissible discounts must also be addressed. What is the retailer's cost per item (including handling)? What forms of payment are permitted (cash and credit)? What discounts are given? Retailers' purchase prices are often discounted for early payments ("2/10/net 30" means there is a 2 percent discount if the full bill is paid in 10 days; the full bill is due in 30 days), support activities (setting up displays), and quantity purchases. Stipulations are needed for the form of delivery (truck, rail, and so on) and the party responsible for shipping fees (FOB factory—free on board—means a supplier places merchandise with the shipper, but the retailer pays the freight). Last, the point of transfer of title—when ownership changes from supplier to buyer—must be stated in a contract.

To learn more about the slotting allowance controversy, visit this Web site (www.ftc.gov/opa/2003/11/slottingallowance.htm).

Special clauses may be inserted by either party. Sometimes, they are beneficial to both parties (such as an agreement about the advertising support each party provides). Other times, the clauses are inserted by the more powerful party. As noted in Chapter 1, a major disagreement between vendors and large retailers is the latter's increasing use of **slotting allowances**—payments that retailers require of vendors for providing shelf space:

> It's a fierce war for shelf space with regular negotiations between manufacturers and retailers for a limited number of inches. More facings for a product equal more sales. A small percentage increase in sales can mean millions of dollars for a large manufacturer. Retailers know this and often charge a luxury tax to the manufacturer for the shelf space known in the industry as a slotting fee. A slotting fee system is a practice seldom talked about beyond retailers' sales negotiation meetings.[8]

Unlike many other retailers, industry leader Wal-Mart does not charge any slotting allowances and often gets new products first from suppliers as a result of this policy.

Concluding Purchases

Many medium-sized and large retailers use computers to complete and process orders (based on electronic data interchange [EDI] and quick response [QR] inventory planning), and each purchase is fed into a computer data bank. Smaller retailers often write up and process orders manually, and purchase amounts are added to their inventory in the same way. Yet, with the advances in computerized ordering software, even small retailers may have the capability of placing orders electronically—especially if they buy from large wholesalers that use EDI and QR systems.

There is EDI/QR software (http://edi.gxs.com) to fit almost any budget.

Multi-unit retailers must determine whether the final purchase decision is made by central or regional management or by local managers. Advantages and disadvantages accrue to each approach.

Several alternatives are possible regarding the transfer of title between parties. The retailer's responsibilities and rights differ in each of these situations:

- The retailer takes title immediately on purchase.
- The retailer assumes ownership after items are loaded onto the mode of transportation.

Ken Nisch: JGA

Ken Nisch, a registered architect, is chairman of JGA (www.jga.com), one of the leading retail-design and branding-strategy firms in the United States. JGA has been honored with prestigious awards in design competitions; and the firm has been featured in *New York Times*, *Wall Street Journal*, *Chain Store Age*, and *Women's Wear Daily*.

JGA's clients include such diverse companies as Bassett Furniture, Diesel, Dress Barn, Estée Lauder, Hickey Freeman, Sears, Tommy Hilfiger (whose brand is now sold exclusively at Macy's), and Vitamin World. Unlike some design firms that provide a limited range of services, JGA's list of activities include design strategy, construction management, and fixture, furniture, and material purchases.

JGA uses a team approach in its design planning and deploys selected individuals from among its 50 associates. Some of its innovative solutions include the use of detailed fitting rooms with oversized mirrors for Dress Barn, a huge staircase leading to a second floor for Hickey Freeman, and graphic display walls for Verizon Wireless.

Nisch is carefully tracking two trends that will have a large impact on his business. One is the increased tendency of chief marketing officers to be more concerned with expense control than image building. The second involves innovations in online retailing. Some of these innovations may be able to be adapted for use in a store-based retail environment.

Source: Janet Groeber, "Bigger Isn't Always Better," www.stores.org (April 2011).

- The retailer takes title when a shipment is received.
- The retailer does not take title until the end of a billing cycle, when the supplier is paid.
- The retailer accepts merchandise on consignment and does not own the items. The supplier is paid after merchandise is sold.

A consignment or memorandum deal may be possible if a vendor is in a weak position and wants to persuade retailers to carry its items. In a **consignment purchase,** a retailer has no risk because title is not taken; the supplier owns the goods until sold. An electronic version (scan-based trading) is being tried at some supermarkets. It saves time and money for all parties due to paperless steps in a purchase. In a **memorandum purchase,** risk is still low, but a retailer takes title on delivery and is responsible for damages. In both cases, retailers do not pay for items until they are sold and can return them.

Receiving and Stocking Merchandise

The retailer is now ready to receive and handle items. This involves receiving and storing, checking and paying invoices, price and inventory marking, setting up displays, figuring on-floor assortments, completing transactions, arranging delivery or pickup, processing returns and damaged goods, monitoring pilferage, and controlling merchandise. See Figure 15-6. Good distribution management is key.

Items may be shipped from suppliers to warehouses (for storage and disbursement) or directly to retailers' store(s). The Walgreens drugstore chain has fully automated warehouses that stock thousands of products and speed their delivery to stores. Amazon.com uses U.S. and international fulfillment centers and warehouses that it operates itself, as well as fulfillment centers that are operated under co-sourcing arrangements.

One important emerging technology that may greatly advance the merchandise tracking and handling process for retailers involves an **RFID (radio frequency identification)** system—a method of storing and remotely retrieving data using devices called RFID tags or transponders. In an RFID system, information is sent via RFID tags by a reader that uses radio waves. In a passive system, which is the most often utilized, an RFID reader provides the power for the tag to communicate with the reader. In an active system, a battery in the RFID tag boosts the effective geographic range of the tag and supports other features not available with passive tags, such as sensing temperature changes in the environment. Data from RFID tags goes through communication interfaces to host computers in a manner similar to that involving barcode labels—with data sent to computer systems to interpret, store, and act upon.

These are some of the key benefits of RFID systems: "Passive smart-label RFID systems offer unique capabilities as an automatic data-capture system. They provide real-time, wireless

FIGURE 15-6

Receiving and Verifying Merchandise

With advances in portable computer technology, it is now simpler and more accurate to verify that the correct merchandise has been received before placing it on the selling floor.

Source: Voznikevich Konstantin/Shutterstock.com. Reprinted by permission.

data transmission without human intervention; do not require line-of-site scanners for operation; allow stored data to be altered during sorting or allow work-flow process information to be captured with the data; and work effectively in harsh environments with excessive dirt, dust, moisture, and extreme temperature."[9]

At present, RFID use is limited. It is too early to predict how widespread RFID use will be or how long it will take to be accepted by most retailers and their suppliers. Suppliers are responsible for most of the work and costs. The current costs for an RFID system range from under $100,000 to $300,000 for a small or medium-sized supplier to several million dollars for a large supplier. But the benefits are clear:

> Wal-Mart and several other major U.S. retailers are moving forward with projects that use RFID to track apparel items in stores. Wal-Mart is working with suppliers of men's jeans and basics (socks, undershirts, and underwear) to track items with RFID tags. At the same time, some forward-looking apparel manufacturers are choosing to adopt RFID in their manufacturing and distribution facilities. Momentum is growing for item-level tagging. Tags costs have fallen up to 40 percent over the past 18 months, and technological advances have addressed concerns about tag readability.[10]

When orders are received, they must be checked for completeness and product condition. Invoices must be reviewed for accuracy and payments made as specified. This step cannot be taken for granted.

Seagull Scientific (www.seagullscientific.com) markets popular labeling software.

At this point, prices and inventory information are marked on merchandise. Supermarkets estimate that price marking on individual items costs them an amount equal to their annual profits. Marking can be done in various ways. Small firms may hand-post prices and manually keep inventory records. Some retailers use their own computer-generated price tags and rely on preprinted UPC data on packages to keep records. Others buy tags, with computer- and human-readable price and inventory data, from outside suppliers. Still others expect vendors to provide source tagging. An inventory system works best when there is more data on labels or tags. With portable devices, hand-held devices print UPC-based labels and can be connected to store computers.

Store displays and on-floor quantities and assortments depend on the retailer and products involved. Supermarkets usually have bin-and-rack displays and place most inventory on the sales floor. Traditional department stores have all kinds of interior displays and place a lot of inventory in the back room, off the sales floor. See Figure 15-7. Displays and on-floor merchandising are discussed in Chapter 18.

FIGURE 15-7

On-Floor Assortments and Men's Shirts

On-floor inventory planning is complicated for items such as men's shirts—due to the choices that must be offered and the various sizes that must be readily available.

Source: Rob Bouwman/ Shutterstock.com. Reprinted by permission.

Merchandise handling is not complete until the customer buys and receives it from a retailer. This means order taking, credit or cash transactions, packaging, and delivery or pickup. Automation has improved retailer performance in each of these areas.

A procedure for processing returns and damaged goods is also needed. The retailer must determine the party responsible for customer returns (supplier or retailer) and the situations in which damaged goods would be accepted for refund or exchange (such as the length of time a warranty is honored).

As discussed later in the chapter, more retailers are taking aggressive actions to monitor and reduce inventory losses. This is a major problem due to the high costs of merchandise theft.

Merchandise control involves assessing sales, profits, turnover, inventory shortages, seasonality, and costs for each product category and item carried. Control is usually achieved by preparing computerized inventory data and doing physical inventories. A physical inventory must be adjusted to reflect damaged goods, pilferage, customer returns, and other factors. See Figure 15-8. A discussion of this topic appears in Chapter 16.

Merchandise receiving and handling is covered further later in this chapter.

Reordering Merchandise

Four factors are critical in reordering merchandise that the retailer purchases more than once: order and delivery time, inventory turnover, financial outlays, and inventory versus ordering costs.

How long does it take for a retailer to process an order and a supplier to fulfill and deliver it? It is possible for delivery time to be so lengthy that a retailer must reorder while having a full inventory. On the other hand, overnight delivery may be available for some items.

How long does it take for a retailer to sell out inventory? A fast-selling product gives a retailer two choices: (1) order a surplus of items and spread out reorder periods or (2) keep a low inventory and order frequently. A slow-selling item may let a retailer reduce its initial inventory and spread out reorders.

What are the financial outlays under various purchase options? A large order, with a quantity discount, may require a big cash outlay. A small order, while more expensive per item, results in lower total costs at any one time since less inventory is held.

There are trade-offs between inventory holding and ordering costs. A large inventory fosters customer satisfaction, volume discounts, low per-item shipping costs, and easier handling. It also means high investments; greater obsolescence and damages; and storage, insurance, and

LXE'S HANDS-FREE PLATFORM ALLOWS:

- Real-time inventory updates
- Real-time selection and let-downs
- Easy management of product shortages as they occur
- Automatic priority updates for replenishments to short picked locations
- Support for multi-language environments
- Automatic or manual assignment by selection zone
- Ability to send the order-picker back to short picked locations that have been replenished
- Picking activity information to be captured, such as assignment times, end times and status
- Reactions to changing distribution needs through the availability of real-time data.
- Much more...

FIGURE 15-8
State-of-the-Art Inventory Control

Source: Reprinted by permission of LXE, now part of Honeywell.

opportunity costs. Placing many orders and keeping a small inventory mean a low investment, low opportunity costs, low storage costs, and little obsolescence. Yet, there may be disappointed customers if items are out of stock, higher unit costs, adverse effects from order delays, a need for partial shipments, service charges, and complex handling. Retailers try to hold enough stock to satisfy customers while not having a high surplus. Quick response inventory planning lowers inventory and ordering costs via close retailer–supplier relationships.

Re-evaluating on a Regular Basis

A merchandising plan should be re-evaluated regularly, with management reviewing the buying organization and that organization assessing the implementation. The overall procedure, as well as the handling of individual goods and services, should be monitored. Conclusions during this stage become part of the information-gathering stage for future efforts.

LOGISTICS

Logistics is the total process of planning, implementing, and coordinating the physical movement of merchandise from manufacturer (wholesaler) to retailer to customer in the most timely, effective, and cost-efficient manner possible. Logistics regards order processing and fulfillment, transportation, warehousing, customer service, and inventory management as interdependent functions in the value delivery chain. If a logistics system works well, firms reduce stockouts, hold down inventories, and improve customer service—all at the same time. See Figure 15-9.

Logistics can also be quite challenging. Consider the case of Supervalu, the grocery wholesaler and retailer (which owns Acme, Albertsons, Cub Farm Fresh, Save-A-Lot, and other chains):

> We are the product-supply lifeline for more than 5,000 retail end points from coast to coast. Our network of 35 distribution centers provides order accuracy and exceptional service while meeting tight delivery schedules. We operate a supply chain network with more than 21 million square feet of facilities. These distribution centers offer complete support for these departments: grocery, meat, produce, dairy, frozen foods, floral, bakery, deli, home and beauty care, general merchandise, and pharmacy. Customer service professionals work around the clock to support distribution customers. The center in Denver handles more than 85,000 customer contacts monthly.[11]

FIGURE 15-9
The Multi-Faceted Nature of Logistics

Logistics has a lot of pieces that must be coordinated and timed right to be effective.

Source: Login/Shutterstock.com. Reprinted by permission.

Upcycling: A Form of Green Marketing

In recycling (also known as "downcycling"), a product is broken down and then reconstituted as another product. This process requires the expenditure of energy. In contrast, "upcycling" transforms an otherwise disposable good into something of higher quality.

Looptworks (www.looptworks.com), an example of a firm engaged in upcycling, was formed by three partners with considerable apparel industry experience. Looptworks makes its fashion accessories, gear, and apparel from factory textile waste fabrics that would otherwise be burned or placed in garbage dumps.

Among the items made from these "pre-consumer excess" materials are a neon-orange-colored laptop sleeve composed from wetsuit material (priced at $30), and a patchwork sweatshirt vest made with "rescued" buttons (priced at $120.) The limited nature of Looptworks' production runs makes the items more appealing and costly. In its first two years of business, Looptworks employed 12 full- and part-time employees and produced close to 50 different items. Looptworks estimates that it saved about 16 million gallons of water.

Hermès (www.hermes.com), the luxury fashion accessory firm, has an upcycling operation called "petit h" that makes home furnishings and accessories from leftover scraps and damaged goods. According to one analyst, Hermès' involvement proves that luxury goods can be both sustainable and yet still expensive.

Source: Jennifer Wang, "One Man's Trash," www.entrepreneur.com (April 2011).

In this section, we discuss these logistics concepts: performance goals, the supply chain, order processing and fulfillment, transportation and warehousing, and customer transactions and customer service. Inventory management is covered in the final section of this chapter.

Performance Goals

Among retailers' major logistics goals are to:

- Match the costs incurred to specific logistics activities, thereby fulfilling all activities as economically as possible, given the firms' other performance objectives.
- Place and receive orders as easily, accurately, and satisfactorily as possible.
- Minimize the time between ordering and receiving merchandise.
- Coordinate shipments from various suppliers.
- Have enough merchandise on hand to satisfy customer demand, without having so much inventory that heavy markdowns will be necessary.
- Place merchandise on the sales floor efficiently.
- Process customer orders efficiently and in a manner satisfactory to customers.
- Work collaboratively and communicate regularly with other supply chain members.
- Handle returns effectively and minimize damaged products.
- Monitor logistics performance.
- Have backup plans in case of breakdowns in the system.

At Sears, there is an entire division devoted to logistics. Sears Logistics Services (SLS) is the sole point of contact for virtually all logistical activity at Sears: It "arranges the home delivery of appliances, electronics, furniture, and home improvement products from more than 2,500 Sears locations. In addition, SLS handles the transportation of apparel and other products from manufacturers' facilities to store shelves and manages other transportation and warehousing services for the Sears retail network."[12]

Bon-Ton (http://logistics.bonton.com) is very serious about maximizing its logistics performance.

The Bon-Ton department store chain's *Merchandise Logistical Standards* guide is posted online (http://logistics.bonton.com/pdfs/2008MerchandiseLogisticalStandards.pdf):

> Every vendor relationship is important. As in any working relationship, it is critical to clearly define expectations. Product quality, shipping windows, production, and product availability are just some of the expectations that we define. Additionally, critical consideration must be given to the environmental impact (including the impact of fuel costs) of processes upon the supply chain. As an organization, we have developed specific vendor and transportation requirements. These provisions allow us to minimize costs and receive and process merchandise in a timely cost-effective manner, thus assuring a continuous flow of merchandise to the selling floor.

Supply Chain Management

The **supply chain** is the logistics aspect of a value delivery chain. It comprises all of the parties that participate in the retail logistics process: manufacturers, wholesalers, third-party specialists (shippers, order-fulfillment houses, and so forth), and the retailer. For numerous links related to supply chain management, visit our Web site (www.pearsonhighered.com/bermanevans).

The CPFR Committee (www.vics.org/committees/cpfr) is actively working to expand the use of integrated supply chain planning.

Many retailers and suppliers are seeking closer logistical relationships. One technique for larger retailers is **collaborative planning, forecasting, and replenishment (CPFR)**—a holistic approach to supply chain management among a network of trading partners. According to the Voluntary Interindustry Commerce Standards Association, hundreds of leading manufacturers, service providers, and retailers (including Best Buy, Kohl's, Macy's, J.C. Penney, QVC, Safeway, Staples, Target, Walgreens, and Wal-Mart) have participated in CPFR programs. Nonetheless, CPFR has not been an unqualified success:

> CPFR enables supply chain integration across organizational boundaries. Aligning business goals can be challenging, since this often means that practices benefiting one party must be discontinued or modified if they're not rewarding to a partner. Examples include "channel stuffing," wherein a retailer is persuaded to periodically absorb larger-than-needed replenishment orders to help a supplier. In collaborative alliances, such practices are impractical. Many studies detail the effectiveness of CPFR relationships and of positive financial and intangible benefits by both trading partners. Such benefits may seem tempting, but it's also important to weigh the costs and requirements of engaging in CPFR relationships.[13]

Third-party logistics (outsourcing) is now more popular. For example, many retailers (including online firms) rely on UPS Supply Chain Solutions, a division of United Parcel Service, as their logistics specialist: "In a retail environment where it is more difficult to show a competitive advantage while maintaining profit margins, you need to focus on your retail strategy rather than deal with supply chain issues." At UPS Supply Chain Solutions, "experienced professionals work closely with retail businesses to improve service, optimize distribution and transportation networks, and streamline their global supply chains."[14] Logistics specialists work with retailers of all sizes to ship and warehouse merchandise.

Target's Partners Online program (www.partnersonline.com) is a proactive relationship retailing activity.

The Web is a growing force in supplier–retailer communications. A number of manufacturers and retailers have set up dedicated sites exclusively to interact with their channel partners. For confidential information exchanges, passwords and secure encryption technology are utilized. Target Corporation has a very advanced Web site called Partners Online, which took several years to develop and test. At the Web site, vendors can access sales data and inventory reports, accounts payable figures, invoices, and report cards on their performance. There are also manuals and newsletters.

Order Processing and Fulfillment

To optimize order processing and fulfillment, many firms now engage in **quick response (QR) inventory planning**, by which a retailer reduces the amount of inventory it holds by ordering more frequently and in lower quantity. A QR system requires a retailer to have good relationships with suppliers, coordinate shipments, monitor inventory levels closely to avoid stockouts, and regularly communicate with suppliers by electronic data interchange (via the Web or direct PC connections) and other means.

For the retailer, a QR system reduces inventory costs, minimizes the space required for storage, and lets the firm better match orders with market conditions—by replenishing stock more quickly. For the manufacturer, a QR system can also improve inventory turnover and better match supply and demand by giving the vendor the data to track actual sales. These data were less available in the past. In addition, an effective QR system makes it more unlikely that a retailer would switch suppliers. The most active users of QR are department stores, full-line discount stores, apparel stores, home centers, supermarkets, and drugstores. Among the firms using QR are Dillard's, Giant Food, Home Depot, Limited Brands, Macy's, J.C. Penney, Sears, Target Corporation, and Wal-Mart.

A QR system works best in conjunction with floor-ready merchandise, lower minimum order sizes, properly formatted store fixtures, and electronic data interchange (EDI). **Floor-ready merchandise** refers to items that are received at the store in condition to be put directly on display without any preparation by retail workers. For example, in this approach, apparel manufacturers are responsible for pre-ticketing garments (with information specified by the retailer) and placing them on hangers. At Saks Fifth Avenue, "Merchandise is 'floor ready' when it is received with accurate coding at our distribution centers ready to be placed directly on the selling floor or in our Saks Direct on-line store." These are some of Saks' floor-ready requirements: "Merchandise must be ticketed prior to receipt at our distribution facilities with our price or a suggested retail price. If your merchandise is sized, a size on your UPC ticket is required. All merchandise displayed hanging on our selling floor must be shipped on a SFA-approved floor-ready hanger, packed to prevent wrinkling. You must be able to receive or transmit an EDI purchase order. An expense offset fee will be assessed for merchandise not in compliance. The purpose is not to chargeback your company, but to achieve compliance so we can move merchandise to the selling floor quickly."[15]

Quick response also means suppliers need to rethink the minimum order sizes they will accept. Although a minimum order size of 12 for a given size or color was once required by sheet and towel makers, minimum order size is now as low as 2 units. Minimum order sizes for men's shirts have been reduced from six to as few as two units. The lower order sizes have led some retailers to refixture in-store departments. Previously, fixtures were often configured on the basis of a retailer's stocking full inventories. Today, the retailer must make a visual impact with smaller inventories.

Electronic data interchange (EDI, described in Chapter 8), lets retailers do QR inventory planning efficiently—via a paperless, computer-to-computer relationship between retailers and vendors. Research suggests that retail prices could be reduced by an average of 10 percent with the industrywide usage of QR and EDI. This illustration shows the value of QR and EDI:

> Lean management provides quick, flexible response to customer demand. Wal-Mart is the world's grand champion of lean supply chains. While advanced information technology gets most of the credit, collaboration is the foundation. Wal-Mart's 2,000-odd suppliers near the retailer's Bentonville, Arkansas, headquarters maintain multi-functional teams on site. Daily, along with their Wal-Mart counterparts, they work out pricing, packaging, logistics, promotions, product options, product coding, weights, and measures by sharing actual and forecast demand data, and so forth. The on-site team from each supplier must get itself together at home before it can present itself collaboratively with Wal-Mart.[16]

ECR Europe (www.ecr-all.org) has taken a lead role in trying to popularize this business tool.

Many firms in the food sector of retailing are using **efficient consumer response (ECR)** planning, which permits supermarkets to incorporate aspects of quick response inventory planning, electronic data interchange, and logistics planning. The aim is "to develop a responsive, consumer-driven system in which manufacturers, brokers, and distributors work together to maximize consumer value and minimize supply chain cost. To meet this goal, we need a smooth, continual product flow matched to consumer consumption. And to support the flow of products, we need timely, accurate data flowing through a paperless system between retail checkout and manufacturing line."[17] Although ECR has enabled supermarkets to cut tens of billions of dollars in distribution costs, applying it has not been easy. Many supermarkets are still unwilling to trade their ability to negotiate short-term purchase terms with vendors in return for routine order fulfillment without special deals.

Retailers are also addressing two other aspects of order processing and fulfillment. (1) With *advanced ship notices*, retailers that utilize QR and EDI receive an alert when bills of lading are sent electronically as soon as a shipment leaves the vendor. This gives the retailers more time to efficiently receive and allocate merchandise. (2) Because more retailers are buying from multiple suppliers, from multi-location sources, and from overseas, they must better coordinate order placement and fulfillment. Home Depot, among others, has added an import logistics group to coordinate overseas forecasting, ordering, sourcing, and logistics; and Supervalu is addressing the complexity of buying products from so many different countries around the globe.

Sometimes, the order-processing-and-fulfillment process can be especially challenging:

> Some flowers are sent packed flat. This enables large amounts of flowers to ship in small spaces like aircraft holds. Other flowers cannot survive for long without water. They are either sent with their own little water holders on each stem end—for more expensive or tropical flowers—or are shipped in buckets of water. This extends the life of flowers and

reduces labor time as flowers are ready for sale, but also reduces the amount of flowers that can be transported as they are heavier than dry-packed flowers and air transportation charges are higher.[18]

Transportation and Warehousing

Several transportation decisions are necessary:

- How often will merchandise be shipped to the retailer?
- How will small order quantities be handled?
- What shipper will be used (the manufacturer, the retailer, or a third-party specialist)? See Figure 15-10.
- What transportation form will be used? Are multiple forms required (such as manufacturer trucks to retailer warehouses and retailer trucks to individual stores)?
- What are the special considerations for perishables and expensive merchandise?
- How often will special shipping arrangements be necessary (such as rush orders)?
- How are shipping terms negotiated with suppliers?
- What delivery options will be available for the retailer's customers? This is a critical decision for nonstore retailers, especially those selling through the Web.

Transportation effectiveness is influenced by the caliber of the logistics infrastructure (including access to refrigerated trucks, airports, waterway docking, and superhighways), traffic congestion, parking, and other factors. Retailers operating outside the United States must come to grips with the logistical problems in many foreign countries, where the transportation network and the existence of modern technology may be severely lacking.

With regard to warehousing, some retailers focus on warehouses as central or regional distribution centers. Products are sent from suppliers to these warehouses, and then they are allotted and shipped to individual stores. Claire's Stores has its central buying and store operations offices, as well as its North American distribution center, in Hoffman Estates, Illinois. The distribution facility has over 370,000 square feet of space. Toys "R" Us has separate regional distribution centers for U.S. Toys "R" Us stores and its international Toys "R" Us stores. Most centers are owned; some are leased.

HighJump (www.highjump.com) offers integrated DSD software. Click on "Solutions."

Other retailers, including many supermarket chains, do not rely as much on central or regional warehouses. Instead, they have at least some goods shipped right from suppliers to individual stores through **direct store delivery (DSD).** This approach works best with retailers that also utilize EDI. It is a way to move high turnover, high bulk, perishable products from the manufacturer directly to the store. The items most apt to involve DSD (such as beverages, bread,

FIGURE 15-10

Shipping Possibilities

A lot of merchandise is transported by at least two types of transportation—such as train and truck or air and truck. These shipments must be delivered as scheduled for the retail supply chain to operate well. With the growth of foreign suppliers, this is tougher to accomplish.

Source: Digital Genetics/Shutterstock.com. Reprinted by permission.

TECHNOLOGY IN RETAILING

Online Inventory Planning Comes to Nordstrom

Nordstrom (www.nordstrom.com) has developed a new online inventory planning system that enables customers to see whether a favorite designer jacket or other product is available at a nearby store. The system goes across multiple channels so that a Web-based customer can examine whether an item is in stock at all of Nordstrom's nearly 120 traditional retail stores.

Nordstrom is using this online inventory system to encourage multiple-channel activity among its shoppers. According to Jamie Nordstrom, president of Nordstrom Direct, multi-channel shoppers spend four times more, on average, than single-source shoppers. In the first year after Nordstrom implemented the new inventory system, the chain's same-store sales increased an average of 8 percent. This was significantly higher than the average department store's performance during the same time period. Online inventory planning also means that Nordstrom's inventory turnover is higher and sold at higher average prices. Nordstrom's inventory turnover has gone from 4.8 in 2005 to more than 5.4 today, an all-time high for the company. In addition, markdowns have been reduced.

Wal-Mart (www.walmart.com) and Target (www.target.com) both use aspects of Nordstrom's online inventory planning strategy. Wal-Mart's system enables its Web-based shoppers to ship items to a nearby store. However, even though Target.com shows which stores carry specific items, it did not set up its system so that customers could purchase these items through the Web for pickup at the store. Target.com does offer free shipping and allows returns to be made at the store.

Sources: Stephanie Clifford, "Nordstrom Links Online Inventory to Real World," www.nytimes.com (August 23, 2010); and "About Nordstrom," http://shop.nordstrom.com/c/about-us (May 26, 2012).

and snack foods) typically have shelf lives of 60 days or less, while warehoused items have an average shelf life of one year or more.[19] More than one-quarter of the typical supermarket's sales are from items with DSD.

The advantages of central warehousing are the efficiency in transportation and storage, mechanized processing of goods, improved security, efficient merchandise marking, ease of returns, and coordinated merchandise flow. Key disadvantages are the excessive centralized control, extra handling of perishables, high costs for small retailers, and potential ordering delays. Centralized warehousing may also reduce the capability of QR systems by adding another step. These are some pros and cons of DSD:

> It makes sense when control of deliveries and customer service are important. If you have tight delivery windows at certain times of day, this requires a lot of scheduling precision. Another consideration is whether your market share is threatened by not being on store shelves. Lastly, if you are challenged with security and product theft—especially for high-value goods like alcohol and jewelry—a direct-to-store model can help mitigate risks. However, determining optimal routes for deliveries to multiple retail outlets can be complicated. There are many variables to consider, such as traffic patterns, speed limits, distance, and time calculations.[20]

Customer Transactions and Customer Service

Retailers must plan for outbound logistics (as well as inbound logistics): completing transactions by turning over merchandise to customers. This can be as simple as having a shopper take an item from a display area to the checkout counter or driving his or her car to a loading area. It can also be as complex as concluding a Web transaction that entails shipments from multiple vendors to the customer. A shopper's purchase of a computer, a tablet, and a refrigerator from Buy.com may result in three separate shipments. That is why UPS, Federal Express, and others are doing more home deliveries of packages. They can readily handle the diversity of shipping requests that retailers often cannot.

Even basic deliveries can have a breakdown. Think of the local pharmacy whose high school delivery person fails to come to work one day—or the pizzeria that gets no customer orders between 2:00 P.M. and 5:00 P.M. and 25 delivery orders between 5:00 P.M. and 7:00 P.M.

There are considerable differences between store-based and nonstore retailers. Most retail stores know that the customer wants to take the purchase or to pick it up when it is ready (such as a new car). All direct marketers, including Web retailers, are responsible for ensuring that products are delivered to the shopper's door or another convenient nearby location.

Customer service expectations are affected by logistical effectiveness. That is why Amazon.com emphasizes excellent logistics and fulfills orders in many ways, "including through U.S. and international fulfillment centers and warehouses that we operate, co-sourced and outsourced arrangements in certain countries, and digital delivery. We operate customer service centers globally, supplemented by co-sourced arrangements. If we do not adequately predict customer demand or otherwise optimize and operate our fulfillment centers, it could result in excess or insufficient inventory, increased costs, impairment charges, or harm our business in other ways."[21]

INVENTORY MANAGEMENT

As part of its logistics efforts, a retailer utilizes **inventory management** to acquire and maintain a proper merchandise assortment while ordering, shipping, handling, storing, displaying, and selling costs are kept in check. First, a retailer places an order based on a sales forecast or actual customer behavior. Both the number of items and their variety are requested when ordering. Order size and frequency depend on quantity discounts and inventory costs. Second, a supplier fills the order and sends merchandise to a warehouse or directly to the store(s). Third, the retailer receives products, makes items available for sale (by removing them from packing, marking prices, and placing them on the sales floor), and completes customer transactions. Some transactions are not concluded until items are delivered to the customer. The cycle starts anew as a retailer places another order. Let's look at these aspects of inventory management: retailer tasks, inventory levels, merchandise security, reverse logistics, and inventory analysis.

Retailer Tasks

Due to the comprehensive nature of inventory management, and to be more cost-effective, some retailers now expect suppliers to perform more tasks, or they outsource at least part of their inventory management activities: "In 1990, producers shipped products to retailers in a *warehouse-ready* mode. Retailers then reprocessed merchandise to package and price it for sale in the store where consumers purchase. Today, in the era of *floor-ready*, producers ship products that have been packaged and prepared for immediate movement to the sales floor. In the future, there will be a shift to *consumer-ready* manufacturing where the links between producer and consumer are even more direct."[22] Here are some examples:

- Wal-Mart and other retailers count on key suppliers to participate in their inventory management programs. Industrywide, this practice is known as **vendor-managed inventory (VMI).** Procter & Gamble even has its own employees stationed at Wal-Mart headquarters to manage the inventory replenishment of that manufacturer's products.[23]
- Target Corporation is at the forefront of another trend—store-based retailers doing their own customer order fulfillment for their online businesses (as those businesses grow): "Establishing a new platform for Target.com allows Target to reinvent our guests' online environment and create a more user-friendly, reliable experience," says Steve Eastman, president of Target.com. The launch of the redesigned site marks the end of Target's relationship with Amazon.com. Target.com ran on Amazon's E-commerce platform for 10 years; and the chain also used Amazon.com services for fulfillment and Web hosting. The outsourcing cost Target a hefty commission on online sales, an amount estimated at $100 million annually." Toys "R" Us has also moved away from Amazon.com.[24]
- According to the National Association for Retail Merchandising Services (www.narms.com), well over $3 billion annually in retail merchandising services—ranging from reordering to display design—are provided by specialized firms. An example is New Concepts in Marketing, which has provided ordering and inventory control, promotional selling, display placement, and other services for such clients as Babies "R" Us, Kmart, Publix, and Sam's Clubs.

The National Association for Retailing Merchandising Services offers a national online "JobBank" (www.narms.com/jobbank.html) by category and job location.

One contentious inventory management activity involves who is responsible for source tagging, the manufacturer or the retailer. In *source tagging*, anti-theft tags are put on items when they are produced, rather than at the store. Although both sides agree on the benefits of this, in terms of the reduced costs and the floor-readiness of merchandise, there are disagreements about who should pay for the tags.

Inventory Levels

Having the proper inventory on hand is a difficult balancing act:

1. The retailer wants to be appealing and never lose a sale by being out of stock. Yet, it does not want to be "stuck" with excess merchandise that must be marked down drastically.
2. The situation is more complicated for retailers that carry fad merchandise, handle new items for which there is no track record, and operate in new business formats where demand estimates are often inaccurate. Thus, inventory levels must be planned in relation to the products involved: staples, assortment merchandise, fashion merchandise, fads, and best-sellers.
3. Customer demand is *never* completely predictable—even for staple items. Weather, special sales, and other factors can have an impact on even the most stable items.
4. Shelf space allocations should be linked to current revenues, which means that allocations must be regularly reviewed and adjusted.

One of the advantages of QR and EDI is that retailers hold "leaner" inventories because they receive new merchandise more often. Yet, when merchandise is especially popular or the supply chain breaks down, stockouts may still occur. A Food Marketing Institute study found that even supermarkets, which carry more staples than most other retailers, lose 3 percent of sales due to out-of-stock goods.

This illustration shows just how tough inventory management can be. Longo Brothers Fruit Markets (www.longos.com) is a family-owned chain of 24 grocery stores [as of 2012] in the Toronto, Canada, area. Superior inventory management is essential for the profitability of the firm. At one point, it had difficulties in this area due to the different systems employed:

> Shelf pricing and register pricing are contained in two different applications, but changes on the shelf weren't always reflected accurately at the cash register, leading to price checks and dissatisfied customers. The inventory system wasn't integrated, causing stores to run out of stock. That problem was aggravated by letting customers order over the Internet and shipping goods directly from a store, not from a central warehouse. Company officials decided to purchase Tomax software, designed to integrate different systems. Now, all Longo's has to do is enter price changes one time and the system coordinates shelf, register, and online pricing.[25]

Inventory level planning is discussed further in the next chapter.

Merchandise Security

Each year, $45 billion in U.S. retail sales—and about $120 billion worldwide—are lost due to **inventory shrinkage** caused by employee theft, customer shoplifting, vendor fraud, and administrative errors. Of the global amount, employees account for 35 percent, customers 43 percent,

Asia's Uniglo Revamps Its Merchandising

Uniglo (www.uniglo.com) is Asia's largest clothing retailer. Fast Retailing, Uniglo's parent company, has doubled its sales in the past five years and is seeking to increase sales an additional six times (to $60 billion U.S.). Outside of its home market of Japan, Uniglo operates more than 150 stores in China, Great Britain, France, Singapore, Russia, Taiwan, Malaysia, South Korea, and the United States. Many of its new stores will be located in China and Southeast Asia, and at least another 200 stores will open in the United States by 2020.

Despite its successes, Uniglo has recently encountered several major problems. While it has been traditionally known for basic items, it recently began to stress more fashionable items. Not only did the newer items not sell as well, but the company also devoted too little space to basic items that were frequently out of stock. As a result, Uniglo plans to place more emphasis on its basic product lines such as denim and lightweight Heattech apparel (that absorbs and retains heat).

Uniglo now further faces competition with other apparel retailers seeking international growth such as the Zara stores brand (www.zara.com) from Spain's Inditex and Swedish-based Hennes & Mauritz, also known as H&M (www.hm.com). For example, Zara currently has more than 70 outlets in Japan; H&M has a dozen stores located there.

Sources: Naoko Fujimura and Shunichi Ozasa, "Uniglo: Asia's Top Clothier Goes Back to Basics," www.businessweek.com (January 6, 2011); and Zara and H&M Web sites (January 9, 2012).

vendors 6 percent, and administrative errors (faulty paperwork and computer entries) 16 percent. As the figures show, shopper theft is much higher than employee theft. Shrinkage typically ranges from under 1 percent of sales to more than 3 percent of sales at retail stores. The global figure is 1.45 percent of sales. This means a small store with $500,000 in annual sales might lose up to $15,000 or more due to shrinkage, and a large store with $3 million in sales might lose up to $90,000 or more due to shrinkage. Thus, some form of merchandise security is needed by all retailers; and each year, nearly $30 billion is spent by retailers worldwide to prevent theft.[26]

To reduce merchandise theft, there are three key points to consider: (1) Loss prevention measures should be incorporated as stores are designed and built. The placement of entrances, dressing rooms, and delivery areas is critical. (2) A combination of security measures should be enacted, such as employee background checks, in-store guards, electronic security equipment, and merchandise tags. (3) Retailers must communicate the importance of loss prevention to employees, customers, and vendors—and the actions they are prepared to take to reduce losses (such as firing workers and prosecuting shoplifters).

Here are some activities that are reducing losses from merchandise theft:

- Product tags, guards, video cameras, point-of-sale computers, employee surveillance, and burglar alarms are being used by more firms. Storefront protection is also popular. See Figure 15-11A.
- Many general merchandise retailers and some supermarkets use **electronic article surveillance**—whereby special tags are attached to products so that the tags can be sensed by electronic security devices at store exits. If the tags are not removed by store personnel or desensitized by scanning equipment, an alarm goes off. Retailers also have access to nonelectronic tags. These are snugly attached to products and must be removed by special detachers; otherwise products are unusable. Dye tags permanently stain products, if not removed properly. See Figure 15-11B.

Sensormatic (www.sensormatic.com) is a leader in electronic security.

- A number of retailers do detailed background checks for each prospective new employee. Some use loss prevention software that detects suspicious employee behavior.
- Various retailers have employee training programs and offer incentives for reducing merchandise losses. Others use written policies on ethical behavior that are signed by all personnel, including senior management. Target has enrolled managers at problem stores in a Stock Shortage Institute. Neiman Marcus has shown workers a film with interviews of convicted shoplifters in prison to highlight the problem's seriousness.
- More retailers are apt to fire employees and prosecute shoplifters involved with theft. Courts are imposing stiffer penalties; in some areas, store detectives are empowered by police to

FIGURE 15-11

Store and Merchandise Security

(A) Retailers are concerned about store security during the hours when they are closed. (B) They also want to make sure that individual items of merchandise are protected from theft.

Sources: (A) Alis Leonte/Shutterstock.com. Reprinted by permission. (B) Rob Bryan/Shutterstock.com. Reprinted by permission.

FIGURE 15-12
Ways Retailers Can Deter Employee and Shopper Theft

A. Employee Theft
- Use honesty tests as employee screening devices.
- Lock up trash to prevent merchandise from being thrown out and then retrieved.
- Verify through cameras and undercover personnel whether all sales are rung up.
- Centrally control all exterior doors to monitor opening and closing.
- Divide responsibilities—have one employee record sales and another make deposits.
- Give rewards for spotting thefts.
- Have training programs.
- Vigorously investigate all known losses and fire offenders immediately.

B. Shopper Theft While Store Is Open
- Use uniformed guards.
- Set up cameras and mirrors to increase visibility—especially in low-traffic areas.
- Use electronic article surveillance for high-value and theft-prone goods.
- Develop comprehensive employee training programs.
- Offer employee bonuses based on an overall reduction in shortages.
- Inspect all packages brought into store.
- Use self-locking showcases for high-value items such as jewelry.
- Attach expensive clothing together.
- Alternate the direction of hangers on clothing near doors.
- Limit the number of entrances and exits to the store, and the dollar value and quantity of merchandise displayed near exits.
- Prosecute all individuals charged with theft.

C. Employee/Shopper Theft While Store Is Closed
- Conduct a thorough building check at night to make sure no one is left in store.
- Lock all exits, even fire exits.
- Utilize ultrasonic/infrared detectors, burglar alarm traps, or guards with dogs.
- Place valuables in a safe.
- Install shatterproof glass and/or iron gates on windows and doors to prevent break-ins.
- Make sure exterior lighting is adequate.
- Periodically test burglar alarms.

make arrests. In more than 40 states, there are civil restitution laws; shoplifters must pay for stolen goods or face arrests and criminal trials. In most states, fines are higher if goods are not returned or are damaged. Shoplifters must also contribute to court costs.

- Some mystery shoppers are hired to watch for shoplifting, not just to research behavior.

Figure 15-12 presents a list of tactics retailers can use to combat employee and shopper theft, by far the leading causes of losses.

When devising a merchandise security plan, a retailer must assess the plan's impact on its image, employee morale, shopper comfort, and vendor relations. By setting strict rules for fitting rooms (by limiting the number of garments) or placing chains on very expensive coats, a retailer may cause some shoppers to avoid this merchandise—or visit another store.

Reverse Logistics

The term **reverse logistics** encompasses all merchandise flows from the customer and/or the retailer back through the supply channel. It typically involves items returned because of shopper second thoughts, damaged or defective products, or retailer overstocking. In the United States, customer returns alone are estimated by the National Retail Federation at about 9 percent of total retail sales, with $15 billion of returns being fraudulent. Sometimes, retailers may use closeout firms that buy back unpopular merchandise (at a fraction of the original cost) that suppliers will not take back; these firms then resell the goods at a deep discount. To avoid channel conflicts, the conditions for reverse logistics should be specified in advance. U.S. firms spend more than $50 billion per year for the handling, transportation, and processing costs associated with returns.[27]

These are among the decisions that must be made for reverse logistics:

The Reverse Logistics Association (www.reverselogisticstrends.com) presents a lot of good information on this topic at its Web site.

- Under what conditions (the permissible time, the condition of the product, and so forth) are customer returns accepted by the retailer and by the manufacturer?
- What is the customer refund policy? Is there a fee for returning an opened package?
- What party is responsible for shipping a returned product to the manufacturer?
- What customer documentation is needed to prove the date of purchase and the price paid?
- How are customer repairs handled (an immediate exchange, a third-party repair, or a refurbished product sent by the manufacturer)?
- To what extent are employees empowered to process customer returns?

Inventory Analysis

Inventory status and performance must be analyzed regularly to gauge the success of inventory management. Recent advances in computer software have made such analysis much more accurate and timely. According to surveys of retailers, these are the elements of inventory performance that are deemed most important: gross margin dollars, inventory turnover, gross profit percentage, gross margin return on inventory, the weeks of supply available, and the average in-stock position.

Inventory analysis is discussed further in the next chapter.

Chapter Summary

1. *To describe the steps in the implementation of merchandise plans.*

(a) Information is gathered about target market needs and prospective suppliers. Data about shopper needs can come from customers, suppliers, personnel, competitors, and others. A want book (want slip) is helpful. To acquire information about suppliers, the retailer can talk to prospects, attend trade shows, visit merchandise marts, and search the Web.

(b) The retailer chooses firm-owned; outside, regularly used; and/or outside, new supply sources. Relationships may become strained with suppliers because their goals differ from those of retailers.

(c) The merchandise under consideration is evaluated by inspection, sampling, and/or description. The method depends on the product and situation.

(d) Purchase terms may be negotiated (as with opportunistic buying) or uniform contracts may be used. Terms must be clear, including the delivery date, quantity purchased, price and payment arrangements, discounts, form of delivery, and point of transfer. There may also be special provisions.

(e) The purchase is concluded automatically or manually. Sometimes, management approval is needed. The transfer of title may take place as soon as the order is shipped or not until after merchandise is sold by the retailer.

(f) Handling involves receiving and storing, price and inventory marking, displays, floor stocking, customer transactions, delivery or pickup, returns and damaged goods, monitoring pilferage, and control. RFID (radio frequency identification) is an emerging technology in this area.

(g) Reorder procedures depend on order and delivery time, inventory turnover, financial outlays, and inventory versus ordering costs.

(h) Both the overall merchandising procedure and specific goods and services must be reviewed.

2. *To examine the prominent roles of logistics and inventory management in the implementation of merchandise plans.* Logistics includes planning, implementing, and coordinating the movement of merchandise from supplier to retailer to customer. Logistics goals are to relate costs to activities, accurately place and receive orders, minimize ordering/receiving time, coordinate shipments, have proper merchandise levels, place merchandise on the sales floor, process customer orders, work well in the supply chain, handle returns effectively and minimize damaged goods, monitor performance, and have backup plans.

A supply chain covers all parties in the logistics process. Collaborative planning, forecasting, and replenishment (CPFR) uses a holistic approach. Third-party logistics is more popular than before. Many manufacturers and retailers have Web sites to interact with channel partners.

Some retailers engage in QR inventory planning. Floor-ready merchandise is received at the store ready to be displayed. EDI lets retailers use QR planning through computerized supply chain relationships. Numerous supermarkets use efficient consumer response. Several transportation decisions are needed, as are warehousing choices. Certain retailers have goods shipped by direct store delivery. Retailers must also plan outbound logistics: completing transactions by turning over merchandise to the customer.

As part of logistics, a retailer uses inventory management. Due to its complexity, and to reduce costs, retailers may expect suppliers to perform more tasks or they may outsource some inventory activities. Vendor-managed inventory (VMI) is growing in popularity.

Having the proper inventory is a balancing act: The retailer does not want to lose sales due to being out of stock. It also does not want to be stuck with excess merchandise. Each year, $40 billion in U.S. retail sales are lost due to employee theft, customer shoplifting, vendor fraud, and administrative errors. Many retailers use electronic article surveillance, with special tags attached to products.

Reverse logistics involves all merchandise flows from the customer and/or the retailer back through a supply channel. It includes returns due to damages, defects, or poor retail sales.

Inventory performance must be analyzed regularly.

Key Terms

want book (want slip) (p. 376)
chargebacks (p. 378)
opportunistic buying (p. 381)
slotting allowances (p. 381)
consignment purchase (p. 382)
memorandum purchase (p. 382)
RFID (radio frequency identification) (p. 382)
logistics (p. 386)
supply chain (p. 388)
collaborative planning, forecasting, and replenishment (CPFR) (p. 388)
quick response (QR) inventory planning (p. 388)
floor-ready merchandise (p. 388)
efficient consumer response (ECR) (p. 389)
direct store delivery (DSD) (p. 390)
inventory management (p. 392)
vendor-managed inventory (VMI) (p. 392)
inventory shrinkage (p. 393)
electronic article surveillance (p. 394)
reverse logistics (p. 395)

Questions for Discussion

1. What information should a department store gather before adding a new watch brand to its product mix?
2. What are the pros and cons of a retailer's relying too much on a want book?
3. Cite the advantages and disadvantages associated with these merchandise sources for your regular fast-food outlet. How would your answers differ for a global apparel chain?
   a. Company-owned.
   b. Outside, regularly used.
   c. Outside, new.
4. Devise a checklist a retailer could use to negotiate opportunistic buying terms with suppliers.
5. Under what circumstances should a retailer try to charge slotting allowances? How may this strategy backfire?
6. Which is more difficult, implementing a merchandise plan for a small bookstore or Costco? Explain your answer.
7. Distinguish between these two terms: *logistics* and *inventory management.* Give an example of each.
8. What are the benefits of quick response inventory planning? What do you think are the risks?
9. Why are some retailers convinced that distribution centers must be used as the shipping points for merchandise from manufacturers while other retailers favor direct store delivery?
10. How could a neighborhood pizzeria be prepared for the variations in customer demand for home delivery during the day?
11. What is vendor-managed inventory? How do both manufacturers and retailers benefit from its use?
12. Present a seven-item checklist for a retailer to use with its reverse logistics.

Web-Based Exercise

Visit the "Business Solutions" section of the U.S. Postal Service's Web site (www.usps.com/business/business-solutions.htm). Describe the services that it offers that are appropriate for retailers. What are the benefits of a retailer's using the U.S. Postal Service?

Note: Also stop by our Web site (www.pearsonhighered.com/bermanevans) to experience a number of highly interactive, appealing Web exercises based on actual company demonstrations and sample materials related to retailing.

16 Financial Merchandise Management

Chapter Objectives

1. To describe the major aspects of financial merchandise planning and management
2. To explain the cost and retail methods of accounting
3. To study the merchandise forecasting and budgeting process
4. To examine alternative methods of inventory unit control
5. To integrate dollar and unit merchandising control concepts

Although it is pretty clear that social media provide a number of advantages for retailers in their merchandising efforts, a key question has not been adequately addressed (except by companies such as Express that actually sell through social media): How can you ensure that social media have a significant positive impact on a retailer's financial performance?

Consider the observations of Deb Scott and Thomas Scott about social media and retail franchising:

> Social media aren't a fad. The majority of us know our customers use these networks and spend a lot of time on them. But, social media take time, distract from other work, and for all the hype, most companies can't seem to harness the potential. It is absolutely possible to grow by leveraging social media; and smart companies are learning how. This is the trick to producing profit: do not shortcut engagement. Either customers are truly engaged or they are not. Fail at engagement and social media efforts will fail as well.

So, what should retailers do? According to Deb Scott and Thomas Scott, franchisors and franchisees can utilize (leverage) social media to increase profitability. These retailers can interact with potential customers and stimulate them to think more highly of their brands; and they can establish stronger long-term relationships with existing customers, thus, generating more brand loyalty. This will enable the retailers to capitalize on the influence of social media-driven customer reviews and ratings. As the Scotts suggest, by supplying customers with a steady flow of honest and positive messages, the customers will often jump into the conversation and be supportive of the firms and their message. In turn, profitability is improved. The Scotts also recommend using social media to help grow franchise revenues by "emotionally engaging franchise candidates." This can be a very powerful tool at the individual franchisee level.[1]

Source: BeTA-Artworks / fotolia.com.

Overview

Sage ERP Accpac (www.sageaccpac.com/Products/Sage-ERP-Accpac) is one of many firms that offer integrated accounting software that is widely used by retailers.

Through **financial merchandise management**, a retailer specifies which products (goods and services) are purchased, when products are purchased, and how many products are purchased. **Dollar control** involves planning and monitoring a retailer's financial investment in merchandise over a stated period. **Unit control** relates to the quantities of merchandise a retailer handles during a stated period. Dollar investment is determined before assortment decisions are made.

Well-structured financial merchandise plans offer these benefits:

- The value and amount of inventory in each department and/or store unit during a given period are delineated. Stock is balanced, and fewer markdowns may be necessary.
- The amount of merchandise (in terms of investment) a buyer can purchase during a given period is stipulated. This gives a buyer direction.
- The inventory investment in relation to planned and actual revenues is studied. This improves the return on investment.
- The retailer's space requirements are partly determined by estimating beginning-of-month and end-of-month inventory levels.
- A buyer's performance is rated. Various measures may be used to set standards.
- Stock shortages are determined, and bookkeeping errors and pilferage are uncovered.
- Slow-moving items are classified—leading to increased sales efforts or markdowns.
- A proper balance between inventory and out-of-stock conditions is maintained.

Yet, "many companies suffer from poor inventory control which leads to inefficiency and wasted expenditures on goods that sit on the shelf." With the right software and techniques, a firm "can optimize inventory levels, eliminate stockouts, increase sales, and squeeze the most out of a supply chain."[2]

This chapter divides financial merchandise management into four areas: methods of accounting, merchandise forecasting and budgeting, unit control systems, and financial inventory control. The hypothetical Handy Hardware Store illustrates the concepts.

INVENTORY VALUATION: THE COST AND RETAIL METHODS OF ACCOUNTING

This site (www.ssinet.com/accounting/docs/imcd.pdf) has an excellent guide on inventory management.

Retail inventory accounting systems can be complex because they entail a great deal of data (due to the number of items sold). A typical retailer's dollar control system must provide such data as the sales and purchases made by that firm during a budget period, the value of beginning and ending inventory, markups and markdowns, and merchandise shortages.

Table 16-1 shows a profit-and-loss statement for Handy Hardware Store for January 1, 2012, through June 30, 2012. The sales amount is total receipts over this time. Beginning inventory was computed by counting merchandise in stock on January 1, 2012—recorded at cost. Purchases (at cost) and transportation charges (costs incurred in shipping items from suppliers to the retailer) were derived by adding invoice slips for all merchandise bought by Handy in the period.

Together, beginning inventory, purchases, and transportation charges equal the cost of **merchandise available for sale.** The **cost of goods sold** equals the cost of merchandise available for sale minus the cost value of ending inventory. Sales less cost of goods sold yields **gross profit**, while **net profit** is gross profit minus retail operating expenses. Because Handy does a physical inventory twice yearly, ending inventory was figured by counting the items in stock on June 30, 2012—recorded at cost (Handy codes each item).

Retailers have different data needs than manufacturers. Assortments are larger. Costs cannot be printed on cartons unless coded (due to customer inspection). Stock shortages are higher. Sales are more frequent. Retailers require monthly, not quarterly, profit data.

Two inventory accounting systems are available: (1) The cost accounting system values merchandise at cost plus inbound transportation charges. (2) The retail accounting system values merchandise at current retail prices. Let's study both methods in terms of the frequency with which data are obtained, the difficulties of a physical inventory and record keeping, the ease of settling insurance claims (if there is inventory damage), the extent to which shortages can be computed, and system complexities.

TABLE 16-1 Handy Hardware Store Profit-and-Loss Statement, January 1, 2012–June 30, 2012

Sales		$417,460
Less cost of goods sold:		
Beginning inventory (at cost)	$ 44,620	
Purchases (at cost)	289,400	
Transportation charges	2,600	
Merchandise available for sale	$336,620	
Ending inventory (at cost)	90,500	
Cost of goods sold		246,120
Gross profit		$171,340
Less operating expenses:		
Salaries	$70,000	
Advertising	25,000	
Rental	16,000	
Other	26,000	
Total operating expenses		137,000
Net profit before taxes		$ 34,340

At our Web site (www.pearsonhighered.com/bermanevans), there are a number of links related to retail accounting and inventory valuation, including several from the Internal Revenue Service.

The Cost Method

With the **cost method of accounting**, the cost to the retailer of each item is recorded on an accounting sheet and/or is coded on a price tag or merchandise container. As a physical inventory is done, item costs must be learned, the quantity of every item in stock counted, and total inventory value at cost calculated. One way to code merchandise cost is to use a 10-letter equivalency system, such as M = 0, N = 1, O = 2, P = 3, Q = 4, R = 5, S = 6, T = 7, U = 8, and V = 9. An item coded with STOP has a cost value of $67.23. This technique is useful as an accounting tool and for retailers that allow price bargaining by customers (profit per item is easy to compute).

Bryan Prince: Loving Books and Bookkeeping

In 2010, Bryan Prince completed the sale of his Bryan Prince Bookseller shop (www.princebooks.net) in Ontario, Canada, to two long-time employees. The new owners are making two changes: (1) placing greater emphasis on attracting younger shoppers and (2) adding some books in French. They still plan to sell no other product categories besides books.

Like other retail business, the book business is undergoing topsy-turvy times as a result of such factors as the dominance of megastores and Amazon.com (www.amazon.com), the popularity of E-books, and the tough economy. In the past, the Prince store was able to effectively compete by providing high levels of personal service. For example, employees can locate a book title based on a theme, an author's name, or even a publisher's name. Bryan Prince Bookseller also has strong roots in the community.

Reflecting on his 23 years in the book business, Bryan Prince noted: "It's better to go a little early than a little late. I'm leaving the business financially healthy, debt free, and in the black. I wanted to turn it over while it's still in good shape." He added: "In this business, you have to turn it over while it's still in good shape."

Source: Steve Arnold, "Bryan Prince Closes the Book on Retail Career," www.thespec.com (February 19, 2011).

A retailer can use the cost method as it does physical or book inventories. A physical inventory means an actual merchandise count; a book inventory relies on record keeping.

A PHYSICAL INVENTORY SYSTEM USING THE COST METHOD In a **physical inventory system**, ending inventory—recorded at cost—is measured by counting the merchandise in stock at the close of a selling period. Gross profit is not computed until ending inventory is valued. A retailer using the cost method along with a physical inventory system derives gross profit only as often as it performs a full merchandise count. Because most firms do so just once or twice yearly, a physical inventory system alone imposes limits on planning. In addition, a firm might be unable to compute inventory shortages (due to pilferage and unrecorded breakage) because ending inventory value is set by adding the costs of all items in stock. It does not compute what the ending inventory *should be.*

CAM Commerce (www.camcommerce.com) software facilitates inventory calculations. Type "perpetual inventory" in the search box.

A BOOK INVENTORY SYSTEM USING THE COST METHOD A **book (perpetual) inventory system** avoids the problem of infrequent financial analysis by keeping a running total of the value of all inventory on hand at cost at a given time. End-of-month inventory values can be computed without a physical inventory, and frequent financial statements can be prepared. In addition, a book inventory lets a retailer uncover stock shortages by comparing projected inventory values with actual inventory values through a physical inventory.[3]

A book inventory is kept by regularly recording purchases and adding them to existing inventory value; sales are subtracted to arrive at the new current inventory value (all at cost). Table 16-2 shows Handy Hardware's book inventory system for July 1, 2012, through December 31, 2012; the beginning inventory in Table 16-2 is the ending inventory from Table 16-1. Table 16-2 assumes that merchandise costs are rather constant and monthly sales at cost are easy to compute. Yet, suppose merchandise costs rise. How would inventory value then be computed?

At its Web site, SourceCorp provides good background information on LIFO (www.lifochannel.com).

FIFO and LIFO are two ways to value inventory. The **FIFO (first-in-first-out) method** logically assumes old merchandise is sold first, while newer items remain in inventory. The **LIFO (last-in-first-out) method** assumes new merchandise is sold first, while older stock remains in inventory. FIFO matches inventory value with the current cost structure—the goods in inventory are the ones bought most recently, while LIFO matches current sales with the current cost structure—the goods sold first are the ones bought most recently. When inventory values rise, LIFO offers retailers a tax advantage because lower profits are shown.

In Figure 16-1, the FIFO and LIFO methods are illustrated for Handy Hardware's snow blowers for 2012; the store carries only one model of snow blower. Handy knows that it sold 220 snow blowers in 2012 at an average price of $320. It began 2012 with an inventory of 30 snow blowers, purchased for $150 each. During January 2012, it bought 100 snow blowers at $175 each; from October to December 2012, Handy bought another 150 snow blowers for $225 apiece. Because Handy sold 220 snow blowers in 2012, as of the close of business on December 31, it had 60 units remaining.

With the FIFO method, Handy assumes its beginning inventory and initial purchases were sold first. The 60 snow blowers remaining in inventory would have a cost value of $225 each, a total cost of goods sold of $42,250, and a gross profit of $28,150. With the LIFO method, Handy assumes the most recently purchased items were sold first and the remaining inventory would consist of

TABLE 16-2 Handy Hardware Store Perpetual Inventory System, July 1, 2012–December 31, 2012[a]

Date	Beginning-of-Month Inventory (at Cost)	+	Net Monthly Purchases (at Cost)	–	Monthly Sales (at Cost)	=	End-of-Month Inventory (at Cost)
7/1/12	$90,500		$ 40,000		$ 62,400		$ 68,100
8/1/12	68,100		28,000		38,400		57,700
9/1/12	57,700		27,600		28,800		56,500
10/1/12	56,500		44,000		28,800		71,700
11/1/12	71,700		50,400		40,800		81,300
12/1/12	81,300		15,900		61,200		36,000
		Total	$205,900		$260,400		(as of 12/31/12)

[a] Transportation charges are not included in computing inventory value in this table.

FIGURE 16-1
Applying FIFO and LIFO Inventory Methods to Handy Hardware, January 1, 2012–December 31, 2012

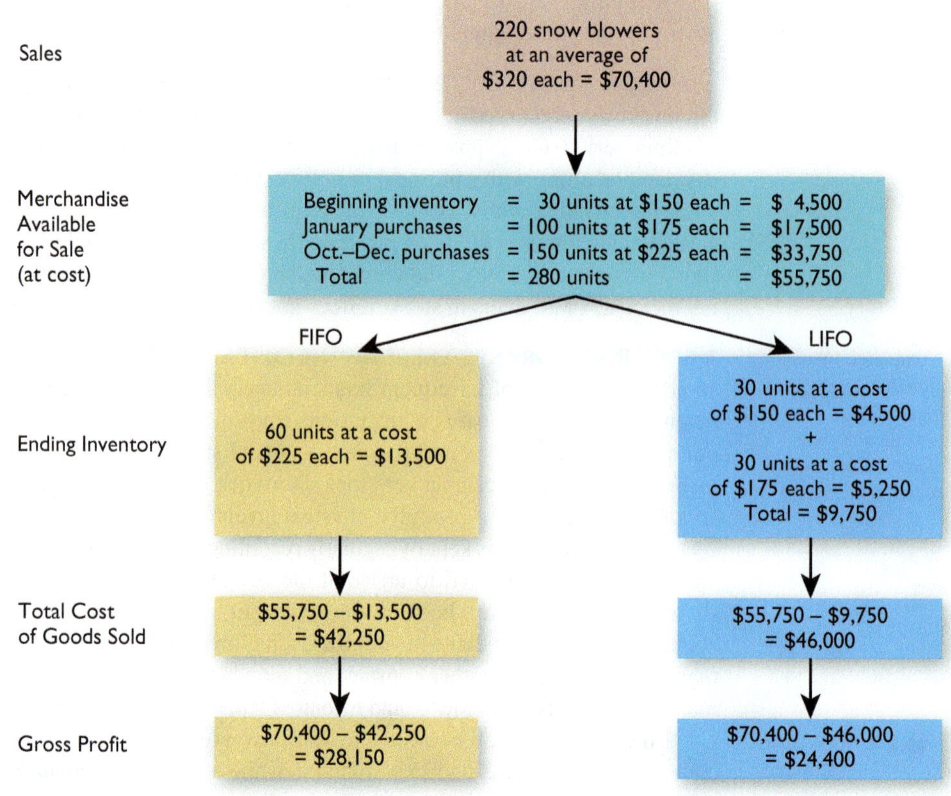

beginning goods and early purchases. Of the snow blowers remaining in inventory, 30 would have a cost value of $150 each and 30 a cost value of $175 apiece, resulting in a total cost of goods sold of $46,000 and a gross profit of $24,400. The FIFO method presents a more accurate picture of the cost of goods sold and the true cost value of ending inventory. The LIFO method indicates a lower profit, leading to the payment of lower taxes but an understated ending inventory value at cost.

The retail method of inventory, which combines FIFO and LIFO concepts, is explained shortly.

DISADVANTAGES OF COST-BASED INVENTORY SYSTEMS Cost-based physical and book systems have significant disadvantages. First, both require that a cost be assigned to each item in stock (and to each item sold). When merchandise costs change, cost-based valuation systems work best for firms with low inventory turnover, limited assortments, and high average prices—such as car dealers.

Second, neither cost-based method adjusts inventory values to reflect style changes, end-of-season markdowns, or sudden surges of demand (which may raise prices). Thus, ending inventory value based on merchandise cost may not reflect its actual worth. This discrepancy could be troublesome if inventory value is used in filing insurance claims for losses.

Despite these factors, retailers that make the products they sell—such as bakeries, restaurants, and furniture showrooms—often keep records on a cost basis. A department store with these operations can use the cost method for them and the retail method for other areas.

The Retail Method

With the **retail method of accounting**, closing inventory value is determined by calculating the average relationship between the cost and retail values of merchandise available for sale during a period. Although the retail method overcomes the disadvantages of the cost method, it requires detailed records and is more complex because ending inventory is first valued in retail dollars and then converted to compute gross margin (gross profit).

There are three basic steps to determine ending inventory value by the retail method:

1. Calculating the cost complement.
2. Calculating deductions from retail value.
3. Converting retail inventory value to cost.

TABLE 16-3 Handy Hardware Store, Calculating Merchandise Available for Sale at Cost and at Retail, July 1, 2012–December 31, 2012

	At Cost	At Retail
Beginning inventory	$ 90,500	$139,200
Net purchases	205,900	340,526
Additional markups	—	16,400
Transportation charges	3,492	—
Total merchandise available for sale	$299,892	$496,126

CALCULATING THE COST COMPLEMENT The value of beginning inventory, net purchases, additional markups, and transportation charges are all included in the retail method. Beginning inventory and net purchase amounts (purchases less returns) are recorded at both cost and retail levels. Additional markups represent the extra revenues received when a retailer increases selling prices, due to inflation or unexpectedly high demand. Transportation charges are the retailer's costs for shipping the goods it buys from suppliers to the retailer. Table 16-3 shows the total merchandise available for sale at cost and at retail for Handy Hardware from July 1, 2012, through December 31, 2012, using the costs in Table 16-2.

By using Table 16-3 data, the average relationship of cost to retail value for all merchandise available for sale by Handy Hardware—the **cost complement**—can be computed:

$$\text{Cost complement} = \frac{\text{Total cost valuation}}{\text{Total retail valuation}}$$

$$= \frac{\$299{,}892}{\$496{,}126} = 0.6045$$

Because the cost complement is 0.6045 (60.45 percent), on average, 60.45 cents of every retail sales dollar went to cover Handy Hardware's merchandise cost.

CALCULATING DEDUCTIONS FROM RETAIL VALUE The ending retail value of inventory must reflect all deductions from the total merchandise available for sale at retail. Besides sales, deductions include markdowns (for special sales and end-of-season goods), employee discounts, and stock shortages (due to pilferage and unrecorded breakage). Although sales, markdowns, and employee discounts can be recorded throughout an accounting period, a physical inventory is needed to learn about stock shortages.

From Table 16-3, it is known that Handy Hardware had a retail value of merchandise available for sale of $496,126 for the period from July 1, 2012, through December 31, 2012. As shown in Table 16-4, this was reduced by sales of $422,540 and recorded markdowns and employee discounts of $14,034. The ending book value of inventory at retail as of December 31, 2012, was $59,552.

TABLE 16-4 Handy Hardware Store, Computing Ending Retail Book Value, as of December 31, 2012

Merchandise available for sale (at retail)		$496,126
Less deductions:		
Sales	$422,540	
Markdowns	11,634	
Employee discounts	2,400	
Total deductions		436,574
Ending retail book value of inventory		$ 59,552

TABLE 16-5 Handy Hardware Store, Computing Stock Shortages and Adjusting Retail Book Value, as of December 31, 2012

Ending retail book value of inventory	$59,552
Physical inventory (at retail)	56,470
Stock shortages (at retail)	3,082
Adjusted ending retail book value of inventory	$56,470

To compute stock shortages, the retail book value of ending inventory is compared with the actual physical ending inventory at retail. If book inventory exceeds physical inventory, a shortage exists. Table 16-5 shows the results of Handy's physical inventory. Shortages were $3,082 (at retail), and book value was adjusted accordingly. Although Handy knows the shortages were from pilferage, bookkeeping errors, and overshipments not billed to customers, it cannot learn the proportion of shortages from each factor.

Occasionally, a physical inventory may reveal a stock overage—an excess of physical inventory value over book value. This may be due to errors in a physical inventory or in keeping a book inventory. If overages occur, ending retail book value is adjusted upward. Inasmuch as a retailer has to conduct a physical inventory to compute shortages (overages), and a physical inventory is usually taken only once or twice a year, shortages (overages) are often estimated for monthly merchandise budgets.

CONVERTING RETAIL INVENTORY VALUE TO COST The retailer must next convert the adjusted ending retail book value of inventory to cost so as to compute dollar gross profit (gross margin). The ending inventory at cost equals the adjusted ending retail book value multiplied by the cost complement. For Handy Hardware, this was:

$$\text{Ending inventory (at cost)} = \text{Adjusted ending retail book value} \times \text{Cost complement}$$
$$= \$56{,}470 \times .6045 = \$34{,}136$$

This computation does not yield the exact inventory cost. It shows the average relationship between cost and the retail selling price for all merchandise available for sale.

The adjusted ending inventory at cost can be used to find gross profit. As Table 16-6 shows, Handy's six-month cost of goods sold was $265,756, resulting in gross profit of $156,784. By deducting operating expenses of $139,000, Handy learns that the net profit before taxes for this period was $17,784.

TABLE 16-6 Handy Hardware Store Profit-and-Loss Statement, July 1, 2012–December 31, 2012

Sales		$422,540
Less cost of goods sold:		
Total merchandise available for sale (at cost)	$299,892	
Adjusted ending inventory (at cost)[a]	34,136	
Cost of goods sold		265,756
Gross profit		$156,784
Less operating expenses:		
Salaries	$ 70,000	
Advertising	25,000	
Rental	16,000	
Other	28,000	
Total operating expenses		139,000
Net profit before taxes		$ 17,784

[a] Adjusted ending inventory (at cost) = Adjusted retail book value × Cost complement = $56,470 × 0.6045 = $34,136

Go here (www.jdapos.com/retail-point-of-sale-solutions/microsoft-rms) to download a good discussion on "Numbers That Matter in Retailing."

ADVANTAGES OF THE RETAIL METHOD Compared with other techniques, there are several advantages to the retail method of accounting:

- Valuation errors are reduced when conducting a physical inventory because merchandise value is recorded at retail and costs do not have to be decoded.
- Because the process is simpler, a physical inventory can be completed more often. This lets a firm be more aware of slow-moving items and stock shortages.
- The physical inventory method at cost requires a physical inventory to prepare a profit-and-loss statement. The retail method lets a firm set up a profit-and-loss statement based on book inventory. The retailer can then estimate the stock shortages between physical inventories and study departmental profit trends.
- A complete record of ending book values helps determine insurance coverage and settle insurance claims. The retail book method gives an estimate of inventory value throughout the year. Because physical inventories are usually taken when merchandise levels are low, the book value at retail lets retailers plan insurance coverage for peak periods and shows the values of goods on hand. The retail method is accepted in insurance claims.

LIMITATIONS OF THE RETAIL METHOD The greatest weakness is the bookkeeping burden of recording data. Ending book inventory figures can be correctly computed only if the following are accurately noted: the value of beginning inventory (at cost and at retail), purchases (at cost and at retail), shipping charges, markups, markdowns, employee discounts, transfers from other departments or stores, returns, and sales. Although personnel are freed from taking many physical inventories, ending book value at retail may be inaccurate unless all required data are precisely recorded. With computerization, this potential problem is lessened.

Another limitation is that the cost complement is an average based on the total cost of merchandise available for sale and total retail value. The ending cost value only approximates the true inventory value. This may cause misinformation if fast-selling items have different markups from slow-selling items or if there are wide variations among the markups of different goods.

Familiarity with the retail and cost methods of inventory is essential for understanding the financial merchandise management material described in the balance of this chapter.

MERCHANDISE FORECASTING AND BUDGETING: DOLLAR CONTROL

As we noted earlier, dollar control entails planning and monitoring a firm's inventory investment over time. Figure 16-2 shows the six-step dollar control process for merchandise forecasting and budgeting. This process should be followed sequentially since a change in one stage affects all the stages after it. If a sales forecast is too low, a firm may run out of items because it does not plan to have enough merchandise during a selling season and planned purchases will also be too low.

Visit our Web site (www.pearsonhighered.com/bermanevans) for a detailed listing of links related to both dollar control and unit control in merchandise management.

Designating Control Units

Merchandise forecasting and budgeting requires the selection of **control units**, the merchandise categories for which data are gathered. Such classifications must be narrow enough to isolate opportunities and problems with specific merchandise lines. A retailer wishing to control goods within departments must record data on dollar allotments separately for each category.

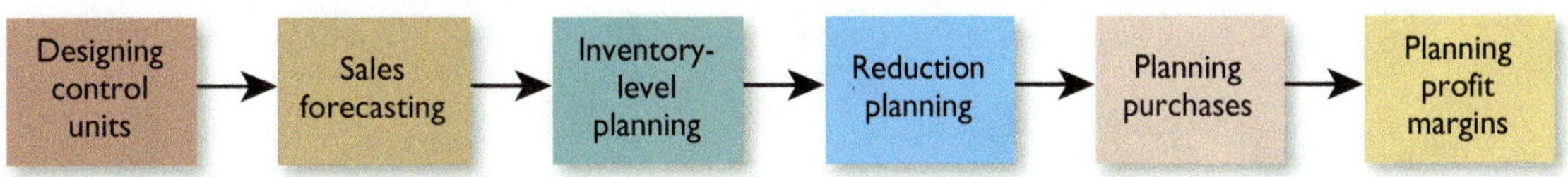

FIGURE 16-2
The Merchandise Forecasting and Budgeting Process: Dollar Control

Retailer Collaborations to Reduce Merchandise Theft

Organized retail crime (ORC) accounts for between $15 billion and $30 billion in U.S. retail theft per year according to estimates by the FBI and other organizations. Two-thirds of the 90 percent of retailers that reported being victimized by organized crime have stated that they had either identified or recovered stolen merchandise and/or gift cards that were offered for sale in online channels such as eBay.

To combat the sales of stolen merchandise, eBay (www.ebay.com) hired Paul Jones, who previously managed loss prevention for Limited Brands (www.limited.com) and Sunglass Hut (www.sunglasshut.com), as the senior director of its global asset protection program (PROACT).

CVS Caremark (www.caremark.com), Kroger (www.kroger.com), and Home Depot (www.homedepot.com) have joined PROACT to deter fraudulent online sales by identifying criteria that help recognize suspicious sellers even before they could list an item for sale. PROACT now has more than 300 retail members representing 166,000 store units.

One warning flag of stolen merchandise being offered for sales is when an item is priced significantly below its normal wholesale cost. When a suspicious lot of goods is found, eBay contacts the seller to verify that the products were bought through legitimate channels. eBay not only bars stolen merchandise from being offered for sale, but it will also contact the legitimate supplier to pursue legal action.

Source: Liz Parks, "Shaking Hands, Not Fists," www.stores.org (April 2011).

Knowing that total markdowns in a department are 20 percent above last year's level is less valuable than knowing the specific merchandise lines in which large markdowns are being taken. A retailer can broaden its control system by combining categories that comprise a department. However, a broad category cannot be broken down into components.

It is helpful to select control units consistent with other company and trade association data. Internal comparisons are meaningful only when categories are stable. Classifications that shift over time do not permit comparisons. External comparisons are not meaningful if control units are dissimilar for a retailer and its trade associations. Control units may be based on departments, classifications within departments, price line classifications, and standard merchandise classifications. A discussion of each follows.

The broadest practical classification for financial records is the department, which lets a retailer assess each general merchandise grouping or buyer. Even small Handy Hardware needs departmental data (tools and equipment, supplies, housewares, and so on) for buying, inventory control, and markdown decisions. For more financial data, **classification merchandising** can be used, with each department subdivided into further categories for related types of merchandise. In planning its tools and equipment department, Handy Hardware can keep financial records on both overall departmental performance and the results of such categories as lawn mowers/snow blowers, power tools, hand tools, and ladders.

A special form of classification merchandising uses *price line classifications*—sales, inventories, and purchases are analyzed by price category. This helps if different models of a product are sold at different prices to different target markets (such as Handy's having $20 power tools for do-it-yourselfers and $135 models for contractors). Retailers with deep assortments most often use price line control.

To best contrast its data with industry averages, a firm's merchandise categories should conform to those cited in trade publications. The National Retail Federation devised a *standard merchandise classification* with common reporting categories for a range of retailers and products. It annually produces *Retail Horizons* (www.nrffoundation.com/retail-horizons), using its classifications. Specific classifications are also popular for some retailers. *Progressive Grocer* regularly publishes data based on standard classifications for supermarkets.

Once appropriate dollar control units are set, all transactions—including sales, purchases, transfers, markdowns, and employee discounts—must be recorded under the proper classification number. Thus, if house paint is Department 25 and brushes are 25-1, all transactions must carry these designations.

Sales Forecasting

Brooks Brothers succeeds with SAS software (www.sas.com/success/brooksbros.html).

A retailer estimates its expected future revenues for a given period by *sales forecasting*. Forecasts may be companywide, departmental, and for individual merchandise classifications. Perhaps the most important step in financial merchandise planning is accurate sales forecasting, because an incorrect projection of sales throws off the entire process. That is why many retailers use state-of-the-art forecasting software. Brooks Brothers has dramatically improved its inventory productivity by using such software from SAS.[4]

Larger retailers often forecast total and department sales by techniques such as trend analysis, time series analysis, and multiple regression analysis. A discussion of these techniques is beyond the scope of this book. Small retailers rely more on "guesstimates," projections based on experience. Even for larger firms, sales forecasting for merchandise classifications within departments (or price lines) relies on more qualitative methods. One way to forecast sales for narrow categories is first to project sales on a company basis and by department and then to break down figures judgmentally into merchandise classifications.

External factors, internal company factors, and seasonal trends must be anticipated and taken into account. Among the external factors that can affect projected sales are consumer trends, competitors' actions, the state of the economy, the weather, and new supplier offerings. For example, Planalytics offers a patented methodology to analyze and forecast the relationship among consumer demand, store traffic, and the weather.[5] Internal company factors that can affect future sales include additions and deletions of merchandise lines, revised promotion and credit policies, changes in hours, new outlets, and store remodeling. With many retailers, seasonality must be considered in setting monthly or quarterly sales forecasts. Handy's yearly snow blower sales should not be estimated from December sales alone.

A sales forecast can be developed by examining past trends and projecting future growth (based on external and internal factors). Table 16-7 shows a sales forecast for Handy Hardware. It is an estimate, subject to revisions. Various factors may be hard to incorporate when devising a forecast, such as merchandise shortages, consumer reactions to new products, the rate of inflation, and new government legislation. That is why a financial merchandise plan needs some flexibility.

After a yearly forecast is derived, it should be broken into quarters or months. In retailing, monthly forecasts are usually required. Jewelry stores know December accounts for nearly one-quarter of annual sales, while drugstores know December sales are slightly better than average. Stationery stores and card stores realize that Christmas and other holiday cards generate more than 60 percent of seasonal greeting card sales, while Valentine's Day cards are second with about 25 percent.[6]

To acquire more specific estimates, a retailer could use a **monthly sales index**, which divides each month's actual sales by average monthly sales and multiplies the results by 100. Table 16-8 shows Handy Hardware's 2012 actual monthly sales and monthly sales indexes. The store is seasonal, with peaks in late spring and early summer (for lawn mowers, garden supplies, and so on), as well as December (for lighting fixtures, snow blowers, and gifts). Average monthly 2012 sales were $70,000 ($840,000/12). Thus, the monthly sales index for January is 67

TABLE 16-7 Handy Hardware Store, A Simple Sales Forecast Using Product Control Units

Product Control Units	Actual Sales 2012	Projected Growth/ Decline (%)	Sales Forecast 2013
Lawn mowers/snow blowers	$200,000	+10.0	$220,000
Paint and supplies	128,000	+3.0	131,840
Hardware supplies	108,000	+8.0	116,640
Plumbing supplies	88,000	−4.0	84,480
Power tools	88,000	+6.0	93,280
Garden supplies/chemicals	68,000	+4.0	70,720
Housewares	48,000	−6.0	45,120
Electrical supplies	40,000	+4.0	41,600
Ladders	36,000	+6.0	38,160
Hand tools	36,000	+9.0	39,240
Total year	$840,000	+4.9[a]	$881,080

[a] There is a small rounding error.

TABLE 16-8 Handy Hardware Store, 2012 Sales by Month

Month	Monthly Actual Sales	Sales Index[a]
January	$ 46,800	67
February	40,864	58
March	48,000	69
April	65,600	94
May	112,196	160
June	103,800	148
July	104,560	149
August	62,800	90
September	46,904	67
October	46,800	67
November	66,884	96
December	94,792	135
Total yearly sales	$840,000	
Average monthly sales	$ 70,000	
Average monthly index		100

[a] Monthly sales index = (Monthly sales/Average monthly sales) × 100

[($46,800/$70,000) × 100]; other monthly indexes are computed similarly. Each monthly index shows the percentage deviation of that month's sales from the average month. A May index of 160 means May sales are 60 percent higher than average. An October index of 67 means sales in October are 33 percent below average.

Once monthly sales indexes are determined, a retailer can forecast monthly sales, based on the yearly sales forecast. Table 16-9 shows how Handy's 2013 monthly sales can be forecast if average monthly sales are expected to be $73,423.

TABLE 16-9 Handy Hardware Store, 2013 Sales Forecast by Month

Month	Actual Sales 2012	Monthly Sales Index	Monthly Sales Forecast for 2013[a]	
January	$ 46,800	67	$73,423 × 0.67 =	$ 49,193
February	40,864	58	73,423 × 0.58 =	42,585
March	48,000	69	73,423 × 0.69 =	50,662
April	65,600	94	73,423 × 0.94 =	69,018
May	112,196	160	73,423 × 1.60 =	117,477
June	103,800	148	73,423 × 1.48 =	108,666
July	104,560	149	73,423 × 1.49 =	109,400
August	62,800	90	73,423 × 0.90 =	66,081
September	46,904	67	73,423 × 0.67 =	49,193
October	46,800	67	73,423 × 0.67 =	49,193
November	66,884	96	73,423 × 0.96 =	70,486
December	94,792	135	73,423 × 1.35 =	99,121
Total sales	$840,000		Total sales forecast	$881,080[b]
Average monthly sales	$ 70,000		Average monthly forecast	$ 73,423

[a] Monthly sales forecast = Average monthly forecast × (Monthly index/100). In this equation, the monthly index is computed as a fraction of 1.00 rather than 100.

[b] There is a small rounding error.

Inventory-Level Planning

IBM ILOG Inventory Analyst (www.bpdi.pl/en/products/14-ibm-ilog-inventory-analyst) software enhances inventory planning.

At this point, a retailer plans its inventory. The level must be sufficient to meet sales expectations, allowing a margin for error. Techniques to plan inventory levels are the basic stock, percentage variation, weeks' supply, and stock-to-sales methods.

With the **basic stock method**, a retailer carries more items than it expects to sell over a specified period. There is a cushion if sales are more than anticipated, shipments are delayed, or customers want to select from a variety of items. It is best when inventory turnover is low or sales are erratic over the year. Beginning-of-month planned inventory equals planned sales plus a basic stock amount:

$$\text{Basic stock (at retail)} = \text{Average monthly stock at retail} - \text{Average monthly sales}$$

$$\text{Beginning-of-month planned inventory level (at retail)} = \text{Planned monthly sales} + \text{Basic stock}$$

If Handy Hardware, with an average monthly 2013 forecast of $73,423, wants extra stock equal to 10 percent of its average monthly forecast and expects January 2013 sales to be $49,193:

$$\text{Basic stock (at retail)} = (\$73{,}423 \times 1.10) - \$73{,}423 = \$7{,}342$$

$$\text{Beginning-of-January planned inventory level (at retail)} = \$49{,}193 + \$7{,}342 = \$56{,}535$$

In the **percentage variation method**, beginning-of-month planned inventory during any month differs from planned average monthly stock by only one-half of that month's variation from estimated average monthly sales. This method is recommended if stock turnover is more than six times a year or relatively stable, since it results in planned inventories closer to the monthly average than other techniques:

$$\text{Beginning-of-month planned inventory level (at retail)} = \text{Planned average monthly stock at retail} \times 1/2\,[1 + (\text{Estimated monthly sales}/\text{Estimated average monthly sales})]$$

If Handy Hardware plans average monthly stock of $80,765 and November 2013 sales are expected to be 4 percent less than average monthly sales of $73,423, the store's planned inventory level at the beginning of November 2013 would be:

$$\text{Beginning-of-November planned inventory level (at retail)} = \$80{,}765 \times 1/2\,[1 + (\$70{,}487/\$73{,}423)] = \$79{,}150$$

TECHNOLOGY IN RETAILING — POS: Not Your Father's (Or Mother's) Cash Register

A major development with point-of-sale (POS) systems is their evolution from being used as traditional cash registers to being interconnected with other software systems and portable data storage devices. Many retailers use POS systems to manage their inventory across multiple channels. And they check their sales figures via smart phones; and they analyze sales associate performance in up-selling activities.

Here's how selected retailers are using their POS systems in unconventional ways:

- Big Drop NYC (www.bigdropnyc.com), an online women's apparel retailer, uses Visual Retail Plus (www.visualretailplus.com) to manage its entire inventory in all of its locations. Its POS system tracks sales, develops loss prevention reports, and forecasts sales at the store level. In addition, the software enables customers to track their online sales, as well as to review past orders.
- The Ultimate Look, a local apparel store in Jackson Heights, New York, uses Visual Retail Plus to evaluate sales, returned items, and peak sales periods—based on fabric and style dimensions such as long sleeve, casual dressy, long dress, and other factors.
- J. McLaughlin (www.jmclaughlin.com), a multi-channel apparel retailer, uses Celerant Command POS (www.celerant.com) to capture information on consumers' past purchases. The system also lets the retailer ship merchandise to a customer even when the closest warehouse does not have the particular item in stock.

Source: Jordan K. Speer, "You Say You Want a (POS) Evolution," *Apparel Magazine* (February 2011), pp. 16–18.

Handy Hardware should not use this method due to its variable sales. If it did, Handy would plan a beginning-of-December 2013 inventory of $94,899, less than expected sales ($99,121).

The **weeks' supply method** forecasts average sales weekly, so beginning inventory equals several weeks' expected sales. It assumes inventory is in proportion to sales. Too much merchandise may be stocked in peak periods and too little during slow periods:

$$\begin{array}{c}\text{Beginning-of-Month}\\ \text{planned inventory level}\\ \text{(at retail)}\end{array} = \begin{array}{c}\text{Average estimated}\\ \text{weekly sales}\end{array} \times \begin{array}{c}\text{Number of weeks}\\ \text{to be stocked}\end{array}$$

If Handy Hardware forecasts average weekly sales of $10,956.92 from January 1, 2013, through March 31, 2013, and it wants to stock 13 weeks of merchandise (based on expected turnover), beginning inventory would be $142,440:

$$\begin{array}{c}\text{Beginning-of-January}\\ \text{planned inventory level}\\ \text{(at retail)}\end{array} = \$10{,}956.92 \times 13 = \$142{,}440$$

With the **stock-to-sales method**, a retailer wants to maintain a specified ratio of goods on hand to sales. A ratio of 1.3 means that if Handy Hardware plans sales of $69,018 in April 2013, it should have $89,723 worth of merchandise (at retail) available during the month. Like the weeks' supply method, this approach tends to adjust inventory more drastically than changes in sales require.

Yearly stock-to-sales ratios by retail type are provided by sources such as *Industry Norms & Key Business Ratios* (New York: Dun & Bradstreet) and *Annual Statement Studies* (Philadelphia: RMA). A retailer can, thus, compare its ratios with other firms'.

Reduction Planning

Besides forecasting sales, a firm should estimate its expected **retail reductions**, which represent the difference between beginning inventory plus purchases during the period and sales plus ending inventory. Planned reductions incorporate anticipated markdowns (discounts to stimulate sales), employee and other discounts (price cuts to employees, senior citizens, and others), and stock shortages (pilferage, breakage, and bookkeeping errors):

$$\text{Planned reductions} = \begin{array}{l}\text{(Beginning inventory + Planned purchases)}\\ -\text{ (Planned sales + Ending inventory)}\end{array}$$

Reduction planning revolves around two key factors: estimating expected total reductions by budget period and assigning the estimates monthly. The following should be considered in planning reductions: past experience, markdown data for similar retailers, changes in company policies, merchandise carryover from one budget period to another, price trends, and stock-shortage trends.

Past experience is a good starting point. This information can then be compared with the performance of similar firms—by reviewing data on markdowns, discounts, and stock shortages in trade publications. A retailer with higher markdowns than competitors could investigate and correct the situation by adjusting its buying practices and price levels or training sales personnel better.

A retailer must consider its own procedures in reviewing reductions. Policy changes often affect the quantity and timing of markdowns. If a firm expands its assortment of seasonal and fashion merchandise, this would probably lead to a rise in markdowns.

Merchandise carryover, price trends, and stock-shortage trends also affect planning. If such items as gloves and antifreeze are stocked in off seasons, markdowns are often not used to clear out inventory. Yet, the carryover of fad items merely postpones reductions. Price trends of product categories have a strong impact on reductions. Many full computer systems now sell for less than $1,000, down considerably from prior years. This means higher-priced computers must be marked down. Recent stock shortage trends (determined by comparing prior book and physical inventory values) can be used to project future reductions due to employee, customer, and vendor theft; breakage; and bookkeeping mistakes. If a firm has total stock shortages of less than 2 percent of annual sales, it is usually deemed to be doing well. Figure 16-3 shows a checklist to reduce shortages from clerical and handling errors. Suggestions for reducing shortages from theft were covered in Chapter 15.

After determining total reductions, they must be planned by month because reductions as a percentage of sales are not the same during each month. Stock shortages may be much higher during busy periods, when stores are more crowded and transactions happen more quickly.

FIGURE 16-3
A Checklist to Reduce Inventory Shortages Due to Clerical and Handling Errors

Answer yes or no to each of the following questions. A no means corrective action must be taken.

Buying

1. Is the exact quantity of merchandise purchased always specified in the contract?
2. Are special purchase terms clearly noted?
3. Are returns to the vendor recorded properly?

Marking

4. Are retail prices clearly and correctly marked on merchandise?
5. Are markdowns and additional markups recorded by item number and quantity?
6. Does a cashier check with a manager if a price is not marked on an item?
7. Are old price tags removed when an item's price changes?

Handling

8. After receipt, are purchase quantities checked against the order?
9. Is merchandise handled in a systematic manner?
10. Are items sold in bulk (such as produce, sugar, candy) measured accurately?
11. Are damaged, soiled, returned, or other special goods handled separately?

Selling

12. Do sales personnel know correct prices or have easy access to them?
13. Are mis-rings by cashiers made on a very small percentage of sales?
14. Are special terms noted on sales receipts (such as employee discounts)?
15. Are sales receipts numbered and later checked for missing invoices?

Inventory Planning

16. Is a physical inventory conducted at least annually and is a book inventory kept throughout the year?
17. Are the differences between physical inventory and book inventory always explained?

Accounting

18. Are permanent records on all transactions kept and monitored for accuracy?
19. Are both retail and cost data maintained?
20. Are inventory shortages compared with industry averages?

Planning Purchases

The formula for calculating planned purchases for a period is:

$$\text{Planned purchases (at retail)} = \text{Planned sales for the month} + \text{Planned reductions for the month} + \text{Planned end-of-month stock} - \text{Beginning-of-month stock}$$

If Handy Hardware projects June 2013 sales to be $108,666 and total planned reductions to be 5 percent of sales, plans end-of-month inventory at retail to be $72,000, and has a beginning-of-month inventory at retail of $80,000, planned purchases for June are:

$$\text{Planned purchases (at retail)} = \$108{,}666 + \$5{,}433 + \$72{,}000 - \$80{,}000 = \$106{,}099$$

Because Handy Hardware expects 2013 merchandise costs to be about 60 percent of retail selling price, its plan is to purchase $63,659 of goods at cost in June 2013:

$$\text{Planned purchases (at cost)} = \text{Planned purchases at retail} \times \text{Merchandise costs as a percentage of selling price}$$

$$= \$106{,}99 \times 0.60 = \$63{,}659$$

The OTB Book (www.otb-retail.com) is easy-to-use inexpensive software.

Open-to-buy is the difference between planned purchases and the purchase commitments already made by a buyer for a given period, often a month. It represents the amount the buyer has left to spend for that month and is reduced each time a purchase is made. At the beginning of a month, a firm's planned purchases and open-to-buy are equal if no purchase commitments have been made before that month starts. Open-to-buy is recorded at cost.

At Handy Hardware, the buyer has made purchase commitments for June 2013 in the amount of $55,000 at retail. Accordingly, Handy's open-to-buy at retail for June is $51,099:

$$\begin{array}{c}\text{Open-to-buy}\\ \text{(at retail)}\end{array} = \begin{array}{l}\text{Planned purchases for the month}\\ -\ \text{Purchase commitments for that month}\end{array}$$

$$= \$106{,}099 - \$55{,}000 = \$51{,}099$$

To calculate the June 2013 open-to-buy at cost, $51,099 is multiplied by Handy Hardware's merchandise costs as a percentage of selling price:

$$\begin{array}{c}\text{Open-to-buy}\\ \text{(at cost)}\end{array} = \begin{array}{l}\text{Open-to-buy at retail}\\ \times\ \text{Merchandise costs as a percentage of selling price}\end{array}$$

$$= \$51{,}099 \times 0.60 = \$30{,}659$$

The open-to-buy concept has two major strengths: (1) It maintains a specified relationship between inventory and planned sales; this avoids overbuying and underbuying. (2) It lets a firm adjust purchases to reflect changes in sales, markdowns, and so on. If Handy revises its June 2013 sales forecast to $120,000 (from $108,666), it automatically increases planned purchases and open-to-buy by $11,334 at retail and $6,800 at cost.

It is advisable for a retailer to keep at least a small open-to-buy figure for as long as possible—to take advantage of special deals, purchase new models when introduced, and fill in items that sell out. An open-to-buy limit sometimes must be exceeded due to underestimated demand (low sales forecasts). A retailer should not be so rigid that merchandising personnel are unable to have the discretion (employee empowerment) to purchase below-average-priced items when the open-to-buy is not really open.

Planning Profit Margins

In preparing a profitable merchandise budget, a retailer must consider planned net sales, retail operating expenses, profit, and retail reductions in pricing merchandise:

$$\begin{array}{c}\text{Required initial}\\ \text{markup percentage}\end{array} = \frac{\text{Planned retail expenses} + \text{Planned profit} + \text{Planned reductions}}{\text{Planned net sales} + \text{Planned reductions}}$$

The required markup is a companywide average. Individual items may be priced according to demand and other factors, as long as the average is met. A fuller markup discussion is in Chapter 17. The concept of initial markup is introduced here for continuity in the description of merchandise budgeting.

Handy has an overall 2013 sales forecast of $881,080 and expects annual expenses to be $290,000. Reductions are projected at $44,000. The total net dollar profit margin goal is $60,000 (6.8 percent of sales). Its required initial markup is 42.6 percent:

$$\begin{array}{c}\text{Required initial}\\ \text{markup percentage}\end{array} = \frac{\$290{,}000 + \$60{,}000 + \$44{,}000}{\$881{,}080 + \$44{,}000} = 42.6\%$$

$$\begin{array}{c}\text{Required initial}\\ \text{markup percentage}\\ \text{(all factors expressed}\\ \text{as a percentage of}\\ \text{net sales)}\end{array} = \frac{32.9\% + 6.8\% + 5.0\%}{100.0\% + 5.0\%} = 42.6\%$$

UNIT CONTROL SYSTEMS

Inventory Magic (www.excelmagic.com) offers unit control capabilities in its spreadsheet-based software.

Unit control systems deal with quantities of merchandise in units rather than in dollars. Information typically reveals:

- Items selling well and those selling poorly.
- Opportunities and problems in terms of price, color, style, size, and so on.

- The quantity of goods on hand (if book inventory is used). This minimizes overstocking and understocking.
- An indication of inventory age, highlighting candidates for markdowns or promotions.
- The optimal time to reorder merchandise.
- Experiences with alternative sources (vendors) when problems arise.
- The level of inventory and sales for each item in every store branch. This improves the transfer of goods between branches and alerts salespeople as to which branches have desired products. Also, less stock can be held in individual stores, reducing costs.

Physical Inventory Systems

A *physical inventory unit control system* is similar to a physical inventory dollar control system. However, the latter is concerned with the financial value of inventory, while a unit control system looks at the number of units by item classification. With unit control, inventory levels are monitored either by visual inspection or actual count. See Figure 16-4.

In a visual inspection system, merchandise is placed on pegboard (or similar) displays, with each item numbered on the back or on a stock card. Minimum inventory quantities are noted, and sales personnel reorder when inventory reaches the minimum level. This is accurate only if items are placed in numerical order on displays (and sold accordingly). The system is used in the housewares and hardware displays of various discount and hardware stores. Although easy to maintain and inexpensive, it does not provide data on the rate of sales of individual items. And minimum stock quantities may be arbitrarily defined and not drawn from in-depth analysis.

The other physical inventory system, actual counting, means regularly compiling the number of units on hand. This approach records—in units—inventory on hand, purchases, sales volume, and shortages during specified periods. A stock-counting system requires more clerical work but lets a firm obtain sales data for given periods and stock-to-sales relationships as of the time of each count. A physical system is not as sophisticated as a book system. It is more useful

FIGURE 16-4

The Time-Consuming Nature of Physical Inventory Systems

Conducting a physical inventory can be extremely time consuming. Think about how much effort an apparel and accessories retailer with a large merchandise mix, such as the one depicted here, would have to exert.

Source: monika3steps/ Shutterstock.com. Reprinted by permission

with low-value items having predictable sales. Handy Hardware could use the system for its insulation tape:

	Number of Rolls of Tape for the Period 12/1/12–12/31/12
Beginning inventory, December 1, 2012	100
Total purchases for period	70
Total units available for sale	170
Closing inventory, December 31, 2012	60
Sales and shortages for period	110

Perpetual Inventory Systems

A *perpetual inventory unit control system* keeps a running total of the number of units handled by a retailer through record keeping entries that adjust for sales, returns, transfers to other departments or stores, receipt of shipments, and other transactions. All additions to and subtractions from beginning inventory are recorded. Such a system can be applied manually, use merchandise tags processed by computers, or rely on point-of-sale devices such as optical scanners.

Point-of-sale (POS) systems—which are widely used today, even by many small retailers—feed data from merchandise tags or product labels directly to in-store computers for immediate data processing. Computer-based systems are quicker, more accurate, and of higher quality than manual ones. A manual system requires employees to gather data by examining sales checks, merchandise receipts, transfer requests, and other documents. Data are then coded and tabulated. A merchandise tagging system relies on pre-printed tags with data by department, classification, vendor, style, date of receipt, color, and/or material. When an item is sold, a copy of the tag is removed and sent to a tabulating facility for computer analysis. Since pre-printed tags are processed in batches, they can be used by smaller retailers that subscribe to service bureaus and by branches of chains (with data processed at a central location).

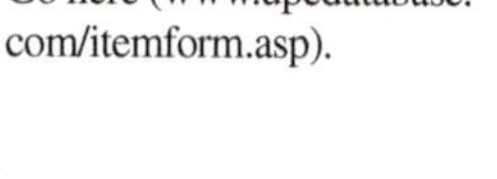

Current POS systems are easy to network, have battery backup capabilities, and run with standard PCs and software. Many of these systems use optical scanners to transfer data from products to computers by wands or other devices that pass over sensitized strips on the items. Figure 16-5 shows how barcoding works. As noted earlier, the UPC is the dominant format for coding data onto merchandise. This is how to interpret a barcode:

1. The *numbering system* contains two (or possibly three) digits to identify the nation (or region) that assigns the manufacturer codes in that geographic area. In the typical UPC code, the initial number digit is 0—which is not shown on a label.
2. The *manufacturer code* is a series of distinctive numbers assigned to specific manufacturers by the coding authority of the nation or region. All of a given company's products get the same manufacturer code—which is usually 5 numbers.

Internationally, the Cost of Living Varies Widely

According to ECA International (www.eca-international.com), a global human resources firm, in 2011, six Australian cities were among the top 30 most costly cities in the world. This is surprising, since not long ago, not one Australian city ranked in the top 100 in costs. The rapid cost increase in these cities was due to the strength of the Australian dollar, as well as rapidly rising prices for food and energy.

Other places where the cost of living has increased significantly are Singapore, which rose to number 36 in 2011 from 68 in 2010 (based on the strength of the Singapore dollar); and Caracas, Venezuela, which rose from number 91 to number 14 (due to rapid inflation). In comparison, due to a weak U.S. dollar, no United States city ranked in the top 30. Manhattan, New York, the country's most costly city, fell to number 44 in 2011 from number 28 in 2010. Honolulu, the second most costly U.S. city dropped to number 62 in 2011 from number 40 in 2010. At the same time, the cost for a movie ticket in U.S. dollars was $24 in Tokyo, Japan.

ECA International's ranking is based on comparing the cost of living for expatriates living abroad. The survey includes food and beverages, basic goods and services, and some entertainment items; but it specifically does not include housing, utilities, car purchases, and school expenses.

Source: Venessa Wong, "Which City in the World Has $24 Movie Tickets?" www.businessweek.com (June 10, 2011).

FIGURE 16-5

How Does a UPC-Based Scanner System Work?

As described by eHow (www.ehow.com/how-does_4909785_how-grocery-scanners-work.html): "A grocery store scanner can read, decode, and charge consumers in a matter of seconds. Every grocery store scanner is a bar code scanner equipped with a laser beam light that translates the binary code of every UPC into its coinciding price. When the items are scanned at the register, the UPC code is identified from the data base and the price is entered into the register, almost simultaneously. Each UPC code has been assigned a price that has been stored into the grocer's data base."

Source: scyther5/Shutterstock.com. Reprinted by permission.

3. The *product code* is determined by each manufacturer—which can assign any 5-digit product codes that it wants to designate different products by that company.
4. The *check digit* is an additional number that helps to verify that a specific barcode is scanned accurately. It is based on the other digits of a barcode.[7]

Many retailers combine perpetual and physical systems, whereby items accounting for a large proportion of sales are controlled by a perpetual system and other items are controlled by a physical inventory system. Thus, attention is properly placed on the retailer's most important products.

Unit Control Systems in Practice

Conducting a physical inventory is extremely time-consuming and labor-intensive. It is also crucial: "Having too much stock, or too little, is costly." The First Insight, the consulting firm, has found that each year U.S. retailers lose about $280 billion due to holding excessive inventory.[8] And the costs of not having sufficient inventory on hand are estimated to be more than $50 billion annually.

Consider this: According to Ted Hurlbut, writing in *Inc.*, retailers—especially smaller ones—need to take into account much more than invoice and freight costs. They need to look at inventory-carrying costs, theft rates, product obsolescence if items are not sold quickly, and the cost of lost sales. Together, these inventory-related costs can mount up and have a big impact on profits. Having too much inventory can be as big a problem (or worse) than running out of merchandise, due to both the costs and the markdowns that might be necessary. As Hulbert says:

> When stores are overstocked, it's harder for customers to find what they came in for and more likely they'll leave without it. Aisles can become narrower, discouraging customers from exploring deeper into the store. If displays are overstuffed, customers become afraid to touch, afraid of breaking or starting an avalanche on a display piled too high. When there are too many things from which to choose, customers can become paralyzed. If the retailer hasn't been able to focus the assortment, how can the customer know with confidence that they'll be happy with what they purchase?[9]

FINANCIAL INVENTORY CONTROL: INTEGRATING DOLLAR AND UNIT CONCEPTS

Oracle (www.oracle.com/oms/retail) markets sophisticated inventory analysis software.

Until now, we have discussed dollar and unit control separately. In practice, they are linked. A decision on how many units to buy is affected by dollar investments, inventory turnover, quantity discounts, warehousing and insurance costs, and so on. Three aspects of financial inventory control are covered next: stock turnover and gross margin return on investment, when to reorder, and how much to reorder.

Stock Turnover and Gross Margin Return on Investment

Stock turnover represents the number of times during a specific period, usually one year, that the average inventory on hand is sold. It can be measured by store, product line, department, and vendor. With high turnover, inventory investments are productive on a per-dollar basis, items are fresh, there are fewer losses due to changes in styles, and interest, insurance, breakage, and warehousing costs are reduced. A retailer can raise stock turnover by reducing its assortment, eliminating or having little inventory for slow-selling items, buying in a timely way, applying quick response (QR) inventory planning, and using reliable suppliers.

Stock turnover can be computed in units or dollars (at retail or cost). The choice of a formula depends on the retailer's accounting system:

$$\begin{array}{c}\text{Annual rate of}\\ \text{stock turnover}\\ \text{(in units)}\end{array} = \frac{\text{Number of units sold during year}}{\text{Average inventory on hand (in units)}}$$

$$\begin{array}{c}\text{Annual rate of}\\ \text{stock turnover}\\ \text{(in retail dollars)}\end{array} = \frac{\text{Net yearly sales}}{\text{Average inventory on hand (at retail)}}$$

$$\begin{array}{c}\text{Annual rate of}\\ \text{stock turnover}\\ \text{(at cost)}\end{array} = \frac{\text{Cost of goods sold during the year}}{\text{Average inventory on hand (at cost)}}$$

In computing turnover, the average inventory for the entire period needs to be reflected. Turnover rates are invalid if the true average is not used, as occurs if a firm mistakenly views the inventory level of a peak or slow month as the yearly average. Table 16-10 shows annual turnover rates for various retailers. Gasoline service stations, convenience stores, and grocery stores have the highest rates. They rely on sales volume for their success. Jewelry stores, shoe stores,

TABLE 16-10 Annual Median Stock Turnover Rates for Selected Types of Retailers, 2011

Type of Retailer	Annual Median Stock Turnover Rate (Times)
Car dealers (new)	5.4
Convenience stores	23.4
Department stores	3.4
Drug and proprietary stores	11.3
Family clothing stores	3.1
Florists	6.2
Furniture stores	3.4
Gasoline service stations	42.6
Gift stores	3.1
Grocery stores	14.5
Hardware stores	2.6
Home centers	5.4
Household appliance stores	4.5
Jewelry stores	1.3
Lumber and other materials dealers	5.7
Men's and boys' clothing stores	2.5
Online retailers	6.2
Shoe stores	2.5
Women's clothing stores	4.3

Source: Extracted and compiled by the authors from www.retailowner.com/StoreBenchmarkRatios.aspx, based on data in *Annual Statement Studies* (Philadelphia: RMA, 2011–2012).

hardware stores, and some clothing stores have very low rates. They require larger profit margins on each item sold and maintain a sizable assortment.

Despite the advantages of high turnover, buying items in small amounts may also result in the loss of quantity discounts and in higher transportation charges. Because high turnover might be due to a limited assortment, some sales may be lost, and profits may be lower if prices are reduced to move inventory quickly. The return on investment depends on both turnover and profit per unit.

Learn more about GMROI (www.jewelerprofit.com/GMROI_Worksheet.html).

Gross margin return on investment (GMROI) shows the relationship between the gross margin in dollars (total dollar operating profits) and the average inventory investment (at cost) by combining profitability and sales-to-stock measures:

$$\text{GMROI} = \frac{\text{Gross margin in dollars}}{\text{Net sales}} \times \frac{\text{Net sales}}{\text{Average inventory at cost}}$$

$$= \frac{\text{Gross margin in dollars}}{\text{Average inventory at cost}}$$

The gross margin in dollars equals net sales minus the cost of goods sold. The gross margin percentage is derived by dividing dollar gross margin by net sales. A sales-to-stock ratio is derived by dividing net sales by average inventory at cost. That ratio may be converted to stock turnover by multiplying it by [(100 – Gross margin percentage)/100].

GMROI is a useful concept for several reasons:

- It shows how diverse retailers can prosper. A supermarket may have a gross margin of 20 percent and a sales-to-stock ratio of 15—a GMROI of 300 percent. A women's clothing store may have a gross margin of 50 percent and a sales-to-stock ratio of 6—a GMROI of 300 percent. Both firms have the same GMROI due to the trade-off between item profitability and turnover.
- It is a good indicator of a manager's performance because it focuses on factors controlled by that person. Interdepartmental comparisons can also be made.
- It is simple to plan and understand, and data collection is easy.
- It can be determined if GMROI performance is consistent with other company goals.

The gross margin percentage and the sales-to-stock ratio must be studied individually. If only overall GMROI is reviewed, performance may be assessed improperly.

When to Reorder

One way to control inventory investment is to systematically set stock levels at which new orders must be placed. Such a stock level is called a **reorder point**, and it is based on three factors. **Order lead time** is the period from the date an order is placed by a retailer to the date merchandise is ready for sale (received, price-marked, and put on the selling floor). **Usage rate** refers to average sales per day, in units, of merchandise. **Safety stock** is the extra inventory that protects against out-of-stock conditions due to unexpected demand and delays in delivery. It depends on the firm's policy toward running out of items.

This is the formula for a retailer that does not plan to carry safety stock. It believes customer demand is stable and that its orders are promptly filled by suppliers:

$$\text{Reorder point} = \text{Usage rate} \times \text{Lead time}$$

If Handy Hardware sells 10 paintbrushes a day and needs 8 days to order, receive, and display them, it has a reorder point of 80 brushes. It would reorder brushes once inventory on hand reaches 80. By the time brushes from that order are placed on shelves (8 days later), stock on hand will be zero, and the new stock will replenish the inventory.

This strategy is proper only when Handy has a steady customer demand of 10 paintbrushes daily and it takes exactly 8 days to complete all stages in the ordering process. This does not normally occur. If customers buy 15 brushes per day during the month, Handy would run out of stock in 5-1/3 days and be without brushes for 2-2/3 days. If an order takes 10 days to process, Handy would have no brushes for 2 days, despite correctly estimating demand. Figure 16-6 shows how stockouts may occur.

FIGURE 16-6
How Stockouts May Occur

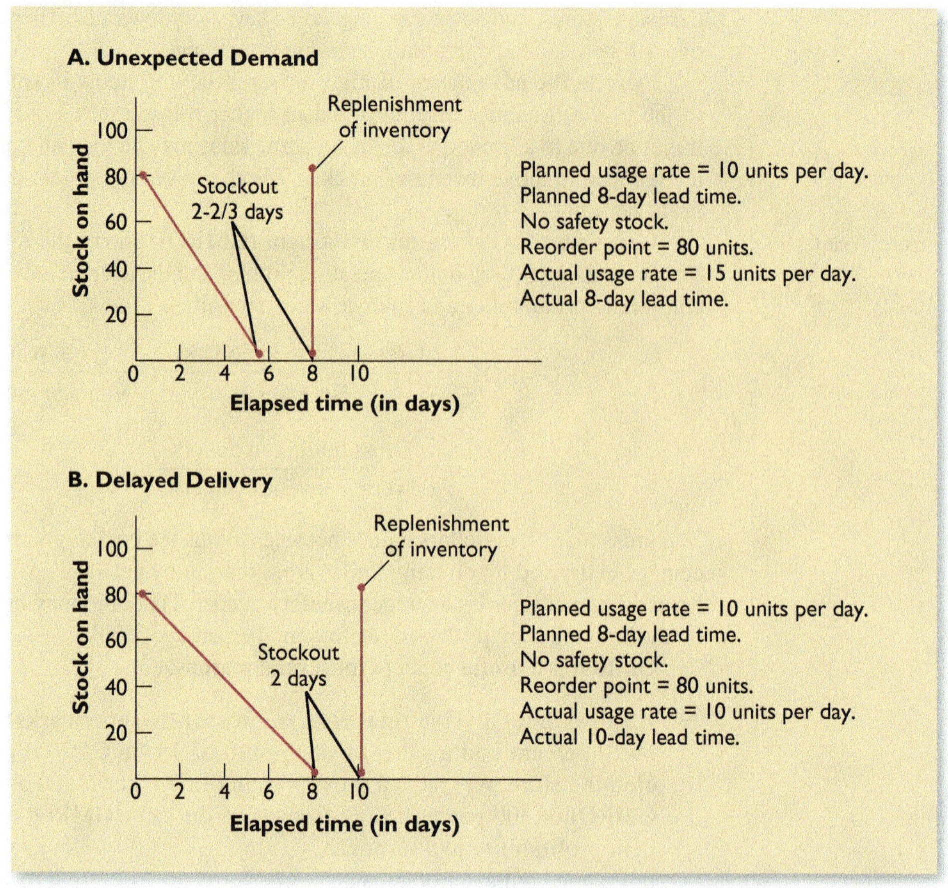

For a retailer interested in keeping a safety stock, the reorder formula becomes:

$$\text{Reorder point} = (\text{Usage rate} \times \text{Lead time}) + \text{Safety stock}$$

Suppose Handy Hardware decides on safety stock of 30 percent for paintbrushes; its reorder point is $(10 \times 8) + (0.30 \times 80) = 80 + 24 = 104$. Handy still expects to sell an average of 10 brushes per day and receive orders in an average of 8 days. The safety stock of 24 extra brushes is kept on hand to protect against unexpected demand or a late shipment.

By combining a perpetual inventory system and reorder point calculations, ordering can be computerized and an **automatic reordering system** can be mechanically activated when stock-on-hand reaches the reorder point. However, intervention by a buyer or manager must be possible, especially if monthly sales fluctuate greatly.

How Much to Reorder

A firm placing large orders generally reduces ordering costs but increases inventory-holding costs. A firm placing small orders often minimizes inventory-holding costs while ordering costs may rise (unless EDI and a QR inventory system are used).

Economic order quantity (EOQ) is the quantity per order (in units) that minimizes the total costs of processing orders and holding inventory. Order-processing costs include computer time, order forms, labor, and handling new goods. Holding costs include warehousing, inventory investment, insurance, taxes, depreciation, deterioration, and pilferage. EOQ calculations can be done by large and small firms.

As Figure 16-7 shows, order-processing costs drop as the order quantity (in units) goes up because fewer orders are needed for the same total annual quantity, and inventory-holding costs rise as the order quantity goes up because more units must be held in inventory and they are

FIGURE 16-7
Economic Order Quantity

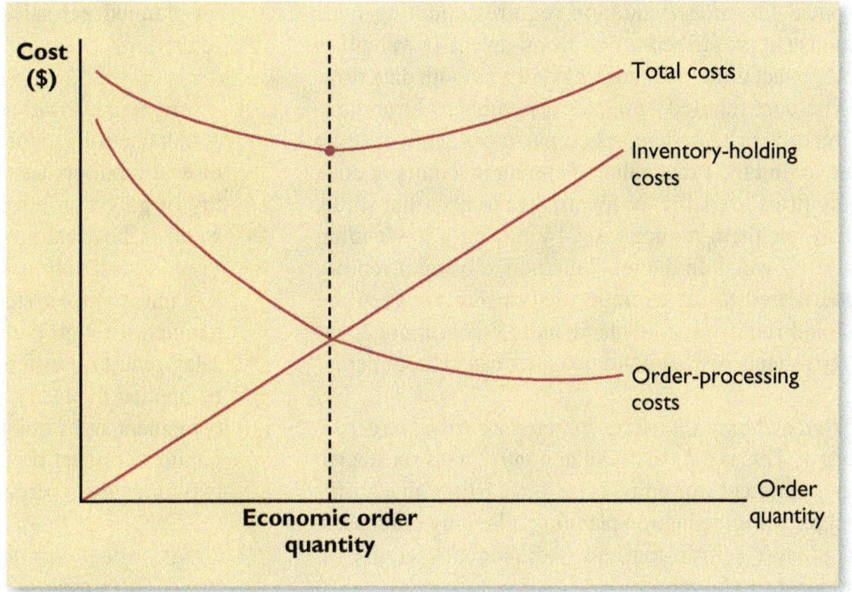

kept for longer periods. The two costs are summed into a total cost curve. Mathematically, the economic order quantity is:

$$EOQ = \sqrt{\frac{2DS}{IC}}$$

where
EOQ = quantity per order (in units)
D = annual demand (in units)
S = costs to place an order (in dollars)
I = percentage of annual carrying cost to unit cost
C = unit cost of an item (in dollars)

Handy estimates it can sell 150 power tool sets per year. They cost $90 each. Breakage, insurance, tied-up capital, and pilferage equal 10 percent of the costs of the sets (or $9 each). Order costs are $25 per order. The economic order quantity is 29:

$$EOQ = \sqrt{\frac{2(150)(\$25)}{(0.10)(\$90)}} = \sqrt{\frac{\$7{,}500}{\$9}} = 29$$

The EOQ formula must often be modified to take into account changes in demand, quantity discounts, and variable ordering and holding costs.

Chapter Summary

1. *To describe the major aspects of financial merchandise planning and management.* The purpose of financial merchandise management is to stipulate which products are bought by the retailer, when, and in what quantity. Dollar control monitors inventory investment, while unit control relates to the amount of merchandise handled. Financial merchandise management encompasses accounting methods, merchandise forecasts and budgets, unit control, and integrated dollar and unit controls.

2. *To explain the cost and retail methods of accounting.* The two accounting techniques for retailers are the cost and retail methods of inventory valuation. Physical and book (perpetual) procedures are possible with each.

Physical inventory valuation requires counting merchandise at prescribed times. Book inventory valuation relies on accurate bookkeeping and a smooth data flow.

The cost method obligates a retailer to have careful records or to code costs on packages. This must be done to find the exact value of ending inventory at cost. Many firms use LIFO accounting to project that value, which lets them reduce taxes by having a low ending inventory value. In the retail method, closing inventory value is tied to the average relationship between the cost and retail value of merchandise. That more accurately reflects market conditions but can be complex.

3. *To study the merchandise forecasting and budgeting process.* This is a form of dollar control with six stages: designating control units, sales forecasting, inventory-level planning, reduction planning, planning purchases, and planning profit margins. Adjustments require all later stages to be modified.

   Control units—merchandise categories for which data are gathered—must be narrow to isolate problems and opportunities with specific product lines. Sales forecasting may be the key stage in the merchandising and budgeting process. Through inventory-level planning, a firm sets merchandise quantities for specified periods through the basic stock, percentage variation, weeks' supply, and/or stock-to-sales methods. Reduction planning estimates expected markdowns, discounts, and stock shortages. Planned purchases are linked to planned sales, reductions, and ending and beginning inventory. Profit margins depend on planned net sales, operating expenses, profit, and reductions.

4. *To examine alternative methods of inventory unit control.* A unit control system involves physical units of merchandise. It monitors best-sellers and poor-sellers, the quantity of goods on hand, inventory age, reorder time, and so on. A physical inventory unit control system may use visual inspection or stock counting. A perpetual inventory unit control system keeps a running total of the units handled through record keeping entries that adjust for sales, returns, transfers, and so on. A perpetual system can be applied manually, by merchandise tags processed by computers, or by point-of-sale devices. Virtually all larger retailers conduct regular complete physical inventories; two-thirds use a perpetual inventory system.

5. *To integrate dollar and unit merchandising control concepts.* Three aspects of financial inventory management integrate dollar and unit control concepts: stock turnover and gross margin return on investment, when to reorder, and how much to reorder. Stock turnover is the number of times during a period that average inventory on hand is sold. Gross margin return on investment shows the relationship between gross margin in dollars (total dollar operating profits) and average inventory investment (at cost). A reorder point calculation—when to reorder—includes the retailer's usage rate, order lead time, and safety stock. The economic order quantity—how much to reorder—shows how big an order to place, based on both ordering and inventory costs.

Key Terms

financial merchandise management (p. 399)
dollar control (p. 399)
unit control (p. 399)
merchandise available for sale (p. 399)
cost of goods sold (p. 399)
gross profit (p. 399)
net profit (p. 399)
cost method of accounting (p. 400)
physical inventory system (p. 401)
book inventory system (perpetual inventory system) (p. 401)
FIFO (first-in-first-out) method (p. 401)
LIFO (last-in-first-out) method (p. 401)
retail method of accounting (p. 402)
cost complement (p. 403)
control units (p. 405)
classification merchandising (p. 406)
monthly sales index (p. 407)
basic stock method (p. 409)
percentage variation method (p. 409)
weeks' supply method (p. 410)
stock-to-sales method (p. 410)
retail reductions (p. 410)
open-to-buy (p. 411)
stock turnover (p. 416)
gross margin return on investment (GMROI) (p. 417)
reorder point (p. 417)
order lead time (p. 417)
usage rate (p. 417)
safety stock (p. 417)
automatic reordering system (p. 418)
economic order quantity (EOQ) (p. 418)

Questions for Discussion

1. Which retailers can best use a perpetual inventory system based on the cost method? Explain your answer.
2. The FIFO method seems more logical than the LIFO method, because it assumes the first merchandise purchased is the first merchandise sold. So, why do more retailers use LIFO?
3. Explain the basic premise of the retail method of accounting. Present an example.
4. Why should a local appliance store designate control units, even though this may be time-consuming?
5. Why use sophisticated weather forecasting services if daily weather predictions tend to be inaccurate?

6. Contrast the weeks' supply method and the percentage variation method of merchandise planning.
7. Present two situations in which it would be advisable for a retailer to take a markdown instead of carry over merchandise from one budget period to another.
8. A retailer has yearly sales of $900,000. Inventory on January 1 is $360,000 (at cost). During the year, $660,000 of merchandise (at cost) is purchased. The ending inventory is $325,000 (at cost). Operating costs are $90,000. Calculate the cost of goods sold and net profit, and set up a profit-and-loss statement. There are no retail reductions in this problem.
9. A retailer has a beginning monthly inventory valued at $100,000 at retail and $61,000 at cost. Net purchases during the month are $190,000 at retail and $115,000 at cost. Transportation charges are $10,500. Sales are $225,000. Markdowns and discounts equal $30,000. A physical inventory at the end of the month shows merchandise valued at $15,000 (at retail) on hand. Compute the following:
   a. Total merchandise available for sale—at cost and at retail.
   b. Cost complement.
   c. Ending retail book value of inventory.
   d. Stock shortages.
   e. Adjusted ending retail book value.
   f. Gross profit.
10. The sales of a full-line discount store are listed. Calculate the monthly sales indexes. What do they mean?

January	$300,000	May	$360,000	September	$360,000
February	315,000	June	330,000	October	300,000
March	315,000	July	270,000	November	390,000
April	360,000	August	330,000	December	510,000

11. If the planned average monthly stock for the discount store in Question 10 is $420,000 (at retail), how much inventory should be planned for August if the retailer uses the percentage variation method? Comment on this retailer's choice of the percentage variation method.
12. The store in Questions 10 and 11 knows its cost complement for all merchandise purchased last year was 0.61; it projects this to remain constant. It expects to begin and end December with inventory valued at $140,000 at retail and estimates December reductions to be $18,000. The firm already has purchase commitments for December worth $50,000 (at retail). What is the open-to-buy at cost for December?

Note: At our Web site (www.pearsonhighered.com/bermanevans), there are several math problems related to the material in this chapter so that you may review these concepts.

Web-Based Exercise

Visit the benchmarking section of the Retail Owners Institute Web site (www.retailowner.com/StoreBenchmarkRatios.aspx). Describe how a department store executive could use the information found at the site in its financial merchandise management efforts. Describe how a gift store could use the information found at the site.

Note: Also stop by our Web site (www.pearsonhighered.com/bermanevans) to experience a number of highly interactive, appealing Web exercises based on actual company demonstrations and sample materials related to retailing.

17 Pricing in Retailing

Chapter Objectives

1. To describe the role of pricing in a retail strategy and to show that pricing decisions must be made in an integrated and adaptive manner

2. To examine the impact of consumers; government; manufacturers, wholesalers, and other suppliers; and current and potential competitors on pricing decisions

3. To present a framework for developing a retail price strategy: objectives, broad policy, basic strategy, implementation, and adjustments

Retail price setting can take one of several approaches. Some retailers offer deep discounts and no-frills shopping (think Costco), others offer everyday low pricing (think Wal-Mart), others offer mid-level prices and promote special sales (think Macy's), and still others set prices that are rarely discounted (think Apple stores). A new entrant to the retail pricing mix is the "real-time deal," whereby online firms, usually driven by social media, offer deals for consumers willing to make a purchase during a defined—and short—time period.

Real-time deal revenues have skyrocketed in recent years and now generate billions of dollars in annual sales. Here's how the process works: (1) A social media firm sets up a site and invites people to sign up for shopping privileges and to ask friends to join. (2) The firm arranges with local retailers to give a discount of 25 to 75 percent off the regular price for one good or service. (3) Consumers are sent an E-mail or other online message to visit the social media firm's site and buy the "deal of the day," which often lasts for 24 hours or less. (4) The consumers buy a certificate for the good or service from the social media firm and then redeem it. (5) The social media firm gets a fee from the retailer.

Among the leaders in this field are Groupon (www.groupon.com), LivingSocial (www.livingsocial.com), and Gilt City (www.giltcity.com) with deals by geographic area. Consumers are attracted by the large discount on a price that may regularly be $25, $50, $100, or even more. Retailers are attracted because they can gain new customers. But the times ahead will prove to be more difficult for individual social media firms due to the growth in competition. And this critique by Wharton professor David Reibstein is also important: "The very loyal customer who pays full retail price will start to resent [those who are getting the discount], particularly if you go to a restaurant [and you are] willing to pay the full retail price. If everybody else has a discount coupon and is paying less, you will feel like an idiot. So retailers start developing some of that resentment in their best customers."[1]

Source: BeTA-Artworks / fotolia.com.

Overview

Learn about the complexities of setting prices (www.ehow.com/how_4473994_set-retail-prices.html).

Goods and services must be priced in a way that both achieves profitability for the retailer and satisfies customers. A pricing strategy must be consistent with the retailer's overall image (positioning), sales, profit, and return on investment goals.

There are three basic pricing options for a retailer: (1) A *discount orientation* uses low prices as the major competitive advantage. A low-price image, fewer shopping frills, and low per-unit profit margins mean a target market of price-oriented customers, low operating costs, and high inventory turnover. Off-price retailers and full-line discount stores are in this category. (2) With an *at-the-market orientation*, the retailer has average prices. It offers solid service and a nice atmosphere to middle-class shoppers. Margins are moderate to good, and average to above-average quality products are stocked. This firm may find it hard to expand its price range, and it may be squeezed by retailers positioned as discounters or prestige stores. Traditional department stores and many drugstores are in this category. (3) Through an *upscale orientation*, a prestigious image is the retailer's major competitive advantage. A smaller target market, higher expenses, and lower turnover mean customer loyalty, distinctive services and products, and high per-unit profit margins. Upscale department stores and specialty stores are in this category.

Nordstrom is one of the world's largest online shoe retailers (http://shop.nordstrom.com/c/shoes), with its usual upscale prices and service.

A key to successful retailing is offering a good *value* in the consumer's mind—for the price orientation chosen. At Sports Authority, "Our customers are passionate about sports they pursue. We understand the passion that comes with being dedicated to a goal. We are dedicated to providing customers with the best shopping experience possible by consistently providing great brands at great values. We are dedicated to increasing value by providing industry-leading customer service and product knowledge. We are dedicated to you, and helping you take your game to the next level."[2]

Every customer, whether buying an inexpensive $4 ream of paper or a $40 ream of embossed, personalized stationery, wants to feel his or her purchase represents a good value. The consumer is not necessarily looking only for the best price. He or she is often interested in the best value—which may be reflected in a superior shopping experience. See Figures 17-1 and 17-2.

FIGURE 17-1
At Barnes & Noble: A Huge Selection and Special Discounts for Members

Source: Reprinted by permission of Susan V. Berry, Retail Image Consulting, Inc.

FIGURE 17-2

Feeling Ripped Off

Consumers do not like feeling overcharged, whether it's for a gallon of gas or a new car or a lawn care service. They want to believe that they are getting a fair value.

Source: Laura Gangi Pond/Shutterstock.com. Reprinted by permission.

Consider this analysis of H&M's strategy:

> Customers are fashionable and trendy, and they see shopping as a social activity. They buy fashionable clothes each season and want to follow trends without spending a lot of money. To fulfill customer needs, H&M launched everyday-low-price products. It also invited top designers such as Karl Lagerfeld to be partners in a new collection. We believe H&M is successfully combining the best design with an inexpensive clothing label. To maintain low prices, H&M has to give up some customer service. Cashiers usually have long lines. Sales staff is relatively less. It is not easy to get help for problems.[3]

Another factor shaping today's pricing environment for retailers of all types is the ease by which a shopper can compare prices on the Web. When a consumer could only do price comparisons by visiting individual stores, the process was time-consuming—which limited many people's willingness to shop around. Now, with a few clicks of a computer mouse, a shopper can quickly gain online price information from several retailers in just minutes—without leaving home. Web sites such as PriceGrabber.com, NexTag, Shopping.com, and Mysimon.com make comparison shopping very simple: As the Smarter.com Web site notes: "Thanks for visiting Smarter.com—your one-stop shopping tool for finding the best deals on a great selection of products from trustworthy Web sites. By displaying product information from hundreds of online merchants, Smarter.com helps you save time and money while you shop the products you want and need—all in one place. Our mission is to help you make smart buying decisions so you can make the most of your time and money."[4]

The interaction of price with other retailing mix elements can be illustrated by BE's Toy City, a hypothetical discounter. It has a broad strategy consisting of:

- A target market of price-conscious families that shop for inexpensive toys ($9 to $12).
- A limited range of merchandise quality (mostly end-of-season closeouts and manufacturer overruns).
- Self-service in an outlet mall location.
- A good assortment supported by quantity purchases at deep discounts from suppliers.
- An image of efficiency and variety.

In this chapter, we divide retail pricing into two major sections: the external factors affecting a price strategy and the steps in a price strategy. At our site (www.pearsonhighered.com/bermanevans), there are several links to information on setting a price strategy.

EXTERNAL FACTORS AFFECTING A RETAIL PRICE STRATEGY

Several factors (discussed next) have an impact on a retail pricing strategy, as shown in Figure 17-3. Sometimes, the factors have a minor effect. In other cases, they severely restrict a firm's pricing options.

The Consumer and Retail Pricing[5]

Retailers should understand the **price elasticity of demand**—the sensitivity of customers to price changes in terms of the quantities they will buy—because there is often a relationship between price and consumer purchases and perceptions. If small percentage changes in price lead to substantial percentage changes in the number of units bought, demand is *price elastic.* This occurs when the urgency to purchase is low or there are acceptable substitutes. If large percentage changes in price lead to small percentage changes in the number of units bought, demand is *price inelastic.* Then purchase urgency is high or there are no acceptable substitutes (as takes place with brand or retailer loyalty). *Unitary elasticity* occurs when percentage changes in price are directly offset by percentage changes in quantity.

One look at Godiva's Web site (www.godiva.com) and you'll know why demand for its products is inelastic.

Price elasticity is computed by dividing the percentage change in the quantity demanded by the percentage change in the price charged. Because purchases generally decline as prices go up, elasticity tends to be a negative number:

$$\text{Elasticity} = \frac{\dfrac{\text{Quantity 1} - \text{Quantity 2}}{\text{Quantity 1} + \text{Quantity 2}}}{\dfrac{\text{Price 1} - \text{Price 2}}{\text{Price 1} + \text{Price 2}}}$$

Table 17-1 shows price elasticity for a 1,000-seat movie theater (with elasticities converted to positive numbers) that offers second-run films. The quantity demanded (tickets sold) declines at each price from $6.00 to $10.00. Demand is inelastic from $6.00 to $7.00 and $7.00 to $8.00; ticket receipts rise since the percentage price change is more than the percentage change in

FIGURE 17-3
Factors Affecting a Retail Price Strategy

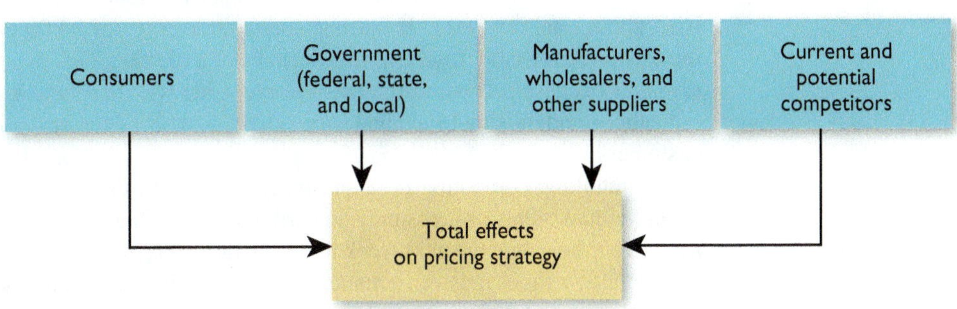

Game Stores: Africa's Largest Discount Retailer

Game Stores' (www.game.co.za) first outlet opened in South Africa and offered a wide variety of national brands at discount prices. In 1998, at a time when Game had 28 stores, the chain was acquired by Massmart (www.massmart.co.za), a wholesale-and-retail conglomerate. As of 2012, there were 80 Game stores in South Africa. In addition, the chain operates around a dozen other stores in 10 major African markets—including Ghana, Mozambique, Namibia, Nigeria, Uganda, and Zambia.

Game responded well to the recent recession in South Africa by building upon its portfolio of private-label products that were sold at lower price points than national brands. Private labels now make up 11.4 percent of Game's sales. Its medium-term goal is for private label to make up 15 percent of its total sales.

Game has improved its supply chain efficiency. It has consolidated the logistics operations by using regional distribution centers (RDCs). Its Western Cape stores that are supplied by an RDC have 1 to 2 percent better in-stock positions than those stores that are supplied by either off-site facilities or direct supplier deliveries. The RDCs even enable Game to deliver goods to its stores within 48 hours of their being shipped to an RDC.

Source: Bryan Roberts, "Game On: the Scope and Scale of 'Africa's Largest Discounter,' " www.kantarretailiq.com (February 18, 2011).

TABLE 17-1 A Movie Theater's Elasticity of Demand

Price	Tickets Sold (Saturday Night)	Total Ticket Receipts	Elasticity of Demand[a]
$ 6.00	1,000	$6,000	
			E = 0.68
7.00	900	6,300	
			E = 0.79
8.00	810	6,480	
			E = 1.00
9.00	720	6,480	
			E = 2.54
10.00	550	5,500	

Computation example ($6.00 to $7.00 price range) $= \dfrac{\dfrac{1{,}000 - 900}{1{,}000 + 900}}{\dfrac{\$6.00 - \$7.00}{\$6.00 + \$7.00}} = 0.68$

[a] Expressed as a positive number.

tickets sold. At $8.00 to $9.00, demand is unitary; ticket receipts are constant since the percentage change in tickets sold exactly offsets the percentage price change. Demand is elastic from $9.00 to $10.00; ticket receipts fall since the percentage change in tickets sold is greater than the percentage change in price.

For our movie theater example, total ticket receipts are highest at $8.00 or at $9.00. But what about total revenues? If patrons spend an average of $4.00 each at the concession stand, the best price is $6.00 (total overall revenues of $10,000). This theater is most interested in total revenues because its operating costs are the same whether there are 1,000 or 550 patrons. But typically, retailers should evaluate the costs, as well as the revenues, from serving additional customers.

In retailing, computing price elasticity is difficult. First, as with the movie theater, demand for individual events or items may be hard to predict. One week, the theater may attract 1,000 patrons to a movie, and the next week it may attract 400 patrons to a different movie. Second, many retailers carry thousands of items and cannot possibly compute elasticities for every one. As a result, they usually rely on average markup pricing, competition, tradition, and industrywide data to indicate price elasticity.

Dell (www.dell.com/us/p) appeals to multiple consumer segments—from novice to advanced computer user, with prices set accordingly.

Price sensitivity varies by market segment, based on shopping orientation. After identifying potential segments, retailers determine which of them form their target market:

- *Economic consumers.* They perceive competing retailers as similar and shop around for the lowest possible prices. This segment has grown dramatically in recent years.
- *Status-oriented consumers.* They perceive competing retailers as quite different. They are more interested in upscale retailers with prestige brands and strong customer service than in price.
- *Assortment-oriented consumers.* They seek retailers with a strong selection in the product categories being considered. They want fair prices.
- *Personalizing consumers.* They shop where they are known and feel a bond with employees and the firm itself. These shoppers will pay slightly above-average prices.
- *Convenience-oriented consumers.* They shop because they must, want nearby stores with long hours, and may use catalogs or the Web. These people will pay higher prices for convenience.

The Government and Retail Pricing

Three levels of government may affect domestic retail pricing decisions: federal, state, and local. When laws are federal, they apply to interstate commerce. A retailer operating only within the boundaries of one state may not be restricted by some federal legislation. Major government rules relate to horizontal price fixing, vertical price fixing, price discrimination, minimum price levels, unit pricing, item price removal, and price advertising. For retailers operating outside their home countries, a fourth level of government comes into play: international jurisdictions.

HORIZONTAL PRICE FIXING An agreement among manufacturers, among wholesalers, or among retailers to set prices is known as **horizontal price fixing**. Such agreements are illegal under the Sherman Antitrust Act and the Federal Trade Commission Act, regardless of how "reasonable" prices may be. It is also illegal for retailers to get together regarding the use of coupons, rebates, or other price-oriented tactics.

Although few large-scale legal actions have been taken in recent years, the penalties for horizontal price fixing can be severe. A decade ago, two popular long-time auction companies, Sotheby's and Christie's, "pled guilty to colluding to fix commission fees in the 1990s. The two firms paid more than $600 million in fines and to settle civil lawsuit damages. After a high-profile trial, Sotheby's Alfred Taubman cooled his heels in prison for ten months and Diana Brooks languished under house arrest in Manhattan."[6]

VERTICAL PRICE FIXING When manufacturers or wholesalers seek to control the retail prices of their goods and services, **vertical price fixing** occurs. Until 2007, retailers in the United States could not be forced to adhere to *minimum retail prices* set by manufacturers and wholesalers. Federal laws banning this practice were intended to encourage price competition among retailers and lower prices for consumers. However, as a result of a 2007 Supreme Court ruling, the situation changed significantly. Manufacturers and wholesalers can now enforce minimum prices at the retail level. Nonetheless, most suppliers choose not to do so since they do not want to eliminate business with discounters such as Wal-Mart, Target, and Costco. Consider the observations of one major law firm about the legal ramifications of the Supreme Court's decision:

> Minimum resale price agreements are most often found anti-competitive when they are viewed as facilitating a horizontal conspiracy—at the retailer or supplier level. Evidence tending to demonstrate a retail-level conspiracy typically includes proof that a group of retailers communicated among themselves, and then approached a common supplier to impose minimum resale prices or discipline price-cutting retailers. Two other instances where minimum resale price maintenance may fail are (1) where it is sought by a dominant retailer to harm horizontal competitors and (2) where a dominant supplier uses the agreement to foreclose competitors from access to distribution.[7]

Manufacturers and wholesalers can also legally control retail prices by one of these methods: They can screen retailers. They can set realistic list prices. They can pre-print prices on products (which retailers do not have to use). They can set regular prices that are accepted by consumers (such as 75 cents for a newspaper). They can use consignment selling, whereby the supplier owns items until they are sold and assumes costs normally associated with the retailer. They can own retail facilities. They can refuse to sell to retailers that advertise discount prices in violation of written policies. A supplier has a right to announce a policy for dealer pricing and can refuse to sell to those that do not comply. It cannot use coercion to prohibit a retailer from advertising low prices.

PRICE DISCRIMINATION The **Robinson-Patman Act** bars manufacturers and wholesalers from discriminating in price or purchase terms in selling to individual retailers if these retailers are purchasing products of "like quality" and the effect of such discrimination is to injure competition. The intent of this Act is to stop large retailers from using their power to gain discounts not justified by the cost savings achieved by suppliers due to big orders. There are exceptions that allow justifiable price discrimination when:

- Products are physically different.
- The retailers paying different prices are not competitors.
- Competition is not injured.
- Price differences are due to differences in supplier costs.
- Market conditions change—costs rise or fall or competing suppliers shift their prices.

Discounts are not illegal, as long as suppliers follow the preceding rules, make discounts available to competing retailers on an equitable basis, and offer discounts sufficiently graduated so small retailers can also qualify. Discounts for cumulative purchases (total yearly orders) and for multistore purchases by chains may be hard to justify.

Although the Robinson-Patman Act restricts sellers more than buyers, retailers are covered under Section 2(F): "It shall be unlawful for any person engaged in commerce, in the course of such commerce, knowingly to induce or receive a discrimination in price which is prohibited in this section." Thus, a retail buyer must try to get the lowest prices charged to any competitor, yet not bargain so hard that discounts cannot be justified by acceptable exceptions.

MINIMUM-PRICE LAWS Nearly one-half of the states have **minimum-price laws** that prevent retailers from selling certain items for less than their cost plus a fixed percentage to cover overhead. Besides general laws, some state rules set minimum prices for specific products. For instance, in New Jersey and Connecticut, the retail price of liquor cannot be less than the wholesale cost (including taxes and delivery charges).

Minimum-price laws protect small retailers from **predatory pricing**, in which large retailers seek to reduce competition by selling goods and services at very low prices, thus causing small retailers to go out of business. In one widely watched case, three pharmacies in Arkansas filed a suit claiming Wal-Mart had sold selected items below cost in an attempt to reduce competition. Wal-Mart agreed it had priced some items below cost to meet or beat rivals' prices but not to harm competitors. The Arkansas Supreme Court ruled that Wal-Mart did not use predatory pricing since the three pharmacies were still profitable.

With **loss leaders**, retailers price selected items below cost to lure more customer traffic for those retailers. Supermarkets and other retailers use loss leaders to increase overall sales and profits because people buy more than one item once in a store: "This strategy is used primarily to attract customers to your business through the introduction of a bargain. Such bargains may result in no profit being made but will be made up through the sale of other goods/services that may or may not be related to the product. Implementing the loss leader strategy can be risky and therefore needs to be considered that it is the right approach to penetrating the market."[8]

UNIT PRICING In some states, the proliferation of package sizes has led to **unit pricing** laws—whereby some retailers must express both the total price of an item and its price per unit of measure. Food stores are most affected by unit price rules because grocery items are more regulated than nongrocery items.[9] There are exemptions for firms with low sales. The aim of unit pricing is to enable consumers to compare prices of products available in many sizes. Thus, a 5-ounce can of tuna fish priced at $1.35 would also have a shelf label showing this as 27 cents per ounce. And a person learns that a 20-ounce bottle of soda selling for $1.00 (5 cents per ounce) costs more than a 67.6-ounce—2-liter—bottle for $1.49 (2.2 cents per ounce).

Retailer costs include computing per-unit prices, printing product and shelf labels, and keeping computer records. These costs are influenced by the way prices are attached to goods (by the supplier or the retailer), the number of items subject to unit pricing, the frequency of price changes, sales volume, and the number of stores in a chain.

Unit pricing can be a good strategy for retailers to follow, even when not required. At many supermarkets, the unit pricing system more than pays for itself because of decreased price-marking errors, better inventory control, and improved space management.

ITEM PRICE REMOVAL The boom in computerized checkout systems has led many firms, especially supermarkets, to push for **item price removal**—whereby prices are marked only on shelves or signs and not on individual items. Instead of the costly price marking of individual items, retailers want to rely on scanning equipment that reads pre-marked product codes and enters price data at the checkout counter. Their efforts have been successful; in 2011, Michigan removed its law—leaving Massachusetts as the only place in the United States with a statewide ban on item price removal. Shelf pricing is now more widely accepted.

Why have retailers opposed item pricing laws? "In the eyes of the typical retailer, these laws are relics of a bygone era, inappropriate for the world of scanners and shelf labeling, electronic or manual. And instead of serving customers and cutting costs, employees are forced to work the aisles with a sticker gun." Yet, consumerists supported them: "Price tags help people shop and help reduce checkout errors. Consumers have the right to compare a price tag to the amount charged at the checkout."[10]

PRICE ADVERTISING The FTC has guidelines pertaining to advertising price reductions, advertising prices in relation to competitors' prices, and bait-and-switch advertising. To access several FTC publications on acceptable pricing practices, visit our Web site (www.pearsonhighered.com/bermanevans).

A retailer cannot claim or imply that a price has been reduced from some former level (a suggested list price) unless the former price was one that the retailer had actually offered for a good or service on a regular basis during a reasonably substantial, recent period of time.

When a retailer says its prices are lower than its competitors, it must make certain that its comparisons pertain to firms selling large quantities in the same trading area. A somewhat controversial, but legal, practice is price matching. For the most part, a retailer makes three assumptions when it "guarantees to match the lowest price" of any competing retailer: (1) This guarantee gives shoppers the impression that a firm always offers low prices or else it would not make such a commitment. (2) Most shoppers will not return to a store after a purchase even if they see a lower price advertised elsewhere. (3) The guarantee may exclude most deep discounters and online firms by stating that they are not really competitors.

Bait-and-switch advertising is an illegal practice in which a retailer lures a customer by advertising goods and services at exceptionally low prices; once the customer contacts the retailer (by entering a store, calling a toll-free number, or going to a Web site), he or she is told the good/service of interest is out of stock or of inferior quality. A salesperson (or Web script) tries to convince the person to buy a more costly substitute. The retailer does not intend to sell the advertised item. In deciding if a promotion uses bait-and-switch advertising, the FTC considers how many transactions are made at the advertised price, whether sales commissions are excluded on sale items, and total sales relative to advertising costs.

Manufacturers, Wholesalers, and Other Suppliers—and Retail Pricing

There may be conflicts between manufacturers (and other suppliers) and retailers in setting final prices; each would like some control. Manufacturers usually want a certain image and to enable all retailers, even inefficient ones, to earn profits. Most retailers want to set prices based on their own image, goals, and so forth. A supplier can best control prices by using exclusive distribution, not selling to price-cutting retailers, or being its own retailer. A retailer can best gain control by being a vital customer, threatening to stop carrying suppliers' lines, stocking private brands, or selling gray market goods.

Many manufacturers set their prices to retailers by estimating final retail prices and then subtracting required retailer and wholesaler profit margins. In the men's apparel industry, the common retail markup is 50 percent of the final price. Thus, a man's shirt retailing at $50 can be sold to the retailer for no more than $25. If a wholesaler is involved, the manufacturer's wholesale price must be far less than $25.

Retailers sometimes carry manufacturers' brands and place high prices on them so rival brands (such as private labels) can be sold more easily. This is called "selling against the brand" and is disliked by manufacturers because sales of their brands are apt to decline. Some retailers

Trust and Fairness in Revenue Management

Revenue management systems seek to maximize a retailer's profits by constantly changing the mix of prices. An airline might have multiple prices for adjacent seats on the same plane based on when the seats were purchased. A restaurant might offer selective discounts on its Web site at times when its reservation schedule indicates a low table utilization rate. Consumers who did not reserve their seats online might be unaware of the discount.

The impact of revenue management policies on consumer perceptions of trust is unclear. Some researchers state that revenue management systems might undermine a consumer's trust in a retail organization. The lack of trust is based on the distinct conflict between revenue management systems that seek to maximize profits and relationship marketing concepts that stress the lifetime revenue per loyal customer.

Consumers may perceive a price as "fair" if it is based on an increase in the seller's costs, but as "unfair" if it is due to increased demand for the good or service. Another explanation for when a consumer may accept price differentials is that they understand the benefits of certain types of price differentials—such as lower prices to reduce unsold hotel rooms in off-season time periods.

Source: Una McMahon-Beattie, "Trust, Fairness, and Justice in Revenue Management: Creating Value for the Customer," *Journal of Revenue and Pricing Management*, Vol. 10 (No. 1, 2011), pp. 44–46.

also sell **gray market goods**, brand-name products bought in foreign markets or goods transshipped from other retailers. Manufacturers dislike gray market goods because they are often sold at low prices by unauthorized dealers. They may sue gray market goods resellers on the basis of copyright and trademark infringement.

When suppliers are unknown or products are new, retailers may seek price guarantees. For example, to get its radios stocked, a new supplier might have to guarantee the $30 suggested retail price. If the retailers cannot sell the radios for $30, the manufacturer pays a refund. Should the retailers have to sell the radios at $25, the manufacturer gives back $5. Another guarantee is one in which a supplier tells the retailer that no competitor can buy an item for a lower price. If anyone does, the retailer gets a rebate. The relative power of the retailer and its suppliers determines whether such guarantees are provided.

A retailer also has other suppliers: employees, fixtures manufacturers, landlords, and outside parties (such as ad agencies). Each has an effect on price because of their costs to the retailer.

Competition and Retail Pricing

See how Auto-by-Tel (www.autobytel.com) and CarsDirect.com (www.carsdirect.com) approach the selling of cars.

Market pricing occurs when shoppers have a large choice of retailers. In this instance, retailers often price similarly to each other and have less control over price because consumers can easily shop around. Supermarkets, fast-food restaurants, and gas stations may use market pricing due to their competitive industries. Demand for specific retailers may be weak enough so that some customers would switch to a competitor if prices are raised much.

With *administered pricing*, firms seek to attract consumers on the basis of distinctive retailing mixes. This occurs when people consider image, assortment, service, and so forth to be important and they are willing to pay above-average prices to unique retailers. Upscale department stores, fashion apparel stores, and expensive restaurants are among those with unique offerings and solid control over their prices.

Most price-oriented strategies can be quickly imitated. Thus, the reaction of competitors is predictable if the leading firm is successful. This means a price strategy should be viewed from both short-run and long-run perspectives. If competition becomes too intense, a price war may erupt—whereby various firms continually lower prices below regular amounts and sometimes below their cost to lure consumers from competitors. Price wars are sometimes difficult to end and can lead to low profits, losses, or even bankruptcy for some competitors. This is especially so for Web retailers.

DEVELOPING A RETAIL PRICE STRATEGY

As Figure 17-4 shows, a retail price strategy has five steps: objectives, policy, strategy, implementation, and adjustments. Pricing policies must be integrated with the total retail mix, which occurs in the second step. The process can be complex due to the often erratic nature of demand, the number of items carried, and the impact of the external factors already noted.

FIGURE 17-4
A Framework for Developing a Retail Price Strategy

Retail Objectives and Pricing

Revionics software (www.revionics.com/pricing-software.aspx) can assist retailers in price optimization.

A retailer's pricing strategy has to reflect its overall goals and be related to sales and profits. There must also be specific pricing goals to avoid such potential problems as confusing people by having too many prices, spending too much time bargaining with customers, offering frequent discounts to stimulate customer traffic, having low profit margins, and placing too much focus on price.

SecondSpin.com (www.secondspin.com) sells used CDs and DVDs at a discount. Tiffany (www.tiffany.com) has great jewelry—although it can be a little pricey.

OVERALL OBJECTIVES AND PRICING Sales goals may be stated in terms of revenues and/or unit volume. An aggressive strategy, known as **market penetration pricing**, is used when a retailer seeks large revenues by setting low prices and selling many units. Profit per unit is low, but total profit is high if sales projections are reached. This approach is proper if customers are price sensitive, low prices discourage actual and potential competition, and retail costs do not rise much with volume.

With a **market skimming pricing** strategy, a firm sets premium prices and attracts customers less concerned with price than service, assortment, and prestige. It usually does not maximize sales but does achieve high profit per unit. It is proper if the targeted segment is price insensitive, new competitors are unlikely to enter the market, and added sales will greatly increase retail costs. See Figure 17-5.

Return on investment and early recovery of cash are other possible profit-based goals for retailers using a market skimming strategy. *Return on investment* is sought if a retailer wants profit to be a certain percentage of its investment, such as 20 percent of inventory investment. *Early recovery of cash* is used by retailers that may be short on funds, wish to expand, or be uncertain about the future.

FIGURE 17-5
Ferragamo's Market Skimming Approach

Salvatore Ferragamo (http://group.ferragamo.com/en) is "one of the major players in the luxury goods industry, which focuses on the creation, manufacture, and sale of footwear, leather goods, clothing, silk products, other accessories, and perfumes for men and women, all made in Italy. The firm's "unique, exclusive design is obtained by combining style, creativity, and innovation with the quality and craftsmanship typical of Italian-made goods." The store shown here is in Valencia, Spain.

Source: Tupungato/Shutterstock.com. Reprinted by permission.

TABLE 17-2 BE's Toy City: Demand, Costs, Profit, and Return on Inventory Investment[a]

Selling Price ($)	Demand (units)	Total Sales Revenue ($)	Average Cost of Goods ($)	Total Cost of Goods ($)	Total Operating Costs ($)	Total Costs ($)	Average Total Costs ($)	Total Profit ($)
9.00	114,000	1,026,000	7.60	866,400	104,000	970,400	8.51	55,600
10.00	104,000	1,040,000	7.85	816,400	94,000	910,400	8.75	129,600
11.00	80,000	880,000	8.25	660,000	88,000	748,000	9.35	132,000
12.00	60,000	720,000	8.75	525,000	80,000	605,000	10.08	115,000

Selling Price ($)	Profit/ Unit ($)	Markup at Retail (%)	Profit/ Sales (%)	Average Inventory on Hand (units)	Inventory Turnover (units)	Average Inventory Investment at Cost ($)	Inventory Turnover ($)	Return-on-Inventory Investment (%)
9.00	0.49	16	5.4	12,000	9.5	91,200	9.5	61
10.00	1.25	22	12.5	13,000	8.0	102,050	8.0	127
11.00	1.65	25	15.0	14,000	5.7	115,500	5.7	114
12.00	1.92	27	16.0	16,000	3.8	140,000	3.8	82

Note: The average cost of goods reflects quantity discounts. Total operating costs include all retail operating expenses.

[a] Numbers have been rounded.

BE's Toy City, the discounter we introduced earlier in this chapter, may be used to illustrate how a retailer sets sales, profit, and return-on-investment goals. The firm sells inexpensive toys and overruns to avoid competing with mainstream toy stores, has one price for all toys (to be set within the $9 to $12 range), minimizes operating costs, encourages self-service, and carries a good selection. Table 17-2 has data on BE's Toy City pertaining to demand, costs, profit, and return-on-inventory investment at prices from $9 to $12. The firm must select the best price within that range. Table 17-3 shows how the figures in Table 17-2 were derived. Several conclusions can be drawn from Table 17-2:

- A sales goal would lead to a price of $10. Total sales are highest ($1,040,000).
- A dollar profit goal would lead to a price of $11. Total profit is highest ($132,000).

TABLE 17-3 Derivation of BE's Toy City Data

Column in Table 17-2	Source of Information or Method of Computation
Selling price	Trade data, comparison shopping, experience
Demand (in units) at each price	Consumer surveys, trade data, experience
Total sales revenue	Selling price × Quantity demanded
Average cost of goods	Supplier contacts, quantity discount structure, estimates of order sizes
Total cost of goods	Average cost of goods × Quantity demanded
Total operating costs	Experience, trade data, estimation of individual retail expenses
Total costs	Total cost of goods + Total operating costs
Average total costs	Total costs/Quantity demanded
Total profit	Total sales revenue – Total costs
Profit per unit	Total profit/Quantity demanded
Markup (at retail)	(Selling price – Average cost of goods)/Selling price
Profit as a percentage of sales	Total profit/Total sales revenue
Average inventory on hand	Trade data, inventory turnover data (in units), experience
Inventory turnover (in units)	Quantity demanded/Average inventory on hand (in units)
Average inventory investment (at cost)	Average cost of goods × Average inventory on hand (in units)
Inventory turnover (in $)	Total cost of goods/Average inventory investment (at cost)
Return-on-inventory investment	Total profit/Average inventory investment (at cost)

- A return-on-inventory investment goal would lead to a price of $10. Return on inventory investment is 127 percent.
- Although the most items can be sold at $9, that price would lead to the least profit ($55,600).
- A price of $12 would yield the highest profit per unit ($1.92) and as a percentage of sales, but total dollar profit is not maximized at this price.
- The highest inventory turnover (16,000 units at $12.00) would not lead to the highest total profits.

As a result, BE's Toy City decides on a price of $11 because it would earn the highest dollar profits, while generating good profit per unit and good profit as a percentage of sales.

SPECIFIC PRICING OBJECTIVES Figure 17-6 lists specific pricing goals other than sales and profits. Each retailer must determine their relative importance given its situation—and plan accordingly. Some goals may be incompatible, such as "to not encourage shoppers to be overly price-conscious" and a "'we-will-not-be-undersold" philosophy.

Broad Price Policy

KSS Fuels (www.kssfuels.com) offers a lot of software solutions that enable convenience store and grocery retailers to better integrate their price strategies.

Through a broad price policy, a retailer generates an integrated price plan with short- and long-run perspectives (balancing immediate and future goals) and a consistent image (vital for chains and franchises). The retailer interrelates its price policy with the target market, the retail image, and the other elements of the retail mix. These are some of the price policies from which a firm could choose:

- No competitors will have lower prices, no competitors will have higher prices (for prestige purposes), or prices will be consistent with competitors'.
- All items will be priced independently, depending on the demand for each, or the prices for all items will be interrelated to maintain an image and ensure proper markups.
- Price leadership will be exerted, competitors will be price leaders and set prices first, or prices will be set independently of competitors.
- Prices will be constant over a year or season, or prices will change if costs change.

FIGURE 17-6
Specific Pricing Objectives from Which Retailers May Choose

- ✓ To maintain a proper image.
- ✓ To encourage shoppers not to be overly price-conscious.
- ✓ To be perceived as fair by all parties (including suppliers, employees, and customers).
- ✓ To be consistent in setting prices.
- ✓ To increase customer traffic during slow periods.
- ✓ To clear out seasonal merchandise.
- ✓ To match competitors' prices without starting a price war.
- ✓ To promote a "we-will-not-be-undersold" philosophy.
- ✓ To be regarded as the price leader in the market area by consumers.
- ✓ To provide ample customer service.
- ✓ To minimize the chance of government actions relating to price advertising and antitrust matters.
- ✓ To discourage potential competitors from entering the marketplace.
- ✓ To create and maintain customer interest.
- ✓ To encourage repeat business.

Price Strategy

See how retailers can improve pricing decisions (www.gofso.com/Premium/BS/fg/fg-Pricing.html).

In **demand-oriented pricing**, a retailer sets prices based on consumer desires. It determines the range of prices acceptable to the target market. The top of this range is the demand ceiling, the most that people will pay for a good or service. With **cost-oriented pricing**, a retailer sets a price floor, the minimum price acceptable to the firm so it can reach a specified profit goal. A retailer usually computes merchandise and operating costs and adds a profit margin to these figures. For **competition-oriented pricing**, a retailer sets its prices in accordance with competitors'. The price levels of key competitors are studied and applied.

As a rule, retailers should combine these approaches in enacting a price strategy. The approaches should not be viewed as operating independently.

DEMAND-ORIENTED PRICING Retailers use demand-oriented pricing to estimate the quantities that customers would buy at various prices. This approach studies customer interests and the psychological implications of pricing. Two aspects of psychological pricing are the price–quality association and prestige pricing.

According to the **price–quality association** concept, many consumers feel high prices connote high quality and low prices connote low quality. This association is especially important if competing firms or products are hard to judge on bases other than price, consumers have little experience or confidence in judging quality (as with a new retailer), shoppers perceive large differences in quality among retailers or products, and brand names are insignificant in product choice. Although various studies have documented a price–quality relationship, research also indicates that if other quality cues, such as retailer atmospherics, customer service, and popular brands, are involved, these cues may be more important than price in a person's judgment of overall retailer or product quality.

Prestige pricing—which assumes that consumers will not buy goods and services at prices deemed too low—is based on the price–quality association. Its premise is that consumers may feel too low a price means poor quality and status. Some people look for prestige pricing when selecting retailers and do not patronize those with prices viewed as too low. Saks Fifth Avenue and Neiman Marcus do not generally carry low-end items because their customers may feel they are inferior. Prestige pricing does not apply to all shoppers. Some people may be economizers and always shop for bargains; and neither the price–quality association nor prestige pricing may be applicable for them.

COST-ORIENTED PRICING One form of cost-oriented pricing, markup pricing, is the most widely used pricing technique. In **markup pricing**, a retailer sets prices by adding per-unit merchandise costs, retail operating expenses, and desired profit. The difference between merchandise costs and selling price is the **markup.** If a retailer buys a desk for $200 and sells it for $300, the extra $100 covers operating costs and profit. The markup is 33-1/3 percent at retail or 50 percent at cost. The markup level depends on a product's traditional markup, the supplier's suggested list price, inventory turnover, competition, rent and other overhead costs, the extent to which the product must be serviced, and the selling effort.

Markups can be computed on the basis of retail selling price or cost but are typically calculated using the retail price. Why? (1) Retail expenses, markdowns, and profit are always stated as a percentage of sales. Thus, markups expressed as a percentage of sales are more meaningful. (2) Manufacturers quote selling prices and discounts to retailers as percentage reductions from retail list prices. (3) Retail price data are more readily available than cost data. (4) Profitability seems smaller if expressed on the basis of price. This can be useful in communicating with the government, employees, and consumers.

This is how a **markup percentage** is calculated. The difference is in the denominator:

$$\text{Markup percentage (at retail)} = \frac{\text{Retail selling price} - \text{Merchandise cost}}{\text{Retail selling price}}$$

$$\text{Markup percentage (at cost)} = \frac{\text{Retail selling price} - \text{Merchandise cost}}{\text{Merchandise cost}}$$

Table 17-4 shows several markup percentages at retail and at cost. As markups go up, the disparity between the percentages grows. Suppose a retailer buys a watch for $20 and considers

TABLE 17-4 Markup Equivalents

Percentage at Retail	Percentage at Cost
10.0	11.1
20.0	25.0
30.0	42.9
40.0	66.7
50.0	100.0
60.0	150.0
70.0	233.3
80.0	400.0
90.0	900.0

whether to sell it for $25, $40, or $100. The $25 price yields a markup of 20 percent at retail and 25 percent at cost, the $40 price a markup of 50 percent at retail and 100 percent at cost, and the $100 price a markup of 80 percent at retail and 400 percent at cost.

These three examples indicate the usefulness of the markup concept in planning:

1. A discount clothing store can buy a shipment of men's long-sleeve shirts at $12 each and wants a 30 percent markup at retail.[11] What retail price should the store charge to achieve this markup?

$$\text{Markup percentage (at retail)} = \frac{\text{Retail selling price} - \text{Merchandise cost}}{\text{Retail selling price}}$$

$$0.30 = \frac{\text{Retail selling price} - \$12.00}{\text{Retail selling price}}$$

$$\text{Retail selling price} = \$17.14$$

2. A stationery store desires a minimum 40 percent markup at retail.[12] If standard envelopes retail at $7.99 per box, what is the maximum price the store should pay for each box?

$$\text{Markup percentage (at retail)} = \frac{\text{Retail selling price} - \text{Merchandise cost}}{\text{Retail selling price}}$$

$$0.40 = \frac{\$7.99 - \text{Merchandise cost}}{\$\,7.99}$$

$$\text{Merchandise cost} = \$4.794$$

3. A sporting goods store has been offered a closeout purchase for bicycles. The cost of each bike is $105, and it should retail for $160. What markup percentage at retail would the store obtain?

$$\text{Markup percentage (at retail)} = \frac{\text{Retail selling price} - \text{Merchandise cost}}{\text{Retail selling price}}$$

$$= \frac{\$160.00 - \$105.00}{\$160.00} = 34.4$$

A retailer's markup percentage may also be determined by examining planned retail operating expenses, profit, and net sales. Suppose a florist estimates yearly operating expenses to be $55,000. The desired profit is $50,000 per year, including the owner's salary. Net sales are forecast to be $250,000. The planned markup percentage would be:

$$\text{Markup percentage (at retail)} = \frac{\text{Planned retail operating expenses} + \text{Planned profit}}{\text{Planned net sales}}$$

$$= \frac{\$55,000 + \$50,000}{\$250,000} = 42$$

If potted plants cost the florist \$8.00 each, the retailer's selling price would be:

$$\text{Retail selling price} = \frac{\text{Merchandise cost}}{1 - \text{Markup}}$$

$$= \frac{\$8.00}{1 - 0.42} = \$13.79$$

The florist must sell about 18,129 plants (assuming that this is the only item it carries) at \$13.79 apiece to achieve sales and profit goals. To reach these goals, all plants must be sold at the \$13.79 price.

Because it is rare to sell all items in stock at their original prices, initial markup, maintained markup, and gross margin should each be computed. **Initial markup** is based on the original retail value assigned to merchandise less the costs of the merchandise. **Maintained markup** is based on the actual prices received for merchandise sold during a time period less merchandise cost. Maintained markups relate to actual prices received, so they can be hard to predict. The difference between initial and maintained markups is that the latter reflect adjustments for markdowns, added markups, shortages, and discounts.

The initial markup percentage depends on planned retail operating expenses, profit, reductions, and net sales:

$$\text{Initial markup percentage (at retail)} = \frac{\text{Planned retail operating expenses} + \text{Planned profit} + \text{Planned retail reductions}}{\text{Planned net sales} + \text{Planned retail reductions}}$$

If planned retail reductions are 0, the initial markup percentage equals planned retail operating expenses plus profit, both divided by planned net sales. To resume the florist example, suppose the firm projects that retail reductions will be 20 percent of estimated sales, or \$50,000. To reach its goals, the initial markup and the original selling price would be:

$$\text{Initial markup percentage (at retail)} = \frac{\$55{,}000 + \$50{,}000 + \$50{,}000}{\$250{,}000 + \$50{,}000} = 51.7$$

$$\text{Retail selling price} = \frac{\text{Merchandise cost}}{1 - \text{Markup}} = \frac{\$8.00}{1 - 0.517} = \$16.56$$

The original retail value of 18,129 plants is about \$300,000. Retail reductions of \$50,000 lead to net sales of \$250,000. Thus, the retailer must begin by selling plants at \$16.56 apiece if it wants an average selling price of \$13.79 and a maintained markup of 42 percent.

The maintained markup percentage is:

$$\text{Maintained markup percentage (at retail)} = \frac{\text{Actual retail operation expenses} + \text{Actual profit}}{\text{Actual net sales}}$$

or

$$\text{Maintained markup percentage (at retail)} = \frac{\text{Average selling price} - \text{Merchandise cost}}{\text{Average selling price}}$$

Gross margin is the difference between net sales and the total cost of goods sold (which adjusts for cash discounts and additional expenses):

$$\text{Gross margin (in \$)} = \text{Net sales} - \text{Total cost of goods}$$

The florist's gross margin (the dollar equivalent of maintained markup) is roughly \$105,000.

Although a retailer must set a companywide markup goal, markups for categories of merchandise or individual products may differ—sometimes dramatically. At many full-line discount stores, maintained markup as a percentage of sales ranges from under 20 percent for consumer electronics to as much as 30 to 40 percent or more for jewelry and watches.

New Uses for Credit and Debit Cards

According to a leading research and consulting firm, the sales of pre-paid credit and debit cards were forecast to grow from $12 billion in 2007 to more than $200 billion in 2013. This high growth rate can be explained by two developments: the increase in the gift card market and the increased numbers of consumers who do not have traditional bank accounts.

Firms such as Home Depot (www.homedepot.com), Gap (www.gap.com), and Nike (www.nike.com) offer closed-loop (firm-specific) gift cards. Visa (www.visa.com), MasterCard (www.mastercard.com), Discover (www.discovercard.com), and American Express (www.americanexpress.com) are among those that offer open-loop gift cards that can be redeemed at any merchant.

The growth in pre-paid calling cards and gift cards has encouraged convenience stores to enter the banking business. Stripes (www.stripesstores.com), which operates about 525 convenience stores—primarily in New Mexico, Oklahoma, and Texas—has introduced a pre-paid credit card in conjunction with nFinanSe (www.nfinanse.com), a financial services company. For a $2.95 monthly maintenance fee, Stripes customers can participate in the firm's credit card programs. This fee entitles users to an unlimited number of purchase transactions, no-cost direct deposit of payroll checks, and 24/7 customer support. The card is particularly attractive to Stripes as it operates in markets where a high percentage of consumers do not have traditional bank accounts.

Source: W. B. King, "Reloadable Profit," www.csnews.com (May 2, 2011).

With a **variable markup policy,** a retailer purposely adjusts markups by merchandise category. Such a policy:

- Recognizes that the costs of different goods/service categories may fluctuate widely. Some items require alterations or installation. Even within a product line, expensive items may require greater end-of-year markdowns than inexpensive ones. The high-priced line needs a larger initial markup.
- Allows for differences in product investments. For major appliances, where the retailer orders regularly from a wholesaler, lower markups are needed than with fine jewelry, where the retailer must have a complete stock of unique merchandise.
- Accounts for differences in sales efforts and merchandising skills. A feature-laden food processor may require a substantial effort, whereas a standard toaster involves much less effort.
- May help a retailer to generate more customer traffic by advertising certain products at deep discounts. This entails leader pricing (discussed later in the chapter).

One way to plan variable markups is **direct product profitability (DPP),** a technique that enables a retailer to find the profitability of each category of merchandise by computing adjusted per-unit gross margin and assigning direct product costs for such expense categories as warehousing, transportation, handling, and selling. The proper markup for each category or item is then set. DPP is used by some supermarkets, discounters, and other retailers. However, it is complex to assign costs.

Figure 17-7 illustrates DPP for two items with a selling price of $20. The retailer pays $12 for Item A, whose per-unit gross margin is $8. Since the retailer gets a $1 per unit allowance to set up a special display, the adjusted gross margin is $9. Total direct retail costs are estimated at $5. Direct product profit is $4 (20 percent of sales). The retailer pays $10 for Item B, whose per-unit gross margin is $10. There are no special discounts or allowances. Because Item B needs more selling effort, total direct retail costs are $6. The direct profit is $4 (20 percent of sales). To attain the same direct profit per unit, Item A needs a 40 percent markup (per-unit gross margin/selling price), and Item B needs 50 percent.

Cost-oriented (markup) pricing is popular among retailers. It is simple, because a retailer can apply a standard markup for a product category more easily than it can estimate demand at various prices. The firm can also adjust prices according to demand or segment its customers. Markup pricing has a sense of equity given that the retailer earns a fair profit. When retailers have similar markups, price competition is reduced. Markup pricing is efficient if it takes into account competition, seasonal factors, and the intricacies in selling some products.

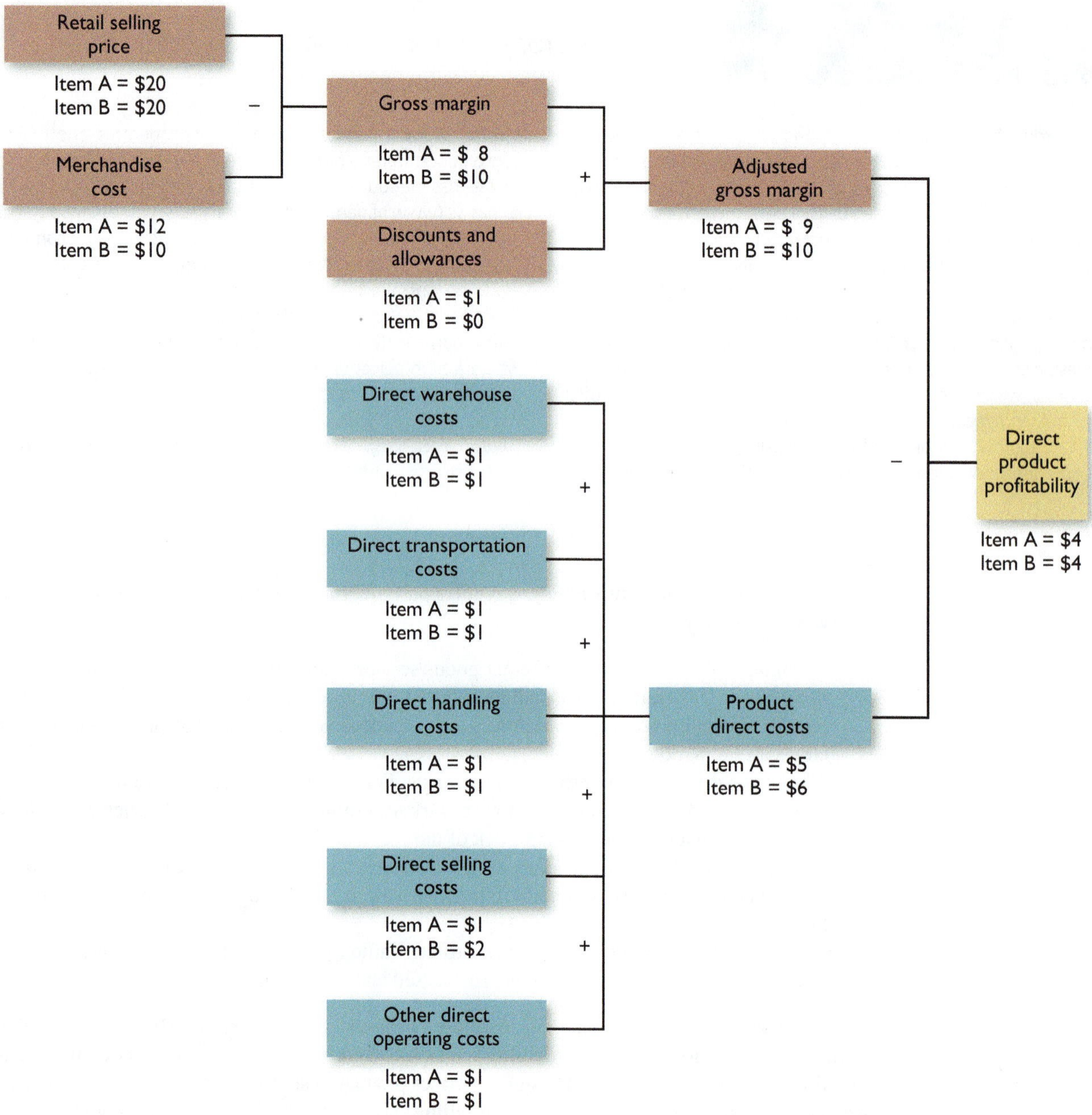

FIGURE 17-7
How to Determine Direct Product Profitability

COMPETITION-ORIENTED PRICING A retailer can use competitors' prices as a guide. That firm might not alter prices in reaction to changes in demand or costs unless competitors alter theirs. Similarly, it might change prices when competitors do, even if demand or costs remain the same.

As shown in Table 17-5, a competition-oriented retailer can price below, at, or above the market. A firm with a strong location, superior service, good assortments, a favorable image, and exclusive brands can set prices above competitors. However, above-market pricing is not suitable for a retailer that has an inconvenient location, relies on self-service, is not innovative, and offers no real product distinctiveness.

Competition-oriented pricing does not require calculations of demand curves or price elasticity. The average market price is assumed to be fair for both the consumer and the retailer. Pricing at the market level does not disrupt competition and therefore does not usually lead to retaliation.

TABLE 17-5 Competition-Oriented Pricing Alternatives

	Alternative Price Strategies		
Retail Mix Variable	Pricing Below the Market	Pricing At the Market	Pricing Above the Market
Location	Poor, inconvenient site; low rent	Close to competitors, no location advantage	Few strong competitors, convenient to consumers
Customer service	Self-service, little salesperson support, limited displays	Moderate assistance by sales personnel	High levels of personal selling, delivery, etc.
Product assortment	More emphasis on best-sellers	Medium or large assortment	Small or large assortment
Atmosphere	Inexpensive fixtures, racks for merchandise	Moderate atmosphere	Attractive and pleasant decor
Innovativeness in assortment	Follower, conservative	Concentration on best-sellers	Quite innovative
Special services	Not available	Not available or extra fee	Included in price
Product lines carried	Some name brands, private labels, closeouts	Selection of name brands, private labels	Exclusive name brands and private labels

INTEGRATION OF APPROACHES TO PRICE STRATEGY To properly integrate the three approaches, questions such as these should be addressed:

- If prices are reduced, will revenues increase greatly? (Demand orientation)
- Should different prices be charged for a product based on negotiations with customers, seasonality, and so on? (Demand orientation)
- Will a given price level allow a traditional markup to be attained? (Cost orientation)
- What price level is needed for an item with special buying, selling, or delivery costs? (Cost orientation)
- What price levels are competitors setting? (Competitive orientation)
- Can above-market prices be set due to a superior image? (Competitive orientation)

Implementation of Price Strategy

Implementing a price strategy involves a variety of separate but interrelated specific decisions, in addition to those broad concepts already discussed. A checklist of selected decisions is shown in Figure 17-8. In this section, the specifics of a pricing strategy are detailed.

FIGURE 17-8
A Checklist of Selected Specific Pricing Decisions

- ✓ How important is price stability? How long should prices be maintained?
- ✓ Is everyday low pricing desirable?
- ✓ Should prices change if costs and/or customer demand vary?
- ✓ Should the same prices be charged to all customers buying under the same conditions?
- ✓ Should customer bargaining be permitted?
- ✓ Should odd pricing be used?
- ✓ Should leader pricing be utilized to draw customer traffic? If yes, should leader prices be above, at, or below costs?
- ✓ Should consumers be offered discounts for purchasing in quantity?
- ✓ Should price lining be used to provide a price range and price points within that range?
- ✓ Should pricing practices vary by department or product line?

CUSTOMARY AND VARIABLE PRICING With **customary pricing**, a retailer sets prices for goods and services and seeks to maintain them for an extended period. Examples of items with customary prices are newspapers, candy, arcade games, vending machine items, and foods on restaurant menus. In each case, the retailer wants to establish set prices and have consumers take them for granted.

Bi-Lo (www.bi-lo.com), the southeastern supermarket chain, offers both everyday low prices and regular promotions.

A version of customary pricing is **everyday low pricing (EDLP)**, in which a retailer strives to sell its goods and services at consistently low prices throughout the selling season. Low prices are set initially; and there are few or no advertised specials, except on discontinued items or end-of-season closeouts. The retailer reduces its advertising and product re-pricing costs, and this approach increases the credibility of its prices in the consumer's mind. On the other hand, with EDLP, suppliers may eliminate special trade allowances designed to encourage retailers to offer price promotions during the year. Wal-Mart, McDonald's, and Ikea are among the retailers successfully using EDLP. See Figure 17-9.

In many instances, a retailer cannot or should not use customary pricing. A firm *cannot* maintain constant prices if its costs are rising. A firm *should not* hold prices constant if customer demand varies. Under **variable pricing**, a retailer alters its prices to coincide with fluctuations in costs or consumer demand. Variable pricing may also provide excitement due to special sales opportunities for customers.

FIGURE 17-9

McDonald's and Everyday Low Prices

A major factor in McDonald's worldwide growth, highlighted here by its store in Copenhagen, Denmark, is its everyday value menu. Many patrons are attracted by the many low-priced items on the menu.

Source: Tupungato/Shutterstock.com. Reprinted by permission.

Cost fluctuations can be seasonal or trend-related. Supermarket and florist prices vary over the year due to the seasonal nature of many food and floral products. When seasonal items are scarce, the cost to the retailer goes up. If costs continually rise (as with luxury cars) or fall (as with computers), the retailer must change prices permanently (unlike temporary seasonal changes).

Demand fluctuations can be place- or time-based. Place-based fluctuations exist for retailers selling seat locations (such as concert halls) or room locations (such as hotels). Different prices can be charged for different locations, such as tickets close to the stage commanding higher prices. Time-based fluctuations occur if consumer demand differs by hour, day, or season. Demand for a movie theater is greater on Saturday than on Wednesday. Prices should be lower during periods of less demand.

Yield management pricing is a computerized, demand-based, variable pricing technique, whereby a retailer (typically a service firm) determines the combination of prices that yield the greatest total revenues for a given period. It is widely used by airlines and hotels. A crucial airline decision is how many first-class, full-coach, and discount tickets to sell on each flight. With this approach, an airline offers fewer discount tickets for flights in peak periods than flights in off-peak times. The airline has two goals: fill as many seats as possible on every flight and sell as many full-fare tickets as it can ("You don't want to sell a seat for $99 if someone will pay $599"). Yield management pricing may be too complex for small firms and requires software. Our Web site (www.pearsonhighered.com/bermanevans) has links that illustrate the uses of yield management and other pricing software.

It is possible to combine customary and variable pricing. A movie theater can charge $5 every Wednesday night and $9 every Saturday. A bookstore can lower prices by 20 percent for best-sellers that have been on shelves for three months.

ONE-PRICE POLICY AND FLEXIBLE PRICING Under a **one-price policy,** a retailer charges the same price to all customers buying an item under similar conditions. This policy may be used together with customary pricing or variable pricing. With variable pricing, all customers interested in a particular section of concert seats would pay the same price. This approach is easy to manage, does not require skilled salespeople, makes shopping quicker, permits self-service, puts consumers under less pressure, and is tied to price goals. One-price policies are the rule for most U.S. retailers, and bargaining is often not permitted.

Looking to bargain? Go to eBay (www.pages.ebay.com/help/buy) or uBid (www.ubid.com).

Flexible pricing lets consumers bargain over prices; those who are good at it obtain lower prices. Jewelry stores, car dealers, and others use flexible pricing. They do not clearly post final prices; shoppers need prior knowledge to bargain well. Flexible pricing encourages consumers to spend more time, gives an impression the firm is discount-oriented, and generates high margins from shoppers who do not like haggling. It requires high initial prices and good salespeople.[13]

Carol Meyrowitz: TJX Companies

TJX (www.tjx.com) is the largest off-price retailer specializing in apparel and home fashions in the United States, where it operates T.J. Maxx (www.tjmaxx.com), Marshalls (www.marshallsonline.com), and HomeGoods (www.homegoods.com). It also operates stores internationally, including T.K. Maxx (www.tkmaxx.com).

Carol Meyrowitz has been the chief executive of TJX since January 2007 and a member of the firm's board of directors since September 2006; and she was president from 2005 until assuming her current position. Meyrowitz's career includes holding senior management positions with former divisions of TJX, consulting work for a private-equity firm, and as an executive vice-president of TJX. Her experience encompasses a broad understanding of distribution, real-estate, finance, and international operations. In 2010, her total compensation exceeded $17 million, of which $1.5 million was base salary and $7.7 million for stock options that were exercised by her.

TJX's companywide strategy is to price its fashionable, brand-name merchandise at 20 to 60 percent less than at department and specialty stores. It has successfully implemented this strategy through opportunistic buying (purchasing bankrupt lots and cancelled orders), high inventory turnover (due to low prices), a treasure hunt atmosphere (shoppers never know what they can find in the store), and being fast to react to unique buying opportunities (a buyer can be summoned out of town on virtually no notice).

Source: "Carol M. Meyrowitz Profile," http://people.forbes.com/profile/print/carol-m-meyrowitz/79325 (January 29, 2012).

A special form of flexible pricing is **contingency pricing**, whereby a service retailer does not get paid until after the service is performed and payment is contingent on the service's being satisfactory. In some cases, such as real-estate, consumers like contingency payments so they know the service is done properly. This represents some risk to the retailer since a lot of time and effort may be spent without payment. A real-estate broker may show a house 25 times, not sell it, and, therefore, not be paid.

ODD PRICING In **odd pricing**, retail prices are set at levels below even dollar values, such as $0.49, $4.98, and $199. The assumption is that people feel these prices represent discounts or that the amounts are beneath consumer price ceilings. Odd pricing is a form of psychological pricing.[14] Realtors hope consumers with a price ceiling of less than $350,000 are attracted to houses selling for $349,500. See Figure 17-10.

Odd prices that are 1 cent or 2 cents below the next highest even price ($0.29, $0.99, $2.98) are common up to $10.00. Beyond that point and up to $50.00, 5-cent reductions from the highest even price ($19.95, $49.95) are more usual. For more expensive items, prices are in dollars ($399, $4,995).

LEADER PRICING In **leader pricing**, a retailer advertises and sells selected items in its goods/service assortment at less than the usual profit margins. The goal is to increase customer traffic for the retailer so that it can sell regularly priced goods and services in addition to the specially priced items. This is different from bait-and-switch, in which sale items are not sold.

Leader pricing typically involves frequently purchased, nationally branded, high turnover goods and services because it is easy for customers to detect low prices. Supermarkets, home centers, discount stores, drugstores, and fast-food restaurants are just some of the retailers that utilize leader pricing to draw shoppers. There are two kinds of leader pricing: loss leaders and sales at lower than regular prices (but higher than cost). Loss leaders are regulated in some states under minimum-price laws.

MULTIPLE-UNIT PRICING With **multiple-unit pricing**, a retailer offers discounts to customers who buy in quantity or who buy a product bundle. By pricing items at two for $0.75, a retailer attempts to sell more products than at $0.39 each. There are three reasons to use multiple-unit pricing: (1) A firm could seek to have shoppers increase their total purchases of an item. (If people buy multiple units to stockpile them, instead of consuming more, the firm's overall sales do not increase.) (2) This approach can help sell slow-moving and end-of-season merchandise. (3) Price bundling may increase sales of related items.

In **bundled pricing**, a retailer combines several elements in one basic price. A digital camera bundle could include a camera, batteries, a telephoto lens, a case, and a tripod for $229. This approach increases overall sales and offers people a discount over unbundled prices. However, it is unresponsive to the needs of different customers. As an alternative, many retailers use **unbundled pricing**—they charge separate prices for each item sold. A TV rental firm could charge separately for TV set rental, home delivery, and a monthly service contract. This closely links prices with costs and gives people more choice. Unbundled pricing may be harder to manage and may lead to people buying fewer related items.[15]

With its many hotel brands (www.marriott.com/corporateinfo/glance.mi), Marriott International really knows how to use price lining.

PRICE LINING Rather than stock merchandise at all different price levels, retailers often employ **price lining** and sell merchandise at a limited range of price points, with each point representing a distinct level of quality. Retailers first determine their price floors and ceilings in each product category. They then set a limited number of price points within the range. Department stores generally carry good, better, and best versions of merchandise consistent with their overall price policy—and set individual prices accordingly.

Price lining benefits both consumers and retailers. If the price range for a box of handkerchiefs is $6 to $15 and the price points are $6, $9, and $15, consumers know that distinct product qualities exist. However, should a retailer have prices of $6, $7, $8, $9, $10, $11, $12, $13, $14, and $15, the consumer may be confused about product differences. For retailers, price lining aids merchandise planning. Retail buyers can seek those suppliers carrying products at appropriate prices, and they can better negotiate with suppliers. They can automatically disregard products not fitting within price lines and thereby reduce inventory investment. Also, stock turnover goes up when the number of models carried is limited.

FIGURE 17-10

Odd Pricing: A Popular Retailing Tactic

Around the world, regardless of the currency, odd pricing is a popular retailing tactic. (A) In U.S. dollars; (B) in European euros; (C) in Japanese yen.

Sources: (A) Reprinted by permission of Susan V. Berry, Retail Image Consulting, Inc. (B) hunta/Shutterstock.com. Reprinted by permission. (C) C./Shutterstock.com. Reprinted by permission.

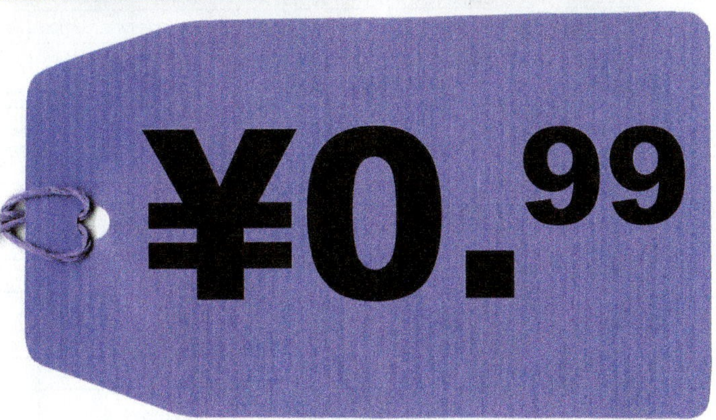

Difficulties do exist: (1) Depending on the price points selected, price lining may leave excessive gaps. A parent shopping for a graduation gift might find a $30 briefcase to be too cheap and a $200 one to be too expensive. (2) Inflation can make it tough to keep price points and price ranges. (3) Markdowns may disrupt the balance in a price line, unless all items in a line are reduced proportionally. (4) Price lines must be coordinated for complementary product categories, such as blazers, skirts, and shoes.

Price Adjustments

Retailers needs to be focused in making price adjustments (www.bizmove.com/general/m6h4.htm).

Price adjustments enable retailers to use price as an adaptive mechanism. Markdowns and additional markups may be needed due to competition, seasonality, demand patterns, merchandise costs, and pilferage. Figure 17-11 shows a price change authorization form.

A **markdown** from an item's original price is used to meet the lower price of another retailer, adapt to inventory overstocking, clear out shopworn merchandise, reduce assortments of odds and ends, and increase customer traffic. An **additional markup** increases an item's original price because demand is unexpectedly high or costs are rising. In today's competitive marketplace, markdowns are applied much more frequently than additional markups.

A third price adjustment, the employee discount, is noted here because it may affect the computation of markdowns and additional markups. Although an employee discount is not an adaptive mechanism, it influences morale. Some firms give employee discounts on all items and also let workers buy sale items before they are made available to the general public.

COMPUTING MARKDOWNS AND ADDITIONAL MARKUPS Markdowns and additional markups can be expressed in dollars or percentages.

The **markdown percentage** is the total dollar markdown as a percentage of net sales (in dollars):

$$\text{Markdown percentage} = \frac{\text{Total dollar markdown}}{\text{Net sales (in \$)}}$$

Although it is simple to compute, this formula does not enable a retailer to learn the percentage of items that are marked down relative to those sold at the original price.

A complementary measure is the **off-retail markdown percentage**, which looks at the markdown for each item or category of items as a percentage of original retail price. The markdown percentage for every item can be computed, as well as the percentage of items marked down:

$$\text{Off-retail markdown percentage} = \frac{\text{Original price} - \text{New price}}{\text{Original price}}$$

FIGURE 17-11
A Price Change Authorization Form

PRICE CHANGE AUTHORIZATION 418651

MARK THE BLANK BOX TO THE LEFT OF EACH STORE AFFECTED WITH AN "X"

HQ | SC | WE | PA | VS | RF | BS | ST | CO | WH

ALL (SOUTH ONLY) | ME | CH | UD | NE | MO | KP | EC | LA | OX | GR

TYPE OF PRICE CHANGE: MARK "X" NEXT TO TYPE

MARKDOWN 1 | MARKDOWN CANCELLATION 2 | MARKUP 3 | MARKUP CANCELLATION 4 | ACTION DATE MM DD YY | DEPT

MARKING INSTRUCTIONS: NEW TICKET 1 PEN 2 CHANGE CHECKS 3
POS FROM BEFORE AND AFTER COUNTS 2 POS FROM SALESCHECKS 3

□ PERMANENT
□ TEMPORARY

DIVISION 1

REASON FOR PRICE CHANGE/ ORIGINAL AUTHORIZATION NO.

AD MERCHANDISE □ NO □ YES

DATES OF SALE FROM / TO /

STOCK STATUS DEPARTMENTS: CIRCLE ONE CODE ONLY FOR ALL STYLES
1 TO BE REPORTED IN REGULAR SELECTION OF STOCK STATUS
3 TO BE REPORTED IN MARKDOWN SECTION OF STOCK STATUS

SPECIAL INSTRUCTIONS

	% OFF	MERCHANDISE DESCRIPTION (CC 1-31)	CLASS	SKU NUMBER VENDOR	SKU NUMBER STYLE	UNIT RETAIL OLD	UNIT RETAIL NEW	CHANGE PER UNIT	EST COUNT (ALL STORES)	TOTAL DOLLARS
01			10							
02			10							
03			10							
04			10							
05			10							
06			10							
07			10							
08			10							
09			10							

REASON (CIRCLE)	LEAD TIME	REASON (CIRCLE)	LEAD TIME
1. COMPETITION	2 DAYS	5. NORMAL CLEARANCE	5 DAYS
2. STOREWIDE EVENTS DIV/DEPT SALE	5 DAYS	6. SLOW SELLING LIQUIDATION	5 DAYS
3. EQUALIZATION	5 DAYS	7. CURRENT RECEIPTS NOT SELLING	4 DAYS
4. MARKOUT/SALVAGE BREAKAGE	5 DAYS		

MEMO TOTAL

BUYER | DATE | BUYER EXT | DIV MDSE MGR | DATE | GEN MDSE MGR | DATE | PRICE CHANGE CONTROL | DATE

PRICE CHANGE CONTROL COPY

Suppose a gas barbecue grill sells for \$400 at the beginning of the summer and is reduced to \$280 at the end of the summer. The off-retail markdown is 30 percent [(\$400 – \$280)/\$400]. If 100 grills are sold at the original price and 20 are sold at the sale price, the percentage of items marked down is 17 percent, and the total dollar markdown is \$2,400.

The **additional markup percentage** looks at total dollar additional markups as a percentage of net sales, while the **addition to retail percentage** measures a price rise as a percentage of the original price:

$$\text{Additional markup percentage} = \frac{\text{Total dollar additional markups}}{\text{Net sales (in \$)}}$$

$$\text{Addition to retail percentage} = \frac{\text{New price} - \text{Original price}}{\text{Original price}}$$

Retailers must realize that many more customers would have to buy at reduced prices for those retailers to have a total gross profit equal to that at higher prices. A retailer's judgment regarding price adjustments is affected by its operating expenses at various sales volumes and customer price elasticities. The true impact of a markdown or an additional markup can be learned from this formula:

$$\text{Unit sales required to earn the same total gross profit with a price adjustment} = \frac{\text{Original markup (\%)}}{\text{Original markup (\%)} +/- \text{Price change (\%)}} \times \text{Expected unit sales at original price}$$

Suppose a Hewlett-Packard printer with a cost of \$50 has an original retail price of \$100 (a markup of 50 percent). A retailer expects to sell 500 units over the next year, generating a total gross profit of \$25,000 (\$50 x 500). How many units does the retailer have to sell if it reduces the price to \$85 or raises it to \$110—and still earn a \$25,000 gross profit? Here are the answers:

$$\text{Unit sales required (at \$85)} = \frac{50\%}{50\% - 15\%} \times 500 = 1.43 \times 500 = 714$$

$$\text{Unit sales required (at \$110)} = \frac{50\%}{50\% - 10\%} \times 500 = 0.83 \times 500 = 417$$

MARKDOWN CONTROL Through markdown control, a retailer evaluates the number of markdowns, the proportion of sales involving markdowns, and the causes. The control must be such that buying plans can be altered in later periods to reflect markdowns. A good way to evaluate the cause of markdowns is to have retail buyers record the reasons for each markdown and then examine them periodically. Possible buyer notations are "end of season," "to match the price of a competitor," and "obsolete style."

Through markdown control, a retailer can monitor its policies, such as the way items are displayed. Careful planning may also enable a retailer to avoid some markdowns by running more ads, training workers better, shipping goods more efficiently among branch units, and returning items to vendors.

The need for markdown control should not be interpreted as meaning that all markdowns can or should be minimized or eliminated. In fact, too low a markdown percentage may indicate that a retailer's buyers have not assumed enough risk in purchasing goods.

TIMING MARKDOWNS There are different perspectives among retailers about the best markdown timing sequence, but much can be said about the benefits of an *early markdown policy*: It requires lower markdowns to sell products than markdowns late in the season. Merchandise is offered at reduced prices while demand is still fairly active. Early markdowns free selling space for new merchandise. The retailer's cash flow position can be improved. The main advantage of a *late markdown policy* is that a retailer gives itself every opportunity to sell merchandise at original prices. Yet, the advantages associated with an early markdown policy cannot be achieved under a late markdown policy.

Retailers can also use a *staggered markdown policy* and discount prices throughout a selling period. One pre-planned staggered markdown policy is an *automatic markdown plan*, in which the amount and timing of markdowns are controlled by the length of time merchandise remains in stock.

A *storewide clearance*, conducted once or twice a year, is another way to time markdowns. It often takes place after peak selling periods such as Christmas and Mother's Day. The goal is to clean out merchandise before taking a physical inventory and beginning the next season. The advantages of a storewide clearance are that a longer period is provided for selling merchandise at original prices and that frequent markdowns can destroy a consumer's confidence in regular prices: "Why buy now, when it will be on sale next week?" Clearance sales limit bargain hunting to once or twice a year.

In the past, many retailers would introduce merchandise at high prices and then mark down many items by as much as 60 percent to increase store traffic and improve inventory turnover. This caused customers to wait for price reductions and treat initial prices skeptically. Today, more retailers start out with lower prices and try to run fewer sales and apply fewer markdowns than before. Nonetheless, a big problem facing some retailers is that they have gotten consumers too used to buying when items are discounted.

One interesting example of markdown management support is the Markdown Manager software that eBay offers as a service for its sellers (http://pages.ebay.com/help/sell/items_on_sale.html).

Chapter Summary

1. *To describe the role of pricing in a retail strategy and to show that pricing decisions must be made in an integrated and adaptive manner.* Pricing is crucial to a retailer because of its interrelationship with overall objectives and the other components of the retail strategy. A price plan must be integrated and responsive—and provide a good value to customers.

2. *To examine the impact of consumers; government; manufacturers, wholesalers, and other suppliers; and current and potential competitors on pricing decisions.* Before designing a price plan, a retailer must study the factors affecting its decisions. Sometimes, the factors have a minor effect on pricing discretion; other times, they severely limit pricing options.

   Retailers should be familiar with the price elasticity of demand and the different market segments that are possible. Government restrictions deal with price fixing, price discrimination, minimum prices, unit pricing, item price removal, and price advertising. There may be conflicts about which party controls retail prices; and manufacturers, wholesalers, and other suppliers may be asked to provide price guarantees (if they are in a weak position). The competitive environment may foster market pricing, lead to price wars, or allow administered pricing.

3. *To present a framework for developing a retail price strategy.* This framework consists of five stages: objectives, broad price policy, price strategy, implementation of price strategy, and price adjustments.

   Retail pricing goals can be chosen from among sales, dollar profits, return on investment, and early recovery of cash. Next, a broad policy outlines a coordinated series of actions, consistent with the retailer's image and oriented to the short and long run.

   A good price strategy incorporates demand, cost, and competitive concepts. Each of these orientations must be understood separately and jointly. Psychological pricing; markup pricing; alternative ways of computing markups; gross margin; direct product profitability; and pricing below, at, or above the market are among the key aspects of strategy planning.

   When enacting a price strategy, specific tools can be used to supplement the broad base of the strategy. Retailers should know when to use customary and variable pricing, one-price policies and flexible pricing, odd pricing, leader pricing, multiple-unit pricing, and price lining.

   Price adjustments may be required to adapt to internal and external conditions. Adjustments include markdowns, additional markups, and employee discounts. It is important that adjustments are controlled by a budget, the causes of markdowns are noted, future company buying reflects prior performance, adjustments are properly timed, and excessive discounting is avoided.

Key Terms

price elasticity of demand (p. 425)
horizontal price fixing (p. 427)
vertical price fixing (p. 427)
Robinson-Patman Act (p. 428)
minimum-price laws (p. 428)
predatory pricing (p. 428)
loss leaders (p. 428)
unit pricing (p. 428)
item price removal (p. 429)

bait-and-switch advertising (p. 429)
gray market goods (p. 430)
market penetration pricing (p. 431)
market skimming pricing (p. 431)
demand-oriented pricing (p. 434)
cost-oriented pricing (p. 434)
competition-oriented pricing (p. 434)
price–quality association (p. 434)
prestige pricing (p. 434)
markup pricing (p. 434)
markup (p. 434)
markup percentage (p. 434)
initial markup (p. 436)
maintained markup (p. 436)
gross margin (p. 436)
variable markup policy (p. 437)
direct product profitability (DPP) (p. 437)
customary pricing (p. 440)
everyday low pricing (EDLP) (p. 440)
variable pricing (p. 440)
yield management pricing (p. 441)
one-price policy (p. 441)
flexible pricing (p. 441)
contingency pricing (p. 442)
odd pricing (p. 442)
leader pricing (p. 442)
multiple-unit pricing (p. 442)
bundled pricing (p. 442)
unbundled pricing (p. 442)
price lining (p. 442)
markdown (p. 444)
additional markup (p. 444)
markdown percentage (p. 444)
off-retail markdown percentage (p. 444)
additional markup percentage (p. 445)
addition to retail percentage (p. 445)

Questions for Discussion

1. Why is it important for retailers to understand the concept of price elasticity even if they are unable to compute it?
2. Comment on each of the following from the perspective of a small retailer:
   a. Horizontal price fixing.
   b. Vertical price fixing.
   c. Price discrimination.
   d. Minimum-price laws.
   e. Unit pricing.
3. Give an example of a price strategy that integrates demand, cost, and competitive criteria.
4. Explain why markups are usually computed as a percentage of selling price rather than of cost.
5. A floor tile retailer wants to receive a 35 percent markup (at retail) for all merchandise. If one style of tile retails for $11 per tile, what is the maximum that the retailer would be willing to pay for a tile?
6. A car dealer purchases multiple-disk CD players for $100 each and desires a 35 percent markup (at retail). What retail price should be charged?
7. A gift store charges $25.00 for a ceramic figurine; its cost is $14.00. What is the markup percentage (at cost and at retail)?
8. A firm has planned operating expenses of $200,000, a profit goal of $130,000, and planned reductions of $35,000, and it expects sales of $700,000. Compute the initial markup percentage.
9. At the end of the year, the retailer in Question 8 determines that actual operating expenses are $160,000, actual profit is $120,000, and actual sales are $650,000. What is the maintained markup percentage? Explain the difference in your answers to Questions 8 and 9.
10. What are the pros and cons of everyday low pricing to a retailer? To a manufacturer?
11. Under what circumstances do you think unbundled pricing is a good idea? A poor idea? Why?
12. A retailer buys items for $65. At an original retail price of $89, it expects to sell 1,000 units.
    a. If the price is marked down to $79, how many units must the retailer sell to earn the same total gross profit it would attain with an $89 price?
    b. If the price is marked up to $99, how many units must the retailer sell to earn the same total gross profit it would attain with an $89 price?

Note: At our Web site (www.pearsonhighered.com/bermanevans), there are several math problems related to the material in this chapter so that you may review these concepts.

Web-Based Exercise

Visit the Web site of Neiman Marcus (www.neimanmarcus.com). What are the least expensive consumer products sold through this site? The most expensive? Do you feel that this price range is consistent with Neiman Marcus as an upscale retailer? Explain your answer.

Note: Also stop by our Web site (www.pearsonhighered.com/bermanevans) to experience a number of highly interactive, appealing Web exercises based on actual company demonstrations and sample materials related to retailing.

PART 6 Short Cases

Case 1: Making McDonald's Recession-Resistant[c-1]

As its chief executive likes to say, McDonald's (www.mcdonalds.com) is "recession-resistant" as opposed to "recession-proof." Nonetheless, the retailer has outperformed many other retailers during the recent tough economic times. The nation's leading fast-food chain has even managed to report comparable store sales growth in many quarters—due to the strong growth in its McCafé beverages, its new fruit-and-maple oatmeal, expanded sales of healthier foods, and its everyday value pricing menu.

Both the McCafé line of beverages and the fruit-and-maple oatmeal were developed to bolster McDonald's weakest meal—breakfast. In May 2009, McDonald's launched its McCafé beverages as an addition to its traditional coffee segment. According to Ashlee Yingling, a company spokesperson: "It continues to evolve as we look at espresso-based drinks." Additional coffee products may make McDonald's a destination retailer of coffees, which Dunkin' Donuts (www.dunkindonuts.com) has accomplished.

McDonald's, which is best known for its burgers, milk shakes, and French fries, is now also featuring healthier foods. Although mostly perceived as a breakfast item, McDonald's fruit-and-maple oatmeal is available all day long. And unlike other products that have been criticized as being unhealthy, the fruit-and-maple oatmeal is available with or without brown sugar, provides the equivalent of two servings of whole grain, and comprises 20 percent of the daily requirements for fiber. The fruit-and-maple oatmeal was developed in association with the Whole Grains Council.

While McDonald's has had salads on its menu since 2003 and snack wraps since 2006, today it also offers small food portions, grilled versus fried alternatives, and a "made for you" platform in which consumers can order any item on the menu to their liking (such as a burger without cheese or oatmeal without brown sugar). Yingling says: "It's not about categorizing it as 'healthier,' it's about providing options customers feel good about eating."

Instead of offering a constant stream of promotions (such as buy a burger and fries and get a free soda) and price reductions, McDonald's is more committed to providing everyday value to its customers. The use of everyday value pricing reduces advertising costs, makes sales forecasting more predictable, avoids excessive peaks and valleys in sales, and is not reliant on a franchisee's joining each promotion.

McDonald's product-planning process seeks to eliminate duplication between existing and new products. Thus, the Big N' Tasty burger was eliminated after the Angus Third Pounder was developed. Similarly, the Mac Snack Wrap was discontinued once the Angus Snack Wrap was commercialized. As Ashlee Yingling notes: "It's just about realizing the similarities in menu items, then a decision has to be made about keeping both or not—but it is not a decision that we take lightly." The introduction of five new products in a year does not mean that five existing products need to be eliminated.

Some retail analysts are concerned that McDonald's stream of new products will reduce its ability to quickly deliver hot-and-tasty foods. Yingling counters this criticism by stating that all of the chain's new products must meet the criteria of being served within 1½ minutes of a customer's initial order.

Questions

1. Evaluate the appropriateness of the McCafé line of coffees and the fruit-and-maple oatmeal to McDonald's overall merchandising strategy.
2. Discuss the pros and cons of McDonald's use of an everyday value pricing strategy versus a constant stream of promotions.
3. Describe the pitfalls associated with McDonald's having too many products.
4. Develop a system for McDonald's to use to eliminate duplication among new and existing products.

Case 2: The Merchandising of Private Brands[c-2]

At one point, product planning decisions by retailers for their private-label brands was a simple process. The retailers simply contracted with national brand manufacturers or with a private-label producer to make a special private-label product version. The retailers then placed the private-label brand on their store shelves. Now, retailers are much more involved with planning the specifications of their private-label products, with designing distinctive logos and labels, and with even managing "good, better, and best" versions of their private-label brands.

Many retail analysts agree that retailers need to develop a strong product-placement strategy for their private-label products so that consumers can more easily locate these items in the store. According to one consumer packaged goods executive: "While innovation is important, the fundamentals of having the right products in stock—in sight and in the right locations with the right message to offer—are key to driving shopper loyalty."

To add to today's complexity in the placement of private-label products, many retailers offer different levels of quality (such as premium products and organics) within a single private-label brand. As a result, promotions for each version need to stress price-based appeals for low-cost private-label goods and a private label's unique characteristics for upscale product categories (such as more chocolate chips than a national brand for a premium chocolate chip cookie or the use of organic ingredients for soup).

Product-placement decisions also need to reflect shelf-height decisions. Duane Reade (www.duanereade.com), a New York–based drugstore chain, places its premium cookies at eye level (the most preferred space), its value-oriented

[c-1]The material in this case is drawn from Renée M. Covino, "Lessons from the 'Big Mac,' " www.csnews.com (March 14, 2011).

[c-2]The material in this case is drawn from Kathie Canning, "Set the Stage," *Progressive Grocer Store Brands* (May 2011), pp. 16–20.

private-label brand of cookies below eye level, and the national brands of cookies at the poorest locations on its store shelves.

The traditional shelf location for private-label brands has been to the right of national brands on the same shelf. This accomplishes several objectives. It enables shoppers to compare price and quantity levels between different types of brands. In many cases, shoppers may elect to buy the private label based on its low cost, similar ingredients, or larger package size as compared with the national brand. The strategy also gives shoppers a better idea of the comprehensive selection available for a store's private labels. Some retailers use endcaps (end-of-aisle displays) for their private labels. These locations have more visibility and greater store traffic than mid-aisle displays. Some retailers give premium space to new national brands based on slotting fees paid by the national brands for preferred product placement.

In addition to shelf placement, merchandising programs for private labels need to engage shoppers. Trader Joe's (www.traderjoes.com) offers sampling stations where employees prepare light snacks using their private-label goods. These snacks are generally easy to prepare, and they stimulate the sales of multiple private-label ingredients to follow the recipes.

Retailers need to be aware of merchandising pitfalls associated with private labels. One common error is not to view the private label as a real brand. Retailers falling victim to this problem area may not give the private label prominent shelf placement or they may fail to make the brand easy to locate. Another merchandising pitfall is for retailers to promote their private-label brands solely on the basis of price.

Questions

1. What factors are behind the shift to an increased role of retailers in the development and promotion of private labels?
2. Provide examples of how a retailer can offer different versions of its private-label chicken soup.
3. What is the impact of a retailer's offering multiple versions of a private label on a manufacturer's brand strategy?
4. Develop a merchandising program for a new private-label line of healthy snacks at a specialty food store chain.

Case 3: Destocking as a Strategy[c-3]

Due to the recent weak economic environment, many retailers have been reluctant to order too many goods, fearing that they will not sell. Among the economic indicators that most concern retailers' stocking approach are high unemployment levels, high foreclosure rates in the housing market, fluctuations in the stock market, and gasoline price levels that deter shopping. As a result of these concerns, some retailers would rather risk lost sales due to stockouts than have to heavily mark down goods that were ordered in too large quantities. Analysts attribute this low-inventory strategy to retailers' remembering the 2008–2009 recession peak when too many retailers were burdened with high inventories.

To reduce inventory risk, some retailers have begun to carefully evaluate such tactics as their "back-to-school" sales. For a number of retailers, this is the second most critical season (after Christmas) in terms of sales. Other retailers have added alternate suppliers to serve as backups in the case of high demand levels. Macy's (www.macys.com) has effectively reduced inventory requirements by working with suppliers to get more store-ready merchandise that does not require distribution centers operated by the retailer. Macy's has also lowered its inventory-holding costs by combining store and online inventories in one facility, instead of maintaining separate warehouses for each channel. These changes resulted in Macy's saving $5 million in 2010 alone.

These shifts in inventory planning are reflected in the retail business inventory-to-sales ratio, which was at 1.33 as of mid-2011, the lowest for this time period since 1992. As a vice-president for the National Retail Federation says: "With rising gas prices and challenges in the labor and housing markets, consumer spending has slowed and retailers have adjusted their inventory levels accordingly."

The inventory-to-sales ratios for manufacturers and wholesalers have shown similar declines. This indicates that these supply chain members are not necessarily holding excess inventories for rapid delivery to retailers with low stock on hand, which is opposite to what the retailers are assuming.

The downside of having too little inventory on hand—a negative impact on revenue—was experienced by Wal-Mart when that retailer reduced inventory selections as a means of lessening inventory-holding costs and improving supply-chain efficiency. Unfortunately, Wal-Mart's sales performance suffered when customers found that their favorite brands were no longer stocked. Another potential problem associated with low inventories is the difficulty in dealing with supply-chain disruptions, such as the 2011 earthquake in Japan.

Sharen Turney, the chief executive of Victoria's Secret (www.victoriassecret.com), understands the need to weigh the benefits of minimizing inventory-holding costs against the possibility of lost sales. Turney says that Victoria's Secret is seeking a "balanced approach between managing the business with optimism and staying conservative on our inventory and expense plans."

In addition to lost sales, too little inventory is typically associated with the need for frequent ordering, the need for emergency shipments, high ordering costs, and less ability to receive quantity discounts. In contrast, too high an inventory is normally associated with high holding costs, the need for markdowns to clear out unsold inventory, and too much dated merchandise.

Questions

1. List five tactics that retailers can use to reduce their inventory levels while keeping the chance of stockouts low.
2. Discuss the supply-chain implications of retailers having low inventory-to-sales ratios if the inventory-to-sales ratios of manufacturers and wholesalers are high.
3. What are the dangers of frequent small orders and the use of emergency shipments as a means of reducing inventory requirements?
4. How could Wal-Mart have foreseen and avoided the negative impact on revenues of pruning its merchandise selection?

[c-3]The material in this case is drawn from Joseph Bonney, "From Restocking to Destocking," *Journal of Commerce* (June 27, 2011), pp. 10–16.

Case 4: Cheap Chic from Forever 21[c-4]

Forever 21 (www.forever21.com) is a retailer that operates various store brands. It generates $3 billion a year in sales, has more than 480 stores, and employs 35,000 people. Forever 21 has grown so quickly that it opened 100 stores in 2010; and during one two-week period in 2011, Forever 21 opened three stores. In the past several years, Forever 21 has increased its square footage of store space from 1 million square feet to 10 million square feet, and from one private-label brand to six such brands. Even with this expansion, Forever 21 has been profitable. Its overall growth has been accomplished with no advertising, almost no marketing effort, and infrequent efforts of the chain's management to introduce themselves to their customers.

Early in their career as merchants, Do Won and Jin Sook Chang, the founders of Forever 21, began to order only small quantities of each style they offered for sale. To reduce their inventory risk and minimize markdowns, they planned to quickly reorder fast-selling clothing and discontinue styles that did not sell well. According to one research analyst: "A typical Forever 21 has inventory turnover of 20 percent per week, about two times the level of apparel manufacturers."

Forever 21 has been quick to capitalize on location opportunities generated by store closings and bankruptcies of other retailers. These include locations that were abandoned by Sears, Saks, Circuit City, Dillards, and Mervyn's. In addition, Forever 21 has locations on Fifth Avenue in New York City, on London's Oxford Street, and in Tokyo's Shibuya district.

Forever 21's growth has not been controversy-free. Even though the owners of the chain have never been found guilty of copyright infringement in court, between 2006 and 2010, about 50 designer brands—including Diane von Furstenberg, Anna Sui, and Anthropologie—individually sued Forever 21. While U.S. copyright law protects original prints and graphics (as opposed to the design itself), these three firms won out-of-court settlements against Forever 21 (the results of this litigation are confidential).

In commenting on the Anthropologie case, a U.S. District Court judge said: "We note the extraordinary litigating history of this company, which raises the most serious questions as to whether it is a business that is predicated in large measure on the systematic infringement of competitors' intellectual property." Similarly, a copyright law expert stated: "Illegal copying has been incorporated into their business model. But it's not necessarily a terrible result for designers who do receive payment."

Another designer who received payment from Forever 21 was Virginia Johnson. The original Johnson skirt was sold for $175; Forever 21's clone was priced at less than $18. In this instance, Forever 21 paid $9,000 (22.5 percent of sales) for a licensing agreement.

Another criticism of Forever 21 involves its history of using suppliers that underpay their workers. As one attorney who successfully sued Forever 21 concluded: "Forever 21 is not a victim of the industry. They create and demand these conditions. They squeeze their suppliers and make it necessary for them to get things done as quickly and as cheaply as possible, no matter what the cost to the workers."

Questions

1. Comment on the statement that Forever 21 "began to order only small quantities of each style offered for sale. They figured that they could quickly reorder fast selling clothing and drop styles that did not sell well to minimize their inventory risk."
2. Legal issues aside, evaluate Forever 21's strategy of making low-cost versions of successful designs by famous designers.
3. What do you recommend that Forever 21 should do in the future to avoid the controversies cited in this case?
4. From a merchandising perspective, what are the pros and cons of Forever 21's fast-growth strategy?

[c-4]The material in this case is drawn from Susan Berfield, "Forever 21's Fast (and Loose) Fashion Empire," www.businessweek.com (January 20, 2011).

PART 6 Comprehensive Case

The Unique Merchandising Strategy of eBay*

Introduction

eBay is known for operating the online marketplace eBay.com (www.ebay.com). The company's marketplace is where third-party buyers and sellers can conduct transactions involving a very wide variety of products, including clothing, electronics, media, collectibles, automobiles, and many other types of merchandise.

In addition to eBay.com, the company operates other online commerce platforms such as Half.com, Rent.com, Shopping.com, and classifieds Web sites. eBay also makes money through its global payments platform called PayPal (www.paypal.com). PayPal enables secure, easy, quick, and cost-effective transfers of payments online.

During 2011, eBay acquired GSI Commerce (www.gsicommerce.com) for $2.4 billion. This deal allows eBay to enable more merchants of all sizes to conduct E-commerce and to compete more effectively with online retailers such as Amazon.com. This deal is one of the biggest for eBay since its 2005 acquisition of Skype for $2.5 billion. [After not meeting eBay's expectations, Skype was sold to Microsoft in 2011.] GSI Commerce will make eBay's marketplace more attractive for large retailers that prefer selling at fixed prices. eBay and GSI aim to move toward a common platform to serve retailers of all sizes across eBay, Paypal, and GSI. eBay hopes this acquisition will add to the bottom line from 2012 onward, even though it may put negative pressure on its operating profits in the short term.

Drivers of Success and Trends

With regard to eBay Marketplaces, the "transaction take rate" is quite important. This is eBay's commission on the items sold. It is projected that the take rate for eBay Marketplaces will decrease from about 8 percent in 2010 to 7.6 percent by 2018. A big challenge for eBay is to try to stabilize the take-out rate. It is also expected that the profit margins for eBay Marketplaces will drop by 3 percent between 2010 and 2018.

At PayPal, eBay's other main business, it is forecast that the average number of payments per customer PayPal account will remain flat from 2010 to 2018. On the positive side, it is projected that PayPal profit margins will increase by 6 percent from 2010 to 2018.

eBay Marketplaces is the more valuable business segment for these reasons: The Marketplaces' take rate (8.2 percent in 2011 is higher than PayPal's take rate of 3.5 percent in 2011). Marketplaces' profit margins are substantially higher than PayPal's profit margins.

In looking to the future, eBay recognizes the following factors as keys to success:

- The conversion rate is a key focus area for eBay, as it seeks to increase the success of sellers in converting listed items to sold items. eBay has implemented a number of features to increase the conversion rate on Marketplaces. One of the more important changes it has made is improving functionality and stepping up efforts related to trust and safety.
- PayPal users will continue to grow as eBay continues to integrate PayPal into its adjacent Marketplaces platforms such as Shopping.com and Rent.com—and through increased penetration of PayPal on third-party merchant platforms, as eBay increases its focus on small and medium-size sellers.
- Google Checkout and credit card merchants will limit eBay's ability to raise revenues by increasing its commission on PayPal transactions. They will hold down PayPal's take rate.

Table 1 contains financial data on eBay overall, as well as for each of its three businesses: eBay Marketplaces, PayPal, and Advertising & Marketing.

eBay Marketplaces

The most important factors for the eBay Marketplaces business are the average selling price of merchandise on eBay, eBay's transaction take rate, the listings-to-sales conversion rate for merchandise offered at eBay, the number of merchandise listings on eBay, and profit margins. The top of Table 2 highlights several key trends for eBay Marketplaces.

eBay's Marketplaces' average selling price includes the merchandise sold on these eBay properties: eBay.com, Half.com, Rent.com, and Shopping.com. The average price incorporates the wide range of prices found on eBay—from low-priced merchandise to expensive electronics, motor vehicles, and boats.

The average selling price of merchandise on eBay is very much a function of the items listed and sold. The average selling price declined from around $60 in 2007 to $51 in 2009, before bouncing back to $65 in 2010. It was expected that the average price will be $64 or less through 2012, and then rise to $76 by 2018. The 2009 selling price was impacted negatively as higher-priced auto sales were decimated by macroeconomic factors and declines in consumer spending.

As previously noted, the eBay transaction take rate represents eBay's commission on items sold. The take rates are primarily a function of pricing actions initiated by eBay to drive higher-priced listings and higher conversion rates on their platforms. After experiencing growth in prior years, eBay witnessed a stagnation in its take rate from 2007 to 2009 due to the weak economy and competition. It is projected that the transaction take rate will increase to 8.2 to 8.3 percent through 2014 and then drop to 7.6 as of 2018.

There is a strategic trade-off between volume and price. eBay has shown the willingness to use pricing as a means to bring more sellers on board, as well as to provide incentives for sellers to enhance the user experience by engaging in safer, simpler transactions. This should continue to be the case. Furthermore, higher-priced products have lower take rates;

*The material in this case is adapted by the authors from *Trefis Analysis for eBay* (Boston, MA: Insight Guru Inc., July 21, 2011). Reprinted by permission of Trefis.com.

TABLE 1 A Financial Summary for eBay

	2007	2008	2009	2010	2011	2012	2013	2014	2015	2016	2017	2018
Total Revenues (Bil $)	7.29	7.99	8.15	9.15	10.82	12.66	14.26	15.92	17.59	19.46	21.47	23.71
eBay Marketplaces	4.68	4.71	4.46	4.80	5.51	6.48	7.05	7.67	8.34	8.99	9.68	10.40
PayPal	1.84	2.32	2.64	3.26	3.87	4.51	5.35	6.20	7.05	8.02	9.12	10.40
Marketing & Advertising	0.77	0.96	1.05	1.09	1.44	1.67	1.86	2.05	2.25	2.45	2.67	2.91
Revenues by Business (% of total company)												
eBay Marketplaces	64.2	59.0	54.7	52.4	50.9	51.2	49.5	48.2	47.3	46.2	45.1	44.0
PayPal	25.2	29.0	32.4	35.6	35.7	35.6	37.5	39.0	40.0	41.2	42.5	43.7
Marketing & Advertising	10.6	12.0	12.9	12.0	13.3	13.2	13.0	12.9	12.7	12.6	12.4	12.3
Total Expenses (Bil $)	4.99	7.27	6.80	7.99	9.35	10.83	12.08	13.36	14.69	16.08	17.73	19.80
eBay Marketplaces	2.97	4.05	3.43	3.92	4.51	5.16	5.56	6.00	6.49	6.96	7.48	8.14
PayPal	1.54	2.44	2.60	3.18	3.68	4.32	5.03	5.73	6.42	7.19	8.15	9.35
Marketing & Advertising	0.48	0.78	0.77	0.89	1.16	1.35	1.49	1.63	1.78	1.93	2.10	2.31
Expenses by Business (% of total company)												
eBay Marketplaces	59.5	55.7	50.4	49.1	48.2	47.6	46.0	44.9	44.2	43.3	42.2	41.1
PayPal	30.9	33.6	38.2	39.8	39.4	39.9	41.6	42.9	43.7	44.7	46.0	47.2
Marketing & Advertising	9.6	10.7	11.3	11.1	12.4	12.5	12.3	12.2	12.1	12.0	11.8	11.7
Gross Profits (Bil $)[a]	2.86	2.45	1.98	2.68	2.74	3.28	3.70	4.16	4.66	5.18	5.68	6.25
eBay Marketplaces	2.07	1.68	1.38	1.68	1.64	2.06	2.25	2.44	2.66	2.86	3.08	3.32
PayPal	0.44	0.38	0.24	0.62	0.64	0.71	0.89	1.10	1.32	1.58	1.79	2.04
Marketing & Advertising	0.35	0.39	0.36	0.38	0.46	0.51	0.56	0.62	0.68	0.74	0.81	0.89
Gross Profits by Business (% of total company)												
eBay Marketplaces (% of total)	72.3	68.6	69.7	62.5	59.9	63.0	60.7	58.7	57.1	55.2	54.2	53.2
PayPal (% of total)	15.4	15.7	12.1	23.2	23.5	21.6	24.1	26.3	28.3	30.4	31.5	32.6
Marketing & Advertising (% of total)	12.3	15.8	18.2	14.3	16.6	15.5	15.3	15.0	14.7	14.3	14.3	14.2
Gross Profits (% of total revenues by segment)	39.2	30.7	24.3	29.3	25.3	25.9	25.9	26.1	26.5	26.6	26.5	26.4
eBay Marketplaces	44.2	35.7	30.9	35.0	29.8	31.8	31.9	31.8	31.9	31.8	31.8	31.9
PayPal	23.9	16.4	9.1	19.0	16.5	15.7	16.6	17.7	18.7	19.7	19.6	19.6
Marketing & Advertising	45.5	40.6	34.3	34.9	31.9	30.5	30.1	30.2	30.2	30.2	30.3	30.6

[a] Gross profits = Total revenues – Direct expenses

Note: There are some rounding errors in this table.

TABLE 2 A Closer Look at eBay Marketplaces and PayPal

	2007	2008	2009	2010	2011	2012	2013	2014	2015	2016	2017	2018
eBay Marketplaces												
Number of Merchandise Listings on eBay (Bil)	2.34	2.69	2.87	3.06	3.26	3.48	3.71	3.96	4.23	4.51	4.81	5.14
Listings-to-Sales Conversion Rate for Merchandise on eBay (%)	42.0	39.0	39.0	31.0	33.0	35.0	35.0	35.0	35.0	35.0	35.0	35.0
Average Selling Price of Merchandise on eBay ($)	60.4	56.9	51.1	65.2	62.2	64.0	65.9	67.9	69.9	72.0	74.2	76.4
eBay Transaction Take Rate (%)	7.88	7.90	7.80	8.03	8.23	8.31	8.23	8.15	8.07	7.91	7.75	7.59
PayPal												
Average Payment Size on PayPal ($)	68.0	67.7	64.1	63.5	65.5	66.5	67.8	69.2	70.6	72.0	73.4	74.9
Number of Accounts on PayPal (Mil)	44.3	63.2	76.9	94.4	105	120	141	162	182	205	231	261
PayPal Payment Take Rate (%)	3.78	3.85	3.69	3.55	3.45	3.38	3.31	3.24	3.18	3.11	3.05	2.99

and competition from Amazon—as well as brick-and-mortar stalwarts like Wal-Mart—to make continued efforts to expand and improve their online presence. Finally, eBay will continue providing more discounts to "power sellers," as it improves its service levels.

The listings-to-sales conversion rate for merchandise on eBay represents the percentage of items for sale listed on eBay that are actually sold. If the conversion rate is increasing while total listings remain the same or continue to increase, this means that the number of items sold on eBay has increased. The listings-to-sales conversion rate has stayed more or less in a tight range of 39 to 43 percent over the years, which is expected to continue.

To lift the conversion rate, eBay has introduced a few programs like eBay Bucks in which shoppers can earn 2 percent of the purchase value of qualified items; they are issued an eBay Bucks certificate at the end of each quarter. According to eBay's management, more than 3 million shoppers have enrolled in the eBay Bucks program and spent five times more than those not enrolled. eBay has also introduced ratings-based fee incentives for sellers to motivate them to exceed buyer expectations in all respects. To inspire more customer confidence, eBay continuously updates its fraud detection software.

Although the positive factors just mentioned may initially increase conversion rates, such initiatives over the long run may not necessarily translate into a higher sales-to-listing ratio, because more listings are likely to be added, putting downward pressure on the ratio.

The number of merchandise listings on eBay represents the number of items for sale listed on eBay's properties, including eBay.com, Half.com, and Shopping.com. The number of listings have steadily increased from 2.4 billion in 2006 to 3.3 billion in 2011. This figure is expected to reach 5.1 billion as of 2018. Traditional retail players, such as Great Britain's Saville Row, Jigsaw, and Ed Hardy have started to list their merchandise on eBay. This trend will benefit eBay dramatically. Global Internet users have increased from 700 million in 2003 to around 2 billion by the end of 2010. This rapid increase will continue globally in the future. eBay had 100 million active users in 2011 as compared to 48 million in 2004. Nonetheless, the number of merchandise listings per active user has gone up in response to efforts put in place by eBay to simplify the fee structure. eBay has made significant reductions in the insertion fee for fixed-price listings.

Gross profit margins steadily decreased from 2007 to 2011. They were expected to rise slightly in 2011 and to stay at that level to 2018. Expenses need to be controlled. Lower fees will drive an increase in sellers and listings. However, to drive conversion of those listings into eventual sales, eBay has a lot of work ahead to facilitate a more enriched buyer experience on the site, which would mean continued investments in research and development to improve the seller and customer experience.

PayPal

The most important factors for the PayPal business are the average payment size on PayPal, the PayPal payment take rate, the number of accounts on PayPal, payments per account on PayPal, and PayPal's profit margins. The bottom of Table 2 highlights some key trends for PayPal.

The average payment size on PayPal declined from a peak of $68 in 2007 to $64 in 2010, owing to the weak economy. It is projected that the average payment size on PayPal will increase in the future, reaching $75 by 2018. From 2007 through 2009, the average payment size for PayPal was higher than the average selling price on eBay Marketplaces. However, from 2010 to 2018, the averages are projected to be much closer together.

The percentage of PayPal's total payment volume (TPV) that is generated from the eBay platform declined from around 64 percent in 2006 to 44 percent in 2009. The average price of items sold on non-eBay platforms is higher. Since PayPal's penetration of non-eBay could continue to increase, this situation will create an upward bias in the overall average prices for PayPal.

PayPal's payment take rate represents the average commission made by PayPal on each transaction. The PayPal payment take rate remained in a range of 3.5 to 3.9 percent from 2003 to 2011. However, it is expected that the take rate will be under downward pressure going forward as a result of increased competition. eBay faces a range of competitors in the payment segments, including Google Checkout, credit-card merchant processors like Amex, First Data, Amazon payments, and money remittance companies like Western Union. The competitive nature of payments will ensure that take rates face a gradual compression in the future.

The number of accounts on PayPal has been growing at a tremendous pace for many years. The figure increased from around 31 million in 2006 to 77 million by 2009 and 105 million as of 2011. The growth is a reflection of eBay's concerted efforts to integrate PayPal into its Marketplaces segment and forge strategic relationships with a diversified group of leading online commerce portals like Blue Nile and Toys "R" Us. The growth rate in user accounts is expected to continue at a double-digit pace in both the United States and international markets for the foreseeable future, with the number of accounts reaching more than 260 million by 2018.

PayPal increased its total payment volume from eBay Marketplaces from $24 billion in 2006 to around $31 billion in 2009. This growth was slower than the growth of PayPal's overall TPV, which increased from $38 billion in 2006 to $72 billion in 2009. It is projected that the TPV from eBay Marketplaces continue to increase going forward, as eBay continues to integrate PayPal into its adjacent marketplaces platforms like Shopping.com and Rent.com. In addition, eBay's focus on buyer protection programs will increase and enhance PayPal's use on the platform.

PayPal's TPV penetration of third-party merchants has steadily increased, going from 36 percent in 2006 to 56 percent in 2009. PayPal has already forged relationships with leading E-commerce Web sites such as Blue Nile, Southwest Airlines, Barnes & Noble, and Toys "R" Us. Growth in this segment should continue as eBay focuses more on small and medium businesses, as well as sole proprietors.

Payments per account on PayPal represent the number of transactions per PayPal user per month. The transactions per account declined from 1.7 in 2005 to less than 1.2 in 2010. The payments per account are expected to stabilize and reach 1.5 transactions per month as of 2018. This will be due to eBay's expanding its partnerships with more third-party sites to use PayPal. However, many of the new customers of PayPal may be marginal users who infrequently shop with that payment service; they are not as likely to be heavy users of E-commerce functionality as early adopters generally are.

Gross profit margins at PayPal are lower than for eBay's other businesses; and they steadily decreased from 2007 to 2012, falling to as low as 9 percent of sales in 2009—down from 24 percent in 2007. But gross profit margins are expected to grow in the future and level off at 20 percent of sales through 2018. Nonetheless, because PayPal's share of eBay's overall revenues will continue to rise (to rough equivalence with eBay Marketplaces by 2018, from less than one-half of the revenues of eBay Marketplaces in 2007), companywide gross profit margins will drop—from 39 percent in 2007 to 26 percent as of 2018.

These two dynamics will impact the operating margins going forward. One, given that the payments business is significantly more competitive than Marketplaces, regular investments will be necessary. Yet, given that a significant majority of the business comes from eBay, that part of the business is shielded from competitive threats, which will marginalize the threat of competition. Two, as an offset to competition, eBay will be shifting its current mix of transactions on PayPal. This will likely involve a switch from credit card–based to bank account or direct PayPal account–based payments, which are higher margin. Competition and the transaction mix factors should offset each other.

Marketing & Advertising

The most important factors for the Marketing & Advertising business are revenue and profit margins.

Revenues from Marketing & Advertising are derived from the sale of advertisements on Marketplaces, as well as from classifieds fees. Revenues from comparison-shopping site Shopping.com are also included. Overall marketing and ad revenue as a percentage of eBay's companywide revenue increased from nearly 9 percent in 2004 to almost 17 percent in 2011. Although revenue growth is expected to continue until 2018 (rising from $1.4 billion in 2011 to $2.91 billion in 2018), the share of companywide revenues will drop—largely due to the boom period for PayPal.

As eBay better monetizes its vast user base and traffic through text and graphical ads, revenues will rise. E-commerce will drive growth in adjacent markets, such as online comparison-shopping sites, including as eBay's Shopping.com. eBay makes money from Shopping.com primarily through advertising, but also through referral fees paid by retailers whose traffic and sales come from Shopping.com.

Gross profit margins for the Marketing and Advertising business are much higher than for PayPal and comparable with eBay Marketplaces. Yet, from 46 percent of revenues in 2007 to 32 percent of revenues in 2011, the gross profit percentage fell steadily. The figure is expected to be 30 to 31 percent in 2018. While marketing and advertising revenues are expected to grow in the low double-digit annual percentage rate, it is also predicted that costs will increase proportionally. This will keep a tab on gross profit margins in the future.

Questions

1. What can *any* retailer learn from this case?
2. Describe and analyze eBay's overall merchandising strategy.
3. Discuss the pros and cons of eBay's huge product assortment to eBay.
4. Today, eBay offers products in two ways: through auctions and through set prices. Comment on this approach.
5. What policies would you set for eBay in deciding which products and sellers are to be listed at the Web site?
6. Evaluate the data in Table 1.
7. Evaluate the data in Table 2.

PART 7

Communicating with the Customer

In Part Seven, the elements involved in how a retailer communicates with its customers are discussed. First, we look at the role of a retail image and how it is developed and sustained. Various aspects of a promotional strategy are then detailed.

Chapter 18 discusses the importance of communications for a retailer. We review the significance of image in the communications effort and the components of a retailer's image. The creation of an image depends heavily on a retailer's atmosphere—which is comprised of all of its physical characteristics, such as the store exterior, the general interior, layouts, and displays. This applies to both store and nonstore retailers. Ways of encouraging customers to spend more time shopping and the value of community relations are also described.

Chapter 19 focuses on the promotional strategy, specifically how a retailer can inform, persuade, and remind the target market about its strategic mix. In the first part of the chapter, we deal with the four basic types of retail promotion: advertising, public relations, personal selling, and sales promotion. The second part describes the steps in a promotional strategy: objectives, budget, mix of forms, implementation of mix, and review and revision of the plan.

Source: cdsk/Shutterstock.com. Reprinted by permission.

18 Establishing and Maintaining a Retail Image

Chapter Objectives

1. To show the importance of communicating with customers and examine the concept of retail image
2. To describe how a retail store image is related to the atmosphere it creates via its exterior, general interior, layout, and displays, and to look at the special case of nonstore atmospherics
3. To discuss ways of encouraging customers to spend more time shopping
4. To consider the impact of community relations on a retailer's image

As we discuss in Chapter 18, a retailer must have a strong communications strategy to properly position itself in customers' minds—and to nurture their shopping behavior. Once customers are attracted, the retailer must strive to create a proper shopping mood for them. Social media can play a major role in this endeavor.

J. Walter Thompson (JWT), a leading media company, has developed a 12-item social media checklist that is quite applicable to retail communications efforts. Here are a few examples:

- *Does the company have social vibrancy? Do customers talk much about it?* The My Starbucks Idea (http://mystarbucksidea.com) Web site stimulates customers to send in any comments related to the retailer. People are able to view and discuss these comments, and participate in polls. Starbucks then publicizes which ideas it will be enacting as new or revised practices. This makes the site a "crowdsourcing" and marketing research tool that helps uncover consumer priorities and shares them with an online community: "It works because Starbucks is the kind of dominant brand that inspires strong opinions among its customers."
- *How do you adapt the firm's voice to social media? As whom are you speaking?* CEO Tony Hsieh of Zappos serves as the leading voice for his firm's main Twitter page (http://twitter.com/zappos). Yet, Zappos—the online shoe-and-apparel retailer—also empowers its employees to use Twitter. So more than 400 of them are Tweeting. Hsieh's Twitter page is linked to each employee page: "Instead of touting products or offering customer service, employees just Tweet for the sake of it. This helps to put human faces on the brand and gives outsiders access to the quirky company culture, helping to strengthen fans' ties to the brand."
- *What's the value exchange?* Ikea used a social media campaign when it opened a new Swedish store. The campaign featured Facebook and included the store manager's profile, complete with 12 images of Ikea showrooms linked to his photo albums: "The first person to tag a product would win it. It took little effort for Facebook members to participate, but as they did, pictures spread around the site via news feeds, profile pages, and links, and participants became Ikea promoters."[1]

Source: BeTA-Artworks / fotolia.com.

Overview

A retailer needs a superior communications strategy to properly position itself in customers' minds, as well as to nurture their shopping behavior. Once customers are attracted, the retailer must strive to create a proper shopping mood for them. Various physical and symbolic cues can be used to do this. See Figure 18-1. It is imperative to maximize the total retail experience for shoppers:

There are many trade associations in the retail image arena. Visit a few online (http://vmsd.com/associations).

> Some firms have gotten distracted by technology. Yet, consumers are still "looking for real-world connections," says Jo Murphy of GDR Creative Intelligence. "Although many use multiple social media platforms, the experience of interacting face-to-face with friends and like-minded strangers is an integral part of the social experience," she says. "Retail space can facilitate these interactions—serving as a community hub and gathering point." So, the future of stores seems to be playing up the tangible strengths of physical stores through experiences that stimulate, educate, and inspire, while integrating digital and technology strategies in complementary ways.[2]

FIGURE 18-1

Positioning and Retail Image

Polaris Fashion Place is the premier shopping center in Central Ohio—and its "look" reinforces this retail image. The shopping center has six anchor stores (Saks Fifth Avenue, Von Maur, Macy's, Sears, J.C. Penney, and Great Indoors), as well as more than 150 specialty stores. Dining options include Brio Tuscan Grille, Molly Woo's, California Pizza Kitchen, and Cheesecake Factory.

Source: Reprinted by permission of Susan V. Berry, Retail Image Consulting, Inc.

This chapter describes how to establish and maintain an image. Retail atmosphere, storefronts, store layouts, and displays are examined. We also explore the challenge of how to encourage people to spend more time shopping and the role of community relations. Chapter 19 focuses on the common promotional tools available to retailers: advertising, public relations, personal selling, and sales promotion.

Though our discussion looks more at store retailers, the basic principles apply to nonstore retailers. For a mail-order firm, the catalog cover is its storefront, and the interior layouts and displays are the pages devoted to product categories and the individual items within them. For a Web retailer, the home page is its storefront, and interior layouts and displays are represented by links within the site.

THE SIGNIFICANCE OF RETAIL IMAGE

Display & Design Ideas (www.ddionline.com) is a leading trade magazine that often deals with retail image topics. Click on "Magazine."

As defined in Chapter 3, *image* refers to how a retailer is perceived by customers and others, and *positioning* refers to how a firm devises its strategy so as to project an image relative to its retail category and its competitors—and to elicit a positive consumer response. To succeed, a retailer must communicate a distinctive, clear, and consistent image. Once its image is established in consumers' minds, a retailer is placed in a niche relative to competitors. For global retailers, it can be challenging to convey a consistent image worldwide, given the different backgrounds of consumers.

Today's extensive use of social media by all parties—including customers, the general public, the media, suppliers, brands, and retailers themselves—must be thoroughly understood by retailers and proper strategies proactively enacted. No firm, of any size or type, is immune from the impact of social media content—pro and con—on its image. That is why we feature an opening vignette in every chapter of this book. To paraphrase what we said at the beginning of Chapter 1, **social media** encompass online technology tools that allow vast numbers of people to easily communicate with one another via the Internet and mobile devices. Through social media, messages, audio, video, photos, podcasts, and other multimedia communications are possible. Social media are discussed further in Chapter 19.

Components of a Retail Image

Just like the image of the Disney Store has evolved, so has its Web site (www.disneystore.com).

Many factors contribute to a retailer's image; it is the totality of them that forms an overall image. See Figure 18-2. We studied these factors in earlier chapters: target market, retail positioning, customer service, store location, merchandise attributes, and pricing. Our focus in Chapters 18 and 19 is attributes of physical facilities, shopping experiences, community service, advertising, public relations, personal selling, and sales promotion.

FIGURE 18-2
The Elements of a Retail Image

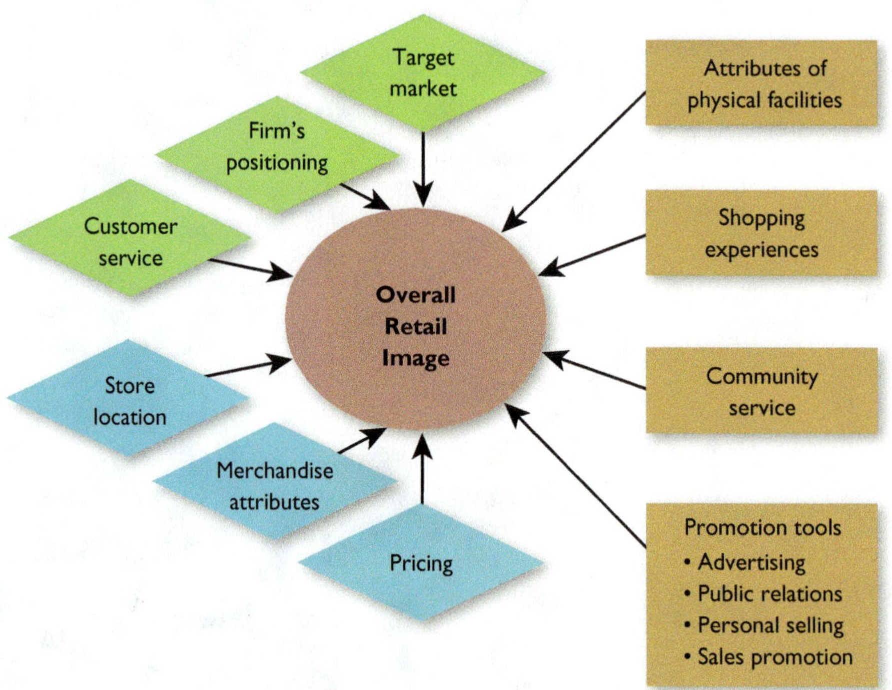

TECHNOLOGY IN RETAILING

Enhancing the Retail Experience

Retailers are increasingly utilizing new digital technologies such as touch-screen screens, facial recognition software, and social media (including Facebook and Twitter) to enable customers to create a customized store experience. These technologies provide personalization, social elements, and fun.

Through personalization, a retailer can make suitable recommendations to shoppers based on their demographics. For example, JR East (www.jreast.co.jp/e) has launched a touch-screen vending machine in Tokyo with an embedded camera and facial-recognition software to determine a consumer's age and gender. These characteristics are then used by the machine to recommend suitable soft drinks.

We (http://twitter.com/wefashion), an international fashion brand, uses a Twitter Mirror in its dressing rooms that enables shoppers to post photos of themselves modeling garments at Twitter. In addition, a touch-screen scanner at the store lets shoppers ascertain the availability of different sizes and colors in the store and on the Web.

American Eagle's 77 kids (http://www.ae.com/77kids) flagship store for children's clothing uses interactive screens to increase the children's involvement in clothing shopping. These young shoppers can select in-store music, play games, try on clothing in a virtual environment, and even take and print photos of themselves.

Source: Sheena Patel, "Digital Engagement," *Display & Design Ideas* (April–May 2011), pp. 28–32.

The Dynamics of Creating and Maintaining a Retail Image

Creating and maintaining a retail image is a complex, multi-step, ongoing process. It encompasses far more than store "atmosphere," which is discussed shortly. Furthermore, with so many people having little time for shopping and others having less interest in it, more retailers understand that may have to *entertain* shoppers to draw their business.

Consider all of the steps that have gone into transforming the Disney Store concept. According to Paul Gainer, the senior vice-president for Disney Store North America, the company has a three-faceted approach. It builds new stores, remodels existing ones, and relocates mall stores to better spots—complete with a full renovation. The goal is to provide "the best 30 minutes of a child's day:

> We focus on creating a magical experience for a child in the store, and the entire family. A pixie path navigates shoppers through the store and into different neighborhoods. In the *Princess* neighborhood, a child can wave a Cinderella wand at the magic mirror, and Cinderella appears in the mirror. Boys can enter the *Cars* neighborhood and build their own car. The Disney Theater has a 12-foot curved screen and a kind of a jumbo iPod device that lets children select what they see. There are many other experiences that allow children to connect with their favorite characters.[3]

And let's highlight the approaches of two other retailers:

> Jungle Jim's International Market has grown over the years from a simple roadside stand to a 300,000-square-foot food extravaganza and tourist destination, offering 150,000 different items from over 75 countries around the globe and employing an average of 350 employees. Jungle Jim's is noted for having one of the largest wine collections in the United States, live seafood tanks, and an in-store cooking school, in addition to a 1,000-person Event Center. Each week, the store is visited by approximately 50,000 shoppers, who are known as "Foodies."[4]

> Gap has been redesigning hundreds of Old Navy locations to emphasize ensembles and outfits rather than deep discounts. The new design includes a smaller layout with brighter design—rearranging displays into areas based on outfit types paired with matching attire and accessories; relocating changing rooms from the back of the store to the middle along with installation of several "Quick Change" booths throughout the store; replacing the cash registers in the front section with attractive merchandise displays and creating a checkout area in mid-store; and adding a small play area for toddlers with digital projectors.[5]

Alan Treadgold, global head of retail strategy at Leo Burnett/Arc Wordwide, has identified six major retail image positions that firms stake out:

- *Price Led*—Low prices are critical, and self-service can be a way to accomplish this. These retailers are "perceived as offering convenience and good return policies. However, the store environment tends to lack inspiration, and service can be lackluster." At these retailers, in-store shopping does not go much beyond what consumers can experience online. Examples: Wal-Mart, CVS
- *All About Ease*—These retailers provide locations that are convenient locations. It is "all about getting the products you need in a very timely manner, which may include self-service check-out." Often, they do not offer liberal return policies or present innovative products or displays; but that does not concern their customer base. Examples: Dollar General, local grocery store
- *All About Atmosphere*—This type of retailer creates an "extraordinary in-store experience, often with a special theme, where consumers are more likely to think it's fun to go." These firms typically do not carry a wide assortment of merchandise, and prices tend to be on the high side. Examples: Tiffany, Abercrombie & Fitch
- *Ideas Led*—These retailers have attractive and appealing displays. "They offer fresh ideas of products to buy; and often these are unique to that particular firm." Examples: Whole Foods, Hallmark/Gold Crown
- *Price Plus*—Such retailers "offer a good value on the items they sell and are also an interesting place to shop." But, they are not as exciting as *All About Atmosphere* or *Ideas Led* retailers. These firms add new items on a regular basis and encourage shoppers to spend more time. They do a good job in coordinating in-store and online shopping experiences. Examples: Kohl's, Bed Bath & Beyond
- *Efficient Errands*—These companies provide "convenient locations to get the products that shoppers need with decent service." The sales staff has some product expertise, and information is easy to acquire. This type of retailer does not have a very exciting in-store environment. It is a good place to buy items that are planned in advance. Examples: AutoZone, Lowe's[6]

See Figure 18-3.

A key goal for chain retailers, franchisors, and global retailers is to maintain a consistent image among all branches. Yet, despite the best planning, a number of factors may vary widely among branch stores and affect the image. They include management and employee performance, consumer profiles, competitors, the convenience in reaching stores, parking, safety, the ease of finding merchandise, language and cultural diversity among customers in different countries, and the qualities of the surrounding area. Sometimes, retailers with good images receive negative publicity. This must be countered in order for them to maintain their desired standing with the public.

FIGURE 18-3

Shopping at Costco: Not Just a Price Leader

Besides its everyday low prices, Costco is a big believer in providing value-added services for its customers.

Source: Reprinted by permission of Susan V. Berry, Retail Image Consulting, Inc.

ATMOSPHERE

VMSD (http://vmsd.com/projects) provides many examples of excellence in retail atmospherics.

A retailer's image depends heavily on its "atmosphere," the psychological feeling a customer gets when visiting that retailer. It is the personality of a store, catalog, vending machine, or Web site. "Retail image" is a much broader and all-encompassing term relative to the communication tools a retailer uses to position itself. For a store-based retailer, **atmosphere (atmospherics)** refers to the store's physical characteristics that project an image and draw customers. For a nonstore-based firm, atmosphere refers to the physical characteristics of catalogs, vending machines, Web sites, and so forth. A retailer's sights, sounds, smells, and other physical attributes all contribute to customer perceptions.

A retailer's atmosphere often influences people's shopping enjoyment, as well as their time spent browsing, willingness to converse with personnel, tendency to spend more than originally planned, and likelihood of future patronage. Many people even form impressions of a retailer before entering its facilities (due to the store location, storefront, and other factors) or just after entering (due to displays, width of aisles, and other things). They often judge the firm prior to examining merchandise and prices.

Check out the advantages of visualization technology (www.facit.co.uk/retail.htm) in planning atmospherics.

When a retailer takes a proactive, integrated atmospherics approach to create a certain "look," properly display products, stimulate shopping behavior, and enhance the physical environment, it engages in **visual merchandising**. This includes everything from store display windows to aisle width to the materials used for fixtures to merchandise presentation:

> From your in-store layout and product merchandising to housekeeping, lighting, music, price tickets, posters and graphics, window displays and props, the color you paint your walls, and the fixtures you use to sell, all of these elements—and how you visually organize them and how often you rotate them within your retail space—encompass visual merchandising. Whether you're an up-market fashion chain or the local hardware store (it doesn't matter what you sell), if you have a retail space, and open your doors for trade, you are conducting "visual merchandising" on some level.[7]

See Figure 18-4.

Visit our Web site (www.pearsonhighered.com/bermanevans) for visual merchandising links.

A Store-Based Retailing Perspective

Store atmosphere (atmospherics) can be divided into these key elements: exterior, general interior, store layout, and displays. Figure 18-5 contains a detailed breakdown of them.

FIGURE 18-4

Visual Merchandising and Shopping Centers

Visual merchandising is not just important to the individual retailer, but also to the shopping centers in which they are located. Appealing atmospherics add to the shopping experience.

Source: Mirenska Olga/ Shutterstock.com. Reprinted by permission.

FIGURE 18-5
The Elements of Atmosphere

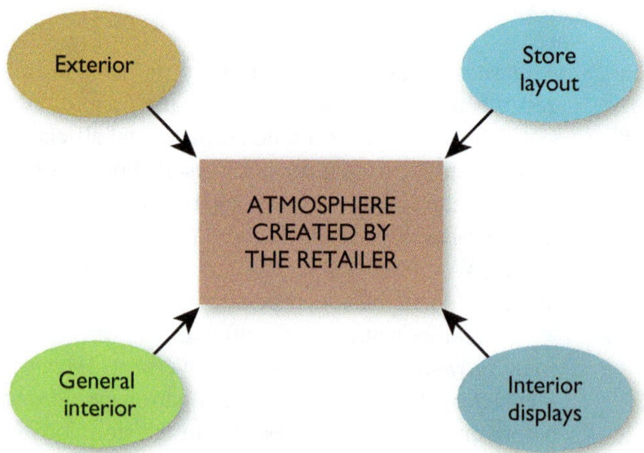

EXTERIOR A store's exterior has a powerful impact on its image and should be planned accordingly.

A **storefront** is the total physical exterior of the store itself. It includes the marquee, entrances, windows, lighting, and construction materials. With its storefront, a retailer can present a conservative, trendy, upscale, discount, or other image. Consumers who pass through an unfamiliar business district or shopping center often judge a store by its exterior. Besides the storefront itself, atmosphere can be enhanced by trees, fountains, and benches in front of the store. These intensify consumer feelings about shopping and about the store by establishing a relaxed environment. There are various alternatives in planning a basic storefront. Here are a few of them:

- Modular structure—a one-piece rectangle or square that may attach several stores.
- Prefabricated (prefab) structure—a frame built in a factory and assembled at the site.
- Prototype store—used by franchisors and chains to foster a consistent atmosphere.
- Recessed storefront—lures people by being recessed from the level of other stores. Customers must walk in a number of feet to examine the storefront.
- Unique building design—a round structure, for example.

A **marquee** is a sign that displays the store's name. It can be painted or a neon light, printed or script, and set alone or mixed with a slogan (trademark) and other information. The marquee should attract attention, as Best Buy's colorful logo on the front of each of its stores does. See Figure 18-6. Image is influenced because a marquee can be gaudy and flashy or subdued and subtle. The world's best-known marquee is McDonald's golden arches.

FIGURE 18-6
Using a Marquee to Generate a Powerful Retail Image

Best Buy's marquee is widely known and can be seen from a considerable distance—even in the dark.

Source: Reprinted by permission of Susan V. Berry, Retail Image Consulting, Inc.

Store entrances require three major decisions. First, the number of entrances is determined. Many small stores have only one entrance. Department stores may have four to eight or more entrances. A store hoping to draw both vehicular and pedestrian traffic may need at least two entrances (one for pedestrians, another near the parking lot). Because front and back entrances serve different purposes, they should be designed separately. A factor that may limit the number of entrances is potential pilferage.

Second, the type of entrance(s) is chosen. The doorway can be revolving; electric, self-opening; regular, push-pull; or climate-controlled. The latter is an open entrance with a curtain of warm or cold air, set at the same temperature as inside the store. Entrance flooring can be cement, tile, or carpeting. Lighting can be traditional or fluorescent, white or colors, and/or flashing or constant. At Apple stores, the exterior entrance and displays are inviting and designed to reinforce its image, as depicted in Figure 18-7.

Third, walkways are considered. A wide, lavish walkway creates a different atmosphere and mood than a narrow one. Large window displays may be attractive, but customers would not be pleased if there is insufficient space for a comfortable entry into the store.

Display windows have two main purposes: (1) to identify the store and its offerings and (2) to induce people to enter. By showing a representative merchandise offering, a store can create an overall mood. By showing fashion or seasonal goods, it can show it is contemporary. By showing sale items, a store can lure price-conscious consumers. By showing eye-catching displays that have little to do with its merchandise offering, a store can attract pedestrians' attention. By showing public service messages (such as a sign for the Special Olympics), the store can indicate its community involvement.

A lot of planning is needed to develop good display windows, which leads many retailers to hire outside specialists. Decisions include the number, size, shape, color, and themes of display windows—and the frequency of changes per year. Retailers in shopping malls may not use display windows for the side of the building facing the parking lot; there are solid building exteriors. They feel vehicular patrons are not lured by expensive outside windows; they invest in displays for storefronts inside the malls.

Exterior building height can be disguised or nondisguised. With disguised building height, part of a store or shopping center is beneath ground level. Such a building is not as intimidating to people who dislike a large structure. With nondisguised building height, the entire store or center can be seen by pedestrians. An intimate image cannot be fostered with a block-long building, nor can a department store image be linked to a small site.

FIGURE 18-7

The Apple Store: Drawing in Shoppers

At the Ridgedale Center in Minnesota, the Apple store's open entrance and exterior displays are certainly a customer traffic draw.

Source: Michael Rubin/ Shutterstock.com. Reprinted by permission.

CAREERS IN RETAILING

Joseph Bona: Retail Division, CBX

Joseph Bona is president of the retail division of CBX (www.cbx.com), a firm that specializes in store design. As head of this division, he is responsible for leading a team of designer professionals who work in all retail formats—from convenience stores to apparel and lifestyle-based retailers.

CBX's mission is to communicate a retailer's image from the store's exterior. As an example of this strategy, it changed Petro-Canada's Neighbours concept (http://neighbours.petro-canada.ca) convenience store image to more closely resemble a Panera Bread or a hybrid corner store and café. In the store's food section, all workers are dressed like chefs and all face the customers from a kitchen area. Although no cooking is done at these stores, the workers reheat and assemble "restaurant-quality" sandwiches and grilled paninis. In addition, these locations feature both dining areas and outside patios for customers who want to eat in the store.

Bona's educational background includes an architecture degree from Fullerton College and advanced classwork at the National Academy of Design. At graduation, he became a retail planner and project manager at Hickory Farms (www.hickoryfarms.com), a specialty food retailer of fruits, nuts, cheeses, and sausages. He later worked for CDI Group (www.cdigroupinc.com), a design consulting and project management company, for more than twenty years.

Sources: Janet Groeber, "Designed to Transform," www.stores.com (July 2010); and "Our Work: Petro-Canada," www.cbx.com (May 9, 2012).

Few firms succeed with poor visibility. This means pedestrian and/or vehicular traffic must clearly see storefronts or marquees. A store located behind a bus stop has poor visibility for vehicular traffic and pedestrians across the street. Many retailers near highways use billboards since drivers go by quickly.

In every case, the goal is to have the store or center appear unique and catch the shopper's eye. A distinctive storefront, an elaborate marquee, recessed open-air entrances, decorative windows, and unusual building height and size are one set of features that could attract consumers by their uniqueness. Nonetheless, uniqueness may not be without its shortcomings. An example is the multi-level "shopping-center-in-the-round." Because this center (which often occupies a square city block) is round, parking on each floor level makes the walking distances very short. Yet, a rectangular center may have greater floor space on a lot of the same size, on-floor parking may reduce shopping on other floors, added entrances increase chances for pilferage, many people dislike circular driving, and architectural costs are higher.

As a retailer plans its exterior, the nearby stores and the surrounding area should be studied. Nearby stores present image cues due to their price range, level of service, and so on. The surrounding area reflects the demographics and lifestyles of those who live nearby. An overall area image rubs off on individual retailers because people tend to have a general perception of a shopping center or a business district. An unfavorable atmosphere would exist if vandalism and crime are high, people living near the store are not in the target market, and the area is rundown.

Parking facilities can add to or detract from store atmosphere. Plentiful, free, nearby parking creates a more positive image than scarce, costly, distant parking. Some potential shoppers may never enter a store if they must drive around for parking. Other customers may rush in and out of a store to finish shopping before parking meters expire. A related potential problem is that of congestion. Atmospherics are diminished if the parking lot, sidewalks, and/or entrances are jammed. Consumers who feel crushed in the crowd spend less time shopping and are in poorer moods than those who feel comfortable.

GENERAL INTERIOR Once customers are in a store, various elements affect their perceptions. Retailers must plan accordingly:

- At Dairy Queen, many stores have been remodeled to be more appealing. At one store, "double-door cake freezers line a new wall that was built to separate the dining area from the counter and to showcase novelty ice-cream cakes. Prior to the remodeling, the cake freezers were in two separate areas of the store, which were ineffective at times because customers could miss one or the other. Also new to the store is a self-serve drink station. In the dining area, customers now have the option of booths or dining tables compared to the previous booth-only seating. They are more family-friendly and we have one extra-large booth."[8]

- Apple store interior design varies by locale: "Some include movie theaters with podiums for training sessions, product promotion, and special events. Others have areas for children to play games and use educational software. However, one of the most iconic fixtures is the Genius Bar, where users can get their Apple hardware and software problems fixed by company-certified repair technicians. It takes customer relationships one step beyond what Apple originally intended with the unrealized cyber café concept by supporting those who have already bought into the firm's product ecosystem."[9]
- The Toys "R" Us Times Square store in New York City attracts "kids and kids at heart who come from all over the world to marvel at the many attractions at the Center of the Toy Universe, take a ride on the 60-foot Ferris wheel, hear the roar of the life-sized T-Rex dinosaur, or make themselves at home in the 4,000-square-foot Barbie dollhouse. And, with dedicated areas for interactive play, boutiques displaying the hottest toys, and electronics for kids of all ages and spectacular views of the crossroads of the world, this store is a 'must see' destination."[10]

The general interior elements of store atmosphere were cited in Figure 18-5. They are described next.

Maxey Hayse Design Studios (www.maxeyhayse.com/design_portfolio.html) has designed interiors for a variety of retailers. Several are profiled here.

Flooring can be cement, wood, linoleum, carpet, and so on. A plush, thick carpet creates one kind of atmosphere and a concrete floor another. Thus, 90 percent of specialty apparel stores have carpeted floors, 70 percent of home centers have concrete floors, and two-thirds of big-box stores have vinyl floors.[11]

Bright, vibrant colors contribute to a different atmosphere than light pastels or plain white walls. Lighting can be direct or indirect, white or colors, constant or flashing. See Figure 18-8. A teen-oriented apparel boutique might use bright colors and vibrant, flashing lights to foster one atmosphere, and a maternity dress shop could use pastel colors and indirect lighting to form a different atmosphere. Sometimes, when colors are changed, customers may be initially uncomfortable until they get used to the new scheme.

Scents and sounds influence the customer's mood. A restaurant can use food aromas to increase people's appetites. A cosmetics store can use an array of perfume scents to attract shoppers. A pet store can let its animals' natural scents and sounds woo customers. A beauty salon can play soft music or rock, depending on its customers. Slow-tempo music in supermarkets encourages people to move more slowly.

Store fixtures can be planned on the basis of both their utility and aesthetics. Pipes, plumbing, beams, doors, storage rooms, and display racks and tables should be considered part of interior decorating. An upscale store usually dresses up its fixtures and disguises them. A discount store might leave fixtures exposed because this portrays the desired image.

FIGURE 18-8

The Impact of Lighting and Flooring

At this store in Kiev, Ukraine, the bright lighting and linoleum flooring both contribute to a discount image for the retailer—as do the plain fixtures and displays.

Source: joyfull/Shutterstock.com. Reprinted by permission.

Wall textures enhance or diminish atmospherics. Prestigious stores often use raised wallpaper. Department stores are more apt to use flat wallpaper, while discount stores may have barren walls. Chic stores might have chandeliers, while discounters have fluorescent lighting.

The customer's mood is affected by the store's temperature and how it is achieved. Insufficient heat in winter and no air-conditioning in summer can shorten a shopping trip. And image is influenced by the use of central air-conditioning, unit air-conditioning, fans, or open windows.

Wide, uncrowded aisles create a better atmosphere than narrow, crowded ones. People shop longer and spend more if they are not pushed while walking or looking at merchandise. Although in-store kiosks have proven very popular, they sometimes cause overcrowding in tight retail spaces or create customer lines if there are not enough kiosks to handle the number of shoppers.

Dressing facilities can be elaborate, plain, or nonexistent. An upscale store has carpeted, private dressing rooms. An average-quality store has linoleum-floored, semiprivate rooms. A discount store has small stalls or no facilities. For some apparel shoppers, dressing facilities are a factor in store selection.

Multi-level stores must have vertical transportation: elevator, escalator, and/or stairs. Larger stores may have a combination of all three. Traditionally, finer stores relied on operator-run elevators and discount stores on stairs. Today, escalators are quite popular. They provide shoppers with a quiet ride and a panoramic view of the store. Finer stores decorate their escalators with fountains, shrubs, and trees. Stairs remain important for some discount and smaller stores.

Light fixtures, wood or metal beams, doors, rest rooms, dressing rooms, and vertical transportation can cause **dead areas** for the retailer. These are awkward spaces where normal displays cannot be set up. Sometimes, it is not possible for such areas to be deployed profitably or attractively. However, retailers have learned to use dead areas better. Mirrors are attached to exit doors. Vending machines are located near restrooms. Ads appear in dressing rooms. One creative use of a dead area involves the escalator. It lets shoppers view each floor, and sales of impulse items go up when placed at the escalator entrance or exit. Many firms plan escalators so customers must get off at each floor and pass by appealing displays to get to the next level.

Polite, well-groomed, knowledgeable personnel generate a positive atmosphere. Ill-mannered, poorly groomed, uninformed personnel engender a negative one. A store using self-service minimizes its personnel and creates a discount, impersonal image. A store cannot develop an upscale image if it is set up for self-service. As one expert puts it, "15 feet, 15 seconds. That's how quickly your customers should be greeted, welcomed, and treated like a guest in your store."[12]

The merchandise a retailer sells influences its image. Top-line items yield one kind of image, and lower-quality items yield another. The mood of the customer is affected accordingly.

Price levels foster a perception of retail image in consumers' minds; and the way prices are displayed is a vital part of atmosphere. Upscale stores have few or no price displays, rely on discrete price tags, and place cash registers in inconspicuous areas behind posts or in employee rooms. Discounters accentuate price displays, show prices in large print, and locate cash registers centrally, with signs pointing to them.

A store with state-of-the-art technology impresses people with its operations efficiency and speed. One with slower, older technology may have impatient shoppers. A store with a modern building (new storefront and marquee) and new fixtures (lights, floors, and walls) fosters a more favorable atmosphere than one with older facilities. Remodeling can improve store appearance, update facilities, and reallocate space. It typically results in strong sales and profit increases after completion.

Last, but certainly not least, there must be a plan for keeping the store clean. No matter how impressive the exterior and interior, an unkempt store will be perceived poorly. According to a recent survey, "99 percent of U.S. adults say that any poor cleanliness issue would negatively affect their perception of a retail store, with dirty rest rooms and unpleasant odors topping the list of annoyances over poor customer service."[13]

STORE LAYOUT At this point, the specifics of store layout are *sequentially* planned and enacted.

ALLOCATION OF FLOOR SPACE. Each store has a total amount of floor space to allot to selling, merchandise, personnel, and customers. Without this allocation, the retailer would have no idea of the space available for displays, signs, rest rooms, and so on:

- *Selling space* is used for displays of merchandise, interactions between salespeople and customers, demonstrations, and so on. Self-service retailers apportion most space to selling.

Promoting Global Corporate Social Responsibility

Hyatt Hotels Corporation (www.hyatt.com) has established a global sustainability and community service operation called Hyatt Thrive (www.hyattthrive.com). This program utilizes a common platform to promote local efforts among Hyatt's employees, investors, business partners, and guests. This program is operational at Hyatt's more than 450 hotel properties in 43 countries.

Hyatt Thrive is based on the firm's contributing to four specific areas: environmental sustainability, economic development, education and personal achievement, and health and wellness. According to Hyatt's vice-president of corporate responsibility: "One thing we're trying to emphasize is by all of us focusing on these goals, there's a huge opportunity to move the needle as a company."

The Hyatt Thrive program was launched on a global basis in June 2011. Among its initial activities were having employees from Hyatt's corporate headquarters and Chicago-area hotels paint and landscape a local school; employees from Hyatt's Regency New Orleans improve a local playground; and employees of the Grand Hyatt Shanghai clean trash along the Hangpu River.

In addition to its community-based efforts, Hyatt has set up internal sustainability goals as part of this program. Hyatt measures energy consumption, water usage, and carbon emission levels at specific hotel, regional, and global levels. Hyatt also monitors volunteer activity on an hourly basis.

Source: Piet Levy, "Hyatt Unites Employees Through CSR Program," www.marketingpower.com (July 21, 2011).

- *Merchandise space* is used to stock nondisplayed items. At a traditional shoe store, this area takes up a large percentage of total space.
- *Personnel space* is set aside for employees to change clothes, to take lunch and coffee breaks, and for restrooms. Because retail space is valuable, personnel space is strictly controlled. Yet, a retailer should consider the effect on employee morale.
- *Customer space* contributes to the shopping mood. It can include a lounge, benches and/or chairs, dressing rooms, rest rooms, a restaurant, a nursery, parking, and wide aisles. Discounters are more apt to skimp on these areas.

Visit Shelf Logic (www.shelflogic.com/movies.htm) and click on "Creating a Planogram" to learn more about this tool.

More firms now use planograms to assign space. A **planogram** is a visual (graphical) representation of the space for selling, merchandise, personnel, and customers—as well as for product categories. It also lays out their in-store placement. A planogram may be hand-drawn or computer-generated. Visit our Web site (www.pearsonhighered.com/bermanevans) for several planogram links.

CLASSIFICATION OF STORE OFFERINGS. A store's offerings are next classified into product groupings. Many retailers use a combination of groupings and plan store layouts accordingly. Special provisions are needed to minimize shoplifting and pilferage. This means placing vulnerable products away from corners and doors. Four types of groupings (and combinations of them) are the most common:

- **Functional product groupings** display merchandise by common end use. A men's clothing store might group shirts, ties, cuff links, and tie pins; shoes, shoe trees, and shoe polish; T-shirts, undershorts, and socks; suits; and sports jackets and slacks.
- **Purchase motivation product groupings** appeal to the consumer's urge to buy products and the amount of time he or she is willing to spend on shopping. A committed customer with time to shop will visit a store's upper floors; a disinterested person with less time will look at displays on the first floor. Look at the first level of a department store. It includes impulse products and other rather quick purchases. The third floor has items encouraging and requiring more thoughtful shopping.
- **Market segment product groupings** place together various items that appeal to a given target market. A women's apparel store divides products into juniors', misses', and ladies' apparel. A music store separates CDs into rock, jazz, classical, R&B, country, and other sections. An art gallery places paintings into different price groups.
- **Storability product groupings** may be used for products needing special handling. A supermarket has freezer, refrigerator, and room-temperature sections. A florist keeps some flowers refrigerated and others at room temperature as do a bakery and a fruit store.

FIGURE 18-9
How a Supermarket Uses a Straight (Gridiron) Traffic Pattern

Source: Illustration by Steve Cowden for *Progressive Grocer*. Reprinted by permission.

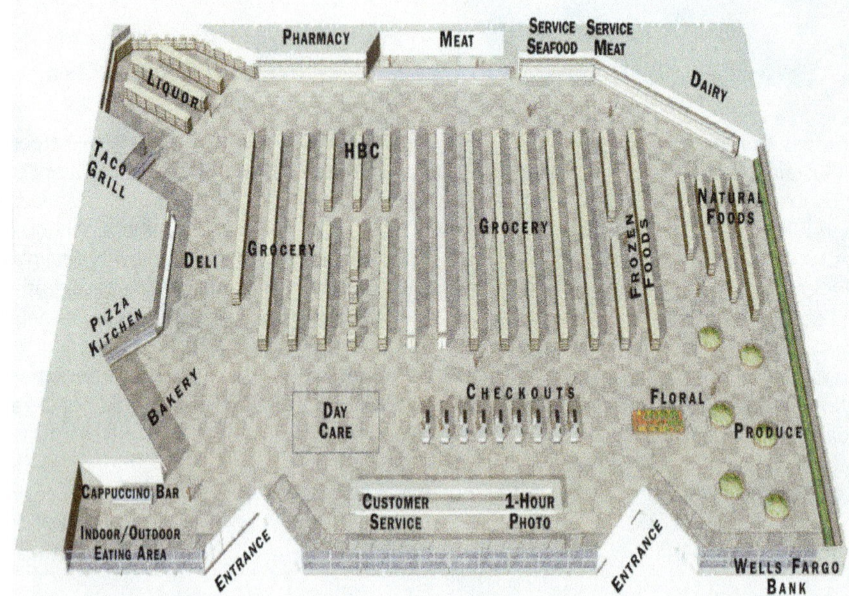

DETERMINATION OF A TRAFFIC-FLOW PATTERN. The traffic-flow pattern of the store is then set. A **straight (gridiron) traffic flow** places displays and aisles in a rectangular or gridiron pattern, as shown in Figure 18-9. A **curving (free-flowing) traffic flow** places displays and aisles in a free-flowing pattern, as shown in Figure 18-10.

FIGURE 18-10
How a Department Store Uses a Curving (Free-Flowing) Traffic Pattern

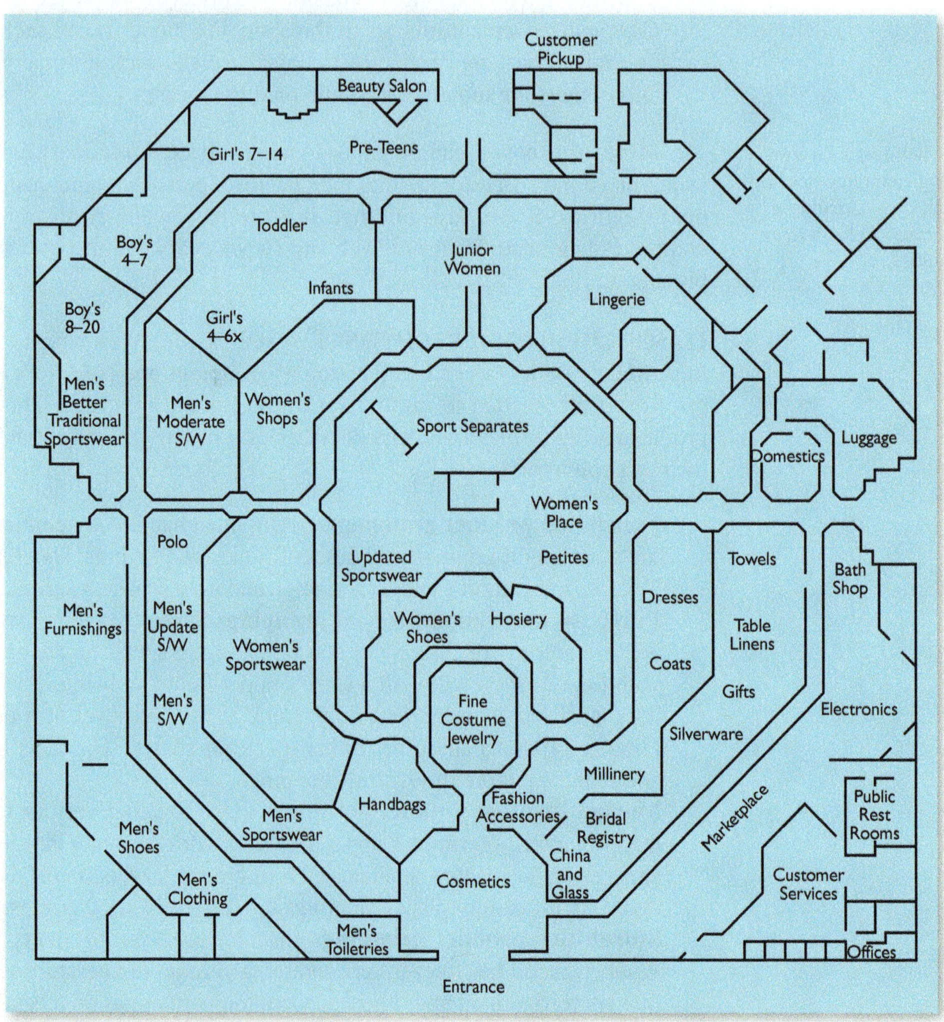

A straight traffic pattern is often used by food retailers, discount stores, drugstores, hardware stores, and stationery stores. It has several advantages:

- An efficient atmosphere is created.
- More floor space is devoted to product displays.
- People can shop quickly.
- Inventory control and security are simplified.
- Self-service is easy, thereby reducing labor costs.

The disadvantages are the impersonal atmosphere, more limited browsing by customers, and rushed shopping behavior.

A curving traffic pattern is used by department stores, apparel stores, and other shopping-oriented stores. This approach has several benefits:

- A friendly atmosphere is presented.
- Shoppers do not feel rushed and will browse around.
- People are encouraged to walk through the store in any direction or pattern.
- Impulse or unplanned purchases are enhanced.

The disadvantages are the possible customer confusion, wasted floor space, difficulties in inventory control, higher labor intensity, and potential loitering. Also, the displays often cost more.

DETERMINATION OF SPACE NEEDS. The space for each product category is now calculated, with both selling and nonselling space considered. There are two different approaches: the model stock method and the space–productivity ratio.

The **model stock approach** determines the floor space necessary to carry and display a proper merchandise assortment. Apparel stores and shoe stores are among those using this method. The **sales–productivity ratio** assigns floor space on the basis of sales or profit per foot. Highly profitable product categories get large chunks of space; marginally profitable categories get less. Food stores and bookstores are among those that use this technique.

MAPPING OUT IN-STORE LOCATIONS. At this juncture, department locations are mapped out. For multi-level stores, that means assigning departments to floors and laying out individual floors. What products should be on each floor? What should be the layout of each floor? A single-level store addresses only the second question. These are some questions to consider:

- What items should be placed on the first floor, on the second floor, and so on?
- How should groupings be placed relative to doors, vertical transportation, and so on?
- Where should impulse products and convenience products be situated?
- How should associated product categories be aligned?
- Where should seasonal and off-season products be placed?
- Where should space-consuming categories such as furniture be located?
- How close should product displays and stored inventory be to each other?
- What shopping patterns do consumers follow once they enter the store?
- How can the overall appearance of store crowding be averted?

ARRANGEMENT OF INDIVIDUAL PRODUCTS. The last step in store layout planning is arranging individual products. The most profitable items and brands could be placed in the best locations, and products could be arranged by package size, price, color, brand, level of personal service required, and/or customer interest. End-aisle display positions, eye-level positions, and checkout counter positions are the most likely to increase sales for individual items. Continuity of locations is also important; shifts in store layout may decrease sales by confusing shoppers. The least desirable display position is often knee or ankle level, because consumers do not like to bend down.

Although large retailers may sometimes use video-tracking equipment to study shoppers' in-store traffic patterns, that is not feasible for small retailers. Instead, this is recommended:

> When customers walk into your store, where do they look? If they look at a display, do their eyes start at the top and work down to the bottom, or vice-versa? If a customer looked at the top of the display first, you know that is the best place to put new products. Watch where in your store customers pick up products. Are there areas that customers shop from more often? If so, place items there that you want to increase sales. Consider every comment, every smile, smirk, or sigh as a sign of what a customer is thinking.[14]

Retailer goals often differ from their manufacturers. While the latter want to maximize their brands' sales and push for eye-level, full-shelf, end-aisle locations, retailers seek to maximize total store sales and profit, regardless of brand. Self-service retailers have special considerations. Besides using a gridiron layout to minimize shopper confusion, they must clearly mark aisles, displays, and merchandise.

Consider some of the tactics that supermarkets have employed:

- Many have produce near the entrance; some others have flowers. "The idea is to tantalize the customer, to draw you in with eye-catching displays."
- "Cereal theory" means placing boxes on lower shelves, which are at eye level for children.
- People buy more soup if the varieties are not shelved in alphabetical order.
- Store brands do better when located to the left of manufacturer brands. "After seeing the name brand, the eye automatically moves left (as if on a new page) to compare prices."
- Because "the best viewing angle is 15 degrees below the horizontal, the choicest display level has been measured at 51 to 53 inches off the floor."
- Virtually all stores place smaller impulse-type purchases near cash registers, "as customers often make last-minute purchases while they're waiting in line to pay."[15]

Cahill specializes in creative retail displays (www.cahilldisplay.com).

INTERIOR (POINT-OF-PURCHASE) DISPLAYS Once the store layout is fully detailed, a retailer devises its interior displays. Each **point-of-purchase (POP) display** provides shoppers with information, adds to store atmosphere, and serves a substantial promotional role. Here's what the Global Association for Marketing at Retail has said about marketing at retail:

- *It is persuasive.* When located near checkout counters, "it is the only mass medium executed at the critical point where products, consumers, and the money to purchase all meet at the same time."
- *It is a silent salesperson.* "Displays and in-store media educate and draw attention to consumers about a product's availability and attributes."
- *It is flexible.* "It can convey the same overall strategic message in differing languages to varying audiences in the same village, city, or region."
- *It enhances the overall shopping experience.* It can "overhaul a store's image, re-direct store traffic, and bolster merchandising plans."[16]

Several types of displays are described here. Most retailers use a combination of them.

At this site (http://dir.yahoo.com/Business_and_Economy), retailers can choose from many display firms. Click on "Business to Business," "Retail Management," and then "Point of Purchase Displays."

An **assortment display** exhibits a wide range of merchandise. With an *open assortment*, the customer is encouraged to feel, look at, and/or try on products. Greeting cards, books, magazines, and apparel are the kinds of products for which retailers use open assortments. In addition, food stores have expanded their open displays for fruit, vegetables, and candy; some department stores have open displays for cosmetics and perfume. With a *closed assortment*, the customer is encouraged to look at merchandise but not touch it or try it on. Computer software, CDs, and DVDs are pre-packaged items that cannot be opened before buying. Jewelry is usually kept in closed glass cases that employees must unlock.

A **theme-setting display** depicts a product offering in a thematic manner and sets a specific mood. Retailers often vary their displays to reflect seasons or special events; some even have employees dress for the occasion. All or part of a store may be adapted to a theme, such as Presidents' Day, Valentine's Day, or another concept. Each special theme seeks to attract attention and make shopping more fun.

With an **ensemble display,** a complete product bundle (ensemble) is presented—rather than showing merchandise in separate categories (such as a shoe department, sock department, pants department, shirt department, and sports jacket department). Thus, a mannequin may be dressed in a matching combination of shoes, socks, pants, shirt, and sports jacket, and these items would be available in one department or adjacent departments. Customers like the ease of a purchase and envisioning an entire product bundle.

A **rack display** has a primarily functional use: to neatly hang or present products. It is often used by apparel retailers, housewares retailers, and others. This display must be carefully maintained because it may lead to product clutter and shoppers' returning items to the wrong place. Current technology enables retailers to use sliding, disconnecting, contracting/expanding, lightweight, attractive rack displays. A **case display** exhibits heavier, bulkier items than racks hold. DVD sets, books, pre-packaged goods, and sweaters typically appear in case displays.

A **cut case** is an inexpensive display that leaves merchandise in the original carton. Supermarkets and discount stores frequently use cut cases, which do not create a warm atmosphere. Neither does a **dump bin**—a case that holds piles of sale clothing, marked-down books, or other products. Dump bins have open assortments of roughly handled items. Both cut cases and dump bins reduce display costs and project a low-price image.

Posters, signs, and cards can dress up all types of displays, including cut cases and dump bins. They provide information about product locations and stimulate customers to shop. A mobile, a hanging display with parts that move in response to air currents, serves the same purpose—but stands out more. Electronic displays are also widely used today. They can be interactive, be tailored to individual stores, provide product demonstrations, answer customer questions, and incorporate the latest in multimedia capabilities. These displays are much easier to reprogram than traditional displays are to remodel.

A Nonstore-Based Retailing Perspective

Try out this demo E-store (http://sm.kemford.com/webstore/store) to experience many of the components of online retailing.

Many atmospherics principles apply to both store and nonstore retailers. However, there are also some distinctions. Let's look at the storefront, general interior, store layout, displays, and checkout counter from the vantage point of one type of direct marketer, the Web retailer.

STOREFRONT The storefront for a Web retailer is the home page. Thus, it is important that the home page:

- Prominently show the company name and indicate the positioning of the firm.
- Be inviting. A "virtual storefront" must encourage customers to enter.
- Make it easy to go into the store.
- Show the product lines carried.
- Use graphics as display windows and icons as access points.
- Have a distinctive look and feel.
- Include the retailer's E-mail address, mailing address, and phone number.
- Indicate that the retailer is involved with social media.
- Be listed at various search engines.

See Figure 18-11.

FIGURE 18-11
The Importance of Web Site Design

It is imperative that an online retailer devote the proper attention to designing and implementing a well-conceived Web site. Although content may be king, the visual effects and ease of use are also crucial.

Source: Angela Waye/Shutterstock.com. Reprinted by permission.

GENERAL INTERIOR As with store retailers, a Web retailer's general interior sets a shopping mood. Colors run the gamut from plain white backgrounds to stylish black backgrounds. Some firms use audio to generate shopper interest. "Fixtures" relate to how simple or elaborate the Web site looks. "Width of aisles" means how cluttered the site appears and the size of the text and images. The general interior also involves these elements:

- Instructions about how to use the site.
- Information about the company.
- Product icons.
- News items.
- The shopping cart (how orders are placed).
- A product search engine.
- Locations of physical stores (for multi-channel retailers).
- A shopper login for firms that use loyalty programs and track their customers.

STORE LAYOUT A Web retailer's store layout has two components: the layout of each individual Web page and the links to move from page to page. Web retailers spend a lot of time planning the traffic flow for their stores. Online consumers want to shop efficiently, and they get impatient if the "store" is not laid out properly.

Some online firms use a gridiron approach, while others have more free-flowing Web pages and links. Web companies often have a directory on the home page that indicates product categories. Shoppers click on an icon to enter the area of the site housing the category (department) of interest. Many retailers encourage customers to shop for any product from any section of the Web site by providing an interactive search engine. In that case, a person types in the product name or category and is automatically sent to the relevant Web page. As with physical stores, online retailers allocate more display space to popular product categories and brands—and give them a better position. On pages that require scrolling down, best-sellers usually appear at the top of the page and slower-sellers at the bottom.

DISPLAYS Web retailers can display full product assortments or let shoppers choose from tailored assortments. This decision affects the open or cluttered appearance of a site, the level of choice, and possible shopper confusion. Online firms often use special themes, such as Valentine's Day. It is easy for them to show ensembles—and for shoppers to interactively mix and match to create their own ensembles. Through graphics and photos, a site can give the appearance of cut cases and dump bins for items on sale.

CHECKOUT COUNTER A Web checkout counter can be complex: (1) Online shoppers worry more about the security and privacy of purchase transactions than those buying in a store. (2) Online shoppers often work harder to complete transactions. They must carefully enter the model number and quantity, as well as their shipping address, E-mail address, shipping preference, and credit card number. They may also be asked for their phone number, job title, and so on, because some retailers want to build their data bases. (3) Online shoppers may feel surprised by shipping and handling fees, if these fees are not revealed until they go to checkout.

To simplify matters, Amazon.com has a patented checkout process—a major competitive advantage. Amazon.com's "1-Click" program lets shoppers securely store their shipping address, preferred shipping method, and credit card information. Each purchase requires just one click to set up an order form.

Learn how Amazon.com (www.amazon.com) enables shoppers to use "1-Click Settings" for easy ordering. Click on "Help" and then "Placing an Order."

SPECIAL CONSIDERATIONS Let's examine two other issues: how to set up a proper Web site and the advantages and disadvantages of Web atmospherics versus those of traditional stores.

New online retailers often have little experience with Web design or the fundamentals of store design and layout. These firms typically hire specialists to design their sites. When business grows, they may take Web design in-house. These are a few firms that design online stores for small retailers: Easy Store Creator (www.easystorecreator.com), Volusion (www.volusion.com/web_design.asp), Webfodder (www.webfodder.com), and Yahoo! Small Business (http://smallbusiness.yahoo.com/ecommerce). The Yahoo! design and hosting costs are as low as $29.97 monthly (for the first three months and $39.95 per month thereafter).

Compared with physical stores, online stores have several advantages. A Web site:

- Has almost unlimited space to present product assortments, displays, and information.
- Can be tailored to the individual customer.
- Can be modified daily (or even hourly) to reflect changes in demand, new offerings from suppliers, and competitors' actions.
- Can promote cross-merchandising and impulse purchases with little shopper effort.
- Enables a shopper to enter and exit an online store in a matter of minutes.
- Is a good gateway to company-run social media sites.

Online stores also have potential disadvantages. A Web site:

- Can be slow for dialup shoppers. The situation worsens as more graphics and video clips are added. [Note: With the widespread use of broadband connections, this is much less of an issue today.]
- Can be confusing. How many clicks must a shopper make from the time he or she enters a site until a purchase is made?
- Cannot display the three-dimensional aspects of products as well as physical stores.
- Requires constant updating to reflect stockouts, new merchandise, and price changes.
- Is more likely to be exited without a purchase. It is easy to visit another Web site.

ENCOURAGING CUSTOMERS TO SPEND MORE TIME SHOPPING

Underhill's Envirosell Inc. (www.envirosell.com) is a leader in shopping behavior research.

Paco Underhill, a pioneer in retail anthropology, has a simple explanation for why consumers should be encouraged to spend more time shopping: "The amount of minutes a shopper spends in a store (shopping, not waiting in a line) is important in determining how much she or he will buy. Over and over again, our studies have shown a direct relationship between these numbers. In an electronics store we studied, nonbuyers spent 5 minutes and 6 seconds in the store, compared to 9 minutes and 29 seconds for buyers. In a toy store, buyers spent over 17 minutes, compared to 10 for nonbuyers. In some stores, buyers spend three or four times as much time as nonbuyers."[17] Our Web site (www.pearsonhighered.com/bermanevans) has links to research projects and video clips from Underhill's company Envirosell.

Among the tactics to persuade people to spend more time shopping are experiential merchandising, solutions selling, an enhanced shopping experience, retailer co-branding, and wish list programs.

The aim of **experiential merchandising** is to convert shopping from a passive activity into a more interactive one, by better engaging customers. See Figure 18-12. A number of retailers are doing so:

> American Girl stores celebrate girls' interests with engaging products and experiences. Located at eleven premier shopping and entertainment destinations nationwide, American Girl stores have been praised as leading models for experiential retail and provide a special place for girls to make lasting memories with their families and friends. Girls ages 3 and up can explore our popular historical and contemporary dolls, browse our award-winning library, enjoy a delicious meal in the on-site restaurant, and treat their doll to a new look in the salon. Engaging programs and special events for girls are also held throughout the year.[18]

> Urban Outfitters operates more than 130 stores in the United States, Canada, and Europe, all offering an eclectic mix of merchandise. We stock our stores with what we love, calling on our—and our customer's—interest in contemporary art, music, and fashion. From men's and women's apparel and accessories to items for the apartment, we offer a lifestyle-specific shopping experience for the educated, urban-minded individual in the 18- to 30-year-old range—both online and in our stores, as well as through our catalog.[19]

> Various tactics keep shoppers in stores longer. Williams-Sonoma hosts cooking classes, and Guitar Center offers weekly recording lessons for customers. Small businesses, like a beauty store, have a makeup artist come in to show customers new products while they shop. Free food samples, live music, light aroma sprays, and product demos can entice customers and keep them in the spending mood. Some stores spray aromas in various parts of their stores. For example, the infant apparel section may get the baby powder scent, and a swimwear section may be filled with the scent of coconut.[20]

FIGURE 18-12
Making the Shopping Experience More Entertaining
Neiman Marcus regularly participates in fashion shows, some of which draw thousands of attendees.

Source: Doug James/ Shutterstock.com. Reprinted by permission.

Solutions selling takes a customer-centered approach and presents "solutions" rather than "products." It goes a step beyond cross-merchandising. At holiday times, some retailers group gift items by price ("under $25, under $50, under $100, $100 and above") rather than by product category. This provides a solution for the shopper who has a budget to spend but a fuzzy idea of what to buy. Many supermarkets sell fully prepared, complete meals that just have to be heated and served. This solves the problem of "What's for dinner?" without requiring the consumer to shop for meal components.

See how retailers can create an enhanced shopping experience (www.merchandiseconcepts.com/blog).

An *enhanced shopping experience* means the retailer does everything possible to minimize annoyances and to make the shopping trip pleasant. Given all of the retail choices facing consumers, retailers must do all they can so that shoppers do not have unpleasant experiences. For example, shoppers often dislike waiting in line to check out. As one retailing expert says:

ETHICS IN RETAILING

Social Media Guidelines

Potential legal problems (such as defamation, trademark and copyright infringement, and overtime concerns) associated with social media can be minimized or avoided by developing and implementing social media guidelines. These include policies regarding professionalism, tie-ins with existing policies, controls, restrictions, defamation of competitors, and after-hours participation:

- *Professionalism*—Employees need to be advised as to what communication is appropriate and what is not. They also need to be informed to contact a manager when in doubt.
- *Tie-in with existing policies*—A retailer's policies relating to professional conduct, anti-harassment, and protection of trade secrets are applicable to social media communications.
- *Controls*—Standards relating to professionalism, customer service, and follow-up procedures apply to all communications, including social media.
- *Restrictions*—Employees should not reveal trade secrets, copy information from another source, use trademarks or logos of others, or use photos of consumers without their written permission.
- *Defamation of competitors*—Employees should not discuss competitors. Employees should also provide a disclaimer that their statements are their own views, not the retailer's.
- *After-hours participation*—Off-the-job work on social media projects is conducted on a voluntary basis and is not part of an employee's work-related responsibilities.

Source: Michael Charapp, "Socially Acceptable Tips," *Ward's Dealer Business* (June 2011), p. 39.

"Think of your most frustrating experience while waiting in a retail line. Remember how you felt standing with products in hand and some unseen impediment ahead costing valuable time and draining your patience? Now, picture that same experience, but imagine a manager who greets you in a friendly tone and offers you a drink or a warm chocolate-chip cookie. The latter may seem rosy or downright silly, but smart retailers use queue times to connect with shoppers in a highly memorable way—whether with warm cookies or simply good, attentive customer service."[21]

Retailers can also provide an enhanced shopping experience by setting up wider aisles so people do not feel cramped, adding benches and chairs so those accompanying the main shopper can relax, using kiosks to stimulate impulse purchases and answer questions, having activities for children (such as Ikea's playroom), and opening more checkout counters. What decades-old shopping accessory is turning out to be one of the greatest enhancements of all? It is the humble shopping cart, as highlighted in Figure 18-13:

> Target recently hired Boston-based Design Continuum to rethink the shopping cart—a big deal in an industry that typically buys generic carts from manufacturers. The new cart uses lightweight recyclable material, with interchangeable plastic parts. Rust isn't a concern, repairs are easy, and scanning cart contents is a breeze. Even the color, Target's trademark cheery tomato red, now plays a starring role.[22]

More firms participate in *co-branding*, whereby two or more well-known retailers situate under the same roof (or at one Web site) to share costs, stimulate consumers to visit more often, and attract people shopping together who have different preferences. Here are several examples: Subway in Wal-Mart stores, Starbucks in Barnes & Noble stores, joint Dunkin' Donuts and Baskin-Robbins outlets, and numerous small retailers that sell their merchandise through Amazon.com. This illustrates why co-branding is growing in popularity: By locating together,

FIGURE 18-13

The Shopping Cart's Role in an Enhanced Shopping Experience

Consider shopping in a large home center and NOT finding a shopping cart to enhance the in-store experience. Many people would buy less.

Source: Helder Almeida/ Shutterstock.com. Reprinted by permission.

"two or more fast-food chains can share facilities like dining rooms and help minimize some of their joint business expenses. At the same time, they attract customers who enjoy the ability to order food from two different menus under the same roof, increasing the possibility of groups of customers choosing them rather than a chain operating alone."[23]

Another tactic being implemented by a growing number of retailers is the *wish list program*. It is a technique that expands upon the long-standing concept of a wedding registry, and it can be used with virtually any products or life events. Wish lists are being used to great effect by Web retailers (and multi-channel retailers) to enable customers to prepare shopping lists for gift items they'd like to receive from a particular store or shopping center. At Amazon.com:

> *Wish Lists* ensure that gifts are sent to the right place and that the recipient doesn't receive more than he or she wants. Through the Amazon.com *Baby Registry*, gift givers can easily find any active baby registry, select an item, and have it shipped. At *Amazon Wedding*, guests can find a couple's registry, select a gift, and have it wrapped and shipped. We'll make sure the gift is delivered to the couple, even if you don't know their address. Couples will find everything they need—registry checklists, comprehensive planning guides, and interactive tools.[24]

COMMUNITY RELATIONS

The way that retailers interact with the communities around them can have a significant impact on both their image and performance. Their stature can be enhanced by engaging in such community-oriented actions as these:

- Making sure that stores are barrier-free for disabled shoppers and strictly enforcing handicapped parking rules.
- Showing a concern for the environment by recycling trash and cleaning streets.
- Supporting charities and noting that support at the company Web site.
- Participating in antidrug programs.
- Employing area residents.
- Running special sales for senior citizens and other groups.
- Sponsoring Little League and other youth activities.
- Cooperating with neighborhood planning groups.
- Donating money and/or equipment to schools.
- Carefully checking IDs for purchases with age minimums.

Each year, 7-Eleven makes substantial charitable contributions of cash and goods to support programs addressing issues such as literacy, reading, crime, and multicultural understanding. It also donates hundreds of thousands of pounds of food to local food banks throughout the United States. Wal-Mart, Kmart, and Big Lots are among the numerous retailers participating in some type of antidrug program. Barnes & Noble, Target, and others participate in national literacy programs. Safeway and Giant Food are just two of the supermarket chains that give money or equipment to schools in their neighborhoods.

As with any aspect of retail strategy planning, community relations efforts can be undertaken by retailers of any size and format. Sleep Country is a Northwest chain that supports efforts to assist foster children. In one recent year,

> people donated 2,800 pairs of new shoes, over 12,000 clothing items, 56,000 school supply items, and 9,000 warm coats. Your gift of thousands of toys helped make birthdays and holidays that much brighter. Thanks to your support, Sleep Country gave local foster children over 2,300 tickets to fun events and raised over $140,000 through donations and the Foster Kids Pajama Bowl. The holidays should be a magical time for a child; and your generosity provided over 15,500 holiday gifts for local foster children. On behalf of Sleep Country and foster children in your neighborhood, thank you![25]

Chapter Summary

1. *To show the importance of communicating with customers and examine the concept of retail image.* Customer communications are crucial for a store or nonstore retailer to position itself in customers' minds. Various physical and symbolic cues can be used.

Presenting the proper image—the way a firm is perceived by its customers and others—is an essential aspect of the retail strategy mix. And the growing impact of social media on a retailer's image must be appreciated. The components of a firm's image are its target market characteristics, retail positioning and reputation, store location, merchandise assortment, price levels, physical facilities, shopping experiences, community service, advertising, public relations, personal selling, and sales promotion. A retail image requires a multi-step, ongoing approach. For chains, there must be a consistent image among branches.

2. *To describe how a retail store image is related to the atmosphere it creates via its exterior, general interior, layout, and displays, and to look at the special case of nonstore atmospherics.* For a store retailer, atmosphere (atmospherics) is based on the physical attributes of the store utilized to develop an image; it is composed of the exterior, general interior, store layout, and displays. For a nonstore firm, physical attributes of such factors as catalogs, vending machines, and Web sites affect image.

The store exterior is comprised of the storefront, marquee, entrances, display windows, building height and size, visibility, uniqueness, surrounding stores and area, parking, and congestion. It sets a mood before a prospective customer even enters a store.

The general interior of a store encompasses its flooring, colors, lighting, scents and sounds, fixtures, wall textures, temperature, width of aisles, dressing facilities, vertical transportation, dead areas, personnel, self-service, merchandise, price displays, cash register placement, technology/modernization, and cleanliness. An upscale retailer's interior is far different from a discounter's—reflecting the image desired and the costs of doing business.

In laying out a store interior, six steps are necessary: (a) Floor space is allocated among selling, merchandise, personnel, and customers based on a firm's overall strategy. More firms now use planograms. (b) Product groupings are set, based on function, purchase motivation, market segment, and/or storability. (c) Traffic flows are planned, using a straight or curving pattern. (d) Space per product category is computed by a model stock approach or sales–productivity ratio. (e) Departments are located. (f) Individual products are arranged within departments.

Interior (point-of-purchase) displays provide information for consumers, add to the atmosphere, and have a promotional role. Interior display possibilities include assortment displays, theme displays, ensemble displays, rack and case displays, cut case and dump bin displays, posters, mobiles, and electronic displays.

For Web retailers, many principles of atmospherics are similar to those for store retailers. There are also key differences. The home page is the storefront. The general interior consists of site instructions, company information, product icons, the shopping cart, the product search engine, and other factors. The store layout includes individual Web pages, as well as the links that connect them. Displays can feature full or more selective assortments. Sales are lost if the checkout counter does not function well. There are specialists that help in Web site design. Compared with traditional stores, Web stores have various pros and cons.

3. *To discuss ways of encouraging customers to spend more time shopping.* To persuade consumers to devote more time with the retailer, these tactics are often employed: experiential merchandising, solutions selling, enhancing the shopping experience, retailer co-branding, and wish list programs.

4. *To consider the impact of community relations on a retailer's image.* Consumers react favorably to retailers involved in such activities as establishing stores that are barrier-free for persons with disabilities, supporting charities, and running special sales for senior citizens.

Key Terms

social media (p. 458)
atmosphere (atmospherics) (p. 461)
visual merchandising (p. 461)
storefront (p. 462)
marquee (p. 462)
dead areas (p. 466)
planogram (p. 467)
functional product groupings (p. 467)
purchase motivation product groupings (p. 467)
market segment product groupings (p. 467)
storability product groupings (p. 467)
straight (gridiron) traffic flow (p. 468)
curving (free-flowing) traffic flow (p. 468)
model stock approach (p. 469)
sales–productivity ratio (p. 469)
point-of-purchase (POP) display (p. 470)
assortment display (p. 470)

theme-setting display (p. 470)
ensemble display (p. 470)
rack display (p. 470)
case display (p. 470)
cut case (p. 471)
dump bin (p. 471)
experiential merchandising (p. 473)
solutions selling (p. 474)

Questions for Discussion

1. Why is it sometimes difficult for a retailer to convey its image to consumers? Give an example of a restaurant with a fuzzy image.
2. How could a store selling new computers project a value-based retail image? How could a store selling used computers project such an image?
3. Define the concept of *atmosphere*. How does this differ from that of *visual merchandising*?
4. Which aspects of a store's exterior are controllable by a retailer? Which are uncontrollable?
5. What are meant by *selling*, *merchandise*, *personnel*, and *customer space*?
6. Present a planogram for a nearby bank.
7. Develop a purchase motivation product grouping for an online men's apparel retailer.
8. Which stores should *not* use a curving (free-flowing) layout? Explain your answer.
9. Visit the Web site of PetsMart (www.petsmart.com), and then comment on its storefront, general interior, store layout, displays, and checkout counter.
10. How could a neighborhood paint supply store engage in solutions selling?
11. Do you agree with upscale retailers' decision not to provide in-store shopping carts? What realistic alternatives would you suggest? Explain your answers.
12. Present a community relations program for an optical chain.

Web-Based Exercise

Visit the Web site of Johnny Rockets (www.johnnyrockets.com). How would you rate the atmospherics and ambience of this site? What do you like most and least about the site? Explain your answers.

Note: Also stop by our Web site (www.pearsonhighered.com/bermanevans) to experience a number of highly interactive, appealing Web exercises based on actual company demonstrations and sample materials related to retailing.

19 Promotional Strategy

For retailers, the main elements of their promotion strategy are advertising, public relations, personal selling, and sales promotion—topics we cover in Chapter 19. Let's see how Cyriac Roeding, founder of mobile shopping application "shopkick" (www.shopkick.com), has devised his app to assist retailers in their promotion efforts.

According to Roeding, the biggest challenge that every retailer encounters is "getting people through the door." He says that 20 to 95 percent of those who enter a physical store, depending on the type of retailer, make a purchase. In contrast, he says that only one-half of 1 percent to 3 percent of online shoppers make a purchase when visiting a Web site. As a result, Roeding believes that retailers should reward people for visiting their stores. However, unless a person makes a purchase, the retailer typically does not know that he or she dropped by.

To address this issue, the shopkick mobile app was invented. Here's how it works:

> Shopkick delivers "kickbucks" rewards to all registered iPhone and Android users who enter a participating store. Kickbucks can be collected and redeemed across any partner store and turned into gift cards, discounts, song downloads, movie tickets, Facebook credits, or charitable donations. Roeding states: "We're tackling a huge market with a big problem, and we're offering them a solution that works. Our vision is to transform shopping into a personal, rewarding, and fun experience for everyone. Shopkick is built around the act of shopping. It's not about letting your friends know where you are."

In the short time that it has been available, shopkick has proven to be quite popular. Already, it has ties to 2,000 individual U.S. retail outlets and 100 shopping centers with such retail partners as American Eagle, Best Buy, Crate & Barrel, Macy's, Sports Authority, Target, Toys "R" Us, and Wet Seal, and mall operator Simon Property. According to shopkick's Web site, shopper activity involves 75,000+ store "favorites" daily—accounting for 2 million retail walk-ins during the first year of operation.[1]

Chapter Objectives

1. To explore the scope of retail promotion
2. To study the elements of retail promotion: advertising, public relations, personal selling, and sales promotion
3. To discuss the strategic aspects of retail promotion: objectives, budgeting, the mix of forms, implementing the mix, and reviewing and revising the plan

Source: BeTA-Artworks / fotolia.com.

Overview

Sephora, the European and U.S. beauty chain, has a well-integrated promotion plan—from its colorful Web site (www.sephora.com) to its stores.

Retail promotion includes any communication by a retailer that informs, persuades, and/or reminds the target market about any aspect of that firm. In the first part of this chapter, the elements of retail promotion are detailed. The second part centers on strategic aspects of promotion.

Consider the effort that Best Buy puts into its promotion strategy:

> Our competitive advantage requires us to have highly trained and engaged employees. District managers monitor operations and meet regularly with store managers to discuss merchandising, sales promotions, customer loyalty programs, and more. Corporate management for each private brand generally controls advertising. Our plans also allow external vendors and retailers to sell through our Web sites. Advertising costs consist primarily of print and television advertisements, as well as promotional events.[2]

Best Buy's approach is largely influenced by its retail positioning strategy and the competitive marketplace that it faces: "We compete for customers, employees, locations, and products with many other local, regional, national, and international retailers, as well as our vendors that offer products directly to the consumer."[3]

ELEMENTS OF THE RETAIL PROMOTIONAL MIX

This site (www.managementhelp.org/marketing/advertising) provides an overview on promotion planning. Click on a topic in the menu.

Advertising, public relations, personal selling, and sales promotion are the elements of promotion. In this section, we discuss each in terms of goals, advantages and disadvantages, and basic forms. A good plan integrates these elements—based on the overall strategy. A movie theater concentrates on ads and sales promotion (food displays), while an upscale specialty store stresses personal selling. See Figure 19-1.

Retailers devote significant sums to promotion. For example, a typical department store spends up to 4 to 5 percent of sales on ads and 8 to 10 percent on personal selling and support services. And most department store chains also invest heavily in sales promotions and use public relations to generate favorable publicity and reply to media information requests. We have more than a dozen links related to the retail promotion mix at our Web site (www.pearsonhighered.com/bermanevans).

Advertising

Advertising is paid, nonpersonal communication transmitted through out-of-store mass media by an identified sponsor. Four aspects of this definition merit clarification:

1. *Paid form.* This distinguishes advertising from publicity (an element of public relations), for which no payment is made by the retailer for the time or space used to convey a message.
2. *Nonpersonal presentation.* A standard message is delivered to the entire audience, and it cannot be adapted to individual customers (except with the Web).
3. *Out-of-store mass media.* These include newspapers, radio, TV, the Web, and other mass channels, rather than personal contacts. In-store communications (such as displays) are considered sales promotion.
4. *Identified sponsor.* The sponsor's name is clearly divulged, unlike publicity. See Figure 19-2.

Wal-Mart has the highest annual dollar advertising expenditures among U.S. retailers—$2.1 billion. However, this represents just 0.6 percent of U.S. sales. Wal-Mart also relies more on word of mouth, in-store events, and everyday low prices. Sears Holdings (which includes Sears and Kmart) has the second-highest annual dollar expenditures among U.S. retailers—$1.8 billion, about 4.1 percent of its U.S. sales. Macy's spends nearly 6 percent of its revenues on advertising.[4] Table 19-1 shows advertising ratios for several retailing categories.

DIFFERENCES BETWEEN RETAILER AND MANUFACTURER ADVERTISING STRATEGIES Retailers—other than national chains—usually have more geographically concentrated target markets than manufacturers. This means they can adapt better to local needs, habits, and preferences. However, those retailers cannot utilize national media as readily as manufacturers. Only the largest retail chains and franchises can advertise on national TV programs. An exception is direct marketing (including the World Wide Web) because trading areas for even small firms can then be geographically dispersed.

FIGURE 19-1

The Retail Promotion Mix in Action

As this montage shows, the retail promotion mix is wide reaching and includes customer relations (A), advertising (B), personal selling (C), sales promotion (D), and more.

Sources: (A) Steve Mann/Shutterstock.com. Reprinted by permission. (B) iQoncept/Shutterstock.com. Reprinted by permission. (C) Monkey Business Images/Shutterstock.com. Reprinted by permission. (D) iQoncept/Shutterstock.com. Reprinted by permission.

FIGURE 19-2

Advertising and Harrods

Harrods, the British retailer, uses all kinds of advertising media to get out its messages—including a billboard ad on the side of a London bus.

Source: Ahmad Faisal Yahya/Shutterstock.com. Reprinted by permission.

TABLE 19-1 Selected U.S. Advertising-to-Sales Ratios by Type of Retailer

Type of Retailer	Advertising Dollars as Percentage of Sales Dollars[a]	Advertising Dollars as Percentage of Margin[b]
Amusement parks	5.5	11.1
Apparel and accessories stores	3.7	8.2
Auto and home supply stores	1.3	2.6
Department stores	4.4	10.8
Drug and proprietary stores	0.7	3.6
Eating places	2.2	8.0
Family clothing stores	1.7	4.3
Food stores	5.5	15.0
Grocery stores	0.8	2.9
Hobby, toy, and game shops	3.3	9.0
Hotels and motels	1.8	9.4
Jewelry stores	5.3	10.3
Lumber and building materials	1.4	3.9
Movie theaters	0.7	3.5
Radio, TV, and consumer electronics stores	2.1	7.1
Real-estate agents and managers	4.5	13.0
Shoe stores	3.2	8.0
Variety stores	1.1	4.0
Video rental	5.6	9.2

[a] Advertising dollars as percentage of sales = Advertising expenditures/Net company sales

[b] Advertising dollars as percentage of margin = Advertising expenditures/(Net company sales – Cost of goods sold)

Source: Schonfeld & Associates, "2011 Advertising-to-Sales Ratios for 200 Largest Ad Spending Industries," www.saiBooks.com. Reprinted by permission.

Retail ads stress immediacy. Individual items are placed for sale and advertised over short time periods. Manufacturers are more often concerned with developing favorable attitudes.

Many retailers stress prices in ads, whereas manufacturers usually emphasize key product attributes. In addition, retailers often display several different products in one ad, whereas manufacturers tend to minimize the number of products mentioned in a single ad.

Media rates tend to be lower for retailers. Because of this, and the desire of many manufacturers and wholesalers for wide distribution, the costs of retail advertising are sometimes shared by manufacturers or wholesalers and their retailers. Two or more retailers may also share costs. Both of these approaches entail **cooperative advertising.**

Find out how to devise good ads (www.inc.com/advertising).

OBJECTIVES A retailer would select one or more of these goals and base advertising efforts on it (them):

- To grow short-term sales.
- To increase customer traffic.
- To develop and/or reinforce a retail image.
- To inform customers about goods and services and/or company attributes.
- To ease the job for sales personnel.
- To stimulate demand for private brands.

ADVANTAGES AND DISADVANTAGES The major advantages of advertising are that:

- A large audience is attracted. For print media, circulation is supplemented by the passing of a copy from one reader to another.
- The costs per viewer, reader, or listener are low.

CAREERS IN RETAILING

Jordan Zimmerman: Zimmerman Advertising

Jordan Zimmerman opened his advertising agency in 1984 with a $10,000 investment in a South Florida strip mall location. As of 2012, Zimmerman Advertising (www.zadv.com) employed 1,100 associates, operated more than twenty offices, and had annual billings of $3 billion.

Zimmerman Advertising specializes in developing and implementing promotional strategies for retail clients that include such major retail accounts such as Party City (www.partycity.com), White Castle (www.whitecastle.com), Lane Bryant (www.lanebryant.com), and Papa John's (www.papajohns.com). One of the key success stories involves Papa John's. With Domino's having a huge market share in the delivery sector and Pizza Hut's dominating eat-in service, Jordan Zimmerman needed a noteworthy promotional strategy for this client. So, he came up with "Better Ingredients. Better Pizza," and began to feature founder "Papa John" Schlatter in TV commercials for added credibility. The campaign was a huge success.

Since many of Zimmerman's large retail accounts have thousands of stores, Zimmerman's staff reviews performance on a store-by-store basis. This enables Zimmerman's staff to determine if a holiday promotion is effective two weeks after its airing. Sales performance for each store is rated on a ten-point scale, reflecting a major problem or opportunity. Based on the importance of each issue, Zimmerman schedules at least 10 meetings per day, about 15 minutes each.

Sources: Leigh Buchanan, "The Iron Man: Jordan Zimmerman of Zimmerman Advertising," www.inc.com (March 2010); and "Zimmerman Advertising," www.linkedin.com/company/zimmerman-advertising (May 9, 2012).

- A number of alternative media are available (including social media), so a retailer can match a medium to the target market.
- The retailer has control over message content, graphics, timing, and size (or length), so a standardized message in a chosen format can be delivered to the entire audience.
- In print media, a message can be studied and restudied by the target market.
- Editorial content (a TV show, a news story, and so on) often surrounds an ad. This may increase its credibility or the probability it will be read.
- Self-service or reduced-service operations are possible since a customer becomes aware of a retailer and its offerings before shopping.

The major disadvantages of advertising are that:

- Standardized messages lack flexibility (except for the Web and its interactive nature). They do not focus on the needs of individual customers.
- Some media require large investments. This may reduce the access of small firms.
- Media may reach large geographic areas, and for retailers, this may be wasteful. A small supermarket chain might find that only 40 percent of an audience resides in its trading area.
- Some media require a long lead time for placing ads. This reduces the ability to advertise fad items or to react to some current events themes.
- Some media have a high throwaway rate. Circulars may be discarded without being read.
- A 30-second TV commercial or small newspaper ad does not have many details.

The preceding are broad generalities. The pros and cons of specific media are covered next.

MEDIA Retailers can choose from the media highlighted in Table 19-2 and described here.

Papers (dailies, weeklies, and shoppers) represent the most preferred medium for many retailers, having the advantages of market coverage, short lead time, reasonable costs, flexibility, longevity, graphics, and editorial association (ads near columns or articles). Disadvantages include the possible waste (circulation to a wider area than necessary), the competition among retailers, the black-and-white format, and the appeal to fewer senses than TV. To maintain a dominant position, many papers have revamped their graphics, and some run color ads. Free-distribution shopper papers ("penny savers"), with little news content and delivery to all households in a geographic area, are popular today.

The Yellow Pages (www.yellowpages.com) remains a key medium for retailers.

In a White Pages phone directory, retailers get free alphabetical listings along with all other phone subscribers, commercial and noncommercial. The major advantage of the White over the Yellow Pages is that those who know a firm's name are not exposed to competitors. The major disadvantage, in contrast with the Yellow Pages, is the alphabetical rather than type-of-business listing. A person unfamiliar with repair services will usually look in the Yellow Pages under

TABLE 19-2 Advertising Media Comparison Chart

Medium	Market Coverage	Particular Suitability
Daily papers	Single community or entire metro area; local editions may be available.	All larger retailers.
Weekly papers	Single community usually; may be a metro area.	Retailers with a strictly local market.
Shopper papers	Most households in one community; chain shoppers can cover a metro area.	Neighborhood retailers and service businesses.
Phone directories	Geographic area or occupational field served by a directory.	All types of goods and service-oriented retailers.
Direct mail	Controlled by the retailer.	New and expanding firms, those using coupons or special offers, mail order.
Radio	Definable market area surrounding the station.	Retailers focusing on identifiable segments.
TV	Definable market area surrounding the station.	Retailers of goods and services with wide appeal.
World Wide Web	Global.	All types of goods and service-oriented retailers.
Transit	Urban or metro community served by transit system.	Retailers near transit routes, especially those appealing to commuters.
Outdoor	Entire metro area or single neighborhood.	Amusement and tourist-oriented retailers, well-known firms.
Local magazines	Entire metro area or region, zoned editions sometimes available.	Restaurants, entertainment-oriented firms, specialty shops, mail-order firms.
Flyers/circulars	Single neighborhood.	Restaurants, dry cleaners, service stations, and other neighborhood firms.

"Repair." In the Yellow Pages, firms pay for listings (and display ads, if desired) in their category. Most retailers advertise in the Yellow Pages. The advantages include widespread usage by people ready to shop and their long life (one year or more). The disadvantages are that retailer awareness may not be gained and there is a lengthy lead time for new ads. Note: There has been a dramatic shift to online directories and away from printed ones.

With direct mail, retailers send catalogs or ads to customers by the mail (including E-mail) or private delivery firms. Advantages are a targeted audience, tailored format, controlled costs, quick feedback, and tie-ins (including ads with bills). Among the disadvantages are the high throwaway rate ("junk mail"), poor image to some people, low response rate, and outdated mailing lists (addressees may have moved).

Radio is used by a variety of retailers. Advantages are the relatively low costs, its value as a medium for car drivers and passengers, its ability to use segmentation, its rather short lead time, and its wide reach. Disadvantages include no visual impact, the need for repetition, the need for brevity, and waste. The use of radio by retailers has gone up in recent years.

TV ads, although increasing due to the rise of national and regional retailers, are far behind papers in retail promotion expenditures. Among the advantages are the dramatic effects of messages, the large market coverage, creativity, and program affiliation (for sponsors). Disadvantages include high minimum costs, audience waste, the need for brevity and repetition, and the limited availability of popular times for nonsponsors. Because cable TV is more focused than conventional stations, it appeals to local retailers.

From an advertising perspective, retailers use the Web to provide information to customers about store locations, to describe the products carried, to let people order catalogs, and so forth. Retailers have two opportunities to reach customers: advertising on search engines and other firms' Web sites; and communicating with customers at their own sites. Web-based advertising has been growing at a fast pace—and will continue to do so for the foreseeable future. See Figure 19-3.

Transit advertising is used in areas with mass transit systems. Ads are displayed on buses and in trains and taxis. Advantages are the captive audience, mass market, high level of repetitiveness, and geographically defined market. Disadvantages are the ad clutter, distracted audience,

FIGURE 19-3

Using the Internet to Draw New Customers

Retailers such as real-estate brokers, hotel chains, repair services, restaurants, and others find Web advertising to be a very good way to attract new customers.

Source: iQoncept/ Shutterstock.com. Reprinted by permission.

lack of availability in small areas, restricted travel paths, and graffiti. Many retailers also advertise on their delivery vehicles.

At the Outdoor Advertising Association Web site (www.oaaa.org), type in "Retail."

Outdoor (billboard) advertising is sometimes used by retailers. Posters and signs may be displayed in public places, on buildings, and alongside highways. Advantages are the large size of the ads, the frequency of exposure, the relatively low costs, and the assistance in directing new customers. Disadvantages include the clutter of ads, a distracted audience, the limited information, and some legislation banning outdoor ads.

Magazine usage (in print and online) is valuable for three reasons: the rise in larger retail chains, the creation of regional and local editions, and the use by nonstore and multichannel retailers. Advantages are tailoring to specific markets, creative options, editorial associations, message longevity, and color. Disadvantages include long lead time, less sense of consumer urgency, waste, and declining readership.

Single-page (flyers) or multiple-page (circulars) ads are distributed in parking lots or to consumer homes. Advantages include the targeted audience, low costs, flexibility, and speed. Among the disadvantages are the level of throwaways, the poor image to some, and clutter. Flyers are good for smaller firms, while circulars are used by larger ones.

TYPES Advertisements can be classified by content and payment method. See Figure 19-4.

Pioneer ads have awareness as a goal and offer information (usually on new firms, products, or locations). *Competitive ads* have persuasion as a goal. *Reminder ads* are geared to loyal customers and stress attributes that have made retailers successful. *Institutional ads* seek to keep retailer names before the public without emphasizing the sale of goods or services. Public service messages are institutional.

Retailers may pay their own way or seek cooperative ventures in placing ads. Firms paying their own way have total control and incur all costs. With cooperative ventures, two or more parties share the costs and the decision making.[5] Billions of dollars are spent yearly on U.S. cooperative advertising, most in vertical agreements. Newspapers are preferred over other media for cooperative ads related to retailing.

FIGURE 19-4
Types of Advertising

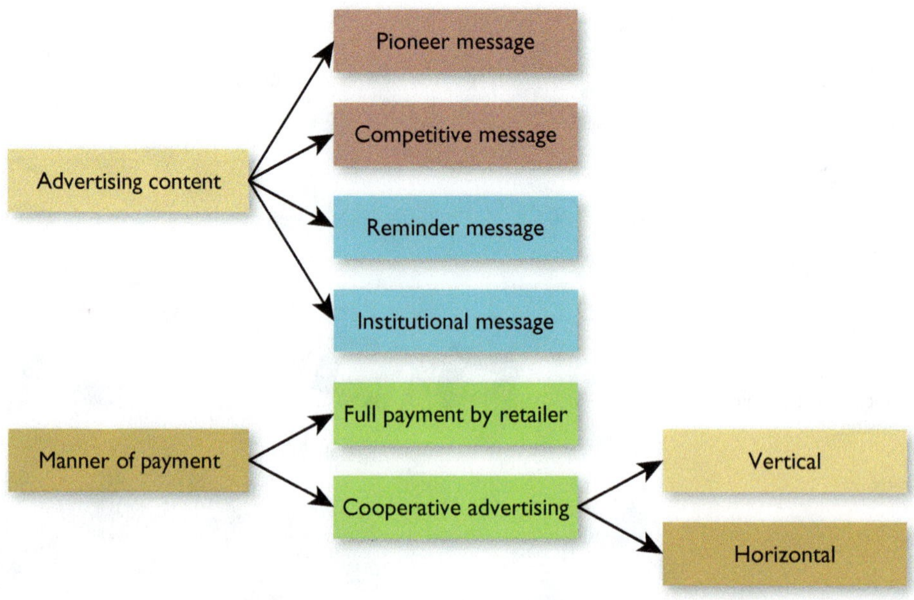

In a **vertical cooperative advertising agreement**, a manufacturer and a retailer or a wholesaler and a retailer share an ad. Responsibilities are specified contractually, and retailers are typically not reimbursed until after ads run. Vertical cooperative advertising is subject to the Robinson-Patman Act; similar arrangements must be offered to all retailers on a proportional basis. Advantages to a retailer are the reduced ad costs, assistance in preparing ads, greater market coverage, and less planning time. Disadvantages to a retailer include less control, flexibility, and distinctiveness. Some retailers are concerned about the eligibility requirements to participate and the emphasis on the supplier's name in ads. In response, manufacturers and other suppliers are now more flexible and understanding.

Carol Wright (www.carolwright.com) is a leader in horizontal cooperative promotions.

With a **horizontal cooperative advertising agreement**, two or more retailers share an ad. A horizontal agreement is most often used by small noncompeting retailers (such as independent hardware stores), retailers in a shopping center, and franchisees of a given firm. Advantages and disadvantages are similar to those in a vertical agreement. Two further benefits are the bargaining power of retailers in dealing with the media and the synergies when multiple retailers work together.

When planning a cooperative strategy, these questions should be considered:

- What ads qualify, in terms of merchandise and special requirements?
- What percentage of advertising is paid by each party?
- When can ads be run? In what media?
- Are there special provisions regarding message content?
- What documentation is required for reimbursement?
- How does each party benefit?
- Do cooperative ads obscure the image of individual retailers?

Public Relations

At Wendy's (www.wendys.com), public relations means community relations. After entering the site, select "Responsibility."

Public relations entails any communication that fosters a favorable image for the retailer among its publics (consumers, investors, government, channel members, employees, and the general public). It may be nonpersonal or personal, paid or nonpaid, and sponsor controlled or not controlled. **Publicity** is any nonpersonal form of public relations whereby messages are transmitted through mass media, the time or space provided by the media is not paid for, and there is no identified commercial sponsor.

The basic distinction between advertising and publicity is that publicity is nonpaid. Thus, it is not as readily controllable. A story on a store opening may not appear, appear after the fact, or not appear in the form desired. Yet, to shoppers, publicity is often more credible and valuable. Advertising and publicity (public relations) should complement one another. Therefore, on some occasions, it may be a good idea to try to gain positive publicity before placing ads.

Public relations can benefit both large and small retailers. Although the former often spend a lot of money to publicize events such as the Macy's Thanksgiving Day Parade, small firms can creatively generate attention for themselves on a limited budget. They can feature book signings by authors, sponsor school sports teams, donate goods and services to charities, and so forth.

Today, social media have a huge impact on a retailer's public relations efforts and on the publicity it receives. Consider the influence of highly interactive blogging sites (some operated by retailers themselves), which now number more than 100 million worldwide and rapidly spread information. Each year, Technorati reports on the state of blogging. Here are some findings from a recent blogger survey:

- Bloggers may be classified as hobbyists (60 percent), professional bloggers (18 percent), company bloggers who blog on behalf of firms for whom they work (9 percent), and entrepreneurs who blog on behalf of their own firms (13 percent).
- Sixty-eight percent of all bloggers say they are influenced by what they read at other blogs; and 65 percent use social media to follow companies and brands.
- Thirty-eight percent of all bloggers write about companies and brands that they love or hate.
- Thirty-four percent of all bloggers post reviews about companies and products; and 17 percent do so at least monthly.
- Twenty-seven percent of all bloggers write about their own everyday experiences with stores or customer care.
- Twenty-two percent of bloggers have their own blogs. [This number may be overstated due to terms in the study methodology.]
- Twelve percent of all bloggers write about company information or gossip they hear.[6]

OBJECTIVES Public relations seeks to accomplish one or more of these goals:

- Increase awareness of the retailer and its strategy mix.
- Maintain or improve the company image.
- Show the retailer as a contributor to the community's quality of life.
- Demonstrate innovativeness.
- Present a favorable message in a highly believable manner.
- Minimize total promotion costs.

ADVANTAGES AND DISADVANTAGES The major advantages of public relations are that:

- An image can be presented or enhanced.
- A more credible source presents the message (such as a good restaurant review).
- There are no costs for message time or space.
- A mass audience is addressed.
- Carryover effects are possible (if a retailer is perceived as community-oriented, its value positioning is more apt to be perceived favorably).
- People pay more attention to independent (third-party) sources than to clearly identified ads.

The major disadvantages of public relations are that:

- Some retailers do not believe in spending any funds on image-related communication.
- There is little retailer control over a publicity message and its timing, placement, and coverage by a given medium (particularly with social media).
- It may be more suitable for short-run, rather than long-run, planning.
- Although there are no media costs for publicity, there are costs for a public relations staff, planning activities, and the activities themselves (such as store openings).
- The Internet has the capability of quickly turning a negative local story into a worldwide media blitz.

TYPES Public relations can be planned or unexpected and image enhancing or image detracting.

With planned public relations, a retailer outlines its activities in advance, strives to have media report on them, and anticipates certain coverage. Community services, such as donations and special sales; parades on holidays (such as the Macy's Thanksgiving Day Parade); the introduction of "hot" new goods and services; and a new store opening are activities a retailer hopes will gain media coverage. The release of quarterly sales figures and publication of the annual report are events a retailer knows will be covered.

When unexpected publicity occurs, the media report on a company without its having advance notice. TV, newspaper, magazine, Internet, and other reporters may anonymously visit retail stores and Web sites or call customer service representatives to rate their performance and quality. A fire, an employee strike, or other newsworthy event may be mentioned in a story. Investigative reports on company practices—such as using suppliers with under-age workers—may appear.

There is positive publicity when media reports are complimentary, with regard to the excellence of a retailer's practices, its community efforts, and so on. However, the media may also provide negative publicity. A story could describe a store opening in less than glowing terms, rap a firm's environmental record, or otherwise be critical. That is why public relations must be viewed as a component of the promotion mix, not as the whole mix.

Personal Selling

The communication tips at this Web site (www.inc.com/guides/sales/23032.html) are quite helpful.

Personal selling involves oral communication with one or more prospective customers for the purpose of making a sale. The level of personal selling used by a retailer depends on the image it wants to convey, the products sold, the amount of self-service, and the interest in long-term customer relationships—as well as customer expectations. Retail salespeople may work in a store, visit consumer homes or places of work, or engage in telemarketing.

J.C. Penney believes in training superior sales associates. Why? First, higher levels of selling are needed to reinforce its image as a fashion-oriented department store. Unlike self-service discounters, Penney wants its sales staff to advise customers. Second, Penney wants to stimulate cross-selling, whereby associates recommend related items to customers. Third, Penney wants sales associates to "save the sale," by suggesting that customers who return merchandise try different colors, styles, or quality. Four, Penney believes it can foster customer loyalty. Figure 19-5 highlights J.C. Penney's sales associate tips.

OBJECTIVES The goals of personal selling are to:

- Persuade customers to buy (since they often enter a store after seeing an ad).
- Stimulate sales of impulse items or products related to customers' basic purchases.
- Complete customer transactions.
- Feed back information to company decision makers.
- Provide proper levels of customer service.
- Improve and maintain customer satisfaction.
- Create awareness of items also marketed through the Web, mail, and telemarketing.

ADVANTAGES AND DISADVANTAGES The advantages of selling relate to its personal nature:

- A salesperson can adapt a message to the needs of the individual customer.
- A salesperson can be flexible in offering ways to address customer needs.
- The attention span of the customer is higher than with advertising.
- There is less waste; most people who walk into a store are potential customers.
- Customers respond more often to personal selling than to ads.
- Immediate feedback is provided.

FIGURE 19-5
J.C. Penney's Tips for Sales Associates

Source: J.C. Penney.

- ✓ Greet the customer. This sets the tone for the customer's visit to your department.
- ✓ Listen to customers to determine their needs.
- ✓ Know your merchandise. For example, describe the quality features of Penney's private brands.
- ✓ Know merchandise in related departments. This can increase sales and lessen a customer's shopping time.
- ✓ Learn to juggle several shoppers at once.
- ✓ Pack merchandise carefully. Ask if customer wants an item on a hanger to prevent creasing.
- ✓ Constantly work at keeping the department looking its best.
- ✓ Refer to the customer by his or her name; this can be gotten from the person's credit card.
- ✓ Stress Penney's "hassle-free" return policy.

The major disadvantages of personal selling are that:

- Only a limited number of customers can be handled at a given time.
- The costs of interacting with each customer can be high.
- Customers are not initially lured into a store through personal selling.
- Self-service may be discouraged.
- Some customers may view salespeople as unhelpful and as too aggressive.

TYPES Most sales positions involve either order taking or order getting. An **order-taking salesperson** performs routine clerical and sales functions—setting up displays, stocking shelves, answering simple questions, and ringing up sales. This type of selling is most likely in stores that are strong in self-service but also have some personnel on the floor. An **order-getting salesperson** is actively involved with informing and persuading customers and in closing sales. This is a true "sales" employee. Order getters usually sell higher-priced or complex items, such as real-estate, autos, and consumer electronics. They are more skilled and better paid than order takers. See Figure 19-6.

A manufacturer may sometimes help fund personal selling by providing **PMs (promotional or push monies)** for retail salespeople selling its brand. PMs are in addition to regular salesperson compensation. Many retailers dislike this practice because their salespeople may be less responsive to actual customer desires (if customers desire brands not yielding PMs).

FUNCTIONS Store sales personnel may be responsible for all or many of the tasks shown in Figure 19-7 and described next. Nonstore sales personnel may also have to generate customer leads (by knocking on doors in residential areas or calling people who are listed in a local phone directory).

On entering a store or a department in it (or being contacted at home), a salesperson greets the customer. Typical in-store greetings are: "Hello, may I help you?" "Hi, is there anything in particular you are looking for?" With any greeting, the salesperson seeks to put the customer at ease and build rapport.

The salesperson next finds out what the person wants: Is the person just looking, or is there a specific good or service in mind? For what purpose is the item to be used? Is there a price range in mind? What other information can the shopper provide to help the salesperson?

At this point, the salesperson may show merchandise. He or she selects the product most apt to satisfy the customer. The salesperson may try to trade up (discuss a more expensive version) or offer a substitute (if the retailer does not carry or is out of the requested item).

FIGURE 19-6

Personal Selling: Catering to the Customer

Even in a small food store, personal selling and good customer service are essential—maybe, especially in a small store.

Source: corepics/ Shutterstock.com. Reprinted by permission.

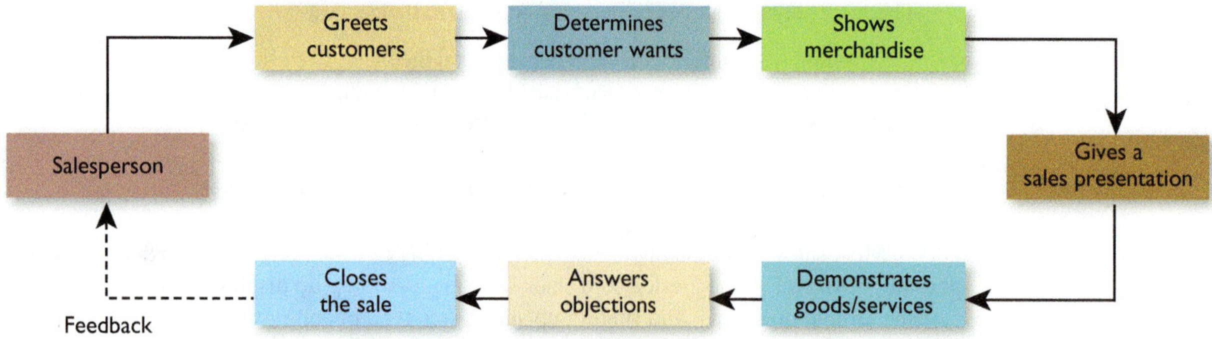

FIGURE 19-7
Typical Personal Selling Functions

The salesperson now makes a sales presentation to motivate the customer to purchase. The **canned sales presentation** is a memorized, repetitive speech given to all customers interested in a particular item. It works best if shoppers require little assistance and sales force turnover is high. The **need-satisfaction approach** is based on the principle that each customer has different wants; thus, a sales presentation should be geared to the demands of the individual customer. It is being used more in retailing.

A demonstration can show the utility of an item and allow customer participation. Demonstrations are often used with stereos, autos, health clubs, and watches.

A customer may have questions, and the salesperson must address them. Once all questions are answered, the salesperson tries to close the sale and get the shopper to buy. Typical closing lines are: "Will you take it with you or have it delivered?" "Cash or charge?" "Would you like this gift wrapped?"

For personal selling to work well, salespeople must be enthusiastic, knowledgeable, interested in customers, and good communicators. Figure 19-8 cites several ways that retail sales can be lost through poor personal selling and how to avoid these problems.[7]

Sales Promotion

Promo magazine (www.promomagazine.com) is a leading source of information about sales promotion.

Sales promotion encompasses the paid communication activities other than advertising, public relations, and personal selling that stimulate consumer purchases and dealer effectiveness. It includes displays, contests, sweepstakes, coupons, frequent shopper programs, prizes, samples, demonstrations, referral gifts, and other limited-time selling efforts outside of the ordinary promotion routine. The value and evolving nature of sales promotion are clear from these commentaries:

FIGURE 19-8
Selected Reasons Retail Sales Are Lost—and How to Avoid Them

- ✗ *Poor qualification of the customer.* ✓ Obtain information from the customer so the sales presentation is properly tailored.
- ✗ *Salespersons not demonstrating the good or service.* ✓ Show the good or service in use so that benefits are visualized.
- ✗ *Failure to put feeling into the presentation.* ✓ Encourage salespeople to be sincere and consumer-oriented.
- ✗ *Poor knowledge.* ✓ Train salespeople to know the major advantages and disadvantages of the goods and services, as well as competitors', and be able to answer questions.
- ✗ *Arguing with a customer.* ✓ Avoid arguments in handling customer objections, even if the customer is wrong.
- ✗ *No suggestion selling.* ✓ Attempt to sell related items (such as service contracts, product supplies, and installation).
- ✗ *Giving up too early.* ✓ Try again if an attempt to close a sale is unsuccessful.
- ✗ *Inflexibility.* ✓ Be creative in offering alternative solutions to a customer's needs.
- ✗ *Poor follow-up.* ✓ Be sure that orders are correctly written, that deliveries arrive on time, and that customers are satisfied.

The purpose of a promotional campaign is to build sales in the short term—or, sometimes, as a long-term strategy of constant promotional pushes to reach sales goals. Because sales promotions are so easy to set up, they are well-suited to small- or medium-sized companies. This is not to say that larger firms don't use promotions, of course, and many rely heavily on promotions in tandem with larger regional or national ad campaigns.[8]

The SmartSource portfolio of in-store media, placed in food, drug, mass, and office supply stores, reaches up to 75 million households monthly. Our at-shelf advertising program delivers four-color signage in front of a brand. Our pamphlet dispenser delivers information, recipes, rebates, and sweepstakes forms at the shelf. Our at-shelf display program attaches product packaging directly in front of a brand. Our coupon dispenser delivers at-shelf incentives to consumers. Our shopping cart advertising delivers throughout the store. Our video unit delivers 32 seconds of television-like advertising at the shelf. Our billboard-sized advertising adheres directly to the store's floor.[9]

OBJECTIVES Sales promotion goals include:

- Increasing short-term sales volume.
- Maintaining customer loyalty.
- Emphasizing novelty.
- Complementing other promotion tools.

ADVANTAGES AND DISADVANTAGES The major advantages of sales promotion are that:

- It often has eye-catching appeal.
- Themes and tools can be distinctive.
- The consumer may receive something of value, such as coupons or free merchandise.
- It helps draw customer traffic and maintain loyalty to the retailer.
- Impulse purchases are increased.
- Customers can have fun, particularly with promotion tools such as contests and demonstrations.

The major disadvantages of sales promotion are that:

- It may be hard to terminate certain promotions without adverse customer reactions.
- The retailer's image may be hurt if trite promotions are used.
- Frivolous selling points may be stressed rather than the retailer's product assortment, prices, customer services, and other factors.
- Many sales promotions have only short-term effects.
- It should be used mostly as a supplement to other promotional forms.

Questionable Uses of Multiple-Unit Pricing

Retailers are now more closely examining loyalty card and other data to encourage consumers to purchase larger quantities. As an executive vice-president for merchandising and marketing at the Great Atlantic and Pacific Tea (A&P) Company (www.aptea.com) stated: "We look at the customer buying behavior, and that's how we land at multiples—to get customers to buy a little higher than their typical purchase rate."

Supervalu (www.supervalu.com), the parent company of Cub Foods (www.cub.com) and other grocery chains, tested 10 for $10 deals versus five for $5 on the same items and in the same markets. Its research indicated that its consumers generally purchased two or more items when the promotion was 10 for $10. Question: Does this pricing strategy encourage consumers to overbuy?

As a result of this research, grocery stores are increasingly using such multiple prices as 10 cans of tuna for $10 or six ears of corn for $2. They are doing this even though there is no real savings to shoppers based on the larger quantities they buy. Consumers seeking to purchase one can of tuna or one ear of corn would pay $1 or 33 cents per ear of corn. According to John T. Gourville, a Harvard Business School professor, "Even though shoppers do not have to buy the suggested amount to get the discount, they do anyway."

Source: Stephanie Clifford, "At Stores, Making 5 for $5 a Bigger Draw Than 1 for $1," www.nytimes.com (July 17, 2011).

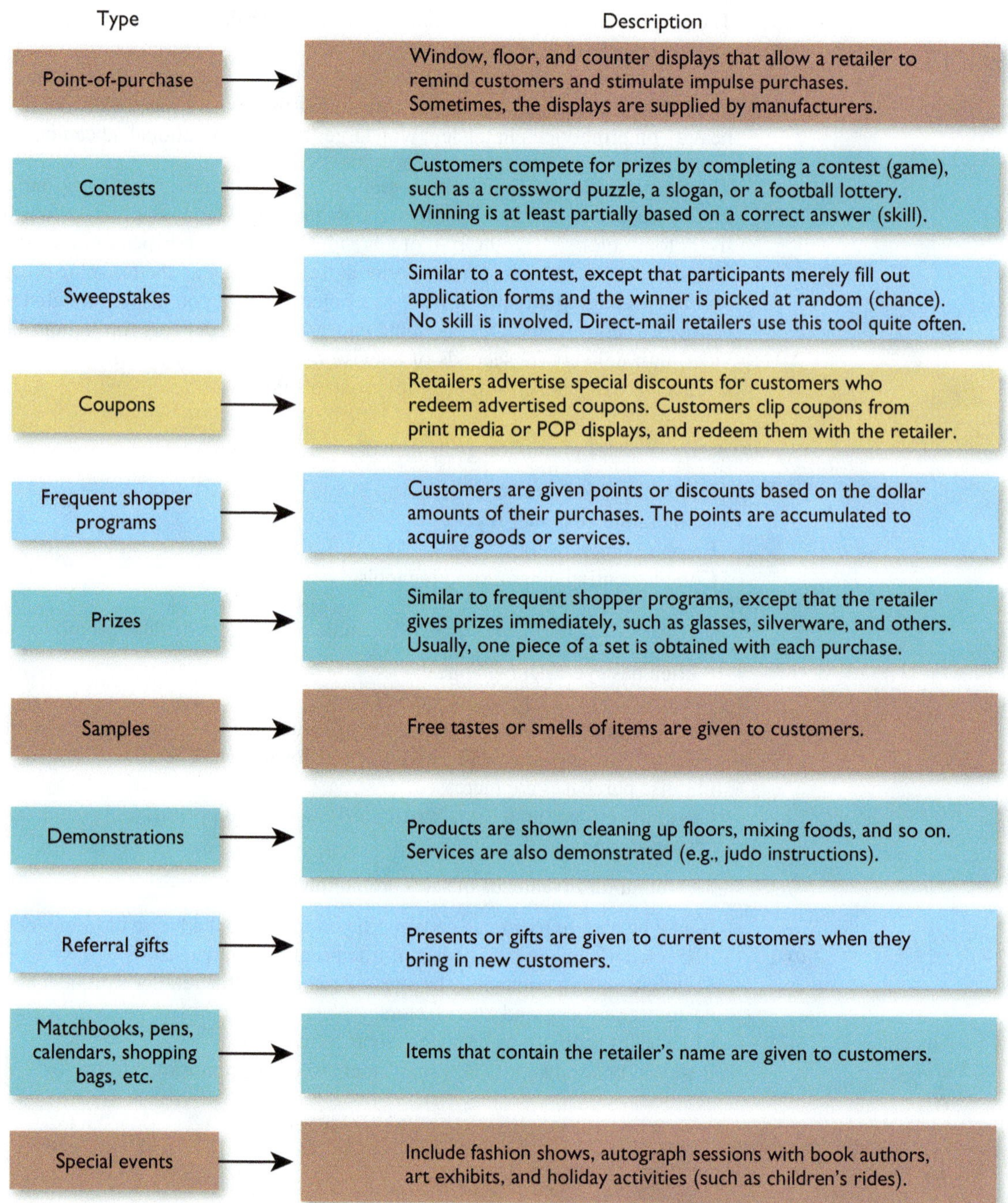

FIGURE 19-9
Types of Sales Promotion

Visit the site of the leading point-of-purchase trade association (www.popai.org).

TYPES Figure 19-9 describes the major types of sales promotions. Each is explained here.

Point-of-purchase promotion consists of in-store displays designed to lift sales. Displays may remind customers, stimulate impulse behavior, facilitate self-service, and reduce retailer costs if manufacturers provide the displays. See Figure 19-10. These data show the extent of displays:

- U.S. manufacturers and retailers together annually spend more than $20 billion on in-store displays, with retailers using about two-thirds of all displays provided by manufacturers.
- Virtually all retailers have some type of POP display.
- Restaurants, apparel stores, music/video stores, toy stores, and sporting goods stores are among the retail categories with above-average use of in-store displays.

FIGURE 19-10

Best Sales Promotion Theme?

For value-conscious customers, it's hard to top this in-store promotion—unless the retailer loses money.

Source: Selena/Shutterstock.com. Reprinted by permission.

- Retailers spend one-sixth of their sales promotion budgets on displays.
- Display ads appear on shopping carts in most U.S. supermarkets. And thousands of supermarkets have electronic signs above their aisles promoting well-known brands.

Contests and sweepstakes are similar; they seek to attract customers who participate in events with large prizes. A contest requires a customer to show some skill. A sweepstakes only requires participation, with the winner chosen at random. Disadvantages of contests and sweepstakes are their costs, customer reliance on these tools for continued patronage, the customer effort, and entries by nonshoppers. Together, U.S. manufacturers and retailers spend $2 billion yearly on contests and sweepstakes.

Each year, hundreds of billions of dollars in coupons—discounts from regular selling prices—are distributed in the United States, with grocery products accounting for two-thirds of them. Consumers actually redeem $4 billion in coupons annually; retailers receive several hundred million dollars for processing coupon redemptions. Coupons are offered through freestanding inserts in Sunday papers and placements in daily papers, direct mail, Web sites, smart phones, regular magazines, and Sunday newspaper magazines. They are also placed in or on packages and dispensed from in-store machines.

Coupons have four key advantages: (1) In many cases, manufacturers pay to advertise and redeem them. (2) According to surveys, more than 80 percent of consumers redeem coupons at least once during the year. (3) They contribute to the consumer's perception that a retailer offers good value. (4) Ad effectiveness can be measured by counting redeemed coupons. Disadvantages include the possible negative effect on the retailer's image, consumers shopping only if coupons are available, the low redemption rates, the clutter of coupons, retailer and consumer fraud, and handling costs. Less than 3 percent of coupons are redeemed by consumers due to the large number of them that are received.

Frequent shopper programs foster customer relationships by awarding discounts or prizes to people for continued patronage. In most programs, customers accumulate points (or their equivalent)—which are redeemed for cash, discounts, or prizes. Programs that follow these principles are most apt to succeed:

1. Regularly collect customer data. This enables the retailer to tailor rewards on the basis of customer preferences and past purchases. When there are many "lapsed customers" in the data base, it may be a good tactic to offer an instant reward to encourage these former shoppers to return.
2. A loyalty program's format, rewards, and manner of communications have to be relevant to the specific customer group, "based upon their attitudes, behaviors, and demographics."
3. A membership card in a shopper's wallet can be a constant reminder of the benefits of the loyalty program of a given retailer.
4. A good loyalty program "builds excitement by letting customers know exactly what rewards they can expect and how to earn them."
5. For a loyalty program to reach a high level of customer participation, "make your rewards readily obtainable and graduate them so you transform a higher percentage of your customers from low value to high value."
6. Many people "love to brag about reaching special membership status that provides them incentives that only few receive." This propels even more repeat business and may politely nudge those who are in a lower reward category.
7. A loyalty program can be used as part of regular E-mails with customers. A retailer can "send follow-up messages after each purchase and communicate frequently to introduce new perks and special offers.[10]

All sorts of retailers participate in online loyalty programs, such as e-Rewards (www.e-rewards.com).

The advantages of frequent shopper programs for retailers are the loyalty (customers amass points only by shopping at a specific firm or firms), the increased shopping, and the competitive edge for a retailer similar to others. However, some consumers feel these programs are not really free and would rather shop at lower-priced stores without loyalty programs, it may take a while for shoppers to gather enough points to earn meaningful gifts, and retail profit margins may be smaller if firms with these programs try to price competitively with those without the programs.

Prizes are similar to frequent shopper programs, but they are given with each purchase. They are most effective when sets of glasses, silverware, dishes, place mats, and so on are distributed one at a time to shoppers. These encourage loyalty. Problems are the cost of prizes, the difficulty of termination, and the possible impact on image.

Free samples (food tastings) and demonstrations (cooking lessons) can complement personal selling. About $2.5 billion is spent annually on sampling and demonstrations in U.S. stores—mostly at supermarkets, membership clubs, specialty stores, and department stores. They are effective because customers become involved and impulse purchases increase. Loitering and costs may be problems.

Referral gifts may encourage existing customers to bring in new ones. Direct marketers, such as book and music clubs, often use this tool. It is a technique that has no important shortcomings and recognizes the value of friends in influencing purchases.

Matchbooks, pens, calendars, and shopping bags may be given to customers. They differ from prizes because they promote retailers' names. These items should be used as supplements. The advantage is longevity. There is no real disadvantage.

Retailers may use special events to generate consumer enthusiasm. Events can range from store grand openings to fashion shows. When new McDonald's stores open, there are typically giveaways and children's activities, and there is a guest appearance by Ronald McDonald (a human in a costume). Generally, in choosing a special event, the potential increase in consumer awareness and store traffic needs to be weighed against that event's costs. See Figure 19-11.

FIGURE 19-11
Driving Business Through Special Events

Source: Reprinted by permission of Susan V. Berry, Retail Image Consulting, Inc.

PLANNING A RETAIL PROMOTIONAL STRATEGY

A systematic approach to promotional planning is shown in Figure 19-12 and explained next. Our Web site (www.pearsonhighered.com/bermanevans) has links related to several aspects of promotional strategy, including word of mouth.

Determining Promotional Objectives

A retailer's broad promotional goals are typically drawn from this list:

- Increase sales.
- Stimulate impulse and reminder buying.
- Raise customer traffic.
- Get leads for sales personnel.

FIGURE 19-12
Planning a Retail Promotional Strategy

- Present and reinforce the retailer image.
- Inform customers about goods and services.
- Popularize new stores and Web sites.
- Capitalize on manufacturer support.
- Enhance customer relations.
- Maintain customer loyalty.
- Have consumers pass along positive information to friends and others.

In developing a promotional strategy, the firm must determine which of these are most important.

It is vital to state goals as precisely as possible to give direction to the choice of promotional types, media, and messages. Increasing sales is not a specific goal. However, increasing sales by 10 percent is directional, quantitative, and measurable. With that goal, a firm would be able to prepare a thorough promotional plan and evaluate its success. McDonald's, which has won numerous awards for creative advertising, wants its ads and promotions to support its franchisees, drive sales, introduce new products, push special offers, create an emotional bond with customers, and deflect criticism about fast food:

> As a franchisee, McDonald's field operations and franchising staff work directly with you from the moment you enter training. Their job is to prepare you to maximize quality, service, and cleanliness in order to optimize sales and profits. To take advantage of our leadership position, each restaurant is required to spend a minimum of 4 percent of gross sales annually on advertising and promotion. This buying power has helped McDonald's create a worldwide brand unmatched in the foodservice industry. We pay particular attention to our offerings for children and how we communicate about them to both kids and parents.[11]

See what tactics facilitate good WOM (www.squidoo.com/word-of-mouth-advertising).

Perhaps the most vital long-term promotion goal for any retailer is to gain positive **word of mouth (WOM)**, which occurs when one consumer talks to others—in person, on the phone, by E-mail, through social media, or in some other format. If a satisfied customer refers friends to a retailer, this can build into a chain of customers. No retailer can succeed if it receives extensive negative WOM (such as "The hotel advertised that everything was included in the price. Yet it cost me another $50 to play golf"). Negative WOM will cause a firm to lose substantial business.

Both goods- and services-oriented retailers must have positive word of mouth to attract and retain customers. They need WOM referrals to generate new customers. Consider these observations from a travel industry expert:

> Customers, for better or worse, are going to talk about their experiences. However, that does not mean word of mouth is out of your control and cannot be managed. You can

Burberry's Promotion Strategy in China

Winning over young customers is a key part of Burberry's (www.burberry.com) Chinese promotion strategy. Seventy-three percent of China's luxury buyers are under 45 years old, versus 50 percent in the United States. And as many as 45 percent of China's high-end consumers are under 35 years old, versus 28 percent in Europe. In an attempt to reposition its image as a younger person's clothing store, Burberry Group PLC has outfitted its 60 Chinese stores with touch screens for customers and iPads for its staff.

Touch screens, which are the size of a full-length mirror, enable Burberry to display its special collections, fashion shows streamed from other countries, and events from Burberry-produced entertainment venues. All employees in Burberry's Chinese stores will have iPads to assist customers in ordering special sizes, as well as some of the 5,000 items in Burberry's portfolio that are not stocked in its Chinese stores.

To celebrate the opening of Burberry's new flagship store in Beijing, the company held an event at the Beijing Television Center for more than 1,000 guests. The models wore clothes from Burberry's new fall collection. Using holograms, projections, and animations, the models almost magically changed clothing or were transformed into snow or red dust.

Sources: Laurie Burkitt, "Burberry Dresses China Stores with Digital Strategy," www.wallstreetjournal.com (April 14, 2011); and Lara Farrar, "Burberry's Beijing Blowout," www.wwd.com (April 14, 2011), 201 (77), p. 4.

promote your brand through a good word-of-mouth campaign. By cultivating your message, you can help ensure that when people talk about you, they say things you want the market to hear. Word of mouth is no more than consumers providing information about you to other consumers. Smart word-of-mouth marketing encourages and gives people a reason to talk about you and your goods and services.[12]

Establishing an Overall Promotional Budget

There are five main procedures for setting the size of a retail promotional budget. Retailers should weigh the strengths and weaknesses of each technique in relation to their own requirements and constraints. To assist firms in their efforts, there is now computer software available.

With the **all-you-can-afford method**, a retailer first allots funds for each element of the retail strategy mix except promotion. The remaining funds go to promotion. This is the weakest technique. Its shortcomings are that little emphasis is placed on promotion as a strategic variable; expenditures are not linked to goals; and if little or no funds are left over, the promotion budget is too small or nonexistent. The method is used predominantly by small, conservative retailers.

The **incremental method** relies on prior promotion budgets to allocate funds. A percentage is either added to or subtracted from one year's budget to determine the next year's. If this year's promotion budget is \$100,000, next year's would be calculated by adjusting that amount. A 10 percent rise means that next year's budget would be \$110,000. This technique is useful for a small retailer. It provides a reference point. The budget is adjusted based on the firm's feelings about past successes and future trends. It is easy to apply. Yet, the budget is rarely tied to specific goals. "Gut feelings" are used.

With the **competitive parity method**, a retailer's promotion budget is raised or lowered based on competitors' actions. If the leading competitor raises its budget, other retailers in the area may follow. This method is useful for small and large firms, uses a comparison point, and is market-oriented and conservative. It is also imitative, takes for granted that tough-to-get competitive data are available, and assumes competitors are similar (as to years in business, size, customers, location, merchandise, prices, and so on). That last point is critical because competitors often need very different promotional budgets.

In the **percentage-of-sales method**, a retailer ties its promotion budget to revenue. A promotion-to-sales ratio is developed. Then, during succeeding years, this ratio remains constant. A firm could set promotion costs at 10 percent of sales. If this year's sales are \$600,000, there is a \$60,000 promotion budget. If next year's sales are estimated at \$720,000, a \$72,000 budget is planned. This process uses sales as a base, is adaptable, and correlates promotion and sales. Nonetheless, there is no relation to goals (for an established firm, sales growth may not require increased promotion); promotion is not used to lead sales; and promotion drops during poor periods, when increases might be helpful. This technique provides excess financing in times of high sales and too few funds in periods of low sales.

Under the **objective-and-task method**, a retailer clearly defines its promotion goals and prepares a budget to satisfy them. A goal might be to have 70 percent of the people in its trading area know a retailer's name by the end of a one-month promotion campaign, up from 50 percent. To do so, it would determine the tasks and costs required to achieve that goal:

Objective	Task	Cost
1. Gain awareness of working women.	Use eight 1/4-page ads in four successive Sunday editions of two area papers.	$20,000
2. Gain awareness of motorists.	Use twenty 30-second radio ads during prime time on local radio stations.	$12,000
3. Gain awareness of pedestrians.	Give away 5,000 shopping bags.	$15,000
	Total budget	$47,000

The objective-and-task method is the best budgeting technique. Goals are clear, spending relates to goal-oriented tasks, and performance can be assessed. It can be time-consuming and complex to set goals and specific tasks, especially for small retailers.

Selecting the Promotional Mix

After a budget is set, the promotional mix is determined: the retailer's combination of advertising, public relations, personal selling, and sales promotion. A firm with a limited budget may rely on store displays, flyers, targeted direct mail, and publicity to generate customer traffic. One with a large budget may rely more on newspaper and TV ads. Retailers often use an assortment of forms to reinforce each other. A melding of media ads and POP displays may be more effective than either form alone. See Figure 19-13.

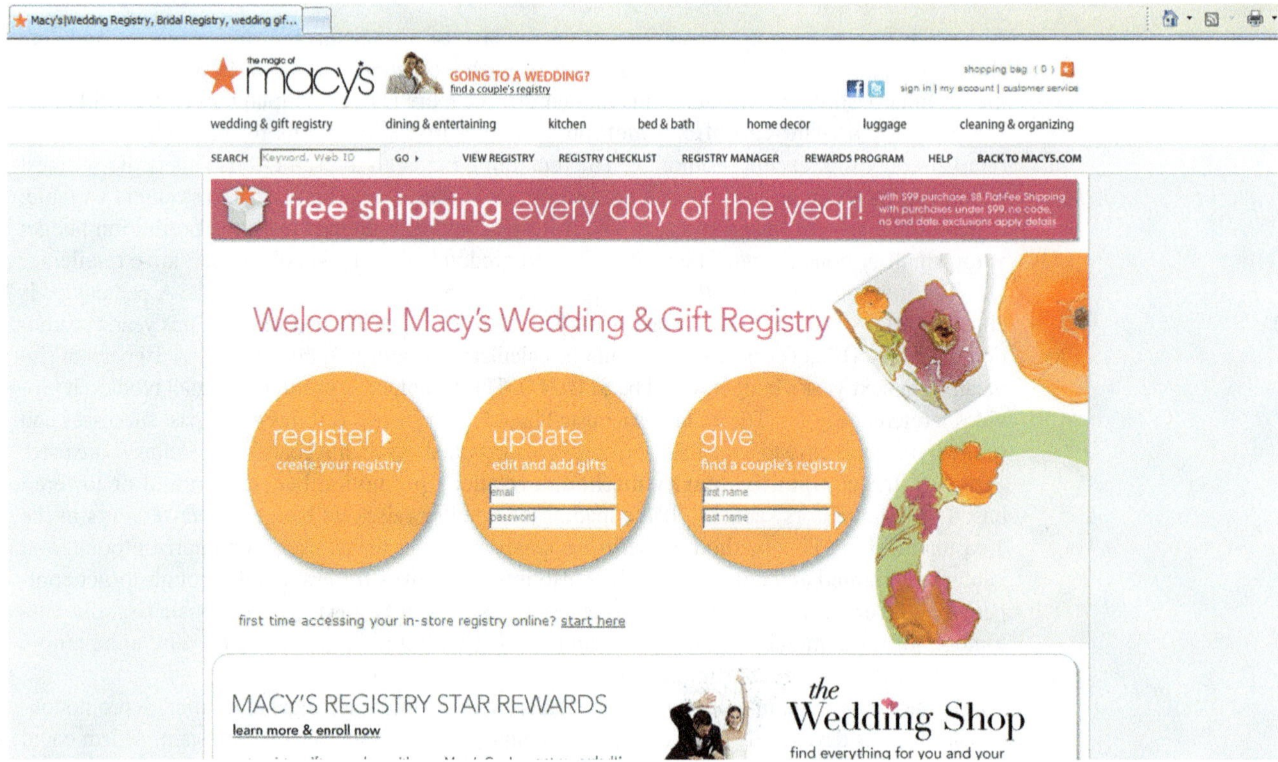

FIGURE 19-13

An Integrated Promotional Approach

Macy's has a well-integrated Wedding & Gift Registry (www.macys.com/registry) program. People can sign up for the registry and then post a list of merchandise from which family and friends can select and buy gifts. If the couple has a Macy's card, they can sign up for Macy's Registry Star Rewards and receive rewards based on the dollar amount of the gifts bought through the registry. This is a real win-win. Macy's generates more business and customer loyalty; and the registrants receive dollar rewards from family and friend purchases.

Source: Used with permission of Macy's, Inc.

TABLE 19-3 The Promotional Mixes of Selected Small Retailers

Type of Retailer	Favorite Media	Personal Selling Emphasis	Special Considerations	Promotional Opportunities
Apparel store	Weekly papers; direct mail; radio; Internet; exterior signs.	High	Cooperative ads available from manufacturers.	Fashion shows for community groups and charities; social media.
Auto supply store	Local papers; Yellow Pages; POP displays; Internet; exterior signs.	Moderate	Cooperative ads available from manufacturers.	Direct mail.
Bookstore	Local papers; Yellow Pages; radio; Internet; exterior signs.	Moderate	Cooperative ads available from publishers.	Author-signing events; retailer blog.
Coin-operated laundry	Yellow Pages; flyers in area; local direct mail; exterior signs.	None	None.	Coupons in newspaper ads.
Gift store	Weekly papers; Yellow Pages; direct mail; Internet; exterior signs.	Moderate	None.	Special events; Web ads.
Hair grooming/ beauty salon	Yellow Pages; mentions in feature articles; exterior signs.	Moderate	Word-of-mouth communication key.	Participation in fashion shows; free beauty clinics.
Health food store	Local papers; shoppers; POP displays; Internet; exterior signs.	Moderate	None.	Display windows.
Restaurant	Newspapers; radio; Yellow Pages; entertainment guides; Internet; exterior signs.	Moderate	Word-of-mouth communication key.	Write-ups in critics' columns; special events.

Freestanding inserts offer retailers many possibilities. Visit Valassis (www.valassis.com), click on "Products," and choose "Freestanding Inserts."

The promotional mix is affected by the type of retailer involved. In supermarkets, sampling, frequent shopper promotions, theme sales, and bonus coupons are among the techniques used most. At upscale stores, there is more attention to personal selling and less to advertising and sales promotion as compared with discounters. Table 19-3 shows a number of small-retailer promotional mixes.

In reacting to a retailer's communication efforts, consumers often go through a sequence of steps known as the **hierarchy of effects**, which takes them from awareness to knowledge to liking to preference to conviction to purchase. Different promotional mixes are needed in each step. Ads and public relations are best to develop awareness; personal selling and sales promotion are best in changing attitudes and stimulating desires. This is especially true for expensive, complex goods and services. See Figure 19-14.

Implementing the Promotional Mix

The implementation of a promotional mix involves choosing which specific media to use (such as Newspaper A and Newspaper B), timing, message content, the makeup of the sales force, specific sales promotion tools, and the responsibility for coordination. Here is an example:

> If you own an upscale jewelry store, you know from your sales history that your target market is consumers earning more than $75,000 per year. Any print advertising should thus appear in publications in which readership income exceeds $75,000. To introduce new customers to your products, a direct-marketing technique, such as a direct-mail letter with a money-saving offer to first-time customers, might work. Or you can try a sales promotion, such as a free gift with a minimum purchase of $250. If your target market has a misconception about you, this can be corrected by providing comparisons or testimonials.[13]

Is 3D shopping on the Web ahead of its time or on target (www.3dshopper.net)?

MEDIA DECISIONS The choice of specific media is based on their overall costs, efficiency (the cost to reach the target market), lead time, and editorial content. Overall costs are important since

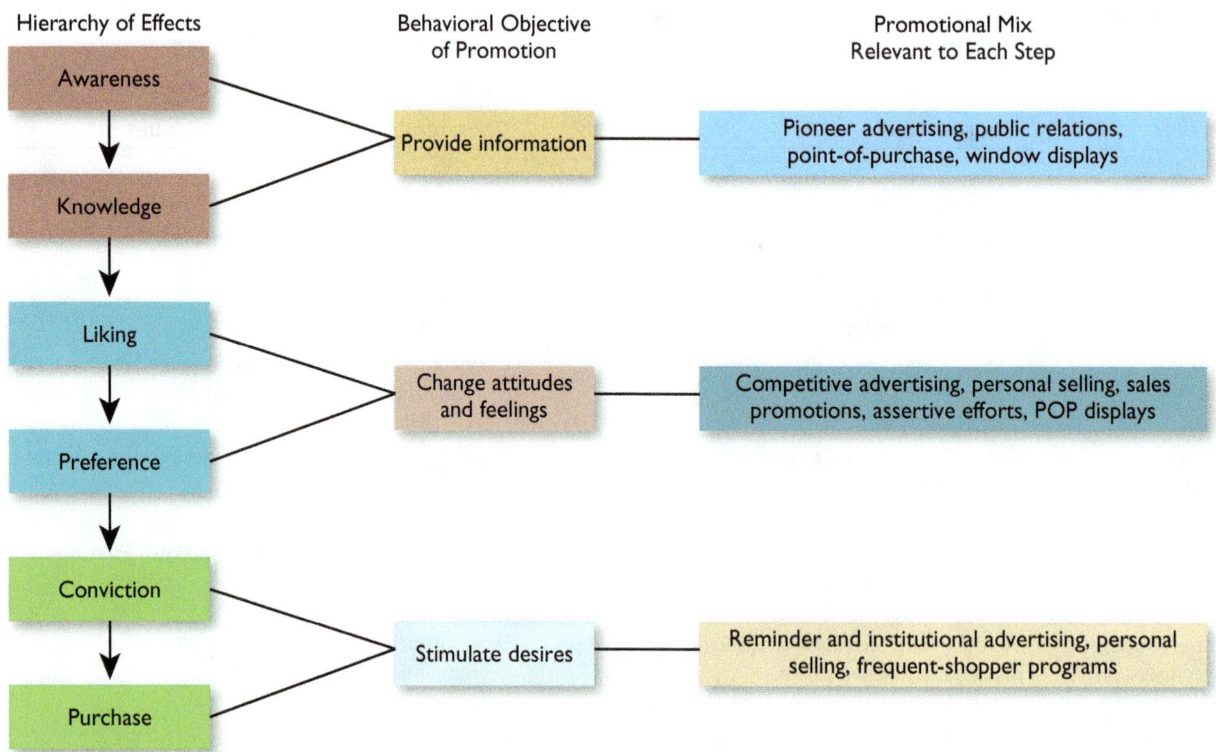

FIGURE 19-14
Promotion and the Hierarchy of Effects

heavy use of one expensive medium may preclude a balanced promotional mix, and a firm may not be able to repeat a message in a costly medium.

A medium's efficiency relates to the cost of reaching a given number of target customers. Media rates are often expressed in terms of cost per 1,000 readers, watchers, or listeners:

$$\text{Cost per thousand} = \frac{\text{Cost per message} \times 1{,}000}{\text{Circulation}}$$

A newspaper with a circulation of 400,000 and a one-page advertising rate of $10,000 has a per-page cost per thousand of $25.

In this computation, total circulation is used to measure efficiency. Yet, because a retailer usually appeals to a limited target market, only the relevant portion of circulation should be considered. If 70 percent of readers are target customers for a particular firm (and the other 30 percent live outside the trading area), the real cost per thousand is:

$$\begin{aligned}\text{Cost per thousand (target market)} &= \frac{\text{Cost per page} \times 1{,}000}{\text{Circulation} \times \dfrac{\text{Target market}}{\text{Circulation}}} \\ &= \frac{\$10{,}000 \times 1{,}000}{400{,}000 \times 0.70} = \$35.71\end{aligned}$$

Different media require different lead times. A newspaper ad can be placed shortly before publication and an online ad can sometimes go "live" almost immediately, whereas a print magazine ad sometimes must be placed months in advance. In addition, the retailer must decide what kind of editorial content it wants near ads (such as a sports story or a personal-care column).

Media decisions are not simple. Despite spending billions of dollars on TV and radio commercials, banner ads at search engines, and other media, many Web retailers have found that the most valuable medium for them is E-mail. It is fast, inexpensive, and targeted. Consider the following.

To generate greater *awareness* of Web retailers, costly advertising may be necessary in today's competitive and cluttered landscape. At Netflix, "we obtain new subscribers through our online marketing efforts, including paid search listings, banner ads, text links, and permission-based E-mails, as well as our active affiliate program. We also engage our consumer electronics partners to generate new subscribers for us. In addition, we have engaged in offline marketing programs, including TV and radio advertising, direct mail and print campaigns, and mailing inserts. We maintain an active public relations program to increase awareness of our service and drive subscriber acquisition."[14] Once customers have visited a Web site, E-mail can help *sustain relationships*:

> Opt-in marketing involves the customer giving permission for the retailer to send marketing materials. The customer is more likely to "read," "hear," or "see" a marketing message if he/she has already given prior permission to do so. In the highest form, opt-in E-mail marketing involves an ongoing, evolving relationship between the retailer and the customer. The relationship is one that becomes increasingly focused, with the relevant exchange of information and value. In order to retain customers, the retailer must continually offer value. Customer loyalty cannot be taken for granted, it has to be earned.[15]

TIMING OF THE PROMOTIONAL MIX **Reach** refers to the number of distinct people exposed to a retailer's promotion efforts in a specific period. **Frequency** is the average number of times each person reached is exposed to a retailer's promotion efforts in a specific period. A retailer can advertise extensively or intensively. Extensive media coverage often means ads reach many people but with relatively low frequency. Intensive media coverage generally means ads are placed in selected media and repeated frequently. Repetition is important, particularly for a retailer seeking to develop an image or sell new goods or services.

Decisions are needed about how to address peak selling seasons and whether to mass or distribute efforts. When peak seasons occur, all elements of the promotional mix are usually utilized; in slow periods, promotional efforts are typically reduced. A **massed promotion effort** is used by retailers, such as toy retailers, that promote seasonally. A **distributed promotion effort** is used by retailers, such as fast-food restaurants, that promote throughout the year. Although they are not affected by seasonality in the same way as other retailers, massed advertising is practiced by supermarkets, many of which use Wednesday or Thursday for weekly newspaper ads. This takes advantage of the fact that a high proportion of their consumers make their major shopping trip on Friday, Saturday, or Sunday.

Sales force size can vary by time (morning versus evening), day (weekdays versus weekends), and month (December versus January). Sales promotions also vary in their timing. Store openings and holidays are especially good times for sales promotions (and public relations).

The CarMax (www.carmax.com) message—"The way car buying should be"—is clear and information packed. Click on "Why CarMax" at the bottom of the screen.

CONTENT OF MESSAGES Whether written or spoken, personally or impersonally delivered, message content is important. Advertising themes, wording, headlines, use of color, size, layout, and placement must be selected. Publicity releases must be written. In personal selling, the greeting,

TECHNOLOGY IN RETAILING

Video in a Broadband Era

German-based Max Röhner Leather Goods is a retailer specializing in high-quality pocketbooks, wallets, and leather accessories. The chain has five brick-and-mortar stores, as well as an online division, Profibag.de (www.profibag.de). The Profibag.de Web site has had close to a 50 percent increase in its conversion rate (the percentage of viewers that actually purchase) since it incorporated an automated product video technology that was developed by Treepodia (www.treepodia.com).

The owner and manager of Max Röhner Leather Goods provided product images, descriptions, prices, and promotional materials to Treepodia, which then developed hundreds of video templates for the retailer's staff to select. These templates were customized to fit with the retailer's image. Röhner now has video templates for about 200 of its 1,100 products. Price changes, special promotions, and customer product reviews can also be easily uploaded to keep the site current.

An important feature of this system is a module that can measure the effectiveness of each video. This component allows a retailer to determine which of several videos results in the greatest sales level. In one case, a video version that included subtitles generated a 9.1 percent conversion rate, versus a 0.8 percent conversion rate for the video without subtitles.

Source: Liz Parks, "The Power of Video," www.stores.org (September 2010).

sales presentation, demonstration, and closing need to be applied. With sales promotion, the firm's message must be composed and placed on the promotional device.

To a large extent, the characteristics of the promotional form influence the message. A shopping bag often contains no more than a retailer's name, and a billboard (seen at 55 miles per hour) is good for visual effect but can hold only limited information. Yet, a salesperson may be able to hold a customer's attention for a while. A number of shopping centers use a glossy magazine—in print and online—to communicate a community-oriented image, introduce new stores to consumers, and promote the goods and services carried at stores in the center. Cluttered ads displaying many products suggest a discounter's orientation, while fine pencil drawings and selective product displays suggest a specialty store focus.

Some retailers use comparative advertising to contrast their offerings with competitors'. These ads help position a retailer relative to competitors, increase awareness of the firm, maximize the efficiency of a limited budget, and offer credibility. Yet, they provide visibility for competitors, may confuse people, and may lead to legal action. Fast-food and off-price retailers are among those using comparative ads.

MAKEUP OF SALES FORCE Sales personnel qualifications must be detailed; and these personnel must be recruited, selected, trained, compensated, supervised, and monitored. Personnel should also be classified as order takers or order getters and assigned to the appropriate departments.

SALES PROMOTION TOOLS Specific sales promotion tools must be chosen from among those cited in Figure 19-9. The combination of tools depends on short-term goals and the other aspects of the promotion mix. If possible, cooperative ventures should be sought. Tools inconsistent with the firm's image should never be used; and retailers should recognize the types of promotions that customers really want. For example, Target "has restrictions on all in-store promotions, and everything that comes along with them from point-of-purchase materials to large-scale holiday displays to motion-activated TVs that call out 'hello' as a customer walks by." Target is one of a growing number of retailers that "want to protect their own brands and differentiate themselves from competitors by limiting and controlling the marketing in their stores. Retailers often want control over color, design, placement, and creative look and feel."[16]

RESPONSIBILITY FOR COORDINATION Regardless of the retailer's size or format, someone must be responsible for the promotion function. Larger retailers often assign this job to a vice-president, who oversees display personnel, works with the firm's ad agency, supervises the firm's advertising department (if there is one), and supplies branch outlets with POP materials. In a large retail store, personal selling is usually under the jurisdiction of the store manager. For a promotional strategy to succeed, its components have to be coordinated with other retail mix elements. Sales personnel must be informed of special sales and know product attributes; featured items must be received, marked, and displayed; and accounting entries must be made. Often, a shopping center or a shopping district runs theme promotions, such as "Back to School." In those instances, someone must coordinate the activities of all participating retailers.

Reviewing and Revising the Promotional Plan

An analysis of the success of a promotional plan depends on its objectives. Revisions should be made if pre-set goals are not achieved. Here are some ways to test the effectiveness of a promotional effort:

Examples of Retail Promotion Goals	Approaches for Evaluating Promotion Effectiveness
Inform current customers about new credit plans; acquaint potential customers with new offerings.	Study company and product awareness before and after promotion; evaluate size of audience.
Develop and reinforce a particular image; maintain customer loyalty.	Study image through surveys before and after public relations and other promotion efforts.
Increase customer traffic; get leads for salespeople; increase revenues above last year's; reduce customer returns from prior year's.	Evaluate sales performance and the number of inquiries; study customer intentions to buy before and after promotion; study customer trading areas and average purchases; review coupon redemption.

Smart Brief (www.smartbrief.com/news/iab) presents insights on the current status of online advertising.

Although it may at times be tough to assess promotion efforts (e.g., increased revenues might be due to several factors, not just promotion), it is crucial for retailers to systematically study and adapt their promotional mixes. Wal-Mart provides suppliers with store-by-store data and sets up-front goals for cooperative promotion programs. Actual sales are then compared against the goals. Lowe's, the home center chain, applies computerized testing to review thousands of different ideas affecting the design of circulars and media mix options. And consider this:

> In a suburb of Minneapolis, Supervalu runs a "lab store," a model store not open to the public where the company can test how new products look on its shelves and experiment with seasonal displays. On endcaps, best-selling items often go on the larger shelves near the floor to grab people's attention from farther away. Employees experiment with which size and shape products look best together. When a product sits on an endcap, its sales can increase three-fold.[17]

Chapter Summary

1. *To explore the scope of retail promotion.* Any communication by a retailer that informs, persuades, and/or reminds the target market about any aspect of the retailer through ads, public relations, personal selling, and sales promotion is retail promotion.

2. *To study the elements of retail promotion: advertising, public relations, personal selling, and sales promotion.* Advertising involves paid, nonpersonal communication. It has a large audience, low costs per person, many alternative media, and other factors. It also involves message inflexibility, high absolute costs, and a wasted portion of the audience. Key advertising media are papers, phone directories, direct mail, radio, TV, the Web, transit, outdoor, magazines, and flyers/circulars. Especially useful are cooperative ads, in which a retailer shares costs and messages with manufacturers, wholesalers, or other retailers.

   Public relations includes all communications fostering a favorable image. It may be nonpersonal or personal, paid or nonpaid, and sponsor controlled or not controlled. Publicity is the nonpersonal, nonpaid form of public relations. Public relations creates awareness, enhances the image, involves credible sources, and has no message costs. It also has little control over messages, is short term, and can entail nonmedia costs. Publicity can be expected or unexpected and positive or negative.

   Personal selling uses oral communication with one or more potential customers and is critical for persuasion and in closing sales. It is adaptable, flexible, and provides immediate feedback. The audience is small, per-customer costs are high, and shoppers are not lured into the store. Order-taking and/or order-getting salespeople can be employed. Functions include greeting the customer, determining wants, showing merchandise, making a sales presentation, demonstrating products, answering objections, and closing the sale.

   Sales promotion comprises the paid communication activities other than advertising, public relations, and personal selling. It may be eye-catching, unique, and valuable to the customer. It also may be hard to end, have a negative effect on image, and rely on frivolous selling points. Tools include POP displays, contests and sweepstakes, coupons, frequent shopper programs, prizes, samples, demonstrations, referral gifts, matchbooks, pens, calendars, shopping bags, and special events.

3. *To discuss the strategic aspects of retail promotion.* There are five steps in a promotion strategy: (a) Goals are stated in specific and measurable terms. Positive word of mouth (WOM) is an important long-term goal. (b) An overall promotion budget is set on the basis of one of these techniques: all you can afford, incremental, competitive parity, percentage of sales, and objective and task. (c) The promotional mix is outlined, based on the budget, the type of retailing, the coverage of the media, and the hierarchy of effects. (d) The promotional mix is enacted. Included are decisions involving specific media, promotional timing, message content, sales force composition, sales promotion tools, and the responsibility for coordination. (e) The retailer systematically reviews and adjusts the promotional plan, consistent with pre-set goals.

Key Terms

retail promotion (p. 480)
advertising (p. 480)
cooperative advertising (p. 482)
vertical cooperative advertising agreement (p. 486)
horizontal cooperative advertising agreement (p. 486)
public relations (p. 486)
publicity (p. 486)
personal selling (p. 488)
order-taking salesperson (p. 489)
order-getting salesperson (p. 489)
PMs (promotional or push monies) (p. 489)
canned sales presentation (p. 490)
need-satisfaction approach (p. 490)
sales promotion (p. 490)
word of mouth (WOM) (p. 496)
all-you-can-afford method (p. 497)
incremental method (p. 497)
competitive parity method (p. 497)
percentage-of-sales method (p. 497)
objective-and-task method (p. 497)
hierarchy of effects (p. 499)
reach (p. 501)
frequency (p. 501)
massed promotion effort (p. 501)
distributed promotion effort (p. 501)

Questions for Discussion

1. How would an advertising plan for an online-only cosmetics retailer differ from that for a bricks-and-clicks cosmetics store chain?
2. How do manufacturer and retailer cooperative advertising goals overlap? How do they differ?
3. How can a local beauty salon try to generate positive publicity?
4. Are there any retailers that should *not* use personal selling? Explain your answer.
5. Are there any retailers that should *not* use sales promotion? Explain your answer.
6. How can advertising, public relations, personal selling, and sales promotion complement each other for a retailer?
7. What are the pros and cons of coupons?
8. Develop sales promotions for each of the following:
   a. A nearby regional shopping center.
   b. A 30-year-old restaurant.
   c. A discount online furniture retailer.
9. Which method of promotional budgeting should a small retailer use? A large retailer? Why?
10. Explain the hierarchy of effects from a retail perspective. Apply your answer to a new auto dealer.
11. Develop a checklist for an upscale sporting goods chain to coordinate its promotional plan.
12. For each of these promotional goals, explain how to evaluate promotional effectiveness:
    a. To increase impulse purchases of magazines.
    b. To project an innovative image.
    c. To maintain customer loyalty rates.

Web-Based Exercise

Visit this Web site (www.businessknowhow.com/marketing/24waysto.htm). What could a small store-based retailer learn by surfing this site?

Note: Also stop by our Web site (www.pearsonhighered.com/bermanevans) to experience a number of highly interactive, appealing Web exercises based on actual company demonstrations and sample materials related to retailing.

PART 7 Short Cases

Case 1: Making Every Day Seem Special[c-1]

While the expression "Christmas in July" may mean one thing to consumers (a sale), to retailers it reflects "Christmas creep," the practice of shifting holiday sales to earlier time periods. Worried about the effects of the recession and its aftermath on sales, retailers have increasingly pushed Christmas sales periods to the summer months. They are hoping to extend the Christmas buying season and to encourage consumers to increase their total expenditures. Among the retailers that have launched sales in summer months are Kmart (www.kmart.com), Target (www.target.com), and Toys "R" Us (www.toysrus.com). Stephen Hoch, a Wharton marketing professor, notes that this seasonal shift has spread across all retail formats—from luxury department stores to value-based retailers.

Erin Armendiner, managing director of the Baker Retailing Initiative at Wharton, views the situation as similar to a game of "chicken" with the retailers offering moderate price reductions for as long as possible, hoping to sell goods at or near full retail price. In turn, consumers have delayed their purchases in an attempt to force the retailers into providing additional markdowns. Armendiner says: "It's this game of who was going to break down first."

One retail consultant believes that successful early seasonal sales by one retailer may encourage other retailers to match or even beat the first retailer's price. "If [one chain] moves its [sale] three days ahead, then [a competitor will jump] a week ahead. Then they go 10 days ahead, and you go two weeks ahead … and it just keeps going." As a result, a tongue-in-cheek comment is that next year's Christmas season will start "in the middle of January clearance at the rate they are going."

The Christmas creep phenomenon has some interesting implications for retailers beyond the changes in their markdown and promotional activity. In the past, retailers would change displays on a given day to reflect the beginning of a new selling season. Now, many retailers are offering a balance of clothing from shorts and bathing suits to cotton and wool sweaters and corduroy slacks to reflect both seasons. In contrast, many consumers have taken the opposite approach by delaying the purchase of seasonal goods. Some retailers, including Abercrombie & Fitch (www.abercrombie.com), have resisted the use of extensive markdowns. Instead, they have lowered their initial price levels.

Several experts expect the Christmas creep phenomenon to be a long-term development that will continue even following the after-effects of the recession. Due to the heavy use of discounting, many consumers are becoming increasingly wary of purchasing goods that are not on sale. As one consultant says: "If you stop doing it [conducting sales early in the buying season], people will stop buying. It's like a drug that you can't get off of."

Questions

1. What is the effect of a retailer's strategy of extensive use of markdowns on its overall retail image?
2. Discuss the impact of "Christmas creep" on a retailer's overall promotional strategy.
3. How can retailers address the impact of the game of chicken in the timing of their promotions?
4. Do you agree that the Christmas creep phenomenon will be a long-term phenomenon? Why or why not? What do you recommend that retailers do?

Case 2: Shopper Marketing Ramps Up[c-2]

Retail experts may disagree as to an exact definition of "shopper marketing." However, most agree that it encompasses in-store deals, promotions that are not store-based, and even digital coupons. Shopper marketing includes promotional activity by retailers and manufacturers before a shopper enters the store (such as a Web-based search), as well as in-store promotions. According to the director of integrated shopper marketing at Campbell Soup (www.campbellsoup.com): "Shopper marketing is bigger than just customer marketing because it takes into account what the consumer is thinking when he or she is outside the store and not planning an immediate purchase."

In many cases, shopper marketing is conducted in a coordinated manner by manufacturers and retailers. A marketing manager at General Mills (www.generalmills.com) says that by working closely with retailers, it helps "them win their share of wallet, align with their programs, and offer solutions that are going to ultimately benefit them [the retailers] the most."

Both manufacturers and retailers can gain from working together in shopper marketing activities. Manufacturers may be able to limit competition from retailers' private brands or to ensure that its second- and third-tier brands get adequate promotion. Retailers may want to use shopper marketing to access new technologies developed by manufacturers, such as in-store couponing via a consumer's smart phone.

Nonetheless, there are major obstacles that need to be overcome for shopper marketing to reach its full potential. In the past, many retailers and manufacturers did not work together on joint promotions. Sometimes, shopper marketing is impeded by channel conflict among channel members, such as when retailers have insisted on obtaining slotting fees, trade allowances, and promotional reimbursements.

An executive at a firm that manufactures private-label products suggests that: "If you continue with the mode of accepting money as a trade allowance [absent other changes], the reality is you are actually letting a national manufacturer control your store environment."

Another major impediment to shopper marketing is the control of prime shelf space by retailers. Wal-Mart

[c-1]The material in this case is drawn from "A Seasonal Shift: For Bargain Hunters, Retailers Make Every Day Feel like Christmas," http://knowledge.wharton.upenn.edu (August 18, 2010).

[c-2]The material in this case is drawn from "Free Mug with Purchase: Retailers and Manufacturers Ramp Up 'Shopper' Marketing," http://knowledge.wharton.upenn.edu (February 16, 2011).

(www.walmart.com) and other major retailers tightly control the amount of shelf space allocated to each brand, as well as their location on a shelf. In general, eye-level locations and end-of-aisle end-cap locations are preferable to ankle-level and mid-aisle locations. Some retailers will give the best locations to either the best-selling national brands or their own private-label products. Changing this culture may be very difficult.

The increased utilization of the Web, including social media, has had a major influence on shopper marketing. A study by the Grocery Manufacturers Association (www.gmaonline.org) found that 62 percent of shoppers now look for deals online before at least one-half of their shopping trips. This behavior shifts channel power to manufacturers by influencing shoppers through discount coupons and other special incentives. Manufacturers such as General Mills have also become more adept at reaching shoppers by using social media and other digital tools. The goal for General Mills is to "build a relationship with them [consumers] so that they take that relationship into the stores and you don't have to work as hard to win in that moment when they're at the shelf."

Questions

1. Provide three of your own examples of shopper marketing that are beneficial for both manufacturers and retailers.
2. Differentiate between shopper marketing and cooperative advertising.
3. Is a retailer's desire to build up its private-label brands an inevitable source of channel conflict? Explain your answer.
4. Describe how digital coupons offered by manufacturers shift channel power to the manufacturer.

Case 3: Best Buy: Promoting Its Insignia Consumer Electronics Brand[c-3]

As the manager of Best Buy's (www.bestbuy.com) in-store network, Paul Flanigan has the responsibility of developing and implementing a strategy that increases both brand awareness and sales for Insignia, Best Buy's flagship private label. (Best Buy also has Dynex, a second-tier private brand). A specific objective for Best Buy's promotional efforts is to make its Insignia brand a direct competitor to such popular brands as Sony, LG, and Samsung.

Best Buy wants the advertising approach to the Insignia brand to focus on how consumers use this brand, not on the brand itself. Thus, Best Buy wants promotions to highlight families watching favorite TV shows in their dens, rather than showing a TV hanging on a wall to make a den look high-tech.

Best Buy's Flanigan reviewed ads from Insignia's major competitors in an effort to better understand how their promotional messages connected to their target customers. One competing brand's advertising showed its television hanging on the wall, while an ad for another brand showed how a large screen can get you close to the sports-related action. Neither of these ads was created especially for in-store networks; and they were 30-second broadcast ads. Based on the review of these and other ads, Flanigan and his team developed a two-tier advertising strategy for the Insignia brand, with the first step focusing on generating brand awareness and the second step portraying the desired lifestyle message.

The first ad created for this campaign had a running time of 31 seconds and was totally visual (with no audio commentary). This approach enables a consumer to get the full message in a noisy store or in stores that do not play the audio portions of ads to reduce noise levels. The ad portrayed several home environments for Insignia products. While each video stressed Insignia HDTVs, Blu-ray DVD players were also included to show an enhanced product line for the brand. Insignia ads were timed to run every 10 to 12 minutes; other brands ran less often because they had to pay for these in-store promotions.

This campaign was highly successful. For a two-month period after the initial in-store promotion, sales for every Insignia-branded model increased (including an older-model 720p plasma model that had seen two months of declining sales). One Insignia model's sales increased by 149 percent, a second by 116 percent, and a third by 69 percent.

The second Insignia ad featured a real family going through the process of purchasing and installing an Insignia HDTV, and then watching a movie in their home on this television. While the running time of the ad was 74 seconds, it was seen on-screen for only 10 seconds.

Paul Flanigan believes that one of the factors accounting for the success of each campaign was that they were created especially for Best Buy's in-store network. Flanigan also feels that traditional broadcast commercials will not engage an in-store customer; to be most effective, ads must show the relationship of the product to a customer's lifestyle—as opposed to merely focusing on a product's features.

Questions

1. Develop five measures of brand awareness that can serve as objectives for Best Buy's advertising efforts for Insignia products.
2. How would advertising developed specifically for an in-store network differ from traditional television-based network advertising for Insignia?
3. Should the Insignia brand be promoted through over-the-air TV ads, as well as in-store ads? Why or why not?
4. What sales promotions should Best Buy use for the Insignia brand? Explain your answer.

Case 4: Coupons in the Digital Era[c-4]

After a 14-year decline in coupon redemption among consumer packaged goods (with coupon volume falling from its peak level of 7.7 billion redemptions in 1992 to 2.6 billion in 2006), redemptions rebounded somewhat and increased to 3.3 billion coupons in 2010. As an executive at one large market research firm observed, until the recession, "it wasn't cool to clip coupons. Digital is making it cool."

Although mobile and social media and other platforms are exciting, print coupons are still the most important coupon type in terms of marketing expenditures and redemption

[c-3]The material in this case is drawn from Paul Flanigan, "Best Buy's Insignia Brand Content Awareness Case Study," www.plattretailinstitute.com (March 4, 2011).

[c-4]The material in this case is drawn from Piet Levy, "Cashing in on the Coupon Comeback," *Marketing News*, www.marketingpower.com (March 15, 2011).

value. An industry executive who specializes in coupons states that free-standing inserts (FSI) still command 90 percent of the coupon market. Marketers spent $19.9 billion for FSI coupon distribution in 2010, a 5 percent increase from the 2009 level. A significant problem with FSI distribution is the poor redemption rate, 0.7 percent in 2010.

A significant trend is the increased use of targeted coupons by retailers. Many of these retailers now use in-store couponing programs in which coupon distribution is based on a customer's purchase history. For example, a customer who is a loyal Maxwell House coffee drinker may get a Folger's coupon. Some manufacturers have increased their use of themed coupon pages that highlight multiple brands, such as the P&G Brand Saver (http://pgeverydaysolutions.com/pgeds/brandsaver-coupons.jsp) that appears as a coupon book in many Sunday newspapers. P&G has also developed a coupon book especially for Wal-Mart (www.walmart.com).

Another recent development is the use of digital coupons that are promoted and distributed by coupon sites, social media sites, and E-mail. One research study found that 290 manufacturers distributed digital coupons in 2010, a 17.4 percent increase from 2009. Despite this high growth rate, digital coupons still accounted for only 1 percent of U.S. coupon distribution in 2010. On a positive note, the distribution redemption share of total coupons was 9.8 percent in 2009 (up from 1.1 percent in 2006).

Cold Stone Creamery (www.coldstonecreamery.com), the ice cream chain, began to use digital coupons in 2010 through an association with Coupons.com (www.coupons.com), an online coupon aggregator. Twenty percent of Cold Stone Creamery's couponing budget was invested in digital couponing. The retailer's couponing for ice cream cakes was promoted on Coupons.com's Web site, at Facebook (www.facebook.com/coldstonecreamery), and via E-mail. Its digital coupons had a 14 percent redemption rate, far in excess of the firm's traditional 0.2 percent redemption rate. Cold Stone attributes the success of this program to the large number of Facebook and E-mail account holders who are loyal Cold Stone users. Cold Stone's digital coupon audience is also younger, more affluent, and more highly educated than those who typically redeem its print-based coupons.

Mobile coupons currently account for less than 1 percent of all coupons issued. However, with 68 percent of all U.S. households having a smart phone, this medium will grow very quickly for coupons. Stop & Shop (www.stopandshop.com) uses mobile devices to produce coupons for customers based on the location of their shopping carts (by aisle) in the supermarket. This makes purchasing the relevant product relatively easy. One limiting factor to the growth of mobile couponing is the need to update a store's POS system to be able to read digital coupons.

Questions

1. What factors account for the large increase in coupon redemptions? Will the growth continue? Why or why not?
2. Are manufacturer-based coupons an example of channel cooperation or channel conflict? Explain your answer.
3. Describe several tactics that a retailer can use to increase its in-store coupon redemption rate.
4. Discuss the pros and cons of digital coupons versus print-based coupons from a retailer's perspective.

PART 7 Comprehensive Case

Evolving Communication Channels and Tools*

Introduction

Highly sophisticated and accessible technologies are reshaping the retail experience for today's consumer. Now armed with nearly limitless information, consumers expect to conduct their business transactions when, where, and how they choose. In this new environment, the consumer is in control and dictates the way that companies (retailers) do business.

The Advances in Retail Communication

The consumer's embrace of personal technologies has accelerated the evolution of retailing. Just as shopping malls and big-box formats changed where consumers shopped, personal technologies have disrupted how consumers shop and how they are informed about products and retail options. The traditional model of business to consumer (B2C), where the retailer controls the offers and interactions, has flipped: Consumer to business (C2B) is now ruling the retailing world.

What does this consumer-driven marketplace mean in terms of consumer behavior? It features a more discretionary and less loyal public, always looking for ways to save more and spend less. According to a recent consumer survey by NCR Corporation, more than one-half (58 percent) of the respondents would switch between retailers to get better prices, deals, or more loyalty rewards, and nearly two-thirds (65 percent) of respondents use the Internet more frequently to research products and prices before making a purchasing decision.

Consider how much NCR itself has changed over the years from manufacturing traditional cash registers (its name was originally National Cash Register, before the conversion to all letters). Take a look at the NCR timeline in Table 1 to see how far that technology has advanced.

As NCR now says at its company Web site (www.ncr.com):

> Welcome to a new world of interaction; where you [the retailer] can serve your customers how, when, and where they choose across point-of-service, mobile, and online channels. Our goal is to enable partners to run their businesses faster and more efficiently than ever before. It's possible to achieve this when you partner with NCR. Learn how our legacy of breakthrough continuous innovation and global reach can transform your business. Embrace the future of self-service technology with NCR. It's from this unique position that NCR boldly invites businesses and consumers to "Experience a new world of interaction."

Digitally enabled and empowered by the information at their fingertips, consumers are forcing retail businesses to deliver targeted and personalized messages, making the shopping experience more enjoyable, convenient, and relevant.

Consumers are embracing the personalization and convenience afforded by technology, using multiple channels (such as social media, smart phones, location-based services, and so forth) to gather information, formulate purchasing decisions, and even make payments. Furthermore, a growing number of people expect retailers to communicate and interact with them through the channel—or channels—that they prefer. Known best as "converged retailing," because transactions involve multiple channels of shopping and communication, this model plays out in people's daily shopping routines, making them more efficient and personalized.

Example: Converged Retailing—A Day in the Life

The typical day for a busy mom can be made easier with personalized communication tools. For instance, she begins her day by using the Internet to update her shopping lists, to research options, to review opinions/comments, to find coupons, and to check prices. After she determines which stores she will go to, she can share her lists and preferences with those retailers to see what personalized offers they may have for her. Family members can also access the shopping list online and add their wishes to the list. She takes her smart phone and heads out. The smart phone helps her locate the stores she'd like to go to and alerts her to sales along the way.

As she approaches a store, the store detects her presence and notifies her of the day's specials. Using grocery shopping as an illustration, once in the store, she will have the capability to print the grocery list that she made at home—and coupons can be automatically added to her card. At the checkout, the self-checkout device will recognize her, apply discounts, and notify her of additional promotions, such as a DVD rental discount.

Recent NCR consumer research provides evidence that these technologies are poised to take hold and expand. According to the survey results, 44 percent of respondents would like to download coupons to redeem when checking out, and 43 percent of respondents would like to use the camera on their mobile phone to scan barcodes and get the best prices.

This consumer has just experienced converged retailing—a shopping experience using multiple channels based on her presence and her preference. Retailers across all industries must find a way to provide customers with this personalized service, or risk losing out to competitors. In fact, 83 percent of consumers are more likely to choose one retailer over another if it makes it easier to personalize and control when, where, and how they interact through preferred channel combinations—online, in-store, mobile, or self-service device.

The physical store has been augmented by the potential for retailers to interact day or night with the shopper, breaking down the traditional shopping patterns. The opportunity now exists to have a dialog with consumers throughout their daily lives, whether they are in-store, near store, or out of store. Nearly one-half (46 percent) of the consumers responding to the NCR survey currently use a smart phone, providing the

* The material in this case is adapted by the authors from Rick Chavie, "Converged Retailing: Communication Channels and Tools Evolve in the Age of Consumer-Driven Retail," *Journal of Retail Analytics* (Quarter 1, 2011), pp. 23–29. Reprinted by permission. Article provided by the Platt Retail Institute, LLC.

TABLE 1 A Selected NCR Timeline

Year	Event
1884	John H. Patterson founded the National Cash Register Company, maker of the first mechanical cash registers.
1893	NCR opened the first sales training school.
1906	Charles F. Kettering designed the first cash register powered by an electric motor.
1914	NCR developed one of the first automated credit systems.
1952	NCR acquired Computer Research Corporation (CRC), of Hawthorne, California, which produced a line of digital computers with applications in aviation.
1953	NCR established the Electronics Division to continue to pursue electronic applications for business machines.
1957	NCR announced the first fully transistorized business computer, the NCR 304.
1968	NCR's John L. Janning invented liquid crystal displays (LCD).
1974	Company changed its name to NCR Corporation.
1974	NCR commercialized the first barcode scanners.
1982	The first NCR Tower super-microcomputer system was launched, establishing NCR as a pioneer in bringing industry standards and open systems architecture to the computer market.
1991–1997	NCR was acquired by AT&T. Spun off at the end of 1996. Name changed to NCR Corporation.
1997	Signaling its evolution from a hardware-only company to a full solutions provider, NCR purchased Compris Technologies, Inc., a leading provider of store automation and management software for the food-service industry, and Dataworks, which develops check-processing software.
1998	NCR sold its computer hardware manufacturing assets, confirming its commitment to concentrate on the market-differentiated software and services components of its solutions portfolios.
2000	NCR acquired CRM (customer retention management) provider Ceres Integrated Solutions and services company 4Front Technologies, deepening NCR's solutions offerings in key markets.
2005	Following the 2004 acquisition of travel self-service leader Kinetics, NCR further strengthens its self-service portfolio by acquiring Galvanon, a leading provider of health-care solutions.
2007–present	The "new" NCR focuses on how the world connects, interacts, and transacts with business. "NCR is at the center of the self-service revolution, strategically poised between consumers who demand fast, easy, and convenient options, and businesses intent on increasing revenues, building customer loyalty, reaching the contemporary consumer, and lowering their cost of operations."

Source: Adapted by the authors from "NCR History/Timeline," www.ncr.com/about-ncr/company-overview/history-timeline (May 9, 2012); and other sections of the NCR Web site.

means for robust interaction with customers at the time and place of their choosing.

Consumers now have access to an expansive amount of information before they even visit a store. Whether they research a product, a service, or a retailer, they can arm themselves with the information they want to see. They are also sharing information with other shoppers through social media and expect retailers to participate: nearly one-half (44 percent) of survey respondents admit that they would like retail businesses to offer social media sites to recognize them as an individual customer, including their unique preferences so they can get personalized information and service. In addition, 85 percent of customers believe organizations need to do more to ensure social media activities are properly integrated with all other forms of interaction, such as Web site, E-mail, and information at physical locations.

Not only are they sharing, a global Nielsen survey of Internet consumers says that the most trusted source of advertising, at 90 percent of respondents, is recommendations from personal acquaintances or opinions posted by consumers online (from Nielsen's annual online consumer survey of more than 25,000 Internet consumers representing 50 countries around the world).

Customer Touch Points

The consumer purchasing process can involve three unique spaces: out of store, near store, and in-store. Each provides its own opportunity for personalized communication based on the consumer's presence in a channel and his or her preferences for interaction.

Out of Store

From the comfort of their own homes, consumers use the Internet to research product options, compare prices, learn about special offers, and read peer reviews via blogs or other social media platforms. All of this information will influence which vendor (retailer) the consumer ultimately chooses. In fact, according to a 2010 independent Forrester Research report, "By 2014, 53 percent of total retail sales will be affected by the Web." And with the advent of tablets, shoppers have a more visual experience than with their smart phones. See Figure 1.

FIGURE 1

Consumers Love Their Tablets

With the growing popularity of touch-screen tablets, people are better able to visualize products, online stores, customer reviews, recipes, and more. This is a great way for retailers to communicate with their customers, and for people to interact with one another.

Source: Reinhold Foeger/ Shutterstock.com. Reprinted by permission.

Near Store

The rapid adoption of mobile technologies has made transactions more convenient for today's time-starved consumer and has created a new type of communication touch point. Fewer shoppers are willing to stroll through store after store to find what they are looking for. They want what they want, when they want it, and will search for the best price. Mobile devices deliver an expansive suite of applications that help consumers locate stores or restaurants, as well as provide access to promotions, price comparisons, and peer reviews while the consumer is on the go.

Busy parents can use their mobile devices to perform transactions including reservations and take-out dinner orders, scheduling a grooming appointment for a pet, and even receive a text message on their smart phone when the pet is ready for pick-up—all while running errands, watching football practice, waiting for piano lessons to end, or any number of other activities. Mobile transactions are predicted to expand, according to an ABI study that found that in 2010, overall U.S. consumer purchases (in dollars) using their mobile phones were double the amount spent compared with 2009. These figures will continue rising at a good clip for the foreseeable future—around the globe. And more and more consumers will be using their smart phones to find information, the location of the retailer with the best prices, scan in QR (quick response) codes, and communicate with their friends.

In-Store

Even though there is double-digit growth in Web retailing and even higher growth potential in mobile retailing, the fact remains that the *completion* of retail transactions still occurs in the store for over 95 percent of sales in markets across the world. Once within the store walls, engaged customers are likely to purchase more products than they would online. In fact, according to an RSR Research survey of retailers, 54 percent say that more personalized attention from store employees is an absolutely vital component to differentiate the store experience from an online retail transaction.

Investment in the physical store is seen as advantageous among most retailers. Technologies to build an associate base that drives value and preference for the in-store shopping experience is a priority in improvement plans among retailers. According to the RSR Research:

- Seventy-three percent will focus on a more convenient customer experience.
- Fifty-four percent will focus on more personalized attention from employees.
- Fifty percent will find ways to make employees more productive.
- Forty-nine percent will educate and empower in-store employees using technology.
- Forty-two percent will provide the ability to locate and sell merchandise from anywhere in the company.

A Food-Service Example

The convergence of channels is also seen in restaurants. In this example, a customer is able to define how she wants to connect and interact with her favorite restaurant.

First, she logs on to the restaurant's Web site from home and enrolls in its "mobile meal" program, entering her personal preferences. Throughout a typical day, she is on the go, so the savvy food-service provider will adapt to her schedule and habits. At 11:30 A.M. she receives a text message on her mobile phone with information about the closest restaurant location. She acknowledges the information and indicates she'll be visiting this site for lunch. A GPS map to the location and her default meal order appears on her screen. She makes any required changes, places the order, and selects the pre-pay option with her preferred method of payment.

As she is driving to pick up her food, the store is alerted that she is within a mile of the site. This triggers a production order and meal preparation begins. As she pulls into the site, GPS (global positioning system) software alerts the staff to begin final preparations like bagging and adding preferred condiments. When she enters the store, the digital menu board acknowledges her presence and confirms that her order is ready. Once she receives her meal, she decides to redeem the mobile coupon for a dessert item and pays for it at the self-checkout.

Enhancing the In-Store Experience

As social media and mobile devices take hold among shoppers, retailers are recognizing the value of equipping associates with similar mobile tools to provide improved customer care to their better informed and demanding customers who opt in for more personalized attention.

Retailers also will continue to improve the in-store experience for use by both sales associates and shoppers by investing in self-serve technologies including kiosks, point-of-sale terminals and applications, assisted devices, self-checkout technology, and digital signage that enable personalized communication. Through advanced analytics, retailers can deliver the information that shoppers want and need by applying individual customers' preferences based on information submitted by the individual (at home or in the store), whether they use the technologies or do so with the help of an associate.

While customers enter stores armed with a solid knowledge base needed to make their decisions attained through online research at home or via a quick mobile search en route to or inside the store, empowering associates with technology can help them be a vital part of the personalized and convenient experience customers demand.

Self-service kiosks also converge information channels, allowing customers to browse online catalogs, review product details, and view real-time inventory information and store maps. The next generation of kiosk applications also allow customers to take control of the transaction process by placing orders (which ship right to their homes), redeeming loyalty rewards, downloading multimedia content, scanning merchandise using a built-in barcode scanner, swiping a credit card to pay, and printing receipts or sending them to their smart phones.

Digital signage is another solution that offers multiple touch points and opportunities for retailers to engage and influence consumers' purchasing decisions throughout the store. Rich multimedia content (HD graphics, video, and music) efficiently delivers targeted information where it is needed. Giving customers real-time information when they are in the store improves their ability to make informed decisions. Digital signage can also become more interactive, providing the functionality of a kiosk with touch-screen graphics.

Empowered by the greater access to information made possible through advanced technologies, today's busy consumers are more accessible and more demanding than ever. Their purchasing options are expansive, making them less loyal to a particular brand or retailer. This landscape means retailers must take advantage of the software and hardware available to communicate targeted, personalized messages to consumers beyond the store walls. The latest touch-point solutions are effective, converged retailing solutions—available to assist retailers as they step up to meet the consumer-driven reality that is mapping the future of retail.

Questions

1. What can *any* retailer learn from this case?
2. What is converged retailing? Why have many retailers not adopted it yet?
3. From a retailer's perspective, discuss the advantages and disadvantages of consumer-driven personal technologies.
4. Describe the kinds of activities in which retailers can engage to foster their image in this high-tech era.
5. What is the current role of each of the traditional communications tools for retailers: advertising, public relations, personal selling, and sales promotion?
6. Comment on NCR's technology evolution as highlighted in Table 1.
7. Cite five ways in which a gourmet food store can be involved with social media.

PART 8

Putting It All Together

In Part Eight, we "put it all together."

Chapter 20 connects the elements of a retail strategy that have been described throughout this book. We examine planning and opportunity analysis, productivity, performance measures, and scenario analysis. The value of data comparisons (benchmarking and gap analysis) is highlighted. Strategic control via the retail audit is covered.

Source: iQoncept/Shutterstock.com. Reprinted by permission.

20 Integrating and Controlling the Retail Strategy

Chapter Objectives

1. To demonstrate the importance of integrating a retail strategy

2. To examine four key factors in the development and enactment of an integrated retail strategy: planning procedures and opportunity analysis, defining productivity, performance measures, and scenario analysis

3. To show how industry and company data can be used in strategy planning and analysis (benchmarking and gap analysis)

4. To show the value of a retail audit

One of the greatest challenges that retailers face with social media relates to negative customer postings. Such postings can rapidly spread, whether true or not; and they can have an impact on a retailer's image and performance. So, both the ramifications of negative customer posts and the proper strategy to handle them must be understood.

Sean Fitzgerald, a vice-president at franchisor Wireless Zone (www.wirelesszone.com), frames the potential problems well: "When someone else controls the message, you can lose control. Many people's first impression may be established by what they find surfing the Web. Negative posts could be their first and only impression of you, regardless of whether these posts are credible or not. When negativity builds and your prospect experiences the negative, it will serve as an influencer."

According to a research study by RightNow, there are several issues that retailers need to address:

- *Pay attention to negative comments on social media.* If retailers listen to and are proactive in responding to social media, they have a better chance of turning unhappy consumers into company evangelists. RightNow found that, "of those who received a reply to a negative review, 33 percent turned around and posted a positive review and 34 percent deleted their original negative review."
- *Unfortunately, people have low expectations that retailers will respond to negative posts.* "Among the consumers not receiving a response to their negative review, 61 percent say they would have been shocked if a retailer responded to their negative comments."
- *Customer experiences shape their decisions whether or not to buy from a given retailer.* "One-half of consumers cited great customer service and/or a previous positive experience as influencing their decision to buy from a specific online retailer."
- *To support consumer brand advocacy, retailers must ensure that information on their Web site is accurate and consistent.* A major frustration that shoppers had when buying online was the "lack of consistent information. Specifically, 22 percent were frustrated by information that was inconsistent between the retailer's Web site and customer service agents."[1]

Source: BeTA-Artworks/ fotolia.com.

Overview

This site (www.bizmove.com/marketing/m2c.htm) raises a lot of good questions for retailers to think about in integrating their strategies.

This chapter focuses on integrating and controlling a retail strategy. We tie together the material detailed previously, show why retailers need coordinated strategies, and describe how to assess performance.

By integrating and regularly monitoring their strategies, firms of any size or format can take a proper view of the retailing concept and create a superior total retail experience. Consider how Dollar Tree competes with Wal-Mart—which is more than 80 times larger. Dollar Tree's biggest competitive strength is its strategy to price all products at $1.

> The company sustains its discount pricing structure by strategic initiatives, including buying in huge quantities, maintaining strong relationships with vendors and suppliers, and purchasing manufacturer overruns. Dollar Tree purchases about 55 to 60 percent of merchandise domestically and imports the rest from low-cost countries like China. At any point in time, Dollar Tree carries roughly 6,100 items in stores. Around 2,700 of its basic, everyday products are automatically replenished. The extensive network of stores provides easy access to customers across geographic areas. It is trying to make shopping at Dollar Tree easier and more fun-filled.[2]

As today's retailers look to the future, they must deal with new strategic choices due to the globalization of world markets, economic uncertainty, evolving consumer lifestyles, competition among formats, and rapid technology changes such as the advances in social media. See Figure 20-1.

They would also be wise to study the strategies of both successful firms and those facing significant challenges. Consider Borders' demise. The firm was once one of the two largest U.S. bookstore chains:

> It clung to an outdated strategy way too long and reacted slowly as more nimble competitors took business away. During most of the 2000s, Borders focused on its store-based strategy, investing money to improve the in-store experience for shoppers, add cafés, experiment with new concepts, and expand internationally. It might have worked a decade or two earlier, but Borders was investing in physical real-estate at a time that shoppers were flocking to the Internet. That left Borders with a muddled, conflicted strategy. Borders' failure is a cautionary tale about staying relevant.[3]

FIGURE 20-1

eBay: Ever Evolving

Since its founding in 1995, San Jose, California-based eBay has recognized the importance of planning for the future. When it began, eBay (www.ebay.com) was the pioneer in online auctions. Founder Pierre Omidyar wrote the computer code, which he called his "experiment." Omidyar tested the online auction concept by "selling a broken laser pointer, which he was about to throw away. And to his surprise, a collector bought it for $14.83." Today, eBay still hosts auctions. But, its merchants also sell fixed-priced merchandise and include some very large traditional retailers. eBay acquired StubHub ("where fans buy and sell tickets") and owns and operates the PayPal payment company, among other businesses.

Source: goldenangel1/Shutterstock.com. Reprinted by permission.

INTEGRATING THE RETAIL STRATEGY

A major goal of *Retail Management* has been to describe the relationships among the elements of a retail strategy and show the need to act in an integrated way. Figure 20-2 highlights the integrated strategy of Coach, the accessories and gifts retailer. Coach has been cited as a "high performance retailer"—and it outperforms most retailers. From fiscal 2007 through fiscal 2011, Coach's sales rose every year; and, despite price pressures from the weak economy, its gross margins and profits remained strong.[4] At our Web site (www.pearsonhighered.com/bermanevans), there are links to several integrated retail strategies using Bplans.com software templates.

Four fundamental factors especially need to be taken into account in devising and enacting an integrated retail strategy: planning procedures and opportunity analysis, properly defining productivity, performance measures, and scenario analysis. These factors are discussed next.

Planning Procedures and Opportunity Analysis

Planning procedures are enhanced by undertaking three coordinated activities. The process is then more systematic and reflects input from multiple parties:

1. Senior executives outline the firm's overall direction and goals. This provides written guidelines for middle- and lower-level managers, who get input from various internal and external sources. These managers are encouraged to generate ideas at an early stage.
2. Top-down plans and bottom-up or horizontal plans are combined.
3. Specific plans are enacted, including checkpoints and dates.

Opportunities need to be studied with regard to their impact on overall strategy and not in an isolated manner. See Figure 20-3. As noted by *Chain Store Age*: "Amid an uneven and slow recovery at home and financial volatility in established European markets, U.S. chain retailers are increasingly looking to emerging global markets to expand operations, increase overall revenues, and gain a competitive advantage. Consumer spending is on the rise in many of these areas, boosted by a growing middle class. Equally important, emerging markets present significant opportunities for store growth."[5]

A useful retailer tool for evaluating opportunities is the **sales opportunity grid**, which rates the promise of new and established goods, services, procedures, and/or store outlets across a variety of criteria. Opportunities can be rated in terms of the integrated strategies the firms would follow if those options are pursued. Computer software makes it easy to use such a grid.

Table 20-1 shows a sales opportunity grid for a supermarket deciding which of two salad dressings to stock. Brand A is established; Brand B is new. Due to newness, the store believes initial Brand B sales would be lower, but first-year sales would be similar. The brands would be priced the same and occupy identical space. Brand B requires higher display costs but offers a

The Store Associate of the Future

In the "new" retail environment, customers will be even better armed with customer reviews, product specifications that can be downloaded from manufacturer Web sites, and even prices at competing retailers. What's different is that customers can have timely access to all of that information as a result of their use of smart phones, handheld computers, and tablets.

The customer's expanded pre-store shopping-trip knowledge base is changing the nature of a salesperson from an educational resource to a vital cog in the retail supply chain. According to an executive with a consulting firm, "The expectations of the store associate have started to change. The retail associate is now interacting with customers who are just as intelligent as they are about products."

Mobile applications also benefit personnel at individual stores, because they can obtain information that formerly was only available in retail corporate offices or distribution centers. Store personnel can now determine inventory availability at other store locations, track packages, and even calculate international shipping rates and duties.

Some barriers to the use of this new technology are the need to update a firm's technology to accommodate mobile applications, the difficulties involved with monitoring cross-channel sales, and the training costs. Retailers need to shift their focus from point-of-sales to mobile supply techniques.

Source: M. V. Greene, "The Changing Face of Retail," www.stores.org (April 2010).

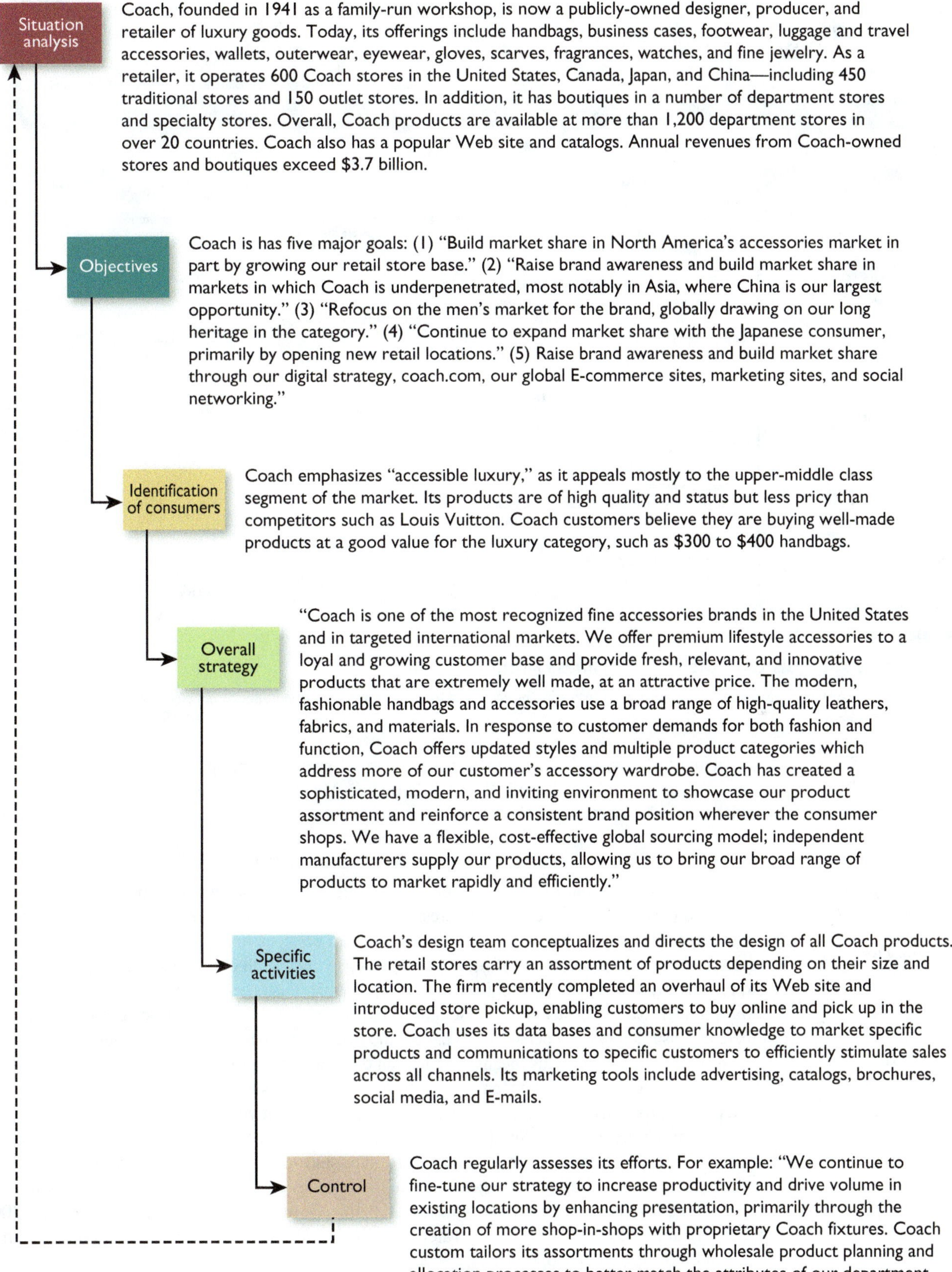

FIGURE 20-2

The Integrated Strategy of Coach

Sources: Figure developed by the authors based on data from the *Coach Inc. 2011 Annual Report* and Web site, www.coach.com (May 9, 2012).

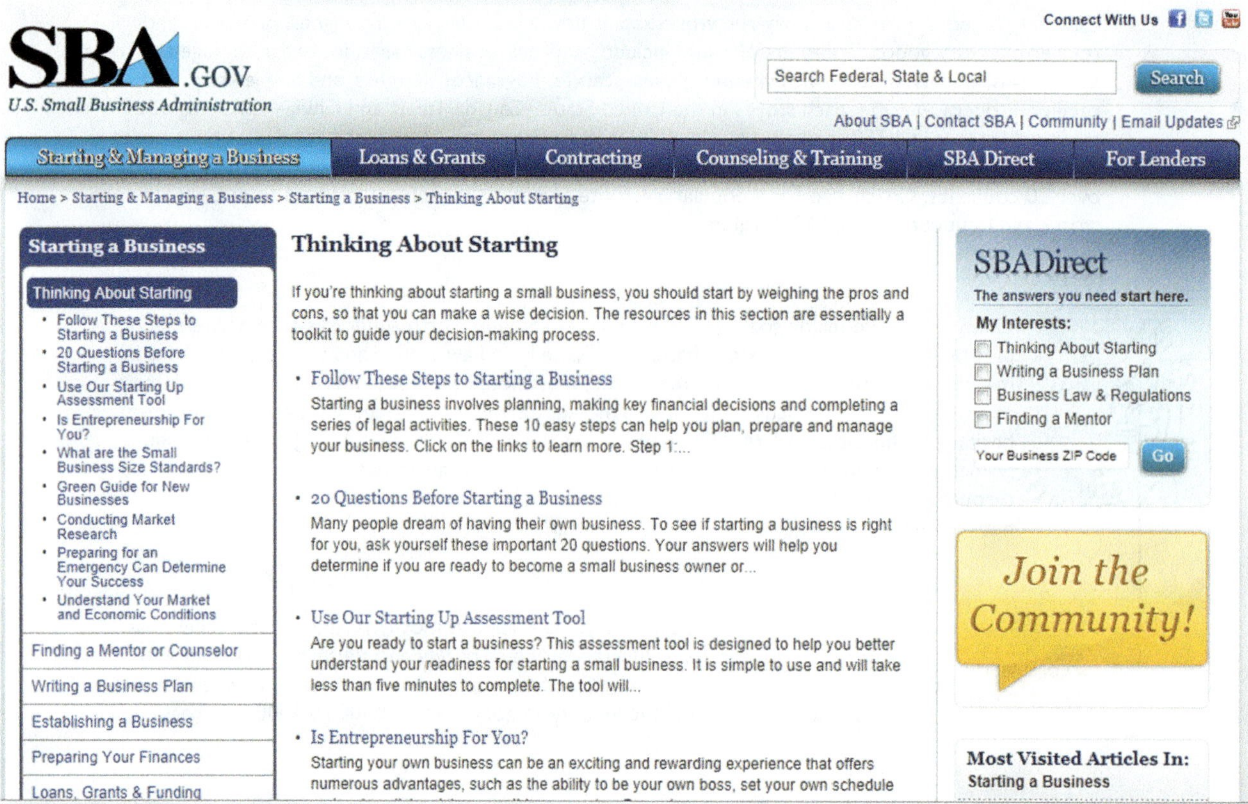

FIGURE 20-3

Opportunity Analysis with the Small Business Administration

Go to www.sba.gov/category/navigation-structure/starting-managing-business and learn more about the opportunities and challenges in starting and running a business.

larger markup. Brand B would have a greater gross profit and net profit by the end of the first year. Based on the overall grid, Brand B is picked. Yet, if the store is more concerned about a quick profit, Brand A might be chosen.

Defining Productivity in a Manner Consistent with the Strategy

XJ Technologies (www.xjtek.com/anylogic/articles/16) shows how to improve a retailer's productivity.

As we noted in Chapters 12 and 13, productivity refers to the efficiency with which a retail strategy is carried out; it is in any retailer's interest to reach sales and profit goals while keeping control over costs. On the one hand, a retailer looks to avoid unnecessary costs. It does not want eight salespeople working at one time if four can satisfactorily handle all customers. And it does not want to pay high rent for a site in a regional shopping center if customers would willingly travel a few miles farther to a less costly site. On the other hand, a firm is not looking to lose customers because there are insufficient sales personnel to handle the rush of shoppers during peak hours. It also does not want a low rent site if this means a significant drop in customer traffic. See Figure 20-4.

Potential trade-offs often mean neither the least expensive strategy nor the most expensive one is the most productive strategy; the former approach might not adequately service customers and the latter might be wasteful. An upscale retailer could not succeed with self-service, and it would be unnecessary for a discounter to have a large sales staff. The most productive approach applies a specific integrated retail strategy (such as a full-service jewelry store) as efficiently as possible.

Food Lion (part of the Brussels-based Delhaize Group) is a leading retailer—with 1,300 supermarkets—due to its well-integrated, productive strategy. Its supermarkets are directly owned or affiliates. They operate:

> under the names of Food Lion, Bloom, Bottom Dollar, Harveys, and Reid's. These stores meet local customer needs and preferences for the freshest and best-quality products in 11 Southeastern and Mid-Atlantic states. Stores offer nationally and regionally advertised brand name products, as well as a growing number of high-quality

TABLE 20-1 Supermarket's Sales Opportunity Grid for Two Brands of Salad Dressing

Criteria	Brand A (established)	Brand B (new)
Retail price	$2.58/8-ounce bottle	$2.58/8-ounce bottle
Floor space needed	8 square feet	8 square feet
Display costs	$10.00/month	$20.00/month for 6 months $10.00/month thereafter
Operating costs	$0.12/unit	$0.12/unit
Markup	19%	22%
Sales estimate		
During first month		
Units	250	50
Dollars	$645	$129
During first six months		
Units	1,400	500
Dollars	$3,612	$1,290
During first year		
Units	2,500	2,750
Dollars	$6,450	$7,095
Gross profit estimate		
During first month	$123	$28
During first six months	$686	$284
During first year	$1,226	$1,561
Net profit estimate		
During first month	$83	$2
During first six months	$458	$104
During first year	$806	$1,051

Example 1:

Gross profit estimate = Sales estimate − [(1.00 − Markup percentage) × (Sales estimate)]

Brand A gross profit estimate during first six months = $3,612 − [(1.00 − 0.19) × ($3,612)] = $686

Example 2:

Net profit estimate = Gross profit estimate − (Display costs + Operating costs)

Brand A net profit estimate during first six months = $686 − ($60 + $168) = $458

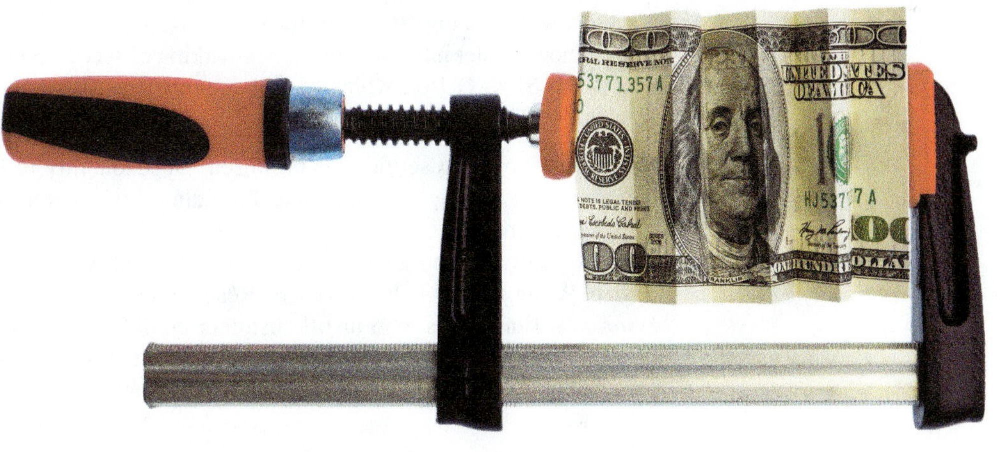

FIGURE 20-4

The Delicate Balance with Activities Intended to Improve Productivity

This is the productivity dilemma: Cut costs too much and shoppers will surely notice and not be happy with fewer salespeople, longer checkout lines, less clean restrooms, and so forth. Cut costs too little and the retailer may have to raise prices or suffer low profits. Striking a balance is tough to do.

Source: Gina Sanders/ Shutterstock.com. Reprinted by permission.

private-label products made and packaged for Food Lion. The company maintains its great prices and quality assurance through technological advances and operating efficiencies such as standard store formats, innovative warehouse design, and management; energy-efficient facilities and data synchronization; and integration with suppliers.[6]

Performance Measures

By outlining relevant **performance measures**—the criteria used to assess effectiveness—and setting standards (goals) for each of them, a retailer can better develop and integrate its strategy. Among the measures frequently used by retailers are total sales, average sales per store, sales by goods/service category, sales per square foot, gross margins, gross margin return on investment, operating income, inventory turnover, markdown percentages, employee turnover, financial ratios, and profitability.

A retailer can gain insights on benchmarking from this site (www.rbabenchmarking.com).

To properly gauge a strategy's effectiveness, a firm should use **benchmarking**, whereby the retailer sets standards and measures its performance based on the achievements of its sector of retailing, specific competitors, high-performance firms, and/or the prior actions of the firm itself: "What company sets the standards in your industry, and what can you learn from them? Many executives sit around the table, beginning the budgeting process for the fiscal year and comparing performance from year to year. That is a good start but not enough. It is necessary to look at internal, as well as external, standards. The goal of benchmarking is to use peer operating results to improve the performance of all business processes."[7]

A good free source is the "Monthly & Annual Retail Trade" section of the U.S. Census Bureau's Web site (www.census.gov/retail). It shows about 20 years of data involving a monthly comparison of sales, purchases, gross margins, inventories, and inventory-to-sales ratios by retail category. In addition to monthly and annual store data, quarterly E-commerce data are reported.

Learn about best practices in retailing (http://retailindustry.about.com/od/retailbestpractices).

Retailers of varying sizes—and in different goods or service lines—can also obtain comparative data from such sources as the Small Business Administration, Internal Revenue Service, *Progressive Grocer, Stores, Chain Store Age, Retailing Today*, BizMiner, Dun & Bradstreet, the National Retail Federation, RMA, and annual reports. Those retailers can then compare their performance with others.

Table 20-2 contains revenue, expense, and income benchmarking data for small retailers in 14 different business categories. The cost of goods sold as a percentage of revenues is highest for gas stations and food and beverage stores, gross profit is greatest for hotels and motels, operating expenses are also the most for hotels and motels, and net income is highest for personal and laundry services.

A popular, independent, ongoing benchmarking survey is the American Customer Satisfaction Index (ACSI). It addresses two questions: (1) Are customer satisfaction and evaluations of quality improving or declining in the United States? (2) Are they improving or declining for particular sectors of industry and for specific companies? The index is based on a scale of 0 to 100, with 100 the highest possible score. A national sample of more than 70,000 people takes part in phone interviews, with 250 interviews of current customers for each of the firms studied (www.theacsi.org). Table 20-3 shows that the highest score by any listed retailer was 86 for Amazon.com, while the lowest was 70 for Wal-Mart.

There is now greater interest in the benchmarking of service retailing. One well-known measurement tool is SERVQUAL, which lets service retailers assess their quality by asking customers to react to a series of statements in five areas of performance:

- *Reliability*. Providing services as promised. Dependability in handling service problems. Performing services right the first time. Providing services at the promised time. Maintaining error-free records.
- *Responsiveness*. Keeping customers informed about when services will be done. Prompt service. Willingness to help customers. Readiness to act on customer requests.
- *Assurance*. Employees who instill customer confidence and make customers feel safe in transactions. Employees who are consistently courteous and have the knowledge to answer questions.

TABLE 20-2 Benchmarking Through Annual Operating Statements of Typical Sole Proprietors, 2008 (Expressed in Terms of Revenues = 100%)

Type of Retailer	Total Revenues	Gross Profit	Cost of Goods Sold	Total Operating Expenses	Net Income
Apparel and accessory stores	100	56.5	43.5	32.3	11.2
Auto repair shops	100	37.6	62.4	45.8	16.6
Building materials/garden equipment	100	61.7	38.3	25.9	12.4
Eating and drinking places	100	41.5	58.5	47.1	11.4
Electronics and appliance stores	100	58.5	41.5	30.1	11.4
Food and beverage stores	100	71.7	28.3	21.9	6.4
Furniture and home furnishings stores	100	46.6	53.4	35.9	17.5
Gas stations	100	87.3	12.7	10.7	2.0
General merchandise stores	100	66.9	33.1	24.1	9.0
Health and personal care stores	100	59.7	40.3	25.2	15.1
Hotel and motels	100	7.0	93.0	73.4	19.6
Nonstore	100	42.1	57.9	31.3	26.6
Personal and laundry services	100	9.1	90.9	50.3	40.6
Sporting goods/hobby/book/ music stores	100	60.9	39.1	26.2	12.9

Source: Computed by the authors from U.S. Internal Revenue Service data, as compiled by www.bizstats.com (May 11, 2012).

- *Empathy.* Giving customers individual attention in a caring way. Having the customer's best interest at heart. Employees who understand the needs of their customers. Convenient business hours.
- *Tangibles.* Modern equipment. Visually appealing facilities. Employees who have a neat, professional appearance. Visually appealing materials associated with the service.[8]

TABLE 20-3 Benchmarking Through the American Customer Satisfaction Index (Ranked by Most Recent Scores)

Retailer	1995 Index Score	1999 Index Score	2003 Index Score	2007 Index Score	2011 Index Score
Department/Discount Stores	75	72	76	73	76
Nordstrom	83	76	—	80	84
J.C. Penney	77	75	77	77	82
Kohl's	—	—	79	79	81
Target	76	74	75	77	80
Dollar General	—	—	—	78	78
Macy's	71	68	71	75	77
Sears	71	74	75	73	76
Wal-Mart	81	72	75	68	70
Internet Retail	—	—	84	83	81
Amazon.com	—	—	88	88	86
Newegg	—	—	—	87	85
Overstock.com	—	—	—	80	83
eBay	—	—	82	81	81
Netflix	—	—	—	84	74

(Continued)

TABLE 20-3 Benchmarking Through the American Customer Satisfaction Index (Ranked by Most Recent Scores) (*Continued*)

Retailer	1995 Index Score	1999 Index Score	2003 Index Score	2007 Index Score	2011 Index Score
Limited-Service Restaurants	**70**	**69**	**74**	**77**	**79**
Pizza Hut	66	68	75	72	81
Starbucks	—	—	—	78	80
Papa John's	—	76	76	77	79
Wendy's	73	71	74	78	77
Taco Bell	66	64	68	69	76
Burger King	65	66	68	69	75
KFC	68	64	71	71	75
McDonald's	63	61	64	64	72
Specialty Retail Stores	**—**	**79**	**74**	**75**	**79**
Costco	—	79	80	81	83
Sam's Club	—	78	77	77	81
Barnes & Noble	—	—	—	83	79
Lowe's	—	—	77	75	79
Staples	—	—	—	77	79
Home Depot	—	—	73	67	78
TJX	—	—	—	74	78
Best Buy	—	—	72	74	77
Gap, Inc.	—	—	—	75	77
Supermarkets	**75**	**74**	**74**	**76**	**76**
Publix	82	82	82	83	84
Whole Foods	—	—	—	73	80
Kroger	76	74	71	75	79
Safeway	75	71	73	71	75
Winn-Dixie	73	72	71	72	75
Supervalu	77	75	77	74	74

— = insufficient data.

Source: University of Michigan Ross School of Business, American Society for Quality Control, and CFI Group, "ACSI Scores & Commentary," www.theacsi.org (March 30, 2012). Reprinted by permission.

In reviewing the performance of others, firms should look at the *best practices* in retailing—whether involving companies in their own business sector or other sectors. For example, the Supply Chain Consortium (www.supplychainconsortium.com) includes a number of retailers. By joining the consortium, member companies get information that help them address issues such as these:

> *Economic Impact*—How do I stack up to my peers? Where can I improve? *Costs*—Are my supply chain costs competitive? *Operations*—How do my operating characteristics compare to my peers? *Performance Measurement*—How do my peers measure supply chain performance? Where do they stand in achieving their goals? *Collaboration*—How much collaboration is there with supply chain firms? *Outsourcing*—Where and why do my peers use outsourcing? *Technology*—What technologies are my peers using in their supply chain operations? What is working and what is not? *Organization*—How does my organization structure compare to my peers?[9]

For those retailers that are expanding internationally, A.T. Kearney (www.atkearney.com), the consulting firm, has devised a **global retail development index (GRDI)**. It measures the retail

ETHICS IN RETAILING

Why Do Poor Ethics Occur?

In two experts' experience in teaching sales executives, a common problem encountered is that sales forces seek to maximize sales, not profits. Many sales incentive programs are also based on rewarding sales, instead of profits. These experts say that too many sales managers are guilty of rewarding results as opposed to rewarding high-quality decisions. A memorable example of this error occurred several years ago when Sears (www.sears.com) in the 1990s gave its auto mechanics a sales goal of $147 per hour. Rather than work faster, the mechanics overcharged consumers by "repairing" parts that were not broken.

Retailers can avoid ethical breakdowns by being mindful of "motivated blindness" and letting their managers know if such ethical dilemmas exist. However, rather than just making the managers aware of potential conflicts, top management should completely remove these obstacles from the organization.

Another type of ethical breakdown results from "indirect blindness," when sales managers might tell their subordinates to "do whatever it takes" to achieve a sale or reach a quota. An example of indirect blindness is producing goods in offshore locations with lower environmental and worker safety standards and trying to sell them as American made.

Managers need to be on the constant lookout for a "slippery slope," which is the gradual acceptance of unethical behavior over time. To avoid the slippery slope, trivial infractions need to be investigated and addressed.

Source: Max H. Bazerman and Ann E. Tenbrunsel, "Ethical Breakdowns," *Harvard Business Review*, Vol. 89 (April 2011), pp. 58–66.

prospects in emerging countries with regard to four factors: market attractiveness, country risk, market saturation, and time pressure. These factors are equally weighted in computing a GRDI score:

- Market attractiveness—based on retail sales per capita, population size, the level of urbanization, and the ease of doing business.
- Country risk—based on political risk, economic performance, debt indicators, and credit ratings, as well as the business costs of crime, violence, and corruption.
- Market saturation—based on the share of retail sales made through a modern distribution format, and the number of international retailers and their market share.
- Time pressure—based on how rapidly sales through modern retail formats have grown, which is an indicator of the time until the market is saturated.

According to the 2011 GRDI, Brazil, Uruguay, Chile, India, Kuwait, and China are rated highest.[10]

What makes a good retail Web site? Companies can close the gap by looking at what Ikea does (www.bytelevel.com/news/IKEA_article.pdf).

A retailer can also benchmark its own internal performance, conduct gap analysis, and plan for the future. Through **gap analysis**, a company compares its actual performance against its potential performance and then determines the areas in which it must improve. As Figure 20-5 indicates, gap analysis has four main steps.

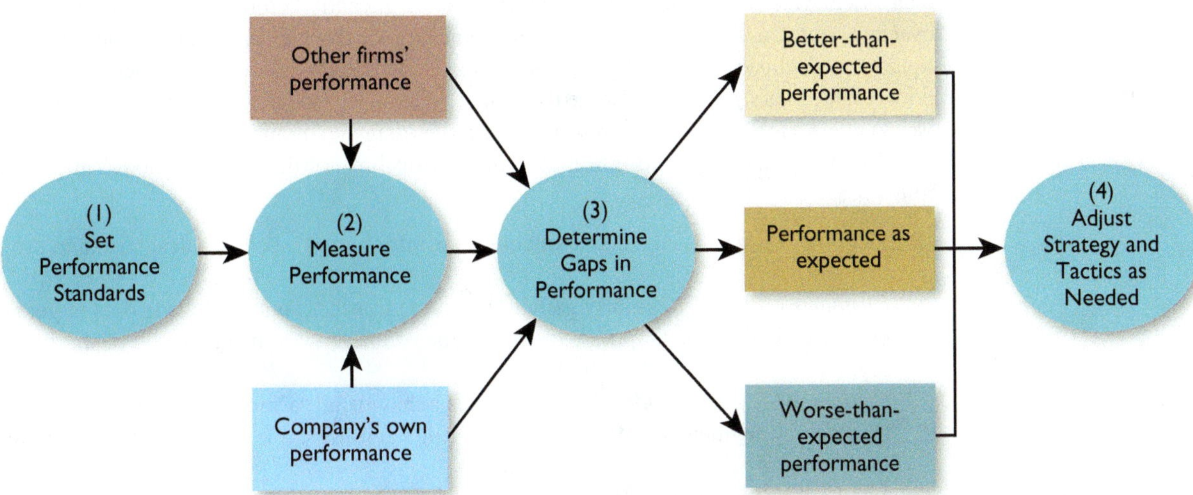

FIGURE 20-5
Utilizing Gap Analysis

TABLE 20-4 Home Depot: Internal Benchmarking and Gap Analysis

	Fiscal Year Ending Jan 30, 2004	Fiscal Year Ending Jan. 29, 2006	Fiscal Year Ending Feb. 3, 2008	Fiscal Year Ending Jan. 3, 2011
Statement of Earnings Data				
Net sales (in millions)	$63,660	$77,019	$77,349	$67,997
Earnings before taxes (in millions)	$ 6,762	$ 8,967	$ 6,620	$ 5,273
Net earnings (in millions)	$ 4,253	$ 5,641	$ 4,210	$ 3,338
Gross margin (% of sales)	31.7	33.7	33.6	34.3
Total operating expenses (% of sales)	21.1	21.9	24.3	25.7
Net earnings (% of sales)	6.7	7.3	5.4	4.9
Balance Sheet Data and Financial Ratios				
Total assets (in millions)	$34,437	$44,405	$44,323	$40,125
Working capital (in millions)	$ 3,774	$ 2,563	$ 1,968	$ 3,357
Merchandise inventories (in millions)	$ 9,076	$11,401	$11,731	$10,625
Current ratio (times)	1.40	1.20	1.15	1.33
Inventory turnover (times)	5.0	4.7	4.2	4.1
Return on invested capital (%)	19.2	20.4	13.9	12.8
Customer and Store Data				
Number of stores	1,707	2,042	2,234	2,248
Total square footage (in millions)	183	215	235	235
Number of customer transactions (in millions)	1,246	1,330	1,336	1,306
Average sale per transaction	$ 51.15	$ 57.98	$ 57.48	$ 51.93
Comparable-store sales change from prior year (%)	+3.7	+3.1	−6.7	+2.9[a]
Weighted-average sales per square foot	$ 371	$ 377	$ 332	$ 289

[a] Sales in the prior two fiscal years were $71.29 billion (2009) and $66.18 billion (2010).

Source: Compiled by the authors from *Home Depot Annual Reports*.

Let us apply gap analysis to Home Depot. Table 20-4 indicates its financial results for fiscal years that ended in January 30, 2004 through January 3, 2011. The data in the table may be used to benchmark Home Depot in terms of its own performance. Between 2004 and 2011, Home Depot saw sales growth slow and then decline; and profitability leveled off and then declined. The gross margin as a percent of sales remained strong, while operating expenses as a percent of sales rose. Although total assets were strong, working capital dropped significantly before rising again. Inventory turnover and return on invested capital both fell. Home Depot continued to open new stores; but sales per square foot declined dramatically. Overall, Home Depot's 2004–2011 performance was not up to its prior results. This signaled that Home Depot had "gaps" to fix and that competition and the economy had an effect. Home Depot must resolve these issues to regain momentum.

To ensure that gaps are minimized in relationship retailing, firms should undertake the following:

1. *Customer insight.* Analyze known consumer information, such as sales, cost, and profits by segment.
2. *Customer profiling.* Regularly gather and merge transaction and lifestyle data to get a fuller picture of individual shoppers. Identify noncustomers who fit the profile of the firm's best segment.
3. *Customer life-cycle model.* Study shopper behavior at various life stages. Look at demographics by segment. Find the cost of serving each life cycle within each segment and the resultant profitability.
4. *Extended business model.* Based on steps 3 and 4, draw conclusions about which customers to focus on, the best ways to interact with them, and the best strategy to foster relationships. Survey individual customers to find out how to tailor the retail strategy to best satisfy their needs.

5. *Relationship program planning and design.* Identify all points of contact (in person, pickup, delivery, kiosk, phone, fax, computer, tablet) between the firm and its customers, and the communications that should flow back and forth during each contact. Select processes that please existing customers and attract new ones, promote retention, increase spending, and lift profitability per customer.
6. *Implementation.* Integrate marketing, customer service, and selling efforts.[11]

At our Web site (www.pearsonhighered.com/bermanevans), we have a number of links related to benchmarking and gap analysis.

Scenario Analysis

Visit this site (www.watt-works.com/consulting) and click "Scenario Planning" on the left toolbar.

In **scenario analysis,** a retailer projects the future by studying factors that affect long-run performance and then forms contingency ("what if") plans based on alternate scenarios (such as low, moderate, and high levels of competition). Planning for the future is not easy:

> Not only has there been significant change, but the rate of change itself is dizzying. The new challenge is striking the balance between getting the day-to-day affairs done while also looking out for those things on the horizon that could alter established processes. Many things that are on the minds and the "worry lists" of retailers have been there for awhile: integrating channels, delivering a consistent customer experience, and providing quality customer service. But, there are some new elements that are still of indeterminate impact: social media, apps, new marketing tools such as Groupon, and the like.[12]

> Because the U.S. market is extremely competitive, retailers—especially department stores—have come to rely on frequent price promotions to attract customers, who now expect low prices. This keeps a lid on profits. Reinforcing this trend is Wal-Mart, with its "everyday low prices" policy. Due to its size, Wal-Mart has gained power in its relationships with manufacturers and squeezes vendors for the greatest possible discount. The combination of a mature, highly saturated market, a slow sales growth environment, and merchants' inability to raise prices makes it imperative to drive down costs and/or improve economies of scale.[13]

> While Zara and H&M have found success by mastering fast fashion—churning out knockoffs of hot trends in as little as two weeks after they create buzz in runway shows—Benetton has stuck with creating its own designs and changes them only seasonally: "Benetton has missed out on the mass fashion wave of the past 10 years," says analyst Luca Solca. Others say larger European mass fashion merchandisers are more vertically integrated than Benetton—tightly controlling everything from design to manufacturing to selling at retail—and have been quicker to shift production to lower-cost countries.[14]

Predicting the future is not simple (www.futurist.com/blog).

In planning for its future, Kohl's (www.kohls.com) has a well-conceived—and widely praised—strategic plan. Here are selected elements of that plan:

- *Organizational mission and positioning.* Kohl's positions as a family-oriented department store chain. It offers moderately priced apparel, footwear, and accessories for women, men, and children; soft goods such as sheets and pillows; and housewares. Stores typically stock a consistent assortment of merchandise assortment with some differences regionally. Kohl's "features private and exclusive brands ('Only at Kohl's'), as well as national brands." Its slogan is "expect great things."
- *Goals.* There are several strategic goals that Kohl's believes are necessary for long-term success. Among these goals are: To consistently provide "a great shopping experience throughout the country at all times—every customer, every time, every store." To have the proper inventory mix that is available in stores at the necessary time. "When cost effective, to use products with recycled content."
- *Basic strategy.* Kohl's operates clean, bright stores that focus on a mix of family, value, and national brands. It also does a lot of business online by selling "the best merchandise at the best prices" with a positive shopping experience.
- *Merchandising.* About one-half of Kohl's annual sales are from private and exclusive brands, the other one-half from national brands. In the early 2000s, 75 percent of Kohl's sales were

Ikea's Multi-Country Approach

The Swedish-based Ikea (www.ikea.com) furniture chain has often been characterized as a global retailer that uses a standardized approach in all of its markets. One recent research study examined the actual degree of standardization (and adaptation) of Ikea with regard to four elements of retailing: merchandise, location and store format, the selling and service environment, and market communication within three countries—Sweden, Great Britain, and China. The findings were based on personal interviews with senior Ikea managers, consumer research, and secondary data from company documents, consulting reports, newspaper and magazine articles, and published academic case studies.

This study found that although Ikea generally utilizes a standardized approach, it has adapted its customer-facing elements, as well as the supporting "back-office" processes. In each of these three markets, for example, the room settings are adjusted to fit with the local tastes and the size of rooms in the markets. Furthermore, the catalog varies from being a major part of Ikea's communication strategy in Sweden and Great Britain to playing a minor part in China. The supply chain and sourcing operations significantly differ by location. As an example, Chinese customers would face high prices and out-of-stock situations if standard European sourcing activities were applied there.

Source: Steve Burt, Ulf Johansson, and Asa Thelander, "Standardized Marketing Strategies in Retailing? Ikea's Marketing Strategies in Sweden, the UK, and China," *Journal of Retailing and Consumer Services*, Vol. 18 (Number 3, 2011), pp. 183–193.

from national brands. Its private brands "represent the absolute best value in our stores." Its exclusive brands "are developed through exclusive license agreements with world class partners." Among its new exclusive brands are women's apparel under the Jennifer Lopez label and menswear under the Marc Anthony label.

- *Marketing.* Kohl's utilizes its own "nine-box merchandising grid" ("lifestyle matrix") to focus its offerings and promotion strategy in a way that relates to both consumer lifestyles and price points.[15]

At our Web site (www.pearsonhighered.com/bermanevans), there are several links related to scenario analysis and future planning.

CONTROL: USING THE RETAIL AUDIT

After a retail strategy is devised and enacted, it must be continuously assessed and necessary adjustments made. A vital evaluation tool is the **retail audit**, which systematically examines and evaluates a firm's total retailing effort or a specific aspect of it. The purpose of an audit is to study what a retailer is presently doing, appraise performance, and make recommendations for the future. An audit investigates a retailer's objectives, strategy, implementation, and organization. Goals are reviewed and evaluated for their clarity, consistency, and appropriateness. The strategy and the methods for deriving it are analyzed. The application of the strategy and how it is received by customers are reviewed. The organizational structure is analyzed with regard to lines of command and other factors.

Good auditing includes these elements: Audits are conducted regularly. In-depth analysis is involved. Data are amassed and analyzed systematically. An open-minded, unbiased perspective is maintained. There is a willingness to uncover weaknesses to be corrected, as well as strengths to be exploited. After an audit is completed, decision makers are responsive to the recommendations made in the audit report.

Undertaking an Audit

There are six steps in retail auditing. See Figure 20-6 for an overview of the six-step retail auditing process, which is described next: (1) Determine who does an audit. (2) Decide when and how often an audit is done. (3) Establish the areas to be audited. (4) Develop audit form(s). (5) Conduct the audit. (6) Report to management.

DETERMINING WHO DOES THE AUDIT One or a combination of three parties can be involved: a company audit specialist, a company department manager, and/or an outside auditor.

A company audit specialist is an internal employee whose prime responsibility is the retail audit. The advantages of this person include the auditing expertise, thoroughness, level of

FIGURE 20-6
The Retail Audit Process

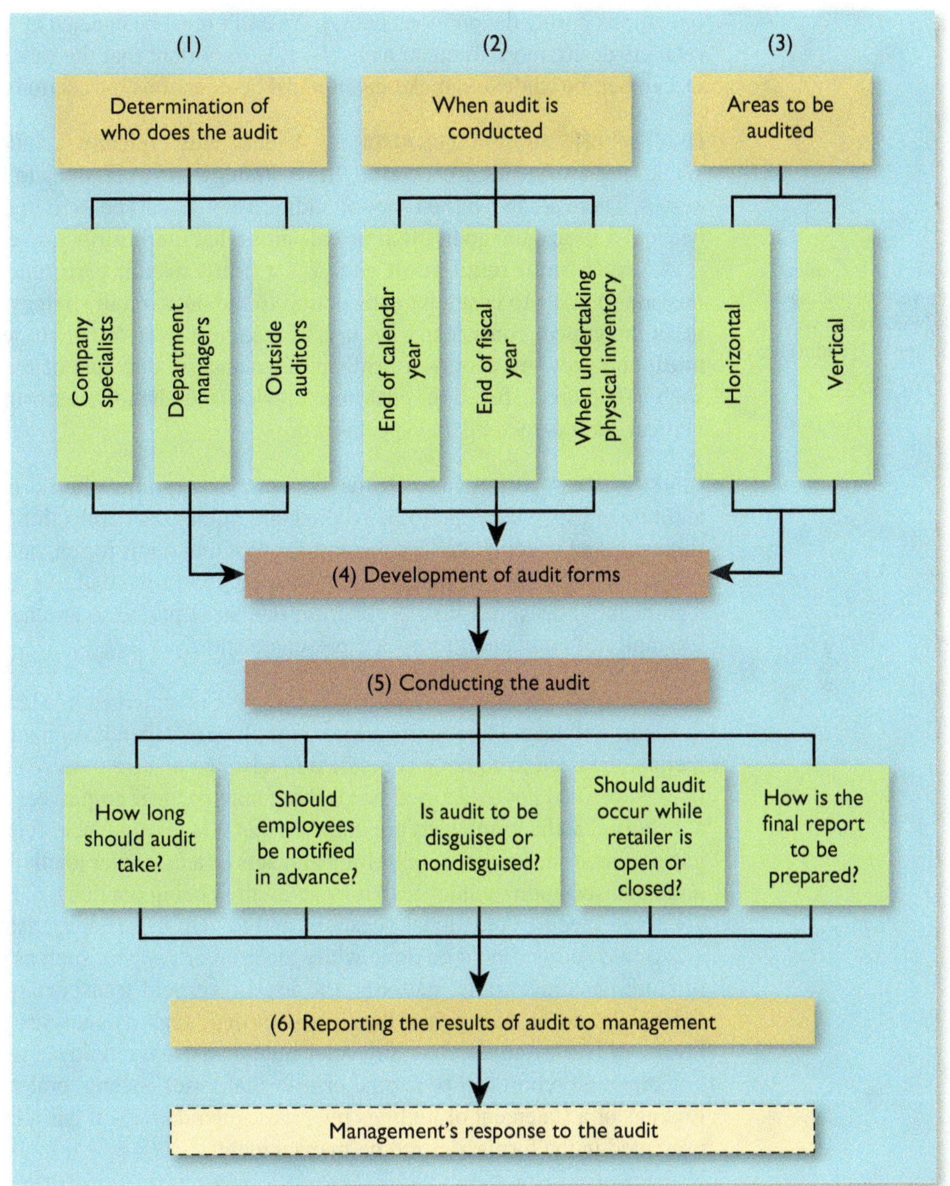

knowledge about the firm, and ongoing nature (no time lags). Disadvantages include the costs (especially for retailers that do not need full-time auditors) and the auditor's limited independence.

A company department manager is an internal employee whose prime job is operations management; that manager may also be asked to participate in the retail audit. The advantages are that there are no added personnel expenses and that the manager is knowledgeable about the firm and its operations. Disadvantages include the manager's time away from the primary job, the potential lack of objectivity, time pressure, and the complexity of companywide audits.

An outside auditor is not a retailer's employee but a paid consultant. Advantages are the auditor's broad experience, objectivity, and thoroughness. Disadvantages are the high costs per day or hour (for some retailers, it may be cheaper to hire per-diem consultants than full-time auditors; the opposite is true for larger firms), the time lag while a consultant gains familiarity with the firm, the failure of some firms to use outside specialists continuously, and the reluctance of some employees to cooperate.

DETERMINING WHEN AND HOW OFTEN THE AUDIT IS CONDUCTED Logical times for auditing are the end of the calendar year, the end of the retailer's annual reporting year (fiscal year), or when a complete physical inventory is conducted. Each of these is appropriate for evaluating a retailer's operations during the previous period. An audit must be enacted at least annually, although some retailers desire more frequent analysis. It is important that the same period(s), such as January–December, be studied to make meaningful comparisons, projections, and adjustments.

DETERMINING AREAS TO BE AUDITED A retail audit typically includes more than financial analysis; it reviews various aspects of a firm's strategy and operations to identify strengths and weaknesses. There are two basic types of audits. They should be used in conjunction with one another because a horizontal audit often reveals areas that merit further investigation by a vertical audit.

This site has a detailed online vertical pricing audit (www.bizmove.com/marketing/m2y3.htm) for retailers.

A **horizontal retail audit** analyzes a firm's overall performance, from the organizational mission to goals to customer satisfaction to the basic retail strategy mix and its implementation in an integrated, consistent way. It is also known as a "retail strategy audit." A **vertical retail audit** analyzes—in depth—a firm's performance in one area of the strategy mix or operations, such as the credit function, customer service, merchandise assortment, or interior displays. A vertical audit is focused and specialized.

DEVELOPING AUDIT FORMS To be systematic, a retailer should use detailed audit forms. An audit form lists the area(s) to be studied and guides data collection. It usually resembles a questionnaire and is completed by the auditor. Without audit forms, analysis is more haphazard and subjective. Key questions may be omitted or poorly worded. Auditor biases may appear. Most significantly, questions may differ from one audit period to another, which limits comparisons. Examples of retail audit forms are presented shortly.

CONDUCTING THE AUDIT Next, the audit itself is undertaken. Management specifies how long the audit will take. Prior notification of employees depends on management's perception of two factors: the need to compile some data in advance to save time versus the desire to get an objective picture and not a distorted one (which may occur if employees have too much notice). With a disguised audit, employees are unaware that it is taking place. It is useful if the auditor investigates an area such as personal selling and acts as a customer to elicit employee responses. With a nondisguised audit, employees know an audit is being conducted. This is desirable if employees are asked specific operational questions and to help in gathering data.

Some audits should be done while the retailer is open, such as assessing parking adequacy, in-store customer traffic patterns, the use of vertical transportation, and customer relations. Others should be done when the firm is closed, such as analyses of the condition of fixtures, inventory levels and turnover, financial statements, and employee records.

An audit report can be formal or informal, brief or long, oral or written, and a statement of findings or a statement of findings plus recommendations. It has a better chance of acceptance if presented in the format desired by management.

REPORTING AUDIT FINDINGS AND RECOMMENDATIONS TO MANAGEMENT The last auditing step is to present findings and recommendations to management. It is the role of management—not the auditor—to see what adjustments (if any) to make. Decision makers must read the report thoroughly, consider each point, and enact the needed strategic changes. They should treat each audit seriously and react accordingly. No matter how well an audit is done, it is not a worthwhile activity if management fails to enact recommendations.

Responding to an Audit

TJX (www.tjx.com/about.asp) is very open about its performance. Click "Our Businesses" and see how much information is available about the firm's plans and results.

After management studies audit findings, appropriate actions are taken. Areas of strength are continued and areas of weakness are revised. The actions must be consistent with the retail strategy and noted in the firm's retail information system (for further reference).

Consider these observations by Booz & Company (www.booz.com), a leading consulting firm:

> To get the most out of their stores, retailers will need to tailor them to better reflect local tastes. They will have to accurately answer tough questions: How many and which SKUs in each category should each store carry? How should product assortment in each store differ by region and by the unique demographics and characteristics of the area? How much space should be dedicated to one category or product versus others? What should be the base price of SKUs in a given category? How should they be promoted and when? There are a vast number of choices.[16]

TECHNOLOGY IN RETAILING

What's Ahead for Smart Retailers

When asked a series of questions regarding future developments in retailing, a panel of retail experts concurred that a large factor in the future growth of E-commerce will be driven by smart phone applications. In particular, the panel cited applications that give consumers the ability to shop for the best prices and then order these goods online or in-store.

Here are some of the conclusions by panel members:

- Retailers will increasingly use social networking sites such as YouTube (www.youtube.com) and Facebook (www.facebook.com) to advertise instead of spending millions of dollars on print and broadcast media.
- Although "stores won't go away," successful firms will use apps that get a shopper from a Web site into a store.
- When consumers make their way into a store, retailers will have to find a way to make their shopping experience very personal versus simply "buying through a phone."
- Retailers of all kinds and sizes will need to be sure to create an experience on the Web that balances content and design. Content will more frequently be conveyed through an interactive experience, including videos and fashion shows that make a site more exciting to the consumer.

Source: Liz Parks, "The Future of Retailing," *Apparel Magazine* (February 2011), pp. 4–5.

Possible Difficulties in Conducting a Retail Audit

AuditNet (www.auditnet.org) has a number of good resources on auditing. Click "Virtual Library" on the left toolbar.

Several obstacles may occur in doing a retail audit. A retailer should be aware of them:

- An audit may be costly.
- It may be quite time-consuming.
- Performance measures may be inaccurate.
- Employees may feel threatened and not cooperate as much as desired.
- Incorrect data may be collected.
- Management may not be responsive to the findings.

At present, many retailers—particularly small ones—do not understand or perform systematic retail audits. But this must change if they are to assess themselves properly and plan correctly for the future.

Illustrations of Retail Audit Forms

Here, we present a management audit form and a retailing effectiveness checklist to show how small and large retailers can inexpensively, yet efficiently, conduct retail audits. An internal or external auditor (or department manager) could periodically complete one of these forms and then discuss the findings with management. The examples noted are both horizontal audits. A vertical audit would involve an in-depth analysis of any one area in the forms.

A MANAGEMENT AUDIT FORM FOR SMALL RETAILERS Under the auspices of the U.S. Small Business Administration, a *Marketing Checklist for Small Retailers* was developed. Although written for small firms, it is a comprehensive horizontal audit applicable to all retailers. Figure 20-7 shows selected questions from this audit form. "Yes" is the desired answer to each question. For questions answered negatively, the firm must learn the causes and adjust its strategy.

A RETAILING EFFECTIVENESS CHECKLIST Figure 20-8 has another type of audit form to assess performance and prepare for the future: a retailing effectiveness checklist. It can be used by small and large firms alike. The checklist is more strategic than the *Management Audit for Small Retailers*—which is more tactical. Unlike the yes–no answers in Figure 20-7, the checklist lets a retailer rate its performance from 1 to 5 in each area; this provides more in-depth information. However, a total score should not be computed (unless items are weighted), because all items are not equally important. A simple summation would not be a meaningful score.

Planning

1. Have you thought about the long-term direction of your business? ______
2. Have you developed a realistic set of plans for the year's operations? ______
3. Do your plans provide methods to deal with competition? ______
4. Is there a system for auditing your objectives? ______

Customer Analysis (Who are your target customers and what are they seeking from you?)

1. Have you profiled your customers by age, income, education, occupation, etc.? ______
2. Are you aware of the reasons why customers shop with you? ______
3. Do you ask your customers for suggestions on ways to improve your operation? ______
4. Do you know what goods and services your customers most prefer? ______

Organization and Human Resources

1. Are job descriptions and authority for responsibilities clearly stated? ______
2. Have you an effective system for communication with employees? ______
3. Do you have a formal program for motivating employees? ______
4. Have you taken steps to minimize shoplifting and internal theft? ______

Operations and Special Services

1. Do you monitor every facet of your operations in terms of specific goals? ______
2. Do you provide time-saving services for greater customer convenience? ______
3. Do you have a policy for handling merchandise returned by customers? ______
4. Do you get feedback through customer surveys? ______

Financial Analysis and Control

1. Do your financial records give you the information to make sound decisions? ______
2. Can sales be broken down by department? ______
3. Do you understand the pros and cons of the retail method of accounting? ______
4. Have you taken steps to minimize shoplifting and internal theft? ______

Buying

1. Do you have a merchandise budget (planned purchases) for each season that is broken down by department and merchandise classification? ______
2. Does it take into consideration planned sales, planned gross margin, planned inventory turnover, and planned markdowns? ______
3. Do you plan exclusive or private brand programs? ______
4. Do you take advantage of cash discounts and allowances offered by your vendor/supplier? ______

Pricing

1. Have you determined whether to price below, at, or above the market? ______
2. Do you set specific markups for each product category? ______
3. Do you know which products are slow-movers and which are fast? ______
4. Have you developed a markdown policy? ______

Atmospherics

1. Are the unique appeals of your business reflected in your image? ______
2. Have you figured out the best locations for displays? ______
3. Do you know which items are bought on "impulse?" ______
4. Do you use signs to aid your customers in shopping? ______

Promotion

1. Are you familiar with the strengths and weaknesses of various promotional methods? ______
2. Do you participate in cooperative advertising? ______
3. Do you ask customers to refer your business to friends and relatives? ______
4. Do you make use of community projects or publicity? ______

FIGURE 20-7

A Management Audit Form for Small Retailers—Selected Questions

These questions cover areas that are the basis for retailing. You can use this form to evaluate your current status and, perhaps, to rethink certain decisions. Answer YES or NO to each question.

Source: Adapted by the authors from Michael W. Little, *Marketing Checklist for Small Retailers* (Washington, DC: U.S. Small Business Administration, Management Aids Number 4.012).

- ✓ A long-term organizational mission is clearly articulated. ____
- ✓ The current status of the firm is taken into consideration when setting future plans. ____
- ✓ Sustainable competitive advantages are actively pursued. ____
- ✓ Company weaknesses have been identified and minimized. ____
- ✓ The management style is compatible with the firm's way of doing business. ____
- ✓ There is a logical short-run and long-run approach to the firm's chosen line of business. ____
- ✓ There are specific, realistic, and measurable short- and long-term goals. ____
- ✓ These goals guide strategy development and resource allocation. ____
- ✓ The characteristics and needs of the target market are known. ____
- ✓ The strategy is tailored to the chosen target market. ____
- ✓ Customers are extremely loyal. ____
- ✓ There are systematic plans prepared for each element of the strategy mix. ____
- ✓ All important uncontrollable factors are monitored. ____
- ✓ The overall strategy is integrated. ____
- ✓ Short-, moderate-, and long-term plans are compatible. ____
- ✓ The firm knows how each merchandise line, for-sale service, and business format stands in the marketplace. ____
- ✓ Tactics are carried out in a manner consistent with the strategic plan. ____
- ✓ The strategic plan and its elements are adequately communicated. ____
- ✓ Unbiased feedback is regularly sought for each aspect of the strategic plan. ____
- ✓ Information about new opportunities and threats is sought out. ____
- ✓ After enacting a strategic plan, company strengths and weaknesses, as well as successes and failures, are studied on an ongoing basis. ____
- ✓ Results are studied in a manner that reduces the firm's chances of overreacting to a situation. ____
- ✓ Strategic modifications are made when needed and before crises occur. ____
- ✓ The firm avoids strategy flip-flops (that confuse customers, employees, suppliers, and others). ____
- ✓ The company has a well-executed Web site or plans to have one shortly. ____

FIGURE 20-8

A Retailing Effectiveness Checklist

Rate your company's effectiveness in each of the following areas on a scale of 1 to 5, with 1 being strongly agree (excellent effort) and 5 being strongly disagree (poor effort). An answer of 3 or higher signifies that improvements are necessary.

Chapter Summary

1. *To demonstrate the importance of integrating a retail strategy.* This chapter shows why retailers need to plan and apply coordinated strategies, and it describes how to assess success or failure. The stages of a retail strategy must be viewed as an ongoing, integrated system of interrelated steps.

2. *To examine four key factors in the development and enactment of an integrated retail strategy: planning procedures and opportunity analysis, defining productivity, performance measures, and scenario analysis.* Planning procedures can be optimized by adhering to a series of specified actions, from situation analysis to control. Opportunities need to be studied in terms of their impact on overall strategy. The sales opportunity grid is good for comparing various strategic options.

   To maximize productivity, retailers need to define exactly what productivity represents to them when they enact their strategies. Although firms should be efficient, this does not necessarily mean having the lowest possible operating costs (which may lead to customer dissatisfaction) but rather keying spending to the performance standards required by a retailer's chosen niche (such as upscale versus discount).

   By applying the right performance measures and setting standards for them, a retailer can better integrate its strategy. Measures include total sales, average sales per store, sales by goods/service category, sales per square foot, gross margins, gross margin return on investment, operating income, inventory turnover, markdown percentages, employee turnover, financial ratios, and profitability. A.T. Kearney's global retail development index is good for reviewing the retailing prospects in developing countries.

With scenario analysis, a retailer projects the future by examining the major factors that will have an impact on its long-term performance. Contingency plans are then keyed to alternative scenarios. This is not easy.

3. *To show how industry and company data can be used in strategy planning and analysis (benchmarking and gap analysis).* With benchmarking, a retailer sets its own standards and measures performance based on the achievements of its sector of retailing, specific competitors, the best companies, and/or its own prior actions. Through gap analysis, a retailer can compare its actual performance against its potential performance and see the areas in which it must improve.

4. *To show the value of a retail audit.* A retail strategy must be regularly monitored, evaluated, and fine-tuned or revised. The retail audit is one way to do this. It is a systematic, thorough, and unbiased review and appraisal.

The audit process has six sequential steps: (a) determining who does the audit, (b) deciding when and how often it is conducted, (c) setting the areas to be audited, (d) preparing forms, (e) conducting the audit, and (f) reporting results and recommendations to management. After the right executives read the audit report, necessary revisions in strategy should be made.

In a horizontal audit, a retailer's overall strategy and performance are assessed. In a vertical audit, one element of a strategy is reviewed in detail. Among the potential difficulties of auditing are the costs, the time commitment, the inaccuracy of performance standards, the poor cooperation from some employees, the collection of incorrect data, and unresponsive management. Some firms do not conduct audits; thus, they may find it difficult to evaluate their positions and plan for the future.

Two audit forms are presented in this chapter: a management audit for retailers and a retailing effectiveness checklist.

Key Terms

sales opportunity grid (p. 516)
performance measures (p. 520)
benchmarking (p. 520)
global retail development index (GRDI) (p. 522)
gap analysis (p. 523)
scenario analysis (p. 525)
retail audit (p. 526)
horizontal retail audit (p. 528)
vertical retail audit (p. 528)

Questions for Discussion

1. Why is it imperative for a firm to view its strategy as an integrated and ongoing process?
2. Develop a sales opportunity grid for a supermarket planning to add a Redbox DVD rental machine to its services mix.
3. Cite five performance measures commonly used by retailers, and explain what can be learned by studying each.
4. What is benchmarking? Present a five-step procedure to do retail benchmarking.
5. What is the value of the global retail development index?
6. How are the terms *gap analysis* and *scenario analysis* interrelated?
7. Distinguish between horizontal and vertical retail audits. Develop a vertical audit form for an auto repair retailer.
8. What are the attributes of good retail auditing?
9. Distinguish among these auditors. Under what circumstances would each be preferred?
   a. Outside auditor.
   b. Company audit specialist.
   c. Company department manager.
10. Under what circumstances should a disguised audit be used?
11. How should management respond to the findings of an audit? What can happen if the findings are ignored?
12. Why do many retailers not conduct any form of retail audit? Are these reasons valid? Explain your answer.

Web-Based Exercise

Visit the Web site of the American Customer Satisfaction Index (www.theacsi.org), click on "ACSI Results," and then "Scores by Industry." Go into each of the retailing industry links. What do you conclude from reviewing these scores? Comment on both the most recent results and how these results have changed over time.

Note: Also stop by our Web site (www.pearsonhighered.com/bermanevans) to experience a number of highly interactive, appealing Web exercises based on actual company demonstrations and sample materials related to retailing.

PART 8 Short Cases

Case 1: After the Recession: Preparing for a Brighter Retail Future[c-1]

This case summarizes some predictions by *Stores* magazine's editor with regard to major developments and trends that are involved with the consumer, the store experience, the economy, information technology, marketing, mobile and social media, and E-commerce.

The Consumer

Consumer values will change as people work to get their household budgets balanced by reducing debt and by more use of debit cards instead of credit cards (to stay within their spending limits). Consumers will also look for value in purchases by focusing on product quality, longevity, and price. There are signs that more affluent consumers are already spending more freely. This bodes well for luxury-based retailers.

The Store Experience

Stores will decrease in size as retailers seek to reduce operating expenses and seek opportunities for fill-in sites. Pop-up stores will be used due to the large number of retail vacancies and the availability of clearance merchandise from cancelled orders and retail bankruptcies. Retailers will also seek to increase the quality of the in-store experience via demonstrations, sampling stations, and better sales support.

The Economy

High unemployment and housing foreclosure rates will continue to have a major effect on consumer confidence and the retail sales climate. Unemployment will particularly affect low- and middle-income consumers. Value-based retailers (such as discounters and factory outlets) will increase their market share. Retailers with the most promising outlook include Web-based firms, limited-assortment food stores (such as Aldi and Trader Joe's), and experience-based retailers. *Stores* magazine expects sales to rise between 2.5 and 3.5 percent annually.

Information Technology (IT)

IT will be used to increase in-store productivity by better inventory rationalization and better matching worker availability and store sales by hour and day. IT will also be used to better understand consumer segments and show how consumer behavior varies among a chain's locations. IT infrastructure needs to be upgraded to reflect the number of people with in-store Wi-Fi access, tablets, and smart phones.

Marketing

There will be additional use of Facebook promotions and more mobile and smart-phone promotions and couponing. Value will be defined in terms of a brand or store experience, not just a low price. Stores will increasingly promote their sustainability efforts and achievements.

Mobile and Social Media

Shoppers may trust their favorite brands; but they trust customer ratings even more. Shoppers will increasingly look up prices, research items, and read product and store reviews via smart-phone apps. QR codes will be increasingly used in ads and commercials.

E-Commerce

"Searchandising," the merger of search technologies and merchandising capabilities, will occur more often. This is the next logical step for the use of Web analytics and product recommendations by progressive retailers. Online sales will grow significantly. Some analysts believe E-commerce will eventually account for 20 percent of total retail revenues as shoppers spend more money online.

Questions

1. How can a retailer respond to the trends identified in this case to best reach consumers who are still having a tough time as a result of weak economic conditions?
2. What other trends should retailers consider in planning for the future?
3. Discuss the pros and cons of enhanced technology from both retailer and customer perspectives.
4. Describe how a conventional supermarket can upgrade its in-store experience.

Case 2: Fixing the Gap[c-2]

In 1997, Gap Inc. (www.gapinc.com) was designated as *Advertising Age's* "Marketer of the Year." *Advertising Age* recognized the firm for its success with integrating its marketing and merchandising strategy, in building its brands via TV, and for its message of selling casual and comfortable clothing. The company was (is) the parent of such chains as Gap (www.gap.com), Banana Republic (www.bananarepublic.com), and Old Navy (www.oldnavy.com).

However, the firm's fortunes have declined in recent years. As one retail analyst noted in 2011, the company's management "will need to rekindle the Gap brand. This has been a challenge facing [the company] since 1998, the last time the Gap brand was hot."

Let's look at some evidence of Gap Inc.'s current problems. Between 2006 and 2010, its net sales declined by 8 percent. This was during a time when the retailer's total square footage declined by 1.3 percent and the number of company-operated stores was reduced by more than 2 percent. Over the 2009 through 2010 period, same-store sales were down by 5.0 percent. In contrast, 2010 sales were down 1.4 percent at Coldwater Creek (www.coldwatercreek.com), down 2.6 percent at Urban Outfitters (www.urbanoutfitters.com), up 6.1

[c-1]The material in this case is drawn from Susan Reda, "Opportunity Comes Calling," www.stores.com (December 2010).

[c-2]The material in this case is drawn from Natalie Zmuda, "Under New Management, Gap Must Figure Out a Way to Fix a Faded Icon," www.adage.com (February 7, 2011); *Gap Inc. 2011 Annual Report*; and *Standard & Poor's Apparel & Footwear: Retailers & Brands* (September 1, 2011).

percent at Chico's (www.chicos.com), and up 10.0 percent at Aeropostale (www.aeropostale.com). Ross Stores (www.rossstores.com) and TJX (www.tjx.com) both had a 6.0 percent same-store sales increase.

Although Gap Inc. has had many successes over the years, these have been too few in the twenty-first century. Its early denim collection was highly successful (forty years ago), the firm was among the first retailers to launch an iPad app, and the August 2011 edition of *Apparel* magazine named the Gap store brand (not Gap Inc.) as the tenth-largest retail brand in terms of popularity on Facebook, with 1.7 million fans. The number of fans now exceeds 2 million people.

Some experts believe that the Gap store brand poor performance in particular has been due to a number of factors: too broad a target market (ranging from babies to men and teens to pregnant women), product designs that have been erratic, and even a change in the corporate logo—which was restored to its former status after irking many consumers.

According to Jeff Jones, president of an advertising and public relations firm and a former Gap executive: "Gap is way too big and broad in today's specialty retail business. Are we trying to sell to my wife or my teenage daughter or both? I don't think you can do both. The hard marketing decision, business decision, is it needs to be really clear who it's for." Jones adds that "Gap has to shrink to regain relevance. On paper, it still has several hundred too many locations." And too many locations means that anything too fashion-forward may be unappealing because its customers are more mass market oriented.

In 2011, Gap made some major structural changes involving its top management and its advertising agency. Art Peck, who was previously the president of Gap Inc.'s outlet business, became the new president of Gap North America (the Gap store brand). Ogilvy & Mather (www.ogilvy.com) was also named its new ad agency. And the former worldwide managing director at Ogilvy & Mather became the Gap store brand's first global chief marketing officer. Gap also announced that its global marketing operation would be located in New York. This operation manages Gap's Global Creative Center with centralized global public relations, design, and production. The Gap brand is now sold in 90 countries, up from 25 at the beginning of 2010.

Questions

1. Why do you think that so many other apparel retailers have outperformed Gap?
2. Visit the Web sites of Gap, Banana Republic, and Old Navy. Describe the positioning of each brand.
3. What are the pros and cons of the Gap store brand's broad target market strategy?
4. What do you think should be done to revitalize the Gap store brand over the next three years?

PART 8 Comprehensive Case

Assessing Best Buy's Long-Term Business Plan*

Introduction

Best Buy is the largest specialty retailer of consumer electronics in the United States, selling a variety of brands of electronic devices such as TVs, home theater systems, cameras, appliances, computers, mobile phones, video games, software, and repair and installation services to consumers across the country and internationally under different store brands. As the firm's Web site (www.bestbuy.com) notes: "With operations in the United States, Canada, Europe, China, and Mexico, Best Buy is a multinational retailer of technology and entertainment products and services with a commitment to growth and innovation." At the start of 2011, in the United States alone, Best Buy employed 165,000 people and operated 1,320 stores (including standalone mobile stores). The retailer utilizes a clicks-and-mortar strategy, wherein it uses an online channel as an effective way to boost store sales and allocates any sales made online to its stores.

Circuit City Stores, the only direct national competitor of Best Buy, went out of business in 2009—largely due to miscalculations in the chain's retail strategy. It had been the second-largest electronics retailer in the United States. Today, Best Buy's greatest competition comes from such retailers as Wal-Mart, Amazon.com, Target, and Costco.

It is estimated that average annual revenue per square foot for big-box Best Buy U.S. stores will decline from $874 in 2010 to $782 in 2018 as competitors take some share from Best Buy. In addition, the number of U.S. Best Buy big-box stores will grow at a very slow pace compared to the historical rate. With regard to SG&A (selling, general, and administrative) expenses, it is expected that this cost category will slightly increase and then stabilize as a percentage of revenues. This could potentially happen due to Best Buy spending a lot more on sales staff and marketing as competition rises.

Background Information

Best Buy U.S. is the primary source of value for Best Buy for the following reasons:

- The larger number of Best Buy U.S. stores compared to international stores—Best Buy has many more stores in the United States than internationally, where there were 465 stores in 2001. Best Buy had previously acquired Carphone Warehouse and the Phone House, two European small-format retail store chains focusing on mobile phones and accessories. With these acquisitions, Best Buy now operates about 2,440 mobile phone stores in Europe. Due to their smaller size, these mobile phone stores do not generate as much in sales as a typical large-format Best Buy store would.
- The larger average size and number of U.S. and international stores compared with mobile phone stores—In addition to the mobile phone stores that Best Buy operates in Europe (through Carphone Warehouse and the Phone House), the company had more than 325 standalone Best Buy mobile stores in the United States during 2011. Best Buy also has some of its U.S. mobile stores integrated into large-format Best Buy stores. On average, Best Buy's U.S. and international mobile phone stores are less than 2,000 square feet in size. In comparison, Best Buy stores tend to be 30,000 to 40,000 square feet in size. Due to the large difference in store size, Best Buy stores generated significantly more in sales revenue compared to a mobile phone store.

These are some of the key trends that Best Buy must contend with in its strategic planning and in the execution of these plans:

- The shifting competition from specialty retailers to big general merchandise players such as Wal-Mart—As noted, Circuit City was the only significant national direct competitor to Best Buy. However, due to Circuit City's demise, its $11 billion annual revenue base was left for grabs. This has stimulated competition among big retail chains including Wal-Mart, Costco, Target, and Amazon.com, which are trying to tap this remaining market.
- The greater emphasis on discounting—Wal-Mart, Amazon.com, and others are posing especially stiff competition due to their deep-discounting strategies and attractive shipping offers, combined with Best Buy's missteps with inventory in 2010 and 2011. This has led to Best Buy's losing some market share.
- The convergence of phones with other consumer electronics to drive sales—Best Buy Mobile is a concept that goes beyond selling just mobile phones. As technology convergence continues and connectivity improves, electronic goods that cater to connecting consumers are expected to drive sales. The company maintains that if a device has the potential to connect consumers, then it will have that device in its stores.
- Growth in mobile computing challenging Best Buy's advantage—Mobile computing has grown rapidly in recent times driven by smart phone adoption and increasingly popular tablets. This has further stimulated usage of the Internet; and consumers can now research products they want to buy, from anywhere and even on the go. This empowerment is challenging the unique advantage that Best Buy has enjoyed until now: Its trained staff that educates consumers about new products to make a better purchase decision. If this trend really picks up, it could further hamper Best Buy's sales as consumers can research products on the Internet and buy them at a cheaper outlet of their choice.

Stores in the United States

The most important factors to review with regard to Best Buy's U.S. stores business are revenue per square foot, the number of U.S. Best Buy stores, the square footage per Best Buy store, and the gross profit margin.

*The material in this case is adapted by the authors from *Trefis Analysis for Best Buy* (Boston, MA: Insight Guru Inc., September 14, 2011). Reprinted by permission of Trefis.com.

The revenue per square foot refers to the average annual revenue per square foot of retail store space for stores operating in the United States under the Best Buy brand. This is an important metric to measure retail sale success and a factor that drives operating margins. This also includes revenue from online sales since Best Buy allocates any sales made via the online channel to its stores.

Best Buy has seen a decline in revenue per square foot for its Best Buy U.S. stores in recent years. This figure dropped from $953 in 2006 to $874 in 2010, partially driven by comparable store sales declines and lower-than-average performance of new stores opened. Here, "comparable store sales" refers to the sales from the Best Buy stores that have been in operation for more than 14 months. We expect this figure will continue to decline in the future. Retailers such as Wal-Mart are increasingly focusing on consumer electronics and pose an immense challenge due to their low-cost strategy. This was visible during the last holiday season when both Wal-Mart and Amazon.com actually gained share while Best Buy lost some. This can be particularly damaging if consumers decide to educate themselves at a Best Buy store and purchase products from Wal-Mart and Amazon.com.

Among the reasons for weak holiday sales for Best Buy were its misplaced confidence in newer technologies like 3-D TVs and in its inventory management. Such devices sold lower than expected. In the future, it is expected that Best Buy will learn from its mistakes and better forecast demand and manage inventory. This will be aided by an improving economy and increased consumer spending.

Multi-channel customers are very important to Best Buy, and the company is taking initiatives to promote multi-channel sales. For Best Buy U.S., multi-channel customers transact twice as much as single-channel customers, spending 95 percent more and contributing 80 percent more to margins. Best Buy has been launching several applications for the Web and for mobile phones, the latter being developed by Google, to drive sales. Digital music downloads will overtake CD sales in the near term, and Best Buy is already capitalizing on the trend. The firm bought Napster in 2008 to strengthen its position in digital music offerings and currently holds the third position in terms of download volume.

The number of Best Buy U.S. stores reflects the total amount of retail stores operating in the United States under the Best Buy brand at the end of the fiscal year. Best Buy U.S. has integrated some of its standalone stores within Best Buy stores to provide a store-within-a-store experience. These stores are typically large-format stores. Despite the recessionary economy, the number of Best Buy U.S. stores consistently rose from 742 in 2005 to 1,100 in 2010. It is expected that Best Buy's U.S. store expansion will significantly slow down in the future.

With Circuit City (the biggest direct competitor) going out of business in 2009, there was ample opportunity for Best Buy to grab former Circuit City customers who looked for alternative places to shop. However, many analysts believe that this opportunity is over now with the share being distributed among retailers like Best Buy, Wal-Mart, Target, and Amazon.com. Thus, the future expansion of Best Buy may not be rapid. For example, compared to about 30 new store openings in 2010, Best Buy opened fewer than ten new stores in 2011. This move comes as a response to unfavorable trends in comparable store sales and Best Buy realizing that it may not be in its best interest to continue with new openings. The company will focus on improving the performance of its current stores. Best Buy has already opened its stores across all the states in the United States.

Square footage per Best Buy store refers to the average retail space area per store measured in terms of square feet. This typically depends on store formats. For example, Best Buy stores are large-format stores with wider aisles and more space for demonstrating certain types of products. Historically, the square footage per U.S. Best Buy store has declined slightly as the company has modeled its stores more efficiently. It is expected that the current average will continue to 2018.

Gross margin represents gross profit as a percentage of revenue. Gross profit is determined as revenue minus the cost of goods and services sold. At Best Buy, the cost of goods includes the goods that are sold online, since the revenue and cost of these goods are allocated to the stores by the company.

The gross profit margin for Best Buy U.S. has remained relatively stable. The figure was about 24.6 percent for 2008, an increase of 0.1 percent over 2007; this figure then further increased to 25.2 percent in 2010 after a slight dip in 2009. It is expected that the profit margins will remain range-bound around current levels through 2018.

Both positive and negative factors will contribute to Best Buy's profit margin stability:

- Positive—Because retail chains were severely hit by the recessionary environment, especially those catering to consumer electronics, there are fewer traditional competitors. Thus, the remaining retailers should have more say in deals with electronics vendors, which will have positive implications on margins. Best Buy mobile stores are also helping to improve margins. As the company continues its in-store expansion in the mobile and connected devices segment, its margins are likely to be aided. In addition, new technologies present the opportunity for higher margins; but the adoption rate for some new technologies, such as 3-D TVs, has been slow.
- Negative—Wal-Mart has indicated that it plans to slow down the industrywide growth of gross margin. Consequently, Wal-Mart has been slashing prices on consumer electronic goods as well. Best Buy, though it caters to a more premium segment, will have to be competitive in prices in order to compete. TV sales comprise a major chunk of Best Buy's annual revenues. However, the average selling prices of TVs have been falling, and, if this continues, Best Buy may not be able to maintain its margins on TV sales, which in turn will affect its overall margins.

International Stores

The most important factors for Best Buy's international stores are the revenue per square foot for Best Buy International, the number of Best Buy International stores, square footage per store, and the gross profit margin.

The revenue per square foot for Best Buy International refers to the average annual revenue per square foot of retail store space for international stores operating under these main brands: Best Buy, Future Shop, and Five Star across Canada, China, and Mexico, respectively. This is an important metric to measure retail sales success and a factor that drives operating margins. Again, this also includes revenue from online sales since Best Buy allocates any sales made via the online channel to its stores. However, Carphone Warehouse and the Phone House stores in Europe are not included here, since they are considered under the division Best Buy Mobile.

Best Buy International has seen a strong increase in revenue per square foot. This figure increased from $540 in 2006 to $822 in 2010 as a result of success in Canada and China. However, it is expected the amount will remain around current levels until 2018. Revenue per square foot for Canada is already quite high, and Best Buy would like to optimize sales productivity in other regions as well.

Although Best Buy is expanding both in Europe and Canada, the majority of international expansion in terms of square footage is expected to come from China, which has typically had much lower revenue per square foot (about one-fourth of that in Canada). Because Best Buy's market share in the huge Chinese market is quite low, the company has a huge opportunity in terms of gaining market share. Best Buy is planning to open several hundred stores there in the next decade.

The number of Best Buy International stores—which include the units operating under the Best Buy, Future Shop, and Five Star names across Canada, China, and Mexico—increased from 304 in 2006 to about 415 in 2010 and 465 in 2011, led by expansion in Canada and China. Best Buy is expected to continue its expansion in these countries, as well as Mexico.

As previously noted, developing economies like China present a major opportunity for Best Buy International. Taking a broad view, Best Buy has accounted for only about 2 percent of international consumer electronics sales (excluding the United States). This means there are many global expansion possibilities for Best Buy.

Leveraging already acquired brands would be helpful in expansion. Best Buy acquired Future Shop in Canada and Five Star in China, which are already established brands among consumers. Best Buy will continue to open new stores under local acquired brand names, but it recently decided to exit its Best Buy brand from China and Turkey.

Despite questions about choosing the worst possible economic timing to grow in Europe, Best Buy remains confident of its plans. It plans to focus on expansion in Great Britain before spreading to the rest of Europe. Best Buy maintains that its level of customer service is much better than any of the main British competitors, such as DSGi and Comet. Best Buy stores have a much broader assortment compared to stores in Great Britain, making it attractive to different customer groups.

The square footage per Best Buy store refers to the average retail space area per store measured in terms of square feet. As in the United States, this typically depends on store formats. Best Buy stores are large-format stores, while Future Shop stores are comparatively smaller. Historically, the square footage per store for Best Buy International has ranged between roughly 30,000 and 32,000 square feet per store, with slight declines seen in recent times. This trend is expected to continue as Best Buy optimizes its store size for better productivity.

Best Buy International's gross profit margin (excluding mobile phone stores) improved from 21.6 percent in 2007 to about 23.2 percent in 2010. It is expected that the profit margin will stabilize at this amount through 2018. Again, Best Buy International faces two trade-offs in looking to the future. On the one hand, the company's gross profit margins are strengthened by Best Buy International's better promotional control and profit optimization initiatives in China. Gross profit margins in Canada have been relatively stable. On the other hand, Chinese stores will continue to operate at lower margins.

Standalone Mobile Phone Stores

The most important factors for the standalone mobile phone store business are the revenue per square foot for European standalone stores, the square footage per store for European standalones, and the gross profit margin.

The revenue per square foot for European standalone stores refers to average annual revenue per square foot of retail store space for Carphone Warehouse (CPW) and the Phone House (PH) stores in Europe. Best Buy formed a joint venture with CPW in Europe by acquiring a 50 percent stake in 2008.

CPW's revenue per square foot is higher when compared to Best Buy Mobile's U.S. stores primarily due to the very small size of CPW stores, which are typically spread across 600 square feet—compared to 1,400 to 1,500 square feet for Best Buy Mobile. Revenue per square foot for European standalone CPW and PH stores was about $1,900 in 2010—compared to $850 for Best Buy Mobile. Both Best Buy Mobile and its European counterparts are positioned well to capitalize on the convergence trend and drive future sales. CPW can benefit from the joint venture by adopting best practices and building upon Best Buy's strengths. For example, Best Buy's customer-service levels are much higher than European stores.

The square footage per store for European standalones typically depends on store formats. For example, Best Buy Mobile stores are larger than CPW and PH stores. This will continue as Best Buy has no plans to open bigger stores under the CPW and PH brands or remodel previous stores into bigger formats.

The gross profit margin for Best Buy Mobile has been about the same as the domestic margin for Best Buy. However, with the CPW acquisition, the overall standalone mobile phone store gross margin (including all mobile store brands) increased to about 31 percent in 2010. This overall level is expected to continue to 2018.

Pacific Sales and Magnolia Audio Video

The most important factors for the Pacific Sales and Magnolia Audio Video stores are revenue per square foot for Pacific Sales, the number of Pacific Sales stores, and Pacific Sales and Magnolia Audio Video gross profit margin. Best Buy acquired Pacific Sales in 2007.

The revenue per square foot for Pacific Sales refers to the average annual revenue per square foot of retail store space for stores operating in the United States under the brand Pacific Sales. This also includes revenue from online sales. The revenue per square foot saw a downward trend, declining from about $696 in 2006 to $443 in 2008. This was primarily attributable to the weakening economy. However, since then, sales per square foot have picked up—amounting to $473 in 2010 and $492 in 2011. This figure is projected to continue increasing and reach slightly more than $600 in 2018.

Pacific Sales is primarily involved in the sale of appliances, which has been an underperforming category for Best Buy. The company has been losing market share in appliances and has witnessed low double-digit comparable store sales declines in recent times. Best Buy accounts for less than 10 percent of the U.S. retail appliance market, which is quite low compared to its share of 20 percent in the U.S. consumer electronics market.

The long-term outlook is positive. Best Buy has the capability to provide customers with complete package solutions for their home, including installation and repair services, thus, adding value. The company has one of the best customer-service standards and is likely to maintain this in the premium segment. It plans to invest in new store openings to reach an untapped customer base.

The number of Pacific Sales stores refers to the number of stores operating under this brand. Pacific Sales specializes in the sale of ultra-premium and mass-premium kitchen appliances, plumbing fixtures, and home entertainment products. The number of stores increased from 14 in 2007 to 35 at the end of 2010. It is forecast that Best Buy will continue increasing the number of Pacific Sales stores in the future because it wants to capitalize on the high-end segment of the U.S. home market. Pacific Sales is also vital due to appliances being an underperforming category for Best Buy.

The gross profit margin for Pacific Sales and Magnolia Audio Video has been stable at about 25 percent of revenues. It should remain at 25 to 26 percent through 2018. Note: In 2010, Pacific Sales' total revenues were 13 times those of Magnolia. As of 2018, they will be 24 times higher due to Pacific Sales' strong revenue growth and Magnolia's stagnant revenues.

Tables 1 and 2 contain financial data regarding Best Buy and its business units.

Questions

1. What can *any* retailer learn from this case?
2. Based on the information in the case, would you consider Best Buy to be a high-performing retailer? Why or why not?
3. What are the major types of retailers with which Best Buy competes? How should best Buy deal with each type?
4. Analyze the data in Table 1.
5. Analyze the data in Table 2.
6. Develop a 10-item retail audit form for Best Buy to use in assessing the performance of its sales personnel.
7. As it looks to the future, what opportunities and threats does Best Buy need to recognize and act upon?

TABLE 1 A Financial Summary for Best Buy

	2007	2008	2009	2010	2011	2012	2013	2014	2015	2016	2017	2018
Total Revenues (Bil $)	40.0	45.0	49.6	50.3	51.0	51.2	51.7	52.2	52.8	53.4	54.1	54.7
U.S. stores	32.9	34.6	36.8	36.5	36.0	35.0	34.5	34.3	34.3	34.2	34.2	34.2
International stores	6.7	7.7	9.5	10.2	11.2	12.1	12.7	13.2	13.6	14.1	14.5	14.9
Standalone mobile phone stores	0.0	2.3	2.8	3.0	3.3	3.5	3.7	3.9	4.0	4.2	4.3	4.4
Pacific Sales and Magnolia Audio Video	0.4	0.4	0.5	0.5	0.5	0.6	0.7	0.8	0.9	1.0	1.1	1.1
Revenues by Business (% of total company)												
U.S. stores	82.3	76.9	74.2	72.7	70.5	68.3	66.8	65.7	64.9	64.1	63.3	62.5
International stores	16.8	17.1	19.2	20.3	22.0	23.6	24.6	25.3	25.8	26.3	26.8	27.3
Standalone mobile phone stores	0.0	5.1	5.6	6.0	6.4	6.9	7.2	7.5	7.6	7.8	7.9	8.1
Pacific Sales and Magnolia Audio Video	1.0	0.9	1.0	1.0	1.1	1.2	1.4	1.5	1.7	1.8	2.0	2.1
Total Expenses (Bil $)	39.1	45.1	48.2	49.9	49.0	49.8	50.3	50.8	51.4	52.0	52.7	53.2
U.S. stores	32.1	34.7	35.7	36.3	34.6	34.0	33.6	33.4	33.3	33.3	33.3	33.3
International stores	6.6	7.7	9.3	10.1	10.8	11.8	12.4	12.8	13.3	13.7	14.2	14.5
Standalone mobile phone stores	0.0	2.3	2.7	3.0	3.1	3.4	3.6	3.8	3.9	4.0	4.2	4.3
Pacific Sales and Magnolia Audio Video	0.4	0.4	0.5	0.5	0.5	0.6	0.7	0.8	0.9	1.0	1.0	1.1
Expenses by Business (% of total company)												
U.S. stores	82.1	76.9	74.1	72.7	70.6	68.3	66.8	65.7	64.8	64.0	63.2	62.6
International stores	16.9	17.1	19.3	20.2	22.0	23.7	24.7	25.2	25.9	26.3	26.9	27.3
Standalone mobile phone stores	0.0	5.1	5.6	6.0	6.3	6.8	7.2	7.5	7.6	7.7	8.0	8.1
Pacific Sales and Magnolia Audio Video	1.0	0.9	1.0	1.0	1.0	1.2	1.4	1.6	1.8	1.9	1.9	2.1
Gross Profits(Bil $)[a]	9.5	10.9	12.0	12.6	12.8	12.9	13.0	13.1	13.3	13.4	13.6	13.8
U.S. stores	8.1	8.5	8.9	9.2	9.1	8.8	8.7	8.6	8.6	8.6	8.6	8.6
International stores	1.4	1.7	2.2	2.4	2.6	2.8	2.9	3.1	3.2	3.3	3.4	3.5
Standalone mobile phone stores	0.0	0.6	0.8	0.9	1.0	1.1	1.2	1.2	1.3	1.3	1.3	1.4
Pacific Sales and Magnolia Audio Video	0.0	0.1	0.1	0.1	0.1	0.2	0.2	0.2	0.2	0.2	0.3	0.3

[a] Gross profits = Total revenues – Direct expenses

TABLE 2 Selected Data by Best Buy Business Category

	2007	2008	2009	2010	2011	2012	2013	2014	2015	2016	2017	2018
Best Buy U.S.												
Square footage per store (000s)	40.1	39.3	38.7	38.6	38.5	38.4	38.3	38.3	38.3	38.3	38.3	38.3
Revenue per square foot ($)	939	905	910	874	847	822	806	798	794	790	786	782
Gross profits (% of sales)	24.6	24.6	24.2	25.2	25.3	25.1	25.2	25.1	25.1	25.1	25.1	25.1
Best Buy International												
Square footage per store (000s)	31.7	32.2	31.8	31.2	31.0	30.9	30.7	30.6	30.4	30.3	30.1	30.0
Revenue per square foot ($)	653	670	796	822	822	822	822	822	822	822	822	822
Gross profits (% of sales)	20.9	22.1	23.2	23.5	23.2	23.1	22.8	23.5	23.5	23.4	23.4	23.5
Standalone Mobile Phone Stores												
U.S. stores (Best Buy Mobile)												
Square footage per store	1,500	1,570	1,510	1,410	1,410	1,410	1,410	1,410	1,410	1,410	1,410	1,410
Revenue per square foot ($)	600	700	770	850	920	1,000	1,050	1,100	1,110	1,110	1,110	1,110
European stores												
Square footage per store	NA	597	603	616	616	616	616	616	616	616	616	616
Revenue per square foot ($)	NA	1,540	1,860	1,900	1,940	2,000	2,040	2,080	2,120	2,160	2,210	2,250
Overall gross profits (% of sales)	NA	27.9	28.0	31.1	31.1	30.9	30.9	31.0	30.9	30.9	30.9	30.9
Pacific Sales and Magnolia Audio Video												
Pacific Sales												
Square footage per store (000s)	34.8	29.5	27.0	27.0	27.2	27.2	27.2	27.2	27.2	27.2	27.2	27.2
Revenue per square foot ($)	550	443	455	473	492	516	542	558	570	581	593	604
Magnolia Audio Video												
Square footage per store (000s)	11.6	13.0	13.0	13.0	13.0	13.0	13.0	13.0	13.0	13.0	13.0	13.0
Revenue per square foot ($)	635	480	510	499	489	480	480	480	480	480	480	480
Overall gross profits (% of sales)	24.3	24.1	24.3	24.7	25.0	24.8	25.1	25.2	25.1	25.1	24.9	25.1

Appendix Careers in Retailing

Overview

A person looking for a career in retailing has two broad possibilities: owning a business or working for a retailer. One alternative does not preclude the other. Many people open their own retail businesses after getting experience as employees. A person can also choose franchising, which has elements of both entrepreneurship and managerial assistance (as discussed in Chapter 4).

Regardless of the specific retail career path chosen, recent college graduates often gain personnel and profit-and-loss responsibilities faster in retailing than in any other major sector of business. After an initial training program, an entry-level manager supervises personnel, works on in-store displays, interacts with customers, and reviews sales and other data on a regular basis. An assistant buyer helps in planning merchandise assortments, interacting with suppliers, and outlining the promotion effort. Our Web site (**www.pearsonhighered.com/bermanevans**) has loads of career-related materials: We

- Have a table describing dozens of positions in retailing.
- Present career paths for several leading retailers across a variety of formats.
- Offer advice on résumé writing (complete with a sample résumé), interviewing, and internships.
- Highlight retailing-related information from the *Occupational Outlook Handbook.*
- Present links to a number of popular career sites, including 200 retailers' sites.

THE BRIGHT FUTURE OF A CAREER IN RETAILING

Consider these observations from Careers-in-Marketing.com, Macy's, and the National Retail Federation. According to Careers-in-Marketing.com:

> Retail is one of the largest, most dynamic parts of the world economy. In good economic times, jobs in the retail sector are numerous and many entry-level positions are easy to get. Even during economic contractions, when some retailing sectors suffer, others—like groceries, drugstores, and discounters—thrive. Careers in retail are people-oriented, fast-paced, and have room for creativity. Retailing jobs are worth taking a good look at, particularly if you want a service-oriented, entrepreneurial profession. Options are many, including store management, buying, merchandising, and central management. There's also the booming area of E-tailing (online retail).[1]

Macy's, Inc. operates hundreds of Macy's and Bloomingdale's stores, runs online businesses, and is avidly engaged in social media. The company has one of the best training programs in the industry; some call it the "graduate school of retail." When a person works at Macy's, Inc., he or she is involved with a *Fortune 100* firm. This means that there are a lot of different career possibilities and opportunities.[2]

At Macy's, new college graduates with diverse backgrounds and interests can succeed: "Whether your passion is in management, finance, product development, logistics, human resources, or some other aspect of business, you can help shape a unique opportunity at Macy's and Bloomingdale's."[3] Consider two of Macy's various career path opportunities:

- The Executive Development Program includes a 10-week training component that exposes new employees to various functional areas. It "focuses on store business trend analysis, the customer, the team, and the functions within the stores." Next, the person is assigned to another merchandise category (and maybe a different store) for 1 to 4 months. At this point, the person becomes a Sales Manager—while continuing in the development program—and oversees "a multi-million dollar business and the profitability of that business," as well as customer service efforts and a team of 10 to 20 associates.[4]

- The Product Development Executive Development Program (EDP) provides new employees with the "fundamental tools and strategies needed in your first position as a product assistant. This layered program provides formal training classes that supplement hands-on experience." In this program, there is interaction with designers, buyers, product managers, planners, and vendors so that each person "learns how to develop, source, negotiate, produce, and sell a specific brand classification within the total $3.7 billion private-brand business." Each person is also involved with other functional areas, such as store operations, marketing, merchandising, information systems, and more. Macy's Merchandising Group (MMG) is engaged with every aspect of private brands, such as Alfani, The Cellar, Charter Club/Club Room, I•N•C, Greendog, Style & Co., Tools of the Trade, American Rag, Martha Stewart, Jenni, and Hotel Collection.[5]

The National Retail Federation offers a lot of valuable advice and resources at its "Retail Careers Center" Web site (**www.nrffoundation.com/content/retail-careers-center**):

> Connect with our employer partners, find retail training classes, and read our blog (**http://blog.nrffoundation.com**). With so many career paths, retailing gives everyone the opportunity to explore their passion and interests. Watch our video (**www.nrffoundation.com/content/go-retail-video**), designed to promote retail as a high energy and fast-growing industry. It features interviews from retail CEOs and corporate employees and covers a wide array of career choices. Explore opportunities in marketing/advertising; store operations; loss prevention; store management; finance; human resources; IT and E-commerce; sales and sales-related fields; distribution, logistics, and supply chain management; merchandise buying/planning; and entrepreneurship.[6]

OWNING A BUSINESS

Owning a retail business is popular, and many opportunities exist. Most retail outlets are sole proprietorships; and many of today's giants began as independents, including Wal-Mart, Home Depot, J.C. Penney, McDonald's, Sears, Cheesecake Factory, and Mrs. Fields. Consider the saga of Wendy's (**www.wendys.com/about_us/story.jsp**):

> When Dave Thomas opened the first Wendy's Old Fashioned Hamburgers restaurant, he had created something new and different—high-quality food made with the freshest ingredients, served the way the customer wanted. Quality was so important to Dave that he put the phrase "Quality is our Recipe" on the logo. Today, that passion for quality remains our number one priority at every Wendy's around the world. And it all began in 1969 with one restaurant in Columbus, Ohio.

Today, Wendy's is the third-largest fast-food chain (after McDonald's and Subway) with more than 6,600 restaurants and systemwide sales of $9 billion. Wendy's surpassed Burger King for the number three spot in 2011.

Too often, people overlook the possibility of owning a retail business. Initial investments can be quite modest (several thousand dollars). Direct marketing (both mail order and online retailing), direct selling, and service retailing often require relatively low initial investments—as do various franchises. Financing may also be available from banks, suppliers, store-fixture firms, and equipment companies.

OPPORTUNITIES AS A RETAIL EMPLOYEE

As we've noted before, in the United States, 25 million people are employed by traditional retailers. This does not include millions of others employed by firms such as banks, insurance companies, and airlines. More people work in retailing than in any other industry.

Career opportunities are plentiful because of the number of new retail businesses that open and the labor intensity of retailing. Thousands of new outlets open each year in the United States, and certain segments of retailing are growing at particularly rapid rates. Retailers such as Wal-Mart and Costco also plan to open many new stores in foreign markets. The increased employment from new store openings and the sales growth of retail formats (such as supercenters) also mean there are significant opportunities for personal advancement for talented retail personnel.

Every time a chain opens a new outlet, there is a need for a store manager and other management-level people.

Selected retailing positions, career paths, and compensation ranges are described next.

Types of Positions in Retailing

Employment is not confined to buying and merchandising. Retail career opportunities also encompass advertising, public relations, credit analysis, marketing research, warehouse management, data processing, personnel management, accounting, and real-estate. Look at the table ("Selected Positions in Retailing") in the career section of our Web site for a list and description of a wide range of retailing positions. Some highly specialized jobs may be available only in large retail firms.

The type of position a person seeks should be matched with the type of retailer likely to have such a position. Chain stores and franchises typically have real-estate divisions. Department stores and chain stores usually have large human resource departments. Mail-order firms often have advertising production departments. If one is interested in travel, a buying position or a job with a retailer having geographically dispersed operations should be sought.

Career Paths and Compensation in Retailing

For college graduates, executive training programs at larger retailers offer good learning experiences and advancement potential. These firms often offer careers in merchandising and nonmerchandising areas.

Here is how a new college graduate could progress in a career path at a typical department store or specialty store chain: He or she usually begins with a training program (lasting from three months to a year or more) on how to run a merchandise department. That program often involves on-the-job and classroom experiences. On-the-job training includes working with records, reordering stock, planning displays, and supervising salespeople. Classroom activities include learning how to evaluate vendors, analyze computer reports, forecast fashion trends, and administer store policy.

After initial training, the person becomes an entry-level operations manager (often called a sales manager, assistant department manager, or department manager—depending on the firm) or an assistant buyer. An entry-level manager or assistant buyer works under the direction of a seasoned department (group) manager or buyer and analyzes sales, assists in purchasing goods, handles reorders, and helps with displays. The new manager supervises personnel and learns store operations; the assistant buyer is more involved in purchases than operations. Depending on the retailer, either person may follow the same type of career path, or the entry-level operations manager may progress up the store management ladder and the assistant buyer up the buying ladder.

During this time, the responsibilities and duties depend on the department (group) manager's or buyer's willingness to delegate and teach. In a situation where a manager or buyer has authority to make decisions, the entry-level manager or assistant buyer will usually be given more responsibility. If a firm has centralized management, a manager (buyer) is more limited in his or her responsibilities, as is the entry-level manager or assistant buyer. Further, an assistant buyer will gain more experience if he or she is in a firm near a wholesale market center and can make trips to the market to buy merchandise.

The next step in a department store or specialty store chain's career path is promotion to department (group) manager or buyer. This position is entrepreneurial—running a business. The manager or buyer selects merchandise, develops a promotional campaign, decides which items to reorder, and oversees personnel and record keeping. For some retailers, *manager* and *buyer* are synonymous. For others, the distinction is as just explained for entry-level positions. Generally, a person is considered for promotion to manager or buyer after two years.

Large department store and specialty store chains have additional levels of personnel to plan, supervise, and assess merchandise departments. On the store management side, there can be group managers, store managers, branch vice-presidents, and others. On the buying side, there can be divisional managers, merchandising vice-presidents, and others.

At many firms, advancement is indicated by specific career paths. This lets employees monitor their performance, know the next career step, and progress in a clear manner. Several retail career paths are shown in the careers section of our Web site.

Table 1 lists compensation ranges for personnel in various retailing positions.

TABLE 1 Typical Compensation Ranges for Personnel in Selected Retailing Positions

Position	Compensation Range
Operations	
Customer service representative	$ 25,000 – $ 50,000+
Department manager—soft-line retailer	$ 30,000 – $ 35,000+
Store management trainee	$ 30,000 – $ 35,000+
Department manager—department store	$ 30,000 – $ 35,000+
Department manager—mass merchandiser	$ 30,000 – $ 35,000+
Department manager—hard-line retailer	$ 30,000 – $ 35,000+
Warehouse director	$ 30,000 – $ 90,000+
Store manager—specialty store, home center, drugstore	$ 32,000 – $ 70,000+
Store manager—soft-line retailer	$ 35,000 – $ 75,000+
Customer service supervisor	$ 40,000 – $ 60,000+
Security director	$ 42,000 – $ 70,000+
Store manager—department store	$ 45,000 – $ 85,000+
Operations director	$ 60,000 – $ 100,000+
Merchandising	
Assistant buyer	$ 25,000 – $ 40,000+
Buyer—specialty store, home center, drugstore, department store	$ 35,000 – $ 80,000+
Buyer—discount store	$ 35,000 – $ 85,000+
Buyer—national chain	$ 45,000 – $ 85,000+
Divisional merchandise manager	$ 60,000 – $ 100,000+
General merchandise manager—drugstore, home center	$ 65,000 – $ 100,000+
General merchandise manager—specialty store, department store	$ 70,000 – $ 125,000+
General merchandise manager—discount store, national chain	$ 70,000 – $ 125,000+
Senior merchandising executive	$ 80,000 – $ 250,000+
Marketing Research	
Market research junior analyst	$ 30,000 – $ 35,000+
Market research analyst	$ 30,000 – $ 45,000+
Market research senior analyst	$ 40,000 – $ 55,000+
Market research assistant director	$ 45,000 – $ 65,000+
Market research director	$ 55,000 – $ 75,000+
Top Management	
Senior human resources executive	$ 60,000 – $ 140,000+
Senior advertising executive	$ 65,000 – $ 110,000+
Senior real-estate executive	$ 65,000 – $ 120,000+
Senior financial executive	$ 85,000 – $ 200,000+
President	$250,000 – $ 3,000,000+
Chairman of the board	$350,000 – $10,000,000+
Other	
Public relations specialist	$ 35,000 – $ 85,000+
Retail sales analyst	$ 38,000 – $ 90,000+
Supply chain specialist	$ 40,000 – $ 60,000+

Source: Estimated by the authors from various sources.

GETTING YOUR FIRST POSITION AS A RETAIL PROFESSIONAL

The key steps in getting your first professional position in retailing are the search for opportunities, interview preparation, and the evaluation of options. You must devote sufficient time to these steps so your job hunt progresses as well as possible.

Searching for Career Opportunities in Retailing

Various sources should be consulted. These include your school placement office, company directories and Web sites, ads in your local newspapers, Web networking and job sites (such as **www.linkedin.com**), and networking (with professors, friends, neighbors, and family members). Here are some hints to consider:

- *Do not "place all your eggs in one basket."* Do not rely too much on friends and relatives. They may be able to get you an interview but not a guaranteed job offer.
- *Be serious and systematic in your career search.* Plan in advance and do not wait until the recruiting season starts at your school to generate a list of retail employers.
- *Use directories with lists of retailers and current job openings.* Online listings include CareerBuilder.com Retail Jobs (**http://retail.careerbuilder.com**), AllRetailJobs.com (**www.allretailjobs.com**), Work in Retail.com (**www.workinretail.com**), and I Hire Retail (**www.ihireretail.com**). Also visit our Web site (**www.pearsonhighered.com/bermanevans**) and blog (**www.bermanevansretail.com**).
- *Rely on the "law of large numbers."* In sending out résumés, you may have to contact at least 10 to 20 retailers to get just two to four interviews.
- *Make sure your résumé and cover letter highlight your best qualities.* These may include school honors, officer status in an organization, work experience, computer skills, and the proportion of college tuition you paid. Our Web site shows a sample résumé for an entry-level position in retailing.
- *Show your résumé to at least one professor or other advisor.* Be receptive to constructive comments. Remember, your professor's goal is to help you get the best possible first job.
- *Be professional at social media sites.* Companies may look you up at Facebook, LinkedIn, and other social media sites. Be careful what you have posted—including the pictures you display.

Preparing for the Interview

The initial and subsequent interviews for a position, which may last for 20 to 30 minutes or longer, play a large part in determining if you get a job offer. For that reason, you should be prepared for all interviews:

- *Adequately research each firm.* Be aware of its goods/service category, current size, overall retail strategy, competitive developments, and so on.
- *Anticipate questions and plan general responses.* "Tell me about yourself." "Why are you interested in a retailing career?" "Why do you want a job with us?" "What are your major strengths?" "Your major weaknesses?" "What do you want to be doing five years from now?" "What would your prior boss say about you?" In preparation, role-play your answers to these questions with someone.
- *Treat every interview as if it is the most important one.* Otherwise, you may not be properly prepared if the position turns out to be more desirable than you originally thought. And remember that you represent both your college and yourself at all interviews.
- *Be prepared to raise your own questions when asked to do so in the interview.* They should relate to career paths, training, and opportunities for advancement.
- *Dress appropriately and be well groomed.*
- *Verify the date and place of the interview.* Be prompt.
- *Have a pen and pad (or PDA/smart phone) available to record information after the interview is over.*
- *Write a note to the interviewer within a week to thank him or her for spending time with you and to express a continuing interest in the company.*

Evaluating Retail Career Opportunities

Job seekers often place too much emphasis on initial salary or the firm's image in assessing career opportunities. Many other factors should be considered, as well:

- What activities do you like?
- What are your personal strengths and weaknesses?
- What are your current and long-term goals?
- Do you want to work for an independent, a chain, or a franchise operation?
- Does the opportunity offer an acceptable and clear career path?
- Does the opportunity include a formal training program?
- Will the opportunity enable you to be rewarded for good performance?
- Will you have to relocate?
- Will each promotion in the company result in greater authority and responsibility?
- Is the compensation level fair relative to other offers?
- Can a good employee move up the career path much faster than an average one?
- If owning a retail firm is a long-term goal, which opportunity is the best preparation?

Glossary

Additional Markup Increase in a retail price above the original markup when demand is unexpectedly high or costs are rising.

Additional Markup Percentage Looks at total dollar additional markups as a percentage of net sales:

$$\text{Additional markup percentage} = \frac{\text{Total dollar additional markups}}{\text{Net sales (in \$)}}$$

Addition to Retail Percentage Measures a price rise as a percentage of the original price:

$$\text{Addition to retail percentage} = \frac{\text{New price} - \text{Original price}}{\text{Original price}}$$

Advertising Paid, nonpersonal communication transmitted through out-of-store mass media by an identified sponsor.

Affinity Exists when the stores at a given location complement, blend, and cooperate with one another, and each benefits from the others' presence.

All-You-Can-Afford Method Promotional budgeting procedure in which a retailer first allots funds for each element of the strategy mix except promotion. The funds that are left go to the promotional budget.

Americans with Disabilities Act (ADA) Mandates that persons with disabilities be given appropriate access to retailing facilities.

Analog Model Computerized site selection tool in which potential sales for a new store are estimated based on sales of similar stores in existing areas, competition at a prospective location, the new store's expected market share at that location, and the size and density of a location's primary trading area.

Application Blank Usually the first tool used to screen applicants. It provides data on education, experience, health, reasons for leaving prior jobs, outside activities, hobbies, and references.

Assets Any items a retailer owns with a monetary value.

Asset Turnover Performance measure based on a retailer's net sales and total assets. It is equal to net sales divided by total assets.

Assortment Selection of merchandise carried by a retailer. It includes both the breadth of product categories and the variety within each category.

Assortment Display An open or closed display in which a retailer exhibits a wide range of merchandise.

Assortment Merchandise Apparel, furniture, autos, and other products for which the retailer must carry a variety of products in order to give customers a proper selection.

Atmosphere (Atmospherics) Reflection of a store's physical characteristics that are used to develop an image and draw customers. The concept is also applicable to nonstore retailers.

Attitudes (Opinions) Positive, neutral, or negative feelings a person has about different topics.

Augmented Customer Service Encompasses the actions that enhance the shopping experience and give retailers a competitive advantage.

Automatic Reordering System Computerized approach that combines a perpetual inventory and reorder point calculations.

Bait-and-Switch Advertising Illegal practice in which a retailer lures a customer by advertising goods and services at exceptionally low prices and then tries to convince the person to buy a better, more expensive substitute that is available. The retailer has no intention of selling the advertised item.

Balanced Tenancy Occurs when stores in a planned shopping center complement each other as to the quality and variety of their product offerings.

Balance Sheet Itemizes a retailer's assets, liabilities, and net worth at a specific time—based on the principle that assets equal liabilities plus net worth.

Basic Stock List Specifies the inventory level, color, brand, style category, size, package, and so on for every staple item carried by a retailer.

Basic Stock Method Inventory level planning tool wherein a retailer carries more items than it expects to sell over a specified period:

$$\text{Basic stock} = \text{Average monthly stock at retail} - \text{Average monthly sales}$$

Battle of the Brands The competition between manufacturers and retailers for shelf space and profits, whereby manufacturer, private, and generic brands fight each other for more space and control.

Benchmarking Occurs when the retailer sets its own standards and measures performance based on the achievements in its sector, specific competitors, high-performance firms, and/or its own prior actions.

Bifurcated Retailing Denotes the decline of middle-of-the-market retailing due to the popularity of both mass merchandising and niche retailing.

Book Inventory System Keeps a running total of the value of all inventory at cost as of a given time. This is done by recording purchases and adding them to existing inventory value; sales are subtracted to arrive at the new current inventory value (all at cost). It is also known as a perpetual inventory system.

Bottom-Up Space Management Approach Exists when planning starts at the individual product level and then proceeds to the category, total store, and overall company levels.

Box (Limited-Line) Store Food-based discounter that focuses on a small selection of items, moderate hours of operation (compared with supermarkets), few services, and limited manufacturer brands.

Budgeting Outlines a retailer's planned expenditures for a given time based on expected performance.

Bundled Pricing Involves a retailer combining several elements in one basic price.

Business Format Franchising Arrangement in which the franchisee receives assistance in site location, quality control, accounting, startup practices, management training, and responding to problems—besides the right to sell goods and services.

Buyer Person responsible for selecting the merchandise to be carried by a retailer and setting a strategy to market that merchandise.

Canned Sales Presentation Memorized, repetitive speech given to all customers interested in a particular item.

Capital Expenditures Retail expenditures that are long-term investments in fixed assets.

Case Display Interior display that exhibits heavier, bulkier items than racks hold.

Cash Flow Relates the amount and timing of revenues received to the amount and timing of expenditures made during a specific time.

Category Killer (Power Retailer) Very large specialty store featuring an enormous selection in its product category and relatively low prices. It draws consumers from wide geographic areas.

Category Management Merchandising technique that improves productivity. It focuses on product category results rather than the performance of individual brands or models.

Census of Population Supplies a wide range of demographic data for all U.S. cities and surrounding vicinities. These data are organized on a geographic basis.

Central Business District (CBD) Hub of retailing in a city. It is synonymous with "downtown." The CBD has the greatest density of office buildings and stores.

Chain Retailer that operates multiple outlets (store units) under common ownership. It usually engages in some level of centralized (or coordinated) purchasing and decision making.

Channel Control Occurs when one member of a distribution channel can dominate the decisions made in that channel by the power it possesses.

Channel of Distribution All of the businesses and people involved in the physical movement and transfer of ownership of goods and services from producer to consumer.

Chargebacks Practice of retailers, at their discretion, making deductions in the manufacturers' bills for infractions ranging from late shipments to damaged and expired merchandise.

Class Consciousness Extent to which a person desires and pursues social status.

Classification Merchandising Allows firms to obtain more financial data by subdividing each specified department into further categories for related types of merchandise.

Cognitive Dissonance Doubt that occurs after a purchase is made, which can be alleviated by customer after-care, money-back guarantees, and realistic sales presentations and advertising campaigns.

Collaborative Planning, Forecasting, and Replenishment (CPFR) Emerging technique for larger firms whereby there is a holistic approach to supply chain management among a network of trading partners.

Combination Store Unites supermarket and general merchandise sales in one facility, with general merchandise typically accounting for 25 to 40 percent of total sales.

Community Shopping Center Moderate-sized, planned shopping facility with a branch department store and/or a category killer store, in addition to several smaller stores. About 20,000 to 100,000 people, who live or work within 10 to 20 minutes of the center, are served by this location.

Compensation Includes direct monetary payments to employees (such as salaries, commissions, and bonuses) and indirect payments (such as paid vacations, health and life insurance benefits, and retirement plans).

Competition-Oriented Pricing Approach in which a firm sets prices in accordance with competitors'.

Competitive Advantages Distinct competencies of a retailer relative to competitors.

Competitive Parity Method Promotional budgeting procedure by which a retailer's budget is raised or lowered based on competitors' actions.

Computerized Checkout Used by large and small retailers to efficiently process transactions and monitor inventory. Cashiers ring up sales or pass items by scanners. Computerized registers instantly record and display sales, customers get detailed receipts, and inventory data are stored in a memory bank.

Concentrated Marketing Selling goods and services to one specific group.

Consignment Purchase Items not paid for by a retailer until they are sold. The retailer can return unsold merchandise. Title is not taken by the retailer; the supplier owns the goods until sold.

Constrained Decision Making Limits franchisee involvement in the strategic planning process.

Consumer Behavior The process by which people determine whether, what, when, where, how, from whom, and how often to purchase goods and services.

Consumer Cooperative Retail firm owned by its customer members. A group of consumers invests in the company, elects officers, manages operations, and shares the profits or savings that accrue.

Consumer Decision Process Stages a consumer goes through in buying a good or service: stimulus, problem awareness, information search, evaluation of alternatives, purchase, and post-purchase behavior. Demographics and lifestyle factors affect this decision process.

Consumerism Involves the activities of government, business, and other organizations that protect people from practices infringing on their rights as consumers.

Consumer Loyalty (Frequent Shopper) Programs Reward a retailer's best customers, those with whom it wants long-lasting relationships.

Contingency Pricing Arrangement by which a service retailer does not get paid until after the service is satisfactorily performed. This is a special form of flexible pricing.

Control Phase in the evaluation of a firm's strategy and tactics in which a semiannual or annual review of the retailer takes place.

Controllable Variables Aspects of business that the retailer can directly affect (such as hours of operation and sales personnel).

Control Units Merchandise categories for which data are gathered.

Convenience Store Well-located food-oriented retailer that is open long hours and carries a moderate number of items. It is small, with average to above-average prices and average atmosphere and services.

Conventional Supermarket Departmentalized food store with a wide range of food and related products; sales of general merchandise are rather limited.

Cooperative Advertising Occurs when manufacturers or wholesalers and their retailers, or two or more retailers, share the costs of retail advertising.

Cooperative Buying Procedure used when a group of retailers make quantity purchases from suppliers.

Core Customers Consumers with whom retailers seek to nurture long relationships. They should be singled out in a firm's data base.

Corporation Retail firm that is formally incorporated under state law. It is a legal entity apart from individual officers (or stockholders).

Cost Complement Average relationship of cost to retail value for all merchandise available for sale during a given time period.

Cost Method of Accounting Requires the retailer's cost of each item to be recorded on an accounting sheet and/or coded on a price tag or merchandise container. When a physical inventory is done, item costs must be learned, the quantity of every item in stock counted, and total inventory value at cost calculated.

Cost of Goods Sold Amount a retailer has paid to acquire the merchandise sold during a given time period. It equals the cost of merchandise available for sale minus the cost value of ending inventory.

Cost-Oriented Pricing Approach in which a retailer sets a price floor, the minimum price acceptable to the firm so it can reach a specified profit goal. A retailer usually computes merchandise and retail operating costs and adds a profit margin to these figures.

Cross-Merchandising Exists when a retailer carries complementary goods and services so that shoppers are encouraged to buy more.

Cross-Shopping Occurs when consumers shop for a product category through more than one retail format during the year or visit multiple retailers on one shopping trip.

Cross-Training Enables personnel to learn tasks associated with more than one job.

Culture Distinctive heritage shared by a group of people. It passes on beliefs, norms, and customs.

Curving (Free-Flowing) Traffic Flow Presents displays and aisles in a free-flowing pattern.

Customary Pricing Used when a retailer sets prices for goods and services and seeks to maintain them for an extended period.

Customer Loyalty Exists when a person regularly patronizes a particular retailer (store or nonstore) that he or she knows, likes, and trusts.

Customer Satisfaction Occurs when the value and customer service provided through a retailing experience meet or exceed consumer expectations.

Customer Service Identifiable, but sometimes intangible, activities undertaken by a retailer in conjunction with the basic goods and services it sells.

Cut Case Inexpensive display in which merchandise is left in the original carton.

Data-Base Management Procedure a retailer uses to gather, integrate, apply, and store information related to specific subject areas. It is a key element in a retail information system.

Data-Base Retailing Way to collect, store, and use relevant information on customers.

Data Mining Involves the in-depth analysis of information so as to gain specific insights about customers, product categories, vendors, and so forth.

Data Warehousing Advance in data-base management whereby copies of all the data bases in a company are maintained in one location and accessible to employees at any locale.

Dead Areas Awkward spaces where normal displays cannot be set up.

Debit Card System Computerized process whereby the purchase price of a good or service is immediately deducted from a consumer's bank account and entered into a retailer's account.

Demand-Oriented Pricing Approach by which a retailer sets prices based on consumer desires. It determines the range of prices acceptable to the target market.

Demographics Objective, quantifiable, easily identifiable, and measurable population data.

Department Store Large store with an extensive assortment (width and depth) of goods and services that has separate departments for purposes of buying, promotion, customer service, and control.

Depth of Assortment The variety in any one goods/service category (product line) with which a retailer is involved.

Destination Retailer Firm that consumers view as distinctive enough to become loyal to it. Consumers go out of their way to shop there.

Destination Store Retail outlet with a trading area much larger than that of a competitor with a less unique appeal. It offers a better merchandise assortment in its product category(ies), promotes more extensively, and/or creates a stronger image.

Differentiated Marketing Aims at two or more distinct consumer groups, with different retailing approaches for each group.

Direct Marketing Form of retailing in which a customer is first exposed to a good or service through a nonpersonal medium and then orders by mail, phone, or fax—and increasingly by computer, phone, or tablet.

Direct Product Profitability (DPP) Method for planning variable markups whereby a retailer finds the profitability of each category or unit of merchandise by computing adjusted per-unit gross margin and assigning direct product costs for such expenses as warehousing, transportation, handling, and selling.

Direct Selling Includes both personal contact with consumers in their homes (and other nonstore locations such as offices) and phone solicitations initiated by a retailer.

Direct Store Delivery (DSD) Exists when retailers have at least some goods shipped directly from suppliers to individual stores. It works best with retailers that also utilize EDI.

Discretionary Income Money left after paying taxes and buying necessities.

Distributed Promotion Effort Used by retailers that promote throughout the year.

Diversification Way in which retailers become active in business outside their normal operations—and add stores in different goods/service categories.

Diversified Retailer Multi-line firm with central ownership. It is also known as a retail conglomerate.

Dollar Control Planning and monitoring the financial merchandise investment over a stated period.

Downsizing Unprofitable stores closed or divisions sold off by retailers unhappy with performance.

Dual Marketing Involves firms engaged in more than one type of distribution arrangement. This enables those firms to appeal to different consumers, increase sales, share some costs, and maintain a good degree of strategic control.

Dump Bin Case display that houses piles of sale clothing, marked-down books, or other products.

Ease of Entry Occurs due to low capital requirements and no, or relatively simple, licensing provisions.

Economic Base Area's industrial and commercial structure—the companies and industries that residents depend on to earn a living.

Economic Order Quantity (EOQ) Quantity per order (in units) that minimizes the total costs of processing orders and holding inventory:

$$\text{EOQ} = \sqrt{\frac{2DS}{IC}}$$

Efficient Consumer Response (ECR) Form of order processing and fulfillment by which supermarkets are incorporating aspects of quick response inventory planning, electronic data interchange, and logistics planning.

Electronic Article Surveillance Involves special tags that are attached to products so that the tags can be sensed by electronic security devices at store exits.

Electronic Banking Includes both automatic teller machines (ATMs) and the instant processing of retail purchases.

Electronic Data Interchange (EDI) Lets retailers and suppliers regularly exchange information through their computers with regard to inventory levels, delivery times, unit sales, and so on, of particular items.

Electronic Point-of-Sale System Performs all the tasks of a computerized checkout and also verifies check and charge transactions, provides instantaneous sales reports, monitors and changes prices, sends intra- and inter-store messages, evaluates personnel and profitability, and stores data.

Employee Empowerment Way of improving customer service in which workers have discretion to do what they feel is needed—within reason—to satisfy the customer, even if this means bending some rules.

Ensemble Display Interior display whereby a complete product bundle (ensemble) is presented rather than showing merchandise in separate categories.

Equal Store Organization Centralizes the buying function. Branch stores become sales units with equal operational status.

Ethics Involves activities that are trustworthy, fair, honest, and respectful for each retailer constituency.

Evaluation of Alternatives Stage in the decision process where a consumer selects one good or service to buy from a list of alternatives.

Everyday Low Pricing (EDLP) Version of customary pricing whereby a retailer strives to sell its goods and services at consistently low prices throughout the selling season.

Exclusive Distribution Takes place when suppliers enter agreements with one or a few retailers to designate the latter as the only firms in specified geographic areas to carry certain brands or product lines.

Expected Customer Service Level of service that customers want to receive from any retailer, such as basic employee courtesy.

Experiential Merchandising Tactic whose intent is to convert shopping from a passive activity into a more interactive one, by better engaging the customer.

Experiment Type of research in which one or more elements of a retail strategy mix are manipulated under controlled conditions.

Extended Decision Making Occurs when a consumer makes full use of the decision process, usually for expensive, complex items with which the person has had little or no experience.

External Secondary Data Available from sources outside a firm.

Factory Outlet Manufacturer-owned store selling its closeouts, discontinued merchandise, irregulars, canceled orders, and, sometimes, in-season, first-quality merchandise.

Fad Merchandise Items that generate a high level of sales for a short time.

Family Life Cycle How a traditional family moves from bachelorhood to children to solitary retirement.

Fashion Merchandise Products that may have cyclical sales due to changing tastes and lifestyles.

Feedback Signals or cues as to the success or failure of part of a retail strategy.

FIFO (First In, First Out) Method Logically assumes old merchandise is sold first, while newer items remain in inventory. It matches inventory value with the current cost structure.

Financial Leverage Performance measure based on the relationship between a retailer's total assets and net worth. It is equal to total assets divided by net worth.

Financial Merchandise Management Occurs when a retailer specifies exactly which products (goods and services) are purchased, when products are purchased, and how many products are purchased.

Flea Market Location where many vendors offer a range of products at discount prices in plain surroundings. Many flea markets are located in nontraditional sites not normally associated with retailing.

Flexible Pricing Strategy that lets consumers bargain over selling prices; those consumers who are good at bargaining obtain lower prices than those who are not.

Floor-Ready Merchandise Items that are received at the store in condition to be put directly on display without any preparation by retail workers.

Food-Based Superstore Retailer that is larger and more diversified than a conventional supermarket but usually smaller and less diversified than a combination store. It caters to consumers' complete grocery needs and offers them the ability to buy fill-in general merchandise.

Forecasts Projections of expected retail sales for given time periods.

Franchising Contractual arrangement between a franchisor (a manufacturer, a wholesaler, or a service sponsor) and a retail franchisee, which allows the franchisee to conduct a given form of business under an established name and according to a given pattern of business.

Frequency Average number of times each person who is reached by a message is exposed to a retailer's promotion efforts in a specific period.

Fringe Trading Area Includes customers not found in primary and secondary trading areas. These are the most widely dispersed customers.

Full-Line Discount Store Type of department store with a broad, low-priced product assortment; all of the range of products expected at department stores; centralized checkout service; self-service; private-brand nondurables and well-known manufacturer-brand durables; less fashion-sensitive merchandise; relatively inexpensive building, equipment, and fixtures; and less emphasis on credit.

Functional Product Groupings Categorize and display a store's merchandise by common end use.

Gap Analysis Enables a company to compare its actual performance against its potential performance and then determine the areas in which it must improve.

Generic Brands No-frills goods stocked by some retailers. These items usually receive secondary shelf locations, have little or no promotion support, are sometimes of less quality than other brands, are stocked in limited assortments, and have plain packages. They are a form of private brand.

Geographic Information System (GIS) Combines digitized mapping with key locational data to graphically depict such trading-area characteristics as the demographic attributes of the population; data on customer purchases; and listings of current, proposed, and competitor locations.

Global Retail Development Index (GRDI) Measures the retail prospects in emerging countries with regard to four factors: market attractiveness, country risk, market saturation, and time pressure.

Goal-Oriented Job Description Enumerates a position's basic functions, the relationship of each job to overall goals, the interdependence of positions, and information flows.

Goods Retailing Focuses on the sale of tangible (physical) products.

Goods/Service Category Retail firm's line of business.

Graduated Lease Calls for precise rent increases over a stated period of time.

Gravity Model Computerized site selection tool based on the premise that people are drawn to stores that are closer and more attractive than competitors'.

Gray Market Goods Brand-name products bought in foreign markets or goods transshipped from other retailers. They are often sold at low prices by unauthorized dealers.

Gross Margin Difference between net sales and the total cost of goods sold. It is also called gross profit.

Gross Margin Return on Investment (GMROI) Shows the relationship between total dollar operating profits and the average inventory investment (at cost) by combining profitability and sales-to-stock measures:

$$\text{GMROI} = \frac{\text{Gross margin in dollars}}{\text{Net sales}} \times \frac{\text{Net sales}}{\text{Average inventory at cost}} = \frac{\text{Gross margin in dollars}}{\text{Average inventory at cost}}$$

Gross Profit Difference between net sales and the total cost of goods sold. It is also known as *gross margin*.

Hidden Assets Depreciated assets, such as store buildings and warehouses, that are reflected on a retailer's balance sheet at low values relative to their actual worth.

Hierarchy of Authority Outlines the job interactions within a company by describing the reporting relationships among employees. Coordination and control are provided.

Hierarchy of Effects Sequence of steps a consumer goes through in reacting to retail communications, which leads him or her from awareness to knowledge to liking to preference to conviction to purchase.

Horizontal Cooperative Advertising Agreement Enables two or more retailers (most often small, situated together, or franchisees of the same company) to share an ad.

Horizontal Price Fixing Agreement among manufacturers, among wholesalers, or among retailers to set certain prices. This is illegal, regardless of how "reasonable" prices may be.

Horizontal Retail Audit Analyzes a retail firm's overall performance, from mission to goals to customer satisfaction to basic retail strategy mix and its implementation in an integrated, consistent way.

Household Life Cycle Incorporates the life stages of both family and nonfamily households.

Huff's Law of Shopper Attraction Delineates trading areas on the basis of the product assortment carried at various shopping locations, travel times from the shopper's home to alternative locations, and the sensitivity of the kind of shopping to travel time.

Human Resource Management Recruiting, selecting, training, compensating, and supervising personnel in a manner consistent with the retailer's organization structure and strategy mix.

Human Resource Management Process Consists of these interrelated activities: recruitment, selection, training, compensation, and supervision. The goals are to obtain, develop, and retain employees.

Hypermarket Combination store pioneered in Europe that blends an economy supermarket with a discount department store. It is even larger than a supercenter.

Image Represents how a given retailer is perceived by consumers and others.

Impulse Purchases Occur when consumers buy products and/or brands they had not planned to before entering a store, reading a catalog, seeing a TV shopping show, turning to the Web, and so forth.

Incremental Budgeting Process whereby a firm uses current and past budgets as guides and adds to or subtracts from them to arrive at the coming period's expenditures.

Incremental Method Promotional budgeting procedure by which a percentage is either added to or subtracted from one year's budget to determine the next year's.

Independent Retailer that owns one retail unit.

Infomercial Program-length TV commercial (most often, 30 minutes in length) for a specific good or service that airs on cable television or on broadcast television, often at a fringe time. It is particularly worthwhile for products that benefit from visual demonstrations.

Information Search Consists of two parts: determining alternatives to solve the problem at hand (and where they can be bought) and learning the characteristics of alternatives. It may be internal or external.

Initial Markup (at Retail) Based on the original retail value assigned to merchandise less the merchandise costs, expressed as a percentage of the original retail price:

$$\text{Initial markup percentage (at retail)} = \frac{\text{Planned retail operating expenses} + \text{Planned profit} + \text{Planned retail reductions}}{\text{Planned net sales} + \text{Planned retail reductions}}$$

Intensive Distribution Takes place when suppliers sell through as many retailers as possible. This often maximizes suppliers' sales and lets retailers offer many brands and product versions.

Internal Secondary Data Available within a company, sometimes from the data bank of a retail information system.

Internet Global electronic superhighway of computer networks that use a common protocol and that are linked by telecommunications lines and satellite.

Inventory Management Process whereby a firm seeks to acquire and maintain a proper merchandise assortment while ordering, shipping, handling, storing, displaying, and selling costs are kept in check.

Inventory Shrinkage Encompasses employee theft, customer shoplifting, vendor fraud, and administrative errors.

Isolated Store Freestanding retail outlet located on either a highway or a street. There are no adjacent retailers with which this type of store shares traffic.

Issue (Problem) Definition Step in the marketing research process that involves a clear statement of the topic to be studied.

Item Price Removal Practice whereby prices are marked only on shelves or signs and not on individual items. It is banned in several states and local communities.

Job Analysis Consists of gathering information about each job's functions and requirements: duties, responsibilities, aptitude, interest, education, experience, and physical tasks.

Job Motivation Drive within people to attain work-related goals.

Job Standardization Keeps tasks of employees with similar positions in different departments rather uniform.

Leader Pricing Occurs when a retailer advertises and sells selected items in its goods/service assortment at less than the usual profit margins. The goal is to increase customer traffic so as to sell regularly priced goods and services in addition to the specially priced items.

Leased Department Site in a retail store—usually a department, discount, or specialty store—that is rented to an outside party.

Liabilities Financial obligations a retailer incurs in operating a business.

Lifestyle Center An open-air shopping site that typically includes 150,000 to 500,000 square feet of space dedicated to upscale, well-known specialty stores.

Lifestyles Ways that individual consumers and families (households) live and spend time and money.

LIFO (Last In, First Out) Method Assumes new merchandise is sold first, while older stock remains in inventory. It matches current sales with the current cost structure.

Limited Decision Making Occurs when a consumer uses every step in the purchase process but does not spend a great deal of time on each of them.

Logistics Total process of planning, enacting, and coordinating the physical movement of merchandise from supplier to retailer to customer in the most timely, effective, and cost-efficient manner possible.

Loss Leaders Items priced below cost to lure more customer traffic. Loss leaders are restricted by some state minimum-price laws.

Maintained Markup (at Retail) Based on the actual prices received for merchandise sold during a time period less merchandise cost, expressed as a percentage:

$$\text{Maintained markup percentage (at retail)} = \frac{\text{Actual retail operating expenses} + \text{Actual profit}}{\text{Actual net sales}}$$

or

$$\frac{\text{Average selling price} - \text{Merchandise cost}}{\text{Average selling price}}$$

Maintenance-Increase-Recoupment Lease Has a provision allowing rent to increase if a property owner's taxes, heating bills, insurance, or other expenses rise beyond a certain point.

Manufacturer (National) Brands Produced and controlled by manufacturers. They are usually well known, supported by manufacturer ads, somewhat pre-sold to consumers, require limited retailer investment in marketing, and often represent maximum product quality to consumers.

Markdown Reduction from the original retail price of an item to meet the lower price of another retailer, adapt to inventory overstocking, clear out shopworn merchandise, reduce assortments of odds and ends, and increase customer traffic.

Markdown Percentage Total dollar markdown as a percentage of net sales (in dollars):

$$\text{Markdown percentage} = \frac{\text{Total dollar markdown}}{\text{Net sales (in \$)}}$$

Marketing Research in Retailing Collection and analysis of information relating to specific issues or problems facing a retailer.

Marketing Research Process Embodies a series of activities: defining the issue or problem, examining secondary data, generating primary data (if needed), analyzing data, making recommendations, and implementing findings.

Market Penetration Pricing Strategy in which a retailer seeks to achieve large revenues by setting low prices and selling a high unit volume.

Market Segment Product Groupings Place together various items that appeal to a given target market.

Market Skimming Pricing Strategy wherein a firm charges premium prices and attracts customers less concerned with price than service, assortment, and status.

Markup Difference between merchandise costs and retail selling price.

Markup Percentage (at Cost) Difference between retail price and merchandise cost expressed as a percentage of merchandise cost:

$$\text{Markup percentage (at cost)} = \frac{\text{Retail selling price} - \text{Merchandise cost}}{\text{Merchandise cost}}$$

Markup Percentage (at Retail) Difference between retail price and merchandise cost expressed as a percentage of retail price:

$$\text{Markup percentage (at retail)} = \frac{\text{Retail selling price} - \text{Merchandise cost}}{\text{Retail selling price}}$$

Markup Pricing Form of cost-oriented pricing in which a retailer sets prices by adding per-unit merchandise costs, retail operating expenses, and desired profit.

Marquee Sign used to display a store's name and/or logo.

Massed Promotion Effort Used by retailers that promote mostly in one or two seasons.

Mass Marketing Selling goods and services to a broad spectrum of consumers.

Mass Merchandising Positioning approach whereby retailers offer a discount or value-oriented image, a wide and/or deep merchandise selection, and large store facilities.

Mazur Plan Divides all retail activities into four functional areas: merchandising, communications, store management, and financial accounting. [modern view]

Megamall Enormous planned shopping center with at least 1 million square feet of retail space, multiple anchor stores, up to several hundred specialty stores, food courts, and entertainment facilities.

Membership (Warehouse) Club Appeals to price-conscious consumers, who must be members to shop.

Memorandum Purchase Occurs when items are not paid for by the retailer until they are sold. The retailer can return unsold merchandise. However, it takes title on delivery and is responsible for damages.

Merchandise Available for Sale Equals beginning inventory, purchases, and transportation charges.

Merchandising Activities involved in acquiring particular goods and/or services and making them available at the places, times, and prices and in the quantity to enable a retailer to reach its goals.

Merchandising Philosophy Sets the guiding principles for all the merchandise decisions a retailer makes.

Mergers The combinations of separately owned retail firms.

Micromarketing Application of data mining whereby the retailer uses differentiated marketing and focused strategy mixes for specific segments, sometimes fine-tuned for the individual shopper.

Micromerchandising Strategy whereby a retailer adjusts its shelf-space allocations to respond to customer and other differences among local markets.

Minimum-Price Laws State regulations preventing retailers from selling certain items for less than their cost plus a fixed percentage to cover overhead. These laws restrict loss leaders and predatory pricing.

Model Stock Approach Method of determining the amount of floor space necessary to carry and display a proper merchandise assortment.

Model Stock Plan Planned composition of fashion goods, which reflects the mix of merchandise available based on expected sales. It indicates product lines, colors, and size distributions.

Monthly Sales Index Measure of sales seasonality that is calculated by dividing each month's actual sales by average monthly sales and then multiplying the results by 100.

Motives Reasons for consumer behavior.

Multi-Channel Retailing A distribution approach whereby a retailer sells to consumers through multiple retail formats (points of contact).

Multiple-Unit Pricing Discounts offered to customers who buy in quantity or who buy a product bundle.

Mystery Shoppers People hired by retailers to pose as customers and observe their operations, from sales presentations to how well displays are maintained to service calls.

Need-Satisfaction Approach Sales technique based on the principle that each customer has a different set of wants; thus, a sales presentation should be geared to the demands of the individual customer.

Neighborhood Business District (NBD) Unplanned shopping area that appeals to the convenience shopping and service needs of a single residential area. The leading retailer is typically a supermarket or a large drugstore, and it is situated on the major street(s) of its residential area.

Neighborhood Shopping Center Planned shopping facility with the largest store being a supermarket or a drugstore. It serves 3,000 to 50,000 people within a 15-minute drive (usually less than 10 minutes).

Net Lease Calls for all maintenance costs, such as heating, electricity, insurance, and interior repair, to be paid by the retailer.

Net Profit Equals gross profit minus retail operating expenses.

Net Profit After Taxes The profit earned after all costs and taxes have been deducted.

Net Profit Margin Performance measure based on a retailer's net profit and net sales. It is equal to net profit divided by net sales.

Net Sales Revenues received by a retailer during a given time period after deducting customer returns, markdowns, and employee discounts.

Net Worth Retailer's assets minus its liabilities.

Never-Out List Used when a retailer plans stock levels for best-sellers. The goal is to purchase enough of these products so they are always in stock.

Niche Retailing Enables retailers to identify customer segments and deploy unique strategies to address the desires of those segments.

Nongoods Services Area of service retailing in which intangible personal services are offered to consumers—who experience the services rather than possess them.

Nonprobability Sample Approach in which stores, products, or customers are chosen by the researcher—based on judgment or convenience.

Nonstore Retailing Utilizes strategy mixes that are not store-based to reach consumers and complete transactions. It occurs via direct marketing, direct selling, and vending machines.

Objective-and-Task Method Promotional budgeting procedure by which a retailer clearly defines its promotional goals and prepares a budget to satisfy them.

Objectives Long-term and short-term performance targets that a retailer hopes to attain. Goals can involve sales, profit, satisfaction of publics, and image.

Observation Form of research in which present behavior or the results of past behavior are observed and recorded. It can be human or mechanical.

Odd Pricing Retail prices set at levels below even dollar values, such as $0.49, $4.98, and $199.

Off-Price Chain Features brand-name apparel and accessories, footwear, linens, fabrics, cosmetics, and/or housewares and sells them at everyday low prices in an efficient, limited-service environment.

Off-Retail Markdown Percentage Markdown for each item or category of items computed as a percentage of original retail price:

$$\text{Off-retail markdown percentage} = \frac{\text{Original price} - \text{New price}}{\text{Original price}}$$

One-Hundred Percent Location Optimum site for a particular store. A location labeled as 100 percent for one firm may be less than optimal for another.

One-Price Policy Strategy wherein a retailer charges the same price to all customers buying an item under similar conditions.

Open Credit Account Requires a consumer to pay his or her bill in full when it is due.

Open-to-Buy Difference between planned purchases and the purchase commitments already made by a buyer for a given time period, often a month. It represents the amount the buyer has left to spend for that month and is reduced each time a purchase is made.

Operating Expenditures (Expenses) Short-term selling and administrative costs of running a business.

Operations Blueprint Systematically lists all the operating functions to be performed, their characteristics, and their timing.

Operations Management Process used to efficiently and effectively enact the policies and tasks to satisfy a firm's customers, employees, and management (and stockholders, if a publicly owned company).

Opportunistic Buying Negotiates low prices for merchandise whose sales have not met expectations, end-of-season goods, items returned to the manufacturer or another retailer, and closeouts.

Opportunities Marketplace openings that exist because other retailers have not yet capitalized on them.

Opportunity Costs Possible benefits a retailer forgoes if it invests in one opportunity rather than another.

Option Credit Account Form of revolving account that allows partial payments. No interest is assessed if a person pays a bill in full when it is due.

Order-Getting Salesperson Actively involved with informing and persuading customers, and in closing sales. This is a true "sales" employee.

Order Lead Time Period from when an order is placed by a retailer to the date merchandise is ready for sale (received, price marked, and put on the selling floor).

Order-Taking Salesperson Engages in routine clerical and sales functions, such as setting up displays, placing inventory on shelves, answering simple questions, filling orders, and ringing up sales.

Organizational Mission Retailer's commitment to a type of business and a distinctive marketplace role. It is reflected in the attitude to consumers, employees, suppliers, competitors, government, and others.

Organization Chart Graphically displays the hierarchical relationships within a firm.

Outshopping When a person goes out of his or her hometown to shop.

Outsourcing Situation whereby a retailer pays an outside party to undertake one or more operating tasks.

Overstored Trading Area Geographic area with so many stores selling a specific good or service that some retailers will be unable to earn an adequate profit.

Owned-Goods Services Area of service retailing in which goods owned by consumers are repaired, improved, or maintained.

Parasite Store Outlet that does not create its own traffic and has no real trading area of its own.

Partnership Unincorporated retail firm owned by two or more persons, each with a financial interest.

Perceived Risk Level of risk a consumer believes exists regarding the purchase of a specific good or service from a given retailer, whether or not the belief is actually correct.

Percentage Lease Stipulates that rent is related to a retailer's sales or profits.

Percentage-of-Sales Method Promotional budgeting method in which a retailer ties its budget to revenue.

Percentage Variation Method Inventory level planning method where beginning-of-month planned inventory during any month differs from planned average monthly stock by only one-half of that month's variation from estimated average monthly sales. Under this method:

$$\text{Beginning-of-month planned inventory level (at retail)} = \text{Planned average monthly stock at retail} \times 1/2\,[1 + (\text{Estimated monthly sales}/\text{Estimated average monthly sales})]$$

Performance Measures Criteria used to assess effectiveness, including total sales, sales per store, sales by product category, sales per square foot, gross margins, gross margin return on investment, operating income, inventory turnover, markdown percentages, employee turnover, financial ratios, and profitability.

Personality Sum total of an individual's traits, which make that individual unique.

Personal Selling Oral communication with one or more prospective customers to make sales.

Physical Inventory System Actual counting of merchandise. A firm using the cost method of inventory valuation and relying on a physical inventory can derive gross profit only when it does a full inventory.

Planned Shopping Center Group of architecturally unified commercial facilities on a site that is centrally owned or managed, designed and operated as a unit, based on balanced tenancy, and accompanied by parking.

Planogram Visual (graphical) representation of the space for selling, merchandise, personnel, and customers—as well as for product categories.

PMs Promotional money, push money, or prize money that a manufacturer provides for retail salespeople selling that manufacturer's brand.

Point of Indifference Geographic breaking point between two cities (communities), so that the trading area of each can be determined. At this point, consumers would be indifferent to shopping at either area.

Point-of-Purchase (POP) Display Interior display that provides shoppers with information, adds to store atmosphere, and serves a substantial promotional role.

Positioning Enables a retailer to devise its strategy in a way that projects an image relative to its retail category and its competitors, and elicits consumer responses to that image.

Post-Purchase Behavior Further purchases or re-evaluation based on a purchase.

Power Center Shopping site with (1) up to a half dozen or so category killer stores and a mix of smaller stores or (2) several complementary stores specializing in one product category.

Predatory Pricing Involves large retailers that seek to reduce competition by selling goods and services at very low prices, thus causing small retailers to go out of business.

Prestige Pricing Assumes consumers will not buy goods and services at prices deemed too low. It is based on the price-quality association.

Pre-Training Indoctrination on the history and policies of the retailer and a job orientation on hours, compensation, the chain of command, and job duties.

Price Elasticity of Demand Sensitivity of customers to price changes in terms of the quantities bought:

$$\text{Elasticity} = \frac{\dfrac{\text{Quantity 1} - \text{Quantity 2}}{\text{Quantity 1} + \text{Quantity 2}}}{\dfrac{\text{Price 1} - \text{Price 2}}{\text{Price 1} + \text{Price 2}}}$$

Price Lining Practice whereby retailers sell merchandise at a limited range of price points, with each point representing a distinct level of quality.

Price–Quality Association Concept stating that many consumers feel high prices connote high quality and low prices connote low quality.

Primary Data Those collected to address the specific issue or problem under study. This type of data may be gathered via surveys, observations, experiments, and simulation.

Primary Trading Area Encompasses 50 to 80 percent of a store's customers. It is the area closest to the store and possesses the highest density of customers to population and the highest per capita sales.

Private (Dealer, Store) Brands Contain names designated by wholesalers or retailers, are more profitable to retailers, are better controlled by retailers, are not sold by competing retailers, are less expensive for consumers, and lead to customer loyalty to retailers (rather than to manufacturers).

Probability (Random) Sample Approach whereby every store, product, or customer has an equal or known chance of being chosen for study.

Problem Awareness Stage in the decision process at which the consumer not only has been aroused by social, commercial, and/or physical stimuli, but also recognizes that the good or service under consideration may solve a problem of shortage or unfulfilled desire.

Productivity Efficiency with which a retail strategy is carried out.

Product Life Cycle Shows the expected behavior of a good or service over its life. The traditional cycle has four stages: introduction, growth, maturity, and decline.

Product/Trademark Franchising Arrangement in which the franchisee acquires the identity of the franchisor by agreeing to sell the latter's products and/or operate under the latter's name.

Profit-and-Loss (Income) Statement Summary of a retailer's revenues and expenses over a particular period of time, usually a month, quarter, or year.

Prototype Stores Used with an operations strategy that requires multiple outlets in a chain to conform to relatively uniform construction, layout, and operations standards.

Publicity Any nonpersonal form of public relations whereby messages are transmitted by mass media, the time or space provided by the media is not paid for, and there is no identified commercial sponsor.

Public Relations Any communication that fosters a favorable image for the retailer among its publics (consumers, investors, government, channel members, employees, and the general public).

Purchase Act Exchange of money or a promise to pay for the ownership or use of a good or service. Purchase variables include the place of purchase, terms, and availability of merchandise.

Purchase Motivation Product Groupings Appeal to the consumer's urge to buy products and the amount of time he or she is willing to spend in shopping.

Quick Response (QR) Inventory Planning Enables a retailer to reduce the amount of inventory it keeps on hand by ordering more frequently and in lower quantity.

Rack Display Interior display that neatly hangs or presents products.

Rationalized Retailing Combines a high degree of centralized management control with strict operating procedures for every phase of business.

Reach Number of distinct people exposed to a retailer's promotional efforts during a specified period.

Recruitment Activity whereby a retailer generates a list of job applicants.

Reference Groups Influence people's thoughts and behavior. They may be classified as aspirational, membership, and dissociative.

Regional Shopping Center Large, planned shopping facility appealing to a geographically dispersed market. It has at least one or two full-sized department stores and 50 to 150 or more smaller retailers. The market for this center is 100,000+ people who live or work up to a 30-minute drive time from the center.

Regression Model Computerized site selection tool that uses equations showing the association between potential store sales and several independent variables at each location under consideration.

Reilly's Law of Retail Gravitation Traditional means of trading-area delineation that establishes a point of indifference between two cities or communities, so the trading area of each can be determined.

Relationship Retailing Exists when retailers seek to establish and maintain long-term bonds with customers, rather than act as if each sales transaction is a completely new encounter with them.

Rented-Goods Services Area of service retailing in which consumers lease and use goods for specified periods of time.

Reorder Point Stock level at which new orders must be placed:

$$\text{Reorder point} = (\text{Usage rate} \times \text{Lead time}) + \text{Safety stock}$$

Resident Buying Office Inside or outside buying organization used when a retailer wants to keep in close touch with market trends and cannot do so with just its headquarters buying staff. Such offices are usually situated in important merchandise centers (sources of supply) and provide valuable data and contacts.

Retail Audit Systematically examines the total retailing effort or a specific aspect of it to study what a retailer is presently doing, appraise how well it is performing, and make recommendations.

Retail Balance The mix of stores within a district or shopping center.

Retail Information System (RIS) Anticipates the information needs of managers; collects, organizes, and stores relevant data on a continuous basis; and directs the flow of information to proper decision makers.

Retailing Business activities involved in selling goods and services to consumers for their personal, family, or household use.

Retailing Concept An approach to business that is customer-oriented, coordinated, value-driven, and goal-oriented.

Retail Institution Basic format or structure of a business. Institutions can be classified by ownership, store-based retail strategy mix, and nonstore-based, electronic, and nontraditional retailing.

Retail Life Cycle Theory asserting that institutions—like the goods and services they sell—pass through identifiable life stages: introduction (early growth), growth (accelerated development), maturity, and decline.

Retail Method of Accounting Determines closing inventory value by calculating the average relationship between the cost and retail values of merchandise available for sale during a period.

Retail Organization How a firm structures and assigns tasks, policies, resources, authority, responsibilities, and rewards so as to efficiently and effectively satisfy the needs of its target market, employees, and management.

Retail Promotion Any communication by a retailer that informs, persuades, and/or reminds the target market about any aspect of that firm.

Retail Reductions Difference between beginning inventory plus purchases during the period and sales plus ending inventory. They encompass anticipated markdowns, employee and other discounts, and stock shortages.

Retail Strategy Overall plan guiding a retail firm. It influences the firm's business activities and its response to market forces, such as competition and the economy.

Return on Assets (ROA) Performance ratio based on net sales, net profit, and total assets:

$$\frac{\text{Return}}{\text{on assets}} = \frac{\text{Net profit}}{\text{Net sales}} \times \frac{\text{Net sales}}{\text{Total assets}} = \frac{\text{Net profit}}{\text{Total assets}}$$

Return on Net Worth (RONW) Performance measure based on net profit, net sales, total assets, and net worth:

$$\frac{\text{Return on}}{\text{net worth}} = \frac{\text{Net profit}}{\text{Net sales}} \times \frac{\text{Net sales}}{\text{Total assets}} \times \frac{\text{Total assets}}{\text{Net worth}}$$

Reverse Logistics Encompasses all merchandise flows from the customer and/or the retailer back through the supply channel.

Revolving Credit Account Allows a customer to charge items and be billed monthly on the basis of the outstanding cumulative balance.

RFID (Radio Frequency Identifaction) A method of storing and remotely retrieving data using devices called RFID tags or transponders.

Robinson-Patman Act Bars manufacturers and wholesalers from discriminating in price or purchase terms in selling to individual retailers if these retailers are purchasing products of "like quality" and the effect of such discrimination is to injure competition.

Routine Decision Making Takes place when a consumer buys out of habit and skips steps in the purchase process.

Safety Stock Extra inventory to protect against out-of-stock conditions due to unexpected demand and delays in delivery.

Sales Manager Person who typically supervises the on-floor selling and operational activities for a specific retail department.

Sales Opportunity Grid Rates the promise of new and established goods, services, procedures, and/or store outlets across a variety of criteria.

Sales–Productivity Ratio Method for assigning floor space on the basis of sales or profit per foot.

Sales Promotion Encompasses the paid communication activities other than advertising, public relations, and personal selling that stimulate consumer purchases and dealer effectiveness.

Saturated Trading Area Geographic area with the proper amount of retail facilities to satisfy the needs of its population for a specific good or service, as well as to enable retailers to prosper.

Scenario Analysis Lets a retailer project the future by studying factors that affect long-term performance and then forming contingency plans based on alternate scenarios.

Scrambled Merchandising Occurs when a retailer adds goods and services that may be unrelated to each other and to the firm's original business.

Seasonal Merchandise Products that sell well over nonconsecutive time periods.

Secondary Business District (SBD) Unplanned shopping area in a city or town that is usually bounded by the intersection of two major streets. It has at least a junior department store and/or some larger specialty stores—in addition to many smaller stores.

Secondary Data Those gathered for purposes other than addressing the issue or problem currently under study.

Secondary Trading Area Geographic area that contains an additional 15 to 25 percent of a store's customers. It is located outside the primary area, and customers are more widely dispersed.

Selective Distribution Takes place when suppliers sell through a moderate number of retailers. This lets suppliers have higher sales than in exclusive distribution and lets retailers carry some competing brands.

Self-Scanning Enables the consumer himself or herself to scan the items being purchased at a checkout counter, pay electronically by credit or debit card, and bag the items.

Semantic Differential Disguised or nondisguised survey technique, whereby a respondent is asked to rate one or more retailers on several criteria; each criterion is evaluated along a bipolar adjective scale.

Service Retailing Involves transactions in which consumers do not purchase or acquire ownership of tangible products. It encompasses rented goods, owned goods, and nongoods.

Simulation Type of experiment whereby a computer program is used to manipulate the elements of a retail strategy mix rather than test them in a real setting.

Single-Channel Retailing A distribution approach whereby a retailer sells to consumers through one retail format.

Situation Analysis Candid evaluation of the opportunities and threats facing a prospective or existing retailer.

Slotting Allowances Payments that retailers require of vendors for providing shelf space in stores.

Social Class Informal ranking of people based on income, occupation, education, and other factors.

Social Media Encompass online technology tools that allow vast numbers of people to easily communicate with one another via the Internet and mobile devices. Through social media, messages, audio, video, photos, podcasts, and other multimedia communications are possible.

Social Responsibility Occurs when a retailer acts in society's best interests—as well as its own. The challenge is to balance corporate citizenship with fair profits.

Sole Proprietorship Unincorporated retail firm owned by one person.

Solutions Selling Takes a customer-centered approach and presents "solutions" rather than "products." It goes a step beyond cross-merchandising.

Sorting Process Involves the retailer's collecting an assortment of goods and services from various sources, buying them in large quantity, and offering to sell them in small quantities to consumers.

Specialog Enables a retailer to cater to the specific needs of customer segments, emphasize a limited number of items, and reduce catalog production and postage costs.

Specialty Store Retailer that concentrates on selling one goods or service line.

Staple Merchandise Consists of the regular products carried by a retailer.

Stimulus Cue (social or commercial) or a drive (physical) meant to motivate or arouse a person to act.

Stock-to-Sales Method Inventory level planning technique wherein a retailer wants to maintain a specified ratio of goods on hand to sales.

Stock Turnover Number of times during a specific period, usually one year, that the average inventory on hand is sold. It can be computed in units or dollars (at retail or cost):

$$\text{Annual rate of stock turnover (in units)} = \frac{\text{Number of units sold during year}}{\text{Average inventory on hand (in units)}}$$

$$\text{Annual rate of stock turnover (in retail dollars)} = \frac{\text{Net yearly sales}}{\text{Average inventory on hand (at retail)}}$$

$$\text{Annual rate of stock turnover (at cost)} = \frac{\text{Cost of goods sold during year}}{\text{Average inventory on hand (at cost)}}$$

Storability Product Groupings Used for products that need special handling.

Storefront Total physical exterior of a store, including the marquee, entrances, windows, lighting, and construction materials.

Store Maintenance Encompasses all the activities in managing a retailer's physical facilities.

Straight (Gridiron) Traffic Flow Presents displays and aisles in a rectangular or gridiron pattern.

Straight Lease Requires the retailer to pay a fixed dollar amount per month over the life of a lease. It is the simplest, most direct leasing arrangement.

Strategic Profit Model Expresses the numerical relationship among net profit margin, asset turnover, and financial leverage. It can be used in planning or controlling a retailer's assets.

Strategy Mix Firm's particular combination of store location, operating procedures, goods/services offered, pricing tactics, store atmosphere and customer services, and promotional methods.

String Unplanned shopping area comprising a group of retail stores, often with similar or compatible product lines, located along a street or highway.

Supercenter Combination store blending an economy supermarket with a discount department store.

Supermarket Self-service food store with grocery, meat, and produce departments and minimum annual sales of

$2 million. The category includes conventional supermarkets, food-based superstores, combination stores, box (limited-line) stores, and warehouse stores.

Supervision Manner of providing a job environment that encourages employee accomplishment.

Supply Chain Logistics aspect of a value delivery chain. It comprises all of the parties that participate in the retail logistics process: manufacturers, wholesalers, third-party specialists, and the retailer.

Survey Research technique that systematically gathers information from respondents by communicating with them.

Tactics Actions that encompass a retailer's daily and short-term operations.

Target Market Customer group that a retailer seeks to attract and satisfy.

Taxes The portion of revenues turned over to the federal, state, and/or local government.

Terms of Occupancy Consist of ownership versus leasing, the type of lease, operations and maintenance costs, taxes, zoning restrictions, and voluntary regulations.

Theme-Setting Display Interior display that depicts a product offering in a thematic manner and portrays a specific atmosphere or mood.

Threats Environmental and marketplace factors that can adversely affect retailers if they do not react to them (and sometimes, even if they do).

Top-Down Space Management Approach Exists when a retailer starts with its total available store space, divides the space into categories, and then works on in-store product layouts.

Total Retail Experience All the elements in a retail offering that encourage or inhibit consumers during their contact with a retailer.

Trading Area Geographical area containing the customers and potential customers of a particular retailer or group of retailers for specific goods or services.

Trading-Area Overlap Occurs when the trading areas of stores in different locations encroach on one another. In the overlap area, the same customers are served by both stores.

Traditional Department Store Type of department store in which merchandise quality ranges from average to quite good, pricing is moderate to above average, and customer service ranges from medium levels of sales help, credit, delivery, and so forth to high levels of each.

Traditional Job Description Contains each position's title, supervisory relationships (superior and subordinate), committee assignments, and the specific ongoing roles and tasks.

Training Programs Used to teach new (and existing) personnel how best to perform their jobs or how to improve themselves.

Unbundled Pricing Involves a retailer's charging separate prices for each item sold.

Uncontrollable Variables Aspects of business to which the retailer must adapt (such as competition, the economy, and laws).

Understored Trading Area Geographic area that has too few stores selling a specific good or service to satisfy the needs of its population.

Unit Control Looks at the quantities of merchandise a retailer handles during a stated period.

Unit Pricing Practice required by many states, whereby retailers (mostly food stores) must express both the total price of an item and its price per unit of measure.

Universal Product Code (UPC) Classification for coding data onto products via a series of thick and thin vertical lines. It lets retailers record information instantaneously on a product's model number, size, color, and other factors when it is sold, as well as send the information to a computer that monitors unit sales, inventory levels, and other factors. The UPC is not readable by humans.

Unplanned Business District Type of retail location where two or more stores situate together (or nearby) in such a way that the total arrangement or mix of stores is not due to prior long-range planning.

Usage Rate Average sales per day, in units, of merchandise.

Value Embodied by the activities and processes (a value chain) that provide a given level of value for the consumer—from manufacturer, wholesaler, and retailer perspectives. From the customer's perspective, it is the perception the shopper has of a value chain.

Value Chain Total bundle of benefits offered to consumers through a channel of distribution.

Value Delivery System All the parties that develop, produce, deliver, and sell and service particular goods and services.

Variable Markup Policy Strategy whereby a firm purposely adjusts markups by merchandise category.

Variable Pricing Strategy wherein a retailer alters prices to coincide with fluctuations in costs or consumer demand.

Variety Store Outlet that handles a wide assortment of inexpensive and popularly priced goods and services, such as apparel and accessories, costume jewelry, notions and small wares, candy, toys, and other items in the price range.

Vending Machine Format involving the cash- or card-operated dispensing of goods and services. It eliminates the use of sales personnel and allows around-the-clock sales.

Vendor-Managed Inventory (VMI) Practice of retailers counting on key suppliers to actively participate in their inventory management programs. Suppliers have their own employees stationed at retailers' headquarters to manage the inventory replenishment of the suppliers' products.

Vertical Cooperative Advertising Agreement Enables a manufacturer and a retailer or a wholesaler and a retailer to share an ad.

Vertical Marketing System All the levels of independently owned businesses along a channel of distribution. Goods and services are normally distributed through one of three types of systems: independent, partially integrated, and fully integrated.

Vertical Price Fixing Occurs when manufacturers or wholesalers seek to control the retail prices of their goods and services.

Vertical Retail Audit Analyzes—in depth—performance in one area of the strategy mix or operations.

Video Kiosk Freestanding, interactive, electronic computer terminal that displays products and related information on a video screen; it often uses a touch screen for consumers to make selections.

Visual Merchandising Proactive, integrated approach to atmospherics taken by a retailer to create a certain "look," properly display products, stimulate shopping, and enhance the physical environment.

Want Book Notebook in which retail store employees record requests for unstocked or out-of-stock merchandise.

Want Slip Slip on which retail store employees enter requests for unstocked or out-of-stock merchandise.

Warehouse Store Food-based discounter offering a moderate number of food items in a no-frills setting.

Weeks' Supply Method An inventory level planning method wherein beginning inventory equals several weeks' expected sales. It assumes inventory is in direct proportion to sales. Under this method:

$$\text{Beginning-of-month planned inventory level (at retail)} = \text{Average estimated weekly sales} \times \text{Number of weeks to be stocked}$$

Weighted Application Blank Form whereby criteria best correlating with job success get more weight than others. A minimum total score becomes a cutoff point for hiring.

Wheel of Retailing Theory stating that retail innovators often first appear as low-price operators with low costs and low profit margins. Over time, they upgrade the products carried and improve facilities and customer services. They then become vulnerable to new discounters with lower cost structures.

Width of Assortment Number of distinct goods/service categories (product lines) a retailer carries.

Word of Mouth (WOM) Occurs when one consumer talks to others—in person, on the phone, by E-mail, through social media, or in some other format.

World Wide Web (Web) Way of accessing the Internet, whereby people work with easy-to-use Web addresses and pages. Users see words, colorful charts, pictures, and video and hear audio.

Yield Management Pricing Computerized, demand-based, variable pricing technique whereby a retailer (typically a service firm) determines the combination of prices that yield the greatest total revenues for a given period.

Zero-Based Budgeting Practice followed when a firm starts each new budget from scratch and outlines the expenditures needed to reach that period's goals. All costs are justified each time a budget is done.

Endnotes

Chapter 1

1. Alison Doyle, "Social Media Definition," http://jobsearch.about.com (April 9, 2012); and Barbara Farfan, "Social Media Study Reveals the One-Night Stand Approach Doesn't Get Retail Customers," http://retailindustry.about.com (April 29, 2011).
2. Estimated by the authors from data in Deloitte, "2011 Global Powers of Retailing," *Stores* (January 2011), special section.
3. "Monthly & Annual Retail Trade," www.census.gov/retail (March 19, 2012); and retailer annual reports.
4. The material in this section is drawn from various Target Corporation online sources, including http://investors.target.com; http://pressroom.target.com; www.target.com; *Target Corporation 2010 Annual Report*; "Target Corporation," www.hoovers.com (February 9, 2012); *Trefis Analysis for Target Corporation* (Boston, MA: Insight Guru Inc., September 7, 2011); Kathie Canning, "Aiming for the Bull's-eye," www.progressivegrocer.com (April 2011); and Matt Townsend, "Target's Cheap-Chic Glamour Is Fading," www.businessweek.com (September 22, 2011),
5. "Best Retail Brands 2011," www.interbrand.eu/en/BestRetailBrands/2011.aspx.
6. Shari Waters, "Top 10 Ways to Turn Off Customers," http://retail.about.com/od/storedesign/tp/store_donts.htm?p=1 (July 16, 2011).
7. "Build-A-Bear Workshop, Inc.," www.buildabear.com/html/en_US/aboutus/ourcompany/factSheet.pdf (March 2, 2012).
8. Susan Reda, "Saving Customer Service: Are Retailers Up to the Challenge?" http://www.treosystems.com/Welcome%20to%20STORES.htm (January 2001).
9. Jessica Swanson, "Is the Customer Always Right?" www.solo-e.com/blog/2011/07/is-the-customer-always-right.html (July 10, 2011).

Chapter 1 Appendix

1. Dana Mattioli, "Joyless Holiday Retail Forecast," *Wall Street Journal* (September 21, 2011), pp. B1, B2.
2. Conor Dougherty, "Income Slides to 1996 Levels," *Wall Street Journal* (September 14, 2011), pp. A1, A4.
3. Ibid.
4. Ellen Byron, "As Middle Class Shrinks, P&G Aims High and Low," *Wall Street Journal* (September 12, 2011), pp. A1, A16.
5. Doug Short, "Conference Board: Consumer Confidence Does a Cliff Dive," http://wallstreetsectorselector.com/2011/08/conference-board-consumer-confidence-does-a-cliff-dive/ (August 30, 2011).
6. Timothy Homan, "U.S. Consumer Confidence Rises More Than Estimated on Outlook for Economy," www.bloomberg.com (September 16, 2011).
7. Nick Timiraos, "Home Forecast Calls for Pain," *Wall Street Journal* (September 21, 2011), pp. A1, A2.
8. Ian Talley, "IMF Cuts Growth Forecast," *Wall Street Journal* (September 21, 2011), p. A15.
9. Simon Kennedy and Fabio Benedetti-Valentini, "Now It's a European Banking Crisis," *Bloomberg Business Week* (May 3, 2101), pp. 11–12.
10. Jason Asaeda, "Retailing: General," *Standard & Poor's* (May 26, 2011), p. 2; and Michael Souers, "Retailing: Specialty," *Standard & Poor's* (September 8, 2011), p. 11.
11. Ann Zimmerman, " 'Frontiers of Frugality' Shoppers Unable to Trade Back Up," *Wall Street Journal* (October 4, 2011), pp. B1, B7.
12. Annie Lowrey, "Readers Without Borders," www.slate.com (July 20, 2011).
13. "A&P Files for Chapter 11 Protection," *Food Logistics* (January/February 2011), p. 6.
14. Joseph Agnese, "Supermarkets & Drugstores," *Standard & Poor's Industry Surveys* (July 21, 2011), pp. 6–7.
15. Mattioli, "Joyless Holiday Retail Forecast."
16. "Coupon Trend Reports," www.santella.com (January 9, 2012).
17. Zimmerman, " 'Frontiers of Frugality' Shoppers Unable to Trade Back Up."
18. Miguiel Bustillo, "How Bad Is the Economy? Wal-Mart Revives Layaway," *Wall Street Journal* (September 9, 2011), pp. B1, B2.
19. Andrea Chang, "Wal-Mart's Layaway Program Returning," *Los Angeles Times* (September 11, 2011).

Chapter 2

1. Awareness, Inc., *A Marketer's Guide to Social Media: Developing and Implementing a Social Media Marketing Strategy* (Burlington, MA, 2011).
2. "About GameStop," www.gamestopcorp.com (April 2, 2011).
3. Retail Forward, *Retailing 2005*, p. 9.
4. Hansen Lieu, "Customer Satisfaction and Customer Loyalty: It's Like 'Like vs. Love,'" www.business2community.com/loyalty-marketing (October 20, 2011).
5. "Dealer-Chic," http://trendwatching.com/trends/12trends2012/?dealerchic (November 2011).
6. "Should You Use a Shotgun or a Sniper Approach to Internet Marketing?" www.thefasttracktowealth.com/2008/08/should-you-use-a-shotgun-or-a-sniper-approach-to (August 13, 2008).
7. "Our Company, Our Culture," www.autozoneinc.com/about_us/our_company (March 2, 2012).
8. "America's Best Drugstores," http://pressroom.consumerreports.org/pressroom/2011/04 (April 2011).
9. "Our Culture," http://about.nordstrom.com/careers/culture.asp (April 12, 2011).
10. Anika Anand, "Major Grocer Getting Rid of Self-Checkout Lanes," www.msnbc.msn.com (July 10, 2011).

11. Rose Otieno, Chris Harrow, and Gaynor Lea-Greenwood, "The Unhappy Shopper, A Retail Experience: Exploring Fashion, Fit, and Affordability," *International Journal of Retail & Distribution Management*, Vol. 33 (Number 4, 2005), pp. 298–309.
12. "Customer Satisfaction Survey," www.statpac.com/online-surveys/Customer_Satisfaction.htm (April 12, 2011)
13. Bryant Ott, "Making Company Loyalty Programs Work," http://gmj.gallup.com/content/149570/making-loyalty-programs-work.aspx#1 (October 10, 2011).
14. Lars Meyer Waarden and Christophe Benavent, "Rewards That Reward," http://online.wsj.com/article/SB122160028857244783.html (September 17, 2008).
15. "Becoming a Wal-Mart or Sam's Club Supplier," www.walmartstores.com/download/2048.pdf (April 11, 2012).
16. "Ace Hardware Stores," www.nbfranchise.com/franchisedetail/ace_hardware_corporation.html (April 11, 2012).
17. Leonard L. Berry, "Relationship Marketing of Services—Growing Interest, Emerging Prospects," *Journal of the Academy of Marketing Science*, Vol. 23 (Fall 1995), pp. 237–238. See also Charlene Pleger Bebko, "Service Intangibility and Its Impact on Consumer Expectations of Service Quality," *Journal of Services Marketing*, Vol. 14 (Number 1, 2000), pp. 9–26.
18. "Global ATM Clock," www.atmia.com/mig/globalatmclock (January 26, 2012).
19. "Smart Card FAQ," www.smartcardalliance.org/pages/smart-cards-faq (January 30, 2012).
20. "Definition of Self-Checkout," www.pcmag.com/encyclopedia_term/0,2542,t=self-scanning+checkout&i=51072,00.asp (February 3, 2012).
21. Grant Thornton, "Gift Cards: Opportunities and Issues for Retailers," www.grantthornton.com (2011).
22. Curt Hopkins, "First All-Automated Hotel Opens in Norway," www.readwriteweb.com/archives/first_all-automated_hotel_opens.php (January 21, 2011).
23. "About Us," www.chaindrugstore.net (February 15, 2012).
24. *Direct Marketing Association's Guidelines for Ethical Business Practices*, www.dmaresponsibility.org/guidelines (revised May 2011).
25. "Sustainability," http://walmartstores.com/Sustainability (February 16, 2012).
26. "About Hannaford," www.hannaford.com (February 16, 2012).
27. Susan Haller, "Privacy: What Every Manager Should Know," *Information Management Journal*, Vol. 36 (May–June 2002), pp. 38–39.
28. JCPenney, public relations.
29. Giant Food, public relations.

Chapter 2 Appendix

1. Estimated by the authors based on data in *2012 Statistical Abstract*, www.census.gov/compendia/statab; and *Industry Statistics Sampler*, www.census.gov/econ/industry (July 13, 2011).
2. Young Namkung, SooCheong (Shawn) Jang, and Soo Keun Choi, "Customer Complaints in Restaurants: Do They Differ by Service Stages and Loyalty Levels?" *International Journal of Hospitality Management* 30 (2011), pp. 495–502.
3. Yi-Shun Wang, Shun-Cheng Wu, Hsin-Hui Lin, and Yu-Yin Wang, "The Relationship of Service Failure Severity, Service Recovery Justice and Perceived Switching Costs with Customer Loyalty in the Context of E-Tailing," *International Journal of Information Management* 31 (2011), pp. 350–359.
4. Karen Holcombe Ehrhart, L.A. Witt, Benjamin Schneider, and Sara Jansen Perry, "Service Employees Give as They Get: Internal Service as a Moderator of the Service Climate-Service Outcomes Link," *Journal of Applied Psychology*, Vol. 96 (No. 2, 2011), pp. 423–431.
5. Leonard L. Berry and Manjit S. Yadav, "Capture and Communicate Value in the Pricng of Services," *Sloan Management Review*, Vol. 37 (Summer 1996), pp. 41–51.
6. The material in this section is drawn from Robin Lee Allen, " Model of Efficiency," Nation's *Restaurant News* (April 4, 2011), p. 24; Sam Smith, "The One-Key Theory," *Restaurant Business* (August 2011), p. 1; and Pal's Sudden Service, www.palsweb.com (March 7, 2012).

Chapter 3

1. Ellen Byron, "In-Store Sales Begin at Home," http://online.wsj.com (April 25, 2011).
2. "Why Do You Need One?" www.sba.gov/content/why-do-you-need-one (April 3, 2012).
3. "Values in Practice," www.aboutmcdonalds.com/mcd/csr/about/values.html (April 3, 2012); "PetSmart Company Information," http://phx.corporate-ir.net/phoenix.zhtml?c=93506&p=irol-homeprofile (April 3, 2012); and "About Zumiez," www.zumiez.com/help/information (April 3, 2012).
4. For additional information about business ownership formats, go to *Inc.*'s "Know Your Options: Choosing a Corporate Form" site (www.inc.com/guides/start_biz/20676.html).
5. "Choosing an Entity for Your Business," www.360financialliteracy.org/Topics/Owning-a-Business/Starting-a-Business/Choosing-an-entity-for-your-business (April 3, 2012).
6. Estimated by the authors from data in *2012 Statistical Abstract of the United States*, www.census.gov/compendia/statab.
7. *2011 Kroger Co. 10K*, p. 4.
8. "About bebe," www.bebe.com (April 5, 2012).
9. "How We Do Business," www.traderjoes.com/how_we_do_biz.html (April 6, 2009).

Chapter 3 Appendix

1. *World Factbook*, https://www.cia.gov/library/publications/the-world-factbook (February 15, 2012); and "Retail Industry Global Report: 2010," www.clearwatercf.com/documents/sectors/IMAP_Retail_Report_2010.pdf.

2. "2011 Global Retail Development Index," www.atkearney.com/index.php/Publications/global-retail-development-index.html.
3. "Deloitte: Leaving Home: Global Powers of Retailing 2011," *Stores* (January 2011), pp. G8–9.
4. Alicia Fiorletta, "Cultural Adaptation Facilitates Retail Success Abroad," www.retailtouchpoints.com (July 14, 2011).
5. "Global Powers of Retailing," *Chain Store Age* (January 2008), pp. G44–G46.
6. "About Toys "R" Us International," www.toysrusinc.com/our-brands/international (February 15, 2012).
7. "About McDonald's," www.aboutmcdonalds.com (February 15, 2011); and "McDonald's in Russia—Defeated Communism with a 'Happy' Meal," www.businesstoday-eg.com/case-studies/case-studies (September 14, 2011).
8. "Ikea: Facts & Figures," www.ikea.com/ms/en_US/about_ikea/facts_and_figures/facts_figures.html (October 7, 2011).
9. "About Us," www.ahold.com/en/about/key-facts (October 7, 2011).
10. "Luxottica Retail," www.luxottica.com/en/retail (February 16, 2012).

Chapter 4

1. "Small Businesses Focus Social Efforts on Top Sites," www.emarketer.com (June 6, 2011); and "Social Marketing's Benefits Rival E-Mail for Small Businesses," www.emarketer.com (April 26, 2011).
2. *2012 Statistical Abstract of the United States*, www.census.gov/compendia/statab.
3. "Pathways to Getting Ahead," www.bos.frb.org/consumer/pathways/knowledge.htm (March 4, 2012).
4. Tom Dorr, "The Hidden Truths of Small Business Ownership," http://bbjtoday.com/blog/hidden-truths-small-business-ownership/10138# (February 8, 2011).
5. For a good overview of franchising and franchising opportunities, see *Entrepreneur's* "Annual Franchise 500" issue (www.entrepreneur.com/franchise500), which appears each January.
6. The material in this section is estimated by the authors based on data in "Franchise Business Economic Outlook: 2011," www.franchise.org.
7. For more information on leased departments, see Kinshuk Jerath and Z. John Zhang, "Store Within a Store," *Journal of Marketing Research*, Vol. 47 (August 2010), pp. 748–763.
8. Kit R. Roane, "Stores Within Stores," http://money.cnn.com/2011/01/24/news/companies/retail_stores_inside_stores.fortune (January 24, 2011).
9. "CPI: About Us," www.cpicorp.com/Pages/CPI_About_Us.html (April 25, 2012).
10. *Sherwin-Williams 2011 Annual Report*, http://investors.sherwin-williams.com/annual-reports.
11. For more information on cooperatives, visit these Web sites: National Cooperative Business Association (www.ncba.coop); National Cooperative Grocers Association (http://ncga.coop); and Go.coop (www.go.coop).

Chapter 4 Appendix

1. "Who We Are," www.ediblearrangements.com/About/WhoWeAre.aspx (April 2, 2012).
2. "Dunkin Brands—Eat, Drink, Think," www.dunkinfranchising.com (March 29, 2012).
3. Robert McIntosh, "Self-Evaluation: Is Franchising for You?" www.franchise.org/FranchiseeSecondary.aspx?id=10010 (March 29, 2012).
4. "Franchising System Support," www.aboutmcdonalds.com/mcd/franchising/us_franchising/why_mcdonalds/system_support.html (March 29, 2012).
5. "Become a TJ's Franchisee," www.tacojohns.com/aboutus/becomeafranchisee (March 30, 2012).
6. "CPR Procedure for Resolution of Franchise Disputes Franchise Mediation Program," www.cpradr.org/Resources/ALLCPRArticles/tabid/265/ID/628/CPR-Procedure-for-Resolution-of-Franchise-Disputes.aspx (March 28, 2012).

Chapter 5

1. Alida Destrempe, "Safeway's Four Tiers of Digital Development," www.kantarretailiq.com (February 8, 2011).
2. The pioneering works on the wheel of retailing are Malcolm P. McNair, "Significant Trends and Developments in the Postwar Period," in A. B. Smith (Editor), *Competitive Distribution in a Free High Level Economy and Its Implications for the University* (Pittsburgh: University of Pittsburgh Press, 1958), pp. 17–18; and Stanley Hollander, "The Wheel of Retailing," *Journal of Marketing*, Vol. 25 (July 1960), pp. 37–42. For further analysis of the concept, see Stephen Brown, "The Wheel of Retailing: Past and Future," *Journal of Retailing*, Vol. 66 (Summer 1990), pp. 143–149; Stephen Brown, "Postmodernism, the Wheel of Retailing, and Will to Power," *International Review of Retail, Distribution, and Consumer Research*, Vol. 5 (July 1995), pp. 387–414; Don E. Schultz, "Another Turn of the Wheel," *Marketing Management* (March–April 2002), pp. 8–9; Susan D. Sampson, "Category Killers and Big-Box Retailing: Their Historical Impact on Retailing in the USA," *International Journal of Retail & Distribution Management*, Vol. 36 (No. 1, 2008), pp. 17–31; and Victor J. Massad, Mary Beth Nein, and Joanne M. Tucker, "The Wheel of Retailing Revisited: Toward a 'Wheel of E-Tailing,' " *Journal of Management and Marketing Research*, Vol. 8 (September 2011), www.aabri.com/manuscripts/11838.pdf.
3. "Ries' Pieces: The Sad Saga of Sears," http://ries.typepad.com/ries_blog/2008/01/with-the-kmart.html (January 29, 2008).
4. See Jonathan Reynolds, Elizabeth Howard, Christine Cuthbertson and Latchezar Hristov, "Perspectives on Retail Format Innovation: Relating Theory and Practice," *International Journal of Retail & Distribution Management*, Vol. 35 (No. 8, 2007), pp. 647–660; and Lai Ngun Sun, Robert Kay, and Matthew Chew, "Development of a Retail Life Cycle:

The Case of Hong Kong's Department Store Industry," *Asia Pacific Business Review*, Vol. 15 (January 2009), pp. 107–121.
5. "Unlimited TV Episodes & Movies Over the Internet," www.netflix.com/HowItWorks (April 11, 2012).
6. See www.kioskmarketplace.com for an overview of kiosks.
7. "Last Catalog Showroom Retailer Now in Liquidation," *Knight Ridder/Tribune Business News* (February 3, 2002); and "Argos," www.argos.co.uk (April 11, 2012).
8. "Retailing: General," *Standard & Poor's Industry Surveys* (November 24, 2011), pp. 11–12.
9. Ibid., pp. 18–19.
10. John Lofstock, "Convenience Store Sales Show Strong Growth in 2010," www.csdecisions.com (April 6, 2011).
11. Various issues of *Progressive Grocer* www.progressivegrocer.com; Food Marketing Institute, "Facts & Figures," www.fmi.org/facts_figs; and author's estimates.
12. Ibid.
13. Ibid.
14. Ibid.
15. Ibid.
16. Estimated by the authors from "Retailing: Specialty," *Standard & Poor's Industry Surveys* (September 8, 2011); "Apparel & Footwear: Retailers & Brands," *Standard & Poor's Industry Surveys* (September 1, 2011).
17. "Sephora," www.sephora.com/help/about_sephora.jhtml?location=sephora (July 2011).
18. "Retailing: Specialty," p. 21.
19. Estimated by the authors from "Retailing: General," *Standard & Poor's Industry Surveys*; and "Department—USA Overview and Growth Forecast," www.kantarretailiq.com (February 19, 2012).
20. Elizabeth Holmes and Ann Zimmerman, "Department Stores Regain Momentum," www.wsj.com (August 4, 2011).
21. Estimated by the authors from Wal-Mart, Target, and Kmart company Web sites (February 20, 2012).
22. Estimated by the authors from Dollar General, Family Dollar, and Big Lots company Web sites (February 20, 2012).
23. "About Us," www.tjx.com/about.asp (February 23, 2012).
24. "Outlook Facts," www.valueretailnews.com/about.php (February 25, 2012).
25. "Industry Outlook: Warehouse Clubs," www.kantarretailiq.com (March 2011).
26. Adapted by the authors from "Rose Bowl Flea Market Selling Information," www.rgcshows.com/RoseBowl.aspx (February 27, 2012).

Chapter 6

1. Verdict Research, "Evolution of Social Media in Retail," http://about.datamonitor.com/media/archives/5702 (June 10, 2011).
2. "For Small-Business Marketers, Are Fewer Channels Better?" www.emarketer.com (May 23, 2011).
3. Chris Cunnane, "The State of Multi-Channel Retail Marketing," www.aberdeen.com (June 2011).
4. Authors' estimates, based on information from www.the-dma.org, www.emarketer.com, and other sources.
5. "What Is the Direct Marketing Association?" www.the-dma.org/aboutdma/whatisthedma.shtml (March 18, 2012).
6. David Danziger, "Transform Your Customer Database Into a Goldmine," www.chiefmarketer.com (July 19, 2011).
7. "The REI Story," www.rei.com/jobs/story.html (March 20, 2012).
8. "QVC at a Glance," www.qvc.com (March 25, 2012); and "About HSNI," www.hsn.com/corp/info/default.aspx (March 25, 2012).
9. "Top Ten Infomercial Products," www.toptenz.net/top-10-most-popular-infomercial-products.php (March 26, 2012).
10. International Direct Marketing Federation, www.idmf.com (March 27, 2012); and Federation of European Direct and Interactive Marketing, www.fedma.org (March 27, 2012).
11. "Fact Sheet: U.S. Direct Selling in 2010," http://dsa.org/research/industry-statistics/10gofactsheet.pdf; and "Global Statistical Report 2010," www.wfdsa.org/files/pdf/global-stats/Global_Statistical_Report_11311.pdf.
12. *Vending Times 2011 Census of the Industry*, www.vendingtimes.com.
13. Authors' estimates, based on information from "Internet World Stats," www.internetworldstats.com/stats.htm (March 28, 2012); Deena M. Amato-McCoy, "M-Commerce Outlook," www.chainstoreage.com (August–September 2011); and "Global Trends in Online Shopping," www.nielsen.com (June 2010).
14. John Stanley, "Retailers—Click into Action," www.toptenwholesale.com (July 1, 2011).
15. Betsy Bugg Holloway and Sharon E. Beatty, "Satisfiers and Dissatisfiers in the Online Environment: A Critical Incident Assessment," *Journal of Service Research*, Vol. 10 (May 2008), p. 356.
16. See, for example, Elias G. Carayannis, Jeffrey Alexander, and Hal Kirkwood, "Electronic Commerce," www.referenceforbusiness.com/management/De-Ele/Electronic-Commerce.html (March 30, 2012).
17. Jodi Mardesich, "The Web Is No Shopper's Paradise," *Fortune* (November 8, 1999), pp. 188–198.
18. "Amazon.com, Inc.," www.hoovers.com (March 27, 2012).
19. "SeamlessWeb," www.seamless.com (March 27, 2012).
20. "Newegg Fact Sheet," www.newegg.com/Info/FactSheet.aspx (March 29, 2012).
21. "Wi-Fi (United States)," www.starbucks.com/coffeehouse/wireless-internet (March 29, 2012).
22. Authors' estimates, based on information from www.kioskmarketplace.com and others sources (March 30, 2012); and Lee Holman and Greg Buzek, *Market Study: 2011 North American Self-Service Kiosks* (Franklin, TN: IHL Group, June 29, 2011).

23. "Interactive Kiosks," www.wirespring.com/Solutions/interactive_kiosks.html (March 30, 2012).
24. "A Small-Box Renaissance at the Big Boxes," *Retailing Today* (August 11, 2008), p. 15.
25. Authors' estimates, based on a variety of sources.
26. Authors' estimates, based on *Airports Council International 2011 Annual Report*, www.aci.aero; and *Airport Revenue News 2011 Fact Book*, www.airport revenuenews.com.
27. Stephanie Clifford, "The Airport Experience Now Includes Shopping for the Family," www.nytimes.com (August 1, 2011).

Chapter 6 Appendix

1. *Cabela's 2011 Annual Report* and "Cabela's Inc.," www.zacks.com (November 29, 2011).
2. Chris Daniels, "Furniture Titans Face Off with Multichannel Tactics Despite Housing Crisis," www.dmnews.com (August 1, 2011).
3. Dana Mattioli, "Tablets: Ultimate Buying Machines," www.wsj.com (September 28, 2011), pp. B1, B6.
4. Scott A. Neslin and Venkatesh Shankar, "Key Issues in Multichannel Customer Management: Current Knowledge and Future Directions," *Journal of Interactive Marketing*, Vol. 23 (No. 1, 2009), pp. 70–81.
5. Chris Daniels, "Retailers Testing Out E-Catalog Versions," www.dmnews.com (January 1, 2011).
6. "Multi-Channel Retailing: Bring All Sales Channels Under One Umbrella," *Marketing Week* (January 28, 2010), p. 24.
7. Andrea Syverson, "The Sins of Silos," www.multichannelmerchant.com (July–August 2010).
8. Jim Tierney, "Pier 1 Returning to E-Commerce with Site-to-Store Model," www.multi channelmerchant.com (September 2010).
9. Susan Reda, "E-Commerce Elite," www.stores.org (September 2011).
10. Jie Zhanh, Paul W, Farris, John W. Irvin, Tarun Kushwaha, Thomas J. Steenburgh, and Barton A. Weitz, "Crafting Integrated Multichannel Retailing Strategies," Harvard Business School Working Paper 09-127 (Cambridge, MA: 2010), p. 10.
11. Glanda Shasho Jones, "Brand Alignment Across Channels," www.multichannelmerchant.com (February 2011).

Chapter 7

1. eMarketer, "How Moms of All Ages Use Smart Phones in Shopping," www.emarketer.com (May 26, 2011); and eMarketer, "How Moms Keep Connected Using Smart Phones," www.emarketer.com (April 14, 2011).
2. Sarah Kellett, "Why Are My Customers So Disloyal?" www.fujitsu.com/downloads/EU/uk/pdf/insights/customer-loyalty.pdf (Spring 2008).
3. Authors' estimates, based on data from the U.S. Census Bureau (www.census.gov) and the U.S. Bureau of Labor (www.bls.gov) Web sites (April 23, 2012).
4. Jack Neff, "Time to Rethink Your Message: Now the Cart Belongs to Daddy," http://adage.com (January 17, 2011.
5. "No Longer Simply 'Chic,' Cheap Is Now a Badge of Honor," http://knowledge.wharton.upenn.edu (New York, NY: 2008), p. 2.
6. Pamela N. Danziger, "The Lure of Shopping," *American Demographics* (July–August 2002), p. 46.
7. WSL Strategic Retail, *How America Shops 1998* (New York, NY: 1998).
8. Karen Knodilis, "What Women Want," www.retail-merchandisers.com (May–June 2011).
9. "Hispanics Are Key Demographic for Retailers & Brands," http://retailsails.com (March 31, 2011).
10. "Nielsen MyBestSegments," www.claritas.com/MyBestSegments/Default.jsp (March 1, 2012).
11. Matt Carmichael, "The New Necessities: What Products and Services Can Consumers Not Live Without?" www.adage.com (November 14, 2011).
12. Paul Keegan, "Extreme Couponing: Student Saves $300 a Month," http://money.cnn.com (July 20, 2011).
13. "About Toys "R" Us, Inc., www.toysrusinc.com/about-us (April 19, 2012).
14. Cathy Hart, Andrew M. Farrell, Grazyna Stachow, Gary Reed, and John W. Cadogan, "Enjoyment of the Shopping Experience: Impact on Customers' Repatronage Intentions and Gender Influence," *Service Industries Journal*, Vol. 27 (July 2007), p. 599.
15. Hye-Young Kim and Youn-Kyung Kim, "Shopping Enjoyment and Store Shopping: The Moderating Influence of Chronic Time Pressure Modes," *Journal of Retailing and Consumer Services*, Vol. 15 (September 2008), p. 417.
16. "Retailing: General," *Standard & Poor's Industry Surveys* (November 24, 2011), p. 19; and "Retailing: Specialty," *Standard & Poor's Industry Surveys* (September 8, 2011), p. 11.
17. Kurt Salmon Associates, "Which Way to the Emerald City?" *Perspective* (February 2000), p. 3.
18. Don Peppers, "Retailers Emphasize Customer Knowledge," www.1to1.com/View.aspx?DocID=28792 (April 4, 2005).
19. "Store Brands Achieving New Heights of Consumer Popularity and Growth," http://plma.com/storeBrands/sbt11.html (December 29, 2011).
20. Rafe Ring, "Turning Shoppers into Buyers," www.wpp.com/wpp/marketing/branding/turning-shoppers-into-buyers.htm (December 16, 2011).
21. Ibid.
22. "Times Are Tough, But Shoppers Are as Impulsive as Ever," www.shoppercentric.com (June 2011); and Matt Townsend, "Retailers Woo the 'Mission Shoppers,'" www.businessweek.com (November 10, 2011).
23. Barry Kirk, "The Four Tiers of Loyalty: Where Do Your Customers Fit?" www.promomagazine.com (October 4, 2011).
24. Lars Meyer-Waarden and Christophe Benavent, "Rewards That," *The Wall Street Journal* (September 22, 2008), p. R5.

25. "Company Overview," http://news.walgreens.com/article_display.cfm?article_id=1046 (March 29, 2012).
26. "Corporate Profile," www.kohlscorporation.com/InvestorRelations/Investor01.htm (March 29, 2012).
27. "Family Dollar Stores, Inc.," www.hoovers.com (March 29, 2012); and "Family Dollar Profile," http://corporate.familydollar.com/pages/investors.aspx (March 29, 2012).
28. "Wet Seal," www.wetsealinc.com/corpinfo/corpinfo.asp?id=3 (March 30, 2012).
29. "Foot Locker, Inc.," www.footlocker-inc.com (March 30, 2012).
30. "Gap: Our Brands," www.gapinc.com/content/gapinc/html/aboutus/ourbrands.html (March 30, 2012).
31. "Standard of Living," www.encyclopedia.com/doc/1E1-stndliv.html (December 27, 2008).
32. "Mintel Reveals Consumer Trends for 2011," www.mintel.com (October 2010).

Chapter 8

1. Kristi Hines, "How to Gain Competitive Insight with Social Media," www.socialmediaexaminer.com (January 17, 2011); and Monika Jansen, "Using Social Media for Competitive Research," www.networksolutions.com/blog (April 14, 2011).
2. Debra Hazel, "Know Your Business," www.chainstoreage.com (April–May 2011).
3. D. Gail Fleenor, "What Customers Think . . . Right Now!" www.stores.com (February 2011).
4. Nick Allen, "Seeing the Value in Supplier Relations," www.supplychainstandard.com (September 27, 2011).
5. "Becoming a Wal-Mart or Sam's Club Supplier," www.walmartstores.com/download/2048.pdf (April 27, 2012).
6. Jeff Haefner, "How Much Should I Spend on a POS/Retail Management System?" www.possoftwareguide.com/articles/pos-costs.html (December 30, 2011).
7. "Retail Pro," www.expressiontech.com/retailpro.html (April 30, 2012).
8. "MicroStrategy Desktop," www.microstrategy.com/Software/Products/User_Interfaces/Desktop (April 30, 2012).
9. "Brinker Features WebFOCUS on Its Enterprise Reporting Menu," www.informationbuilders.com/applications/brinker (April 30, 2012).
10. "Pitney Bowes Business Insight Demographic Content," www.anysiteonline.com/available_data.htm (May 1, 2012).
11. Adapted by the authors from "Data Management Checklist: The Long Version," http://dataservices.gmu.edu/data-management/data-management-checklist (May 2, 2012); and Jeff St. Onge, "Direct Marketing Credos for Today's Banking," www.allbusiness.com/marketing/direct-marketing/267104-1.html (March 1999).
12. "Data Warehouse Definition," www.1keydata.com/datawarehousing/data-warehouse-definition.html (May 2, 2012).
13. Dan Ross, "Retail Data Warehousing—State of the Art," www.b-eye-network.com/view/769 (April 19, 2005).
14. "Customer Profile: Helzberg Diamonds," www.informationbuilders.com (December 9, 2011).
15. SAS, "Unlocking Analytics in the Grocery Channel: How to Connect Data to Decisions," www.chainstoreage.com (May 9, 2011).
16. Sandy Smith, "What Shoppers Want," www.stores.org (May 2011).
17. "Universal Product Code," www.gs1us.org/about_us/history/the_universal_product_code (May 2, 2012).
18. Jon Roberts, "Why EDI Is Retail's Trading Foundation," www.multichannelmerchant.com (July 4, 2011).
19. "Web EDI," http://edi.gxs.com/types_of_edi/web_edi (May 3, 2012).
20. "Who Are Michelson & Associates' Mystery Shoppers?" www.michelson.com/mystery/ourshoppers.html (May 4, 2012).
21. "Virtual Shopping," www.visioncritical.com/what-we-do/products/virtual-shopping (February 27, 2012).

Chapter 9

1. eMarketer, "Interest Builds for Location-Based Services Beyond the Check-In," www.emarketer.com (June 6, 2011); and Alida Destrempe, "Safeway 'Checks-In' to Foursquare," www.kantarretailiq.com (March 28, 2011).
2. Marianne Wilson, "Aldi Steps Out—Into the Mall," www.chainstoreage.com (August–September 2011).
3. "Dictionary," www.marketingpower.com/_layouts/Dictionary.aspx?dLetter=T (March 30, 2012).
4. See "GIS Lounge," http://gislounge.com/web-based-gis, for more information about the technical aspects of geographic information systems.
5. Erin Harris, "Inside Starbucks' GIS Strategy," www.retailsolutionsonline.com (May 2011).
6. GFK GeoMarketing, "Geomarketing in Practice," www.gfk-regiograph.com (2011).
7. For a good overview of trading-area analysis, see Jean-Paul Rodrigue, "Market Areas Analysis," http://people.hofstra.edu/geotrans/eng/ch7en/meth7en/ch7m2en.html (January 6, 2012). Click on the images on the right side of this Web site.
8. William J. Reilly, *Method for the Study of Retail Relationships*, Research Monograph No. 4 (Austin: University of Texas Press, 1929), University of Texas Bulletin No. 2944. See also MacKenzie S. Bottum, "Reilly's Law," *Appraisal Journal*, Vol. 57 (April 1989), pp. 166–172; Michael D. D'Amico, Jon M. Hawes, and Dale M. Lewison, "Determining a Hospital's Trading Area: An Application of Reilly's Law," *Journal of Hospital Marketing*, Vol. 8 (No. 2, 1994), pp. 121–129; and Matt T. Rosenberg, "Gravity Models," http://geography.about.com/library/weekly/aa031601a.htm (March 25, 2012).
9. See, for example, Matt T. Rosenberg, "Reilly's Law of Retail Gravitation," http://geography.about.com/cs/citiesurbangeo/a/aa041403a.htm (March 25, 2012).

10. David L. Huff, "Defining and Estimating a Trading Area," *Journal of Marketing*, Vol. 28 (July 1964), pp. 34–38; and David L. Huff and Larry Blue, *A Programmed Solution for Estimating Retail Sales Potential* (Lawrence: University of Kansas, 1966). See also Ela Dramowicz, "Retail Trade Area Analysis Using the Huff Model," www.directionsmag.com/printer.php?article_id=896 (July 2, 2005); David Huff and Bradley M. McCallum, "Calibrating the Huff Model Using ArcGIS Business Analyst," www.esri.com/library/whitepapers/pdfs/calibrating-huff-model.pdf (September 25, 2008); and Pan-Jin Kim1, Wanki Kim, Won-Ki Chung, and Myoung-Kil Youn, "Using New Huff Model for Predicting Potential Retail Market in South Korea," www.academicjournals.org/AJBM (March 4, 2011).
11. David A. Gautschi, "Specification of Patronage Models for Retail Center Choice," *Journal of Marketing Research*, Vol. 18 (May 1981), pp. 162–174; Glen E. Weisbrod, Robert J. Parcells, and Clifford Kern, "A Disaggregate Model for Predicting Shopping Area Market Attraction," *Journal of Retailing*, Vol. 60 (Spring 1984), pp. 65–83; Paul LeBlang, "A Theoretical Approach for Predicting Sales at a New Department-Store Location Via Lifestyles," *Direct Marketing*, Vol. 7 (Autumn 1993), pp. 70–74; Isabel P. Albaladejo-Pina and Joaquin Aranda-Gallego, "A Measure of Trade Centre Position," *European Journal of Marketing*, Vol. 32 (No. 5–6, 1998), pp. 464–479; David R. Bell, Teck-Hua Ho, and Christopher S. Tang, "Determining Where to Shop: Fixed and Variable Costs of Shopping," *Journal of Marketing Research*, Vol. 35 (August 1998), pp. 352–369; David S. Rogers, "Developing a Location Research Methodology," *Journal of Targeting, Measurement & Analysis for Marketing*, Vol. 13 (March 2005), pp. 201–208; Howard Smith and Donald Hay, "Streets, Malls, and Supermarkets," *Journal of Economics & Management Strategy*, Vol. 14 (March 2005), pp. 29–59; Charles ReVelle, Alan T. Murray, and Daniel Serra, "Location Models for Ceding Market Share and Shrinking Services," *Omega*, Vol. 35 (2007), pp. 533–540; Steve Wood and Sue Browne, "Convenience Store Location Planning and Forecasting: A Practical Research Agenda," *International Journal of Retail & Distribution Management*, Vol. 35 (No. 4, 2007), pp. 233–255; Vien Chau, Stephanie Diep, and Jillian C. Sweeney, "Shopping Trip Value: Do Stores and Products Matter?" *Journal of Retailing and Consumer Services*, Vol. 15 (2008), pp. 399–409; Rajagopal, "Determinants of Shopping Behavior of Urban Consumers," *Journal of International Consumer Marketing*, Vol. 23 (No. 2, 2011), pp. 83–104; and Scott E. Russell and C. Patrick Heidkamp, "'Food Desertification': The Loss of a Major Supermarket in New Haven, Connecticut," *Applied Geography*, Vol. 31 (2011), pp. 1197–1209.
12. Katherine Field, "Focus on: Site Selection and Optimization," www.chainstoreage.com (January 2011); *AutoZone 2011 Annual Report*; *Collective Brands 2011 Annual Report*; and *Dollar General 2011 Annual Report*.
13. "Retail Pharmacy," http://phx.corporate-ir.net/phoenix.zhtml?c=183405&p=irol-faq (March 21, 2012).
14. *Kroger 2011 Annual Report*.
15. *Kohl's 2011 Annual Report*.

Chapter 10

1. Katherine Field, "Focus on Social Media: Malls Take Their Communications and Promotions Online," www.chainstoreage.com (February 2011); and "Forest City and PlaceWise Media Introduce Shoptopia Network," www.chainstoreage.com (April 5, 2011).
2. "Five Tips for Retail Sites Selection," www.progressivegrocer.com (May 15,2011).
3. "Census 2010: Why the Urban Core Matters," www.metrojacksonville.com (April 12, 2011).
4. "Urban Exploration 2011," www.downtowndenver.com/LinkClick.aspx?fileticket=hMbT%2F4f7AHA%3D&tabid=263.
5. "Faneuil Hall Marketplace," www.faneuilhallmarketplace.com (March 15, 2012).
6. Author projections, based on International Council of Shopping Centers' data in "2011 Economic Impact of Shopping Centers," www.icsc.org/ICSC%20PressKit_FINAL_11_9_11.pdf.
7. "The Mall at Partridge Creek," www.shoppartridgecreek.com/about_the_mall (March 19, 2012).
8. *Radio Shack 2011 Annual Report*; and Jennifer Hopfinger, "Radio Shack's Revamp Starts to Pay Dividends," *Shopping Centers Today* (December 2008).
9. *Guitar Center Holding 2011 10-Q* (September 30, 2011).
10. *Apple Inc. 2011 Annual Report*.
11. *Home Depot 2011 Annual Report*.
12. See "Lease Terminology," www.realtechre.com/terminology.htm (April 3, 2012).
13. Julie Zeveloff, "The Most Expensive Shopping Streets in the World," www.businessinsider.com (September 1, 2011).
14. "Store Size Caps," www.newrules.org/retail/rules/store-size-caps (April 3, 2012).

Chapter 11

1. Sandy Smith, "Culture Club," http://www.stores.org/print/book/export/html/6393 (May 2011); and "Reward Your People, Reward Business," http://peoplematter.com/solutions/engage/rewards (February 16, 2012).
2. "Driving Success: The Incredible Power of Company-Wide Goal Alignment," www.successfactors.com (2011).
3. Adapted and updated by the authors from Paul M. Mazur, *Principles of Organization Applied to Modern Retailing* (New York: Harper & Brothers, 1927).
4. "Target Careers: Culture," http://sites.target.com/site/en/company/page.jsp?contentId=WCMP04-031452 (May 11, 2012).
5. "Management Opportunities," www.unos.com/mgmtJobs.html (May 11, 2012).
6. "Our Structure," http://about.nordstrom.com/careers/structure.asp (May 11, 2012).

7. "Career Paths," www.wholefoodsmarket.com/careers/paths.php (May 11, 2012).
8. "National Hiring Partnerships," https://careers.homedepot.com/cg/content.do?p=nhp (May 12, 2012).
9. "2011 Catalyst Census: *Fortune 500* Women Board Directors," http://www.catalyst.org/file/533/2011_fortune_500_census_wbd.pdf (December 2011).
10. "Katherine Krill: Executive Profile & Biography," http://investing.businessweek.com (January 5, 2012).
11. "Rite Aid Board of Directors: Mary F. Sammons," www.riteaid.com/company/about/board_directors.jsf#2 (January 8, 2012).
12. "Top Companies: Most Diverse," http://money.cnn.com/magazines/fortune/bestcompanies/2011/minorities (February 7, 2011).
13. "CarMax: Our Commitment to Diversity," http://www.carmax.com/enus/company-info/diversity.html (April 19, 2012); "Whole Foods: Our Mission and Culture," www.wholefoodsmarket.com/careers/workhere2.php (April 19, 2012); and "Zappos Family Core Values," http://about.zappos.com/our-unique-culture/zappos-core-values (April 19, 2012).
14. "Wal-Mart 2010 Work Diversity Report," http://walmartstores.com/Diversity; "Enterprise Rent-A-Car Careers," www.erac.com/our-culture/diversity.aspx (April 19, 2012); and "Walgreens Commitment to Diversity," www.walgreens.com/topic/sr/sr_diversity_commit.jsp (April 19, 2012).
15. For a good illustration of the testing resources available for retailers, visit the Web site of Employee Selection & Development Inc. (www.employeeselect.com/selectTests.htm).
16. Judith Brown, "Employee Orientation: Keeping New Employees on Board," http://humanresources.about.com/od/retention/a/keepnewemployee.htm (April 20, 2012).
17. "The Container Store," http://company.monster.com/container.aspx (April 20, 2012).
18. Stephenie Overman, "On the Right Track," *HR Magazine* (April 2011), pp. 74–75.
19. Adapted by the authors from Anthony J. Rucci, Steven P. Kirn, and Richard T. Quinn, "The Employee-Customer-Profit Chain at Sears," *Harvard Business Review*, Vol. 76 (January–February 1998), pp. 82–97.
20. Adapted by the authors from Ed Sykes, "Jump Start Your Employee Motivation," www.thesykesgrp.com/MotivateTeamJumpstart01.htm (October 9, 2011).

Chapter 12

1. Lauri Giesen, "You've Got a Friend," www.stores.org/print/book/export/html/6357 (April 2011); and Scott Thompson, "PayPal Unveils the Future of Shopping," www.thepaypalblog.com (September 14, 2011).
2. See "20 Straightforward Ways to Improve Retail Profit Margins," www.ideaanglers.com/20-straightforward-ways-to-improve-retail-profit-margins (September 9, 2011).
3. *Industry Norms & Key Business Ratios* (New York: Dun & Bradstreet, 2011–12).
4. Jenn Abelson, "Retail Sales Surge, But Not the Profits," www.bostonglobe.com/business (January 6, 2012).
5. "Report: U.S. Retail Availability Expected to Decline in 2012," www.chainstoreage.com (November 21, 2011).
6. "Retail-Focused REIT Fairly Resilient," www.iproperty.com.my (January 6, 2012).
7. "How to Cash in on IPOs," www.kiplinger.com (January 2010); and "IPO Central," www.hoovers.com (April 29, 2012).
8. Michael J. de la Merced and Stephanie Clifford, "Limited Brands to Cut Ties to The Limited," www.nytimes.com (June 16, 2010).
9. Rachel Dodes, Ann Zimmerman, and Jeffrey McCracken, "Retailers Brace for Major Change—Chain Stores See a Future with Fewer Outlets, Brands—and Thinner Profits," www.wallstreetjournal.com (December 27, 2008).
10. Michael Hartnett, "Value of Chapter 11 Protections for Retailers Sparks Sharp Debate," *Stores* (April 1999), p. 92.
11. Harry & David Holdings, Inc., "Results of Operations—Management Discussion and Analysis for the First Quarter Ended October 1, 2011," www.hndcorp.com.
12. "Former CFO of National Auto Parts Retailer Pleads Guilty to Scheme to Manipulate Corporate Earnings," www.justice.gov/opa/pr/2011/May/11-crm-618.html (May 13, 2011).
13. "Appendix: Code of Ethics for Senior Financial Officers," http://ir.homedepot.com/phoenix.zhtml?c=63646&p=irol-govconduct (December 2011).
14. See "How to Better Manage Your Cash Flow," www.entrepreneur.com/article/66008 (January 30, 2012); and "Ten Ways to Keep Cash-Flow Problems from Putting You Out of Business," www.greenhousemanagementonline.com/ten-ways-cash-flow-problems.aspx (December 18, 2011).
15. Computed by the authors from Marianne Wilson, "2011 Annual Store Construction & Outfitting Survey," www.chainstoreage.com.
16. Company annual reports.
17. "Corporate Information," http://shop.tuesdaymorning.com/index.asp (April 30, 2012).
18. Craig R. Johnson, "Profitable Productivity," *Chain Store Age* (July 2007), p. 154.

Chapter 13

1. Susan Reda, "Game Changer," www.stores.org/print/book/export/html/5649 (October 2010); and Bernie Brennan and Lori Schafer, *Branded!: How Retailers Engage Consumers with Social Media and Mobility* (Hoboken, NJ: Wiley, 2010).
2. See Mary Jo Bitner, Amy L. Ostrom, and Felicia N. Morgan, "Service Blueprinting: A Practical Technique for Service Innovation," *California Management Review*, Vol. 50 (Spring 2008), pp. 66–94; and Gillian Guthrie, Van Luong, Camille Neubauer, and Emily Steyer, "A Service Blueprint of Brassfield's Salon and Day Spa," www.plu.edu/~guthrigm/doc/brassfieldsppt.ppt (December 2008).
3. *Tiffany & Co. 2011 Annual Report*, pp. K-19, K-25.

4. "Average Life Span of Store-Outfitting Systems," www.chainstoreage.com (July 2008).
5. Janet Groeber, "Green Grand Slam," www.stores.org (May 2011).
6. Juan Martinez, "In-Store Digital Upgrades Integral to Macy's $400 Million Renovation," www.dmnews.com (November 1, 2011).
7. Bill Zalud, "Retail's Wholesale Use of Security Video," www.securitymagazine.com (April 2011).
8. David Bodamer, "Talking Points," *Retail Traffic* (January 2008), p. 23.
9. Compiled from various sources by the authors. See www.creditcards.com for a lot of information on transaction methods.
10. "Merchant Credit-Card Processing," www.elavon.com/acquiring/costco (February 2, 2009).
11. Marianne Crowe, "Emerging Payments—The Changing Landscape," www.bos.frb.org/economic/eprg/presentations/2008/crowe04151708.pdf (2008).
12. "Is Retail Growth Ready to Accelerate in 2012?" www.tompkinsinc.com (May 20, 2012).
13. "Fresh Market Manager; Perishable Inventory Management," www.parkcitygroup.com/business-suite/fresh-market-manager (May 22, 2012).
14. "Barcode Scanners," www.posguys.com/barcode-scanner_3 (May 22, 2012).
15. "Self-Checkout Moves into the Mainstream," www.rbrlondon.com/retail (October 31, 2011.)
16. "Outsourcing for the Retail Industry," www.accenture.com/us-en/Pages/service-retail-outsourcing-summary.aspx (May 27, 2012).
17. CFO Innovation Asia Staff, "Auditors Declare Three Imperatives for Crisis Management in 2012," www.cfoinnovation.com (October 3, 2011).
18. Victoria Duff, "What Is a Business Contingency Plan?" http://smallbusiness.chron.com/business-contingency-plan-1081.html (May 27, 2012).

Chapter 14

1. Fiona Soltes, "The Tastemakers," www.stores.org (May 2011).
2. Ted Hurlbut, "Merchandising Strategy for Independent Retailers," www.articlesbase.com/small-business-articles (July 22, 2009).
3. Janet Groeber, "Resetting Priorities: Winston Retail Solutions' Jan Croatt," www.stores.org (May 2010).
4. PwC, "What's in Store? Rethinking the Supply Chain," www.pwc.co.uk (June 2011).
5. Sally Furrer, "Merchandising from a Clean Slate—Part One," www.theinstoreshow.com/component/k2/item/64-sally-furrer-clean-slate-part1 (January 2, 2011).
6. *Costco 2011 Annual Report.*
7. "Keep Your Finger on the Pulse," www.7thonline.com/public/publilocalization.shtm (May 27, 2012).
8. Amanda Baltazar, "Cross-Merchandising Done Right," http://pharmacy.about.com/od/Operations (May 28, 2012).
9. "Zara," www.inditex.com/en/who_we_are/concepts/zara (June 1, 2012).
10. *Ross Stores 2011 Annual Report.*
11. "Corporate Information," www.doneger.com/web/89357.htm (June 1, 2012).
12. "Fashion Consulting Buying Office," www.vibitalia.com (June 2, 2012).
13. "United We Stand," www.twice.com (March 2011).
14. "FPN History—Who We Are," www.fpn.org/groups.html (June 2, 2012).
15. "Executive Board," www.jcpenney.net/about/executives.aspx (June 2, 2012).
16. "Collateral: Ikea Revamps Supply Chain Strategy with Demand and Fulfillment Solutions from JDA," www.jda.com (October 2010); and "Corporate Ikea," www.ikea.com/us/en/customerservices/faq (May 27, 2012).
17. "About Brookstone," www.brookstone.com (May 27, 2012); and "About Us" http://corp.7-eleven.com (May 27, 2012).
18. "About Us," www.dollartree.com (May 27, 2012).
19. Fred Minnick, "Cracking the Assortment Planning Code," www.stores.org (June 2011).
20. Gary Rodkin, "A Balancing Act," *Progressive Grocer* (June 1999), p. 29.
21. "Private Label Market Share Sets a New Record," www.storebrandsdecisions.com (June 28, 2011); and "Retail Private Label Brands in Europe," www.symphonyiri.eu (December 2011).
22. "Retail Private Label Brands in Europe," www.symphonyiri.com (December 15, 2011).
23. "H.T. Traders," www.harristeeter.com/in_our_stores/our_brands/harris_teeter.aspx (May 29, 2012).
24. Laurie Sullivan, "Retailers Ply Their Own Brands," *Information Week* (April 18, 2005), pp. 61–65.
25. "What Is Category Management?" www.catmanplus.com/whatis.html (May 29, 2012).
26. Al Heller, "Consumer-Centric Category Management a Fresh Spin on Maximizing Performance," www.acnielsen.com (Fourth Quarter 2005).
27. Information Resources, Inc., "Manufacturer and Retailer Report Cards," *NeoBrief* (Issue 1, 1999), pp. 3–6.
28. "MicroStrategy Selected by Groupon for Detailed Insights into Consumer Purchasing Trends," www.microstrategy.com (March 30, 2011).
29. "Shoe Retailer DSW Optimizes Fixed Store Capacities with Help from JDA," www.jda.com/file_bin/casestudies/dsw_case-study.pdf (2011).
30. "Forecasting Software," www.sas.com/technologies/analytics/forecasting (May 29, 2012).
31. "Turning on the Spigot of Ideas at O.co," http://info.spigit.com/rs/spigit/images/Overstock-Case-Study.pdf (2011).
32. "Fast, Accurate Merchandising," www.sas.com/success/sportchalet.html (May 30, 2012).
33. "Allocation & Replenishment," www.justenough.com/retail/allocation-replenishment/allocation (May 30, 2012).

Chapter 15

1. Juan Martinez, "Express Launches Social Shopping Catalog," www.dmnews.com (May 3, 2011); and "Express Puts Entire Product Lines on Its Facebook Page," www.chainstoreage.com (May 3, 2011).

2. Shveta Aror and Krishna Raghavulu, "Grocery Retail: The Next Level of Inventory Management," www.retail-merchandiser.com (May–June 2011).
3. "Real 3-D Virtual Trade Shows," www.goexhibit.com/GoExhibit/shockwave (April 19, 2012).
4. *Big Lots 2011 Annual Report.*
5. Steve Keifer, "Chargebacks and Deductions in the Retail Supply Channel," www.gxsblogs.com/keifers (August 26, 2010).
6. Justin Horwath, "Report: Apple to Open Stores within Select Target Locations," www.bizjournals.com/twincities/news (January 2012).
7. *TJX Companies 2011 Annual Report.*
8. "Practicing Shelf-Awareness at the Grocery Store," www.gatewaycitysavers.com (August 15, 2011).
9. "RFID Basics," www.zebra.com/id/zebra/na/en/index/rfid/faqs/rfid_basics.html (March 25, 2012).
10. "How to RFID-Tag Apparel and Benefit Internally," www.rfidjournalevents.com/live/howto.php (2011).
11. "Supply Chain Capabilities," www.supervalu.com/sv-webapp/supply/capabilities.jsp (March 26, 2012).
12. "Sears Logistics Services," http://biz.yahoo.com/ic/108/108358.html (March 27, 2012).
13. Jerry Andrews, "CPFR: Considering the Options, Advantages, and Pitfalls," www.sdcexec.com/publication/index.jsp?issueId=86 (April–May 2008).
14. "Retail," http://ups-scs.com/solutions/retail.html (March 29, 2012).
15. "Saks Fifth Avenue Vendor Standards Manual," www.saksincorporated.com/vendorrelations/documents/SFAVSM01-05-12.pdf (January 5, 2012).
16. Richard Schonberger, "The Skinny on Lean Management," www.superfactory.com/articles/featured/2009/0109-schonberger-skinny-lean-management.html (January 2009).
17. "What Is Efficient Consumer Response?" www.ecr.ca/en/ecrinfo.html (March 29, 2012).
18. "What Is Perishable," www.perishablelogisticsalliance.com/eng/whatis.asp (March 30, 2012).
19. Guy Toksoy, "Weighing the Direct-to-Store Delivery Model," www.stores.org (October 2010).
20. Ibid.
21. *Amazon.com 2011 Annual Report.*
22. Kurt Salmon Associates, "Vision for the New Millennium," *KSA Brochure* (n.d.).
23. See Jeremy B. Thompson, "Inventory Control Through Vendor Managed Inventories: A Sure Way to Reduce Stock Cost," http://ezinearticles.com (November 21, 2011).
24. Allison Enright, "Target Redesigns Its E-commerce Site," www.internetretailer.com (August 23, 2011).
25. Phil Britt, "Retailers Look to KM to Drive Business," *KM World* (January 2009), pp. 114–115.
26. "Global Theft Barometer 2011," www.retailresearch.org/grtb_currentsurvey.php; and "Retail Theft Goes Global," www.securitymagazine.com (February 2011).
27. "2011 Customer Returns in the Retail Industry," www.theretailequation.com; and Andrew K. Reese, "Meeting the Reverse Logistics Challenge," www.sdcexec.com (August 24, 2011).

Chapter 16

1. Deb Evans and Thomas Scott, "Turning Social Media into Profit," *Franchising World* (March 2011), pp. 46–48.
2. "Inventory Management Software," www.logisense.com/billing_cpe.html (April 17, 2012).
3. For more information on inventory valuat ion, visit the Investopedia.com Web site, www.investopedia.com/terms/p/perpetualinventory.asp.
4. "Brooks Brothers Uses SAS to Drive Global Customer Satisfaction and Profitability," www.sas.com/success/brooksbros.html (April 18, 2012).
5. "A Solution for Every Season," www.planalytics.com/index.php?p=retail_products (April 18, 2012).
6. "The Facts About Greeting Cards," http://www.greetingcard.org/AbouttheIndustry/tabid/58/Default.aspx (April 20, 2012).
7. Adapted by the authors from "EAN-13 Background Information," www.barcodeisland.com/ean13.phtml (April 18, 2012).
8. First Insight, "Weeding Out the Weak: Real-Time Insight from Customers Who Know," www.firstinsight.com/files/WeedingDownTheWeak-Fall11.pdf (Fall 2011).
9. Ted Hurlbut, "The True Cost of Retail Inventory," www.hurlbutassociates.com/The-True-Cost-of-Retail-Inventory (May 18, 2007).

Chapter 17

1. "Groupon Now and the Rise of the Real-Time Deal," www.entrepreneur.com (July 2011); and "How Sustainable Is Groupon's Business Model?" http://knowledge.wharton.upenn.edu (May 25, 2011).
2. "Sports Authority: About Us," www.sportsauthority.com/corp/index.jsp (April 22, 2012).
3. "H&M Vs. Marks & Spencer," www.g-cem.org (January 13, 2012).
4. "Why Use Smarter.com to Shop Online?" www.smarter.com (April 23, 2012).
5. See Bob Sherlock, "What Matters Most in Pricing?" www.brickmeetsclick.com/what-matters-most-in-pricing- (December 19, 2011); Jeffrey Helbling, Josh Leibowitz, and Aaron Rettaliata, "The Value Proposition in Multi-Channel Retailing," www.mckinseyquarterly.com (May 2011); and Mark Striving, "Four Rules for Pricing Products," www.entrepreneur.com (November 15, 2011).
6. Julie Creswell, "Sotheby's Is Back in Auction," *Fortune* (September 20, 2004), p. 18.
7. Tucker, Ellis, & West LLP, "Minimum Resale Price Maintenance After Leegin," www.tuckerellis.com (October 2009).
8. "The Loss Leader," www.bizhelp24.com/marketing/the-loss-leader.html (April 9, 2012).
9. See "A Guide to Retail Pricing Laws and Regulations," www.nist.gov/pml/wmd/metric/pricing-laws.cfm (December 15, 2011).
10. Ken Clark, "Sticker Shock," *Chain Store Age* (September 2000), p. 88. See also David C. Wyld, "Back to the Future?: Why 'Old School' Item Pricing Laws May Hold Back the Use of RFID in Retail Settings," www.coastal.edu/business/cbj/pdfs/articles/spring2008/wyld.pdf (Spring 2008).

11. Selling price may also be computed by transposing the markup formula into

$$\text{Retail selling price} = \frac{\text{Merchandise cost}}{1 - \text{Markup}} = \$17.14$$

12. Merchandise cost may also be computed by transposing the markup formula into

$$\text{Merchandise cost} = (\text{Retail selling price})(1 - \text{Markup}) = \$4.794$$

13. See Robert Frick, "You Can Haggle for That!" www.kiplinger.com/magazine (January 2011).
14. See Paul-Valentin Ngobo, Patrick Legohérel, and Nicolas Guéguen, "A Cross-Category Investigation into the Effects of Nin-Ending Pricing on Brand Choice," *Journal of Retailing and Consumer Services*, Vol. 17 (2010), pp. 374–385.
15. See Ruiliang Yan and Subir Bandyopadhyay, "The Profit Benefits of Bundle Pricing of Complementary Products," *Journal of Retailing and Consumer Services*, Vol. 18 (2011), pp. 355–361.

Chapter 18

1. J. Walter Thompson Company, "Social Media Checklist," http://02a6614.netsolhost.com/production/JWT_SocialMediaChecklist.ppt (March 2011).
2. Jill Rivkin, "A Future in Store," www.bevindustry.com (June 20, 2011).
3. Paul Gainer, "Growing Disney's Best 30 Minutes," www.chainstoreage.com (August-September 2011).
4. "Jungle Jim's Overview," www.junglejims.com/about/aboutus.asp (March 7, 2012).
5. "Gap to Redesign Old Navy Stores," www.kantarretailiq.com (June 7, 2011).
6. Alan Treadgold, "Engaging Your Shopper," www.retail-merchandiser.com (March–April 2011).
7. "What Is Visual Merchandising?" www.ausvm.com.au/whatisvisualmerchandising.html (March 9, 2012).
8. Ana Anthony, "Dairy Queen Welcomes New Store Interior," www.dglobe.com (January 8, 2012).
9. Josh Lowenstein, "How Apple's Stores Turned into a Retail Juggernaut," http://news.cnet.com (May 19, 2011).
10. "About Toys "R" Us Times Square," www.toysrusinc.com/about-us/times-square (April 9, 2012).
11. Leo J. Shapiro & Associates, "Types of Flooring Used," www.chainstoreage.com (July 2011).
12. Steven Zarwell, "What's on Your Front Door?" *Dealernews* (March 2005), p. 38.
13. "Dirty Stores Kiss Sales Goodbye," www.progressivegrocer.com (January 23, 2011).
14. Samantha Hadley, "Tracking Customers Shopping Habits Can Increase Sales Part One," www.businessfinancestore.com (December 22, 2011).
15. Jack Hitt, "The Theory of Supermarkets," *New York Times Magazine* (March 10, 1996), pp. 56–61, 94, 98; and Jennifer Lonoff Schiff, "The Layout of the Land," www.multichannelmerchant.com (December 2007).
16. "The Marketing at Retail Industry," www.popai.com (April 30, 2009).
17. Paco Underhill, *Why We Buy: Updated and Revised* (New York: Simon & Schuster, 2009).
18. "American Girl Place," www.americangirl.com/corp/corporate.php?section=about&id=14 (March 12, 2012).
19. "Urban Outfitters," www.urbn.com/profileurban.html (May 12, 2012).
20. Alicia Johnston, "Retailers: Tips to Keep Your Shoppers In-Store Longer," www.maxpointinteractive.com/onpoint-blog (September 20, 2011).
21. James Bickers, "A Wait They Won't Hate," www.retailcustomerexperience.com/article.php?id=440 (June 20, 2008).
22. Kim Cook, "Shopping Cart Advances Just Keep Rolling Along," www.msnbc.msn.com (September 7, 2011).
23. "What Is Co-Branding?" www.wisegeek.com/what-is-co-branding.htm (March 12, 2012).
24. "Wish Lists and Baby & Wedding Registries," www.amazon.com (March 12, 2012).
25. "Help Local Foster Kids," www.sleepcountry.com/local-foster-kids.aspx (March 13, 2012).

Chapter 19

1. Jason Ankeny, "Innovator: Shopkick's Cyriac Roeding Reinvents Retail," www.entrepreneur.com/article/218157 (March 2011); and "Shopkick Turns 1!" www.shopkick.com (January 31, 2012).
2. *Best Buy 2011 Annual Report*.
3. Ibid.
4. Computed by the authors from data in "100 Leading National Advertisers," www.adage.com (June 20, 2011); and company annual reports.
5. See "Co-Op Advertising," www.entrepreneur.com/encyclopedia/term/82096.html (May 3, 2012).
6. "State of the Blogosphere 2011," http://technorati.com/state-of-the-blogosphere (November 4, 2011).
7. See also Mark Smock, "Don't Make These Top 10 Selling Mistakes!" www.woopidoo.com/articles/smock/selling-mistakes.htm (May 3, 2012).
8. "What Is the Difference between Advertising and Promotion?" www.wisegeek.com (February 7, 2012).
9. "Reach Consumers in Store," www.newsamerica.com/productsandservices/instore (May 6, 2012).
10. "Loyalty/Rewards Program Module," www.managemore.com/rewards/rewards-tips.htm (2009).
11. "Why McDonald's," www.mcdonalds.ca/ca/en/our_story/corporate_info.html (May 8, 2012); and "Nutrition and Well Being," www.aboutmcdonalds.com/mcd/sustainability.html (May 8, 2012).
12. Richard Earls, "A 2012 Marketing Plan—Word-of-Mouth Marketing," www.travelresearchonline.com/blog (December 12, 2011).
13. Morey Stettner, "How to Establish a Promotion Mix," http://edwardlowe.org/index.elf?page=sserc&storyid=8816&function=story (2000).
14. *Netflix 2011 Annual Report*.
15. Evelyn Lim, "How Opt-in E-mail Marketing Helps You in Your Online Business," www.seotoday.net (January 5, 2006).
16. Patricia Odell, "Workarounds for Clean Store Policies," www.promomagazine.com (October 27, 2011).
17. Sarah Nassauer, "A Season (Or 13) for Shopping," www.wallstreetjournal.com (August 17, 2011).

Chapter 20

1. Sean Fitzgerald, "Reacting, Responding, and Preparing for Negative Social Media Postings," www.franchise.org (February 2011); and RightNow, "The Retail Consumer Report," www.rightnow.com/files/Retail-Consumer-Report.pdf (2011).
2. "Dollar Tree Stores: Company Profile," *Datamonitor* (November 29, 2011).
3. Rick Newman, "4 Lessons From the Demise of Borders," www.usnews.com (July 20, 2011).
4. *Coach Inc. 2011 Annual Report.*
5. Marianne Wilson, "Global Expansion," www.chainstoreage.com (November 2011).
6. "Food Lion's History," www.foodlion.com/Corporate/History (May 20, 2012).
7. Thomas Angell, "Benchmarking Strategy Vital to Business Performance," *Financial Executive* (June 2005), p. 16.
8. A. Parasuraman, Valarie A. Zeithaml, and Leonard L. Berry, "Alternative Scales for Measuring Service Quality: A Comparative Assessment Based on Psychometric and Diagnostic Criteria," *Journal of Retailing*, Vol. 70 (Fall 1994), pp. 201–230. See also Lisa J. Morrison Coulthard, "Measuring Service Quality," *International Journal of Market Research*, Vol. 46 (Quarter 4, 2004), pp. 479–497; François A. Carrillat, Fernando Jaramillo, and Jay P. Mulki, "The Validity of the SERVQUAL and SERVPERF Scales," *International Journal of Service Industry Management*, Vol. 18 (December 2007), pp. 472–490; Riadh Ladhari, "Developing E-Service Quality Scales: A Literature Review," *Journal of Retailing and Consumer Services*, Vol. 10 (2010), pp. 464–477; and Hokey Min and Hyesung Min, "Benchmarking the Service Quality of Fast-Food Restaurant Franchises in the USA: A Longitudinal Study," *Benchmarking: An International Journal*, Vol. 18 (April 2011), pp. 282–300.
9. "Supply Chain Overview," www.supplychainconsortium.com/resource_center_process_overview.asp (May 22, 2012).
10. "The 2011 A.T. Kearney Global Retail Development Index," www.atkearney.com (2011).
11. Austen Mulinder, "Hear Today … Or Gone Tomorrow? Winners Listen to Customers," *Retailing Issues Letter* (September 1999), p. 5.
12. "2011 Top 100: Retailers, Issues, and Trends That Are Making an Impact," www.retailcustomerexperience.com (2011).
13. "Retailing General," *Standard & Poor's Industry Surveys* (November 24, 2011), p. 11.
14. Armorel Kenna, "Benetton: A Must-Have Becomes a Has-Been," www.businessweek.com (March 10, 2011).
15. *Kohl's 2011 Annual Report*; and *Kohl's 2011 Fact Book.*
16. Nicholas Hodson, Karla Martin, Deniz Caglar, and Marcelo TauJane Stevenson, "2012 Retail Industry Perspective," www.booz.com (December 7, 2011).

Appendix

1. "Retailing: Overview," www.careers-in-marketing.com/rt.htm (May 13, 2012).
2. "About Macy's Jobs," www.macysjobs.com/about (May 13, 2012).
3. "Careers After College," www.macyscollege.com/college (May 13, 2012).
4. "Store Management," www.macyscollege.com/college/careers/edp/storemanagement.aspx (May 13, 2012).
5. "Product Development," www.macyscollege.com/college/careers/edp/productdevelopment.aspx (May 13, 2012).
6. "Experience Retail," www.nrffoundation.com/content/retail-careers-center (May 13, 2012).

Name Index

Subject Index

D

E

Q

R

T

U

W

Z